Introduction to 3D GAME PROGRAMMING WITH DIRECTX® 12

LICENSE, DISCLAIMER OF LIABILITY, AND LIMITED WARRANTY

By purchasing or using this book (the "Work"), you agree that this license grants permission to use the contents contained herein, but does not give you the right of ownership to any of the textual content in the book or ownership to any of the information or products contained in it. *This license does not permit uploading of the Work onto the Internet or on a network (of any kind) without the written consent of the Publisher.* Duplication or dissemination of any text, code, simulations, images, etc. contained herein is limited to and subject to licensing terms for the respective products, and permission must be obtained from the Publisher or the owner of the content, etc., in order to reproduce or network any portion of the textual material (in any media) that is contained in the Work.

MERCURY LEARNING AND INFORMATION ("MLI" or "the Publisher") and anyone involved in the creation, writing, or production of the companion disc, accompanying algorithms, code, or computer programs ("the software"), and any accompanying Web site or software of the Work, cannot and do not warrant the performance or results that might be obtained by using the contents of the Work. The author, developers, and the Publisher have used their best efforts to insure the accuracy and functionality of the textual material and/or programs contained in this package; we, however, make no warranty of any kind, express or implied, regarding the performance of these contents or programs. The Work is sold "as is" without warranty (except for defective materials used in manufacturing the book or due to faulty workmanship).

The author, developers, and the publisher of any accompanying content, and anyone involved in the composition, production, and manufacturing of this work will not be liable for damages of any kind arising out of the use of (or the inability to use) the algorithms, source code, computer programs, or textual material contained in this publication. This includes, but is not limited to, loss of revenue or profit, or other incidental, physical, or consequential damages arising out of the use of this Work.

The sole remedy in the event of a claim of any kind is expressly limited to replacement of the book, and only at the discretion of the Publisher. The use of "implied warranty" and certain "exclusions" vary from state to state, and might not apply to the purchaser of this product.

Companion disc files are available for download from the publisher by writing to info@merclearning.com.

Introduction to 3D GAME PROGRAMMING WITH DIRECTX® 12

Frank D. Luna

MERCURY LEARNING AND INFORMATION

Dulles, Virginia
Boston, Massachusetts
New Delhi

Copyright ©2016 by MERCURY LEARNING AND INFORMATION LLC. All rights reserved.

This publication, portions of it, or any accompanying software may not be reproduced in any way, stored in a retrieval system of any type, or transmitted by any means, media, electronic display or mechanical display, including, but not limited to, photocopy, recording, Internet postings, or scanning, without prior permission in writing from the publisher.

Publisher: David Pallai
MERCURY LEARNING AND INFORMATION
22841 Quicksilver Drive
Dulles, VA 20166
info@merclearning.com
www.merclearning.com
(800) 232-0223

Frank D. Luna. *Introduction to 3D GAME PROGRAMMING WITH DIRECTX 12*
ISBN: 978-1-942270-06-5

The publisher recognizes and respects all marks used by companies, manufacturers, and developers as a means to distinguish their products. All brand names and product names mentioned in this book are trademarks or service marks of their respective companies. Any omission or misuse (of any kind) of service marks or trademarks, etc. is not an attempt to infringe on the property of others.

Library of Congress Control Number: 2015957713

161718321   This book is printed on acid-free paper.

Our titles are available for adoption, license, or bulk purchase by institutions, corporations, etc. For additional information, please contact the Customer Service Dept. at 800-232-0223(toll free).

All of our titles are available in digital format at authorcloudware.com and other digital vendors. Companion files for this title are available by contacting info@merclearning.com. The sole obligation of MERCURY LEARNING AND INFORMATION to the purchaser is to replace the book or disc, based on defective materials or faulty workmanship, but not based on the operation or functionality of the product.

*To my nieces and nephews,
Marrick, Hans, Max, Anna, Augustus, Presley, and Elyse*

Contents

Dedication   v

Acknowledgments   xxii

Introduction   xxv
    Intended Audience   xxvi
    Prerequisites   xxvi
    Required Development Tools and Hardware   xxvii
    Using the DirectX SDK Documentation and SDK Samples   xxvii
    Clarity   xxix
    Sample Programs and Online Supplements   xxix
    Demo Project Setup in Visual Studio 2010   xxix
        Download the Book's Source Code   xxx
        Create a Win32 Project   xxx
        Linking the DirectX Libraries   xxxi
        Adding the Source Code and Building the Project   xxxii

PART I   MATHEMATICAL PREREQUISITES

Chapter 1   Vector Algebra   3

    1.1   Vectors   4
        1.1.1   Vectors and Coordinate Systems   5
        1.1.2   Left-Handed Versus Right-Handed Coordinate Systems   6
        1.1.3   Basic Vector Operations   7
    1.2   Length and Unit Vectors   9
    1.3   The Dot Product   10
        1.3.1   Orthogonalization   13
    1.4   The Cross Product   14
        1.4.1   Pseudo 2D Cross Product   16
        1.4.2   Orthogonalization with the Cross Product   16

1.5	Points	17
1.6	DirectX Math Vectors	18
	1.6.1 Vector Types	19
	1.6.2 Loading and Storage Methods	21
	1.6.3 Parameter Passing	21
	1.6.4 Constant Vectors	23
	1.6.5 Overloaded Operators	24
	1.6.6 Miscellaneous	24
	1.6.7 Setter Functions	25
	1.6.8 Vector Functions	26
	1.6.9 Floating-Point Error	30
1.7	Summary	31
1.8	Exercises	33

Chapter 2 Matrix Algebra 37

2.1	Definition	38
2.2	Matrix Multiplication	40
	2.2.1 Definition	40
	2.2.2 Vector-Matrix Multiplication	41
	2.2.3 Associativity	42
2.3	The Transpose of a Matrix	42
2.4	The Identity Matrix	43
2.5	The Determinant of a Matrix	44
	2.5.1 Matrix Minors	45
	2.5.2 Definition	45
2.6	The Adjoint of a Matrix	47
2.7	The Inverse of a Matrix	47
2.8	DirectX Math Matrices	49
	2.8.1 Matrix Types	50
	2.8.2 Matrix Functions	52
	2.8.3 DirectX Math Matrix Sample Program	53
2.9	Summary	54
2.10	Exercises	55

Chapter 3 Transformations 59

3.1	Linear Transformations	60
	3.1.1 Definition	60
	3.1.2 Matrix Representation	60
	3.1.3 Scaling	61
	3.1.4 Rotation	63

3.2 Affine Transformations 66
    3.2.1 Homogeneous Coordinates 66
    3.2.2 Definition and Matrix Representation 67
    3.2.3 Translation 67
    3.2.4 Affine Matrices for Scaling and Rotation 70
    3.2.5 Geometric Interpretation of an Affine Transformation Matrix 70
3.3 Composition of Transformations 72
3.4 Change of Coordinate Transformations 73
    3.4.1 Vectors 74
    3.4.2 Points 74
    3.4.3 Matrix Representation 75
    3.4.4 Associativity and Change of Coordinate Matrices 76
    3.4.5 Inverses and Change of Coordinate Matrices 77
3.5 Transformation Matrix versus Change of Coordinate Matrix 78
3.6 DirectX Math Transformation Functions 79
3.7 Summary 80
3.8 Exercises 82

PART II   DIRECT 3D FOUNDATIONS

Chapter 4   Direct3D Initialization   89

4.1 Preliminaries 90
    4.1.1 Direct3D 12 Overview 90
    4.1.2 COM 90
    4.1.3 Textures Formats 91
    4.1.4 The Swap Chain and Page Flipping 93
    4.1.5 Depth Buffering 93
    4.1.6 Resources and Descriptors 96
    4.1.7 Multisampling Theory 98
    4.1.8 Multisampling in Direct3D 99
    4.1.9 Feature Levels 101
    4.1.10 DirectX Graphics Infrastructure 101
    4.1.11 Checking Feature Support 105
    4.1.12 Residency 107
4.2 CPU/GPU Interaction 107
    4.2.1 The Command Queue and Command Lists 108
    4.2.2 CPU/GPU Synchronization 112

	4.2.3 Resource Transitions	114
	4.2.4 Multithreading with Commands	116
4.3	Initializing Direct3D	116
	4.3.1 Create the Device	117
	4.3.2 Create the Fence and Descriptor Sizes	118
	4.3.3 Check 4X MSAA Quality Support	119
	4.3.4 Create Command Queue and Command List	119
	4.3.5 Describe and Create the Swap Chain	120
	4.3.6 Create the Descriptor Heaps	122
	4.3.7 Create the Render Target View	123
	4.3.8 Create the Depth/Stencil Buffer and View	125
	4.3.9 Set the Viewport	129
	4.3.10 Set the Scissor Rectangles	131
4.4	Timing and Animation	131
	4.4.1 The Performance Timer	132
	4.4.2 Game Timer Class	133
	4.4.3 Time Elapsed Between Frames	134
	4.4.4 Total Time	136
4.5	The Demo Application Framework	139
	4.5.1 D3DApp	139
	4.5.2 Non-Framework Methods	142
	4.5.3 Framework Methods	143
	4.5.4 Frame Statistics	145
	4.5.5 The Message Handler	146
	4.5.6 The "Init Direct3D" Demo	149
4.6	Debugging Direct3D Applications	153
4.7	Summary	155

Chapter 5   The Rendering Pipeline   159

5.1	The 3D Illusion	160
5.2	Model Representation	162
5.3	Basic Computer Color	163
	5.3.1 Color Operations	164
	5.3.2 128-Bit Color	165
	5.3.3 32-Bit Color	165
5.4	Overview of the Rendering Pipeline	167
5.5	The Input Assembler Stage	168
	5.5.1 Vertices	168
	5.5.2 Primitive Topology	169
	5.5.2.1 Point List	170

		5.5.2.2	Line Strip	170
		5.5.2.3	Line List	170
		5.5.2.4	Triangle Strip	170
		5.5.2.5	Triangle List	171
		5.5.2.6	Primitives with Adjacency	171
		5.5.2.7	Control Point Patch List	172
	5.5.3	Indices		172
5.6	The Vertex Shader Stage			175
	5.6.1	Local Space and World Space		175
	5.6.2	View Space		179
	5.6.3	Projection and Homogeneous Clip Space		182
		5.6.3.1	Defining a Frustum	183
		5.6.3.2	Projecting Vertices	184
		5.6.3.3	Normalized Device Coordinates (NDC)	185
		5.6.3.4	Writing the Projection Equations with a Matrix	186
		5.6.3.5	Normalized Depth Value	187
		5.6.3.6	XMMatrixPerspectiveFovLH	189
5.7	The Tessellation Stages			190
5.8	The Geometry Shader Stage			191
5.9	Clipping			191
5.10	The Rasterization Stage			193
	5.10.1 Viewport Transform			193
	5.10.2 Backface Culling			194
	5.10.3 Vertex Attribute Interpolation			195
5.11	The Pixel Shader Stage			196
5.12	The Output Merger Stage			197
5.13	Summary			197
5.14	Exercises			198

Chapter 6 Drawing in Direct3D   203

6.1	Vertices and Input Layouts			203
6.2	Vertex Buffers			207
6.3	Indices and Index Buffers			212
6.4	Example Vertex Shader			216
	6.4.1	Input Layout Description and Input Signature Linking		219
6.5	Example Pixel Shader			222
6.6	Constant Buffers			224
	6.6.1	Creating Constant Buffers		224

	6.6.2	Updating Constant Buffers	227
	6.6.3	Upload Buffer Helper	227
	6.6.4	Constant Buffer Descriptors	230
	6.6.5	Root Signature and Descriptor Tables	232
6.7	Compiling Shaders		235
	6.7.1	Offline Compilation	237
	6.7.2	Generated Assembly	239
	6.7.3	Using Visual Studio to Compile Shaders Offline	241
6.8	Rasterizer State		242
6.9	Pipeline State Object		243
6.10	Geometry Helper Structure		247
6.11	Box Demo		249
6.12	Summary		259
6.13	Exercises		260

Chapter 7 Drawing in Direct 3D Part II — 265

7.1	Frame Resources		266
7.2	Render Items		269
7.3	Pass Constants		270
7.4	Shape Geometry		273
	7.4.1	Generating a Cylinder Mesh	275
		7.4.1.1 Cylinder Side Geometry	275
		7.4.1.2 Cap Geometry	278
	7.4.2	Generating a Sphere Mesh	279
	7.4.3	Generating a Geosphere Mesh	279
7.5	Shapes Demo		281
	7.5.1	Vertex and Index Buffers	282
	7.5.2	Render Items	286
	7.5.3	Frame Resources and Constant Buffer Views	288
	7.5.4	Drawing the Scene	290
7.6	More on Root Signatures		293
	7.6.1	Root Parameters	293
	7.6.2	Descriptor Tables	295
	7.6.3	Root Descriptors	297
	7.6.4	Root Constants	298
	7.6.5	A More Complicated Root Signature Example	299
	7.6.6	Root Parameter Versioning	300
7.7	Land and Waves Demo		301
	7.7.1	Generating the Grid Vertices	302

	7.7.2	Generating the Grid Indices	304
	7.7.3	Applying the Height Function	305
	7.7.4	Root CBVs	307
	7.7.5	Dynamic Vertex Buffers	309
7.8	Summary		311
7.9	Exercises		313

Chapter 8 Lighting   315

8.1	Light and Material Interaction		316
8.2	Normal Vectors		318
	8.2.1	Computing Normal Vectors	319
	8.2.2	Transforming Normal Vectors	321
8.3	Important Vectors in Lighting		323
8.4	Lambert's Cosine Law		323
8.5	Diffuse Lighting		325
8.6	Ambient Lighting		326
8.7	Specular Lighting		327
	8.7.1	Fresnel Effect	328
	8.7.2	Roughness	330
8.8	Lighting Model Recap		333
8.9	Implementing Materials		334
8.10	Parallel Lights		339
8.11	Point Lights		339
	8.11.1	Attenuation	340
8.12	Spotlights		341
8.13	Lighting Implementation		342
	8.13.1	Light Structure	342
	8.13.2	Common Helper Functions	344
	8.13.3	Implementing Directional Lights	346
	8.13.4	Implementing Point Lights	346
	8.13.5	Implementing Spotlights	347
	8.13.6	Accumulating Multiple Lights	348
	8.13.7	The Main HLSL File	349
8.14	Lighting Demo		351
	8.14.1	Vertex Format	352
	8.14.2	Normal Computation	352
	8.14.3	Updating the Light Direction	354
	8.14.4	Update to Root Signature	356
8.15	Summary		356
8.16	Exercises		357

Chapter 9 Texturing — 359

- 9.1 Texture and Resource Recap — 360
- 9.2 Texture Coordinates — 362
- 9.3 Texture Data Sources — 364
    - 9.3.1 DDS Overview — 365
    - 9.3.2 Creating DDS Files — 366
- 9.4 Creating and Enabling a Texture — 367
    - 9.4.1 Loading DDS Files — 367
    - 9.4.2 SRV Heap — 368
    - 9.4.3 Creating SRV Descriptors — 368
    - 9.4.4 Binding Textures to the Pipeline — 370
- 9.5 Filters — 373
    - 9.5.1 Magnification — 373
    - 9.5.2 Minification — 375
    - 9.5.3 Anisotropic Filtering — 376
- 9.6 Address Modes — 376
- 9.7 Sampler Objects — 378
    - 9.7.1 Creating Samplers — 379
    - 9.7.2 Static Samplers — 381
- 9.8 Sampling Textures in a Shader — 384
- 9.9 Crate Demo — 385
    - 9.9.1 Specifying Texture Coordinates — 385
    - 9.9.2 Creating the Texture — 386
    - 9.9.3 Setting the Texture — 386
    - 9.9.4 Updated HLSL — 387
- 9.10 Transforming Textures — 389
- 9.11 Textured Hills and Waves Demo — 390
    - 9.11.1 Grid Texture Coordinate Generation — 391
    - 9.11.2 Texture Tiling — 392
    - 9.11.3 Texture Animation — 393
- 9.12 Summary — 393
- 9.13 Exercises — 394

Chapter 10 Blending — 397

- 10.1 The Blending Equation — 398
- 10.2 Blend Operations — 399
- 10.3 Blend Factors — 400
- 10.4 Blend State — 401
- 10.5 Examples — 404
    - 10.5.1 No Color Write — 404

	10.5.2	Adding/Subtracting	405
	10.5.3	Multiplying	405
	10.5.4	Transparency	406
	10.5.5	Blending and the Depth Buffer	407
10.6	Alpha Channels	408
10.7	Clipping Pixels	408
10.8	Fog	410
10.9	Summary	416
10.10	Exercises	417

Chapter 11 Stenciling 419

11.1	Depth/Stencil Formats and Clearing	420
11.2	The Stencil Test	421
11.3	Describing the Depth/Stencil State	422
	11.3.1	Depth Settings	423
	11.3.2	Stencil Settings	423
	11.3.3	Creating and Binding a Depth/Stencil State	425
11.4	Implementing Planar Mirrors	426
	11.4.1	Mirror Overview	426
	11.4.2	Defining the Mirror Depth/Stencil States	429
	11.4.3	Drawing the Scene	430
	11.4.4	Winding Order and Reflections	431
11.5	Implementing Planar Shadows	432
	11.5.1	Parallel Light Shadows	433
	11.5.2	Point Light Shadows	434
	11.5.3	General Shadow Matrix	435
	11.5.4	Using the Stencil Buffer to Prevent Double Blending	436
	11.5.5	Shadow Code	437
11.6	Summary	438
11.7	Exercises	439

Chapter 12 The Geometry Shader 445

12.1	Programming Geometry Shaders	446
12.2	Tree Billboards Demo	451
	12.2.1	Overview	451
	12.2.2	Vertex Structure	453
	12.2.3	The HLSL File	454
	12.2.4	SV_PrimitiveID	458
12.3	Texture Arrays	459
	12.3.1	Overview	459

	12.3.2 Sampling a Texture Array	460
	12.3.3 Loading Texture Arrays	461
	12.3.4 Texture Subresources	462
12.4	Alpha-to-Coverage	463
12.5	Summary	464
12.6	Exercises	465

Chapter 13 The Compute Shader   469

13.1	Threads and Thread Groups	471
13.2	A Simple Compute Shader	472
	13.2.1 Compute PSO	473
13.3	Data Input and Output Resources	474
	13.3.1 Texture Inputs	474
	13.3.2 Texture Outputs and Unordered Access Views (UAVs)	474
	13.3.3 Indexing and Sampling Textures	477
	13.3.4 Structured Buffer Resources	479
	13.3.5 Copying CS Results to System Memory	482
13.4	Thread Identification System Values	485
13.5	Append and Consume Buffers	486
13.6	Shared Memory and Synchronization	487
13.7	Blur Demo	489
	13.7.1 Blurring Theory	489
	13.7.2 Render-to-Texture	493
	13.7.3 Blur Implementation Overview	495
	13.7.4 Compute Shader Program	501
13.8	Further Resources	505
13.9	Summary	506
13.10	Exercises	508

Chapter 14 The Tessellation Stages   513

14.1	Tessellation Primitive Types	514
	14.1.1 Tessellation and the Vertex Shader	515
14.2	The Hull Shader	516
	14.2.1 Constant Hull Shader	516
	14.2.2 Control Point Hull Shader	518
14.3	The Tessellation Stage	520
	14.3.1 Quad Patch Tessellation Examples	520
	14.3.2 Triangle Patch Tessellation Examples	521
14.4	The Domain Shader	521
14.5	Tessellating a Quad	522

14.6	Cubic Bézier Quad Patches		526
	14.6.1 Bézier Curves		527
	14.6.2 Cubic Bézier Surfaces		529
	14.6.3 Cubic Bézier Surface Evaluation Code		530
	14.6.4 Defining the Patch Geometry		532
14.7	Summary		534
14.8	Exercises		536

PART III   TOPICS

Chapter 15   Building a First Person Camera and Dynamic Indexing   539

15.1	View Transform Review	540
15.2	The Camera Class	541
15.3	Selected Method Implementations	543
	15.3.1 XMVECTOR Return Variations	543
	15.3.2 SetLens	543
	15.3.3 Derived Frustum Info	544
	15.3.4 Transforming the Camera	544
	15.3.5 Building the View Matrix	546
15.4	Camera Demo Comments	547
15.5	Dynamic Indexing	548
15.6	Summary	555
15.7	Exercises	556

Chapter 16   Instancing and Frustum Culling   557

16.1	Hardware Instancing	557
	16.1.1 Drawing Instanced Data	558
	16.1.2 Instance Data	559
	16.1.3 Creating the Instanced Buffer	564
16.2	Bounding Volumes and Frustums	566
	16.2.1 DirectX Math Collision	566
	16.2.2 Boxes	566
	16.2.2.1 Rotations and Axis-Aligned Bounding Boxes	568
	16.2.3 Spheres	570
	16.2.4 Frustums	571
	16.2.4.1 Constructing the Frustum Planes	571
	16.2.4.2 Frustum/Sphere Intersection	574
	16.2.4.3 Frustum/AABB Intersection	575

16.3	Frustum Culling	576
16.4	Summary	579
16.5	Exercises	580

Chapter 17 Picking   583

17.1	Screen to Projection Window Transform	585
17.2	World/Local Space Picking Ray	588
17.3	Ray/Mesh Intersection	589
	17.3.1 Ray/AABB Intersection	591
	17.3.2 Ray/Sphere Intersection	591
	17.3.3 Ray/Triangle Intersection	592
17.4	Demo Application	594
17.5	Summary	596
17.6	Exercises	596

Chapter 18 Cube Mapping   597

18.1	Cube Mapping	597
18.2	Environment Maps	599
	18.2.1 Loading and Using Cube Maps in Direct3D	601
18.3	Texturing a Sky	602
18.4	Modeling Reflections	606
18.5	Dynamic Cube Maps	609
	18.5.1 Dynamic Cube Map Helper Class	610
	18.5.2 Building the Cube Map Resource	611
	18.5.3 Extra Descriptor Heap Space	612
	18.5.4 Building the Descriptors	613
	18.5.5 Building the Depth Buffer	614
	18.5.6 Cube Map Viewport and Scissor Rectangle	615
	18.5.7 Setting up the Cube Map Camera	615
	18.5.8 Drawing into the Cube Map	617
18.6	Dynamic Cube Maps with the Geometry Shader	620
18.7	Summary	623
18.8	Exercises	624

Chapter 19 Normal Mapping   627

19.1	Motivation	628
19.2	Normal Maps	629
19.3	Texture/Tangent Space	631
19.4	Vertex Tangent Space	633

19.5	Transforming Between Tangent Space and Object Space	633
19.6	Normal Mapping Shader Code	635
19.7	Summary	639
19.8	Exercises	640

Chapter 20 Shadow Mapping — 643

20.1	Rendering Scene Depth	644
20.2	Orthographic Projections	646
20.3	Projective Texture Coordinates	649
	20.3.1 Code Implementation	651
	20.3.2 Points Outside the Frustum	651
	20.3.3 Orthographic Projections	652
20.4	Shadow Mapping	653
	20.4.1 Algorithm Description	653
	20.4.2 Biasing and Aliasing	654
	20.4.3 PCF Filtering	657
	20.4.4 Building the Shadow Map	660
	20.4.5 The Shadow Factor	665
	20.4.6 The Shadow Map Test	667
	20.4.7 Rendering the Shadow Map	667
20.5	Large PCF Kernels	668
	20.5.1 The DDX and DDY Functions	669
	20.5.2 Solution to the Large PCF Kernel Problem	669
	20.5.3 An Alternative Solution to the Large PCF Kernel Problem	671
20.6	Summary	673
20.7	Exercises	674

Chapter 21 Ambient Occlusion — 675

21.1	Ambient Occlusion via Ray Casting	676
21.2	Screen Space Ambient Occlusion	680
	21.2.1 Render Normals and Depth Pass	680
	21.2.2 Ambient Occlusion Pass	681
	21.2.2.1 Reconstruct View Space Position	682
	21.2.2.2 Generate Random Samples	683
	21.2.2.3 Generate the Potential Occluding Points	685
	21.2.2.4 Perform the Occlusion Test	685
	21.2.2.5 Finishing the Calculation	686
	21.2.2.6 Implementation	686

	21.2.3	Blur Pass	690
	21.2.4	Using the Ambient Occlusion Map	694
21.3	Summary		695
21.4	Exercises		695

Chapter 22   Quaternions   697

22.1	Review of the Complex Numbers		698
	22.1.1	Definitions	698
	22.1.2	Geometric Interpretation	699
	22.1.3	Polar Representation and Rotations	700
22.2	Quaternion Algebra		701
	22.2.1	Definition and Basic Operations	701
	22.2.2	Special Products	702
	22.2.3	Properties	703
	22.2.4	Conversions	703
	22.2.5	Conjugate and Norm	704
	22.2.6	Inverses	705
	22.2.7	Polar Representation	706
22.3	Unit Quaternions and Rotations		707
	22.3.1	Rotation Operator	707
	22.3.2	Quaternion Rotation Operator to Matrix	709
	22.3.3	Matrix to Quaternion Rotation Operator	710
	22.3.4	Composition	712
22.4	Quaternion Interpolation		713
22.5	DirectX Math Quaternion Functions		718
22.6	Rotation Demo		719
22.7	Summary		723
22.8	Exercises		724

Chapter 23   Character Animation   727

23.1	Frame Hierarchies		728
	23.1.1	Mathematical Formulation	729
23.2	Skinned Meshes		731
	23.2.1	Definitions	731
	23.2.2	Reformulating the Bones To-Root Transform	732
	23.2.3	The Offset Transform	732
	23.2.4	Animating the Skeleton	733
	23.2.5	Calculating the Final Transform	735
23.3	Vertex Blending		737

23.4		Loading Animation Data from File	740
	23.4.1	Header	740
	23.4.2	Materials	741
	23.4.3	Subsets	741
	23.4.4	Vertex Data and Triangles	742
	23.4.5	Bone Offset Transforms	743
	23.4.6	Hierarchy	743
	23.4.7	Animation Data	743
	23.4.8	M3DLoader	746
23.5		Character Animation Demo	747
23.6		Summary	750
23.7		Exercises	751

Appendix A: Introduction to Windows Programming 753

A.1		Overview	754
	A.1.1	Resources	754
	A.1.2	Events, the Message Queue, Messages, and the Message Loop	754
	A.1.3	GUI	755
	A.1.4	Unicode	757
A.2		Basic Windows Application	757
A.3		Explaining the Basic Windows Application	761
	A.3.1	Includes, Global Variables, and Prototypes	761
	A.3.2	WinMain	762
	A.3.3	WNDCLASS and Registration	763
	A.3.4	Creating and Displaying the Window	765
	A.3.5	The Message Loop	767
	A.3.6	The Window Procedure	768
	A.3.7	The MessageBox Function	770
A.4		A Better Message Loop	770
A.5		Summary	771
A.6		Exercises	772

Appendix B: High Level Shader Language Reference 773

Variable Types	
Scalar Types	773
Vector Types	773
Swizzles	774
Matrix Types	775
Arrays	776

Variable Types — 773

		Structures	776
		The `typedef` Keyword	777
		Variable Prefixes	777
		Casting	777
	Keywords and Operators		778
		Keywords	778
		Operators	778
	Program Flow		780
	Functions		781
		User Defined Functions	781
		Built-in Functions	782
		Constant Buffer Packing	785

Appendix C: Some Analytic Geometry — 789

C.1	Rays, Lines, and Segments		789
C.2	Parallelograms		790
C.3	Triangles		791
C.4	Planes		792
	C.4.1	DirectX Math Planes	793
	C.4.2	Point/Plane Spatial Relation	793
	C.4.3	Construction	794
	C.4.4	Normalizing a Plane	795
	C.4.5	Transforming a Plane	795
	C.4.6	Nearest Point on a Plane to a Given Point	795
	C.4.7	Ray/Plane Intersection	796
	C.4.8	Reflecting Vectors	797
	C.4.9	Reflecting Points	797
	C.4.10	Reflection Matrix	797
C.5	Exercises		799

Appendix D: Solutions to Selected Exercises — 801

Appendix E: Bibliography and Further Reading — 803

Index — 809

Acknowledgments

I would like to thank Rod Lopez, Jim Leiterman, Hanley Leung, Rick Falck, Tybon Wu, Tuomas Sandroos, Eric Sandegren, Jay Tennant and William Goschnick for reviewing earlier editions of the book. I want to thank Tyler Drinkard for building some of the 3D models and textures used in some of the demo programs available on the book's website. I also want to thank Dale E. La Force, Adam Hoult, Gary Simmons, James Lambers, and William Chin for their assistance in the past. In addition, I want to thank Matt Sandy for getting me on the DirectX 12 beta, and the rest of the DirectX team that helped answer questions for beta users. Finally, I want to thank the staff at Mercury Learning and Information, in particular, David Pallai, the publisher, and Jennifer Blaney, who guided the book through production.

INTRODUCTION

Direct3D 12 is a rendering library for writing high-performance 3D graphics applications using modern graphics hardware on various Windows 10 platforms (Windows Desktop, Mobile, and Xbox One). Direct3D is a low-level library in the sense that its application programming interface (API) closely models the underlying graphics hardware it controls. The predominant consumer of Direct3D is the games industry, where higher level rendering engines are built on top of Direct3D. However, other industries need high performance interactive 3D graphics as well, such as medical and scientific visualization and architectural walkthrough. In addition, with every new PC being equipped with a modern graphics card, non-3D applications are beginning to take advantage of the GPU (graphics processing unit) to offload work to the graphics card for intensive calculations; this is known as *general purpose GPU computing*, and Direct3D provides the compute shader API for writing general purpose GPU programs. Although Direct3D 12 is usually programmed from native C++, the SharpDX team (http://sharpdx.org/) is working on .NET wrappers so that you can access this powerful 3D graphics API from managed applications.

    This book presents an introduction to programming interactive computer graphics, with an emphasis on game development, using Direct3D 12. It teaches the fundamentals of Direct3D and shader programming, after which the reader will be prepared to go on and learn more advanced techniques. The book is divided into three main parts. Part I explains the mathematical tools that will be used throughout this book. Part II shows how to implement fundamental tasks in Direct3D, such as initialization; defining 3D geometry; setting up cameras; creating vertex, pixel, geometry, and compute shaders; lighting; texturing; blending; stenciling; and tessellation. Part III is largely about applying Direct3D to implement a variety of interesting techniques and special effects, such as working with animated character meshes, picking, environment mapping, normal mapping, real-time shadows, and ambient occlusion.

For the beginner, this book is best read front to back. The chapters have been organized so that the difficulty increases progressively with each chapter. In this way, there are no sudden jumps in complexity leaving the reader lost. In general, for a particular chapter, we will use the techniques and concepts previously developed. Therefore, it is important that you have mastered the material of a chapter before continuing. Experienced readers can pick the chapters of interest.

Finally, you may be wondering what kinds of games you can develop after reading this book. The answer to that question is best obtained by skimming through this book and seeing the types of applications that are developed. From that you should be able to visualize the types of games that can be developed based on the techniques taught in this book and some of your own ingenuity.

INTENDED AUDIENCE

This book was designed with the following three audiences in mind:

1. Intermediate level C++ programmers who would like an introduction to 3D programming using the latest iteration of Direct3D.
2. 3D programmers experienced with an API other than DirectX (e.g., OpenGL) who would like an introduction to Direct3D 12
3. Experienced Direct3D programmers wishing to learn the latest version of Direct3D.

PREREQUISITES

It should be emphasized that this is an introduction to Direct3D 12, shader programming, and 3D game programming; it is *not* an introduction to general computer programming. The reader should satisfy the following prerequisites:

1. High School mathematics: algebra, trigonometry, and (mathematical) functions, for example.
2. Competence with Visual Studio: should know how to create projects, add files, and specify external libraries to link, for example.

3. Intermediate C++ and data structure skills: comfortable with pointers, arrays, operator overloading, linked lists, inheritance and polymorphism, for example.
4. Familiarity with Windows programming with the Win32 API is helpful, but not required; we provide a Win32 primer in Appendix A.

REQUIRED DEVELOPMENT TOOLS AND HARDWARE

The following are needed to program Direct3D 12 applications:

1. Windows 10.
2. Visual Studio 2015 or later.
3. A graphics card that supports Direct3D 12. The demos in this book were tested on a Geforce GTX 760.

USING THE DIRECTX SDK DOCUMENTATION AND SDK SAMPLES

Direct3D is a huge API and we cannot hope to cover all of its details in this one book. Therefore, to obtain extended information it is imperative that you learn how to use the DirectX SDK documentation. The most up to date documentation will be available on MSDN:

https://msdn.microsoft.com/en-us/library/windows/desktop/ dn899121%28v=vs.85%29.aspx

Figure 1 shows a screenshot of the online documentation.

The DirectX documentation covers just about every part of the DirectX API; therefore it is very useful as a reference, but because the documentation doesn't go into much depth or assumes some previous knowledge, it isn't the best learning tool. However, it does get better and better with every new DirectX version released.

As said, the documentation is primarily useful as a reference. Suppose you come across a DirectX related type or function, say the function `ID3D12Device::CreateCommittedResource`, which you would like more information on. You simply do a search in the documentation and get a description of the object type, or in this case function; see Figure 2.

In this book we may direct you to the documentation for further details from time to time.

Figure 1. Direct3D Programming Guide in the DirectX documentation.

Figure 2. Getting documentation of a function.

We would also like to point out the available Direct3D 12 sample programs that are available online:

https://github.com/Microsoft/DirectX-Graphics-Samples

More samples should come in the future, and also be on the lookout for Direct3D 12 samples on NVIDIA's, AMD's, and Intel's websites.

CLARITY

Although we strive to write efficient code and follow best Direct3D 12 programming practices, the main goal of each sample program is to demonstrate Direct3D concepts or graphics programming techniques. Writing the most optimal code was not the goal, and would likely obfuscate the ideas trying to be illustrated. Keep this in mind if you are using any of the sample code in your own projects, as you may wish to rework it for better efficiency. Moreover, in order to focus on the Direct3D API, we have built minimal infrastructure on top of Direct3D. This means we hardcode values and define things in the source code that might normally be data driven. In a large 3D application, you will likely implement a rendering engine on top of Direct3D; however, the topic of this book is the Direct3D API, not rendering engine design.

SAMPLE PROGRAMS AND ONLINE SUPPLEMENTS

The website for this book (*www.d3dcoder.net* and *www.merclearning.com*) plays an integral part in getting the most out of this book. On the website you will find the complete source code and project files for every samples in this book. In many cases, DirectX programs are too large to fully embed in a textbook; therefore, we only embed relevant code fragments based on the ideas being shown. It is highly recommended that the reader study the corresponding demo code to see the program in its entirety. (We have aimed to make the demos small and focused for easy study.) As a general rule, the reader should be able to implement a chapter's demo(s) on his or her own after reading the chapter and spending some time studying the demo code. In fact, a good exercise is trying to implement the samples on your own using the book and sample code as a reference.

DEMO PROJECT SETUP IN VISUAL STUDIO 2010

The demos for this book can be opened simply by double clicking the corresponding project file (.vcxproj) or solution file (.sln). This section describes how to create and build a project from scratch using the book's demo application framework using Visual Studio 2015 (VS15). As a working example, we will show how to recreate and build the "Box" demo of Chapter 6.

Download the Book's Source Code

First, download the book's source code to some folder on your hard drive. For the sake of discussion, we will assume this folder is *C:\d3d12book*. In the source code folder, you will see a list of folders for each chapter. Each folder contains the code projects for the given chapter. Note also a folder called *Common*; this folder contains shared source code that is reused in all of the demo projects. Now, in the source code folder, create a new folder where you want to store your demos. For example, *C:\d3d12book\MyDemos*. This folder is where you will create new projects based on the book's sample framework.

This directory structure is not completely necessary, but it is the structure the book demos follow. If you are comfortable with setting additional include paths, you can put your demo projects anywhere so long as you direct Visual Studio how to find the source code in the Common directory.

Create a Win32 Project

First launch VS15, then go to the main menu and select **File->New->Project,** as shown in Figure 3.

The New Project dialog box will appear (Figure 4). Select **Visual C++ > Win32** from the Visual C++ Project Types tree control on the left. On the right, select **Win32 Project.** Next, give the project a name and specify the location you wish to store the project folder. Also uncheck **Create directory for solution,** if it is initially checked by default. Now hit **OK**.

A new dialog box will appear. On the left, there are two options: Overview and Application Settings. Select **Application Settings,** which produces the dialog box shown in Figure 5. From here, be sure that **Windows application** is chosen, and the **Empty project** box is checked. Now press the **Finish** button. At this point, you have successfully created an empty Win32 project, but there are still some things to do before you can build a DirectX project demo.

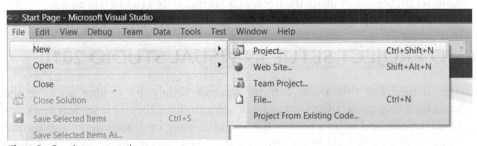
Figure 3. Creating a new project.

INTRODUCTION xxxi

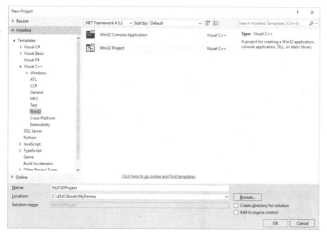

Figure 4. New Project settings.

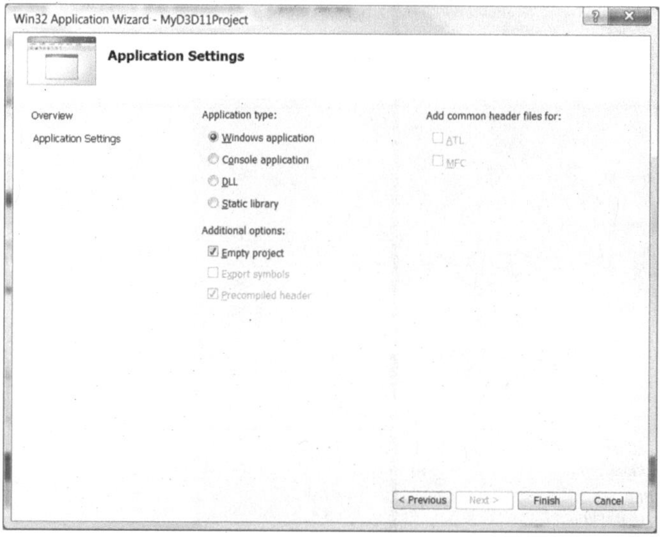

Figure 5. Application settings.

Linking the DirectX Libraries

We link the necessary library files through the source code using `#pragma`s in *Common/d3dApp.h* like so:

```
// Link necessary d3d12 libraries.
#pragma comment(lib,"d3dcompiler.lib")
#pragma comment(lib, "D3D12.lib")
#pragma comment(lib, "dxgi.lib")
```

For making demo applications, this saves us from the additional step of opening the project property pages and specifying additional dependencies under the Linker settings.

Adding the Source Code and Building the Project

Finally, our project setup is complete. We can now add our source code files to the project and build it. First, copy the "Box" demo source code (*d3d12book\Chapter 6 Drawing in Direct3D\Box*) *BoxApp.cpp* and the *Shaders* folder to your project's directory.

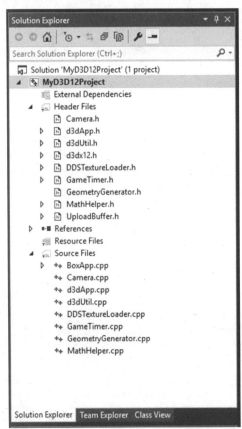

Figure 6. Solution Explorer after adding the required source code files for the "Box" demo.

After you copy the files, follow these steps to add the code to your project.

1. Right click on the project name under the Solution Explorer and select **Add > Existing Item…** from the dropdown menu, and add *BoxApp.cpp* to the project.

2. Right click on the project name under the Solution Explorer and select **Add > Existing Item…** from the dropdown menu, navigate to where you placed the book's *Common* directory code, and add all the *.h/.cpp* files from that directory to the project. Your solution explorer should look like Figure 6.

3. Right click on the project name under the Solution Explorer and select **Properties** from the context menu. Under **Configuration Properties > General** tab, make sure the **Target Platform Version** is set to version **10.x** to target Windows 10. Then click **Apply**.

4. The source code files are now part of the project, and you can now go to the main menu, and select **Debug->Start Debugging** to compile, link, and execute the demo. The application in Figure 7 should appear.

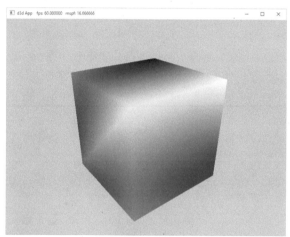

Figure 7. Screenshot of the "Box" demo.

A lot of the code in the Common directory is built up over the course of the book. So we recommend that you do not start looking through the code. Instead, wait until you are reading the chapter in the book where that code is covered.

Part 1 MATHEMATICAL PREREQUISITES

"For the things of this world cannot be made known without a knowledge of mathematics."

Roger Bacon, Opus Majus part 4 Distinctia Prima cap 1, 1267.

Video games attempt to simulate a virtual world. However, computers, by their very nature, crunch numbers. Thus the problem of how to convey a world to a computer arises. The answer is to describe our worlds, and the interactions therein, completely mathematically. Consequently, mathematics plays a fundamental role in video game development.

In this prerequisites part, we introduce the mathematical tools that will be used throughout this book. The emphasis is on vectors, coordinate systems, matrices, and transformations, as these tools are used in just about every sample program of this book. In addition to the mathematical explanations, a survey and demonstration of the relevant classes and functions from the DirectX Math library are provided.

Note that the topics covered here are only those essential to understanding the rest of this book; it is by no means a comprehensive treatment of video game mathematics, as entire books are devoted to this topic. For readers desiring a more complete reference to video game mathematics, we recommend [Verth04] and [Lengyel02].

Chapter 1, Vector Algebra: Vectors are, perhaps, the most fundamental mathematical objects used in computer games. We use vectors to represent positions, displacements, directions, velocities, and forces, for example. In this chapter, we study vectors and the operations used to manipulate them.

Chapter 2, Matrix Algebra: Matrices provide an efficient and compact way of representing transformations. In this chapter, we become familiar with matrices and the operations defined on them.

Chapter 3, Transformations: This chapter examines three fundamental geometric transformations: scaling, rotation, and translation. We use these transformations to manipulate 3D objects in space. In addition, we explain change of coordinate transformations, which are used to transform coordinates representing geometry from one coordinate system into another.

Chapter 1: Vector Algebra

Vectors play a crucial role in computer graphics, collision detection, and physical simulation, all of which are common components in modern video games. Our approach here is informal and practical; for a book dedicated to 3D game/graphics math, we recommend [Verth04]. We emphasize the importance of vectors by noting that they are used in just about every demo program in this book.

Objectives:

1. To learn how vectors are represented geometrically and numerically.
2. To discover the operations defined on vectors and their geometric applications.
3. To become familiar with the vector functions and classes of the DirectXMath library.

1.1 VECTORS

A *vector* refers to a quantity that possesses both magnitude and direction. Quantities that possess both magnitude and direction are called *vector-valued quantities*. Examples of vector-valued quantities are forces (a force is applied in a particular direction with a certain strength—magnitude), displacements (the net direction and distance a particle moved), and velocities (speed and direction). Thus, vectors are used to represent forces, displacements, and velocities. In addition, we also use vectors to specify pure directions, such as the direction the player is looking in a 3D game, the direction a polygon is facing, the direction in which a ray of light travels, or the direction in which a ray of light reflects off a surface.

A first step in characterizing a vector mathematically is geometrically: We graphically specify a vector by a directed line segment (see Figure 1.1), where the length denotes the magnitude of the vector and the aim denotes the direction of the vector. We note that the location in which we draw a vector is immaterial because changing the location does not change the magnitude or direction (the two properties a vector possesses). Therefore, we say two vectors are equal if and only if they have the same length and they point in the same direction. Thus, the vectors **u** and **v** drawn in Figure 1.1a are actually equal because they have the same length and point in the same direction. In fact, because location is unimportant for vectors, we can always translate a vector without changing its meaning (since a translation changes neither length nor direction). Observe that we could translate **u** such that it completely overlaps with **v** (and conversely), thereby making them indistinguishable—hence their equality. As a physical example, the vectors **u** and **v** in Figure 1.1b both tell the ants at two different points A and B to move north ten

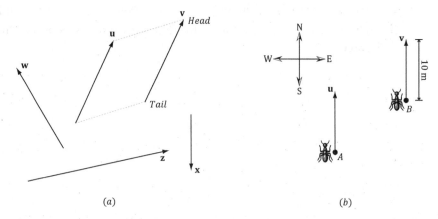

Figure 1.1. (a) Vectors drawn on a 2D plane. (b) Vectors instructing ants to move 10 meters north.

meters from where they are. Again we have that **u** = **v**. The vectors themselves are independent of position; they simply instruct the ants how to move from where they are. In this example, they tell the ants to move north (direction) ten meters (length).

1.1.1 Vectors and Coordinate Systems

We could now define useful geometric operations on vectors, which can then be used to solve problems involving vector-valued quantities. However, since the computer cannot work with vectors geometrically, we need to find a way of specifying vectors numerically instead. So what we do is introduce a 3D coordinate system in space, and translate all the vectors so that their tails coincide with the origin (Figure 1.2). Then we can identify a vector by specifying the coordinates of its head, and write **v** = (x, y, z) as shown in Figure 1.3. Now we can represent a vector with three `float`s in a computer program.

If working in 2D, then we just use a 2D coordinate system and the vector only has two coordinates: **v** = (x, y) *and we can represent a vector with two* `float`s *in a computer program.*

Consider Figure 1.4, which shows a vector **v** and two frames in space. (Note that we use the terms *frame*, *frame of reference*, *space*, and *coordinate system* to all mean the same thing in this book.) We can translate **v** so that it is in standard position in either of the two frames. Observe, however, that the coordinates of the vector **v** relative to frame *A* are different than the coordinates of the vector **v** relative to frame *B*. In other words, the *same* vector **v** has a different coordinate representation for distinct frames.

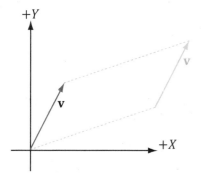

Figure 1.2. We translate **v** so that its tail coincides with the origin of the coordinate system. When a vector's tail coincides with the origin, we say that it is in *standard position*.

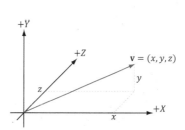

Figure 1.3. A vector specified by coordinates relative to a coordinate system.

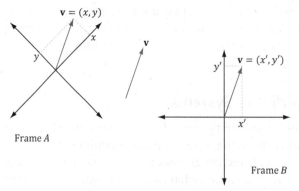

Figure 1.4. The same vector **v** has different coordinates when described relative to different frames.

The idea is analogous to, say, temperature. Water boils at 100° Celsius or 212° Fahrenheit. The physical temperature of boiling water is the *same* no matter the scale (i.e., we can't lower the boiling point by picking a different scale), but we assign a different scalar number to the temperature based on the scale we use. Similarly, for a vector, its direction and magnitude, which are embedded in the directed line segment, does not change; only the coordinates of it change based on the frame of reference we use to describe it. This is important because it means whenever we identify a vector by coordinates, those coordinates are relative to some frame of reference. Often in 3D computer graphics, we will utilize more than one frame of reference and, therefore, we will need to keep track of which frame a vector's coordinates are relative to; additionally, we will need to know how to convert vector coordinates from one frame to another.

 We see that both vectors and points can be described by coordinates (x, y, z) relative to a frame. However, they are not the same; a point represents a location in 3-space, whereas a vector represents a magnitude and direction. We will have more to say about points in §1.5.

1.1.2 Left-Handed Versus Right-Handed Coordinate Systems

Direct3D uses a so-called left-handed coordinate system. If you take your left hand and aim your fingers down the positive x-axis, and then curl your fingers towards the positive y-axis, your thumb points roughly in the direction of the positive z-axis. Figure 1.5 illustrates the differences between a left-handed and right-handed coordinate system.

Observe that for the right-handed coordinate system, if you take your right hand and aim your fingers down the positive x-axis, and then curl your fingers towards the positive y-axis, your thumb points roughly in the direction of the positive z-axis.

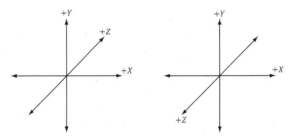

Figure 1.5. On the left we have a left-handed coordinate system. Observe that the positive z-axis goes into the page. On the right we have a right-handed coordinate system. Observe that the positive z-axis comes out of the page.

1.1.3 Basic Vector Operations

We now define equality, addition, scalar multiplication, and subtraction on vectors using the coordinate representation. For these four definitions, let $\mathbf{u} = (u_x, u_y, u_z)$ and $\mathbf{v} = (v_x, v_y, v_z)$.

1. Two vectors are equal if and only if their corresponding components are equal. That is, $\mathbf{u} = \mathbf{v}$ if and only if $u_x = v_x, u_y = v_y,$ and $u_z = v_z$.
2. We add vectors component-wise: $\mathbf{u} + \mathbf{v} = (u_x + v_x, u_y + v_y, u_z + v_z)$. Observe that it only makes sense to add vectors of the same dimension.
3. We can multiply a scalar (i.e., a real number) and a vector and the result is a vector. Let k be a scalar, then $k\mathbf{u} = (ku_x, ku_y, ku_z)$. This is called *scalar multiplication*.
4. We define subtraction in terms of vector addition and scalar multiplication. That is, $\mathbf{u} - \mathbf{v} = \mathbf{u} + (-1 \cdot \mathbf{v}) = \mathbf{u} + (-\mathbf{v}) = (u_x - v_x, u_y - v_y, u_z - v_z)$.

☞ Example 1.1

Let $\mathbf{u} = (1, 2, 3), \mathbf{v} = (1, 2, 3), \mathbf{w} = (3, 0, -2),$ and $k = 2$. Then,

1. $\mathbf{u} + \mathbf{w} = (1, 2, 3) + (3, 0, -2) = (4, 2, 1)$;
2. $\mathbf{u} = \mathbf{v}$;
3. $\mathbf{u} - \mathbf{v} = \mathbf{u} + (-\mathbf{v}) = (1, 2, 3) + (-1, -2, -3) = (0, 0, 0) = \mathbf{0}$;
4. $k\mathbf{w} = 2(3, 0, -2) = (6, 0, -4)$

The difference in the third bullet illustrates a special vector, called the *zero-vector*, which has zeros for all of its components and is denoted by $\mathbf{0}$.

☞ Example 1.2

We will illustrate this example with 2D vectors to make the drawings simpler. The ideas are the same as in 3D; we just work with one less component in 2D.

1. Let $\mathbf{v} = (2, 1)$ How do $\mathbf{v}$ and $-\frac{1}{2}\mathbf{v}$ compare geometrically? We note that $-\frac{1}{2}\mathbf{v} = \left(-1, -\frac{1}{2}\right)$. Graphing both $\mathbf{v}$ and $-\frac{1}{2}\mathbf{v}$ (Figure 1.6a), we notice that $-\frac{1}{2}\mathbf{v}$ is in the direction directly opposite of $\mathbf{v}$ and its length is 1/2 that of $\mathbf{v}$. Thus, geometrically, negating a vector can be thought of as "flipping" its direction, and scalar multiplication can be thought of as scaling the length of a vector.

2. Let $\mathbf{u} = \left(2, \frac{1}{2}\right)$ and $\mathbf{v} = (1, 2)$. Then $\mathbf{u} + \mathbf{v} = \left(3, \frac{5}{2}\right)$. Figure 1.6b shows what vector addition means geometrically: We parallel translate $\mathbf{u}$ so that its *tail* coincided with the *head* of $\mathbf{v}$. Then, the sum is the vector originating at the tail of $\mathbf{v}$ and ending at the head of the translated $\mathbf{u}$. (We get the same result if we keep $\mathbf{u}$ fixed and translate $\mathbf{v}$ so that its tail coincided with the head of $\mathbf{u}$. In this case, $\mathbf{u} + \mathbf{v}$ would be the vector originating at the tail of $\mathbf{u}$ and ending at the head of the translated $\mathbf{v}$.) Observe also that our rules of vector addition agree with what we would intuitively expect to happen physically when we add forces together to produce a net force: If we add two forces (vectors) in the same direction, we get another stronger net force (longer vector) in that direction. If we add two forces (vectors) in opposition to each other, then we get a weaker net force (shorter vector). Figure 1.7 illustrates these ideas.

3. Let $\mathbf{u} = \left(2, \frac{1}{2}\right)$ and $\mathbf{v} = (1, 2)$. Then $\mathbf{v} - \mathbf{u} = \left(-1, \frac{3}{2}\right)$. Figure 1.6c shows what vector subtraction means geometrically. Essentially, the difference $\mathbf{v} - \mathbf{u}$ gives us a vector aimed from the head of $\mathbf{u}$ to the head of $\mathbf{v}$. If we instead interpret $\mathbf{u}$ and $\mathbf{v}$ as points, then $\mathbf{v} - \mathbf{u}$ gives us a vector aimed from the point $\mathbf{u}$ to the point $\mathbf{v}$; this interpretation is important as we will often want the vector

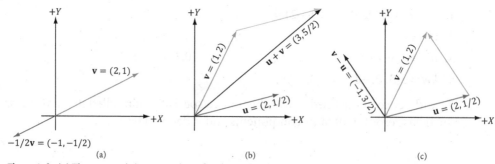

Figure 1.6. (a) The geometric interpretation of scalar multiplication. (b) The geometric interpretation of vector addition. (c) The geometric interpretation of vector subtraction.

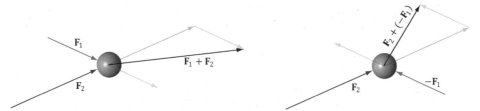

Figure 1.7. Forces applied to a ball. The forces are combined using vector addition to get a net force.

aimed from one point to another. Observe also that the length of **v** − **u** is the distance from **u** to **v**, when thinking of **u** and **v** as points.

1.2 LENGTH AND UNIT VECTORS

Geometrically, the magnitude of a vector is the length of the directed line segment. We denote the magnitude of a vector by double vertical bars (e.g., ||**u**|| denotes the magnitude of **u**). Now, given a vector **u** = (x, y, z), we wish to compute its magnitude algebraically. The magnitude of a 3D vector can be computed by applying the Pythagorean theorem twice; see Figure 1.8.

First, we look at the triangle in the xz-plane with sides x, z, and hypotenuse a. From the Pythagorean theorem, we have $a = \sqrt{x^2 + z^2}$. Now look at the triangle with sides a, y, and hypotenuse ||**u**||. From the Pythagorean theorem again, we arrive at the following magnitude formula:

$$\|\mathbf{u}\| = \sqrt{y^2 + a^2} = \sqrt{y^2 + \left(\sqrt{x^2 + z^2}\right)^2} = \sqrt{x^2 + y^2 + z^2} \quad \text{(eq. 1.1)}$$

For some applications, we do not care about the length of a vector because we want to use the vector to represent a pure direction. For such direction-only

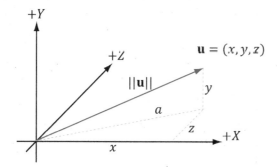

Figure 1.8. The 3D length of a vector can be computed by applying the Pythagorean theorem twice.

vectors, we want the length of the vector to be exactly 1. When we make a vector unit length, we say that we are *normalizing* the vector. We can normalize a vector by dividing each of its components by its magnitude:

$$\hat{\mathbf{u}} = \frac{\mathbf{u}}{\|\mathbf{u}\|} = \left(\frac{x}{\|\mathbf{u}\|}, \frac{y}{\|\mathbf{u}\|}, \frac{z}{\|\mathbf{u}\|}\right) \qquad \text{(eq. 1.2)}$$

To verify that this formula is correct, we can compute the length of $\hat{\mathbf{u}}$:

$$\|\hat{\mathbf{u}}\| = \sqrt{\left(\frac{x}{\|\mathbf{u}\|}\right)^2 + \left(\frac{y}{\|\mathbf{u}\|}\right)^2 + \left(\frac{z}{\|\mathbf{u}\|}\right)^2} = \frac{\sqrt{x^2 + y^2 + z^2}}{\sqrt{\|\mathbf{u}\|^2}} = \frac{\|\mathbf{u}\|}{\|\mathbf{u}\|} = 1$$

So $\hat{\mathbf{u}}$ is indeed a unit vector.

☞ Example 1.3

Normalize the vector $\mathbf{v} = (-1, 3, 4)$. We have $\|\mathbf{v}\| = \sqrt{(-1)^2 + 3^2 + 4^2} = \sqrt{26}$. Thus,

$$\hat{\mathbf{v}} = \frac{\mathbf{v}}{\|\mathbf{v}\|} = \left(-\frac{1}{\sqrt{26}}, \frac{3}{\sqrt{26}}, \frac{4}{\sqrt{26}}\right).$$

To verify that $\hat{\mathbf{v}}$ is indeed a unit vector, we compute its length:

$$\|\hat{\mathbf{v}}\| = \sqrt{\left(-\frac{1}{\sqrt{26}}\right)^2 + \left(\frac{3}{\sqrt{26}}\right)^2 + \left(\frac{4}{\sqrt{26}}\right)^2} = \sqrt{\frac{1}{26} + \frac{9}{26} + \frac{16}{26}} = \sqrt{1} = 1.$$

1.3 THE DOT PRODUCT

The *dot product* is a form of vector multiplication that results in a scalar value; for this reason, it is sometimes referred to as the *scalar product*. Let $\mathbf{u} = (u_x, u_y, u_z)$ and $\mathbf{v} = (v_x, v_y, v_z)$, then the dot product is defined as follows:

$$\mathbf{u} \cdot \mathbf{v} = u_x v_x + u_y v_y + u_z v_z \qquad \text{(eq. 1.3)}$$

In words, the dot product is the sum of the products of the corresponding components.

The dot product definition does not present an obvious geometric meaning. Using the law of cosines (see Exercise 10), we can find the relationship,

$$\mathbf{u} \cdot \mathbf{v} = \|\mathbf{u}\| \|\mathbf{v}\| \cos\theta \qquad \text{(eq. 1.4)}$$

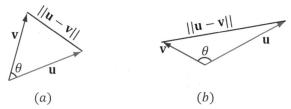

Figure 1.9. In the left figure, the angle θ between **u** and **v** is an acute angle. In the right figure, the angle θ between **u** and **v** is an obtuse angle. When we refer to the angle between two vectors, we always mean the smallest angle, that is, the angle θ such that $0 \leq \theta \leq \pi$.

where θ is the angle between the vectors **u** and **v** such that $0 \leq \theta \leq \pi$; see Figure 1.9. So, Equation 1.4 says that the dot product between two vectors is the cosine of the angle between them scaled by the vectors' magnitudes. In particular, if both **u** and **v** are unit vectors, then **u** · **v** is the cosine of the angle between them (i.e., **u** · **v** = cos θ).

Equation 1.4 provides us with some useful geometric properties of the dot product:

1. If **u** · **v** = 0, then **u** ⊥ **v** (i.e., the vectors are orthogonal).
2. If **u** · **v** > 0, then the angle θ between the two vectors is less than 90 degrees (i.e., the vectors make an acute angle).
3. If **u** · **v** < 0, the angle θ between the two vectors is greater than 90 degrees (i.e., the vectors make an obtuse angle).

 The word "orthogonal" can be used as a synonym for "perpendicular."

☞ Example 1.4

Let **u** = (1, 2, 3) and **v** = (−4, 0, −1). Find the angle between **u** and **v**. First we compute:

$$\mathbf{u} \cdot \mathbf{v} = (1, 2, 3) \cdot (-4, 0, -1) = -4 - 3 = -7$$

$$\|\mathbf{u}\| = \sqrt{1^2 + 2^2 + 3^2} = \sqrt{14}$$

$$\|\mathbf{v}\| = \sqrt{(-4)^2 + 0^2 + (-1)^2} = \sqrt{17}$$

Now, applying Equation 1.4 and solving for theta, we get:

$$\cos\theta = \frac{\mathbf{u} \cdot \mathbf{v}}{\|\mathbf{u}\|\|\mathbf{v}\|} = \frac{-7}{\sqrt{14}\sqrt{17}}$$

$$\theta = \cos^{-1}\frac{-7}{\sqrt{14}\sqrt{17}} \approx 117°$$

Example 1.5

Consider Figure 1.10. Given **v** and the *unit* vector **n**, find a formula for **p** in terms of **v** and **n** using the dot product.

First, observe from the figure that there exists a scalar k such that $\mathbf{p} = k\mathbf{n}$; moreover, since we assumed $||\mathbf{n}|| = 1$, we have $||\mathbf{p}|| = ||k\mathbf{n}|| = |k|\,||\mathbf{n}|| = |k|$. (Note that k may be negative if and only if **p** and **n** aim in opposite directions.) Using trigonometry, we have that $k = ||\mathbf{v}||\cos\theta$; therefore, $\mathbf{p} = k\mathbf{n} = (||\mathbf{v}||\cos\theta)\mathbf{n}$. However, because **n** is a unit vector, we can say this in another way:

$$\mathbf{p} = (||\mathbf{v}||\cos\theta)\mathbf{n} = (||\mathbf{v}||\cdot 1\cos\theta)\mathbf{n} = (||\mathbf{v}||\,||\mathbf{n}||\cos\theta)\mathbf{n} = (\mathbf{v}\cdot\mathbf{n})\mathbf{n}$$

In particular, this shows $k = \mathbf{v}\cdot\mathbf{n}$, and this illustrates the geometric interpretation of $\mathbf{v}\cdot\mathbf{n}$ when **n** is a unit vector. We call **p** the *orthogonal projection* of **v** on **n**, and it is commonly denoted by

$$\mathbf{p} = \text{proj}_{\mathbf{n}}(\mathbf{v})$$

If we interpret **v** as a force, **p** can be thought of as the portion of the force **v** that acts in the direction **n**. Likewise, the vector $\mathbf{w} = \text{perp}_{\mathbf{n}}(\mathbf{v}) = \mathbf{v} - \mathbf{p}$ is the portion of the force **v** that acts orthogonal to the direction **n** (which is why we also denote it by $\text{perp}_{\mathbf{n}}(\mathbf{v})$ for perpendicular). Observe that $\mathbf{v} = \mathbf{p} + \mathbf{w} = \text{proj}_{\mathbf{n}}(\mathbf{v}) + \text{perp}_{\mathbf{n}}(\mathbf{v})$, which is to say we have decomposed the vector **v** into the sum of two orthogonal vectors **p** and **w**.

If **n** is not of unit length, we can always normalize it first to make it unit length. Replacing **n** by the unit vector $\frac{\mathbf{n}}{||\mathbf{n}||}$ gives us the more general projection formula:

$$\mathbf{p} = \text{proj}_{\mathbf{n}}(\mathbf{v}) = \left(\mathbf{v}\cdot\frac{\mathbf{n}}{||\mathbf{n}||}\right)\frac{\mathbf{n}}{||\mathbf{n}||} = \frac{(\mathbf{v}\cdot\mathbf{n})}{||\mathbf{n}||^2}\mathbf{n}$$

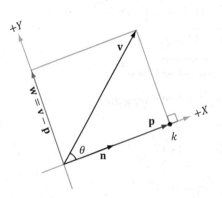
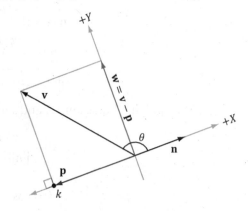

Figure 1.10. The *orthogonal projection* of **v** on **n**.

1.3.1 Orthogonalization

A set of vectors $\{\mathbf{v}_0, ..., \mathbf{v}_{n-1}\}$ is called *orthonormal* if the vectors are mutually orthogonal (every vector in the set is orthogonal to every other vector in the set) and unit length. Sometimes we have a set of vectors that are almost orthonormal, but not quite. A common task is to orthogonalize the set and make it orthonormal. In 3D computer graphics we might start off with an orthonormal set, but due to numerical precision issues, the set gradually becomes un-orthonormal. We are mainly concerned with the 2D and 3D cases of this problem (that is, sets that contain two and three vectors, respectively).

We examine the simpler 2D case first. Suppose we have the set of vectors $\{\mathbf{v}_0, \mathbf{v}_1\}$ that we want to orthogonalize into an orthonormal set $\{\mathbf{w}_0, \mathbf{w}_1\}$ as shown in Figure 1.11. We start with $\mathbf{w}_0 = \mathbf{v}_0$ and modify $\mathbf{v}_1$ to make it orthogonal to $\mathbf{w}_0$; this is done by subtracting out the portion of $\mathbf{v}_1$ that acts in the $\mathbf{w}_0$ direction:

$$\mathbf{w}_1 = \mathbf{v}_1 - \text{proj}_{\mathbf{w}_0}(\mathbf{v}_1)$$

We now have a mutually orthogonal set of vectors $\{\mathbf{w}_0, \mathbf{w}_1\}$; the last step to constructing the orthonormal set is to normalize $\mathbf{w}_0$ and $\mathbf{w}_1$ to make them unit length.

The 3D case follows in the same spirit as the 2D case, but with more steps. Suppose we have the set of vectors $\{\mathbf{v}_0, \mathbf{v}_1, \mathbf{v}_2\}$ that we want to orthogonalize into an orthonormal set $\{\mathbf{w}_0, \mathbf{w}_1, \mathbf{w}_2\}$ as shown in Figure 1.12. We start with $\mathbf{w}_0 = \mathbf{v}_0$ and modify $\mathbf{v}_1$ to make it orthogonal to $\mathbf{w}_0$; this is done by subtracting out the portion of $\mathbf{v}_1$ that acts in the $\mathbf{w}_0$ direction:

$$\mathbf{w}_1 = \mathbf{v}_1 - \text{proj}_{\mathbf{w}_0}(\mathbf{v}_1)$$

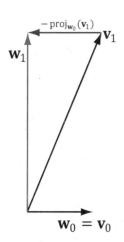

Figure 1.11. 2D orthogonalization.

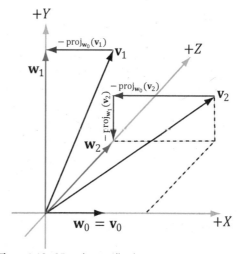

Figure 1.12. 3D orthogonalization.

Next, we modify $\mathbf{v}_2$ to make it orthogonal to *both* $\mathbf{w}_0$ and $\mathbf{w}_1$. This is done by subtracting out the portion of $\mathbf{v}_2$ that acts in the $\mathbf{w}_0$ direction and the portion of $\mathbf{v}_2$ that acts in the $\mathbf{w}_1$ direction:

$$\mathbf{w}_2 = \mathbf{v}_2 - \mathrm{proj}_{\mathbf{w}_0}(\mathbf{v}_2) - \mathrm{proj}_{\mathbf{w}_1}(\mathbf{v}_2)$$

We now have a mutually orthogonal set of vectors $\{\mathbf{w}_0, \mathbf{w}_1, \mathbf{w}_2\}$; the last step to constructing the orthonormal set is to normalize $\mathbf{w}_0, \mathbf{w}_1$ and $\mathbf{w}_2$ to make them unit length.

For the general case of n vectors $\{\mathbf{v}_0, ..., \mathbf{v}_{n-1}\}$ that we want to orthogonalize into an orthonormal set $\{\mathbf{w}_0, ..., \mathbf{w}_{n-1}\}$, we have the following procedure commonly called the *Gram-Schmidt Orthogonalization* process:

Base Step: Set $\mathbf{w}_0 = \mathbf{v}_0$

For $1 \le i \le n-1$, Set $\mathbf{w}_i = \mathbf{v}_i - \sum_{j=0}^{i-1} \mathrm{proj}_{\mathbf{w}_j}(\mathbf{v}_i)$

Normalization Step: Set $\mathbf{w}_i = \dfrac{\mathbf{w}_i}{\|\mathbf{w}_i\|}$

Again, the intuitive idea is that when we pick a vector $\mathbf{v}_i$ from the input set to add to the orthonormal set, we need to subtract out the components of $\mathbf{v}_i$ that act in the directions of the other vectors ($\mathbf{w}_0, \mathbf{w}_1, ..., \mathbf{w}_{i-1}$) that are already in the orthonormal set to ensure the new vector being added is orthogonal to the other vectors already in the orthonormal set.

1.4 THE CROSS PRODUCT

The second form of multiplication vector math defines is the *cross product*. Unlike the dot product, which evaluates to a scalar, the cross product evaluates to another vector; moreover, the cross product is only defined for 3D vectors (in particular, there is no 2D cross product). Taking the cross product of two 3D vectors $\mathbf{u}$ and $\mathbf{v}$ yields another vector, $\mathbf{w}$ that is mutually orthogonal to $\mathbf{u}$ and $\mathbf{v}$. By that we mean $\mathbf{w}$ is orthogonal to $\mathbf{u}$, and $\mathbf{w}$ is orthogonal to $\mathbf{v}$; see Figure 1.13. If $\mathbf{u} = (u_x, u_y, u_z)$ and $\mathbf{v} = (v_x, v_y, v_z)$, then the cross product is computed like so:

$$\mathbf{w} = \mathbf{u} \times \mathbf{v} = (u_y v_z - u_z v_y, u_z v_x - u_x v_z, u_x v_y - u_y v_x) \qquad \text{(eq. 1.5)}$$

If you are working in a right-handed coordinate system, then you use the right-hand-thumb rule: If you take your right hand and aim the fingers in the direction of the first vector $\mathbf{u}$, and then curl your fingers toward $\mathbf{v}$ along an angle $0 \le \theta \le \pi$, then your thumb roughly points in the direction of $\mathbf{w} = \mathbf{u} \times \mathbf{v}$.

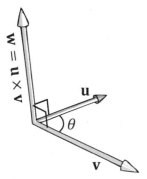

Figure 1.13. The cross product of two 3D vectors **u** and **v** yields another vector **w** that is mutually orthogonal to **u** and **v**. If you take your left hand and aim the fingers in the direction of the first vector **u**, and then curl your fingers toward **v** along an angle $0 \leq \theta \leq \pi$, then your thumb roughly points in the direction of **w** = **u** × **v**; this is called the *left-hand-thumb rule*.

☞ Example 1.6

Let **u** = (2, 1, 3) and **v** = (2, 0, 0). Compute **w** = **u** × **v** and **z** = **v** × **u**, and then verify that **w** is orthogonal to **u** and that **w** is orthogonal to **v**. Applying Equation 1.5 we have,

$$\begin{aligned} \mathbf{w} &= \mathbf{u} \times \mathbf{v} \\ &= (2, 1, 3) \times (2, 0, 0) \\ &= (1 \cdot 0 - 3 \cdot 0, 3 \cdot 2 - 2 \cdot 0, 2 \cdot 0 - 1 \cdot 2) \\ &= (0, 6, -2) \end{aligned}$$

And

$$\begin{aligned} \mathbf{z} &= \mathbf{v} \times \mathbf{u} \\ &= (2, 0, 0) \times (2, 1, 3) \\ &= (0 \cdot 3 - 0 \cdot 1, 0 \cdot 2 - 2 \cdot 3, 2 \cdot 1 - 0 \cdot 2) \\ &= (0, -6, 2) \end{aligned}$$

This result makes one thing clear, generally speaking **u** × **v** ≠ **v** × **u**. Therefore, we say that the cross product is anti-commutative. In fact, it can be shown that **u** × **v** = − **v** × **u**. You can determine the vector returned by the cross product by the *left-hand thumb* rule. If you first aim your fingers in the direction of the first vector, and then curl your fingers towards the second vector (always take the path with the smallest angle), your thumb points in the direction of the returned vector, as shown in Figure 1.11.

To show that **w** is orthogonal to **u** and that **w** is orthogonal to **v**, we recall from §1.3 that if **u** · **v** = 0, then **u** ⊥ **v** (i.e., the vectors are orthogonal). Because

$$\mathbf{w} \cdot \mathbf{u} = (0, 6, -2) \cdot (2, 1, 3) = 0 \cdot 2 + 6 \cdot 1 + (-2) \cdot 3 = 0$$

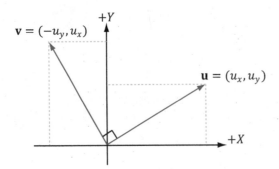

Figure 1.14. The 2D Pseudo Cross Product of a vector **u** evaluates to an orthogonal vector **v**.

and

$$\mathbf{w} \cdot \mathbf{v} = (0,6,-2) \cdot (2,0,0) = 0 \cdot 2 + 6 \cdot 0 + (-2) \cdot 0 = 0$$

we conclude that **w** is orthogonal to **u** and that **w** is orthogonal to **v**.

1.4.1 Pseudo 2D Cross Product

The cross product allows us to find a vector orthogonal to two given 3D vectors. In 2D we do not quite have the same situation, but given a 2D vector $\mathbf{u} = (u_x, u_y)$ it can be useful to find a vector **v** orthogonal to **u**. Figure 1.14 shows the geometric setup from which it is suggested that $\mathbf{v} = (-u_y, u_x)$. The formal proof is straightforward:

$$\mathbf{u} \cdot \mathbf{v} = (u_x, u_y) \cdot (-u_y, u_x) = -u_x u_y + u_y u_x = 0$$

Thus $\mathbf{u} \perp \mathbf{v}$. Observe that $\mathbf{u} \cdot -\mathbf{v} = u_x u_y + u_y (-u_x) = 0$, too, so we also have that $\mathbf{u} \perp -\mathbf{v}$.

1.4.2 Orthogonalization with the Cross Product

In §1.3.1, we looked at a way to orthogonalize a set of vectors using the *Gram-Schmidt* process. For 3D, there is another strategy to orthogonalize a set of vectors $\{\mathbf{v}_0, \mathbf{v}_1, \mathbf{v}_2\}$ that are almost orthonormal, but perhaps became un-orthonormal due to accumulated numerical precision errors, using the cross product. Refer to Figure 1.15 for the geometry of this process:

1. Set $\mathbf{w}_0 = \dfrac{\mathbf{v}_0}{\|\mathbf{v}_0\|}$.

2. Set $\mathbf{w}_2 = \dfrac{\mathbf{w}_0 \times \mathbf{v}_1}{\|\mathbf{w}_0 \times \mathbf{v}_1\|}$

3. Set $\mathbf{w}_1 = \mathbf{w}_2 \times \mathbf{w}_0$ By Exercise 14, $\|\mathbf{w}_2 \times \mathbf{w}_0\| = 1$ because $\mathbf{w}_2 \perp \mathbf{w}_0$ and $\|\mathbf{w}_2\| = \|\mathbf{w}_0\| = 1$, so we do not need to do any normalization in this last step.

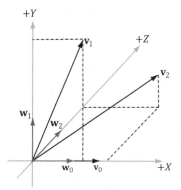

Figure 1.15. 3D orthogonalization with the cross product.

At this point, the set of vectors $\{\mathbf{w}_0, \mathbf{w}_1, \mathbf{w}_2\}$ is orthonormal.

 In the above example, we started with $\mathbf{w}_0 = \dfrac{\mathbf{v}_0}{\|\mathbf{v}_0\|}$ which means we did not change the direction when going from $\mathbf{v}_0$ to $\mathbf{w}_0$; we only changed the length. However, the directions of $\mathbf{w}_1$ and $\mathbf{w}_2$ could be different from $\mathbf{v}_1$ and $\mathbf{v}_2$, respectively. Depending on the specific application, the vector you choose not to change the direction of might be important. For example, later in this book we represent the orientation of the camera with three orthonormal vectors $\{\mathbf{v}_0, \mathbf{v}_1, \mathbf{v}_2\}$ where the third vector $\mathbf{v}_2$ describes the direction the camera is looking. When orthogonalizing these vectors, we often do not want to change the direction we are looking, and so we will start the above algorithm with $\mathbf{v}_2$ and modify $\mathbf{v}_0$ and $\mathbf{v}_1$ to orthogonalize the vectors.

1.5 POINTS

So far we have been discussing vectors, which do not describe positions. However, we will also need to specify positions in our 3D programs, for example, the position of 3D geometry and the position of the 3D virtual camera. Relative to a coordinate system, we can use a vector in standard position (Figure 1.16) to represent a 3D position in space; we call this a *position vector*. In this case, the location of the tip of the vector is the characteristic of interest, not the direction or magnitude. We will use the terms "position vector" and "point" interchangeably since a position vector is enough to identify a point.

One side effect of using vectors to represent points, especially in code, is that we can do vector operations that do not make sense for points; for instance, geometrically, what should the sum of two points mean? On the other hand, some operations can be extended to points. For example, we define the difference of two points $\mathbf{q} - \mathbf{p}$ to be the vector from $\mathbf{p}$ to $\mathbf{q}$. Also, we define a point $\mathbf{p}$ plus a vector $\mathbf{v}$ to

18 MATHEMATICAL PREREQUISITES

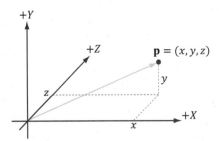

Figure 1.16. The position vector, which extends from the origin to the point, fully describes where the point is located relative to the coordinate system.

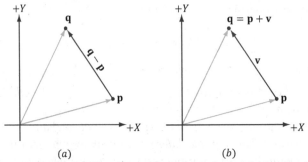

Figure 1.17. (a) The difference **q** − **p** between two points is defined as the vector from **p** to **q**. (b) A point **p** plus the vector **v** is defined to be the point **q** obtained by displacing **p** by the vector **v**.

be the point **q** obtained by displacing **p** by the vector **v**. Conveniently, because we are using vectors to represent points relative to a coordinate system, no extra work needs to be done for the point operations just discussed, as the vector algebra framework already takes care of them; see Figure 1.17.

 Actually there is a geometric meaningful way to define a special sum of points, called an affine combination, which is like a weighted average of points.

1.6 DIRECTX MATH VECTORS

For Windows 8 and above, DirectX Math is a 3D math library for Direct3D application that is part of the Windows SDK. The library uses the SSE2 (Streaming SIMD Extensions 2) instruction set. With 128-bit wide SIMD (single instruction multiple data) registers, SIMD instructions can operate on four 32-bit `floats` or `ints` with one instruction. This is very useful for vector calculations; for example, if you look at vector addition:

$$\mathbf{u} + \mathbf{v} = (u_x + v_x, u_y + v_y, u_z + v_z)$$

we see that we just add corresponding components. By using SIMD, we can do 4D vector addition with one SIMD instruction instead of four scalar instructions. If we only required three coordinates for 3D work, we can still use SIMD, but we would just ignore the fourth coordinate; likewise, for 2D we would ignore the third and fourth coordinates.

Our coverage of the DirectX Math library is not comprehensive, and we only cover the key parts needed for this book. For all the details, we recommend the online documentation [DirectXMath]. For readers wishing to understand how an SIMD vector library might be developed optimally, and, perhaps, to gain some insight why the DirectX Math library made some of the design decisions that it did, we recommend the article *Designing Fast Cross-Platform SIMD Vector Libraries* by [Oliveira2010].

To use the DirectX Math library, you need to `#include <DirectXMath.h>`, and for some additional data types `#include <DirectXPackedVector.h>`. There are no additional library files, as all the code is implemented inline in the header file. The DirectXMath.h code lives in the `DirectX` namespace, and the DirectXPackedVector.h code lives in the `DirectX::PackedVector` namespace. In addition, for the x86 platform you should enable SSE2 (**Project Properties > Configuration Properties > C/C++ > Code Generation > Enable Enhanced Instruction Set**), and for all platforms you should enable the fast floating point model /fp:fast (**Project Properties > Configuration Properties > C/C++ > Code Generation > Floating Point Model**). You do not need to enable SSE2 for the x64 platform because all x64 CPUs support SSE2 (http://en.wikipedia.org/wiki/SSE2).

1.6.1 Vector Types

In DirectX Math, the core vector type is `XMVECTOR`, which maps to SIMD hardware registers. This is a 128-bit type that can process four 32-bit floats with a single SIMD instruction. When SSE2 is available, it is defined like so for x86 and x64 platforms:

```
typedef __m128 XMVECTOR;
```

where __m128 is a special SIMD type. When doing calculations, vectors must be of this type to take advantage of SIMD. As already mentioned, we still use this type for 2D and 3D vectors to take advantage of SIMD, but we just zero out the unused components and ignore them.

`XMVECTOR` needs to be 16-byte aligned, and this is done automatically for local and global variables. For class data members, it is recommended to use `XMFLOAT2` (2D), `XMFLOAT3` (3D), and `XMFLOAT4` (4D) instead; these structures are defined below:

```cpp
struct XMFLOAT2
{
    float x;
    float y;

    XMFLOAT2() {}
    XMFLOAT2(float _x, float _y) : x(_x), y(_y) {}
    explicit XMFLOAT2(_In_reads_(2) const float *pArray) :
      x(pArray[0]), y(pArray[1]) {}

    XMFLOAT2& operator= (const XMFLOAT2& Float2)
    { x = Float2.x; y = Float2.y; return *this; }
};

struct XMFLOAT3
{
    float x;
    float y;
    float z;

    XMFLOAT3() {}
    XMFLOAT3(float _x, float _y, float _z) : x(_x), y(_y), z(_z) {}
    explicit XMFLOAT3(_In_reads_(3) const float *pArray) :
      x(pArray[0]), y(pArray[1]), z(pArray[2]) {}

    XMFLOAT3& operator= (const XMFLOAT3& Float3)
    { x = Float3.x; y = Float3.y; z = Float3.z; return *this; }
};

struct XMFLOAT4
{
    float x;
    float y;
    float z;
    float w;

    XMFLOAT4() {}
    XMFLOAT4(float _x, float _y, float _z, float _w) :
      x(_x), y(_y), z(_z), w(_w) {}
    explicit XMFLOAT4(_In_reads_(4) const float *pArray) :
      x(pArray[0]), y(pArray[1]), z(pArray[2]), w(pArray[3]) {}

    XMFLOAT4& operator= (const XMFLOAT4& Float4)
    { x = Float4.x; y = Float4.y; z = Float4.z; w = Float4.w; return
      *this; }
};
```

However, if we use these types directly for calculations, then we will not take advantage of SIMD. In order to use SIMD, we need to convert instances of these types into the XMVECTOR type. This is done with the DirectX Math loading functions. Conversely, DirectX Math provides storage functions which are used to convert data from XMVECTOR into the XMFLOATn types above.

To summarize,

1. Use XMVECTOR for local or global variables.
2. Use XMFLOAT2, XMFLOAT3, and XMFLOAT4 for class data members.
3. Use loading functions to convert from XMFLOATn to XMVECTOR before doing calculations.
4. Do calculations with XMVECTOR instances.
5. Use storage functions to convert from XMVECTOR to XMFLOATn.

1.6.2 Loading and Storage Methods

We use the following methods to load data from XMFLOATn into XMVECTOR:

```
// Loads XMFLOAT2 into XMVECTOR
XMVECTOR XM_CALLCONV XMLoadFloat2(const XMFLOAT2 *pSource);

// Loads XMFLOAT3 into XMVECTOR
XMVECTOR XM_CALLCONV XMLoadFloat3(const XMFLOAT3 *pSource);

// Loads XMFLOAT4 into XMVECTOR
XMVECTOR XM_CALLCONV XMLoadFloat4(const XMFLOAT4 *pSource);
```

We use the following methods to store data from XMVECTOR into XMFLOATn:

```
// Loads XMVECTOR into XMFLOAT2
void XM_CALLCONV XMStoreFloat2(XMFLOAT2 *pDestination, FXMVECTOR V);

// Loads XMVECTOR into XMFLOAT3
void XM_CALLCONV XMStoreFloat3(XMFLOAT3 *pDestination, FXMVECTOR V);

// Loads XMVECTOR into XMFLOAT4
void XM_CALLCONV XMStoreFloat4(XMFLOAT4 *pDestination, FXMVECTOR V);
```

Sometimes we just want to get or set one component of an XMVECTOR; the following getter and setter functions facilitate this:

```
float XM_CALLCONV XMVectorGetX(FXMVECTOR V);
float XM_CALLCONV XMVectorGetY(FXMVECTOR V);
float XM_CALLCONV XMVectorGetZ(FXMVECTOR V);
float XM_CALLCONV XMVectorGetW(FXMVECTOR V);

XMVECTOR XM_CALLCONV XMVectorSetX(FXMVECTOR V, float x);
XMVECTOR XM_CALLCONV XMVectorSetY(FXMVECTOR V, float y);
XMVECTOR XM_CALLCONV XMVectorSetZ(FXMVECTOR V, float z);
XMVECTOR XM_CALLCONV XMVectorSetW(FXMVECTOR V, float w);
```

1.6.3 Parameter Passing

For efficiency purposes, XMVECTOR values can be passed as arguments to functions in SSE/SSE2 registers instead of on the stack. The number of arguments that can be passed this way depends on the platform (e.g., 32-bit Windows, 64-bit Windows, and Windows RT) and compiler. Therefore, to be platform/compiler independent, we use the types FXMVECTOR, GXMVECTOR, HXMVECTOR and CXMVECTOR for passing XMVECTOR parameters; these are defined to the right type based on the platform and compiler. Furthermore, the calling convention annotation XM_CALLCONV must be specified before the function name so that the proper calling convention is used, which again depends on the compiler version.

Now the rules for passing XMVECTOR parameters are as follows:

1. The first three XMVECTOR parameters should be of type FXMVECTOR;
2. The fourth XMVECTOR should be of type GXMVECTOR;
3. The fifth and sixth XMVECTOR parameter should be of type HXMVECTOR;
4. Any additional XMVECTOR parameters should be of type CXMVECTOR.

We illustrate how these types are defined on 32-bit Windows with a compiler that supports the __fastcall calling convention and a compiler that supports the newer __vectorcall calling convention:

```
// 32-bit Windows __fastcall passes first 3 XMVECTOR arguments
// via registers, the remaining on the stack.
typedef const XMVECTOR FXMVECTOR;
typedef const XMVECTOR& GXMVECTOR;
typedef const XMVECTOR& HXMVECTOR;
typedef const XMVECTOR& CXMVECTOR;

// 32-bit Windows __vectorcall passes first 6 XMVECTOR arguments
// via registers, the remaining on the stack.
typedef const XMVECTOR FXMVECTOR;
typedef const XMVECTOR GXMVECTOR;
typedef const XMVECTOR HXMVECTOR;
typedef const XMVECTOR& CXMVECTOR;
```

For the details on how these types are defined for the other platforms, see "Calling Conventions" under "Library Internals" in the DirectX Math documentation [DirectXMath]. The exception to these rules is with constructor methods. [DirectXMath] recommends using FXMVECTOR for the first three XMVECTOR parameters and CXMVECTOR for the rest when writing a constructor that takes XMVECTOR parameters. Furthermore, do not use the annotation XM_CALLCONV for constructors

Here is an example from the DirectXMath library:

```
inline XMMATRIX XM_CALLCONV XMMatrixTransformation(
    FXMVECTOR ScalingOrigin,
    FXMVECTOR ScalingOrientationQuaternion, .
    FXMVECTOR Scaling,
    GXMVECTOR RotationOrigin,
    HXMVECTOR RotationQuaternion,
    HXMVECTOR Translation);
```

This function takes 6 XMVECTOR parameters, but following the parameter passing rules, it uses FXMVECTOR for the first three parameters, GXMVECTOR for the fourth, and HXMVECTOR for the fifth and sixth.

You can have non-XMVECTOR parameters between XMVECTOR parameters. The same rules apply and the XMVECTOR parameters are counted as if the non-XMVECTOR parameters were not there. For example, in the following function, the first three XMVECTOR parameters are of type FXMVECTOR as and the fourth XMVECTOR parameter is of type GXMVECTOR.

```
inline XMMATRIX XM_CALLCONV XMMatrixTransformation2D(
    FXMVECTOR ScalingOrigin,
    float    ScalingOrientation,
    FXMVECTOR Scaling,
    FXMVECTOR RotationOrigin,
    float    Rotation,
    GXMVECTOR Translation);
```

The rules for passing XMVECTOR parameters apply to "input" parameters. "Output" XMVECTOR parameters (XMVECTOR& or XMVECTOR*) will not use the SSE/SSE2 registers and so will be treated like non-XMVECTOR parameters.

1.6.4 Constant Vectors

Constant XMVECTOR instances should use the XMVECTORF32 type. Here are some examples from the DirectX SDK's CascadedShadowMaps11 sample:

```
static const XMVECTORF32 g_vHalfVector = { 0.5f, 0.5f, 0.5f, 0.5f };
static const XMVECTORF32 g_vZero = { 0.0f, 0.0f, 0.0f, 0.0f };

XMVECTORF32 vRightTop = {
vViewFrust.RightSlope,
vViewFrust.TopSlope,
1.0f,1.0f
};

XMVECTORF32 vLeftBottom = {
vViewFrust.LeftSlope,
vViewFrust.BottomSlope,
1.0f,1.0f
};
```

Essentially, we use XMVECTORF32 whenever we want to use initialization syntax. XMVECTORF32 is a 16-byte aligned structure with a XMVECTOR conversion operator; it is defined as follows:

```
// Conversion types for constants
__declspec(align(16)) struct XMVECTORF32
{
  union
```

```
{
  float f[4];
  XMVECTOR v;
};

inline operator XMVECTOR() const { return v; }
inline operator const float*() const { return f; }
#if !defined(_XM_NO_INTRINSICS_) && defined(_XM_SSE_INTRINSICS_)
inline operator __m128i() const { return _mm_castps_si128(v); }
inline operator __m128d() const { return _mm_castps_pd(v); }
#endif
};
```

You can also create a constant XMVECTOR of integer data using XMVECTORU32:

```
static const XMVECTORU32 vGrabY = {
0x00000000,0xFFFFFFFF,0x00000000,0x00000000
};
```

1.6.5 Overloaded Operators

The XMVECTOR has several overloaded operators for doing vector addition, subtraction, and scalar multiplication.

```
XMVECTOR   XM_CALLCONV    operator+ (FXMVECTOR V);
XMVECTOR   XM_CALLCONV    operator- (FXMVECTOR V);

XMVECTOR&  XM_CALLCONV    operator+= (XMVECTOR& V1, FXMVECTOR V2);
XMVECTOR&  XM_CALLCONV    operator-= (XMVECTOR& V1, FXMVECTOR V2);
XMVECTOR&  XM_CALLCONV    operator*= (XMVECTOR& V1, FXMVECTOR V2);
XMVECTOR&  XM_CALLCONV    operator/= (XMVECTOR& V1, FXMVECTOR V2);

XMVECTOR&  operator*= (XMVECTOR& V, float S);
XMVECTOR&  operator/= (XMVECTOR& V, float S);

XMVECTOR   XM_CALLCONV    operator+ (FXMVECTOR V1, FXMVECTOR V2);
XMVECTOR   XM_CALLCONV    operator- (FXMVECTOR V1, FXMVECTOR V2);
XMVECTOR   XM_CALLCONV    operator* (FXMVECTOR V1, FXMVECTOR V2);
XMVECTOR   XM_CALLCONV    operator/ (FXMVECTOR V1, FXMVECTOR V2);
XMVECTOR   XM_CALLCONV    operator* (FXMVECTOR V, float S);
XMVECTOR   XM_CALLCONV    operator* (float S, FXMVECTOR V);
XMVECTOR   XM_CALLCONV    operator/ (FXMVECTOR V, float S);
```

1.6.6 Miscellaneous

The DirectX Math library defined the following constants useful for approximating different expressions involving π:

```
const float XM_PI       = 3.141592654f;
const float XM_2PI      = 6.283185307f;
const float XM_1DIVPI   = 0.318309886f;
const float XM_1DIV2PI  = 0.159154943f;
```

```
const float XM_PIDIV2    = 1.570796327f;
const float XM_PIDIV4    = 0.785398163f;
```

In addition, it defines the following inline functions for converting between radians and degrees:

```
inline float XMConvertToRadians(float fDegrees)
{ return fDegrees * (XM_PI / 180.0f); }
inline float XMConvertToDegrees(float fRadians)
{ return fRadians * (180.0f / XM_PI); }
```

It also defines min/max functions:

```
template<class T> inline T XMMin(T a, T b) { return (a < b) ? a : b; }
template<class T> inline T XMMax(T a, T b) { return (a > b) ? a : b; }
```

1.6.7 Setter Functions

DirectX Math provides the following functions to set the contents of an XMVECTOR:

```
// Returns the zero vector 0
XMVECTOR XM_CALLCONV XMVectorZero();

// Returns the vector (1, 1, 1, 1)
XMVECTOR XM_CALLCONV XMVectorSplatOne();

// Returns the vector (x, y, z, w)
XMVECTOR XM_CALLCONV XMVectorSet(float x, float y, float z, float w);

// Returns the vector (s, s, s, s)
XMVECTOR XM_CALLCONV XMVectorReplicate(float Value);

// Returns the vector (v_x, v_x, v_x, v_x)
XMVECTOR XM_CALLCONV XMVectorSplatX(FXMVECTOR V);

// Returns the vector (v_y, v_y, v_y, v_y)
XMVECTOR XM_CALLCONV XMVectorSplatY(FXMVECTOR V);

// Returns the vector (v_z, v_z, v_z, v_z)
XMVECTOR XM_CALLCONV XMVectorSplatZ(FXMVECTOR V);
```

The following program illustrates most of these functions:

```
#include <windows.h> // for XMVerifyCPUSupport
#include <DirectXMath.h>
#include <DirectXPackedVector.h>
#include <iostream>
using namespace std;
using namespace DirectX;
using namespace DirectX::PackedVector;

// Overload the "<<" operators so that we can use cout to
// output XMVECTOR objects.
```

```
ostream& XM_CALLCONV operator<<(ostream& os, FXMVECTOR v)
{
  XMFLOAT3 dest;
  XMStoreFloat3(&dest, v);

  os << "(" << dest.x << ", " << dest.y << ", " << dest.z << ")";
  return os;
}

int main()
{
  cout.setf(ios_base::boolalpha);

  // Check support for SSE2 (Pentium4, AMD K8, and above).
  if (!XMVerifyCPUSupport())
  {
    cout << "directx math not supported" << endl;
    return 0;
  }

  XMVECTOR p = XMVectorZero();
  XMVECTOR q = XMVectorSplatOne();
  XMVECTOR u = XMVectorSet(1.0f, 2.0f, 3.0f, 0.0f);
  XMVECTOR v = XMVectorReplicate(-2.0f);
  XMVECTOR w = XMVectorSplatZ(u);

  cout << "p = " << p << endl;
  cout << "q = " << q << endl;
  cout << "u = " << u << endl;
  cout << "v = " << v << endl;
  cout << "w = " << w << endl;

  return 0;
}
```

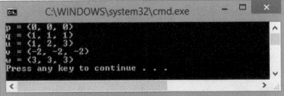

Figure 1.18. Output for the above program.

1.6.8 Vector Functions

DirectX Math provides the following functions to do various vector operations. We illustrate with the 3D versions, but there are analogous versions for 2D and 4D; the 2D and 4D versions have the same names as the 3D versions, with the exception of a 2 and 4 substituted for the 3, respectively.

```
XMVECTOR XM_CALLCONV XMVector3Length(    // Returns ||v||
    FXMVECTOR V);                         // Input v
```

```
XMVECTOR XM_CALLCONV XMVector3LengthSq(      // Returns ||v||²
    FXMVECTOR V);                             // Input v

XMVECTOR XM_CALLCONV XMVector3Dot(            // Returns v₁·v₂
    FXMVECTOR V1,                             // Input v₁
    FXMVECTOR V2);                            // Input v₂

XMVECTOR XM_CALLCONV XMVector3Cross(          // Returns v₁ × v₂
    FXMVECTOR V1,                             // Input v₁
    FXMVECTOR V2);                            // Input v₂

XMVECTOR XM_CALLCONV XMVector3Normalize(      // Returns v/||v||
    FXMVECTOR V);                             // Input v

XMVECTOR XM_CALLCONV XMVector3Orthogonal(     // Returns a vector orthogonal to v
    FXMVECTOR V);                             // Input v

XMVECTOR XM_CALLCONV
XMVector3AngleBetweenVectors(                 // Returns the angle between v₁ and v₂
    FXMVECTOR V1,                             // Input v₁
    FXMVECTOR V2);                            // Input v₂

void XM_CALLCONV XMVector3ComponentsFromNormal(
    XMVECTOR* pParallel,                      // Returns projₙ(v)
    XMVECTOR* pPerpendicular,                 // Returns perpₙ(v)
    FXMVECTOR V,                              // Input v
    FXMVECTOR Normal);                        // Input n

bool XM_CALLCONV XMVector3Equal(              // Returns v₁ = v₂
    FXMVECTOR V1,                             // Input v₁
    FXMVECTOR V2);                            // Input v₂

bool XM_CALLCONV XMVector3NotEqual(           // Returns v₁ ≠ v₂
    FXMVECTOR V1,                             // Input v₁
    FXMVECTOR V2);                            // Input v₂
```

Note: *Observe that these functions return* XMVECTOR*s even for operations that mathematically return a scalar (for example, the dot product* $k = \mathbf{v}_1 \cdot \mathbf{v}_2$*). The scalar result is replicated in each component of the* XMVECTOR*. For example, for the dot product, the returned vector would be* $(\mathbf{v}_1 \cdot \mathbf{v}_2, \mathbf{v}_1 \cdot \mathbf{v}_2, \mathbf{v}_1 \cdot \mathbf{v}_2, \mathbf{v}_1 \cdot \mathbf{v}_2)$*. One reason for this is to minimize mixing of scalar and SIMD vector operations; it is more efficient to keep everything SIMD until you are done with your calculations.*

The following demo program shows how to use most of these functions, as well as some of the overloaded operators:

```
#include <windows.h> // for XMVerifyCPUSupport
```

```cpp
#include <DirectXMath.h>
#include <DirectXPackedVector.h>
#include <iostream>
using namespace std;
using namespace DirectX;
using namespace DirectX::PackedVector;

// Overload the "<<" operators so that we can use cout to
// output XMVECTOR objects.
ostream& XM_CALLCONV operator<<(ostream& os, FXMVECTOR v)
{
  XMFLOAT3 dest;
  XMStoreFloat3(&dest, v);

  os << "(" << dest.x << ", " << dest.y << ", " << dest.z << ")";
  return os;
}

int main()
{
  cout.setf(ios_base::boolalpha);

  // Check support for SSE2 (Pentium4, AMD K8, and above).
  if (!XMVerifyCPUSupport())
  {
    cout << "directx math not supported" << endl;
    return 0;
  }

  XMVECTOR n = XMVectorSet(1.0f, 0.0f, 0.0f, 0.0f);
  XMVECTOR u = XMVectorSet(1.0f, 2.0f, 3.0f, 0.0f);
  XMVECTOR v = XMVectorSet(-2.0f, 1.0f, -3.0f, 0.0f);
  XMVECTOR w = XMVectorSet(0.707f, 0.707f, 0.0f, 0.0f);

  // Vector addition: XMVECTOR operator +
  XMVECTOR a = u + v;

  // Vector subtraction: XMVECTOR operator -
  XMVECTOR b = u - v;

  // Scalar multiplication: XMVECTOR operator *
  XMVECTOR c = 10.0f*u;

  // ||u||
  XMVECTOR L = XMVector3Length(u);

  // d = u / ||u||
  XMVECTOR d = XMVector3Normalize(u);

  // s = u dot v
  XMVECTOR s = XMVector3Dot(u, v);

  // e = u x v
  XMVECTOR e = XMVector3Cross(u, v);
```

```cpp
    // Find proj_n(w) and perp_n(w)
    XMVECTOR projW;
    XMVECTOR perpW;
    XMVector3ComponentsFromNormal(&projW, &perpW, w, n);

    // Does projW + perpW == w?
    bool equal = XMVector3Equal(projW + perpW, w) != 0;
    bool notEqual = XMVector3NotEqual(projW + perpW, w) != 0;

    // The angle between projW and perpW should be 90 degrees.
    XMVECTOR angleVec = XMVector3AngleBetweenVectors(projW, perpW);
    float angleRadians = XMVectorGetX(angleVec);
    float angleDegrees = XMConvertToDegrees(angleRadians);

    cout << "u                = " << u << endl;
    cout << "v                = " << v << endl;
    cout << "w                = " << w << endl;
    cout << "n                = " << n << endl;
    cout << "a = u + v        = " << a << endl;
    cout << "b = u - v        = " << b << endl;
    cout << "c = 10 * u       = " << c << endl;
    cout << "d = u / ||u||    = " << d << endl;
    cout << "e = u x v        = " << e << endl;
    cout << "L = ||u||        = " << L << endl;
    cout << "s = u.v          = " << s << endl;
    cout << "projW            = " << projW << endl;
    cout << "perpW            = " << perpW << endl;
    cout << "projW + perpW == w = " << equal << endl;
    cout << "projW + perpW != w = " << notEqual << endl;
    cout << "angle            = " << angleDegrees << endl;

    return 0;
}
```

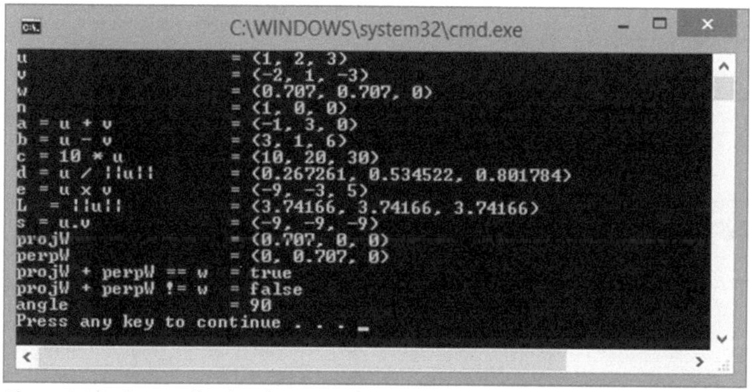

```
u                = (1, 2, 3)
v                = (-2, 1, -3)
w                = (0.707, 0.707, 0)
n                = (1, 0, 0)
a = u + v        = (-1, 3, 0)
b = u - v        = (3, 1, 6)
c = 10 * u       = (10, 20, 30)
d = u / ||u||    = (0.267261, 0.534522, 0.801784)
e = u x v        = (-9, -3, 5)
L = ||u||        = (3.74166, 3.74166, 3.74166)
s = u.v          = (-9, -9, -9)
projW            = (0.707, 0, 0)
perpW            = (0, 0.707, 0)
projW + perpW == w = true
projW + perpW != w = false
angle            = 90
Press any key to continue . . .
```

Figure 1.19. Output for the above program.

30 Mathematical Prerequisites

Note: *The DirectX Math library also includes some estimation methods, which are less accurate but faster to compute. If you are willing to sacrifice some accuracy for speed, then use the estimate methods. Here are two examples of estimate functions:*

```
XMVECTOR XM_CALLCONV XMVector3LengthEst(       // Returns estimated ||v||
    FXMVECTOR V);                              // Input v

XMVECTOR XM_CALLCONV XMVector3NormalizeEst(    // Returns estimated v/||v||
    FXMVECTOR V);                              // Input v
```

1.6.9 Floating-Point Error

While on the subject of working with vectors on a computer, we should be aware of the following. When comparing floating-point numbers, care must be taken due to floating-point imprecision. Two floating-point numbers that we expect to be equal may differ slightly. For example, mathematically, we'd expect a normalized vector to have a length of 1, but in a computer program, the length will only be approximately 1. Moreover, mathematically, $1^p = 1$ for any real number p, but when we only have a numerical approximation for 1, we see that the approximation raised to the pth power increases the error; thus, numerical error also accumulates. The following short program illustrates these ideas:

```cpp
#include <windows.h> // for XMVerifyCPUSupport
#include <DirectXMath.h>
#include <DirectXPackedVector.h>
#include <iostream>
using namespace std;
using namespace DirectX;
using namespace DirectX::PackedVector;

int main()
{
  cout.precision(8);

  // Check support for SSE2 (Pentium4, AMD K8, and above).
  if (!XMVerifyCPUSupport())
  {
    cout << "directx math not supported" << endl;
    return 0;
  }

  XMVECTOR u = XMVectorSet(1.0f, 1.0f, 1.0f, 0.0f);
  XMVECTOR n = XMVector3Normalize(u);

  float LU = XMVectorGetX(XMVector3Length(n));

  // Mathematically, the length should be 1. Is it numerically?
```

```
cout << LU << endl;
if (LU == 1.0f)
  cout << "Length 1" << endl;
else
  cout << "Length not 1" << endl;

// Raising 1 to any power should still be 1. Is it?
float powLU = powf(LU, 1.0e6f);
cout << "LU^(10^6) = " << powLU << endl;
}
```

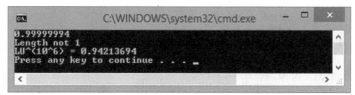

Figure 1.20. Output for the above program.

To compensate for floating-point imprecision, we test if two floating-point numbers are approximately equal. We do this by defining an Epsilon constant, which is a very small value we use as a "buffer." We say two values are approximately equal if their distance is less than Epsilon. In other words, Epsilon gives us some tolerance for floating-point imprecision. The following function illustrates how Epsilon can be used to test if two floating-point values are equal:

```
const float Epsilon = 0.001f;
bool Equals(float lhs, float rhs)
{
   // Is the distance between lhs and rhs less than EPSILON?
    return fabs(lhs - rhs) < Epsilon ? true : false;
}
```

The DirectX Math library provides the XMVector3NearEqual function when testing the equality of vectors with an allowed tolerance Epsilon parameter:

```
// Returns
//   abs(U.x - V.x) <= Epsilon.x &&
//   abs(U.y - V.y) <= Epsilon.y &&
//   abs(U.z - V.z) <= Epsilon.z
XMFINLINE bool XM_CALLCONV XMVector3NearEqual(
   FXMVECTOR U,
   FXMVECTOR V,
   FXMVECTOR Epsilon);
```

1.7 SUMMARY

1. Vectors are used to model physical quantities that possess both magnitude and direction. Geometrically, we represent a vector with a directed line segment.

A vector is in standard position when it is translated parallel to itself so that its tail coincides with the origin of the coordinate system. A vector in standard position can be described numerically by specifying the coordinates of its head relative to a coordinate system.

2. If $\mathbf{u} = (u_x, u_y, u_z)$ and $\mathbf{v} = (v_x, v_y, v_z)$, then we have the following vector operations:

   (a) Addition: $\mathbf{u} + \mathbf{v} = (u_x + v_x, u_y + v_y, u_z + v_z)$

   (b) Subtraction: $\mathbf{u} - \mathbf{v} = (u_x - v_x, u_y - v_y, u_z - v_z)$

   (c) Scalar Multiplication: $k\mathbf{u} = (ku_x, ku_y, ku_z)$

   (d) Length: $\|\mathbf{u}\| = \sqrt{x^2 + y^2 + z^2}$

   (e) Normalization: $\hat{\mathbf{u}} = \dfrac{\mathbf{u}}{\|\mathbf{u}\|} = \left(\dfrac{x}{\|\mathbf{u}\|}, \dfrac{y}{\|\mathbf{u}\|}, \dfrac{z}{\|\mathbf{u}\|}\right)$

   (f) Dot Product: $\mathbf{u} \cdot \mathbf{v} = \|\mathbf{u}\|\|\mathbf{v}\|\cos\theta = u_x v_x + u_y v_y + u_z v_z$

   (g) Cross Product: $\mathbf{u} \times \mathbf{v} = (u_y v_z - u_z v_y, u_z v_x - u_x v_z, u_x v_y - u_y v_x)$

3. We use the DirectX Math XMVECTOR type to describe vectors efficiently in code using SIMD operations. For class data members, we use the XMFLOAT2, XMFLOAT3, and XMFLOAT4 classes, and then use the loading and storage methods to convert back and forth between XMVECTOR and XMFLOAT*n*. Constant vectors that require initialization syntax should use the XMVECTORF32 type.

4. For efficiency purposes, XMVECTOR values can be passed as arguments to functions in SSE/SSE2 registers instead of on the stack. To do this in a platform independent way, we use the types FXMVECTOR, GXMVECTOR, HXMVECTOR and CXMVECTOR for passing XMVECTOR parameters. Then the rule for passing XMVECTOR parameters is that the first three XMVECTOR parameters should be of type FXMVECTOR; the fourth XMVECTOR should be of type GXMVECTOR; the fifth and sixth XMVECTOR parameter should be of type HXMVECTOR; and any additional XMVECTOR parameters should be of type CXMVECTOR.

5. The XMVECTOR class overloads the arithmetic operators to do vector addition, subtraction, and scalar multiplication. Moreover, the DirectX Math library provides the following useful functions for computing the length of a vector, the squared length of a vector, computing the dot product of two vectors, computing the cross product of two vectors, and normalizing a vector:

```
XMVECTOR XM_CALLCONV XMVector3Length(FXMVECTOR V);
XMVECTOR XM_CALLCONV XMVector3LengthSq(FXMVECTOR V);
XMVECTOR XM_CALLCONV XMVector3Dot(FXMVECTOR V1, FXMVECTOR V2);
XMVECTOR XM_CALLCONV XMVector3Cross(FXMVECTOR V1, FXMVECTOR V2);
XMVECTOR XM_CALLCONV XMVector3Normalize(FXMVECTOR V);
```

1.8 EXERCISES

1. Let $\mathbf{u} = (1, 2)$ and $\mathbf{v} = (3, -4)$. Perform the following computations and draw the vectors relative to a 2D coordinate system.
   (a) $\mathbf{u} + \mathbf{v}$
   (b) $\mathbf{u} - \mathbf{v}$
   (c) $2\mathbf{u} + \frac{1}{2}\mathbf{v}$
   (d) $-2\mathbf{u} + \mathbf{v}$

2. Let $\mathbf{u} = (-1, 3, 2)$ and $\mathbf{v} = (3, -4, 1)$. Perform the following computations.
   (a) $\mathbf{u} + \mathbf{v}$
   (b) $\mathbf{u} - \mathbf{v}$
   (c) $3\mathbf{u} + 2\mathbf{v}$
   (d) $-2\mathbf{u} + \mathbf{v}$

3. This exercise shows that vector algebra shares many of the nice properties of real numbers (this is not an exhaustive list). Assume $\mathbf{u} = (u_x, u_y, u_z)$, $\mathbf{v} = (v_x, v_y, v_z)$, and $\mathbf{w} = (w_x, w_y, w_z)$. Also assume that c and k are scalars. Prove the following vector properties.
   (a) $\mathbf{u} + \mathbf{v} = \mathbf{v} + \mathbf{u}$ (Commutative Property of Addition)
   (b) $\mathbf{u} + (\mathbf{v} + \mathbf{w}) = (\mathbf{u} + \mathbf{v}) + \mathbf{w}$ (Associative Property of Addition)
   (c) $(ck)\mathbf{u} = c(k\mathbf{u})$ (Associative Property of Scalar Multiplication)
   (d) $k(\mathbf{u} + \mathbf{v}) = k\mathbf{u} + k\mathbf{v}$ (Distributive Property 1)
   (e) $\mathbf{u}(k + c) = k\mathbf{u} + c\mathbf{u}$ (Distributive Property 2)

   Just use the definition of the vector operations and the properties of real numbers. For example,

   $$\begin{aligned}(ck)\mathbf{u} &= (ck)(u_x, u_y, u_z) \\ &= ((ck)u_x, (ck)u_y, (ck)u_z) \\ &= (c(ku_x), c(ku_y), c(ku_z)) \\ &= c(ku_x, ku_y, ku_z) \\ &= c(k\mathbf{u})\end{aligned}$$

4. Solve the equation $2((1, 2, 3) - \mathbf{x}) - (-2, 0, 4) = -2(1, 2, 3)$ for $\mathbf{x}$.
5. Let $\mathbf{u} = (-1, 3, 2)$ and $\mathbf{v} = (3, -4, 1)$. Normalize $\mathbf{u}$ and $\mathbf{v}$.
6. Let k be a scalar and let $\mathbf{u} = (u_x, u_y, u_z)$. Prove that $\|k\mathbf{u}\| = |k|\|\mathbf{u}\|$.
7. Is the angle between $\mathbf{u}$ and $\mathbf{v}$ orthogonal, acute, or obtuse?
   (a) $\mathbf{u} = (1, 1, 1), \mathbf{v} = (2, 3, 4)$
   (b) $\mathbf{u} = (1, 1, 0), \mathbf{v} = (-2, 2, 0)$

(c) $\mathbf{u} = (-1, -1, -1)$, $\mathbf{v} = (3, 1, 0)$

8. Let $\mathbf{u} = (-1, 3, 2)$ and $\mathbf{v} = (3, -4, 1)$. Find the angle θ between $\mathbf{u}$ and $\mathbf{v}$.

9. Let $\mathbf{u} = (u_x, u_y, u_z)$, $\mathbf{v} = (v_x, v_y, v_z)$, and $\mathbf{w} = (w_x, w_y, w_z)$. Also let c and k be scalars. Prove the following dot product properties.

    (a) $\mathbf{u} \cdot \mathbf{v} = \mathbf{v} \cdot \mathbf{u}$
    (b) $\mathbf{u} \cdot (\mathbf{v} + \mathbf{w}) = \mathbf{u} \cdot \mathbf{v} + \mathbf{u} \cdot \mathbf{w}$
    (c) $k(\mathbf{u} \cdot \mathbf{v}) = (k\mathbf{u}) \cdot \mathbf{v} = \mathbf{u} \cdot (k\mathbf{v})$
    (d) $\mathbf{v} \cdot \mathbf{v} = \|\mathbf{v}\|^2$
    (e) $\mathbf{0} \cdot \mathbf{v} = 0$

Just use the definitions, for example,

$$\mathbf{v} \cdot \mathbf{v} = v_x v_x + v_y v_y + v_z v_z$$
$$= v_x^2 + v_y^2 + v_z^2$$
$$= \left(\sqrt{v_x^2 + v_y^2 + v_z^2}\right)^2$$
$$= \|\mathbf{v}\|^2$$

10. Use the law of cosines ($c^2 = a^2 + b^2 - 2ab\cos\theta$), where a, b, and c are the lengths of the sides of a triangle and θ is the angle between sides a and b) to show

$$u_x v_x + u_y v_y + u_z v_z = \|\mathbf{u}\| \|\mathbf{v}\| \cos\theta$$

Consider Figure 1.9 and set $c^2 = \|\mathbf{u} - \mathbf{v}\|$, $a^2 = \|\mathbf{u}\|^2$ and $b^2 = \|\mathbf{v}\|^2$, and use the dot product properties from the previous exercise.

11. Let $\mathbf{n} = (-2, 1)$. Decompose the vector $\mathbf{g} = (0, -9.8)$ into the sum of two orthogonal vectors, one parallel to $\mathbf{n}$ and the other orthogonal to $\mathbf{n}$. Also, draw the vectors relative to a 2D coordinate system.

12. Let $\mathbf{u} = (-2, 1, 4)$ and $\mathbf{v} = (3, -4, 1)$. Find $\mathbf{w} = \mathbf{u} \times \mathbf{v}$, and show $\mathbf{w} \cdot \mathbf{u} = 0$ and $\mathbf{w} \cdot \mathbf{v} = 0$.

13. Let the following points define a triangle relative to some coordinate system: $A = (0, 0, 0)$, $B = (0, 1, 3)$, and $C = (5, 1, 0)$. Find a vector orthogonal to this triangle.

Find two vectors on two of the triangle's edges and use the cross product.

14. Prove that $\|\mathbf{u} \times \mathbf{v}\| = \|\mathbf{u}\| \|\mathbf{v}\| \sin\theta$.

Start with $\|\mathbf{u}\|\|\mathbf{v}\|\|\sin\theta\|$ *and use the trigonometric identity* $\cos^2\theta + \sin^2\theta = 1 \Rightarrow \sin\theta = \sqrt{1-\cos^2\theta}$, *then apply Equation 1.4.*

15. Prove that $\|\mathbf{u}\times\mathbf{v}\|$ gives the area of the parallelogram spanned by $\mathbf{u}$ and $\mathbf{v}$; see Figure 1.21.

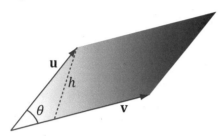

Figure 1.21. Parallelogram spanned by two 3D vectors $\mathbf{u}$ and $\mathbf{v}$; the parallelogram has base $\|\mathbf{v}\|$ and height *h*

16. Give an example of 3D vectors $\mathbf{u}$, $\mathbf{v}$, and $\mathbf{w}$ such that $\mathbf{u}\times(\mathbf{v}\times\mathbf{w}) \neq (\mathbf{u}\times\mathbf{v})\times\mathbf{w}$. This shows the cross product is generally not associative.

Consider combinations of the simple vectors $\mathbf{i} = (1, 0, 0)$, $\mathbf{j} = (0, 1, 0)$, *and* $\mathbf{k} = (0, 0, 1)$.

17. Prove that the cross product of two nonzero parallel vectors results in the null vector; that is, $\mathbf{u} \times k\mathbf{u} = \mathbf{0}$.

Just use the cross product definition.

18. Orthonormalize the set of vectors $\{(1, 0, 0), (1, 5, 0), (2, 1, -4)\}$ using the Gram-Schmidt process.

19. Consider the following program and output. Make a conjecture of what each `XMVector*` function does; then look up each function in the DirectXMath documentation.

```
#include <windows.h> // for XMVerifyCPUSupport
#include <DirectXMath.h>
#include <DirectXPackedVector.h>
#include <iostream>
using namespace std;
using namespace DirectX;
using namespace DirectX::PackedVector;

// Overload the "<<" operators so that we can use cout to
// output XMVECTOR objects.
ostream& XM_CALLCONV operator<<(ostream& os, FXMVECTOR v)
{
  XMFLOAT4 dest;
```

```cpp
    XMStoreFloat4(&dest, v);

    os << "(" << dest.x << ", " << dest.y << ", "
       << dest.z << ", " << dest.w << ")";
    return os;
}

int main()
{
    cout.setf(ios_base::boolalpha);

    // Check support for SSE2 (Pentium4, AMD K8, and above).
    if (!XMVerifyCPUSupport())
    {
        cout << "directx math not supported" << endl;
        return 0;
    }

    XMVECTOR p = XMVectorSet(2.0f, 2.0f, 1.0f, 0.0f);
    XMVECTOR q = XMVectorSet(2.0f, -0.5f, 0.5f, 0.1f);
    XMVECTOR u = XMVectorSet(1.0f, 2.0f, 4.0f, 8.0f);
    XMVECTOR v = XMVectorSet(-2.0f, 1.0f, -3.0f, 2.5f);
    XMVECTOR w = XMVectorSet(0.0f, XM_PIDIV4, XM_PIDIV2, XM_PI);

    cout << "XMVectorAbs(v)          = " << XMVectorAbs(v) << endl;
    cout << "XMVectorCos(w)          = " << XMVectorCos(w) << endl;
    cout << "XMVectorLog(u)          = " << XMVectorLog(u) << endl;
    cout << "XMVectorExp(p)          = " << XMVectorExp(p) << endl;

    cout << "XMVectorPow(u, p)       = " << XMVectorPow(u, p) << endl;
    cout << "XMVectorSqrt(u)         = " << XMVectorSqrt(u) << endl;

    cout << "XMVectorSwizzle(u, 2, 2, 1, 3) = "
         << XMVectorSwizzle(u, 2, 2, 1, 3) << endl;
    cout << "XMVectorSwizzle(u, 2, 1, 0, 3) = "
         << XMVectorSwizzle(u, 2, 1, 0, 3) << endl;

    cout << "XMVectorMultiply(u, v)  = " << XMVectorMultiply(u, v) <<
        endl;
    cout << "XMVectorSaturate(q)     = " << XMVectorSaturate(q) << endl;
    cout << "XMVectorMin(p, v)       = " << XMVectorMin(p, v) << endl;
    cout << "XMVectorMax(p, v)       = " << XMVectorMax(p, v) << endl;

    return 0;
}
```

Figure 1.22. Output for the above program.

Chapter 2: Matrix Algebra

In 3D computer graphics, we use matrices to compactly describe geometric transformations such as scaling, rotation, and translation, and also to change the coordinates of a point or vector from one frame to another. This chapter explores the mathematics of matrices.

Objectives:

1. To obtain an understanding of matrices and the operations defined on them.
2. To discover how a vector-matrix multiplication can be viewed as a linear combination.
3. To learn what the identity matrix is, and what the transpose, determinant, and inverse of a matrix are.
4. To become familiar with the subset of classes and functions provided by the DirectX Math library used for matrix mathematics.

2.1 DEFINITION

An *m* × *n* **matrix** **M** is a rectangular array of real numbers with m rows and n columns. The product of the number of rows and columns gives the dimensions of the matrix. The numbers in a matrix are called *elements or entries*. We identify a matrix element by specifying the row and column of the element using a double subscript notation M_{ij}, where the first subscript identifies the row and the second subscript identifies the column.

☞ Example 2.1

Consider the following matrices:

$$\mathbf{A} = \begin{bmatrix} 3.5 & 0 & 0 & 0 \\ 0 & 1 & 0 & 0 \\ 0 & 0 & 0.5 & 0 \\ 2 & -5 & \sqrt{2} & 1 \end{bmatrix} \quad \mathbf{B} = \begin{bmatrix} B_{11} & B_{12} \\ B_{21} & B_{22} \\ B_{31} & B_{32} \end{bmatrix} \quad \mathbf{u} = [u_1, u_2, u_3] \quad \mathbf{v} = \begin{bmatrix} 1 \\ 2 \\ \sqrt{3} \\ \pi \end{bmatrix}$$

1. The matrix **A** is a 4 × 4 matrix; the matrix **B** is a 3 × 2 matrix; the matrix **u** is a 1 × 3 matrix; and the matrix **v** is a 4 × 1 matrix.

2. We identify the element in the fourth row and second column of the matrix **A** by $A_{42} = -5$. We identify the element in the second row and first column of the matrix **B** by B_{21}.

3. The matrices **u** and **v** are special matrices in the sense that they contain a single row or column, respectively. We sometimes call these kinds of matrices row vectors or column vectors because they are used to represent a vector in matrix form (e.g., we can freely interchange the vector notations (x, y, z) and $[x, y, z]$). Observe that for row and column vectors, it is unnecessary to use a double subscript to denote the elements of the matrix—we only need one subscript.

Occasionally we like to think of the rows of a matrix as vectors. For example, we might write:

$$\begin{bmatrix} A_{11} & A_{12} & A_{13} \\ A_{21} & A_{22} & A_{23} \\ A_{31} & A_{32} & A_{33} \end{bmatrix} = \begin{bmatrix} \leftarrow \mathbf{A}_{1,*} \rightarrow \\ \leftarrow \mathbf{A}_{2,*} \rightarrow \\ \leftarrow \mathbf{A}_{3,*} \rightarrow \end{bmatrix}$$

where $\mathbf{A}_{1,*} = [A_{11}, A_{12}, A_{13}]$, $\mathbf{A}_{2,*} = [A_{21}, A_{22}, A_{23}]$, and $\mathbf{A}_{3,*} = [A_{31}, A_{32}, A_{33}]$. In this notation, the first index specifies the row, and we put a '*' in the second index to indicate that we are referring to the entire row vector. Likewise, we like to do the same thing for the columns:

$$\begin{bmatrix} A_{11} & A_{12} & A_{13} \\ A_{21} & A_{22} & A_{23} \\ A_{31} & A_{32} & A_{33} \end{bmatrix} = \begin{bmatrix} \uparrow & \uparrow & \uparrow \\ \mathbf{A}_{*,1} & \mathbf{A}_{*,2} & \mathbf{A}_{*,3} \\ \downarrow & \downarrow & \downarrow \end{bmatrix}$$

where

$$\mathbf{A}_{*,1} = \begin{bmatrix} A_{11} \\ A_{21} \\ A_{31} \end{bmatrix}, \ \mathbf{A}_{*,2} = \begin{bmatrix} A_{12} \\ A_{22} \\ A_{32} \end{bmatrix}, \ \mathbf{A}_{*,3} = \begin{bmatrix} A_{13} \\ A_{23} \\ A_{33} \end{bmatrix}$$

In this notation, the second index specifies the column, and we put a '*' in the first index to indicate that we are referring to the entire column vector.

We now define equality, addition, scalar multiplication, and subtraction on matrices.

1. Two matrices are equal if and only if their corresponding elements are equal; as such, two matrices must have the same number of rows and columns in order to be compared.
2. We add two matrices by adding their corresponding elements; as such, it only makes sense to add matrices that the same number of rows and columns.
3. We multiply a scalar and a matrix by multiplying the scalar with every element in the matrix.
4. We define subtraction in terms of matrix addition and scalar multiplication. That is, $\mathbf{A} - \mathbf{B} = \mathbf{A} + (-1 \cdot \mathbf{B}) = \mathbf{A} + (-\mathbf{B})$.

☞ Example 2.2

Let

$$\mathbf{A} = \begin{bmatrix} 1 & 5 \\ -2 & 3 \end{bmatrix}, \ \mathbf{B} = \begin{bmatrix} 6 & 2 \\ 5 & -8 \end{bmatrix}, \ \mathbf{C} = \begin{bmatrix} 1 & 5 \\ -2 & 3 \end{bmatrix}, \ \mathbf{D} = \begin{bmatrix} 2 & 1 & -3 \\ -6 & 3 & 0 \end{bmatrix}$$

Then,

(i) $\quad \mathbf{A} + \mathbf{B} = \begin{bmatrix} 1 & 5 \\ -2 & 3 \end{bmatrix} + \begin{bmatrix} 6 & 2 \\ 5 & -8 \end{bmatrix} = \begin{bmatrix} 1+6 & 5+2 \\ -2+5 & 3+(-8) \end{bmatrix} = \begin{bmatrix} 7 & 7 \\ 3 & -5 \end{bmatrix}$

(ii) $\quad \mathbf{A} = \mathbf{C}$

(iii) $\quad 3\mathbf{D} = 3 \begin{bmatrix} 2 & 1 & -3 \\ -6 & 3 & 0 \end{bmatrix} = \begin{bmatrix} 3(2) & 3(1) & 3(-3) \\ 3(-6) & 3(3) & 3(0) \end{bmatrix} = \begin{bmatrix} 6 & 3 & -9 \\ -18 & 9 & 0 \end{bmatrix}$

(iv) $\quad \mathbf{A} - \mathbf{B} = \begin{bmatrix} 1 & 5 \\ -2 & 3 \end{bmatrix} - \begin{bmatrix} 6 & 2 \\ 5 & -8 \end{bmatrix} = \begin{bmatrix} 1-6 & 5-2 \\ -2-5 & 3-(-8) \end{bmatrix} = \begin{bmatrix} -5 & 3 \\ -7 & 11 \end{bmatrix}$

Because addition and scalar multiplication is done element-wise, matrices essentially inherit the following addition and scalar multiplication properties from real numbers:

1. $\mathbf{A} + \mathbf{B} = \mathbf{B} + \mathbf{A}$ — Commutative law of addition
2. $(\mathbf{A} + \mathbf{B}) + \mathbf{C} = \mathbf{A} + (\mathbf{B} + \mathbf{C})$ — Associative law of addition
3. $r(\mathbf{A} + \mathbf{B}) = r\mathbf{A} + r\mathbf{B}$ — Scalar distribution over matrices
4. $(r + s)\mathbf{A} = r\mathbf{A} + s\mathbf{A}$ — Matrix distribution over scalars

2.2 MATRIX MULTIPLICATION

2.2.1 Definition

If A is a $m \times n$ matrix and **B** is a $n \times p$ matrix, then the product **AB** is defined and is a $m \times p$ matrix **C**, where the ijth entry of the product **C** is given by taking the dot product of the ith row vector in **A** with the jth column vector in **B**, that is,

$$C_{ij} = \mathbf{A}_{i,*} \cdot \mathbf{B}_{*,j} \qquad \text{(eq. 2.1)}$$

So note that in order for the matrix product **AB** to be defined, we require that the number of columns in **A** equal the number of rows in **B**, which is to say, we require that the dimension of the row vectors in **A** equal the dimension of the column vectors in **B**. If these dimensions did not match, then the dot product in Equation 2.1 would not make sense.

☞ Example 2.3

Let

$$\mathbf{A} = \begin{bmatrix} 1 & 5 \\ -2 & 3 \end{bmatrix} \quad \text{and} \quad \mathbf{B} = \begin{bmatrix} 2 & -6 \\ 1 & 3 \\ -3 & 0 \end{bmatrix}$$

The product **AB** is not defined since the row vectors in **A** have dimension 2 and the column vectors in **B** have dimension 3. In particular, we cannot take the dot product of the first row vector in **A** with the first column vector in **B** because we cannot take the dot product of a 2D vector with a 3D vector.

☞ Example 2.4

Let

$$A = \begin{bmatrix} -1 & 5 & -4 \\ 3 & 2 & 1 \end{bmatrix} \text{ and } B = \begin{bmatrix} 2 & 1 & 0 \\ 0 & -2 & 1 \\ -1 & 2 & 3 \end{bmatrix}$$

We first point out that the product **AB** is defined (and is a 2 × 3 matrix) because the number of columns of **A** equals the number of rows of **B**. Applying Equation 2.1 yields:

$$\begin{aligned}
AB &= \begin{bmatrix} -1 & 5 & -4 \\ 3 & 2 & 1 \end{bmatrix} \begin{bmatrix} 2 & 1 & 0 \\ 0 & -2 & 1 \\ -1 & 2 & 3 \end{bmatrix} \\
&= \begin{bmatrix} (-1,5,-4)\cdot(2,0,-1) & (-1,5,-4)\cdot(1,-2,2) & (-1,5,-4)\cdot(0,1,3) \\ (3,2,1)\cdot(2,0,-1) & (3,2,1)\cdot(1,-2,2) & (3,2,1)\cdot(0,1,3) \end{bmatrix} \\
&= \begin{bmatrix} 2 & -19 & -7 \\ 5 & 1 & 5 \end{bmatrix}
\end{aligned}$$

Observe that the product **BA** is not defined because the number of columns in **B** does *not* equal the number of rows in **A**. This demonstrates that, in general, matrix multiplication is not commutative; that is, **AB** ≠ **BA**.

2.2.2 Vector-Matrix Multiplication

Consider the following vector-matrix multiplication:

$$\mathbf{uA} = [x,y,z] \begin{bmatrix} A_{11} & A_{12} & A_{13} \\ A_{21} & A_{22} & A_{23} \\ A_{31} & A_{32} & A_{33} \end{bmatrix} = [x,y,z] \begin{bmatrix} \uparrow & \uparrow & \uparrow \\ \mathbf{A}_{*,1} & \mathbf{A}_{*,2} & \mathbf{A}_{*,3} \\ \downarrow & \downarrow & \downarrow \end{bmatrix}$$

Observe that **uA** evaluates to a 1×3 row vector in this case. Now, applying Equation 2.1 gives:

$$\mathbf{uA} = \begin{bmatrix} \mathbf{u} \cdot \mathbf{A}_{*,1} & \mathbf{u} \cdot \mathbf{A}_{*,2} & \mathbf{u} \cdot \mathbf{A}_{*,3} \end{bmatrix}$$
$$= \begin{bmatrix} xA_{11} + yA_{21} + zA_{31}, & xA_{12} + yA_{22} + zA_{32}, & xA_{13} + yA_{23} + zA_{33} \end{bmatrix}$$
$$= \begin{bmatrix} xA_{11}, xA_{12}, xA_{13} \end{bmatrix} + \begin{bmatrix} yA_{21}, yA_{22}, yA_{23} \end{bmatrix} + \begin{bmatrix} zA_{31}, zA_{32}, zA_{33} \end{bmatrix}$$
$$= x\begin{bmatrix} A_{11}, A_{12}, A_{13} \end{bmatrix} + y\begin{bmatrix} A_{21}, A_{22}, A_{23} \end{bmatrix} + z\begin{bmatrix} A_{31}, A_{32}, A_{33} \end{bmatrix}$$
$$= x\mathbf{A}_{1,*} + y\mathbf{A}_{2,*} + z\mathbf{A}_{3,*}$$

Thus,

$$\mathbf{uA} = x\mathbf{A}_{1,*} + y\mathbf{A}_{2,*} + z\mathbf{A}_{3,*} \qquad \text{(eq. 2.2)}$$

Equation 2.2 is an example of a *linear combination*, and it says that the vector-matrix product **uA** is equivalent to a linear combination of the row vectors of the matrix **A** with scalar coefficients x, y, and z given by the vector **u**. Note that, although we showed this for a 1×3 row vector and a 3×3 matrix, the result is true in general. That is, for a $1 \times n$ row vector **u** and a $n \times m$ matrix **A**, we have that **uA** is a linear combination of the row vectors in **A** with scalar coefficients given by **u**:

$$\begin{bmatrix} u_1, \ldots, u_n \end{bmatrix} \begin{bmatrix} A_{11} & \cdots & A_{1m} \\ \vdots & \ddots & \vdots \\ A_{n1} & \cdots & A_{nm} \end{bmatrix} = u_1 \mathbf{A}_{1,*} + \ldots + u_n \mathbf{A}_{n,*} \qquad \text{(eq. 2.3)}$$

2.2.3 Associativity

Matrix multiplication has some nice algebraic properties. For example, matrix multiplication distributes over addition: **A(B + C) = AB + AC** and **(A + B)C = AC + BC**. In particular, however, we will use the associative law of matrix multiplication from time to time, which allows us to choose the order we multiply matrices:

$$\mathbf{(AB)C = A(BC)}$$

2.3 THE TRANSPOSE OF A MATRIX

The *transpose* of a matrix is found by interchanging the rows and columns of the matrix. Thus the transpose of an $m \times n$ matrix is an $n \times m$ matrix. We denote the transpose of a matrix **M** as $\mathbf{M}^T$.

☞ Example 2.5

Find the transpose for the following three matrices:

$$\mathbf{A} = \begin{bmatrix} 2 & -1 & 8 \\ 3 & 6 & -4 \end{bmatrix}, \quad \mathbf{B} = \begin{bmatrix} a & b & c \\ d & e & f \\ g & h & i \end{bmatrix}, \quad \mathbf{C} = \begin{bmatrix} 1 \\ 2 \\ 3 \\ 4 \end{bmatrix}$$

To reiterate, the transposes are found by interchanging the rows and columns, thus

$$\mathbf{A}^T = \begin{bmatrix} 2 & 3 \\ -1 & 6 \\ 8 & -4 \end{bmatrix}, \quad \mathbf{B}^T = \begin{bmatrix} a & d & g \\ b & e & h \\ c & f & i \end{bmatrix}, \quad \mathbf{C}^T = \begin{bmatrix} 1 & 2 & 3 & 4 \end{bmatrix}$$

The transpose has the following useful properties:

1. $(\mathbf{A}+\mathbf{B})^T = \mathbf{A}^T + \mathbf{B}^T$
2. $(c\mathbf{A})^T = c\mathbf{A}^T$
3. $(\mathbf{AB})^T = \mathbf{B}^T\mathbf{A}^T$
4. $(\mathbf{A}^T)^T = \mathbf{A}$
5. $(\mathbf{A}^{-1})^T = (\mathbf{A}^T)^{-1}$

2.4 THE IDENTITY MATRIX

There is a special matrix called the *identity matrix*. The identity matrix is a square matrix that has zeros for all elements except along the main diagonal; the elements along the main diagonal are all ones.

For example, below are 2×2, 3×3 and 4×4 identity matrices.

$$\begin{bmatrix} 1 & 0 \\ 0 & 1 \end{bmatrix}, \quad \begin{bmatrix} 1 & 0 & 0 \\ 0 & 1 & 0 \\ 0 & 0 & 1 \end{bmatrix}, \quad \begin{bmatrix} 1 & 0 & 0 & 0 \\ 0 & 1 & 0 & 0 \\ 0 & 0 & 1 & 0 \\ 0 & 0 & 0 & 1 \end{bmatrix}$$

The identity matrix acts as a multiplicative identity; that is, if $\mathbf{A}$ is an $m \times n$ matrix, $\mathbf{B}$ is an $n \times p$ matrix, and $\mathbf{I}$ is the $n \times n$ identity matrix, then

$$\mathbf{AI} = \mathbf{A} \quad \text{and} \quad \mathbf{IB} = \mathbf{B}$$

In other words, multiplying a matrix by the identity matrix does not change the matrix. The identity matrix can be thought of as the number 1 for matrices. In particular, if **M** is a square matrix, then multiplication with the identity matrix is commutative:

$$\mathbf{MI} = \mathbf{IM} = \mathbf{M}$$

☞ Example 2.6

Let $\mathbf{M} = \begin{bmatrix} 1 & 2 \\ 0 & 4 \end{bmatrix}$ and let $\mathbf{I} = \begin{bmatrix} 1 & 0 \\ 0 & 1 \end{bmatrix}$. Verify that $\mathbf{MI} = \mathbf{IM} = \mathbf{M}$.

Applying Equation 2.1 yields:

$$\mathbf{MI} = \begin{bmatrix} 1 & 2 \\ 0 & 4 \end{bmatrix}\begin{bmatrix} 1 & 0 \\ 0 & 1 \end{bmatrix} = \begin{bmatrix} (1,2)\cdot(1,0) & (1,2)\cdot(0,1) \\ (0,4)\cdot(1,0) & (0,4)\cdot(0,1) \end{bmatrix} = \begin{bmatrix} 1 & 2 \\ 0 & 4 \end{bmatrix}$$

and

$$\mathbf{IM} = \begin{bmatrix} 1 & 0 \\ 0 & 1 \end{bmatrix}\begin{bmatrix} 1 & 2 \\ 0 & 4 \end{bmatrix} = \begin{bmatrix} (1,0)\cdot(1,0) & (1,0)\cdot(2,4) \\ (0,1)\cdot(1,0) & (0,1)\cdot(2,4) \end{bmatrix} = \begin{bmatrix} 1 & 2 \\ 0 & 4 \end{bmatrix}$$

Thus it is true that $\mathbf{MI} = \mathbf{IM} = \mathbf{M}$.

☞ Example 2.7

Let $\mathbf{u} = \begin{bmatrix} -1, 2 \end{bmatrix}$ and let $\mathbf{I} = \begin{bmatrix} 1 & 0 \\ 0 & 1 \end{bmatrix}$. Verify that $\mathbf{uI} = \mathbf{u}$.

Applying Equation 2.1 yields:

$$\mathbf{uI} = \begin{bmatrix} -1, & 2 \end{bmatrix}\begin{bmatrix} 1 & 0 \\ 0 & 1 \end{bmatrix} = \begin{bmatrix} (-1,2)\cdot(1,0), & (-1,2)\cdot(0,1) \end{bmatrix} = \begin{bmatrix} -1, & 2 \end{bmatrix}$$

Note that we cannot take the product **Iu** because the matrix multiplication is not defined.

2.5 THE DETERMINANT OF A MATRIX

The determinant is a special function which inputs a square matrix and outputs a real number. The determinant of a square matrix **A** is commonly denoted by det **A**. It can be shown that the determinant has a geometric interpretation related to volumes of boxes and that the determinant provides information on how volumes change under linear transformations. In addition, determinants are used to solve systems of linear equations using Cramer's Rule. However, for our purposes, we are mainly motivated to study the determinant because it gives us an explicit formula for finding the inverse of a matrix (the topic of §2.7). In addition, it can be proved that: *A square matrix* **A** *is invertible if and only if* det **A** $\neq$ 0. This fact is useful because it gives us a computational tool for determining if a matrix is invertible. Before we can define the determinant, we first introduce the concept of matrix minors.

2.5.1 Matrix Minors

Given an $n \times n$ matrix **A**, the *minor matrix* $\overline{\mathbf{A}}_{ij}$ is the $(n-1) \times (n-1)$ matrix found by deleting the ith row and jth column of **A**.

☞ Example 2.8

Find the minor matrices $\overline{\mathbf{A}}_{11}, \overline{\mathbf{A}}_{22}$, and $\overline{\mathbf{A}}_{13}$ of the following matrix:

$$\mathbf{A} = \begin{bmatrix} A_{11} & A_{12} & A_{13} \\ A_{21} & A_{22} & A_{23} \\ A_{31} & A_{32} & A_{33} \end{bmatrix}$$

For $\overline{\mathbf{A}}_{11}$ we eliminate the first row and first column to obtain:

$$\overline{\mathbf{A}}_{11} = \begin{bmatrix} A_{22} & A_{23} \\ A_{32} & A_{33} \end{bmatrix}$$

For $\overline{\mathbf{A}}_{22}$ we eliminate the second row and second column to obtain:

$$\overline{\mathbf{A}}_{22} = \begin{bmatrix} A_{11} & A_{13} \\ A_{31} & A_{33} \end{bmatrix}$$

For $\overline{\mathbf{A}}_{13}$ we eliminate the first row and third column to obtain:

$$\overline{\mathbf{A}}_{13} = \begin{bmatrix} A_{21} & A_{22} \\ A_{31} & A_{32} \end{bmatrix}$$

2.5.2 Definition

The determinant of a matrix is defined recursively; for instance, the determinant of a 4×4 matrix is defined in terms of the determinant of a 3×3 matrix, and the determinant of a 3×3 matrix is defined in terms of the determinant of a 2×2 matrix, and the determinant of a 2×2 matrix is defined in terms of the determinant of a 1×1 matrix (the determinant of a 1×1 matrix $\mathbf{A} = [A_{11}]$ is trivially defined to be $\det[A_{11}] = A_{11}$).

Let $\mathbf{A}$ be an $n \times n$ matrix. Then for $n > 1$ we define:

$$\det \mathbf{A} = \sum_{j=1}^{n} A_{1j}(-1)^{1+j} \det \overline{\mathbf{A}}_{1j} \qquad \text{(eq. 2.4)}$$

Recalling the definition of the minor matrix $\overline{\mathbf{A}}_{ij}$, for 2×2 matrices, this gives the formula:

$$\det \begin{bmatrix} A_{11} & A_{12} \\ A_{21} & A_{22} \end{bmatrix} = A_{11} \det[A_{22}] - A_{12} \det[A_{21}] = A_{11}A_{22} - A_{12}A_{21}$$

For 3×3 matrices, this gives the formula:

$$\det \begin{bmatrix} A_{11} & A_{12} & A_{13} \\ A_{21} & A_{22} & A_{23} \\ A_{31} & A_{32} & A_{33} \end{bmatrix}$$

$$= A_{11} \det \begin{bmatrix} A_{22} & A_{23} \\ A_{32} & A_{33} \end{bmatrix} - A_{12} \det \begin{bmatrix} A_{21} & A_{23} \\ A_{31} & A_{33} \end{bmatrix} + A_{13} \det \begin{bmatrix} A_{21} & A_{22} \\ A_{31} & A_{32} \end{bmatrix}$$

And for 4×4 matrices, this gives the formula:

$$\det \begin{bmatrix} A_{11} & A_{12} & A_{13} & A_{14} \\ A_{21} & A_{22} & A_{23} & A_{24} \\ A_{31} & A_{32} & A_{33} & A_{34} \\ A_{41} & A_{42} & A_{43} & A_{44} \end{bmatrix} = A_{11} \det \begin{bmatrix} A_{22} & A_{23} & A_{24} \\ A_{32} & A_{33} & A_{34} \\ A_{42} & A_{43} & A_{44} \end{bmatrix} - A_{12} \det \begin{bmatrix} A_{21} & A_{23} & A_{24} \\ A_{31} & A_{33} & A_{34} \\ A_{41} & A_{43} & A_{44} \end{bmatrix}$$

$$+ A_{13} \det \begin{bmatrix} A_{21} & A_{22} & A_{24} \\ A_{31} & A_{32} & A_{34} \\ A_{41} & A_{42} & A_{44} \end{bmatrix} - A_{14} \det \begin{bmatrix} A_{21} & A_{22} & A_{23} \\ A_{31} & A_{32} & A_{33} \\ A_{41} & A_{42} & A_{43} \end{bmatrix}$$

In 3D graphics, we primarily work with 4×4 matrices, and so we do not need to continue generating explicit formulas for $n > 4$.

☞ Example 2.9

Find the determinant of the matrix

$$\mathbf{A} = \begin{bmatrix} 2 & -5 & 3 \\ 1 & 3 & 4 \\ -2 & 3 & 7 \end{bmatrix}$$

We have that:

$$\det \mathbf{A} = A_{11} \det \begin{bmatrix} A_{22} & A_{23} \\ A_{32} & A_{33} \end{bmatrix} - A_{12} \det \begin{bmatrix} A_{21} & A_{23} \\ A_{31} & A_{33} \end{bmatrix} + A_{13} \det \begin{bmatrix} A_{21} & A_{22} \\ A_{31} & A_{32} \end{bmatrix}$$

$$\det \mathbf{A} = 2 \det \begin{bmatrix} 3 & 4 \\ 3 & 7 \end{bmatrix} - (-5) \det \begin{bmatrix} 1 & 4 \\ -2 & 7 \end{bmatrix} + 3 \det \begin{bmatrix} 1 & 3 \\ -2 & 3 \end{bmatrix}$$

$$= 2(3 \cdot 7 - 4 \cdot 3) + 5(1 \cdot 7 - 4 \cdot (-2)) + 3(1 \cdot 3 - 3 \cdot (-2))$$

$$= 2(9) + 5(15) + 3(9)$$

$$= 18 + 75 + 27$$

$$= 120$$

2.6 THE ADJOINT OF A MATRIX

Let $\mathbf{A}$ be an $n \times n$ matrix. The product $C_{ij} = (-1)^{i+j} \det \overline{\mathbf{A}}_{ij}$ is called the *cofactor of* A_{ij}. If we compute C_{ij} and place it in the ijth position of a corresponding matrix $\mathbf{C_A}$ for every element in $\mathbf{A}$, we obtain the *cofactor matrix of* $\mathbf{A}$:

$$\mathbf{C_A} = \begin{bmatrix} C_{11} & C_{12} & \cdots & C_{1n} \\ C_{21} & C_{22} & \cdots & C_{2n} \\ \vdots & \vdots & \ddots & \vdots \\ C_{n1} & C_{n2} & \cdots & C_{nn} \end{bmatrix}$$

If we take the transpose of $\mathbf{C_A}$ we get a matrix that is called *adjoint of* $\mathbf{A}$, which we denote by

$$\mathbf{A}^* = \mathbf{C_A}^T \qquad \text{(eq. 2.5)}$$

In the next section, we learn that the adjoint enables us to find an explicit formula for computing matrix inverses.

2.7 THE INVERSE OF A MATRIX

Matrix algebra does not define a division operation, but it does define a multiplicative inverse operation. The following list summarizes the important information about inverses:

1. Only square matrices have inverses; therefore, when we speak of matrix inverses, we assume we are dealing with a square matrix.

2. The inverse of an $n \times n$ matrix **M** is an $n \times n$ matrix denoted by $\mathbf{M}^{-1}$.
3. Not every square matrix has an inverse. A matrix that does have an inverse is said to be *invertible*, and a matrix that does not have an inverse is said to be *singular*.
4. The inverse is unique when it exists.
5. Multiplying a matrix with its inverse results in the identity matrix: $\mathbf{MM}^{-1} = \mathbf{M}^{-1}\mathbf{M} = \mathbf{I}$. Note that multiplying a matrix with its own inverse is a case when matrix multiplication is commutative.

Matrix inverses are useful when solving for other matrices in a matrix equation. For example, suppose that we are given the matrix equation $\mathbf{p}' = \mathbf{pM}$. Further suppose that we are given $\mathbf{p}'$ and $\mathbf{M}$, and want to solve for $\mathbf{p}$. Assuming that $\mathbf{M}$ is invertible (i.e., $\mathbf{M}^{-1}$ exists), we can solve for $\mathbf{p}$ like so:

$\mathbf{p}' = \mathbf{pM}$
$\mathbf{p}'\mathbf{M}^{-1} = \mathbf{pMM}^{-1}$ Multiplying both sides of the equation by $\mathbf{M}^{-1}$
$\mathbf{p}'\mathbf{M}^{-1} = \mathbf{pI}$ $\mathbf{MM}^{-1} = \mathbf{I}$, by definition of inverse.
$\mathbf{p}'\mathbf{M}^{-1} = \mathbf{p}$ $\mathbf{pI} = \mathbf{p}$, by definition of the identity matrix.

A formula for finding inverses, which we do not prove here but should be proved in any college level linear algebra text, can be given in terms of the adjoint and determinant:

$$\mathbf{A}^{-1} = \frac{\mathbf{A}^*}{\det \mathbf{A}} \qquad \text{(eq. 2.6)}$$

☞ Example 2.10

Find a general formula for the inverse of a 2×2 matrix $\mathbf{A} = \begin{bmatrix} A_{11} & A_{12} \\ A_{21} & A_{22} \end{bmatrix}$, and use this formula to find the inverse of the matrix $\mathbf{M} = \begin{bmatrix} 3 & 0 \\ -1 & 2 \end{bmatrix}$.
We have that

$\det \mathbf{A} = A_{11}A_{22} - A_{12}A_{21}$

$\mathbf{C_A} = \begin{bmatrix} (-1)^{1+1} \det \overline{\mathbf{A}}_{11} & (-1)^{1+2} \det \overline{\mathbf{A}}_{12} \\ (-1)^{2+1} \det \overline{\mathbf{A}}_{21} & (-1)^{2+2} \det \overline{\mathbf{A}}_{22} \end{bmatrix} = \begin{bmatrix} A_{22} & -A_{21} \\ -A_{12} & A_{11} \end{bmatrix}$

Therefore,

$$\mathbf{A}^{-1} = \frac{\mathbf{A}^*}{\det \mathbf{A}} = \frac{\mathbf{C}_\mathbf{A}^T}{\det \mathbf{A}} = \frac{1}{A_{11}A_{22} - A_{12}A_{21}} \begin{bmatrix} A_{22} & -A_{12} \\ -A_{21} & A_{11} \end{bmatrix}$$

Now we apply this formula to invert $\mathbf{M} = \begin{bmatrix} 3 & 0 \\ -1 & 2 \end{bmatrix}$:

$$\mathbf{M}^{-1} = \frac{1}{3 \cdot 2 - 0 \cdot (-1)} \begin{bmatrix} 2 & 0 \\ 1 & 3 \end{bmatrix} = \begin{bmatrix} 1/3 & 0 \\ 1/6 & 1/2 \end{bmatrix}$$

To check out work we verify $\mathbf{MM}^{-1} = \mathbf{M}^{-1}\mathbf{M} = \mathbf{I}$:

$$\begin{bmatrix} 3 & 0 \\ -1 & 2 \end{bmatrix} \begin{bmatrix} 1/3 & 0 \\ 1/6 & 1/2 \end{bmatrix} = \begin{bmatrix} 1 & 0 \\ 0 & 1 \end{bmatrix} = \begin{bmatrix} 1/3 & 0 \\ 1/6 & 1/2 \end{bmatrix} \begin{bmatrix} 3 & 0 \\ -1 & 2 \end{bmatrix}$$

> **Note:** *For small matrices (sizes 4×4 and smaller), the adjoint method is computationally efficient. For larger matrices, other methods are used like Gaussian elimination. However, the matrices we are concerned about in 3D computer graphics have special forms, which enable us to determine the inverse formulas ahead of time, so that we do not need to waste CPU cycles finding the inverse of a general matrix. Consequently, we rarely need to apply Equation 2.6 in code.*

To conclude this section on inverses, we present the following useful algebraic property for the inverse of a product:

$$(\mathbf{AB})^{-1} = \mathbf{B}^{-1}\mathbf{A}^{-1}$$

This property assumes both **A** and **B** are invertible and that they are both square matrices of the same dimension. To prove that $\mathbf{B}^{-1}\mathbf{A}^{-1}$ is the inverse of **AB**, we must show $(\mathbf{AB})(\mathbf{B}^{-1}\mathbf{A}^{-1}) = \mathbf{I}$ and $(\mathbf{B}^{-1}\mathbf{A}^{-1})(\mathbf{AB}) = \mathbf{I}$. This is done as follows:

$$(\mathbf{AB})(\mathbf{B}^{-1}\mathbf{A}^{-1}) = \mathbf{A}(\mathbf{BB}^{-1})\mathbf{A}^{-1} = \mathbf{AIA}^{-1} = \mathbf{AA}^{-1} = \mathbf{I}$$
$$(\mathbf{B}^{-1}\mathbf{A}^{-1})(\mathbf{AB}) = \mathbf{B}^{-1}(\mathbf{A}^{-1}\mathbf{A})\mathbf{B} = \mathbf{B}^{-1}\mathbf{IB} = \mathbf{B}^{-1}\mathbf{B} = \mathbf{I}$$

2.8 DIRECTX MATH MATRICES

For transforming points and vectors, we use 1×4 row vectors and 4×4 matrices. The reason for this will be explained in the next chapter. For now, we just concentrate on the DirectX Math types used to represent 4×4 matrices.

2.8.1 Matrix Types

To represent 4 × 4 matrices in DirectX math, we use the XMMATRIX class, which is defined as follows in the *DirectXMath.h* header file (with some minor adjustments we have made for clarity):

```
#if (defined(_M_IX86) || defined(_M_X64) || defined(_M_ARM)) && 
defined(_XM_NO_INTRINSICS_)
struct XMMATRIX
#else
__declspec(align(16)) struct XMMATRIX
#endif
{
  // Use 4 XMVECTORs to represent the matrix for SIMD.
  XMVECTOR r[4];

  XMMATRIX() {}

  // Initialize matrix by specifying 4 row vectors.
  XMMATRIX(FXMVECTOR R0, FXMVECTOR R1, FXMVECTOR R2, CXMVECTOR R3)
    { r[0] = R0; r[1] = R1; r[2] = R2; r[3] = R3; }

  // Initialize matrix by specifying 4 row vectors.
  XMMATRIX(float m00, float m01, float m02, float m03,
      float m10, float m11, float m12, float m13,
      float m20, float m21, float m22, float m23,
      float m30, float m31, float m32, float m33);

  // Pass array of sixteen floats to construct matrix.
  explicit XMMATRIX(_In_reads_(16) const float *pArray);

  XMMATRIX&  operator= (const XMMATRIX& M)
    { r[0] = M.r[0]; r[1] = M.r[1]; r[2] = M.r[2]; r[3] = M.r[3];
    return *this; }

  XMMATRIX  operator+ () const { return *this; }
  XMMATRIX  operator- () const;

  XMMATRIX&  XM_CALLCONV   operator+= (FXMMATRIX M);
  XMMATRIX&  XM_CALLCONV   operator-= (FXMMATRIX M);
  XMMATRIX&  XM_CALLCONV   operator*= (FXMMATRIX M);
  XMMATRIX&  operator*= (float S);
  XMMATRIX&  operator/= (float S);

  XMMATRIX  XM_CALLCONV   operator+ (FXMMATRIX M) const;
  XMMATRIX  XM_CALLCONV   operator- (FXMMATRIX M) const;
  XMMATRIX  XM_CALLCONV   operator* (FXMMATRIX M) const;
  XMMATRIX  operator* (float S) const;
  XMMATRIX  operator/ (float S) const;

  friend XMMATRIX   XM_CALLCONV   operator* (float S, FXMMATRIX M);
};
```

As you can see, XMMATRIX uses four XMVECTOR instances to use SIMD. Moreover, XMMATRIX provides overloaded operators for matrix arithmetic.

In addition to using the various constructors, an XMMATRIX instance can be created using the XMMatrixSet function:

```
XMMATRIX XM_CALLCONV XMMatrixSet(
  float m00, float m01, float m02, float m03,
  float m10, float m11, float m12, float m13,
  float m20, float m21, float m22, float m23,
  float m30, float m31, float m32, float m33);
```

Just as we use XMFLOAT2 (2D), XMFLOAT3 (3D), and XMFLOAT4 (4D) when storing vectors in a class, it is recommended, by the DirectXMath documentation to use the XMFLOAT4X4 type to store matrices as class data members.

```
struct XMFLOAT4X4
{
  union
  {
    struct
    {
      float _11, _12, _13, _14;
      float _21, _22, _23, _24;
      float _31, _32, _33, _34;
      float _41, _42, _43, _44;
    };
    float m[4][4];
  };

  XMFLOAT4X4() {}
  XMFLOAT4X4(float m00, float m01, float m02, float m03,
      float m10, float m11, float m12, float m13,
      float m20, float m21, float m22, float m23,
      float m30, float m31, float m32, float m33);
  explicit XMFLOAT4X4(_In_reads_(16) const float *pArray);

  float   operator() (size_t Row, size_t Column) const { return m[Row]
    [Column]; }
  float&  operator() (size_t Row, size_t Column) { return m[Row]
    [Column]; }

  XMFLOAT4X4& operator= (const XMFLOAT4X4& Float4x4);
},
```

We use the following method to load data from XMFLOAT4X4 into XMMATRIX:

```
inline XMMATRIX XM_CALLCONV
XMLoadFloat4x4(const XMFLOAT4X4* pSource);
```

We use the following method to store data from XMMATRIX into XMFLOAT4X4:

```
inline void XM_CALLCONV
XMStoreFloat4x4(XMFLOAT4X4* pDestination, FXMMATRIX M);
```

2.8.2 Matrix Functions

The DirectX Math library includes the following useful matrix related functions:

```
XMMATRIX XM_CALLCONV XMMatrixIdentity();    // Returns the identity matrix I

bool XM_CALLCONV XMMatrixIsIdentity(        // Returns true if M is the identity matrix
    FXMMATRIX M);                           // Input M

XMMATRIX XM_CALLCONV XMMatrixMultiply(      // Returns the matrix product AB
    FXMMATRIX A,                            // Input A
    CXMMATRIX B);                           // Input B

XMMATRIX XM_CALLCONV XMMatrixTranspose(     // Returns M^T
    FXMMATRIX M);                           // Input M

XMVECTOR XM_CALLCONV XMMatrixDeterminant(   // Returns (det M, det M, det M, det M)
    FXMMATRIX M);                           // Input M

XMMATRIX XM_CALLCONV XMMatrixInverse(       // Returns M^-1
    XMVECTOR* pDeterminant,                 // Input (det M, det M, det M, det M)
    FXMMATRIX M);                           // Input M
```

When we declare a XMMATRIX parameter to a function, we use the same rules we used when passing XMVECTOR parameters (see §1.6.3), except that an XMMATRIX counts as four XMVECTOR parameters. Assuming there are no more than two additional FXMVECTOR parameters in total to the function, the first XMMATRIX should be of type FXMMATRIX, and any other XMMATRIX should be of type CXMMATRIX. We illustrate how these types are defined on 32-bit Windows with a compiler that supports the __fastcall calling convention and a compiler that supports the newer __vectorcall calling convention:

```
// 32-bit Windows __fastcall passes first 3 XMVECTOR arguments
// via registers, the remaining on the stack.
typedef const XMMATRIX& FXMMATRIX;
typedef const XMMATRIX& CXMMATRIX;

// 32-bit Windows __vectorcall passes first 6 XMVECTOR arguments
// via registers, the remaining on the stack.
typedef const XMMATRIX FXMMATRIX;
typedef const XMMATRIX& CXMMATRIX;
```

Observe that on 32-bit Windows with __fastcall, a XMMATRIX cannot be passed through SSE/SSE2 registers because only three XMVECTOR arguments via registers are supported, and a XMMATRIX requires four; thus the matrix is just passed on the stack by reference. For the details on how these types are defined for the other platforms, see "Calling Conventions" under "Library Internals" in the DirectXMath documentation [DirectXMath]. The exception to these rules is with constructor methods. [DirectXMath] recommends always using CXMMATRIX for constructors that takes XMMATRIX parameters. Furthermore, do not use the annotation XM_CALLCONV for constructors.

2.8.3 DirectX Math Matrix Sample Program

The following code provides some examples on how to use the `XMMATRIX` class and most of the functions listed in the previous section.

```cpp
#include <windows.h> // for XMVerifyCPUSupport
#include <DirectXMath.h>
#include <DirectXPackedVector.h>
#include <iostream>
using namespace std;
using namespace DirectX;
using namespace DirectX::PackedVector;

// Overload the "<<" operators so that we can use cout to
// output XMVECTOR and XMMATRIX objects.
ostream& XM_CALLCONV operator << (ostream& os, FXMVECTOR v)
{
  XMFLOAT4 dest;
  XMStoreFloat4(&dest, v);

  os << "(" << dest.x << ", " << dest.y << ", " << dest.z << ", " <<
    dest.w << ")";
  return os;
}

ostream& XM_CALLCONV operator << (ostream& os, FXMMATRIX m)
{
  for (int i = 0; i < 4; ++i)
  {
    os << XMVectorGetX(m.r[i]) << "\t";
    os << XMVectorGetY(m.r[i]) << "\t";
    os << XMVectorGetZ(m.r[i]) << "\t";
    os << XMVectorGetW(m.r[i]);
    os << endl;
  }
  return os;
}

int main()
{
  // Check support for SSE2 (Pentium4, AMD K8, and above).
  if (!XMVerifyCPUSupport())
  {
    cout << "directx math not supported" << endl;
    return 0;
  }

  XMMATRIX A(1.0f, 0.0f, 0.0f, 0.0f,
    0.0f, 2.0f, 0.0f, 0.0f,
    0.0f, 0.0f, 4.0f, 0.0f,
    1.0f, 2.0f, 3.0f, 1.0f);

  XMMATRIX B = XMMatrixIdentity();
```

54 MATHEMATICAL PREREQUISITES

```
    XMMATRIX C = A * B;

    XMMATRIX D = XMMatrixTranspose(A);

    XMVECTOR det = XMMatrixDeterminant(A);
    XMMATRIX E = XMMatrixInverse(&det, A);

    XMMATRIX F = A * E;

    cout << "A = " << endl << A << endl;
    cout << "B = " << endl << B << endl;
    cout << "C = A*B = " << endl << C << endl;
    cout << "D = transpose(A) = " << endl << D << endl;
    cout << "det = determinant(A) = " << det << endl << endl;
    cout << "E = inverse(A) = " << endl << E << endl;
    cout << "F = A*E = " << endl << F << endl;

    return 0;
}
```

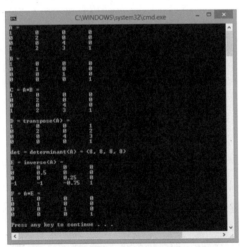

Figure 2.1. Output of the above program.

2.9 SUMMARY

1. An $m \times n$ matrix **M** is a rectangular array of real numbers with m rows and n columns. Two matrices of the same dimensions are equal if and only if their corresponding components are equal. We add two matrices of the same dimensions by adding their corresponding elements. We multiply a scalar and a matrix by multiplying the scalar with every element in the matrix.

2. If **A** is a $m \times n$ *matrix and* **B** is a $n \times p$ matrix, then the product **AB** is defined and is a $m \times p$ *matrix* **C**, where the *ijth entry of the product* **C** is given by taking the dot product of the *ith row vector in* **A** with the *jth column vector in* **B**, that is, $C_{ij} = \mathbf{A}_{i,*} \cdot \mathbf{B}_{*,j}$.

3. Matrix multiplication is not commutative (i.e., **AB** ≠ **BA**, in general). Matrix multiplication is associative: $(\mathbf{AB})\mathbf{C} = \mathbf{A}(\mathbf{BC})$.

4. The transpose of a matrix is found by interchanging the rows and columns of the matrix. Thus the transpose of an $m \times n$ matrix is an $n \times m$ matrix. We denote the transpose of a matrix **M** as $\mathbf{M}^T$.

5. The identity matrix is a square matrix that has zeros for all elements except along the main diagonal, and the elements along the main diagonal are all ones.

6. The determinant, det **A**, is a special function which inputs a square matrix and outputs a real number. A square matrix **A** is invertible if and only if det **A** ≠ 0. The determinant is used in the formula for computing the inverse of a matrix.

7. Multiplying a matrix with its inverse results in the identity matrix: $\mathbf{MM}^{-1} = \mathbf{M}^{-1}\mathbf{M} = \mathbf{I}$. The inverse of a matrix, if it exists, is unique. Only square matrices have inverses and even then, a square matrix may not be invertible. The inverse of a matrix can be computed with the formula: $\mathbf{A}^{-1} = \mathbf{A}^* / \det \mathbf{A}$, where $\mathbf{A}^*$ is the adjoint (transpose of the cofactor matrix of **A**).

8. We use the DirectX Math XMMATRIX type to describe 4 × 4 matrices efficiently in code using SIMD operations. For class data members, we use the XMFLOAT4X4 class, and then use the loading (XMLoadFloat4x4) and storage (XMStoreFloat4x4) methods to convert back and forth between XMMATRIX and XMFLOAT4X4. The XMMATRIX class overloads the arithmetic operators to do matrix addition, subtraction, matrix multiplication, and scalar multiplication. Moreover, the DirectX Math library provides the following useful matrix functions for computing the identity matrix, product, transpose, determinant, and inverse:

```
XMMATRIX XM_CALLCONV XMMatrixIdentity();
XMMATRIX XM_CALLCONV XMMatrixMultiply(FXMMATRIX A, CXMMATRIX B);
XMMATRIX XM_CALLCONV XMMatrixTranspose(FXMMATRIX M);
XMVECTOR XM_CALLCONV XMMatrixDeterminant(FXMMATRIX M);
XMMATRIX XM_CALLCONV XMMatrixInverse(XMVECTOR* pDeterminant,
   FXMMATRIX M);
```

2.10 EXERCISES

1. Solve the following matrix equation for **X**: $3\left(\begin{bmatrix} -2 & 0 \\ 1 & 3 \end{bmatrix} - 2\mathbf{X}\right) = 2\begin{bmatrix} -2 & 0 \\ 1 & 3 \end{bmatrix}$.

2. Compute the following matrix products:

(a) $\begin{bmatrix} -2 & 0 & 3 \\ 4 & 1 & -1 \end{bmatrix} \begin{bmatrix} 2 & -1 \\ 0 & 6 \\ 2 & -3 \end{bmatrix}$,

(b) $\begin{bmatrix} 1 & 2 \\ 3 & 4 \end{bmatrix} \begin{bmatrix} -2 & 0 \\ 1 & 1 \end{bmatrix}$

(c) $\begin{bmatrix} 2 & 0 & 2 \\ 0 & -1 & -3 \\ 0 & 0 & 1 \end{bmatrix} \begin{bmatrix} 1 \\ 2 \\ 1 \end{bmatrix}$

3. Compute the transpose of the following matrices:

(a) $\begin{bmatrix} 1, & 2, & 3 \end{bmatrix}$,

(b) $\begin{bmatrix} x & y \\ z & w \end{bmatrix}$,

(c) $\begin{bmatrix} 1 & 2 \\ 3 & 4 \\ 5 & 6 \\ 7 & 8 \end{bmatrix}$

4. Write the following linear combinations as vector-matrix products:

(a) $\mathbf{v} = 2(1, 2, 3) - 4(-5, 0, -1) + 3(2, -2, 3)$

(b) $\mathbf{v} = 3(2, -4) + 2(1, 4) - 1(-2, -3) + 5(1, 1)$

5. Show that

$$\mathbf{AB} = \begin{bmatrix} A_{11} & A_{12} & A_{13} \\ A_{21} & A_{22} & A_{23} \\ A_{31} & A_{32} & A_{33} \end{bmatrix} \begin{bmatrix} B_{11} & B_{12} & B_{13} \\ B_{21} & B_{22} & B_{23} \\ B_{31} & B_{32} & B_{33} \end{bmatrix} = \begin{bmatrix} \leftarrow \mathbf{A}_{1,*}\mathbf{B} \rightarrow \\ \leftarrow \mathbf{A}_{2,*}\mathbf{B} \rightarrow \\ \leftarrow \mathbf{A}_{3,*}\mathbf{B} \rightarrow \end{bmatrix}$$

6. Show that

$$\mathbf{Au} = \begin{bmatrix} A_{11} & A_{12} & A_{13} \\ A_{21} & A_{22} & A_{23} \\ A_{31} & A_{32} & A_{33} \end{bmatrix} \begin{bmatrix} x \\ y \\ z \end{bmatrix} = x\mathbf{A}_{*,1} + y\mathbf{A}_{*,2} + z\mathbf{A}_{*,3}$$

7. Prove that the cross product can be expressed by the matrix product:

$$\mathbf{u} \times \mathbf{v} = \begin{bmatrix} v_x & v_y & v_z \end{bmatrix} \begin{bmatrix} 0 & u_z & -u_y \\ -u_z & 0 & u_x \\ u_y & -u_x & 0 \end{bmatrix}$$

8. Let $= \begin{bmatrix} 2 & 0 & 1 \\ 0 & -1 & -3 \\ 0 & 0 & 1 \end{bmatrix}$. Is $\mathbf{B} = \begin{bmatrix} 1/2 & 0 & -1/2 \\ 0 & -1 & -3 \\ 0 & 0 & 1 \end{bmatrix}$ the inverse of **A**?

9. Let $\mathbf{A} = \begin{bmatrix} 1 & 2 \\ 3 & 4 \end{bmatrix}$. Is $\mathbf{B} = \begin{bmatrix} -2 & 1 \\ 3/2 & 1/2 \end{bmatrix}$ the inverse of **A**?

10. Find the determinants of the following matrices:

$$\begin{bmatrix} 21 & -4 \\ 10 & 7 \end{bmatrix} \qquad \begin{bmatrix} 2 & 0 & 0 \\ 0 & 3 & 0 \\ 0 & 0 & 7 \end{bmatrix}$$

11. Find the inverse of the following matrices:

$$\begin{bmatrix} 21 & -4 \\ 10 & 7 \end{bmatrix} \qquad \begin{bmatrix} 2 & 0 & 0 \\ 0 & 3 & 0 \\ 0 & 0 & 7 \end{bmatrix}$$

12. Is the following matrix invertible?

$$\begin{bmatrix} 1 & 2 & 3 \\ 0 & 4 & 5 \\ 0 & 0 & 0 \end{bmatrix}$$

13. Show that $(\mathbf{A}^{-1})^T = (\mathbf{A}^T)^{-1}$, assuming **A** is invertible.

14. Let **A** and **B** be $n \times n$ matrices. A fact proved in linear algebra books is that $\det(\mathbf{AB}) = \det \mathbf{A} \cdot \det \mathbf{B}$. Use this fact along with the fact that $\det \mathbf{I} = 1$ to prove $\det \mathbf{A}^{-1} = \dfrac{1}{\det \mathbf{A}}$, assuming **A** is invertible.

15. Prove that the 2D determinant $\begin{bmatrix} u_x & u_y \\ v_x & v_y \end{bmatrix}$ gives the signed area of the parallelogram spanned by $\mathbf{u} = (u_x, u_y)$ and $\mathbf{v} = (v_x, v_y)$. The result is positive if $\mathbf{u}$ can be rotated counterclockwise to coincide with $\mathbf{v}$ by an angle $\theta \in (0, \pi)$, and negative otherwise.

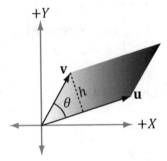

16. Find the area of the parallelogram spanned by:
    (a) $\mathbf{u} = (3, 0)$ band $\mathbf{v} = (1, 1)$
    (b) $\mathbf{u} = (-1, -1)$ and $\mathbf{v} = (0, 1)$

17. Let $\mathbf{A} = \begin{bmatrix} A_{11} & A_{12} \\ A_{21} & A_{22} \end{bmatrix}$, $\mathbf{B} = \begin{bmatrix} B_{11} & B_{12} \\ B_{21} & B_{22} \end{bmatrix}$, and $\mathbf{C} = \begin{bmatrix} C_{11} & C_{12} \\ C_{21} & C_{22} \end{bmatrix}$. Show that $\mathbf{A}(\mathbf{BC}) = (\mathbf{AB})\mathbf{C}$. This shows that matrix multiplication is associative for 2×2 matrices. (In fact, matrix multiplication is associative for general sized matrices, whenever the multiplication is defined.)

18. Write a computer program that computes the transpose of an $m \times n$ matrix without using DirectX Math (just use an array of arrays in C++).

19. Write a computer program that computes the determinant and inverse of 4×4 matrices without using DirectX Math (just use an array of arrays in C++).

Chapter 3 TRANSFORMATIONS

We describe objects in our 3D worlds geometrically; that is, as a collection of triangles that approximate the exterior surfaces of the objects. It would be an uninteresting world if our objects remained motionless. Thus we are interested in methods for transforming geometry; examples of geometric transformations are translation, rotation, and scaling. In this chapter, we develop matrix equations, which can be used to transform points and vectors in 3D space.

Objectives:

1. To understand how linear and affine transformations can be represented by matrices.
2. To learn the coordinate transformations for scaling, rotating, and translating geometry.
3. To discover how several transformation matrices can be combined into one net transformation matrix through matrix-matrix multiplication.
4. To find out how we can convert coordinates from one coordinate system to another, and how this change of coordinate transformation can be represented by a matrix.
5. To become familiar with the subset of functions provided by the DirectX Math library used for constructing transformation matrices.

3.1 LINEAR TRANSFORMATIONS

3.1.1 Definition

Consider the mathematical function $\tau(\mathbf{v}) = \tau(x, y, z) = (x', y', z')$. This function inputs a 3D vector and outputs a 3D vector. We say that τ is a *linear transformation* if and only if the following properties hold:

$$\tau(\mathbf{u}+\mathbf{v}) = \tau(\mathbf{u}) + \tau(\mathbf{v})$$
$$\tau(k\mathbf{u}) = k\tau(\mathbf{u})$$
(eq. 3.1)

where $\mathbf{u} = (u_x, u_y, u_z)$ and $\mathbf{v} = (v_x, v_y, v_z)$ are any 3D vectors, and k is a scalar.

Note: *A linear transformation can consist of input and output values other than 3D vectors, but we do not need such generality in a 3D graphics book.*

☞ Example 3.1

Define the function $\tau(x, y, z) = (x^2, y^2, z^2)$; for example, $\tau(1, 2, 3) = (1, 4, 9)$. This function is not linear since, for $k = 2$ and $\mathbf{u} = (1, 2, 3)$ we have:

$$\tau(k\mathbf{u}) = \tau(2, 4, 6) = (4, 16, 36)$$

but

$$k\tau(\mathbf{u}) = 2(1, 4, 9) = (2, 8, 18)$$

So property 2 of Equation 3.1 is not satisfied.
If τ is linear, then it follows that:

$$\begin{aligned}\tau(a\mathbf{u}+b\mathbf{v}+c\mathbf{w}) &= \tau(a\mathbf{u}+(b\mathbf{v}+c\mathbf{w})) \\ &= a\tau(\mathbf{u}) + \tau(b\mathbf{v}+c\mathbf{w}) \\ &= a\tau(\mathbf{u}) + b\tau(\mathbf{v}) + c\tau(\mathbf{w})\end{aligned}$$
(eq. 3.2)

We will use this result in the next section.

3.1.2 Matrix Representation

Let $\mathbf{u} = (x, y, z)$. Observe that we can always write this as:

$$\mathbf{u} = (x, y, z) = x\mathbf{i} + y\mathbf{j} + z\mathbf{k} = x(1, 0, 0) + y(0, 1, 0) + z(0, 0, 1)$$

The vectors $\mathbf{i} = (1, 0, 0)$, $\mathbf{j} = (0, 1, 0)$, and $\mathbf{k} = (0, 0, 1)$, which are unit vectors that aim along the working coordinate axes, respectively, are called the *standard basis*

Figure 3.1. The left pawn is the original object. The middle pawn is the original pawn scaled 2 units on the *y*-axis making it taller. The right pawn is the original pawn scaled 2 units on the *x*-axis making it fatter.

vectors for $\mathbb{R}^3$. ($\mathbb{R}^3$ denotes the set of all 3D coordinate vectors (x, y, z)). Now let τ be a linear transformation; by linearity (i.e., Equation 3.2), we have:

$$\tau(\mathbf{u}) = \tau(x\mathbf{i} + y\mathbf{j} + z\mathbf{k}) = x\tau(\mathbf{i}) + y\tau(\mathbf{j}) + z\tau(\mathbf{k}) \qquad \text{(eq. 3.3)}$$

Observe that this is nothing more than a linear combination, which, as we learned in the previous chapter, can be written by a vector-matrix multiplication. By Equation 2.2 we may rewrite Equation 3.3 as:

$$\tau(\mathbf{u}) = x\tau(\mathbf{i}) + y\tau(\mathbf{j}) + z\tau(\mathbf{k})$$

$$= \mathbf{u}\mathbf{A} = \begin{bmatrix} x & y & z \end{bmatrix} \begin{bmatrix} \leftarrow \tau(\mathbf{i}) \rightarrow \\ \leftarrow \tau(\mathbf{j}) \rightarrow \\ \leftarrow \tau(\mathbf{k}) \rightarrow \end{bmatrix} = \begin{bmatrix} x & y & z \end{bmatrix} \begin{bmatrix} A_{11} & A_{12} & A_{13} \\ A_{21} & A_{22} & A_{23} \\ A_{31} & A_{32} & A_{33} \end{bmatrix} \qquad \text{(eq. 3.4)}$$

where $\tau(\mathbf{i}) = (A_{11}, A_{12}, A_{13})$, $\tau(\mathbf{j}) = (A_{21}, A_{22}, A_{23})$, and $\tau(\mathbf{k}) = (A_{31}, A_{32}, A_{33})$. We call the matrix **A** the matrix representation of the linear transformation τ.

3.1.3 Scaling

Scaling refers to changing the size of an object as shown in Figure 3.1. We define the scaling transformation by:

$$S(x, y, z) = (s_x x, s_y y, s_z z)$$

This scales the vector by s_x units on the *x*-axis, s_y units on the *y*-axis, and s_z units on the *z*-axis, relative to the origin of the working coordinate system. We now show that S is indeed a linear transformation. We have that:

$$S(\mathbf{u} + \mathbf{v}) = \left(s_x(u_x + v_x), s_y(u_y + v_y), s_z(u_z + v_z)\right)$$

$$= \left(s_x u_x + s_x v_x, s_y u_y + s_y v_y, s_z u_z + s_z v_z\right)$$

$$= (s_x u_x, s_y u_y, s_z u_z) + (s_x v_x, s_y v_y, s_z v_z)$$
$$= S(\mathbf{u}) + S(\mathbf{v})$$
$$S(k\mathbf{u}) = (s_x k u_x, s_y k u_y, s_z k u_z)$$
$$= k(s_x u_x, s_y u_y, s_z u_z)$$
$$= k S(\mathbf{u})$$

Thus both properties of Equation 3.1 are satisfied, so S is linear, and thus there exists a matrix representation. To find the matrix representation, we just apply S to each of the standard basis vectors, as in Equation 3.3, and then place the resulting vectors into the rows of a matrix (as in Equation 3.4):

$$S(\mathbf{i}) = (s_x \cdot 1, s_y \cdot 0, s_z \cdot 0) = (s_x, 0, 0)$$
$$S(\mathbf{j}) = (s_x \cdot 0, s_y \cdot 1, s_z \cdot 0) = (0, s_y, 0)$$
$$S(\mathbf{k}) = (s_x \cdot 0, s_y \cdot 0, s_z \cdot 1) = (0, 0, s_z)$$

Thus the matrix representation of S is:

$$\mathbf{S} = \begin{bmatrix} s_x & 0 & 0 \\ 0 & s_y & 0 \\ 0 & 0 & s_z \end{bmatrix}$$

We call this matrix the *scaling matrix*.

The inverse of the scaling matrix is given by:

$$\mathbf{S}^{-1} = \begin{bmatrix} 1/s_x & 0 & 0 \\ 0 & 1/s_y & 0 \\ 0 & 0 & 1/s_z \end{bmatrix}$$

☞ Example 3.2

Suppose we have a square defined by a minimum point $(-4, -4, 0)$ and a maximum point $(4, 4, 0)$. Suppose now that we wish to scale the square 0.5 units on the x-axis, 2.0 units on the y-axis, and leave the z-axis unchanged. The corresponding scaling matrix is:

$$\mathbf{S} = \begin{bmatrix} 0.5 & 0 & 0 \\ 0 & 2 & 0 \\ 0 & 0 & 1 \end{bmatrix}$$

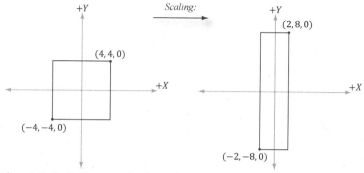

Figure 3.2. Scaling by one-half units on the x-axis and two units on the y-axis. Note that when looking down the negative z-axis, the geometry is basically 2D since z = 0.

Now to actually scale (transform) the square, we multiply both the minimum point and maximum point by this matrix:

$$[-4,-4,0]\begin{bmatrix} 0.5 & 0 & 0 \\ 0 & 2 & 0 \\ 0 & 0 & 1 \end{bmatrix} = [-2,-8,0] \quad [4,4,0]\begin{bmatrix} 0.5 & 0 & 0 \\ 0 & 2 & 0 \\ 0 & 0 & 1 \end{bmatrix} = [2,8,0]$$

The result is shown in Figure 3.2.

3.1.4 Rotation

In this section, we describe rotating a vector **v** about an axis **n** by an angle θ; see Figure 3.3. Note that we measure the angle clockwise when looking down the axis **n**; moreover, we assume $\|\mathbf{n}\| = 1$.

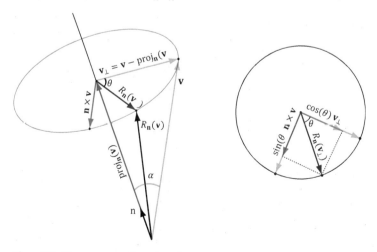

Figure 3.3. The geometry of rotation about a vector **n**.

First, decompose **v** into two parts: one part parallel to **n** and the other part orthogonal to **n**. The parallel part is just $\text{proj}_\mathbf{n}(\mathbf{v})$ (recall Example 1.5); the orthogonal part is given by $\mathbf{v}_\perp = \text{perp}_\mathbf{n}(\mathbf{v}) = \mathbf{v} - \text{proj}_\mathbf{n}(\mathbf{v})$. (Recall, also from Example 1.5, that since **n** is a unit vector, we have $\text{proj}_\mathbf{n}(\mathbf{v}) = (\mathbf{n} \cdot \mathbf{v})\mathbf{n}$.) The key observation is that the part $\text{proj}_\mathbf{n}(\mathbf{v})$ that is parallel to **n** is invariant under the rotation, so we only need to figure out how to rotate the orthogonal part. That is, the rotated vector $R_\mathbf{n}(\mathbf{v}) = \text{proj}_\mathbf{n}(\mathbf{v}) + R_\mathbf{n}(\mathbf{v}_\perp)$, by Figure 3.3.

To find $R_\mathbf{n}(\mathbf{v}_\perp)$, we set up a 2D coordinate system in the plane of rotation. We will use $\mathbf{v}_\perp$ as one reference vector. To get a second reference vector orthogonal to $\mathbf{v}_\perp$ and **n** we take the cross product $\mathbf{n} \times \mathbf{v}$ (left-hand-thumb rule). From the trigonometry of Figure 3.3 and Exercise 14 of Chapter 1, we see that

$$\|\mathbf{n} \times \mathbf{v}\| = \|\mathbf{n}\| \|\mathbf{v}\| \sin\alpha = \|\mathbf{v}\| \sin\alpha = \|\mathbf{v}_\perp\|$$

where α is the angle between **n** and **n**. So both reference vectors have the same length and lie on the circle of rotation. Now that we have set up these two reference vectors, we see from trigonometry that:

$$R_\mathbf{n}(\mathbf{v}_\perp) = \cos\theta \mathbf{v}_\perp + \sin\theta (\mathbf{n} \times \mathbf{v})$$

This gives us the following rotation formula:

$$\begin{aligned}R_\mathbf{n}(\mathbf{v}) &= \text{proj}_\mathbf{n}(\mathbf{v}) + R_\mathbf{n}(\mathbf{v}_\perp) \\ &= (\mathbf{n} \cdot \mathbf{v})\mathbf{n} + \cos\theta \mathbf{v}_\perp + \sin\theta(\mathbf{n} \times \mathbf{v}) \\ &= (\mathbf{n} \cdot \mathbf{v})\mathbf{n} + \cos\theta(\mathbf{v} - (\mathbf{n} \cdot \mathbf{v})\mathbf{n}) + \sin\theta(\mathbf{n} \times \mathbf{v}) \\ &= \cos\theta\mathbf{v} + (1-\cos\theta)(\mathbf{n} \cdot \mathbf{v})\mathbf{n} + \sin\theta(\mathbf{n} \times \mathbf{v})\end{aligned} \quad \text{(eq. 3.5)}$$

We leave it as an exercise to show that this is a linear transformation. To find the matrix representation, we just apply $R_\mathbf{n}$ to each of the standard basis vectors, as in Equation 3.3, and then place the resulting vectors into the rows of a matrix (as in Equation 3.4). The final result is:

$$\mathbf{R}_\mathbf{n} = \begin{bmatrix} c+(1-c)x^2 & (1-c)xy+sz & (1-c)xz-sy \\ (1-c)xy-sz & c+(1-c)y^2 & (1-c)yz+sx \\ (1-c)xz+sy & (1-c)yz-sx & c+(1-c)z^2 \end{bmatrix}$$

where we let $c = \cos\theta$ and $s = \sin\theta$.

The rotation matrices have an interesting property. Each row vector is unit length (verify) and the row vectors are mutually orthogonal (verify). Thus the row vectors are *orthonormal* (i.e., mutually orthogonal and unit length). A matrix whose rows are orthonormal is said to be an *orthogonal matrix*. An orthogonal matrix has the attractive property that its inverse is actually equal to its transpose. Thus, the inverse of R_n is:

$$\mathbf{R}_n^{-1} = \mathbf{R}_n^T = \begin{bmatrix} c+(1-c)x^2 & (1-c)xy-sz & (1-c)xz+sy \\ (1-c)xy+sz & c+(1-c)y^2 & (1-c)yz-sx \\ (1-c)xz-sy & (1-c)yz+sx & c+(1-c)z^2 \end{bmatrix}$$

In general, orthogonal matrices are desirable to work with since their inverses are easy and efficient to compute.

In particular, if we choose the x-, y-, and z-axes for rotation (i.e., **n** = (1, 0, 0), **n** = (0, 1, 0), and **n** = (0, 0, 1), respectively), then we get the following rotation matrices which rotate about the x-, y-, and z-axis, respectively:

$$\mathbf{R}_x = \begin{bmatrix} 1 & 0 & 0 & 0 \\ 0 & \cos\theta & \sin\theta & 0 \\ 0 & -\sin\theta & \cos\theta & 0 \\ 0 & 0 & 0 & 1 \end{bmatrix}, \mathbf{R}_y = \begin{bmatrix} \cos\theta & 0 & -\sin\theta & 0 \\ 0 & 1 & 0 & 0 \\ \sin\theta & 0 & \cos\theta & 0 \\ 0 & 0 & 0 & 1 \end{bmatrix}, \mathbf{R}_z = \begin{bmatrix} \cos\theta & \sin\theta & 0 & 0 \\ -\sin\theta & \cos\theta & 0 & 0 \\ 0 & 0 & 1 & 0 \\ 0 & 0 & 0 & 1 \end{bmatrix}$$

☞ Example 3.3

Suppose we have a square defined by a minimum point (−1, 0, −1) and a maximum point (1, 0, 1). Suppose now that we wish to rotate the square −30° clockwise about the y-axis (i.e., 30° counterclockwise). In this case, **n** = (0, 1, 0), which simplifies $\mathbf{R}_n$ considerably; the corresponding y-axis rotation matrix is:

$$\mathbf{R}_y = \begin{bmatrix} \cos\theta & 0 & -\sin\theta \\ 0 & 1 & 0 \\ \sin\theta & 0 & \cos\theta \end{bmatrix} = \begin{bmatrix} \cos(-30°) & 0 & -\sin(-30°) \\ 0 & 1 & 0 \\ \sin(-30°) & 0 & \cos(-30°) \end{bmatrix} = \begin{bmatrix} \frac{\sqrt{3}}{2} & 0 & \frac{1}{2} \\ 0 & 1 & 0 \\ -\frac{1}{2} & 0 & \frac{\sqrt{3}}{2} \end{bmatrix}$$

Now to actually rotate (transform) the square, we multiply both the minimum point and maximum point by this matrix:

$$[-1,0,-1] \begin{bmatrix} \frac{\sqrt{3}}{2} & 0 & \frac{1}{2} \\ 0 & 1 & 0 \\ -\frac{1}{2} & 0 & \frac{\sqrt{3}}{2} \end{bmatrix} \approx [-0.36, 0, -1.36] \quad [1,0,1] \begin{bmatrix} \frac{\sqrt{3}}{2} & 0 & \frac{1}{2} \\ 0 & 1 & 0 \\ -\frac{1}{2} & 0 & \frac{\sqrt{3}}{2} \end{bmatrix} \approx [0.36, 0, 1.36]$$

The result is shown in Figure 3.4.

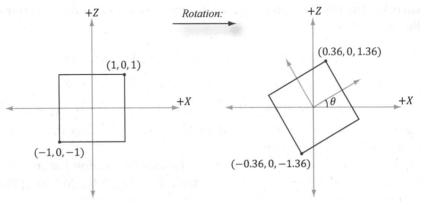

Figure 3.4. Rotating −30° clockwise around the y-axis. Note that when looking down the positive y-axis, the geometry is basically 2D since y = 0.

3.2 AFFINE TRANSFORMATIONS

3.2.1 Homogeneous Coordinates

We will see in the next section that an affine transformation is a linear transformation combined with a translation. However, translation does not make sense for vectors because a vector only describes direction and magnitude, independent of location; in other words, vectors should be unchanged under translations. Translations should only be applied to points (i.e., position vectors). *Homogeneous coordinates* provide a convenient notational mechanism that enables us to handle points and vectors uniformly. With homogeneous coordinates, we augment to 4-tuples and what we place in the fourth w-coordinate depends on whether we are describing a point or vector. Specifically, we write:

1. $(x, y, z, 0)$ for vectors
2. $(x, y, z, 1)$ for points

We will see later that setting $w = 1$ for points allows translations of points to work correctly, and setting $w = 0$ for vectors prevents the coordinates of vectors from being modified by translations (we do not want to translate the coordinates of a vector, as that would change its direction and magnitude—translations should not alter the properties of vectors).

The notation of homogeneous coordinates is consistent with the ideas shown in Figure 1.17. That is, the difference between two points $\mathbf{q} - \mathbf{p} = (q_x, q_y, q_z, 1) - (p_x, p_y, p_z, 1) = (q_x - p_x, q_y - p_y, q_z - p_z, 0)$ *results in a vector, and a point plus a vector* $\mathbf{p} + \mathbf{v} = (p_x, p_y, p_z, 1) + (v_x, v_y, v_z, 1) = (p_x + v_x, p_y + v_y, p_z + v_z, 1)$ *results in a point.*

3.2.2 Definition and Matrix Representation

A linear transformation cannot describe all the transformations we wish to do; therefore, we augment to a larger class of functions called affine transformations. An affine transformation is a linear transformation plus a translation vector **b**; that is:

$$\alpha(\mathbf{u}) = \tau(\mathbf{u}) + \mathbf{b}$$

Or in matrix notation:

$$\alpha(\mathbf{u}) = \mathbf{u}\mathbf{A} + \mathbf{b} = \begin{bmatrix} x & y & z \end{bmatrix} \begin{bmatrix} A_{11} & A_{12} & A_{13} \\ A_{21} & A_{22} & A_{23} \\ A_{31} & A_{32} & A_{33} \end{bmatrix} + \begin{bmatrix} b_x & b_y & b_z \end{bmatrix} = \begin{bmatrix} x' & y' & z' \end{bmatrix}$$

where **A** is the matrix representation of a linear transformation.

If we augment to homogeneous coordinates with $w = 1$, then we can write this more compactly as:

$$\begin{bmatrix} x & y & z & 1 \end{bmatrix} \begin{bmatrix} A_{11} & A_{12} & A_{13} & 0 \\ A_{21} & A_{22} & A_{23} & 0 \\ A_{31} & A_{32} & A_{33} & 0 \\ b_x & b_y & b_z & 1 \end{bmatrix} = \begin{bmatrix} x' & y' & z' & 1 \end{bmatrix} \quad \text{(eq. 3.6)}$$

The 4 × 4 matrix in Equation 3.6 is called the matrix representation of the affine transformation.

Observe that the addition by **b** is essentially a translation (i.e., change in position). We do not want to apply this to vectors because vectors have no position. However, we still want to apply the linear part of the affine transformation to vectors. If we set $w = 0$ in the fourth component for vectors, then the translation by **b** is *not* applied (verify by doing the matrix multiplication).

Note: *Because the dot product of the row vector with the fourth column of the above 4 × 4 affine transformation matrix is: [x, y, z, w]·[0, 0, 0, 1] = w, this matrix does not modify the w-coordinate of the input vector.*

3.2.3 Translation

The *identity transformation* is a linear transformation that just returns its argument; that is, $I(\mathbf{u}) = \mathbf{u}$. It can be shown that the matrix representation of this linear transformation is the identity matrix.

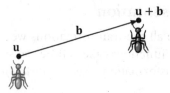

Figure 3.5. Displacing the position of the ant by some displacement vector **b**.

Now, we define the translation transformation to be the affine transformation whose linear transformation is the identity transformation; that is,

$$\tau(\mathbf{u}) = \mathbf{u}\mathbf{I} + \mathbf{b} = \mathbf{u} + \mathbf{b}$$

As you can see, this simply translates (or displaces) point **u** by **b**. Figure 3.5 illustrates how this could be used to displace objects—we translate every point on the object by the same vector **b** to move it.

By Equation 3.6, τ has the matrix representation:

$$\mathbf{T} = \begin{bmatrix} 1 & 0 & 0 & 0 \\ 0 & 1 & 0 & 0 \\ 0 & 0 & 1 & 0 \\ b_x & b_y & b_z & 1 \end{bmatrix}$$

This is called the *translation matrix*.

The inverse of the translation matrix is given by:

$$\mathbf{T}^{-1} = \begin{bmatrix} 1 & 0 & 0 & 0 \\ 0 & 1 & 0 & 0 \\ 0 & 0 & 1 & 0 \\ -b_x & -b_y & -b_z & 1 \end{bmatrix}$$

☞ Example 3.4

Suppose we have a square defined by a minimum point (−8, 2, 0) and a maximum point (−2, 8, 0). Suppose now that we wish to translate the square 12 units on the x-axis, −10.0 units on the y-axis, and leave the z-axis unchanged. The corresponding translation matrix is:

$$\mathbf{T} = \begin{bmatrix} 1 & 0 & 0 & 0 \\ 0 & 1 & 0 & 0 \\ 0 & 0 & 1 & 0 \\ 12 & -10 & 0 & 1 \end{bmatrix}$$

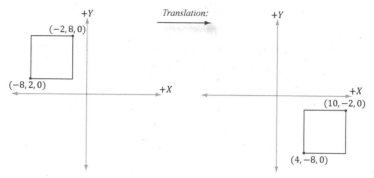

Figure 3.6. Translating 12 units on the x-axis and −10 units on the y-axis. Note that when looking down the negative z-axis, the geometry is basically 2D since z = 0.

Now to actually translate (transform) the square, we multiply both the minimum point and maximum point by this matrix:

$$[-8,\ 2,\ 0,\ 1]\begin{bmatrix} 1 & 0 & 0 & 0 \\ 0 & 1 & 0 & 0 \\ 0 & 0 & 1 & 0 \\ 12 & -10 & 0 & 1 \end{bmatrix} = [4,\ -8\ 0,\ 1]$$

$$[-2,\ 8,\ 0,\ 1]\begin{bmatrix} 1 & 0 & 0 & 0 \\ 0 & 1 & 0 & 0 \\ 0 & 0 & 1 & 0 \\ 12 & -10 & 0 & 1 \end{bmatrix} = [10,\ -2,\ 0,\ 1]$$

The result is shown in Figure 3.6.

Note:
> Let **T** be a transformation matrix, and recall that we transform a point/vector by computing the product **vT** = **v**′. Observe that if we transform a point/vector by **T** and then transform it again by the inverse **T**⁻¹ we end up with the original vector: **vTT**⁻¹ = **vI** = **v**. In other words, the inverse transformation undoes the transformation. For example, if we translate a point 5 units on the x-axis, and then translate by the inverse -5 units on the x-axis, we end up where we started. Likewise, if we rotate a point 30° about the y-axis, and then rotate by the inverse −30° about the y-axis, then we end up with our original point. In summary, the inverse of a transformation matrix does the opposite transformation such that the composition of the two transformations leaves the geometry unchanged.

3.2.4 Affine Matrices for Scaling and Rotation

Observe that if $\mathbf{b} = \mathbf{0}$, the affine transformation reduces to a linear transformation. Thus we can express any linear transformation as an affine transformation with $\mathbf{b} = \mathbf{0}$. This, in turn, means we can represent any linear transformation by a 4×4 affine matrix. For example, the scaling and rotation matrices written using 4×4 matrices are given as follows:

$$\mathbf{S} = \begin{bmatrix} s_x & 0 & 0 & 0 \\ 0 & s_y & 0 & 0 \\ 0 & 0 & s_z & 0 \\ 0 & 0 & 0 & 1 \end{bmatrix}$$

$$\mathbf{R_n} = \begin{bmatrix} c+(1-c)x^2 & (1-c)xy+sz & (1-c)xz-sy & 0 \\ (1-c)xy-sz & c+(1-c)y^2 & (1-c)yz+sx & 0 \\ (1-c)xz+sy & (1-c)yz-sx & c+(1-c)z^2 & 0 \\ 0 & 0 & 0 & 1 \end{bmatrix}$$

In this way, we can express all of our transformations consistently using 4×4 matrices and points and vectors using 1×4 homogeneous row vectors.

3.2.5 Geometric Interpretation of an Affine Transformation Matrix

In this section, we develop some intuition of what the numbers inside an affine transformation matrix mean geometrically. First, let us consider a *rigid body transformation*, which is essentially a shape preserving transformation. A real world example of a rigid body transformation might be picking a book off your desk and placing it on a bookshelf; during this process you are translating the book from your desk to the bookshelf, but also very likely changing the orientation of the book in the process (rotation). Let τ be a rotation transformation describing how we want to rotate an object and let $\mathbf{b}$ define a displacement vector describing how we want to translate an object. This rigid body transform can be described by the affine transformation:

$$\alpha(x,y,z) = \tau(x,y,z) + \mathbf{b} = x\tau(\mathbf{i}) + y\tau(\mathbf{j}) + z\tau(\mathbf{k}) + \mathbf{b}$$

In matrix notation, using homogeneous coordinates ($w = 1$ for points and $w = 0$ for vectors so that the translation is not applied to vectors), this is written as:

$$[x, \ y, \ z, \ w] \begin{bmatrix} \leftarrow \tau(\mathbf{i}) \rightarrow \\ \leftarrow \tau(\mathbf{j}) \rightarrow \\ \leftarrow \tau(\mathbf{k}) \rightarrow \\ \leftarrow \mathbf{b} \rightarrow \end{bmatrix} = [x', \ y', \ z', \ w] \qquad \text{(eq. 3.7)}$$

Now, to see what this equation is doing geometrically, all we need to do is graph the row vectors in the matrix (see Figure 3.7). Because τ is a rotation transformation it preserves lengths and angles; in particular, we see that τ is just rotating the standard basis vectors $\mathbf{i}$, $\mathbf{j}$, and $\mathbf{k}$ into a new orientation $\tau(\mathbf{i})$, $\tau(\mathbf{j})$, and $\tau(\mathbf{k})$. The vector $\mathbf{b}$ is just a position vector denoting a displacement from the origin. Now Figure 3.7 shows how the transformed point is obtained geometrically when $\alpha(x, y, z) = x\tau(\mathbf{i}) + y\tau(\mathbf{j}) + z\tau(\mathbf{k}) + \mathbf{b}$ is computed.

The same idea applies to scaling or skew transformations. Consider the linear transformation τ that warps a square into a parallelogram as shown in Figure 3.8. The warped point is simply the linear combination of the warped basis vectors.

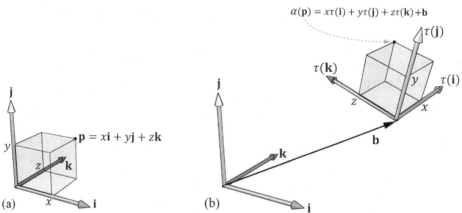

Figure 3.7. The geometry of the rows of an affine transformation matrix. The transformed point, $\alpha(\mathbf{p})$, is given as a linear combination of the transformed basis vectors $\tau(\mathbf{i})$, $\tau(\mathbf{j})$, $\tau(\mathbf{k})$, and the offset $\mathbf{b}$.

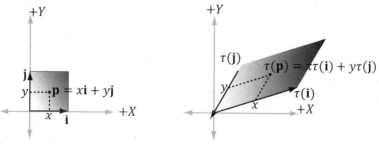

Figure 3.8. For a linear transformation that warps a square into a parallelogram, the transformed point $\tau(\mathbf{p}) = (x, y)$ is given as a linear combination of the transformed basis vectors $\tau(\mathbf{i})$, $\tau(\mathbf{j})$.

3.3 COMPOSITION OF TRANSFORMATIONS

Suppose **S** is a scaling matrix, **R** is a rotation matrix, and **T** is a translation matrix. Assume we have a cube made up of eight vertices $\mathbf{v}_i$ for $i = 0, 1, \ldots, 7$, and we wish to apply these three transformations to each vertex successively. The obvious way to do this is step-by-step:

$$((\mathbf{v}_i \mathbf{S})\mathbf{R})\mathbf{T} = (\mathbf{v}'_i \mathbf{R})\mathbf{T} = \mathbf{v}''_i \mathbf{T} = \mathbf{v}'''_i \quad \text{for } i = 0,1,\ldots,7$$

However, because matrix multiplication is associative, we can instead write this equivalently as:

$$\mathbf{v}_i(\mathbf{SRT}) = \mathbf{v}'''_i \quad \text{for } i = 0,1,\ldots,7$$

We can think of the matrix **C** = **SRT** as a matrix that encapsulates all three transformations into one net transformation matrix. In other words, matrix-matrix multiplication allows us to concatenate transforms.

This has performance implications. To see this, assume that a 3D object is composed of 20,000 points and that we want to apply these three successive geometric transformations to the object. Using the step-by-step approach, we would require 20,000 × 3 vector-matrix multiplications. On the other hand, using the combined matrix approach requires 20,000 vector-matrix multiplications and 2 matrix-matrix multiplications. Clearly, two extra matrix-matrix multiplications is a cheap price to pay for the large savings in vector-matrix multiplications.

> *Again we point out that matrix multiplication is not commutative. This is even seen geometrically. For example, a rotation followed by a translation, which we can describe by the matrix product* **RT**, *does not result in the same transformation as the same translation followed by the same rotation, that is,* **TR**. *Figure 3.9 demonstrates this.*

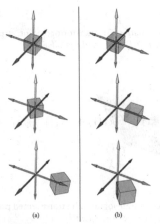

Figure 3.9. (a) Rotating first and then translating. (b) Translating first and then rotating.

3.4 CHANGE OF COORDINATE TRANSFORMATIONS

The scalar 100°C represents the temperature of boiling water relative to the Celsius scale. How do we describe the *same* temperature of boiling water relative to the Fahrenheit scale? In other words, what is the scalar, relative to the Fahrenheit scale, that represents the temperature of boiling water? To make this conversion (or change of frame), we need to know how the Celsius and Fahrenheit scales relate. They are related as follows: $T_F = \frac{9}{5}T_C + 32°$. Therefore, the temperature of boiling water relative to the Fahrenheit scale is given by $T_F = \frac{9}{5}(100)° + 32° = 212°F$.

This example illustrates that we can convert a scalar k that describes some quantity relative to a frame A into a new scalar k' that describes the *same* quantity relative to a different frame B, provided that we knew how frame A and B were related. In the following subsections, we look at a similar problem, but instead of scalars, we are interested in how to convert the coordinates of a point/vector relative to one frame into coordinates relative to a different frame (see Figure 3.10). We call the transformation that converts coordinates from one frame into coordinates of another frame a *change of coordinate transformation*.

It is worth emphasizing that in a change of coordinate transformation, we do not think of the geometry as changing; rather, we are changing the frame of reference, which thus changes the coordinate representation of the geometry. This is in contrast to how we usually think about rotations, translations, and scaling, where we think of actually physically moving or deforming the geometry.

In 3D computer graphics, we employ multiple coordinate systems, so we need to know how to convert from one to another. Because location is a property of

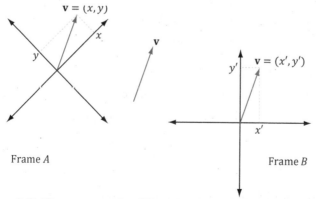

Figure 3.10. The *same* vector **v** has different coordinates when described relative to different frames. It has coordinates (x, y) relative to frame A and coordinates (x', y') relative to frame B.

points, but not of vectors, the change of coordinate transformation is different for points and vectors.

3.4.1 Vectors

Consider Figure 3.11, in which we have two frames A and B and a vector $\mathbf{p}$. Suppose we are given the coordinates $\mathbf{p}_A = (x, y)$ of $\mathbf{p}$ relative to frame A, and we wish to find the coordinates $\mathbf{p}_B = (x', y')$ of $\mathbf{p}$ relative to frame B. In other words, given the coordinates identifying a vector relative to one frame, how do we find the coordinates that identify the same vector relative to a different frame?

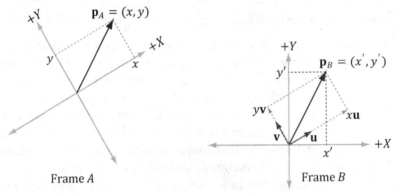

Figure 3.11. The geometry of finding the coordinates of $\mathbf{p}$ relative to frame B.

From Figure 3.11, it is clear that

$$\mathbf{p} = x\mathbf{u} + y\mathbf{v}$$

where $\mathbf{u}$ and $\mathbf{v}$ are unit vectors which aim, respectively, along the x- and y-axes of frame A. Expressing each vector in the above equation in frame B coordinates we get:

$$\mathbf{p}_B = x\mathbf{u}_B + y\mathbf{v}_B$$

Thus, if we are given $\mathbf{p}_A = (x, y)$ and we know the coordinates of the vectors $\mathbf{u}$ and $\mathbf{v}$ relative to frame B, that is if we know $\mathbf{u}_B = (u_x, u_y)$ and $\mathbf{v}_B = (v_x, v_y)$, then we can always find $\mathbf{p}_B = (x', y')$.

Generalizing to 3D, if $\mathbf{p}_A = (x, y, z)$, then

$$\mathbf{p}_B = x\mathbf{u}_B + y\mathbf{v}_B + z\mathbf{w}_B$$

where $\mathbf{u}$, $\mathbf{v}$, and $\mathbf{w}$ are unit vectors which aim, respectively, along the x-, y- and z-axes of frame A.

3.4.2 Points

The change of coordinate transformation for points is slightly different than it is for vectors; this is because location is important for points, so we cannot translate points as we translated the vectors in Figure 3.11.

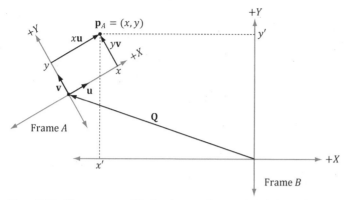

Figure 3.12. The geometry of finding the coordinates of **p** relative to frame B.

Figure 3.12 shows the situation, and we see that the point **p** can be expressed by the equation:

$$\mathbf{p} = x\mathbf{u} + y\mathbf{v} + \mathbf{Q}$$

where **u** and **v** are unit vectors which aim, respectively, along the x- and y-axes of frame A, and **Q** is the origin of frame A. Expressing each vector/point in the above equation in frame B coordinates we get:

$$\mathbf{p}_B = x\mathbf{u}_B + y\mathbf{v}_B + \mathbf{Q}_B$$

Thus, if we are given $\mathbf{p}_A = (x, y)$ and we know the coordinates of the vectors **u** and **v**, and origin **Q** relative to frame B, that is if we know $\mathbf{u}_B = (u_x, u_y)$, $\mathbf{v}_B = (v_x, v_y)$, and $\mathbf{Q}_B = (Q_x, Q_y)$, then we can always find $\mathbf{p}_B = (x', y')$.

Generalizing to 3D, if $\mathbf{p}_A = (x, y, z)$, then

$$\mathbf{p}_B = x\mathbf{u}_B + y\mathbf{v}_B + z\mathbf{w}_B + \mathbf{Q}_B$$

where **u**, **v**, and **w** are unit vectors which aim, respectively, along the x-, y- and z-axes of frame A, and **Q** is the origin of frame A.

3.4.3 Matrix Representation

To review so far, the vector and point change of coordinate transformations are:

$(x', y', z') = x\mathbf{u}_B + y\mathbf{v}_B + z\mathbf{w}_B$ for vectors
$(x', y', z') = x\mathbf{u}_B + y\mathbf{v}_B + z\mathbf{w}_B + \mathbf{Q}_B$ for points

If we use homogeneous coordinates, then we can handle vectors and points by one equation:

$$(x', y', z', w) = x\mathbf{u}_B + y\mathbf{v}_B + z\mathbf{w}_B + w\mathbf{Q}_B \quad \textbf{(eq. 3.8)}$$

If $w = 0$, then this equation reduces to the change of coordinate transformation for vectors; if $w = 1$, then this equation reduces to the change of coordinate transformation for points. The advantage of Equation 3.8 is that it works for both vectors and points, provided we set the *w*-coordinates correctly; we no longer need two equations (one for vectors and one for points). Equation 2.3 says that we can write Equation 3.8 in the language of matrices:

$$[x', y', z', w] = [x, y, z, w] \begin{bmatrix} \leftarrow \mathbf{u}_B \rightarrow \\ \leftarrow \mathbf{v}_B \rightarrow \\ \leftarrow \mathbf{w}_B \rightarrow \\ \leftarrow \mathbf{Q}_B \rightarrow \end{bmatrix}$$

$$= [x, y, z, w] \begin{bmatrix} u_x & u_y & u_z & 0 \\ v_x & v_y & v_z & 0 \\ w_x & w_y & w_z & 0 \\ Q_x & Q_y & Q_z & 1 \end{bmatrix} \quad \text{(eq. 3.9)}$$

$$= x\mathbf{u}_B + y\mathbf{v}_B + z\mathbf{w}_B + w\mathbf{Q}_B$$

where $\mathbf{Q}_B = (Q_x, Q_y, Q_z, 1)$, $\mathbf{u}_B = (u_x, u_y, u_z, 0)$, $\mathbf{v}_B = (v_x, v_y, v_z, 0)$, and $\mathbf{w}_B = (w_x, w_y, w_z, 0)$ describe the origin and axes of frame *A* with homogeneous coordinates relative to frame *B*. We call the 4 × 4 matrix in Equation 3.9 a *change of coordinate matrix* or *change of frame matrix*, and we say it converts (or maps) frame *A* coordinates into frame *B* coordinates.

3.4.4 Associativity and Change of Coordinate Matrices

Suppose now that we have three frames *F*, *G*, and *H*. Moreover, let **A** be the change of frame matrix from *F* to *G*, and let **B** be the change of frame matrix from *G* to *H*. Suppose we have the coordinates $\mathbf{p}_F$ of a vector relative to frame *F* and we want the coordinates of the same vector relative to frame *H*, that is, we want $\mathbf{p}_H$. One way to do this is step-by-step:

$$(\mathbf{p}_F \mathbf{A})\mathbf{B} = \mathbf{p}_H$$
$$(\mathbf{p}_G)\mathbf{B} = \mathbf{p}_H$$

However, because matrix multiplication is associative, we can instead rewrite $(\mathbf{p}_F\mathbf{A})\mathbf{B} = \mathbf{p}_H$ as:

$$\mathbf{p}_F(\mathbf{AB}) = \mathbf{p}_H$$

In this sense, the matrix product $\mathbf{C} = \mathbf{AB}$ can be thought of as the change of frame matrix from *F* directly to *H*; it combines the affects of **A** and **B** into a net matrix. (The idea is like composition of functions.)

This has performance implications. To see this, assume that a 3D object is composed of 20,000 points and that we want to apply two successive change of frame transformation to the object. Using the step-by-step approach, we would require 20,000 × 2 vector-matrix multiplications. On the other hand, using the combined matrix approach requires 20,000 vector-matrix multiplications and 1 matrix-matrix multiplication to combine the two change of frame matrices. Clearly, one extra matrix-matrix multiplication is a cheap price to pay for the large savings in vector-matrix multiplications.

Again, matrix multiplication is not commutative, so we expect that **AB** *and* **BA** *do not represent the same composite transformation. More specifically, the order in which you multiply the matrices is the order in which the transformations are applied, and in general, it is not a commutative process.*

3.4.5 Inverses and Change of Coordinate Matrices

Suppose that we are given $\mathbf{p}_B$ (the coordinates of a vector $\mathbf{p}$ relative to frame B), and we are given the change of coordinate matrix $\mathbf{M}$ from frame A to frame B; that is, $\mathbf{p}_B = \mathbf{p}_A \mathbf{M}$. We want to solve for $\mathbf{p}_A$. In other words, instead of mapping from frame A into frame B, we want the change of coordinate matrix that maps us from B into A. To find this matrix, suppose that $\mathbf{M}$ is invertible (i.e., $\mathbf{M}^{-1}$ exists). We can solve for $\mathbf{p}_A$ like so:

$\mathbf{p}_B = \mathbf{p}_A \mathbf{M}$

$\mathbf{p}_B \mathbf{M}^{-1} = \mathbf{p}_A \mathbf{M} \mathbf{M}^{-1}$ Multiplying both sides of the equation by $\mathbf{M}^{-1}$

$\mathbf{p}_B \mathbf{M}^{-1} = \mathbf{p}_A \mathbf{I}$ $\mathbf{M} \mathbf{M}^{-1} = \mathbf{I}$, by definition of inverse.

$\mathbf{p}_B \mathbf{M}^{-1} = \mathbf{p}_A$ $\mathbf{p}_A \mathbf{I} = \mathbf{p}_A$, by definition of the identity matrix.

Thus the matrix $\mathbf{M}^{-1}$ is the change of coordinate matrix from B into A.

Figure 3.13 illustrates the relationship between a change of coordinate matrix and its inverse. Also note that all of the change of frame mappings that we do in this book will be invertible, so we won't have to worry about whether the inverse exists.

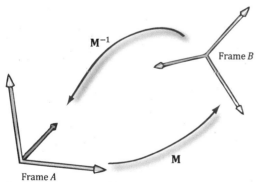

Figure 3.13. **M** maps A into B and $\mathbf{M}^{-1}$ maps from B into A.

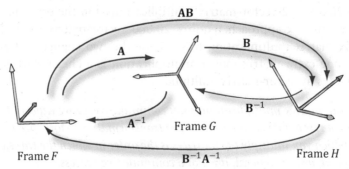

Figure 3.14. **A** maps from F into G, **B** maps from G into H, and **AB** maps from F directly into H. **B**$^{-1}$ maps from H into G, **A**$^{-1}$ maps from G into F and **B**$^{-1}$**A**$^{-1}$ maps from H directly into F.

Figure 3.14 shows how the matrix inverse property $(\mathbf{AB})^{-1} = \mathbf{B}^{-1}\mathbf{A}^{-1}$ can be interpreted in terms of change of coordinate matrices.

3.5 TRANSFORMATION MATRIX VERSUS CHANGE OF COORDINATE MATRIX

So far we have distinguished between "active" transformations (scaling, rotation, translation) and change of coordinate transformations. We will see in this section that mathematically, the two are equivalent, and an active transformation can be interpreted as a change of coordinate transformation, and conversely.

Figure 3.15 shows the geometric resemblance between the rows in Equation 3.7 (rotation followed by translation affine transformation matrix) and the rows in Equation 3.9 (change of coordinate matrix).

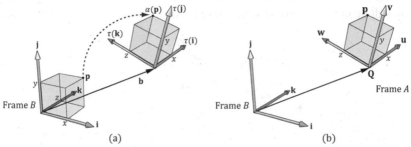

Figure 3.15. We see that $\mathbf{b} = \mathbf{Q}$, $\tau(\mathbf{i}) = \mathbf{u}$, $\tau(\mathbf{j}) = \mathbf{v}$, and $\tau(\mathbf{k}) = \mathbf{w}$. (a) We work with one coordinate system, call it frame B, and we apply an affine transformation to the cube to change its position and orientation relative to frame B: $\alpha(x, y, z, w) = x\tau(\mathbf{i}) + y\tau(\mathbf{j}) + z\tau(\mathbf{k}) + w\mathbf{b}$. (b) We have two coordinate systems called frame A and frame B. The points of the cube relative to frame A can be converted to frame B coordinates by the formula $\mathbf{p}_B = x\mathbf{u}_B + y\mathbf{v}_B + z\mathbf{w}_B + w\mathbf{Q}_B$, where $\mathbf{p}_A = (x, y, z, w)$. In both cases, we have $\alpha(\mathbf{p}) = (x', y', z', w) = \mathbf{p}_B$ with coordinates relative to frame B.

If we think about this, it makes sense. For with a change of coordinate transformation, the frames differ in position and orientation. Therefore, the mathematical conversion formula to go from one frame to the other would require rotating and translating the coordinates, and so we end up with the same mathematical form. In either case, we end up with the same numbers; the difference is the way we interpret the transformation. For some situations, it is more intuitive to work with multiple coordinate systems and convert between the systems where the object remains unchanged, but its coordinate representation changes since it is being described relative to a different frame of reference (this situation corresponds with Figure 3.15b). Other times, we want to transform an object inside a coordinate system without changing our frame of reference (this situation corresponds with Figure 3.15a).

In particular, this discussion shows that we can interpret a composition of active transformations (scaling, rotation, translation) as a change of coordinate transformation. This is important because we will often define our world space (Chapter 5) change of coordinate matrix as a composition of scaling, rotation, and translation transformations.

3.6 DIRECTX MATH TRANSFORMATION FUNCTIONS

We summarize the DirectX Math related transformation functions for reference.

```
// Constructs a scaling matrix:
XMMATRIX XM_CALLCONV XMMatrixScaling(
float ScaleX,
float ScaleY,
float ScaleZ);                         // Scaling factors

// Constructs a scaling matrix from components in vector:
XMMATRIX XM_CALLCONV XMMatrixScalingFromVector(
FXMVECTOR Scale);                      // Scaling factors (sx, sy, sz)

// Constructs a x-axis rotation matrix Rx:
XMMATRIX XM_CALLCONV XMMatrixRotationX(
     float Angle);                     // Clockwise angle θ to rotate

// Constructs a y-axis rotation matrix Ry:
XMMATRIX XM_CALLCONV XMMatrixRotationY(
     float Angle);                     // Clockwise angle θ to rotate

// Constructs a z-axis rotation matrix Rz:
XMMATRIX XM_CALLCONV XMMatrixRotationZ(
     float Angle);                     // Clockwise angle θ to rotate
```

```cpp
// Constructs an arbitrary axis rotation matrix R_n:
XMMATRIX XM_CALLCONV XMMatrixRotationAxis(
    FXMVECTOR Axis,          // Axis n to rotate about
    float Angle);            // Clockwise angle θ to rotate

Constructs a translation matrix:
XMMATRIX XM_CALLCONV XMMatrixTranslation(
    float OffsetX,
    float OffsetY,
    float OffsetZ);          // Translation factors

Constructs a translation matrix from components in a vector:
XMMATRIX XM_CALLCONV XMMatrixTranslationFromVector(
    FXMVECTOR Offset);       // Translation factors (t_x, t_y, t_z)

// Computes the vector-matrix product vM where v_w = 1 for transforming points:
XMVECTOR XM_CALLCONV XMVector3TransformCoord(
    FXMVECTOR V,             // Input v
    CXMMATRIX M);            // Input M

// Computes the vector-matrix product vM where v_w = 0 for transforming vectors:
XMVECTOR XM_CALLCONV XMVector3TransformNormal(
    FXMVECTOR V,             // Input v
    CXMMATRIX M);            // Input M
```

For the last two functions `XMVector3TransformCoord` and `XMVector3TransformNormal`, you do not need to explicitly set the *w* coordinate. The functions will always use $v_w = 1$ and $v_w = 0$ for `XMVector3TransformCoord` and `XMVector3TransformNormal`, respectively.

3.7 SUMMARY

1. The fundamental transformation matrices—scaling, rotation, and translation—are given by:

$$\mathbf{S} = \begin{bmatrix} s_x & 0 & 0 & 0 \\ 0 & s_y & 0 & 0 \\ 0 & 0 & s_z & 0 \\ 0 & 0 & 0 & 1 \end{bmatrix} \quad \mathbf{T} = \begin{bmatrix} 1 & 0 & 0 & 0 \\ 0 & 1 & 0 & 0 \\ 0 & 0 & 1 & 0 \\ b_x & b_y & b_z & 1 \end{bmatrix}$$

$$\mathbf{R_n} = \begin{bmatrix} c+(1-c)x^2 & (1-c)xy+sz & (1-c)xz-sy & 0 \\ (1-c)xy-sz & c+(1-c)y^2 & (1-c)yz+sx & 0 \\ (1-c)xz+sy & (1-c)yz-sx & c+(1-c)z^2 & 0 \\ 0 & 0 & 0 & 1 \end{bmatrix}$$

2. We use 4×4 matrices to represent transformations and 1×4 homogeneous coordinates to describe points and vectors, where we denote a point by setting the fourth component to $w = 1$ and a vector by setting $w = 0$. In this way, translations are applied to points but not to vectors.

3. A matrix is orthogonal if all of its row vectors are of unit length and mutually orthogonal. An orthogonal matrix has the special property that its inverse is equal to its transpose, thereby making the inverse easy and efficient to compute. All the rotation matrices are orthogonal.

4. From the associative property of matrix multiplication, we can combine several transformation matrices into one transformation matrix, which represents the net effect of applying the individual matrices sequentially.

5. Let $\mathbf{Q}_B$, $\mathbf{u}_B$, $\mathbf{v}_B$, and $\mathbf{W}_B$ describe the origin, x-, y-, and z-axes of frame A with coordinates relative to frame B, respectively. If a vector/point $\mathbf{p}$ has coordinates $\mathbf{p}_A = (x, y, z)$ relative to frame A, then the same vector/point relative to frame B has coordinates:

   (a) $\mathbf{p}_B = (x', y', z') = x\mathbf{u}_B + y\mathbf{v}_B + z\mathbf{w}_B$ For vectors (direction and magnitude)
   (b) $\mathbf{p}_B = (x', y', z') = \mathbf{Q}_B + x\mathbf{u}_B + y\mathbf{v}_B + z\mathbf{w}_B$ For position vectors (points)

   These change of coordinate transformations can be written in terms of matrices using homogeneous coordinates.

6. Suppose we have three frames, F, G, and H, and let $\mathbf{A}$ be the change of frame matrix from F to G, and let $\mathbf{B}$ be the change of frame matrix from G to H. Using matrix-matrix multiplication, the matrix $\mathbf{C} = \mathbf{AB}$ can be thought of as the change of frame matrix F directly to H; that is, matrix-matrix multiplication combines the effects of $\mathbf{A}$ and $\mathbf{B}$ into one net matrix, and so we can write: $\mathbf{p}_F(\mathbf{AB}) = \mathbf{p}_H$.

7. If the matrix $\mathbf{M}$ maps frame A coordinates into frame B coordinates, then the matrix $\mathbf{M}^{-1}$ maps frame B coordinates into frame A coordinates.

8. An active transformation can be interpreted as a change of coordinate transformation, and conversely. For some situations, it is more intuitive to work with multiple coordinate systems and convert between the systems where the object remains unchanged, but its coordinate representation changes since it is being described relative to a different frame of reference. Other times, we want to transform an object inside a coordinate system without changing our frame of reference of reference.

3.8 EXERCISES

1. Let $\tau: \mathbb{R}^3 \to \mathbb{R}^3$ be defined by $\tau(x, y, z) = (x + y, x - 3, z)$. Is τ a linear transformation? If it is, find its standard matrix representation.
2. Let $\tau: \mathbb{R}^3 \to \mathbb{R}^3$ be defined by $\tau(x, y, z) = (3x + 4z, 2x - z, x + y + z)$. Is τ a linear transformation? If it is, find its standard matrix representation.
3. Assume that $\tau: \mathbb{R}^3 \to \mathbb{R}^3$ is a linear transformation. Further suppose that $\tau(1, 0, 0) = (3, 1, 2)$, $\tau(0, 1, 0) = (2, -1, 3)$, and $\tau(0, 0, 1) = (4, 0, 2)$. Find $\tau(1, 1, 1)$.
4. Build a scaling matrix that scales 2 units on the x-axis, -3 units on the y-axis, and keeps the z-dimension unchanged.
5. Build a rotation matrix that rotates 30° along the axis $(1, 1, 1)$.
6. Build a translation matrix that translates 4 units on the x-axis, no units on the y-axis, and -9 units on the z-axis.
7. Build a single transformation matrix that first scales 2 units on the x-axis, -3 units on the y-axis, and keeps the z-dimension unchanged, and then translates 4 units on the x-axis, no units on the y-axis, and -9 units on the z-axis.
8. Build a single transformation matrix that first rotates 45° about the y-axis and then translates -2 units on the x-axis, 5 units on the y-axis, and 1 unit on the z-axis.
9. Redo Example 3.2, but this time scale the square 1.5 units on the x-axis, 0.75 units on the y-axis, and leave the z-axis unchanged. Graph the geometry before and after the transformation to confirm your work.
10. Redo Example 3.3, but this time rotate the square $-45°$ clockwise about the y-axis (i.e., 45° counterclockwise). Graph the geometry before and after the transformation to confirm your work.
11. Redo Example 3.4, but this time translate the square -5 units on the x-axis, -3.0 units on the y-axis, and 4.0 units on the z-axis. Graph the geometry before and after the transformation to confirm your work.
12. Show that $R_n(\mathbf{v}) = \cos\theta \mathbf{v} + (1 - \cos\theta)(\mathbf{n} \cdot \mathbf{v})\mathbf{n} + \sin\theta(\mathbf{n} \times \mathbf{v})$ is a linear transformation and find its standard matrix representation.
13. Prove that the rows of $\mathbf{R}_y$ are orthonormal. For a more computational intensive exercise, the reader can do this for the general rotation matrix (rotation matrix about an arbitrary axis), too.
14. Prove the matrix $\mathbf{M}$ is orthogonal if and only if $\mathbf{M}^T = \mathbf{M}^{-1}$.

15. Compute:

$$[x,y,z,1]\begin{bmatrix} 1 & 0 & 0 & 0 \\ 0 & 1 & 0 & 0 \\ 0 & 0 & 1 & 0 \\ b_x & b_y & b_z & 1 \end{bmatrix} \text{ and } [x,y,z,0]\begin{bmatrix} 1 & 0 & 0 & 0 \\ 0 & 1 & 0 & 0 \\ 0 & 0 & 1 & 0 \\ b_x & b_y & b_z & 1 \end{bmatrix}$$

Does the translation translate points? Does the translation translate vectors? Why does it not make sense to translate the coordinates of a vector in standard position?

16. Verify that the given scaling matrix inverse is indeed the inverse of the scaling matrix; that is, show, by directly doing the matrix multiplication, $\mathbf{SS}^{-1} = \mathbf{S}^{-1}\mathbf{S} = \mathbf{I}$. Similarly, verify that the given translation matrix inverse is indeed the inverse of the translation matrix; that is, show that $\mathbf{TT}^{-1} = \mathbf{T}^{-1}\mathbf{T} = \mathbf{I}$.

17. Suppose that we have frames A and B. Let $\mathbf{p}_A = (1, -2, 0)$ and $\mathbf{q}_A = (1, 2, 0)$ represent a point and force, respectively, relative to frame A. Moreover, let $\mathbf{Q}_B = (-6, 2, 0)$, $\mathbf{u}_B = \left(\frac{1}{\sqrt{2}}, \frac{1}{\sqrt{2}}, 0\right)$, $\mathbf{v}_B = \left(-\frac{1}{\sqrt{2}}, \frac{1}{\sqrt{2}}, 0\right)$, and $\mathbf{w}_B = (0, 0, 1)$ describe frame A with coordinates relative to frame B. Build the change of coordinate matrix that maps frame A coordinates into frame B coordinates, and find $\mathbf{p}_B = (x, y, z)$ and $\mathbf{q}_B = (x, y, z)$. Draw a picture on graph paper to verify that your answer is reasonable.

18. The analog for points to a linear combination of vectors is an *affine combination*: $\mathbf{p} = a_1\mathbf{p}_1 + \ldots + a_n\mathbf{p}_n$ where $a_1 + \ldots + a_n = 1$ and $\mathbf{p}_1, \ldots, \mathbf{p}_n$ are points. The scalar coefficient a_k can be thought of as a "point" weight that describe how much influence the point $\mathbf{p}_k$ has in determining $\mathbf{p}$; loosely speaking, the closer a_k is to 1, the closer $\mathbf{p}$ will be to $\mathbf{p}_k$, and a negative a_k "repels" $\mathbf{p}$ from $\mathbf{p}_k$. (The next exercise will help you develop some intuition on this.) The weights are also known as *barycentric coordinates*. Show that an affine combination can be written as a point plus a vector:

$$\mathbf{p} = \mathbf{p}_1 + a_2(\mathbf{p}_2 - \mathbf{p}_1) + \ldots + a_n(\mathbf{p}_n - \mathbf{p}_1)$$

19. Consider the triangle defined by the points $\mathbf{p}_1 = (0, 0, 0)$, $\mathbf{p}_2 = (0, 1, 0)$, and $\mathbf{p}_3 = (2, 0, 0)$. Graph the following points:

(a) $\frac{1}{3}\mathbf{p}_1 + \frac{1}{3}\mathbf{p}_2 + \frac{1}{3}\mathbf{p}_3$

(b) $0.7\mathbf{p}_1 + 0.2\mathbf{p}_2 + 0.1\mathbf{p}_3$

(c) $0.0\mathbf{p}_1 + 0.5\mathbf{p}_2 + 0.5\mathbf{p}_3$
(d) $-0.2\mathbf{p}_1 + 0.6\mathbf{p}_2 + 0.6\mathbf{p}_3$
(e) $0.6\mathbf{p}_1 + 0.5\mathbf{p}_2 - 0.1\mathbf{p}_3$
(f) $0.8\mathbf{p}_1 - 0.3\mathbf{p}_2 + 0.5\mathbf{p}_3$

What is special about the point in part (a)? What would be the barycentric coordinates of $\mathbf{p}_2$ and the point $(1, 0, 0)$ in terms of $\mathbf{p}_1, \mathbf{p}_2, \mathbf{p}_3$? Can you make a conjecturer about where the point $\mathbf{p}$ will be located relative to the triangle if one of the barycentric coordinates is negative?

20. One of the defining factors of an affine transformation is that it preserves affine combinations. Prove that the affine transformation $\alpha(\mathbf{u})$ preserves affine transformations; that is, $\alpha(a_1\mathbf{p}_1 + \ldots + a_n\mathbf{p}_n) = a_1\alpha(\mathbf{p}_1) + \ldots + a_n\alpha(\mathbf{p}_n)$ where $a_1 + \ldots + a_n = 1$.

21. Consider Figure 3.16. A common change of coordinate transformation in computer graphics is to map coordinates from frame A (the square $[-1, 1]^2$) to frame B (the square $[0, 1]^2$ where the y-axes aims opposite to the one in Frame A). Prove that the change of coordinate transformation from Frame A to Frame B is given by:

$$[x, \; y, \; 0 \; 1] \begin{bmatrix} 0.5 & 0 & 0 & 0 \\ 0 & -0.5 & 0 & 0 \\ 0 & 0 & 1 & 0 \\ 0.5 & 0.5 & 0 & 1 \end{bmatrix} = [x', \; y', \; 0 \; 1]$$

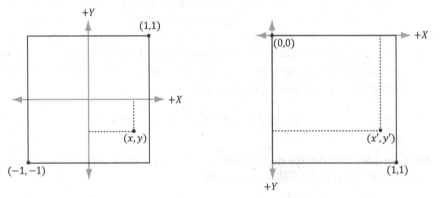

Figure 3.16. Change of coordinates from frame A (the square $[-1, 1]^2$) to frame B (the square $[0, 1]^2$ where the y-axes aims opposite to the one in Frame A).

22. It was mentioned in the last chapter that the determinant was related to the change in volume of a box under a linear transformation. Find the determinant of the scaling matrix and interpret the result in terms of volume.

23. Consider the transformation τ that warps a square into a parallelogram given by:

$$\tau(x, y) = (3x + y, x + 2y)$$

Find the standard matrix representation of this transformation, and show that the determinant of the transformation matrix is equal to the area of the parallelogram spanned by τ(**i**) and τ(**j**).

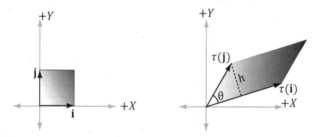

Figure 3.17. Transformation that maps square into parallelogram.

24. Show that the determinant of the y-axis rotation matrix is 1. Based on the above exercise, explain why it makes sense that it is 1. For a more computational intensive exercise, the reader can show the determinant of the general rotation matrix (rotation matrix about an arbitrary axis) is 1.

25. A rotation matrix can be characterized algebraically as an orthogonal matrix with determinant equal to 1. If we reexamine Figure 3.7 along with Exercise 24 this makes sense; the rotated basis vectors τ(**i**) , τ(**j**), and τ(**k**) are unit length and mutually orthogonal; moreover, rotation does not change the size of the object, so the determinant should be 1. Show that the product of two rotation matrices $R_1 R_2 = R$ is a rotation matrix. That is, show $RR^T = R^T R = I$ (to show **R** is orthogonal), and show det **R** = 1.

26. Show that the following properties hold for a rotation matrix **R**:
    (a) (**uR**) · (**vR**) = **u** · **v**   Preservation of dot product
    (b) ||**uR**|| = ||**u**|| Preservation of length
    (c) θ(**uR**, **vR**) = θ(**u**, **v**)   Preservation of angle, where θ(**x**, **y**) evaluates to the angle between **x** and **y**:

$$\theta(\mathbf{x}, \mathbf{y}) = \cos^{-1} \frac{\mathbf{x} \cdot \mathbf{y}}{\|\mathbf{x}\| \|\mathbf{y}\|}$$

Explain why all these properties make sense for a rotation transformation.

27. Find a scaling, rotation, and translation matrix whose product transforms the line segment with start point $\mathbf{p} = (0, 0, 0)$ and endpoint $\mathbf{q} = (0, 0, 1)$ into the line segment with length 2, parallel to the vector $(1, 1, 1)$, with start point $(3, 1, 2)$.

28. Suppose we have a box positioned at (x, y, z). The scaling transform we have defined uses the origin as a reference point for the scaling, so scaling this box (not centered about the origin) has the side effect of translating the box (Figure 3.18); this can be undesirable in some situations. Find a transformation that scales the box relative to its center point.

 Change coordinates to the box coordinate system with origin at the center of the box, scale the box, then transform back to the original coordinate system.

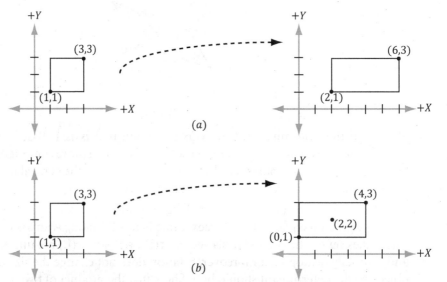

Figure 3.18. (a) Scaling 2-units on the x-axis relative to the origin results in a translation of the rectangle. (b) Scaling 2-units on the x-axis relative to the center of the rectangle does not result in a translation (the rectangle maintains its original center point).

Part 2 DIRECT3D FOUNDATIONS

In this part, we study fundamental Direct3D concepts and techniques that are used throughout the rest of this book. With these fundamentals mastered, we can move on to writing more interesting applications. A brief description of the chapters in this part follows.

Chapter 4, Direct3D Initialization: In this chapter, we learn what Direct3D is about and how to initialize it in preparation for 3D drawing. Basic Direct3D topics are also introduced, such as surfaces, pixel formats, page flipping, depth buffering, and multisampling. We also learn how to measure time with the performance counter, which we use to compute the frames rendered per second. In addition, we give some tips on debugging Direct3D applications. We develop and use our own application framework—not the SDK's framework.

Chapter 5, The Rendering Pipeline: In this long chapter, we provide a thorough introduction to the rendering pipeline, which is the sequence of steps necessary to generate a 2D image of the world based on what the virtual camera sees. We learn how to define 3D worlds, control the virtual camera, and project 3D geometry onto a 2D image plane.

Chapter 6, Drawing in Direct3D: This chapter focuses on the Direct3D API interfaces and methods needed to define 3D geometry, configure the rendering pipeline, create vertex and pixel shaders, and submit geometry to the rendering pipeline for drawing. By the end of this chapter, you will be able to draw a 3D box and transform it.

Chapter 7, Drawing in Direct3D Part II: This chapter introduces a number of drawing patterns that will be used throughout the remainder of the book. From improving the workload balance between CPU and GPU, to organizing how our renderer draws objects. The chapter concludes by showing how to draw more complicated objects like grids, spheres, cylinders, and an animated wave simulation.

Chapter 8, Lighting: This chapter shows how to create light sources and define the interaction between light and surfaces via materials. In particular, we show how to implement directional lights, point lights, and spotlights with vertex and pixel shaders.

Chapter 9, Texturing: This chapter describes texture mapping, which is a technique used to increase the realism of the scene by mapping 2D image data onto a 3D primitive. For example, using texture mapping, we can model a brick wall by applying a 2D brick wall image onto a 3D rectangle. Other key texturing topics covered include texture tiling and animated texture transformations.

Chapter 10, Blending: Blending allows us to implement a number of special effects like transparency. In addition, we discuss the intrinsic clip function, which enables us to mask out certain parts of an image from showing up; this can be used to implement fences and gates, for example. We also show how to implement a fog effect.

Chapter 11, Stenciling: This chapter describes the stencil buffer, which, like a stencil, allows us to block pixels from being drawn. Masking out pixels is a useful tool for a variety of situations. To illustrate the ideas of this chapter, we include a thorough discussion on implementing planar reflections and planar shadows using the stencil buffer.

Chapter 12, The Geometry Shader: This chapter shows how to program geometry shaders, which are special because they can create or destroy entire geometric primitives. Some applications include billboards, fur rendering, subdivisions, and particle systems. In addition, this chapter explains primitive IDs and texture arrays.

Chapter 13, The Compute Shader: The Compute Shader is a programmable shader Direct3D exposes that is not directly part of the rendering pipeline. It enables applications to use the graphics processing unit (GPU) for general purpose computation. For example, an imaging application can take advantage of the GPU to speed up image processing algorithms by implementing them with the compute shader. Because the Compute Shader is part of Direct3D, it reads from and writes to Direct3D resources, which enables us integrate results directly to the rendering pipeline. Therefore, in addition to general purpose computation, the compute shader is still applicable for 3D rendering.

Chapter 14, The Tessellation Stages: This chapter explores the tessellation stages of the rendering pipeline. Tessellation refers to subdividing geometry into smaller triangles and then offsetting the newly generated vertices in some way. The motivation to increase the triangle count is to add detail to the mesh. To illustrate the ideas of this chapter, we show how to tessellate a quad patch based on distance, and we show how to render cubic Bézier quad patch surfaces.

Chapter 4

DIRECT3D INITIALIZATION

The initialization process of Direct3D requires us to be familiar with some basic Direct3D types and basic graphics concepts; the first and second sections of this chapter address these requirements. We then detail the necessary steps to initialize Direct3D. Next, a small detour is taken to introduce accurate timing and the time measurements needed for real-time graphics applications. Finally, we explore the sample framework code, which is used to provide a consistent interface that all demo applications in this book follow.

Objectives:

1. To obtain a basic understanding of Direct3D's role in programming 3D hardware.
2. To understand the role COM plays with Direct3D.
3. To learn fundamental graphics concepts, such as how 2D images are stored, page flipping, depth buffering, multi-sampling, and how the CPU and GPU interact.
4. To learn how to use the performance counter functions for obtaining high-resolution timer readings.
5. To find out how to initialize Direct3D.
6. To become familiar with the general structure of the application framework that all the demos of this book employ.

4.1 PRELIMINARIES

The Direct3D initialization process requires us to be familiar with some basic graphics concepts and Direct3D types. We introduce these ideas and types in this section, so that we do not have to digress when we cover the initialization process.

4.1.1 Direct3D 12 Overview

Direct3D is a low-level graphics API (application programming interface) used to control and program the GPU (graphics processing unit) from our application, thereby allowing us to render virtual 3D worlds using hardware acceleration. For example, to submit a command to the GPU to clear a render target (e.g., the screen), we would call the Direct3D method `ID3D12CommandList::ClearRenderTargetView`. The Direct3D layer and hardware drivers will translate the Direct3D commands into native machine instructions understood by the system's GPU; thus, we do not have to worry about the specifics of the GPU, so long as it supports the Direct3D version we are using. To make this work, GPU vendors like NVIDIA, Intel, and AMD must work with the Direct3D team and provide compliant Direct3D drivers.

Direct3D 12 adds some new rendering features, but the main improvement over the previous version is that it has been redesigned to significantly reduce CPU overhead and improve multi-threading support. In order to achieve these performance goals, Direct3D 12 has become a much lower level API than Direct3D 11; it has less abstraction, requires additional manual "bookkeeping" from the developer, and more closely mirrors modern GPU architectures. The improved performance is, of course, the reward for using this more difficult API.

4.1.2 COM

Component Object Model (COM) is the technology that allows DirectX to be programming-language independent and have backwards compatibility. We usually refer to a COM object as an interface, which for our purposes can be thought of and used as a C++ class. Most of the details of COM are hidden to us when programming DirectX with C++. The only thing that we must know is that we obtain pointers to COM interfaces through special functions or by the methods of another COM interface—we do not create a COM interface with the C++ `new` keyword. In addition, COM objects are reference counted; when we are done with an interface we call its `Release` method (all COM interfaces inherit functionality from the `IUnknown` COM interface, which provides the `Release` method) rather than `delete` it—COM objects will free their memory when their reference count goes to 0.

To help manage the lifetime of COM objects, the Windows Runtime Library (WRL) provides the `Microsoft::WRL::ComPtr` class (`#include <wrl.h>`), which can be thought of as a smart pointer for COM objects. When a `ComPtr` instance goes out of scope, it will automatically call `Release` on the underlying COM object, thereby saving us from having to manually call `Release`. The three main `ComPtr` methods we use in this book are:

1. `Get`: Returns a pointer to the underlying COM interface. This is often used to pass arguments to functions that take a raw COM interface pointer. For example:

   ```
   ComPtr<ID3D12RootSignature> mRootSignature;
   ...
   // SetGraphicsRootSignature expects ID3D12RootSignature* argument.
   mCommandList->SetGraphicsRootSignature(mRootSignature.Get());
   ```

2. `GetAddressOf`: Returns the address of the pointer to the underlying COM interface. This is often used to return a COM interface pointer through a function parameter. For example:

   ```
   ComPtr<ID3D12CommandAllocator> mDirectCmdListAlloc;
   ...
   ThrowIfFailed(md3dDevice->CreateCommandAllocator(
       D3D12_COMMAND_LIST_TYPE_DIRECT,
       mDirectCmdListAlloc.GetAddressOf()));
   ```

3. `Reset`: Sets the `ComPtr` instance to `nullptr` and decrements the reference count of the underlying COM interface. Equivalently, you can assign `nullptr` to a `ComPtr` instance.

There is, of course, much more to COM, but more detail is not necessary for using DirectX effectively.

 COM interfaces are prefixed with a capital I. For example, the COM interface that represents a command list is called `ID3D12GraphicsCommandList`.

4.1.3 Textures Formats

A 2D texture is a matrix of data elements. One use for 2D textures is to store 2D image data, where each element in the texture stores the color of a pixel. However, this is not the only usage; for example, in an advanced technique called normal mapping, each element in the texture stores a 3D vector instead of a color. Therefore, although it is common to think of textures as storing image data, they are really more general purpose than that. A 1D texture is like a 1D array of data elements, a 2D texture is like a 2D array of data elements, and a 3D texture is like a 3D array of data elements. As will be discussed in later chapters, textures are actually more than just arrays of data; they can have mipmap levels, and the GPU can do special operations on them, such as apply filters and multi-sampling. In addition, a texture cannot store arbitrary kinds of data elements; it can only store certain kinds of data element formats, which are described by the DXGI_FORMAT enumerated type. Some example formats are:

1. DXGI_FORMAT_R32G32B32_FLOAT: Each element has three 32-bit floating-point components.
2. DXGI_FORMAT_R16G16B16A16_UNORM: Each element has four 16-bit components mapped to the [0, 1] range.
3. DXGI_FORMAT_R32G32_UINT: Each element has two 32-bit unsigned integer components.
4. DXGI_FORMAT_R8G8B8A8_UNORM: Each element has four 8-bit unsigned components mapped to the [0, 1] range.
5. DXGI_FORMAT_R8G8B8A8_SNORM: Each element has four 8-bit signed components mapped to the [-1, 1] range.
6. DXGI_FORMAT_R8G8B8A8_SINT: Each element has four 8-bit signed integer components mapped to the [-128, 127] range.
7. DXGI_FORMAT_R8G8B8A8_UINT: Each element has four 8-bit unsigned integer components mapped to the [0, 255] range.

Note that the R, G, B, A letters are used to stand for red, green, blue, and alpha, respectively. Colors are formed as combinations of the basis colors red, green, and blue (e.g., equal red and equal green makes yellow). The alpha channel or alpha component is generally used to control transparency. However, as we said earlier, textures need not store color information even though the format names suggest that they do; for example, the format

```
DXGI_FORMAT_R32G32B32_FLOAT
```

has three floating-point components and can therefore store any 3D vector with floating-point coordinates. There are also *typeless* formats, where we just reserve memory and then specify how to reinterpret the data at a later time (sort of like a C++ reinterpret cast) when the texture is bound to the pipeline; for example, the following typeless format reserves elements with four 16-bit components, but does not specify the data type (e.g., integer, floating-point, unsigned integer):

```
DXGI_FORMAT_R16G16B16A16_TYPELESS
```

We will see in Chapter 6 that the DXGI_FORMAT enumerated type is also used to describe vertex data formats and index data formats.

4.1.4 The Swap Chain and Page Flipping

To avoid flickering in animation, it is best to draw an entire frame of animation into an off-screen texture called the back buffer. Once the entire scene has been drawn to the back buffer for the given frame of animation, it is presented to the screen as one complete frame; in this way, the viewer does not watch as the frame gets drawn—the viewer only sees complete frames. To implement this, two texture buffers are maintained by the hardware, one called the *front buffer* and a second called the *back buffer*. The front buffer stores the image data currently being displayed on the monitor, while the next frame of animation is being drawn to the back buffer. After the frame has been drawn to the back buffer, the roles of the back buffer and front buffer are reversed: the back buffer becomes the front buffer and the front buffer becomes the back buffer for the next frame of animation. Swapping the roles of the back and front buffers is called *presenting*. Presenting is an efficient operation, as the pointer to the current front buffer and the pointer to the current back buffer just need to be swapped. Figure 4.1 illustrates the process.

The front and back buffer form a *swap chain*. In Direct3D, a swap chain is represented by the `IDXGISwapChain` interface. This interface stores the front and back buffer textures, as well as provides methods for resizing the buffers (`IDXGISwapChain::ResizeBuffers`) and presenting (`IDXGISwapChain::Present`).

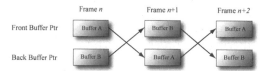

Figure 4.1. For frame n, Buffer A is currently being displayed and we render the next frame to Buffer B, which is serving as the current back buffer. Once the frame is completed, the pointers are swapped and Buffer B becomes the front buffer and Buffer A becomes the new back buffer. We then render the next frame n+1 to Buffer A. Once the frame is completed, the pointers are swapped and Buffer A becomes the front buffer and Buffer B becomes the back buffer again.

Using two buffers (front and back) is called *double buffering*. More than two buffers can be employed; using three buffers is called *triple buffering*. Two buffers are usually sufficient, however.

 Even though the back buffer is a texture (so an element should be called a texel), we often call an element a pixel since, in the case of the back buffer, it stores color information. Sometimes people will call an element of a texture a pixel, even if it doesn't store color information (e.g., "the pixels of a normal map").

4.1.5 Depth Buffering

The *depth buffer* is an example of a texture that does not contain image data, but rather depth information about a particular pixel. The possible depth values range

Figure 4.2. A group of objects that partially obscure each other.

from 0.0 to 1.0, where 0.0 denotes the closest an object in the view frustum can be to the viewer and 1.0 denotes the farthest an object in the view frustum can be from the viewer. There is a one-to-one correspondence between each element in the depth buffer and each pixel in the back buffer (i.e., the *ij*th element in the back buffer corresponds to the *ij*th element in the depth buffer). So if the back buffer had a resolution of 1280×1024, there would be 1280×1024 depth entries.

Figure 4.2 shows a simple scene, where some objects partially obscure the objects behind them. In order for Direct3D to determine which pixels of an object are in front of another, it uses a technique called *depth buffering* or *z-buffering*. Let us emphasize that with depth buffering, the order in which we draw the objects does not matter.

To handle the depth problem, one might suggest drawing the objects in the scene in the order of farthest to nearest. In this way, near objects will be painted over far objects, and the correct results should be rendered. This is how a painter would draw a scene. However, this method has its own problems—sorting a large data set in back-to-front order and intersecting geometry. Besides, the graphics hardware gives us depth buffering for free.

To illustrate how depth buffering works, let us look at an example. Consider Figure 4.3, which shows the volume the viewer sees and a 2D side view of that volume. From the figure, we observe that three different pixels compete to be rendered onto the pixel *P* on the view window. (Of course, we know the closest pixel should be rendered to *P* since it obscures the ones behind it, but the computer does not.) First, before any rendering takes place, the back buffer is cleared to a default color, and the depth buffer is cleared to a default value—usually 1.0 (the farthest depth value a pixel can have). Now, suppose that the objects are rendered in the order of cylinder, sphere, and cone. The following table summarizes how

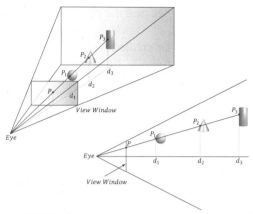

Figure 4.3. The view window corresponds to the 2D image (back buffer) we generate of the 3D scene. We see that three different pixels can be projected to the pixel P. Intuition tells us that P_1 should be written to P since it is closer to the viewer and blocks the other two pixels. The depth buffer algorithm provides a mechanical procedure for determining this on a computer. Note that we show the depth values relative to the 3D scene being viewed, but they are actually normalized to the range [0.0, 1.0] when stored in the depth buffer.

the pixel P and its corresponding depth value d are updated as the objects are drawn; a similar process happens for the other pixels.

Operation	P	d	Description
Clear Operation	Black	1.0	Pixel and corresponding depth entry initialized.
Draw Cylinder	P_3	d_3	Since $d_3 \leq d = 1.0$ the depth test passes and we update the buffers by setting $P = P_3$ and $d = d_3$.
Draw Sphere	P_1	d_1	Since $d_1 \leq d = d_3$ the depth test passes and we update the buffers by setting $P = P_1$ and $d = d_1$.
Draw Cone	P_1	d_1	Since $d_2 > d = d_1$ the depth test fails and we do not update the buffers.

As you can see, we only update the pixel and its corresponding depth value in the depth buffer when we find a pixel with a smaller depth value. In this way, after all is said and done, the pixel that is closest to the viewer will be the one rendered. (You can try switching the drawing order around and working through this example again if you are still not convinced.)

To summarize, depth buffering works by computing a depth value for each pixel and performing a depth test. The depth test compares the depths of pixels competing to be written to a particular pixel location on the back buffer. The pixel with the depth value closest to the viewer wins, and that is the pixel that gets written to the back buffer. This makes sense because the pixel closest to the viewer obscures the pixels behind it.

The depth buffer is a texture, so it must be created with certain data formats. The formats used for depth buffering are as follows:

1. DXGI_FORMAT_D32_FLOAT_S8X24_UINT: Specifies a 32-bit floating-point depth buffer, with 8-bits (unsigned integer) reserved for the stencil buffer mapped to the [0, 255] range and 24-bits not used for padding.
2. DXGI_FORMAT_D32_FLOAT: Specifies a 32-bit floating-point depth buffer.
3. DXGI_FORMAT_D24_UNORM_S8_UINT: Specifies an unsigned 24-bit depth buffer mapped to the [0, 1] range with 8-bits (unsigned integer) reserved for the stencil buffer mapped to the [0, 255] range.
4. DXGI_FORMAT_D16_UNORM: Specifies an unsigned 16-bit depth buffer mapped to the [0, 1] range.

An application is not required to have a stencil buffer, but if it does, the stencil buffer is always attached to the depth buffer. For example, the 32-bit format

DXGI_FORMAT_D24_UNORM_S8_UINT

uses 24-bits for the depth buffer and 8-bits for the stencil buffer. For this reason, the depth buffer is better called the depth/stencil buffer. Using the stencil buffer is a more advanced topic and will be explained in Chapter 11.

4.1.6 Resources and Descriptors

During the rendering process, the GPU will write to resources (e.g., the back buffer, the depth/stencil buffer), and read from resources (e.g., textures that describe the appearance of surfaces, buffers that store the 3D positions of geometry in the scene). Before we issue a draw command, we need to *bind* (or link) the resources to the rendering pipeline that are going to be referenced in that draw call. Some of the resources may change per draw call, so we need to update the bindings per draw call if necessary. However, GPU resources are not bound directly. Instead, a resource is referenced through a *descriptor* object, which can be thought of as lightweight structure that describes the resource to the GPU. Essentially, it is a level of indirection; given a resource descriptor, the GPU can get the actual resource data and know the necessary information about it. We bind resources to the rendering pipeline by specifying the descriptors that will be referenced in the draw call.

Why go to this extra level of indirection with descriptors? The reason is that GPU resources are essentially generic chunks of memory. Resources are kept generic so they can be used at different stages of the rendering pipeline; a common example is to use a texture as a render target (i.e., Direct3D draws into the texture) and later as a shader resource (i.e., the texture will be sampled and serve as input data for a shader). A resource by itself does not say if it is being used as a render target, depth/stencil buffer, or shader resource. Also, perhaps we only want to bind a subregion of the resource data to the rendering pipeline—how can we do that given the whole resource? Moreover, a resource can be created with a typeless format, so the GPU would not even know the format of the resource.

This is where descriptors come in. In addition to identifying the resource data, descriptors describe the resource to the GPU: they tell Direct3D how the resource will be used (i.e., what stage of the pipeline you will bind it to), where applicable we can specify a subregion of the resource we want to bind in the descriptor, and if the resource format was specified as typeless at creation time, then we must now state the type when creating the descriptor.

A view is a synonym for descriptor. The term "view" was used in previous versions of Direct3D, and it is still used in some parts of the Direct3D 12 API. We use both interchangeably in this book; for example, constant buffer view and constant buffer descriptor mean the same thing.

Descriptors have a type, and the type implies how the resource will be used. The types of descriptors we use in this book are:

1. CBV/SRV/UAV descriptors describe constant buffers, shader resources and unordered access view resources.
2. Sampler descriptors describe sampler resources (used in texturing).
3. RTV descriptors describe render target resources.
4. DSV descriptors describe depth/stencil resources.

A *descriptor heap* is an array of descriptors; it is the memory backing for all the descriptors of a particular type your application uses. You will need a separate descriptor heap for each type of descriptor. You can also create multiple heaps of the same descriptor type.

We can have multiple descriptors referencing the same resource. For example, we can have multiple descriptors referencing different subregions of a resource. Also, as mentioned, resources can be bound to different stages of the rendering pipeline. For each stage, we need a separate descriptor. For the example of using a texture as a render target and shader resource, we would need to create two descriptors: an RTV typed descriptor, and an SRV typed descriptor. Similarly, if you create a resource with a typeless format, it is possible for the elements of a texture to be viewed as floating-point values or as integers, for example; this would require two descriptors, where one descriptor specifies the floating-point format, and the other the integer format.

Descriptors should be created at initialization time. This is because there is some type checking and validation that occurs, and it is better to do this at initialization time rather than runtime.

 The August 2009 SDK documentation says: "Creating a fully-typed resource restricts the resource to the format it was created with. This enables the runtime to optimize access [...]." Therefore, you should only create a typeless resource if you really need the flexibility they provide (the ability to reinterpret the data in multiple ways with multiple views); otherwise, create a fully typed resource.

4.1.7 Multisampling Theory

Because the pixels on a monitor are not infinitely small, an arbitrary line cannot be represented perfectly on the computer monitor. Figure 4.4 illustrates a "stair-step" (*aliasing*) effect, which can occur when approximating a line by a matrix of pixels. Similar aliasing effects occur with the edges of triangles.

Shrinking the pixel sizes by increasing the monitor resolution can alleviate the problem significantly to where the stair-step effect goes largely unnoticed.

When increasing the monitor resolution is not possible or not enough, we can apply *antialiasing* techniques. One technique, called *supersampling*, works by making the back buffer and depth buffer 4X bigger than the screen resolution. The 3D scene is then rendered to the back buffer at this larger resolution. Then, when it comes time to present the back buffer to the screen, the back buffer is *resolved* (or downsampled) such that 4 pixel block colors are averaged together to get an averaged pixel color. In effect, supersampling works by increasing the resolution in software.

Supersampling is expensive because it increases the amount of pixel processing and memory by fourfold. Direct3D supports a compromising antialiasing technique called *multisampling*, which shares some computational information across subpixels making it less expensive than supersampling. Assuming we are using 4X multisampling (4 subpixels per pixel), multisampling also uses a back

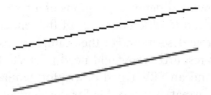

Figure 4.4. On the top we observe aliasing (the stairstep effect when trying to represent a line by a matrix of pixels) On the bottom, we see an antialiased line, which generates the final color of a pixel by sampling and using its neighboring pixels; this results in a smoother image and dilutes the stairstep effect.

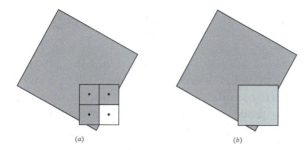

(a)   (b)

Figure 4.5. We consider one pixel that crosses the edge of a polygon. (a) The green color evaluated at the pixel center is stored in the three visible subpixels that are covered by the polygon. The subpixel in the fourth quadrant is not covered by the polygon and so does not get updated with the green color—it just keeps its previous color computed from previously drawn geometry or the Clear operation. (b) To compute the resolved pixel color, we average the four subpixels (three green pixels and one white pixel) to get a light green along the edge of the polygon. This results in a smoother looking image by diluting the stairstep effect along the edge of the polygon.

buffer and depth buffer 4X bigger than the screen resolution; however, instead of computing the image color for each subpixel, it computes it only once per pixel, at the pixel center, and then shares that color information with its subpixels based on visibility (the depth/stencil test is evaluated per subpixel) and coverage (does the subpixel center lie inside or outside the polygon?). Figure 4.5 shows an example.

 Observe the key difference between supersampling and multisampling. With supersampling, the image color is computed per subpixel, and so each subpixel could potentially be a different color. With multisampling (Figure 4.5), the image color is computed once per pixel and that color is replicated into all visible subpixels that are covered by the polygon. Because computing the image color is one of the most expensive steps in the graphics pipeline, the savings from multisampling over supersampling is significant. On the other hand, supersampling is more accurate.

In Figure 4.5, we show a pixel subdivided into four subpixels in a uniform grid pattern. The actual pattern used (the points where the subpixels are positioned) can vary across hardware vendors, as Direct3D does not define the placement of the subpixels. Some patterns do better than others in certain situations.

4.1.8 Multisampling in Direct3D

In the next section, we will be required to fill out a DXGI_SAMPLE_DESC structure. This structure has two members and is defined as follows:

```
typedef struct DXGI_SAMPLE_DESC
{
```

```
  UINT Count;
  UINT Quality;
} DXGI_SAMPLE_DESC;
```

The `Count` member specifies the number of samples to take per pixel, and the `Quality` member is used to specify the desired quality level (what "quality level" means can vary across hardware manufacturers). Higher sample counts or higher quality is more expensive to render, so a tradeoff between quality and speed must be made. The range of quality levels depends on the texture format and the number of samples to take per pixel.

We can query the number of quality levels for a given texture format and sample count using the `ID3D12Device::CheckFeatureSupport` method like so:

```
typedef struct D3D12_FEATURE_DATA_MULTISAMPLE_QUALITY_LEVELS {
  DXGI_FORMAT                              Format;
  UINT                                     SampleCount;
  D3D12_MULTISAMPLE_QUALITY_LEVELS_FLAG    Flags;
  UINT                                     NumQualityLevels;
} D3D12_FEATURE_DATA_MULTISAMPLE_QUALITY_LEVELS;

D3D12_FEATURE_DATA_MULTISAMPLE_QUALITY_LEVELS msQualityLevels;
msQualityLevels.Format = mBackBufferFormat;
msQualityLevels.SampleCount = 4;
msQualityLevels.Flags = D3D12_MULTISAMPLE_QUALITY_LEVELS_FLAG_NONE;
msQualityLevels.NumQualityLevels = 0;
ThrowIfFailed(md3dDevice->CheckFeatureSupport(
    D3D12_FEATURE_MULTISAMPLE_QUALITY_LEVELS,
    &msQualityLevels,
    sizeof(msQualityLevels)));
```

Note that the second parameter is both an input and output parameter. For the input, we must specify the texture format, sample count, and flag we want to query multisampling support for. The function will then fill out the quality level as the output. Valid quality levels for a texture format and sample count combination range from zero to `NumQualityLevels-1`.

The maximum number of samples that can be taken per pixel is defined by:

```
#define D3D11_MAX_MULTISAMPLE_SAMPLE_COUNT    ( 32 )
```

However, a sample count of 4 or 8 is common in order to keep the performance and memory cost of multisampling reasonable. If you do not wish to use multisampling, set the sample count to 1 and the quality level to 0. All Direct3D 11 capable devices support 4X multisampling for all render target formats.

 A `DXGI_SAMPLE_DESC` structure needs to be filled out for both the swap chain buffers and the depth buffer. Both the back buffer and depth buffer must be created with the same multisampling settings.

4.1.9 Feature Levels

Direct3D 11 introduces the concept of feature levels (represented in code by the `D3D_FEATURE_LEVEL` enumerated type), which roughly correspond to various Direct3D versions from version 9 to 11:

```
enum D3D_FEATURE_LEVEL
{
    D3D_FEATURE_LEVEL_9_1       = 0x9100,
    D3D_FEATURE_LEVEL_9_2       = 0x9200,
    D3D_FEATURE_LEVEL_9_3       = 0x9300,
    D3D_FEATURE_LEVEL_10_0      = 0xa000,
    D3D_FEATURE_LEVEL_10_1      = 0xa100,
    D3D_FEATURE_LEVEL_11_0      = 0xb000,
    D3D_FEATURE_LEVEL_11_1      = 0xb100
} D3D_FEATURE_LEVEL;
```

Feature levels define a strict set of functionality (see the SDK documentation for the specific capabilities each feature level supports). For example, a GPU that supports feature level 11 must support the entire Direct3D 11 capability set, with few exceptions (some things like the multisampling count still need to be queried, as they are allowed to vary between different Direct3D 11 hardware). Feature sets make development easier—once you know the supported feature set, you know the Direct3D functionality you have at your disposal.

If a user's hardware did not support a certain feature level, the application could fallback to an older feature level. For example, to support a wider audience, an application might support Direct3D 11, 10, and 9.3 level hardware. The application would check feature level support from newest to oldest: That is, the application would first check if Direct3D 11 is supported, second Direct3D 10, and finally Direct3D 9.3. In this book, we always require support for feature level `D3D_FEATURE_LEVEL_11_0`. However, real-world applications do need to worry about supporting older hardware to maximize their audience.

4.1.10 DirectX Graphics Infrastructure

DirectX Graphics Infrastructure (DXGI) is an API used along with Direct3D. The basic idea of DXGI is that some graphics related tasks are common to multiple graphics APIs. For example, a 2D rendering API would need swap chains and page flipping for smooth animation just as much as a 3D rendering API; thus the swap chain interface `IDXGISwapChain` (§4.1.4) is actually part of the DXGI API. DXGI handles other common graphical functionality like full-screen mode transitions, enumerating graphical system information like display adapters, monitors, and supported display modes (resolution, refresh rate, and such); it also defines the various supported surface formats (DXGI_FORMAT).

We briefly describe some DXGI concepts and interfaces that will be used during our Direct3D initialization. One of the key DXGI interfaces is the IDXGIFactory interface, which is primarily used to create the IDXGISwapChain interface and enumerate display adapters. Display adapters implement graphical functionality. Usually, the *display adapter* is a physical piece of hardware (e.g., graphics card); however, a system can also have a software display adapter that emulates hardware graphics functionality. A system can have several adapters (e.g., if it has several graphics cards). An adapter is represented by the IDXGIAdapter interface. We can enumerate all the adapters on a system with the following code:

```
void D3DApp::LogAdapters()
{
  UINT i = 0;
  IDXGIAdapter* adapter = nullptr;
  std::vector<IDXGIAdapter*> adapterList;
  while(mdxgiFactory->EnumAdapters(i, &adapter) != DXGI_ERROR_NOT_
    FOUND)
  {
    DXGI_ADAPTER_DESC desc;
    adapter->GetDesc(&desc);

    std::wstring text = L"***Adapter: ";
    text += desc.Description;
    text += L"\n";

    OutputDebugString(text.c_str());

    adapterList.push_back(adapter);

    ++i;
  }

  for(size_t i = 0; i < adapterList.size(); ++i)
  {
    LogAdapterOutputs(adapterList[i]);
    ReleaseCom(adapterList[i]);
  }
}
```

An example of the output from this method is the following:

```
***Adapter: NVIDIA GeForce GTX 760
***Adapter: Microsoft Basic Render Driver
```

The "Microsoft Basic Render Driver" is a software adapter included with Windows 8 and above.

A system can have several monitors. A monitor is an example of a *display output*. An output is represented by the IDXGIOutput interface. Each adapter is associated with a list of outputs. For instance, consider a system with two graphics cards and three monitors, where two monitors are hooked up to one graphics card, and the third monitor is hooked up to the other graphics card. In this case, one adapter has two outputs associated with it, and the other adapter has one output associated with it. We can enumerate all the outputs associated with an adapter with the following code:

```
void D3DApp::LogAdapterOutputs(IDXGIAdapter* adapter)
{
  UINT i = 0;
  IDXGIOutput* output = nullptr;
  while(adapter->EnumOutputs(i, &output) != DXGI_ERROR_NOT_FOUND)
  {
    DXGI_OUTPUT_DESC desc;
    output->GetDesc(&desc);

    std::wstring text = L"***Output: ";
    text += desc.DeviceName;
    text += L"\n";
    OutputDebugString(text.c_str());

    LogOutputDisplayModes(output, DXGI_FORMAT_B8G8R8A8_UNORM);

    ReleaseCom(output);

    ++i;
  }
}
```

Note that, per the documentation, the "Microsoft Basic Render Driver" has no display outputs.

Each monitor has a set of display modes it supports. A display mode refers to the following data in `DXGI_MODE_DESC`:

```
typedef struct DXGI_MODE_DESC
{
  UINT Width;                       // Resolution width
  UINT Height;                      // Resolution height
  DXGI_RATIONAL RefreshRate;
  DXGI_FORMAT Format;               // Display format
  DXGI_MODE_SCANLINE_ORDER ScanlineOrdering; //Progressive vs.
    interlaced
  DXGI_MODE_SCALING Scaling;        // How the image is stretched
                                    // over the monitor.

} DXGI_MODE_DESC;

typedef struct DXGI_RATIONAL
{
  UINT Numerator;
  UINT Denominator;
} DXGI_RATIONAL;
```

```
typedef enum DXGI_MODE_SCANLINE_ORDER
{
  DXGI_MODE_SCANLINE_ORDER_UNSPECIFIED       = 0,
  DXGI_MODE_SCANLINE_ORDER_PROGRESSIVE       = 1,
  DXGI_MODE_SCANLINE_ORDER_UPPER_FIELD_FIRST = 2,
  DXGI_MODE_SCANLINE_ORDER_LOWER_FIELD_FIRST = 3
} DXGI_MODE_SCANLINE_ORDER;

typedef enum DXGI_MODE_SCALING
{
  DXGI_MODE_SCALING_UNSPECIFIED = 0,
  DXGI_MODE_SCALING_CENTERED    = 1,
  DXGI_MODE_SCALING_STRETCHED   = 2
} DXGI_MODE_SCALING;
```

Fixing a display mode format, we can get a list of all supported display modes an output supports in that format with the following code:

```
void D3DApp::LogOutputDisplayModes(IDXGIOutput* output, DXGI_FORMAT format)
{
  UINT count = 0;
  UINT flags = 0;

  // Call with nullptr to get list count.
  output->GetDisplayModeList(format, flags, &count, nullptr);

  std::vector<DXGI_MODE_DESC> modeList(count);
  output->GetDisplayModeList(format, flags, &count, &modeList[0]);

  for(auto& x : modeList)
  {
    UINT n = x.RefreshRate.Numerator;
    UINT d = x.RefreshRate.Denominator;
    std::wstring text =
      L"Width = " + std::to_wstring(x.Width) + L" " +
      L"Height = " + std::to_wstring(x.Height) + L" " +
      L"Refresh = " + std::to_wstring(n) + L"/" + std::to_wstring(d) +
      L"\n";

    ::OutputDebugString(text.c_str());
  }
}
```

An example of some of the output from this code is as follows:

```
***Output: \\.\DISPLAY2
...
Width = 1920 Height = 1080 Refresh = 59950/1000
Width = 1920 Height = 1200 Refresh = 59950/1000
```

Enumerating display modes is particularly important when going into full-screen mode. In order to get optimal full-screen performance, the specified display mode (including refresh rate), must match exactly a display mode the monitor supports. Specifying an enumerated display mode guarantees this.

For more reference material on DXGI, we recommend reading the following articles "DXGI Overview," "DirectX Graphics Infrastructure: Best Practices," and "DXGI 1.4 Improvements" available online at:

DXGI Overview: http://msdn.microsoft.com/en-us/library/windows/desktop/bb205075(v=vs.85).aspx
DirectX Graphics Infrastructure: Best Practices: http://msdn.microsoft.com/en-us/library/windows/desktop/ee417025(v=vs.85).aspx
DXGI 1.4 Improvements: https://msdn.microsoft.com/en-us/library/windows/desktop/mt427784%28v=vs.85%29.aspx

4.1.11 Checking Feature Support

We already used the `ID3D12Device::CheckFeatureSupport` method to check multisampling support by the current graphics driver. However, that is just one feature support we can check for with this function. The prototype of this method is as follows:

```
HRESULT ID3D12Device::CheckFeatureSupport(
  D3D12_FEATURE Feature,
  void *pFeatureSupportData,
  UINT FeatureSupportDataSize);
```

1. `Feature`: A member of the `D3D12_FEATURE` enumerated type identifying the type of features we want to check the support:

    a) `D3D12_FEATURE_D3D12_OPTIONS`: Checks support for various Direct3D 12 features.
    b) `D3D12_FEATURE_ARCHITECTURE`: Checks support for hardware architecture features.
    c) `D3D12_FEATURE_FEATURE_LEVELS`: Checks feature level support.
    d) `D3D12_FEATURE_FORMAT_SUPPORT`: Check feature support for a given texture format (e.g., can the format be used as a render target, can the format be used with blending).
    e) `D3D12_FEATURE_MULTISAMPLE_QUALITY_LEVELS`: Check multisampling feature support.

2. `pFeatureSupportData`: Pointer to a data structure to retrieve the feature support information. The type of structure you use depends on what you specified for the `Feature` parameter:

    a) If you specified `D3D12_FEATURE_D3D12_OPTIONS`, then pass an instance of `D3D12_FEATURE_DATA_D3D12_OPTIONS`.

b) If you specified `D3D12_FEATURE_ARCHITECTURE`, then pass an instance of `D3D12_FEATURE_DATA_ARCHITECTURE`.

c) If you specified `D3D12_FEATURE_FEATURE_LEVELS`, then pass an instance of `D3D12_FEATURE_DATA_FEATURE_LEVELS`.

d) If you specified `D3D12_FEATURE_FORMAT_SUPPORT`, then pass an instance of `D3D12_FEATURE_DATA_FORMAT_SUPPORT`.

e) If you specified `D3D12_FEATURE_MULTISAMPLE_QUALITY_LEVELS`, then pass an instance of `D3D12_FEATURE_DATA_MULTISAMPLE_QUALITY_LEVELS`.

3. `FeatureSupportDataSize`: The size of the data structure passed into `pFeatureSupportData` the parameter.

The `ID3D12Device::CheckFeatureSupport` function checks support for a lot of features, many of which we do not need to check in this book and are advanced; see the SDK documentation for details on the data members for each feature structure. However, as an example, we show below how to check for supported feature levels (§4.1.9):

```
typedef struct D3D12_FEATURE_DATA_FEATURE_LEVELS {
  UINT              NumFeatureLevels;
  const D3D_FEATURE_LEVEL *pFeatureLevelsRequested;
  D3D_FEATURE_LEVEL   MaxSupportedFeatureLevel;
} D3D12_FEATURE_DATA_FEATURE_LEVELS;

D3D_FEATURE_LEVEL featureLevels[3] =
{
  D3D_FEATURE_LEVEL_11_0, // First check D3D 11 support
  D3D_FEATURE_LEVEL_10_0, // Next, check D3D 10 support
  D3D_FEATURE_LEVEL_9_3   // Finally, check D3D 9.3 support
};

D3D12_FEATURE_DATA_FEATURE_LEVELS featureLevelsInfo;
featureLevelsInfo.NumFeatureLevels = 3;
featureLevelsInfo.pFeatureLevelsRequested = featureLevels;
md3dDevice->CheckFeatureSupport(
  D3D12_FEATURE_FEATURE_LEVELS,
  &featureLevelsInfo,
  sizeof(featureLevelsInfo));
```

Note that the second parameter is both an input and output parameter. For the input, we specify the number of elements (`NumFeatureLevels`) in a feature level array, and a pointer to a feature level array (`pFeatureLevelsRequested`) which contains a list of feature levels we want to check hardware support for. The function outputs the maximum supported feature level through the `MaxSupportedFeatureLevel` field.

4.1.12 Residency

A complex game will use a lot of resources such as textures and 3D meshes, but many of these resources will not be needed by the GPU all the time. For example, if we imagine a game with an outdoor forest that has a large cave in it, the cave resources will not be needed until the player enters the cave, and when the player enters the cave, the forest resources will no longer be needed.

In Direct3D 12, applications manage resource residency (essentially, whether a resource is in GPU memory) by evicting resources from GPU memory and then making them resident on the GPU again as needed. The basic idea is to minimize how much GPU memory the application is using because there might not be enough to store every resource for the entire game, or the user has other applications running that require GPU memory. As a performance note, the application should avoid the situation of swapping the same resources in and out of GPU memory within a short time frame, as there is overhead for this. Ideally, if you are going to evict a resource, that resource should not be needed for a while. Game level/area changes are good examples of times to change resource residency.

By default, when a resource is created it is made resident and it is evicted when it is destroyed. However, an application can manually control residency with the following methods:

```
HRESULT ID3D12Device::MakeResident(
    UINT           NumObjects,
    ID3D12Pageable *const *ppObjects);

HRESULT ID3D12Device::Evict(
    UINT           NumObjects,
    ID3D12Pageable *const *ppObjects);
```

For both methods, the second parameter is an array of `ID3D12Pageable` resources, and the first parameter is the number of resources in the array.

In this book, for simplicity and due to our demos being small compared to a game, we do not manage residency. See the documentation on residency for more information: *https://msdn.microsoft.com/en-us/library/windows/desktop/mt186622%28v=vs.85%29.aspx*

4.2 CPU/GPU INTERACTION

We must understand that with graphics programming we have two processors at work: the CPU and GPU. They work in parallel and sometimes need to be synchronized. For optimal performance, the goal is to keep both busy for as long as possible and minimize synchronizations. Synchronizations are undesirable because it means one processing unit is idle while waiting on the other to finish some work; in other words, it ruins the parallelism.

4.2.1 The Command Queue and Command Lists

The GPU has a command queue. The CPU submits commands to the queue through the Direct3D API using command lists (see Figure 4.6). It is important to understand that once a set of commands have been submitted to the command queue, they are not immediately executed by the GPU. They sit in the queue until the GPU is ready to process them, as the GPU is likely busy processing previously inserted commands.

If the command queue gets empty, the GPU will idle because it does not have any work to do; on the other hand, if the command queue gets too full, the CPU will at some point have to idle while the GPU catches up [Crawfis12]. Both of these situations are undesirable; for high performance applications like games, the goal is to keep both CPU and GPU busy to take full advantage of the hardware resources available.

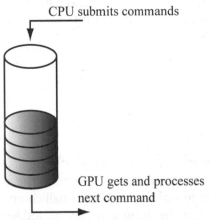

Figure 4.6. The command queue.

In Direct3D 12, the command queue is represented by the ID3D12CommandQueue interface. It is created by filling out a D3D12_COMMAND_QUEUE_DESC structure describing the queue and then calling ID3D12Device::CreateCommandQueue. The way we create our command queue in this book is as follows:

```
Microsoft::WRL::ComPtr<ID3D12CommandQueue> mCommandQueue;
D3D12_COMMAND_QUEUE_DESC queueDesc = {};
queueDesc.Type = D3D12_COMMAND_LIST_TYPE_DIRECT;
queueDesc.Flags = D3D12_COMMAND_QUEUE_FLAG_NONE;
ThrowIfFailed(md3dDevice->CreateCommandQueue(
    &queueDesc, IID_PPV_ARGS(&mCommandQueue)));
```

The `IID_PPV_ARGS` helper macro is defined as:

```
#define IID_PPV_ARGS(ppType) __uuidof(**(ppType)), IID_PPV_ARGS_Helper(ppType)
```

where `__uuidof(**(ppType))` evaluates to the COM interface ID of `(**(ppType))`, which in the above code is `ID3D12CommandQueue`. The `IID_PPV_ARGS_Helper` function essentially casts `ppType` to a `void**`. We use this macro throughout this book, as many Direct3D 12 API calls have a parameter that requires the COM ID of the interface we are creating and take a `void**`.

One of the primary methods of this interface is the `ExecuteCommandLists` method which adds the commands in the command lists to the queue:

```
void ID3D12CommandQueue::ExecuteCommandLists(
  // Number of commands lists in the array
  UINT Count,
  // Pointer to the first element in an array of command lists
  ID3D12CommandList *const *ppCommandLists);
```

The command lists are executed in order starting with the first array element.

As the above method declarations imply, a command list for graphics is represented by the `ID3D12GraphicsCommandList` interface which inherits from the `ID3D12CommandList` interface. The `ID3D12GraphicsCommandList` interface has numerous methods for adding commands to the command list. For example, the following code adds commands that set the viewport, clear the render target view, and issue a draw call:

```
// mCommandList pointer to ID3D12CommandList
mCommandList->RSSetViewports(1, &mScreenViewport);
mCommandList->ClearRenderTargetView(mBackBufferView,
    Colors::LightSteelBlue, 0, nullptr);
mCommandList->DrawIndexedInstanced(36, 1, 0, 0, 0);
```

The names of these methods suggest that the commands are executed immediately, but they are not. The above code just adds commands to the command list. The `ExecuteCommandLists` method adds the commands to the command queue, and the GPU processes commands from the queue. We will learn about the various commands `ID3D12GraphicsCommandList` supports as we progress through this book. When we are done adding commands to a command list, we must indicate that we are finished recording commands by calling the `ID3D12GraphicsCommandList::Close` method:

```
// Done recording commands.
mCommandList->Close();
```

The command list must be closed before passing it off to `ID3D12CommandQueue::ExecuteCommandLists`.

Associated with a command list is a memory backing class called an `ID3D12CommandAllocator`. As commands are recorded to the command list, they will actually be stored in the associated command allocator. When a command list is executed via `ID3D12CommandQueue::ExecuteCommandLists`, the command queue will reference the commands in the allocator. A command allocator is created from the `ID3D12Device`:

```
HRESULT ID3D12Device::CreateCommandAllocator(
  D3D12_COMMAND_LIST_TYPE type,
  REFIID riid,
  void **ppCommandAllocator);
```

1. `type`: The type of command lists that can be associated with this allocator. The two common types we use in this book are:

    a) `D3D12_COMMAND_LIST_TYPE_DIRECT`: Stores a list of commands to directly be executed by the GPU (the type of command list we have been describing thus far).

    b) `D3D12_COMMAND_LIST_TYPE_BUNDLE`: Specifies the command list represents a *bundle*. There is some CPU overhead in building a command list, so Direct3D 12 provides an optimization that allows us to record a sequence of commands into a so-called bundle. After a bundle has been recorded, the driver will preprocess the commands to optimize their execution during rendering. Therefore, bundles should be recorded at initialization time. The use of bundles should be thought of as an optimization to use if profiling shows building particular command lists are taking significant time. The Direct3D 12 drawing API is already very efficient, so you should not need to use bundles often, and you should only use them if you can demonstrate a performance gain by them; that is to say, do not use them by default. We do not use bundles in this book; see the DirectX 12 documentation for further details.

2. `riid`: The COM ID of the `ID3D12CommandAllocator` interface we want to create.
3. `ppCommandAllocator`: Outputs a pointer to the created command allocator.

Command lists are also created from the `ID3D12Device`:

```
HRESULT ID3D12Device::CreateCommandList(
  UINT nodeMask,
  D3D12_COMMAND_LIST_TYPE type,
  ID3D12CommandAllocator *pCommandAllocator,
  ID3D12PipelineState *pInitialState,
  REFIID riid,
  void **ppCommandList);
```

1. `nodeMask`: Set to 0 for single GPU system. Otherwise, the node mask identifies the physical GPU this command list is associated with. In this book we assume single GPU systems.
2. `type`: The type of command list: either `_COMMAND_LIST_TYPE_DIRECT` or `D3D12_COMMAND_LIST_TYPE_BUNDLE`.
3. `pCommandAllocator`: The allocator to be associated with the created command list. The command allocator type must match the command list type.
4. `pInitialState`: Specifies the initial pipeline state of the command list. This can be null for bundles, and in the special case where a command list is executed for initialization purposes and does not contain any draw commands. We discuss `ID3D12PipelineState` in Chapter 6.
5. `riid`: The COM ID of the `ID3D12CommandList` interface we want to create.
6. `ppCommandList`: Outputs a pointer to the created command list.

> **Note:** *You can use the `ID3D12Device::GetNodeCount` method to query the number of GPU adapter nodes on the system.*

You can create multiple command lists associated with the same allocator, but you cannot record at the same time. That is, all command lists must be closed except the one whose commands we are going to record. Thus, all commands from a given command list will be added to the allocator contiguously. Note that when a command list is created or reset, it is in an "open" state. So if we tried to create two command lists in a row with the same allocator, we would get an error:

```
D3D12 ERROR: ID3D12CommandList::{Create,Reset}CommandList: The command
allocator is currently in-use by another command list.
```

After we have called `ID3D12CommandQueue::ExecuteCommandList(C)`, it is safe to reuse the internal memory of C to record a new set of commands by calling the `ID3D12CommandList::Reset` method. The parameters of this method are the same as the matching parameters in `ID3D12Device::CreateCommandList`.

```
HRESULT ID3D12CommandList::Reset(
  ID3D12CommandAllocator *pAllocator,
  ID3D12PipelineState *pInitialState);
```

This method puts the command list in the same state as if it was just created, but allows us to reuse the internal memory and avoid deallocating the old command list and allocating a new one. Note that resetting the command list does not affect the commands in the command queue because the associated command allocator still has the commands in memory that the command queue references.

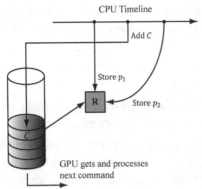

Figure 4.7. This is an error because C draws the geometry with p_2 or draws while R is in the middle of being updated. In any case, this is not the intended behavior.

After we have submitted the rendering commands for a complete frame to the GPU, we would like to reuse the memory in the command allocator for the next frame. The `ID3D12CommandAllocator::Reset` method may be used for this:

```
HRESULT ID3D12CommandAllocator::Reset(void);
```

The idea of this is analogous to calling `std::vector::clear`, which resizes a vector back to zero, but keeps the current capacity the same. However, because the command queue may be referencing data in an allocator, **a command allocator must not be reset until we are sure the GPU has finished executing all the commands in the allocator;** how to do this is covered in the next section.

4.2.2 CPU/GPU Synchronization

Due to having two processors running in parallel, a number of synchronization issues appear.

Suppose we have some resource R that stores the position of some geometry we wish to draw. Furthermore, suppose the CPU updates the data of R to store position p_1 and then adds a drawing command C that references R to the command queue with the intent of drawing the geometry at position p_1. Adding commands to the command queue does not block the CPU, so the CPU continues on. It would be an error for the CPU to continue on and overwrite the data of R to store a new position p_2 before the GPU executed the draw command C (see Figure 4.7).

One solution to this situation is to force the CPU to wait until the GPU has finished processing all the commands in the queue up to a specified fence point. We call this *flushing the command queue*. We can do this using a *fence*. A fence is represented by the `ID3D12Fence` interface and is used to synchronize the GPU and CPU. A fence object can be created with the following method:

```
HRESULT ID3D12Device::CreateFence(
    UINT64 InitialValue,
```

```
    D3D12_FENCE_FLAGS Flags,
    REFIID riid,
    void **ppFence);

// Example
ThrowIfFailed(md3dDevice->CreateFence(
    0,
    D3D12_FENCE_FLAG_NONE,
    IID_PPV_ARGS(&mFence)));
```

A fence object maintains a UINT64 value, which is just an integer to identify a fence point in time. We start at value zero and every time we need to mark a new fence point, we just increment the integer. Now, the following code/comments show how we can use a fence to flush the command queue.

```
UINT64 mCurrentFence = 0;
void D3DApp::FlushCommandQueue()
{
  // Advance the fence value to mark commands up to this fence point.
  mCurrentFence++;

  // Add an instruction to the command queue to set a new fence point.
  // Because we are on the GPU timeline, the new fence point won't be
  // set until the GPU finishes processing all the commands prior to
  // this Signal().
  ThrowIfFailed(mCommandQueue->Signal(mFence.Get(), mCurrentFence));

  // Wait until the GPU has completed commands up to this fence point.
  if(mFence->GetCompletedValue() < mCurrentFence)
  {
    HANDLE eventHandle = CreateEventEx(nullptr, false, false, EVENT_
    ALL_ACCESS);

    // Fire event when GPU hits current fence.
    ThrowIfFailed(mFence->SetEventOnCompletion(mCurrentFence,
    eventHandle));

    // Wait until the GPU hits current fence event is fired.
    WaitForSingleObject(eventHandle, INFINITE);
    CloseHandle(eventHandle);
  }
}
```

Figure 4.8 explains this code graphically.

So in the previous example, after the CPU issued the draw command C, it would flush the command queue before overwriting the data of R to store a new position p_2. This solution is not ideal because it means the CPU is idle while waiting for the GPU to finish, but it provides a simple solution that we will use until Chapter 7. You can flush the command queue at almost any point (not necessarily only once per frame); if you have some initialization GPU commands, you can flush the command queue to execute the initialization before entering the main rendering loop, for example.

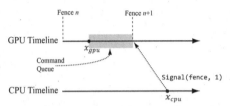

Figure 4.8. At this snapshot, the GPU has processed commands up to x_{gpu} and the CPU has just called the `ID3D12CommandQueue::Signal(fence, n+1)` method. This essentially adds an instruction to the end of the queue to change the fence value to $n+1$. However, `mFence->GetCompletedValue()` will continue to return n until the GPU processes all the commands in the queue that were added prior to the `Signal(fence, n+1)` instruction.

Note that flushing the command queue also can be used to solve the problem we mentioned at the end of the last section; that is, we can flush the command queue to be sure that all the GPU commands have been executed before we reset the command allocator.

4.2.3 Resource Transitions

To implement common rendering effects, it is common for the GPU to write to a resource R in one step, and then, in a later step, read from the resource R. However, it would be a *resource hazard* to read from a resource if the GPU has not finished writing to it or not started writing at all. To solve this problem, Direct3D associates a state to resources. Resources are in a default state when they are created, and it is up to the application to tell Direct3D any state transitions. This enables the GPU to do any work it needs to do to make the transition and prevent resource hazards. For example, if we are writing to a resource, say a texture, we will set the texture state to a render target state; when we need to read the texture, we will change its state to a shader resource state. By informing Direct3D of a transition, the GPU can take steps to avoid the hazard, for example, by waiting for all the write operations to complete before reading from the resource. The burden of resource transition falls on the application developer for performance reasons. The application developer knows when these transitions are happening. An automatic transition tracking system would impose additional overhead.

A resource transition is specified by setting an array of *transition resource barriers* on the command list; it is an array in case you want to transition multiple resources with one API call. In code, a resource barrier is represented by the `D3D12_RESOURCE_BARRIER_DESC` structure. The following helper function (defined in *d3dx12.h*) returns a transition resource barrier description for a given resource, and specifies the before and after states:

```
struct CD3DX12_RESOURCE_BARRIER : public D3D12_RESOURCE_BARRIER
```

```
{
    // [...] convenience methods

    static inline CD3DX12_RESOURCE_BARRIER Transition(
        _In_ ID3D12Resource* pResource,
        D3D12_RESOURCE_STATES stateBefore,
        D3D12_RESOURCE_STATES stateAfter,
        UINT subresource = D3D12_RESOURCE_BARRIER_ALL_SUBRESOURCES,
        D3D12_RESOURCE_BARRIER_FLAGS flags = D3D12_RESOURCE_BARRIER_FLAG_
    NONE)
    {
        CD3DX12_RESOURCE_BARRIER result;
        ZeroMemory(&result, sizeof(result));
        D3D12_RESOURCE_BARRIER &barrier = result;
        result.Type = D3D12_RESOURCE_BARRIER_TYPE_TRANSITION;
        result.Flags = flags;
        barrier.Transition.pResource = pResource;
        barrier.Transition.StateBefore = stateBefore;
        barrier.Transition.StateAfter = stateAfter;
        barrier.Transition.Subresource = subresource;
        return result;
    }

    // [...] more convenience methods
};
```

Observe that CD3DX12_RESOURCE_BARRIER extends D3D12_RESOURCE_BARRIER_DESC and adds convenience methods. Most Direct3D 12 structures have extended helper variations, and we prefer those variations for the convenience. The CD3DX12 variations are all defined in *d3dx12.h*. This file is not part of the core DirectX 12 SDK, but is available for download from Microsoft. For convenience, a copy is included in the *Common* directory of the book's source code.

An example of this function from this chapter's sample application is as follows:

```
mCommandList->ResourceBarrier(1,
    &CD3DX12_RESOURCE_BARRIER::Transition(
        CurrentBackBuffer(),
        D3D12_RESOURCE_STATE_PRESENT,
        D3D12_RESOURCE_STATE_RENDER_TARGET));
```

This code transitions a texture representing the image we are displaying on screen from a presentation state to a render target state. Observe that the resource barrier is added to the command list. You can think of the resource barrier transition as a command itself instructing the GPU that the state of a resource is being transitioned, so that it can take the necessary steps to prevent a resource hazard when executing subsequent commands.

There are other types of resource barriers besides transition types. For now, we only need the transition types. We will introduce the other types when we need them.

4.2.4 Multithreading with Commands

Direct3D 12 was designed for efficient multithreading. The command list design is one way Direct3D takes advantage of multithreading. For large scenes with lots of objects, building the command list to draw the entire scene can take CPU time. So the idea is to build command lists in parallel; for example, you might spawn four threads, each responsible for building a command list to draw 25% of the scene objects.

A few things to note about command list multithreading:

1. Command list are not free-threaded; that is, multiple threads may not share the same command list and call its methods concurrently. So generally, each thread will get its own command list.
2. Command allocators are not free-threaded; that is, multiple threads may not share the same command allocator and call its methods concurrently. So generally, each thread will get its own command allocator.
3. The command queue is free-threaded, so multiple threads can access the command queue and call its methods concurrently. In particular, each thread can submit their generated command list to the thread queue concurrently.
4. For performance reasons, the application must specify at initialization time the maximum number of command lists they will record concurrently.

For simplicity, we will not use multithreading in this book. Once the reader is finished with this book, we recommend they study the Multithreading12 SDK sample to see how command lists can be generated in parallel. Applications that want to maximize system resources should definitely use multithreading to take advantage of multiple CPU cores.

4.3 INITIALIZING DIRECT3D

The following subsections show how to initialize Direct3D for our demo framework. It is a long process, but only needs to be done once. Our process of initializing Direct3D can be broken down into the following steps:

1. Create the `ID3D12Device` using the `D3D12CreateDevice` function.
2. Create an `ID3D12Fence` object and query descriptor sizes.
3. Check 4X MSAA quality level support.
4. Create the command queue, command list allocator, and main command list.
5. Describe and create the swap chain.
6. Create the descriptor heaps the application requires.

7. Resize the back buffer and create a render target view to the back buffer.
8. Create the depth/stencil buffer and its associated depth/stencil view.
9. Set the viewport and scissor rectangles.

4.3.1 Create the Device

Initializing Direct3D begins by creating the Direct3D 12 device (`ID3D12Device`). The device represents a display adapter. Usually, the display adapter is a physical piece of 3D hardware (e.g., graphics card); however, a system can also have a software display adapter that emulates 3D hardware functionality (e.g., the WARP adapter). The Direct3D 12 device is used to check feature support, and create all other Direct3D interface objects like resources, views, and command lists. The device can be created with the following function:

```
HRESULT WINAPI D3D12CreateDevice(
  IUnknown* pAdapter,
  D3D_FEATURE_LEVEL MinimumFeatureLevel,
  REFIID riid, // Expected: ID3D12Device
  void** ppDevice );
```

1. `pAdapter`: Specifies the display adapter we want the created device to represent. Specifying null for this parameter uses the primary display adapter. We always use the primary adapter in the sample programs of this book. §4.1.10 showed how to enumerate all the system's display adapters.

2. `MinimumFeatureLevel`: The minimum feature level our application requires support for; device creation will fail if the adapter does not support this feature level. In our framework, we specify `D3D_FEATURE_LEVEL_11_0` (i.e., Direct3D 11 feature support).

3. `riid`: The COM ID of the `ID3D12Device` interface we want to create.

4. `ppDevice`: Returns the created device.

Here is an example call of this function:

```
#if defined(DEBUG) || defined(_DEBUG)
// Enable the D3D12 debug layer.
{
  ComPtr<ID3D12Debug> debugController;
  ThrowIfFailed(D3D12GetDebugInterface(IID_PPV_
    ARGS(&debugController)));
  debugController->EnableDebugLayer();
}
#endif

ThrowIfFailed(CreateDXGIFactory1(IID_PPV_ARGS(&mdxgiFactory)));

// Try to create hardware device.
```

```
HRESULT hardwareResult = D3D12CreateDevice(
  nullptr,             // default adapter
  D3D_FEATURE_LEVEL_11_0,
  IID_PPV_ARGS(&md3dDevice));

// Fallback to WARP device.
if(FAILED(hardwareResult))
{
  ComPtr<IDXGIAdapter> pWarpAdapter;
  ThrowIfFailed(mdxgiFactory->EnumWarpAdapter(IID_PPV_
    ARGS(&pWarpAdapter)));

  ThrowIfFailed(D3D12CreateDevice(
    pWarpAdapter.Get(),
    D3D_FEATURE_LEVEL_11_0,
    IID_PPV_ARGS(&md3dDevice)));
}
```

Observe that we first enable the debug layer for debug mode builds. When the debug layer is enabled, Direct3D will enable extra debugging and send debug messages to the VC++ output window like the following:

```
D3D12 ERROR: ID3D12CommandList::Reset: Reset fails because the command
list was not closed.
```

Also observe that if our call to `D3D12CreateDevice` fails, we fallback to a WARP device, which is a software adapter. WARP stands for Windows Advanced Rasterization Platform. On Windows 7 and lower, the WARP device supports up to feature level 10.1; on Windows 8, the WARP device supports up to feature level 11.1. In order to create a WARP adapter, we need to create an `IDXGIFactory4` object so that we can enumerate the warp adapter:

```
ComPtr<IDXGIFactory4> mdxgiFactory;
CreateDXGIFactory1(IID_PPV_ARGS(&mdxgiFactory));
mdxgiFactory->EnumWarpAdapter(
  IID_PPV_ARGS(&pWarpAdapter));
```

The `mdxgiFactory` object will also be used to create our swap chain since it is part of the DXGI.

4.3.2 Create the Fence and Descriptor Sizes

After we have created our device, we can create our fence object for CPU/GPU synchronization. In addition, once we get to working with descriptors, we are going to need to know their size. Descriptor sizes can vary across GPUs so we need to query this information. We cache the descriptor sizes so that it is available when we need it for various descriptor types:

```
ThrowIfFailed(md3dDevice->CreateFence(
  0, D3D12_FENCE_FLAG_NONE, IID_PPV_ARGS(&mFence)));
```

```
mRtvDescriptorSize = md3dDevice->GetDescriptorHandleIncrementSize(
    D3D12_DESCRIPTOR_HEAP_TYPE_RTV);
mDsvDescriptorSize = md3dDevice->GetDescriptorHandleIncrementSize(
    D3D12_DESCRIPTOR_HEAP_TYPE_DSV);
mCbvSrvDescriptorSize = md3dDevice->GetDescriptorHandleIncrementSize(
    D3D12_DESCRIPTOR_HEAP_TYPE_CBV_SRV_UAV);
```

4.3.3 Check 4X MSAA Quality Support

In this book, we check support for 4X MSAA. We choose 4X because it gives a good improvement without being overly expensive, and because all Direct3D 11 capable devices support 4X MSAA with all render target formats. Therefore, it is guaranteed to be available on Direct3D 11 hardware and we do not have to verify support for it. However, we do have to check the supported quality level, which can be done with the following method:

```
D3D12_FEATURE_DATA_MULTISAMPLE_QUALITY_LEVELS msQualityLevels;
msQualityLevels.Format = mBackBufferFormat;
msQualityLevels.SampleCount = 4;
msQualityLevels.Flags = D3D12_MULTISAMPLE_QUALITY_LEVELS_FLAG_NONE;
msQualityLevels.NumQualityLevels = 0;
ThrowIfFailed(md3dDevice->CheckFeatureSupport(
    D3D12_FEATURE_MULTISAMPLE_QUALITY_LEVELS,
    &msQualityLevels,
    sizeof(msQualityLevels)));

m4xMsaaQuality = msQualityLevels.NumQualityLevels;
assert(m4xMsaaQuality > 0 && "Unexpected MSAA quality level.");
```

Because 4X MSAA is always supported, the returned quality should always be greater than 0; therefore, we assert that this is the case.

4.3.4 Create Command Queue and Command List

Recall from §4.2.1 that a command queue is represented by the ID3D12CommandQueue interface, a command allocator is represented by the ID3D12CommandAllocator interface, and a command list is represented by the ID3D12GraphicsCommandList interface. The following function shows how we create a command queue, command allocator, and command list:

```
ComPtr<ID3D12CommandQueue> mCommandQueue;
ComPtr<ID3D12CommandAllocator> mDirectCmdListAlloc;
ComPtr<ID3D12GraphicsCommandList> mCommandList;
void D3DApp::CreateCommandObjects()
{
  D3D12_COMMAND_QUEUE_DESC queueDesc = {};
  queueDesc.Type = D3D12_COMMAND_LIST_TYPE_DIRECT;
  queueDesc.Flags = D3D12_COMMAND_QUEUE_FLAG_NONE;
  ThrowIfFailed(md3dDevice->CreateCommandQueue(
    &queueDesc, IID_PPV_ARGS(&mCommandQueue)));
```

```
ThrowIfFailed(md3dDevice->CreateCommandAllocator(
  D3D12_COMMAND_LIST_TYPE_DIRECT,
  IID_PPV_ARGS(mDirectCmdListAlloc.GetAddressOf())));

ThrowIfFailed(md3dDevice->CreateCommandList(
  0,
  D3D12_COMMAND_LIST_TYPE_DIRECT,
  mDirectCmdListAlloc.Get(), // Associated command allocator
  nullptr,                   // Initial PipelineStateObject
  IID_PPV_ARGS(mCommandList.GetAddressOf())));

// Start off in a closed state. This is because the first time we
// refer to the command list we will Reset it, and it needs to be
// closed before calling Reset.
mCommandList->Close();
}
```

Observe that for `CreateCommandList`, we specify null for the pipeline state object parameter. In this chapter's sample program, we do not issue any draw commands, so we do not need a valid pipeline state object. We will discuss pipeline state objects in Chapter 6.

4.3.5 Describe and Create the Swap Chain

The next step in the initialization process is to create the swap chain. This is done by first filling out an instance of the DXGI_SWAP_CHAIN_DESC structure, which describes the characteristics of the swap chain we are going to create. This structure is defined as follows:

```
typedef struct DXGI_SWAP_CHAIN_DESC
{
  DXGI_MODE_DESC BufferDesc;
  DXGI_SAMPLE_DESC SampleDesc;
  DXGI_USAGE BufferUsage;
  UINT BufferCount;
  HWND OutputWindow;
  BOOL Windowed;
  DXGI_SWAP_EFFECT SwapEffect;
  UINT Flags;
} DXGI_SWAP_CHAIN_DESC;
```

The DXGI_MODE_DESC type is another structure, defined as:

```
typedef struct DXGI_MODE_DESC
{
  UINT Width;                // Buffer resolution width
  UINT Height;               // Buffer resolution height
  DXGI_RATIONAL RefreshRate;
  DXGI_FORMAT Format;        // Buffer display format
  DXGI_MODE_SCANLINE_ORDER ScanlineOrdering; //Progressive vs.
    interlaced
```

```
    DXGI_MODE_SCALING Scaling;    // How the image is stretched
                                  // over the monitor.
} DXGI_MODE_DESC;
```

In the following data member descriptions, we only cover the common flags and options that are most important to a beginner at this point. For a description of further flags and options, refer to the SDK documentation.

1. `BufferDesc`: This structure describes the properties of the back buffer we want to create. The main properties we are concerned with are the width and height, and pixel format; see the SDK documentation for further details on the other members.
2. `SampleDesc`: The number of multisamples and quality level; see §4.1.8. For single sampling, specify a sample count of 1 and quality level of 0.
3. `BufferUsage`: Specify `DXGI_USAGE_RENDER_TARGET_OUTPUT` since we are going to be rendering to the back buffer (i.e., use it as a render target).
4. `BufferCount`: The number of buffers to use in the swap chain; specify two for double buffering.
5. `OutputWindow`: A handle to the window we are rendering into.
6. `Windowed`: Specify `true` to run in windowed mode or `false` for full-screen mode.
7. `SwapEffect`: Specify `DXGI_SWAP_EFFECT_FLIP_DISCARD`.
8. `Flags`: Optional flags. If you specify `DXGI_SWAP_CHAIN_FLAG_ALLOW_MODE_SWITCH`, then when the application is switching to full-screen mode, it will choose a display mode that best matches the current application window dimensions. If this flag is not specified, then when the application is switching to full-screen mode, it will use the current desktop display mode.

After we have described out swap chain, we can create it with the `IDXGIFactory::CreateSwapChain` method:

```
HRESULT IDXGIFactory::CreateSwapChain(
    IUnknown *pDevice,             // Pointer to ID3D12CommandQueue.
    DXGI_SWAP_CHAIN_DESC *pDesc,   // Pointer to swap chain description.
    IDXGISwapChain **ppSwapChain); // Returns created swap chain interface.
```

The following code shows how we create the swap chain in our sample framework. Observe that this function has been designed so that it can be called multiple times. It will destroy the old swap chain before creating the new one. This allows us to recreate the swap chain with different settings; in particular, we can change the multisampling settings at runtime.

```
DXGI_FORMAT mBackBufferFormat = DXGI_FORMAT_R8G8B8A8_UNORM;
```

122   Direct3D Foundations

```cpp
void D3DApp::CreateSwapChain()
{
  // Release the previous swapchain we will be recreating.
  mSwapChain.Reset();

  DXGI_SWAP_CHAIN_DESC sd;
  sd.BufferDesc.Width = mClientWidth;
  sd.BufferDesc.Height = mClientHeight;
  sd.BufferDesc.RefreshRate.Numerator = 60;
  sd.BufferDesc.RefreshRate.Denominator = 1;
  sd.BufferDesc.Format = mBackBufferFormat;
  sd.BufferDesc.ScanlineOrdering = DXGI_MODE_SCANLINE_ORDER_
    UNSPECIFIED;
  sd.BufferDesc.Scaling = DXGI_MODE_SCALING_UNSPECIFIED;
  sd.SampleDesc.Count = m4xMsaaState ? 4 : 1;
  sd.SampleDesc.Quality = m4xMsaaState ? (m4xMsaaQuality - 1) : 0;
  sd.BufferUsage = DXGI_USAGE_RENDER_TARGET_OUTPUT;
  sd.BufferCount = SwapChainBufferCount;
  sd.OutputWindow = mhMainWnd;
  sd.Windowed = true;
  sd.SwapEffect = DXGI_SWAP_EFFECT_FLIP_DISCARD;
  sd.Flags = DXGI_SWAP_CHAIN_FLAG_ALLOW_MODE_SWITCH;
  // Note: Swap chain uses queue to perform flush.
  ThrowIfFailed(mdxgiFactory->CreateSwapChain(
    mCommandQueue.Get(),
    &sd,
    mSwapChain.GetAddressOf()));
}
```

4.3.6 Create the Descriptor Heaps

We need to create the descriptor heaps to store the descriptors/views (§4.1.6) our application needs. A descriptor heap is represented by the `ID3D12DescriptorHeap` interface. A heap is created with the `ID3D12Device::CreateDescriptorHeap` method. In this chapter's sample program, we need `SwapChainBufferCount` many render target views (RTVs) to describe the buffer resources in the swap chain we will render into, and one depth/stencil view (DSV) to describe the depth/stencil buffer resource for depth testing. Therefore, we need a heap for storing `SwapChainBufferCount` RTVs, and we need a heap for storing one DSV. These heaps are created with the following code:

```cpp
ComPtr<ID3D12DescriptorHeap> mRtvHeap;
ComPtr<ID3D12DescriptorHeap> mDsvHeap;
void D3DApp::CreateRtvAndDsvDescriptorHeaps()
{
  D3D12_DESCRIPTOR_HEAP_DESC rtvHeapDesc;
  rtvHeapDesc.NumDescriptors = SwapChainBufferCount;
  rtvHeapDesc.Type = D3D12_DESCRIPTOR_HEAP_TYPE_RTV;
  rtvHeapDesc.Flags = D3D12_DESCRIPTOR_HEAP_FLAG_NONE;
    rtvHeapDesc.NodeMask = 0;
```

```
    ThrowIfFailed(md3dDevice->CreateDescriptorHeap(
        &rtvHeapDesc, IID_PPV_ARGS(mRtvHeap.GetAddressOf())));


    D3D12_DESCRIPTOR_HEAP_DESC dsvHeapDesc;
    dsvHeapDesc.NumDescriptors = 1;
    dsvHeapDesc.Type = D3D12_DESCRIPTOR_HEAP_TYPE_DSV;
    dsvHeapDesc.Flags = D3D12_DESCRIPTOR_HEAP_FLAG_NONE;
    dsvHeapDesc.NodeMask = 0;
    ThrowIfFailed(md3dDevice->CreateDescriptorHeap(
        &dsvHeapDesc, IID_PPV_ARGS(mDsvHeap.GetAddressOf())));
}
```

In our application framework, we define

```
static const int SwapChainBufferCount = 2;
int mCurrBackBuffer = 0;
```

and we keep track of the current back buffer index with `mCurrBackBuffer` (recall that the front and back buffers get swapped in page flipping, so we need to track which buffer is the current back buffer so we know which one to render to).

After we create the heaps, we need to be able to access the descriptors they store. Our application references descriptors through handles. A handle to the first descriptor in a heap is obtained with the `ID3D12DescriptorHeap::GetCPUDescriptorHandleForHeapStart` method. The following functions get the current back buffer RTV and DSV, respectively:

```
D3D12_CPU_DESCRIPTOR_HANDLE CurrentBackBufferView()const
{
    // CD3DX12 constructor to offset to the RTV of the current back buffer.
    return CD3DX12_CPU_DESCRIPTOR_HANDLE(
        mRtvHeap->GetCPUDescriptorHandleForHeapStart(),// handle start
        mCurrBackBuffer,    // index to offset
        mRtvDescriptorSize); // byte size of descriptor
}

D3D12_CPU_DESCRIPTOR_HANDLE DepthStencilView()const
{
    return mDsvHeap->GetCPUDescriptorHandleForHeapStart();
}
```

We now see an example of where the descriptor size is needed. In order to offset to the current back buffer RTV descriptor, we need to know the RTV descriptor byte size.

4.3.7 Create the Render Target View

As said in §4.1.6, we do not bind a resource to a pipeline stage directly; instead, we must create a resource view (descriptor) to the resource and bind the view to the pipeline stage. In particular, in order to bind the back buffer to the output merger stage of the pipeline (so Direct3D can render onto it), we need to create a render target view to the back buffer. The first step is to get the buffer resources which are stored in the swap chain:

```
HRESULT IDXGISwapChain::GetBuffer(
    UINT Buffer,
    REFIID riid,
    void **ppSurface);
```

1. `Buffer`: An index identifying the particular back buffer we want to get (in case there is more than one).
2. `riid`: The COM ID of the `ID3D12Resource` interface we want to obtain a pointer to.
3. `ppSurface`: Returns a pointer to an `ID3D12Resource` that represents the back buffer.

The call to `IDXGISwapChain::GetBuffer` increases the COM reference count to the back buffer, so we must release it when we are finished with it. This is done automatically if using a `ComPtr`.

To create the render target view, we use the `ID3D12Device::CreateRenderTargetView` method:

```
void ID3D12Device::CreateRenderTargetView(
    ID3D12Resource *pResource,
    const D3D12_RENDER_TARGET_VIEW_DESC *pDesc,
    D3D12_CPU_DESCRIPTOR_HANDLE DestDescriptor);
```

1. `pResource`: Specifies the resource that will be used as the render target, which, in the example above, is the back buffer (i.e., we are creating a render target view to the back buffer).
2. `pDesc`: A pointer to a `D3D12_RENDER_TARGET_VIEW_DESC`. Among other things, this structure describes the data type (format) of the elements in the resource. If the resource was created with a typed format (i.e., not typeless), then this parameter can be null, which indicates to create a view to the first mipmap level of this resource (the back buffer only has one mipmap level) with the format the resource was created with. (Mipmaps are discussed in Chapter 9.) Because we specified the type of our back buffer, we specify null for this parameter.
3. `DestDescriptor`: Handle to the descriptor that will store the created render target view.

Below is an example of calling these two methods where we create an RTV to each buffer in the swap chain:

```
ComPtr<ID3D12Resource> mSwapChainBuffer[SwapChainBufferCount];
CD3DX12_CPU_DESCRIPTOR_HANDLE rtvHeapHandle(
  mRtvHeap->GetCPUDescriptorHandleForHeapStart());
for (UINT i = 0; i < SwapChainBufferCount; i++)
{
  // Get the ith buffer in the swap chain.
  ThrowIfFailed(mSwapChain->GetBuffer(
    i, IID_PPV_ARGS(&mSwapChainBuffer[i])));

  // Create an RTV to it.
  md3dDevice->CreateRenderTargetView(
    mSwapChainBuffer[i].Get(), nullptr, rtvHeapHandle);

  // Next entry in heap.
  rtvHeapHandle.Offset(1, mRtvDescriptorSize);
}
```

4.3.8 Create the Depth/Stencil Buffer and View

We now need to create the depth/stencil buffer. As described in §4.1.5, the depth buffer is just a 2D texture that stores the depth information of the nearest visible objects (and stencil information if using stenciling). A texture is a kind of GPU resource, so we create one by filling out a D3D12_RESOURCE_DESC structure describing the texture resource, and then calling the ID3D12Device::CreateCommittedResource method. The D3D12_RESOURCE_DESC structure is defined as follows:

```
typedef struct D3D12_RESOURCE_DESC
  {
  D3D12_RESOURCE_DIMENSION Dimension;
  UINT64 Alignment;
  UINT64 Width;
  UINT Height;
  UINT16 DepthOrArraySize;
  UINT16 MipLevels;
  DXGI_FORMAT Format;
  DXGI_SAMPLE_DESC SampleDesc;
  D3D12_TEXTURE_LAYOUT Layout;
  D3D12_RESOURCE_MISC_FLAG MiscFlags;
} D3D12_RESOURCE_DESC;
```

1. Dimension: The dimension of the resource, which is one of the following enumerated types:

```
enum D3D12_RESOURCE_DIMENSION
  {
    D3D12_RESOURCE_DIMENSION_UNKNOWN = 0,
    D3D12_RESOURCE_DIMENSION_BUFFER = 1,
    D3D12_RESOURCE_DIMENSION_TEXTURE1D = 2,
```

```
        D3D12_RESOURCE_DIMENSION_TEXTURE2D = 3,
        D3D12_RESOURCE_DIMENSION_TEXTURE3D = 4
    } D3D12_RESOURCE_DIMENSION;
```

2. `Width`: The width of the texture in texels. For buffer resources, this is the number of bytes in the buffer.

3. `Height`: The height of the texture in texels.

4. `DepthOrArraySize`: The depth of the texture in texels, or the texture array size (for 1D and 2D textures). Note that you cannot have a texture array of 3D textures.

5. `MipLevels`: The number of mipmap levels. Mipmaps are covered in Chapter 9 on texturing. For creating the depth/stencil buffer, our texture only needs one mipmap level.

6. `Format`: A member of the `DXGI_FORMAT` enumerated type specifying the format of the texels. For a depth/stencil buffer, this needs to be one of the formats shown in §4.1.5.

7. `SampleDesc`: The number of multisamples and quality level; see §4.1.7 and §4.1.8. Recall that 4X MSAA uses a back buffer and depth buffer 4X bigger than the screen resolution, in order to store color and depth/stencil information per subpixel. Therefore, the multisampling settings used for the depth/stencil buffer must match the settings used for the render target.

8. `Layout`: A member of the `D3D12_TEXTURE_LAYOUT` enumerated type that specifies the texture layout. For now, we do not have to worry about the layout and can specify `D3D12_TEXTURE_LAYOUT_UNKNOWN`.

9. `MiscFlags`: Miscellaneous resource flags. For a depth/stencil buffer resource, specify `D3D12_RESOURCE_MISC_DEPTH_STENCIL`.

GPU resources live in heaps, which are essentially blocks of GPU memory with certain properties. The `ID3D12Device::CreateCommittedResource` method creates and commits a resource to a particular heap with the properties we specify.

```
HRESULT ID3D12Device::CreateCommittedResource(
    const D3D12_HEAP_PROPERTIES *pHeapProperties,
    D3D12_HEAP_MISC_FLAG HeapMiscFlags,
    const D3D12_RESOURCE_DESC *pResourceDesc,
    D3D12_RESOURCE_USAGE InitialResourceState,
    const D3D12_CLEAR_VALUE *pOptimizedClearValue,
    REFIID riidResource,
    void **ppvResource);

typedef struct D3D12_HEAP_PROPERTIES {
    D3D12_HEAP_TYPE          Type;
    D3D12_CPU_PAGE_PROPERTIES CPUPageProperties;
    D3D12_MEMORY_POOL        MemoryPoolPreference;
```

```
UINT CreationNodeMask;
UINT VisibleNodeMask;
} D3D12_HEAP_PROPERTIES;
```

1. `pHeapProperties`: The properties of the heap we want to commit the resource to. Some of these properties are for advanced usage. For now, the main property we need to worry about is the `D3D12_HEAP_TYPE`, which can be one of the following members of the `D3D12_HEAP_PROPERTIES` enumerated type:

   a) `D3D12_HEAP_TYPE_DEFAULT`: Default heap. This is where we commit resources that will be solely accessed by the GPU. Take the depth/stencil buffer as an example: The GPU reads and writes to the depth/stencil buffer. The CPU never needs access to it, so the depth/stencil buffer would be placed in the default heap.

   b) `D3D12_HEAP_TYPE_UPLOAD`: Upload heap. This is where we commit resources where we need to upload data from the CPU to the GPU resource.

   c) `D3D12_HEAP_TYPE_READBACK`: Read-back heap. This is where we commit resources that need to be read by the CPU.

   d) `D3D12_HEAP_TYPE_CUSTOM`: For advanced usage scenarios—see the MSDN documentation for more information.

2. `HeapMiscFlags`: Additional flags about the heap we want to commit the resource to. This will usually be `D3D12_HEAP_MISC_NONE`.

3. `pResourceDesc`: Pointer to a `D3D12_RESOURCE_DESC` instance describing the resource we want to create.

4. `InitialResourceState`: Recall from §4.2.3 that resources have a current usage state. Use this parameter to set the initial state of the resource when it is created. For the depth/stencil buffer, the initial state will be `D3D12_RESOURCE_USAGE_INITIAL`, and then we will want to transition it to the `D3D12_RESOURCE_USAGE_DEPTH` so it can be bound to the pipeline as a depth/stencil buffer.

5. `pOptimizedClearValue`: Pointer to a `D3D12_CLEAR_VALUE` object that describes an optimized value for clearing resources. Clear calls that match the optimized clear value can potentially be faster than clear calls that do not match the optimized clear value. Null can also be specified for this value to not specify an optimized clear value.

```
struct D3D12_CLEAR_VALUE
{
  DXGI_FORMAT Format;
  union
    {
      FLOAT Color[ 4 ];
      D3D12_DEPTH_STENCIL_VALUE DepthStencil;
    };
}   D3D12_CLEAR_VALUE;
```

6. `riidResource`: The COM ID of the `ID3D12Resource` interface we want to obtain a pointer to.

7. `ppvResource`: Returns pointer to an `ID3D12Resource` that represents the newly created resource.

 Resources should be placed in the default heap for optimal performance. Only use upload or read back heaps if you need those features.

In addition, before using the depth/stencil buffer, we must create an associated depth/stencil view to be bound to the pipeline. This is done similarly to creating the render target view. The following code example shows how we create the depth/stencil texture and its corresponding depth/stencil view:

```
// Create the depth/stencil buffer and view.
D3D12_RESOURCE_DESC depthStencilDesc;
depthStencilDesc.Dimension = D3D12_RESOURCE_DIMENSION_TEXTURE2D;
depthStencilDesc.Alignment = 0;
depthStencilDesc.Width = mClientWidth;
depthStencilDesc.Height = mClientHeight;
depthStencilDesc.DepthOrArraySize = 1;
depthStencilDesc.MipLevels = 1;
depthStencilDesc.Format = mDepthStencilFormat;
depthStencilDesc.SampleDesc.Count = m4xMsaaState ? 4 : 1;
depthStencilDesc.SampleDesc.Quality = m4xMsaaState ? (m4xMsaaQuality - 1) : 0;
depthStencilDesc.Layout = D3D12_TEXTURE_LAYOUT_UNKNOWN;
depthStencilDesc.Flags = D3D12_RESOURCE_FLAG_ALLOW_DEPTH_STENCIL;

D3D12_CLEAR_VALUE optClear;
optClear.Format = mDepthStencilFormat;
optClear.DepthStencil.Depth = 1.0f;
optClear.DepthStencil.Stencil = 0;
ThrowIfFailed(md3dDevice->CreateCommittedResource(
  &CD3DX12_HEAP_PROPERTIES(D3D12_HEAP_TYPE_DEFAULT),
  D3D12_HEAP_FLAG_NONE,
  &depthStencilDesc,
  D3D12_RESOURCE_STATE_COMMON,
  &optClear,
  IID_PPV_ARGS(mDepthStencilBuffer.GetAddressOf())));

// Create descriptor to mip level 0 of entire resource using the
// format of the resource.
md3dDevice->CreateDepthStencilView(
  mDepthStencilBuffer.Get(),
  nullptr,
  DepthStencilView());

// Transition the resource from its initial state to be used as a depth buffer.
mCommandList->ResourceBarrier(
  1,
  &CD3DX12_RESOURCE_BARRIER::Transition(
    mDepthStencilBuffer.Get(),
```

```
D3D12_RESOURCE_STATE_COMMON,
D3D12_RESOURCE_STATE_DEPTH_WRITE));
```

Note that we use the `CD3DX12_HEAP_PROPERTIES` helper constructor to create the heap properties structure, which is implemented like so:

```
explicit CD3DX12_HEAP_PROPERTIES(
    D3D12_HEAP_TYPE type,
    UINT creationNodeMask = 1,
    UINT nodeMask = 1 )
{
  Type = type;
  CPUPageProperty = D3D12_CPU_PAGE_PROPERTY_UNKNOWN;
  MemoryPoolPreference = D3D12_MEMORY_POOL_UNKNOWN;
  CreationNodeMask = creationNodeMask;
  VisibleNodeMask = nodeMask;
}
```

The second parameter of `CreateDepthStencilView` is a pointer to a `D3D12_DEPTH_STENCIL_VIEW_DESC`. Among other things, this structure describes the data type (format) of the elements in the resource. If the resource was created with a typed format (i.e., not typeless), then this parameter can be null, which indicates to create a view to the first mipmap level of this resource (the depth/stencil buffer was created with only one mipmap level) with the format the resource was created with. (Mipmaps are discussed in Chapter 9.) Because we specified the type of our depth/stencil buffer, we specify null for this parameter.

4.3.9 Set the Viewport

Usually we like to draw the 3D scene to the entire back buffer, where the back buffer size corresponds to the entire screen (full-screen mode) or the entire client area of a window. However, sometimes we only want to draw the 3D scene into a subrectangle of the back buffer; see Figure 4.9.

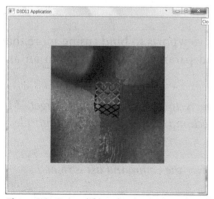

Figure 4.9. By modifying the viewport, we can draw the 3D scene into a subrectangle of the back buffer. The back buffer then gets presented to the client area of the window.

The subrectangle of the back buffer we draw into is called the viewport and it is described by the following structure:

```
typedef struct D3D12_VIEWPORT {
  FLOAT TopLeftX;
  FLOAT TopLeftY;
  FLOAT Width;
  FLOAT Height;
  FLOAT MinDepth;
  FLOAT MaxDepth;
} D3D12_VIEWPORT;
```

The first four data members define the viewport rectangle relative to the back buffer (observe that we can specify fractional pixel coordinates because the data members are of type `float`). In Direct3D, depth values are stored in the depth buffer in a normalized range of 0 to 1. The `MinDepth` and `MaxDepth` members are used to transform the depth interval [0, 1] to the depth interval [`MinDepth`, `MaxDepth`]. Being able to transform the depth range can be used to achieve certain effects; for example, you could set `MinDepth=0` and `MaxDepth=0`, so that all objects drawn with this viewport will have depth values of 0 and appear in front of all other objects in the scene. However, usually `MinDepth` is set to 0 and `MaxDepth` is set to 1 so that the depth values are not modified.

Once we have filled out the `D3D12_VIEWPORT` structure, we set the viewport with Direct3D with the `ID3D12CommandList::RSSetViewports` method. The following example creates and sets a viewport that draws onto the entire back buffer:

```
D3D12_VIEWPORT vp;
vp.TopLeftX = 0.0f;
vp.TopLeftY = 0.0f;
vp.Width    = static_cast<float>(mClientWidth);
vp.Height   = static_cast<float>(mClientHeight);
vp.MinDepth = 0.0f;
vp.MaxDepth = 1.0f;

mCommandList->RSSetViewports(1, &vp);
```

The first parameter is the number of viewports to bind (using more than one is for advanced effects), and the second parameter is a pointer to an array of viewports.

You cannot specify multiple viewports to the same render target. Multiple viewports are used for advanced techniques that render to multiple render targets at the same time.

The viewport needs to be reset whenever the command list is reset.

You could use the viewport to implement split screens for two-player game modes, for example. You would create two viewports, one for the left half of the screen and one for the right half of the screen. Then you would draw the 3D scene from the perspective of Player 1 into the left viewport and draw the 3D scene from the perspective of Player 2 into the right viewport.

4.3.10 Set the Scissor Rectangles

We can define a *scissor rectangle* relative to the back buffer such that pixels outside this rectangle are culled (i.e., not rasterized to the back buffer). This can be used for optimizations. For example, if we know an area of the screen will contain a rectangular UI element on top of everything, we do not need to process the pixels of the 3D world that the UI element will obscure.

A scissor rectangle is defined by a `D3D12_RECT` structure which is `typedef`ed to the following structure:

```
typedef struct tagRECT
{
    LONG    left;
    LONG    top;
    LONG    right;
    LONG    bottom;
} RECT;
```

We set the scissor rectangle with Direct3D with the `ID3D12CommandList::RSSetScissorRects` method. The following example creates and sets a scissor rectangle that covers the upper-left quadrant of the back buffer:

```
mScissorRect = { 0, 0, mClientWidth/2, mClientHeight/2 };
mCommandList->RSSetScissorRects(1, &mScissorRect);
```

Similar to `RSSetViewports`, the first parameter is the number of scissor rectangles to bind (using more than one is for advanced effects), and the second parameter is a pointer to an array of rectangles.

You cannot specify multiple scissor rectangles on the same render target. Multiple scissor rectangles are used for advanced techniques that render to multiple render targets at the same time.

The scissors rectangles need to be reset whenever the command list is reset.

4.4 TIMING AND ANIMATION

To do animation correctly, we will need to keep track of the time. In particular, we will need to measure the amount of time that elapses between frames of animation. If the frame rate is high, these time intervals between frames will be very short; therefore, we need a timer with a high level of accuracy.

4.4.1 The Performance Timer

For accurate time measurements, we use the performance timer (or performance counter). To use the Win32 functions for querying the performance timer, we must `#include <windows.h>`.

The performance timer measures time in units called counts. We obtain the current time value, measured in counts, of the performance timer with the `QueryPerformanceCounter` function like so:

```
__int64 currTime;
QueryPerformanceCounter((LARGE_INTEGER*)&currTime);
```

Observe that this function returns the current time value through its parameter, which is a 64-bit integer value.

To get the frequency (counts per second) of the performance timer, we use the `QueryPerformanceFrequency` function:

```
__int64 countsPerSec;
QueryPerformanceFrequency((LARGE_INTEGER*)&countsPerSec);
```

Then the number of seconds (or fractions of a second) per count is just the reciprocal of the counts per second:

```
mSecondsPerCount = 1.0 / (double)countsPerSec;
```

Thus, to convert a time reading `valueInCounts` to seconds, we just multiply it by the conversion factor `mSecondsPerCount`

```
valueInSecs = valueInCounts * mSecondsPerCount;
```

The values returned by the `QueryPerformanceCounter` function are not particularly interesting in and of themselves. What we do is get the current time value using `QueryPerformanceCounter`, and then get the current time value a little later using `QueryPerformanceCounter` again. Then the time that elapsed between those two time calls is just the difference. That is, we always look at the relative difference between two time stamps to measure time, not the actual values returned by the performance counter. The following better illustrates the idea:

```
__int64 A = 0;
QueryPerformanceCounter((LARGE_INTEGER*)&A);

/* Do work */

__int64 B = 0;
QueryPerformanceCounter((LARGE_INTEGER*)&B);
```

So it took (B-A) counts to do the work, or (B-A)*mSecondsPerCount seconds to do the work.

MSDN has the following remark about `QueryPerformanceCounter`*: "On a multiprocessor computer, it should not matter which processor is called. However, you can get different results on different processors due to bugs in the basic input/output system (BIOS) or the hardware abstraction layer (HAL)." You can use the* `SetThreadAffinityMask` *function so that the main application thread does not get switch to another processor.*

4.4.2 Game Timer Class

In the next two sections, we will discuss the implementation of the following `GameTimer` class.

```
class GameTimer
{
public:
    GameTimer();

    float GameTime()const; // in seconds
    float DeltaTime()const; // in seconds

    void Reset(); // Call before message loop.
    void Start(); // Call when unpaused.
    void Stop();  // Call when paused.
    void Tick();  // Call every frame.

private:
    double mSecondsPerCount;
    double mDeltaTime;

    __int64 mBaseTime;
    __int64 mPausedTime;
    __int64 mStopTime;
    __int64 mPrevTime;
    __int64 mCurrTime;

    bool mStopped;
};
```

The constructor, in particular, queries the frequency of the performance counter. The other member functions are discussed in the next two sections.

```
GameTimer::GameTimer()
: mSecondsPerCount(0.0), mDeltaTime(-1.0), mBaseTime(0),
  mPausedTime(0), mPrevTime(0), mCurrTime(0), mStopped(false)
{
    __int64 countsPerSec;
    QueryPerformanceFrequency((LARGE_INTEGER*)&countsPerSec);
    mSecondsPerCount = 1.0 / (double)countsPerSec;
}
```

The `GameTimer` class and implementations are in the *GameTimer.h* and *GameTimer.cpp* files, which can be found in the *Common* directory of the sample code.

4.4.3 Time Elapsed Between Frames

When we render our frames of animation, we will need to know how much time has elapsed between frames so that we can update our game objects based on how much time has passed. Computing the time elapsed between frames proceeds as follows. Let t_i be the time returned by the performance counter during the ith frame and let t_{i-1} be the time returned by the performance counter during the previous frame. Then the time elapsed between the t_{i-1} reading and the t_i reading is $\Delta t = t_i - t_{i-1}$. For real-time rendering, we typically require at least 30 frames per second for smooth animation (and we usually have much higher rates); thus, $\Delta t = t_i - t_{i-1}$ tends to be a relatively small number.

The following code shows how Δt is computed in code:

```
void GameTimer::Tick()
{
    if( mStopped )
    {
        mDeltaTime = 0.0;
        return;
    }

    // Get the time this frame.
    __int64 currTime;
    QueryPerformanceCounter((LARGE_INTEGER*)&currTime);
    mCurrTime = currTime;

    // Time difference between this frame and the previous.
    mDeltaTime = (mCurrTime - mPrevTime)*mSecondsPerCount;

    // Prepare for next frame.
    mPrevTime = mCurrTime;

    // Force nonnegative. The DXSDK's CDXUTTimer mentions that if the
    // processor goes into a power save mode or we get shuffled to
    // another processor, then mDeltaTime can be negative.
    if(mDeltaTime < 0.0)
    {
        mDeltaTime = 0.0;
    }
}

float GameTimer::DeltaTime()const
{
    return (float)mDeltaTime;
}
```

The function `Tick` is called in the application message loop as follows:

```
int D3DApp::Run()
{
  MSG msg = {0};

  mTimer.Reset();

  while(msg.message != WM_QUIT)
  {
    // If there are Window messages then process them.
    if(PeekMessage( &msg, 0, 0, 0, PM_REMOVE ))
    {
      TranslateMessage( &msg );
      DispatchMessage( &msg );
    }
    // Otherwise, do animation/game stuff.
    else
    {
      mTimer.Tick();

      if( !mAppPaused )
      {
        CalculateFrameStats();
        Update(mTimer);
        Draw(mTimer);
      }
      else
      {
        Sleep(100);
      }
    }
  }

  return (int)msg.wParam;
}
```

In this way, Δt is computed every frame and fed into the `UpdateScene` method so that the scene can be updated based on how much time has passed since the previous frame of animation. The implementation of the `Reset` method is:

```
void GameTimer::Reset()
{
    __int64 currTime;
    QueryPerformanceCounter((LARGE_INTEGER*)&currTime);

    mBaseTime = currTime;
    mPrevTime = currTime;
    mStopTime = 0;
    mStopped = false;
}
```

Some of the variables shown have not been discussed yet (see §4.4.4). However, we see that this initializes `mPrevTime` to the current time when `Reset` is called. It is important to do this because for the first frame of animation, there is no previous frame, and therefore, no previous time stamp t_{i-1}. Thus this value needs to be initialized in the `Reset` method before the message loop starts.

4.4.4 Total Time

Another time measurement that can be useful is the amount of time that has elapsed since the application start, not counting paused time; we will call this *total time*. The following situation shows how this could be useful. Suppose the player has 300 seconds to complete a level. When the level starts, we can get the time t_{start} which is the time elapsed since the application started. Then after the level has started, every so often we can check the time t since the application started. If $t - t_{start} > 300s$ (see Figure 4.10) then the player has been in the level for over 300 seconds and loses. Obviously in this situation, we do not want to count any time the game was paused against the player.

Another application of total time is when we want to animate a quantity as a function of time. For instance, suppose we wish to have a light orbit the scene as a function of time. Its position can be described by the parametric equations:

$$\begin{cases} x = 10\cos t \\ y = 20 \\ z = 10\sin t \end{cases}$$

Here t represents time, and as t (time) increases, the coordinates of the light are updated so that the light moves in a circle with radius 10 in the $y = 20$ plane. For this kind of animation, we also do not want to count paused time; see Figure 4.11.

To implement total time, we use the following variables:

```
__int64 mBaseTime;
__int64 mPausedTime;
__int64 mStopTime;
```

As we saw in §4.4.3, `mBaseTime` is initialized to the current time when `Reset` was called. We can think of this as the time when the application started. In most cases,

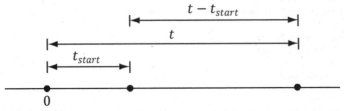

Figure 4.10. Computing the time since the level started. Note that we choose the application start time as the origin (0), and measure time values relative to that frame of reference.

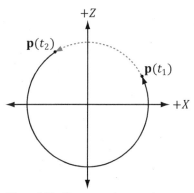

Figure 4.11. If we paused at t_1 and unpaused at t_2, and counted paused time, then when we unpause, the position will jump abruptly from $\mathbf{p}(t_1)$ to $\mathbf{p}(t_2)$.

you will only call `Reset` once before the message loop, so `mBaseTime` stays constant throughout the application's lifetime. The variable `mPausedTime` accumulates all the time that passes while we are paused. We need to accumulate this time so we can subtract it from the total running time, in order to not count paused time. The `mStopTime` variable gives us the time when the timer is stopped (paused); this is used to help us keep track of paused time.

Two important methods of the `GameTimer` class are `Stop` and `Start`. They should be called when the application is paused and unpaused, respectively, so that the `GameTimer` can keep track of paused time. The code comments explain the details of these two methods.

```
void GameTimer::Stop()
{
    // If we are already stopped, then don't do anything.
    if( !mStopped )
    {
        __int64 currTime;
        QueryPerformanceCounter((LARGE_INTEGER*)&currTime);

        // Otherwise, save the time we stopped at, and set
        // the Boolean flag indicating the timer is stopped.
        mStopTime = currTime;
        mStopped = true;
    }
}

void GameTimer::Start()
{
    __int64 startTime;
    QueryPerformanceCounter((LARGE_INTEGER*)&startTime);

    // Accumulate the time elapsed between stop and start pairs.
    //
    //              |<-------d------->|
```

```
//  ---------------*------------------*------------> time
//         mStopTime         startTime

// If we are resuming the timer from a stopped state...
if( mStopped )
{
    // then accumulate the paused time.
    mPausedTime += (startTime - mStopTime);

    // since we are starting the timer back up, the current
    // previous time is not valid, as it occurred while paused.
    // So reset it to the current time.
    mPrevTime = startTime;

    // no longer stopped...
    mStopTime = 0;
    mStopped = false;
}
}
```

Finally, the `TotalTime` member function, which returns the time elapsed since `Reset` was called not counting paused time, is implemented as follows:

```
float GameTimer::TotalTime()const
{
// If we are stopped, do not count the time that has passed
// since we stopped. Moreover, if we previously already had
// a pause, the distance mStopTime - mBaseTime includes paused
// time,which we do not want to count. To correct this, we can
// subtract the paused time from mStopTime:
//
//        previous paused time
//        |<----------->|
// ---*-------------*--------------*-------*-----------*------> time
// mBaseTime        mStopTime     mCurrTime

    if( mStopped )
    {
        return (float)(((mStopTime - mPausedTime)-
            mBaseTime)*mSecondsPerCount);
    }

// The distance mCurrTime - mBaseTime includes paused time,
// which we do not want to count. To correct this, we can subtract
// the paused time from mCurrTime:
//
// (mCurrTime - mPausedTime) - mBaseTime
//
//            |<--paused time-->|
// ----*----------------*------------------*-------------*------> time
// mBaseTime    mStopTime       startTime     mCurrTime

    else
    {
```

```
        return (float)(((mCurrTime-mPausedTime)-
            mBaseTime)*mSecondsPerCount);
    }
}
```

Our demo framework creates an instance of `GameTimer` for measuring the total time since the application started, and the time elapsed between frames; however, you can also create additional instances and use them as generic "stopwatches." For example, when a bomb is ignited, you could start a new `GameTimer`, and when the `TotalTime` reached 5 seconds, you could raise an event that the bomb exploded.

4.5 THE DEMO APPLICATION FRAMEWORK

The demos in this book use code from the *d3dUtil.h, d3dUtil.cpp, d3dApp.h,* and *d3dApp.cpp* files, which can be downloaded from the book's website. The *d3dUtil.h* and *d3dUtil.cpp* files contain useful utility code, and the *d3dApp.h* and *d3dApp.cpp* files contain the core Direct3D application class code that is used to encapsulate a Direct3D sample application. The reader is encouraged to study these files after reading this chapter, as we do not cover every line of code in these files (e.g., we do not show how to create a window, as basic Win32 programming is a prerequisite of this book). The goal of this framework was to hide the window creation code and Direct3D initialization code; by hiding this code, we feel it makes the demos less distracting, as you can focus only on the specific details the sample code is trying to illustrate.

4.5.1 D3DApp

The `D3DApp` class is the base Direct3D application class, which provides functions for creating the main application window, running the application message loop, handling window messages, and initializing Direct3D. Moreover, the class defines the framework functions for the demo applications. Clients are to derive from `D3DApp`, override the virtual framework functions, and instantiate only a single instance of the derived `D3DApp` class. The `D3DApp` class is defined as follows:

```
#include "d3dUtil.h"
#include "GameTimer.h"

// Link necessary d3d12 libraries.
#pragma comment(lib,"d3dcompiler.lib")
#pragma comment(lib, "D3D12.lib")
#pragma comment(lib, "dxgi.lib")

class D3DApp
{
```

```cpp
protected:

    D3DApp(HINSTANCE hInstance);
    D3DApp(const D3DApp& rhs) = delete;
    D3DApp& operator=(const D3DApp& rhs) = delete;
    virtual ~D3DApp();

public:

    static D3DApp* GetApp();

    HINSTANCE AppInst()const;
    HWND      MainWnd()const;
    float     AspectRatio()const;

    bool Get4xMsaaState()const;
    void Set4xMsaaState(bool value);

    int Run();

    virtual bool Initialize();
    virtual LRESULT MsgProc(HWND hwnd, UINT msg, WPARAM wParam, LPARAM
      lParam);

protected:
    virtual void CreateRtvAndDsvDescriptorHeaps();
    virtual void OnResize();
    virtual void Update(const GameTimer& gt)=0;
    virtual void Draw(const GameTimer& gt)=0;

    // Convenience overrides for handling mouse input.
    virtual void OnMouseDown(WPARAM btnState, int x, int y){ }
    virtual void OnMouseUp(WPARAM btnState, int x, int y) { }
    virtual void OnMouseMove(WPARAM btnState, int x, int y){ }

protected:

    bool InitMainWindow();
    bool InitDirect3D();
    void CreateCommandObjects();
    void CreateSwapChain();

    void FlushCommandQueue();

    ID3D12Resource* CurrentBackBuffer()const
    {
      return mSwapChainBuffer[mCurrBackBuffer].Get();
    }

    D3D12_CPU_DESCRIPTOR_HANDLE CurrentBackBufferView()const
    {
      return CD3DX12_CPU_DESCRIPTOR_HANDLE(
        mRtvHeap->GetCPUDescriptorHandleForHeapStart(),
        mCurrBackBuffer,
        mRtvDescriptorSize);
    }
```

```cpp
    D3D12_CPU_DESCRIPTOR_HANDLE DepthStencilView()const
    {
      return mDsvHeap->GetCPUDescriptorHandleForHeapStart();
    }

    void CalculateFrameStats();

    void LogAdapters();
    void LogAdapterOutputs(IDXGIAdapter* adapter);
    void LogOutputDisplayModes(IDXGIOutput* output, DXGI_FORMAT format);

protected:

    static D3DApp* mApp;

    HINSTANCE mhAppInst = nullptr; // application instance handle
    HWND      mhMainWnd = nullptr; // main window handle
    bool      mAppPaused = false;  // is the application paused?
    bool      mMinimized = false;  // is the application minimized?
    bool      mMaximized = false;  // is the application maximized?
    bool      mResizing = false;   // are the resize bars being dragged?
    bool      mFullscreenState = false;// fullscreen enabled

    // Set true to use 4X MSAA (§4.1.8). The default is false.
    bool      m4xMsaaState = false;    // 4X MSAA enabled
    UINT      m4xMsaaQuality = 0;      // quality level of 4X MSAA

    // Used to keep track of the "delta-time" and game time (§4.4).
    GameTimer mTimer;

    Microsoft::WRL::ComPtr<IDXGIFactory4> mdxgiFactory;
    Microsoft::WRL::ComPtr<IDXGISwapChain> mSwapChain;
    Microsoft::WRL::ComPtr<ID3D12Device> md3dDevice;

    Microsoft::WRL::ComPtr<ID3D12Fence> mFence;
    UINT64 mCurrentFence = 0;

    Microsoft::WRL::ComPtr<ID3D12CommandQueue> mCommandQueue;
    Microsoft::WRL::ComPtr<ID3D12CommandAllocator> mDirectCmdListAlloc;
    Microsoft::WRL::ComPtr<ID3D12GraphicsCommandList> mCommandList;

    static const int SwapChainBufferCount = 2;
    int mCurrBackBuffer = 0;
    Microsoft::WRL::ComPtr<ID3D12Resource> mSwapChainBuffer[SwapChainBuf
       ferCount];
    Microsoft::WRL::ComPtr<ID3D12Resource> mDepthStencilBuffer;

    Microsoft::WRL::ComPtr<ID3D12DescriptorHeap> mRtvHeap;
    Microsoft::WRL::ComPtr<ID3D12DescriptorHeap> mDsvHeap;

    D3D12_VIEWPORT mScreenViewport;
    D3D12_RECT mScissorRect;

    UINT mRtvDescriptorSize = 0;
    UINT mDsvDescriptorSize = 0;
```

```
    UINT mCbvSrvDescriptorSize = 0;

    // Derived class should set these in derived constructor to customize
    // starting values.
    std::wstring mMainWndCaption = L"d3d App";
    D3D_DRIVER_TYPE md3dDriverType = D3D_DRIVER_TYPE_HARDWARE;
    DXGI_FORMAT mBackBufferFormat = DXGI_FORMAT_R8G8B8A8_UNORM;
    DXGI_FORMAT mDepthStencilFormat = DXGI_FORMAT_D24_UNORM_S8_UINT;
    int mClientWidth = 800;
    int mClientHeight = 600;
};
```

We have used comments in the above code to describe some of the data members; the methods are discussed in the subsequent sections.

4.5.2 Non-Framework Methods

1. `D3DApp`: The constructor simply initializes the data members to default values.
2. `~D3DApp`: The destructor releases the COM interfaces the `D3DApp` acquires, and flushes the command queue. The reason we need to flush the command queue in the destructor is that we need to wait until the GPU is done processing the commands in the queue before we destroy any resources the GPU is still referencing. Otherwise, the GPU might crash when the application exits.

```
D3DApp::~D3DApp()
{
  if(md3dDevice != nullptr)
    FlushCommandQueue();
}
```

3. `AppInst`: Trivial access function returns a copy of the application instance handle.
4. `MainWnd`: Trivial access function returns a copy of the main window handle.
5. `AspectRatio`: The aspect ratio is defined as the ratio of the back buffer width to its height. The aspect ratio will be used in the next chapter. It is trivially implemented as:

```
float D3DApp::AspectRatio()const
{
  return static_cast<float>(mClientWidth) / mClientHeight;
}
```

6. `Get4xMsaaState`: Returns true is 4X MSAA is enabled and false otherwise.
7. `Set4xMsaaState`: Enables/disables 4X MSAA.
8. `Run`: This method wraps the application message loop. It uses the Win32 `PeekMessage` function so that it can process our game logic when no messages are present. The implementation of this function was shown in §4.4.3.

9. `InitMainWindow`: Initializes the main application window; we assume the reader is familiar with basic Win32 window initialization.
10. `InitDirect3D`: Initializes Direct3D by implementing the steps discussed in §4.3.
11. `CreateSwapChain`: Creates the swap chain (§4.3.5.).
12. `CreateCommandObjects`: Creates the command queue, a command list allocator, and a command list, as described in §4.3.4.
13. `FlushCommandQueue`: Forces the CPU to wait until the GPU has finished processing all the commands in the queue (see §4.2.2).
14. `CurrentBackBuffer`: Returns an `ID3D12Resource` to the current back buffer in the swap chain.
15. `CurrentBackBufferView`: Returns the RTV (render target view) to the current back buffer.
16. `DepthStencilView`: Returns the DSV (depth/stencil view) to the main depth/stencil buffer.
17. `CalculateFrameStats`: Calculates the average frames per second and the average milliseconds per frame. The implementation of this method is discussed in §4.4.4.
18. `LogAdapters`: Enumerates all the adapters on a system (§4.1.10).
19. `LogAdapterOutputs`: Enumerates all the outputs associated with an adapter (§4.1.10).
20. `LogOutputDisplayModes`: Enumerates all the display modes an output supports for a given format (§4.1.10).

4.5.3 Framework Methods

For each sample application in this book, we consistently override six virtual functions of `D3DApp`. These six functions are used to implement the code specific to the particular sample. The benefit of this setup is that the initialization code, message handling, etc., is implemented in the `D3DApp` class, so that the derived class needs to only focus on the specific code of the demo application. Here is a description of the framework methods:

1. `Initialize`: Use this method to put initialization code for the application such as allocating resources, initializing objects, and setting up the 3D scene. The `D3DApp` implementation of this method calls `InitMainWindow` and `InitDirect3D`; therefore, you should call the `D3DApp` version of this method in your derived implementation first like this:

```
bool TestApp::Init()
{
```

```
if(!D3DApp::Init())
  return false;

/* Rest of initialization code goes here */
}
```

so that your initialization code can access the initialized members of `D3DApp`.

2. `MsgProc`: This method implements the window procedure function for the main application window. Generally, you only need to override this method if there is a message you need to handle that `D3DApp::MsgProc` does not handle (or does not handle to your liking). The `D3DApp` implementation of this method is explored in §4.5.5. If you override this method, any message that you do not handle should be forwarded to `D3DApp::MsgProc`.

3. `CreateRtvAndDsvDescriptorHeaps`: Virtual function where you create the RTV and DSV descriptor heaps your application needs. The default implementation creates an RTV heap with `SwapChainBufferCount` many descriptors (for the buffer in the swap chain) and a DSV heap with one descriptor (for the depth/stencil buffer). The default implementation will be sufficient for a lot of our demos; for more advanced rendering techniques that use multiple render targets, we will have to override this method.

4. `OnResize`: This method is called by `D3DApp::MsgProc` when a `WM_SIZE` message is received. When the window is resized, some Direct3D properties need to be changed, as they depend on the client area dimensions. In particular, the back buffer and depth/stencil buffers need to be recreated to match the new client area of the window. The back buffer can be resized by calling the `IDXGISwapChain::ResizeBuffers` method. The depth/stencil buffer needs to be destroyed and then remade based on the new dimension. In addition, the render target and depth/stencil views need to be recreated. The `D3DApp` implementation of `OnResize` handles the code necessary to resize the back and depth/stencil buffers; see the source code for the straightforward details. In addition to the buffers, other properties depend on the size of the client area (e.g., the projection matrix), so this method is part of the framework because the client code may need to execute some of its own code when the window is resized.

5. `Update`: This abstract method is called every frame and should be used to update the 3D application over time (e.g., perform animations, move the camera, do collision detection, check for user input, and etc.).

6. `Draw`: This abstract method is invoked every frame and is where we issue rendering commands to actually draw our current frame to the back buffer. When we are done drawing our frame, we call the `IDXGISwapChain::Present` method to present the back buffer to the screen.

In addition to the above six framework methods, we provide three other virtual functions for convenience to handle the events when a mouse button is pressed, released, and when the mouse moves:

```
virtual void OnMouseDown(WPARAM btnState, int x, int y){ }
virtual void OnMouseUp(WPARAM btnState, int x, int y) { }
virtual void OnMouseMove(WPARAM btnState, int x, int y){ }
```

In this way, if you want to handle mouse messages, you can override these methods instead of overriding the MsgProc *method. The first parameter is the same as the* WPARAM *parameter for the various mouse messages, which stores the mouse button states (i.e., which mouse buttons were pressed when the event was raised). The second and third parameters are the client area (x, y) coordinates of the mouse cursor.*

4.5.4 Frame Statistics

It is common for games and graphics application to measure the number of frames being rendered per second (FPS). To do this, we simply count the number of frames processed (and store it in a variable n) over some specified time period t. Then, the average FPS over the time period t is $fps_{avg} = n/t = n$. If we set $t = 1$, then $fps_{avg} = n/1 = n$. In our code, we use $t = 1$ (second) since it avoids a division, and moreover, one second gives a pretty good average—it is not too long and not too short. The code to compute the FPS is provided by the D3DApp::CalculateFrameStats method:

```
void D3DApp::CalculateFrameStats()
{
    // Code computes the average frames per second, and also the
    // average time it takes to render one frame. These stats
    // are appended to the window caption bar.

    static int frameCnt = 0;
    static float timeElapsed = 0.0f;

    frameCnt++;

    // Compute averages over one second period.
    if( (mTimer.TotalTime() - timeElapsed) >= 1.0f )
    {
        float fps = (float)frameCnt; // fps = frameCnt / 1
        float mspf = 1000.0f / fps;

        wstring fpsStr = to_wstring(fps);
        wstring mspfStr = to_wstring(mspf);

        wstring windowText = mMainWndCaption +
            L"    fps: " + fpsStr +
            L"   mspf: " + mspfStr;
```

```
            SetWindowText(mhMainWnd, windowText.c_str());

            // Reset for next average.
            frameCnt = 0;
            timeElapsed += 1.0f;
        }
    }
```

This method would be called every frame in order to count the frame.

In addition to computing the FPS, the above code also computes the number of milliseconds it takes, on average, to process a frame:

```
    float mspf = 1000.0f / fps;
```

The seconds per frame is just the reciprocal of the FPS, but we multiply by 1000 ms / 1 s to convert from seconds to milliseconds (recall there are 1000 ms per second).

The idea behind this line is to compute the time, in milliseconds, it takes to render a frame; this is a different quantity than FPS (but observe this value can be derived from the FPS). In actuality, the time it takes to render a frame is more useful than the FPS, as we may directly see the increase/decrease in time it takes to render a frame as we modify our scene. On the other hand, the FPS does not immediately tell us the increase/decrease in time as we modify our scene. Moreover, as [Dunlop03] points out in his article *FPS versus Frame Time*, due to the non-linearity of the FPS curve, using the FPS can give misleading results. For example, consider situation (1): Suppose our application is running at 1000 FPS, taking 1 ms (millisecond) to render a frame. If the frame rate drops to 250 FPS, then it takes 4 ms to render a frame. Now consider situation (2): Suppose that our application is running at 100 FPS, taking 10 ms to render a frame. If the frame rate drops to about 76.9 FPS, then it takes about 13 ms to render a frame. In both situations, the rendering per frame increased by 3 ms, and thus both represent the same increase in time it takes to render a frame. Reading the FPS is not as straightforward. The drop from 1000 FPS to 250 FPS seems much more drastic than the drop from 100 FPS to 76.9 FPS; however, as we have just showed, they actually represent the same increase in time it takes to render a frame.

4.5.5 The Message Handler

The window procedure we implement for our application framework does the bare minimum. In general, we won't be working very much with Win32 messages anyway. In fact, the core of our application code gets executed during idle processing (i.e., when no window messages are present). Still, there are some important messages we do need to process. However, because of the length of the window procedure, we do not embed all the code here; rather, we just explain the motivation behind each message we handle. We encourage the reader to download the source code files and spend some time getting familiar with the application framework code, as it is the foundation of every sample for this book.

The first message we handle is the `WM_ACTIVATE` message. This message is sent when an application becomes activated or deactivated. We implement it like so:

```
case WM_ACTIVATE:
  if( LOWORD(wParam) == WA_INACTIVE )
  {
    mAppPaused = true;
    mTimer.Stop();
  }
  else
  {
    mAppPaused = false;
    mTimer.Start();
  }
  return 0;
```

As you can see, when our application becomes deactivated, we set the data member `mAppPaused` to `true`, and when our application becomes active, we set the data member `mAppPaused` to `false`. In addition, when the application is paused, we stop the timer, and then resume the timer once the application becomes active again. If we look back at the implementation to `D3DApp::Run` (§4.4.3), we find that if our application is paused, then we do not update our application code, but instead free some CPU cycles back to the OS; in this way, our application does not hog CPU cycles when it is inactive.

The next message we handle is the `WM_SIZE message`. Recall that this message is called when the window is resized. The main reason for handling this message is that we want the back buffer and depth/stencil dimensions to match the dimensions of the client area rectangle (so no stretching occurs). Thus, every time the window is resized, we want to resize the buffer dimensions. The code to resize the buffers is implemented in `D3DApp::OnResize`. As already stated, the back buffer can be resized by calling the `IDXGISwapChain::ResizeBuffers` method. The depth/stencil buffer needs to be destroyed and then remade based on the new dimensions. In addition, the render target and depth/stencil views need to be recreated. If the user is dragging the resize bars, we must be careful because dragging the resize bars sends continuous `WM_SIZE` messages, and we do not want to continuously resize the buffers. Therefore, if we determine that the user is resizing by dragging, we actually do nothing (except pause the application) until the user is done dragging the resize bars. We can do this by handling the `WM_EXITSIZEMOVE` message. This message is sent when the user releases the resize bars.

```
// WM_ENTERSIZEMOVE is sent when the user grabs the resize bars.
case WM_ENTERSIZEMOVE:
```

```
    mAppPaused = true;
    mResizing = true;
    mTimer.Stop();
    return 0;

// WM_EXITSIZEMOVE is sent when the user releases the resize bars.
// Here we reset everything based on the new window dimensions.
case WM_EXITSIZEMOVE:
    mAppPaused = false;
    mResizing = false;
    mTimer.Start();
    OnResize();
    return 0;
```

The next three messages we handle are trivially implemented and so we just show the code:

```
// WM_DESTROY is sent when the window is being destroyed.
case WM_DESTROY:
    PostQuitMessage(0);
    return 0;

// The WM_MENUCHAR message is sent when a menu is active and the user
// presses a key that does not correspond to any mnemonic or
// accelerator key.
case WM_MENUCHAR:
    // Don't beep when we alt-enter.
    return MAKELRESULT(0, MNC_CLOSE);

// Catch this message to prevent the window from becoming too small.
case WM_GETMINMAXINFO:
    ((MINMAXINFO*)lParam)->ptMinTrackSize.x = 200;
    ((MINMAXINFO*)lParam)->ptMinTrackSize.y = 200;
    return 0;
```

Finally, to support our mouse input virtual functions, we handle the following messages as follows:

```
case WM_LBUTTONDOWN:
case WM_MBUTTONDOWN:
case WM_RBUTTONDOWN:
    OnMouseDown(wParam, GET_X_LPARAM(lParam), GET_Y_LPARAM(lParam));
    return 0;
case WM_LBUTTONUP:
case WM_MBUTTONUP:
case WM_RBUTTONUP:
    OnMouseUp(wParam, GET_X_LPARAM(lParam), GET_Y_LPARAM(lParam));
    return 0;
case WM_MOUSEMOVE:
    OnMouseMove(wParam, GET_X_LPARAM(lParam), GET_Y_LPARAM(lParam));
    return 0;
```

We must #include <Windowsx.h> for the GET_X_LPARAM and GET_Y_LPARAM macros.

4.5.6 The "Init Direct3D" Demo

Now that we have discussed the application framework, let us make a small application using it. The program requires almost no real work on our part since the parent class D3DApp does most of the work required for this demo. The main thing to note is how we derive a class from D3DApp and implement the framework functions, where we will write our sample specific code. All of the programs in this book will follow the same template.

```
#include "../../Common/d3dApp.h"
#include <DirectXColors.h>

using namespace DirectX;

class InitDirect3DApp : public D3DApp
{
public:
    InitDirect3DApp(HINSTANCE hInstance);
    ~InitDirect3DApp();

    virtual bool Initialize()override;

private:
    virtual void OnResize()override;
    virtual void Update(const GameTimer& gt)override;
    virtual void Draw(const GameTimer& gt)override;

};

int WINAPI WinMain(HINSTANCE hInstance, HINSTANCE prevInstance,
                   PSTR cmdLine, int showCmd)
{
    // Enable run-time memory check for debug builds.
#if defined(DEBUG) | defined(_DEBUG)
    _CrtSetDbgFlag( _CRTDBG_ALLOC_MEM_DF | _CRTDBG_LEAK_CHECK_DF );
#endif

    try
    {
        InitDirect3DApp theApp(hInstance);
        if(!theApp.Initialize())
            return 0;

        return theApp.Run();
    }
    catch(DxException& e)
    {
        MessageBox(nullptr, e.ToString().c_str(), L"HR Failed", MB_OK);
        return 0;
    }
}
```

```cpp
InitDirect3DApp::InitDirect3DApp(HINSTANCE hInstance)
: D3DApp(hInstance)
{
}

InitDirect3DApp::~InitDirect3DApp()
{
}

bool InitDirect3DApp::Initialize()
{
  if(!D3DApp::Initialize())
    return false;

  return true;
}

void InitDirect3DApp::OnResize()
{
  D3DApp::OnResize();
}

void InitDirect3DApp::Update(const GameTimer& gt)
{

}

void InitDirect3DApp::Draw(const GameTimer& gt)
{
  // Reuse the memory associated with command recording.
  // We can only reset when the associated command lists have finished
  // execution on the GPU.
  ThrowIfFailed(mDirectCmdListAlloc->Reset());

  // A command list can be reset after it has been added to the
  // command queue via ExecuteCommandList. Reusing the command list
    reuses memory.
  ThrowIfFailed(mCommandList->Reset(
    mDirectCmdListAlloc.Get(), nullptr));

  // Indicate a state transition on the resource usage.
  mCommandList->ResourceBarrier(
    1, &CD3DX12_RESOURCE_BARRIER::Transition(
      CurrentBackBuffer(),
      D3D12_RESOURCE_STATE_PRESENT,
      D3D12_RESOURCE_STATE_RENDER_TARGET));

  // Set the viewport and scissor rect. This needs to be reset
  // whenever the command list is reset.
  mCommandList->RSSetViewports(1, &mScreenViewport);
  mCommandList->RSSetScissorRects(1, &mScissorRect);

  // Clear the back buffer and depth buffer.
  mCommandList->ClearRenderTargetView(
```

```
        CurrentBackBufferView(),
        Colors::LightSteelBlue, 0, nullptr);
    mCommandList->ClearDepthStencilView(
        DepthStencilView(), D3D12_CLEAR_FLAG_DEPTH |
        D3D12_CLEAR_FLAG_STENCIL, 1.0f, 0, 0, nullptr);

    // Specify the buffers we are going to render to.
    mCommandList->OMSetRenderTargets(1, &CurrentBackBufferView(),
        true, &DepthStencilView());

    // Indicate a state transition on the resource usage.
    mCommandList->ResourceBarrier(
        1, &CD3DX12_RESOURCE_BARRIER::Transition(
        CurrentBackBuffer(),
        D3D12_RESOURCE_STATE_RENDER_TARGET,
        D3D12_RESOURCE_STATE_PRESENT));

    // Done recording commands.
    ThrowIfFailed(mCommandList->Close());

    // Add the command list to the queue for execution.
    ID3D12CommandList* cmdsLists[] = { mCommandList.Get() };
    mCommandQueue->ExecuteCommandLists(_countof(cmdsLists), cmdsLists);

    // swap the back and front buffers
    ThrowIfFailed(mSwapChain->Present(0, 0));
    mCurrBackBuffer = (mCurrBackBuffer + 1) % SwapChainBufferCount;

    // Wait until frame commands are complete. This waiting is
    // inefficient and is done for simplicity. Later we will show how to
    // organize our rendering code so we do not have to wait per frame.
    FlushCommandQueue();
}
```

There are some methods we have not yet discussed. The `ClearRenderTargetView` method clears the specified render target to a given color, and the `ClearDepthStencilView` method clears the specified depth/stencil buffer. We always clear the back buffer render target and depth/stencil buffer every frame before drawing to start the image fresh. These methods are declared as follows:

```
void ID3D12GraphicsCommandList::ClearRenderTargetView(
    D3D12_CPU_DESCRIPTOR_HANDLE RenderTargetView,
    const FLOAT ColorRGBA[ 4 ],
    UINT NumRects,
    const D3D12_RECT *pRects);
```

1. `RenderTargetView`: RTV to the resource we want to clear.
2. `ColorRGBA`: Defines the color to clear the render target to.
3. `NumRects`: The number of elements in the `pRects` array. This can be 0.

4. **pRects**: An array of `D3D12_RECT`s that identify rectangle regions on the render target to clear. This can be a `nullptr` to indicate to clear the entire render target.

```
void ID3D12GraphicsCommandList::ClearDepthStencilView(
  D3D12_CPU_DESCRIPTOR_HANDLE DepthStencilView,
  D3D12_CLEAR_FLAGS ClearFlags,
  FLOAT Depth,
  UINT8 Stencil,
  UINT NumRects,
  const D3D12_RECT *pRects);
```

1. **DepthStencilView**: DSV to the depth/stencil buffer to clear.
2. **ClearFlags**: Flags indicating which part of the depth/stencil buffer to clear. This can be either `D3D12_CLEAR_FLAG_DEPTH`, `D3D12_CLEAR_FLAG_STENCIL`, or both bitwised ORed together.
3. **Depth**: Defines the value to clear the depth values to.
4. **Stencil**: Defines the value to clear the stencil values to.
5. **NumRects**: The number of elements in the `pRects` array. This can be 0.
6. **pRects**: An array of `D3D12_RECT`s that identify rectangle regions on the render target to clear. This can be a `nullptr` to indicate to clear the entire render target.

Another new method is the `ID3D12GraphicsCommandList::OMSetRenderTargets` method. This method sets the render target and depth/stencil buffer we want to use to the pipeline. For now, we want to use the current back buffer as a render target and our main depth/stencil buffer. Later in this book, we will look at techniques that use multiple render targets. This method has the following prototype:

```
void ID3D12GraphicsCommandList::OMSetRenderTargets(
  UINT NumRenderTargetDescriptors,
  const D3D12_CPU_DESCRIPTOR_HANDLE *pRenderTargetDescriptors,
  BOOL RTsSingleHandleToDescriptorRange,
  const D3D12_CPU_DESCRIPTOR_HANDLE *pDepthStencilDescriptor);
```

1. **NumRenderTargetDescriptors**: Specifies the number of RTVs we are going to bind. Using multiple render targets simultaneously is used for some advanced techniques. For now, we always use one RTV.
2. **pRenderTargetDescriptors**: Pointer to an array of RTVs that specify the render targets we want to bind to the pipeline.
3. **RTsSingleHandleToDescriptorRange**: Specify true if all the RTVs in the previous array are contiguous in the descriptor heap. Otherwise, specify false.
4. **pDepthStencilDescriptor**: Pointer to a DSV that specifies the depth/stencil buffer we want to bind to the pipeline.

Finally, the `IDXGISwapChain::Present` method swaps the back and front buffers. When we `Present` the swap chain to swap the front and back buffers, we have to update the index to the current back buffer as well so that we render to the new back buffer on the subsequent frame:

```
ThrowIfFailed(mSwapChain->Present(0, 0));
mCurrBackBuffer = (mCurrBackBuffer + 1) % SwapChainBufferCount;
```

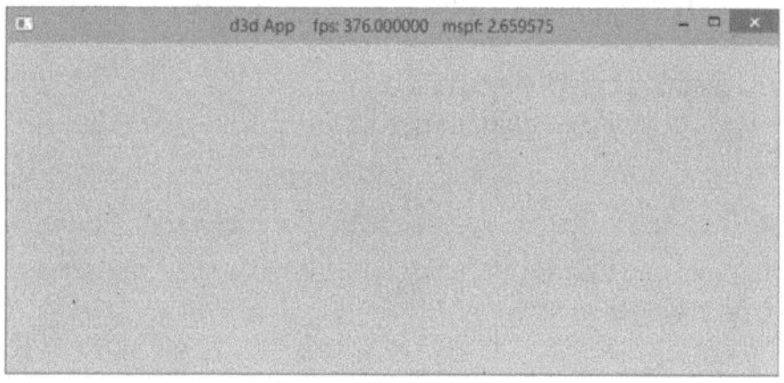

Figure 4.12. A screenshot of the sample program for Chapter 4.

4.6 DEBUGGING DIRECT3D APPLICATIONS

Many Direct3D functions return HRESULT error codes. For our sample programs, we use a simple error handling system where we check a returned HRESULT, and if it failed, we throw an exception that stores the error code, function name, filename, and line number of the offending call. This is done with the following code in *d3dUtil.h*:

```
class DxException
{
public:
  DxException() = default;
  DxException(HRESULT hr, const std::wstring& functionName,
    const std::wstring& filename, int lineNumber);

  std::wstring ToString()const;

  HRESULT ErrorCode = S_OK;
  std::wstring FunctionName;
  std::wstring Filename;
  int LineNumber = -1;
};

#ifndef ThrowIfFailed
#define ThrowIfFailed(x) \
{ \
  HRESULT hr__ = (x); \
  std::wstring wfn = AnsiToWString(__FILE__); \
  if(FAILED(hr__)) { throw DxException(hr__, L#x, wfn, __LINE__); } \
}
#endif
```

Observe that `ThrowIfFailed` must be a macro and not a function; otherwise __FILE__ and __LINE__ would refer to the file and line of the function implementation instead of the file and line where `ThrowIfFailed` was written.

The `L#x` turns the `ThrowIfFailed` macro's argument token into a Unicode string. In this way, we can output the function call that caused the error to the message box.

For a Direct3D function that returns an `HRESULT`, we use the macro like so:

```
ThrowIfFailed(md3dDevice->CreateCommittedResource(
  &CD3D12_HEAP_PROPERTIES(D3D12_HEAP_TYPE_DEFAULT),
  D3D12_HEAP_MISC_NONE,
  &depthStencilDesc,
  D3D12_RESOURCE_USAGE_INITIAL,
  IID_PPV_ARGS(&mDepthStencilBuffer)));
```

Our entire application exists in a try/catch block:

```
try
{
  InitDirect3DApp theApp(hInstance);
  if(!theApp.Initialize())
    return 0;

  return theApp.Run();
}
catch(DxException& e)
{
  MessageBox(nullptr, e.ToString().c_str(), L"HR Failed", MB_OK);
  return 0;
}
```

If an `HRESULT` fails, an exception is thrown, we output information about it via the `MessageBox` function, and then exit the application. For example, if we pass an invalid argument to `CreateCommittedResource`, we get the following message box:

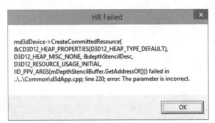

Figure 4.13. Example of the error message box shown when an HRESULT fails.

4.7 SUMMARY

1. Direct3D can be thought of as a mediator between the programmer and the graphics hardware. For example, the programmer calls Direct3D functions to bind resource views to the hardware rendering pipeline, to configure the output of the rendering pipeline, and to draw 3D geometry.
2. Component Object Model (COM) is the technology that allows DirectX to be language independent and have backwards compatibility. Direct3D programmers don't need to know the details of COM and how it works; they need only to know how to acquire COM interfaces and how to release them.
3. A 1D texture is like a 1D array of data elements, a 2D texture is like a 2D array of data elements, and a 3D texture is like a 3D array of data elements. The elements of a texture must have a format described by a member of the `DXGI_FORMAT` enumerated type. Textures typically contain image data, but they can contain other data, too, such as depth information (e.g., the depth buffer). The GPU can do special operations on textures, such as filter and multisample them.
4. To avoid flickering in animation, it is best to draw an entire frame of animation into an off-screen texture called the back buffer. Once the entire scene has been drawn to the back buffer for the given frame of animation, it is presented to the screen as one complete frame; in this way, the viewer does not watch as the frame gets drawn. After the frame has been drawn to the back buffer, the roles of the back buffer and front buffer are reversed: the back buffer becomes the front buffer and the front buffer becomes the back buffer for the next frame of animation. Swapping the roles of the back and front buffers is called presenting. The front and back buffer form a swap chain, represented by the `IDXGISwapChain` interface. Using two buffers (front and back) is called double buffering.
5. Assuming opaque scene objects, the points nearest to the camera occlude any points behind them. Depth buffering is a technique for determining the points in the scene nearest to the camera. In this way, we do not have to worry about the order in which we draw our scene objects.
6. In Direct3D, resources are not bound to the pipeline directly. Instead, we bind resources to the rendering pipeline by specifying the descriptors that will be referenced in the draw call. A descriptor object can be thought of as lightweight structure that identifies and describes a resource to the GPU. Different descriptors of a single resource may be created. In this way, a single resource may be viewed in different ways; for example, bound to different

stages of the rendering pipeline or have its bits interpreted as a different `DXGI_FORMAT`. Applications create descriptor heaps which form the memory backing of descriptors.

7. The `ID3D12Device` is the chief Direct3D interface that can be thought of as our software controller of the physical graphics device hardware; through it, we can create GPU resources, and create other specialized interfaces used to control the graphics hardware and instruct it to do things.

8. The GPU has a command queue. The CPU submits commands to the queue through the Direct3D API using command lists. A command instructs the GPU to do something. Submitted commands are not executed by the GPU until they reach the front of the queue. If the command queue gets empty, the GPU will idle because it does not have any work to do; on the other hand, if the command queue gets too full, the CPU will at some point have to idle while the GPU catches up. Both of these scenarios underutilize the system's hardware resources.

9. The GPU is a second processor in the system that runs in parallel with the CPU. Sometimes the CPU and GPU will need to be synchronized. For example, if the GPU has a command in its queue that references a resource, the CPU must not modify or destroy that resource until the GPU is done with it. Any synchronization methods that cause one of the processors to wait and idle should be minimized, as it means we are not taking full advantage of the two processors.

10. The performance counter is a high-resolution timer that provides accurate timing measurements needed for measuring small time differentials, such as the time elapsed between frames. The performance timer works in time units called *counts*. The `QueryPerformanceFrequency` outputs the counts per second of the performance timer, which can then be used to convert from units of counts to seconds. The current time value of the performance timer (measured in counts) is obtained with the `QueryPerformanceCounter` function.

11. To compute the average frames per second (FPS), we count the number of frames processed over some time interval Δt. Let n be the number of frames counted over time Δt, then the average frames per second over that time interval is $fps_{avg} = \frac{n}{\Delta t}$. The frame rate can give misleading conclusions about performance; the time it takes to process a frame is more informative. The amount of time, in seconds, spent processing a frame is the reciprocal of the frame rate, i.e., $1/fps_{avg}$.

12. The sample framework is used to provide a consistent interface that all demo applications in this book follow. The code provided in the *d3dUtil.h, d3dUtil.*

cpp, *d3dApp.h* and *d3dApp.cpp* files, wrap standard initialization code that every application must implement. By wrapping this code up, we hide it, which allows the samples to be more focused on demonstrating the current topic.

13. For debug mode builds, we enable the debug layer (`debugController->EnableDebugLayer()`). When the debug layer is enabled, Direct3D will send debug messages to the VC++ output window.

Chapter 5: The Rendering Pipeline

The primary theme of this chapter is the rendering pipeline. Given a geometric description of a 3D scene with a positioned and oriented virtual camera, the *rendering pipeline* refers to the entire sequence of steps necessary to generate a 2D image based on what the virtual camera sees (Figure 5.1). This chapter is mostly theoretical—the next chapter puts the theory into practice as we learn to draw with Direct3D. Before we begin coverage of the rendering pipeline, we have two short stops: First, we discuss some elements of the 3D illusion (i.e., the illusion that we are looking into a 3D world through a flat 2D monitor screen); and second, we explain how colors will be represented and worked with mathematically and in Direct3D code.

Objectives:

1. To discover several key signals used to convey a realistic sense of volume and spatial depth in a 2D image.
2. To find out how we represent 3D objects in Direct3D.
3. To learn how we model the virtual camera.
4. To understand the rendering pipeline—the process of taking a geometric description of a 3D scene and generating a 2D image from it.

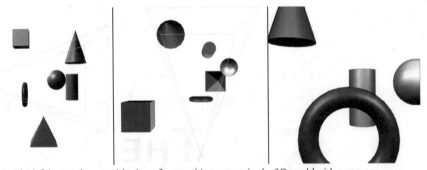

Figure 5.1. The left image shows a side view of some objects setup in the 3D world with a camera positioned and aimed; the middle image shows the same scene, but from a top-down view. The "pyramid" volume specifies the volume of space that the viewer can see; objects (and parts of objects) outside this volume are not seen. The image on the right shows the 2D image created based on what the camera "sees."

5.1 THE 3D ILLUSION

Before we embark on our journey of 3D computer graphics, a simple question remains outstanding: How do we display a 3D world with depth and volume on a flat 2D monitor screen? Fortunately for us, this problem has been well studied, as artists have been painting 3D scenes on 2D canvases for centuries. In this section, we outline several key techniques that make an image look 3D, even though it is actually drawn on a 2D plane.

Suppose that you have encountered a railroad track that doesn't curve, but goes along a straight line for a long distance. Now the railroad rails remain parallel to each other for all time, but if you stand on the railroad and look down its path, you will observe that the two railroad rails get closer and closer together as their distance from you increases, and eventually they converge at an infinite distance. This is one observation that characterizes our human viewing system: parallel lines of vision converge to a *vanishing point*; see Figure 5.2.

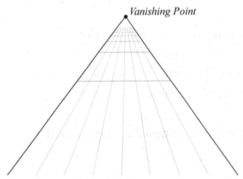

Figure 5.2. Parallel lines of vision converge to a vanishing point. Artists sometimes call this *linear perspective*.

Figure 5.3. Here, all the columns are of the same size, but a viewer observes a diminishing in size with respect to depth phenomenon.

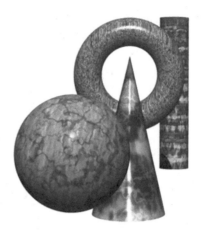

Figure 5.4. A group of objects that partially obscure each other because one is in front of the other, etc. (they overlap).

Another simple observation of how humans see things is that the size of an object appears to diminish with depth; that is, objects near us look bigger than objects far away. For example, a house far away on a hill will look very small, while a tree near us will look very large in comparison. Figure 5.3 shows a simple scene where parallel rows of columns are placed behind each other, one after another. The columns are actually all the same size, but as their depths increase from the viewer, they get smaller and smaller. Also notice how the columns are converging to the vanishing point at the horizon.

We all experience *object overlap* (Figure 5.4), which refers to the fact that opaque objects obscure parts (or all) of the objects behind them. This is an important perception, as it conveys the depth ordering relationship of the objects in the scene. We already discussed (Chapter 4) how Direct3D uses a depth buffer to figure out which pixels are being obscured and thus should not be drawn.

Consider Figure 5.5. On the left we have an unlit sphere, and on the right, we have a lit sphere. As you can see, the sphere on the left looks rather flat—maybe it

Figure 5.5. (a) An unlit sphere that looks 2D. (b) A lit sphere that looks 3D.

Figure 5.6. A spaceship and its shadow. The shadow implies the location of the light source in the scene and also gives an idea of how high off the ground the spaceship is.

is not even a sphere at all, but just a textured 2D circle! Thus, lighting and shading play a very important role in depicting the solid form and volume of 3D objects.

Finally, Figure 5.6 shows a spaceship and its shadow. The shadow serves two key purposes. First, it tells us the origin of the light source in the scene. And secondly, it provides us with a rough idea of how high off the ground the spaceship is.

The observations just discussed, no doubt, are intuitively obvious from our day-to-day experiences. Nonetheless, it is helpful to explicitly state what we know and to keep these observations in mind as we study and work on 3D computer graphics.

5.2 MODEL REPRESENTATION

A solid 3D *object* is represented by a *triangle mesh* approximation, and consequently, triangles form the basic building blocks of the objects we model. As Figure 5.7 implies, we can approximate any real-world 3D object by a triangle mesh. In general, the more triangles you use to approximate an object, the better the approximation, as you can model finer details. Of course, the more triangles we use, the more processing power is required, and so a balance must be made based on the hardware power of the application's target audience. In addition to triangles, it is sometimes useful to draw lines or points. For example, a curve could be graphically drawn by a sequence of short line segments a pixel thick.

The large number of triangles used in Figure 5.7 makes one thing clear: It would be extremely cumbersome to manually list the triangles of a 3D model. For all but the simplest models, special 3D applications called *3D modelers* are used to generate and manipulate 3D objects. These modelers allow the user to build complex and realistic meshes in a visual and interactive environment with a rich tool set, thereby making the entire modeling process much easier. Examples of popular modelers used for game development are 3D Studio Max (*http://usa.autodesk.com/3ds-max/*), LightWave 3D (*https://www.lightwave3d.com/*), Maya

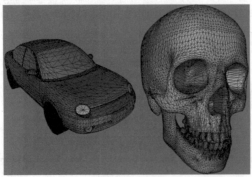

Figure 5.7. (Left) A car approximated by a triangle mesh. (Right) A skull approximated by a triangle mesh.

(*http://usa.autodesk.com/maya/*), Softimage|XSI (www.softimage.com), and Blender (*www.blender.org/*). (Blender has the advantage for hobbyists of being open source and free.) Nevertheless, for the first part of this book, we will generate our 3D models manually by hand, or via a mathematical formula (the triangle list for cylinders and spheres, for example, can easily be generated with parametric formulas). In the third part of this book, we show how to load and display 3D models exported from 3D modeling programs.

5.3 BASIC COMPUTER COLOR

Computer monitors emit a mixture of red, green, and blue light through each pixel. When the light mixture enters the eye and strikes an area of the retina, cone receptor cells are stimulated and neural impulses are sent down the optic nerve toward the brain. The brain interprets the signal and generates a color. As the light mixture varies, the cells are stimulated differently, which in turn generates a different color in the mind. Figure 5.8 shows some examples of mixing red, green, and blue to get different colors; it also shows different intensities of red. By using different intensities for each color component and mixing them together, we can describe all the colors we need to display realistic images.

The best way to get comfortable with describing colors by RGB (red, green, blue) values is to use a paint program like Adobe Photoshop, or even the Win32 `ChooseColor` dialog box (Figure 5.9), and experiment with different RGB combinations to see the colors they produce.

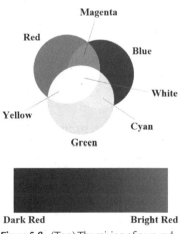

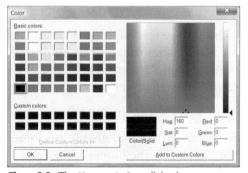

Figure 5.8. (Top) The mixing of pure red, green, and blue colors to get new colors. (Bottom) Different shades of red found by controlling the intensity of red light.

Figure 5.9. The `ChooseColor` dialog box.

A monitor has a maximum intensity of red, green, and blue light it can emit. To describe the intensities of light, it is useful to use a normalized range from 0 to 1. 0 denotes no intensity and 1 denotes the full intensity. Intermediate values denote intermediate intensities. For example, the values (0.25, 0.67, 1.0) mean the light mixture consists of 25% intensity of red light, 67% intensity of green light, and 100% intensity of blue light. As the example just stated implies, we can represent a color by a 3D color vector (r, g, b), where $0 \leq r, g, b \leq 1$, and each color component describes the intensity of red, green, and blue light in the mixture.

5.3.1 Color Operations

Some vector operations also apply to color vectors. For example, we can add color vectors to get new colors:

$$(0.0, 0.5, 0) + (0, 0.0, 0.25) = (0.0, 0.5, 0.25)$$

By combining a medium intensity green color with a low intensity blue color, we get a dark-green color.

Colors can also be subtracted to get new colors:

$$(1, 1, 1) - (1, 1, 0) = (0, 0, 1)$$

That is, we start with white and subtract out the red and green parts, and we end up with blue.

Scalar multiplication also makes sense. Consider the following:

$$0.5(1, 1, 1) = (0.5, 0.5, 0.5)$$

That is, we start with white and multiply by 0.5, and we end up with a medium shade of gray. On the other hand, the operation $2(0.25, 0, 0) = (0.5, 0, 0)$ doubles the intensity of the red component.

Obviously expressions like the dot product and cross product do not make sense for color vectors. However, color vectors do get their own special color operation called *modulation* or *componentwise* multiplication. It is defined as:

$$(c_r, c_g, c_b) \otimes (k_r, k_g, k_b) = (c_r k_r, c_g k_g, c_b k_b)$$

This operation is mainly used in lighting equations. For example, suppose we have an incoming ray of light with color (r, g, b) and it strikes a surface which reflects 50% red light, 75% green light, and 25% blue light, and absorbs the rest. Then the color of the reflected light ray is given by:

$$(r, g, b) \otimes (0.5, 0.75, 0.25) = (0.5r, 0.75g, 0.25b)$$

So we can see that the light ray lost some intensity when it struck the surface, since the surface absorbed some of the light.

When doing color operation, it is possible that your color components go outside the [0, 1] interval; consider the equation, (1, 0.1, 0.6) + (0, 0.3, 0.5) = (1, 0.4, 1.1), for example. Since 1.0 represents the maximum intensity of a color component, you cannot become more intense than it. Thus 1.1 is just as intense as 1.0. So what we do is clamp 1.1 → 1.0. Likewise, a monitor cannot emit negative light, so any negative color component (which could result from a subtraction operation) should be clamped to 0.0.

5.3.2 128-Bit Color

It is common to incorporate an additional color component, called the *alpha component*. The alpha component is often used to denote the opacity of a color, which is useful in blending (Chapter 10). (Since we are not using blending yet, just set the alpha component to 1 for now.) Including the alpha component, means we can represent a color by a 4D color vector (r, g, b, a) where $0 \leq r, g, b, a \leq 1$. To represent a color with 128-bits, we use a floating-point value for each component. Because mathematically a color is just a 4D vector, we can use the XMVECTOR type to represent a color in code, and we gain the benefit of SIMD operations whenever we use the DirectXMath vector functions to do color operations (e.g., color addition, subtraction, scalar multiplication). For componentwise multiplication, the DirectX Math library provides the following function:

```
XMVECTOR XM_CALLCONV XMColorModulate( // Returns c₁ ⊗ c₂
    FXMVECTOR C1,
    FXMVECTOR C2);
```

5.3.3 32-Bit Color

To represent a color with 32-bits, a byte is given to each component. Since each color is given an 8-bit byte, we can represent 256 different shades for each color component—0 being no intensity, 255 being full intensity, and intermediate values being intermediate intensities. A byte per color component may seem small, but when we look at all the combinations ($256 \times 256 \times 256 = 16,777,216$), we see millions of distinct colors can be represented. The DirectX Math library (*#include <DirectXPackedVector.h>*) provides the following structure, in the DirectX::PackedVector namespace, for storing a 32-bit color:

```
namespace DirectX
{
namespace PackedVector
{
// ARGB Color; 8-8-8-8 bit unsigned normalized integer components packed
// into a 32 bit integer. The normalized color is packed into 32 bits
// using 8 bit unsigned, normalized integers for the alpha, red, green,
// and blue components.
```

```
// The alpha component is stored in the most significant bits and the
// blue component in the least significant bits (A8R8G8B8):
// [32] aaaaaaaa rrrrrrrr gggggggg bbbbbbbb [0]
struct XMCOLOR
{
  union
  {
    struct
    {
      uint8_t b; // Blue:  0/255 to 255/255
      uint8_t g; // Green: 0/255 to 255/255
      uint8_t r; // Red:   0/255 to 255/255
      uint8_t a; // Alpha: 0/255 to 255/255
    };
    uint32_t c;
  };

  XMCOLOR() {}
  XMCOLOR(uint32_t Color) : c(Color) {}
  XMCOLOR(float _r, float _g, float _b, float _a);
  explicit XMCOLOR(_In_reads_(4) const float *pArray);

  operator uint32_t () const { return c; }

  XMCOLOR& operator= (const XMCOLOR& Color) { c = Color.c; return
    *this; }
  XMCOLOR& operator= (const uint32_t Color) { c = Color; return *this;
    }
};
} // end PackedVector namespace
} // end DirectX namespace
```

A 32-bit color can be converted to a 128-bit color by mapping the integer range [0, 255] onto the real-valued interval [0, 1]. This is done by dividing by 255. That is, if $0 \leq n \leq 255$ is an integer, then $0 \leq \frac{n}{255} \leq 1$ gives the intensity in the normalized range from 0 to 1. For example, the 32-bit color (80, 140, 200, 255) becomes:

$$(80, 140, 200, 255) \rightarrow \left(\frac{80}{255}, \frac{140}{255}, \frac{200}{255}, \frac{255}{255}\right) \approx (0.31, 0.55, 0.78, 1.0)$$

On the other hand, a 128-bit color can be converted to a 32-bit color by multiplying each component by 255 and rounding to the nearest integer. For example:

$$(0.3, 0.6, 0.9, 1.0) \rightarrow (0.3 \cdot 255, 0.6 \cdot 255, 0.9 \cdot 255, 1.0 \cdot 255) = (77, 153, 230, 255)$$

Additional bit operations must usually be done when converting a 32-bit color to a 128-bit color and conversely because the 8-bit color components are usually packed into a 32-bit integer value (e.g., an unsigned int), as it is in XMCOLOR. The

Figure 5.10. A 32-bit color, where a byte is allocated for each color component alpha, red, green, and blue.

DirectXMath library defines the following function which takes a XMCOLOR and returns an XMVECTOR from it:

```
XMVECTOR XM_CALLCONV PackedVector::XMLoadColor(
    const XMCOLOR* pSource);
```

Figure 5.10 shows how the 8-bit color components are packed into a UINT. Note that this is just one way to pack the color components. Another format might be ABGR or RGBA, instead of ARGB; however, the XMCOLOR class uses the ARGB layout. The DirectX Math library also provides a function to convert an XMVECTOR color to a XMCOLOR:

```
void XM_CALLCONV PackedVector::XMStoreColor(
    XMCOLOR* pDestination,
    FXMVECTOR V);
```

Typically, 128-bit colors values are used where high precision color operations are needed (e.g., in a pixel shader); in this way, we have many bits of accuracy for the calculations so arithmetic error does not accumulate too much. The final pixel color, however, is usually stored in a 32-bit color value in the back buffer; current physical display devices cannot take advantage of the higher resolution color [Verth04].

5.4 OVERVIEW OF THE RENDERING PIPELINE

Given a geometric description of a 3D scene with a positioned and oriented virtual camera, the *rendering pipeline* refers to the entire sequence of steps necessary to generate a 2D image based on what the virtual camera sees. Figure 5.11 shows a diagram of the stages that make up the rendering pipeline, as well as GPU memory resources off to the side. An arrow going from the resource memory pool to a stage means the stage can access the resources as input; for example, the pixel shader stage may need to read data from a texture resource stored in memory in order to do its work. An arrow going from a stage to memory means the stage writes to GPU resources; for example, the output merger stage writes data to textures such as the back buffer and depth/stencil buffer. Observe that the arrow for the output merger stage is bidirectional (it reads and writes to GPU resources). As we can see, most stages do not write to GPU resources. Instead, their output is just fed in as input to the next stage of the pipeline; for example, the Vertex Shader

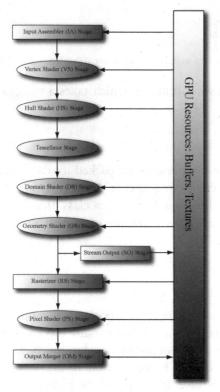

Figure 5.11. The stages of the rendering pipeline.

stage inputs data from the Input Assembler stage, does its own work, and then outputs its results to the Geometry Shader stage. The subsequent sections give an overview of each stage of the rendering pipeline.

5.5 THE INPUT ASSEMBLER STAGE

The *input assembler* (IA) stage reads geometric data (vertices and indices) from memory and uses it to assemble geometric primitives (e.g., triangles, lines). (Indices are covered in a later subsection, but briefly, they define how the vertices should be put together to form the primitives.)

5.5.1 Vertices

Mathematically, the vertices of a triangle are where two edges meet; the vertices of a line are the endpoints; for a single point, the point itself is the vertex. Figure 5.12 illustrates vertices pictorially.

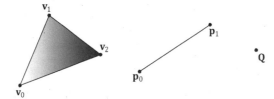

Figure 5.12. A triangle defined by the three vertices v_0, v_1, v_2; a line defined by the two vertices p_0, p_1; a point defined by the vertex **Q**.

From Figure 5.12, it seems that a vertex is just a special point in a geometric primitive. However, in Direct3D, vertices are much more general than that. Essentially, a vertex in Direct3D can consist of additional data besides spatial location, which allows us to perform more sophisticated rendering effects. For example, in Chapter 8, we will add normal vectors to our vertices to implement lighting, and in Chapter 9, we will add texture coordinates to our vertices to implement texturing. Direct3D gives us the flexibility to define our own vertex formats (i.e., it allows us to define the components of a vertex), and we will see the code used to do this in the next chapter. In this book, we will define several different vertex formats based on the rendering effect we are doing.

5.5.2 Primitive Topology

Vertices are bound to the rendering pipeline in a special Direct3D data structure called a *vertex buffer*. A vertex buffer just stores a list of vertices in contiguous memory. However, it does not say how these vertices should be put together to form geometric primitives. For example, should every two vertices in the vertex buffer be interpreted as a line or should every three vertices in the vertex buffer be interpreted as a triangle? We tell Direct3D how to form geometric primitives from the vertex data by specifying the *primitive topology*:

```
void ID3D12GraphicsCommandList::IASetPrimitiveTopology(
  D3D_PRIMITIVE_TOPOLOGY Topology);

typedef enum D3D_PRIMITIVE_TOPOLOGY
{
  D3D_PRIMITIVE_TOPOLOGY_UNDEFINED = 0,
  D3D_PRIMITIVE_TOPOLOGY_POINTLIST = 1,
  D3D_PRIMITIVE_TOPOLOGY_LINELIST = 2,
  D3D_PRIMITIVE_TOPOLOGY_LINESTRIP = 3,
  D3D_PRIMITIVE_TOPOLOGY_TRIANGLELIST = 4,
  D3D_PRIMITIVE_TOPOLOGY_TRIANGLESTRIP = 5,
  D3D_PRIMITIVE_TOPOLOGY_LINELIST_ADJ = 10,
  D3D_PRIMITIVE_TOPOLOGY_LINESTRIP_ADJ = 11,
  D3D_PRIMITIVE_TOPOLOGY_TRIANGLELIST_ADJ = 12,
  D3D_PRIMITIVE_TOPOLOGY_TRIANGLESTRIP_ADJ = 13,
  D3D_PRIMITIVE_TOPOLOGY_1_CONTROL_POINT_PATCHLIST = 33,
```

```
                D3D_PRIMITIVE_TOPOLOGY_2_CONTROL_POINT_PATCHLIST = 34,
                    .
                    .
                    .
                D3D_PRIMITIVE_TOPOLOGY_32_CONTROL_POINT_PATCHLIST = 64,
            } D3D_PRIMITIVE_TOPOLOGY;
```

All subsequent drawing calls will use the currently set primitive topology until the topology is changed via the command list. The following code illustrates:

```
mCommandList->IASetPrimitiveTopology(
  D3D_PRIMITIVE_TOPOLOGY_LINELIST);
/* ...draw objects using line list... */

mCommandList->IASetPrimitiveTopology(
  D3D_PRIMITIVE_TOPOLOGY_TRIANGLELIST);
/* ...draw objects using triangle list... */

mCommandList->IASetPrimitiveTopology(
  D3D_PRIMITIVE_TOPOLOGY_TRIANGLESTRIP);
/* ...draw objects using triangle strip... */
```

The following subsections elaborate on the different primitive topologies. In this book, we mainly use triangle lists exclusively with few exceptions.

5.5.2.1 Point List

A point list is specified by `D3D_PRIMITIVE_TOPOLOGY_POINTLIST`. With a point list, every vertex in the draw call is drawn as an individual point, as shown in Figure 5.13a.

5.5.2.2 Line Strip

A line strip is specified by `D3D_PRIMITIVE_TOPOLOGY_LINESTRIP`. With a line strip, the vertices in the draw call are connected to form lines (see Figure 5.13b); so $n + 1$ vertices induce n lines.

5.5.2.3 Line List

A line list is specified by `D3D_PRIMITIVE_TOPOLOGY_LINELIST`. With a line list, every two vertices in the draw call forms an individual line (see Figure 5.13c); so $2n$ vertices induce n lines. The difference between a line list and strip is that the lines in the line list may be disconnected, whereas a line strip automatically assumes they are connected; by assuming connectivity, fewer vertices can be used since each interior vertex is shared by two lines.

5.5.2.4 Triangle Strip

A triangle strip is specified by `D3D_PRIMITIVE_TOPOLOGY_TRIANGLESTRIP`. With a triangle strip, it is assumed the triangles are connected as shown in Figure 5.13d to form a strip. By assuming connectivity, we see that vertices are shared between adjacent triangles, and n vertices induce $n - 2$ triangles.

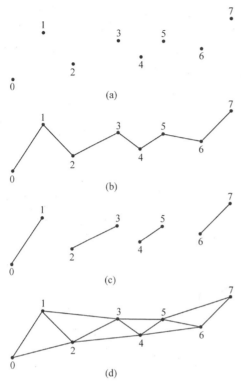

Figure 5.13. (a) A point list; (b) a line strip; (c) a line list; (d) a triangle strip.

Observe that the winding order for even triangles in a triangle strip differs from the odd triangles, thereby causing culling issues (see §5.10.2). To fix this problem, the GPU internally swaps the order of the first two vertices of even triangles, so that they are consistently ordered like the odd triangles.

5.5.2.5 Triangle List

A triangle list is specified by `D3D_PRIMITIVE_TOPOLOGY_TRIANGLELIST`. With a triangle list, every three vertices in the draw call forms an individual triangle (see Figure 5.14a); so $3n$ vertices induce n triangles. The difference between a triangle list and strip is that the triangles in the triangle list may be disconnected, whereas a triangle strip assumes they are connected.

5.5.2.6 Primitives with Adjacency

A triangle list with adjacency is where, for each triangle, you also include its three neighboring triangles called *adjacent triangles*; see Figure 5.14b to observe how these triangles are defined. This is used for the geometry shader, where certain geometry shading algorithms need access to the adjacent triangles. In order for the geometry shader to get those adjacent triangles, the adjacent triangles need

172   DIRECT3D FOUNDATIONS

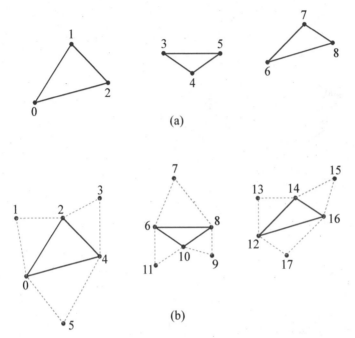

Figure 5.14. (a) A triangle list; (b) A triangle list with adjacency—observe that each triangle requires 6 vertices to describe it and its adjacent triangles. Thus $6n$ vertices induce n triangles with adjacency info.

to be submitted to the pipeline in the vertex/index buffers along with the triangle itself, and the `D3D_PRIMITIVE_TOPOLOGY_TRIANGLELIST_ADJ` topology must be specified so that the pipeline knows how construct the triangle and its adjacent triangles from the vertex buffer. Note that the vertices of adjacent primitives are only used as input into the geometry shader—they are not drawn. If there is no geometry shader, the adjacent primitives are still not drawn.

It is also possible to have a line list with adjacency, line strip with adjacency, and triangle with strip adjacency primitives; see the SDK documentation for details.

5.5.2.7 Control Point Patch List

The `D3D_PRIMITIVE_TOPOLOGY_N_CONTROL_POINT_PATCHLIST` topology type indicates that the vertex data should be interpreted as a patch lists with N control points. These are used in the (optional) tessellation stage of the rendering pipeline, and therefore, we will postpone a discussion of them until Chapter 14.

5.5.3 Indices

As already mentioned, triangles are the basic building blocks for solid 3D objects. The following code shows the vertex arrays used to construct a quad and octagon using triangle lists (i.e., every three vertices form a triangle).

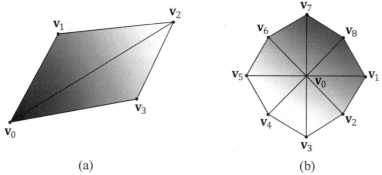

Figure 5.15. (a) A quad built from two triangles. (b) An octagon built from eight triangles.

```
Vertex quad[6] = {
    v0, v1, v2, // Triangle 0
    v0, v2, v3, // Triangle 1
};

Vertex octagon[24] = {
    v0, v1, v2, // Triangle 0
    v0, v2, v3, // Triangle 1
    v0, v3, v4, // Triangle 2
    v0, v4, v5, // Triangle 3
    v0, v5, v6, // Triangle 4
    v0, v6, v7, // Triangle 5
    v0, v7, v8, // Triangle 6
    v0, v8, v1 // Triangle 7
};
```

The order in which you specify the vertices of a triangle is important and is called the *winding order*; see §5.10.2 for details.

As Figure 5.15 illustrates, the triangles that form a 3D object share many of the same vertices. More specifically, each triangle of the quad in Figure 5.15a shares the vertices $\mathbf{v}_0$ and $\mathbf{v}_2$. While duplicating two vertices is not too bad, the duplication is worse in the octagon example (Figure 5.15b), as every triangle duplicates the center vertex $\mathbf{v}_0$, and each vertex on the perimeter of the octagon is shared by two triangles. In general, the number of duplicate vertices increases as the detail and complexity of the model increases.

There are two reasons why we do not want to duplicate vertices:

1. Increased memory requirements. (Why store the same vertex data more than once?)

2. Increased processing by the graphics hardware. (Why process the same vertex data more than once?)

Triangle strips can help the duplicate vertex problem in some situations, provided the geometry can be organized in a strip like fashion. However, triangle lists are more flexible (the triangles need not be connected), and so it is worth devising a method to remove duplicate vertices for triangle lists. The solution is to use *indices*. It works like this: We create a vertex list and an index list. The vertex list consists of all the *unique* vertices and the index list contains values that index into the vertex list to define how the vertices are to be put together to form triangles. Returning to the shapes in Figure 5.15, the vertex list of the quad would be constructed as follows:

```
Vertex v[4] = {v0, v1, v2, v3};
```

Then the index list needs to define how the vertices in the vertex list are to be put together to form the two triangles.

```
UINT indexList[6] = {0, 1, 2, // Triangle 0
                     0, 2, 3}; // Triangle 1
```

In the index list, every three elements define a triangle. So the above index list says, "form triangle 0 by using the vertices `v[0]`, `v[1]`, and `v[2]`, and form triangle 1 by using the vertices `v[0]`, `v[2]`, and `v[3]`."

Similarly, the vertex list for the circle would be constructed as follows:

```
Vertex v [9] = {v0, v1, v2, v3, v4, v5, v6, v7, v8};
```

and the index list would be:

```
UINT indexList[24] = {
  0, 1, 2, // Triangle 0
  0, 2, 3, // Triangle 1
  0, 3, 4, // Triangle 2
  0, 4, 5, // Triangle 3
  0, 5, 6, // Triangle 4
  0, 6, 7, // Triangle 5
  0, 7, 8, // Triangle 6
  0, 8, 1  // Triangle 7
};
```

After the unique vertices in the vertex list are processed, the graphics card can use the index list to put the vertices together to form the triangles. Observe that we have moved the "duplication" over to the index list, but this is not bad since:

1. Indices are simply integers and do not take up as much memory as a full vertex structure (and vertex structures can get big as we add more components to them).

2. With good vertex cache ordering, the graphics hardware won't have to process duplicate vertices (too often).

5.6 THE VERTEX SHADER STAGE

After the primitives have been assembled, the vertices are fed into the vertex shader stage. The vertex shader can be thought of as a function that inputs a vertex and outputs a vertex. Every vertex drawn will be pumped through the vertex shader; in fact, we can conceptually think of the following happening on the hardware:

```
for(UINT i = 0; i < numVertices; ++i)
    outputVertex[i] = VertexShader( inputVertex[i] );
```

The vertex shader function is something we implement, but it is executed by the GPU for each vertex, so it is very fast.

Many special effects can be done in the vertex shader such as transformations, lighting, and displacement mapping. Remember that not only do we have access to the input vertex data, but we also can access textures and other data stored in GPU memory such as transformation matrices, and scene lights.

We will see many examples of different vertex shaders throughout this book; so by the end, you should have a good idea of what can be done with them. For our first code example, however, we will just use the vertex shader to transform vertices. The following subsections explain the kind of transformations that generally need to be done.

5.6.1 Local Space and World Space

Suppose for a moment that you are working on a film and your team has to construct a miniature version of a train scene for some special effect shots. In particular, suppose that you are tasked with making a small bridge. Now, you would not construct the bridge in the middle of the scene, where you would likely have to work from a difficult angle and be careful not to mess up the other miniatures that compose the scene. Instead, you would work on the bridge at your workbench away from the scene. Then when it is all done, you would place the bridge at its correct position and angle in the scene.

3D artists do something similar when constructing 3D objects. Instead of building an object's geometry with coordinates relative to a global scene coordinate system (*world space*), they specify them relative to a local coordinate system (*local space*); the local coordinate system will usually be some convenient coordinate system located near the object and axis-aligned with the object. Once the vertices of the 3D model have been defined in local space, it is placed in the global scene. In order to do this, we must define how the local space and world space are related; this is done by specifying where we want the origin and axes of the local space coordinate system relative to the global scene coordinate system, and executing a change of coordinate transformation (see Figure 5.16 and recall

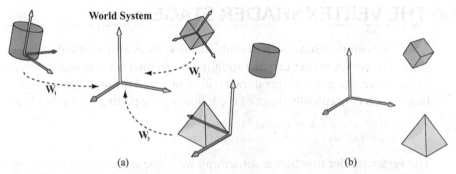

Figure 5.16. (a) The vertices of each object are defined with coordinates relative to their own local coordinate system. In addition, we define the position and orientation of each local coordinate system relative to the world space coordinate system based on where we want the object in the scene. Then we execute a change of coordinate transformation to make all coordinates relative to the world space system. (b) After the world transform, the objects' vertices have coordinates all relative to the same world system.

§3.4). The process of changing coordinates relative to a local coordinate system into the global scene coordinate system is called the *world transform*, and the corresponding matrix is called the *world matrix*. Each object in the scene has its own world matrix. After each object has been transformed from its local space to the world space, then all the coordinates of all the objects are relative to the same coordinate system (the world space). If you want to define an object directly in the world space, then you can supply an identity world matrix.

Defining each model relative to its own local coordinate system has several advantages:

1. It is easier. For instance, usually in local space the object will be centered at the origin and symmetrical with respect to one of the major axes. As another example, the vertices of a cube are much easier to specify if we choose a local coordinate system with origin centered at the cube and with axes orthogonal to the cube faces; see Figure 5.17.

2. The object may be reused across multiple scenes, in which case it makes no sense to hardcode the object's coordinates relative to a particular scene. Instead, it is better to store its coordinates relative to a local coordinate system and then define, via a change of coordinate matrix, how the local coordinate system and world coordinate system are related for each scene.

3. Finally, sometimes we draw the same object more than once in a scene, but in different positions, orientations, and scales (e.g., a tree object may be reused several times to build a forest). It would be wasteful to duplicate the object's vertex and index data for each instance. Instead, we store a single copy of the geometry (i.e., vertex and index lists) relative to its local space. Then we draw the object several times, but each time with a different world matrix to specify

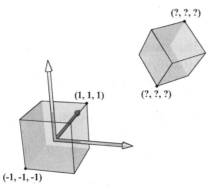

Figure 5.17. The vertices of a cube are easily specified when the cube is centered at the origin and axis-aligned with the coordinate system. It is not so easy to specify the coordinates when the cube is at an arbitrary position and orientation with respect to the coordinate system. Therefore, when we construct the geometry of an object, we usually always choose a convenient coordinate system near the object and aligned with the object, from which to build the object around.

the position, orientation, and scale of the instance in the world space. This is called *instancing*.

As §3.4.3 shows, the world matrix for an object is given by describing its local space with coordinates relative to the world space, and placing these coordinates in the rows of a matrix. If $\mathbf{Q}_w = (Q_x, Q_y, Q_z, 1)$, $\mathbf{u}_w = (u_x, u_y, u_z, 0)$, $\mathbf{v}_w = (v_x, v_y, v_z, 0)$, and $\mathbf{w}_w = (w_x, w_y, w_z, 0)$ describe, respectively, the origin, x-, y-, and z-axes of a local space with homogeneous coordinates relative to world space, then we know from §3.4.3 that the change of coordinate matrix from local space to world space is:

$$\mathbf{W} = \begin{bmatrix} u_x & u_y & u_z & 0 \\ v_x & v_y & v_z & 0 \\ w_x & w_y & w_z & 0 \\ Q_x & Q_y & Q_z & 1 \end{bmatrix}$$

We see that to construct a world matrix, we must directly figure out the coordinates of the local space origin and axes relative to the world space. This is sometimes not that easy or intuitive. A more common approach is to define $\mathbf{W}$ as a sequence of transformations, say $\mathbf{W} = \mathbf{SRT}$, the product of a scaling matrix $\mathbf{S}$ to scale the object into the world, followed by a rotation matrix $\mathbf{R}$ to define the orientation of the local space relative to the world space, followed by a translation matrix $\mathbf{T}$ to define the origin of the local space relative to the world space. From §3.5, we know that this sequence of transformations may be interpreted as a change of coordinate transformation, and that the row vectors of $\mathbf{W} = \mathbf{SRT}$ store the homogeneous coordinates of the x-axis, y-axis, z-axis and origin of the local space relative to the world space.

☞ Example

Suppose we have a unit square defined relative to some local space with minimum and maximum points (−0.5, 0, −0.5) and (0.5, 0, 0.5), respectively. Find the world matrix such that the square has a length of 2 in world space, the square is rotated 45° clockwise in the *xz*-plane of the world space, and the square is positioned at (10, 0, 10) in world space. We construct **S**, **R**, **T**, and **W** as follows:

$$S = \begin{bmatrix} 2 & 0 & 0 & 0 \\ 0 & 1 & 0 & 0 \\ 0 & 0 & 2 & 0 \\ 0 & 0 & 0 & 1 \end{bmatrix} \quad R = \begin{bmatrix} \sqrt{2}/2 & 0 & -\sqrt{2}/2 & 0 \\ 0 & 1 & 0 & 0 \\ \sqrt{2}/2 & 0 & \sqrt{2}/2 & 0 \\ 0 & 0 & 0 & 1 \end{bmatrix} \quad T = \begin{bmatrix} 1 & 0 & 0 & 0 \\ 0 & 1 & 0 & 0 \\ 0 & 0 & 1 & 0 \\ 10 & 0 & 10 & 1 \end{bmatrix}$$

$$W = SRT = \begin{bmatrix} \sqrt{2} & 0 & -\sqrt{2} & 0 \\ 0 & 1 & 0 & 0 \\ \sqrt{2} & 0 & \sqrt{2} & 0 \\ 10 & 0 & 10 & 1 \end{bmatrix}$$

Now from §3.5, the rows in **W** describe the local coordinate system relative to the world space; that is, $\mathbf{u}_W = (\sqrt{2}, 0, -\sqrt{2}, 0)$, $\mathbf{v}_W = (0, 1, 0, 0)$, $\mathbf{w}_W = (\sqrt{2}, 0, \sqrt{2}, 0)$, and $\mathbf{Q}_W = (10, 0, 10, 1)$. When we change coordinates from the local space to the world space with **W**, the square end up in the desired place in world space (see Figure 5.18).

$$[-0.5, \ 0, \ -0.5, \ 1]W = [10-\sqrt{2}, \ 0, \ 0, \ 1]$$
$$[-0.5, \ 0, \ +0.5, \ 1]W = [0, \ 0, \ 10+\sqrt{2}, \ 1]$$
$$[+0.5, \ 0, \ +0.5, \ 1]W = [10+\sqrt{2}, \ 0, \ 0, \ 1]$$
$$[+0.5, \ 0, \ -0.5, \ 1]W = [0, \ 0, \ 10-\sqrt{2}, \ 1]$$

The point of this example is that instead of figuring out $\mathbf{Q}_W$, $\mathbf{u}_W$, $\mathbf{v}_W$, and $\mathbf{w}_W$ directly to form the world matrix, we were able to construct the world matrix by compositing a sequence of simple transforms. This is often much easier than figuring out $\mathbf{Q}_W$, $\mathbf{u}_W$, $\mathbf{v}_W$, and $\mathbf{w}_W$ directly, as we need only ask: what size do we want the object in world space, at what orientation do we want the object in world space, and at what position do we want the object in world space.

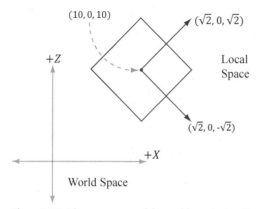

Figure 5.18. The row vectors of the world matrix describe the local coordinate system with coordinates relative to the world coordinate system.

Another way to consider the world transform is to just take the local space coordinates and treat them as world space coordinates (this is equivalent to using an identity matrix as the world transform). Thus if the object is modeled at the center of its local space, the object is just at the center of the world space. In general, the center of the world is probably not where we want to position all of our objects. So now, for each object, just apply a sequence of transformations to scale, rotation, and position the object where you want in the world space. Mathematically, this will give the same world transform as building the change of coordinate matrix from local space to world space.

5.6.2 View Space

In order to form a 2D image of the scene, we must place a virtual camera in the scene. The camera specifies what volume of the world the viewer can see and thus what volume of the world we need to generate a 2D image of. Let us attach a local coordinate system (called *view space*, *eye space*, or *camera space*) to the camera as shown in Figure 5.19; that is, the camera sits at the origin looking down the

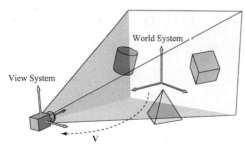

Figure 5.19. Convert the coordinates of vertices relative to the world space to make them relative to the camera space.

positive z-axis, the x-axis aims to the right of the camera, and the y-axis aims above the camera. Instead of describing our scene vertices relative to the world space, it is convenient for later stages of the rendering pipeline to describe them relative to the camera coordinate system. The change of coordinate transformation from world space to view space is called the *view transform*, and the corresponding matrix is called the *view matrix*.

If $\mathbf{Q}_W = (Q_x, Q_y, Q_z, 1)$, $\mathbf{u}_W = (u_x, u_y, u_z, 0)$, $\mathbf{v}_W = (v_x, v_y, v_z, 0)$, and $\mathbf{w}_W = (w_x, w_y, w_z, 0)$ describe, respectively, the origin, x-, y-, and z-axes of view space with homogeneous coordinates relative to world space, then we know from §3.4.3 that the change of coordinate matrix from view space to world space is:

$$\mathbf{W} = \begin{bmatrix} u_x & u_y & u_z & 0 \\ v_x & v_y & v_z & 0 \\ w_x & w_y & w_z & 0 \\ Q_x & Q_y & Q_z & 1 \end{bmatrix}$$

However, this is not the transformation we want. We want the reverse transformation from world space to view space. But recall from §3.4.5 that reverse transformation is just given by the inverse. Thus $\mathbf{W}^{-1}$ transforms from world space to view space.

The world coordinate system and view coordinate system generally differ by position and orientation only, so it makes intuitive sense that $\mathbf{W} = \mathbf{RT}$ (i.e., the world matrix can be decomposed into a rotation followed by a translation). This form makes the inverse easier to compute:

$$\mathbf{V} = \mathbf{W}^{-1} = (\mathbf{RT})^{-1} = \mathbf{T}^{-1}\mathbf{R}^{-1} = \mathbf{T}^{-1}\mathbf{R}$$

$$= \begin{bmatrix} 1 & 0 & 0 & 0 \\ 0 & 1 & 0 & 0 \\ 0 & 0 & 1 & 0 \\ -Q_x & -Q_y & -Q_z & 1 \end{bmatrix} \begin{bmatrix} u_x & v_x & w_x & 0 \\ u_y & v_y & w_y & 0 \\ u_z & v_z & w_z & 0 \\ 0 & 0 & 0 & 1 \end{bmatrix} = \begin{bmatrix} u_x & v_x & w_x & 0 \\ u_y & v_y & w_y & 0 \\ u_z & v_z & w_z & 0 \\ -\mathbf{Q}\cdot\mathbf{u} & -\mathbf{Q}\cdot\mathbf{v} & -\mathbf{Q}\cdot\mathbf{w} & 1 \end{bmatrix}$$

So the view matrix has the form:

$$\mathbf{V} = \begin{bmatrix} u_x & v_x & w_x & 0 \\ u_y & v_y & w_y & 0 \\ u_z & v_z & w_z & 0 \\ -\mathbf{Q}\cdot\mathbf{u} & -\mathbf{Q}\cdot\mathbf{v} & -\mathbf{Q}\cdot\mathbf{w} & 1 \end{bmatrix}$$

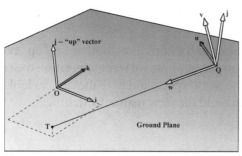

Figure 5.20. Constructing the camera coordinate system given the camera position, a target point, and a world "up" vector.

We now show an intuitive way to construct the vectors needed to build the view matrix. Let **Q** be the position of the camera and let **T** be the target point the camera is aimed at. Furthermore, let **j** be the unit vector that describes the "up" direction of the world space. (In this book, we use the world xz-plane as our world "ground plane" and the world y-axis describes the "up" direction; therefore, $\mathbf{j} = (0, 1, 0)$ is just a unit vector parallel to the world y-axis. However, this is just a convention, and some applications might choose the xy-plane as the ground plane, and the z-axis as the "up" direction.) Referring to Figure 5.20, the direction the camera is looking is given by:

$$\mathbf{w} = \frac{\mathbf{T} - \mathbf{Q}}{\|\mathbf{T} - \mathbf{Q}\|}$$

This vector describes the local z-axis of the camera. A unit vector that aims to the "right" of **w** is given by:

$$\mathbf{u} = \frac{\mathbf{j} \times \mathbf{w}}{\|\mathbf{j} \times \mathbf{w}\|}$$

This vector describes the local x-axis of the camera. Finally, a vector that describes the local y-axis of the camera is given by:

$$\mathbf{v} = \mathbf{w} \times \mathbf{u}$$

Since **w** and **u** are orthogonal unit vectors, $\mathbf{w} \times \mathbf{u}$ is necessarily a unit vector, and so it does not need to be normalized.

Thus, given the position of the camera, the target point, and the world "up" direction, we were able to derive the local coordinate system of the camera, which can be used to form the view matrix.

The DirectXMath library provides the following function for computing the view matrix based on the just described process:

```
XMMATRIX XM_CALLCONV XMMatrixLookAtLH(          // Outputs view matrix V
    FXMVECTOR EyePosition,                      // Input camera position Q
```

```
                FXMVECTOR FocusPosition,              // Input target point T
                FXMVECTOR UpDirection);               // Input world up direction j
```

Usually the world's *y*-axis corresponds to the "up" direction, so the "up" vector is usually always **j** = (0, 1, 0). As an example, suppose we want to position the camera at the point (5, 3, −10) relative to the world space, and have the camera look at the origin of the world (0, 0, 0). We can build the view matrix by writing:

```
XMVECTOR pos    = XMVectorSet(5, 3, -10, 1.0f);
XMVECTOR target = XMVectorZero();
XMVECTOR up     = XMVectorSet(0.0f, 1.0f, 0.0f, 0.0f);

XMMATRIX V = XMMatrixLookAtLH(pos, target, up);
```

5.6.3 Projection and Homogeneous Clip Space

So far we have described the position and orientation of the camera in the world, but there is another component to a camera, which is the volume of space the camera sees. This volume is described by a frustum (Figure 5.21).

Our next task is to project the 3D geometry inside the frustum onto a 2D projection window. The projection must be done in such a way that parallel lines converge to a vanishing point, and as the 3D depth of an object increases, the size of its projection diminishes; a perspective projection does this, and is illustrated in Figure 5.22. We call the line from a vertex to the eye point the *vertex's line of projection*. Then we define the *perspective projection transformation* as the transformation that transforms a 3D vertex **v** to the point **v'** where its line of projection intersects the 2D projection plane; we say that **v'** is the projection of **v**. The projection of a 3D object refers to the projection of all the vertices that make up the object.

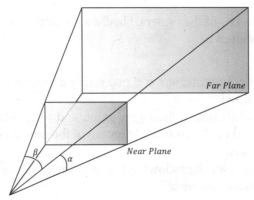

Eye / Center of Projection

Figure 5.21. A frustum defines the volume of space that the camera "sees."

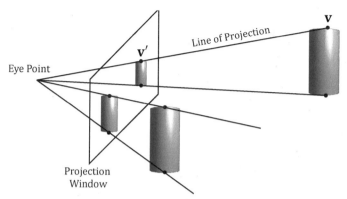

Figure 5.22. Both cylinders in 3D space are the same size but are placed at different depths. The projection of the cylinder closer to the eye is bigger than the projection of the farther cylinder. Geometry inside the frustum is projected onto a projection window; geometry outside the frustum, gets projected onto the projection plane, but will lie outside the projection window.

5.6.3.1 Defining a Frustum

We can define a frustum in view space, with center of projection at the origin and looking down the positive z-axis, by the following four quantities: a near plane n, far plane f, vertical field of view angle α, and aspect ratio r. Note that in view space, the near plane and far plane are parallel to the xy-plane; thus we simply specify their distance from the origin along the z-axis. The aspect ratio is defined by $r = w/h$ where w is the width of the projection window and h is the height of the projection window (units in view space). The projection window is essentially the 2D image of the scene in view space. The image here will eventually be mapped to the back buffer; therefore, we like the ratio of the projection window dimensions to be the same as the ratio of the back buffer dimensions. So the ratio of the back buffer dimensions is usually specified as the aspect ratio (it is a ratio so it has no units). For example, if the back buffer dimensions are 800 × 600, then we specify $r = \frac{800}{600} \approx 1.333$. If the aspect ratio of the projection window and the back buffer were not the same, then a non-uniform scaling would be necessary to map the projection window to the back buffer, which would cause distortion (e.g., a circle on the projection window might get stretched into an ellipse when mapped to the back buffer).

We label the horizontal field of view angle β, and it is determined by the vertical field of view angle α and aspect ratio r. To see how r helps us find β, consider Figure 5.23. Note that the actual dimensions of the projection window are not important, just the aspect ratio needs to be maintained. Therefore, we will choose the convenient height of 2, and thus the width must be:

$$r = \frac{w}{h} = \frac{w}{2} \Rightarrow w = 2r$$

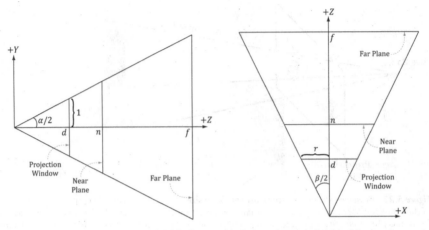

Figure 5.23. Deriving the horizontal field of view angle β given the vertical field of view angle α and the aspect ratio r.

In order to have the specified vertical field of view α, the projection window must be placed a distance d from the origin:

$$\tan\left(\frac{\alpha}{2}\right) = \frac{1}{d} \Rightarrow d = \cot\left(\frac{\alpha}{2}\right)$$

We have now fixed the distance d of the projection window along the z-axis to have a vertical field of view α when the height of the projection window is 2. Now we can solve for β. Looking at the xz-plane in Figure 5.23, we now see that:

$$\tan\left(\frac{\beta}{2}\right) = \frac{r}{d} = \frac{r}{\cot\left(\frac{\alpha}{2}\right)}$$

$$= r \cdot \tan\left(\frac{\alpha}{2}\right)$$

So given the vertical field of view angle α and the aspect ratio r, we can always get the horizontal field of view angle β:

$$\beta = 2\tan^{-1}\left(r \cdot \tan\left(\frac{\alpha}{2}\right)\right)$$

5.6.3.2 Projecting Vertices

Refer to Figure 5.24. Given a point (x, y, z), we wish to find its projection (x', y', d), on the projection plane $z = d$. By considering the x- and y-coordinates separately and using similar triangles, we find:

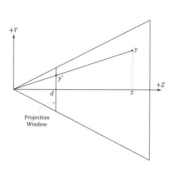
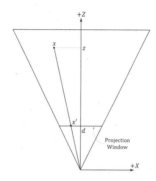

Figure 5.24. Similar triangles.

$$\frac{x'}{d} = \frac{x}{z} \Rightarrow x' = \frac{xd}{z} = \frac{x\cot(\alpha/2)}{z} = \frac{x}{z\tan(\alpha/2)}$$

and

$$\frac{y'}{d} = \frac{y}{z} \Rightarrow y' = \frac{yd}{z} = \frac{y\cot(\alpha/2)}{z} = \frac{y}{z\tan(\alpha/2)}$$

Observe that a point (x, y, z) is inside the frustum if and only if

$$-r \le x' \le r$$
$$-1 \le y' \le 1$$
$$n \le z \le f$$

5.6.3.3 Normalized Device Coordinates (NDC)

The coordinates of the projected points in the preceding section are computed in view space. In view space, the projection window has a height of 2 and a width of $2r$, where r is the aspect ratio. The problem with this is that the dimensions depend on the aspect ratio. This means we would need to tell the hardware the aspect ratio, since the hardware will later need to do some operations that involve the dimensions of the projection window (such as map it to the back buffer). It would be more convenient if we could remove this dependency on the aspect ratio. The solution is to scale the projected x-coordinate from the interval $[-r, r]$ to $[-1, 1]$ like so:

$$-r \le x' \le r$$
$$-1 \le x'/r \le 1$$

After this mapping, the *x*- and *y*-coordinates are said to be *normalized device coordinates* (NDC) (the *z*-coordinate has not yet been normalized), and a point (x, y, z) is inside the frustum if and only if

$$-1 \leq x'/r \leq 1$$
$$-1 \leq y' \leq 1$$
$$n \leq z \leq f$$

The transformation from view space to NDC space can be viewed as a unit conversion. We have the relationship that one NDC unit equals *r* units in view space (i.e., 1ndc = *r* vs) on the *x*-axis. So given *x* view space units, we can use this relationship to convert units:

$$x \text{ vs} \cdot \frac{1 \text{ ndc}}{r \text{ vs}} = \frac{x}{r} \text{ ndc}$$

We can modify our projection formulas to give us the projected *x*- and *y*-coordinates directly in NDC coordinates:

$$x' = \frac{x}{rz \tan(\alpha/2)}$$
$$y' = \frac{y}{z \tan(\alpha/2)}$$ (eq. 5.1)

Note that in NDC coordinates, the projection window has a height of 2 and a width of 2. So now the dimensions are fixed, and the hardware need not know the aspect ratio, but it is our responsibility to always supply the projected coordinates in NDC space (the graphics hardware assumes we will).

5.6.3.4 Writing the Projection Equations with a Matrix

For uniformity, we would like to express the projection transformation by a matrix. However, Equation 5.1 is nonlinear, so it does not have a matrix representation. The "trick" is to separate it into two parts: a linear part and a nonlinear part. The nonlinear part is the divide by *z*. As will be discussed in the next section, we are going to normalize the *z*-coordinate; this means we will not have the original *z*-coordinate around for the divide. Therefore, we must save the input *z*-coordinate before it is transformed; to do this, we take advantage of homogeneous coordinates and copy the input *z*-coordinate to the output *w*-coordinate. In terms of matrix multiplication, this is done by setting entry [2][3] = 1 and entry [3][3] = 0 (zero-based indices). Our projection matrix looks like this:

$$\mathbf{P} = \begin{bmatrix} \frac{1}{r\tan(\alpha/2)} & 0 & 0 & 0 \\ 0 & \frac{1}{\tan(\alpha/2)} & 0 & 0 \\ 0 & 0 & A & 1 \\ 0 & 0 & B & 0 \end{bmatrix}$$

Note that we have placed constants (to be determined in the next section) A and B into the matrix; these constants will be used to transform the input z-coordinate into the normalized range. Multiplying an arbitrary point $(x, y, z, 1)$ by this matrix gives:

$$[x, y, z, 1] \begin{bmatrix} \frac{1}{r\tan(\alpha/2)} & 0 & 0 & 0 \\ 0 & \frac{1}{\tan(\alpha/2)} & 0 & 0 \\ 0 & 0 & A & 1 \\ 0 & 0 & B & 0 \end{bmatrix} \quad \text{(eq. 5.2)}$$

$$= \left[\frac{x}{r\tan(\alpha/2)}, \frac{y}{\tan(\alpha/2)}, Az + B, z \right]$$

After multiplying by the projection matrix (the linear part), we complete the transformation by dividing each coordinate by $w = z$ (the nonlinear part):

$$\left[\frac{x}{r\tan(\alpha/2)}, \frac{y}{\tan(\alpha/2)}, Az + B, z \right] \xrightarrow{\text{divide by } w} \left[\frac{x}{rz\tan(\alpha/2)}, \frac{y}{z\tan(\alpha/2)}, A + \frac{B}{z}, 1 \right] \quad \text{(eq. 5.3)}$$

Incidentally, you may wonder about a possible divide by zero; however, the near plane should be greater than zero, so such a point would be clipped (§5.9). The divide by w is sometimes called the *perspective divide* or *homogeneous divide*. We see that the projected x- and y-coordinates agree with Equation 5.1.

5.6.3.5 Normalized Depth Value

It may seem like after projection, we can discard the original 3D z-coordinate, as all the projected points now lay on the 2D projection window, which forms the 2D image seen by the eye. However, we still need 3D depth information around for the depth buffering algorithm. Just like Direct3D wants the projected x- and

y-coordinates in a normalized range, Direct3D wants the depth coordinates in the normalized range [0, 1]. Therefore, we must construct an order preserving function $g(z)$ that maps the interval $[n, f]$ onto [0, 1]. Because the function is order preserving, if $z_1, z_2 \in [n, f]$ and $z_1 < z_2$, then $g(z_1) < g(z_2)$; so even though the depth values have been transformed, the relative depth relationships remain intact, so we can still correctly compare depths in the normalized interval, which is all we need for the depth buffering algorithm.

Mapping $[n, f]$ onto [0, 1] can be done with a scaling and translation. However, this approach will not integrate into our current projection strategy. We see from Equation 5.3, that the z-coordinate undergoes the transformation:

$$g(z) = A + \frac{B}{z}$$

We now need to choose A and B subject to the constraints:

Condition 1: $g(n) = A + B/n = 0$ (the near plane gets mapped to zero)
Condition 2: $g(f) = A + B/f = 1$ (the far plane gets mapped to one)

Solving condition 1 for B yields: $B = -An$. Substituting this into condition 2 and solving for A gives:

$$A + \frac{-An}{f} = 1$$

$$\frac{Af - An}{f} = 1$$

$$Af - An = f$$

$$A = \frac{f}{f-n}$$

Therefore,

$$g(z) = \frac{f}{f-n} - \frac{nf}{(f-n)z}$$

A graph of g (Figure 5.25) shows it is strictly increasing (order preserving) and nonlinear. It also shows that most of the range is "used up" by depth values close to the near plane. Consequently, the majority of the depth values get mapped to a small subset of the range. This can lead to depth buffer precision problems (the computer can no longer distinguish between slightly different transformed depth values due to finite numerical representation). The general advice is to make the near and far planes as close as possible to minimize depth precision problems.

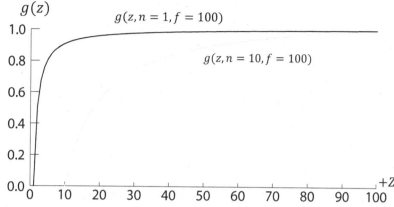

Figure 5.25. Graph of g(z) for different near planes.

Now that we have solved for A and B, we can state the full *perspective projection matrix*:

$$\mathbf{P} = \begin{bmatrix} \dfrac{1}{r\tan(\alpha/2)} & 0 & 0 & 0 \\ 0 & \dfrac{1}{\tan(\alpha/2)} & 0 & 0 \\ 0 & 0 & \dfrac{f}{f-n} & 1 \\ 0 & 0 & \dfrac{-nf}{f-n} & 0 \end{bmatrix}$$

After multiplying by the projection matrix, but before the perspective divide, geometry is said to be in *homogeneous clip space* or *projection space*. After the perspective divide, the geometry is said to be in normalized device coordinates (NDC).

5.6.3.6 XMMatrixPerspectiveFovLH

A perspective projection matrix can be built with the following DirectX Math function:

```
// Returns the projection matrix
XMMATRIX XM_CALLCONV XMMatrixPerspectiveFovLH(
    float FovAngleY,    // vertical field of view angle in radians
    float Aspect,       // aspect ratio = width / height
    float NearZ,        // distance to near plane
    float FarZ);        // distance to far plane
```

The following code snippet illustrates how to use `XMMatrixPerspectiveFovLH`. Here, we specify a 45° vertical field of view, a near plane at $z = 1$ and a far plane at $z = 1000$ (these lengths are in view space).

```
XMMATRIX P = XMMatrixPerspectiveFovLH(0.25f*XM_PI,
  AspectRatio(), 1.0f, 1000.0f);
```

The aspect ratio is taken to match our window aspect ratio:

```
float D3DApp::AspectRatio()const
{
  return static_cast<float>(mClientWidth) / mClientHeight;
}
```

5.7 THE TESSELLATION STAGES

Tessellation refers to subdividing the triangles of a mesh to add new triangles. These new triangles can then be offset into new positions to create finer mesh detail (see Figure 5.26).

There are a number of benefits to tessellations:

1. We can implement a level-of-detail (LOD) mechanism, where triangles near the camera are tessellated to add more detail, and triangles far away from the camera are not tessellated. In this way, we only use more triangles where the extra detail will be noticed.
2. We keep a simpler *low-poly* mesh (low-poly means low triangle count) in memory, and add the extra triangles on the fly, thus saving memory.
3. We do operations like animation and physics on a simpler low-poly mesh, and only use the tessellated high-poly mesh for rendering.

The tessellation stages are new to Direct3D 11, and they provide a way to tessellate geometry on the GPU. Before Direct3D 11, if you wanted to implement a form of tessellation, it would have to be done on the CPU, and then the new tessellated

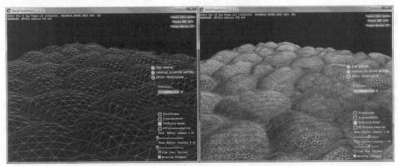

Figure 5.26. The left image shows the original mesh. The right image shows the mesh after tessellation.

geometry would have to be uploaded back to the GPU for rendering. However, uploading new geometry from CPU memory to GPU memory is slow, and it also burdens the CPU with computing the tessellation. For this reason, tessellation methods have not been very popular for real-time graphics prior to Direct3D 11. Direct3D 11 provides an API to do tessellation completely in hardware with a Direct3D 11 capable video card. This makes tessellation a much more attractive technique. The tessellation stages are optional (you only need to use it if you want tessellation). We defer our coverage of tessellation until Chapter 14.

5.8 THE GEOMETRY SHADER STAGE

The geometry shader stage is optional, and we do not use it until Chapter 12, so we will be brief here. The geometry shader inputs entire primitives. For example, if we were drawing triangle lists, then the input to the geometry shader would be the three vertices defining the triangle. (Note that the three vertices will have already passed through the vertex shader.) The main advantage of the geometry shader is that it can create or destroy geometry. For example, the input primitive can be expanded into one or more other primitives, or the geometry shader can choose not to output a primitive based on some condition. This is in contrast to a vertex shader, which cannot create vertices: it inputs one vertex and outputs one vertex. A common example of the geometry shader is to expand a point into a quad or to expand a line into a quad.

We also notice the "stream-out" arrow from Figure 5.11. That is, the geometry shader can stream-out vertex data into a buffer in memory, which can later be drawn. This is an advanced technique, and will be discussed in a later chapter.

 Vertex positions leaving the geometry shader must be transformed to homogeneous clip space.

5.9 CLIPPING

Geometry completely outside the viewing frustum needs to be discarded, and geometry that intersects the boundary of the frustum must be clipped, so that only the interior part remains; see Figure 5.27 for the idea illustrated in 2D.

We can think of the frustum as being the region bounded by six planes: the top, bottom, left, right, near, and far planes. To clip a polygon against the frustum, we clip it against each frustum plane one-by-one. When clipping a polygon against a plane (Figure 5.28), the part in the positive half-space of the plane is kept, and the

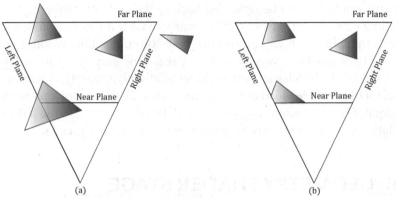

Figure 5.27. (a) Before clipping. (b) After clipping.

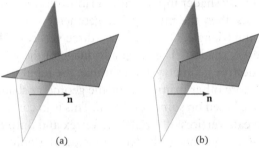

Figure 5.28. (a) Clipping a triangle against a plane. (b) The clipped triangle. Note that the clipped triangle is not a triangle, but a quad. Thus the hardware will need to triangulate the resulting quad, which is straightforward to do for convex polygons.

part in the negative half space is discarded. Clipping a convex polygon against a plane will always result in a convex polygon. Because the hardware does clipping for us, we will not cover the details here; instead, we refer the reader to the popular Sutherland-Hodgeman clipping algorithm [Sutherland74]. It basically amounts to finding the intersection points between the plane and polygon edges, and then ordering the vertices to form the new clipped polygon.

[Blinn78] describes how clipping can be done in 4D homogeneous space. After the perspective divide, points $\left(\frac{x}{w}, \frac{y}{w}, \frac{z}{w}, 1\right)$ inside the view frustum are in normalized device coordinates and bounded as follows:

$$-1 \leq x/w \leq 1$$
$$-1 \leq y/w \leq 1$$
$$0 \leq z/w \leq 1$$

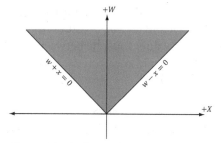

Figure 5.29. The frustum boundaries in the *xw*-plane in homogeneous clip space.

So in homogeneous clip space, before the divide, 4D points (x, y, z, w) inside the frustum are bounded as follows:

$$-w \leq x \leq w$$
$$-w \leq y \leq w$$
$$0 \leq z \leq w$$

That is, the points are bounded by the simple 4D planes:

Left: $w = -x$
Right: $w = x$
Bottom: $w = -y$
Top: $w = y$
Near: $z = 0$
Far: $z = w$

Once we know the frustum plane equations in homogeneous space, we can apply a clipping algorithm (such as Sutherland-Hodgeman). Note that the mathematics of the segment/plane intersection test generalizes to $\mathbb{R}^4$, so we can do the test with 4D points and the 4D planes in homogeneous clip space.

5.10 THE RASTERIZATION STAGE

The main job of the rasterization stage is to compute pixel colors from the projected 3D triangles.

5.10.1 Viewport Transform

After clipping, the hardware can do the perspective divide to transform from homogeneous clip space to normalized device coordinates (NDC). Once vertices are in NDC space, the 2D *x*- and *y*- coordinates forming the 2D image are transformed to a rectangle on the back buffer called the viewport (recall §4.3.9). After this transform, the *x*- and *y*-coordinates are in units of pixels. Usually the viewport transformation does not modify the *z*-coordinate, as it is used for depth buffering, but it can by modifying the MinDepth and MaxDepth values of the D3D12_VIEWPORT structure. The MinDepth and MaxDepth values must be between 0 and 1.

5.10.2 Backface Culling

A triangle has two sides. To distinguish between the two sides we use the following convention. If the triangle vertices are ordered $\mathbf{v}_0$, $\mathbf{v}_1$, $\mathbf{v}_2$ then we compute the triangle normal **n** like so:

$$\mathbf{e}_0 = \mathbf{v}_1 - \mathbf{v}_0$$
$$\mathbf{e}_1 = \mathbf{v}_2 - \mathbf{v}_0$$
$$\mathbf{n} = \frac{\mathbf{e}_0 \times \mathbf{e}_1}{\|\mathbf{e}_0 \times \mathbf{e}_1\|}$$

The side the normal vector emanates from is the *front side* and the other side is the *back side*. Figure 5.30 illustrates this.

We say that a triangle is *front-facing* if the viewer sees the front side of a triangle, and we say a triangle is *back-facing* if the viewer sees the back side of a triangle. From our perspective of Figure 5.30, the left triangle is front-facing while the right triangle is back-facing. Moreover, from our perspective, the left triangle is ordered clockwise while the right triangle is ordered counterclockwise. This is no coincidence: with the convention we have chosen (i.e., the way we compute the triangle normal), a triangle ordered clockwise (with respect to that viewer) is front-facing, and a triangle ordered counterclockwise (with respect to that viewer) is back-facing.

Now, most objects in 3D worlds are enclosed solid objects. Suppose we agree to construct the triangles for each object in such a way that the normals are always aimed outward. Then, the camera does not see the back-facing triangles of a solid object because the front-facing triangles occlude the back-facing triangles; Figure 5.31 illustrates this in 2D and 5.32 in 3D. Because the front-facing triangles occlude the back-facing triangles, it makes no sense to draw them. *Backface culling*

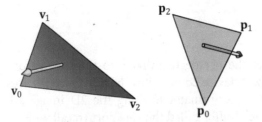

Figure 5.30. The left triangle is front-facing from our viewpoint, and the right triangle is back-facing from our viewpoint.

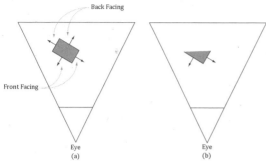

Figure 5.31. (a) A solid object with front-facing and back-facing triangles. (b) The scene after culling the back-facing triangles. Note that backface culling does not affect the final image since the back-facing triangles are occluded by the front-facing ones.

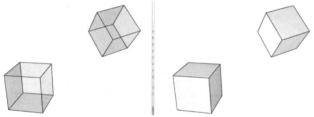

Figure 5.32. (Left) We draw the cubes with transparency so that you can see all six sides. (Right) We draw the cubes as solid blocks. Note that we do not see the three back-facing sides since the three front-facing sides occlude them—thus the back-facing triangles can actually be discarded from further processing and no one will notice.

refers to the process of discarding back-facing triangles from the pipeline. This can potentially reduce the amount of triangles that need to be processed by half.

By default, Direct3D treats triangles with a clockwise winding order (with respect to the viewer) as front-facing, and triangles with a counterclockwise winding order (with respect to the viewer) as back-facing. However, this convention can be reversed with a Direct3D render state setting.

5.10.3 Vertex Attribute Interpolation

Recall that we define a triangle by specifying its vertices. In addition to position, we can attach attributes to vertices such as colors, normal vectors, and texture coordinates. After the viewport transform, these attributes need to be interpolated for each pixel covering the triangle. In addition to vertex attributes, vertex depth values need to get interpolated so that each pixel has a depth value for the depth buffering algorithm. The vertex attributes are interpolated in screen space in such a way that the attributes are interpolated linearly across the triangle in 3D space (Figure 5.33); this requires the so-called *perspective correct interpolation*. Essentially, interpolation allows us to use the vertex values to compute values for the interior pixels.

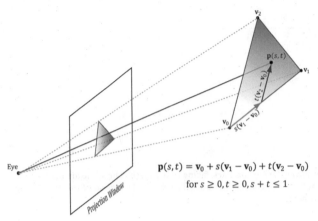

Figure 5.33. An attribute value **p**(s, t) on a triangle can be obtained by linearly interpolating between the attribute values at the vertices of the triangle.

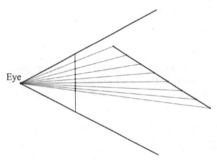

Figure 5.34. A 3D line is being projected onto the projection window (the projection is a 2D line in screen space). We see that taking uniform step sizes along the 3D line corresponds to taking non-uniform step sizes in 2D screen space. Therefore to do linear interpolation in 3D space, we need to do nonlinear interpolation in screen space.

The mathematical details of perspective correct attribute interpolation are not something we need to worry about since the hardware does it; the interested reader may find the mathematical derivation in [Eberly01]. However, Figure 5.34 gives the basic idea of what is going on.

5.11 THE PIXEL SHADER STAGE

Pixel shaders are programs we write that are executed on the GPU. A pixel shader is executed for each pixel fragment and uses the interpolated vertex attributes as input to compute a color. A pixel shader can be as simple as returning a constant color, to doing more complicated things like per-pixel lighting, reflections and shadowing effects.

5.12 THE OUTPUT MERGER STAGE

After pixel fragments have been generated by the pixel shader, they move onto the output merger (OM) stage of the rendering pipeline. In this stage, some pixel fragments may be rejected (e.g., from the depth or stencil buffer tests). Pixel fragments that are not rejected are written to the back buffer. Blending is also done in this stage, where a pixel may be blended with the pixel currently on the back buffer instead of overriding it completely. Some special effects like transparency are implemented with blending; Chapter 10 is devoted to blending.

5.13 SUMMARY

1. We can simulate 3D scenes on 2D images by employing several techniques based on the way we see things in real life. We observe parallel lines converge to vanishing points, the size of objects diminishes with depth, objects obscure the objects behind them, lighting and shading depict the solid form and volume of 3D objects, and shadows imply the location of light sources and indicate the position of objects relative to other objects in the scene.

2. We approximate objects with triangle meshes. We can define each triangle by specifying its three vertices. In many meshes, vertices are shared among triangles; indexed lists can be used to avoid vertex duplication.

3. Colors are described by specifying an intensity of red, green, and blue. The additive mixing of these three colors at different intensities allows us to describe millions of colors. To describe the intensities of red, green, and blue, it is useful to use a normalized range from 0 to 1. 0 denotes no intensity, 1 denotes the full intensity, and intermediate values denote intermediate intensities. It is common to incorporate an additional color component, called the *alpha component*. The alpha component is often used to denote the opacity of a color, which is useful in blending. Including the alpha component, means we can represent a color by a 4D color vector (r, g, b, a) where $0 \leq r, g, b, a \leq 1$. Because the data needed to represent a color is a 4D vector, we can use the XMVECTOR type to represent a color in code, and we gain the benefit of SIMD operations whenever use the DirectX Math vector functions to do color operations. To represent a color with 32-bits, a byte is given to each component; the DirectXMath library provides the XMCOLOR structure for storing a 32-bit color. Color vectors are added, subtracted, and scaled just like regular vectors, except that we must clamp their components to the [0, 1] interval (or [0, 255] for 32-bit colors). The other vector operations such

as the dot product and cross product do not make sense for color vectors. The symbol ⊗ denotes component-wise multiplication and it is defined as: $(c_1,c_2,c_3,c_4) \otimes (k_1,k_2,k_3,k_4) = (c_1 k_1, c_2 k_2, c_3 k_3, c_4 k_4)$.

4. Given a geometric description of a 3D scene and a positioned and aimed virtual camera in that scene, the *rendering pipeline* refers to the entire sequence of steps necessary to generate a 2D image that can be displayed on a monitor screen based on what the virtual camera sees.

5. The rendering pipeline can be broken down into the following major stages. The input assembly (IA) stage; the vertex shader (VS) stage; the tessellation stages; the geometry shader (GS) stage; the clipping stage; the rasterization stage (RS); the pixel shader (PS) stage; and the output merger (OM) stage.

5.14 EXERCISES

1. Construct the vertex and index list of a pyramid, as shown in Figure 5.35.

Figure 5.35. The triangles of a pyramid.

2. Consider the two shapes shown in Figure 5.36. Merge the objects into one vertex and index list. (The idea here is that when you append the second index list to the first, you will need to update the appended indices since they reference vertices in the original vertex list, not the merged vertex list.)

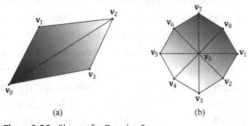

Figure 5.36. Shapes for Exercise 2.

3. Relative to the world coordinate system, suppose that the camera is positioned at (−20, 35, -50) and looking at the point (10, 0, 30). Compute the view matrix assuming (0, 1, 0) describes the "up" direction in the world.

4. Given that the view frustum has a vertical field of view angle $\theta = 45°$, the aspect ratio is $a = 4/3$, the near plane is $n = 1$, and the far plane is $f = 100$, find the corresponding perspective projection matrix.

5. Suppose that the view window has height 4. Find the distance d from the origin the view window must be to create a vertical field of view angle $\theta = 60°$.

6. Consider the following perspective projection matrix:

$$\begin{bmatrix} 1.86603 & 0 & 0 & 0 \\ 0 & 3.73205 & 0 & 0 \\ 0 & 0 & 1.02564 & 1 \\ 0 & 0 & 5.12821 & 0 \end{bmatrix}$$

Find the vertical field of view angle α the aspect ratio r, and the near and far plane values that were used to build this matrix.

7. Suppose that you are given the following perspective projection matrix with fixed A, B, C, D:

$$\begin{bmatrix} A & 0 & 0 & 0 \\ 0 & B & 0 & 0 \\ 0 & 0 & C & 1 \\ 0 & 0 & D & 0 \end{bmatrix}$$

Find the vertical field of view angle α the aspect ratio r, and the near and far plane values that were used to build this matrix in terms of A, B, C, D. That is, solve the following equations:

(a) $A = \dfrac{1}{r \tan(\alpha/2)}$

(b) $B = \dfrac{1}{\tan(\alpha/2)}$

(c) $C = \dfrac{f}{f-n}$

(d) $D = \dfrac{-nf}{f-n}$

Solving these equations will give you formulas for extracting the vertical field of view angle α the aspect ratio r, and the near and far plane values from any perspective projection matrix of the kind described in this book.

8. For projective texturing algorithms, we multiply an affine transformation matrix **T** after the projection matrix. Prove that it does not matter if we do the perspective divide before or after multiplying by **T**. Let, **v** be a 4D vector, **P** be a projection matrix, **T** be a 4×4 affine transformation matrix, and let a w subscript denote the w-coordinate of a 4D vector, prove:

$$\left(\frac{\mathbf{vP}}{(\mathbf{vP})_w}\right)\mathbf{T} = \frac{(\mathbf{vPT})}{(\mathbf{vPT})_w}$$

9. Prove that the inverse of the projection matrix is given by:

$$\mathbf{P}^{-1} = \begin{bmatrix} r\tan\left(\frac{\alpha}{2}\right) & 0 & 0 & 0 \\ 0 & \tan\left(\frac{\alpha}{2}\right) & 0 & 0 \\ 0 & 0 & 0 & -\frac{f-n}{nf} \\ 0 & 0 & 1 & \frac{1}{n} \end{bmatrix}$$

10. Let $[x, y, z, 1]$ be the coordinates of a point in view space, and let $[x_{ndc}, y_{ndc}, z_{ndc}, 1]$ be the coordinates of the same point in NDC space. Prove that you can transform from NDC space to view space in the following way:

$$[x_{ndc}, y_{ndc}, z_{ndc}, 1]\mathbf{P}^{-1} = \left[\frac{x}{z}, \frac{y}{z}, 1, \frac{1}{z}\right] \xrightarrow{\text{divide by } w} [x, y, z, 1]$$

Explain why you need the division by w. Would you need the division by w if you were transforming from homogeneous clip space to view space?

11. Another way to describe the view frustum is by specifying the width and height of the view volume at the near plane. Given the width w and height h of the view volume at the near plane, and given the near plane n and far plane f show that the perspective projection matrix is given by:

$$\mathbf{P} = \begin{bmatrix} \frac{2n}{w} & 0 & 0 & 0 \\ 0 & \frac{2n}{h} & 0 & 0 \\ 0 & 0 & \frac{f}{f-n} & 1 \\ 0 & 0 & \frac{-nf}{f-n} & 0 \end{bmatrix}$$

12. Given a view frustum with vertical field of view angle θ, aspect ratio is a, near plane n, and far plane f, find the 8 vertex corners of the frustum.

13. Consider the 3D shear transform given by $S_{xy}(x, y, z) = (x + zt_x, y + zt_y, z)$. This transformation is illustrated in Figure 5.37. Prove that this is a linear transformation and has the following matrix representation:

$$\mathbf{S}_{xy} = \begin{bmatrix} 1 & 0 & 0 \\ 0 & 1 & 0 \\ t_x & t_y & 1 \end{bmatrix}$$

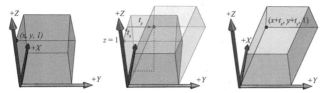

Figure 5.37. The x- and y-coordinates sheared by the z-coordinate. The top face of the box lies in the $z = 1$ plane. Observe that the shear transform translates points in this plane.

14. Consider 3D points in the plane $z = 1$; that is, points of the form $(x, y, 1)$. Observe that transforming a point $(x, y, 1)$ by the shear transformation $\mathbf{S}_{xy}$ given in the previous exercise amounts to a 2D translation in the $z = 1$ plane:

$$\begin{bmatrix} x & y & 1 \end{bmatrix} \begin{bmatrix} 1 & 0 & 0 \\ 0 & 1 & 0 \\ t_x & t_y & 1 \end{bmatrix} = \begin{bmatrix} x + t_x & y + t_y & 1 \end{bmatrix}$$

If we are working on a 2D application, we could use 3D coordinates, but where our 2D universe always lies on the plane $z = 1$; then we could use $\mathbf{S}_{xy}$ to do translations in our 2D space.

Conclude the following generalizations:

a. Just as a plane in 3D space is a 2D space, a plane in 4D space is a 3D space. When we write homogeneous points $(x, y, z, 1)$ we are working in the 3D space that lives in the 4D plane $w = 1$.

b. The translation matrix is the matrix representation of the 4D shear transformation $S_{xyz}(x, y, z, w) = (x + wt_x, y + wt_y, z + wt_z, w)$. The 4D shear transformation has the effect of translating points in the plane $w = 1$.

Chapter 6
Drawing in Direct3D

In the previous chapter, we mostly focused on the conceptual and mathematical aspects of the rendering pipeline. This chapter, in turn, focuses on the Direct3D API interfaces and methods needed to configure the rendering pipeline, define vertex and pixel shaders, and submit geometry to the rendering pipeline for drawing. By the end of this chapter, you will be able to draw a 3D box with solid coloring or in wireframe mode.

Objectives:

1. To discover the Direct3D interfaces methods for defining, storing, and drawing geometric data.
2. To learn how to write basic vertex and pixel shaders.
3. To find out how to configure the rendering pipeline with pipeline state objects.
4. To understand how to create and bind constant buffer data to the pipeline, and to become familiar with the root signature.

6.1 VERTICES AND INPUT LAYOUTS

Recall from §5.5.1 that a vertex in Direct3D can consist of additional data besides spatial location. To create a custom vertex format, we first create a structure that holds the vertex data we choose. For instance, the following illustrates two different kinds of vertex formats; one consists of position and color, and the second consists of position, normal vector, and two sets of 2D texture coordinates.

```
struct Vertex1
{
  XMFLOAT3 Pos;
  XMFLOAT4 Color;
};

struct Vertex2
{
  XMFLOAT3 Pos;
  XMFLOAT3 Normal;
  XMFLOAT2 Tex0;
  XMFLOAT2 Tex1;
};
```

Once we have defined a vertex structure, we need to provide Direct3D with a description of our vertex structure so that it knows what to do with each component. This description is provided to Direct3D in the form of an *input layout description* which is represented by the D3D12_INPUT_LAYOUT_DESC structure:

```
typedef struct D3D12_INPUT_LAYOUT_DESC
{
  const D3D12_INPUT_ELEMENT_DESC *pInputElementDescs;
  UINT NumElements;
} D3D12_INPUT_LAYOUT_DESC;
```

An input layout description is simply an array of D3D12_INPUT_ELEMENT_DESC elements, and the number of elements in the array.

Each element in the D3D12_INPUT_ELEMENT_DESC array describes and corresponds to one component in the vertex structure. So if the vertex structure has two components, then the corresponding D3D12_INPUT_ELEMENT_DESC array will have two elements. The D3D12_INPUT_ELEMENT_DESC structure is defined as:

```
typedef struct D3D12_INPUT_ELEMENT_DESC
{
  LPCSTR SemanticName;
  UINT SemanticIndex;
  DXGI_FORMAT Format;
  UINT InputSlot;
  UINT AlignedByteOffset;
  D3D12_INPUT_CLASSIFICATION InputSlotClass;
  UINT InstanceDataStepRate;
} D3D12_INPUT_ELEMENT_DESC;
```

1. SemanticName: A string to associate with the element. This can be any valid variable name. Semantics are used to map elements in the vertex structure to elements in the vertex shader input signature; see Figure 6.1.

```
struct Vertex
{
    XMFLOAT3 Pos;
    XMFLOAT3 Normal;
    XMFLOAT2 Tex0;
    XMFLOAT2 Tex1;
};

D3D11_INPUT_ELEMENT_DESC vertexDesc[] =
{
    {"POSITION", 0, DXGI_FORMAT_R32G32B32_FLOAT, 0, 0,
        D3D11_INPUT_PER_VERTEX_DATA, 0},
    {"NORMAL", 0, DXGI_FORMAT_R32G32B32_FLOAT, 0, 12,
        D3D11_INPUT_PER_VERTEX_DATA, 0},
    {"TEXCOORD", 0, DXGI_FORMAT_R32G32_FLOAT, 0, 24,
        D3D11_INPUT_PER_VERTEX_DATA, 0},
    {"TEXCOORD", 1, DXGI_FORMAT_R32G32_FLOAT, 0, 32,
        D3D11_INPUT_PER_VERTEX_DATA, 0}
};

VertexOut VS(float3 iPos    : POSITION,
             float3 iNormal : NORMAL,
             float2 iTex0   : TEXCOORD0,
             float2 iTex1   : TEXCOORD1)
```

Figure 6.1. Each element in the vertex structure is described by a corresponding element in the D3D12_INPUT_ELEMENT_DESC array. The semantic name and index provides way for mapping vertex elements to the corresponding parameters of the vertex shader.

2. SemanticIndex: An index to attach to a semantic. The motivation for this is illustrated in Figure 6.1, where, for example, a vertex structure may have more than one set of texture coordinates; so rather than introducing a new semantic name, we can just attach an index to the end to distinguish the two texture coordinate sets. A semantic with no index specified in the shader code defaults to index zero; for instance, POSITION is equivalent to POSITION0 in Figure 6.1.

3. Format: A member of the DXGI_FORMAT enumerated type specifying the format (i.e., the data type) of this vertex element to Direct3D; here are some common examples of formats used:

```
DXGI_FORMAT_R32_FLOAT         // 1D 32-bit float scalar
DXGI_FORMAT_R32G32_FLOAT      // 2D 32-bit float vector
DXGI_FORMAT_R32G32B32_FLOAT   // 3D 32-bit float vector
DXGI_FORMAT_R32G32B32A32_FLOAT // 4D 32-bit float vector

DXGI_FORMAT_R8_UINT           // 1D 8-bit unsigned integer scalar
DXGI_FORMAT_R16G16_SINT       // 2D 16-bit signed integer vector
DXGI_FORMAT_R32G32B32_UINT    // 3D 32-bit unsigned integer vector
DXGI_FORMAT_R8G8B8A8_SINT     // 4D 8-bit signed integer vector
DXGI_FORMAT_R8G8B8A8_UINT     // 4D 8-bit unsigned integer vector
```

4. `InputSlot`: Specifies the input slot index this element will come from. Direct3D supports sixteen input slots (indexed from 0-15) through which you can feed vertex data. For now, we will only be using input slot 0 (i.e., all vertex elements come from the same input slot); Exercise 2 asks you to experiment with multiple input slots.

5. `AlignedByteOffset`: The offset, in bytes, from the start of the C++ vertex structure of the specified input slot to the start of the vertex component. For example, in the following vertex structure, the element `Pos` has a 0-byte offset since its start coincides with the start of the vertex structure; the element `Normal` has a 12-byte offset because we have to skip over the bytes of `Pos` to get to the start of `Normal`; the element `Tex0` has a 24-byte offset because we need to skip over the bytes of `Pos` and `Normal` to get to the start of `Tex0`; the element `Tex1` has a 32-byte offset because we need to skip over the bytes of `Pos`, `Normal`, and `Tex0` to get to the start of `Tex1`.

```
struct Vertex2
{
  XMFLOAT3 Pos;    // 0-byte offset
  XMFLOAT3 Normal; // 12-byte offset
  XMFLOAT2 Tex0;   // 24-byte offset
  XMFLOAT2 Tex1;   // 32-byte offset
};
```

6. `InputSlotClass`: Specify `D3D12_INPUT_PER_VERTEX_DATA` for now; the other option is used for the advanced technique of instancing.

7. `InstanceDataStepRate`: Specify 0 for now; other values are only used for the advanced technique of instancing.

For the previous two example vertex structures, `Vertex1` and `Vertex2`, the corresponding input layout descriptions would be:

```
D3D12_INPUT_ELEMENT_DESC desc1[] =
{
  {"POSITION", 0, DXGI_FORMAT_R32G32B32_FLOAT, 0, 0,
    D3D12_INPUT_PER_VERTEX_DATA, 0},
  {"COLOR", 0, DXGI_FORMAT_R32G32B32A32_FLOAT, 0, 12,
    D3D12_INPUT_PER_VERTEX_DATA, 0}
};

D3D12_INPUT_ELEMENT_DESC desc2[] =
{
  {"POSITION", 0, DXGI_FORMAT_R32G32B32_FLOAT, 0, 0,
    D3D12_INPUT_PER_VERTEX_DATA, 0},
  {"NORMAL", 0, DXGI_FORMAT_R32G32B32_FLOAT, 0, 12,
    D3D12_INPUT_PER_VERTEX_DATA, 0},
  {"TEXCOORD", 0, DXGI_FORMAT_R32G32_FLOAT, 0, 24,
    D3D12_INPUT_PER_VERTEX_DATA, 0},
  {"TEXCOORD", 1, DXGI_FORMAT_R32G32_FLOAT, 0, 32,
    D3D12_INPUT_PER_VERTEX_DATA, 0}
};
```

6.2 VERTEX BUFFERS

In order for the GPU to access an array of vertices, they need to be placed in a GPU resource (ID3D12Resource) called a *buffer*. We call a buffer that stores vertices a *vertex buffer*. Buffers are simpler resources than textures; they are not multidimensional, and do not have mipmaps, filters, or multisampling support. We will use buffers whenever we need to provide the GPU with an array of data elements such as vertices.

As we did in §4.3.8, we create an ID3D12Resource object by filling out a D3D12_RESOURCE_DESC structure describing the buffer resource, and then calling the ID3D12Device::CreateCommittedResource method. See §4.3.8 for a description of all the members of the D3D12_RESOURCE_DESC structure. Direct3D 12 provides a C++ wrapper class CD3DX12_RESOURCE_DESC, which derives from D3D12_RESOURCE_DESC and provides convenience constructors and methods. In particular, it provides the following method that simplifies the construction of a D3D12_RESOURCE_DESC describing a buffer:

```
static inline CD3DX12_RESOURCE_DESC Buffer(
    UINT64 width,
    D3D12_RESOURCE_FLAGS flags = D3D12_RESOURCE_FLAG_NONE,
    UINT64 alignment = 0 )
{
    return CD3DX12_RESOURCE_DESC( D3D12_RESOURCE_DIMENSION_BUFFER,
        alignment, width, 1, 1, 1,
        DXGI_FORMAT_UNKNOWN, 1, 0,
        D3D12_TEXTURE_LAYOUT_ROW_MAJOR, flags );
}
```

For a buffer, the *width* refers to the number of bytes in the buffer. For example, if the buffer stored 64 `float`s, then the width would be `64*sizeof(float)`.

The CD3DX12_RESOURCE_DESC *class also provides convenience methods for constructing a* D3D12_RESOURCE_DESC *that describes texture resources and querying information about the resource:*

1. CD3DX12_RESOURCE_DESC::Tex1D
2. CD3DX12_RESOURCE_DESC::Tex2D
3. CD3DX12_RESOURCE_DESC::Tex3D

Recall from Chapter 4 that the depth/stencil buffer, which was a 2D texture was also represented by an ID3D12Resource *object. All resources in Direct3D 12 are represented by the* ID3D12Resource *interface. This is in contrast to Direct3D 11 which had different interfaces for various resources like* ID3D11Buffer *and* ID3D11Texture2D. *The type of resource is specified by the* D3D12_RESOURCE_

`DESC::D3D12_RESOURCE_DIMENSION` *field. For example, buffers have dimension* `D3D12_RESOURCE_DIMENSION_BUFFER` *and 2D textures have dimension* `D3D12_RESOURCE_DIMENSION_TEXTURE2D`.

For static geometry (i.e., geometry that does not change on a per-frame basis), we put vertex buffers in the default heap (`D3D12_HEAP_TYPE_DEFAULT`) for optimal performance. Generally, most geometry in a game will be like this (e.g., trees, buildings, terrain, characters). After the vertex buffer has been initialized, only the GPU needs to read from the vertex buffer to draw the geometry, so the default heap makes sense. However, if the CPU cannot write to the vertex buffer in the default heap, how do we initialize the vertex buffer?

In addition to creating the actual vertex buffer resource, we need to create an intermediate *upload* buffer resource with heap type `D3D12_HEAP_TYPE_UPLOAD`. Recall from §4.3.8 that we commit a resource to the upload heap when we need to copy data from CPU to GPU memory. After we create the upload buffer, we copy our vertex data from system memory to the upload buffer, and then we copy the vertex data from the upload buffer to the actual vertex buffer.

Because an intermediate upload buffer is required to initialize the data of a default buffer (buffer with heap type `D3D12_HEAP_TYPE_DEFAULT`), we build the following utility function in *d3dUtil.h/.cpp* to avoid repeating this work every time we need a default buffer:

```
Microsoft::WRL::ComPtr<ID3D12Resource> d3dUtil::CreateDefaultBuffer(
  ID3D12Device* device,
  ID3D12GraphicsCommandList* cmdList,
  const void* initData,
  UINT64 byteSize,
  Microsoft::WRL::ComPtr<ID3D12Resource>& uploadBuffer)
{
  ComPtr<ID3D12Resource> defaultBuffer;

  // Create the actual default buffer resource.
  ThrowIfFailed(device->CreateCommittedResource(
    &CD3DX12_HEAP_PROPERTIES(D3D12_HEAP_TYPE_DEFAULT),
    D3D12_HEAP_FLAG_NONE,
    &CD3DX12_RESOURCE_DESC::Buffer(byteSize),
    D3D12_RESOURCE_STATE_COMMON,
    nullptr,
    IID_PPV_ARGS(defaultBuffer.GetAddressOf())));

  // In order to copy CPU memory data into our default buffer, we need
  // to create an intermediate upload heap.
  ThrowIfFailed(device->CreateCommittedResource(
    &CD3DX12_HEAP_PROPERTIES(D3D12_HEAP_TYPE_UPLOAD),
    D3D12_HEAP_FLAG_NONE,
    &CD3DX12_RESOURCE_DESC::Buffer(byteSize),
    D3D12_RESOURCE_STATE_GENERIC_READ,
```

```
        nullptr,
        IID_PPV_ARGS(uploadBuffer.GetAddressOf())));


    // Describe the data we want to copy into the default buffer.
    D3D12_SUBRESOURCE_DATA subResourceData = {};
    subResourceData.pData = initData;
    subResourceData.RowPitch = byteSize;
    subResourceData.SlicePitch = subResourceData.RowPitch;

    // Schedule to copy the data to the default buffer resource.
    // At a high level, the helper function UpdateSubresources
    // will copy the CPU memory into the intermediate upload heap.
    // Then, using ID3D12CommandList::CopySubresourceRegion,
    // the intermediate upload heap data will be copied to mBuffer.
    cmdList->ResourceBarrier(1,
        &CD3DX12_RESOURCE_BARRIER::Transition(defaultBuffer.Get(),
        D3D12_RESOURCE_STATE_COMMON,
        D3D12_RESOURCE_STATE_COPY_DEST));
    UpdateSubresources<1>(cmdList,
        defaultBuffer.Get(), uploadBuffer.Get(),
        0, 0, 1, &subResourceData);
    cmdList->ResourceBarrier(1,
        &CD3DX12_RESOURCE_BARRIER::Transition(defaultBuffer.Get(),
        D3D12_RESOURCE_STATE_COPY_DEST,
        D3D12_RESOURCE_STATE_GENERIC_READ));

    // Note: uploadBuffer has to be kept alive after the above function
    // calls because the command list has not been executed yet that
    // performs the actual copy.
    // The caller can Release the uploadBuffer after it knows the copy
    // has been executed.
    return defaultBuffer;
}
```

The D3D12_SUBRESOURCE_DATA structure is defined as follows:

```
typedef struct D3D12_SUBRESOURCE_DATA
{
  const void *pData;
  LONG_PTR RowPitch;
  LONG_PTR SlicePitch;
} D3D12_SUBRESOURCE_DATA;
```

1. pData: A pointer to a system memory array which contains the data to initialize the buffer with. If the buffer can store *n* vertices, then the system array must contain at least *n* vertices so that the entire buffer can be initialized.
2. RowPitch: For buffers, the size of the data we are copying in bytes.
3. SlicePitch: For buffers, the size of the data we are copying in bytes.

The following code shows how this class would be used to create a default buffer that stored the 8 vertices of a cube, where each vertex had a different color associated with it:

```
Vertex vertices[] =
{
  { XMFLOAT3(-1.0f, -1.0f, -1.0f), XMFLOAT4(Colors::White) },
  { XMFLOAT3(-1.0f, +1.0f, -1.0f), XMFLOAT4(Colors::Black) },
  { XMFLOAT3(+1.0f, +1.0f, -1.0f), XMFLOAT4(Colors::Red) },
  { XMFLOAT3(+1.0f, -1.0f, -1.0f), XMFLOAT4(Colors::Green) },
  { XMFLOAT3(-1.0f, -1.0f, +1.0f), XMFLOAT4(Colors::Blue) },
  { XMFLOAT3(-1.0f, +1.0f, +1.0f), XMFLOAT4(Colors::Yellow) },
  { XMFLOAT3(+1.0f, +1.0f, +1.0f), XMFLOAT4(Colors::Cyan) },
  { XMFLOAT3(+1.0f, -1.0f, +1.0f), XMFLOAT4(Colors::Magenta) }
};

const UINT64 vbByteSize = 8 * sizeof(Vertex);

ComPtr<ID3D12Resource> VertexBufferGPU = nullptr;
ComPtr<ID3D12Resource> VertexBufferUploader = nullptr;
VertexBufferGPU = d3dUtil::CreateDefaultBuffer(md3dDevice.Get(),
  mCommandList.Get(), vertices, vbByteSize, VertexBufferUploader);
```

where the `Vertex` type and colors are defined as follows:

```
struct Vertex
{
  XMFLOAT3 Pos;
  XMFLOAT4 Color;
};
```

In order to bind a vertex buffer to the pipeline, we need to create a vertex buffer view to the vertex buffer resource. Unlike an RTV (render target view), we do not need a descriptor heap for a vertex buffer view. A vertex buffer view is represented by the `D3D12_VERTEX_BUFFER_VIEW_DESC` structure:

```
typedef struct D3D12_VERTEX_BUFFER_VIEW
{
  D3D12_GPU_VIRTUAL_ADDRESS BufferLocation;
  UINT SizeInBytes;
  UINT StrideInBytes;
} D3D12_VERTEX_BUFFER_VIEW;
```

1. `BufferLocation`: The virtual address of the vertex buffer resource we want to create a view to. We can use the `ID3D12Resource::GetGPUVirtualAddress` method to get this.
2. `SizeInBytes`: The number of bytes to view in the vertex buffer starting from `BufferLocation`.
3. `StrideInBytes`: The size of each vertex element, in bytes.

After a vertex buffer has been created and we have created a view to it, we can bind it to an input slot of the pipeline to feed the vertices to the input assembler stage of the pipeline. This can be done with the following method:

```
void ID3D12GraphicsCommandList::IASetVertexBuffers(
  UINT StartSlot,
  UINT NumBuffers,
  const D3D12_VERTEX_BUFFER_VIEW *pViews);
```

1. `StartSlot`: The input slot to start binding vertex buffers to. There are 16 input slots indexed from 0-15.
2. `NumBuffers`: The number of vertex buffers we are binding to the input slots. If the start slot has index k and we are binding n buffers, then we are binding buffers to input slots $I_k, I_{k+1},\ldots,I_{k+n-1}$.
3. `pViews`: Pointer to the first element of an array of vertex buffers views.

Below is an example call:

```
D3D12_VERTEX_BUFFER_VIEW vbv;
vbv.BufferLocation = VertexBufferGPU->GetGPUVirtualAddress();
vbv.StrideInBytes = sizeof(Vertex);
vbv.SizeInBytes = 8 * sizeof(Vertex);

D3D12_VERTEX_BUFFER_VIEW vertexBuffers[1] = { vbv };
mCommandList->IASetVertexBuffers(0, 1, vertexBuffers);
```

The `IASetVertexBuffers` method may seem a little complicated because it supports setting an array of vertex buffers to various input slots. However, we will only use one input slot. An end-of-chapter exercise gives you some experience working with two input slots.

A vertex buffer will stay bound to an input slot until you change it. So you may structure your code like this, if you are using more than one vertex buffer:

```
ID3D12Resource* mVB1; // stores vertices of type Vertex1
ID3D12Resource* mVB2; // stores vertices of type Vertex2

D3D12_VERTEX_BUFFER_VIEW_DESC mVBView1; // view to mVB1
D3D12_VERTEX_BUFFER_VIEW_DESC mVBView2; // view to mVB2

/*...Create the vertex buffers and views...*/

mCommandList->IASetVertexBuffers(0, 1, &VBView1);
/* ...draw objects using vertex buffer 1... */

mCommandList->IASetVertexBuffers(0, 1, &mVBView2);
/* ...draw objects using vertex buffer 2... */
```

Setting a vertex buffer to an input slot does not draw them; it only makes the vertices ready to be fed into the pipeline. The final step to actually draw the vertices is done with the `ID3D12GraphicsCommandList::DrawInstanced` method:

```
void ID3D12CommandList::DrawInstanced(
  UINT VertexCountPerInstance,
  UINT InstanceCount,
  UINT StartVertexLocation,
  UINT StartInstanceLocation);
```

1. `VertexCountPerInstance`: The number of vertices to draw (per instance).
2. `InstanceCount`: Used for an advanced technique called instancing; for now, set this to 1 as we only draw one instance.
3. `StartVertexLocation`: specifies the index (zero-based) of the first vertex in the vertex buffer to begin drawing.
4. `StartInstanceLocation`: Used for an advanced technique called instancing; for now, set this to 0.

The two parameters `VertexCountPerInstance` and `StartVertexLocation` define a contiguous subset of vertices in the vertex buffer to draw; see Figure 6.2.

Figure 6.2. `StartVertexLocation` specifies the index (zero-based) of the first vertex in the vertex buffer to begin drawing. `VertexCountPerInstance` specifies the number of vertices to draw.

The `DrawInstanced` method does not specify what kind of primitive the vertices define. Should they be drawn as points, line lists, or triangle lists? Recall from §5.5.2 that the primitive topology state is set with the `ID3D12GraphicsCommandList::IASetPrimitiveTopology` method. Here is an example call:

```
cmdList->IASetPrimitiveTopology(D3D_PRIMITIVE_TOPOLOGY_TRIANGLELIST);
```

6.3 INDICES AND INDEX BUFFERS

Similar to vertices, in order for the GPU to access an array of indices, they need to be placed in a buffer GPU resource (`ID3D12Resource`). We call a buffer that stores indices an *index buffer*. Because our `d3dUtil::CreateDefaultBuffer` function works with generic data via a `void*`, we can use this same function to create an index buffer (or any default buffer).

In order to bind an index buffer to the pipeline, we need to create an index buffer view to the index buffer resource. As with vertex buffer views, we do not need a descriptor heap for an index buffer view. An index buffer view is represented by the `D3D12_INDEX_BUFFER_VIEW` structure:

```
typedef struct D3D12_INDEX_BUFFER_VIEW
{
  D3D12_GPU_VIRTUAL_ADDRESS BufferLocation;
  UINT SizeInBytes;
  DXGI_FORMAT Format;
} D3D12_INDEX_BUFFER_VIEW;
```

1. `BufferLocation`: The virtual address of the vertex buffer resource we want to create a view to. We can use the `ID3D12Resource::GetGPUVirtualAddress` method to get this.
2. `SizeInBytes`: The number of bytes to view in the index buffer starting from `BufferLocation`.
3. `Format`: The format of the indices which must be either `DXGI_FORMAT_R16_UINT` for 16-bit indices or `DXGI_FORMAT_R32_UINT` for 32-bit indices. You should use 16-bit indices to reduce memory and bandwidth, and only use 32-bit indices if you have index values that need the extra 32-bit range.

As with vertex buffers, and other Direct3D resource for that matter, before we can use it, we need to bind it to the pipeline. An index buffer is bound to the input assembler stage with the `ID3D12CommandList::SetIndexBuffer` method. The following code shows how to create an index buffer defining the triangles of a cube, create a view to it, and bind it to the pipeline:

```
std::uint16_t indices[] = {
  // front face
  0, 1, 2,
  0, 2, 3,

  // back face
  4, 6, 5,
  4, 7, 6,

  // left face
  4, 5, 1,
  4, 1, 0,

  // right face
  3, 2, 6,
  3, 6, 7,

  // top face
  1, 5, 6,
  1, 6, 2,
```

```cpp
    // bottom face
    4, 0, 3,
    4, 3, 7
};

const UINT ibByteSize = 36 * sizeof(std::uint16_t);

ComPtr<ID3D12Resource> IndexBufferGPU = nullptr;
ComPtr<ID3D12Resource> IndexBufferUploader = nullptr;
IndexBufferGPU = d3dUtil::CreateDefaultBuffer(md3dDevice.Get(),
   mCommandList.Get(), indices), ibByteSize, IndexBufferUploader);

D3D12_INDEX_BUFFER_VIEW ibv;
ibv.BufferLocation = IndexBufferGPU->GetGPUVirtualAddress();
ibv.Format = DXGI_FORMAT_R16_UINT;
ibv.SizeInBytes = ibByteSize;

mCommandList->IASetIndexBuffer(&ibv);
```

Finally, when using indices, we must use the `ID3D12GraphicsCommandList::DrawIndexedInstanced` method instead of `DrawInstanced`:

```cpp
void ID3D12GraphicsCommandList::DrawIndexedInstanced(
   UINT IndexCountPerInstance,
   UINT InstanceCount,
   UINT StartIndexLocation,
   INT BaseVertexLocation,
   UINT StartInstanceLocation);
```

1. `IndexCountPerInstance`: The number of indices to draw (per instance).
2. `InstanceCount`: Used for an advanced technique called instancing; for now, set this to 1 as we only draw one instance.
3. `StartIndexLocation`: Index to an element in the index buffer that marks the starting point from which to begin reading indices.
4. `BaseVertexLocation`: An integer value to be added to the indices used in this draw call before the vertices are fetched.
5. `StartInstanceLocation`: Used for an advanced technique called instancing; for now, set this to 0.

To illustrate these parameters, consider the following situation. Suppose we have three objects: a sphere, box, and cylinder. At first, each object has its own vertex buffer and its own index buffer. The indices in each local index buffer are relative to the corresponding local vertex buffer. Now suppose that we concatenate the vertices and indices of the sphere, box, and cylinder into one global vertex and index buffer, as shown in Figure 6.3. (One might concatenate vertex and index buffers because there is some API overhead when changing the vertex and index buffers. Most likely this will not be a bottleneck, but if you have many small vertex and index buffers that could be easily merged, it may be worth doing so for

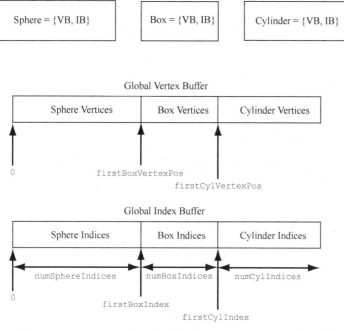

Figure 6.3. Concatenating several vertex buffers into one large vertex buffer, and concatenating several index buffers into one large index buffer.

performance reasons.) After this concatenation, the indices are no longer correct, as they store index locations relative to their corresponding local vertex buffers, not the global one; thus the indices need to be recomputed to index correctly into the global vertex buffer. The original box indices were computed with the assumption that the box's vertices ran through the indices

```
0, 1, ..., numBoxVertices-1
```

But after the merger, they run from

```
firstBoxVertexPos,
firstBoxVertexPos+1,
...,
firstBoxVertexPos+numBoxVertices-1
```

Therefore, to update the indices, we need to add `firstBoxVertexPos` to every box index. Likewise, we need to add `firstCylVertexPos` to every cylinder index. Note that the sphere's indices do not need to be changed (since the first sphere vertex position is zero). Let us call the position of an object's first vertex relative to the global vertex buffer its *base vertex location*. In general, the new indices of an object are computed by adding its base vertex location to each index. Instead of having to compute the new indices ourselves, we can let Direct3D do it by passing the base vertex location to the fourth parameter of `DrawIndexedInstanced`.

We can then draw the sphere, box, and cylinder one-by-one with the following three calls:

```
mCmdList->DrawIndexedInstanced(
    numSphereIndices, 1, 0, 0, 0);
mCmdList->DrawIndexedInstanced(
    numBoxIndices, 1, firstBoxIndex, firstBoxVertexPos, 0);
mCmdList->DrawIndexedInstanced(
    numCylIndices, 1, firstCylIndex, firstCylVertexPos, 0);
```

The "Shapes" demo project in the next chapter uses this technique.

6.4 EXAMPLE VERTEX SHADER

Below in an implementation of the simple vertex shader (recall §5.6):

```
cbuffer cbPerObject : register(b0)
{
    float4x4 gWorldViewProj;
};

void VS(float3 iPosL : POSITION,
        float4 iColor : COLOR,
        out float4 oPosH : SV_POSITION,
        out float4 oColor : COLOR)
{
    // Transform to homogeneous clip space.
    oPosH = mul(float4(iPosL, 1.0f), gWorldViewProj);

    // Just pass vertex color into the pixel shader.
    oColor = iColor;
}
```

Shaders are written in a language called the *high level shading language* (HLSL), which has similar syntax to C++, so it is easy to learn. Appendix B provides a concise reference to the HLSL. Our approach to teaching the HLSL and programming shaders will be example based. That is, as we progress through the book, we will introduce any new HLSL concepts we need in order to implement the demo at hand. Shaders are usually written in text-based files with a .hlsl extension.

The vertex shader is the function called vs. Note that you can give the vertex shader any valid function name. This vertex shader has four parameters; the first two are *input* parameters, and the last two are output parameters (indicated by the out keyword). The HLSL does not have references or pointers, so to return multiple values from a function, you need to either use structures or out parameters. In HLSL, functions are always inlined.

```
struct Vertex
{
    XMFLOAT3 Pos;
    XMFLOAT4 Color;
};

D3D11_INPUT_ELEMENT_DESC vertexDesc[] =
{
    {"POSITION", 0, DXGI_FORMAT_R32G32B32_FLOAT, 0, 0,
        D3D11_INPUT_PER_VERTEX_DATA, 0},
    {"COLOR",    0, DXGI_FORMAT_R32G32B32A32_FLOAT, 0, 12,
        D3D11_INPUT_PER_VERTEX_DATA, 0}
};

void VS(float3 iPosL : POSITION,
        float4 iColor : COLOR,
        out float4 oPosH : SV_POSITION,
        out float4 oColor : COLOR)
{
    // Transform to homogeneous clip space.
    oPosH = mul(float4(iPosL, 1.0f), gWorldViewProj);

    // Just pass vertex color into the pixel shader.
    oColor = iColor;
}
```

Figure 6.4. Each vertex element has an associated semantic specified by the D3D12_INPUT_ELEMENT_DESC array. Each parameter of the vertex shader also has an attached semantic. The semantics are used to match vertex elements with vertex shader parameters.

The first two input parameters form the *input signature* of the vertex shader and correspond to data members in our custom vertex structure we are using for the draw. The parameter semantics ":POSITION" and ":COLOR" are used for mapping the elements in the vertex structure to the vertex shader input parameters, as Figure 6.4 shows.

The output parameters also have attached semantics (":SV_POSITION" and ":COLOR"). These are used to map vertex shader outputs to the corresponding inputs of the next stage (either the geometry shader or pixel shader). Note that the SV_POSITION semantic is special (SV stands for *system value*). It is used to denote the vertex shader output element that holds the vertex position in homogeneous clip space. We must attach the SV_POSITION semantic to the position output because the GPU needs to be aware of this value because it is involved in operations the other attributes are not involved in, such as clipping, depth testing and rasterization. The semantic name for output parameters that are not system values can be any valid semantic name.

The first line transforms the vertex position from local space to homogeneous clip space by multiplying by the 4 × 4 matrix gWorldViewProj:

```
// Transform to homogeneous clip space.
oPosH = mul(float4(iPosL, 1.0f), gWorldViewProj);
```

The constructor syntax `float4(iPosL, 1.0f)` constructs a 4D vector and is equivalent to `float4(iPosL.x, iPosL.y, iPosL.z, 1.0f)`; because we know the position of vertices are points and not vectors, we place a 1 in the fourth component ($w = 1$). The `float2` and `float3` types represent 2D and 3D vectors, respectively. The matrix variable `gWorldViewProj` lives in what is called a constant buffer, which will be discussed in the next section. The built-in function `mul` is used for the vector-matrix multiplication. Incidentally, the `mul` function is overloaded for matrix multiplications of different sizes; for example, you can use it to multiply two 4 × 4 matrices, two 3 × 3 matrices, or a 1 × 3 vector and a 3 × 3 matrix. The last line in the shader body just copies the input color to the output parameter so that the color will be fed into the next stage of the pipeline:

```
oColor = iColor;
```

We can equivalently rewrite the above vertex shader above using structures for the return type and input signature (as opposed to a long parameter list):

```
cbuffer cbPerObject : register(b0)
{
  float4x4 gWorldViewProj;
};

struct VertexIn
{
  float3 PosL  : POSITION;
  float4 Color : COLOR;
};

struct VertexOut
{
  float4 PosH  : SV_POSITION;
  float4 Color : COLOR;
};

VertexOut VS(VertexIn vin)
{
  VertexOut vout;

  // Transform to homogeneous clip space.
  vout.PosH = mul(float4(vin.PosL, 1.0f), gWorldViewProj);

  // Just pass vertex color into the pixel shader.
  vout.Color = vin.Color;

  return vout;
}
```

Drawing in Direct3D

Note: *If there is no geometry shader (geometry shaders are covered in Chapter 12), then the vertex shader must output the vertex position in homogenous clip space with the* `SV_POSITION` *semantic because this is the space the hardware expects the vertices to be in when leaving the vertex shader (if there is no geometry shader). If there is a geometry shader, the job of outputting the homogenous clip space position can be deferred to the geometry shader.*

Note: *A vertex shader (or geometry shader) does not do the perspective divide; it just does the projection matrix part. The perspective divide will be done later by the hardware.*

6.4.1 Input Layout Description and Input Signature Linking

Note from Figure 6.4 that there is a linking between the attributes of the vertices being fed into the pipeline, which is defined by the input layout description. If you feed in vertices that do not supply all the inputs a vertex shader expects, an error will result. For example, the following vertex shader input signature and vertex data are incompatible:

```
//--------------
// C++ app code
//--------------
struct Vertex
{
  XMFLOAT3 Pos;
  XMFLOAT4 Color;
};

D3D12_INPUT_ELEMENT_DESC desc[] =
{
  {"POSITION", 0, DXGI_FORMAT_R32G32B32_FLOAT, 0, 0,
    D3D12_INPUT_PER_VERTEX_DATA, 0},
  {"COLOR", 0, DXGI_FORMAT_R32G32B32A32_FLOAT, 0, 12,
    D3D12_INPUT_PER_VERTEX_DATA, 0}
};

//--------------
// Vertex shader
//--------------
struct VertexIn
{
  float3 PosL   : POSITION;
  float4 Color  : COLOR;
  float3 Normal : NORMAL;
};

struct VertexOut
{
```

```
    float4 PosH  : SV_POSITION;
    float4 Color : COLOR;
};

VertexOut VS(VertexIn vin) { ... }
```

As we will see in §6.9, when we create an `ID3D12PipelineState` object, we must specify both the input layout description and the vertex shader. Direct3D will then validate that the input layout description and vertex shader are compatible.

The vertex data and input signature do not need to match exactly. What is needed is for the vertex data to provide all the data the vertex shader expects. Therefore, it is allowed for the vertex data to provide additional data the vertex shader does not use. That is, the following are compatible:

```
//---------------
// C++ app code
//---------------
struct Vertex
{
  XMFLOAT3 Pos;
  XMFLOAT4 Color;
  XMFLOAT3 Normal;
};

D3D12_INPUT_ELEMENT_DESC desc[] =
{
  {"POSITION", 0, DXGI_FORMAT_R32G32B32_FLOAT, 0, 0,
    D3D12_INPUT_PER_VERTEX_DATA, 0},
  {"COLOR", 0, DXGI_FORMAT_R32G32B32A32_FLOAT, 0, 12,
    D3D12_INPUT_PER_VERTEX_DATA, 0},
  { "NORMAL", 0, DXGI_FORMAT_R32G32B32_FLOAT, 0, 28,
    D3D12_INPUT_PER_VERTEX_DATA, 0 }
};

//---------------
// Vertex shader
//---------------
struct VertexIn
{
  float3 PosL  : POSITION;
  float4 Color : COLOR;
};

struct VertexOut
{
  float4 PosH  : SV_POSITION;
  float4 Color : COLOR;
};

VertexOut VS(VertexIn vin) { ... }
```

Now consider the case where the vertex structure and input signature have matching vertex elements, but the types are different for the color attribute:

```
//--------------
// C++ app code
//--------------
struct Vertex
{
  XMFLOAT3 Pos;
  XMFLOAT4 Color;
};

D3D12_INPUT_ELEMENT_DESC desc[] =
{
  {"POSITION", 0, DXGI_FORMAT_R32G32B32_FLOAT, 0, 0,
    D3D12_INPUT_PER_VERTEX_DATA, 0},
  {"COLOR", 0, DXGI_FORMAT_R32G32B32A32_FLOAT, 0, 12,
    D3D12_INPUT_PER_VERTEX_DATA, 0}
};

//--------------
// Vertex shader
//--------------
struct VertexIn
{
  float3 PosL  : POSITION;
  int4 Color : COLOR;
};

struct VertexOut
{
  float4 PosH : SV_POSITION;
  float4 Color : COLOR;
};

VertexOut VS(VertexIn vin) { ... }
```

This is actually legal because Direct3D allows the bits in the input registers to be reinterpreted. However, the VC++ debug output window gives the following warning:

```
D3D12 WARNING: ID3D11Device::CreateInputLayout: The provided input
signature expects to read an element with SemanticName/Index: 'COLOR'/0
and component(s) of the type 'int32'. However, the matching entry in
the Input Layout declaration, element[1], specifies mismatched format:
'R32G32B32A32_FLOAT'. This is not an error, since behavior is well
defined: The element format determines what data conversion algorithm
gets applied before it shows up in a shader register. Independently,
the shader input signature defines how the shader will interpret the
data that has been placed in its input registers, with no change in the
bits stored. It is valid for the application to reinterpret data as
a different type once it is in the vertex shader, so this warning is
issued just in case reinterpretation was not intended by the author.
```

6.5 EXAMPLE PIXEL SHADER

As discussed in §5.10.3, during rasterization vertex attributes output from the vertex shader (or geometry shader) are interpolated across the pixels of a triangle. The interpolated values are then fed into the pixel shader as input (§5.11). Assuming there is no geometry shader, Figure 6.5 illustrates the path vertex data takes up to now.

A pixel shader is like a vertex shader in that it is a function executed for each pixel fragment. Given the pixel shader input, the job of the pixel shader is to calculate a color value for the pixel fragment. We note that the pixel fragment may not survive and make it onto the back buffer; for example, it might be clipped in the pixel shader (the HLSL includes a `clip` function which can discard a pixel fragment from further processing), occluded by another pixel fragment with a smaller depth value, or the pixel fragment may be discarded by a later pipeline test

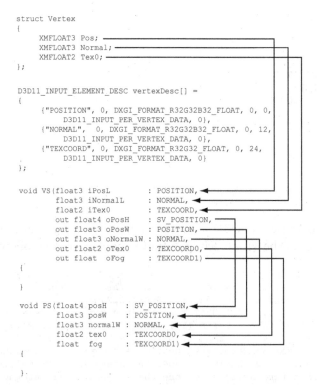

Figure 6.5. Each vertex element has an associated semantic specified by the `D3D12_INPUT_ELEMENT_DESC` array. Each parameter of the vertex shader also has an attached semantic. The semantics are used to match vertex elements with vertex shader parameters. Likewise, each output from the vertex shader has an attached semantic, and each pixel shader input parameter has an attached semantics. These semantics are used to map vertex shader outputs into the pixel shader input parameters.

like the stencil buffer test. Therefore, a pixel on the back buffer may have several pixel fragment candidates; this is the distinction between what is meant by "pixel fragment" and "pixel," although sometimes the terms are used interchangeably, but context usually makes it clear what is meant.

 As a hardware optimization, it is possible that a pixel fragment is rejected by the pipeline before making it to the pixel shader (e.g., early-z rejection). This is where the depth test is done first, and if the pixel fragment is determined to be occluded by the depth test, then the pixel shader is skipped. However, there are some cases that can disable the early-z rejection optimization. For example, if the pixel shader modifies the depth of the pixel, then the pixel shader has to be executed because we do not really know what the depth of the pixel is before the pixel shader if the pixel shader changes it.

Below is a simple pixel shader which corresponds to the vertex shader given in §6.4. For completeness, the vertex shader is shown again.

```
cbuffer cbPerObject : register(b0)
{
    float4x4 gWorldViewProj;
};

void VS(float3 iPos : POSITION, float4 iColor : COLOR,
        out float4 oPosH : SV_POSITION,
        out float4 oColor : COLOR)
{
    // Transform to homogeneous clip space.
    oPosH = mul(float4(iPos, 1.0f), gWorldViewProj);

    // Just pass vertex color into the pixel shader.
    oColor = iColor;
}

float4 PS(float4 posH : SV_POSITION, float4 color : COLOR) : SV_Target
{
    return pin.Color;
}
```

In this example, the pixel shader simply returns the interpolated color value. Notice that the pixel shader input exactly matches the vertex shader output; this is a requirement. The pixel shader returns a 4D color value, and the SV_TARGET semantic following the function parameter listing indicates the return value type should match the render target format.

We can equivalently rewrite the above vertex and pixel shaders using input/output structures. The notation varies in that we attach the semantics to the members of the input/output structures, and that we use a return statement for output instead of output parameters.

```hlsl
cbuffer cbPerObject : register(b0)
{
    float4x4 gWorldViewProj;
};

struct VertexIn
{
  float3 Pos   : POSITION;
  float4 Color : COLOR;
};

struct VertexOut
{
  float4 PosH  : SV_POSITION;
  float4 Color : COLOR;
};

VertexOut VS(VertexIn vin)
{
  VertexOut vout;

  // Transform to homogeneous clip space.
  vout.PosH = mul(float4(vin.Pos, 1.0f), gWorldViewProj);

  // Just pass vertex color into the pixel shader.
  vout.Color = vin.Color;

  return vout;
}

float4 PS(VertexOut pin) : SV_Target
{
  return pin.Color;
}
```

6.6 CONSTANT BUFFERS

6.6.1 Creating Constant Buffers

A constant buffer is an example of a GPU resource (ID3D12Resource) whose data contents can be referenced in shader programs. As we will learn throughout this book, textures and other types of buffer resources can also be referenced in shader programs. The example vertex shader in the §6.4 had the code:

```hlsl
cbuffer cbPerObject : register(b0)
{
   float4x4 gWorldViewProj;
};
```

This code refers to a cbuffer object (constant buffer) called cbPerObject. In this example, the constant buffer stores a single 4 × 4 matrix called gWorldViewProj, representing the combined world, view, and projection matrices used to transform a point from local space to homogeneous clip space. In HLSL, a 4 × 4 matrix is declared by the built-in `float4x4` type; to declare a 3 × 4 matrix and 2 × 4 matrix, for example, you would use the `float3x4` and `float2x2` types, respectively.

Unlike vertex and index buffers, constant buffers are usually updated once per frame by the CPU. For example, if the camera is moving every frame, the constant buffer would need to be updated with the new view matrix every frame. Therefore, we create constant buffers in an upload heap rather than a default heap so that we can update the contents from the CPU.

Constant buffers also have the special hardware requirement that their size must be a multiple of the minimum hardware allocation size (256 bytes).

Often we will need multiple constant buffers of the same type. For example, the above constant buffer `cbPerObject` stores constants that vary per object, so if we have *n* objects, then we will need *n* constant buffers of this type. The following code shows how we create a buffer that stores `NumElements` many constant buffers:

```
struct ObjectConstants
{
   DirectX::XMFLOAT4X4 WorldViewProj = MathHelper::Identity4x4();
};

UINT elementByteSize = d3dUtil::CalcConstantBufferByteSize(sizeof(Objec
   tConstants));

ComPtr<ID3D12Resource> mUploadCBuffer;
device->CreateCommittedResource(
   &CD3DX12_HEAP_PROPERTIES(D3D12_HEAP_TYPE_UPLOAD),
   D3D12_HEAP_FLAG_NONE,
   &CD3DX12_RESOURCE_DESC::Buffer(mElementByteSize * NumElements),
   D3D12_RESOURCE_STATE_GENERIC_READ,
   nullptr,
   IID_PPV_ARGS(&mUploadCBuffer));
```

We can think of the `mUploadCBuffer` as storing an array of constant buffers of type `ObjectConstants` (with padding to make a multiple of 256 bytes). When it comes time to draw an object, we just bind a constant buffer view (CBV) to a subregion of the buffer that stores the constants for that object. Note that we will often call the buffer `mUploadCBuffer` a constant buffer since it stores an array of constant buffers.

The utility function `d3dUtil::CalcConstantBufferByteSize` does the arithmetic to round the byte size of the buffer to be a multiple of the minimum hardware allocation size (256 bytes):

```
UINT d3dUtil::CalcConstantBufferByteSize(UINT byteSize)
{
   // Constant buffers must be a multiple of the minimum hardware
   // allocation size (usually 256 bytes). So round up to nearest
```

```
            // multiple of 256. We do this by adding 255 and then masking off
            // the lower 2 bytes which store all bits < 256.
            // Example: Suppose byteSize = 300.
            // (300 + 255) & ~255
            // 555 & ~255
            // 0x022B & ~0x00ff
            // 0x022B & 0xff00
            // 0x0200
            // 512
            return (byteSize + 255) & ~255;
        }
```

Even though we allocate constant data in multiples of 256, it is not necessary to explicitly pad the corresponding constant data in the HLSL structure because it is done implicitly:

```
// Implicitly padded to 256 bytes.
cbuffer cbPerObject : register(b0)
{
   float4x4 gWorldViewProj;
};

// Explicitly padded to 256 bytes.
cbuffer cbPerObject : register(b0)
{
   float4x4 gWorldViewProj;
   float4x4 Pad0;
   float4x4 Pad1;
   float4x4 Pad1;
};
```

To avoid dealing with rounding constant buffer elements to a multiple of 256 bytes, you could explicitly pad all your constant buffer structures to always be a multiple of 256 bytes.

Direct3D 12 introduced shader model 5.1. Shader model 5.1 has introduced an alternative HLSL syntax for defining a constant buffer which looks like this:

```
struct ObjectConstants
{
   float4x4 gWorldViewProj;
   uint matIndex;
};
ConstantBuffer<ObjectConstants> gObjConstants : register(b0);
```

Here the data elements of the constant buffer are just defined in a separate structure, and then a constant buffer is created from that structure. Fields of the constant buffer are then accessed in the shader using data member syntax:

```
uint index = gObjConstants.matIndex;
```

6.6.2 Updating Constant Buffers

Because a constant buffer is created with the heap type D3D12_HEAP_TYPE_UPLOAD, we can upload data from the CPU to the constant buffer resource. To do this, we first must obtain a pointer to the resource data, which can be done with the Map method:

```
ComPtr<ID3D12Resource> mUploadBuffer;
BYTE* mMappedData = nullptr;
mUploadBuffer->Map(0, nullptr, reinterpret_cast<void**>(&mMappedData));
```

The first parameter is a subresource index identifying the subresource to map. For a buffer, the only subresource is the buffer itself, so we just set this to 0. The second parameter is an optional pointer to a D3D12_RANGE structure that describes the range of memory to map; specifying null maps the entire resource. The second parameter returns a pointer to the mapped data. To copy data from system memory to the constant buffer, we can just do a memcpy:

```
memcpy(mMappedData, &data, dataSizeInBytes);
```

When we are done with a constant buffer, we should Unmap it before releasing the memory:

```
if(mUploadBuffer != nullptr)
  mUploadBuffer->Unmap(0, nullptr);

mMappedData = nullptr;
```

The first parameter to Unmap is a subresource index identifying the subresource to map, which will be 0 for a buffer. The second parameter to Unmap is an optional pointer to a D3D12_RANGE structure that describes the range of memory to unmap; specifying null unmaps the entire resource.

6.6.3 Upload Buffer Helper

It is convenient to build a light wrapper around an upload buffer. We define the following class in *UploadBuffer.h* to make working with upload buffers easier. It handles the construction and destruction of an upload buffer resource for us, handles mapping and unmapping the resource, and provides the CopyData method to update a particular element in the buffer. We use the CopyData method when we need to change the contents of an upload buffer from the CPU (e.g., when the view matrix changes). Note that this class can be used for any upload buffer, not necessarily a constant buffer. If we do use it for a constant buffer, however, we need to indicate so via the isConstantBuffer constructor parameter. If it is storing a constant buffer, then it will automatically pad the memory to make each constant buffer a multiple of 256 bytes.

```cpp
template<typename T>
class UploadBuffer
{
public:
  UploadBuffer(ID3D12Device* device, UINT elementCount, bool
   isConstantBuffer) :
    mIsConstantBuffer(isConstantBuffer)
  {
    mElementByteSize = sizeof(T);

    // Constant buffer elements need to be multiples of 256 bytes.
    // This is because the hardware can only view constant data
    // at m*256 byte offsets and of n*256 byte lengths.
    // typedef struct D3D12_CONSTANT_BUFFER_VIEW_DESC {
    // UINT64 OffsetInBytes; // multiple of 256
    // UINT   SizeInBytes;   // multiple of 256
    // } D3D12_CONSTANT_BUFFER_VIEW_DESC;
    if(isConstantBuffer)
      mElementByteSize = d3dUtil::CalcConstantBufferByteSize(sizeof
    (T));

    ThrowIfFailed(device->CreateCommittedResource(
      &CD3DX12_HEAP_PROPERTIES(D3D12_HEAP_TYPE_UPLOAD),
      D3D12_HEAP_FLAG_NONE,
      &CD3DX12_RESOURCE_DESC::Buffer(mElementByteSize*elementCount),
          D3D12_RESOURCE_STATE_GENERIC_READ,
      nullptr,
      IID_PPV_ARGS(&mUploadBuffer)));

    ThrowIfFailed(mUploadBuffer->Map(0, nullptr, reinterpret_
    cast<void**>(&mMappedData)));

    // We do not need to unmap until we are done with the resource.
    // However, we must not write to the resource while it is in use by
    // the GPU (so we must use synchronization techniques).
  }

  UploadBuffer(const UploadBuffer& rhs) = delete;
  UploadBuffer& operator=(const UploadBuffer& rhs) = delete;
  ~UploadBuffer()
  {
    if(mUploadBuffer != nullptr)
      mUploadBuffer->Unmap(0, nullptr);

    mMappedData = nullptr;
  }

  ID3D12Resource* Resource()const
  {
    return mUploadBuffer.Get();
  }

  void CopyData(int elementIndex, const T& data)
  {
    memcpy(&mMappedData[elementIndex*mElementByteSize], &data,
    sizeof(T));
```

```
    }

private:
  Microsoft::WRL::ComPtr<ID3D12Resource> mUploadBuffer;
  BYTE* mMappedData = nullptr;

  UINT mElementByteSize = 0;
  bool mIsConstantBuffer = false;
};
```

Typically, the world matrix of an object will change when it moves/rotates/scales, the view matrix changes when the camera moves/rotates, and the projection matrix changes when the window is resized. In our demo for this chapter, we allow the user to rotate and move the camera with the mouse, and we update the combined world-view-projection matrix with the new view matrix every frame in the Update function:

```
void BoxApp::OnMouseMove(WPARAM btnState, int x, int y)
{
  if((btnState & MK_LBUTTON) != 0)
  {
    // Make each pixel correspond to a quarter of a degree.
    float dx = XMConvertToRadians(0.25f*static_cast<float>
    (x - mLastMousePos.x));
    float dy = XMConvertToRadians(0.25f*static_cast<float>
    (y - mLastMousePos.y));

    // Update angles based on input to orbit camera around box.
    mTheta += dx;
    mPhi += dy;

    // Restrict the angle mPhi.
    mPhi = MathHelper::Clamp(mPhi, 0.1f, MathHelper::Pi - 0.1f);
  }
  else if((btnState & MK_RBUTTON) != 0)
  {
    // Make each pixel correspond to 0.005 unit in the scene.
    float dx = 0.005f*static_cast<float>(x - mLastMousePos.x);
    float dy = 0.005f*static_cast<float>(y - mLastMousePos.y);

    // Update the camera radius based on input.
    mRadius += dx - dy;

    // Restrict the radius.
    mRadius = MathHelper::Clamp(mRadius, 3.0f, 15.0f);
  }

  mLastMousePos.x = x;
  mLastMousePos.y = y;
}

void BoxApp::Update(const GameTimer& gt)
{
```

```
// Convert Spherical to Cartesian coordinates.
float x = mRadius*sinf(mPhi)*cosf(mTheta);
float z = mRadius*sinf(mPhi)*sinf(mTheta);
float y = mRadius*cosf(mPhi);

// Build the view matrix.
XMVECTOR pos = XMVectorSet(x, y, z, 1.0f);
XMVECTOR target = XMVectorZero();
XMVECTOR up = XMVectorSet(0.0f, 1.0f, 0.0f, 0.0f);

XMMATRIX view = XMMatrixLookAtLH(pos, target, up);
XMStoreFloat4x4(&mView, view);

XMMATRIX world = XMLoadFloat4x4(&mWorld);
XMMATRIX proj = XMLoadFloat4x4(&mProj);
XMMATRIX worldViewProj = world*view*proj;

// Update the constant buffer with the latest worldViewProj matrix.
ObjectConstants objConstants;
XMStoreFloat4x4(&objConstants.WorldViewProj,
    XMMatrixTranspose(worldViewProj));
mObjectCB->CopyData(0, objConstants);
}
```

6.6.4 Constant Buffer Descriptors

Recall from §4.1.6 that we bind a resource to the rendering pipeline through a descriptor object. So far we have used descriptors/views for render targets, depth/stencil buffers, and vertex and index buffers. We also need descriptors to bind constant buffers to the pipeline. Constant buffer descriptors live in a descriptor heap of type D3D12_DESCRIPTOR_HEAP_TYPE_CBV_SRV_UAV. Such a heap can store a mixture of constant buffer, shader resource, and unordered access descriptors. To store these new types of descriptors we will need to create a new descriptor heap of this type:

```
D3D12_DESCRIPTOR_HEAP_DESC cbvHeapDesc;
cbvHeapDesc.NumDescriptors = 1;
cbvHeapDesc.Type = D3D12_DESCRIPTOR_HEAP_TYPE_CBV_SRV_UAV;
cbvHeapDesc.Flags = D3D12_DESCRIPTOR_HEAP_FLAG_SHADER_VISIBLE;
cbvHeapDesc.NodeMask = 0;

ComPtr<ID3D12DescriptorHeap> mCbvHeap
md3dDevice->CreateDescriptorHeap(&cbvHeapDesc,
    IID_PPV_ARGS(&mCbvHeap));
```

This code is similar to how we created the render target and depth/stencil buffer descriptor heaps. However, one important difference is that we specify the D3D12_DESCRIPTOR_HEAP_FLAG_SHADER_VISIBLE flag to indicate that these descriptors will be accessed by shader programs. In the demo for his chapter, we have no SRV or

UAV descriptors, and we are only going to draw one object; therefore, we only need 1 descriptor in this heap to store 1 CBV.

A constant buffer view is created by filling out a D3D12_CONSTANT_BUFFER_VIEW_DESC instance and calling ID3D12Device::CreateConstantBufferView:

```
// Constant data per-object.
struct ObjectConstants
{
  XMFLOAT4X4 WorldViewProj = MathHelper::Identity4x4();
};

// Constant buffer to store the constants of n object.
std::unique_ptr<UploadBuffer<ObjectConstants>> mObjectCB = nullptr;
mObjectCB = std::make_unique<UploadBuffer<ObjectConstants>>(
  md3dDevice.Get(), n, true);

UINT objCBByteSize = d3dUtil::CalcConstantBufferByteSize(sizeof(ObjectC
    onstants));

// Address to start of the buffer (0th constant buffer).
D3D12_GPU_VIRTUAL_ADDRESS cbAddress = mObjectCB->Resource()-
    >GetGPUVirtualAddress();

// Offset to the ith object constant buffer in the buffer.
int boxCBufIndex = i;
cbAddress += boxCBufIndex*objCBByteSize;

D3D12_CONSTANT_BUFFER_VIEW_DESC cbvDesc;
cbvDesc.BufferLocation = cbAddress;
cbvDesc.SizeInBytes = d3dUtil::CalcConstantBufferByteSize(sizeof(Object
    Constants));

md3dDevice->CreateConstantBufferView(
  &cbvDesc,
  mCbvHeap->GetCPUDescriptorHandleForHeapStart());
```

The D3D12_CONSTANT_BUFFER_VIEW_DESC structure describes a subset of the constant buffer resource to bind to the HLSL constant buffer structure. As mentioned, typically a constant buffer stores an array of per-object constants for *n* objects, but we can get a view to the *i*th object constant data by using the BufferLocation and SizeInBytes. The D3D12_CONSTANT_BUFFER_VIEW_DESC::SizeInBytes and D3D12_CONSTANT_BUFFER_VIEW_DESC::OffsetInBytes members must by a multiple of 256 bytes due to hardware requirements. For example, if you specified 64, then you would get the following debug errors:

```
D3D12 ERROR: ID3D12Device::CreateConstantBufferView: SizeInBytes of 64
is invalid. Device requires SizeInBytes be a multiple of 256.

D3D12 ERROR: ID3D12Device:: CreateConstantBufferView: OffsetInBytes of
64 is invalid. Device requires OffsetInBytes be a multiple of 256.
```

6.6.5 Root Signature and Descriptor Tables

Generally, different shader programs will expect different resources to be bound to the rendering pipeline before a draw call is executed. Resources are bound to particular register slots, where they can be accessed by shader programs. For example, the previous vertex and pixel shader expected only a constant buffer to be bound to register b0. A more advanced set of vertex and pixel shaders that we use later in this book expect several constant buffers, textures, and samplers to be bound to various register slots:

```
// Texture resource bound to texture register slot 0.
Texture2D  gDiffuseMap : register(t0);

// Sampler resources bound to sampler register slots 0-5.
SamplerState gsamPointWrap        : register(s0);
SamplerState gsamPointClamp       : register(s1);
SamplerState gsamLinearWrap       : register(s2);
SamplerState gsamLinearClamp      : register(s3);
SamplerState gsamAnisotropicWrap  : register(s4);
SamplerState gsamAnisotropicClamp : register(s5);

// cbuffer resource bound to cbuffer register slots 0-2
cbuffer cbPerObject : register(b0)
{
  float4x4 gWorld;
  float4x4 gTexTransform;
};

// Constant data that varies per material.
cbuffer cbPass : register(b1)
{
  float4x4 gView;
  float4x4 gProj;
  [...] // Other fields omitted for brevity.
};

cbuffer cbMaterial : register(b2)
{
  float4  gDiffuseAlbedo;
  float3  gFresnelR0;
  float   gRoughness;
  float4x4 gMatTransform;
};
```

The *root signature* defines what resources the application will bind to the rendering pipeline before a draw call can be executed and where those resources get mapped to shader input registers. The root signature must be compatible with the shaders it will be used with (i.e., the root signature must provide all the resources the shaders expect to be bound to the rendering pipeline before a draw call can be executed); this will be validated when the pipeline state object is created (§6.9).

Different draw calls may use a different set of shader programs, which will require a different root signature.

Note: *If we think of the shader programs as a function, and the input resources the shaders expect as function parameters, then the root signature can be thought of as defining a function signature (hence the name root signature). By binding different resources as arguments, the shader output will be different. So, for example, a vertex shader will depend on the actual vertex being input to the shader, and also the bound resources.*

A root signature is represented in Direct3D by the ID3D12RootSignature interface. It is defined by an array of root parameters that describe the resources the shaders expect for a draw call. A *root parameter* can be a *root constant, root descriptor,* or *descriptor table*. We will discuss root constants and root descriptors in the next chapter; in this chapter, we will just use descriptor tables. A descriptor table specifies a contiguous range of descriptors in a descriptor heap.

The following code below creates a root signature that has one root parameter that is a descriptor table large enough to store one CBV (constant buffer view):

```
// Root parameter can be a table, root descriptor or root constants.
CD3DX12_ROOT_PARAMETER slotRootParameter[1];

// Create a single descriptor table of CBVs.
CD3DX12_DESCRIPTOR_RANGE cbvTable;
cbvTable.Init(
    D3D12_DESCRIPTOR_RANGE_TYPE_CBV,
    1, // Number of descriptors in table
    0);// base shader register arguments are bound to for this root
      parameter

slotRootParameter[0].InitAsDescriptorTable(
    1,    // Number of ranges
    &cbvTable); // Pointer to array of ranges

// A root signature is an array of root parameters.
CD3DX12_ROOT_SIGNATURE_DESC rootSigDesc(1, slotRootParameter, 0,
    nullptr,
    D3D12_ROOT_SIGNATURE_FLAG_ALLOW_INPUT_ASSEMBLER_INPUT_LAYOUT);

// create a root signature with a single slot which points to a
// descriptor range consisting of a single constant buffer.
ComPtr<ID3DBlob> serializedRootSig = nullptr;
ComPtr<ID3DBlob> errorBlob = nullptr;
HRESULT hr = D3D12SerializeRootSignature(&rootSigDesc,
    D3D_ROOT_SIGNATURE_VERSION_1,
    serializedRootSig.GetAddressOf(),
    errorBlob.GetAddressOf());
```

```
ThrowIfFailed(md3dDevice->CreateRootSignature(
    0,
    serializedRootSig->GetBufferPointer(),
    serializedRootSig->GetBufferSize(),
    IID_PPV_ARGS(&mRootSignature)));
```

We will describe `CD3DX12_ROOT_PARAMETER` and `CD3DX12_DESCRIPTOR_RANGE` more in the next chapter, but for now just understand that the code

```
CD3DX12_ROOT_PARAMETER slotRootParameter[1];

CD3DX12_DESCRIPTOR_RANGE cbvTable;
cbvTable.Init(
    D3D12_DESCRIPTOR_RANGE_TYPE_CBV, // table type
    1, // Number of descriptors in table
    0);// base shader register arguments are bound to for this root
       parameter

slotRootParameter[0].InitAsDescriptorTable(
    1,    // Number of ranges
    &cbvTable); // Pointer to array of ranges
```

creates a root parameter that expects a descriptor table of 1 CBV that gets bound to constant buffer register 0 (i.e., `register(b0)` in the HLSL code).

Our root signature example in this chapter is very simple. We will see lots of examples of root signatures throughout this book, and they will grow in complexity as needed.

The root signature only defines what resources the application will bind to the rendering pipeline; it does not actually do any resource binding. Once a root signature has been set with a command list, we use the `ID3D12GraphicsCommandList::SetGraphicsRootDescriptorTable` to bind a descriptor table to the pipeline:

```
void ID3D12GraphicsCommandList::SetGraphicsRootDescriptorTable(
    UINT RootParameterIndex,
    D3D12_GPU_DESCRIPTOR_HANDLE BaseDescriptor);
```

1. `RootParameterIndex`: Index of the root parameter we are setting.
2. `BaseDescriptor`: Handle to a descriptor in the heap that specifies the first descriptor in the table being set. For example, if the root signature specified that this table had five descriptors, then `BaseDescriptor` and the next four descriptors in the heap are being set to this root table.

The following code sets the root signature and CBV heap to the command list, and sets the descriptor table identifying the resource we want to bind to the pipeline:

```
mCommandList->SetGraphicsRootSignature(mRootSignature.Get());
ID3D12DescriptorHeap* descriptorHeaps[] = { mCbvHeap.Get() };
```

```
mCommandList->SetDescriptorHeaps(_countof(descriptorHeaps),
    descriptorHeaps);

// Offset the CBV we want to use for this draw call.
CD3DX12_GPU_DESCRIPTOR_HANDLE cbv(mCbvHeap
    ->GetGPUDescriptorHandleForHeapStart());
cbv.Offset(cbvIndex, mCbvSrvUavDescriptorSize);

mCommandList->SetGraphicsRootDescriptorTable(0, cbv);
```

 For performance, make the root signature as small as possible, and try to minimize the number of times you change the root signature per rendering frame.

 The contents of the Root Signature (the descriptor tables, root constants and root descriptors) that the application has bound automatically get versioned by the D3D12 driver whenever any part of the contents change between draw/dispatch calls. So each draw/dispatch gets a unique full set of Root Signature state.

 If you change the root signature then you lose all the existing bindings. That is, you need to rebind all the resources to the pipeline the new root signature expects.

6.7 COMPILING SHADERS

In Direct3D, shader programs must first be compiled to a portable bytecode. The graphics driver will then take this bytecode and compile it again into optimal native instructions for the system's GPU [ATI1]. At runtime, we can compile a shader with the following function:

```
HRESULT D3DCompileFromFile(
  LPCWSTR pFileName,
  const D3D_SHADER_MACRO *pDefines,
  ID3DInclude *pInclude,
  LPCSTR pEntrypoint,
  LPCSTR pTarget,
  UINT Flags1,
  UINT Flags2,
  ID3DBlob **ppCode,
  ID3DBlob **ppErrorMsgs);
```

1. `pFileName`: The name of the .hlsl file that contains the HLSL source code we want to compile.

2. `pDefines`: Advanced option we do not use; see the SDK documentation. We always specify null in this book.

3. `pInclude`: Advanced option we do not use; see the SDK documentation. We always specify null in this book.
4. `pEntrypoint`: The function name of the shader's entry point. A .hlsl can contain multiple shaders programs (e.g., one vertex shader and one pixel shader), so we need to specify the entry point of the particular shader we want to compile.
5. `pTarget`: A string specifying the shader program type and version we are using. In this book, we target versions 5.0 and 5.1.
   a) `vs_5_0` and `vs_5_1`: Vertex shader 5.0 and 5.1, respectively.
   b) `hs_5_0` and `hs_5_1`: Hull shader 5.0 and 5.1, respectively.
   c) `ds_5_0` and `ds_5_1`: Domain shader 5.0 and 5.1, respectively.
   d) `gs_5_0` and `gs_5_1`: Geometry shader 5.0 and 5.1, respectively.
   e) `ps_5_0` and `ps_5_1`: Pixel shader 5.0 and 5.1, respectively.
   f) `cs_5_0` and `cs_5_1`: Compute shader 5.0 and 5.1, respectively.
6. `Flags1`: Flags to specify how the shader code should be compiled. There are quite a few of these flags listed in the SDK documentation, but the only two we use in this book are:
   a) `D3DCOMPILE_DEBUG`: Compiles the shaders in debug mode.
   b) `D3DCOMPILE_SKIP_OPTIMIZATION`: Instructs the compiler to skip optimizations (useful for debugging).
7. `Flags2`: Advanced effect compilation options we do not use; see the SDK documentation.
8. `ppCode`: Returns a pointer to a `ID3DBlob` data structure that stores the compiled shader object bytecode.
9. `ppErrorMsgs`: Returns a pointer to a `ID3DBlob` data structure that stores a string containing the compilation errors, if any.

The type `ID3DBlob` is just a generic chunk of memory that has two methods:
   a) `LPVOID GetBufferPointer`: Returns a void* to the data, so it must be casted to the appropriate type before use (see the example below).
   b) `SIZE_T GetBufferSize`: Returns the byte size of the buffer.

To support error output, we implement the following helper function to compile shaders at runtime in *d3dUtil.h/.cpp*:

```
ComPtr<ID3DBlob> d3dUtil::CompileShader(
    const std::wstring& filename,
    const D3D_SHADER_MACRO* defines,
    const std::string& entrypoint,
    const std::string& target)
{
    // Use debug flags in debug mode.
```

```
    UINT compileFlags = 0;
#if defined(DEBUG) || defined(_DEBUG)
    compileFlags = D3DCOMPILE_DEBUG | D3DCOMPILE_SKIP_OPTIMIZATION;
#endif

    HRESULT hr = S_OK;

    ComPtr<ID3DBlob> byteCode = nullptr;
    ComPtr<ID3DBlob> errors;
    hr = D3DCompileFromFile(filename.c_str(), defines, D3D_COMPILE_
       STANDARD_FILE_INCLUDE,
        entrypoint.c_str(), target.c_str(), compileFlags, 0, &byteCode,
       &errors);

    // Output errors to debug window.
    if(errors != nullptr)
        OutputDebugStringA((char*)errors->GetBufferPointer());

    ThrowIfFailed(hr);

    return byteCode;
}
Here is an example of calling this function:
ComPtr<ID3DBlob> mvsByteCode = nullptr;
ComPtr<ID3DBlob> mpsByteCode = nullptr;
mvsByteCode = d3dUtil::CompileShader(L"Shaders\\color.hlsl",
    nullptr, "VS", "vs_5_0");
mpsByteCode = d3dUtil::CompileShader(L"Shaders\\color.hlsl",
    nullptr, "PS", "ps_5_0");
```

HLSL errors and warnings will be returned through the `ppErrorMsgs` parameter. For example, if we misspelled the `mul` function, then we get the following error output to the debug window:

```
Shaders\color.hlsl(29,14-55): error X3004: undeclared identifier 'mu'
```

Compiling a shader does not bind it to the rendering pipeline for use. We will see how to do that in §6.9.

6.7.1 Offline Compilation

Instead of compiling shaders at runtime, we can compile them offline in a separate step (e.g., a build step, or as part of an asset content pipeline process). There are a few reasons to do this:

1. For complicated shaders, compilation can take a long time. Therefore, compiling offline will make your loading times faster.
2. It is convenient to see shader compilation errors earlier in the build process rather than at runtime.
3. Windows 8 Store apps must use offline compilation.

It is the common practice to use the .cso (compiled shader object) extension for compiled shaders.

To compile shaders offline we use the *FXC* tool that comes with DirectX. This is a command line tool. To compile a vertex and pixel shader stored in *color.hlsl* with entry points VS and PS, respectively, with debugging we would write:

```
fxc "color.hlsl" /Od /Zi /T vs_5_0 /E "VS" /Fo "color_vs.cso" /Fc "color_vs.asm"
fxc "color.hlsl" /Od /Zi /T ps_5_0 /E "PS" /Fo "color_ps.cso" /Fc "color_ps.asm"
```

To compile a vertex and pixel shader stored in *color.hlsl* with entry points VS and PS, respectively, for *release* we would write:

```
fxc "color.hlsl" /T vs_5_0 /E "VS" /Fo "color_vs.cso" /Fc "color_vs.asm"
fxc "color.hlsl" /T ps_5_0 /E "PS" /Fo "color_ps.cso" /Fc "color_ps.asm"
```

Parameter	Description
/Od	Disables optimizations (useful for debugging).
/Zi	Enables debug information.
/T \<string\>	Shader type and target version.
/E \<string\>	Shader entry point.
/Fo \<string\>	Compiled shader object bytecode.
/Fc \<string\>	Outputs an assembly file listing (useful for debugging, checking instruction counts, seeing what kind of code is being generated).

If you try to compile a shader with a syntax error, FXC will output the error/warning to the command window. For example, if we misname a variable in the color.hlsl effect file:

```
// Should be gWorldViewProj, not worldViewProj!
vout.PosH = mul(float4(vin.Pos, 1.0f), worldViewProj);
```

Then we get quite a few errors from this one mistake (the top error being the key one to fix) listed in the debut output window:

```
color.hlsl(29,42-54): error X3004: undeclared identifier
   'worldViewProj'
color.hlsl(29,14-55): error X3013: 'mul': no matching 2 parameter
   intrinsic function
color.hlsl(29,14-55): error X3013: Possible intrinsic functions are:
color.hlsl(29,14-55): error X3013:    mul(float|half...
```

Getting the error messages at compile time is much more convenient than runtime.

We have shown how to compile our vertex and pixel shaders offline to .cso files. Therefore, we no longer need to do it at runtime (i.e., we do not need to call D3DCompileFromFile). However, we still need to load the compiled shader object bytecode from the .cso files into our app. This can be done using standard C++ file input mechanisms like so:

```cpp
ComPtr<ID3DBlob> d3dUtil::LoadBinary(const std::wstring& filename)
{
  std::ifstream fin(filename, std::ios::binary);

  fin.seekg(0, std::ios_base::end);
  std::ifstream::pos_type size = (int)fin.tellg();
  fin.seekg(0, std::ios_base::beg);

  ComPtr<ID3DBlob> blob;
  ThrowIfFailed(D3DCreateBlob(size, blob.GetAddressOf()));

  fin.read((char*)blob->GetBufferPointer(), size);
  fin.close();

  return blob;
}
...
ComPtr<ID3DBlob> mvsByteCode = d3dUtil::LoadBinary(L"Shaders\\color_vs.cso");
ComPtr<ID3DBlob> mpsByteCode = d3dUtil::LoadBinary(L"Shaders\\color_ps.cso");
```

6.7.2 Generated Assembly

The /Fc optional parameter to FXC generates the generated portable assembly code. Looking at the assembly of your shaders from time to time is useful to check shader instruction counts, and to see what kind of code is being generated—sometimes it might be different than what you expect. For example, if you have a conditional statement in your HLSL code, then you might expect there to be a branching instruction in the assembly code. In the early days of programmable GPUs, branching in shaders used to be expensive, and so sometimes the compiler will flatten a conditional statement by evaluating both branches and then interpolate between the two to pick the right answer. That is, the following codes will give the same answer:

Conditional	Flattened
`float x = 0;`	`float a = 2*y;`
	`float b = sqrt(y);`
`// s == 1 (true) or s == 0 (false)`	`float x = a + s*(b-a);`
`if( s )`	
`  x = sqrt(y);`	`// s == 1: x = a + b - a = b = sqrt(y)`
`else`	
`  x = 2*y;`	`// s == 0: x = a + 0*(b-a) = a = 2*y`

So the flattened method gives us the same result without any branching, but without looking at the assembly code, we would not know if flattening was happening, or if a true branch instruction was generated. The point being that sometimes you want to look at the assembly to see what is really going on. The following is an example of the assembly generated for the vertex shader in color.hlsl:

```
//
// Generated by Microsoft (R) HLSL Shader Compiler 6.4.9844.0
//
//
// Buffer Definitions:
//
// cbuffer cbPerObject
// {
//
//   float4x4 gWorldViewProj;           // Offset:    0 Size:    64
//
// }
//
//
// Resource Bindings:
//
// Name                                 Type  Format         Dim Slot Elements
// ------------------------------ ---------- ------- ----------- ---- --------
// cbPerObject                       cbuffer      NA          NA    0        1
//
//
//
// Input signature:
//
// Name                 Index   Mask Register SysValue  Format   Used
// -------------------- ----- ------ -------- -------- ------- ------
// POSITION                 0   xyz        0     NONE   float   xyz
// COLOR                    0   xyzw       1     NONE   float   xyzw
//
//
// Output signature:
//
// Name                 Index   Mask Register SysValue  Format   Used
// -------------------- ----- ------ -------- -------- ------- ------
// SV_POSITION              0   xyzw       0      POS   float   xyzw
// COLOR                    0   xyzw       1     NONE   float   xyzw
//
vs_5_0
dcl_globalFlags refactoringAllowed | skipOptimization
dcl_constantbuffer cb0[4], immediateIndexed
dcl_input v0.xyz
dcl_input v1.xyzw
dcl_output_siv o0.xyzw, position
dcl_output o1.xyzw
dcl_temps 2
//
// Initial variable locations:
```

```
//   v0.x <- vin.PosL.x; v0.y <- vin.PosL.y; v0.z <- vin.PosL.z;
//   v1.x <- vin.Color.x; v1.y <- vin.Color.y; v1.z <- vin.Color.z; v1.w
     <- vin.Color.w;
//   o1.x <- <VS return value>.Color.x;
//   o1.y <- <VS return value>.Color.y;
//   o1.z <- <VS return value>.Color.z;
//   o1.w <- <VS return value>.Color.w;
//   o0.x <- <VS return value>.PosH.x;
//   o0.y <- <VS return value>.PosH.y;
//   o0.z <- <VS return value>.PosH.z;
//   o0.w <- <VS return value>.PosH.w;
//
#line 29 "color.hlsl"
mov r0.xyz, v0.xyzx
mov r0.w, l(1.000000)
dp4 r1.x, r0.xyzw, cb0[0].xyzw // r1.x <- vout.PosH.x
dp4 r1.y, r0.xyzw, cb0[1].xyzw // r1.y <- vout.PosH.y
dp4 r1.z, r0.xyzw, cb0[2].xyzw // r1.z <- vout.PosH.z
dp4 r1.w, r0.xyzw, cb0[3].xyzw // r1.w <- vout.PosH.w

#line 32
mov r0.xyzw, v1.xyzw // r0.x <- vout.Color.x; r0.y <- vout.Color.y;
                     // r0.z <- vout.Color.z; r0.w <- vout.Color.w
mov o0.xyzw, r1.xyzw
mov o1.xyzw, r0.xyzw
ret
// Approximately 10 instruction slots used
```

6.7.3 Using Visual Studio to Compile Shaders Offline

Visual Studio 2013 has some integrated support for compiling shader programs. You can add .hlsl files to your project, and Visual Studio (VS) will recognize them and provide compilation options (see Figure 6.6). These options provide a UI for

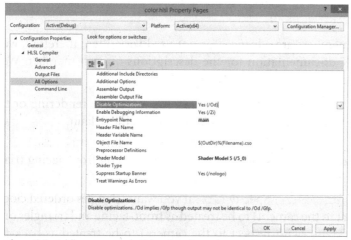

Figure 6.6. Adding a custom build tool to the project.

the FXC parameters. When you add a HLSL file to your VS project, it will become part of the build process, and the shader will be compiled with FXC.

One downside to using the VS integrated HLSL support is that it only supports one shader program per file. Therefore, you cannot store both a vertex and pixel shader in one file. Moreover, sometimes we want to compile the same shader program with different preprocessor directives to get different variations of a shader. Again, this will not be possible using the integrated VS support since it is one .cso output per .hlsl input.

6.8 RASTERIZER STATE

While many parts of the rendering pipeline are programmable, some parts are only configurable. The *rasterizer state* group, represented by the `D3D12_RASTERIZER_DESC` structure, is used to configure the rasterization stage of the rendering pipeline:

```
typedef struct D3D12_RASTERIZER_DESC {
    D3D12_FILL_MODE FillMode;          // Default: D3D12_FILL_SOLID
    D3D12_CULL_MODE CullMode;          // Default: D3D12_CULL_BACK
    BOOL FrontCounterClockwise;        // Default: false
    INT DepthBias;                     // Default: 0
    FLOAT DepthBiasClamp;              // Default: 0.0f
    FLOAT SlopeScaledDepthBias;        // Default: 0.0f
    BOOL DepthClipEnable;              // Default: true
    BOOL ScissorEnable;                // Default: false
    BOOL MultisampleEnable;            // Default: false
    BOOL AntialiasedLineEnable;        // Default: false
    UINT ForcedSampleCount;            // Default: 0

    // Default: D3D12_CONSERVATIVE_RASTERIZATION_MODE_OFF
    D3D12_CONSERVATIVE_RASTERIZATION_MODE ConservativeRaster;
} D3D12_RASTERIZER_DESC;
```

Most of these members are advanced or not used very often; therefore, we refer you to the SDK documentation for the descriptions of each member. We only describe four here.

1. `FillMode`: Specify `D3D12_FILL_WIREFRAME` for wireframe rendering or `D3D12_FILL_SOLID` for solid rendering. Solid rendering is the default.
2. `CullMode`: Specify `D3D12_CULL_NONE` to disable culling, `D3D12_CULL_BACK` to cull back-facing triangles, or `D3D12_CULL_FRONT` to cull front-facing triangles. Back-facing triangles are culled by default.
3. `FrontCounterClockwise`: Specify `false` if you want triangles ordered clockwise (with respect to the camera) to be treated as front-facing and triangles ordered counterclockwise (with respect to the camera) to be treated as back-facing.

Specify `true` if you want triangles ordered counterclockwise (with respect to the camera) to be treated as front-facing and triangles ordered clockwise (with respect to the camera) to be treated as back-facing. This state is false by default.

4. `ScissorEnable`: Specify true to enable the scissor test (§4.3.10) and false to disable it. The default is false.

The following code shows how to create a rasterize state that turns on wireframe mode and disables backface culling:

```
CD3DX12_RASTERIZER_DESC rsDesc(D3D12_DEFAULT);
rsDesc.FillMode = D3D12_FILL_WIREFRAME;
rsDesc.CullMode = D3D12_CULL_NONE;
```

`CD3DX12_RASTERIZER_DESC` is a convenience class that extends `D3D12_RASTERIZER_DESC` and adds some helper constructors. In particular, it has a constructor that takes an object of type `CD3D12_DEFAULT`, which is just a dummy type used for overloading to indicate the rasterizer state members should be initialized to the default values. `CD3D12_DEFAULT` and `D3D12_DEFAULT` are defined like so:

```
struct CD3D12_DEFAULT {};
extern const DECLSPEC_SELECTANY CD3D12_DEFAULT D3D12_DEFAULT;
```

`D3D12_DEFAULT` is used in several of the Direct3D convenience classes.

6.9 PIPELINE STATE OBJECT

We have shown, for example, how to describe an input layout description, how to create vertex and pixel shaders, and how to configure the rasterizer state group. However, we have not yet shown how to bind any of these objects to the graphics pipeline for actual use. Most of the objects that control the state of the graphics pipeline are specified as an aggregate called a *pipeline state object* (PSO), which is represented by the `ID3D12PipelineState` interface. To create a PSO, we first describe it by filling out a `D3D12_GRAPHICS_PIPELINE_STATE_DESC` instance:

```
typedef struct D3D12_GRAPHICS_PIPELINE_STATE_DESC
{
  ID3D12RootSignature *pRootSignature;
  D3D12_SHADER_BYTECODE VS;
  D3D12_SHADER_BYTECODE PS;
  D3D12_SHADER_BYTECODE DS;
  D3D12_SHADER_BYTECODE HS;
  D3D12_SHADER_BYTECODE GS;
  D3D12_STREAM_OUTPUT_DESC StreamOutput;
  D3D12_BLEND_DESC BlendState;
  UINT SampleMask;
```

```
    D3D12_RASTERIZER_DESC RasterizerState;
    D3D12_DEPTH_STENCIL_DESC DepthStencilState;
    D3D12_INPUT_LAYOUT_DESC InputLayout;
    D3D12_PRIMITIVE_TOPOLOGY_TYPE PrimitiveTopologyType;
    UINT NumRenderTargets;
    DXGI_FORMAT RTVFormats[8];
    DXGI_FORMAT DSVFormat;
    DXGI_SAMPLE_DESC SampleDesc;
} D3D12_GRAPHICS_PIPELINE_STATE_DESC;
```

1. pRootSignature: Pointer to the root signature to be bound with this PSO. The root signature must be compatible with the shaders specified with this PSO.

2. VS: The vertex shader to bind. This is specified by the D3D12_SHADER_BYTECODE structure which is a pointer to the compiled bytecode data, and the size of the bytecode data in bytes.

```
typedef struct D3D12_SHADER_BYTECODE {
  const BYTE *pShaderBytecode;
  SIZE_T     BytecodeLength;
} D3D12_SHADER_BYTECODE;
```

3. PS: The pixel shader to bind.

4. DS: The domain shader to bind (we will discuss this type of shader in a later chapter).

5. HS: The hull shader to bind (we will discuss this type of shader in a later chapter).

6. GS: The geometry shader to bind (we will discuss this type of shader in a later chapter).

7. StreamOutput: Used for an advanced technique called stream-out. We just zero-out this field for now.

8. BlendState: Specifies the blend state which configures blending. We will discuss this state group in a later chapter; for now, specify the default CD3DX12_BLEND_DESC(D3D12_DEFAULT).

9. SampleMask: Multisampling can take up to 32 samples. This 32-bit integer value is used to enable/disable the samples. For example, if you turn off the 5th bit, then the 5th sample will not be taken. Of course, disabling the 5th sample only has any consequence if you are actually using multisampling with at least 5 samples. If an application is using single sampling, then only the first bit of this parameter matters. Generally the default of 0xffffffff is used, which does not disable any samples.

10. RasterizerState: Specifies the rasterization state which configures the rasterizer.

11. `DepthStencilState`: Specifies the depth/stencil state which configures the depth/stencil test. We will discuss this state group in a later chapter; for now, specify the default `CD3DX12_DEPTH_STENCIL_DESC(D3D12_DEFAULT)`.
12. InputLayout: An input layout description which is simply an array of `D3D12_INPUT_ELEMENT_DESC` elements, and the number of elements in the array.

    ```
    typedef struct D3D12_INPUT_LAYOUT_DESC
    {
      const D3D12_INPUT_ELEMENT_DESC *pInputElementDescs;
      UINT NumElements;
    } D3D12_INPUT_LAYOUT_DESC;
    ```
13. `PrimitiveTopologyType`: Specifies the primitive topology type.

    ```
    typedef enum D3D12_PRIMITIVE_TOPOLOGY_TYPE {
      D3D12_PRIMITIVE_TOPOLOGY_TYPE_UNDEFINED = 0,
      D3D12_PRIMITIVE_TOPOLOGY_TYPE_POINT     = 1,
      D3D12_PRIMITIVE_TOPOLOGY_TYPE_LINE      = 2,
      D3D12_PRIMITIVE_TOPOLOGY_TYPE_TRIANGLE  = 3,
      D3D12_PRIMITIVE_TOPOLOGY_TYPE_PATCH     = 4
    } D3D12_PRIMITIVE_TOPOLOGY_TYPE;
    ```
14. `NumRenderTargets`: The number of render targets we are using simultaneously.
15. `RTVFormats`: The render target formats. This is an array to support writing to multiple render targets simultaneously. This should match the settings of the render target we are using the PSO with.
16. `DSVFormat`: The format of the depth/stencil buffer. This should match the settings of the depth/stencil buffer we are using the PSO with.
17. `SampleDesc`: Describes the multisample count and quality level. This should match the settings of the render target we are using.

After we have filled out a `D3D12_GRAPHICS_PIPELINE_STATE_DESC` instance, we create an ID3D12PipelineState object using the `ID3D12Device::CreateGraphicsPipelineState` method:

```
ComPtr<ID3D12RootSignature> mRootSignature;
std::vector<D3D12_INPUT_ELEMENT_DESC> mInputLayout;
ComPtr<ID3DBlob> mvsByteCode;
ComPtr<ID3DBlob> mpsByteCode;
...
D3D12_GRAPHICS_PIPELINE_STATE_DESC psoDesc;
ZeroMemory(&psoDesc, sizeof(D3D12_GRAPHICS_PIPELINE_STATE_DESC));
psoDesc.InputLayout = { mInputLayout.data(), (UINT)mInputLayout.size()
    };
psoDesc.pRootSignature = mRootSignature.Get();
psoDesc.VS =
{
  reinterpret_cast<BYTE*>(mvsByteCode->GetBufferPointer()),
```

```
    mvsByteCode->GetBufferSize()
};
psoDesc.PS =
{
   reinterpret_cast<BYTE*>(mpsByteCode->GetBufferPointer()),
   mpsByteCode->GetBufferSize()
};
psoDesc.RasterizerState = CD3D12_RASTERIZER_DESC(D3D12_DEFAULT);
psoDesc.BlendState = CD3D12_BLEND_DESC(D3D12_DEFAULT);
psoDesc.DepthStencilState = CD3D12_DEPTH_STENCIL_DESC(D3D12_DEFAULT);
psoDesc.SampleMask = UINT_MAX;
psoDesc.PrimitiveTopologyType = D3D12_PRIMITIVE_TOPOLOGY_TYPE_TRIANGLE;
psoDesc.NumRenderTargets = 1;
psoDesc.RTVFormats[0] = mBackBufferFormat;
psoDesc.SampleDesc.Count = m4xMsaaState ? 4 : 1;
psoDesc.SampleDesc.Quality = m4xMsaaState ? (m4xMsaaQuality - 1) : 0;
psoDesc.DSVFormat = mDepthStencilFormat;

ComPtr<ID3D12PipelineState> mPSO;
md3dDevice->CreateGraphicsPipelineState(&psoDesc, IID_PPV_
ARGS(&mPSO)));
```

This is quite a lot of state in one aggregate `ID3D12PipelineState` object. We specify all these objects as an aggregate to the graphics pipeline for performance. By specifying them as an aggregate, Direct3D can validate that all the state is compatible and the driver can generate all the code up front to program the hardware state. In the Direct3D 11 state model, these render states pieces were set separately. However, the states are related; if one piece of state gets changed, it may additionally require the driver to reprogram the hardware for another piece of dependent state. As many states are changed to configure the pipeline, the state of the hardware could get reprogrammed redundantly. To avoid this redundancy, the drivers typically deferred programming the hardware state until a draw call is issued when the entire pipeline state would be known. But this deferral requires additional bookkeeping work by the driver at runtime; it needs to track which states have changed, and then generate the code to program the hardware state at runtime. In the new Direct3D 12 model, the driver can generate all the code needed to program the pipeline state at initialization time because we specify the majority of pipeline state as an aggregate.

> **Note:** *Because PSO validation and creation can be time consuming, PSOs should be generated at initialization time. One exception to this might be to create a PSO at runtime on demand the first time it is referenced; then store it in a collection such as a hash table so it can quickly be fetched for future use.*

Not all rendering states are encapsulated in a PSO. Some states like the viewport and scissor rectangles are specified independently to the PSO. Such state can efficiently be set independently to the other pipeline state, so no advantage was gained by including them in the PSO.

Direct3D is basically a state machine. Things stay in their current state until we change them. If some objects you are drawing use one PSO, and other objects you are drawing require a different PSO, then you need to structure your code like this:

```
// Reset specifies initial PSO.
mCommandList->Reset(mDirectCmdListAlloc.Get(), mPSO1.Get())
/* ...draw objects using PSO 1... */

// Change PSO
mCommandList->SetPipelineState(mPSO2.Get());
/* ...draw objects using PSO 2... */

// Change PSO
mCommandList->SetPipelineState(mPSO3.Get());
/* ...draw objects using PSO 3... */
```

In other words, when a PSO is bound to the command list, it does not change until you overwrite it (or the command list is reset).

PSO state changes should be kept to a minimum for performance. Draw all objects together that can use the same PSO. Do not change the PSO per draw call!

6.10 GEOMETRY HELPER STRUCTURE

It is helpful to create a structure that groups a vertex and index buffer together to define a group of geometry. In addition, this structure can keep a system memory backing of the vertex and index data so that it can be read by the CPU. The CPU will need access to the geometry data for things like picking and collision detection. In addition, the structure caches the important properties of the vertex and index buffers such as the format and strike, and provides methods that return views to the buffers. We use the following MeshGeometry (defined in *d3dUtil.h*) structure throughout the book whenever we define a chunk of geometry.

```
// Defines a subrange of geometry in a MeshGeometry. This is for when
// multiple geometries are stored in one vertex and index buffer. It
// provides the offsets and data needed to draw a subset of geometry
// stores in the vertex and index buffers so that we can implement the
// technique described by Figure 6.3.
struct SubmeshGeometry
{
    UINT IndexCount = 0;
    UINT StartIndexLocation = 0;
```

```cpp
    INT BaseVertexLocation = 0;

    // Bounding box of the geometry defined by this submesh.
    // This is used in later chapters of the book.
    DirectX::BoundingBox Bounds;
};

struct MeshGeometry
{
    // Give it a name so we can look it up by name.
    std::string Name;

    // System memory copies. Use Blobs because the vertex/index format can
    // be generic.
    // It is up to the client to cast appropriately.
    Microsoft::WRL::ComPtr<ID3DBlob> VertexBufferCPU = nullptr;
    Microsoft::WRL::ComPtr<ID3DBlob> IndexBufferCPU = nullptr;

    Microsoft::WRL::ComPtr<ID3D12Resource> VertexBufferGPU = nullptr;
    Microsoft::WRL::ComPtr<ID3D12Resource> IndexBufferGPU = nullptr;

    Microsoft::WRL::ComPtr<ID3D12Resource> VertexBufferUploader = nullptr;
    Microsoft::WRL::ComPtr<ID3D12Resource> IndexBufferUploader = nullptr;

    // Data about the buffers.
    UINT VertexByteStride = 0;
    UINT VertexBufferByteSize = 0;
    DXGI_FORMAT IndexFormat = DXGI_FORMAT_R16_UINT;
    UINT IndexBufferByteSize = 0;

    // A MeshGeometry may store multiple geometries in one vertex/index
    // buffer.
    // Use this container to define the Submesh geometries so we can draw
    // the Submeshes individually.
    std::unordered_map<std::string, SubmeshGeometry> DrawArgs;

    D3D12_VERTEX_BUFFER_VIEW VertexBufferView()const
    {
        D3D12_VERTEX_BUFFER_VIEW vbv;
        vbv.BufferLocation = VertexBufferGPU->GetGPUVirtualAddress();
        vbv.StrideInBytes = VertexByteStride;
        vbv.SizeInBytes = VertexBufferByteSize;

        return vbv;
    }

    D3D12_INDEX_BUFFER_VIEW IndexBufferView()const
    {
        D3D12_INDEX_BUFFER_VIEW ibv;
        ibv.BufferLocation = IndexBufferGPU->GetGPUVirtualAddress();
        ibv.Format = IndexFormat;
        ibv.SizeInBytes = IndexBufferByteSize;

        return ibv;
    }
```

```cpp
    // We can free this memory after we finish upload to the GPU.
    void DisposeUploaders()
    {
      VertexBufferUploader = nullptr;
      IndexBufferUploader = nullptr;
    }
};
```

6.11 BOX DEMO

At last, we have covered enough material to present a simple demo, which renders a colored box. This example essentially puts everything we have discussed in this chapter up to now into a single program. The reader should study the code and refer back to the previous sections of this chapter until every line is understood. Note that the program uses the *Shaders\color.hlsl*, which was shown at the end of §6.5.

```cpp
//***************************************************************************
// BoxApp.cpp by Frank Luna (C) 2015 All Rights Reserved.
//
// Shows how to draw a box in Direct3D 12.
//
// Controls:
//   Hold the left mouse button down and move the mouse to rotate.
//   Hold the right mouse button down and move the mouse to zoom in and
//   out.
//***************************************************************************

#include "../../Common/d3dApp.h"
#include "../../Common/MathHelper.h"
#include "../../Common/UploadBuffer.h"

using Microsoft::WRL::ComPtr;
using namespace DirectX;
using namespace DirectX::PackedVector;

struct Vertex
{
  XMFLOAT3 Pos;
  XMFLOAT4 Color;
};

struct ObjectConstants
{
  XMFLOAT4X4 WorldViewProj = MathHelper::Identity4x4();
};

class BoxApp : public D3DApp
{
public:
  BoxApp(HINSTANCE hInstance);
```

```cpp
    BoxApp(const BoxApp& rhs) = delete;
    BoxApp& operator=(const BoxApp& rhs) = delete;
    ~BoxApp();

    virtual bool Initialize()override;

private:
    virtual void OnResize()override;
    virtual void Update(const GameTimer& gt)override;
    virtual void Draw(const GameTimer& gt)override;

    virtual void OnMouseDown(WPARAM btnState, int x, int y)override;
    virtual void OnMouseUp(WPARAM btnState, int x, int y)override;
    virtual void OnMouseMove(WPARAM btnState, int x, int y)override;

    void BuildDescriptorHeaps();
    void BuildConstantBuffers();
    void BuildRootSignature();
    void BuildShadersAndInputLayout();
    void BuildBoxGeometry();
    void BuildPSO();

private:

    ComPtr<ID3D12RootSignature> mRootSignature = nullptr;
    ComPtr<ID3D12DescriptorHeap> mCbvHeap = nullptr;

    std::unique_ptr<UploadBuffer<ObjectConstants>> mObjectCB = nullptr;

    std::unique_ptr<MeshGeometry> mBoxGeo = nullptr;

    ComPtr<ID3DBlob> mvsByteCode = nullptr;
    ComPtr<ID3DBlob> mpsByteCode = nullptr;

    std::vector<D3D12_INPUT_ELEMENT_DESC> mInputLayout;

    ComPtr<ID3D12PipelineState> mPSO = nullptr;

    XMFLOAT4X4 mWorld = MathHelper::Identity4x4();
    XMFLOAT4X4 mView = MathHelper::Identity4x4();
    XMFLOAT4X4 mProj = MathHelper::Identity4x4();

    float mTheta = 1.5f*XM_PI;
    float mPhi = XM_PIDIV4;
    float mRadius = 5.0f;

    POINT mLastMousePos;
};

int WINAPI WinMain(HINSTANCE hInstance, HINSTANCE prevInstance,
                   PSTR cmdLine, int showCmd)
{
    // Enable run-time memory check for debug builds.
#if defined(DEBUG) | defined(_DEBUG)
```

```cpp
        _CrtSetDbgFlag( _CRTDBG_ALLOC_MEM_DF | _CRTDBG_LEAK_CHECK_DF );
#endif

    try
    {
        BoxApp theApp(hInstance);
        if(!theApp.Initialize())
            return 0;

        return theApp.Run();
    }
    catch(DxException& e)
    {
        MessageBox(nullptr, e.ToString().c_str(), L"HR Failed", MB_OK);
        return 0;
    }
}

BoxApp::BoxApp(HINSTANCE hInstance)
: D3DApp(hInstance)
{
}

BoxApp::~BoxApp()
{
}

bool BoxApp::Initialize()
{
    if(!D3DApp::Initialize())
        return false;

    // Reset the command list to prep for initialization commands.
    ThrowIfFailed(mCommandList->Reset(mDirectCmdListAlloc.Get(),
        nullptr));

    BuildDescriptorHeaps();
    BuildConstantBuffers();
    BuildRootSignature();
    BuildShadersAndInputLayout();
    BuildBoxGeometry();
    BuildPSO();

    // Execute the initialization commands.
    ThrowIfFailed(mCommandList->Close());
    ID3D12CommandList* cmdsLists[] = { mCommandList.Get() };
    mCommandQueue->ExecuteCommandLists(_countof(cmdsLists), cmdsLists);

    // Wait until initialization is complete.
    FlushCommandQueue();

    return true;
}
```

```cpp
void BoxApp::OnResize()
{
    D3DApp::OnResize();

    // The window resized, so update the aspect ratio and recompute the
    // projection matrix.
    XMMATRIX P = XMMatrixPerspectiveFovLH(0.25f*MathHelper::Pi,
        AspectRatio(), 1.0f, 1000.0f);
    XMStoreFloat4x4(&mProj, P);
}

void BoxApp::Update(const GameTimer& gt)
{
    // Convert Spherical to Cartesian coordinates.
    float x = mRadius*sinf(mPhi)*cosf(mTheta);
    float z = mRadius*sinf(mPhi)*sinf(mTheta);
    float y = mRadius*cosf(mPhi);

    // Build the view matrix.
    XMVECTOR pos = XMVectorSet(x, y, z, 1.0f);
    XMVECTOR target = XMVectorZero();
    XMVECTOR up = XMVectorSet(0.0f, 1.0f, 0.0f, 0.0f);

    XMMATRIX view = XMMatrixLookAtLH(pos, target, up);
    XMStoreFloat4x4(&mView, view);

    XMMATRIX world = XMLoadFloat4x4(&mWorld);
    XMMATRIX proj = XMLoadFloat4x4(&mProj);
    XMMATRIX worldViewProj = world*view*proj;

    // Update the constant buffer with the latest worldViewProj matrix.
    ObjectConstants objConstants;
    XMStoreFloat4x4(&objConstants.WorldViewProj, XMMatrixTranspose(world
        ViewProj));
    mObjectCB->CopyData(0, objConstants);
}

void BoxApp::Draw(const GameTimer& gt)
{
    // Reuse the memory associated with command recording.
    // We can only reset when the associated command lists have finished
    // execution on the GPU.
    ThrowIfFailed(mDirectCmdListAlloc->Reset());

    // A command list can be reset after it has been added to the
    // command queue via ExecuteCommandList. Reusing the command
    // list reuses memory.
    ThrowIfFailed(mCommandList->Reset(mDirectCmdListAlloc.Get(), mPSO.
        Get()));

    mCommandList->RSSetViewports(1, &mScreenViewport);
    mCommandList->RSSetScissorRects(1, &mScissorRect);

    // Indicate a state transition on the resource usage.
```

```cpp
    mCommandList->ResourceBarrier(1,
        &CD3DX12_RESOURCE_BARRIER::Transition(CurrentBackBuffer(),
        D3D12_RESOURCE_STATE_PRESENT, D3D12_RESOURCE_STATE_RENDER_TARGET));

    // Clear the back buffer and depth buffer.
    mCommandList->ClearRenderTargetView(CurrentBackBufferView(),
        Colors::LightSteelBlue, 0, nullptr);
    mCommandList->ClearDepthStencilView(DepthStencilView(),
        D3D12_CLEAR_FLAG_DEPTH | D3D12_CLEAR_FLAG_STENCIL,
        1.0f, 0, 0, nullptr);

    // Specify the buffers we are going to render to.
    mCommandList->OMSetRenderTargets(1, &CurrentBackBufferView(),
        true, &DepthStencilView());

    ID3D12DescriptorHeap* descriptorHeaps[] = { mCbvHeap.Get() };
    mCommandList->SetDescriptorHeaps(_countof(descriptorHeaps),
        descriptorHeaps);

    mCommandList->SetGraphicsRootSignature(mRootSignature.Get());

    mCommandList->IASetVertexBuffers(0, 1, &mBoxGeo->VertexBufferView());
    mCommandList->IASetIndexBuffer(&mBoxGeo->IndexBufferView());
    mCommandList->IASetPrimitiveTopology(D3D11_PRIMITIVE_TOPOLOGY_
        TRIANGLELIST);

    mCommandList->SetGraphicsRootDescriptorTable(
        0, mCbvHeap->GetGPUDescriptorHandleForHeapStart());

    mCommandList->DrawIndexedInstanced(
        mBoxGeo->DrawArgs["box"].IndexCount,
        1, 0, 0, 0);

    // Indicate a state transition on the resource usage.
    mCommandList->ResourceBarrier(1,
        &CD3DX12_RESOURCE_BARRIER::Transition(CurrentBackBuffer(),
        D3D12_RESOURCE_STATE_RENDER_TARGET, D3D12_RESOURCE_STATE_PRESENT));

    // Done recording commands.
    ThrowIfFailed(mCommandList->Close());

    // Add the command list to the queue for execution.
    ID3D12CommandList* cmdsLists[] = { mCommandList.Get() };
    mCommandQueue->ExecuteCommandLists(_countof(cmdsLists), cmdsLists);

    // swap the back and front buffers
    ThrowIfFailed(mSwapChain->Present(0, 0));
    mCurrBackBuffer = (mCurrBackBuffer + 1) % SwapChainBufferCount;

    // Wait until frame commands are complete. This waiting is
    // inefficient and is done for simplicity. Later we will show how to
    // organize our rendering code so we do not have to wait per frame.
    FlushCommandQueue();
}
```

```cpp
void BoxApp::OnMouseDown(WPARAM btnState, int x, int y)
{
  mLastMousePos.x = x;
  mLastMousePos.y = y;

  SetCapture(mhMainWnd);
}

void BoxApp::OnMouseUp(WPARAM btnState, int x, int y)
{
  ReleaseCapture();
}

void BoxApp::OnMouseMove(WPARAM btnState, int x, int y)
{
  if((btnState & MK_LBUTTON) != 0)
  {
    // Make each pixel correspond to a quarter of a degree.
    float dx = XMConvertToRadians(0.25f*static_cast<float>(x - mLastMousePos.x));
    float dy = XMConvertToRadians(0.25f*static_cast<float>(y - mLastMousePos.y));

    // Update angles based on input to orbit camera around box.
    mTheta += dx;
    mPhi += dy;

    // Restrict the angle mPhi.
    mPhi = MathHelper::Clamp(mPhi, 0.1f, MathHelper::Pi - 0.1f);
  }
  else if((btnState & MK_RBUTTON) != 0)
  {
    // Make each pixel correspond to 0.005 unit in the scene.
    float dx = 0.005f*static_cast<float>(x - mLastMousePos.x);
    float dy = 0.005f*static_cast<float>(y - mLastMousePos.y);

    // Update the camera radius based on input.
    mRadius += dx - dy;

    // Restrict the radius.
    mRadius = MathHelper::Clamp(mRadius, 3.0f, 15.0f);
  }

  mLastMousePos.x = x;
  mLastMousePos.y = y;
}

void BoxApp::BuildDescriptorHeaps()
{
  D3D12_DESCRIPTOR_HEAP_DESC cbvHeapDesc;
  cbvHeapDesc.NumDescriptors = 1;
  cbvHeapDesc.Type = D3D12_DESCRIPTOR_HEAP_TYPE_CBV_SRV_UAV;
  cbvHeapDesc.Flags = D3D12_DESCRIPTOR_HEAP_FLAG_SHADER_VISIBLE;
    cbvHeapDesc.NodeMask = 0;
  ThrowIfFailed(md3dDevice->CreateDescriptorHeap(&cbvHeapDesc,
```

```cpp
        IID_PPV_ARGS(&mCbvHeap)));
}

void BoxApp::BuildConstantBuffers()
{
  mObjectCB = std::make_unique<UploadBuffer<ObjectConstants>>(md3dDevi
    ce.Get(), 1, true);

  UINT objCBByteSize = d3dUtil::CalcConstantBufferByteSize(sizeof(Objec
    tConstants));

  D3D12_GPU_VIRTUAL_ADDRESS cbAddress = mObjectCB->Resource()-
    >GetGPUVirtualAddress();
  // Offset to the ith object constant buffer in the buffer.
  // Here our i = 0.
  int boxCBufIndex = 0;
  cbAddress += boxCBufIndex*objCBByteSize;

  D3D12_CONSTANT_BUFFER_VIEW_DESC cbvDesc;
  cbvDesc.BufferLocation = cbAddress;
  cbvDesc.SizeInBytes = d3dUtil::CalcConstantBufferByteSize(sizeof(Obje
    ctConstants));

  md3dDevice->CreateConstantBufferView(
    &cbvDesc,
    mCbvHeap->GetCPUDescriptorHandleForHeapStart());
}


void BoxApp::BuildRootSignature()
{
  // Shader programs typically require resources as input (constant
  // buffers, textures, samplers). The root signature defines the
  // resources the shader programs expect. If we think of the shader
  // programs as a function, and the input resources as function
  // parameters, then the root signature can be thought of as defining
  // the function signature.

  // Root parameter can be a table, root descriptor or root constants.
  CD3DX12_ROOT_PARAMETER slotRootParameter[1];

  // Create a single descriptor table of CBVs.
  CD3DX12_DESCRIPTOR_RANGE cbvTable;
  cbvTable.Init(D3D12_DESCRIPTOR_RANGE_TYPE_CBV, 1, 0);
  slotRootParameter[0].InitAsDescriptorTable(1, &cbvTable);

  // A root signature is an array of root parameters.
  CD3DX12_ROOT_SIGNATURE_DESC rootSigDesc(1, slotRootParameter, 0,
    nullptr,
    D3D12_ROOT_SIGNATURE_FLAG_ALLOW_INPUT_ASSEMBLER_INPUT_LAYOUT);

  // create a root signature with a single slot which points to a
  // descriptor range consisting of a single constant buffer
  ComPtr<ID3DBlob> serializedRootSig = nullptr;
  ComPtr<ID3DBlob> errorBlob = nullptr;
```

```cpp
    HRESULT hr = D3D12SerializeRootSignature(&rootSigDesc, D3D_ROOT_
      SIGNATURE_VERSION_1,
      serializedRootSig.GetAddressOf(), errorBlob.GetAddressOf());

    if(errorBlob != nullptr)
    {
      ::OutputDebugStringA((char*)errorBlob->GetBufferPointer());
    }
    ThrowIfFailed(hr);

    ThrowIfFailed(md3dDevice->CreateRootSignature(
      0,
      serializedRootSig->GetBufferPointer(),
      serializedRootSig->GetBufferSize(),
      IID_PPV_ARGS(&mRootSignature)));
}

void BoxApp::BuildShadersAndInputLayout()
{
    HRESULT hr = S_OK;

    mvsByteCode = d3dUtil::CompileShader(L"Shaders\\color.hlsl", nullptr,
      "VS", "vs_5_0");
    mpsByteCode = d3dUtil::CompileShader(L"Shaders\\color.hlsl", nullptr,
      "PS", "ps_5_0");

    mInputLayout =
    {
      { "POSITION", 0, DXGI_FORMAT_R32G32B32_FLOAT, 0, 0,
        D3D12_INPUT_CLASSIFICATION_PER_VERTEX_DATA, 0 },
      { "COLOR", 0, DXGI_FORMAT_R32G32B32A32_FLOAT, 0, 12,
        D3D12_INPUT_CLASSIFICATION_PER_VERTEX_DATA, 0 }
    };
}

void BoxApp::BuildBoxGeometry()
{
    std::array<Vertex, 8> vertices =
    {
      Vertex({ XMFLOAT3(-1.0f, -1.0f, -1.0f), XMFLOAT4(Colors::White) }),
      Vertex({ XMFLOAT3(-1.0f, +1.0f, -1.0f), XMFLOAT4(Colors::Black) }),
      Vertex({ XMFLOAT3(+1.0f, +1.0f, -1.0f), XMFLOAT4(Colors::Red) }),
      Vertex({ XMFLOAT3(+1.0f, -1.0f, -1.0f), XMFLOAT4(Colors::Green) }),
      Vertex({ XMFLOAT3(-1.0f, -1.0f, +1.0f), XMFLOAT4(Colors::Blue) }),
      Vertex({ XMFLOAT3(-1.0f, +1.0f, +1.0f), XMFLOAT4(Colors::Yellow)
      }),
      Vertex({ XMFLOAT3(+1.0f, +1.0f, +1.0f), XMFLOAT4(Colors::Cyan) }),
      Vertex({ XMFLOAT3(+1.0f, -1.0f, +1.0f), XMFLOAT4(Colors::Magenta)
      })
    };

    std::array<std::uint16_t, 36> indices =
    {
      // front face
```

```
    0, 1, 2,
    0, 2, 3,

    // back face
    4, 6, 5,
    4, 7, 6,

    // left face
    4, 5, 1,
    4, 1, 0,

    // right face
    3, 2, 6,
    3, 6, 7,

    // top face
    1, 5, 6,
    1, 6, 2,

    // bottom face
    4, 0, 3,
    4, 3, 7
};

const UINT vbByteSize = (UINT)vertices.size() * sizeof(Vertex);
const UINT ibByteSize = (UINT)indices.size() * sizeof(std::uint16_t);

mBoxGeo = std::make_unique<MeshGeometry>();
mBoxGeo->Name = "boxGeo";

ThrowIfFailed(D3DCreateBlob(vbByteSize, &mBoxGeo->VertexBufferCPU));
CopyMemory(mBoxGeo->VertexBufferCPU->GetBufferPointer(),
    vertices.data(), vbByteSize);

ThrowIfFailed(D3DCreateBlob(ibByteSize, &mBoxGeo->IndexBufferCPU));
CopyMemory(mBoxGeo->IndexBufferCPU->GetBufferPointer(),
    indices.data(), ibByteSize);

mBoxGeo->VertexBufferGPU = d3dUtil::CreateDefaultBuffer(
    md3dDevice.Get(), mCommandList.Get(),
    vertices.data(), vbByteSize,
    mBoxGeo->VertexBufferUploader);

mBoxGeo->IndexBufferGPU = d3dUtil::CreateDefaultBuffer(
    md3dDevice.Get(), mCommandList.Get(),
    indices.data(), ibByteSize,
    mBoxGeo->IndexBufferUploader);

mBoxGeo->VertexByteStride = sizeof(Vertex);
mBoxGeo->VertexBufferByteSize = vbByteSize;
mBoxGeo->IndexFormat = DXGI_FORMAT_R16_UINT;
mBoxGeo->IndexBufferByteSize = ibByteSize;

SubmeshGeometry submesh;
submesh.IndexCount = (UINT)indices.size();
```

```cpp
    submesh.StartIndexLocation = 0;
    submesh.BaseVertexLocation = 0;

    mBoxGeo->DrawArgs["box"] = submesh;
}

void BoxApp::BuildPSO()
{
    D3D12_GRAPHICS_PIPELINE_STATE_DESC psoDesc;
    ZeroMemory(&psoDesc, sizeof(D3D12_GRAPHICS_PIPELINE_STATE_DESC));
    psoDesc.InputLayout = { mInputLayout.data(), (UINT)mInputLayout.
        size() };
    psoDesc.pRootSignature = mRootSignature.Get();
    psoDesc.VS =
        {
            reinterpret_cast<BYTE*>(mvsByteCode->GetBufferPointer()),
            mvsByteCode->GetBufferSize()
        };
    psoDesc.PS =
        {
            reinterpret_cast<BYTE*>(mpsByteCode->GetBufferPointer()),
            mpsByteCode->GetBufferSize()
        };
    psoDesc.RasterizerState = CD3DX12_RASTERIZER_DESC(D3D12_DEFAULT);
    psoDesc.BlendState = CD3DX12_BLEND_DESC(D3D12_DEFAULT);
    psoDesc.DepthStencilState = CD3DX12_DEPTH_STENCIL_DESC(D3D12_
        DEFAULT);
    psoDesc.SampleMask = UINT_MAX;
    psoDesc.PrimitiveTopologyType = D3D12_PRIMITIVE_TOPOLOGY_TYPE_
        TRIANGLE;
    psoDesc.NumRenderTargets = 1;
    psoDesc.RTVFormats[0] = mBackBufferFormat;
    psoDesc.SampleDesc.Count = m4xMsaaState ? 4 : 1;
    psoDesc.SampleDesc.Quality = m4xMsaaState ? (m4xMsaaQuality - 1) : 0;
    psoDesc.DSVFormat = mDepthStencilFormat;
    ThrowIfFailed(md3dDevice->CreateGraphicsPipelineState(&psoDesc, IID_
        PPV_ARGS(&mPSO)));
}
```

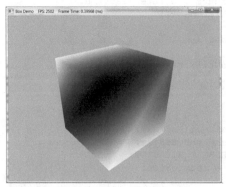

Figure 6.7. Screenshot of the "Box" demo.

6.12 SUMMARY

1. A vertex in Direct3D can consist of additional data besides spatial location. To create a custom vertex format, we first define a structure that holds the vertex data we choose. Once we have defined a vertex structure, we describe it to Direct3D by defining an input layout description (`D3D12_INPUT_LAYOUT_DESC`), which is an array of `D3D12_INPUT_ELEMENT_DESC` elements, and the number of elements in the array. Each element in the `D3D12_INPUT_ELEMENT_DESC` array describes and corresponds to one component in the vertex structure. An input layout description is set as a field in the `D3D12_GRAPHICS_PIPELINE_STATE_DESC` structure, where it becomes part of a PSO, and is validated against the vertex shader input signature. An input layout is bound to the IA stage when the PSO it is part of gets bound.

2. In order for the GPU to access an array of vertices/indices, they need to be placed in a resource called a *buffer*, which is represented by the `ID3D12Resource` interface. A buffer that stores vertices is called a *vertex buffer* and a buffer that stores indices is called an *index buffer*. A buffer resource is created by filling out a `D3D12_RESOURCE_DESC` structure and then calling the `ID3D12Device::CreateCommittedResource` method. A view to a vertex buffer is represented by the `D3D12_VERTEX_BUFFER_VIEW` structure, and a view to an index buffer is represented by the `D3D12_INDEX_BUFFER_VIEW` structure. A vertex buffer is bound to the IA stage with the `ID3D12GraphicsCommandList::IASetVertexBuffers` method, and an index buffer is bound to the IA stage with the `ID3D12GraphicsCommandList::IASetIndexBuffer` method. Non-indexed geometry can be drawn with `ID3D12GraphicsCommandList::DrawInstanced`, and indexed geometry can be drawn with `ID3D12GraphicsCommandList::DrawIndexedInstanced`.

3. A vertex shader is a program written in HLSL, executed on the GPU, which inputs a vertex and outputs a vertex. Every drawn vertex goes through the vertex shader. This enables the programmer to do specialized work on a per vertex basis to achieve various rendering effects. The values output from the vertex shader are passed on to the next stage in the pipeline.

4. A constant buffer is a GPU resource (`ID3D12Resource`) whose data contents can be referenced in shader programs. They are created in an upload heap rather than a default heap so that the application can update the constant buffer data by copying system memory to GPU memory. In this way, the C++ application can communicate with the shader and update the values in the constant buffers the shader uses; for example, the C++ application can change the world-view-projection matrix the shader uses. The general advice

is to create constant buffers based on the frequency in which you need to update their contents. The motivation for dividing the constant buffers up is efficiency. When a constant buffer is updated, all its variables must be updated; therefore, it is efficient to group them based on their update frequency to minimize redundant updates.

5. A pixel shader is a program written in HLSL, executed on the GPU, which inputs interpolated vertex data and outputs a color value. As a hardware optimization, it is possible that a pixel fragment is rejected by the pipeline before making it to the pixel shader (e.g., early-z rejection). Pixel shaders enable the programmer to do specialized work on a per pixel basis to achieve various rendering effects. The values output from the pixel shader are passed on to the next stage in the pipeline.

6. Most of the Direct3D objects that control the state of the graphics pipeline are specified as an aggregate called a pipeline state object (PSO), which is represented by the ID3D12PipelineState interface. We specify all these objects as an aggregate to the graphics pipeline for performance. By specifying them as an aggregate, Direct3D can validate that all the state is compatible and the driver can generate all the code up front to program the hardware state.

6.13 EXERCISES

1. Write down the D3D12_INPUT_ELEMENT_DESC array for the following vertex structure:

```
struct Vertex
{
    XMFLOAT3 Pos;
    XMFLOAT3 Tangent;
    XMFLOAT3 Normal;
    XMFLOAT2 Tex0;
    XMFLOAT2 Tex1;
    XMCOLOR Color;
};
```

2. Redo the Colored Cube demo, but this time use two vertex buffers (and two input slots) to feed the pipeline with vertices, one that stores the position element and the other that stores the color element. For this you will use two vertex structures to store the split data:

```
struct VPosData
{
    XMFLOAT3 Pos;
};
```

```
struct VColorData
{
  XMFLOAT4 Color;
};
```

Your `D3D12_INPUT_ELEMENT_DESC` array will look like this:

```
D3D12_INPUT_ELEMENT_DESC vertexDesc[] =
{
  {"POSITION", 0, DXGI_FORMAT_R32G32B32_FLOAT, 0, 0,
    D3D12_INPUT_PER_VERTEX_DATA, 0},
  {"COLOR",    0, DXGI_FORMAT_R32G32B32A32_FLOAT, 1, 0,
    D3D12_INPUT_PER_VERTEX_DATA, 0}
};
```

The position element is hooked up to input slot 0, and the color element is hooked up to input slot 1. Moreover note that the `D3D12_INPUT_ELEMENT_DESC::AlignedByteOffset` is 0 for both elements; this is because the position and color elements are no longer interleaved in a single input slot. Then use `ID3D12CommandList::IASetVertexBuffers` to bind the two vertex buffers to slots 0 and 1. Direct3D will then use the elements from the different input slots to assemble the vertices. This can be used as an optimization. For example, in the shadow mapping algorithm, we need to draw our scene twice per frame: once from the perspective of the light source (shadow pass) and once from the perspective of the main camera (main pass). The shadow pass only requires the position data and texture coordinates (for alpha tested geometry). So we can split the vertex data into two slots: one slot contains position and texture coordinates, and the other slot contains the other vertex attributes (e.g., normal and tangent vectors). Now we can easily only stream in the vertex data the shadow pass needs (position and texture coordinates), thereby saving data bandwidth for the shadow pass. The main render pass would use both vertex input slots to get all the vertex data it needs. For performance, the advice is to minimize the number of input slots used to a small number less than or equal to 3.

3. Draw

    (a) a point list like the one shown in Figure 5.13*a*.

    (b) a line strip like the one shown in Figure 5.13*b*.

    (c) a line list like the one shown in Figure 5.13*c*.

    (d) a triangle strip like the one shown in Figure 5.13*d*.

    (e) a triangle list like the one shown in Figure 5.14*a*.

4. Construct the vertex and index list of a pyramid, as shown in Figure 6.8, and draw it. Color the base vertices green and the tip vertex red.

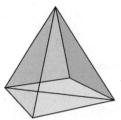

Figure 6.8. The triangles of a pyramid.

5. Run the "Box" demo, and recall that we specified colors at the vertices only. Explain how pixel colors were obtained for each pixel on the triangle.

6. Modify the Box demo by applying the following transformation to each vertex in the vertex shader prior to transforming to world space.

```
vin.PosL.xy += 0.5f*sin(vinL.Pos.x)*sin(3.0f*gTime);
vin.PosL.z *= 0.6f + 0.4f*sin(2.0f*gTime);
```

You will need to add a `gTime` constant buffer variable; this variable corresponds to the current `GameTimer::TotalTime()` value. This will animate the vertices as a function of time by distorting them periodically with the sine function.

7. Merge the vertices of a box and pyramid (Exercise 4) into one large vertex buffer. Also merge the indices of the box and pyramid into one large index buffer (but do not update the index values). Then draw the box and pyramid one-by-one using the parameters of `ID3D12CommandList::DrawIndexedInstanced`. Use the world transformation matrix so that the box and pyramid are disjoint in world space.

8. Modify the Box demo by rendering the cube in wireframe mode.

9. Modify the Box demo by disabling backface culling (`D3D12_CULL_NONE`); also try culling front faces instead of back faces (`D3D12_CULL_FRONT`). Output your results in wireframe mode so that you can more easily see the difference.

10. If vertex memory is significant, then reducing from 128-bit color values to 32-bit color values may be worthwhile. Modify the "Box" demo by using a 32-bit color value instead of a 128-bit color value in the vertex structure. Your vertex structure and corresponding vertex input description will look like this:

```
struct Vertex
{
  XMFLOAT3 Pos;
  XMCOLOR Color;
};

D3D12_INPUT_ELEMENT_DESC vertexDesc[] =
{
  {"POSITION", 0, DXGI_FORMAT_R32G32B32_FLOAT, 0, 0,
    D3D12_INPUT_PER_VERTEX_DATA, 0},
```

```
    {"COLOR",    0, DXGI_FORMAT_B8G8R8A8_UNORM, 0, 12,
     D3D12_INPUT_PER_VERTEX_DATA, 0}
};
```

We use the `DXGI_FORMAT_B8G8R8A8_UNORM` format (8-bits red, green, blue, and alpha). This format corresponds to the common 32-bit graphics color format ARGB, but the `DXGI_FORMAT` symbol lists the bytes as they appear in memory in *little-endian* notation. In little-endian, the bytes of a multi-byte data word are written from least significant byte to most significant byte, which is why ARGB appears in memory as BGRA with the least significant byte at the smallest memory address and the most significant byte at the highest memory address.

11. Consider the following C++ vertex structure:

    ```
    struct Vertex
    {
      XMFLOAT3 Pos;
      XMFLOAT4 Color;
    };
    ```

    (a) Does the input layout description order need to match the vertex structure order? That is, is the following vertex declaration correct for this vertex structure? Do an experiment to find out. Then give reasoning for why you think it works or does not work.

    ```
    D3D11_INPUT_ELEMENT_DESC vertexDesc[] =
    {
      {"COLOR",    0, DXGI_FORMAT_R32G32B32A32_FLOAT, 0, 12,
       D3D11_INPUT_PER_VERTEX_DATA, 0},
      {"POSITION", 0, DXGI_FORMAT_R32G32B32_FLOAT, 0, 0,
       D3D11_INPUT_PER_VERTEX_DATA, 0},
    };
    ```

    (b) Does the corresponding vertex shader structure order need to match the C++ vertex structure order? That is, does the following vertex shader structure work with the above C++ vertex structure? Do an experiment to find out. Then give reasoning for why you think it works or does not work.

    ```
    struct VertexIn
    {
      float4 Color : COLOR;
      float3 Pos   : POSITION;
    };
    ```

12. Set the viewport to the left half of the back buffer.

13. Use the scissor test to cull all pixels outside a rectangle centered about the back buffer with width `mClientWidth/2` and height `mClientHeight/2`. Remember that you also need to enable the scissor test with the rasterizer state group.

14. Pixel shader color tint. Use constant buffer to animate color over time. Use smooth easing function. Do it in vertex shader and pixel shader.
15. Modify the pixel shader in the Box demo to be the following:
    ```
    float4 PS(VertexOut pin) : SV_Target
    {
      clip(pin.Color.r - 0.5f);
      return pin.Color;
    }
    ```
    Run the demo and make a conjecture of what the built-in `clip` function does.
16. Modify the pixel shader in the Box demo to smoothly pulse between the interpolated vertex color and a `gPulseColor` specified through the constant buffer. You will also need to update the constant buffer on the application side. The constant buffer and pixel shader in the HLSL code should look like the following:
    ```
    cbuffer cbPerObject : register(b0)
    {
      float4x4 gWorldViewProj;
      float4 gPulseColor;
      float gTime;
    };

    float4 PS(VertexOut pin) : SV_Target
    {
      const float pi = 3.14159;

      // Oscillate a value in [0,1] over time using a sine function.
      float s = 0.5f*sin(2*gTime - 0.25f*pi)+0.5f;

      // Linearly interpolate between pin.Color and gPulseColor based on
      // parameter s.
      float4 c = lerp(pin.Color, gPulseColor, s);

      return c;
    }
    ```
    The `gTime` variable corresponds to the current `GameTimer::TotalTime()` value.

Chapter 7 Drawing in Direct3D Part II

This chapter introduces a number of drawing patterns that we will use throughout the rest of this book. The chapter begins by introducing a drawing optimization, which we refer to as "frame resources." With frame resources, we modify our render loop so that we do not have to flush the command queue every frame; this improves CPU and GPU utilization. Next we introduce the concept of a render item and explain how we divide up our constant data based on update frequency. In addition, we examine root signatures in more detail and learn about the other root parameter types: root descriptors and root constants. Finally, we show how to draw some more complicated objects; by the end of this chapter, you will be able to draw a surface that resembles hills and valleys, cylinders, spheres, and an animated wave simulation.

Objectives:

1. To understand a modification to our rendering process that does not require us to flush the command queue every frame, thereby improving performance.
2. To learn about the two other types of root signature parameter types: root descriptors and root constants.
3. To discover how to procedurally generate and draw common geometric shapes like grids, cylinders, and spheres.
4. To find out how we can animate vertices on the CPU and upload the new vertex positions to the GPU using dynamic vertex buffers.

7.1 FRAME RESOURCES

Recall from §4.2 that the CPU and GPU work in parallel. The CPU builds and submits command lists (in addition to other CPU work) and the GPU processes commands in the command queue. The goal is to keep both CPU and GPU busy to take full advantage of the hardware resources available on the system. So far in our demos, we have been synchronizing the CPU and GPU once per frame. Two examples of why this is necessary are:

1. The command allocator cannot be reset until the GPU is finished executing the commands. Suppose we did not synchronize so that the CPU could continue on to the next frame $n+1$ before the GPU has finished processing the current frame n: If the CPU resets the command allocator in frame $n+1$, but the GPU is still processing commands from frame n, then we would be clearing the commands the GPU is still working on.

2. A constant buffer cannot be updated by the CPU until the GPU has finished executing the drawing commands that reference the constant buffer. This example corresponds to the situation described in §4.2.2 and Figure 4.7. Suppose we did not synchronize so that the CPU could continue on to the next frame $n + 1$ before the GPU has finished processing the current frame n: If the CPU overwrites the constant buffer data in frame $n+1$, but the GPU has not yet executed the draw call that references the constant buffer in frame n, then the constant buffer contains the wrong data for when the GPU executes the draw call for frame n.

Thus we have been calling `D3DApp::FlushCommandQueue` at the end of every frame to ensure the GPU has finished executing all the commands for the frame. This solution works but is inefficient for the following reasons:

1. At the beginning of a frame, the GPU will not have any commands to process since we waited to empty the command queue. It will have to wait until the CPU builds and submits some commands for execution.

2. At the end of a frame, the CPU is waiting for the GPU to finish processing commands.

So every frame, the CPU and GPU are idling at some point.

One solution to this problem is to create a circular array of the resources the CPU needs to modify each frame. We call such resources *frame resources*, and we usually use a circular array of three frame resource elements. The idea is that for frame n, the CPU will cycle through the frame resource array to get the next available (i.e., not in use by GPU) frame resource. The CPU will then do any resource updates, and build and submit command lists for frame n while the GPU works on previous frames. The CPU will then continue on to frame $n+1$ and repeat. If the frame resource array has three elements, this lets the CPU get up to two frames ahead of the GPU, ensuring that the GPU is kept busy. Below is an example of the frame resource class we use for the "Shapes" demo in this chapter. Because the CPU only needs to modify constant buffers in this demo, the frame resource class only contains constant buffers.

```
// Stores the resources needed for the CPU to build the command lists
// for a frame. The contents here will vary from app to app based on
// the needed resources.
struct FrameResource
{
public:

    FrameResource(ID3D12Device* device, UINT passCount,
      UINT objectCount);
    FrameResource(const FrameResource& rhs) = delete;
    FrameResource& operator=(const FrameResource& rhs) = delete;
    ~FrameResource();

    // We cannot reset the allocator until the GPU is done processing the
    // commands. So each frame needs their own allocator.
    Microsoft::WRL::ComPtr<ID3D12CommandAllocator> CmdListAlloc;

    // We cannot update a cbuffer until the GPU is done processing the
    // commands that reference it. So each frame needs their own cbuffers.
    std::unique_ptr<UploadBuffer<PassConstants>> PassCB = nullptr;
    std::unique_ptr<UploadBuffer<ObjectConstants>> ObjectCB = nullptr;

    // Fence value to mark commands up to this fence point. This lets us
    // check if these frame resources are still in use by the GPU.
    UINT64 Fence = 0;
};

FrameResource::FrameResource(ID3D12Device* device, UINT passCount, UINT
  objectCount)
{
    ThrowIfFailed(device->CreateCommandAllocator(
      D3D12_COMMAND_LIST_TYPE_DIRECT,
      IID_PPV_ARGS(CmdListAlloc.GetAddressOf())));

    PassCB = std::make_unique<UploadBuffer<PassConstants>>(device,
      passCount, true);
    ObjectCB = std::make_unique<UploadBuffer<ObjectConstants>>(device,
      objectCount, true);
}
FrameResource::~FrameResource() { }
```

Our application class will then instantiate a vector of three frame resources, and keep member variables to track the current frame resource:

```
static const int NumFrameResources = 3;
std::vector<std::unique_ptr<FrameResource>> mFrameResources;
FrameResource* mCurrFrameResource = nullptr;
```

```cpp
int mCurrFrameResourceIndex = 0;

void ShapesApp::BuildFrameResources()
{
  for(int i = 0; i < gNumFrameResources; ++i)
  {
    mFrameResources.push_back(std::make_unique<FrameResource>(
      md3dDevice.Get(), 1, (UINT)mAllRitems.size()));
  }
}
```

Now, for CPU frame n, the algorithm works like so:

```cpp
void ShapesApp::Update(const GameTimer& gt)
{
  // Cycle through the circular frame resource array.
  mCurrFrameResourceIndex = (mCurrFrameResourceIndex + 1) %
    NumFrameResources;
  mCurrFrameResource = mFrameResources[mCurrFrameResourceIndex];

  // Has the GPU finished processing the commands of the current frame
  // resource. If not, wait until the GPU has completed commands up to
  // this fence point.
  if(mCurrFrameResource->Fence != 0 &&
    mCommandQueue->GetLastCompletedFence() < mCurrFrameResource->Fence)
  {
    HANDLE eventHandle = CreateEventEx(nullptr, false, false, EVENT_
    ALL_ACCESS);
    ThrowIfFailed(mCommandQueue->SetEventOnFenceCompletion(
      mCurrFrameResource->Fence, eventHandle));
    WaitForSingleObject(eventHandle, INFINITE);
    CloseHandle(eventHandle);
  }

  // [...] Update resources in mCurrFrameResource (like cbuffers).
}

void ShapesApp::Draw(const GameTimer& gt)
{
  // [...] Build and submit command lists for this frame.

  // Advance the fence value to mark commands up to this fence point.
  mCurrFrameResource->Fence = ++mCurrentFence;

  // Add an instruction to the command queue to set a new fence point.
  // Because we are on the GPU timeline, the new fence point won't be
  // set until the GPU finishes processing all the commands prior to
  // this Signal().
  mCommandQueue->Signal(mFence.Get(), mCurrentFence);

  // Note that GPU could still be working on commands from previous
  // frames, but that is okay, because we are not touching any frame
  // resources associated with those frames.
}
```

Note that this solution does not prevent waiting. If one processor is processing frames much faster than the other, one processor will eventually have to wait for the other to catch up, as we cannot let one get too far ahead of the other. If the GPU is processing commands faster than the CPU can submit work, then the GPU will idle. In general, if we are trying to push the graphical limit, we want to avoid this situation, as we are not taking full advantage of the GPU. On the other hand, if the CPU is always processing frames faster than the GPU, then the CPU will have to wait at some point. This is the desired situation, as the GPU is being fully utilized; the extra CPU cycles can always be used for other parts of the game such as AI, physics, and game play logic.

So if multiple frame resources do not prevent any waiting, how does it help us? It helps us keep the GPU fed. While the GPU is processing commands from frame n, it allows the CPU to continue on to build and submit commands for frames $n+1$ and $n+2$. This helps keep the command queue nonempty so that the GPU always has work to do.

7.2 RENDER ITEMS

Drawing an object requires setting multiple parameters such as binding vertex and index buffers, binding object constants, setting a primitive type, and specifying the `DrawIndexedInstanced` parameters. As we begin to draw more objects in our scenes, it is helpful to create a lightweight structure that stores the data needed to draw an object; this data will vary from app to app as we add new features which will require different drawing data. We call the set of data needed to submit a full draw call the rendering pipeline a *render item*. For this demo, our `RenderItem` structure looks like this:

```
// Lightweight structure stores parameters to draw a shape. This will
// vary from app-to-app.
struct RenderItem
{
    RenderItem() = default;

    // World matrix of the shape that describes the object's local space
    // relative to the world space, which defines the position,
    // orientation, and scale of the object in the world.
    XMFLOAT4X4 World = MathHelper::Identity4x4();

    // Dirty flag indicating the object data has changed and we need
    // to update the constant buffer. Because we have an object
    // cbuffer for each FrameResource, we have to apply the
    // update to each FrameResource. Thus, when we modify obect data we
    // should set
    // NumFramesDirty = gNumFrameResources so that each frame resource
    // gets the update.
```

```cpp
    int NumFramesDirty = gNumFrameResources;

    // Index into GPU constant buffer corresponding to the ObjectCB
    // for this render item.
    UINT ObjCBIndex = -1;

    // Geometry associated with this render-item. Note that multiple
    // render-items can share the same geometry.
    MeshGeometry* Geo = nullptr;

    // Primitive topology.
    D3D12_PRIMITIVE_TOPOLOGY PrimitiveType = D3D_PRIMITIVE_TOPOLOGY_
      TRIANGLELIST;

    // DrawIndexedInstanced parameters.
    UINT IndexCount = 0;
    UINT StartIndexLocation = 0;
    int BaseVertexLocation = 0;
};
```

Our application will maintain lists of render items based on how they need to be drawn; that is, render items that need different PSOs will be kept in different lists.

```cpp
// List of all the render items.
std::vector<std::unique_ptr<RenderItem>> mAllRitems;

// Render items divided by PSO.
std::vector<RenderItem*> mOpaqueRitems;
std::vector<RenderItem*> mTransparentRitems;
```

7.3 PASS CONSTANTS

Observe from the previous section that we introduced a new constant buffer in our `FrameResource` class:

```cpp
std::unique_ptr<UploadBuffer<PassConstants>> PassCB = nullptr;
```

In the demos going forward, this buffer stores constant data that is fixed over a given rendering pass such as the eye position, the view and projection matrices, and information about the screen (render target) dimensions; it also includes game timing information, which is useful data to have access to in shader programs. Note that our demos will not necessarily use all this constant data, but it is convenient to have available, and there is little cost providing the extra data. For example, while we do not need the render target sizes now, when we go to implement some post processing effect, having that information will be needed.

```cpp
cbuffer cbPass : register(b1)
{
```

```
    float4x4 gView;
    float4x4 gInvView;
    float4x4 gProj;
    float4x4 gInvProj;
    float4x4 gViewProj;
    float4x4 gInvViewProj;
    float3 gEyePosW;
    float cbPerObjectPad1;
    float2 gRenderTargetSize;
    float2 gInvRenderTargetSize;
    float gNearZ;
    float gFarZ;
    float gTotalTime;
    float gDeltaTime;
};
```

We have also modified our per object constant buffer to only store constants that are associated with an object. So far, the only constant data we associate with an object for drawing is its world matrix:

```
cbuffer cbPerObject : register(b0)
{
    float4x4 gWorld;
};
```

The idea of these changes is to group constants based on update frequency. The per pass constants only need to be updated once per rendering pass, and the object constants only need to change when an object's world matrix changes. If we had a static object in the scene, like a tree, we only need to set its world matrix once to a constant buffer and then never update the constant buffer again. In our demos, we implement the following methods to handle updating the per pass and per object constant buffers. These methods are called once per frame in the Update method.

```
void ShapesApp::UpdateObjectCBs(const GameTimer& gt)
{
    auto currObjectCB = mCurrFrameResource->ObjectCB.get();
    for(auto& e : mAllRitems)
    {
        // Only update the cbuffer data if the constants have changed.
        // This needs to be tracked per frame resource.
        if(e->NumFramesDirty > 0)
        {
            XMMATRIX world = XMLoadFloat4x4(&e->World);

            ObjectConstants objConstants;
            XMStoreFloat4x4(&objConstants.World, XMMatrixTranspose(world));

            currObjectCB->CopyData(e->ObjCBIndex, objConstants);

            // Next FrameResource need to be updated too.
            e->NumFramesDirty--;
```

```
      }
    }
  }

  void ShapesApp::UpdateMainPassCB(const GameTimer& gt)
  {
    XMMATRIX view = XMLoadFloat4x4(&mView);
    XMMATRIX proj = XMLoadFloat4x4(&mProj);

    XMMATRIX viewProj = XMMatrixMultiply(view, proj);
    XMMATRIX invView = XMMatrixInverse(&XMMatrixDeterminant(view), view);
    XMMATRIX invProj = XMMatrixInverse(&XMMatrixDeterminant(proj), proj);
    XMMATRIX invViewProj = XMMatrixInverse(&XMMatrixDeterminant(viewPr
      oj), viewProj);

    XMStoreFloat4x4(&mMainPassCB.View, XMMatrixTranspose(view));
    XMStoreFloat4x4(&mMainPassCB.InvView, XMMatrixTranspose(invView));
    XMStoreFloat4x4(&mMainPassCB.Proj, XMMatrixTranspose(proj));
    XMStoreFloat4x4(&mMainPassCB.InvProj, XMMatrixTranspose(invProj));
    XMStoreFloat4x4(&mMainPassCB.ViewProj, XMMatrixTranspose(viewProj));
    XMStoreFloat4x4(&mMainPassCB.InvViewProj, XMMatrixTranspose(invViewP
      roj));
    mMainPassCB.EyePosW = mEyePos;
    mMainPassCB.RenderTargetSize = XMFLOAT2((float)mClientWidth, (float)
      mClientHeight);
    mMainPassCB.InvRenderTargetSize = XMFLOAT2(1.0f / mClientWidth, 1.0f
      / mClientHeight);
    mMainPassCB.NearZ = 1.0f;
    mMainPassCB.FarZ = 1000.0f;
    mMainPassCB.TotalTime = gt.TotalTime();
    mMainPassCB.DeltaTime = gt.DeltaTime();

    auto currPassCB = mCurrFrameResource->PassCB.get();
    currPassCB->CopyData(0, mMainPassCB);
  }
```

We update our vertex shader accordingly to support these constant buffer changes:

```
VertexOut VS(VertexIn vin)
{
  VertexOut vout;

  // Transform to homogeneous clip space.
  float4 posW = mul(float4(vin.PosL, 1.0f), gWorld);
  vout.PosH = mul(posW, gViewProj);

  // Just pass vertex color into the pixel shader.
  vout.Color = vin.Color;

  return vout;
}
```

The extra vector-matrix multiplication per vertex this adjustment gives is negligible on modern GPUs, which have plenty of computation power.

The resources that our shaders expect have changed; therefore, we need to update the root signature accordingly to take two descriptor tables (we need two tables because the CBVs will be set at different frequencies—the per pass CBV only needs to be set once per rendering pass while the per object CBV needs to be set per render item):

```
CD3DX12_DESCRIPTOR_RANGE cbvTable0;
cbvTable0.Init(D3D12_DESCRIPTOR_RANGE_TYPE_CBV, 1, 0);

CD3DX12_DESCRIPTOR_RANGE cbvTable1;
cbvTable1.Init(D3D12_DESCRIPTOR_RANGE_TYPE_CBV, 1, 1);

// Root parameter can be a table, root descriptor or root constants.
CD3DX12_ROOT_PARAMETER slotRootParameter[2];

// Create root CBVs.
slotRootParameter[0].InitAsDescriptorTable(1, &cbvTable0);
slotRootParameter[1].InitAsDescriptorTable(1, &cbvTable1);

// A root signature is an array of root parameters.
CD3DX12_ROOT_SIGNATURE_DESC rootSigDesc(2, slotRootParameter, 0,
    nullptr,
    D3D12_ROOT_SIGNATURE_FLAG_ALLOW_INPUT_ASSEMBLER_INPUT_LAYOUT);
```

 Do not go overboard with the number of constant buffers in your shaders. [Thibieroz13] recommends you keep them under five for performance.

7.4 SHAPE GEOMETRY

In this section, we show how to create the geometry for ellipsoids, spheres, cylinders and cones. These shapes are useful for drawing sky domes, debugging, visualizing collision detection, and deferred rendering. For example, you might want to render all of your game characters as spheres for a debug test.

We put our procedural geometry generation code in the `GeometryGenerator` class (GeometryGenerator.h/.cpp). `GeometryGenerator` is a utility class for generating simple geometric shapes like grids, sphere, cylinders, and boxes, which we use throughout this book for our demo programs. This class generates the data in system memory, and we must then copy the data we want to our vertex and index buffers. `GeometryGenerator` creates some vertex data that will be used in later chapters. We do not need this data in our current demos, and so we do *not* copy this data into our vertex buffers. The `MeshData` structure is a simple structure nested inside `GeometryGenerator` that stores a vertex and index list:

```
class GeometryGenerator
{
public:
```

```cpp
using uint16 = std::uint16_t;
using uint32 = std::uint32_t;

struct Vertex
{
  Vertex(){}
  Vertex(
    const DirectX::XMFLOAT3& p,
    const DirectX::XMFLOAT3& n,
    const DirectX::XMFLOAT3& t,
    const DirectX::XMFLOAT2& uv) :
    Position(p),
    Normal(n),
    TangentU(t),
    TexC(uv){}
  Vertex(
    float px, float py, float pz,
    float nx, float ny, float nz,
    float tx, float ty, float tz,
    float u, float v) :
    Position(px,py,pz),
    Normal(nx,ny,nz),
    TangentU(tx, ty, tz),
    TexC(u,v){}

  DirectX::XMFLOAT3 Position;
  DirectX::XMFLOAT3 Normal;
  DirectX::XMFLOAT3 TangentU;
  DirectX::XMFLOAT2 TexC;
};
struct MeshData
{
  std::vector<Vertex> Vertices;
  std::vector<uint32> Indices32;

  std::vector<uint16>& GetIndices16()
  {
    if(mIndices16.empty())
    {
      mIndices16.resize(Indices32.size());
      for(size_t i = 0; i < Indices32.size(); ++i)
        mIndices16[i] = static_cast<uint16>(Indices32[i]);
    }

    return mIndices16;
  }

  private:
    std::vector<uint16> mIndices16;
};

...


};
```

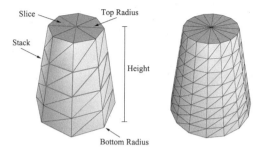

Figure 7.1. In this illustration, the cylinder on the left has eight slices and four stacks, and the cylinder on the right has sixteen slices and eight stacks. The slices and stacks control the triangle density. Note that the top and bottom radii can differ so that we can create cone shaped objects, not just "pure" cylinders.

7.4.1 Generating a Cylinder Mesh

We define a cylinder by specifying its bottom and top radii, its height, and the slice and stack count, as shown in Figure 7.1. We break the cylinder into three parts: 1) the side geometry, 2) the top cap geometry, and 3) the bottom cap geometry.

7.4.1.1 Cylinder Side Geometry

We generate the cylinder centered at the origin, parallel to the *y*-axis. From Figure 7.1, all the vertices lie on the "rings" of the cylinder, where there are *stackCount* + 1 rings, and each ring has *sliceCount* unique vertices. The difference in radius between consecutive rings is Δr = *(topRadius – bottomRadius)/stackCount*. If we start at the bottom ring with index 0, then the radius of the *i*th ring is r_i = *bottomRadius* + $i\Delta r$ and the height of the *i*th ring is $h_i = -\frac{h}{2} + i\Delta h$, where Δh is the stack height and *h* is the cylinder height. So the basic idea is to iterate over each ring, and generate the vertices that lie on that ring. This gives the following implementation:

```
GeometryGenerator::MeshData
GeometryGenerator::CreateCylinder(
  float bottomRadius, float topRadius,
  float height, uint32 sliceCount, uint32 stackCount)
{
  MeshData meshData;

  //
  // Build Stacks.
  //

  float stackHeight = height / stackCount;

  // Amount to increment radius as we move up each stack level from
  // bottom to top.
  float radiusStep = (topRadius - bottomRadius) / stackCount;

  uint32 ringCount = stackCount+1;
```

```cpp
// Compute vertices for each stack ring starting at the bottom and
// moving up.
for(uint32 i = 0; i < ringCount; ++i)
{
  float y = -0.5f*height + i*stackHeight;
  float r = bottomRadius + i*radiusStep;

  // vertices of ring
  float dTheta = 2.0f*XM_PI/sliceCount;
  for(uint32 j = 0; j <= sliceCount; ++j)
  {
    Vertex vertex;

    float c = cosf(j*dTheta);
    float s = sinf(j*dTheta);

    vertex.Position = XMFLOAT3(r*c, y, r*s);

    vertex.TexC.x = (float)j/sliceCount;
    vertex.TexC.y = 1.0f - (float)i/stackCount;

    // Cylinder can be parameterized as follows, where we introduce v
    // parameter that goes in the same direction as the v tex-coord
    // so that the bitangent goes in the same direction as the
    // v tex-coord.
    //   Let r0 be the bottom radius and let r1 be the top radius.
    //  y(v) = h - hv for v in [0,1].
    //  r(v) = r1 + (r0-r1)v
    //
    //  x(t, v) = r(v)*cos(t)
    //  y(t, v) = h - hv
    //  z(t, v) = r(v)*sin(t)
    //
    // dx/dt = -r(v)*sin(t)
    // dy/dt = 0
    // dz/dt = +r(v)*cos(t)
    //
    // dx/dv = (r0-r1)*cos(t)
    // dy/dv = -h
    // dz/dv = (r0-r1)*sin(t)

    // This is unit length.
    vertex.TangentU = XMFLOAT3(-s, 0.0f, c);

    float dr = bottomRadius-topRadius;
    XMFLOAT3 bitangent(dr*c, -height, dr*s);

    XMVECTOR T = XMLoadFloat3(&vertex.TangentU);
    XMVECTOR B = XMLoadFloat3(&bitangent);
    XMVECTOR N = XMVector3Normalize(XMVector3Cross(T, B));
    XMStoreFloat3(&vertex.Normal, N);

    meshData.Vertices.push_back(vertex);
  }
}
```

> **Note:** *Observe that the first and last vertex of each ring is duplicated in position, but the texture coordinates are not duplicated. We have to do this so that we can apply textures to cylinders correctly.*

> **Note:** *The actual method* `GeometryGenerator::CreateCylinder` *creates additional vertex data such as normal vectors and texture coordinates that will be useful for future demos. Do not worry about these quantities for now.*

Observe from Figure 7.2 that there is a quad (two triangles) for each slice in every stack. Figure 7.2 shows that the indices for the ith stack and jth slice are given by:

$$\Delta ABC = \left(i \cdot n + j, (i+1) \cdot n + j, (i+1) \cdot n + j + 1\right)$$

$$\Delta ACD = \left(i \cdot n + j, (i+1) \cdot n + j + 1, i \cdot n + j + 1\right)$$

where n is the number of vertices per ring. So the key idea is to loop over every slice in every stack, and apply the above formulas.

```
// Add one because we duplicate the first and last vertex per ring
// since the texture coordinates are different.
uint32 ringVertexCount = sliceCount+1;

// Compute indices for each stack.
for(uint32 i = 0; i < stackCount; ++i)
{
  for(uint32 j = 0; j < sliceCount; ++j)
  {
    meshData.Indices32.push_back(i*ringVertexCount + j);
    meshData.Indices32.push_back((i+1)*ringVertexCount + j);
    meshData.Indices32.push_back((i+1)*ringVertexCount + j+1);

    meshData.Indices32.push_back(i*ringVertexCount + j);
```

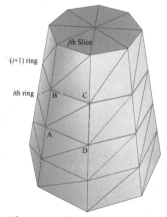

Figure 7.2. The vertices A, B, C, D contained in the ith and i + 1th ring, and jth slice.

```
        meshData.Indices32.push_back((i+1)*ringVertexCount + j+1);
        meshData.Indices32.push_back(i*ringVertexCount + j+1);
    }
}

BuildCylinderTopCap(bottomRadius, topRadius, height,
    sliceCount, stackCount, meshData);
BuildCylinderBottomCap(bottomRadius, topRadius, height,
    sliceCount, stackCount, meshData);

return meshData;
}
```

7.4.1.2 Cap Geometry

Generating the cap geometry amounts to generating the slice triangles of the top and bottom rings to approximate a circle:

```
void GeometryGenerator::BuildCylinderTopCap(
  float bottomRadius, float topRadius, float height,
  uint32 sliceCount, uint32 stackCount, MeshData& meshData)
{
  uint32 baseIndex = (uint32)meshData.Vertices.size();

  float y = 0.5f*height;
  float dTheta = 2.0f*XM_PI/sliceCount;

  // Duplicate cap ring vertices because the texture coordinates and
  // normals differ.
  for(uint32 i = 0; i <= sliceCount; ++i)
  {
    float x = topRadius*cosf(i*dTheta);
    float z = topRadius*sinf(i*dTheta);

    // Scale down by the height to try and make top cap texture coord
    // area proportional to base.
    float u = x/height + 0.5f;
    float v = z/height + 0.5f;

    meshData.Vertices.push_back(
      Vertex(x, y, z, 0.0f, 1.0f, 0.0f, 1.0f, 0.0f, 0.0f, u, v) );
  }

  // Cap center vertex.
  meshData.Vertices.push_back(
    Vertex(0.0f, y, 0.0f, 0.0f, 1.0f, 0.0f, 1.0f, 0.0f, 0.0f, 0.5f,
    0.5f) );

  // Index of center vertex.
  uint32 centerIndex = (uint32)meshData.Vertices.size()-1;

  for(uint32 i = 0; i < sliceCount; ++i)
  {
    meshData.Indices32.push_back(centerIndex);
    meshData.Indices32.push_back(baseIndex + i+1);
```

```
            meshData.Indices32.push_back(baseIndex + i);
        }
    }
```

The bottom cap code is analogous.

7.4.2 Generating a Sphere Mesh

We define a sphere by specifying its radius, and the slice and stack count, as shown in Figure 7.3. The algorithm for generating the sphere is very similar to that of the cylinder, except that the radius per ring changes is a nonlinear way based on trigonometric functions. We will leave it to the reader to study the `GeometryGenerator::CreateSphere` code. Note that we can apply a non-uniform scaling world transformation to transform a sphere into an ellipsoid.

7.4.3 Generating a Geosphere Mesh

Observe from Figure 7.3 that the triangles of the sphere do not have equal areas. This can be undesirable for some situations. A geosphere approximates a sphere using triangles with almost equal areas as well as equal side lengths (see Figure 7.4).

To generate a geosphere, we start with an icosahedron, subdivide the triangles, and then project the new vertices onto the sphere with the given radius. We can repeat this process to improve the tessellation.

Figure 7.5 shows how a triangle can be subdivided into four equal sized triangles. The new vertices are found just by taking the midpoints along the edges of the original triangle. The new vertices can then be projected onto a sphere of

Figure 7.3. The idea of slices and stacks also apply to a sphere to control the level of tessellation.

Figure 7.4. Approximating a geosphere by repeated subdivision and reprojection onto the sphere.

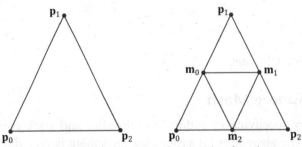

Figure 7.5. Subdividing a triangle into four triangles of equal area.

radius *r* by projecting the vertices onto the unit sphere and then scalar multiplying by $r : \mathbf{v}' = r \frac{\mathbf{v}}{\|\mathbf{v}\|}$.

The code is given below:

```
GeometryGenerator::MeshData
GeometryGenerator::CreateGeosphere(float radius, uint32
    numSubdivisions)
{
  MeshData meshData;

  // Put a cap on the number of subdivisions.
  numSubdivisions = std::min<uint32>(numSubdivisions, 6u);

  // Approximate a sphere by tessellating an icosahedron.

  const float X = 0.525731f;
  const float Z = 0.850651f;

  XMFLOAT3 pos[12] =
  {
    XMFLOAT3(-X, 0.0f, Z),  XMFLOAT3(X, 0.0f, Z),
    XMFLOAT3(-X, 0.0f, -Z), XMFLOAT3(X, 0.0f, -Z),
    XMFLOAT3(0.0f, Z, X),   XMFLOAT3(0.0f, Z, -X),
    XMFLOAT3(0.0f, -Z, X),  XMFLOAT3(0.0f, -Z, -X),
    XMFLOAT3(Z, X, 0.0f),   XMFLOAT3(-Z, X, 0.0f),
    XMFLOAT3(Z, -X, 0.0f),  XMFLOAT3(-Z, -X, 0.0f)
  };

  uint32 k[60] =
  {
    1,4,0,  4,9,0,  4,5,9,  8,5,4,  1,8,4,
    1,10,8, 10,3,8, 8,3,5,  3,2,5,  3,7,2,
    3,10,7, 10,6,7, 6,11,7, 6,0,11, 6,1,0,
    10,1,6, 11,0,9, 2,11,9, 5,2,9,  11,2,7
  };

  meshData.Vertices.resize(12);
  meshData.Indices32.assign(&k[0], &k[60]);

  for(uint32 i = 0; i < 12; ++i)
    meshData.Vertices[i].Position = pos[i];
```

```
  for(uint32 i = 0; i < numSubdivisions; ++i)
    Subdivide(meshData);

  // Project vertices onto sphere and scale.
  for(uint32 i = 0; i < meshData.Vertices.size(); ++i)
  {
    // Project onto unit sphere.
    XMVECTOR n = XMVector3Normalize(XMLoadFloat3(&meshData.Vertices[i].
    Position));

    // Project onto sphere.
    XMVECTOR p = radius*n;

    XMStoreFloat3(&meshData.Vertices[i].Position, p);
    XMStoreFloat3(&meshData.Vertices[i].Normal, n);

    // Derive texture coordinates from spherical coordinates.
    float theta = atan2f(meshData.Vertices[i].Position.z,
              meshData.Vertices[i].Position.x);

    // Put in [0, 2pi].
    if(theta < 0.0f)
      theta += XM_2PI;

    float phi = acosf(meshData.Vertices[i].Position.y / radius);

    meshData.Vertices[i].TexC.x = theta/XM_2PI;
    meshData.Vertices[i].TexC.y = phi/XM_PI;

    // Partial derivative of P with respect to theta
    meshData.Vertices[i].TangentU.x = -radius*sinf(phi)*sinf(theta);
    meshData.Vertices[i].TangentU.y = 0.0f;
    meshData.Vertices[i].TangentU.z = +radius*sinf(phi)*cosf(theta);

    XMVECTOR T = XMLoadFloat3(&meshData.Vertices[i].TangentU);
    XMStoreFloat3(&meshData.Vertices[i].TangentU,
      XMVector3Normalize(T));
  }

  return meshData;
}
```

7.5 SHAPES DEMO

To demonstrate our sphere and cylinder generation code, we implement the "Shapes" demo shown in Figure 7.6. In addition, you will also gain experience positioning and drawing multiple objects in a scene (i.e., creating multiple world transformation matrices). Furthermore, we place all of the scene geometry in one big vertex and index buffer. Then we will use the DrawIndexedInstanced method to draw one object at a time (as the world matrix needs to be changed

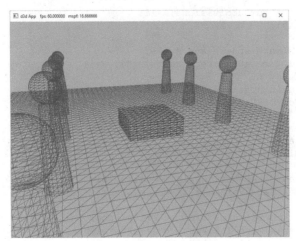

Figure 7.6. Screenshot of the "Shapes" demo.

between objects); so you will see an example of using the `StartIndexLocation` and `BaseVertexLocation` parameters of `DrawIndexedInstanced`.

7.5.1 Vertex and Index Buffers

As Figure 7.6 shows, in this demo we draw a box, grid, cylinders, and sphere. Even though we draw multiple spheres and cylinders in this demo, we only need one copy of the sphere and cylinder geometry. We simply redraw the same sphere and cylinder mesh multiple times, but with different world matrices; this is an example of *instancing* geometry, which saves memory.

We pack all the mesh vertices and indices into one vertex and index buffer. This is done by concatenating the vertex and index arrays. This means that when we draw an object, we are only drawing a subset of the vertex and index buffers. There are three quantities we need to know in order to draw only a subset of the geometry using `ID3D12CommandList::DrawIndexedInstanced` (recall Figure 6.3 and the discussion about it from Chapter 6). We need to know the starting index to the object in the concatenated index buffer, its index count, and we need to know the base vertex location—the index of the object's first vertex relative to the concatenated vertex buffer. Recall that the base vertex location is an integer value added to the indices in a draw call before the vertices are fetched, so that the indices reference the proper subset in the concatenated vertex buffer. (See also Exercise 2 in Chapter 5.)

The code below shows how the geometry buffers are created, how the necessary drawing quantities are cached, and how the objects are drawn.

```
void ShapesApp::BuildShapeGeometry()
{
```

```
GeometryGenerator geoGen;
GeometryGenerator::MeshData box = geoGen.CreateBox(1.5f, 0.5f, 1.5f,
   3);
GeometryGenerator::MeshData grid = geoGen.CreateGrid(20.0f, 30.0f,
   60, 40);
GeometryGenerator::MeshData sphere = geoGen.CreateSphere(0.5f, 20,
   20);
GeometryGenerator::MeshData cylinder = geoGen.CreateCylinder(0.5f,
   0.3f, 3.0f, 20, 20);

//
// We are concatenating all the geometry into one big vertex/index
// buffer. So define the regions in the buffer each submesh covers.
//

// Cache the vertex offsets to each object in the concatenated vertex
// buffer.
UINT boxVertexOffset = 0;
UINT gridVertexOffset = (UINT)box.Vertices.size();
UINT sphereVertexOffset = gridVertexOffset + (UINT)grid.Vertices.
   size();
UINT cylinderVertexOffset = sphereVertexOffset + (UINT)sphere.
   Vertices.size();

// Cache the starting index for each object in the concatenated index
// buffer.
UINT boxIndexOffset = 0;
UINT gridIndexOffset = (UINT)box.Indices32.size();
UINT sphereIndexOffset = gridIndexOffset + (UINT)grid.Indices32.
   size();
UINT cylinderIndexOffset = sphereIndexOffset + (UINT)sphere.Indices32.
   size();

// Define the SubmeshGeometry that cover different
// regions of the vertex/index buffers.

SubmeshGeometry boxSubmesh;
boxSubmesh.IndexCount = (UINT)box.Indices32.size();
boxSubmesh.StartIndexLocation = boxIndexOffset;
boxSubmesh.BaseVertexLocation = boxVertexOffset;

SubmeshGeometry gridSubmesh;
gridSubmesh.IndexCount = (UINT)grid.Indices32.size();
gridSubmesh.StartIndexLocation = gridIndexOffset;
gridSubmesh.BaseVertexLocation = gridVertexOffset;

SubmeshGeometry sphereSubmesh;
sphereSubmesh.IndexCount = (UINT)sphere.Indices32.size();
sphereSubmesh.StartIndexLocation = sphereIndexOffset;
sphereSubmesh.BaseVertexLocation = sphereVertexOffset;

SubmeshGeometry cylinderSubmesh;
cylinderSubmesh.IndexCount = (UINT)cylinder.Indices32.size();
cylinderSubmesh.StartIndexLocation = cylinderIndexOffset;
```

```cpp
cylinderSubmesh.BaseVertexLocation = cylinderVertexOffset;

//
// Extract the vertex elements we are interested in and pack the
// vertices of all the meshes into one vertex buffer.
//

auto totalVertexCount =
  box.Vertices.size() +
  grid.Vertices.size() +
  sphere.Vertices.size() +
  cylinder.Vertices.size();

std::vector<Vertex> vertices(totalVertexCount);

UINT k = 0;
for(size_t i = 0; i < box.Vertices.size(); ++i, ++k)
{
  vertices[k].Pos = box.Vertices[i].Position;
  vertices[k].Color = XMFLOAT4(DirectX::Colors::DarkGreen);
}

for(size_t i = 0; i < grid.Vertices.size(); ++i, ++k)
{
  vertices[k].Pos = grid.Vertices[i].Position;
  vertices[k].Color = XMFLOAT4(DirectX::Colors::ForestGreen);
}

for(size_t i = 0; i < sphere.Vertices.size(); ++i, ++k)
{
  vertices[k].Pos = sphere.Vertices[i].Position;
  vertices[k].Color = XMFLOAT4(DirectX::Colors::Crimson);
}

for(size_t i = 0; i < cylinder.Vertices.size(); ++i, ++k)
{
  vertices[k].Pos = cylinder.Vertices[i].Position;
  vertices[k].Color = XMFLOAT4(DirectX::Colors::SteelBlue);
}

std::vector<std::uint16_t> indices;
indices.insert(indices.end(),
  std::begin(box.GetIndices16()),
  std::end(box.GetIndices16()));
indices.insert(indices.end(),
  std::begin(grid.GetIndices16()),
  std::end(grid.GetIndices16()));
indices.insert(indices.end(),
  std::begin(sphere.GetIndices16()),
  std::end(sphere.GetIndices16()));
indices.insert(indices.end(),
  std::begin(cylinder.GetIndices16()),
  std::end(cylinder.GetIndices16()));
```

```
    const UINT vbByteSize = (UINT)vertices.size() * sizeof(Vertex);
    const UINT ibByteSize = (UINT)indices.size() * sizeof(std::uint16_t);

    auto geo = std::make_unique<MeshGeometry>();
    geo->Name = "shapeGeo";

    ThrowIfFailed(D3DCreateBlob(vbByteSize, &geo->VertexBufferCPU));
    CopyMemory(geo->VertexBufferCPU->GetBufferPointer(), vertices.data(),
      vbByteSize);

    ThrowIfFailed(D3DCreateBlob(ibByteSize, &geo->IndexBufferCPU));
    CopyMemory(geo->IndexBufferCPU->GetBufferPointer(), indices.data(),
      ibByteSize);

    geo->VertexBufferGPU = d3dUtil::CreateDefaultBuffer(md3dDevice.Get(),
      mCommandList.Get(), vertices.data(), vbByteSize, geo-
      >VertexBufferUploader);

    geo->IndexBufferGPU = d3dUtil::CreateDefaultBuffer(md3dDevice.Get(),
      mCommandList.Get(), indices.data(), ibByteSize, geo-
      >IndexBufferUploader);

    geo->VertexByteStride = sizeof(Vertex);
    geo->VertexBufferByteSize = vbByteSize;
    geo->IndexFormat = DXGI_FORMAT_R16_UINT;
    geo->IndexBufferByteSize = ibByteSize;

    geo->DrawArgs["box"] = boxSubmesh;
    geo->DrawArgs["grid"] = gridSubmesh;
    geo->DrawArgs["sphere"] = sphereSubmesh;
    geo->DrawArgs["cylinder"] = cylinderSubmesh;

    mGeometries[geo->Name] = std::move(geo);
}
```

The `mGeometries` variable used in the last line of the above method is defined like so:

```
std::unordered_map<std::string, std::unique_ptr<MeshGeometry>>
    mGeometries;
```

This is a common pattern we employ for the rest of this book. It is cumbersome to create a new variable name for each geometry, PSO, texture, shader, etc., so we use unordered maps for constant time lookup and reference our objects by name. Here are some more examples:

```
std::unordered_map<std::string, std::unique_ptr<MeshGeometry>>
    mGeometries;
std::unordered_map<std::string, ComPtr<ID3DBlob>> mShaders;
std::unordered_map<std::string, ComPtr<ID3D12PipelineState>> mPSOs;
```

7.5.2 Render Items

We now define our scene render items. Observe how all the render items share the same `MeshGeometry`, and we use the `DrawArgs` to get the `DrawIndexedInstanced` parameters to draw a subregion of the vertex/index buffers.

```
// ShapesApp member variable.
std::vector<std::unique_ptr<RenderItem>> mAllRitems;
std::vector<RenderItem*> mOpaqueRitems;

void ShapesApp::BuildRenderItems()
{
  auto boxRitem = std::make_unique<RenderItem>();
  XMStoreFloat4x4(&boxRitem->World,
    XMMatrixScaling(2.0f, 2.0f, 2.0f)*XMMatrixTranslation(0.0f, 0.5f,
    0.0f));
  boxRitem->ObjCBIndex = 0;
  boxRitem->Geo = mGeometries["shapeGeo"].get();
  boxRitem->PrimitiveType = D3D_PRIMITIVE_TOPOLOGY_TRIANGLELIST;
  boxRitem->IndexCount = boxRitem->Geo->DrawArgs["box"].IndexCount;
  boxRitem->StartIndexLocation = boxRitem->Geo->DrawArgs["box"].
    StartIndexLocation;
  boxRitem->BaseVertexLocation = boxRitem->Geo->DrawArgs["box"].
    BaseVertexLocation;
  mAllRitems.push_back(std::move(boxRitem));

  auto gridRitem = std::make_unique<RenderItem>();
  gridRitem->World = MathHelper::Identity4x4();
  gridRitem->ObjCBIndex = 1;
  gridRitem->Geo = mGeometries["shapeGeo"].get();
  gridRitem->PrimitiveType = D3D_PRIMITIVE_TOPOLOGY_TRIANGLELIST;
  gridRitem->IndexCount = gridRitem->Geo->DrawArgs["grid"].IndexCount;
  gridRitem->StartIndexLocation = gridRitem->Geo->DrawArgs["grid"].
    StartIndexLocation;
  gridRitem->BaseVertexLocation = gridRitem->Geo->DrawArgs["grid"].
    BaseVertexLocation;
  mAllRitems.push_back(std::move(gridRitem));

  // Build the columns and spheres in rows as in Figure 7.6.
  UINT objCBIndex = 2;
  for(int i = 0; i < 5; ++i)
  {
    auto leftCylRitem = std::make_unique<RenderItem>();
    auto rightCylRitem = std::make_unique<RenderItem>();
    auto leftSphereRitem = std::make_unique<RenderItem>();
    auto rightSphereRitem = std::make_unique<RenderItem>();

    XMMATRIX leftCylWorld = XMMatrixTranslation(-5.0f, 1.5f, -10.0f +
    i*5.0f);
    XMMATRIX rightCylWorld = XMMatrixTranslation(+5.0f, 1.5f, -10.0f +
    i*5.0f);

    XMMATRIX leftSphereWorld = XMMatrixTranslation(-5.0f, 3.5f, -10.0f +
    i*5.0f);
```

Drawing in Direct3D Part II   287

```cpp
    XMMATRIX rightSphereWorld = XMMatrixTranslation(+5.0f, 3.5f, -10.0f
      + i*5.0f);

    XMStoreFloat4x4(&leftCylRitem->World, rightCylWorld);
    leftCylRitem->ObjCBIndex = objCBIndex++;
    leftCylRitem->Geo = mGeometries["shapeGeo"].get();
    leftCylRitem->PrimitiveType = D3D_PRIMITIVE_TOPOLOGY_TRIANGLELIST;
    leftCylRitem->IndexCount = leftCylRitem->Geo->DrawArgs["cylinder"].
    IndexCount;
    leftCylRitem->StartIndexLocation =
      leftCylRitem->Geo->DrawArgs["cylinder"].StartIndexLocation;
    leftCylRitem->BaseVertexLocation =
      leftCylRitem->Geo->DrawArgs["cylinder"].BaseVertexLocation;

    XMStoreFloat4x4(&rightCylRitem->World, leftCylWorld);
    rightCylRitem->ObjCBIndex = objCBIndex++;
    rightCylRitem->Geo = mGeometries["shapeGeo"].get();
    rightCylRitem->PrimitiveType = D3D_PRIMITIVE_TOPOLOGY_TRIANGLELIST;
    rightCylRitem->IndexCount = rightCylRitem->
    Geo->DrawArgs["cylinder"].
    IndexCount;
    rightCylRitem->StartIndexLocation =
      rightCylRitem->Geo->DrawArgs["cylinder"].StartIndexLocation;
    rightCylRitem->BaseVertexLocation =
      rightCylRitem->Geo->DrawArgs["cylinder"].BaseVertexLocation;

    XMStoreFloat4x4(&leftSphereRitem->World, leftSphereWorld);
    leftSphereRitem->ObjCBIndex = objCBIndex++;
    leftSphereRitem->Geo = mGeometries["shapeGeo"].get();
    leftSphereRitem->PrimitiveType = D3D_PRIMITIVE_TOPOLOGY_
    TRIANGLELIST;
    leftSphereRitem->IndexCount = leftSphereRitem->Geo-
    >DrawArgs["sphere"].
      IndexCount;
    leftSphereRitem->StartIndexLocation =
      leftSphereRitem->Geo->DrawArgs["sphere"].StartIndexLocation;
    leftSphereRitem->BaseVertexLocation =
      leftSphereRitem->Geo->DrawArgs["sphere"].BaseVertexLocation;

    XMStoreFloat4x4(&rightSphereRitem->World, rightSphereWorld);
    rightSphereRitem->ObjCBIndex = objCBIndex++;
    rightSphereRitem->Geo = mGeometries["shapeGeo"].get();
    rightSphereRitem->PrimitiveType = D3D_PRIMITIVE_TOPOLOGY_
    TRIANGLELIST;
    rightSphereRitem->IndexCount = rightSphereRitem->Geo-
    >DrawArgs["sphere"].
      IndexCount;
    rightSphereRitem->StartIndexLocation =
      rightSphereRitem->Geo->DrawArgs["sphere"].StartIndexLocation;
    rightSphereRitem->BaseVertexLocation =
      rightSphereRitem->Geo->DrawArgs["sphere"].BaseVertexLocation;

    mAllRitems.push_back(std::move(leftCylRitem));
    mAllRitems.push_back(std::move(rightCylRitem));
```

```
    mAllRitems.push_back(std::move(leftSphereRitem));
    mAllRitems.push_back(std::move(rightSphereRitem));
  }

  // All the render items are opaque in this demo.
  for(auto& e : mAllRitems)
    mOpaqueRitems.push_back(e.get());
}
```

7.5.3 Frame Resources and Constant Buffer Views

Recall that we have a vector of `FrameResource`s, and each `FrameResource` has an upload buffer for storing the pass constants and constant buffers for every render item in the scene.

```
std::unique_ptr<UploadBuffer<PassConstants>> PassCB = nullptr;
std::unique_ptr<UploadBuffer<ObjectConstants>> ObjectCB = nullptr;
```

If we have 3 frame resources and n render items, then we have three $3n$ object constant buffers and 3 pass constant buffers. Hence we need $3(n+1)$ constant buffer views (CBVs). Thus we will need to modify our CBV heap to include the additional descriptors:

```
void ShapesApp::BuildDescriptorHeaps()
{
  UINT objCount = (UINT)mOpaqueRitems.size();

  // Need a CBV descriptor for each object for each frame resource,
  // +1 for the perPass CBV for each frame resource.
  UINT numDescriptors = (objCount+1) * gNumFrameResources;

  // Save an offset to the start of the pass CBVs. These are the last 3
    descriptors.
  mPassCbvOffset = objCount * gNumFrameResources;

  D3D12_DESCRIPTOR_HEAP_DESC cbvHeapDesc;
  cbvHeapDesc.NumDescriptors = numDescriptors;
  cbvHeapDesc.Type = D3D12_DESCRIPTOR_HEAP_TYPE_CBV_SRV_UAV;
  cbvHeapDesc.Flags = D3D12_DESCRIPTOR_HEAP_FLAG_SHADER_VISIBLE;
  cbvHeapDesc.NodeMask = 0;
  ThrowIfFailed(md3dDevice->CreateDescriptorHeap(&cbvHeapDesc,
    IID_PPV_ARGS(&mCbvHeap)));
}
```

Now, we can populate the CBV heap with the following code where descriptors 0 to n-1 contain the object CBVs for the 0th frame resource, descriptors n to $2n$-1 contains the object CBVs for 1st frame resource, descriptors $2n$ to $3n$-1 contain the objects CBVs for the 2nd frame resource, and descriptors $3n$, $3n$+1, and $3n$+2 contain the pass CBVs for the 0th, 1st, and 2nd frame resource, respectively:

```
void ShapesApp::BuildConstantBufferViews()
{
```

```cpp
UINT objCBByteSize = d3dUtil::CalcConstantBufferByteSize(sizeof
  (ObjectConstants));

UINT objCount = (UINT)mOpaqueRitems.size();

// Need a CBV descriptor for each object for each frame resource.
for(int frameIndex = 0; frameIndex < gNumFrameResources;
  ++frameIndex)
{
  auto objectCB = mFrameResources[frameIndex]->ObjectCB->Resource();
  for(UINT i = 0; i < objCount; ++i)
  {
    D3D12_GPU_VIRTUAL_ADDRESS cbAddress = objectCB-
    >GetGPUVirtualAddress();

    // Offset to the ith object constant buffer in the current buffer.
    cbAddress += i*objCBByteSize;

    // Offset to the object CBV in the descriptor heap.
    int heapIndex = frameIndex*objCount + i;
    auto handle = CD3DX12_CPU_DESCRIPTOR_HANDLE(
      mCbvHeap->GetCPUDescriptorHandleForHeapStart());
    handle.Offset(heapIndex, mCbvSrvUavDescriptorSize);

    D3D12_CONSTANT_BUFFER_VIEW_DESC cbvDesc;
    cbvDesc.BufferLocation = cbAddress;
    cbvDesc.SizeInBytes = objCBByteSize;

    md3dDevice->CreateConstantBufferView(&cbvDesc, handle);
  }
}

UINT passCBByteSize = d3dUtil::CalcConstantBufferByteSize(sizeof
  (PassConstants));

// Last three descriptors are the pass CBVs for each frame resource.
for(int frameIndex = 0; frameIndex < gNumFrameResources;
  ++frameIndex)
{
  auto passCB = mFrameResources[frameIndex]->PassCB->Resource();

  // Pass buffer only stores one cbuffer per frame resource.
  D3D12_GPU_VIRTUAL_ADDRESS cbAddress = passCB-
  >GetGPUVirtualAddress();

  // Offset to the pass cbv in the descriptor heap.
  int heapIndex = mPassCbvOffset + frameIndex;
  auto handle = CD3DX12_CPU_DESCRIPTOR_HANDLE(
    mCbvHeap->GetCPUDescriptorHandleForHeapStart());
  handle.Offset(heapIndex, mCbvSrvUavDescriptorSize);

  D3D12_CONSTANT_BUFFER_VIEW_DESC cbvDesc;
  cbvDesc.BufferLocation = cbAddress;
  cbvDesc.SizeInBytes = passCBByteSize;
```

```
        md3dDevice->CreateConstantBufferView(&cbvDesc, handle);
    }
}
```

Recall that we can get a handle to the first descriptor in a heap with the `ID3D12 DescriptorHeap::GetCPUDescriptorHandleForHeapStart` method. However, now that our heap has more than one descriptor, this method is no longer sufficient. We need to be able to offset to other descriptors in the heap. To do this, we need to know the size to increment in the heap to get to the next descriptor. This is hardware specific, so we have to query this information from the device, and it depends on the heap type. Recall that our `D3DApp` class caches this information:

```
mRtvDescriptorSize = md3dDevice->GetDescriptorHandleIncrementSize(
    D3D12_DESCRIPTOR_HEAP_TYPE_RTV);
mDsvDescriptorSize = md3dDevice->GetDescriptorHandleIncrementSize(
    D3D12_DESCRIPTOR_HEAP_TYPE_DSV);
mCbvSrvUavDescriptorSize = md3dDevice->GetDescriptorHandleIncrementSize(
    D3D12_DESCRIPTOR_HEAP_TYPE_CBV_SRV_UAV);
```

Once we know the descriptor increment size, we can use one of the two `CD3DX12_CPU_DESCRIPTOR_HANDLE::Offset` methods to offset the handle by *n* descriptors:

```
// Specify the number of descriptors to offset times the descriptor
// Offset by n descriptors:
CD3DX12_CPU_DESCRIPTOR_HANDLE handle = mCbvHeap->GetCPUDescriptorHandle
    ForHeapStart();
handle.Offset(n * mCbvSrvDescriptorSize);

// Or equivalently, specify the number of descriptors to offset,
// followed by the descriptor increment size:
CD3DX12_CPU_DESCRIPTOR_HANDLE handle = mCbvHeap->GetCPUDescriptorHandle
    ForHeapStart();
handle.Offset(n, mCbvSrvDescriptorSize);
```

 `CD3DX12_GPU_DESCRIPTOR_HANDLE` has the same `Offset` methods.

7.5.4 Drawing the Scene

At last we can draw our render items. Perhaps the only tricky part is offsetting to the correct CBV in the heap for the object we want to draw. Notice how a render item stores an index to the constant buffer that is associated with the render item.

```
void ShapesApp::DrawRenderItems(
  ID3D12GraphicsCommandList* cmdList,
  const std::vector<RenderItem*>& ritems)
{
  UINT objCBByteSize = d3dUtil::CalcConstantBufferByteSize(sizeof(Objec
    tConstants));
```

```cpp
    auto objectCB = mCurrFrameResource->ObjectCB->Resource();

    // For each render item...
    for(size_t i = 0; i < ritems.size(); ++i)
    {
      auto ri = ritems[i];

      cmdList->IASetVertexBuffers(0, 1, &ri->Geo->VertexBufferView());
      cmdList->IASetIndexBuffer(&ri->Geo->IndexBufferView());
      cmdList->IASetPrimitiveTopology(ri->PrimitiveType);

      // Offset to the CBV in the descriptor heap for this object and
      // for this frame resource.
      UINT cbvIndex = mCurrFrameResourceIndex*(UINT)mOpaqueRitems.size()
        + ri->ObjCBIndex;
      auto cbvHandle = CD3DX12_GPU_DESCRIPTOR_HANDLE(
        mCbvHeap->GetGPUDescriptorHandleForHeapStart());
      cbvHandle.Offset(cbvIndex, mCbvSrvUavDescriptorSize);

      cmdList->SetGraphicsRootDescriptorTable(0, cbvHandle);

      cmdList->DrawIndexedInstanced(ri->IndexCount, 1,
        ri->StartIndexLocation, ri->BaseVertexLocation, 0);
    }
}
```

The `DrawRenderItems` method is invoked in the main `Draw` call:

```cpp
void ShapesApp::Draw(const GameTimer& gt)
{
    auto cmdListAlloc = mCurrFrameResource->CmdListAlloc;

    // Reuse the memory associated with command recording.
    // We can only reset when the associated command lists have
    // finished execution on the GPU.
    ThrowIfFailed(cmdListAlloc->Reset());

    // A command list can be reset after it has been added to the
    // command queue via ExecuteCommandList.
    // Reusing the command list reuses memory.
    if(mIsWireframe)
    {
      ThrowIfFailed(mCommandList->Reset(
        cmdListAlloc.Get(), mPSOs["opaque_wireframe"].Get()));
    }
    else
    {
      ThrowIfFailed(mCommandList->Reset(cmdListAlloc.Get(),
      mPSOs["opaque"].Get()));
    }

    mCommandList->RSSetViewports(1, &mScreenViewport);
    mCommandList->RSSetScissorRects(1, &mScissorRect);

    // Indicate a state transition on the resource usage.
```

```cpp
    mCommandList->ResourceBarrier(1,
      &CD3DX12_RESOURCE_BARRIER::Transition(CurrentBackBuffer(),
      D3D12_RESOURCE_STATE_PRESENT,
      D3D12_RESOURCE_STATE_RENDER_TARGET));

    // Clear the back buffer and depth buffer.
    mCommandList->ClearRenderTargetView(CurrentBackBufferView(),
      Colors::LightSteelBlue, 0, nullptr);
    mCommandList->ClearDepthStencilView(DepthStencilView(),
      D3D12_CLEAR_FLAG_DEPTH | D3D12_CLEAR_FLAG_STENCIL,
      1.0f, 0, 0, nullptr);

    // Specify the buffers we are going to render to.
    mCommandList->OMSetRenderTargets(1, &CurrentBackBufferView(),
      true, &DepthStencilView());

    ID3D12DescriptorHeap* descriptorHeaps[] = { mCbvHeap.Get() };
    mCommandList->SetDescriptorHeaps(_countof(descriptorHeaps),
      descriptorHeaps);

    mCommandList->SetGraphicsRootSignature(mRootSignature.Get());

    int passCbvIndex = mPassCbvOffset + mCurrFrameResourceIndex;
    auto passCbvHandle = CD3DX12_GPU_DESCRIPTOR_HANDLE(
      mCbvHeap->GetGPUDescriptorHandleForHeapStart());
    passCbvHandle.Offset(passCbvIndex, mCbvSrvUavDescriptorSize);
    mCommandList->SetGraphicsRootDescriptorTable(1, passCbvHandle);

    DrawRenderItems(mCommandList.Get(), mOpaqueRitems);

    // Indicate a state transition on the resource usage.
    mCommandList->ResourceBarrier(1,
      &CD3DX12_RESOURCE_BARRIER::Transition(CurrentBackBuffer(),
      D3D12_RESOURCE_STATE_RENDER_TARGET,
      D3D12_RESOURCE_STATE_PRESENT));

    // Done recording commands.
    ThrowIfFailed(mCommandList->Close());

    // Add the command list to the queue for execution.
    ID3D12CommandList* cmdsLists[] = { mCommandList.Get() };
    mCommandQueue->ExecuteCommandLists(_countof(cmdsLists), cmdsLists);

    // Swap the back and front buffers
    ThrowIfFailed(mSwapChain->Present(0, 0));
    mCurrBackBuffer = (mCurrBackBuffer + 1) % SwapChainBufferCount;

    // Advance the fence value to mark commands up to this fence point.
    mCurrFrameResource->Fence = ++mCurrentFence;

    // Add an instruction to the command queue to set a new fence point.
    // Because we are on the GPU timeline, the new fence point won't be
    // set until the GPU finishes processing all the commands prior to
    // this Signal().
    mCommandQueue->Signal(mFence.Get(), mCurrentFence);
}
```

7.6 MORE ON ROOT SIGNATURES

We introduced root signatures in §6.6.5 of the previous chapter. A root signature defines what resources need to be bound to the pipeline before issuing a draw call and how those resources get mapped to shader input registers. What resources need to be bound depends on what resources the current shader programs expect. When the PSO is created, the root signature and shader programs combination will be validated.

7.6.1 Root Parameters

Recall that a root signature is defined by an array of root parameters. Thus far we have only created a root parameter that stores a descriptor table. However, a root parameter can actually be one of three types:

1. *Descriptor Table*: Expects a descriptors table referencing a contiguous range in a heap that identifies the resource to be bound.
2. *Root descriptor (inline descriptor)*: Expects a descriptor to be set directly that identifies the resource to be bound; the descriptor does not need to be in a heap. Only CBVs to constant buffers, and SRV/UAVs to buffers can be bound as a root descriptor. In particular, this means SRVs to textures cannot be bound as a root descriptor.
3. *Root constant*: Expects a list of 32-bit constant values to be bound directly.

For performance, there is a limit of 64 DWORDs that can be put in a root signature. The three types of root parameters have the following costs:

1. Descriptor Table: 1 DWORD
2. Root Descriptor: 2 DWORDs
3. Root Constant: 1 DWORD per 32-bit constant

We can create an arbitrary root signature, provided we do not go over the sixty-four DWORD limit. Root constants are very convenient but their cost adds up quickly. For example, if the only constant data we needed was a world-view-projection matrix, we could use sixteen root constants to store it, which would make us not need to bother with a constant buffer and CBV heap. However, that eats up a quarter of our root signature budget. Using a root descriptor would only be two DWORDs, and a descriptor table is only one DWORD. As our applications become more complex, our constant buffer data will become larger, and it is unlikely we will be able to get away with using only root constants. In a real world application, you will probably use a combination of all three types of root parameters.

In code a root parameter is described by filling out a CD3DX12_ROOT_PARAMETER structure. As we have seen with CD3DX code, the CD3DX12_ROOT_PARAMETER extends D3D12_ROOT_PARAMETER and add some helper initialization functions.

```
typedef struct D3D12_ROOT_PARAMETER
{
  D3D12_ROOT_PARAMETER_TYPE ParameterType;
  union
  {
    D3D12_ROOT_DESCRIPTOR_TABLE DescriptorTable;
    D3D12_ROOT_CONSTANTS Constants;
    D3D12_ROOT_DESCRIPTOR Descriptor;
  };
  D3D12_SHADER_VISIBILITY ShaderVisibility;
} D3D12_ROOT_PARAMETER;
```

1. ParameterType: A member of the following enumerated type indicating the root parameter type (descriptor table, root constant, CBV root descriptor, SRV root descriptor, UAV root descriptor).

   ```
   enum D3D12_ROOT_PARAMETER_TYPE
   {
     D3D12_ROOT_PARAMETER_TYPE_DESCRIPTOR_TABLE = 0,
     D3D12_ROOT_PARAMETER_TYPE_32BIT_CONSTANTS= 1,
     D3D12_ROOT_PARAMETER_TYPE_CBV       = 2,
     D3D12_ROOT_PARAMETER_TYPE_SRV       = 3 ,
     D3D12_ROOT_PARAMETER_TYPE_UAV       = 4
   } D3D12_ROOT_PARAMETER_TYPE;
   ```

2. DescriptorTable/Constants/Descriptor: A structure describing the root parameter. The member of the union you fill out depends on the root parameter type. §7.6.2, §7.6.3, and §7.6.4 discuss these structures.

3. ShaderVisibility: A member of the following enumeration that specifies which shader programs this root parameter is visible to. Usually in this book we specify D3D12_SHADER_VISIBILITY_ALL. However, if we know a resource is only going to be used in a pixel shader, for example, then we can specify D3D12_SHADER_VISIBILITY_PIXEL. Limiting the visibility of a root parameter can potentially lead to some optimizations.

   ```
   enum D3D12_SHADER_VISIBILITY
   {
     D3D12_SHADER_VISIBILITY_ALL      = 0,
     D3D12_SHADER_VISIBILITY_VERTEX   = 1,
     D3D12_SHADER_VISIBILITY_HULL     = 2,
     D3D12_SHADER_VISIBILITY_DOMAIN   = 3,
     D3D12_SHADER_VISIBILITY_GEOMETRY = 4,
     D3D12_SHADER_VISIBILITY_PIXEL    = 5
   }   D3D12_SHADER_VISIBILITY;
   ```

7.6.2 Descriptor Tables

A descriptor table root parameter is further defined by filling out the `DescriptorTable` member of `D3D12_ROOT_PARAMETER`.

```
typedef struct D3D12_ROOT_DESCRIPTOR_TABLE
{
  UINT NumDescriptorRanges;
  const D3D12_DESCRIPTOR_RANGE *pDescriptorRanges;
}   D3D12_ROOT_DESCRIPTOR_TABLE;
```

This simply specifies an array of `D3D12_DESCRIPTOR_RANGE`s and the number of ranges in the array.

The `D3D12_DESCRIPTOR_RANGE` structure is defined like so:

```
typedef struct D3D12_DESCRIPTOR_RANGE
{
  D3D12_DESCRIPTOR_RANGE_TYPE RangeType;
  UINT NumDescriptors;
  UINT BaseShaderRegister;
  UINT RegisterSpace;
  UINT OffsetInDescriptorsFromTableStart;
}   D3D12_DESCRIPTOR_RANGE;
```

1. `RangeType`: A member of the following enumerated type indicating the type of descriptors in this range:

    ```
    enum D3D12_DESCRIPTOR_RANGE_TYPE
    {
      D3D12_DESCRIPTOR_RANGE_TYPE_SRV     = 0,
      D3D12_DESCRIPTOR_RANGE_TYPE_UAV     = 1,
      D3D12_DESCRIPTOR_RANGE_TYPE_CBV     = 2 ,
      D3D12_DESCRIPTOR_RANGE_TYPE_SAMPLER = 3
    } D3D12_DESCRIPTOR_RANGE_TYPE;
    ```

    Sampler descriptors are discussed in the chapter on texturing.

2. `NumDescriptors`: The number of descriptors in the range.

3. `BaseShaderRegister`: Base shader register arguments are bound to. For example, if you set NumDescriptors to 3, BaseShaderRegister to 1 and the range type is CBV (for constant buffers), then you will be binding to HLSL registers

    ```
    cbuffer cbA : register(b1) {...};
    cbuffer cbB : register(b2) {...};
    cbuffer cbC : register(b3) {...};
    ```

4. `RegisterSpace`: This property gives you another dimension to specify shader registers. For example, the following two registers seem to overlap register

slot t0, but they are different registers because they live in different spaces: Texture2D gDiffuseMap : register(t0, space0);

```
Texture2D gNormalMap : register(t0, space1);
```

If no space register is explicitly specified in the shader, it automatically defaults to space0. Usually we use space0, but for arrays of resources it is useful to use multiple spaces, and necessary if the arrays are of an unknown size.

5. `OffsetInDescriptorsFromTableStart`: The offset of this range of descriptors from the start of the table. See the example below.

A slot parameter initialized as a descriptor table takes an array of `D3D12_DESCRIPTOR_RANGE` instances because we can mix various types of descriptors in one table. Suppose we defined a table of six descriptors by the following three ranges in order: two CBVs, three SRVs and one UAV. This table would be defined like so:

```
// Create a table with 2 CBVs, 3 SRVs and 1 UAV.
CD3DX12_DESCRIPTOR_RANGE descRange[3];
descRange[0].Init(
  D3D12_DESCRIPTOR_RANGE_TYPE_CBV, // descriptor type
  2, // descriptor count
  0, // base shader register arguments are bound to for this root
     // parameter
  0, // register space
  0);// offset from start of table
descRange[1].Init(
  D3D12_DESCRIPTOR_RANGE_TYPE_SRV, // descriptor type
  3, // descriptor count
  0, // base shader register arguments are bound to for this root
     // parameter
  0, // register space
  2);// offset from start of table
descRange[2].Init(
  D3D12_DESCRIPTOR_RANGE_TYPE_UAV, // descriptor type
  1, // descriptor count
  0, // base shader register arguments are bound to for this root
     // parameter
  0, // register space
  5);// offset from start of table

slotRootParameter[0].InitAsDescriptorTable(
  3, descRange, D3D12_SHADER_VISIBILITY_ALL);
```

As usual, there is a `CD3DX12_DESCRIPTOR_RANGE` variation that inherits from `D3D12_DESCRIPTOR_RANGE`, and we use the following initialization function:

```
void CD3DX12_DESCRIPTOR_RANGE::Init(
    D3D12_DESCRIPTOR_RANGE_TYPE rangeType,
    UINT numDescriptors,
    UINT baseShaderRegister,
```

```
        UINT registerSpace = 0,
        UINT offsetInDescriptorsFromTableStart =
        D3D12_DESCRIPTOR_RANGE_OFFSET_APPEND);
```

This table covers six descriptors, and the application is expected to bind a contiguous range of descriptors in a descriptor heap that include two CBVs followed by three SRVs followed by one UAV. We see that all the range types start at register 0 but there is no "overlap" conflict because CBVs, SRVs, and UAVs all get bound to different register types, each starting at register 0.

We can have Direct3D compute the `OffsetInDescriptorsFromTableStart` value for us by specifying `D3D12_DESCRIPTOR_RANGE_OFFSET_APPEND`; this instructs Direct3D to use the previous range descriptor counts in the table to compute the offset. Note that the `CD3DX12_DESCRIPTOR_RANGE::Init` method defaults to the register space to 0, and the `OffsetInDescriptorsFromTableStart` to `D3D12_DESCRIPTOR_RANGE_OFFSET_APPEND`.

7.6.3 Root Descriptors

A root descriptor root parameter is further defined by filling out the `Descriptor` member of `D3D12_ROOT_PARAMETER`.

```
typedef struct D3D12_ROOT_DESCRIPTOR
{
  UINT ShaderRegister;
  UINT RegisterSpace;
}D3D12_ROOT_DESCRIPTOR;
```

1. `ShaderRegister`: The shader register the descriptor will be bound to. For example, if you specify 2 and this root parameter is a CBV then the parameter gets mapped to the constant buffer in `register(b2)`:

   ```
   cbuffer cbPass : register(b2) {...};
   ```

2. `RegisterSpace`: See `D3D12_DESCRIPTOR_RANGE::RegisterSpace`.

Unlike descriptor tables which require us to set a descriptor handle in a descriptor heap, to set a root descriptor, we simply bind the virtual address of the resource directly.

```
UINT objCBByteSize = d3dUtil::CalcConstantBufferByteSize(sizeof
  (ObjectConstants));

D3D12_GPU_VIRTUAL_ADDRESS objCBAddress =
    objectCB->GetGPUVirtualAddress();

// Offset to the constants for this object in the buffer.
```

```cpp
objCBAddress += ri->ObjCBIndex*objCBByteSize;

cmdList->SetGraphicsRootConstantBufferView(
    0, // root parameter index
    objCBAddress);
```

7.6.4 Root Constants

A descriptor table root parameter is further defined by filling out the `Constants` member of `D3D12_ROOT_PARAMETER`.

```cpp
typedef struct D3D12_ROOT_CONSTANTS
{
  UINT ShaderRegister;
  UINT RegisterSpace;
  UINT Num32BitValues;
} D3D12_ROOT_CONSTANTS;
```

1. `ShaderRegister`: See `D3D12_ROOT_DESCRIPTOR::ShaderRegister`.
2. `RegisterSpace`: See `D3D12_DESCRIPTOR_RANGE::RegisterSpace`.
3. `Num32BitValues`: The number of 32-bit constants this root parameter expects.

Setting root constants still maps the data to a constant buffer from the shader's perspective. The following example illustrates:

```cpp
// Application code: Root signature definition.
CD3DX12_ROOT_PARAMETER slotRootParameter[1];
slotRootParameter[0].InitAsConstants(12, 0);

// A root signature is an array of root parameters.
CD3DX12_ROOT_SIGNATURE_DESC rootSigDesc(1, slotRootParameter,
    0, nullptr,
    D3D12_ROOT_SIGNATURE_FLAG_ALLOW_INPUT_ASSEMBLER_INPUT_LAYOUT);

// Application code: to set the constants to register b0.
auto weights = CalcGaussWeights(2.5f);
int blurRadius = (int)weights.size() / 2;

cmdList->SetGraphicsRoot32BitConstants(0, 1, &blurRadius, 0);
cmdList->SetGraphicsRoot32BitConstants(0, (UINT)weights.size(),
    weights.data(), 1);

// HLSL code.
cbuffer cbSettings : register(b0)
{
    // We cannot have an array entry in a constant buffer that gets
    // mapped onto root constants, so list each element.

    int gBlurRadius;

    // Support up to 11 blur weights.
    float w0;
```

```
    float w1;
    float w2;
    float w3;
    float w4;
    float w5;
    float w6;
    float w7;
    float w8;
    float w9;
    float w10;
};
```

The `ID3D12GraphicsCommandList::SetGraphicsRoot32BitConstants` method has the following prototype:

```
void ID3D12GraphicsCommandList::SetGraphicsRoot32BitConstants(
    UINT RootParameterIndex,
    UINT Num32BitValuesToSet,
    const void *pSrcData,
    UINT DestOffsetIn32BitValues);
```

1. `RootParameterIndex`: Index of the root parameter we are setting.
2. `Num32BitValuesToSet`: The number of 32-bit values to set.
3. `pSrcData`: Pointer to an array of 32-bit values to set.
4. `DestOffsetIn32BitValues`: Offset in 32-bit values in the constant buffer.

As with root descriptors, setting root constants bypasses the need for a descriptor heap.

7.6.5 A More Complicated Root Signature Example

Consider a shader that expects the following resources:

```
Texture2D gDiffuseMap : register(t0);

cbuffer cbPerObject : register(b0)
{
    float4x4 gWorld;
    float4x4 gTexTransform;
};

cbuffer cbPass : register(b1)
{
    float4x4 gView;
    float4x4 gInvView;
    float4x4 gProj;
    float4x4 gInvProj;
    float4x4 gViewProj;
    float4x4 gInvViewProj;
    float3 gEyePosW;
    float cbPerObjectPad1;
    float2 gRenderTargetSize;
```

```
  float2 gInvRenderTargetSize;
  float gNearZ;
  float gFarZ;
  float gTotalTime;
  float gDeltaTime;
  float4 gAmbientLight;
  Light gLights[MaxLights];
};

cbuffer cbMaterial : register(b2)
{
  float4   gDiffuseAlbedo;
  float3   gFresnelR0;
  float    gRoughness;
  float4x4 gMatTransform;
};
```

The root signature for this shader would be described as follows:

```
CD3DX12_DESCRIPTOR_RANGE texTable;
  texTable.Init(
  D3D12_DESCRIPTOR_RANGE_TYPE_SRV,
  1, // number of descriptors
  0); // register t0

// Root parameter can be a table, root descriptor or root constants.
CD3DX12_ROOT_PARAMETER slotRootParameter[4];

// Perfomance TIP: Order from most frequent to least frequent.
slotRootParameter[0].InitAsDescriptorTable(1,
  &texTable, D3D12_SHADER_VISIBILITY_PIXEL);
slotRootParameter[1].InitAsConstantBufferView(0); // register b0
slotRootParameter[2].InitAsConstantBufferView(1); // register b1
slotRootParameter[3].InitAsConstantBufferView(2); // register b2

// A root signature is an array of root parameters.
CD3DX12_ROOT_SIGNATURE_DESC rootSigDesc(4, slotRootParameter,
  0, nullptr,
  D3D12_ROOT_SIGNATURE_FLAG_ALLOW_INPUT_ASSEMBLER_INPUT_LAYOUT);
```

7.6.6 Root Parameter Versioning

Root arguments refer to the actual values we pass to root parameters. Consider the following code where we change the root arguments (only descriptor table in this case) between draw calls:

```
for(size_t i = 0; i < mRitems.size(); ++i)
{
  const auto& ri = mRitems[i];

  ...

  // Offset to the CBV for this frame and this render item.
```

```
    int cbvOffset = mCurrFrameResourceIndex*(int)mRitems.size();
    cbvOffset += ri.CbIndex;
    cbvHandle.Offset(cbvOffset, mCbvSrvDescriptorSize);

    // Identify descriptors to use for this draw call.
    cmdList->SetGraphicsRootDescriptorTable(0, cbvHandle);

    cmdList->DrawIndexedInstanced(
      ri.IndexCount, 1,
      ri.StartIndexLocation,
      ri.BaseVertexLocation, 0);
  }
```

Each draw call will be executed with the currently set state of the root arguments at the time of the draw call. This works because the hardware automatically saves a snapshot of the current state of the root arguments for each draw call. In other words, the root arguments are automatically versioned for each draw call.

Note that a root signature can provide more fields than a shader uses. For example, if the root signature specifies a root CBV in root parameter 2, but the shader does not use that constant buffer, then this combination is valid as long as the root signature does specify all the resource the shader does use.

For performance, we should aim to keep the root signature small. One reason for this is the automatic versioning of the root arguments per draw call. The larger the root signature, the larger these snapshots of the root arguments will be. Additionally, the SDK documentation advises that root parameters should be ordered in the root signature from most frequently changed to least frequently changed. The Direct3D 12 documentation also advises to avoid switching the root signature when possible, so it is a good idea to share the same root signature across many PSOs you create. In particular, it may be beneficial to have a "super" root signature that works with several shader programs even though not all the shaders uses all the parameters the root signature defines. On the other hand, it also depends how big this "super" root signature has to be for this to work. If it is too big, it could cancel out the gains of not switching the root signature.

7.7 LAND AND WAVES DEMO

In this section, we show how to build the "Land and Waves" demo shown in Figure 7.7. This demo constructs a triangle grid mesh procedurally and offsets the vertex heights to create a terrain. In addition, it uses another triangle grid to represent water, and animates the vertex heights to create waves. This demo also switches to using root descriptors for constant buffers, which allows us to drop support for a descriptor heap for CBVs.

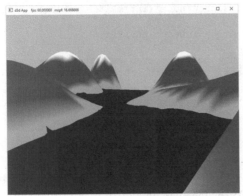

Figure 7.7. Screenshot of the "Lands and Waves" demo. Because we do not have lighting yet, it is difficult to see the shape of the waves. Hold the '1' key down to view the scene in wireframe mode to see the waves better.

The graph of a "nice" real-valued function $y = f(x, z)$ is a surface. We can approximate the surface by constructing a grid in the xz-plane, where every quad is built from two triangles, and then applying the function to each grid point; see Figure 7.8.

7.7.1 Generating the Grid Vertices

So the main task is how to build the grid in the xz-plane. A grid of $m \times n$ vertices induces $(m-1) \times (n-1)$ quads (or cells), as shown in Figure 7.9. Each cell will be covered by two triangles, so there are a total of $2 \cdot (m-1) \times (n-1)$ triangles. If the grid has width w and depth d, the cell spacing along the x-axis is $dx = w/(n-1)$ and the cell spacing along the z-axis is $dz = d/(m-1)$. To generate the vertices, we start at the upper-left corner and incrementally compute the vertex coordinates row-by-row. The coordinates of the ijth grid vertex in the xz-plane are given by:

$$\mathbf{v}_{ij} = [-0.5w + j \cdot dx, \quad 0.0, \quad 0.5d - i \cdot dz]$$

The following code generates the grid vertices:

```
GeometryGenerator::MeshData
GeometryGenerator::CreateGrid(float width, float depth, uint32 m,
    uint32 n)
{
    MeshData meshData;

    uint32 vertexCount = m*n;
    uint32 faceCount   = (m-1)*(n-1)*2;

    float halfWidth = 0.5f*width;
    float halfDepth = 0.5f*depth;

    float dx = width / (n-1);
```

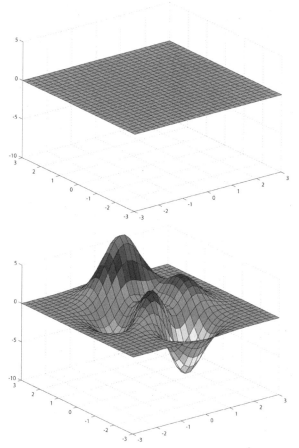

Figure 7.8. (Top) Lay down a grid in the xz-plane. (Bottom) For each grid point, apply the function $f(x, z)$ to obtain the y-coordinate. The plot of the points $(x, f(x, z), z)$ gives the graph of a surface.

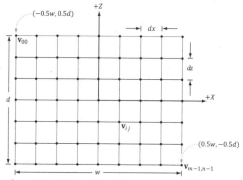

Figure 7.9. Grid construction.

```
        float dz = depth / (m-1);

        float du = 1.0f / (n-1);
        float dv = 1.0f / (m-1);

        meshData.Vertices.resize(vertexCount);
        for(uint32 i = 0; i < m; ++i)
        {
          float z = halfDepth - i*dz;
          for(uint32 j = 0; j < n; ++j)
          {
            float x = -halfWidth + j*dx;

            meshData.Vertices[i*n+j].Position = XMFLOAT3(x, 0.0f, z);
            meshData.Vertices[i*n+j].Normal   = XMFLOAT3(0.0f, 1.0f, 0.0f);
            meshData.Vertices[i*n+j].TangentU = XMFLOAT3(1.0f, 0.0f, 0.0f);

            // Stretch texture over grid.
            meshData.Vertices[i*n+j].TexC.x = j*du;
            meshData.Vertices[i*n+j].TexC.y = i*dv;
          }
        }
```

7.7.2 Generating the Grid Indices

After we have computed the vertices, we need to define the grid triangles by specifying the indices. To do this, we iterate over each quad, again row-by-row starting at the top-left, and compute the indices to define the two triangles of the quad; referring to Figure 7.10, for an $m \times n$ vertex grid, the linear array indices of the two triangles are computed as follows:

$$\Delta ABC = \left(i \cdot n + j, \quad i \cdot n + j + 1, (i+1) \cdot n + j\right)$$

$$\Delta CBD = \left((i+1) \cdot n + j, i \cdot n + j + 1, (i+1) \cdot n + j + 1\right)$$

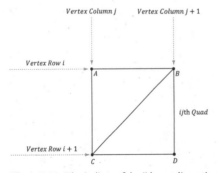

Figure 7.10. The indices of the *ij*th quad's vertices.

The corresponding code:

```
meshData.Indices32.resize(faceCount*3); // 3 indices per face

// Iterate over each quad and compute indices.
uint32 k = 0;
for(uint32 i = 0; i < m-1; ++i)
{
  for(uint32 j = 0; j < n-1; ++j)
  {
    meshData.Indices32[k]   = i*n+j;
    meshData.Indices32[k+1] = i*n+j+1;
    meshData.Indices32[k+2] = (i+1)*n+j;

    meshData.Indices32[k+3] = (i+1)*n+j;
    meshData.Indices32[k+4] = i*n+j+1;
    meshData.Indices32[k+5] = (i+1)*n+j+1;

    k += 6; // next quad
  }
}

return meshData;
}
```

7.7.3 Applying the Height Function

After we have created the grid, we can extract the vertex elements we want from the `MeshData` grid, turn the flat grid into a surface representing hills, and generate a color for each vertex based on the vertex altitude (y-coordinate).

```
// Not to be confused with GeometryGenerator::Vertex.
struct Vertex
{
  XMFLOAT3 Pos;
  XMFLOAT4 Color;
};
void LandAndWavesApp::BuildLandGeometry()
{
  GeometryGenerator geoGen;
  GeometryGenerator::MeshData grid = geoGen.CreateGrid(160.0f, 160.0f,
    50, 50);

  //
  // Extract the vertex elements we are interested and apply the height
  // function to each vertex. In addition, color the vertices based on
  // their height so we have sandy looking beaches, grassy low hills,
  // and snow mountain peaks.
  //

  std::vector<Vertex> vertices(grid.Vertices.size());
  for(size_t i = 0; i < grid.Vertices.size(); ++i)
```

```
{
  auto& p = grid.Vertices[i].Position;
  vertices[i].Pos = p;
  vertices[i].Pos.y = GetHillsHeight(p.x, p.z);

  // Color the vertex based on its height.
  if(vertices[i].Pos.y < -10.0f)
  {
    // Sandy beach color.
    vertices[i].Color = XMFLOAT4(1.0f, 0.96f, 0.62f, 1.0f);
  }
  else if(vertices[i].Pos.y < 5.0f)
  {
    // Light yellow-green.
    vertices[i].Color = XMFLOAT4(0.48f, 0.77f, 0.46f, 1.0f);
  }
  else if(vertices[i].Pos.y < 12.0f)
  {
    // Dark yellow-green.
    vertices[i].Color = XMFLOAT4(0.1f, 0.48f, 0.19f, 1.0f);
  }
  else if(vertices[i].Pos.y < 20.0f)
  {
    // Dark brown.
    vertices[i].Color = XMFLOAT4(0.45f, 0.39f, 0.34f, 1.0f);
  }
  else
  {
    // White snow.
    vertices[i].Color = XMFLOAT4(1.0f, 1.0f, 1.0f, 1.0f);
  }
}

const UINT vbByteSize = (UINT)vertices.size() * sizeof(Vertex);

std::vector<std::uint16_t> indices = grid.GetIndices16();
const UINT ibByteSize = (UINT)indices.size() * sizeof(std::uint16_t);

auto geo = std::make_unique<MeshGeometry>();
geo->Name = "landGeo";

ThrowIfFailed(D3DCreateBlob(vbByteSize, &geo->VertexBufferCPU));
CopyMemory(geo->VertexBufferCPU->GetBufferPointer(), vertices.data(),
  vbByteSize);

ThrowIfFailed(D3DCreateBlob(ibByteSize, &geo->IndexBufferCPU));
CopyMemory(geo->IndexBufferCPU->GetBufferPointer(), indices.data(),
  ibByteSize);

geo->VertexBufferGPU = d3dUtil::CreateDefaultBuffer(md3dDevice.Get(),
  mCommandList.Get(), vertices.data(), vbByteSize, geo-
  >VertexBufferUploader);
```

```cpp
    geo->IndexBufferGPU = d3dUtil::CreateDefaultBuffer(md3dDevice.Get(),
        mCommandList.Get(), indices.data(), ibByteSize,
        geo->IndexBufferUploader);

    geo->VertexByteStride = sizeof(Vertex);
    geo->VertexBufferByteSize = vbByteSize;
    geo->IndexFormat = DXGI_FORMAT_R16_UINT;
    geo->IndexBufferByteSize = ibByteSize;

    SubmeshGeometry submesh;
    submesh.IndexCount = (UINT)indices.size();
    submesh.StartIndexLocation = 0;
    submesh.BaseVertexLocation = 0;

    geo->DrawArgs["grid"] = submesh;

    mGeometries["landGeo"] = std::move(geo);
}
```

The function $f(x, z)$ we have used in this demo is given by:

```cpp
float LandAndWavesApp::GetHeight(float x, float z)const
{
    return 0.3f*(z*sinf(0.1f*x) + x*cosf(0.1f*z));
}
```

Its graph looks like somewhat like a terrain with hills and valleys (see Figure 7.7).

7.7.4 Root CBVs

Another change we make to the "Land and Waves" demo from the previous "Shape" demos is that we use root descriptors so that we can bind CBVs directly without having to use a descriptor heap. Here are the changes that need to be made to do this:

1. The root signature needs to be changed to take two root CBVs instead of two descriptor tables.
2. No CBV heap is needed nor needs to be populated with descriptors.
3. There is new syntax for binding a root descriptor.

The new root signature is defined like so:

```cpp
// Root parameter can be a table, root descriptor or root constants.
CD3DX12_ROOT_PARAMETER slotRootParameter[2];

// Create root CBV.
slotRootParameter[0].InitAsConstantBufferView(0); // per-object CBV
slotRootParameter[1].InitAsConstantBufferView(1); // per-pass CBV

// A root signature is an array of root parameters.
CD3DX12_ROOT_SIGNATURE_DESC rootSigDesc(2, slotRootParameter, 0,
```

```
  nullptr, D3D12_ROOT_SIGNATURE_FLAG_ALLOW_INPUT_ASSEMBLER_INPUT_
    LAYOUT);
```

Observe that we use the `InitAsConstantBufferView` helper method to create root CBV; the parameter specifies the shader register this parameter is bound to (in the above code, shader constant buffer register "b0" and "b1").

Now, we bind a CBV as an argument to a root descriptor using the following method:

```
void
ID3D12GraphicsCommandList::SetGraphicsRootConstantBufferView(
  UINT RootParameterIndex,
  D3D12_GPU_VIRTUAL_ADDRESS BufferLocation);
```

1. `RootParameterIndex`: The index of the root parameter we are binding a CBV to.
2. `BufferLocation`: The virtual address to the resource that contains the constant buffer data.

With this change, our drawing code now looks like this:

```
void LandAndWavesApp::Draw(const GameTimer& gt)
{
  [...]

  // Bind per-pass constant buffer. We only need to do this once per-
  // pass.
  auto passCB = mCurrFrameResource->PassCB->Resource();
  mCommandList->SetGraphicsRootConstantBufferView(1, passCB-
    >GetGPUVirtualAddress());

  DrawRenderItems(mCommandList.Get(), mRitemLayer[(int)
    RenderLayer::Opaque]);

  [...]
}

void LandAndWavesApp::DrawRenderItems(
  ID3D12GraphicsCommandList* cmdList,
  const std::vector<RenderItem*>& ritems)
{
  UINT objCBByteSize = d3dUtil::CalcConstantBufferByteSize(sizeof
    (ObjectConstants));

  auto objectCB = mCurrFrameResource->ObjectCB->Resource();

  // For each render item...
  for(size_t i = 0; i < ritems.size(); ++i)
  {
    auto ri = ritems[i];

    cmdList->IASetVertexBuffers(0, 1, &ri->Geo->VertexBufferView());
    cmdList->IASetIndexBuffer(&ri->Geo->IndexBufferView());
    cmdList->IASetPrimitiveTopology(ri->PrimitiveType);
```

```
    D3D12_GPU_VIRTUAL_ADDRESS objCBAddress =
    objectCB->GetGPUVirtualAddress();
    objCBAddress += ri->ObjCBIndex*objCBByteSize;

    cmdList->SetGraphicsRootConstantBufferView(0, objCBAddress);

    cmdList->DrawIndexedInstanced(ri->IndexCount, 1,
       ri->StartIndexLocation, ri->BaseVertexLocation, 0);
  }
}
```

7.7.5 Dynamic Vertex Buffers

So far we have stored our vertices in a default buffer resource. We use this kind of resource when we want to store static geometry. That is, geometry that we do not change—we set the data, and the GPU reads and draws the data. A dynamic vertex buffer is where we change the vertex data frequently, say per-frame. For example, suppose we are doing a wave simulation, and we solve the wave equation for the solution function $f(x, z, t)$. This function represents the wave height at each point in the xz-plane at time t. If we were to use this function to draw the waves, we would use a triangle grid mesh like we did with the peaks and valleys, and apply $f(x, z, t)$ to each grid point in order to obtain the wave heights at the grid points. Because this function also depends on time t (i.e., the wave surface changes with time), we would need to reapply this function to the grid points a short time later (say every 1/30th of a second) to get a smooth animation. Thus, we need a dynamic vertex buffer in order to update the heights of the triangle grid mesh vertices as time passes. Another situation that leads to dynamic vertex buffers is particle systems with complex physics and collision detection. Each frame we will do the physics and collision detection on the CPU to find the new position of the particles. Because the particle positions are changing each frame, we need a dynamic vertex buffer in order to update the particle positions for drawing each frame.

We have already seen an example of uploading data from the CPU to the GPU per-frame when we used upload buffers to update our constant buffer data. We can apply the same technique and use our `UploadBuffer` class, but instead of storing an array of constant buffers, we store an array of vertices:

```
    std::unique_ptr<UploadBuffer<Vertex>> WavesVB = nullptr;

    WavesVB = std::make_unique<UploadBuffer<Vertex>>(
       device, waveVertCount, false);
```

Because we need to upload the new contents from the CPU to the wave's dynamic vertex buffer every frame, the dynamic vertex buffer needs to be a frame resource. Otherwise we could overwrite the memory before the GPU has finished processing the last frame.

Every frame, we run the wave simulation and update the vertex buffer like so:

```cpp
void LandAndWavesApp::UpdateWaves(const GameTimer& gt)
{
  // Every quarter second, generate a random wave.
  static float t_base = 0.0f;
  if((mTimer.TotalTime() - t_base) >= 0.25f)
  {
    t_base += 0.25f;

    int i = MathHelper::Rand(4, mWaves->RowCount() - 5);
    int j = MathHelper::Rand(4, mWaves->ColumnCount() - 5);

    float r = MathHelper::RandF(0.2f, 0.5f);

    mWaves->Disturb(i, j, r);
  }

  // Update the wave simulation.
  mWaves->Update(gt.DeltaTime());

  // Update the wave vertex buffer with the new solution.
  auto currWavesVB = mCurrFrameResource->WavesVB.get();
  for(int i = 0; i < mWaves->VertexCount(); ++i)
  {
    Vertex v;

    v.Pos = mWaves->Position(i);
    v.Color = XMFLOAT4(DirectX::Colors::Blue);

    currWavesVB->CopyData(i, v);
  }

  // Set the dynamic VB of the wave renderitem to the current frame VB.
  mWavesRitem->Geo->VertexBufferGPU = currWavesVB->Resource();
}
```

> **Note:** We save a reference to the wave render item (`mWavesRitem`) so that we can set its vertex buffer on the fly. We need to do this because its vertex buffer is a dynamic buffer and changes every frame.

There is some overhead when using dynamic buffers, as the new data must be transferred from CPU memory back up to GPU memory. Therefore, static buffers should be preferred to dynamic buffers, provided static buffers will work. Recent versions of Direct3D have introduced new features to lessen the need for dynamic buffers. For instance:

1. Simple animations may be done in a vertex shader.
2. It is possible, through render to texture or compute shaders and vertex texture fetch functionality, to implement a wave simulation like the one described above that runs completely on the GPU.

3. The geometry shader provides the ability for the GPU to create or destroy primitives, a task that would normally need to be done on the CPU without a geometry shader.

4. The tessellation stages can add tessellate geometry on the GPU, a task that would normally need to be done on the CPU without hardware tessellation.

Index buffers can be dynamic, too. However, in the "Land and Waves" demo, the triangle topology remains constant and only the vertex heights change; therefore, only the vertex buffer needs to be dynamic.

The "Waves" demo for this chapter uses a dynamic vertex buffer to implement a simple wave simulation like the one described at the beginning of this section. For this book, we are not concerned with the actual algorithm details for the wave simulation (see [Lengyel02] for that), but more with the process so as to illustrate dynamic buffers: update the simulation on CPU and then update the vertex data using an upload buffer.

We mention again that this demo could be implemented on the GPU using more advanced methods such as render to texture functionality or the compute shader, and vertex texture fetch. Because we have not covered these topics yet, we do the wave simulation on the CPU and update the new vertices using dynamic vertex buffers.

7.8 SUMMARY

1. Waiting for the GPU to finish executing all the commands in the queue every frame is inefficient because it causes both the CPU and GPU to idle at some point. A more efficient technique is to create *frame resources*—a circular array of the resources the CPU needs to modify each frame. This way, the CPU does not need to wait for the GPU to finish before moving on to the next frame; the CPU will just work with the next available (i.e., not in use by GPU) frame resource. If the CPU is always processing frames faster than the GPU, then eventually the CPU will have to wait at some point for the GPU to catch up, but this is the desired situation, as the GPU is being fully utilized; the extra CPU cycles can always be used for other parts of the game such as AI, physics, and game play logic.

2. We can get a handle to the first descriptor in a heap with the `ID3D12Descriptor Heap::GetCPUDescriptorHandleForHeapStart` method. We can get a descriptor size (depends on the hardware and descriptor type) with the `ID3D12Device:: GetDescriptorHandleIncrementSize(DescriptorHeapType type)` method. Once

we know the descriptor increment size, we can use one of the two `CD3DX12_CPU_DESCRIPTOR_HANDLE::Offset` methods to offset the handle by *n* descriptors:

```
// Specify the number of descriptors to offset times the descriptor
// increment size:
D3D12_CPU_DESCRIPTOR_HANDLE handle = mCbvHeap->
    GetCPUDescriptorHandleForHeapStart();
handle.Offset(n * mCbvSrvDescriptorSize);

// Or equivalently, specify the number of descriptors to offset,
// followed by the descriptor increment size:
D3D12_CPU_DESCRIPTOR_HANDLE handle = mCbvHeap->GetCPUDescriptorHandleFo
    rHeapStart();
handle.Offset(n, mCbvSrvDescriptorSize);
The CD3DX12_GPU_DESCRIPTOR_HANDLE type has the same Offset methods.
```

3. A root signature defines what resources need to be bound to the pipeline before issuing a draw call and how those resources get mapped to shader input registers. What resources need to be bound depends on what resources the bound shader programs expect. When the PSO is created, the root signature and shader programs combination will be validated. A root signature is specified as an array of root parameters. A root parameter can be a descriptor table, root descriptor, or root constant. A descriptor table specifies a contiguous range of descriptors in a heap. A root descriptor is used to bind a descriptor directly in the root signature (it does not need to be in a heap). Root constants are used to bind constant values directly in the root signature. For performance, there is a limit of sixty-four DWORDs that can be put in a root signature. Descriptor tables cost one DWORD each, root descriptors cost two DWORDs each, and root constants cost one DWORD for each 32-bit constant. The hardware automatically saves a snapshot of the root arguments for each draw call. Thus we are safe to change root arguments per draw call, however, we should also try to keep the root signatures small so there is less memory to copy.

4. Dynamic vertex buffers are used when the contents of a vertex buffer needs to be updated frequently at runtime (e.g., every frame or every 1/30th of a second). We can use an `UploadBuffer` to implement dynamic vertex buffers, but instead of storing an array of constant buffers, we store an array of vertices. Because we need to upload the new contents from the CPU to the wave's dynamic vertex buffer every frame, the dynamic vertex buffer needs to be a frame resource. There is some overhead when using dynamic vertex buffers, as the new data must be transferred from CPU memory back up to GPU memory. Therefore, static vertex buffers should be preferred to dynamic vertex buffers, provided static vertex buffers will work. Recent versions of Direct3D have introduced new features to lessen the need for dynamic buffers.

7.9 EXERCISES

1. Modify the "Shape" demo to use `GeometryGenerator::CreateGeosphere` instead of `GeometryGenerator::CreateSphere`. Try with 0, 1, 2, and 3 subdivision levels.
2. Modify the "Shapes" demo to use sixteen root constants to set the per-object world matrix instead of a descriptor table.
3. On the DVD, there a file called Models/Skull.txt. This file contains the vertex and index lists needed to render the skull in Figure 7.11. Study the file using a text editor like notepad, and modify the "Shapes" demo to load and render the skull mesh.

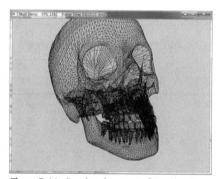

Figure 7.11. Rendered output of Exercise 4.

Chapter 8 LIGHTING

Consider Figure 8.1. On the left we have an unlit sphere, and on the right, we have a lit sphere. As you can see, the sphere on the left looks rather flat—maybe it is not even a sphere at all, but just a 2D circle! On the other hand, the sphere on the right does look 3D—the lighting and shading aid in our perception of the solid form and volume of the object. In fact, our visual perception of the world depends on light and its interaction with materials, and consequently, much of the problem of generating photorealistic scenes has to do with physically accurate lighting models.

Of course, in general, the more accurate the model, the more computationally expensive it is; thus a balance must be reached between realism and speed. For example, 3D special FX scenes for films can be much more complex and utilize very realistic lighting models than a game because the frames for a film are

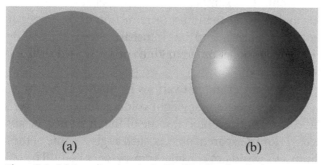

Figure 8.1. (a) An unlit sphere looks 2D. (b) A lit sphere looks 3D.

315

pre-rendered, so they can afford to take hours or days to process a frame. Games, on the other hand, are real-time applications, and therefore, the frames need to be drawn at a rate of at least 30 frames per second.

Note that the lighting model explained and implemented in this book is largely based off the one described in [Möller08].

Objectives:

1. To gain a basic understanding of the interaction between lights and materials
2. To understand the differences between local illumination and global illumination
3. To find out how we can mathematically describe the direction a point on a surface is "facing" so that we can determine the angle at which incoming light strikes the surface
4. To learn how to correctly transform normal vectors
5. To be able to distinguish between ambient, diffuse, and specular light
6. To learn how to implement directional lights, point lights, and spotlights
7. To understand how to vary light intensity as a function of depth by controlling attenuation parameters

8.1 LIGHT AND MATERIAL INTERACTION

When using lighting, we no longer specify vertex colors directly; rather, we specify materials and lights, and then apply a lighting equation, which computes the vertex colors for us based on light/material interaction. This leads to a much more realistic coloring of the object (compare Figure 8.1a and 8.1b again).

Materials can be thought of as the properties that determine how light interacts with a surface of an object. Examples of such properties are the color of light the surface reflects and absorbs, the index of refraction of the material under the surface, how smooth the surface is, and how transparent the surface is. By specifying material properties we can model different kinds of real-world surfaces like wood, stone, glass, metals, and water.

In our model, a light source can emit various intensities of red, green, and blue light; in this way, we can simulate many light colors. When light travels outwards from a source and collides with an object, some of that light may be absorbed and some may be reflected (for transparent objects, such as glass, some of the light passes through the medium, but we do not consider transparency here). The reflected light now travels along its new path and may strike other objects where some light is

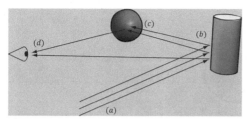

Figure 8.2. (a) Flux of incoming white light. (b) The light strikes the cylinder and some rays are absorbed and other rays are scatted toward the eye and sphere. (c) The light reflecting off the cylinder toward the sphere is absorbed or reflected again and travels into the eye. (d) The eye receives incoming light that determines what the eye sees.

again absorbed and reflected. A light ray may strike many objects before it is fully absorbed. Presumably, some light rays eventually travel into the eye (see Figure 8.2) and strike the light receptor cells (named cones and rods) on the retina.

According to the *trichromatic* theory (see [Santrock03]), the retina contains three kinds of light receptors, each one sensitive to red, green, and blue light (with some overlap). The incoming RGB light stimulates its corresponding light receptors to varying intensities based on the strength of the light. As the light receptors are stimulated (or not), neural impulses are sent down the optic nerve toward the brain, where the brain generates an image in your head based on the stimulus of the light receptors. (Of course, if you close/cover your eyes, the receptor cells receive no stimulus and the brain registers this as black.)

For example, consider Figure 8.2 again. Suppose that the material of the cylinder reflects 75% red light, 75% green light, and absorbs the rest, and the sphere reflects 25% red light and absorbs the rest. Also suppose that pure white light is being emitted from the light source. As the light rays strike the cylinder, all the blue light is absorbed and only 75% red and green light is reflected (i.e., a medium-high intensity yellow). This light is then scattered—some of it travels into the eye and some of it travels toward the sphere. The part that travels into the eye primarily stimulates the red and green cone cells to a semi-high degree; hence, the viewer sees the cylinder as a semi-bright shade of yellow. Now, the other light rays travel toward the sphere and strike it. The sphere reflects 25% red light and absorbs the rest; thus, the diluted incoming red light (medium-high intensity red) is diluted further and reflected, and all of the incoming green light is absorbed. This remaining red light then travels into the eye and primarily stimulates the red cone cells to a low degree. Thus the viewer sees the sphere as a dark shade of red.

The lighting models we (and most real-time applications) adopt in this book are called *local illumination models*. With a local model, each object is lit independently of another object, and only the light directly emitted from light sources is taken into account in the lighting process (i.e., light that has bounced off other scene objects to strikes the object currently being lit is ignored). Figure 8.3 shows a consequence of this model.

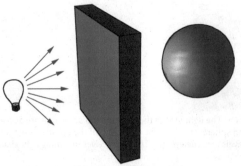

Figure 8.3. Physically, the wall blocks the light rays emitted by the light bulb and the sphere is in the shadow of the wall. However, in a local illumination model, the sphere is lit as if the wall were not there.

On the other hand, global illumination models light objects by taking into consideration not only the light directly emitted from light sources, but also the indirect light that has bounced off other objects in the scene. These are called global illumination models because they take everything in the global scene into consideration when lighting an object. Global illumination models are generally prohibitively expensive for real-time games (but come very close to generating photorealistic scenes). Finding real-time methods for approximating global illumination is an area of ongoing research; see, for example, voxel global illumination [*http://on-demand.gputechconf.com/gtc/2014/presentations/S4552-rt-voxel-based-global-illumination-gpus.pdf*]. Other popular methods are to precompute indirect lighting for static objects (e.g., walls, statues), and then use that result to approximate indirect lighting for dynamic objects (e.g., moving game characters).

8.2 NORMAL VECTORS

A *face normal* is a unit vector that describes the direction a polygon is facing (i.e., it is orthogonal to all points on the polygon); see Figure 8.4a. A *surface normal* is a unit vector that is orthogonal to the tangent plane of a point on a surface; see Figure 8.4b. Observe that surface normals determine the direction a point on a surface is "facing."

For lighting calculations, we need the surface normal at each point on the surface of a triangle mesh so that we can determine the angle at which light strikes the point on the mesh surface. To obtain surface normals, we specify the surface normals only at the vertex points (so-called *vertex normals*). Then, in order to obtain a surface normal approximation at each point on the surface of a triangle mesh, these vertex normals will be interpolated across the triangle during rasterization (recall §5.10.3 and see Figure 8.5).

Lighting

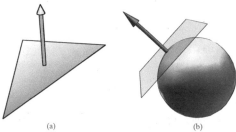

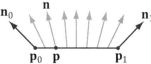

Figure 8.5. The vertex normals n_0 and n_1 are defined at the segment vertex points p_0 and p_1. A normal vector n for a point p in the interior of the line segment is found by linearly interpolating (weighted average) between the vertex normals; that is, $n = n_0 + t(n_1 - n_0)$ where t is such that $p = p_0 + t(p_1 - p_0)$ Although we illustrated normal interpolation over a line segment for simplicity, the idea straightforwardly generalizes to interpolating over a 3D triangle.

Figure 8.4. (a) The face normal is orthogonal to all points on the face. (b) The surface normal is the vector that is orthogonal to the tangent plane of a point on a surface.

 Interpolating the normal and doing lighting calculations per pixel is called pixel lighting or phong lighting. A less expensive, but less accurate, method is doing the lighting calculations per vertex. Then the result of the per vertex lighting calculation is output from the vertex shader and interpolated across the pixels of the triangle. Moving calculations from the pixel shader to the vertex shader is a common performance optimization at the sake of quality and sometimes the visual difference is very subtle making such optimizations very attractive.

8.2.1 Computing Normal Vectors

To find the face normal of a triangle $\Delta p_0, p_1, p_2$ we first compute two vectors that lie on the triangle's edges:

$$u = p_1 - p_0$$
$$v = p_2 - p_0$$

Then the face normal is:

$$n = \frac{u \times v}{\|u \times v\|}$$

Below is a function that computes the face normal of the front side (§5.10.2) of a triangle from the three vertex points of the triangle.

```
XMVECTOR ComputeNormal(FXMVECTOR p0,
          FXMVECTOR p1,
          FXMVECTOR p2)
{
  XMVECTOR u = p1 - p0;
  XMVECTOR v = p2 - p0;

  return XMVector3Normalize(
    XMVector3Cross(u,v));
}
```

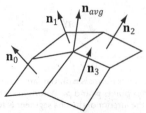

Figure 8.6. The middle vertex is shared by the neighboring four polygons, so we approximate the middle vertex normal by averaging the four polygon face normals.

For a differentiable surface, we can use calculus to find the normals of points on the surface. Unfortunately, a triangle mesh is not differentiable. The technique that is generally applied to triangle meshes is called *vertex normal averaging*. The vertex normal **n** or an arbitrary vertex **v** in a mesh is found by averaging the face normals of every polygon in the mesh that shares the vertex **v**. For example, in Figure 8.6, four polygons in the mesh share the vertex **v** thus, the vertex normal for **v** is given by:

$$\mathbf{n}_{avg} = \frac{\mathbf{n}_0 + \mathbf{n}_1 + \mathbf{n}_2 + \mathbf{n}_3}{\|\mathbf{n}_0 + \mathbf{n}_1 + \mathbf{n}_2 + \mathbf{n}_3\|}$$

In the above example, we do not need to divide by 4, as we would in a typical average, since we normalize the result. Note also that more sophisticated averaging schemes can be constructed; for example, a weighted average might be used where the weights are determined by the areas of the polygons (e.g., polygons with larger areas have more weight than polygons with smaller areas).

The following pseudocode shows how this averaging can be implemented given the vertex and index list of a triangle mesh:

```
// Input:
// 1. An array of vertices (mVertices). Each vertex has a
//    position component (pos) and a normal component (normal).
// 2. An array of indices (mIndices).

// For each triangle in the mesh:
for(UINT i = 0; i < mNumTriangles; ++i)
{
  // indices of the ith triangle
  UINT i0 = mIndices[i*3+0];
  UINT i1 = mIndices[i*3+1];
  UINT i2 = mIndices[i*3+2];

  // vertices of ith triangle
  Vertex v0 = mVertices[i0];
  Vertex v1 = mVertices[i1];
  Vertex v2 = mVertices[i2];

  // compute face normal
  Vector3 e0 = v1.pos - v0.pos;
  Vector3 e1 = v2.pos - v0.pos;
```

```
            Vector3 faceNormal = Cross(e0, e1);

            // This triangle shares the following three vertices,
            // so add this face normal into the average of these
            // vertex normals.
            mVertices[i0].normal += faceNormal;
            mVertices[i1].normal += faceNormal;
            mVertices[i2].normal += faceNormal;
        }

        // For each vertex v, we have summed the face normals of all
        // the triangles that share v, so now we just need to normalize.
        for(UINT i = 0; i < mNumVertices; ++i)
            mVertices[i].normal = Normalize(&mVertices[i].normal));
```

8.2.2 Transforming Normal Vectors

Consider Figure 8.7a where we have a tangent vector $\mathbf{u} = \mathbf{v}_1 - \mathbf{v}_0$ orthogonal to a normal vector $\mathbf{n}$. If we apply a non-uniform scaling transformation $\mathbf{A}$ we see from Figure 8.7b that the transformed tangent vector $\mathbf{uA} = \mathbf{v}_1\mathbf{A} - \mathbf{v}_0\mathbf{A}$ does not remain orthogonal to the transformed normal vector $\mathbf{nA}$.

So our problem is this: Given a transformation matrix $\mathbf{A}$ that transforms points and vectors (non-normal), we want to find a transformation matrix $\mathbf{B}$ that transforms normal vectors such that the transformed tangent vector is orthogonal to the transformed normal vector (i.e., $\mathbf{uA} \cdot \mathbf{nB} = 0$). To do this, let us first start with something we know: we know that the normal vector $\mathbf{n}$ is orthogonal to the tangent vector $\mathbf{u}$:

$\mathbf{u} \cdot \mathbf{n} = 0$	Tangent vector orthogonal to normal vector
$\mathbf{u}\mathbf{n}^T = 0$	Rewriting the dot product as a matrix multiplication
$\mathbf{u}(\mathbf{A}\mathbf{A}^{-1})\mathbf{n}^T = 0$	Inserting the identity matrix $\mathbf{I} = \mathbf{A}\mathbf{A}^{-1}$
$(\mathbf{uA})(\mathbf{A}^{-1}\mathbf{n}^T) = 0$	Associative property of matrix multiplication
$(\mathbf{uA})(\mathbf{A}^{-1}\mathbf{n}^T)^T)^T = 0$	Transpose property $(\mathbf{A}^T)^T = \mathbf{A}$
$(\mathbf{uA})(\mathbf{n}(\mathbf{A}^{-1})^T)^T = 0$	Transpose property $(\mathbf{AB}^T)^T = \mathbf{B}^T\mathbf{A}^T$
$\mathbf{uA} \cdot \mathbf{n}(\mathbf{A}^{-1})^T = 0$	Rewriting the matrix multiplication as a dot product
$\mathbf{uA} \cdot \mathbf{nB} = 0$	Transformed tangent vector orthogonal to transformed normal vector

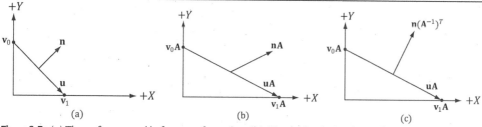

Figure 8.7. (a) The surface normal before transformation. (b) After scaling by 2 units on the x-axis the normal is no longer orthogonal to the surface. (c) The surface normal correctly transformed by the inverse-transpose of the scaling transformation.

Thus $\mathbf{B} = (\mathbf{A}^{-1})^T$ (the inverse transpose of $\mathbf{A}$) does the job in transforming normal vectors so that they are perpendicular to its associated transformed tangent vector $\mathbf{uA}$.

Note that if the matrix is orthogonal ($\mathbf{A}^T = \mathbf{A}^{-1}$), then $\mathbf{B} = (\mathbf{A}^{-1})^T = (\mathbf{A}^T)^T = \mathbf{A}$; that is, we do not need to compute the inverse transpose, since $\mathbf{A}$ does the job in this case. In summary, when transforming a normal vector by a nonuniform or shear transformation, use the inverse-transpose.

We implement a helper function in *MathHelper.h* for computing the inverse-transpose:

```
static XMMATRIX InverseTranspose(CXMMATRIX M)
{
  XMMATRIX A = M;
  A.r[3] = XMVectorSet(0.0f, 0.0f, 0.0f, 1.0f);

  XMVECTOR det = XMMatrixDeterminant(A);
  return XMMatrixTranspose(XMMatrixInverse(&det, A));
}
```

We clear out any translation from the matrix because we use the inverse-transpose to transform vectors, and translations only apply to points. However, from §3.2.1 we know that setting $w = 0$ for vectors (using homogeneous coordinates) prevents vectors from being modified by translations. Therefore, we should not need to zero out the translation in the matrix. The problem is if we want to concatenate the inverse-transpose and another matrix that does not contain non-uniform scaling, say the view matrix $(\mathbf{A}^{-1})^T \mathbf{V}$, the transposed translation in the fourth column of $(\mathbf{A}^{-1})^T$ "leaks" into the product matrix causing errors. Hence, we zero out the translation as a precaution to avoid this error. The proper way would be to transform the normal by: $((\mathbf{AV})^{-1})^T$. Below is an example of a scaling and translation matrix, and what the inverse-transpose looks like with a fourth column not $[0, 0, 0, 1]^T$:

$$\mathbf{A} = \begin{bmatrix} 1 & 0 & 0 & 0 \\ 0 & 0.5 & 0 & 0 \\ 0 & 0 & 0.5 & 0 \\ 1 & 1 & 1 & 1 \end{bmatrix}$$

$$(\mathbf{A}^{-1})^T = \begin{bmatrix} 1 & 0 & 0 & -1 \\ 0 & 2 & 0 & -2 \\ 0 & 0 & 2 & -2 \\ 0 & 0 & 0 & 1 \end{bmatrix}$$

Even with the inverse-transpose transformation, normal vectors may lose their unit length; thus, they may need to be renormalized after the transformation.

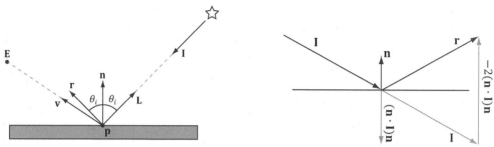

Figure 8.8. Important vectors involved in lighting calculations.   **Figure 8.9.** Geometry of reflection.

8.3 IMPORTANT VECTORS IN LIGHTING

In this section, we summarize some important vectors involved with lighting. Referring to Figure 8.8, **E** is the eye position, and we are considering the point **p** the eye sees along the line of site defined by the unit vector **v**. At the point **p** the surface has normal **n**, and the point is hit by a ray of light traveling with incident direction **I**. The *light vector* **L** is the unit vector that aims in the opposite direction of the light ray striking the surface point. Although it may be more intuitive to work with the direction the light travels **I**, for lighting calculations we work with the light vector **L**; in particular, for calculating Lambert's Cosine Law, the vector **L** is used to evaluate **L·n** = cos θ_i, where θ_i is the angle between **L** and **n**. The reflection vector **r** is the reflection of the incident light vector about the surface normal **n**. The *view vector* (or *to-eye vector*) **v** = normalize(**E** − **p**) is the unit vector from the surface point **p** to the eye point **E** that defines the line of site from the eye to the point on the surface being seen. Sometimes we need to use the vector −**v**, which is the unit vector from the eye to the point on the surface we are evaluating the lighting of.

The reflection vector is given by: **r** = **I** − 2(**n·I**)**n**; see Figure 8.9. (It is assumed that **n** is a unit vector.) However, we can actually use the HLSL intrinsic `reflect` function to compute **r** for us in a shader program.

8.4 LAMBERT'S COSINE LAW

We can think of light as a collection of photons traveling through space in a certain direction. Each photon carries some (light) energy. The amount of (light) energy emitted per second is called *radiant flux*. The density of radiant flux per area (called *irradiance*) is important because that will determine how much light an area on a surface receives (and thus how bright it will appear to the eye). Loosely,

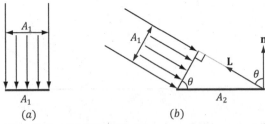

Figure 8.10. (a) A light beam with cross sectional area A_1 strikes a surface head-on. (b) A light beam with cross sectional area A_1 strikes a surface at an angle to cover a larger area A_2 on the surface, thereby spreading the light energy over a larger area, thus making the light appear "dimmer."

we can think of irradiance as the amount of light striking an area on a surface, or the amount of light passing through an imaginary area in space.

Light that strikes a surface head-on (i.e., the light vector **L** equals the normal vector **n**) is more intense than light that glances a surface at an angle. Consider a small light beam with cross sectional area A_1 with radiant flux P passing through it. If we aim this light beam at a surface head-on (Figure 8.10a), then the light beam strikes the area A_1 on the surface and the irradiance at A_1 is $E_1 = P/A_1$. Now suppose we rotate the light beam so that it strikes the surface at an angle (Figure 8.10b), then the light beam covers the larger area A_2 and the irradiance striking this area is $E_2 = P/A_2$. By trigonometry, A_1 and A_2 are related by:

$$\cos\theta = \frac{A_1}{A_2} \Rightarrow \frac{1}{A_2} = \frac{\cos\theta}{A_1}$$

Therefore,

$$E_2 = \frac{P}{A_2} = \frac{P}{A_1}\cos\theta = E_1 \cos\theta = E_1 (\mathbf{n}\cdot\mathbf{L})$$

In other words, the irradiance striking area A_2 is equal to the irradiance at the area A_1 perpendicular to the light direction scaled by $\mathbf{n}\cdot\mathbf{L} = \cos\theta$. This is called *Lambert's Cosine Law*. To handle the case where light strikes the back of the surface (which results in the dot product being negative), we clamp the result with the max function:

$$f(\theta) = \max(\cos\theta, 0) = \max(\mathbf{L}\cdot\mathbf{n}, 0)$$

Figure 8.11 shows a plot of $f(\theta)$ to see how the intensity, ranging from 0.0 to 1.0 (i.e., 0% to 100%), varies with θ.

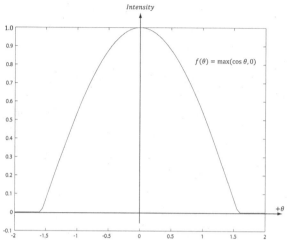

Figure 8.11. Plot of the function $f(\theta) = \max(\cos\theta, 0) = \max(\mathbf{L}\cdot\mathbf{n}, 0)$ for $-2 \leq \theta \leq 2$. Note that $\pi/2 \approx 1.57$.

8.5 DIFFUSE LIGHTING

Consider the surface of an opaque object, as in Figure 8.12. When light strikes a point on the surface, some of the light enters the interior of the object and interacts with the matter near the surface. The light will bounce around in the interior, where some of it will be absorbed and the remaining part scattered out of the surface in every direction; this is called a *diffuse reflection*. For simplification, we assume the light is scattered out at the same point the light entered. The amount of absorption and scattering out depends on the material; for example, wood, dirt, brick, tile, and stucco would absorb/scatter light differently (which is why the materials look different). In our approximation for modeling this kind of light/material interaction, we stipulate that the light scatters out equally in all directions above the surface; consequently, the reflected light will reach the eye

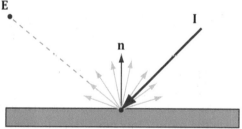

Figure 8.12. Incoming light scatters equally in every direction when striking a diffuse surface. The idea is that light enters the interior of the medium and scatters around under the surface. Some of the light will be absorbed and the remaining will scatter back out of the surface. Because it is difficult to model this subsurface scattering, we assume the re-emitted light scatters out equally in all directions above the surface about the point the light entered.

no matter the viewpoint (eye position). Therefore, we do not need to take the viewpoint into consideration (i.e., the diffuse lighting calculation is viewpoint independent), and the color of a point on the surface will always look the same no matter the viewpoint.

We break the calculation of diffuse lighting into two parts. For the first part, we specify a light color and a *diffuse albedo* color. The diffuse albedo specifies the amount of incoming light that the surface reflects due to diffuse reflectance (by energy conservation, the amount not reflected is absorbed by the material). This is handled with a component-wise color multiplication (because light can be colored). For example, suppose some point on a surface reflects 50% incoming red light, 100% green light, and 75% blue light, and the incoming light color is 80% intensity white light. That is to say, the quantity of incoming light is given by $\mathbf{B}_L = (0.8, 0.8, 0.8)$ and the diffuse albedo is given by $\mathbf{m}_d = (0.5, 1.0, 0.75)$; then the amount of light reflected off the point is given by:

$$c_d = \mathbf{B}_L \otimes \mathbf{m}_d = (0.8, 0.8, 0.8) \otimes (0.5, 1.0, 0.75) = (0.4, 0.8, 0.6)$$

Note that the diffuse albedo components must be in the range 0.0 to 1.0 so that they describe the fraction of light reflected.

The above formula is not quite correct, however. We still need to include Lambert's cosine law (which controls how much of the original light the surface receives based on the angle between the surface normal and light vector). Let $\mathbf{B}_L$ represent the quantity of incoming light, $\mathbf{m}_d$ be the diffuse albedo color, $\mathbf{L}$ be the light vector, and $\mathbf{n}$ be the surface normal. Then the amount of diffuse light reflected off a point is given by:

$$c_d = \max(\mathbf{L} \cdot \mathbf{n}, 0) \cdot \mathbf{B}_L \otimes \mathbf{m}_d \qquad \text{(eq. 8.1)}$$

8.6 AMBIENT LIGHTING

As stated earlier, our lighting model does not take into consideration indirect light that has bounced off other objects in the scenes. However, much light we see in the real world is indirect. For example, a hallway connected to a room might not be in the direct line of site with a light source in the room, but the light bounces off the walls in the room and some of it may make it into the hallway, thereby lightening it up a bit. As a second example, suppose we are sitting in a room with a teapot on a desk and there is one light source in the room. Only one side of the teapot is in the direct line of site of light source; nevertheless, the backside of the teapot would not be completely black. This is because some light scatters off the walls or other objects in the room and eventually strikes the backside of the teapot.

To sort of hack this indirect light, we introduce an ambient term to the lighting equation:

$$c_a = A_L \otimes m_d \qquad \text{(eq. 8.2)}$$

The color A_L specifies the total amount of indirect (ambient) light a surface receives, which may be different than the light emitted from the source due to the absorption that occurred when the light bounced off other surfaces. The diffuse albedo m_d specifies the amount of incoming light that the surface reflects due to diffuse reflectance. We use the same value for specifying the amount of incoming ambient light the surface reflects; that is, for ambient lighting, we are modeling the diffuse reflectance of the indirect (ambient) light. All ambient light does is uniformly brighten up the object a bit—there is no real physics calculation at all. The idea is that the indirect light has scattered and bounced around the scene so many times that it strikes the object equally in every direction.

8.7 SPECULAR LIGHTING

We used diffuse lighting to model diffuse reflection, where light enters a medium, bounces around, some light is absorbed, and the remaining light is scattered out of the medium in every direction. A second kind of reflection happens due to the Fresnel effect, which is a physical phenomenon. When light reaches the interface between two media with different indices of refraction some of the light is reflected and the remaining light is refracted (see Figure 8.13). The index of refraction is a physical property of a medium that is the ratio of the speed of light in a vacuum to the speed of light in the given medium. We refer to this light

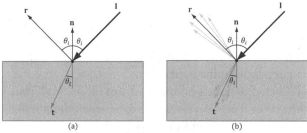

Figure 8.13. (a) The Fresnel effect for a perfectly flat mirror with normal **n**. The incident light **l** is split where some of it reflects in the reflection direction **r** and the remaining light refracts into the medium in the refraction direction **t**. All these vectors are in the same plane. The angle between the reflection vector and normal is always θ_i, which is the same as the angle between the light vector **L** = −**l** and normal **n**. The angle θ_t between the refraction vector and −**n** depends in the indices of refraction between the two mediums and is specified by Snell's Law. (b) Most objects are not perfectly flat mirrors but have microscopic roughness. This causes the reflected and refracted light to spread about the reflection and refraction vectors.

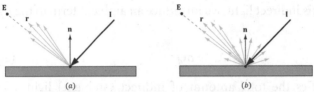

Figure 8.14. (a) Specular light of a rough surface spreads about the reflection vector **r**. (b) The reflected light that makes it into the eye is a combination of specular reflection and diffuse reflection.

reflection process as *specular reflection* and the reflected light as *specular light*. Specular light is illustrated in Figure 8.14a.

If the refracted vector exits the medium (from the other side) and enters the eye, the object appears transparent. That is, light passes through transparent objects. Real-time graphics typically use alpha blending or a post process effect to approximate refraction in transparent objects, which we will explain later in this book. For now, we consider only opaque objects.

For opaque objects, the refracted light enters the medium and undergoes diffuse reflectance. So we can see from Figure 8.14b that for opaque objects, the amount of light that reflects off a surface and makes it into the eye is a combination of body reflected (diffuse) light and specular reflection. In contrast to diffuse light, specular light might not travel into the eye because it reflects in a specific direction; that is to say, the specular lighting calculation is viewpoint dependent. This means that as the eye moves about the scene, the amount of specular light it receives will change.

8.7.1 Fresnel Effect

Let us consider a flat surface with normal **n** that separates two mediums with different indices of refraction. Due to the index of refraction discontinuity at the surface, when incoming light strikes the surface some reflects away from the surface and some refracts into the surface (see Figure 8.13). The *Fresnel equations* mathematically describe the percentage of incoming light that is reflected, $0 \leq \mathbf{R}_F \leq 1$. By conservation of energy, if $\mathbf{R}_F$ is the amount of reflected light then $(1 - \mathbf{R}_F)$ is the amount of refracted light. The value $\mathbf{R}_F$ is an RGB vector because the amount of reflection depends on the light color.

How much light is reflected depends on the medium (some materials will be more reflective than others) and also on the angle θ_i between the normal vector **n** and light vector **L**. Due to their complexity, the full Fresnel equations are not typically used in real-time rendering; instead, the *Schlick approximation* is used:

$$\mathbf{R}_F(\theta_i) = \mathbf{R}_F(0°) + \left(1 - \mathbf{R}_F(0°)\right)\left(1 - \cos\theta_i\right)^5$$

$\mathbf{R}_F(0°)$ is a property of the medium; below are some values for common materials [Möller08]:

Medium	$\mathbf{R}_F(0°)$
Water	(0.02, 0.02, 0.02)
Glass	(0.08, 0.08, 0.08)
Plastic	(0.05, 0.05, 0.05)
Gold	(1.0, 0.71, 0.29)
Silver	(0.95, 0.93, 0.88)
Copper	(0.95, 0.64, 0.54)

Figure 8.15 shows a plot of the Schlick approximation for a couple different $\mathbf{R}_F(0°)$. The key observation is that the amount of reflection increases as $\theta_i \to 90°$. Let us look at a real-world example. Consider Figure 8.16. Suppose we are standing a couple feet deep in a calm pond of relatively clear water. If we look down, we mostly see the bottom sand and rocks of the pond. This is because the light coming down from the environment that reflects into our eye forms a small angle θ_i near $0.0°$; thus, the amount of reflection is low, and, by energy conservation, the amount of refraction high. On the other hand, if we look towards the horizon, we will see a strong reflection in the pond water. This is because the light coming down from the environment that makes it into our eye forms an angle θ_i closer to $90.0°$, thus increasing the amount of reflection. This behavior is often referred to as the *Fresnel effect*. To summarize the Fresnel effect briefly: *the amount of reflected light depends on the material ($\mathbf{R}_F(0°)$) and the angle between the normal and light vector.*

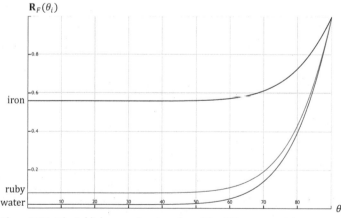

Figure 8.15. The Schlick approximation plotted for different materials: water, ruby, and iron.

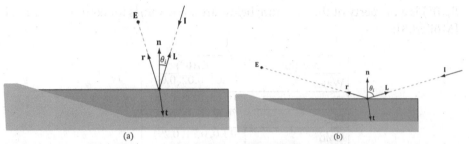

Figure 8.16. (a): Looking down in the pond, reflection is low and refraction high because the angle between **L** and **n** is small. (b) Look towards the horizon and reflection is high and refraction low because the angle between **L** and **n** is closer to 90°.

Metals absorb transmitted light [Möller08], which means they will not have body reflectance. Metals do not appear black, however, as they have high $\mathbf{R}_F(0°)$ values which means they reflect a fair amount of specular light even at small incident angles near 0°.

8.7.2 Roughness

Reflective objects in the real world tend not to be perfect mirrors. Even if an object's surface appears flat, at the microscopic level we can think of it as having *roughness*. Referring to Figure 8.17, we can think of a perfect mirror as having no roughness and its micro-normals all aim in the same direction as the macro-normal. As the roughness increases, the direction of the micro-normals diverge from the macro-normal, causing the reflected light to spread out into a *specular lobe*.

To model roughness mathematically, we employ the *microfacet* model, where we model the microscopic surface as a collection of tiny flat elements called microfacets; the micro-normals are the normals to the microfacets. For a given view **v** and light vector **L**, we want to know the fraction of microfacets that reflect **L** into **v**; in other words, the fraction of microfacets with normal **h** = normalize(**L** + **v**); see Figure 8.18. This will tell us how much light is reflected into the eye from

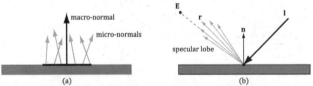

Figure 8.17. (a) The black horizontal bar represents the magnification of a small surface element. At the microscopic level, the area has many micro-normals that aim in different directions due to roughness at the microscopic level. The smoother the surface, the more aligned the micro-normals will be with the macro-normal; the rougher the surface, the more the micro-normals will diverge from the macro-normal. (b) This roughness causes the specular reflected light to spread out. The shape of the of the specular reflection is referred to as the specular lobe. In general, the shape of the specular lobe can vary based on the type of surface material being modeled.

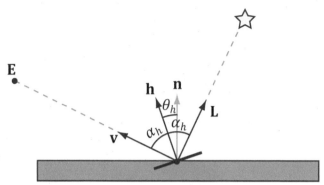

Figure 8.18. The microfacets with normal **h** reflect **L** into **v**.

specular reflection—the more microfacets that reflect **L** into **v** the brighter the specular light the eye sees.

The vector **h** is called the *halfway vector* as it lies halfway between **L** and **v**. Moreover, let us also introduce the angle θ_h between the halfway vector **h** and the macro-normal **n**.

We define the normalized distribution function $\rho(\theta_h) \in [0, 1]$ to denote the fraction of microfacets with normals **h** that make an angle θ_h with the macro-normal **n**. Intuitively, we expect that $\rho(\theta_h)$ achieves its maximum when $\theta_h = 0°$. That is, we expect the microfacet normals to be biased towards the macro-normal, and as θ_h increases (as **h** diverges from the micro-normal **n**) we expect the fraction of microfacets with normal **h** to decrease. A popular controllable function to model $\rho(\theta_h)$ that has the expectations just discussed is:

$$\rho(\theta_h) = \cos^m(\theta_h) \\ = \cos^m(\mathbf{n} \cdot \mathbf{h})$$

Note that $\cos(\theta_h) = (\mathbf{n} \cdot \mathbf{h})$ provided both vectors and unit length. Figure 8.19 shows $\rho(\theta_h) = \cos^m(\theta_h)$ for various m. Here m controls the roughness, which specifies the fraction of microfacets with normals **h** that make an angle θ_h with the macro-normal **n**. As m decreases, the surface becomes rougher, and the microfacet normals increasingly diverge from the macro-normal. As m increases, the surface becomes smoother, and the microfacet normals increasingly converge to the macro-normal.

We can combine $\rho(\theta_h)$ with a normalization factor to obtain a new function that models the amount of specular reflection of light based on roughness:

$$S(\theta_h) = \frac{m+8}{8} \cos^m(\theta_h) \\ = \frac{m+8}{8}(\mathbf{n} \cdot \mathbf{h})^m$$

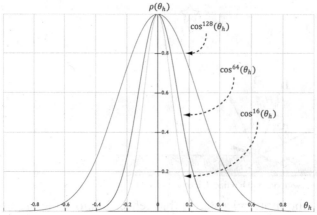

Figure 8.19. A function to model roughness.

Figure 8.20 shows this function for various m. Like before, m controls the roughness, but we have added the $\frac{m+8}{8}$ normalization factor so that light energy is conserved; it is essentially controlling the height of the curve in Figure 8.20 so that the overall light energy is conserved as the specular lobe widens or narrows with m. For a smaller m, the surface is rougher and the specular lobe widens as light energy is more spread out; therefore, we expect the specular highlight to be dimmer since the energy has been spread out. On the other hand, for a larger m, the surface is smoother and the specular lobe is narrower; therefore, we expect the specular highlight to be brighter since the energy has been concentrated. Geometrically, m controls the spread of the specular lobe. To model smooth surfaces (like polished metal) you will use a large m, and for rougher surfaces you will use a small m.

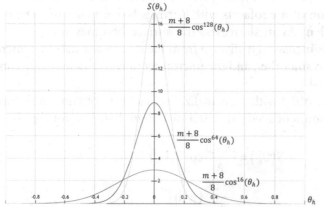

Figure 8.20. A function to model specular reflection of light due to roughness.

To conclude this section, let us combine Fresnel reflection and surface roughness. We are trying to compute how much light is reflected into the view direction **v** (see Figure 8.18). Recall that microfacets with normals **h** reflect light into **v**. Let α_h be the angle between the light vector and half vector **h**, then $R_F(\alpha_h)$ tells us the amount of light reflected about **h** into **v** due to the Fresnel effect. Multiplying the amount of reflected light $R_F(\alpha_h)$ due to the Fresnel effect with the amount of light reflected due to roughness $S(\theta_h)$ gives us the amount of specular reflected light: Let $(\max(\mathbf{L}\cdot\mathbf{n}, 0)\cdot\mathbf{B}_L)$ represent the quantity of incoming light that strikes the surface point we are lighting, then the fraction of $(\max(\mathbf{L}\cdot\mathbf{n}, 0)\cdot\mathbf{B}_L)$ specularly reflected into the eye due to roughness and the Fresnel effect is given by:

$$\mathbf{c}_s = \max(\mathbf{L}\cdot\mathbf{n},0)\cdot\mathbf{B}_L \otimes \mathbf{R}_F(\alpha_h)\frac{m+8}{8}(\mathbf{n}\cdot\mathbf{h})^m \quad \text{(eq. 8.3)}$$

Observe that if $\mathbf{L}\cdot\mathbf{n} \leq 0$ the light strikes the back of the surface we are computing; hence the front-side surface receives no light.

8.8 LIGHTING MODEL RECAP

Bringing everything together, the total light reflected off a surface is a sum of ambient light reflectance, diffuse light reflectance and specular light reflectance:

1. Ambient Light $\mathbf{c}_a$: Models the amount of light reflected off the surface due to indirect light.
2. Diffuse Light $\mathbf{c}_d$: Models light that enters the interior of a medium, scatters around under the surface where some of the light is absorbed and the remaining light scatters back out of the surface. Because it is difficult to model this subsurface scattering, we assume the re-emitted light scatters out equally in all directions above the surface about the point the light entered.
3. Specular Light $\mathbf{c}_s$: Models the light that is reflected off the surface due to the Fresnel effect and surface roughness.

This leads to the lighting equation our shaders implement in this book:

$$\begin{aligned}LitColor &= \mathbf{c}_a + \mathbf{c}_d + \mathbf{c}_s \\ &= \mathbf{A}_L \otimes \mathbf{m}_d + \max(\mathbf{L}\cdot\mathbf{n},0)\cdot\mathbf{B}_L \otimes \left(\mathbf{m}_d + \mathbf{R}_F(\alpha_h)\frac{m+8}{8}(\mathbf{n}\cdot\mathbf{h})^m\right)\end{aligned} \quad \text{(eq. 8.4)}$$

All of the vectors in this equation are assumed to be unit length.

1. **L**: The light vector aims toward the light source.
2. **n**: The surface normal.

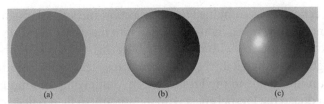

Figure 8.21: (a) Sphere colored with ambient light only, which uniformly brightens it. (b) Ambient and diffuse lighting combined. There is now a smooth transition from bright to dark due to Lambert's cosine law. (c) Ambient, diffuse, and specular lighting. The specular lighting yields a specular highlight.

3. **h**: The halfway vector lies halfway between the light vector and view vector (vector from surface point being lit to the eye point).
4. A_L: Represent the quantity of incoming ambient light.
5. B_L: Represent the quantity of incoming direct light.
6. m_d: Specifies the amount of incoming light light that the surface reflects due to diffuse reflectance.
7. **L·n** : Lambert's Cosine Law.
8. α_h: Angle between the half vector **h** and light vector **L**.
9. $R_F(\alpha_h)$: Specifies the amount of light reflected about **h** into the eye due to the Fresnel effect.
10. *m*: Controls the surface roughness.
11. $(\mathbf{n} \cdot \mathbf{h})^m$: Specifies the fraction of microfacets with normals **h** that make an angle θ_h with the macro-normal **n**.
12. $\frac{m+8}{8}$: Normalization factor to model energy conservation in the specular reflection.

Figure 8.21 shows how these three components work together.

 Equation 4 is a common and popular lighting equation, but it is just a model. Other lighting models have been proposed as well.

8.9 IMPLEMENTING MATERIALS

Our material structure looks like this, and is defined in *d3dUtil.h*:

```
// Simple struct to represent a material for our demos.
struct Material
{
  // Unique material name for lookup.
  std::string Name;

  // Index into constant buffer corresponding to this material.
  int MatCBIndex = -1;
```

```cpp
    // Index into SRV heap for diffuse texture. Used in the texturing
    // chapter.
    int DiffuseSrvHeapIndex = -1;

    // Dirty flag indicating the material has changed and we need to
    // update the constant buffer. Because we have a material constant
    // buffer for each FrameResource, we have to apply the update to each
    // FrameResource. Thus, when we modify a material we should set
    // NumFramesDirty = gNumFrameResources so that each frame resource
    // gets the update.
    int NumFramesDirty = gNumFrameResources;

    // Material constant buffer data used for shading.
    DirectX::XMFLOAT4 DiffuseAlbedo = { 1.0f, 1.0f, 1.0f, 1.0f };
    DirectX::XMFLOAT3 FresnelR0    = { 0.01f, 0.01f, 0.01f };
    float Roughness = 0.25f;
    DirectX::XMFLOAT4X4 MatTransform = MathHelper::Identity4x4();
};
```

Modeling real-world materials will require a combination of setting realistic values for the `DiffuseAlbedo` and `FresnelR0`, and some artistic tweaking. For example, metal conductors absorb refracted light [Möller08] that enters the interior of the metal, which means metals will not have diffuse reflection (i.e., the `DiffuseAlbedo` would be zero). However, to compensate that we are not doing 100% physical simulation of lighting, it may give better artistic results to give a low `DiffuseAlbedo` value rather than zero. The point is: we will try to use physically realistic material values, but are free to tweak the values as we want if the end result looks better from an artistic point of view.

In our material structure, roughness is specified in a normalized floating-point value in the [0, 1] range. A roughness of 0 would indicate a perfectly smooth surface, and a roughness of 1 would indicate the roughest surface physically possible. The normalized range makes it easier to author roughness and compare the roughness between different materials. For example, a material with a roughness of 0.6 is twice as rough as a material with roughness 0.3. In the shader code, we will use the roughness to derive the exponent m used in Equation 8.4. Note that with our definition of roughness, the shininess of a surface is just the inverse of the roughness: *shininess* = 1 − *roughness* ∈ [0, 1].

A question now is at what granularity we should specify the material values? The material values may vary over the surface; that is, different points on the surface may have different material values. For example, consider a car model as shown in Figure 8.22, where the frame, windows, lights, and tires reflect and absorb light differently, and so the material values would need to vary over the car surface.

To implement this variation, one solution might be to specify material values on a per vertex basis. These per vertex materials would then interpolated across the triangle during rasterization, giving us material values for each point on the surface

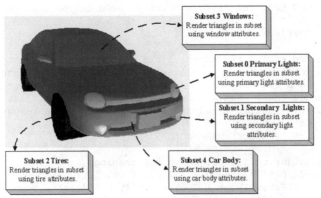

Figure 8.22. A car mesh divided into five material attribute groups.

of the triangle mesh. However, as we saw from the "Hills" demo in Chapter 7, per vertex colors are still too coarse to realistically model fine details. Moreover, per vertex colors add additional data to our vertex structures, and we need to have tools to paint per vertex colors. Instead, the prevalent solution is to use texture mapping, which will have to wait until the next chapter. For this chapter, we allow material changes at the draw call frequency. To do this, we define the properties of each unique material and put them in a table:

```
std::unordered_map<std::string, std::unique_ptr<Material>> mMaterials;

void LitWavesApp::BuildMaterials()
{
  auto grass = std::make_unique<Material>();
  grass->Name = "grass";
  grass->MatCBIndex = 0;
  grass->DiffuseAlbedo = XMFLOAT4(0.2f, 0.6f, 0.6f, 1.0f);
  grass->FresnelR0 = XMFLOAT3(0.01f, 0.01f, 0.01f);
  grass->Roughness = 0.125f;

  // This is not a good water material definition, but we do not have
  // all the rendering tools we need (transparency, environment
  // reflection), so we fake it for now.
  auto water = std::make_unique<Material>();
  water->Name = "water";
  water->MatCBIndex = 1;
  water->DiffuseAlbedo = XMFLOAT4(0.0f, 0.2f, 0.6f, 1.0f);
  water->FresnelR0 = XMFLOAT3(0.1f, 0.1f, 0.1f);
  water->Roughness = 0.0f;

  mMaterials["grass"] = std::move(grass);
  mMaterials["water"] = std::move(water);
}
```

The above table stores the material data in system memory. In order for the GPU to access the material data in a shader, we need to mirror the relevant data in a constant buffer. Just like we did with per-object constant buffers, we add a constant buffer to each `FrameResource` that will store the constants for each material:

```
struct MaterialConstants
{
  DirectX::XMFLOAT4 DiffuseAlbedo = { 1.0f, 1.0f, 1.0f, 1.0f };
  DirectX::XMFLOAT3 FresnelR0 = { 0.01f, 0.01f, 0.01f };
  float Roughness = 0.25f;

  // Used in the chapter on texture mapping.
  DirectX::XMFLOAT4X4 MatTransform = MathHelper::Identity4x4();
};

struct FrameResource
{
public:
  ...

  std::unique_ptr<UploadBuffer<MaterialConstants>> MaterialCB =
    nullptr;

  ...
};
```

Note that the `MaterialConstants` structure contains a subset of the `Material` data; specifically, it contains just the data the shaders need for rendering.

In the update function, the material data is then copied to a subregion of the constant buffer whenever it is changed ("dirty") so that the GPU material constant buffer data is kept up to date with the system memory material data:

```
void LitWavesApp::UpdateMaterialCBs(const GameTimer& gt)
{
  auto currMaterialCB = mCurrFrameResource->MaterialCB.get();
  for(auto& e : mMaterials)
  {
    // Only update the cbuffer data if the constants have changed. If
    // the cbuffer data changes, it needs to be updated for each
    // FrameResource.
    Material* mat = e.second.get();
    if(mat->NumFramesDirty > 0)
    {
      XMMATRIX matTransform = XMLoadFloat4x4(&mat->MatTransform);

      MaterialConstants matConstants;
      matConstants.DiffuseAlbedo = mat->DiffuseAlbedo;
      matConstants.FresnelR0 = mat->FresnelR0;
      matConstants.Roughness = mat->Roughness;

      currMaterialCB->CopyData(mat->MatCBIndex, matConstants);

      // Next FrameResource need to be updated too.
      mat->NumFramesDirty--;
    }
```

        }
    }

Now each render item contains a pointer to a Material. Note that multiple render items can refer to the same Material object; for example, multiple render items might use the same "brick" material. In turn, each Material object has an index that specifies were its constant data is in the material constant buffer. From this, we can offset to the virtual address of the constant data needed for the render item we are drawing, and set it to the root descriptor that expects the material constant data. (Alternatively, we could offset to a CBV descriptor in a heap and set a descriptor table, but we defined our root signature in this demo to take a root descriptor for the material constant buffer instead of a table.) The following code shows how we draw render items with different materials:

```
void LitWavesApp::DrawRenderItems(
    ID3D12GraphicsCommandList* cmdList,
    const std::vector<RenderItem*>& ritems)
{
    UINT objCBByteSize = d3dUtil::CalcConstantBufferByteSize
        (sizeof(ObjectConstants));
    UINT matCBByteSize = d3dUtil::CalcConstantBufferByteSize
        (sizeof(MaterialConstants));

    auto objectCB = mCurrFrameResource->ObjectCB->Resource();
    auto matCB = mCurrFrameResource->MaterialCB->Resource();

    // For each render item...
    for(size_t i = 0; i < ritems.size(); ++i)
    {
        auto ri = ritems[i];

        cmdList->IASetVertexBuffers(0, 1, &ri->Geo->VertexBufferView());
        cmdList->IASetIndexBuffer(&ri->Geo->IndexBufferView());
        cmdList->IASetPrimitiveTopology(ri->PrimitiveType);

        D3D12_GPU_VIRTUAL_ADDRESS objCBAddress =
            objectCB->GetGPUVirtualAddress() +
            ri->ObjCBIndex*objCBByteSize;
        D3D12_GPU_VIRTUAL_ADDRESS matCBAddress =
            matCB->GetGPUVirtualAddress() +
            ri->Mat->MatCBIndex*matCBByteSize;

        cmdList->SetGraphicsRootConstantBufferView(0, objCBAddress);
        cmdList->SetGraphicsRootConstantBufferView(1, matCBAddress);

        cmdList->DrawIndexedInstanced(ri->IndexCount, 1,
            ri->StartIndexLocation, ri->BaseVertexLocation, 0);
    }
}
```

Lighting

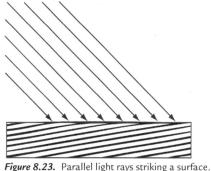

Figure 8.23. Parallel light rays striking a surface.

Figure 8.24. The figure is not drawn to scale, but if you select a small surface area on the Earth, the light rays striking that area are approximately parallel.

We remind the reader that we need normal vectors at each point on the surface of a triangle mesh so that we can determine the angle at which light strikes a point on the mesh surface (for Lambert's cosine law). In order to obtain a normal vector approximation at each point on the surface of the triangle mesh, we specify normals at the vertex level. These vertex normals will be interpolated across the triangle during rasterization.

So far we have discussed the components of light, but we have not discussed specific kinds of light sources. The next three sections describe how to implement, parallel, point, and spot lights.

8.10 PARALLEL LIGHTS

A parallel light (or directional light) approximates a light source that is very far away. Consequently, we can approximate all incoming light rays as parallel to each other (Figure 8.23). Moreover, because the light source is very far away, we can ignore the effects of distance and just specify the light intensity where the light strikes the scene.

A parallel light source is defined by a vector, which specifies the direction the light rays travel. Because the light rays are parallel, they all use the same direction vector. The light vector, aims in the opposite direction the light rays travel. A common example of a light source that can accurately be modeled as a directional light is the sun (Figure 8.24).

8.11 POINT LIGHTS

A good physical example of a point light is a lightbulb; it radiates spherically in all directions (Figure 8.25). In particular, for an arbitrary point **P**, there exists a light ray originating from the point light position **Q** traveling toward the point.

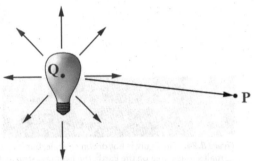

Figure 8.25. Point lights radiate in every direction; in particular, for an arbitrary point **P** there exists a light ray originating from the point source **Q** towards **P**.

As usual, we define the light vector to go in the opposite direction; that is, the direction from the point **P** to the point light source **Q**:

$$\mathbf{L} = \frac{\mathbf{Q} - \mathbf{P}}{\|\mathbf{Q} - \mathbf{P}\|}$$

Essentially, the only difference between point lights and parallel lights is how the light vector is computed—it varies from point to point for point lights, but remains constant for parallel lights.

8.11.1 Attenuation

Physically, light intensity weakens as a function of distance based on the inverse squared law. That is to say, the light intensity at a point a distance d away from the light source is given by:

$$I(d) = \frac{I_0}{d^2}$$

where I_0 is the light intensity at a distance $d = 1$ from the light source. This works well if you set up physically based light values and use HDR (high dynamic range) lighting and tonemapping. However, an easier formula to get started with, and the one we shall use in our demos, is a linear falloff function:

$$\text{att}(d) = \text{saturate}\left(\frac{\text{falloffEnd} - d}{\text{falloffEnd} - \text{falloffStart}}\right)$$

A graph of this function is depicted in Figure 8.26. The `saturate` function clamps the argument to the range [0, 1]:

$$\text{saturate}(x) = \begin{cases} x, & 0 \le x \le 1 \\ 0, & x < 0 \\ 1, & x > 1 \end{cases}$$

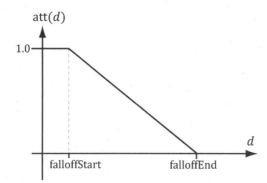

Figure 8.26. The attenuation factor that scales the light value stays at full strength (1.0) until the distance *d* reaches *falloffStart*, it then linearly decays to 0.0 as the distance reaches *falloffEnd*.

The formula for evaluating a point light is the same as Equation 8.4, but we must scale the light source value $\mathbf{B}_L$ by the attenuation factor att(d). Note that attenuation does not affect ambient term, as the ambient term is used to model indirect light that has bounced around.

Using our falloff function, a point whose distance from the light source is greater than or equal to *falloffEnd* receives no light. This provides a useful lighting optimization: in our shader programs, if a point is out of range, then we can return early and skip the lighting calculations with dynamic branching.

8.12 SPOTLIGHTS

A good physical example of a spotlight is a flashlight. Essentially, a spotlight has a position **Q**, is aimed in a direction **d**, and radiates light through a cone (see Figure 8.27).

To implement a spotlight, we begin as we do with a point light: the light vector is given by:

$$\mathbf{L} = \frac{\mathbf{Q} - \mathbf{P}}{\|\mathbf{Q} - \mathbf{P}\|}$$

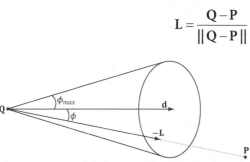

Figure 8.27. A spotlight has a position **Q**, is aimed in a direction **d**, and radiates light through a cone with angle ϕ_{max}.

where **P** is the position of the point being lit and **Q** is the position of the spotlight. Observe from Figure 8.27 that **P** is inside the spotlight's cone (and therefore receives light) if and only if the angle ϕ between $-\mathbf{L}$ and **d** is smaller than the cone angle ϕ_{max}. Moreover, all the light in the spotlight's cone should not be of equal intensity; the light at the center of the cone should be the most intense and the light intensity should fade to zero as ϕ increases from 0 to ϕ_{max}.

So how do we control the intensity falloff as a function of ϕ, and also how do we control the size of the spotlight's cone? We can use a function with the same graph as in Figure 8.19, but replace θ_h with ϕ and m with s:

$$k_{spot}(\phi) = \max(\cos\phi, 0)^s = \max(-\mathbf{L}\cdot\mathbf{d}, 0)^s$$

This gives us what we want: the intensity smoothly fades as ϕ increases; additionally, by altering the exponent s, we can indirectly control ϕ_{max} (the angle the intensity drops to 0); that is to say, we can shrink or expand the spotlight cone by varying s. For example, if we set $s = 8$, the cone has approximately a 45° half angle.

The spotlight equation is just like Equation 8.4, except that we multiply the light source value $\mathbf{B}_L$ by both the attenuation factor att(d) and the spotlight factor k_{spot} to scale the light intensity based on where the point is with respect to the spotlight cone.

We see that a spotlight is more expensive than a point light because we need to compute the additional k_{spot} factor and multiply by it. Similarly, we see that a point light is more expensive than a directional light because the distance d needs to be computed (this is actually pretty expensive because distance involves a square root operation), and we need to compute and multiply by the attenuation factor. To summarize, directional lights are the least expensive light source, followed by point lights, followed by spotlights being the most expensive light source.

8.13 LIGHTING IMPLEMENTATION

This section discusses the details for implementing directional, point, and spot lights.

8.13.1 Light Structure

In *d3dUtil.h*, we define the following structure to support lights. This structure can represent directional, point, or spot lights. However, depending on the light type, some values will not be used; for example, a point light does not use the `Direction` data member.

```
struct Light
{
  DirectX::XMFLOAT3 Strength;  // Light color
  float FalloffStart;          // point/spot light only
  DirectX::XMFLOAT3 Direction;// directional/spot light only
  float FalloffEnd;            // point/spot light only
  DirectX::XMFLOAT3 Position;  // point/spot light only
  float SpotPower;             // spot light only
};
```

The *LightingUtils.hlsl* file defines structures that mirror these:

```
struct Light
{
  float3 Strength;
  float FalloffStart;    // point/spot light only
  float3 Direction;      // directional/spot light only
  float FalloffEnd;      // point/spot light only
  float3 Position;       // point light only
  float SpotPower;       // spot light only
};
```

The order of data members listed in the `Light` structure (and also the `MaterialConstants` structure) is not arbitrary. They are cognizant of the HLSL structure packing rules. See Appendix B ("Structure Packing") for details, but the main idea is that in HLSL, structure padding occurs so that elements are packed into 4D vectors, with the restriction that a single element cannot be split across two 4D vectors. This means the above structure gets nicely packed into three 4D vectors like this:

```
vector 1: (Strength.x, Strength.y, Strength.z, FalloffStart)
vector 2: (Direction.x, Direction.y, Direction.z, FalloffEnd)
vector 3: (Position.x, Position.y, Position.z, SpotPower)
```

On the other hand, if we wrote our `Light` structure like this

```
struct Light
{
  DirectX::XMFLOAT3 Strength;  // Light color
  DirectX::XMFLOAT3 Direction;// directional/spot light only
  DirectX::XMFLOAT3 Position;  // point/spot light only
  float FalloffStart;          // point/spot light only
  float FalloffEnd;            // point/spot light only
  float SpotPower;             // spot light only
};

struct Light
{
  float3 Strength;
  float3 Direction;      // directional/spot light only
  float3 Position;       // point light only
  float FalloffStart;    // point/spot light only
  float FalloffEnd;      // point/spot light only
```

```
        float SpotPower;    // spot light only
    };
```

then it would get packed into four 4D vectors like this:

```
    vector 1: (Strength.x, Strength.y, Strength.z, empty)
    vector 2: (Direction.x, Direction.y, Direction.z, empty)
    vector 3: (Position.x, Position.y, Position.z, empty)
    vector 4: (FalloffStart, FalloffEnd, SpotPower, empty)
```

The second approach takes up more data, but that is not the main problem. The more serious problem is that we have a C++ application side structure that mirrors the HLSL structure, but the C++ structure does not follow the same HLSL packing rules; thus, the C++ and HLSL structure layouts are likely not going to match unless you are careful with the HLSL packing rules and write them so that they do. If the C++ and HLSL structure layouts do not match, then we will get rendering bugs when we upload data from the CPU to GPU constant buffers using `memcpy`.

8.13.2 Common Helper Functions

The below three functions, defined in *LightingUtils.hlsl*, contain code that is common to more than one type of light, and therefore we define in helper functions.

1. `CalcAttenuation`: Implements a linear attenuation factor, which applies to point lights and spot lights.
2. `SchlickFresnel`: The Schlick approximation to the Fresnel equations; it approximates the percentage of light reflected off a surface with normal **n** based on the angle between the light vector **L** and surface normal **n** due to the Fresnel effect.
3. `BlinnPhong`: Computes the amount of light reflected into the eye; it is the sum of diffuse reflectance and specular reflectance.

```
    float CalcAttenuation(float d, float falloffStart, float falloffEnd)
    {
      // Linear falloff.
      return saturate((falloffEnd-d) / (falloffEnd - falloffStart));
    }

    // Schlick gives an approximation to Fresnel reflectance
    // (see pg. 233 "Real-Time Rendering 3rd Ed.").
    // R0 = ( (n-1)/(n+1) )^2, where n is the index of refraction.
    float3 SchlickFresnel(float3 R0, float3 normal, float3 lightVec)
    {
      float cosIncidentAngle = saturate(dot(normal, lightVec));

      float f0 = 1.0f - cosIncidentAngle;
      float3 reflectPercent = R0 + (1.0f - R0)*(f0*f0*f0*f0*f0);
```

```
    return reflectPercent;
}

struct Material
{
    float4 DiffuseAlbedo;
    float3 FresnelR0;

    // Shininess is inverse of roughness: Shininess = 1-roughness.
    float Shininess;
};

float3 BlinnPhong(float3 lightStrength, float3 lightVec,
        float3 normal, float3 toEye, Material mat)
{
    // Derive m from the shininess, which is derived from the roughness.
    const float m = mat.Shininess * 256.0f;
    float3 halfVec = normalize(toEye + lightVec);

    float roughnessFactor = (m + 8.0f)*pow(max(dot(halfVec, normal),
        0.0f), m) / 8.0f;
    float3 fresnelFactor = SchlickFresnel(mat.FresnelR0, halfVec,
        lightVec);

    // Our spec formula goes outside [0,1] range, but we are doing
    // LDR rendering. So scale it down a bit.
    specAlbedo = specAlbedo / (specAlbedo + 1.0f);

    return (mat.DiffuseAlbedo.rgb + specAlbedo) * lightStrength;
}
```

The following intrinsic HLSL functions were used: dot, pow, and max, which are, respectively, the vector dot product function, power function, and maximum function. Descriptions of most of the HLSL intrinsic functions can be found in Appendix B, along with a quick primer on other HLSL syntax. One thing to note, however, is that when two vectors are multiplied with operator*, the multiplication is done component-wise.

Our formula for computing the specular albedo allows for specular values to be greater than 1 which indicates very bright highlights. However, our render target expects color values to be in the low-dynamic-range (LDR) of [0, 1]. Values outside this range will simply get clamped to 1.0 since our render target requires color values to be in the [0, 1] range. Therefore, to get softer specular highlights without a sharp clamp, we need to need to scale down the specular albedo:

```
specAlbedo = specAlbedo / (specAlbedo + 1.0f);
```

High-Dynamic-Range (HDR) lighting uses floating-point render targets that allows light values to go outside the range [0, 1], and then a tonemapping step is performed to remap the high-dynamic-range back to [0, 1] for display, while preserving the details that are important. HDR rendering and tonemapping is a subject on its own—see the textbook by [Reinhard10]. However, [Pettineo12] provides a good introduction and demo to experiment with.

Note: On the PC, HLSL functions are always inlined; therefore, there is no performance overhead for functions or parameter passing.

8.13.3 Implementing Directional Lights

Given the eye position **E** and given a point **p** on a surface visible to the eye with surface normal **n**, and material properties, the following HLSL function outputs the amount of light, from a directional light source, that reflects into the to-eye direction **v** = normalize (**E** − **p**). In our samples, this function will be called in a pixel shader to determine the color of the pixel based on lighting.

```
float3 ComputeDirectionalLight(Light L, Material mat, float3 normal,
float3 toEye)
{
  // The light vector aims opposite the direction the light rays
    travel.
  float3 lightVec = -L.Direction;

  // Scale light down by Lambert's cosine law.
  float ndotl = max(dot(lightVec, normal), 0.0f);
  float3 lightStrength = L.Strength * ndotl;

  return BlinnPhong(lightStrength, lightVec, normal, toEye, mat);
}
```

8.13.4 Implementing Point Lights

Given the eye position **E** and given a point **p** on a surface visible to the eye with surface normal **n**, and material properties, the following HLSL function outputs the amount of light, from a point light source, that reflects into the to-eye direction **v** = normalize (**E** − **p**). In our samples, this function will be called in a pixel shader to determine the color of the pixel based on lighting.

```
float3 ComputePointLight(Light L, Material mat, float3 pos, float3
normal, float3 toEye)
{
  // The vector from the surface to the light.
  float3 lightVec = L.Position - pos;

  // The distance from surface to light.
  float d = length(lightVec);

  // Range test.
  if(d > L.FalloffEnd)
    return 0.0f;
```

```
    // Normalize the light vector.
    lightVec /= d;

    // Scale light down by Lambert's cosine law.
    float ndotl = max(dot(lightVec, normal), 0.0f);
    float3 lightStrength = L.Strength * ndotl;

    // Attenuate light by distance.
    float att = CalcAttenuation(d, L.FalloffStart, L.FalloffEnd);
    lightStrength *= att;

    return BlinnPhong(lightStrength, lightVec, normal, toEye, mat);
}
```

8.13.5 Implementing Spotlights

Given the eye position **E** and given a point **p** on a surface visible to the eye with surface normal **n**, and material properties, the following HLSL function outputs the amount of light, from a spot light source, that reflects into the to-eye direction **v** = normalize (**E** − **p**). In our samples, this function will be called in a pixel shader to determine the color of the pixel based on lighting.

```
float3 ComputeSpotLight(Light L, Material mat, float3 pos, float3
normal, float3 toEye)
{
    // The vector from the surface to the light.
    float3 lightVec = L.Position - pos;

    // The distance from surface to light.
    float d = length(lightVec);

    // Range test.
    if(d > L.FalloffEnd)
        return 0.0f;

    // Normalize the light vector.
    lightVec /= d;

    // Scale light down by Lambert's cosine law.
    float ndotl = max(dot(lightVec, normal), 0.0f);
    float3 lightStrength = L.Strength * ndotl;

    // Attenuate light by distance.
    float att = CalcAttenuation(d, L.FalloffStart, L.FalloffEnd);
    lightStrength *= att;

    // Scale by spotlight
    float spotFactor = pow(max(dot(-lightVec, L.Direction), 0.0f),
      L.SpotPower);
    lightStrength *= spotFactor;

    return BlinnPhong(lightStrength, lightVec, normal, toEye, mat);
}
```

8.13.6 Accumulating Multiple Lights

Lighting is additive, so supporting multiple lights in a scene simply means we need to iterate over each light source and sum its contribution to the point/pixel we are evaluating the lighting of. Our sample framework supports up to sixteen total lights. We can use any combination of directional, point, or spot lights, but the total must not exceed sixteen. Moreover, our code uses the convention that directional lights must come first in the light array, point lights come second, and spot lights come last. The following code evaluates the lighting equation for a point

```
#define MaxLights 16

// Constant data that varies per material.
cbuffer cbPass : register(b2)
{
  ...
// Indices [0, NUM_DIR_LIGHTS) are directional lights;
// indices [NUM_DIR_LIGHTS, NUM_DIR_LIGHTS+NUM_POINT_LIGHTS) are
// point lights;
// indices [NUM_DIR_LIGHTS+NUM_POINT_LIGHTS,
// NUM_DIR_LIGHTS+NUM_POINT_LIGHT+NUM_SPOT_LIGHTS)
// are spot lights for a maximum of MaxLights per object.
  Light gLights[MaxLights];
};

float4 ComputeLighting(Light gLights[MaxLights], Material mat,
          float3 pos, float3 normal, float3 toEye,
          float3 shadowFactor)
{
  float3 result = 0.0f;

  int i = 0;

#if (NUM_DIR_LIGHTS > 0)
  for(i = 0; i < NUM_DIR_LIGHTS; ++i)
  {
    result += shadowFactor[i] * ComputeDirectionalLight(gLights[i],
    mat, normal, toEye);
  }
#endif

#if (NUM_POINT_LIGHTS > 0)
  for(i = NUM_DIR_LIGHTS; i < NUM_DIR_LIGHTS+NUM_POINT_LIGHTS; ++i)
  {
    result += ComputePointLight(gLights[i], mat, pos, normal, toEye);
  }
#endif

#if (NUM_SPOT_LIGHTS > 0)
  for(i = NUM_DIR_LIGHTS + NUM_POINT_LIGHTS;
    i < NUM_DIR_LIGHTS + NUM_POINT_LIGHTS + NUM_SPOT_LIGHTS;
    ++i)
```

```
    {
      result += ComputeSpotLight(gLights[i], mat, pos, normal, toEye);
    }
#endif

    return float4(result, 0.0f);
}
```

Observe that the number of lights for each type is controlled with `#define`s. The idea is for the shader to only do the lighting equation for the number of lights that are actually needed. So if an application only requires three lights, we only do the calculations for three lights. If your application needs to support a different number of lights at different times, then you just generate different shaders using different `#define`s.

The `shadowFactor` parameter will not be used until the chapter on shadowing. So for now, we just set this to the vector (1, 1, 1), which makes the shadow factor have no effect in the equation.

8.13.7 The Main HLSL File

The below code contains the vertex and pixel shaders used for the demo of this chapter, and makes use of the HLSL code in *LightingUtil.hlsl* we have been discussing up to now.

```
//***********************************************************************
// Default.hlsl by Frank Luna (C) 2015 All Rights Reserved.
//
// Default shader, currently supports lighting.
//***********************************************************************

// Defaults for number of lights.
#ifndef NUM_DIR_LIGHTS
    #define NUM_DIR_LIGHTS 1
#endif

#ifndef NUM_POINT_LIGHTS
    #define NUM_POINT_LIGHTS 0
#endif

#ifndef NUM_SPOT_LIGHTS
    #define NUM_SPOT_LIGHTS 0
#endif

// Include structures and functions for lighting.
#include "LightingUtil.hlsl"

// Constant data that varies per frame.

cbuffer cbPerObject : register(b0)
{
```

```hlsl
    float4x4 gWorld;
};

cbuffer cbMaterial : register(b1)
{
    float4 gDiffuseAlbedo;
    float3 gFresnelR0;
    float gRoughness;
    float4x4 gMatTransform;
};

// Constant data that varies per material.
cbuffer cbPass : register(b2)
{
    float4x4 gView;
    float4x4 gInvView;
    float4x4 gProj;
    float4x4 gInvProj;
    float4x4 gViewProj;
    float4x4 gInvViewProj;
    float3 gEyePosW;
    float cbPerObjectPad1;
    float2 gRenderTargetSize;
    float2 gInvRenderTargetSize;
    float gNearZ;
    float gFarZ;
    float gTotalTime;
    float gDeltaTime;
    float4 gAmbientLight;

    // Indices [0, NUM_DIR_LIGHTS) are directional lights;
    // indices [NUM_DIR_LIGHTS, NUM_DIR_LIGHTS+NUM_POINT_LIGHTS) are
    // point lights;
    // indices [NUM_DIR_LIGHTS+NUM_POINT_LIGHTS,
    // NUM_DIR_LIGHTS+NUM_POINT_LIGHT+NUM_SPOT_LIGHTS)
    // are spot lights for a maximum of MaxLights per object.
    Light gLights[MaxLights];
};

struct VertexIn
{
    float3 PosL    : POSITION;
    float3 NormalL : NORMAL;
};

struct VertexOut
{
    float4 PosH    : SV_POSITION;
    float3 PosW    : POSITION;
    float3 NormalW : NORMAL;
};

VertexOut VS(VertexIn vin)
{
```

```
    VertexOut vout = (VertexOut)0.0f;

    // Transform to world space.
    float4 posW = mul(float4(vin.PosL, 1.0f), gWorld);
    vout.PosW = posW.xyz;

    // Assumes nonuniform scaling; otherwise, need to use
    // inverse-transpose of world matrix.
    vout.NormalW = mul(vin.NormalL, (float3x3)gWorld);

    // Transform to homogeneous clip space.
    vout.PosH = mul(posW, gViewProj);

    return vout;
}

float4 PS(VertexOut pin) : SV_Target
{
    // Interpolating normal can unnormalize it, so renormalize it.
    pin.NormalW = normalize(pin.NormalW);

    // Vector from point being lit to eye.
    float3 toEyeW = normalize(gEyePosW - pin.PosW);

    // Indirect lighting.
    float4 ambient = gAmbientLight*gDiffuseAlbedo;

    // Direct lighting.
    const float shininess = 1.0f - gRoughness;
    Material mat = { gDiffuseAlbedo, gFresnelR0, shininess };
    float3 shadowFactor = 1.0f;
    float4 directLight = ComputeLighting(gLights, mat,
        pin.PosW, pin.NormalW, toEyeW, shadowFactor);

    float4 litColor = ambient + directLight;

    // Common convention to take alpha from diffuse material.
    litColor.a = gDiffuseAlbedo.a;

    return litColor;
}
```

8.14 LIGHTING DEMO

The lighting demo builds off the "Waves" demo from the previous chapter. It uses one directional light to represent the sun. The user can rotate the sun position using the left, right, up, and down arrow keys. While we have discussed how material and lights are implemented, the following subsections go over implementation details not yet discussed. Figure 8.28 shows a screen shot of the lighting demo.

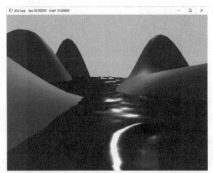

Figure 8.28. Screenshot of the lighting demo.

8.14.1 Vertex Format

Lighting calculations require a surface normal. We define normals at the vertex level; these normals are then interpolated across the pixels of a triangle so that we may do the lighting calculations per pixel. Moreover, we no longer specify a vertex color. Instead, pixel colors are generated by applying the lighting equation for each pixel. To support vertex normals we modify our vertex structures like so:

```
// C++ Vertex structure
struct Vertex
{
  DirectX::XMFLOAT3 Pos;
  DirectX::XMFLOAT3 Normal;
};

// Corresponding HLSL vertex structure
struct VertexIn
{
  float3 PosL    : POSITION;
  float3 NormalL : NORMAL;
};
```

When we add a new vertex format, we need to describe it with a new input layout description:

```
mInputLayout =
{
  { "POSITION", 0, DXGI_FORMAT_R32G32B32_FLOAT, 0, 0,
    D3D12_INPUT_CLASSIFICATION_PER_VERTEX_DATA, 0 },
  { "NORMAL", 0, DXGI_FORMAT_R32G32B32_FLOAT, 0, 12,
    D3D12_INPUT_CLASSIFICATION_PER_VERTEX_DATA, 0 }
};
```

8.14.2 Normal Computation

The shape functions in `GeometryGenerator` already create data with vertex normals, so we are all set there. However, because we modify the heights of the grid in this demo to make it look like terrain, we need to generate the normal vectors for the terrain ourselves.

Because our terrain surface is given by a function $y = f(x, z)$, we can compute the normal vectors directly using calculus, rather than the normal averaging technique described in §8.2.1. To do this, for each point on the surface, we form two tangent vectors in the +x- and +z- directions by taking the partial derivatives:

$$\mathbf{T}_x = \left(1, \frac{\partial f}{\partial x}, 0\right)$$

$$\mathbf{T}_z = \left(0, \frac{\partial f}{\partial z}, 1\right)$$

These two vectors lie in the tangent plane of the surface point. Taking the cross product then gives the normal vector:

$$\mathbf{n} = \mathbf{T}_z \times \mathbf{T}_x = \begin{vmatrix} \mathbf{i} & \mathbf{j} & \mathbf{k} \\ 0 & \frac{\partial f}{\partial z} & 1 \\ 1 & \frac{\partial f}{\partial x} & 0 \end{vmatrix}$$

$$= \left(\begin{vmatrix} \frac{\partial f}{\partial z} & 1 \\ \frac{\partial f}{\partial x} & 0 \end{vmatrix}, -\begin{vmatrix} 0 & 1 \\ 1 & 0 \end{vmatrix}, \begin{vmatrix} 0 & \frac{\partial f}{\partial z} \\ 1 & \frac{\partial f}{\partial x} \end{vmatrix} \right)$$

$$= \left(-\frac{\partial f}{\partial x}, 1, -\frac{\partial f}{\partial z}\right)$$

The function we used to generate the land mesh is:

$$f(x,z) = 0.3z \cdot \sin(0.1x) + 0.3x \cdot \cos(0.1z)$$

The partial derivatives are:

$$\frac{\partial f}{\partial x} = 0.03z \cdot \cos(0.1x) + 0.3\cos(0.1z)$$

$$\frac{\partial f}{\partial z} = 0.3\sin(0.1x) - 0.03x \cdot \sin(0.1z)$$

The surface normal at a surface point $(x, f(x, z), z)$ is thus given by:

$$\mathbf{n}(x,z) = \left(-\frac{\partial f}{\partial x}, 1, -\frac{\partial f}{\partial z}\right) = \begin{bmatrix} -0.03z \cdot \cos(0.1x) - 0.3\cos(0.1z) \\ 1 \\ -0.3\sin(0.1x) + 0.03x \cdot \sin(0.1z) \end{bmatrix}^T$$

We note that this surface normal is not of unit length, so it needs to be normalized before lighting calculations.

In particular, we do the above normal calculation at each vertex point to get the vertex normals:

```
XMFLOAT3 LitWavesApp::GetHillsNormal(float x, float z)const
{
  // n = (-df/dx, 1, -df/dz)
  XMFLOAT3 n(
    -0.03f*z*cosf(0.1f*x) - 0.3f*cosf(0.1f*z),
    1.0f,
    -0.3f*sinf(0.1f*x) + 0.03f*x*sinf(0.1f*z));

  XMVECTOR unitNormal = XMVector3Normalize(XMLoadFloat3(&n));
  XMStoreFloat3(&n, unitNormal);

  return n;
}
```

The normal vectors for the water surface are done in a similar way, except that we do not have a formula for the water. However, tangent vectors at each vertex point can be approximated using a finite difference scheme (see [Lengyel02] or any numerical analysis book).

If your calculus is rusty, do not worry as it will not play a major role in this book. Right now it is useful because we are using mathematical surfaces to generate our geometry so that we have some interesting objects to draw. Eventually, we will load 3D meshes from file that were exported from 3D modeling programs.

8.14.3 Updating the Light Direction

As shown in §8.13.7, our array of Lights is put in the per-pass constant buffer. The demo uses one directional light to represent the sun, and allows the user to rotate the sun position using the left, right, up, and down arrow keys. So every frame, we need to calculate the new light direction from the sun, and set it to the per-pass constant buffer.

We track the sun position in spherical coordinates (ρ, θ, ϕ), but the radius ρ does not matter, because we assume the sun is infinitely far away. In particular, we just use $\rho = 1$ so that it lies on the unit sphere and interpret $(1, \theta, \phi)$ as the direction towards the sun. The direction of the light is just the negative of the direction towards the sun. Below is the relevant code for updating the sun.

```
float mSunTheta = 1.25f*XM_PI;
float mSunPhi = XM_PIDIV4;

void LitWavesApp::OnKeyboardInput(const GameTimer& gt)
{
  const float dt = gt.DeltaTime();

  if(GetAsyncKeyState(VK_LEFT) & 0x8000)
    mSunTheta -= 1.0f*dt;

  if(GetAsyncKeyState(VK_RIGHT) & 0x8000)
    mSunTheta += 1.0f*dt;

  if(GetAsyncKeyState(VK_UP) & 0x8000)
    mSunPhi -= 1.0f*dt;

  if(GetAsyncKeyState(VK_DOWN) & 0x8000)
    mSunPhi += 1.0f*dt;

  mSunPhi = MathHelper::Clamp(mSunPhi, 0.1f, XM_PIDIV2);
}

void LitWavesApp::UpdateMainPassCB(const GameTimer& gt)
{
    ...
    XMVECTOR lightDir = -MathHelper::SphericalToCartesian(1.0f,
      mSunTheta, mSunPhi);

    XMStoreFloat3(&mMainPassCB.Lights[0].Direction, lightDir);
    mMainPassCB.Lights[0].Strength = { 0.8f, 0.8f, 0.7f };

    auto currPassCB = mCurrFrameResource->PassCB.get();
    currPassCB->CopyData(0, mMainPassCB);
}
```

Note: *Putting the* Light *array in the per-pass constant buffer means we cannot have more than sixteen (the maximum number of lights we support) lights per rendering pass. This is more than sufficient for small demos. However, for large game worlds, this would not be enough, as you can imagine game levels with hundreds of lights spread throughout the level. One solution to this is to move the* Light *array to the per-object constant buffer. Then, for each object O, you do a search of the scene and find the lights that affect the object O, and bind those lights to the constant buffer. The lights that would affect O are the lights whose volumes (sphere for point light and cone for spot light) intersect it. Another popular strategy is to use deferred rendering or Forward+ rendering.*

8.14.4 Update to Root Signature

Lighting introduces a new material constant buffer to our shader programs. To support this, we need to update our root signature to support an additional constant buffer. As with per-object constant buffers, we use a root descriptor for the material constant buffer to support binding a constant buffer directly rather than going through a descriptor heap.

8.15 SUMMARY

1. With lighting, we no longer specify per-vertex colors but instead define scene lights and per-vertex materials. Materials can be thought of as the properties that determine how light interacts with a surface of an object. The per-vertex materials are interpolated across the face of the triangle to obtain material values at each surface point of the triangle mesh. The lighting equations then compute a surface color the eye sees based on the interaction between the light and surface materials; other parameters are also involved, such as the surface normal and eye position.

2. A *surface normal* is a unit vector that is orthogonal to the tangent plane of a point on a surface. Surface normals determine the direction a point on a surface is "facing." For lighting calculations, we need the surface normal at each point on the surface of a triangle mesh so that we can determine the angle at which light strikes the point on the mesh surface. To obtain surface normals, we specify the surface normals only at the vertex points (so-called *vertex normals*). Then, in order to obtain a surface normal approximation at each point on the surface of a triangle mesh, these vertex normals will be interpolated across the triangle during rasterization. For arbitrary triangle meshes, vertex normals are typically approximated via a technique called normal averaging. If the matrix $\mathbf{A}$ is used to transform points and vectors (non-normal vectors), then $(\mathbf{A}^{-1})^T$ should be used to transform surface normals.

3. A parallel (directional) light approximates a light source that is very far away. Consequently, we can approximate all incoming light rays as parallel to each other. A physical example of a directional light is the sun relative to the earth. A point light emits light in *every* direction. A physical example of a point light is a light bulb. A spotlight emits light through a cone. A physical example of a spotlight is a flashlight.

4. Due to the Fresnel effect, when light reaches the interface between two media with different indices of refraction some of the light is reflected and the

remaining light is refracted into the medium. How much light is reflected depends on the medium (some materials will be more reflective than others) and also on the angle θ_i between the normal vector **n** and light vector **L**. Due to their complexity, the full Fresnel equations are not typically used in real-time rendering; instead, the *Schlick approximation* is used.

5. Reflective objects in the real-world tend not to be perfect mirrors. Even if an object's surface appears flat, at the microscopic level we can think of it as having *roughness*. We can think of a perfect mirror as having no roughness and its micro-normals all aim in the same direction as the macro-normal. As the roughness increases, the direction of the micro-normals diverge from the macro-normal causing the reflected light to spread out into a *specular lobe*.

6. Ambient light models indirect light that has scattered and bounced around the scene so many times that it strikes the object equally in every direction, thereby uniformly brightening it up. Diffuse light models light that enters the interior of a medium and scatters around under the surface where some of the light is absorbed and the remaining light scatters back out of the surface. Because it is difficult to model this subsurface scattering, we assume the re-emitted light scatters out equally in all directions above the surface about the point the light entered. Specular light models the light that is reflected off the surface due to the Fresnel effect and surface roughness.

8.16 EXERCISES

1. Modify the lighting demo of this chapter so that the directional light only emits mostly red light. In addition, make the strength of the light oscillate as a function of time using the sine function so that the light appears to pulse. Using colored and pulsing lights can be useful for different game moods; for example, a pulsing red light might be used to signify emergency situations.

2. Modify the lighting demo of this chapter by changing the roughness in the materials.

3. Modify the "Shapes" demo from the previous chapter by adding materials and a three-point lighting system. The three-point lighting system is commonly used in film and photography to get better lighting than just one light source can provide; it consists of a primary light source called the *key light*, a secondary *fill light* usually aiming in the side direction from the key light, and a *back light*. We use three-point lighting as a way to fake indirect lighting that gives better object definition than just using the ambient component for indirect lighting. Use three directional lights for the three-point lighting system.

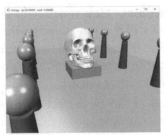

Figure 8.29. Screenshot of the solution to Exercise 3.

4. Modify the solution to Exercise 3 by removing the three-point lighting, and adding a point centered about each sphere above the columns.

5. Modify the solution to Exercise 3 by removing the three-point lighting, and adding a spotlight centered about each sphere above the columns and aiming down.

6. One characteristic of cartoon styled lighting is the abrupt transition from one color shade to the next (in contrast with a smooth transition) as shown in Figure 8.30. This can be implemented by computing k_d and k_s in the usual way, but then transforming them by discrete functions like the following before using them in the pixel shader:

$$k'_d = f(k_d) = \begin{cases} 0.4 & \text{if } -\infty < k_d \leq 0.0 \\ 0.6 & \text{if } 0.0 < k_d \leq 0.5 \\ 1.0 & \text{if } 0.5 < k_d \leq 1.0 \end{cases}$$

$$k'_s = g(k_s) = \begin{cases} 0.0 & \text{if } 0.0 \leq k_s \leq 0.1 \\ 0.5 & \text{if } 0.1 < k_s \leq 0.8 \\ 0.8 & \text{if } 0.8 < k_s \leq 1.0 \end{cases}$$

Modify the lighting demo of this chapter to use this sort of toon shading. (Note: The functions f and g above are just sample functions to start with, and can be tweaked until you get the results you want.)

Figure 8.30. Screenshot of cartoon lighting.

Chapter 9

TEXTURING

Our demos are getting a little more interesting, but real-world objects typically have more details than per-object materials can capture. *Texture mapping* is a technique that allows us to map image data onto a triangle, thereby enabling us to increase the details and realism of our scene significantly. For instance, we can build a cube and turn it into a crate by mapping a crate texture on each side (Figure 9.1).

Objectives:

1. To learn how to specify the part of a texture that gets mapped to a triangle.
2. To find out how to create and enable textures.
3. To learn how textures can be filtered to create a smoother image.

Figure 9.1. The Crate demo creates a cube with a crate texture.

359

4. To discover how to tile a texture several times with address modes.
5. To find out how multiple textures can be combined to create new textures and special effects.
6. To learn how to create some basic effects via texture animation.

9.1 TEXTURE AND RESOURCE RECAP

Recall that we have already been using textures since Chapter 4; in particular, the depth buffer and back buffer are 2D texture objects represented by the `ID3D12Resource` interface with the `D3D12_RESOURCE_DESC::Dimension` of `D3D12_RESOURCE_DIMENSION_TEXTURE2D`. For easy reference, in this first section we review much of the material on textures we have already covered in Chapter 4.

A 2D texture is a matrix of data elements. One use for 2D textures is to store 2D image data, where each element in the texture stores the color of a pixel. However, this is not the only usage; for example, in an advanced technique called normal mapping, each element in the texture stores a 3D vector instead of a color. Therefore, although it is common to think of textures as storing image data, they are really more general purpose than that. A 1D texture (`D3D12_RESOURCE_DIMENSION_TEXTURE1D`) is like a 1D array of data elements, and a 3D texture (`D3D12_RESOURCE_DIMENSION_TEXTURE3D`) is like a 3D array of data elements. The 1D, 2D, and 3D texture interfaces are all represented by the generic `ID3D12Resource`.

Textures are different than buffer resources, which just store arrays of data; textures can have mipmap levels, and the GPU can do special operations on them, such as apply filters and multisampling. Because of these special operations that are supported for texture resources, they are limited to certain kind of data formats, whereas buffer resources can store arbitrary data. The data formats supported for textures are described by the `DXGI_FORMAT` enumerated type. Some example formats are:

1. `DXGI_FORMAT_R32G32B32_FLOAT`: Each element has three 32-bit floating-point components.
2. `DXGI_FORMAT_R16G16B16A16_UNORM`: Each element has four 16-bit components mapped to the [0, 1] range.
3. `DXGI_FORMAT_R32G32_UINT`: Each element has two 32-bit unsigned integer components.
4. `DXGI_FORMAT_R8G8B8A8_UNORM`: Each element has four 8-bit unsigned components mapped to the [0, 1] range.
5. `DXGI_FORMAT_R8G8B8A8_SNORM`: Each element has four 8-bit signed components mapped to the [-1, 1] range.

6. `DXGI_FORMAT_R8G8B8A8_SINT`: Each element has four 8-bit signed integer components mapped to the [−128, 127] range.

7. `DXGI_FORMAT_R8G8B8A8_UINT`: Each element has four 8-bit unsigned integer components mapped to the [0, 255] range.

Note that the R, G, B, A letters are used to stand for red, green, blue, and alpha, respectively. However, as we said earlier, textures need not store color information; for example, the format

`DXGI_FORMAT_R32G32B32_FLOAT`

has three floating-point components and can therefore store a 3D vector with floating-point coordinates (not necessarily a color vector). There are also *typeless* formats, where we just reserve memory and then specify how to reinterpret the data at a later time (sort of like a cast) when the texture is bound to the rendering pipeline; for example, the following typeless format reserves elements with four 8-bit components, but does not specify the data type (e.g., integer, floating-point, unsigned integer):

`DXGI_FORMAT_R8G8B8A8_TYPELESS`

The DirectX 11 SDK documentation says: "Creating a fully-typed resource restricts the resource to the format it was created with. This enables the runtime to optimize access [...]." Therefore, you should only create a typeless resource if you really need it; otherwise, create a fully typed resource.

A texture can be bound to different stages of the rendering pipeline; a common example is to use a texture as a render target (i.e., Direct3D draws into the texture) and as a shader resource (i.e., the texture will be sampled in a shader). A texture can also be used as both a render target and as a shader resource, but not at the same time. Rendering to a texture and then using it as a shader resource, a method called *render-to-texture*, allows for some interesting special effects which we will use later in this book. For a texture to be used as both a render target and a shader resource, we would need to create two descriptors to that texture resource: 1) one that lives in a render target heap (i.e., `D3D12_DESCRIPTOR_HEAP_TYPE_RTV`) and 2) one that lives in a shader resource heap (i.e., `D3D12_DESCRIPTOR_HEAP_TYPE_CBV_SRV_UAV`). (Note that a shader resource heap can also store constant buffer view descriptors and unordered access view descriptors.) Then the resource can be bound as a render target or bound as a shader input to a root parameter in the root signature (but never at the same time):

```
// Bind as render target.
CD3DX12_CPU_DESCRIPTOR_HANDLE rtv = ...;
CD3DX12_CPU_DESCRIPTOR_HANDLE dsv = ...;
cmdList->OMSetRenderTargets(1, &rtv, true, &dsv);
```

```
// Bind as shader input to root parameter.
CD3DX12_GPU_DESCRIPTOR_HANDLE tex = ...;
cmdList->SetGraphicsRootDescriptorTable(rootParamIndex, tex);
```

Resource descriptors essentially do two things: they tell Direct3D how the resource will be used (i.e., what stage of the pipeline you will bind it to), and if the resource format was specified as typeless at creation time, then we must now state the type when creating a view. Thus, with typeless formats, it is possible for the elements of a texture to be viewed as floating-point values in one pipeline stage and as integers in another; this essentially amounts to a reinterpret cast of the data.

In this chapter, we will only be interested in binding textures as shader resources so that our pixel shaders can sample the textures and use them to color pixels.

9.2 TEXTURE COORDINATES

Direct3D uses a texture coordinate system that consists of a u-axis that runs horizontally to the image and a v-axis that runs vertically to the image. The coordinates, (u, v) such that $0 \leq u, v \leq 1$, identify an element on the texture called a *texel*. Notice that the v-axis is positive in the "down" direction (see Figure 9.2). Also, notice the normalized coordinate interval, [0, 1], which is used because it gives Direct3D a dimension independent range to work with; for example, (0.5, 0.5) always specifies the middle texel no matter if the actual texture dimensions are 256 × 256, 512 × 1024 or 2048 × 2048 in pixels. Likewise, (0.25, 0.75) identifies the texel a quarter of the total width in the horizontal direction, and three-quarters of the total height in the vertical direction. For now, texture coordinates are always in the range [0, 1], but later we explain what can happen when you go outside this range.

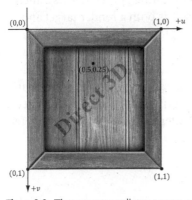

Figure 9.2. The texture coordinate system, sometimes called texture space.

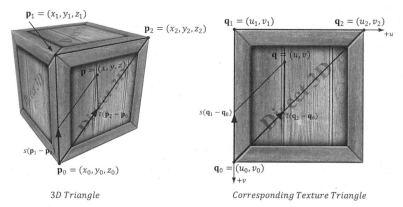

3D Triangle   *Corresponding Texture Triangle*

Figure 9.3. On the left is a triangle in 3D space, and on the right we define a 2D triangle on the texture that is going to be mapped onto the 3D triangle.

For each 3D triangle, we want to define a corresponding triangle on the texture that is to be mapped onto the 3D triangle (see Figure 9.3). Let $\mathbf{p}_0$, $\mathbf{p}_1$, and $\mathbf{p}_2$ be the vertices of a 3D triangle with respective texture coordinates $\mathbf{q}_0$, $\mathbf{q}_1$, and $\mathbf{q}_2$. For an arbitrary point (x, y, z) on the 3D triangle, its texture coordinates (u, v) are found by linearly interpolating the vertex texture coordinates across the 3D triangle by the same s, t parameters; that is, if

$$(x, y, z) = \mathbf{p} = \mathbf{p}_0 + s(\mathbf{p}_1 - \mathbf{p}_0) + t(\mathbf{p}_2 - \mathbf{p}_0)$$

for $s \geq 0, t \geq 0, s + t \leq 1$ then,

$$(u, v) = \mathbf{q} = \mathbf{q}_0 + s(\mathbf{q}_1 - \mathbf{q}_0) + t(\mathbf{q}_2 - \mathbf{q}_0)$$

In this way, every point on the triangle has a corresponding texture coordinate.

To implement this, we modify our vertex structure once again and add a pair of texture coordinates that identify a point on the texture. Now every 3D vertex has a corresponding 2D texture vertex. Thus, every 3D triangle defined by three vertices also defines a 2D triangle in texture space (i.e., we have associated a 2D texture triangle for every 3D triangle).

```
struct Vertex
{
  DirectX::XMFLOAT3 Pos;
  DirectX::XMFLOAT3 Normal;
  DirectX::XMFLOAT2 TexC;
};

std::vector<D3D12_INPUT_ELEMENT_DESC> mInputLayout =
{
  { "POSITION", 0, DXGI_FORMAT_R32G32B32_FLOAT, 0, 0,
    D3D12_INPUT_CLASSIFICATION_PER_VERTEX_DATA, 0 },
```

Figure 9.4. A texture atlas storing four subtextures on one large texture. The texture coordinates for each vertex are set so that the desired part of the texture gets mapped onto the geometry.

```
    { "NORMAL", 0, DXGI_FORMAT_R32G32B32_FLOAT, 0, 12,
      D3D12_INPUT_CLASSIFICATION_PER_VERTEX_DATA, 0 },
    { "TEXCOORD", 0, DXGI_FORMAT_R32G32_FLOAT, 0, 24,
      D3D12_INPUT_CLASSIFICATION_PER_VERTEX_DATA, 0 },
};
```

 You can create "odd" texture mappings where the 2D texture triangle is much different than the 3D triangle. Thus, when the 2D texture is mapped onto the 3D triangle, a lot of stretching and distortion occurs making the results not look good. For example, mapping an acute angled triangle to a right angled triangle requires stretching. In general, texture distortion should be minimized, unless the texture artist desires the distortion look.

Observe that in Figure 9.3, we map the entire texture image onto each face of the cube. This is by no means required. We can map only a subset of a texture onto geometry. In fact, we can place several unrelated images on one big texture map (this is called a *texture atlas*), and use it for several different objects (Figure 9.4). The texture coordinates are what will determine what part of the texture gets mapped on the triangles.

9.3 TEXTURE DATA SOURCES

The most prevalent way of creating textures for games is for an artist to make them in Photoshop or some other image editor, and then save them as an image file like BMP, DDS, TGA, or PNG. Then the game application will load the image data at load time into an ID3D12Resource object. For real-time graphics applications, the

DDS (DirectDraw Surface format) image file format is preferred, as it supports a variety of image formats that are natively understood by the GPU; in particular, it supports compressed image formats that can be natively decompressed by the GPU.

 Artists should not use the DDS format as a working image format. Instead they should use their preferred format for saving work. Then when the texture is complete, they export out to DDS for the game application.

9.3.1 DDS Overview

The DDS format is ideal for 3D graphics because it supports special formats and texture types that are specifically used for 3D graphics. It is essentially an image format built for GPUs. For example, DDS textures support the following features (not yet discussed) used in 3D graphics development:

1. mipmaps
2. compressed formats that the GPU can natively decompress
3. texture arrays
4. cube maps
5. volume textures

The DDS format can support different pixel formats. The pixel format is described by a member of the DXGI_FORMAT enumerated type; however, not all formats apply to DDS textures. Typically, for uncompressed image data you will use the formats:

1. DXGI_FORMAT_B8G8R8A8_UNORM or DXGI_FORMAT_B8G8R8X8_UNORM: For low-dynamic-range images.
2. DXGI_FORMAT_R16G16B16A16_FLOAT: For high-dynamic-range images.

The GPU memory requirements for textures add up quickly as your virtual worlds grow with hundreds of textures (remember we need to keep all these textures in GPU memory to apply them quickly). To help alleviate these memory requirements, Direct3D supports compressed texture formats: BC1, BC2, BC3, BC4, BC5, BC6, and BC7:

1. BC1 (DXGI_FORMAT_BC1_UNORM): Use this format if you need to compress a format that supports three color channels, and only a 1-bit (on/off) alpha component.
2. BC2 (DXGI_FORMAT_BC2_UNORM): Use this format if you need to compress a format that supports three color channels, and only a 4-bit alpha component.
3. BC3 (DXGI_FORMAT_BC3_UNORM): Use this format if you need to compress a format that supports three color channels, and a 8-bit alpha component.

4. BC4 (DXGI_FORMAT_BC4_UNORM): Use this format if you need to compress a format that contains one color channel (e.g., a grayscale image).

5. BC5 (DXGI_FORMAT_BC5_UNORM): Use this format if you need to compress a format that supports two color channels.

6. BC6 (DXGI_FORMAT_BC6_UF16): Use this format for compressed HDR (high dynamic range) image data.

7. BC7 (DXGI_FORMAT_BC7_UNORM): Use this format for high quality RGBA compression. In particular, this format significantly reduces the errors caused by compressing normal maps.

A compressed texture can only be used as an input to the shader stage of the rendering pipeline, not as a render target.

Because the block compression algorithms work with 4 × 4 pixel blocks, the dimensions of the texture must be multiples of 4.

Again, the advantage of these formats is that they can be stored compressed in GPU memory, and then decompressed on the fly by the GPU when needed. An additional advantage of storing your textures compressed in DDS files is that they also take up less hard disk space.

9.3.2 Creating DDS Files

If you are new to graphics programming, you are probably unfamiliar with DDS and are probably more used to using formats like BMP, TGA, or PNG. Here are two ways to convert traditional image formats to the DDS format:

1. NVIDIA supplies a plugin for Adobe Photoshop that can export images to the DDS format. The plugin is available at *https://developer.nvidia.com/nvidia-texture-tools-adobe-photoshop*. Among other options, it allows you to specify the DXGI_FORMAT of the DDS file, and generate mipmaps.

2. Microsoft provides a command line tool called *texconv* that can be used to convert traditional image formats to DDS. In addition, the *texconv* program can be used for more such as resizing images, changing pixel formats, generating mipmaps and even more. You can find the documentation and download link at the following website *https://directxtex.codeplex.com/wikipage?title=Texconv&referringTitle=Documentation*.

The following example inputs a BMP file *bricks.bmp* and outpts a DDS file *bricks.dds* with format BC3_UNORM and generates a mipmaps chain with 10 mipmaps.

```
texconv -m 10 -f BC3_UNORM treeArray.dds
```

TEXTURING 367

Note: *Microsoft provides an additional command line tool called texassemble, which is used to create DDS files that store texture arrays, volume maps, and cube maps. We will need this tool later in the book. Its documentation and download link can be found at https://directxtex.codeplex.com/wikipage?title=Texassemble&referringTitle=Documentation.*

Note: *Visual Studio 2015 has a built-in image editor that supports DDS in addition to other popular formats. You can drag an image into Visual Studio 2015 and it should open it in the image editor. For DDS files, you can view the mipmap levels, change the DDS format, and view the various color channels.*

9.4 CREATING AND ENABLING A TEXTURE

9.4.1 Loading DDS Files

Microsoft provides lightweight source code to load DDS files at:
https://github.com/Microsoft/DirectXTK/wiki/DDSTextureLoader

However, at the time of this writing, the code only supports DirectX 11. We have modified the *DDSTextureLoader.h/.cpp* files and provided an additional method for DirectX 12 (these modified files can be found in the *Common* folder on the DVD or downloadable source):

```
HRESULT DirectX::CreateDDSTextureFromFile12(
    _In_ ID3D12Device* device,
    _In_ ID3D12GraphicsCommandList* cmdList,
    _In_z_ const wchar_t* szFileName,
    _Out_ Microsoft::WRL::ComPtr<ID3D12Resource>& texture,
    _Out_ Microsoft::WRL::ComPtr<ID3D12Resource>& textureUploadHeap);
```

1. `device`: Pointer to the D3D device to create the texture resources.
2. `cmdList`: Command list to submit GPU commands (e.g., copying texture data from an upload heap to a default heap).
3. `szFileName`: Filename of the image to load.
4. `texture`: Returns the texture resource with the loaded image data.
5. `textureUploadHeap`: Returns the texture resource that was used as an upload heap to copy the image data into the default heap texture resource. This resource cannot be destroyed until the GPU finished the copy command.

To create a texture from an image called *WoodCrate01.dds*, we would write the following:

```
struct Texture
```

```
{
  // Unique material name for lookup.
  std::string Name;

  std::wstring Filename;

  Microsoft::WRL::ComPtr<ID3D12Resource> Resource = nullptr;
  Microsoft::WRL::ComPtr<ID3D12Resource> UploadHeap = nullptr;
};

auto woodCrateTex = std::make_unique<Texture>();
woodCrateTex->Name = "woodCrateTex";
woodCrateTex->Filename = L"Textures/WoodCrate01.dds";
ThrowIfFailed(DirectX::CreateDDSTextureFromFile12(
  md3dDevice.Get(), mCommandList.Get(),
  woodCrateTex->Filename.c_str(),
  woodCrateTex->Resource, woodCrateTex->UploadHeap));
```

9.4.2 SRV Heap

Once a texture resource is created, we need to create an SRV descriptor to it which we can set to a root signature parameter slot for use by the shader programs. In order to do that, we first need to create a descriptor heap with `ID3D12Device::CreateDescriptorHeap` to store the SRV descriptors. The following code builds a heap with three descriptors that can store either CBV, SRV, or UAV descriptors, and is visible to shaders:

```
D3D12_DESCRIPTOR_HEAP_DESC srvHeapDesc = {};
srvHeapDesc.NumDescriptors = 3;
srvHeapDesc.Type = D3D12_DESCRIPTOR_HEAP_TYPE_CBV_SRV_UAV;
srvHeapDesc.Flags = D3D12_DESCRIPTOR_HEAP_FLAG_SHADER_VISIBLE;
ThrowIfFailed(md3dDevice->CreateDescriptorHeap(
  &srvHeapDesc, IID_PPV_ARGS(&mSrvDescriptorHeap)));
```

9.4.3 Creating SRV Descriptors

Once we have an SRV heap, we need to create the actual descriptors. An SRV descriptor is described by filling out a `D3D12_SHADER_RESOURCE_VIEW_DESC` object, which describes how the resource is used and other information—its format, dimension, mipmaps count, etc.

```
typedef struct D3D12_SHADER_RESOURCE_VIEW_DESC
{
  DXGI_FORMAT Format;
  D3D12_SRV_DIMENSION ViewDimension;
  UINT Shader4ComponentMapping;
  union
  {
    D3D12_BUFFER_SRV Buffer;
    D3D12_TEX1D_SRV Texture1D;
    D3D12_TEX1D_ARRAY_SRV Texture1DArray;
```

```cpp
    D3D12_TEX2D_SRV Texture2D;
    D3D12_TEX2D_ARRAY_SRV Texture2DArray;
    D3D12_TEX2DMS_SRV Texture2DMS;
    D3D12_TEX2DMS_ARRAY_SRV Texture2DMSArray;
    D3D12_TEX3D_SRV Texture3D;
    D3D12_TEXCUBE_SRV TextureCube;
    D3D12_TEXCUBE_ARRAY_SRV TextureCubeArray;
  };
} D3D12_SHADER_RESOURCE_VIEW_DESC;

typedef struct D3D12_TEX2D_SRV
{
  UINT MostDetailedMip;
  UINT MipLevels;
  UINT PlaneSlice;
  FLOAT ResourceMinLODClamp;
} D3D12_TEX2D_SRV;
```

For 2D textures, we are only interested in the `D3D12_TEX2D_SRV` part of the union.

1. `Format`: The format of the resource. Set this to the `DXGI_FORMAT` of the resource you are creating a view to if the format was non-typeless. If you specified a typeless `DXGI_FORMAT` for the resource during creation, then you must specify a non-typeless format for the view here so that the GPU knows how to interpret the data.
typeless format when creating

2. `ViewDimension`: The resource dimension; for now, we are using 2D textures so we specify `D3D12_SRV_DIMENSION_TEXTURE2D`. Other common texture dimensions would be:
   (a) `D3D12_SRV_DIMENSION_TEXTURE1D`: The resource is a 1D texture.
   (b) `D3D12_SRV_DIMENSION_TEXTURE3D`: The resource is a 3D texture.
   (c) `D3D12_SRV_DIMENSION_TEXTURECUBE`: The resource is a cube texture.

3. `Shader4ComponentMapping`: When a texture is sampled in a shader, it will return a vector of the texture data at the specified texture coordinates. This field provides a way to reorder the vector components returned when sampling the texture. For example, you could use this field to swap the red and green color components. This would be used in special scenarios, which we do not need in this book. So we just specify `D3D12_DEFAULT_SHADER_4_COMPONENT_MAPPING` which will not reorder the components and just return the data in the order it is stored in the texture resource.

4. `MostDetailedMip`: Specifies the index of the most detailed mipmap level to view. This will be a number between 0 and *MipCount*-1.

5. `MipLevels`: The number of mipmap levels to view, starting at `MostDetailedMip`. This field, along with `MostDetailedMip` allows us to specify a subrange of

mipmap levels to view. You can specify -1 to indicate to view all mipmap levels from `MostDetailedMip` down to the last mipmap level.

6. `PlaneSlice`: Plane index.

7. `ResourceMinLODClamp`: Specifies the minimum mipmap level that can be accessed. 0.0 means all the mipmap levels can be accessed. Specifying 3.0 means mipmap levels 3.0 to *MipCount*-1 can be accessed.

The following populates the heap we created in the previous section with actual descriptors to three resources:

```
// Suppose the following texture resources are already created.
// ID3D12Resource* bricksTex;
// ID3D12Resource* stoneTex;
// ID3D12Resource* tileTex;

// Get pointer to the start of the heap.
CD3DX12_CPU_DESCRIPTOR_HANDLE hDescriptor(
  mSrvDescriptorHeap->GetCPUDescriptorHandleForHeapStart());

D3D12_SHADER_RESOURCE_VIEW_DESC srvDesc = {};
srvDesc.Shader4ComponentMapping = D3D12_DEFAULT_SHADER_4_COMPONENT_MAPPING;
srvDesc.Format = bricksTex->GetDesc().Format;
srvDesc.ViewDimension = D3D12_SRV_DIMENSION_TEXTURE2D;
srvDesc.Texture2D.MostDetailedMip = 0;
srvDesc.Texture2D.MipLevels = bricksTex->GetDesc().MipLevels;
srvDesc.Texture2D.ResourceMinLODClamp = 0.0f;
md3dDevice->CreateShaderResourceView(bricksTex.Get(), &srvDesc, hDescriptor);

// offset to next descriptor in heap
hDescriptor.Offset(1, mCbvSrvDescriptorSize);

srvDesc.Format = stoneTex->GetDesc().Format;
srvDesc.Texture2D.MipLevels = stoneTex->GetDesc().MipLevels;
md3dDevice->CreateShaderResourceView(stoneTex.Get(), &srvDesc, hDescriptor);

// offset to next descriptor in heap
hDescriptor.Offset(1, mCbvSrvDescriptorSize);

srvDesc.Format = tileTex->GetDesc().Format;
srvDesc.Texture2D.MipLevels = tileTex->GetDesc().MipLevels;
md3dDevice->CreateShaderResourceView(tileTex.Get(), &srvDesc, hDescriptor);
```

9.4.4 Binding Textures to the Pipeline

Right now we specify materials per draw call by changing the material constant buffer. This means that all geometry in the draw call will have the same material values. This is quite limited as we cannot specify per pixel material variations so our scenes lack detail. The idea of texturing mapping is to get the material data from texture maps instead of the material constant buffer. This allows for per pixel variation which increases the details and realism of our scene, as Figure 9.1 showed.

In this chapter, we add a diffuse albedo texture map to specify the diffuse albedo component of our material. The `FresnelR0` and `Roughness` material values will still be specified at the per draw call frequency via the material constant buffer; however, in the chapter on "Normal Mapping" we will describe how to use texturing to specify roughness at a per-pixel level. Note that with texturing we will still keep the `DiffuseAlbedo` component in the material constant buffer. In fact, we will combine it with the texture diffuse albedo value in the following way in the pixel-shader:

```
// Get diffuse albedo at this pixel from texture.
float4 texDiffuseAlbedo = gDiffuseMap.Sample(
  gsamAnisotropicWrap, pin.TexC);

// Multiple texture sample with constant buffer albedo.
float4 diffuseAlbedo = texDiffuseAlbedo * gDiffuseAlbedo;
```

Usually, we will set `DiffuseAlbedo=(1,1,1,1)` so that to does not modify `texDiffuseAlbedo`. However, sometimes it is useful to slightly tweak the diffuse albedo without having to author a new texture. For example, suppose we had a brick texture and an artist wanted to slightly tint it blue. This could be accomplished by reducing the red and green components by setting `DiffuseAlbedo=(0.9,0.9,1,1)`.

We add an index to our material definition, which references an SRV in the descriptor heap specifying the texture associated with the material:

```
struct Material
{
  ...

  // Index into SRV heap for diffuse texture.
  int DiffuseSrvHeapIndex = -1;

  ...
};
```

Then, assuming the root signature has been defined to expect a table of shader resource views to be bound to the 0th slot parameter, we can draw our render items with texturing using the following code:

```
void CrateApp::DrawRenderItems(
  ID3D12GraphicsCommandList* cmdList,
  const std::vector<RenderItem*>& ritems)
{
  UINT objCBByteSize = d3dUtil::CalcConstantBufferByteSize(sizeof(Objec
    tConstants));
  UINT matCBByteSize = d3dUtil::CalcConstantBufferByteSize(sizeof(Mater
    ialConstants));
```

```cpp
auto objectCB = mCurrFrameResource->ObjectCB->Resource();
auto matCB = mCurrFrameResource->MaterialCB->Resource();

// For each render item...
for(size_t i = 0; i < ritems.size(); ++i)
{
  auto ri = ritems[i];

  cmdList->IASetVertexBuffers(0, 1, &ri->Geo->VertexBufferView());
  cmdList->IASetIndexBuffer(&ri->Geo->IndexBufferView());
  cmdList->IASetPrimitiveTopology(ri->PrimitiveType);

  CD3DX12_GPU_DESCRIPTOR_HANDLE tex(
    mSrvDescriptorHeap->GetGPUDescriptorHandleForHeapStart());
  tex.Offset(ri->Mat->DiffuseSrvHeapIndex, mCbvSrvDescriptorSize);

  D3D12_GPU_VIRTUAL_ADDRESS objCBAddress =
    objectCB->GetGPUVirtualAddress() +
    ri->ObjCBIndex*objCBByteSize;
  D3D12_GPU_VIRTUAL_ADDRESS matCBAddress =
    matCB->GetGPUVirtualAddress() +
    ri->Mat->MatCBIndex*matCBByteSize;

  cmdList->SetGraphicsRootDescriptorTable(0, tex);
  cmdList->SetGraphicsRootConstantBufferView(1, objCBAddress);
  cmdList->SetGraphicsRootConstantBufferView(3, matCBAddress);

  cmdList->DrawIndexedInstanced(ri->IndexCount,
    1, ri->StartIndexLocation,
    ri->BaseVertexLocation, 0);
 }
}
```

Note: *A texture resource can actually be used by any shader (vertex, geometry, or pixel shader). For now, we will just be using them in pixel shaders. As we mentioned, textures are essentially special arrays that support special operations on the GPU, so it is not hard to imagine that they could be useful in other shader programs, too.*

Note: *Texture atlases can improve performance because it can lead to drawing more geometry with one draw call. For example, suppose we used the texture atlas as in Figure 9.4 that contains the crate, grass, and brick textures. Then, by adjusting the texture coordinates for each object to its corresponding subtexture, we could put all the geometry in one render item (assuming no other parameters needed to be changed per object). There is overhead to draw calls, so it is desirable to minimize them with techniques like this, although we note that the overhead has significantly been reduced with Direct3D 12 compared to earlier versions of Direct3D.*

9.5 FILTERS

9.5.1 Magnification

The elements of a texture map should be thought of as discrete color samples from a continuous image; they should not be thought of as rectangles with areas. So the question is: What happens if we have texture coordinates (u, v) that do not coincide with one of the texel points? This can happen in the following situation. Suppose the player zooms in on a wall in the scene so that the wall covers the entire screen. For the sake of example, suppose the monitor resolution is 1024×1024 and the wall's texture resolution is 256×256. This illustrates texture *magnification*—we are trying to cover many pixels with a few texels. In our example, between every texel point lies four pixels. Each pixel will be given a pair of unique texture coordinates when the vertex texture coordinates are interpolated across the triangle. Thus there will be pixels with texture coordinates that do not coincide with one of the texel points. Given the colors at the texels we can approximate the colors between texels using interpolation. There are two methods of interpolation graphics hardware supports: constant interpolation and linear interpolation. In practice, linear interpolation is almost always used.

Figure 9.5 illustrates these methods in 1D: Suppose we have a 1D texture with 256 samples and an interpolated texture coordinate $u = 0.126484375$. This normalized texture coordinate refers to the $0.126484375 \times 256 = 32.38$ texel. Of course, this value lies between two of our texel samples, so we must use interpolation to approximate it.

2D linear interpolation is called bilinear interpolation and is illustrated in Figure 9.6. Given a pair of texture coordinates between four texels, we do two 1D linear interpolations in the u-direction, followed by one 1D interpolation in the v-direction.

Figure 9.7 shows the difference between constant and linear interpolation. As you can see, constant interpolation has the characteristic of creating a blocky

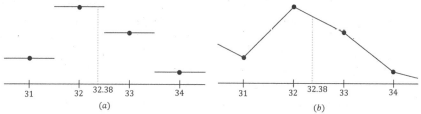

Figure 9.5. (a) Given the texel points, we construct a piecewise constant function to approximate values between the texel points; this is sometimes called *nearest neighbor point sampling*, as the value of the nearest texel point is used. (b) Given the texel points, we construct a piecewise linear function to approximate values between texel points.

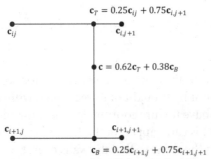

Figure 9.6. Here we have four texel points: c_{ij}, $c_{i,j+1}$, $c_{i+1,j}$, and $c_{i+1,j+1}$. We want to approximate the color of c, which lies between these four texel points, using interpolation; in this example, c lies 0.75 units to the right of c_{ij} and 0.38 units below c_{ij}. We first do a 1D linear interpolation between the top two colors to get c_T. Likewise, we do a 1D linear interpolate between the bottom two colors to get c_B. Finally, we do a 1D linear interpolation between c_T and c_B to get c.

Figure 9.7. We zoom in on a cube with a crate texture so that magnification occurs. On the left we use constant interpolation, which results in a blocky appearance; this makes sense because the interpolating function has discontinuities (Figure 9.5a), which makes the changes abrupt rather than smooth. On the right we use linear filtering, which results in a smoother image due to the continuity of the interpolating function.

looking image. Linear interpolation is smoother, but still will not look as good as if we had real data (e.g., a higher resolution texture) instead of derived data via interpolation.

One thing to note about this discussion is that there is no real way to get around magnification in an interactive 3D program where the virtual eye is free to move around and explore. From some distances, the textures will look great, but will start to break down as the eye gets too close to them. Some games limit how close the virtual eye can get to a surface to avoid excessive magnification. Using higher resolution textures can help.

> In the context of texturing, using constant interpolation to find texture values for texture coordinates between texels is also called **point filtering**. And using linear interpolation to find texture values for texture coordinates between texels is also called called **linear filtering**. Point and linear filtering *is the terminology Direct3D uses.*

9.5.2 Minification

Minification is the opposite of magnification. In minification, too many texels are being mapped to too few pixels. For instance, consider the following situation where we have a wall with a 256 × 256 texture mapped over it. The eye, looking at the wall, keeps moving back so that the wall gets smaller and smaller until it only covers 64 × 64 pixels on screen. So now we have 256 × 256 texels getting mapped to 64 × 64 screen pixels. In this situation, texture coordinates for pixels will still generally not coincide with any of the texels of the texture map, so constant and linear interpolation filters still apply to the minification case. However, there is more that can be done with minification. Intuitively, a sort of average downsampling of the 256 × 256 texels should be taken to reduce it to 64 × 64. The technique of mipmapping offers an efficient approximation for this at the expense of some extra memory. At initialization time (or asset creation time), smaller versions of the texture are made by downsampling the image to create a mipmap chain (see Figure 9.8). Thus the averaging work is precomputed for the mipmap sizes. At runtime, the graphics hardware will do two different things based on the mipmap settings specified by the programmer:

1. Pick and use the mipmap level that best matches the projected screen geometry resolution for texturing, applying constant or linear interpolation as needed. This is called *point filtering* for mipmaps because it is like constant interpolation—you just choose the nearest mipmap level and use that for texturing.

2. Pick the two nearest mipmap levels that best match the projected screen geometry resolution for texturing (one will be bigger and one will be smaller than the screen geometry resolution). Next, apply constant or linear filtering to both of these mipmap levels to produce a texture color for each one. Finally, interpolate between these two texture color results. This is called *linear filtering* for mipmaps because it is like linear interpolation—you linearly interpolate between the two nearest mipmap levels.

By choosing the best texture levels of detail from the mipmap chain, the amount of minification is greatly reduced.

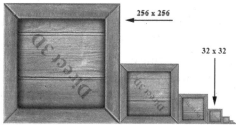

Figure 9.8. A chain of mipmaps; each successive mipmap is half the size, in each dimension, of the previous mipmap level of detail down to 1 × 1.

Figure 9.9. The top face of the crate is nearly orthogonal to the view window. (Left) Using linear filtering the top of the crate is badly blurred. (Right) Anisotropic filtering does a better job at rendering the top face of the crate from this angle.

 As mentioned in §9.3.2, mipmaps can be created using the Photoshop DDS exporter plugin, or using the texconv program. These programs use a downsampling algorithm to generate the lower mipmap levels from the base image data. Sometimes these algorithms do not preserve the details we want and an artist has to manually create/edit the lower mipmap levels to keep the important details.

9.5.3 Anisotropic Filtering

Another type of filter that can be used is called *anisotropic filtering*. This filter helps alleviate the distortion that occurs when the angle between a polygon's normal vector and camera's look vector is wide (e.g., when a polygon is orthogonal to the view window). This filter is the most expensive, but can be worth the cost for correcting the distortion artifacts. Figure 9.9 shows a screenshot comparing anisotropic filtering with linear filtering.

9.6 ADDRESS MODES

A texture, combined with constant or linear interpolation, defines a vector-valued function $T(u, v) = (r, g, b, a)$. That is, given the texture coordinates $(u, v) \in [0, 1]^2$ the texture function T returns a color (r, g, b, a). Direct3D allows us to extend the domain of this function in four different ways (called *address modes*): *wrap*, *border color*, *clamp*, and *mirror*.

1. *wrap* extends the texture function by repeating the image at every integer junction (see Figure 9.10).
2. *border color* extends the texture function by mapping each (u, v) not in $[0, 1]^2$ to some color specified by the programmer (see Figure 9.11).
3. *clamp* extends the texture function by mapping each (u, v) not in $[0, 1]^2$ to the color $T(u_0, v_0)$, where (u_0, v_0) is the nearest point to (u, v) contained in $[0, 1]^2$ (see Figure 9.12).
4. *mirror* extends the texture function by mirroring the image at every integer junction (see Figure 9.13).

Texturing 377

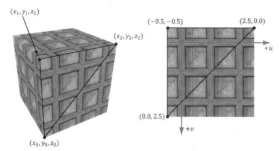

Figure 9.10. Wrap address mode.

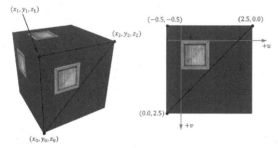

Figure 9.11. Border color address mode.

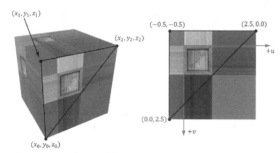

Figure 9.12. Clamp address mode.

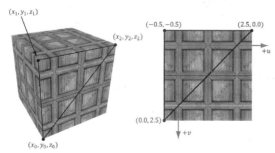

Figure 9.13. Mirror address mode.

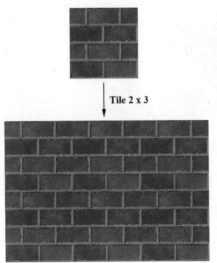

Figure 9.14. A brick texture tiled 2 × 3 times. Because the texture is seamless, the repetition pattern is harder to notice.

An address mode is always specified (wrap mode is the default), so therefore, texture coordinates outside the [0, 1] range are always defined.

The wrap address mode is probably the most often employed; it allows us to tile a texture repeatedly over some surface. This effectively enables us to increase the texture resolution without supplying additional data (although the extra resolution is repetitive). With tiling, it is usually important that the texture is seamless. For example, the crate texture is not seamless, as you can see the repetition clearly. However, Figure 9.14 shows a seamless brick texture repeated 2 × 3 times.

Address modes are described in Direct3D via the D3D12_TEXTURE_ADDRESS_MODE enumerated type:

```
typedef enum D3D12_TEXTURE_ADDRESS_MODE
{
    D3D12_TEXTURE_ADDRESS_MODE_WRAP         = 1,
    D3D12_TEXTURE_ADDRESS_MODE_MIRROR       = 2,
    D3D12_TEXTURE_ADDRESS_MODE_CLAMP        = 3,
    D3D12_TEXTURE_ADDRESS_MODE_BORDER       = 4,
    D3D12_TEXTURE_ADDRESS_MODE_MIRROR_ONCE  = 5
} D3D12_TEXTURE_ADDRESS_MODE;
```

9.7 SAMPLER OBJECTS

From the previous two sections, we see that in addition to texture data, there are two other key concepts involved with using textures: texture filtering and address modes. What filter and address mode to use when sampling a texture resource is defined by a *sampler object*. An application will usually need several sampler objects to sample textures in different ways.

9.7.1 Creating Samplers

As we will see in the next section, samplers are used in shaders. In order to bind samplers to shaders for use, we need to bind descriptors to sampler objects. The following code shows an example root signature such that the second slot takes a table of one sampler descriptor bound to sampler register slot 0.

```
CD3DX12_DESCRIPTOR_RANGE descRange[3];
descRange[0].Init(D3D12_DESCRIPTOR_RANGE_TYPE_SRV, 1, 0);
descRange[1].Init(D3D12_DESCRIPTOR_RANGE_TYPE_SAMPLER, 1, 0);
descRange[2].Init(D3D12_DESCRIPTOR_RANGE_TYPE_CBV, 1, 0);

CD3DX12_ROOT_PARAMETER rootParameters[3];
rootParameters[0].InitAsDescriptorTable(1, &descRange[0], D3D12_SHADER_
   VISIBILITY_PIXEL);
rootParameters[1].InitAsDescriptorTable(1, &descRange[1], D3D12_SHADER_
   VISIBILITY_PIXEL);
rootParameters[2].InitAsDescriptorTable(1, &descRange[2], D3D12_SHADER_
   VISIBILITY_ALL);

CD3DX12_ROOT_SIGNATURE_DESC descRootSignature;
descRootSignature.Init(3, rootParameters, 0, nullptr,
   D3D12_ROOT_SIGNATURE_FLAG_ALLOW_INPUT_ASSEMBLER_INPUT_LAYOUT);
```

If we are going to be setting sampler descriptors, we need a sampler heap. A sampler heap is created by filling out a D3D12_DESCRIPTOR_HEAP_DESC instance and specifying the heap type D3D12_DESCRIPTOR_HEAP_TYPE_SAMPLER:

```
D3D12_DESCRIPTOR_HEAP_DESC descHeapSampler = {};
descHeapSampler.NumDescriptors = 1;
descHeapSampler.Type = D3D12_DESCRIPTOR_HEAP_TYPE_SAMPLER;
descHeapSampler.Flags = D3D12_DESCRIPTOR_HEAP_FLAG_SHADER_VISIBLE;

ComPtr<ID3D12DescriptorHeap> mSamplerDescriptorHeap;
ThrowIfFailed(mDevice->CreateDescriptorHeap(&descHeapSampler,
   __uuidof(ID3D12DescriptorHeap),
   (void**)&mSamplerDescriptorHeap));
```

Once we have a sampler heap, we can create sampler descriptors. It is here that we specify the address mode and filter type, as well as other parameters by filling out a D3D12_SAMPLER_DESC object:

```
typedef struct D3D12_SAMPLER_DESC
{
  D3D12_FILTER Filter;
  D3D12_TEXTURE_ADDRESS_MODE AddressU;
  D3D12_TEXTURE_ADDRESS_MODE AddressV;
```

```
    D3D12_TEXTURE_ADDRESS_MODE AddressW;
    FLOAT MipLODBias;
    UINT MaxAnisotropy;
    D3D12_COMPARISON_FUNC ComparisonFunc;
    FLOAT BorderColor[ 4 ];
    FLOAT MinLOD;
    FLOAT MaxLOD;
} D3D12_SAMPLER_DESC;
```

1. `Filter`: A member of the `D3D12_FILTER` enumerated type to specify the kind of filtering to use.
2. `AddressU`: The address mode in the horizontal *u*-axis direction of the texture.
3. `AddressV`: The address mode in the vertical *v*-axis direction of the texture.
4. `AddressW`: The address mode in the depth *w*-axis direction of the texture (applicable to 3D textures only).
5. `MipLODBias`: A value to bias the mipmap level picked. Specify 0.0 for no bias.
6. `MaxAnisotropy`: The maximum anisotropy value which must be between 1-16 inclusively. This is only applicable for `D3D12_FILTER_ANISOTROPIC` or `D3D12_FILTER_COMPARISON_ANISOTROPIC`. Larger values are more expensive, but can give better results.
7. `ComparisonFunc`: Advanced options used for some specialized applications like shadow mapping. For now, just set to `D3D12_COMPARISON_FUNC_ALWAYS` until the shadow mapping chapter.
8. `BorderColor`: Used to specify the border color for address mode `D3D12_TEXTURE_ADDRESS_MODE_BORDER`.
9. `MinLOD`: Minimum mipmap level that can be selected.
10. `MaxLOD`: Maximum mipmap level that can be selected.

Below are some examples of commonly used `D3D12_FILTER` types:

1. `D3D12_FILTER_MIN_MAG_MIP_POINT`: Point filtering over a texture map, and point filtering across mipmap levels (i.e., the nearest mipmap level is used).
2. `D3D12_FILTER_MIN_MAG_LINEAR_MIP_POINT`: Bilinear filtering over a texture map, and point filtering across mipmap levels (i.e., the nearest mipmap level is used).
3. `D3D12_FILTER_MIN_MAG_MIP_LINEAR`: Bilinear filtering over a texture map, and linear filtering between the two nearest lower and upper mipmap levels. This is often called trilinear filtering.
4. `D3D12_FILTER_ANISOTROPIC`: Anisotropic filtering for minification, magnification, and mipmapping.

You can figure out the other possible permutations from these examples, or you can look up the D3D12_FILTER enumerated type in the SDK documentation.

The following example shows how to create a descriptor to a sampler in the heap that uses linear filtering, wrap address mode, and typical default values for the other parameters:

```
D3D12_SAMPLER_DESC samplerDesc = {};
samplerDesc.Filter = D3D12_FILTER_MIN_MAG_MIP_LINEAR;
samplerDesc.AddressU = D3D12_TEXTURE_ADDRESS_MODE_WRAP;
samplerDesc.AddressV = D3D12_TEXTURE_ADDRESS_MODE_WRAP;
samplerDesc.AddressW = D3D12_TEXTURE_ADDRESS_MODE_WRAP;
samplerDesc.MinLOD = 0;
samplerDesc.MaxLOD = D3D12_FLOAT32_MAX;
samplerDesc.MipLODBias = 0.0f;
samplerDesc.MaxAnisotropy = 1;
samplerDesc.ComparisonFunc = D3D12_COMPARISON_FUNC_ALWAYS;

md3dDevice->CreateSampler(&samplerDesc,
    mSamplerDescriptorHeap->GetCPUDescriptorHandleForHeapStart());
```

The following code shows how to bind a sampler descriptor to a root signature parameter slot for use by the shader programs:

```
commandList->SetGraphicsRootDescriptorTable(1,
    samplerDescriptorHeap->GetGPUDescriptorHandleForHeapStart());
```

9.7.2 Static Samplers

It turns out that a graphics application usually only uses a handful of samplers. Therefore, Direct3D provides a special shortcut to define an array of samplers and set them without going through the process of creating a sampler heap. The Init function of the CD3DX12_ROOT_SIGNATURE_DESC class has two parameters that allow you to define an array of so-called static samplers your application can use. Static samplers are described by the D3D12_STATIC_SAMPLER_DESC structure. This structure is very similar to D3D12_SAMPLER_DESC, with the following exceptions:

1. There are some limitations on what the border color can be. Specifically, the border color of a static sampler must be a member of:

```
enum D3D12_STATIC_BORDER_COLOR
{
  D3D12_STATIC_BORDER_COLOR_TRANSPARENT_BLACK     = 0,
  D3D12_STATIC_BORDER_COLOR_OPAQUE_BLACK    = (
    D3D12_STATIC_BORDER_COLOR_TRANSPARENT_BLACK + 1 ) ,
  D3D12_STATIC_BORDER_COLOR_OPAQUE_WHITE    = (
    D3D12_STATIC_BORDER_COLOR_OPAQUE_BLACK + 1 )
}D3D12_STATIC_BORDER_COLOR;
```

2. It contains additional fields to specify the shader register, register space, and shader visibility, which would normally be specified as part of the sampler heap.

In addition, you can only define 2032 number of static samplers, which is more than enough for most applications. If you do need more, however, you can just use non-static samplers and go through a sampler heap.

We use static samplers in our demos. The following code shows how we define our static samplers. Note that we do not need all these static samplers in our demos, but we define them anyway so that they are there if we do need them. It is only a handful anyway, and it does not hurt to define a few extra samplers that may or may not be used.

```
std::array<const CD3DX12_STATIC_SAMPLER_DESC, 6>
  TexColumnsApp::GetStaticSamplers()
{
  // Applications usually only need a handful of samplers. So just
    define them
  // all up front and keep them available as part of the root
    signature.

  const CD3DX12_STATIC_SAMPLER_DESC pointWrap(
    0, // shaderRegister
    D3D12_FILTER_MIN_MAG_MIP_POINT, // filter
    D3D12_TEXTURE_ADDRESS_MODE_WRAP, // addressU
    D3D12_TEXTURE_ADDRESS_MODE_WRAP, // addressV
    D3D12_TEXTURE_ADDRESS_MODE_WRAP); // addressW

  const CD3DX12_STATIC_SAMPLER_DESC pointClamp(
    1, // shaderRegister
    D3D12_FILTER_MIN_MAG_MIP_POINT, // filter
    D3D12_TEXTURE_ADDRESS_MODE_CLAMP, // addressU
    D3D12_TEXTURE_ADDRESS_MODE_CLAMP, // addressV
    D3D12_TEXTURE_ADDRESS_MODE_CLAMP); // addressW

  const CD3DX12_STATIC_SAMPLER_DESC linearWrap(
    2, // shaderRegister
    D3D12_FILTER_MIN_MAG_MIP_LINEAR, // filter
    D3D12_TEXTURE_ADDRESS_MODE_WRAP, // addressU
    D3D12_TEXTURE_ADDRESS_MODE_WRAP, // addressV
    D3D12_TEXTURE_ADDRESS_MODE_WRAP); // addressW

  const CD3DX12_STATIC_SAMPLER_DESC linearClamp(
    3, // shaderRegister
    D3D12_FILTER_MIN_MAG_MIP_LINEAR, // filter
    D3D12_TEXTURE_ADDRESS_MODE_CLAMP, // addressU
    D3D12_TEXTURE_ADDRESS_MODE_CLAMP, // addressV
    D3D12_TEXTURE_ADDRESS_MODE_CLAMP); // addressW

  const CD3DX12_STATIC_SAMPLER_DESC anisotropicWrap(
    4, // shaderRegister
    D3D12_FILTER_ANISOTROPIC, // filter
    D3D12_TEXTURE_ADDRESS_MODE_WRAP, // addressU
    D3D12_TEXTURE_ADDRESS_MODE_WRAP, // addressV
    D3D12_TEXTURE_ADDRESS_MODE_WRAP, // addressW
    0.0f,           // mipLODBias
```

```cpp
        8);                   // maxAnisotropy

    const CD3DX12_STATIC_SAMPLER_DESC anisotropicClamp(
        5,  // shaderRegister
        D3D12_FILTER_ANISOTROPIC, // filter
        D3D12_TEXTURE_ADDRESS_MODE_CLAMP,  // addressU
        D3D12_TEXTURE_ADDRESS_MODE_CLAMP,  // addressV
        D3D12_TEXTURE_ADDRESS_MODE_CLAMP,  // addressW
        0.0f,                 // mipLODBias
        8);                   // maxAnisotropy

    return {
        pointWrap, pointClamp,
        linearWrap, linearClamp,
        anisotropicWrap, anisotropicClamp };
}

void TexColumnsApp::BuildRootSignature()
{
    CD3DX12_DESCRIPTOR_RANGE texTable;
    texTable.Init(D3D12_DESCRIPTOR_RANGE_TYPE_SRV, 1, 0);

    // Root parameter can be a table, root descriptor or root constants.
    CD3DX12_ROOT_PARAMETER slotRootParameter[4];

    slotRootParameter[0].InitAsDescriptorTable(1,
        &texTable, D3D12_SHADER_VISIBILITY_PIXEL);
    slotRootParameter[1].InitAsConstantBufferView(0);
    slotRootParameter[2].InitAsConstantBufferView(1);
    slotRootParameter[3].InitAsConstantBufferView(2);

    auto staticSamplers = GetStaticSamplers();

    // A root signature is an array of root parameters.
    CD3DX12_ROOT_SIGNATURE_DESC rootSigDesc(4, slotRootParameter,
        (UINT)staticSamplers.size(), staticSamplers.data(),
        D3D12_ROOT_SIGNATURE_FLAG_ALLOW_INPUT_ASSEMBLER_INPUT_LAYOUT);

    // create a root signature with a single slot which points to a
    // descriptor range consisting of a single constant buffer
    ComPtr<ID3DBlob> serializedRootSig = nullptr;
    ComPtr<ID3DBlob> errorBlob = nullptr;
    HRESULT hr = D3D12SerializeRootSignature(&rootSigDesc, D3D_ROOT_
        SIGNATURE_VERSION_1,
        serializedRootSig.GetAddressOf(), errorBlob.GetAddressOf());

    if(errorBlob != nullptr)
    {
        ::OutputDebugStringA((char*)errorBlob->GetBufferPointer());
    }
    ThrowIfFailed(hr);

    ThrowIfFailed(md3dDevice->CreateRootSignature(
        0,
        serializedRootSig->GetBufferPointer(),
```

```
      serializedRootSig->GetBufferSize(),
      IID_PPV_ARGS(mRootSignature.GetAddressOf())));
}
```

9.8 SAMPLING TEXTURES IN A SHADER

A texture object is defined in HLSL and assigned to a texture register with the following syntax:

```
Texture2D gDiffuseMap : register(t0);
```

Note that texture registers use specified by tn where n is an integer identifying the texture register slot. The root signature definition specifies the mapping from slot parameter to shader register; this is how the application code can bind an SRV to a particular `Texture2D` object in a shader.

Similarly, sampler objects are defined HLSL and assigned to a sampler register with the following syntax:

```
SamplerState gsamPointWrap        : register(s0);
SamplerState gsamPointClamp       : register(s1);
SamplerState gsamLinearWrap       : register(s2);
SamplerState gsamLinearClamp      : register(s3);
SamplerState gsamAnisotropicWrap  : register(s4);
SamplerState gsamAnisotropicClamp : register(s5);
```

These samplers correspond to the static sampler array we set in the previous section. Note that texture registers use specified by sn where n is an integer identifying the sampler register slot.

Now, given a pair of texture coordinate (u, v) for a pixel in the pixel shader, we actually sample a texture using the `Texture2D::Sample` method:

```
Texture2D gDiffuseMap : register(t0);

SamplerState gsamPointWrap        : register(s0);
SamplerState gsamPointClamp       : register(s1);
SamplerState gsamLinearWrap       : register(s2);
SamplerState gsamLinearClamp      : register(s3);
SamplerState gsamAnisotropicWrap  : register(s4);
SamplerState gsamAnisotropicClamp : register(s5);

struct VertexOut
{
  float4 PosH    : SV_POSITION;
  float3 PosW    : POSITION;
  float3 NormalW : NORMAL;
  float2 TexC    : TEXCOORD;
};

float4 PS(VertexOut pin) : SV_Target
```

```
{
    float4 diffuseAlbedo = gDiffuseMap.Sample(gsamAnisotropicWrap, pin.
     TexC) * gDiffuseAlbedo;
    ...
```

We pass a `SamplerState` object for the first parameter indicating how the texture data will be sampled, and we pass in the pixel's (u, v) texture coordinates for the second parameter. This method returns the interpolated color from the texture map at the specified (u, v) point using the filtering methods specified by the `SamplerState` object.

9.9 CRATE DEMO

We now review the key points of adding a crate texture to a cube (as shown in Figure 9.1).

9.9.1 Specifying Texture Coordinates

The `GeometryGenerator::CreateBox` generates the texture coordinates for the box so that the entire texture image is mapped onto each face of the box. For brevity, we only show the vertex definitions for the front, back, and top face. Note also that we omit the coordinates for the normal and tangent vectors in the `Vertex` constructor (the texture coordinates are bolded).

```
GeometryGenerator::MeshData GeometryGenerator::CreateBox(
   float width, float height, float depth,
   uint32 numSubdivisions)
{
   MeshData meshData;

   Vertex v[24];

   float w2 = 0.5f*width;
   float h2 = 0.5f*height;
   float d2 = 0.5f*depth;

   // Fill in the front face vertex data.
   v[0] = Vertex(-w2, -h2, -d2, ..., 0.0f, 1.0f);
   v[1] = Vertex(-w2, +h2, -d2, ..., 0.0f, 0.0f);
   v[2] = Vertex(+w2, +h2, -d2, ..., 1.0f, 0.0f);
   v[3] = Vertex(+w2, -h2, -d2, ..., 1.0f, 1.0f);

   // Fill in the back face vertex data.
   v[4] = Vertex(-w2, -h2, +d2, ..., 1.0f, 1.0f);
   v[5] = Vertex(+w2, -h2, +d2, ..., 0.0f, 1.0f);
   v[6] = Vertex(+w2, +h2, +d2, ..., 0.0f, 0.0f);
   v[7] = Vertex(-w2, +h2, +d2, ..., 1.0f, 0.0f);
```

```
// Fill in the top face vertex data.
v[8]  = Vertex(-w2, +h2, -d2, ..., 0.0f, 1.0f);
v[9]  = Vertex(-w2, +h2, +d2, ..., 0.0f, 0.0f);
v[10] = Vertex(+w2, +h2, +d2, ..., 1.0f, 0.0f);
v[11] = Vertex(+w2, +h2, -d2, ..., 1.0f, 1.0f);
```

Refer back to Figure 9.3 if you need help seeing why the texture coordinates are specified this way.

9.9.2 Creating the Texture

We create the texture from file at initialization time as follows:

```
// Helper structure to group data related to the texture.
struct Texture
{
  // Unique material name for lookup.
  std::string Name;

  std::wstring Filename;

  Microsoft::WRL::ComPtr<ID3D12Resource> Resource = nullptr;
  Microsoft::WRL::ComPtr<ID3D12Resource> UploadHeap = nullptr;
};

std::unordered_map<std::string, std::unique_ptr<Texture>> mTextures;

void CrateApp::LoadTextures()
{
  auto woodCrateTex = std::make_unique<Texture>();
  woodCrateTex->Name = "woodCrateTex";
  woodCrateTex->Filename = L"Textures/WoodCrate01.dds";
  ThrowIfFailed(DirectX::CreateDDSTextureFromFile12(md3dDevice.Get(),
    mCommandList.Get(), woodCrateTex->Filename.c_str(),
    woodCrateTex->Resource, woodCrateTex->UploadHeap));

  mTextures[woodCrateTex->Name] = std::move(woodCrateTex);
}
```

We store all of our unique textures in an unordered map so that we can look them up by name. In production code, before loading a texture, you would want to check if the texture data has already been loaded (i.e., is it already contained in the unordered map) so that it does not get loaded multiple times.

9.9.3 Setting the Texture

Once a texture has been created and an SRV has been created for it in a descriptor heap, binding the texture to the pipeline so that it can be used in shader programs is simply a matter of setting it to the root signature parameter that expects the texture:

```
// Get SRV to texture we want to bind.
```

```
CD3DX12_GPU_DESCRIPTOR_HANDLE tex(
mSrvDescriptorHeap->GetGPUDescriptorHandleForHeapStart());
tex.Offset(ri->Mat->DiffuseSrvHeapIndex, mCbvSrvDescriptorSize);

...

// Bind to root parameter 0. The root parameter description specifies which
// shader register slot this corresponds to.
cmdList->SetGraphicsRootDescriptorTable(0, tex);
```

9.9.4 Updated HLSL

Below is the revised Default.hlsl file that now supports texturing (texturing code has been bolded):

```
// Defaults for number of lights.
#ifndef NUM_DIR_LIGHTS
    #define NUM_DIR_LIGHTS 3
#endif

#ifndef NUM_POINT_LIGHTS
    #define NUM_POINT_LIGHTS 0
#endif

#ifndef NUM_SPOT_LIGHTS
    #define NUM_SPOT_LIGHTS 0
#endif

// Include structures and functions for lighting.
#include "LightingUtil.hlsl"

Texture2D gDiffuseMap : register(t0);


SamplerState gsamPointWrap        : register(s0);
SamplerState gsamPointClamp       : register(s1);
SamplerState gsamLinearWrap       : register(s2);
SamplerState gsamLinearClamp      : register(s3);
SamplerState gsamAnisotropicWrap  : register(s4);
SamplerState gsamAnisotropicClamp : register(s5);

// Constant data that varies per frame.
cbuffer cbPerObject : register(b0)
{
    float4x4 gWorld;
    float4x4 gTexTransform;
};

// Constant data that varies per material.
cbuffer cbPass : register(b1)
{
    float4x4 gView;
```

```
    float4x4 gInvView;
    float4x4 gProj;
    float4x4 gInvProj;
    float4x4 gViewProj;
    float4x4 gInvViewProj;
    float3 gEyePosW;
    float cbPerObjectPad1;
    float2 gRenderTargetSize;
    float2 gInvRenderTargetSize;
    float gNearZ;
    float gFarZ;
    float gTotalTime;
    float gDeltaTime;
    float4 gAmbientLight;

    // Indices [0, NUM_DIR_LIGHTS) are directional lights;
    // indices [NUM_DIR_LIGHTS, NUM_DIR_LIGHTS+NUM_POINT_LIGHTS) are
      point lights;
    // indices [NUM_DIR_LIGHTS+NUM_POINT_LIGHTS,
    //    NUM_DIR_LIGHTS+NUM_POINT_LIGHT+NUM_SPOT_LIGHTS)
    // are spot lights for a maximum of MaxLights per object.
    Light gLights[MaxLights];
};

cbuffer cbMaterial : register(b2)
{
    float4   gDiffuseAlbedo;
    float3   gFresnelR0;
    float    gRoughness;
    float4x4 gMatTransform;
};

struct VertexIn
{
    float3 PosL    : POSITION;
    float3 NormalL : NORMAL;
    float2 TexC    : TEXCOORD;
};

struct VertexOut
{
    float4 PosH    : SV_POSITION;
    float3 PosW    : POSITION;
    float3 NormalW : NORMAL;
    float2 TexC    : TEXCOORD;
};

VertexOut VS(VertexIn vin)
{
    VertexOut vout = (VertexOut)0.0f;

    // Transform to world space.
    float4 posW = mul(float4(vin.PosL, 1.0f), gWorld);
    vout.PosW = posW.xyz;
```

```
    // Assumes nonuniform scaling; otherwise, need to use
    // inverse-transpose of world matrix.
    vout.NormalW = mul(vin.NormalL, (float3x3)gWorld);

    // Transform to homogeneous clip space.
    vout.PosH = mul(posW, gViewProj);

    // Output vertex attributes for interpolation across triangle.
    float4 texC = mul(float4(vin.TexC, 0.0f, 1.0f), gTexTransform);
    vout.TexC = mul(texC, gMatTransform).xy;

    return vout;
}

float4 PS(VertexOut pin) : SV_Target
{
    float4 diffuseAlbedo = gDiffuseMap.Sample(gsamAnisotropicWrap, pin.
      TexC) * gDiffuseAlbedo;

    // Interpolating normal can unnormalize it, so renormalize it.
    pin.NormalW = normalize(pin.NormalW);

    // Vector from point being lit to eye.
    float3 toEyeW = normalize(gEyePosW - pin.PosW);

    // Light terms.
    float4 ambient = gAmbientLight*diffuseAlbedo;

    const float shininess = 1.0f - gRoughness;
    Material mat = { diffuseAlbedo, gFresnelR0, shininess };
    float3 shadowFactor = 1.0f;
    float4 directLight = ComputeLighting(gLights, mat, pin.PosW,
       pin.NormalW, toEyeW, shadowFactor);

    float4 litColor = ambient + directLight;

    // Common convention to take alpha from diffuse albedo.
    litColor.a = diffuseAlbedo.a;

    return litColor;
}
```

9.10 TRANSFORMING TEXTURES

Two constant buffer variables we have not discussed are gTexTransform and gMatTransform. These variables are used in the vertex shader to transform the input texture coordinates:

```
    // Output vertex attributes for interpolation across triangle.
    float4 texC = mul(float4(vin.TexC, 0.0f, 1.0f), gTexTransform);
    vout.TexC = mul(texC, gMatTransform).xy;
```

Texture coordinates represent 2D points in the texture plane. Thus, we can translate, rotate, and scale them like we could any other point. Here are some example uses for transforming textures:

1. A brick texture is stretched along a wall. The wall vertices currently have texture coordinates in the range [0, 1]. We scale the texture coordinates by 4 to scale them to the range [0, 4], so that the texture will be repeated four-by-four times across the wall.
2. We have cloud textures stretches over a clear blue sky. By translating the texture coordinates as a function of time, the clouds are animated over the sky.
3. Texture rotation is sometimes useful for particle like effects, where we rotate a fireball texture over time, for example.

In the "Crate" demo, we use an identity matrix transformation so that the input texture coordinates are left unmodified, but in the next section we explain a demo that does use texture transforms.

Note that to transform the 2D texture coordinates by a 4 × 4 matrix, we augment it to a 4D vector:

```
vin.TexC ---> float4(vin.Tex, 0.0f, 1.0f)
```

After the multiplication is done, the resulting 4D vector is cast back to a 2D vector by throwing away the z- and w-components. That is,

```
vout.TexC = mul(float4(vin.TexC, 0.0f, 1.0f), gTexTransform).xy;
```

We use two separate texture transformation matrices `gTexTransform` and `gMatTransform` because sometimes it makes more sense for the material to transform the textures (for animated materials like water), but sometimes it makes more sense for the texture transform to be a property of the object.

Because we are working with 2D texture coordinates, we only care about transformations done to the first two coordinates. For instance, if the texture matrix translated the z-coordinate, it would have no effect on the resulting texture coordinates.

9.11 TEXTURED HILLS AND WAVES DEMO

In this demo, we add textures to our land and water scene. The first key issue is that we tile a grass texture over the land. Because the land mesh is a large surface, if we simply stretched a texture over it, then too few texels would cover each triangle. In other words, there is not enough texture resolution for the surface; we would thus get magnification artifacts. Therefore, we repeat the grass texture over the

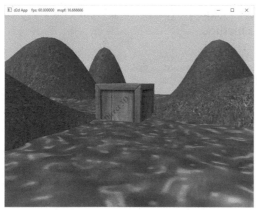

Figure 9.15. Screenshot of the Land Tex demo.

land mesh to get more resolution. The second key issue is that we scroll the water texture over the water geometry as a function of time. This added motion makes the water a bit more convincing. Figure 9.15 shows a screenshot of the demo.

9.11.1 Grid Texture Coordinate Generation

Figure 9.16 shows an $m \times n$ grid in the *xz*-plane and a corresponding grid in the normalized texture space domain $[0, 1]^2$. From the picture, it is clear that the texture coordinates of the *ij*th grid vertex in the *xz*-plane are the coordinates of the *ij*th grid vertex in the texture space. The texture space coordinates of the *ij*th vertex are:

$$u_{ij} = j \cdot \Delta u$$
$$v_{ij} = i \cdot \Delta v$$

where $\Delta u = \dfrac{1}{n-1}$ and $\Delta v = \dfrac{1}{m-1}$.

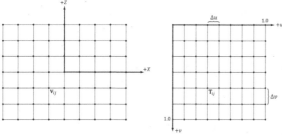

Figure 9.16. The texture coordinates of the grid vertex $\mathbf{v}_{ij}$ in xz-space are given by the *ij*th grid vertex $\mathbf{T}_{ij}$ in *uv*-space.

Thus, we use the following code to generate texture coordinates for a grid in the `GeometryGenerator::CreateGrid` method:

```
GeometryGenerator::MeshData
GeometryGenerator::CreateGrid(float width, float depth, uint32 m, uint32 n)
{
  MeshData meshData;

  uint32 vertexCount = m*n;
  uint32 faceCount   = (m-1)*(n-1)*2;

  float halfWidth = 0.5f*width;
  float halfDepth = 0.5f*depth;

  float dx = width / (n-1);
  float dz = depth / (m-1);

  float du = 1.0f / (n-1);
  float dv = 1.0f / (m-1);

  meshData.Vertices.resize(vertexCount);
  for(uint32 i = 0; i < m; ++i)
  {
    float z = halfDepth - i*dz;
    for(uint32 j = 0; j < n; ++j)
    {
      float x = -halfWidth + j*dx;

      meshData.Vertices[i*n+j].Position = XMFLOAT3(x, 0.0f, z);
      meshData.Vertices[i*n+j].Normal   = XMFLOAT3(0.0f, 1.0f, 0.0f);
      meshData.Vertices[i*n+j].TangentU = XMFLOAT3(1.0f, 0.0f, 0.0f);

      // Stretch texture over grid.
      meshData.Vertices[i*n+j].TexC.x = j*du;
      meshData.Vertices[i*n+j].TexC.y = i*dv;
    }
  }
}
```

9.11.2 Texture Tiling

We said we wanted to tile a grass texture over the land mesh. But so far the texture coordinates we have computed lie in the unit domain $[0, 1]^2$; so no tiling will occur. To tile the texture, we specify the wrap address mode and scale the texture coordinates by 5 using a texture transformation matrix. Thus the texture coordinates are mapped to the domain $[0, 5]^2$ so that the texture is tiled 5×5 times across the land mesh surface:

```
void TexWavesApp::BuildRenderItems()
{
  auto gridRitem = std::make_unique<RenderItem>();
  gridRitem->World = MathHelper::Identity4x4();
```

```
    XMStoreFloat4x4(&gridRitem->TexTransform,
        XMMatrixScaling(5.0f, 5.0f, 1.0f));
    ...
}
```

9.11.3 Texture Animation

To scroll a water texture over the water geometry, we translate the texture coordinates in the texture plane as a function of time in the `AnimateMaterials` method, which gets called every update cycle. Provided the displacement is small for each frame, this gives the illusion of a smooth animation. We use the wrap address mode along with a seamless texture so that we can seamlessly translate the texture coordinates around the texture space plane. The following code shows how we calculate the offset vector for the water texture, and how we build and set the water's texture matrix:

```
void TexWavesApp::AnimateMaterials(const GameTimer& gt)
{
    // Scroll the water material texture coordinates.
    auto waterMat = mMaterials["water"].get();

    float& tu = waterMat->MatTransform(3, 0);
    float& tv = waterMat->MatTransform(3, 1);

    tu += 0.1f * gt.DeltaTime();
    tv += 0.02f * gt.DeltaTime();

    if(tu >= 1.0f)
        tu -= 1.0f;

    if(tv >= 1.0f)
        tv -= 1.0f;

    waterMat->MatTransform(3, 0) = tu;
    waterMat->MatTransform(3, 1) = tv;

    // Material has changed, so need to update cbuffer.
    waterMat->NumFramesDirty = gNumFrameResources;
}
```

9.12 SUMMARY

1. Texture coordinates are used to define a triangle on the texture that gets mapped to the 3D triangle.

2. The most prevalent way of creating textures for games is for an artist to make them in Photoshop or some other image editor, and then save them as an image file like BMP, DDS, TGA, or PNG. Then the game application will load

the image data at load time into an `ID3D12Resource` object. For real-time graphics applications, the DDS (DirectDraw Surface format) image file format is preferred, as it supports a variety of image formats that are natively understood by the GPU; in particular, it supports compressed image formats that can be natively decompressed by the GPU.

3. There are two popular ways to convert traditional image formats to the DDS format: use an image editor that exports to DDS or use a Microsoft command line tool called texconv.

4. We can create textures from image files stored on disk using the `CreateDDSTextureFromFile12` function, which is located on the DVD at *Common/DDSTextureLoader.h/.cpp*.

5. Magnification occurs when we zoom in on a surface and are trying to cover too many screen pixels with a few texels. Minification occurs when we zoom out of a surface and too many texels are trying to cover too few screen pixels. Mipmaps and texture filters are techniques to handle magnification and minification. GPUs support three kinds of texture filtering natively (in order of lowest quality and least expensive to highest quality and most expensive): point, linear, and anisotropic filters.

6. Address modes define what Direct3D is supposed to do with texture coordinates outside the [0, 1] range. For example, should the texture be tiled, mirrored, clamped, etc.?

7. Texture coordinates can be scaled, rotated, and translated just like other points. By incrementally transforming the texture coordinates by a small amount each frame, we animate the texture.

9.13 EXERCISES

1. Experiment with the "Crate" demo by changing the texture coordinates and using different address mode combinations and filtering options. In particular, reproduce the images in Figures 9.7, 9.9, 9.10, 9.11, 9.12, and 9.13.

2. Using the DirectX Texture Tool, we can manually specify each mipmap level (**File->Open Onto This Surface**). Create a DDS file with a mipmap chain like the one in Figure 9.17, with a different textual description or color on each level so that you can easily distinguish between each mipmap level. Modify the Crate demo by using this texture and have the camera zoom in and out so that you can explicitly see the mipmap levels changing. Try both point and linear mipmap filtering.

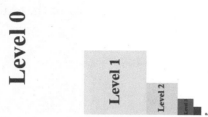

Figure 9.17. A mipmap chain manually constructed so that each level is easily distinguishable.

3. Given two textures of the same size, we can combine them via different operations to obtain a new image. More generally, this is called multitexturing, where multiple textures are used to achieve a result. For example, we can add, subtract, or (component-wise) multiply the corresponding texels of two textures. Figure 9.18 shows the result of component-wise multiplying two textures to get a fireball like result. For this exercise, modify the "Crate" demo by combining the two source textures in Figure 9.18 in a pixel shader to produce the fireball texture over each cube face. (The image files for this exercise may be downloaded from the book's website.) Note that you will have to modify the Default.hlsl to support more than one texture.

Figure 9.18: Component-wise multiplying corresponding texels of two textures to produce a new texture.

4. Modify the solution to Exercise 3 by rotating the fireball texture as a function of time over each cube face.

5. Let $\mathbf{p}_0$, $\mathbf{p}_1$, and $\mathbf{p}_2$ be the vertices of a 3D triangle with respective texture coordinates $\mathbf{q}_0$, $\mathbf{q}_1$, and $\mathbf{q}_2$. Recall from §9.2 that for an arbitrary point on a 3D triangle $\mathbf{p}(s, t) = \mathbf{p}_0 + s(\mathbf{p}_1 - \mathbf{p}_0) + t(\mathbf{p}_2 - \mathbf{p}_0)$ where $s \geq 0$, $t \geq 0$, $s + t \leq 1$, its texture coordinates (u, v) are found by linearly interpolating the vertex texture coordinates across the 3D triangle by the same s, t parameters:

$$(u, v) = \mathbf{q}_0 + s(\mathbf{q}_1 - \mathbf{q}_0) + t(\mathbf{q}_2 - \mathbf{q}_0)$$

(a) Given (u, v) and $\mathbf{q}_0$, $\mathbf{q}_1$, and $\mathbf{q}_2$, solve for (s, t) in terms of u and v (Hint: Consider the vector equation $(u, v) = \mathbf{q}_0 + s(\mathbf{q}_1 - \mathbf{q}_0) + t(\mathbf{q}_2 - \mathbf{q}_0)$.
(b) Express $\mathbf{p}$ as a function of u and v; that is, find a formula $\mathbf{p} = \mathbf{p}(u, v)$.
(c) Compute $\partial \mathbf{p}/\partial u$ and $\partial \mathbf{p}/\partial v$ and give a geometric interpretation of what these vectors mean.

6. Modify the "LitColumns" demo from the previous chapter by adding textures to the ground, columns, and spheres (Figure 9.19). The textures can be found in this chapter's code directory.

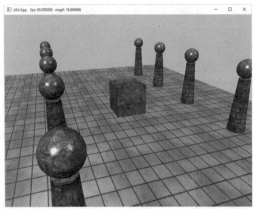

Figure 9.19. Textured column scene.

Chapter 10 BLENDING

Consider Figure 10.1. We start rendering the frame by first drawing the terrain followed by the wooden crate, so that the terrain and crate pixels are on the back buffer. We then draw the water surface to the back buffer using blending, so that the water pixels get blended with the terrain and crate pixels on back buffer in such a way that the terrain and crate shows through the water. In this chapter, we examine *blending* techniques which allow us to blend (combine) the pixels that we are currently rasterizing (so-called *source* pixels) with the pixels that were previously rasterized to the back buffer (so-called *destination* pixels). This technique enables us, among other things, to render semi-transparent objects such as water and glass.

Figure 10.1. A semi-transparent water surface.

Note: *For the sake of discussion, we specifically mention the back buffer as the render target. However, we will show later that we can render to "off screen" render targets as well. Blending applies to these render targets just the same, and the destination pixels are the pixel values that were previously rasterized to these off screen render targets.*

Objectives:

1. To understand how blending works and how to use it with Direct3D
2. To learn about the different blend modes that Direct3D supports
3. To find out how the alpha component can be used to control the transparency of a primitive
4. To learn how we can prevent a pixel from being drawn to the back buffer altogether by employing the HLSL `clip` function

10.1 THE BLENDING EQUATION

Let $\mathbf{C}_{src}$ be the color output from the pixel shader for the *ij*th pixel we are currently rasterizing (source pixel), and let $\mathbf{C}_{dst}$ be the color of the *ij*th pixel currently on the back buffer (destination pixel). Without blending, $\mathbf{C}_{src}$ would overwrite $\mathbf{C}_{dst}$ (assuming it passes the depth/stencil test) and become the new color of the *ij*th back buffer pixel. But with blending, $\mathbf{C}_{src}$ and $\mathbf{C}_{dst}$ are blended together to get the new color $\mathbf{C}$ that will overwrite $\mathbf{C}_{dst}$ (i.e., the blended color $\mathbf{C}$ will be written to the *ij*th pixel of the back buffer). Direct3D uses the following blending equation to blend the source and destination pixel colors:

$$\mathbf{C} = \mathbf{C}_{src} \otimes \mathbf{F}_{src} \boxplus \mathbf{C}_{dst} \otimes \mathbf{F}_{dst}$$

The colors $\mathbf{F}_{src}$ (source blend factor) and $\mathbf{F}_{dst}$ (destination blend factor) may be any of the values described in §10.3, and they allow us modify the original source and destination pixels in a variety of ways, allowing for different effects to be achieved. The $\otimes$ operator means component wise multiplication for color vectors as defined in §5.3.1; the $\boxplus$ operator may be any of the binary operators defined in §10.2.

The above blending equation holds only for the RGB components of the colors. The alpha component is actually handled by a separate similar equation:

$$A = A_{src} F_{src} \boxplus A_{dst} F_{dst}$$

The equation is essentially the same, but it is possible that the blend factors and binary operation are different. The motivation for separating RGB from alpha is simply so that we can process them independently, and hence, differently, which allows for a greater variety of possibilities.

 Blending the alpha component is needed much less frequently than blending the RGB components. This is mainly because we do not care about the back buffer alpha values. Back buffer alpha values are only important if you have some algorithm that requires destination alpha values.

10.2 BLEND OPERATIONS

The binary ⊞ operator used in the blending equation may be one of the following:

```
typedef enum D3D12_BLEND_OP
{
    D3D12_BLEND_OP_ADD          = 1,        C = C_src ⊗ F_src + C_dst ⊗ F_dst
    D3D12_BLEND_OP_SUBTRACT     = 2,        C = C_dst ⊗ F_dst − C_src ⊗ F_src
    D3D12_BLEND_OP_REV_SUBTRACT = 3,        C = C_src ⊗ F_src − C_dst ⊗ F_dst
    D3D12_BLEND_OP_MIN          = 4,        C = min(C_src, C_dst)
    D3D12_BLEND_OP_MAX          = 5,        C = max(C_src, C_dst)
} D3D12_BLEND_OP;
```

 The blend factors are ignored in the min/max operation.

These same operators also work for the alpha blending equation. Also, you can specify a different operator for RGB and alpha. For example, it is possible to add the two RGB terms, but subtract the two alpha terms:

$$\mathbf{C} = \mathbf{C}_{src} \otimes \mathbf{F}_{src} + \mathbf{C}_{dst} \otimes \mathbf{F}_{dst}$$
$$A = A_{dst} F_{dst} - A_{src} F_{src}$$

A feature recently added to Direct3D is the ability to blend the source color and destination color using a logic operator instead of the traditional blending equations above. The available logic operators are given below:

```
typedef
enum D3D12_LOGIC_OP
{
  D3D12_LOGIC_OP_CLEAR = 0,
  D3D12_LOGIC_OP_SET          = ( D3D12_LOGIC_OP_CLEAR + 1 ) ,
  D3D12_LOGIC_OP_COPY         = ( D3D12_LOGIC_OP_SET + 1 ) ,
  D3D12_LOGIC_OP_COPY_INVERTED         = ( D3D12_LOGIC_OP_COPY + 1 ) ,
  D3D12_LOGIC_OP_NOOP         = ( D3D12_LOGIC_OP_COPY_INVERTED + 1 ) ,
  D3D12_LOGIC_OP_INVERT        = ( D3D12_LOGIC_OP_NOOP + 1 ) ,
  D3D12_LOGIC_OP_AND          = ( D3D12_LOGIC_OP_INVERT + 1 ) ,
  D3D12_LOGIC_OP_NAND         = ( D3D12_LOGIC_OP_AND + 1 ) ,
```

```
D3D12_LOGIC_OP_OR       = ( D3D12_LOGIC_OP_NAND + 1 ) ,
D3D12_LOGIC_OP_NOR      = ( D3D12_LOGIC_OP_OR + 1 ) ,
D3D12_LOGIC_OP_XOR      = ( D3D12_LOGIC_OP_NOR + 1 ) ,
D3D12_LOGIC_OP_EQUIV    = ( D3D12_LOGIC_OP_XOR + 1 ) ,
D3D12_LOGIC_OP_AND_REVERSE  = ( D3D12_LOGIC_OP_EQUIV + 1 ) ,
D3D12_LOGIC_OP_AND_INVERTED = ( D3D12_LOGIC_OP_AND_REVERSE + 1 ) ,
D3D12_LOGIC_OP_OR_REVERSE   = ( D3D12_LOGIC_OP_AND_INVERTED + 1 ) ,
D3D12_LOGIC_OP_OR_INVERTED  = ( D3D12_LOGIC_OP_OR_REVERSE + 1 )
} D3D12_LOGIC_OP;
```

Note that you cannot use traditional blending and logic operator blending at the same time; you pick one or the other. Note also that in order to use logic operator blending the render target format must support—it should be a format of the UINT variety, otherwise you will get errors like the following:

```
D3D12 ERROR: ID3D12Device::CreateGraphicsPipelineState: The render
target format at slot 0 is format (R8G8B8A8_UNORM). This format
does not support logic ops. The Pixel Shader output signature
indicates this output could be written, and the Blend State indicates
logic op is enabled for this slot. [ STATE_CREATION ERROR #678:
CREATEGRAPHICSPIPELINESTATE_OM_RENDER_TARGET_DOES_NOT_SUPPORT_LOGIC_
OPS]

D3D12 WARNING: ID3D12Device::CreateGraphicsPipelineState: Pixel Shader
output 'SV_Target0' has type that is NOT unsigned int, while the
corresponding Output Merger RenderTarget slot [0] has logic op enabled.
This happens to be well defined: the raw bits output from the shader
will simply be interpreted as UINT bits in the blender without any data
conversion. This warning is to check that the application developer
really intended to rely on this behavior. [ STATE_CREATION WARNING
#677: CREATEGRAPHICSPIPELINESTATE_PS_OUTPUT_TYPE_MISMATCH]
```

10.3 BLEND FACTORS

By setting different combinations for the source and destination blend factors along with different blend operators, dozens of different blending effects may be achieved. We will illustrate some combinations in §10.5, but you will need to experiment with others to get a feel of what they do. The following list describes the basic blend factors, which apply to both $\mathbf{F}_{src}$ and $\mathbf{F}_{dst}$. See the D3D12_BLEND enumerated type in the SDK documentation for some additional advanced blend factors. Letting $\mathbf{C}_{src} = (r_s, g_s, b_s)$, $A_{src} = a_s$ (the RGBA values output from the pixel shader), $\mathbf{C}_{dst} = (r_d, g_d, b_d)$, $A_{dst} = a_d$ (the RGBA values already stored in the render target), $\mathbf{F}$ being either $\mathbf{F}_{src}$ or $\mathbf{F}_{dst}$ and F being either F_{src} or F_{dst}, we have:

D3D12_BLEND_ZERO: $\mathbf{F} = (0, 0, 0)$ and $F = 0$

D3D12_BLEND_ONE: $\mathbf{F} = (1, 1, 1)$ and $F = 1$

D3D12_BLEND_SRC_COLOR: $\mathbf{F} = (r_s, g_s, b_s)$

D3D12_BLEND_INV_SRC_COLOR: $\mathbf{F}_{src} = (1 - r_s, 1 - g_s, 1 - b_s)$

`D3D12_BLEND_SRC_ALPHA`: $\mathbf{F} = (a_s, a_s, a_s)$ and $F = a_s$
`D3D12_BLEND_INV_SRC_ALPHA`: $\mathbf{F} = (1 - a_s, 1 - a_s, 1 - a_s)$ and $F = (1 - a_s)$
`D3D12_BLEND_DEST_ALPHA`: $\mathbf{F} = (a_d, a_d, a_d)$ and $F = a_d$
`D3D12_BLEND_INV_DEST_ALPHA`: $\mathbf{F} = (1 - a_d, 1 - a_d, 1 - a_d)$ and $F = (1 - a_d)$
`D3D12_BLEND_DEST_COLOR`: $\mathbf{F} = (r_d, g_d, b_d)$
`D3D12_BLEND_INV_DEST_COLOR`: $\mathbf{F} = (1 - r_d, 1 - g_d, 1 - b_d)$
`D3D12_BLEND_SRC_ALPHA_SAT`: $\mathbf{F} = (a'_s, a'_s, a'_s)$ and $F = a'_s$
 where $a'_s = \text{clamp}(a_s, 0, 1)$
`D3D12_BLEND_BLEND_FACTOR`: $\mathbf{F} = (r, g, b)$ and $F = a$, where the color (r, g, b, a) is supplied to the second parameter of the `ID3D12GraphicsCommandList::OMSetBlendFactor` method. This allows you to specify the blend factor color to use directly; however, it is constant until you change the blend state.
`D3D12_BLEND_INV_BLEND_FACTOR`: $\mathbf{F} = (1 - r, 1 - g, 1 - b)$ and $F = 1 - a$, where the color (r, g, b, a) is supplied by the second parameter of the `ID3D12GraphicsCommandList::OMSetBlendFactor` method. This allows you to specify the blend factor color to use directly; however, it is constant until you change the blend state.

All of the above blend factors apply to the RGB blending equation. For the alpha blending equation, blend factors ending with _COLOR are *not allowed*.

The `clamp` *function is defined as:*

$$\text{clamp}(x,a,b) = \begin{cases} x, a \leq x \leq b \\ a, x < a \\ b, x > b \end{cases}$$

We can set the blend factor color with the following function:

```
void ID3D12GraphicsCommandList::OMSetBlendFactor(
   const FLOAT BlendFactor[ 4 ]);
```

Passing a `nullptr` *restores the default blend factor of (1, 1, 1, 1).*

10.4 BLEND STATE

We have talked about the blending operators and blend factors, but where do we set these values with Direct3D? As with other Direct3D state, the blend state is part of the PSO. Thus far we have been using the default blend state, which disables blending:

```
D3D12_GRAPHICS_PIPELINE_STATE_DESC opaquePsoDesc;
ZeroMemory(&opaquePsoDesc, sizeof(D3D12_GRAPHICS_PIPELINE_STATE_DESC));
...
```

```
opaquePsoDesc.BlendState = CD3DX12_BLEND_DESC(D3D12_DEFAULT);
```

To configure a non-default blend state we must fill out a `D3D12_BLEND_DESC` structure. The `D3D12_BLEND_DESC` structure is defined like so:

```
typedef struct D3D12_BLEND_DESC {
  BOOL AlphaToCoverageEnable;  // Default: False
  BOOL IndependentBlendEnable; // Default: False
  D3D11_RENDER_TARGET_BLEND_DESC RenderTarget[8];
} D3D11_BLEND_DESC;
```

1. `AlphaToCoverageEnable`: Specify true to enable alpha-to-coverage, which is a multisampling technique useful when rendering foliage or gate textures. Specify false to disable alpha-to-coverage. Alpha-to-coverage requires multisampling to be enabled (i.e., the back and depth buffer were created with multisampling).

2. `IndependentBlendEnable`: Direct3D supports rendering to up to eight render targets simultaneously. When this flag is set to true, it means blending can be performed for each render target differently (different blend factors, different blend operations, blending disabled/enabled, etc.). If this flag is set to false, it means all the render targets will be blended the same way as described by the first element in the `D3D12_BLEND_DESC::RenderTarget` array. Multiple render targets are used for advanced algorithms; for now, assume we only render to one render target at a time.

3. `RenderTarget`: An array of 8 `D3D12_RENDER_TARGET_BLEND_DESC` elements, where the *i*th element describes how blending is done for the *i*th simultaneous render target. If `IndependentBlendEnable` is set to false, then all the render targets use `RenderTarget[0]` for blending.

The `D3D12_RENDER_TARGET_BLEND_DESC` structure is defined like so:

```
typedef struct D3D12_RENDER_TARGET_BLEND_DESC
{
  BOOL BlendEnable;    // Default: False
  BOOL LogicOpEnable;  // Default: False
  D3D12_BLEND SrcBlend;        // Default: D3D12_BLEND_ONE
  D3D12_BLEND DestBlend;       // Default: D3D12_BLEND_ZERO
  D3D12_BLEND_OP BlendOp;      // Default: D3D12_BLEND_OP_ADD
  D3D12_BLEND SrcBlendAlpha;   // Default: D3D12_BLEND_ONE
  D3D12_BLEND DestBlendAlpha;  // Default: D3D12_BLEND_ZERO
  D3D12_BLEND_OP BlendOpAlpha; // Default: D3D12_BLEND_OP_ADD
  D3D12_LOGIC_OP LogicOp;      // Default: D3D12_LOGIC_OP_NOOP
  UINT8 RenderTargetWriteMask; // Default: D3D12_COLOR_WRITE_ENABLE_ALL
} D3D12_RENDER_TARGET_BLEND_DESC;
```

1. `BlendEnable`: Specify true to enable blending and false to disable it. Note that `BlendEnable` and `LogicOpEnable` cannot both be set to true; you either use regular blending or logic operator blending.

2. `LogicOpEnable`: Specify true to enable a logic blend operation. Note that `BlendEnable` and `LogicOpEnable` cannot both be set to true; you either use regular blending or logic operator blending.
3. `SrcBlend`: A member of the `D3D12_BLEND` enumerated type that specifies the source blend factor $\mathbf{F}_{src}$ for RGB blending.
4. `DestBlend`: A member of the `D3D12_BLEND` enumerated type that specifies the destination blend factor $\mathbf{F}_{dst}$ for RGB blending.
5. `BlendOp`: A member of the `D3D12_BLEND_OP` enumerated type that specifies the RGB blending operator.
6. `SrcBlendAlpha`: A member of the `D3D12_BLEND` enumerated type that specifies the destination blend factor $\mathbf{F}_{src}$ for alpha blending.
7. `DestBlendAlpha`: A member of the `D3D12_BLEND` enumerated type that specifies the destination blend factor $\mathbf{F}_{dst}$ for alpha blending.
8. `BlendOpAlpha`: A member of the `D3D12_BLEND_OP` enumerated type that specifies the alpha blending operator.
9. `LogicOp`: A member of the `D3D12_LOGIC_OP` enumerated type that specifies the logic operator to use for blending the source and destination colors.
10. `RenderTargetWriteMask`: A combination of one or more of the following flags:

```
typedef enum D3D12_COLOR_WRITE_ENABLE {
D3D12_COLOR_WRITE_ENABLE_RED    = 1,
D3D12_COLOR_WRITE_ENABLE_GREEN  = 2,
D3D12_COLOR_WRITE_ENABLE_BLUE   = 4,
D3D12_COLOR_WRITE_ENABLE_ALPHA  = 8,
D3D12_COLOR_WRITE_ENABLE_ALL    =
   ( D3D12_COLOR_WRITE_ENABLE_RED | D3D12_COLOR_WRITE_ENABLE_GREEN |
     D3D12_COLOR_WRITE_ENABLE_BLUE | D3D12_COLOR_WRITE_ENABLE_ALPHA )
} D3D12_COLOR_WRITE_ENABLE;
```

These flags control which color channels in the back buffer are written to after blending. For example, you could disable writes to the RGB channels, and only write to the alpha channel, by specifying `D3D12_COLOR_WRITE_ENABLE_ALPHA`. This flexibility can be useful for advanced techniques. When blending is disabled, the color returned from the pixel shader is used with no write mask applied.

Blending is not free and does require additional per-pixel work, so only enable it if you need it, and turn it off when you are done.

The following code shows example code of creating and setting a blend state:

```
// Start from non-blended PSO
D3D12_GRAPHICS_PIPELINE_STATE_DESC transparentPsoDesc = opaquePsoDesc;
```

```cpp
D3D12_RENDER_TARGET_BLEND_DESC transparencyBlendDesc;
transparencyBlendDesc.BlendEnable = true;
transparencyBlendDesc.LogicOpEnable = false;
transparencyBlendDesc.SrcBlend = D3D12_BLEND_SRC_ALPHA;
transparencyBlendDesc.DestBlend = D3D12_BLEND_INV_SRC_ALPHA;
transparencyBlendDesc.BlendOp = D3D12_BLEND_OP_ADD;
transparencyBlendDesc.SrcBlendAlpha = D3D12_BLEND_ONE;
transparencyBlendDesc.DestBlendAlpha = D3D12_BLEND_ZERO;
transparencyBlendDesc.BlendOpAlpha = D3D12_BLEND_OP_ADD;
transparencyBlendDesc.LogicOp = D3D12_LOGIC_OP_NOOP;
transparencyBlendDesc.RenderTargetWriteMask = D3D12_COLOR_WRITE_ENABLE_
    ALL;

transparentPsoDesc.BlendState.RenderTarget[0] = transparencyBlendDesc;
ThrowIfFailed(md3dDevice->CreateGraphicsPipelineState(
    &transparentPsoDesc, IID_PPV_ARGS(&mPSOs["transparent"])));
```

As with other PSOs, you should create them all at application initialization time, and then just switch between them as needed with the `ID3D12GraphicsCommandList::SetPipelineState` method.

10.5 EXAMPLES

In the following subsections, we look at some blend factor combinations used to get specific effects. In these examples, we only look at RGB blending. Alpha blending is handled analogously.

10.5.1 No Color Write

Suppose that we want to keep the original destination pixel exactly as it is and not overwrite it or blend it with the source pixel currently being rasterized. This can be useful, for example, if you just want to write to the depth/stencil buffer, and not the back buffer. To do this, set the source pixel blend factor to `D3D12_BLEND_ZERO`, the destination blend factor to `D3D12_BLEND_ONE`, and the blend operator to `D3D12_BLEND_OP_ADD`. With this setup, the blending equation reduces to:

$$C = C_{src} \otimes F_{src} \boxplus C_{dst} \otimes F_{dst}$$
$$C = C_{src} \otimes (0,0,0) + C_{dst} \otimes (1,1,1)$$
$$C = C_{dst}$$

This is a contrived example; another way to implement the same thing would be to set the `D3D12_RENDER_TARGET_BLEND_DESC::RenderTargetWriteMask` member to 0, so that none of the color channels are written to.

Figure 10.2. Adding source and destination color. Adding creates a brighter image since color is being added.

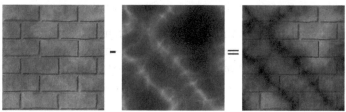

Figure 10.3. Subtracting source color from destination color. Subtraction creates a darker image since color is being removed.

10.5.2 Adding/Subtracting

Suppose that we want to add the source pixels with the destination pixels (see Figure 10.2). To do this, set the source blend factor to D3D12_BLEND_ONE, the destination blend factor to D3D12_BLEND_ONE, and the blend operator to D3D12_BLEND_OP_ADD. With this setup, the blending equation reduces to:

$$\mathbf{C} = \mathbf{C}_{src} \otimes \mathbf{F}_{src} \boxplus \mathbf{C}_{dst} \otimes \mathbf{F}_{dst}$$
$$\mathbf{C} = \mathbf{C}_{src} \otimes (1,1,1) + \mathbf{C}_{dst} \otimes (1,1,1)$$
$$\mathbf{C} = \mathbf{C}_{src} + \mathbf{C}_{dst}$$

We can subtract source pixels from destination pixels by using the above blend factors and replacing the blend operation with D3D12_BLEND_OP_SUBTRACT (Figure 10.3).

10.5.3 Multiplying

Suppose that we want to multiply a source pixel with its corresponding destination pixel (see Figure 10.4). To do this, we set the source blend factor to D3D12_BLEND_ZERO, the destination blend factor to D3D12_BLEND_SRC_COLOR, and the blend operator to D3D12_BLEND_OP_ADD. With this setup, the blending equation reduces to:

$$\mathbf{C} = \mathbf{C}_{src} \otimes \mathbf{F}_{src} \boxplus \mathbf{C}_{dst} \otimes \mathbf{F}_{dst}$$
$$\mathbf{C} = \mathbf{C}_{src} \otimes (0,0,0) + \mathbf{C}_{dst} \otimes \mathbf{C}_{src}$$
$$\mathbf{C} = \mathbf{C}_{dst} \otimes \mathbf{C}_{src}$$

Figure 10.4. Multiplying source color and destination color.

10.5.4 Transparency

Let the source alpha component *as* be thought of as a percent that controls the opacity of the source pixel (e.g., 0 alpha means 0% opaque, 0.4 means 40% opaque, and 1.0 means 100% opaque). The relationship between opacity and transparency is simply $T = 1 - A$, where A is opacity and T is transparency. For instance, if something is 0.4 opaque, then it is $1 - 0.4 = 0.6$ transparent. Now suppose that we want to blend the source and destination pixels based on the opacity of the source pixel. To do this, set the source blend factor to D3D12_BLEND_SRC_ALPHA and the destination blend factor to D3D12_BLEND_INV_SRC_ALPHA, and the blend operator to D3D12_BLEND_OP_ADD. With this setup, the blending equation reduces to:

$$\mathbf{C} = \mathbf{C}_{src} \otimes \mathbf{F}_{src} \boxplus \mathbf{C}_{dst} \otimes \mathbf{F}_{dst}$$
$$\mathbf{C} = \mathbf{C}_{src} \otimes (a_s, a_s, a_s) + \mathbf{C}_{dst} \otimes (1 - a_s, 1 - a_s, 1 - a_s)$$
$$\mathbf{C} = a_s \mathbf{C}_{src} + (1 - a_s) \mathbf{C}_{dst}$$

For example, suppose $a_s = 0.25$, which is to say the source pixel is only 25% opaque. Then when the source and destination pixels are blended together, we expect the final color will be a combination of 25% of the source pixel and 75% of the destination pixel (the pixel "behind" the source pixel), since the source pixel is 75% transparent. The equation above gives us precisely this:

$$\mathbf{C} = a_s \mathbf{C}_{src} + (1 - a_s) \mathbf{C}_{dst}$$
$$\mathbf{C} = 0.25 \mathbf{C}_{src} + 0.75 \mathbf{C}_{dst}$$

Using this blending method, we can draw transparent objects like the one in Figure 10.1. It should be noted that with this blending method, the order that you draw the objects matters. We use the following rule:

Draw objects that do not use blending first. Next, sort the objects that use blending by their distance from the camera. Finally, draw the objects that use blending in a back-to-front order.

The reason for the back-to-front draw order is so that objects are blended with the objects spatially behind them. For if an object is transparent, we can see through it to see the scene behind it. So it is necessary that all the pixels behind the transparent object have already been written to the back buffer, so that we can blend the transparent source pixels with the destination pixels of the scene behind it.

For the blending method in §10.5.1, draw order does not matter since it simply prevents source pixel writes to the back buffer. For the blending methods discussed in §10.5.2 and 10.5.3, we still draw non-blended objects first and blended objects last; this is because we want to first lay all the non-blended geometry onto the back buffer before we start blending. However, we do not need to sort the objects that use blending. This is because the operations are commutative. That is, if you start with a back buffer pixel color **B**, and then do n additive/subtractive/multiplicative blends to that pixel, the order does not matter:

$$\mathbf{B}' = \mathbf{B} + \mathbf{C}_0 + \mathbf{C}_1 + \ldots + \mathbf{C}_{n-1}$$
$$\mathbf{B}' = \mathbf{B} - \mathbf{C}_0 - \mathbf{C}_1 - \ldots - \mathbf{C}_{n-1}$$
$$\mathbf{B}' = \mathbf{B} \otimes \mathbf{C}_0 \otimes \mathbf{C}_1 \otimes \ldots \otimes \mathbf{C}_{n-1}$$

10.5.5 Blending and the Depth Buffer

When blending with additive/subtractive/multiplicative blending, an issue arises with the depth test. For the sake of example, we will explain only with additive blending, but the same idea holds for subtractive/multiplicative blending. If we are rendering a set S of objects with additive blending, the idea is that the objects in S do not obscure each other; instead, their colors are meant to simply accumulate (see Figure 10.5). Therefore, we do not want to perform the depth test between objects in S; for if we did, without a back-to-front draw ordering, one of the objects in S would obscure another object in S, thus causing the pixel fragments to be rejected due to the depth test, which means that object's pixel

Figure 10.5. With additive blending, the intensity is greater near the source point where more particles are overlapping and being added together. As the particles spread out, the intensity weakens because there are less particles overlapping and being added together.

colors would not be accumulated into the blend sum. We can disable the depth test between objects in S by disabling writes to the depth buffer while rendering objects in S. Because depth writes are disabled, the depths of an object in S drawn with additive blending will not be written to the depth buffer; hence, this object will not obscure any later drawn object in S behind it due to the depth test. Note that we only disable depth writes while drawing the objects in S (the set of objects drawn with additive blending). Depth reads and the depth test are still enabled. This is so that non-blended geometry (which is drawn before blended geometry) will still obscure blended geometry behind it. For example, if you have a set of additively blended objects behind a wall, you will not see the blended objects because the solid wall obscures them. How to disable depth writes and, more generally, configure the depth test settings will be covered in the next chapter.

10.6 ALPHA CHANNELS

The example from §10.5.4 showed that source alpha components can be used in RGB blending to control transparency. The source color used in the blending equation comes from the pixel shader. As we saw in the last chapter, we return the diffuse material's alpha value as the alpha output of the pixel shader. Thus the alpha channel of the diffuse map is used to control transparency.

```
float4 PS(VertexOut pin) : SV_Target
{
  float4 diffuseAlbedo = gDiffuseMap.Sample(
    gsamAnisotropicWrap, pin.TexC) * gDiffuseAlbedo;

  ...

  // Common convention to take alpha from diffuse albedo.
  litColor.a = diffuseAlbedo.a;
  return litColor;
}
```

You can generally add an alpha channel in any popular image editing software, such as Adobe Photoshop, and then save the image to an image format that supports an alpha channel like DDS.

10.7 CLIPPING PIXELS

Sometimes we want to completely reject a source pixel from being further processed. This can be done with the intrinsic HLSL `clip(x)` function. This function can only be called in a pixel shader, and it discards the current pixel from

Blending 409

RGB Channels   **Alpha Channel**

Figure 10.6. A wire fence texture with its alpha channel. The pixels with black alpha values will be rejected by the `clip` function and not drawn; hence, only the wire fence remains. Essentially, the alpha channel is used to mask out the non fence pixels from the texture.

further processing if x < 0. This function is useful to render wire fence textures, for example, like the one shown in Figure 10.6. That is, it is useful for rendering pixels were a pixel is either completely opaque or completely transparent.

In the pixel shader, we grab the alpha component of the texture. If it is a small value close to 0, which indicates that the pixel is completely transparent, then we clip the pixel from further processing.

```
float4 PS(VertexOut pin) : SV_Target
{
  float4 diffuseAlbedo = gDiffuseMap.Sample(
    gsamAnisotropicWrap, pin.TexC) * gDiffuseAlbedo;

#ifdef ALPHA_TEST
  // Discard pixel if texture alpha < 0.1. We do this test as soon
  // as possible in the shader so that we can potentially exit the
  // shader early, thereby skipping the rest of the shader code.
  clip(diffuseAlbedo.a - 0.1f);
#endif

  ...

  // Common convention to take alpha from diffuse albedo.
  litColor.a = diffuseAlbedo.a;

  return litColor;
}
```

Observe that we only clip if ALPHA_TEST is defined; this is because we might not want to invoke `clip` for some render items, so we need to be able to switch it on/off by having specialized shaders. Moreover, there is a cost to using alpha testing, so we should only use it if we need it.

Note that the same result can be obtained using blending, but this is more efficient. For one thing, no blending calculation needs to be done (blending can be disabled). Also, the draw order does not matter. And furthermore, by discarding

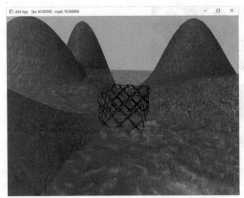

Figure 10.7. Screenshot of the "Blend" demo.

a pixel early from the pixel shader, the remaining pixel shader instructions can be skipped (no point in doing the calculations for a discarded pixel).

Due to filtering, the alpha channel can get blurred a bit, so you should leave some buffer room when clipping pixels. For example, clip pixels with alpha values close to 0, but not necessarily exactly zero.

Figure 10.7 shows a screenshot of the "Blend" demo. It renders semi-transparent water using transparency blending, and renders the wire fenced box using the `clip` test. One other change worth mentioning is that, because we can now see through the box with the fence texture, we want to disable back face culling for alpha tested objects:

```
// PSO for alpha tested objects

D3D12_GRAPHICS_PIPELINE_STATE_DESC alphaTestedPsoDesc = opaquePsoDesc;
alphaTestedPsoDesc.PS =
{
  reinterpret_cast<BYTE*>(mShaders["alphaTestedPS"]-
    >GetBufferPointer()),
    mShaders["alphaTestedPS"]->GetBufferSize()
};
alphaTestedPsoDesc.RasterizerState.CullMode = D3D12_CULL_MODE_NONE;
ThrowIfFailed(md3dDevice->CreateGraphicsPipelineState(
  &alphaTestedPsoDesc, IID_PPV_ARGS(&mPSOs["alphaTested"])));
```

10.8 FOG

To simulate certain types of weather conditions in our games, we need to be able to implement a fog effect; see Figure 10.8. In addition to the obvious purposes of fog, fog provides some fringe benefits. For example, it can mask distant

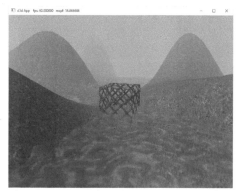

Figure 10.8. Screenshot of the "Blend" demo with fog enabled.

rendering artifacts and prevent *popping*. Popping refers to when an object that was previously behind the far plane all of a sudden comes in front of the frustum, due to camera movement, and thus becomes visible; so it seems to "pop" into the scene abruptly. By having a layer of fog in the distance, the popping is hidden. Note that if your scene takes place on a clear day, you may wish to still include a subtle amount of fog at far distances, because, even on clear days, distant objects such as mountains appear hazier and lose contrast as a function of depth, and we can use fog to simulate this atmospheric perspective phenomenon.

Our strategy for implementing fog works as follows: We specify a fog color, a fog start distance from the camera and a fog range (i.e., the range from the fog start distance until the fog completely hides any objects). Then the color of a point on a triangle is a weighted average of its usual color and the fog color:

$$foggedColor = litColor + s(fogColor - litColor)$$
$$= (1-s) \cdot litColor + s \cdot fogColor$$

The parameter *s* ranges from 0 to 1 and is a function of the distance between the camera position and the surface point. As the distance between a surface point and the eye increases, the point becomes more and more obscured by the fog. The parameter s is defined as follows:

$$s = \text{saturate}\left(\frac{\text{dist}(\mathbf{p},\mathbf{E}) - fogStart}{fogRange}\right)$$

where dist (**p, E**) is the distance between the surface point p and the camera position **E**. The `saturate` function clamps the argument to the range [0, 1]:

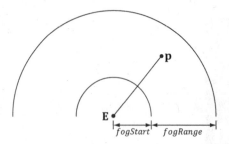

Figure 10.9. The distance of a point from the eye, and the *fogStart* and *fogRange parameters*.

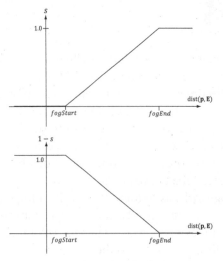

Figure 10.10. (Left): A plot of *s* (the fog color weight) as a function of distance. (Right): A plot of 1 − *s* (the lit color weight) as a function of distance. As *s* increases, (1 − *s*) decreases the same amount.]

$$saturate(x) = \begin{cases} x, 0 \le x \le 1 \\ 0, x < 0 \\ 1, x > 1 \end{cases}$$

Figure 10.10 shows a plot of *s* as a function of distance. We see that when dist(**p**, **E**) ≤ *fogStart*, *s* = 0 and the fogged color is given by:

$$foggedColor = litColor$$

In other words, the fog does not modify the color of vertices whose distance from the camera is less than *fogStart*. This makes sense based on the name "*fogStart*"; the fog does not start affecting the color until the distance from the camera is at least that of *fogStart*.

Let *fogEnd* = *fogStart* + *fogRange*. When dist(**p, E**) ≥ *fogEnd*, $s = 1$ and the fogged color is given by:

$$foggedColor = fogColor$$

In other words, the fog completely hides the surface point at distances greater than or equal to *fogEnd*—so all you see is the fog color.

When *fogStart* < dist(**p, E**) < *fogEnd*, we see that s linearly ramps up from 0 to 1 as dist(**p, E**) increases from *fogStart* to *fogEnd*. This means that as the distance increases, the fog color gets more and more weight while the original color gets less and less weight. This makes sense, of course, because as the distance increases, the fog obscures more and more of the surface point.

The following shader code shows how fog is implemented. We compute the distance and interpolation at the pixel level, after we have computed the lit color.

```
// Defaults for number of lights.
#ifndef NUM_DIR_LIGHTS
    #define NUM_DIR_LIGHTS 3
#endif

#ifndef NUM_POINT_LIGHTS
    #define NUM_POINT_LIGHTS 0
#endif

#ifndef NUM_SPOT_LIGHTS
    #define NUM_SPOT_LIGHTS 0
#endif

// Include structures and functions for lighting.
#include "LightingUtil.hlsl"

Texture2D    gDiffuseMap : register(t0);


SamplerState gsamPointWrap        : register(s0);
SamplerState gsamPointClamp       : register(s1);
SamplerState gsamLinearWrap       : register(s2);
SamplerState gsamLinearClamp      : register(s3);
SamplerState gsamAnisotropicWrap  : register(s4);
SamplerState gsamAnisotropicClamp : register(s5);

// Constant data that varies per frame.
cbuffer cbPerObject : register(b0)
{
    float4x4 gWorld;
    float4x4 gTexTransform;
};

// Constant data that varies per material.
cbuffer cbPass : register(b1)
{
```

```
    float4x4 gView;
    float4x4 gInvView;
    float4x4 gProj;
    float4x4 gInvProj;
    float4x4 gViewProj;
    float4x4 gInvViewProj;
    float3 gEyePosW;
    float cbPerPassPad1;
    float2 gRenderTargetSize;
    float2 gInvRenderTargetSize;
    float gNearZ;
    float gFarZ;
    float gTotalTime;
    float gDeltaTime;
    float4 gAmbientLight;

    // Allow application to change fog parameters once per frame.
    // For example, we may only use fog for certain times of day.
    float4 gFogColor;
    float gFogStart;
    float gFogRange;
    float2 cbPerPassPad2;

    // Indices [0, NUM_DIR_LIGHTS) are directional lights;
    // indices [NUM_DIR_LIGHTS, NUM_DIR_LIGHTS+NUM_POINT_LIGHTS) are
      point lights;
    // indices [NUM_DIR_LIGHTS+NUM_POINT_LIGHTS,
    // NUM_DIR_LIGHTS+NUM_POINT_LIGHT+NUM_SPOT_LIGHTS)
    // are spot lights for a maximum of MaxLights per object.
    Light gLights[MaxLights];
};

cbuffer cbMaterial : register(b2)
{
    float4   gDiffuseAlbedo;
    float3   gFresnelR0;
    float    gRoughness;
    float4x4 gMatTransform;
};

struct VertexIn
{
    float3 PosL    : POSITION;
    float3 NormalL : NORMAL;
    float2 TexC    : TEXCOORD;
};

struct VertexOut
{
    float4 PosH    : SV_POSITION;
    float3 PosW    : POSITION;
    float3 NormalW : NORMAL;
    float2 TexC    : TEXCOORD;
};
```

```
VertexOut VS(VertexIn vin)
{
  VertexOut vout = (VertexOut)0.0f;

  // Transform to world space.
  float4 posW = mul(float4(vin.PosL, 1.0f), gWorld);
  vout.PosW = posW.xyz;

  // Assumes nonuniform scaling; otherwise, need to use inverse-
    transpose
  // of world matrix.
  vout.NormalW = mul(vin.NormalL, (float3x3)gWorld);

  // Transform to homogeneous clip space.
  vout.PosH = mul(posW, gViewProj);

  // Output vertex attributes for interpolation across triangle.
  float4 texC = mul(float4(vin.TexC, 0.0f, 1.0f), gTexTransform);
  vout.TexC = mul(texC, gMatTransform).xy;

  return vout;
}

float4 PS(VertexOut pin) : SV_Target
{
  float4 diffuseAlbedo = gDiffuseMap.Sample(
    gsamAnisotropicWrap, pin.TexC) * gDiffuseAlbedo;

#ifdef ALPHA_TEST
  // Discard pixel if texture alpha < 0.1. We do this test as soon
  // as possible in the shader so that we can potentially exit the
  // shader early, thereby skipping the rest of the shader code.
  clip(diffuseAlbedo.a - 0.1f);
#endif

  // Interpolating normal can unnormalize it, so renormalize it.
  pin.NormalW = normalize(pin.NormalW);

  // Vector from point being lit to eye.
  float3 toEyeW = gEyePosW - pin.PosW;
  float distToEye = length(toEyeW);
  toEyeW /= distToEye; // normalize

  // Light terms.
  float4 ambient = gAmbientLight*diffuseAlbedo;

  const float shininess = 1.0f - gRoughness;
  Material mat = { diffuseAlbedo, gFresnelR0, shininess };
  float3 shadowFactor = 1.0f;
  float4 directLight = ComputeLighting(gLights, mat, pin.PosW,
    pin.NormalW, toEyeW, shadowFactor);

  float4 litColor = ambient + directLight;
```

```
#ifdef FOG
  float fogAmount = saturate((distToEye - gFogStart) / gFogRange);
  litColor = lerp(litColor, gFogColor, fogAmount);
#endif

  // Common convention to take alpha from diffuse albedo.
  litColor.a = diffuseAlbedo.a;

  return litColor;
}
```

Some scenes may not want to use fog; therefore, we make fog optional by requiring FOG to be defined when compiling the shader. This way, if fog is not wanted, then we do not pay the cost of the fog calculations. In our demo, we enable fog by supplying the following `D3D_SHADER_MACRO` to the `CompileShader` function:

```
const D3D_SHADER_MACRO defines[] =
{
  "FOG", "1",
  NULL, NULL
};

mShaders["opaquePS"] = d3dUtil::CompileShader(
  L"Shaders\\Default.hlsl", defines, "PS", "ps_5_0");
```

Observe that in the fog calculation, we use the `distToEye` value, that we also computed to normalize the `toEye` vector. A less optimal implementation would have been to write:

```
float3 toEye = normalize(gEyePosW - pin.PosW);
float distToEye = distance(gEyePosW, pin.PosW);
```

This essentially computes the length of the `toEye` vector twice, once in the `normalize` function, and again in the `distance` function.

10.9 SUMMARY

1. Blending is a technique which allows us to blend (combine) the pixels that we are currently rasterizing (so-called *source* pixels) with the pixels that were previously rasterized to the back buffer (so-called *destination* pixels). This technique enables us, among other things, to render semi-transparent objects such as water and glass.

2. The blending equation is:

$$C = C_{src} \otimes F_{src} \boxplus C_{dst} \otimes F_{dst}$$

$$A = A_{src} F_{src} \boxplus A_{dst} F_{dst}$$

Note that RGB components are blended independently to alpha components. The ⊞ binary operator can be one of the operators defined by the `D3D12_BLEND_OP` enumerated type.

3. $\mathbf{F}_{src}, \mathbf{F}_{dst}$, F_{src}, and F_{dst} are called blend factors, and they provide a means for customizing the blending equation. They can be a member of the `D3D12_BLEND` enumerated type. For the alpha blending equation, blend factors ending with `_COLOR` are *not allowed*.

4. Source alpha information comes from the diffuse material. In our framework, the diffuse material is defined by a texture map, and the texture's alpha channel stores the alpha information.

5. Source pixels can be completely rejected from further processing using the intrinsic HLSL `clip(x)` function. This function can only be called in a pixel shader, and it discards the current pixel from further processing if `x < 0`. Among other things, this function is useful for efficiently rendering pixels were a pixel is either completely opaque or completely transparent (it is used to reject completely transparent pixels—pixels with an alpha value near zero).

6. Use fog to model various weather effects and atmospheric perspective, to hide distant rendering artifacts, and to hide popping. In our linear fog model, we specify a fog color, a fog start distance from the camera and a fog range. The color of a point on a triangle is a weighted average of its usual color and the fog color:

$$foggedColor = litColor + s\left(fogColor - litColor\right)$$
$$= (1-s) \cdot litColor + s \cdot fogColor$$

The parameter *s* ranges from 0 to 1 and is a function of the distance between the camera position and the surface point. As the distance between a surface point and the eye increases, the point becomes more and more obscured by the fog.

10.10 EXERCISES

1. Experiment with different blend operation and blend factor combinations.
2. Modify the "Blend" demo by drawing the water first. Explain the results.
3. Suppose *fogStart* = 10 and *fogRange* = 200. Compute *foggedColor* for when
   (a) dist (**p**, **E**) = 160
   (b) dist (**p**, **E**) = 110

(c) dist $(\mathbf{p}, \mathbf{E}) = 60$

(d) dist $(\mathbf{p}, \mathbf{E}) = 30$

4. Verify the compiled pixel shader without `ALPHA_TEST` defined does not have a `discard` instruction, and the compiled pixel shader with `ALPHA_TEST` does, by looking at the generated shader assembly. The discard instruction corresponds to the HLSL `clip` instruction.

5. Modify the "Blend" demo by creating and applying a blend render state that disables color writes to the red and green color channels.

Chapter 11 STENCILING

The stencil buffer is an off-screen buffer we can use to achieve some special effects. The stencil buffer has the same resolution as the back buffer and depth buffer, such that the *ij*th pixel in the stencil buffer corresponds with the *ij*th pixel in the back buffer and depth buffer. Recall from §4.1.5 that when a stencil buffer is specified, it comes attached to the depth buffer. As the name suggests, the stencil buffer works as a stencil and allows us to block the rendering of certain pixel fragments to the back buffer.

For instance, when implementing a mirror, we need to reflect an object across the plane of the mirror; however, we only want to draw the reflection into the mirror. We can use the stencil buffer to block the rendering of the reflection unless it is being drawn into the mirror (see Figure 11.1).

The stencil buffer (and also the depth buffer) state is configured by filling out a D3D12_DEPTH_STENCIL_DESC instance and assigning it to the D3D12_GRAPHICS_PIPELINE_STATE_DESC::DepthStencilState field of a pipeline state object (PSO). Learning to use the stencil buffer effectively comes best by studying existing example application. Once you understand a few applications of the stencil buffer, you will have a better idea of how it can be used for your own specific needs.

Objectives:

1. To find out how to control the depth and stencil buffer state by filling out the D3D12_DEPTH_STENCIL_DESC field in a pipeline state object.

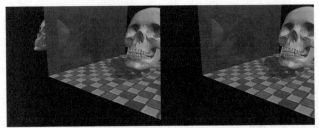

Figure 11.1. (Left) The reflected skull shows properly in the mirror. The reflection does not show through the wall bricks because it fails the depth test in this area. However, looking behind the wall we are able to see the reflection, thus breaking the illusion (the reflection should only show up through the mirror). (Right) By using the stencil buffer, we can block the reflected skull from being rendered unless it is being drawn in the mirror.

2. To learn how to implement mirrors by using the stencil buffer to prevent reflections from being drawn to non-mirror surfaces.

3. To be able to identify double blending and understand how the stencil buffer can prevent it.

4. To explain depth complexity and describe two ways the depth complexity of a scene can to measured.

11.1 DEPTH/STENCIL FORMATS AND CLEARING

Recalling that the depth/stencil buffer is a texture, it must be created with certain data formats. The formats used for depth/stencil buffering are as follows:

1. `DXGI_FORMAT_D32_FLOAT_S8X24_UINT`: Specifies a 32-bit floating-point depth buffer, with 8-bits (unsigned integer) reserved for the stencil buffer mapped to the [0, 255] range and 24-bits not used for padding.

2. `DXGI_FORMAT_D24_UNORM_S8_UINT`: Specifies an unsigned 24-bit depth buffer mapped to the [0, 1] range with 8-bits (unsigned integer) reserved for the stencil buffer mapped to the [0, 255] range.

In our D3DApp framework, when we create the depth buffer, we specify:

```
DXGI_FORMAT mDepthStencilFormat = DXGI_FORMAT_D24_UNORM_S8_UINT;
depthStencilDesc.Format = mDepthStencilFormat;
```

Also, the stencil buffer should be reset to some value at the beginning of each frame. This is done with the following method (which also clears the depth buffer):

```
void ID3D12GraphicsCommandList::ClearDepthStencilView(
    D3D12_CPU_DESCRIPTOR_HANDLE DepthStencilView,
    D3D12_CLEAR_FLAGS ClearFlags,
    FLOAT Depth,
```

```
    UINT8 Stencil,
    UINT NumRects,
    const D3D12_RECT *pRects);
```

1. `DepthStencilView`: Descriptor to the view of the depth/stencil buffer we want to clear.
2. `ClearFlags`: Specify `D3D12_CLEAR_FLAG_DEPTH` to clear the depth buffer only; specify `D3D12_CLEAR_FLAG_STENCIL` to clear the stencil buffer only; specify `D3D12_CLEAR_FLAG_DEPTH | D3D12_CLEAR_FLAG_STENCIL` to clear both.
3. `Depth`: The float-value to set each pixel in the depth buffer to; it must be a floating point number x such that $0 \leq x \leq 1$.
4. `Stencil`: The integer-value to set each pixel of the stencil buffer to; it must be an integer n such that $0 \leq n \leq 255$.
5. `NumRects`: The number of rectangles in the array `pRects` points to.
6. `pRects`: An array of `D3D12_RECT`s marking rectangular regions on the depth/stencil buffer to clear; specify `nullptr` to clear the entire depth/stencil buffer.

We have already been calling this method every frame in our demos. For example:

```
mCommandList->ClearDepthStencilView(DepthStencilView(),
    D3D12_CLEAR_FLAG_DEPTH | D3D12_CLEAR_FLAG_STENCIL,
    1.0f, 0, 0, nullptr);
```

11.2 THE STENCIL TEST

As previously stated, we can use the stencil buffer to block rendering to certain areas of the back buffer. The decision to block a particular pixel from being written is decided by the *stencil test*, which is given by the following:

```
if( StencilRef & StencilReadMask ⊴ Value & StencilReadMask )
    accept pixel
else
    reject pixel
```

The stencil test is performed as pixels get rasterized (i.e., during the output-merger stage), assuming stenciling is enabled, and takes two operands:

1. A left-hand-side (LHS) operand that is determined by ANDing an application-defined *stencil reference value* (`StencilRef`) with an application-defined *masking value* (`StencilReadMask`).
2. A right-hand-side (RHS) operand that is determined by ANDing the entry already in the stencil buffer of the particular pixel we are testing (`Value`) with an application-defined masking value (`StencilReadMask`).

Note that the `StencilReadMask` is the same for the LHS and the RHS. The stencil test then compares the LHS with the RHS as specified an application-chosen *comparison function* ⊴, which returns a true or false value. We write the pixel to the back buffer if the test evaluates to true (assuming the depth test also passes). If the test evaluates to false, then we block the pixel from being written to the back buffer. And of course, if a pixel is rejected due to failing the stencil test, it is not written to the depth buffer either.

The ⊴ operator is any one of the functions defined in the `D3D12_COMPARISON_FUNC` enumerated type:

```
typedef enum D3D12_COMPARISON_FUNC
{
  D3D12_COMPARISON_NEVER = 1,
  D3D12_COMPARISON_LESS = 2,
  D3D12_COMPARISON_EQUAL = 3,
  D3D12_COMPARISON_LESS_EQUAL = 4,
  D3D12_COMPARISON_GREATER = 5,
  D3D12_COMPARISON_NOT_EQUAL = 6,
  D3D12_COMPARISON_GREATER_EQUAL = 7,
  D3D12_COMPARISON_ALWAYS = 8,
} D3D12_COMPARISON_FUNC;
```

1. `D3D12_COMPARISON_NEVER`: The function always returns false.
2. `D3D12_COMPARISON_LESS`: Replace ⊴ with the < operator.
3. `D3D12_COMPARISON_EQUAL`: Replace ⊴ with the == operator.
4. `D3D12_COMPARISON_LESS_EQUAL`: Replace ⊴ with the ≤ operator.
5. `D3D12_COMPARISON_GREATER`: Replace ⊴ with the > operator.
6. `D3D12_COMPARISON_NOT_EQUAL`: Replace ⊴ with the != operator.
7. `D3D12_COMPARISON_GREATER_EQUAL`: Replace ⊴ with the ≥ operator.
8. `D3D12_COMPARISON_ALWAYS`: The function always returns true.

11.3 DESCRIBING THE DEPTH/STENCIL STATE

The depth/stencil state is described by filling out a `D3D12_DEPTH_STENCIL_DESC` instance:

```
typedef struct D3D12_DEPTH_STENCIL_DESC {
  BOOL DepthEnable; // Default True

  // Default: D3D11_DEPTH_WRITE_MASK_ALL
  D3D12_DEPTH_WRITE_MASK DepthWriteMask;

  // Default: D3D11_COMPARISON_LESS
  D3D12_COMPARISON_FUNC DepthFunc;
```

```
    BOOL StencilEnable;             // Default: False
    UINT8 StencilReadMask;          // Default: 0xff
    UINT8 StencilWriteMask;         // Default: 0xff
    D3D12_DEPTH_STENCILOP_DESC FrontFace;
    D3D12_DEPTH_STENCILOP_DESC BackFace;
} D3D12_DEPTH_STENCIL_DESC;
```

11.3.1 Depth Settings

1. `DepthEnable`: Specify true to enable the depth buffering; specify false to disable it. When depth testing is disabled, the draw order matters, and a pixel fragment will be drawn even if it is behind an occluding object (review §4.1.5). If depth buffering is disabled, elements in the depth buffer are *not* updated either, regardless of the `DepthWriteMask` setting.

2. `DepthWriteMask`: This can be either `D3D12_DEPTH_WRITE_MASK_ZERO` or `D3D12_DEPTH_WRITE_MASK_ALL`, but not both. Assuming DepthEnable is set to true, `D3D12_DEPTH_WRITE_MASK_ZERO` disables writes to the depth buffer, but depth testing will still occur. `D3D12_DEPTH_WRITE_MASK_ALL` enables writes to the depth buffer; new depths will be written provided the depth and stencil test both pass. The ability to control depth reads and writes becomes necessary for implementing certain special effects.

3. `DepthFunc`: Specify one of the members of the `D3D12_COMPARISON_FUNC` enumerated type to define the depth test comparison function. Usually this is always `D3D12_COMPARISON_LESS` so that the usual depth test is performed, as described in §4.1.5. That is, a pixel fragment is accepted provided its depth value is less than the depth of the previous pixel written to the back buffer. But as you can see, Direct3D allows you to customize the depth test if necessary.

11.3.2 Stencil Settings

1. `StencilEnable`: Specify true to enable the stencil test; specify false to disable it.

2. `StencilReadMask`: The `StencilReadMask` used in the stencil test:

```
if( StencilRef & StencilReadMask ⊴ Value & StencilReadMask )
    accept pixel
else
    reject pixel
```

The default does not mask any bits:

```
#define     D3D12_DEFAULT_STENCIL_READ_MASK        ( 0xff )
```

3. **StencilWriteMask**: When the stencil buffer is being updated, we can mask off certain bits from being written to with the write mask. For example, if you wanted to prevent the top 4 bits from being written to, you could use the write mask of 0x0f. The default value does not mask any bits:

   ```
   #define       D3D12_DEFAULT_STENCIL_WRITE_MASK       ( 0xff )
   ```

4. **FrontFace**: A filled out D3D12_DEPTH_STENCILOP_DESC structure indicating how the stencil buffer works for front facing triangles.

5. **BackFace**: A filled out D3D12_DEPTH_STENCILOP_DESC structure indicating how the stencil buffer works for back facing triangles.

```
typedef struct D3D12_DEPTH_STENCILOP_DESC {

D3D12_STENCIL_OP StencilFailOp;          // Default: D3D12_STENCIL_OP_KEEP
D3D12_STENCIL_OP StencilDepthFailOp;     // Default: D3D12_STENCIL_OP_KEEP
D3D12_STENCIL_OP StencilPassOp;          // Default: D3D12_STENCIL_OP_KEEP
D3D12_COMPARISON_FUNC StencilFunc;       // Default: D3D12_COMPARISON_ALWAYS
} D3D12_DEPTH_STENCILOP_DESC;
```

1. **StencilFailOp**: A member of the D3D12_STENCIL_OP enumerated type describing how the stencil buffer should be updated when the stencil test fails for a pixel fragment.

2. **StencilDepthFailOp**: A member of the D3D12_STENCIL_OP enumerated type describing how the stencil buffer should be updated when the stencil test passes but the depth test fails for a pixel fragment.

3. **StencilPassOp**: A member of the D3D12_STENCIL_OP enumerated type describing how the stencil buffer should be updated when the stencil test and depth test both pass for a pixel fragment.

4. **StencilFunc**: A member of the D3D12_COMPARISON_FUNC enumerated type to define the stencil test comparison function.

```
typedef
enum D3D12_STENCIL_OP
{
   D3D12_STENCIL_OP_KEEP       = 1,
   D3D12_STENCIL_OP_ZERO       = 2,
   D3D12_STENCIL_OP_REPLACE    = 3,
   D3D12_STENCIL_OP_INCR_SAT   = 4,
   D3D12_STENCIL_OP_DECR_SAT   = 5,
   D3D12_STENCIL_OP_INVERT     = 6,
   D3D12_STENCIL_OP_INCR       = 7,
   D3D12_STENCIL_OP_DECR       = 8
} D3D12_STENCIL_OP;
```

1. **D3D12_STENCIL_OP_KEEP**: Specifies to not change the stencil buffer; that is, keep the value currently there.

2. `D3D12_STENCIL_OP_ZERO`: Specifies to set the stencil buffer entry to zero.
3. `D3D12_STENCIL_OP_REPLACE`: Specifies to replaces the stencil buffer entry with the stencil-reference value (`StencilRef`) used in the stencil test. Note that the `StencilRef` value is set when we bind the depth/stencil state block to the rendering pipeline (§11.3.3).
4. `D3D12_STENCIL_OP_INCR_SAT`: Specifies to increment the stencil buffer entry. If the incremented value exceeds the maximum value (e.g., 255 for an 8-bit stencil buffer), then we clamp the entry to that maximum.
5. `D3D12_STENCIL_OP_DECR_SAT`: Specifies to decrement the stencil buffer entry. If the decremented value is less than zero, then we clamp the entry to zero.
6. `D3D12_STENCIL_OP_INVERT`: Specifies to invert the bits of the stencil buffer entry.
7. `D3D12_STENCIL_OP_INCR`: Specifies to increment the stencil buffer entry. If the incremented value exceeds the maximum value (e.g., 255 for an 8-bit stencil buffer), then we wrap to 0.
8. `D3D12_STENCIL_OP_DECR`: Specifies to decrement the stencil buffer entry. If the decremented values is less than zero, then we wrap to the maximum allowed value.

Observe that the stenciling behavior for front facing and back facing triangles can be different. The `BackFace` *settings are irrelevant in the case that we do not render back facing polygons due to back face culling. However, sometimes we do need to render back facing polygons for certain graphics algorithms, or for transparent geometry (like the wire fence box, where we could see through the box to see the back sides). In these cases, the* `BackFace` *settings are relevant.*

11.3.3 Creating and Binding a Depth/Stencil State

Once we have fully filled out a `D3D12_DEPTH_STENCIL_DESC` instance describing our depth/stencil state, we can assign it to the `D3D12_GRAPHICS_PIPELINE_STATE_DESC::DepthStencilState` field of a PSO. Any geometry drawn with this PSO will be rendered with the depth/stencil settings of the PSO.

One detail we have not mentioned yet is how to set the stencil reference value. The stencil reference value is set with the `ID3D12GraphicsCommandList::OMSetStencilRef` method, which takes a single unsigned integer parameter; for example, the following sets the stencil reference value to 1:

```
mCommandList->OMSetStencilRef(1);
```

11.4 IMPLEMENTING PLANAR MIRRORS

Many surfaces in nature serve as mirrors and allow us to see the reflections of objects. This section describes how we can simulate mirrors for our 3D applications. Note that for simplicity, we reduce the task of implementing mirrors to planar surfaces only. For instance, a shiny car can display a reflection; however, a car's body is smooth, round, and not planar. Instead, we render reflections such as those that are displayed in a shiny marble floor or those that are displayed in a mirror hanging on a wall—in other words, mirrors that lie on a plane.

Implementing mirrors programmatically requires us to solve two problems. First, we must learn how to reflect an object about an arbitrary plane so that we can draw the reflection correctly. Second, we must only display the reflection in a mirror, that is, we must somehow "mark" a surface as a mirror and then, as we are rendering, only draw the reflected object if it is in a mirror. Refer back to Figure 11.1, which first introduced this concept.

The first problem is easily solved with some analytical geometry, and is discussed in Appendix C. The second problem can be solved using the stencil buffer.

11.4.1 Mirror Overview

When we draw the reflection, we also need to reflect the light source across the mirror plane. Otherwise, the lighting in the reflection would not be accurate.

Figure 11.2 shows that to draw a reflection of an object, we just need to reflect it over the mirror plane. However, this introduces the problem shown in Figure 11.1. Namely, the reflection of the object (the skull in this case) is just another object in our scene, and if nothing is occluding it, then the eye will see it. However, the reflection should only be seen through the mirror. We can solve this problem

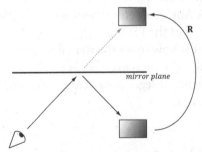

Figure 11.2. The eye sees the box reflection through the mirror. To simulate this, we reflect the box across the mirror plane and render the reflected box as usual.

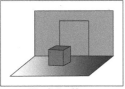
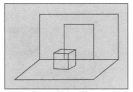

Back buffer   **Stencil buffer**

Figure 11.3. The floor, walls, and skull to the back buffer and the stencil buffer cleared to 0 (denoted by light gray color). The black outlines drawn on the stencil buffer illustrate the relationship between the back buffer pixels and the stencil buffer pixels—they do not indicate any data drawn on the stencil buffer.

using the stencil buffer because the stencil buffer allows us to block rendering to certain areas on the back buffer. Thus we can use the stencil buffer to block the rendering of the reflected skull if it is not being rendered into the mirror. The following outlines the step of how this can be accomplished:

1. Render the floor, walls, and skull to the back buffer as normal (but not the mirror). Note that this step does not modify the stencil buffer.
2. Clear the stencil buffer to 0. Figure 11.3 shows the back buffer and stencil buffer at this point (where we substitute a box for the skull to make the drawing simpler).
3. Render the mirror only to the stencil buffer. We can disable color writes to the back buffer by creating a blend state that sets

   ```
   D3D12_RENDER_TARGET_BLEND_DESC::RenderTargetWriteMask = 0;
   ```

   and we can disable writes to the depth buffer by setting

   ```
   D3D12_DEPTH_STENCIL_DESC::DepthWriteMask = D3D12_DEPTH_WRITE_MASK_ZERO;
   ```

   When rendering the mirror to the stencil buffer, we set the stencil test to always succeed (D3D12_COMPARISON_ALWAYS) and specify that the stencil buffer entry should be replaced (D3D12_STENCIL_OP_REPLACE) with 1 (StencilRef) if the test passes. If the depth test fails, we specify D3D12_STENCIL_OP_KEEP so that the stencil buffer is not changed if the depth test fails (this can happen, for example, if the skull obscures part of the mirror). Since we are only rendering the mirror to the stencil buffer, it follows that all the pixels in the stencil buffer will be 0 except for the pixels that correspond to the visible part of the mirror—they will have a 1. Figure 11.4 shows the updated stencil buffer. Essentially, we are marking the visible pixels of the mirror in the stencil buffer.

It is important to draw the mirror to the stencil buffer after we have drawn the skull so that pixels of the mirror occluded by the skull fail the depth test, and thus do not modify the stencil buffer. We do not want to turn on parts of the stencil buffer that are occluded; otherwise the reflection will show through the skull.

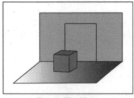
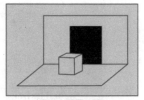

Back Buffer   **Stencil Buffer**

Figure 11.4: Rendering the mirror to the stencil buffer, essentially marking the pixels in the stencil buffer that correspond to the visible parts of the mirror. The solid black area on the stencil buffer denotes stencil entries set to 1. Note that the area on the stencil buffer occluded by the box does not get set to 1 since it fails the depth test (the box is in front of that part of the mirror).

4. Now we render the reflected skull to the back buffer and stencil buffer. But recall that we only will render to the back buffer if the stencil test passes. This time, we set the stencil test to only succeed if the value in the stencil buffer equals 1; this is done using a `StencilRef` of 1, and the stencil operator `D3D12_COMPARISON_EQUAL`. In this way, the reflected skull will only be rendered to areas that have a 1 in their corresponding stencil buffer entry. Since the areas in the stencil buffer that correspond to the visible parts of the mirror are the only entries that have a 1, it follows that the reflected skull will only be rendered into the visible parts of the mirror.

5. Finally, we render the mirror to the back buffer as normal. However, in order for the skull reflection to show through (which lies behind the mirror), we need to render the mirror with transparency blending. If we did not render the mirror with transparency, the mirror would simply occlude the reflection since its depth is less than that of the reflection. To implement this, we simply need to define a new material instance for the mirror; we set the alpha channel of the diffuse component to 0.3 to make the mirror 30% opaque, and we render the mirror with the transparency blend state as described in the last chapter (§10.5.4).

```
auto icemirror = std::make_unique<Material>();
icemirror->Name = "icemirror";
icemirror->MatCBIndex = 2;
icemirror->DiffuseSrvHeapIndex = 2;
icemirror->DiffuseAlbedo = XMFLOAT4(1.0f, 1.0f, 1.0f, 0.3f);
icemirror->FresnelR0 = XMFLOAT3(0.1f, 0.1f, 0.1f);
icemirror->Roughness = 0.5f;
```

These settings give the following blending equation:

$$\mathbf{C} = 0.3 \cdot \mathbf{C}_{src} + 0.7 \cdot \mathbf{C}_{dst}$$

Assuming we have laid down the reflected skull pixels to the back buffer, we see 30% of the color comes from the mirror (source) and 70% of the color comes from the skull (destination).

11.4.2 Defining the Mirror Depth/Stencil States

To implement the previously described algorithm, we need two PSOs. The first is used when drawing the mirror to mark the mirror pixels on the stencil buffer. The second is used to draw the reflected skull so that it is only drawn into the visible parts of the mirror.

```
//
// PSO for marking stencil mirrors.
//

// Turn off render target writes.
CD3DX12_BLEND_DESC mirrorBlendState(D3D12_DEFAULT);
mirrorBlendState.RenderTarget[0].RenderTargetWriteMask = 0;

D3D12_DEPTH_STENCIL_DESC mirrorDSS;
mirrorDSS.DepthEnable = true;
mirrorDSS.DepthWriteMask = D3D12_DEPTH_WRITE_MASK_ZERO;
mirrorDSS.DepthFunc = D3D12_COMPARISON_FUNC_LESS;
mirrorDSS.StencilEnable = true;
mirrorDSS.StencilReadMask = 0xff;
mirrorDSS.StencilWriteMask = 0xff;

mirrorDSS.FrontFace.StencilFailOp = D3D12_STENCIL_OP_KEEP;
mirrorDSS.FrontFace.StencilDepthFailOp = D3D12_STENCIL_OP_KEEP;
mirrorDSS.FrontFace.StencilPassOp = D3D12_STENCIL_OP_REPLACE;
mirrorDSS.FrontFace.StencilFunc = D3D12_COMPARISON_FUNC_ALWAYS;

// We are not rendering backfacing polygons, so these settings do not
// matter.
mirrorDSS.BackFace.StencilFailOp = D3D12_STENCIL_OP_KEEP;
mirrorDSS.BackFace.StencilDepthFailOp = D3D12_STENCIL_OP_KEEP;
mirrorDSS.BackFace.StencilPassOp = D3D12_STENCIL_OP_REPLACE;
mirrorDSS.BackFace.StencilFunc = D3D12_COMPARISON_FUNC_ALWAYS;

D3D12_GRAPHICS_PIPELINE_STATE_DESC markMirrorsPsoDesc = opaquePsoDesc;
markMirrorsPsoDesc.BlendState = mirrorBlendState;
markMirrorsPsoDesc.DepthStencilState = mirrorDSS;
ThrowIfFailed(md3dDevice->CreateGraphicsPipelineState(
    &markMirrorsPsoDesc,
    IID_PPV_ARGS(&mPSOs["markStencilMirrors"])));

//
// PSO for stencil reflections.
//

D3D12_DEPTH_STENCIL_DESC reflectionsDSS;
reflectionsDSS.DepthEnable = true;
reflectionsDSS.DepthWriteMask = D3D12_DEPTH_WRITE_MASK_ALL;
reflectionsDSS.DepthFunc = D3D12_COMPARISON_FUNC_LESS;
reflectionsDSS.StencilEnable = true;
reflectionsDSS.StencilReadMask = 0xff;
reflectionsDSS.StencilWriteMask = 0xff;
```

```cpp
reflectionsDSS.FrontFace.StencilFailOp = D3D12_STENCIL_OP_KEEP;
reflectionsDSS.FrontFace.StencilDepthFailOp = D3D12_STENCIL_OP_KEEP;
reflectionsDSS.FrontFace.StencilPassOp = D3D12_STENCIL_OP_KEEP;
reflectionsDSS.FrontFace.StencilFunc = D3D12_COMPARISON_FUNC_EQUAL;

// We are not rendering backfacing polygons, so these settings do not
// matter.
reflectionsDSS.BackFace.StencilFailOp = D3D12_STENCIL_OP_KEEP;
reflectionsDSS.BackFace.StencilDepthFailOp = D3D12_STENCIL_OP_KEEP;
reflectionsDSS.BackFace.StencilPassOp = D3D12_STENCIL_OP_KEEP;
reflectionsDSS.BackFace.StencilFunc = D3D12_COMPARISON_FUNC_EQUAL;

D3D12_GRAPHICS_PIPELINE_STATE_DESC drawReflectionsPsoDesc =
    opaquePsoDesc;
drawReflectionsPsoDesc.DepthStencilState = reflectionsDSS;
drawReflectionsPsoDesc.RasterizerState.CullMode = D3D12_CULL_MODE_BACK;
drawReflectionsPsoDesc.RasterizerState.FrontCounterClockwise = true;
ThrowIfFailed(md3dDevice->CreateGraphicsPipelineState(
  &drawReflectionsPsoDesc,
  IID_PPV_ARGS(&mPSOs["drawStencilReflections"])));
```

11.4.3 Drawing the Scene

The following code outlines our draw method. We have omitted irrelevant details, such as setting constant buffer values, for brevity and clarity (see the example code for the full details).

```cpp
// Draw opaque items--floors, walls, skull.
auto passCB = mCurrFrameResource->PassCB->Resource();
mCommandList->SetGraphicsRootConstantBufferView(2,
  passCB->GetGPUVirtualAddress());
DrawRenderItems(mCommandList.Get(), mRitemLayer[(int)
    RenderLayer::Opaque]);

// Mark the visible mirror pixels in the stencil buffer with the value 1
mCommandList->OMSetStencilRef(1);
mCommandList->SetPipelineState(mPSOs["markStencilMirrors"].Get());
DrawRenderItems(mCommandList.Get(), mRitemLayer[(int)
    RenderLayer::Mirrors]);

// Draw the reflection into the mirror only (only for pixels where the
// stencil buffer is 1).
// Note that we must supply a different per-pass constant buffer--one
// with the lights reflected.
mCommandList->SetGraphicsRootConstantBufferView(2,
  passCB->GetGPUVirtualAddress() + 1 * passCBByteSize);
mCommandList->SetPipelineState(mPSOs["drawStencilReflections"].Get());
DrawRenderItems(mCommandList.Get(), mRitemLayer[(int)
    RenderLayer::Reflected]);

// Restore main pass constants and stencil ref.
mCommandList->SetGraphicsRootConstantBufferView(2,
  passCB->GetGPUVirtualAddress());
```

```
mCommandList->OMSetStencilRef(0);

// Draw mirror with transparency so reflection blends through.
mCommandList->SetPipelineState(mPSOs["transparent"].Get());
DrawRenderItems(mCommandList.Get(), mRitemLayer[(int)
RenderLayer::Transparent]);
```

One point to note in the above code is how we change the per-pass constant buffer when drawing the `RenderLayer::Reflected` layer. This is because the scene lighting also needs to get reflected when drawing the reflection. The lights are stored in a per-pass constant buffer, so we create an additional per-pass constant buffer that stores the reflected scene lighting. The per-pass constant buffer used for drawing reflections is set in the following method:

```
PassConstants StencilApp::mMainPassCB;
PassConstants StencilApp::mReflectedPassCB;
void StencilApp::UpdateReflectedPassCB(const GameTimer& gt)
{
  mReflectedPassCB = mMainPassCB;

  XMVECTOR mirrorPlane = XMVectorSet(0.0f, 0.0f, 1.0f, 0.0f); // xy plane
  XMMATRIX R = XMMatrixReflect(mirrorPlane);

  // Reflect the lighting.
  for(int i = 0; i < 3; ++i)
  {
    XMVECTOR lightDir = XMLoadFloat3(&mMainPassCB.Lights[i].Direction);
    XMVECTOR reflectedLightDir = XMVector3TransformNormal(lightDir, R);
    XMStoreFloat3(&mReflectedPassCB.Lights[i].Direction,
      reflectedLightDir);
  }

  // Reflected pass stored in index 1
  auto currPassCB = mCurrFrameResource->PassCB.get();
  currPassCB->CopyData(1, mReflectedPassCB);
}
```

11.4.4 Winding Order and Reflections

When a triangle is reflected across a plane, its winding order does not reverse, and thus, its face normal does not reverse. Hence, outward facing normals become inward facing normals (see Figure 11.5), after reflection. To correct this, we tell Direct3D to interpret triangles with a counterclockwise winding order as front-facing and triangles with a clockwise winding order as back-facing (this is the opposite of our usual convention—§5.10.2). This effectively reflects the normal directions so that they are outward facing after reflection. We reverse the winding order convention by setting the following rasterizer properties in the PSO:

```
drawReflectionsPsoDesc.RasterizerState.FrontCounterClockwise = true;
```

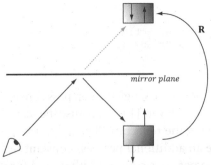

Figure 11.5. The polygon normals do not get reversed with reflection, which makes them inward facing after reflection.

11.5 IMPLEMENTING PLANAR SHADOWS

Portions of this section appeared in the book by Frank D. Luna, Introduction to 3D Game Programming with DirectX 9.0c: A Shader Approach, *2006:* Jones and Bartlett Learning, Burlington, MA. www.jblearning.com. Reprinted with permission.

Shadows aid in our perception of where light is being emitted in a scene and ultimately makes the scene more realistic. In this section, we will show how to implement planar shadows; that is, shadows that lie on a plane (see Figure 11.6).

To implement planar shadows, we must first find the shadow an object casts to a plane and model it geometrically so that we can render it. This can easily be done with some 3D math. We then render the triangles that describe the shadow with a black material at 50% transparency. Rendering the shadow like this can introduce some rendering artifacts called "double blending," which we explain in a few sections; we utilize the stencil buffer to prevent double blending from occurring.

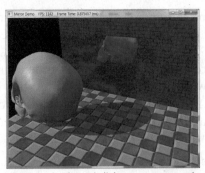

Figure 11.6. The main light source casts a planar shadow in the "Mirror" demo.

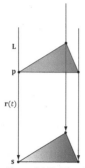

Figure 11.7. The shadow cast with respect to a parallel light source.

11.5.1 Parallel Light Shadows

Figure 11.7 shows the shadow an object casts with respect to a parallel light source. Given a parallel light source with direction **L**, the light ray that passes through a vertex **p** is given by $\mathbf{r}(t) = \mathbf{p} + t\mathbf{L}$. The intersection of the ray $r(t)$ with the shadow plane $(\mathbf{n}, d)$ gives **s**. (The reader can read more about rays and planes in Appendix C.) The set of intersection points found by shooting a ray through each of the object's vertices with the plane defines the projected geometry of the shadow. For a vertex **p**, its shadow projection is given by

$$\mathbf{s} = \mathbf{r}(t_s) = \mathbf{p} - \frac{\mathbf{n} \cdot \mathbf{p} + d}{\mathbf{n} \cdot \mathbf{L}} \mathbf{L} \qquad \text{(eq. 11.1)}$$

The details of the ray/plane intersection test are given in Appendix C.

Equation 11.1 can be written in terms of matrices.

$$\mathbf{s}' = \begin{bmatrix} p_x & p_y & p_z & 1 \end{bmatrix} \begin{bmatrix} \mathbf{n} \cdot \mathbf{L} - L_x n_x & -L_y n_x & -L_z n_x & 0 \\ -L_x n_y & \mathbf{n} \cdot \mathbf{L} - L_y n_y & -L_z n_y & 0 \\ -L_x n_z & -L_y n_z & \mathbf{n} \cdot \mathbf{L} - L_z n_z & 0 \\ -L_x d & -L_y d & -L_z d & \mathbf{n} \cdot \mathbf{L} \end{bmatrix}$$

We call the preceding 4 × 4 matrix the directional shadow matrix and denote it by $\mathbf{S}_{dir}$. To see how this matrix is equivalent to Equation 11.1, we just need to perform the multiplication. First, however, observe that this equation modifies the w-component so that $s_w = \mathbf{n} \cdot \mathbf{L}$. Thus, when the perspective divide (§5.6.3.4) takes place, each coordinate of **s** will be divided by $\mathbf{n} \cdot \mathbf{L}$; this is how we get the division by $\mathbf{n} \cdot \mathbf{L}$ in Equation 11.1 using matrices. Now doing the matrix multiplication to obtain the ith coordinate s'_i for $i \in \{1, 2, 3\}$, followed by the perspective divide we obtain:

$$s_i' = \frac{(\mathbf{n}\cdot\mathbf{L})p_i - L_i n_x p_x - L_i n_y p_y - L_i n_z p_z - L_i d}{\mathbf{n}\cdot\mathbf{L}}$$

$$= \frac{(\mathbf{n}\cdot\mathbf{L})p_i - (\mathbf{n}\cdot\mathbf{p}+d)L_i}{\mathbf{n}\cdot\mathbf{L}}$$

$$= p_i - \frac{\mathbf{n}\cdot\mathbf{p}+d}{\mathbf{n}\cdot\mathbf{L}}L_i$$

This is exactly the ith coordinate of $\mathbf{s}$ in Equation 11.1, so $\mathbf{s}=\mathbf{s}'$.

To use the shadow matrix, we combine it with our world matrix. However, after the world transform, the geometry has not really been projected on to the shadow plane yet because the perspective divide has not occurred yet. A problem arises if $s_w = \mathbf{n}\cdot\mathbf{L} < 0$. because this makes the w-coordinate negative. Usually in the perspective projection process we copy the z-coordinate into the w-coordinate, and a negative w-coordinate would mean the point is not in the view volume and thus is clipped away (clipping is done in homogeneous space before the divide). This is a problem for planar shadows because we are now using the w-coordinate to implement shadows, in addition to the perspective divide. Figure 11.8 shows a valid situation where $\mathbf{n}\cdot\mathbf{L} < 0$, but the shadow will not show up.

To fix this, instead of using the light ray direction $\mathbf{L}$, we should use the vector towards the infinitely far away light source $\tilde{\mathbf{L}} = -\mathbf{L}$. Observe that $\mathbf{r}(t) = \mathbf{p} + t\mathbf{L}$ and $\mathbf{r}(t) = \mathbf{p} + t\tilde{\mathbf{L}}$ define the same 3D line, and the intersection point between the line and the plane will be the same (the intersection parameter t_s will be different to compensate for the sign difference between $\tilde{\mathbf{L}}$ and $\mathbf{L}$). So using $\tilde{\mathbf{L}} = -\mathbf{L}$ gives us the same answer, but with $\mathbf{n}\cdot\mathbf{L} > 0$, which avoids the negative w-coordinate.

11.5.2 Point Light Shadows

Figure 11.9 shows the shadow an object casts with respect to a point light source whose position is described by the point $\mathbf{L}$. The light ray from a point light through

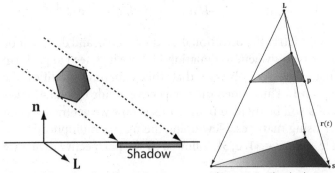

Figure 11.8. A situation where $\mathbf{n}\cdot\mathbf{L} < 0$.

Figure 11.9. The shadow cast with respect to a point light source.

any vertex **p** is given by $\mathbf{r}(t) = \mathbf{p} + t(\mathbf{p} - \mathbf{L})$. The intersection of the ray $\mathbf{r}(t)$ with the shadow plane $(\mathbf{n}, d)$ gives **s**. The set of intersection points found by shooting a ray through each of the object's vertices with the plane defines the projected geometry of the shadow. For a vertex **p**, its shadow projection is given by

$$\mathbf{s} = \mathbf{r}(t_s) = \mathbf{p} - \frac{\mathbf{n} \cdot \mathbf{p} + d}{\mathbf{n} \cdot (\mathbf{p} - \mathbf{L})}(\mathbf{p} - \mathbf{L}) \qquad \text{(eq. 11.2)}$$

Equation 11.2 can also be written by a matrix equation:

$$\mathbf{S}_{point} = \begin{bmatrix} \mathbf{n} \cdot \mathbf{L} + d - L_x n_x & -L_y n_x & -L_z n_x & -n_x \\ -L_x n_y & \mathbf{n} \cdot \mathbf{L} + d - L_y n_y & -L_z n_y & -n_y \\ -L_x n_z & -L_y n_z & \mathbf{n} \cdot \mathbf{L} + d - L_z n_z & -n_z \\ -L_x d & -L_y d & -L_z d & \mathbf{n} \cdot \mathbf{L} \end{bmatrix}$$

To see how this matrix is equivalent to Equation 11.2, we just need to perform the multiplication the same way we did in the previous section. Note that the last column has no zeros and gives:

$$s_w = -p_x n_x - p_y n_y - p_z n_z + \mathbf{n} \cdot \mathbf{L}$$
$$= -\mathbf{p} \cdot \mathbf{n} + \mathbf{n} \cdot \mathbf{L}$$
$$= -\mathbf{n} \cdot (\mathbf{p} - \mathbf{L})$$

This is the negative of the denominator in Equation 11.2, but we can negate the denominator if we also negate the numerator.

*Notice that **L** serves different purposes for point and parallel lights. For point lights we use **L** to define the position of the point light. For parallel lights we use **L** to define the direction towards the infinitely far away light source (i.e., the opposite direction the parallel light rays travel).*

11.5.3 General Shadow Matrix

Using homogeneous coordinates, it is possible to create a general shadow matrix that works for both point and directional lights.

1. If $L_w = 0$ then **L** describes the direction towards the infinitely far away light source (i.e., the opposite direction the parallel light rays travel).
2. If $L_w = 1$ then **L** describes the location of the point light.

Then we represent the transformation from a vertex p to its projection s with the following *shadow matrix:*

$$S = \begin{bmatrix} \mathbf{n} \cdot \mathbf{L} + dL_w - L_x n_x & -L_y n_x & -L_z n_x & -L_w n_x \\ -L_x n_y & \mathbf{n} \cdot \mathbf{L} + dL_w - L_y n_y & -L_z n_y & -L_w n_y \\ -L_x n_z & -L_y n_z & \mathbf{n} \cdot \mathbf{L} + dL_w - L_z n_z & -L_w n_z \\ -L_x d & -L_y d & -L_z d & \mathbf{n} \cdot \mathbf{L} \end{bmatrix}$$

It is easy to see that S reduced to S_{dir} if $L_w = 0$ and S reduces to S_{point} for $L_w = 0$.

The DirectX math library provides the following function to build the shadow matrix given the plane we wish to project the shadow into and a vector describing a parallel light if $w = 0$ or a point light if $w = 1$:

```
inline XMMATRIX XM_CALLCONV XMMatrixShadow(
    FXMVECTOR ShadowPlane,
    FXMVECTOR LightPosition);
```

For further reading, both [Blinn96] and [Möller02] discuss planar shadows.

11.5.4 Using the Stencil Buffer to Prevent Double Blending

When we flatten out the geometry of an object onto the plane to describe its shadow, it is possible (and in fact likely) that two or more of the flattened triangles will overlap. When we render the shadow with transparency (using blending), these areas that have overlapping triangles will get blended multiple times and thus appear darker. Figure 11.10 shows this.

We can solve this problem using the stencil buffer.

1. Assume the stencil buffer pixels where the shadow will be rendered have been cleared to 0. This is true in our mirror demo because we are only casting a shadow onto the ground plane, and we only modified the mirror stencil buffer pixels.

2. Set the stencil test to only accept pixels if the stencil buffer has an entry of 0. If the stencil test passes, then we increment the stencil buffer value to 1.

The first time we render a shadow pixel, the stencil test will pass because the stencil buffer entry is 0. However, when we render this pixel, we also increment

Figure 11.10. Notice the darker "acne" areas of the shadow in the left image; these correspond to areas where parts of the flattened skull overlapped, thus causing a "double blend." The image on the right shows the shadow rendered correctly, without double blending.

the corresponding stencil buffer entry to 1. Thus, if we attempt to *overwrite to an area that has already been rendered to (marked in the stencil buffer with a value of 1), the stencil test will fail.* This prevents drawing over the same pixel more than once, and thus prevents double blending.

11.5.5 Shadow Code

We define a shadow material used to color the shadow that is just a 50% transparent black material:

```
auto shadowMat = std::make_unique<Material>();
shadowMat->Name = "shadowMat";
shadowMat->MatCBIndex = 4;
shadowMat->DiffuseSrvHeapIndex = 3;
shadowMat->DiffuseAlbedo = XMFLOAT4(0.0f, 0.0f, 0.0f, 0.5f);
shadowMat->FresnelR0 = XMFLOAT3(0.001f, 0.001f, 0.001f);
shadowMat->Roughness = 0.0f;
```

In order to prevent double blending we set up the following PSO with depth/stencil state:

```
// We are going to draw shadows with transparency, so base it off
// the transparency description.
D3D12_DEPTH_STENCIL_DESC shadowDSS;
shadowDSS.DepthEnable = true;
shadowDSS.DepthWriteMask = D3D12_DEPTH_WRITE_MASK_ALL;
shadowDSS.DepthFunc = D3D12_COMPARISON_FUNC_LESS;
shadowDSS.StencilEnable = true;
shadowDSS.StencilReadMask = 0xff;
shadowDSS.StencilWriteMask = 0xff;

shadowDSS.FrontFace.StencilFailOp = D3D12_STENCIL_OP_KEEP;
shadowDSS.FrontFace.StencilDepthFailOp = D3D12_STENCIL_OP_KEEP;
shadowDSS.FrontFace.StencilPassOp = D3D12_STENCIL_OP_INCR;
shadowDSS.FrontFace.StencilFunc = D3D12_COMPARISON_FUNC_EQUAL;

// We are not rendering backfacing polygons, so these settings do not
// matter.
shadowDSS.BackFace.StencilFailOp = D3D12_STENCIL_OP_KEEP;
shadowDSS.BackFace.StencilDepthFailOp = D3D12_STENCIL_OP_KEEP;
shadowDSS.BackFace.StencilPassOp = D3D12_STENCIL_OP_INCR;
shadowDSS.BackFace.StencilFunc = D3D12_COMPARISON_FUNC_EQUAL;

D3D12_GRAPHICS_PIPELINE_STATE_DESC shadowPsoDesc = transparentPsoDesc;
shadowPsoDesc.DepthStencilState = shadowDSS;
ThrowIfFailed(md3dDevice->CreateGraphicsPipelineState(
    &shadowPsoDesc,
    IID_PPV_ARGS(&mPSOs["shadow"])));
```

We then draw the skull shadow with the shadow PSO with a `StencilRef` value of 0:

```
// Draw shadows
```

```
mCommandList->OMSetStencilRef(0);
mCommandList->SetPipelineState(mPSOs["shadow"].Get());
DrawRenderItems(mCommandList.Get(), mRitemLayer[(int)
    RenderLayer::Shadow]);
```

where the skull shadow render-item's world matrix is computed like so:

```
// Update shadow world matrix.
XMVECTOR shadowPlane = XMVectorSet(0.0f, 1.0f, 0.0f, 0.0f); // xz plane
XMVECTOR toMainLight = -XMLoadFloat3(&mMainPassCB.Lights[0].Direction);
XMMATRIX S = XMMatrixShadow(shadowPlane, toMainLight);
XMMATRIX shadowOffsetY = XMMatrixTranslation(0.0f, 0.001f, 0.0f);
XMStoreFloat4x4(&mShadowedSkullRitem->World, skullWorld * S * shadowOffsetY);
```

Note that we offset the projected shadow mesh along the y-axis by a small amount to prevent z-fighting so the shadow mesh does not intersect the floor mesh, but lies slightly above it. If the meshes did intersect, then due to limited precision of the depth buffer, we would see flickering artifacts as the floor and shadow mesh pixels compete to be visible.

11.6 SUMMARY

1. The stencil buffer is an off-screen buffer we can use to block the rendering of certain pixel fragments to the back buffer. The stencil buffer is shared with the depth buffer and thus has the same resolution as the depth buffer. Valid depth/stencil buffer formats are `DXGI_FORMAT_D32_FLOAT_S8X24_UINT` and `DXGI_FORMAT_D24_UNORM_S8_UINT`.

2. The decision to block a particular pixel from being written is decided by the stencil test, which is given by the following:

   ```
   if( StencilRef & StencilReadMask ⊴ Value & StencilReadMask )
     accept pixel
   else
     reject pixel
   ```

   where the ⊴ operator is any one of the functions defined in the `D3D12_COMPARISON_FUNC` enumerated type. The `StencilRef`, `StencilReadMask`, `StencilReadMask`, and comparison operator ⊴ are all application-defined quantities set with the Direct3D depth/stencil API. The Value quantity is the current value in the stencil buffer.

3. The depth/stencil state is part of a PSO description. Specifically, the depth/stencil state is configured by filling out the `D3D12_GRAPHICS_PIPELINE_STATE_DESC::DepthStencilState` field, where `DepthStencilState` is of type `D3D12_DEPTH_STENCIL_DESC`.

4. The stencil reference value is set with the ID3D12GraphicsCommandList::OMSetStencilRef method, which takes a single unsigned integer parameter specifying the stencil reference value.

11.7 EXERCISES

1. Prove that the general shadow matrix **S** reduced to $\mathbf{S}_{dir}$ if $L_w = 0$ and **S** reduces to $\mathbf{S}_{point}$ for $L_w = 1$.
2. Prove that $\mathbf{s} = \mathbf{p} - \dfrac{\mathbf{n} \cdot \mathbf{p} + d}{\mathbf{n} \cdot (\mathbf{p} - \mathbf{L})}(\mathbf{p} - \mathbf{L}) = \mathbf{p}\mathbf{S}_{point}$ by doing the matrix multiplication for each component, as was done in §11.5.1 for directional lights.
3. Modify the "Mirror" demo to produce the "Left" image in Figure 11.1.
4. Modify the "Mirror" demo to produce the "Left" image in Figure 11.10.
5. Modify the "Mirror" demo in the following way. First draw a wall with the following depth settings:

```
depthStencilDesc.DepthEnable    = false;
depthStencilDesc.DepthWriteMask = D3D12_DEPTH_WRITE_MASK_ALL;
depthStencilDesc.DepthFunc      = D3D12_COMPARISON_LESS;
```

Next, draw the skull behind the wall with the depth settings:

```
depthStencilDesc.DepthEnable    = true;
depthStencilDesc.DepthWriteMask = D3D12_DEPTH_WRITE_MASK_ALL;
depthStencilDesc.DepthFunc      = D3D12_COMPARISON_LESS;
```

Does the wall occlude the skull? Explain. What happens if you use the following to draw the wall instead?

```
depthStencilDesc.DepthEnable    = true;
depthStencilDesc.DepthWriteMask = D3D12_DEPTH_WRITE_MASK_ALL;
depthStencilDesc.DepthFunc      = D3D12_COMPARISON_LESS;
```

Note that this exercise does not use the stencil buffer, so that should be disabled.

6. Modify the "Mirror" demo by not reversing the triangle winding order convention. Does the reflected teapot render correctly?
7. Modify the "Blend" demo from Chapter 10 to draw a cylinder (with no caps) at the center of the scene. Texture the cylinder with the 60 frame animated electric bolt animation found in this chapter's directory using additive blending. Figure 11.11 shows an example of the output.

Refer back to §10.5.5 for the depth states to use when rendering additive blending geometry.

Figure 11.11. Sample screenshot of the solution to Exercise 7.

8. *Depth complexity* refers to the number of pixel fragments that compete, via the depth test, to be written to a particular entry in the back buffer. For example, a pixel we have drawn may be overwritten by a pixel that is closer to the camera (and this can happen several times before the closest pixel is actually figured out once the entire scene has been drawn). The pixel in Figure 11.12 has a depth complexity of 3 since three pixel fragments compete for the pixel.

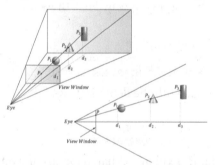

Figure 11.12. Multiple pixel fragments competing to be rendering to a single pixel on the projection window. In this scene, the pixel P has a depth complexity of 3.

Potentially, the graphics card could fill a pixel several times each frame. This *overdraw* has performance implications, as the graphics card is wasting time processing pixels that eventually get overridden and are never seen. Consequently, it is useful to measure the depth complexity in a scene for performance analysis.

We can measure the depth complexity as follows: Render the scene and use the stencil buffer as a counter; that is, each pixel in the stencil buffer is originally cleared to zero, and every time a pixel fragment is processed, we increment its count with `D3D12_STENCIL_OP_INCR`. The corresponding stencil buffer entry should always be incremented for every pixel fragment no matter what, so use the stencil comparison function `D3D12_COMPARISON_ALWAYS`. Then, for example, after the frame has been drawn, if the *ij*th pixel has a corresponding entry of five in the stencil buffer, then we know that that five pixel fragments were processed for that pixel during that frame (i.e., the pixel has a depth complexity of five). Note that when counting the depth complexity, technically you only need to render the scene to the stencil buffer.

To visualize the depth complexity (stored in the stencil buffer), proceed as follows:

a. Associate a color c_k for each level of depth complexity *k*. For example, blue for a depth complexity of one, green for a depth complexity of two, red for a depth complexity of three, and so on. (In very complex scenes where the depth complexity for a pixel could get very large, you probably do not want to associate a color for each level. Instead, you could associate a color for a range of disjoint levels. For example, pixels with depth complexity 1-5 are colored blue, pixels with depth complexity 6-10 are colored green, and so on.)

b. Set the stencil buffer operation to D3D12_STENCIL_OP_KEEP so that we do not modify it anymore. (We modify the stencil buffer with D3D12_STENCIL_OP_INCR when we are counting the depth complexity as the scene is rendered, but when writing the code to visualize the stencil buffer, we only need to *read* from the stencil buffer and we should not *write* to it.)

c. For each level of depth complexity k:

(i) Set the stencil comparison function to D3D12_COMPARISON_EQUAL and set the stencil reference value to *k*.

(ii) draw a quad of color c_k that covers the entire projection window. Note that this will only color the pixels that have a depth complexity of *k* because of the preceding set stencil comparison function and reference value.

With this setup, we have colored each pixel based on its depth complexity uniquely, and so we can easily study the depth complexity of the scene. For this exercise, render the depth complexity of the scene used in the "Blend" demo from Chapter 10. Figure 11.13 shows a sample screenshot.

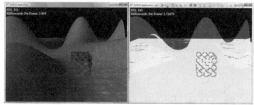

Figure 11.13. Sample screenshot of the solution to Exercise 8.

Note: *The depth test occurs in the output merger stage of the pipeline, which occurs after the pixel shader stage. This means that a pixel fragment is processed through the pixel shader, even if it may ultimately be rejected by the depth test. However, modern hardware does an "early z-test" where the depth test is performed before the pixel shader. This way, a rejected pixel fragment will be discarded before being processed by a potentially expensive pixel shader. To take advantage of this optimization, you should try to render your non-blended game objects in front-to-back order with respect to the camera; in this way, the nearest objects will be drawn first, and objects behind them will fail the early z-test and not be processed further. This can be a significant performance benefit if your scene suffers from lots overdraw due to a high depth complexity. We are not able to control the early z-test through the Direct3D API; the graphics driver is the one that decides if it is possible to perform the early z-test. For example, if a pixel shader modifies the pixel fragment's depth value, then the early z-test is not possible, as the pixel shader must be executed before the depth test since the pixel shader modifies depth values.*

Note: *We mentioned the ability to modify the depth of a pixel in the pixel shader. How does that work? A pixel shader can actually output a structure, not just a single color vector as we have been doing thus far:*

```
struct PixelOut
{
  float4 color : SV_Target;
  float depth : SV_Depth;
};

PixelOut PS(VertexOut pin)
{
  PixelOut pout;

  // ... usual pixel work

  pout.Color = float4(litColor, alpha);

  // set pixel depth in normalized [0, 1] range
  pout.depth = pin.PosH.z - 0.05f;

  return pout;
}
```

The z-coordinate of the `SV_Position` *element (*`pin.PosH.z`*) gives the unmodified pixel depth value. Using the special system value semantic* `SV_Depth`*, the pixel shader can output a modified depth value.*

9. Another way to implement depth complexity visualization is to use additive blending. First clear the back buffer black and disable the depth test. Next, set the source and destination blend factors both to `D3D12_BLEND_ONE`, and the blend operation to `D3D12_BLEND_OP_ADD` so that the blending equation looks like $\mathbf{C} = \mathbf{C}_{src} + \mathbf{C}_{dst}$. Observe that with this formula, for each pixel, we are accumulating the colors of all the pixel fragments written to it. Now render all the objects in the scene with a pixel shader that outputs a low intensity color like (0.05, 0.05, 0.05). The more overdraw a pixel has, the more of these low intensity colors will be summed in, thus increasing the brightness of the pixel. If a pixel was overdrawn ten times, for example, then it will have a color intensity of (0.5, 0.5, 0.5). Thus by looking at the intensity of each pixel after rendering the scene, we obtain an idea of the scene depth complexity. Implement this version of depth complexity measurement using the "Blend" demo from Chapter 10 as a test scene.

10. Explain how you can count the number of pixels that pass the depth test. Explain how you can count the number of pixels that fail the depth test?

11. Modify the "Mirror" demo to reflect the floor into the mirror in addition to the skull.

12. Remove the vertical offset from the world matrix of the shadow render-item so that you can see z-fighting.

Chapter 12　THE GEOMETRY SHADER

Assuming we are not using the tessellation stages, the geometry shader stage is an optional stage that sits between the vertex and pixel shader stages. While the vertex shader inputs vertices, the geometry shader inputs entire primitives. For example, if we were drawing triangle lists, then conceptually the geometry shader program would be executed for each triangle T in the list:

```
for(UINT i = 0; i < numTriangles; ++i)
    OutputPrimitiveList = GeometryShader( T[i].vertexList );
```

Notice the three vertices of each triangle are input into the geometry shader, and the geometry shader outputs a list of primitives. Unlike vertex shaders which cannot destroy or create vertices, the main advantage of the geometry shader is that it can create or destroy geometry; this enables some interesting effects to be implemented on the GPU. For example, the input primitive can be expanded into one or more other primitives, or the geometry shader can choose not to output a primitive based on some condition. Note that the output primitives need not be the same type as the input primitive; for instance, a common application of the geometry shader is to expand a point into a quad (two triangles).

The primitives output from the geometry shader are defined by a vertex list. Vertex positions leaving the geometry shader must be transformed to homogeneous clip space. After the geometry shader stage, we have a list of vertices defining primitives in homogeneous clip space. These vertices are projected (homogeneous divide), and then rasterization occurs as usual.

Objectives:

1. To learn how to program geometry shaders.
2. To discover how billboards can be implemented efficiently using the geometry shader.
3. To recognize auto generated primitive IDs and some of their applications.
4. To find out how to create and use texture arrays, and understand why they are useful.
5. To understand how alpha-to-coverage helps with the aliasing problem of alpha cutouts.

12.1 PROGRAMMING GEOMETRY SHADERS

Programming geometry shaders is a lot like programming vertex or pixel shaders, but there are some differences. The following code shows the general form:

```
[maxvertexcount(N)]
void ShaderName (
  PrimitiveType InputVertexType InputName [NumElements],
  inout StreamOutputObject<OutputVertexType> OutputName)
{
    // Geometry shader body...
}
```

We must first specify the maximum number of vertices the geometry shader will output for a single invocation (the geometry shader is invoked per primitive). This is done by setting the max vertex count before the shader definition using the following *attribute* syntax:

```
[maxvertexcount(N)]
```

where N is the maximum number of vertices the geometry shader will output for a single invocation. The number of vertices a geometry shader can output per invocation is variable, but it cannot exceed the defined maximum. For performance purposes, `maxvertexcount` should be as small as possible; [NVIDIA08] states that peak performance of the GS is achieved when the GS outputs between 1-20 scalars, and performance drops to 50% if the GS outputs between 27-40 scalars. The number of scalars output per invocation is the product of `maxvertexcount` *and* the number of scalars in the output vertex type structure. Working with such restrictions is difficult in practice, so we can either accept lower than peak performance as good enough, or choose an alternative implementation that does not use the geometry shader; however, we must also consider that an alternative implementation may have other drawbacks, which can still make the geometry shader implementation a better choice. Furthermore, the recommendations in [NVIDIA08] are from 2008 (first generation geometry shaders), so things should have improved.

The geometry shader takes two parameters: an input parameter and an output parameter. (Actually, it can take more, but that is a special topic; see §12.2.4.) The input parameter is always an array of vertices that define the primitive—one vertex for a point, two for a line, three for a triangle, four for a line with adjacency, and six for a triangle with adjacency. The vertex type of the input vertices is the vertex type returned by the vertex shader (e.g., `VertexOut`). The input parameter must be prefixed by a primitive type, describing the type of primitives being input into the geometry shader. This can be anyone of the following:

1. `point`: The input primitives are points.
2. `line`: The input primitives are lines (lists or strips).
3. `triangle`: The input primitives triangles (lists or strips).
4. `lineadj`: The input primitives are lines with adjacency (lists or strips).
5. `triangleadj`: The input primitives are triangles with adjacency (lists or strips).

The input primitive into a geometry shader is always a complete primitive (e.g., two vertices for a line, and three vertices for a triangle). Thus the geometry shader does not need to distinguish between lists and strips. For example, if you are drawing triangle strips, the geometry shader is still executed for every triangle in the strip, and the three vertices of each triangle are passed into the geometry shader as input. This entails additional overhead, as vertices that are shared by multiple primitives are processed multiple times in the geometry shader.

The output parameter always has the `inout` modifier. Additionally, the output parameter is always a stream type. A stream type stores a list of vertices which defines the geometry the geometry shader is outputting. A geometry shader adds a vertex to the outgoing stream list using the intrinsic `Append` method:

```
void StreamOutputObject<OutputVertexType>::Append(OutputVertexType v);
```

A stream type is a template type, where the template argument is used to specify the vertex type of the outgoing vertices (e.g., `GeoOut`). There are three possible stream types:

1. `PointStream<OutputVertexType>`: A list of vertices defining a point list.
2. `LineStream<OutputVertexType>`: A list of vertices defining a line strip.
3. `TriangleStream<OutputVertexType>`: A list of vertices defining a triangle strip.

The vertices output by a geometry shader form primitives; the type of output primitive is indicated by the stream type (`PointStream`, `LineStream`, `TriangleStream`). For lines and triangles, the output primitive is always a strip. Line and triangle lists, however, can be simulated by using the intrinsic `RestartStrip` method:

```
void StreamOutputObject<OutputVertexType>::RestartStrip();
```

For example, if you wanted to output triangle lists, then you would call `RestartStrip` every time after three vertices were appended to the output stream.

Below are some specific examples of geometry shader signatures:

```
// EXAMPLE 1: GS ouputs at most 4 vertices. The input primitive is a
// line.
// The output is a triangle strip.
//
[maxvertexcount(4)]
void GS(line VertexOut gin[2],
    inout TriangleStream<GeoOut> triStream)
{
    // Geometry shader body...
}
//
// EXAMPLE 2: GS outputs at most 32 vertices. The input primitive is
// a triangle. The output is a triangle strip.
//
[maxvertexcount(32)]
void GS(triangle VertexOut gin[3],
    inout TriangleStream<GeoOut> triStream)
{
    // Geometry shader body...
}
//
// EXAMPLE 3: GS outputs at most 4 vertices. The input primitive
// is a point. The output is a triangle strip.
//
[maxvertexcount(4)]
void GS(point VertexOut gin[1],
    inout TriangleStream<GeoOut> triStream)
{
    // Geometry shader body...
}
```

The following geometry shader illustrates the `Append` and `RestartStrip` methods; it inputs a triangle, subdivides it (Figure 12.1) and outputs the four subdivided triangles:

```
struct VertexOut
{
    float3 PosL    : POSITION;
    float3 NormalL : NORMAL;
    float2 Tex     : TEXCOORD;
};
```

The Geometry Shader

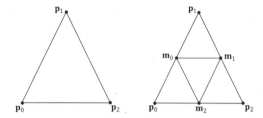

Figure 12.1. Subdividing a triangle into four equally sized triangles. Observe that the three new vertices are the midpoints along the edges of the original triangle.

```
struct GeoOut
{
    float4 PosH    : SV_POSITION;
    float3 PosW    : POSITION;
    float3 NormalW : NORMAL;
    float2 Tex     : TEXCOORD;
    float FogLerp  : FOG;
};

void Subdivide(VertexOut inVerts[3], out VertexOut outVerts[6])
{
    //       1
    //       *
    //      / \
    //     /   \
    //  m0*-----*m1
    //   / \   / \
    //  /   \ /   \
    // *-----*-----*
    // 0     m2    2

    VertexOut m[3];

    // Compute edge midpoints.
    m[0].PosL = 0.5f*(inVerts[0].PosL+inVerts[1].PosL);
    m[1].PosL = 0.5f*(inVerts[1].PosL+inVerts[2].PosL);
    m[2].PosL = 0.5f*(inVerts[2].PosL+inVerts[0].PosL);

    // Project onto unit sphere
    m[0].PosL = normalize(m[0].PosL);
    m[1].PosL = normalize(m[1].PosL);
    m[2].PosL = normalize(m[2].PosL);

    // Derive normals.
    m[0].NormalL = m[0].PosL;
    m[1].NormalL = m[1].PosL;
    m[2].NormalL = m[2].PosL;

    // Interpolate texture coordinates.
    m[0].Tex = 0.5f*(inVerts[0].Tex+inVerts[1].Tex);
    m[1].Tex = 0.5f*(inVerts[1].Tex+inVerts[2].Tex);
    m[2].Tex = 0.5f*(inVerts[2].Tex+inVerts[0].Tex);
```

```
        outVerts[0] = inVerts[0];
        outVerts[1] = m[0];
        outVerts[2] = m[2];
        outVerts[3] = m[1];
        outVerts[4] = inVerts[2];
        outVerts[5] = inVerts[1];
};

void OutputSubdivision(VertexOut v[6],
    inout TriangleStream<GeoOut> triStream)
{
    GeoOut gout[6];

    [unroll]
    for(int i = 0; i < 6; ++i)
    {
        // Transform to world space space.
        gout[i].PosW    = mul(float4(v[i].PosL, 1.0f), gWorld).xyz;
        gout[i].NormalW = mul(v[i].NormalL,
(float3x3)gWorldInvTranspose);

        // Transform to homogeneous clip space.
        gout[i].PosH = mul(float4(v[i].PosL, 1.0f), gWorldViewProj);

        gout[i].Tex     = v[i].Tex;
    }

    //          1
    //          *
    //         / \
    //        /   \
    //    m0*-----*m1
    //     / \   / \
    //    /   \ /   \
    //   *-----*-----*
    //   0     m2    2

    // We can draw the subdivision in two strips:
    //    Strip 1: bottom three triangles
    //    Strip 2: top triangle

    [unroll]
    for(int j = 0; j < 5; ++j)
    {
        triStream.Append(gout[j]);
    }
    triStream.RestartStrip();

    triStream.Append(gout[1]);
    triStream.Append(gout[5]);
    triStream.Append(gout[3]);
}

[maxvertexcount(8)]
```

```
void GS(triangle VertexOut gin[3], inout TriangleStream<GeoOut>)
{
    VertexOut v[6];
    Subdivide(gin, v);
    OutputSubdivision(v, triStream);
}
```

Geometry shaders are compiled very similarly to vertex and pixel shaders. Suppose we have a geometry shader called GS in *TreeSprite.hlsl*, then we would compile the shader to bytecode like so:

```
mShaders["treeSpriteGS"] = d3dUtil::CompileShader(
  L"Shaders\\TreeSprite.hlsl", nullptr, "GS", "gs_5_0");
```

Like vertex and pixel shaders, a given geometry shader is bound to the rendering pipeline as part of a pipeline state object (PSO):

```
D3D12_GRAPHICS_PIPELINE_STATE_DESC treeSpritePsoDesc = opaquePsoDesc;
...
treeSpritePsoDesc.GS =
{
    reinterpret_cast<BYTE*>(mShaders["treeSpriteGS"]-
    >GetBufferPointer()),
    mShaders["treeSpriteGS"]->GetBufferSize()
};
```

Given an input primitive, the geometry shader can choose not to output it based on some condition. In this way, geometry is "destroyed" by the geometry shader, which can be useful for some algorithms.

If you do not output enough vertices to complete a primitive in a geometry shader, then the partial primitive is discarded.

12.2 TREE BILLBOARDS DEMO

12.2.1 Overview

When trees are far away, a *billboarding* technique is used for efficiency. That is, instead of rendering the geometry for a fully 3D tree, a quad with a picture of a 3D tree is painted on it (see Figure 12.2). From a distance, you cannot tell that a billboard is being used. However, the trick is to make sure that the billboard always faces the camera (otherwise the illusion would break).

Assuming the *y*-axis is up and the *xz*-plane is the ground plane, the tree billboards will generally be aligned with the *y*-axis and just face the camera in the *xz*-plane. Figure 12.3 shows the local coordinate systems of several billboards from a bird's eye view—notice that the billboards are "looking" at the camera.

Figure 12.2. A tree billboard texture with alpha channel.

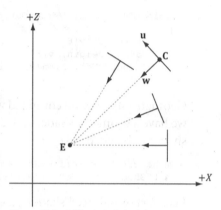

Figure 12.3. Billboards facing the camera.

So given the center position $\mathbf{C} = (C_x, C_y, C_z)$ of a billboard in world space and the position of the camera $\mathbf{E} = (E_x, E_y, E_z)$ in world space, we have enough information to describe the local coordinate system of the billboard relative to the world space:

$$\mathbf{w} = \frac{(E_x - C_x, 0, E_z - C_z)}{\|(E_x - C_x, 0, E_z - C_z)\|}$$

$$\mathbf{v} = (0,1,0)$$

$$\mathbf{u} = \mathbf{v} \times \mathbf{w}$$

Given the local coordinate system of the billboard relative to the world space, and the world size of the billboard, the billboard quad vertices can be obtained as follows (see Figure 12.4):

```
v[0] = float4(gin[0].CenterW - halfWidth*right - halfHeight*up, 1.0f);
v[1] = float4(gin[0].CenterW - halfWidth*right + halfHeight*up, 1.0f);
v[2] = float4(gin[0].CenterW + halfWidth*right - halfHeight*up, 1.0f);
v[3] = float4(gin[0].CenterW + halfWidth*right + halfHeight*up, 1.0f);
```

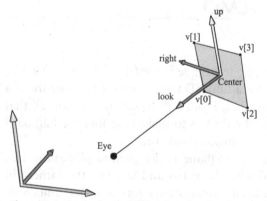

Figure 12.4. Computing the billboard quad vertices from the local coordinate system and world size of the billboard.

Figure 12.5. Screenshot of the tree billboard demo.

Note that the local coordinate system of a billboard differs for each billboard, so it must be computed for each billboard.

For this demo, we will construct a list of point primitives (`D3D12_PRIMITIVE_TOPOLOGY_TYPE_POINT` for the `PrimitiveTopologyType` of the PSO and `D3D_PRIMITIVE_TOPOLOGY_POINTLIST` as the argument for `ID3D12GraphicsCommandList::IASetPrimitiveTopology`) that lie slightly above a land mass. These points represent the centers of the billboards we want to draw. In the geometry shader, we will expand these points into billboard quads. In addition, we will compute the world matrix of the billboard in the geometry shader. Figure 12.5 shows a screenshot of the demo.

As Figure 12.5 shows, this sample builds off the "Blend" demo from Chapter 10.

 A common CPU implementation of billboards would be to use four vertices per billboard in a dynamic vertex buffer (i.e., upload heap). Then every time the camera moved, the vertices would be updated on the CPU and `memcpy`*ed to the GPU buffer so that the billboards face the camera. This approach must submit four vertices per billboard to the IA stage, and requires updating dynamic vertex buffers, which has overhead. With the geometry shader approach, we can use static vertex buffers since the geometry shader does the billboard expansion and makes the billboards face the camera. Moreover, the memory footprint of the billboards is quite small, as we only have to submit one vertex per billboard to the IA stage.*

12.2.2 Vertex Structure

We use the following vertex structure for our billboard points:

```
struct TreeSpriteVertex
{
```

```
    XMFLOAT3 Pos;
    XMFLOAT2 Size;
};

mTreeSpriteInputLayout =
{
    { "POSITION", 0, DXGI_FORMAT_R32G32B32_FLOAT, 0, 0,
      D3D12_INPUT_CLASSIFICATION_PER_VERTEX_DATA, 0 },
    { "SIZE", 0, DXGI_FORMAT_R32G32_FLOAT, 0, 12,
      D3D12_INPUT_CLASSIFICATION_PER_VERTEX_DATA, 0 },
};
```

The vertex stores a point which represents the center position of the billboard in world space. It also includes a size member, which stores the width/height of the billboard (scaled to world space units); this is so the geometry shader knows how large the billboard should be after expansion (Figure 12.6). By having the size vary per vertex, we can easily allow for billboards of different sizes.

Excepting texture arrays (§12.2.4), the other C++ code in the "Tree Billboard" demo should be routine Direct3D code by now (creating vertex buffers, effects, invoking draw methods, etc.). Thus we will now turn our attention to the *TreeSprite.hlsl* file.

12.2.3 The HLSL File

Since this is our first demo with a geometry shader, we will show the entire HLSL file here so that you can see how it fits together with the vertex and pixel shaders. This effect also introduces some new objects that we have not discussed yet (`SV_PrimitiveID` and `Texture2DArray`); these items will be discussed next. For now, mainly focus on the geometry shader program `GS`; this shader expands a point into a quad aligned with the world's *y*-axis that faces the camera, as described in §12.2.1.

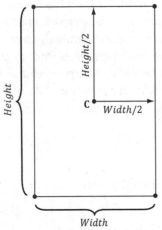

Figure 12.6. Expanding a point into a quad.

```hlsl
//***************************************************************************************
// TreeSprite.hlsl by Frank Luna (C) 2015 All Rights Reserved.
//***************************************************************************************

// Defaults for number of lights.
#ifndef NUM_DIR_LIGHTS
    #define NUM_DIR_LIGHTS 3
#endif

#ifndef NUM_POINT_LIGHTS
    #define NUM_POINT_LIGHTS 0
#endif

#ifndef NUM_SPOT_LIGHTS
    #define NUM_SPOT_LIGHTS 0
#endif

// Include structures and functions for lighting.
#include "LightingUtil.hlsl"

Texture2DArray gTreeMapArray : register(t0);


SamplerState gsamPointWrap        : register(s0);
SamplerState gsamPointClamp       : register(s1);
SamplerState gsamLinearWrap       : register(s2);
SamplerState gsamLinearClamp      : register(s3);
SamplerState gsamAnisotropicWrap  : register(s4);
SamplerState gsamAnisotropicClamp : register(s5);

// Constant data that varies per frame.
cbuffer cbPerObject : register(b0)
{
    float4x4 gWorld;
    float4x4 gTexTransform;
};

// Constant data that varies per material.
cbuffer cbPass : register(b1)
{
    float4x4 gView;
    float4x4 gInvView;
    float4x4 gProj;
    float4x4 gInvProj;
    float4x4 gViewProj;
    float4x4 gInvViewProj;
    float3 gEyePosW;
    float cbPerPassPad1;
    float2 gRenderTargetSize;
    float2 gInvRenderTargetSize;
    float gNearZ;
    float gFarZ;
    float gTotalTime;
    float gDeltaTime;
    float4 gAmbientLight;
```

```
    float4 gFogColor;
    float gFogStart;
    float gFogRange;
    float2 cbPerPassPad2;

    // Indices [0, NUM_DIR_LIGHTS) are directional lights;
    // indices [NUM_DIR_LIGHTS, NUM_DIR_LIGHTS+NUM_POINT_LIGHTS) are point
    // lights;
    // indices [NUM_DIR_LIGHTS+NUM_POINT_LIGHTS,
    // NUM_DIR_LIGHTS+NUM_POINT_LIGHT+NUM_SPOT_LIGHTS)
    // are spot lights for a maximum of MaxLights per object.
    Light gLights[MaxLights];
};

cbuffer cbMaterial : register(b2)
{
    float4   gDiffuseAlbedo;
    float3   gFresnelR0;
    float    gRoughness;
    float4x4 gMatTransform;
};

struct VertexIn
{
    float3 PosW  : POSITION;
    float2 SizeW : SIZE;
};

struct VertexOut
{
    float3 CenterW : POSITION;
    float2 SizeW   : SIZE;
};

struct GeoOut
{
    float4 PosH    : SV_POSITION;
    float3 PosW    : POSITION;
    float3 NormalW : NORMAL;
    float2 TexC    : TEXCOORD;
    uint   PrimID  : SV_PrimitiveID;
};

VertexOut VS(VertexIn vin)
{
    VertexOut vout;

    // Just pass data over to geometry shader.
    vout.CenterW = vin.PosW;
    vout.SizeW   = vin.SizeW;

    return vout;
}
```

```hlsl
 // We expand each point into a quad (4 vertices), so the maximum number of vertices
 // we output per geometry shader invocation is 4.
[maxvertexcount(4)]
void GS(point VertexOut gin[1],
    uint primID : SV_PrimitiveID,
    inout TriangleStream<GeoOut> triStream)
{
  //
  // Compute the local coordinate system of the sprite relative to the world
  // space such that the billboard is aligned with the y-axis and faces the eye.
  //

  float3 up = float3(0.0f, 1.0f, 0.0f);
  float3 look = gEyePosW - gin[0].CenterW;
  look.y = 0.0f; // y-axis aligned, so project to xz-plane
  look = normalize(look);
  float3 right = cross(up, look);

  //
  // Compute triangle strip vertices (quad) in world space.
  //
  float halfWidth  = 0.5f*gin[0].SizeW.x;
  float halfHeight = 0.5f*gin[0].SizeW.y;

  float4 v[4];
  v[0] = float4(gin[0].CenterW + halfWidth*right - halfHeight*up, 1.0f);
  v[1] = float4(gin[0].CenterW + halfWidth*right + halfHeight*up, 1.0f);
  v[2] = float4(gin[0].CenterW - halfWidth*right - halfHeight*up, 1.0f);
  v[3] = float4(gin[0].CenterW - halfWidth*right + halfHeight*up, 1.0f);

  //
  // Transform quad vertices to world space and output
  // them as a triangle strip.
  //

  float2 texC[4] =
  {
    float2(0.0f, 1.0f),
    float2(0.0f, 0.0f),
    float2(1.0f, 1.0f),
    float2(1.0f, 0.0f)
  };

  GeoOut gout;
  [unroll]
  for(int i = 0; i < 4; ++i)
  {
    gout.PosH    = mul(v[i], gViewProj);
    gout.PosW    = v[i].xyz;
    gout.NormalW = look;
    gout.TexC    = texC[i];
    gout.PrimID  = primID;

    triStream.Append(gout);
  }
}
```

```
float4 PS(GeoOut pin) : SV_Target
{
  float3 uvw = float3(pin.TexC, pin.PrimID%3);
  float4 diffuseAlbedo = gTreeMapArray.Sample(
    gsamAnisotropicWrap, uvw) * gDiffuseAlbedo;

#ifdef ALPHA_TEST
  // Discard pixel if texture alpha < 0.1. We do this test as soon
  // as possible in the shader so that we can potentially exit the
  // shader early, thereby skipping the rest of the shader code.
  clip(diffuseAlbedo.a - 0.1f);
#endif

  // Interpolating normal can unnormalize it, so renormalize it.
  pin.NormalW = normalize(pin.NormalW);

  // Vector from point being lit to eye.
  float3 toEyeW = gEyePosW - pin.PosW;
  float distToEye = length(toEyeW);
  toEyeW /= distToEye; // normalize

  // Light terms.
  float4 ambient = gAmbientLight*diffuseAlbedo;

  const float shininess = 1.0f - gRoughness;
  Material mat = { diffuseAlbedo, gFresnelR0, shininess };
  float3 shadowFactor = 1.0f;
  float4 directLight = ComputeLighting(gLights, mat, pin.PosW,
    pin.NormalW, toEyeW, shadowFactor);

  float4 litColor = ambient + directLight;

#ifdef FOG
  float fogAmount = saturate((distToEye - gFogStart) / gFogRange);
  litColor = lerp(litColor, gFogColor, fogAmount);
#endif

  // Common convention to take alpha from diffuse albedo.
  litColor.a = diffuseAlbedo.a;

  return litColor;
}
```

12.2.4 SV_PrimitiveID

The geometry shader in this example takes a special unsigned integer parameter with semantic SV_PrimitiveID.

```
[maxvertexcount(4)]
void GS(point VertexOut gin[1],
    uint primID : SV_PrimitiveID,
    inout TriangleStream<GeoOut> triStream)
```

When this semantic is specified, it tells the input assembler stage to automatically generate a primitive ID for each primitive. When a draw call is executed to draw *n* primitives, the first primitive is labeled 0; the second primitive is labeled 1; and so on, until the last primitive in the draw call is labeled *n*-1. The primitive IDs are only unique for a single draw call. In our billboard example, the geometry shader does not use this ID (although a geometry shader could); instead, the geometry shader writes the primitive ID to the outgoing vertices, thereby passing it on to the pixel shader stage. The pixel shader uses the primitive ID to index into a texture array, which leads us to the next section.

If a geometry shader is not present, the primitive ID parameter can be added to the parameter list of the pixel shader:

```
float4 PS(VertexOut pin, uint primID : SV_PrimitiveID) : SV_Target
{
  // Pixel shader body...
}
```

However, if a geometry shader is present, then the primitive ID parameter must occur in the geometry shader signature. Then the geometry shader can use the primitive ID or pass it on to the pixel shader stage (or both).

It is also possible to have the input assembler generate a vertex ID. To do this, add an additional parameter of type uint *to the vertex shader signature with semantic* SV_VertexID:
The following vertex shader signature shows how this is done:

```
VertexOut VS(VertexIn vin, uint vertID : SV_VertexID)
{
  // vertex shader body...
}
```

For a Draw *call, the vertices in the draw call will be labeled with IDs from 0, 1, ..., n-1, where n is the number of vertices in the draw call. For a* DrawIndexed *call, the vertex IDs correspond to the vertex index values.*

12.3 TEXTURE ARRAYS

12.3.1 Overview

A texture array stores an array of textures. In C++ code, a texture array is represented by the ID3D12Resource interface just like all resources are (textures and buffers). When creating an ID3D12Resource object, there is actually a property called DepthOrArraySize that can be set to specify the number of texture elements the texture stores (or the depth for a 3D texture). When we create our depth/stencil texture in *d3dApp.cpp,* we always set this to 1. If you look at the `CreateD3DResources12` function in Common/DDSTextureLoader.cpp you will see how the code supports creating texture arrays and volume textures. In a HLSL file, a texture array is represented by the `Texture2DArray` type:

```
Texture2DArray gTreeMapArray;
```

Now, you have be wondering why we need texture arrays. Why not just do this:

```
Texture2D TexArray[4];
 ...

float4 PS(GeoOut pin) : SV_Target
{
float4 c = TexArray[pin.PrimID%4].Sample(samLinear, pin.Tex);
```

In shader model 5.1 (new to Direct3D 12), we actually can do this. However, this was not allowed in previous Direct3D versions. Moreover, indexing textures like this may have a little overhead depending on the hardware, so for this chapter we will stick to texture arrays.

12.3.2 Sampling a Texture Array

In the Billboards demo, we sample a texture array with the following code:

```
float3 uvw = float3(pin.Tex, pin.PrimID%4);
float4 diffuseAlbedo = gTreeMapArray.Sample(
  gsamAnisotropicWrap, uvw) * gDiffuseAlbedo;
```

When using a texture array, three texture coordinates are required. The first two texture coordinates are the usual 2D texture coordinates; the third texture coordinate is an index into the texture array. For example, 0 is the index to the first texture in the array, 1 is the index to the second texture in the array, 2 is the index to the third texture in the array, and so on.

In the Billboards demo, we use a texture array with four texture elements, each with a different tree texture (Figure 12.7). However, because we are drawing more than four trees per draw call, the primitive IDs will become greater than three. Thus, we take the primitive ID modulo 4 (`pin.PrimID % 4`) to map the primitive ID to 0, 1, 2, or 3, which are valid array indices for an array with four elements.

One of the advantages with texture arrays is that we were able to draw a collection of primitives, with different textures, in one draw call. Normally, we would have to have a separate render-item for each mesh with a different texture:

```
SetTextureA();
DrawPrimitivesWithTextureA();
```

Figure 12.7. Tree billboard images.
```
SetTextureB();
DrawPrimitivesWithTextureB();

...

SetTextureZ();
DrawPrimitivesWithTextureZ();
```

Each set and draw call has some overhead associated with it. With texture arrays, we could reduce this to one set and one draw call:

```
SetTextureArray();
DrawPrimitivesWithTextureArray();
```

12.3.3 Loading Texture Arrays

Our DDS loading code in *Common/DDSTextureLoader.h/.cpp* supports loading DDS files that store texture arrays. So the key is to create a DDS file that contains a texture array. To do this, we use the *texassemble* tool provided by Microsoft at *https://directxtex.codeplex.com/wikipage?title=Texassemble&referringTitle=Texconv*. The following syntax shows how to create a texture array called *treeArray.dds* from 4 images *t0.dds, t1.dds, t2.dds,* and *t3.dds*:

```
texassemble -array -o treeArray.dds t0.dds t1.dds t2.dds t2.dds
```

Note that when building a texture array with *texassemble*, the input images should only have one mipmap level. After you have invoked *texassemble* to build the texture array, you can use *texconv* (*https://directxtex.codeplex.com/wikipage?title=Texconv*) to generate mipmaps and change the pixel format if needed:

```
texconv -m 10 -f BC3_UNORM treeArray.dds
```

12.3.4 Texture Subresources

Now that we have discussed texture arrays, we can talk about subresources. Figure 12.8 shows an example of a texture array with several textures. In turn, each texture has its own mipmap chain. The Direct3D API uses the term *array slice* to refer to an element in a texture along with its complete mipmap chain. The Direct3D API uses the term *mip slice* to refer to all the mipmaps at a particular level in the texture array. A subresource refers to a single mipmap level in a texture array element.

Given the texture array index, and a mipmap level, we can access a subresource in a texture array. However, the subresources can also be labeled by a linear index; Direct3D uses a linear index ordered as shown in Figure 12.9.

The following utility function is used to compute the linear subresource index given the mip level, array index, and the number of mipmap levels:

```
inline UINT D3D12CalcSubresource( UINT MipSlice, UINT ArraySlice,
   UINT PlaneSlice, UINT MipLevels, UINT ArraySize )
{
   return MipSlice + ArraySlice * MipLevels + PlaneSlice * MipLevels *
     ArraySize;
}
```

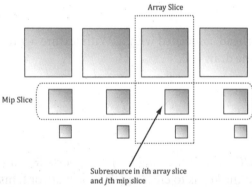

Figure 12.8. A texture array with four textures. Each texture has three mipmap levels.

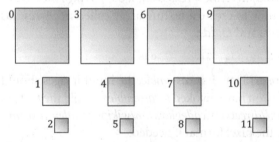

Figure 12.9. Subresources in a texture array labeled with a linear index.

12.4 ALPHA-TO-COVERAGE

When the "Tree Billboard" demo is run, notice that at some distances the edges of the tree billboard cutouts appear blocky. This is caused by the `clip` function, which we use to mask out the pixels of the texture that are not part of the tree; the clip function either keeps a pixel or rejects it—there is no smooth transition. The distance from the eye to the billboard plays a role because the short distances result in magnification, which makes the block artifacts larger, and short distances result in a lower resolution mipmap level being used.

One way to fix this problem is to use transparency blending instead of the alpha test. Due to linear texture filtering, the edge pixels will be blurred slightly making a smooth transition from white (opaque pixels) to black (masked out pixels). The transparency blending will consequently cause a smooth fade out along the edges from opaque pixels to masked pixels. Unfortunately, transparency blending requires sorting and rendering in back-to-front order. The overhead for sorting a small number of tree billboards is not high, but if we are rendering a forest or grass prairie, the sorting can be expensive as it must be done every frame; worse is that rendering in back-to-front order results in massive overdraw (see Exercise 8 in Chapter 11), which can kill performance.

One might suggest that MSAA (multisampling antialiasing—see §4.1.7) can help, as MSAA is used to smooth out blocky edges of polygons. Indeed, it should be able to help, but there is a problem. MSAA executes the pixel shader once per pixel, at the pixel center, and then shares that color information with its subpixels based on visibility (the depth/stencil test is evaluated per subpixel) and coverage (does the subpixel center lie inside or outside the polygon?). The key here is that *coverage is determined at the polygon level*. Therefore, MSAA is not going to detect the edges of the tree billboard cutouts as defined by the alpha channel—it will only look at the edges of the quads the textures are mapped onto. So is there a way to tell Direct3D to take the alpha channel into consideration when calculating coverage? The answer is yes, and it leads us to the technique known as *alpha-to-coverage*.

When MSAA is enabled, and alpha-to-coverage is enabled (a member of `D3D12_BLEND_DESC::AlphaToCoverageEnable = true`), the hardware will look at the alpha value returned by the pixel shader and use that to determine coverage [NVIDIA05]. For example, with 4X MSAA, if the pixel shader alpha is 0.5, then we can assume that two out of the four subpixels are covered and this will create a smooth edge.

The general advice is that you always want to use alpha-to-coverage for alpha masked cut out textures like foliage and fences. However, it does require that MSAA is enabled. Note that in the constructor of our demo application, we set:

```
mEnable4xMsaa = true;
```

This causes our sample framework to create the back and depth buffers with 4X MSAA support.

12.5 SUMMARY

1. Assuming we are not using the tessellation stages, the geometry shader stage is an optional stage that sits between the vertex and pixel shader stages. The geometry shader is invoked for each primitive sent through the input assembler. The geometry shader can output zero, one, or more primitives. The output primitive type may be different from the input primitive type. The vertices of the output primitives should be transformed to homogeneous clip space before leaving the geometry shader. The primitives output from the geometry shader next enter the rasterization stage of the rendering pipeline. Geometry shaders are programmed in effect files, side-by-side vertex and pixel shaders.

2. The billboard technique is where a quad textured with an image of an object is used instead of a true 3D model of the object. For objects far away, the viewer cannot tell a billboard is being used. The advantage of billboards is that the GPU does not have to waste processing time rendering a full 3D object, when a textured quad will suffice. This technique can be useful for rendering forests of trees, where true 3D geometry is used for trees near the camera, and billboards are used for trees in the distance. In order for the billboard trick to work, the billboard must always face the camera. The billboard technique can be implemented efficiently in a geometry shader.

3. A special parameter of type uint and semantic SV_PrimitiveID can be added to the parameter list of a geometry shader as the following example shows:

```
[maxvertexcount(4)]
void GS(point VertexOut gin[1],
        uint primID : SV_PrimitiveID,
        inout TriangleStream<GeoOut> triStream);
```

When this semantic is specified, it tells the input assembler stage to automatically generate a primitive ID for each primitive. When a draw call is executed to draw *n* primitives, the first primitive is labeled 0; the second primitive is labeled 1; and so on, until the last primitive in the draw call is labeled *n*-1. If a geometry shader is not present, the primitive ID parameter can be added to the parameter list of the pixel shader. However, if a geometry shader is present, then the primitive ID parameter must occur in the geometry shader signature. Then the geometry shader can use the primitive ID or pass it on to the pixel shader stage (or both).

4. The input assembler stage can generate a vertex ID. To do this, add an additional parameter of type uint to the vertex shader signature with semantic SV_VertexID. For a Draw call, the vertices in the draw call will be labeled with IDs from 0, 1, ..., *n-1*, where *n* is the number of vertices in the draw call. For a DrawIndexed call, the vertex IDs correspond to the vertex index values.

5. A texture array stores an array of textures. In C++ code, a texture array is represented by the ID3D12Resource interface just like all resources are (textures and buffers). When creating an ID3D12Resource object, there is a property called DepthOrArraySize that can be set to specify the number of texture elements the texture stores (or the depth for a 3D texture). In HLSL, a texture array is represented by the Texture2DArray type. When using a texture array, three texture coordinates are required. The first two texture coordinates are the usual 2D texture coordinates; the third texture coordinate is an index into the texture array. For example, 0 is the index to the first texture in the array, 1 is the index to the second texture in the array, 2 is the index to the third texture in the array, and so on. One of the advantages with texture arrays is that we were able to draw a collection of primitives, with different textures, in one draw call. Each primitive will have an index into the texture array which indicates which texture to apply to the primitive.

6. Alpha-to-coverage instructs the hardware to look at the alpha value returned by the pixel shader when determining subpixel coverage. This enables smooth edges for alpha masked cutout textures like foliage and fences. Alpha-to-coverage is controlled by the D3D12_BLEND_DESC::AlphaToCoverageEnable field in a PSO.

12.6 EXERCISES

1. Consider a circle, drawn with a line strip, in the *xz*-plane. Expand the line strip into a cylinder with no caps using the geometry shader.

2. An icosahedron is a rough approximation of a sphere. By subdividing each triangle (Figure 12.10), and projecting the new vertices onto the sphere, a better approximation is obtained. (Projecting a vertex onto a unit sphere simply amounts to normalizing the position vector, as the heads of all unit vectors coincide with the surface of the unit sphere.) For this exercise, build and render an icosahedron. Use a geometry shader to subdivide the icosahedron based on its distance *d* from the camera. For example, if $d < 15$, then subdivide the original icosahedron twice; if $15 \leq d < 30$, then subdivide the original icosahedron once; if $d \geq 30$, then just render the original icosahedron. The

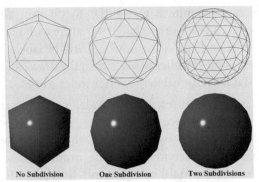

Figure 12.10. Subdivision of an icosahedron with vertices projected onto the unit sphere.

idea of this is to only use a high number of polygons if the object is close to the camera; if the object is far away, then a coarser mesh will suffice, and we need not waste GPU power processing more polygons than needed. Figure 12.10 shows the three LOD levels side-by-side in wireframe and solid (lit) mode. Refer back to §7.4.3 for a discussion on tessellating an icosahedron.

3. A simple explosion effect can be simulated by translating triangles in the direction of their face normal as a function of time. This simulation can be implemented in a geometry shader. For each triangle input into the geometry shader, the geometry shader computes the face normal **n**, and then translates the three triangle vertices, $\mathbf{p}_0$, $\mathbf{p}_1$, and $\mathbf{p}_2$, in the direction **n** based on the time t since the explosion started:

$$\mathbf{p}'_i = \mathbf{p}_i + t\mathbf{n} \quad \text{for} \quad i = 0, 1, 2$$

The face normal **n** need not be unit length, and can be scaled accordingly to control the speed of the explosion. One could even make the scale depend on the primitive ID, so that each primitive travels at a different speed. Use an icosahedron (not subdivided) as a sample mesh for implementing this effect.

4. It can be useful for debugging to visualize the vertex normals of a mesh. Write an effect that renders the vertex normals of a mesh as short line segments. To do this, implement a geometry shader that inputs the point primitives of the mesh (i.e., its vertices with topology `D3D_PRIMITIVE_TOPOLOGY_POINTLIST`), so that each vertex gets pumped through the geometry shader. Now the geometry shader can expand each point into a line segment of some length L. If the vertex has position **p** and normal **n**, then the two endpoints of the line segment representing the vertex normal are **p** and **p** + L**n**. After this is implemented, draw the mesh as normal, and then draw the scene again with the normal vector visualization technique so that the normals are rendered on top of the scene. Use the "Blend" demo as a test scene.

5. Similar to the previous exercise, write an effect that renders the face normals of a mesh as short line segments. For this effect, the geometry shader will input a triangle, calculate its normal, and output a line segment.

6. This exercise shows that for a `Draw` call, the vertices in the draw call will be labeled with IDs from 0, 1, ..., *n*-1, where n is the number of vertices in the draw call, and that for a `DrawIndexed` call, the vertex IDs correspond to the vertex index values.

   Modify the "Tree Billboards" demo in the following way. First, change the vertex shader to the following:

   ```
   VertexOut VS(VertexIn vin, uint vertID : SV_VertexID)
   {
     VertexOut vout;

     // Just pass data over to geometry shader.
     vout.CenterW = vin.PosW;
     vout.SizeW   = float2(2+vertID, 2+vertID);

     return vout;
   }
   ```

   In other words, we size the tree billboard based on the vertex ID of its center. Now run the program; when drawing 16 billboards, the sizes should range from 2 to 17. Now modify the drawing like so: Instead of using a single draw call to draw all 16 points at once, use four like so:

   ```
   cmdList->Draw(4, 0, 0, 0);
   cmdList->Draw(4, 0, 4, 0);
   cmdList->Draw(4, 0, 8, 0);
   cmdList->Draw(4, 0, 12, 0);
   ```

   Now run the program. This time, the sizes should range from 2 to 5. Because each draw call draws 4 vertices, the vertex IDs range from 0-3 for each draw call. Now use an index buffer and four DrawIndexed calls. After running the program, the sizes should return back to the range of 2 to 17. This is because when using DrawIndexed, the vertex IDs correspond to the vertex index values.

7. Modify the "Tree Billboards" demo in the following way. First, remove the "modulo 4" from the pixel shader:

   ```
   float3 uvw = float3(pin.Tex, pin.PrimID);
   ```

   Now run the program. Since we are drawing 16 primitives, with primitive IDs ranging from 0-15, these IDs go outside the array bounds. However, this does not cause an error, as the out-of-bounds index will be clamped to the highest valid index (3 in this case). Now instead of using a single draw call to draw all 16 points at once, use four like so:

   ```
   cmdList->Draw(4, 0, 0, 0);
   cmdList->Draw(4, 0, 4, 0);
   ```

```
cmdList->Draw(4, 0, 8, 0);
cmdList->Draw(4, 0, 12, 0);
```

Run the program again. This time there is no clamping. Because each draw call draws 4 primitives, the primitive IDs range from 0-3 for each draw call. Thus the primitive IDs can be used as indices without going out of bounds. This shows that the primitive ID "count" resets to zero with each draw call.

Chapter 13 THE COMPUTE SHADER

GPUs have been optimized to process a large amount of memory from a single location or sequential locations (so-called *streaming operation*); this is in contrast to a CPU designed for random memory accesses [Boyd10]. Moreover, because vertices and pixels can be independently processed, GPUs have been architected to be massively parallel; for example, the NVIDIA "Fermi" architecture supports up to sixteen streaming multiprocessors of thirty-two CUDA cores for a total of 512 CUDA cores [NVIDIA09].

Obviously, graphics benefit from this GPU architecture, as the architecture was designed for graphics. However, some non-graphical applications benefit from the massive amount of computational power a GPU can provide with its parallel architecture. Using the GPU for non-graphical applications is called *general purpose GPU* (GPGPU) *programming*. Not all algorithms are ideal for a GPU implementation; GPUs need data-parallel algorithms to take advantage of the parallel architecture of the GPU. That is, we need a large amount of data elements that will have similar operations performed on them so that the elements can be processed in parallel. Graphical operations like shading pixels is a good example, as each pixel fragment being drawn is operated on by the pixel shader. As another example, if you look at the code for our wave simulation from the previous chapters, you will see that in the update step, we perform a calculation on each grid element. So this, too, is a good candidate for a GPU implementation, as each grid element can be updated in parallel by the GPU. Particle systems

470 DIRECT3D FOUNDATIONS

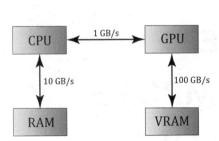

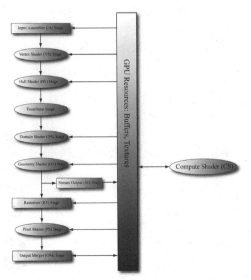

Figure 13.1. Image has been redrawn from [Boyd10]. The relative memory bandwidth speeds between CPU and RAM, CPU and GPU, and GPU and VRAM. These numbers are just illustrative numbers to show the order of magnitude difference between the bandwidths. Observe that transferring memory between CPU and GPU is the bottleneck.

Figure 13.2. The compute shader is not part of the rendering pipeline but sits off to the side. The compute shader can read and write to GPU resources. The compute shader can be mixed with graphics rendering, or used alone for GPGPU programming.

provide yet another example, where the physics of each particle can be computed independently provided we take the simplification that the particles do not interact with each other.

For GPGPU programming, the user generally needs to access the computation results back on the CPU. This requires copying the result from video memory to system memory, which is slow (see Figure 13.1), but may be a negligible issue compared to the speed up from doing the computation on the GPU. For graphics, we typically use the computation result as an input to the rendering pipeline, so no transfer from GPU to CPU is needed. For example, we can blur a texture with the compute shader, and then bind a shader resource view to that blurred texture to a shader as input.

The Compute Shader is a programmable shader Direct3D exposes that is not directly part of the rendering pipeline. Instead, it sits off to the side and can read from GPU resources and write to GPU resources (Figure 13.2). Essentially, the Compute Shader allows us to access the GPU to implement data-parallel algorithms without drawing anything. As mentioned, this is useful for GPGPU programming, but there are still many graphical effects that can be implemented on the compute shader as well—so it is still very relevant for a graphics programmer. And as already mentioned, because the Compute Shader is part of Direct3D, it reads from and writes to Direct3D resources, which enables us to bind the output of a compute shader directly to the rendering pipeline.

Objectives:

1. To learn how to program compute shaders.
2. To obtain a basic high-level understanding of how the hardware processes thread groups, and the threads within them.
3. To discover which Direct3D resources can be set as an input to a compute shader and which Direct3D resources can be set as an output to a compute shader.
4. To understand the various thread IDs and their uses.
5. To learn about shared memory and how it can be used for performance optimizations.
6. To find out where to obtain more detailed information about GPGPU programming.

13.1 THREADS AND THREAD GROUPS

In GPU programming, the number of threads desired for execution is divided up into a grid of *thread groups*. A thread group is executed on a single multiprocessor. Therefore, if you had a GPU with sixteen multiprocessors, you would want to break up your problem into at least sixteen thread groups so that each multiprocessor has work to do. For better performance, you would want at least two thread groups per multiprocessor since a multiprocessor can switch to processing the threads in a different group to hide stalls [Fung10] (a stall can occur, for example, if a shader needs to wait for a texture operation result before it can continue to the next instruction).

Each thread group gets shared memory that all threads in that group can access; a thread cannot access shared memory in a different thread group. Thread synchronization operations can take place amongst the threads in a thread group, but different thread groups cannot be synchronized. In fact, we have no control over the order in which different thread groups are processed. This makes sense as the thread groups can be executed on different multiprocessors.

A thread group consists of n threads. The hardware actually divides these threads up into *warps* (thirty-two threads per warp), and a warp is processed by the multiprocessor in SIMD32 (i.e., the same instructions are executed for the thirty-two threads simultaneously). Each CUDA core processes a thread and recall that a "Fermi" multiprocessor has thirty-two CUDA cores (so a CUDA core is like an SIMD "lane.") In Direct3D, you can specify a thread group size with dimensions that are not multiples of thirty-two, but for performance reasons, the thread group dimensions should always be multiples of the warp size [Fung10].

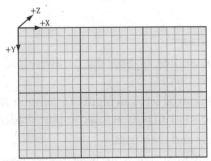

Figure 13.3. Dispatching a grid of 3 × 2 thread groups. Each thread group has 8 × 8 threads.

Thread group sizes of 256 seems to be a good starting point that should work well for various hardware. Then experiment with other sizes. Changing the number of threads per group will change the number of groups dispatched.

 NVIDIA hardware uses warp sizes of thirty-two threads. ATI uses "wavefront" sizes of sixty-four threads, and recommends the thread group size should always be a multiple of the wavefront size [Bilodeau10]. Also, the warp size or wavefront size can change in future generations of hardware.

In Direct3D, thread groups are launched via the following method call:

```
void ID3D12GraphicsCommandList::Dispatch(
  UINT ThreadGroupCountX,
  UINT ThreadGroupCountY,
  UINT ThreadGroupCountZ);
```

This enables you to launch a 3D grid of thread groups; however, in this book we will only be concerned with 2D grids of thread groups. The following example call launches three groups in the *x* direction and two groups in the *y* direction for a total of 3 × 2 = 6 thread groups (see Figure 13.3).

13.2 A SIMPLE COMPUTE SHADER

Below is a simple compute shader that sums two textures, assuming all the textures are the same size. This shader is not very interesting, but it illustrates the basic syntax of writing a compute shader.

```
cbuffer cbSettings
{
   // Compute shader can access values in constant buffers.
};

// Data sources and outputs.
Texture2D gInputA;
```

```
Texture2D gInputB;
RWTexture2D<float4> gOutput;

// The number of threads in the thread group. The threads in a group
    can
// be arranged in a 1D, 2D, or 3D grid layout.
[numthreads(16, 16, 1)]
void CS(int3 dispatchThreadID : SV_DispatchThreadID) // Thread ID
{
  // Sum the xyth texels and store the result in the xyth texel of
  // gOutput.
  gOutput[dispatchThreadID.xy] =
    gInputA[dispatchThreadID.xy] +
    gInputB[dispatchThreadID.xy];
}
```

A compute shader consists of the following components:

1. Global variable access via constant buffers.
2. Input and output resources, which are discussed in the next section.
3. The `[numthreads(X, Y, Z)]` attribute, which specifies the number of threads in the thread group as a 3D grid of threads.
4. The shader body that has the instructions to execute for each thread.
5. Thread identification system value parameters (discussed in §13.4).

Observe that we can define different topologies of the thread group; for example, a thread group could be a single line of *X* threads `[numthreads(X, 1, 1)]` or a single column of *Y* threads `[numthreads(1, Y, 1)]`. 2D thread groups of $X \times Y$ threads can be made by setting the *z*-dimension to 1 like this `[numthreads(X, Y, 1)]`. The topology you choose will be dictated by the problem you are working on. As mentioned in the previous section, the total thread count per group should be a multiple of the warp size (thirty-two for NVIDIA cards) or a multiple of the wavefront size (sixty-four for ATI cards). A multiple of the wavefront size is also a multiple of the warp size, so choosing a multiple of the wavefront size works for both types of cards.

13.2.1 Compute PSO

To enable a compute shader, we use a special "compute pipeline state description." This structure has far fewer fields than `D3D12_GRAPHICS_PIPELINE_STATE_DESC` because the compute shader sits to the side of the graphics pipeline, so all the graphics pipeline state does not apply to compute shaders and thus does not need to be set. Below shows an example of creating a compute pipeline state object:

```
D3D12_COMPUTE_PIPELINE_STATE_DESC wavesUpdatePSO = {};
wavesUpdatePSO.pRootSignature = mWavesRootSignature.Get();
wavesUpdatePSO.CS =
```

```
{
  reinterpret_cast<BYTE*>(mShaders["wavesUpdateCS"]-
    >GetBufferPointer()),
  mShaders["wavesUpdateCS"]->GetBufferSize()
};
wavesUpdatePSO.Flags = D3D12_PIPELINE_STATE_FLAG_NONE;
ThrowIfFailed(md3dDevice->CreateComputePipelineState(
    &wavesUpdatePSO, IID_PPV_ARGS(&mPSOs["wavesUpdate"])));
```

The root signature defines what parameters the shader expects as input (CBVs, SRVs, etc.). The cs field is where we specify the compute shader. The following code shows an example of compiling a compute shader to bytecode:

```
mShaders["wavesUpdateCS"] = d3dUtil::CompileShader(
    L"Shaders\\WaveSim.hlsl", nullptr, "UpdateWavesCS", "cs_5_0");
```

13.3 DATA INPUT AND OUTPUT RESOURCES

Two types of resources can be bound to a compute shader: buffers and textures. We have worked with buffers already such as vertex and index buffers, and constant buffers. We are also familiar with texture resources from Chapter 9.

13.3.1 Texture Inputs

The compute shader defined in the previous section defined two input texture resources:

```
Texture2D gInputA;
Texture2D gInputB;
```

The input textures gInputA and gInputB are bound as inputs to the shader by creating (SRVs) to the textures and passing them as arguments to the root parameters; for example:

```
cmdList->SetComputeRootDescriptorTable(1, mSrvA);
cmdList->SetComputeRootDescriptorTable(2, mSrvB);
```

This is exactly the same way we bind shader resource views to pixel shaders. Note that SRVs are read-only.

13.3.2 Texture Outputs and Unordered Access Views (UAVs)

The compute shader defined in the previous section defined one output resource:

```
RWTexture2D<float4> gOutput;
```

Outputs are treated special and have the special prefix to their type "RW," which stands for read-write, and as the name implies, you can read and write to elements

The Compute Shader

in this resource in the compute shader. In contrast, the textures gInputA and gInputB are read-only. Also, it is necessary to specify the type and dimensions of the output with the template angle brackets syntax <float4>. If our output was a 2D integer like DXGI_FORMAT_R8G8_SINT, then we would have instead written:

```
RWTexture2D<int2> gOutput;
```

Binding an output resource is different than an input, however. To bind a resource that we will write to in a compute shader, we need to bind it using a new view type called an *unordered access view* (UAV), which is represented in code by a descriptor handle and described in code by the D3D12_UNORDERED_ACCESS_VIEW_DESC structure. This is created in a similar way to a shader resource view. Here is an example that creates a UAV to a texture resource:

```
D3D12_RESOURCE_DESC texDesc;
ZeroMemory(&texDesc, sizeof(D3D12_RESOURCE_DESC));
texDesc.Dimension = D3D12_RESOURCE_DIMENSION_TEXTURE2D;
texDesc.Alignment = 0;
texDesc.Width = mWidth;
texDesc.Height = mHeight;
texDesc.DepthOrArraySize = 1;
texDesc.MipLevels = 1;
texDesc.Format = DXGI_FORMAT_R8G8B8A8_UNORM;
texDesc.SampleDesc.Count = 1;
texDesc.SampleDesc.Quality = 0;
texDesc.Layout = D3D12_TEXTURE_LAYOUT_UNKNOWN;
texDesc.Flags = D3D12_RESOURCE_FLAG_ALLOW_UNORDERED_ACCESS;

ThrowIfFailed(md3dDevice->CreateCommittedResource(
    &CD3DX12_HEAP_PROPERTIES(D3D12_HEAP_TYPE_DEFAULT),
    D3D12_HEAP_FLAG_NONE,
    &texDesc,
    D3D12_RESOURCE_STATE_COMMON,
    nullptr,
    IID_PPV_ARGS(&mBlurMap0)));

D3D12_SHADER_RESOURCE_VIEW_DESC srvDesc = {};
srvDesc.Shader4ComponentMapping = D3D12_DEFAULT_SHADER_4_COMPONENT_
    MAPPING;
srvDesc.Format = mFormat;
srvDesc.ViewDimension = D3D12_SRV_DIMENSION_TEXTURE2D;
srvDesc.Texture2D.MostDetailedMip = 0;
srvDesc.Texture2D.MipLevels = 1;

D3D12_UNORDERED_ACCESS_VIEW_DESC uavDesc = {};

uavDesc.Format = mFormat;
uavDesc.ViewDimension = D3D12_UAV_DIMENSION_TEXTURE2D;
uavDesc.Texture2D.MipSlice = 0;

md3dDevice->CreateShaderResourceView(mBlurMap0.Get(),
    &srvDesc, mBlur0CpuSrv);
```

```
md3dDevice->CreateUnorderedAccessView(mBlurMap0.Get(),
    nullptr, &uavDesc, mBlur0CpuUav);
```

Observe that if a texture is going to be bound as UAV, then it must be created with the `D3D12_RESOURCE_FLAG_ALLOW_UNORDERED_ACCESS` flag; in the above example, the texture will be bound as a UAV and as a SRV (but not simultaneously). This is common, as we often use the compute shader to perform some operation on a texture (so the texture will be bound to the compute shader as a UAV), and then after, we want to texture geometry with it, so it will be bound to the vertex or pixel shader as a SRV.

Recall that a descriptor heap of type `D3D12_DESCRIPTOR_HEAP_TYPE_CBV_SRV_UAV` can mix CBVs, SRVs, and UAVs all in the same heap. Therefore, we can put UAV descriptors in that heap. Once they are in a heap, we simply pass the descriptor handles as arguments to the root parameters to bind the resources to the pipeline for a dispatch call. Consider the following root signature for a compute shader:

```
void BlurApp::BuildPostProcessRootSignature()
{
    CD3DX12_DESCRIPTOR_RANGE srvTable;
    srvTable.Init(D3D12_DESCRIPTOR_RANGE_TYPE_SRV, 1, 0);

    CD3DX12_DESCRIPTOR_RANGE uavTable;
    uavTable.Init(D3D12_DESCRIPTOR_RANGE_TYPE_UAV, 1, 0);

    // Root parameter can be a table, root descriptor or root constants.
    CD3DX12_ROOT_PARAMETER slotRootParameter[3];

    // Perfomance TIP: Order from most frequent to least frequent.
    slotRootParameter[0].InitAsConstants(12, 0);
    slotRootParameter[1].InitAsDescriptorTable(1, &srvTable);
    slotRootParameter[2].InitAsDescriptorTable(1, &uavTable);

    // A root signature is an array of root parameters.
    CD3DX12_ROOT_SIGNATURE_DESC rootSigDesc(3, slotRootParameter,
        0, nullptr,
        D3D12_ROOT_SIGNATURE_FLAG_ALLOW_INPUT_ASSEMBLER_INPUT_LAYOUT);

    // create a root signature with a single slot which points to a
    // descriptor range consisting of a single constant buffer
    ComPtr<ID3DBlob> serializedRootSig = nullptr;
    ComPtr<ID3DBlob> errorBlob = nullptr;
    HRESULT hr = D3D12SerializeRootSignature(&rootSigDesc, D3D_ROOT_
        SIGNATURE_VERSION_1,
        serializedRootSig.GetAddressOf(), errorBlob.GetAddressOf());

    if(errorBlob != nullptr)
    {
        ::OutputDebugStringA((char*)errorBlob->GetBufferPointer());
    }
    ThrowIfFailed(hr);
```

```
    ThrowIfFailed(md3dDevice->CreateRootSignature(
      0,
      serializedRootSig->GetBufferPointer(),
      serializedRootSig->GetBufferSize(),
      IID_PPV_ARGS(mPostProcessRootSignature.GetAddressOf())));
}
```

The root signature defines that the shader expects a constant buffer for root parameter slot 0, an SRV for root parameter slot 1, and a UAV for root parameter slot 2. Before a dispatch invocation, we bind the constants and descriptors to use for this dispatch call:

```
cmdList->SetComputeRootSignature(rootSig);

cmdList->SetComputeRoot32BitConstants(0, 1, &blurRadius, 0);
cmdList->SetComputeRoot32BitConstants(0, (UINT)weights.size(), weights.data(), 1);

cmdList->SetComputeRootDescriptorTable(1, mBlur0GpuSrv);
cmdList->SetComputeRootDescriptorTable(2, mBlur1GpuUav);

UINT numGroupsX = (UINT)ceilf(mWidth / 256.0f);
cmdList->Dispatch(numGroupsX, mHeight, 1);
```

13.3.3 Indexing and Sampling Textures

The elements of the textures can be accessed using 2D indices. In the compute shader defined in §13.2, we index the texture based on the dispatch thread ID (thread IDs are discussed in §13.4). Each thread is given a unique dispatch ID.

```
[numthreads(16, 16, 1)]
void CS(int3 dispatchThreadID : SV_DispatchThreadID)
{
  // Sum the xyth texels and store the result in the xyth texel of
  // gOutput.
  gOutput[dispatchThreadID.xy] =
    gInputA[dispatchThreadID.xy] +
    gInputB[dispatchThreadID.xy];
}
```

Assuming that we dispatched enough thread groups to cover the texture (i.e., so there is one thread being executed for one texel), then this code sums the texture images and stores the result in the texture gOutput.

The behavior of out-of-bounds indices are well defined in a compute shader. Out-of-bounds reads return 0, and out-of-bounds writes result in no-ops [Boyd08].

Because the compute shader is executed on the GPU, it has access to the usual GPU tools. In particular, we can sample textures using texture filtering. There are two issues, however. First, we cannot use the Sample method, but instead must use the SampleLevel method. SampleLevel takes an additional third parameter that specifies the mipmap level of the texture; 0 takes the top most level, 1 takes the second mip level, etc., and fractional values are used to interpolate between two mip levels of linear mip filtering is enabled. On the other hand, `Sample` automatically selects the best mipmap level to use based on how many pixels on the screen the texture will cover. Since compute shaders are not used for rendering directly, it does not know how to automatically select a mipmap level like this, and therefore, we must explicitly specify the level with `SampleLevel` in a compute shader. The second issue is that when we sample a texture, we use normalized texture-coordinates in the range $[0, 1]^2$ instead of integer indices. However, the texture size (*width*, *height*) can be set to a constant buffer variable, and then normalized texture coordinates can be derived from the integer indices (x, y):

$$u = \frac{x}{width}$$

$$v = \frac{y}{height}$$

The following code shows a compute shader using integer indices, and a second equivalent version using texture coordinates and `SampleLevel`, where it is assumed the texture size is 512×512 and we only need the top level mip:

```
//
// VERSION 1: Using integer indices.
//

cbuffer cbUpdateSettings
{
    float gWaveConstant0;
    float gWaveConstant1;
    float gWaveConstant2;

    float gDisturbMag;
    int2 gDisturbIndex;
};

RWTexture2D<float> gPrevSolInput : register(u0);
RWTexture2D<float> gCurrSolInput : register(u1);
RWTexture2D<float> gOutput       : register(u2);

[numthreads(16, 16, 1)]
void CS(int3 dispatchThreadID : SV_DispatchThreadID)
{
    int x = dispatchThreadID.x;
    int y = dispatchThreadID.y;

    gNextSolOutput[int2(x,y)] =
        gWaveConstants0*gPrevSolInput[int2(x,y)].r +
        gWaveConstants1*gCurrSolInput[int2(x,y)].r +
        gWaveConstants2*(
```

```
                    gCurrSolInput[int2(x,y+1)].r +
                    gCurrSolInput[int2(x,y-1)].r +
                    gCurrSolInput[int2(x+1,y)].r +
                    gCurrSolInput[int2(x-1,y)].r);
}

//
// VERSION 2: Using SampleLevel and texture coordinates.
//

cbuffer cbUpdateSettings
{
    float gWaveConstant0;
    float gWaveConstant1;
    float gWaveConstant2;

    float gDisturbMag;
    int2 gDisturbIndex;
};

SamplerState samPoint : register(s0);

RWTexture2D<float> gPrevSolInput : register(u0);
RWTexture2D<float> gCurrSolInput : register(u1);
RWTexture2D<float> gOutput       : register(u2);

[numthreads(16, 16, 1)]
void CS(int3 dispatchThreadID : SV_DispatchThreadID)
{
// Equivalently using SampleLevel() instead of operator [].
int x = dispatchThreadID.x;
int y = dispatchThreadID.y;

float2 c = float2(x,y)/512.0f;
float2 t = float2(x,y-1)/512.0;
float2 b = float2(x,y+1)/512.0;
float2 l = float2(x-1,y)/512.0;
float2 r = float2(x+1,y)/512.0;

gNextSolOutput[int2(x,y)] =
    gWaveConstants0*gPrevSolInput.SampleLevel(samPoint, c, 0.0f).r +
    gWaveConstants1*gCurrSolInput.SampleLevel(samPoint, c, 0.0f).r +
    gWaveConstants2*(
        gCurrSolInput.SampleLevel(samPoint, b, 0.0f).r +
        gCurrSolInput.SampleLevel(samPoint, t, 0.0f).r +
        gCurrSolInput.SampleLevel(samPoint, r, 0.0f).r +
        gCurrSolInput.SampleLevel(samPoint, l, 0.0f).r);
}
```

13.3.4 Structured Buffer Resources

The following examples show how structured buffers are defined in the HLSL:

```
struct Data
```

```
{
    float3 v1;
    float2 v2;
};

StructuredBuffer<Data> gInputA : register(t0);
StructuredBuffer<Data> gInputB : register(t1);
RWStructuredBuffer<Data> gOutput : register(u0);
```

A structured buffer is simply a buffer of elements of the same type—essentially an array. As you can see, the type can be a user-defined structure in the HLSL.

A structured buffer used as an SRV can be created just like we have been creating our vertex and index buffers. A structured buffer used as a UAV is almost created the same way, except that we must specify the flag D3D12_RESOURCE_FLAG_ALLOW_UNORDERED_ACCESS, and it is good practice to put it in the D3D12_RESOURCE_STATE_UNORDERED_ACCESS state.

```
struct Data
{
  XMFLOAT3 v1;
  XMFLOAT2 v2;
};

// Generate some data to fill the SRV buffers with.
std::vector<Data> dataA(NumDataElements);
std::vector<Data> dataB(NumDataElements);
for(int i = 0; i < NumDataElements; ++i)
{
    dataA[i].v1 = XMFLOAT3(i, i, i);
    dataA[i].v2 = XMFLOAT2(i, 0);

    dataB[i].v1 = XMFLOAT3(-i, i, 0.0f);
    dataB[i].v2 = XMFLOAT2(0, -i);
}

UINT64 byteSize = dataA.size()*sizeof(Data);

// Create some buffers to be used as SRVs.
mInputBufferA = d3dUtil::CreateDefaultBuffer(
    md3dDevice.Get(),
    mCommandList.Get(),
    dataA.data(),
    byteSize,
    mInputUploadBufferA);

mInputBufferB = d3dUtil::CreateDefaultBuffer(
    md3dDevice.Get(),
    mCommandList.Get(),
    dataB.data(),
    byteSize,
    mInputUploadBufferB);
```

```cpp
// Create the buffer that will be a UAV.
ThrowIfFailed(md3dDevice->CreateCommittedResource(
    &CD3DX12_HEAP_PROPERTIES(D3D12_HEAP_TYPE_DEFAULT),
    D3D12_HEAP_FLAG_NONE,
    &CD3DX12_RESOURCE_DESC::Buffer(byteSize,
        D3D12_RESOURCE_FLAG_ALLOW_UNORDERED_ACCESS),
    D3D12_RESOURCE_STATE_UNORDERED_ACCESS,
    nullptr,
    IID_PPV_ARGS(&mOutputBuffer)));
```

Structured buffers are bound to the pipeline just like textures. We create SRVs or UAV descriptors to them and pass them as arguments to root parameters that take descriptor tables. Alternatively, we can define the root signature to take root descriptors so that we can pass the virtual address of resources directly as root arguments without the need to go through a descriptor heap (this only works for SRVs and UAVs to buffer resource, not textures). Consider the following root signature description:

```cpp
// Root parameter can be a table, root descriptor or root constants.
CD3DX12_ROOT_PARAMETER slotRootParameter[3];

// Perfomance TIP: Order from most frequent to least frequent.
slotRootParameter[0].InitAsShaderResourceView(0);
slotRootParameter[1].InitAsShaderResourceView(1);
slotRootParameter[2].InitAsUnorderedAccessView(0);

// A root signature is an array of root parameters.
CD3DX12_ROOT_SIGNATURE_DESC rootSigDesc(3, slotRootParameter,
    0, nullptr,
    D3D12_ROOT_SIGNATURE_FLAG_NONE);
```

Then we can bind our buffers like so to be used for a dispatch call:

```cpp
mCommandList->SetComputeRootSignature(mRootSignature.Get());

mCommandList->SetComputeRootShaderResourceView(0,
    mInputBufferA->GetGPUVirtualAddress());
mCommandList->SetComputeRootShaderResourceView(1,
    mInputBufferB->GetGPUVirtualAddress());
mCommandList->SetComputeRootUnorderedAccessView(2,
    mOutputBuffer->GetGPUVirtualAddress());

mCommandList->Dispatch(1, 1, 1);
```

There is also such a thing called a raw buffer, which is basically a byte array of data. Byte offsets are used and the data can then be casted to the proper type. This could be useful for storing different data types in the same buffer, for example. To be a raw buffer, the resource must be created with the DXGI_FORMAT_R32_TYPELESS *format, and when creating the UAV we must specify the* D3D12_BUFFER_UAV_FLAG_RAW *flag. We do not use raw buffers in this book; see the SDK documentation for further details.*

13.3.5 Copying CS Results to System Memory

Typically, when we use the compute shader to process a texture, we will display that processed texture on the screen; therefore, we visually see the result to verify the accuracy of our compute shader. With structured buffer calculations, and GPGPU computing in general, we might not display our results at all. So the question is how do we get our results from GPU memory (remember when we write to a structured buffer via a UAV, that buffer is stored in GPU memory) back to system memory. The required way is to create system memory buffer with heap properties `D3D12_HEAP_TYPE_READBACK`. Then we can use the `ID3D12GraphicsCommandList::CopyResource` method to copy the GPU resource to the system memory resource. The system memory resource must be the same type and size as the resource we want to copy. Finally, we can map the system memory buffer with the mapping API to read it on the CPU. From there we can then copy the data into a system memory array for further processing on the CPU side, save the data to file, or what have you.

We have included a structured buffer demo for this chapter called "VecAdd," which simply sums the corresponding vector components stored in two structured buffers:

```
struct Data
{
  float3 v1;
  float2 v2;
};

StructuredBuffer<Data> gInputA : register(t0);
StructuredBuffer<Data> gInputB : register(t1);
RWStructuredBuffer<Data> gOutput : register(u0);

[numthreads(32, 1, 1)]
void CS(int3 dtid : SV_DispatchThreadID)
{
  gOutput[dtid.x].v1 = gInputA[dtid.x].v1 + gInputB[dtid.x].v1;
  gOutput[dtid.x].v2 = gInputA[dtid.x].v2 + gInputB[dtid.x].v2;
}
```

For simplicity, the structured buffers only contain thirty-two elements; therefore, we only have to dispatch one thread group (since one thread group processes thirty-two elements). After the compute shader completes its work for all threads in this demo, we copy the results to system memory and save them to file. The following code shows how to create the system memory buffer and how to copy the GPU results to CPU memory:

```
// Create a system memory version of the buffer to read the
// results back from.
ThrowIfFailed(md3dDevice->CreateCommittedResource(
```

```
    &CD3DX12_HEAP_PROPERTIES(D3D12_HEAP_TYPE_READBACK),
    D3D12_HEAP_FLAG_NONE,
    &CD3DX12_RESOURCE_DESC::Buffer(byteSize),
    D3D12_RESOURCE_STATE_COPY_DEST,
    nullptr,
    IID_PPV_ARGS(&mReadBackBuffer)));

// ...
//
// Compute shader finished!

struct Data
{
    XMFLOAT3 v1;
    XMFLOAT2 v2;
};

// Schedule to copy the data to the default buffer to the readback
//    buffer.
mCommandList->ResourceBarrier(1, &CD3DX12_RESOURCE_BARRIER::Transition(
    mOutputBuffer.Get(),
    D3D12_RESOURCE_STATE_COMMON,
    D3D12_RESOURCE_STATE_COPY_SOURCE));

mCommandList->CopyResource(mReadBackBuffer.Get(), mOutputBuffer.Get());

mCommandList->ResourceBarrier(1, &CD3DX12_RESOURCE_BARRIER::Transition(
    mOutputBuffer.Get(),
    D3D12_RESOURCE_STATE_COPY_SOURCE,
    D3D12_RESOURCE_STATE_COMMON));

// Done recording commands.
ThrowIfFailed(mCommandList->Close());

// Add the command list to the queue for execution.
ID3D12CommandList* cmdsLists[] = { mCommandList.Get() };
mCommandQueue->ExecuteCommandLists(_countof(cmdsLists), cmdsLists);

// Wait for the work to finish.
FlushCommandQueue();

// Map the data so we can read it on CPU.
Data* mappedData = nullptr;
ThrowIfFailed(mReadBackBuffer->Map(0, nullptr,
    reinterpret_cast<void**>(&mappedData)));

std::ofstream fout("results.txt");

for(int i = 0; i < NumDataElements; ++i)
{
    fout << "(" << mappedData[i].v1.x << ", " <<
            mappedData[i].v1.y << ", " <<
            mappedData[i].v1.z <<        ", " <<
            mappedData[i].v2.x << ", " <<
            mappedData[i].v2.y << ")" << std::endl;
```

```
}

mReadBackBuffer->Unmap(0, nullptr);
In the demo, we fill the two input buffers with the following initial
    data:
std::vector<Data> dataA(NumDataElements);
std::vector<Data> dataB(NumDataElements);
for(int i = 0; i < NumDataElements; ++i)
{
  dataA[i].v1 = XMFLOAT3(i, i, i);
  dataA[i].v2 = XMFLOAT2(i, 0);

  dataB[i].v1 = XMFLOAT3(-i, i, 0.0f);
  dataB[i].v2 = XMFLOAT2(0, -i);
}
```

The resulting text file contains the following data, which confirms that the compute shader is working as expected.

```
(0, 0, 0, 0, 0)
(0, 2, 1, 1, -1)
(0, 4, 2, 2, -2)
(0, 6, 3, 3, -3)
(0, 8, 4, 4, -4)
(0, 10, 5, 5, -5)
(0, 12, 6, 6, -6)
(0, 14, 7, 7, -7)
(0, 16, 8, 8, -8)
(0, 18, 9, 9, -9)
(0, 20, 10, 10, -10)
(0, 22, 11, 11, -11)
(0, 24, 12, 12, -12)
(0, 26, 13, 13, -13)
(0, 28, 14, 14, -14)
(0, 30, 15, 15, -15)
(0, 32, 16, 16, -16)
(0, 34, 17, 17, -17)
(0, 36, 18, 18, -18)
(0, 38, 19, 19, -19)
(0, 40, 20, 20, -20)
(0, 42, 21, 21, -21)
(0, 44, 22, 22, -22)
(0, 46, 23, 23, -23)
(0, 48, 24, 24, -24)
(0, 50, 25, 25, -25)
(0, 52, 26, 26, -26)
(0, 54, 27, 27, -27)
(0, 56, 28, 28, -28)
(0, 58, 29, 29, -29)
(0, 60, 30, 30, -30)
(0, 62, 31, 31, -31)
```

From Figure 13.1, we see that copying between CPU and GPU memory is the slowest. For graphics, we never want to do this copy per frame, as it will kill

performance. For GPGPU programming, it is generally required to get the results back on the CPU; however, this is usually not a big deal for GPGPU programming, as the gains of using a GPU outweigh the copy cost from GPU to CPU—moreover, for GPGPU, the copy will be less frequent than "per frame." For example, suppose an application uses GPGPU programming to implement a costly image processing calculation. After the calculation is done the result is copied to the CPU. The GPU is not used again until the user requests another calculation.

13.4 THREAD IDENTIFICATION SYSTEM VALUES

Consider Figure 13.4.

1. Each thread group is assigned an ID by the system; this is called the *group ID* and has the system value semantic SV_GroupID. If $G_x \times G_y \times G_z$ are the number of thread groups dispatched, then the group ID ranges from $(0, 0, 0)$ to $(G_x - 1, G_y - 1, G_z - 1)$.
2. Inside a thread group, each thread is given a unique ID relative to its group. If the thread group has size $X \times Y \times Z$, then the *group thread IDs* will range from $(0, 0, 0)$ to $(X - 1, Y - 1, Z - 1)$. The system value semantic for the group thread ID is SV_GroupThreadID.
3. A Dispatch call dispatches a grid of thread groups. The *dispatch thread ID* uniquely identifies a thread relative to *all* the threads generated by a Dispatch call. In other words, whereas the group thread ID uniquely identifies a thread relative to its thread group, the dispatch thread ID uniquely identifies a thread relative to the union of all the threads from all the thread groups dispatched by a Dispatch call. Let, ThreadGroupSize = (X,Y,Z) be the thread group size,

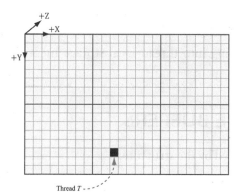

Figure 13.4. Consider the marked thread T. Thread T has thread group ID .(1, 1, 0). It has group thread ID (1, 5, 0). It has dispatch thread ID (1, 1, 0) ⊗ (8, 8, 0) + (2, 5, 0) = (10, 13, 0). It has group index ID 5·8 + 2 = 42.

then the dispatch thread ID can be derived from the group ID and the group thread ID as follows:

```
dispatchThreadID.xyz = groupID.xyz * ThreadGroupSize.xyz +
                       groupThreadID.xyz;
```

The dispatch thread ID has the system value semantic SV_DispatchThreadID. If 3×2 thread groups are dispatched, where each thread group is 10×10, then a total of 60 threads are dispatched and the dispatch thread IDs will range from $(0, 0, 0)$ to $(29, 19, 0)$.

4. A linear index version of the group thread ID is given to us by Direct3D through the SV_GroupIndex system value; it is computed as:

```
groupIndex = groupThreadID.z*ThreadGroupSize.x*ThreadGroupSize.y +
             groupThreadID.y*ThreadGroupSize.x + groupThreadID.x;
```

Regarding the indexing coordinate order, the first coordinate gives the x-position (or column) and the second coordinate gives the y-position (or row). This is in contrast to common matrix notation, where M_{ij} denotes the element in the ith row and jth column.

So why do we need these thread ID values. Well a compute shader generally takes some input data structure and outputs to some data structure. We can use the thread ID values as indexes into these data structures:

```
Texture2D gInputA;
Texture2D gInputB;
RWTexture2D<float4> gOutput;

[numthreads(16, 16, 1)]
void CS(int3 dispatchThreadID : SV_DispatchThreadID)
{
    // Use dispatch thread ID to index into output and input textures.
    gOutput[dispatchThreadID.xy] =
        gInputA[dispatchThreadID.xy] +
        gInputB[dispatchThreadID.xy];
}
```

The SV_GroupThreadID is useful for indexing into thread local storage memory (§13.6).

13.5 APPEND AND CONSUME BUFFERS

Suppose we have a buffer of particles defined by the structure:

```
struct Particle
{
    float3 Position;
    float3 Velocity;
```

```
    float3 Acceleration;
};
```

and we want to update the particle positions based on their constant acceleration and velocity in the compute shader. Moreover, suppose that we do not care about the order the particles are updated nor the order they are written to the output buffer. Consume and append structured buffers are ideal for this scenario, and they provide the convenience that we do not have to worry about indexing:

```
struct Particle
{
    float3 Position;
    float3 Velocity;
    float3 Acceleration;
};

float TimeStep = 1.0f / 60.0f;

ConsumeStructuredBuffer<Particle> gInput;
AppendStructuredBuffer<Particle> gOutput;
[numthreads(16, 16, 1)]
void CS()
{
    // Consume a data element from the input buffer.
    Particle p = gInput.Consume();

    p.Velocity += p.Acceleration*TimeStep;
    p.Position += p.Velocity*TimeStep;

    // Append normalized vector to output buffer.
    gOutput.Append( p );
}
```

Once a data element is consumed, it cannot be consumed again by a different thread; one thread will consume exactly one data element. And again, we emphasize that the order elements are consumed and appended are unknown; therefore, it is generally not the case that the *i*th element in the input buffer gets written to the *i*th element in the output buffer.

Note: *Append structured buffers do not dynamically grow. They must still be large enough to store all the elements you will append to it.*

13.6 SHARED MEMORY AND SYNCHRONIZATION

Thread groups are given a section of so-called shared memory or thread local storage. Accessing this memory is fast and can be thought of being as fast as a hardware cache. In the compute shader code, shared memory is declared like so:

```
groupshared float4 gCache[256];
```

The array size can be whatever you want, but the maximum size of group shared memory is 32kb. Because the shared memory is local to the thread group, it is indexed with the SV_ThreadGroupID; so, for example, you might give each thread in the group access to one slot in the shared memory.

Using too much shared memory can lead to performance issues [Fung10], as the following example illustrates. Suppose a multiprocessor supports 32kb of shared memory, and your compute shader requires 20kb of shared memory. This means that only one thread group will fit on the multiprocessor because there is not enough memory left for another thread group [Fung10], as 20kb + 20kb = 40kb > 32kb. This limits the parallelism of the GPU, as a multiprocessor cannot switch off between thread groups to hide latency (recall from §13.1 that at least two thread groups per multiprocessor is recommended). Thus, even though the hardware technically supports 32kb of shared memory, performance improvements can be achieved by using less.

A common application of shared memory is to store texture values in it. Certain algorithms, such as blurs, require fetching the same texel multiple times. Sampling textures is actually one of the slower GPU operations because memory bandwidth and memory latency have not improved as much as the raw computational power of GPUs [Möller08]. A thread group can avoid redundant texture fetches by preloading all the needed texture samples into the shared memory array. The algorithm then proceeds to look up the texture samples in the shared memory array, which is very fast. Suppose we implement this strategy with the following erroneous code:

```
Texture2D gInput;
RWTexture2D<float4> gOutput;

groupshared float4 gCache[256];

[numthreads(256, 1, 1)]
void CS(int3 groupThreadID : SV_GroupThreadID,
    int3 dispatchThreadID : SV_DispatchThreadID)
{
    // Each thread samples the texture and stores the
    // value in shared memory.
    gCache[groupThreadID.x] = gInput[dispatchThreadID.xy];

    // Do computation work: Access elements in shared memory
    // that other threads stored:

    // BAD!!! Left and right neighbor threads might not have
    // finished sampling tzZhe texture and storing it in shared memory.
    float4 left = gCache[groupThreadID.x - 1];
    float4 right = gCache[groupThreadID.x + 1];

    ...
}
```

A problem arises with this scenario because we have no guarantee that all the threads in the thread group finish at the same time. Thus a thread could go to access a shared memory element that is not yet initialized because the neighboring threads responsible for initializing those elements have not finished yet. To fix this problem, before the compute shader can continue, it must wait until all the threads have done their texture loading into shared memory. This is accomplished by a synchronization command:

```
Texture2D gInput;
RWTexture2D<float4> gOutput;

groupshared float4 gCache[256];

[numthreads(256, 1, 1)]
void CS(int3 groupThreadID : SV_GroupThreadID,
    int3 dispatchThreadID : SV_DispatchThreadID)
{
  // Each thread samples the texture and stores the
  // value in shared memory.
  gCache[groupThreadID.x] = gInput[dispatchThreadID.xy];

  // Wait for all threads in group to finish.
  GroupMemoryBarrierWithGroupSync();

  // Safe now to read any element in the shared memory
  //and do computation work.

  float4 left = gCache[groupThreadID.x - 1];
  float4 right = gCache[groupThreadID.x + 1];

  ...
}
```

13.7 BLUR DEMO

In this section, we explain how to implement a blur algorithm on the compute shader. We begin by describing the mathematical theory of blurring. Then we discuss the technique of technique of render-to-texture, which our demo uses to generate a source image to blur. Finally, we review the code for a compute shader implementation and discuss how to handle certain details that make the implementation a little tricky.

13.7.1 Blurring Theory

The blurring algorithm we use is described as follows: For each pixel P_{ij} in the source image, compute the weighted average of the $m \times n$ matrix of pixels centered

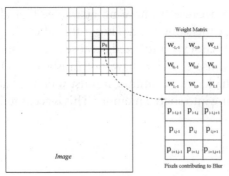

Figure 13.5. To blur the pixel Pij we compute the weighted average of the m × n matrix of pixels centered about the pixel. In this example, the matrix is a square 3 × 3 matrix, with blur radius $a = b = 1$. Observe that the center weight w_{00} aligns with the pixel P_{ij}.

about the pixel P_{ij} (see Figure 13.5); this weighted average becomes the *ij*th pixel in the blurred image. Mathematically,

$$Blur(P_{ij}) = \sum_{r=-a}^{a}\sum_{c=-b}^{b} w_{rc} P_{i+r,j+c} \text{ for } \sum_{r=-a}^{a}\sum_{c=-b}^{b} w_{rc} = 1$$

where $m = 2a + 1$ and $n = 2b + 1$. By forcing *m* and *n* to be odd, we ensure that the m × n matrix always has a natural "center." We call *a* the vertical blur radius and *b* the horizontal blur radius. If $a = b$, then we just refer to the *blur radius* without having to specify the dimension. The m × n matrix of weights is called the *blur kernel*. Observe also that the weights must sum to 1. If the sum of the weights is less than one, the blurred image will appear darker as color has been removed. If the sum of the weights is greater than one, the blurred image will appear brighter as color has been added.

There are various ways to compute the weights so long as they sum to 1. A well-known blur operator found in many image editing programs is the Gaussian blur, which obtains its weights from the Gaussian function $G(x) = \exp\left(-\frac{x^2}{2\sigma^2}\right)$. A graph of this function is shown in Figure 13.6 for different σ.

Let us suppose we are doing a 1 × 5 Gaussian blur (i.e., a 1D blur in the horizontal direction), and let $\sigma = 1$. Evaluating $G(x)$ for $x = -2, -1, 0, 1, 2$ we have:

$$G(-2) = \exp\left(-\frac{(-2)^2}{2}\right) = e^{-2}$$

$$G(-1) = \exp\left(-\frac{(-1)^2}{2}\right) = e^{-\frac{1}{2}}$$

$$G(0) = \exp(0) = 1$$

$$G(1) = \exp\left(-\frac{1^2}{2}\right) = e^{-\frac{1}{2}}$$

$$G(2) = \exp\left(-\frac{2^2}{2}\right) = e^{-2}$$

However, these values are not the weights because they do not sum to 1:

$$\sum_{x=-2}^{x=2} G(x) = G(-2) + G(-1) + G(0) + G(1) + G(2)$$

$$= 1 + 2e^{-\frac{1}{2}} + 2e^{-2}$$

$$\approx 2.48373$$

If we normalize the above equation by dividing by the sum $\sum_{x=-2}^{x=2} G(x)$, then we obtain weights based on the Gaussian function that sum to 1:

$$\frac{G(-2) + G(-1) + G(0) + G(1) + G(2)}{\sum_{x=-2}^{x=2} G(x)} = 1$$

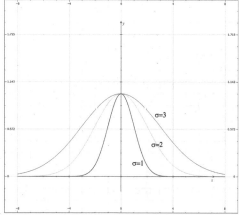

Figure 13.6. Plot of $G(x)$ for σ = 1, 2, 3. Observe that a larger σ flattens the curve out and gives more weight to the neighboring points.

Therefore, the Gaussian blur weights are:

$$w_{-2} = \frac{G(-2)}{\sum_{x=-2}^{x=2} G(x)} = \frac{e^{-2}}{1 + 2e^{-\frac{1}{2}} + 2e^{-2}} \approx 0.0545$$

$$w_{-1} = \frac{G(-1)}{\sum_{x=-2}^{x=2} G(x)} = \frac{e^{-\frac{1}{2}}}{1 + 2e^{-\frac{1}{2}} + 2e^{-2}} \approx 0.2442$$

$$w_{0} = \frac{G(0)}{\sum_{x=-2}^{x=2} G(x)} = \frac{1}{1 + 2e^{-\frac{1}{2}} + 2e^{-2}} \approx 0.4026$$

$$w_{1} = \frac{G(1)}{\sum_{x=-2}^{x=2} G(x)} = \frac{e^{-\frac{1}{2}}}{1 + 2e^{-\frac{1}{2}} + 2e^{-2}} \approx 0.2442$$

$$w_{2} = \frac{G(2)}{\sum_{x=-2}^{x=2} G(x)} = \frac{e^{-2}}{1 + 2e^{-\frac{1}{2}} + 2e^{-2}} \approx 0.0545$$

The Gaussian blur is known to be separable, which means it can be broken up into two 1D blurs as follows.

1. Blur the input image I using a 1D horizontal blur: $I_H = Blur_H(I)$.
2. Blur the output from the previous step using a 1D vertical blur: $Blur(I) = Blur_V(I_H)$.

Written more succinctly, we have:

$$Blur(I) = Blur_V(Blur_H(I))$$

Suppose that the blur kernel is a 9 × 9 matrix, so that we needed a total of 81 samples to do the 2D blur. By separating the blur into two 1D blurs, we only need 9 + 9 = 18 samples. Typically, we will be blurring textures; as mentioned in this chapter, fetching texture samples is expensive, so reducing texture samples by separating a blur is a welcome improvement. Even if a blur is not separable (some blur operators are not), we can often make the simplification and assume it is for the sake of performance, as long as the final image looks accurate enough.

13.7.2 Render-to-Texture

So far in our programs, we have been rendering to the back buffer. But what is the back buffer? If we review our D3DApp code, we see that the back buffer is just a texture in the swap chain:

```
Microsoft::WRL::ComPtr<ID3D12Resource> mSwapChainBuffer[SwapChainBuffe
rCount];
CD3DX12_CPU_DESCRIPTOR_HANDLE rtvHeapHandle(mRtvHeap->GetCPUDescriptorH
    andleForHeapStart());
for (UINT i = 0; i < SwapChainBufferCount; i++)
{
  ThrowIfFailed(mSwapChain->GetBuffer(i,
    IID_PPV_ARGS(&mSwapChainBuffer[i])));
  md3dDevice->CreateRenderTargetView(
    mSwapChainBuffer[i].Get(), nullptr, rtvHeapHandle);
  rtvHeapHandle.Offset(1, mRtvDescriptorSize);
}
```

We instruct Direct3D to render to the back buffer by binding a render target view of the back buffer to the OM stage of the rendering pipeline:

```
// Specify the buffers we are going to render to.
mCommandList->OMSetRenderTargets(1, &CurrentBackBufferView(),
    true, &DepthStencilView());
```

The contents of the back buffer are eventually displayed on the screen when the back buffer is presented via the `IDXGISwapChain::Present` method.

 A texture that will be used as a render target must be created with the flag `D3D12_RESOURCE_FLAG_ALLOW_RENDER_TARGET`.

If we think about this code, there is nothing that stops us from creating another texture, creating a render target view to it, and binding it to the OM stage of the rendering pipeline. Thus we will be drawing to this different "off-screen" texture (possible with a different camera) instead of the back buffer. This technique is known as *render-to-off-screen-texture* or simply *render-to-texture*. The only difference is that since this texture is not the back buffer, it does not get displayed to the screen during presentation.

Consequently, render-to-texture might seem worthless at first as it does not get presented to the screen. But, after we have rendered-to-texture, we can bind the back buffer back to the OM stage, and resume drawing geometry to the back buffer. We can texture the geometry with the texture we generated during the render-to-texture period. This strategy is used to implement a variety of special effects. For example, you can render-to-texture the scene from a bird's eye view to a texture. Then, when drawing to the back buffer, you can draw a quad in the lower-right corner of the screen with the bird's

Figure 13.7. A camera is placed above the player from a bird's eye view and renders the scene into an off-screen texture. When we draw the scene from the player's eye to the back buffer, we map the texture onto a quad in the bottom-right corner of the screen to display the radar map.

eye view texture to simulate a radar system (see Figure 13.7). Other render-to-texture techniques include:

1. Shadow mapping
2. Screen Space Ambient Occlusion
3. Dynamic reflections with cube maps

Using render-to-texture, implementing a blurring algorithm on the GPU would work the following way: render our normal demo scene to an off-screen texture. This texture will be the input into our blurring algorithm that executes on the compute shader. After the texture is blurred, we will draw a full screen quad to the back buffer with the blurred texture applied so that we can see the blurred result to test our blur implementation. The steps are outlined as follows:

1. Draw scene as usual to an off-screen texture.
2. Blur the off-screen texture using a compute shader program.
3. Restore the back buffer as the render target, and draw a full screen quad with the blurred texture applied.

Using render-to-texture to implement a blur works fine, and is the required approach if we want to render the scene to a different sized texture than the back buffer. However, if we make the assumption that our off-screen textures match the format and size of our back buffer, instead of redirecting rendering to our off-screen texture, we can render to the back buffer as usual, and then do a `CopyResource` to copy the back-buffer contents to our off-screen texture. Then we can do our compute work on our off-screen textures, and then draw a full-screen quad to the back buffer with the blurred texture to produce the final screen output.

```
// Copy the input (back-buffer in this example) to BlurMap0.
cmdList->CopyResource(mBlurMap0.Get(), input);
```

This is the technique we will use to implement our blur demo, but Exercise 6 asks you to implement a different filter using render-to-texture.

 The above process requires us to draw with the usual rendering pipeline, switch to the compute shader and do compute work, and finally switch back to the usual rendering pipeline. In general, try to avoid switching back and forth between rendering and doing compute work, as there is overhead due to a context switch [NVIDIA10]. For each frame, try to do all compute work, and then do all rendering work. Sometimes it is impossible; for example, in the process described above, we need to render the scene to a texture, blur it with the compute shader, and then render the blurred results. However, try to minimize the number of switches.

13.7.3 Blur Implementation Overview

We assume that the blur is separable, so we break the blur down into computing two 1D blurs—a horizontal one and a vertical one. Implementing this requires two texture buffers where we can read and write to both; therefore, we need a SRV and UAV to both textures. Let us call one of the textures **A** and the other texture **B**. The blurring algorithm proceeds as follows:

1. Bind the SRV to **A** as an input to the compute shader (this is the input image that will be horizontally blurred).
2. Bind the UAV to **B** as an output to the compute shader (this is the output image that will store the blurred result).
3. Dispatch the thread groups to perform the horizontal blur operation. After this, texture **B** stores the horizontally blurred result $Blur_H(I)$, where I is the image to blur.
4. Bind the SRV to **B** as an input to the compute shader (this is the horizontally blurred image that will next be vertically blurred).
5. Bind the UAV to **A** as an output to the compute shader (this is the output image that will store the final blurred result).
6. Dispatch the thread groups to perform the vertical blur operation. After this, texture **A** stores the final blurred result $Blur(I)$, where I is the image to blur.

This logic implements the separable blur formula $Blur(I) = Blur_V\left(Blur_H(I)\right)$. Observe that both texture **A** and texture **B** serve as an input and an output to the compute shader at some point, but not simultaneously. (It is Direct3D error to bind a resource as an input and output at the same time.) The combined horizontal and vertical blur passes constitute one complete blur pass. The resulting image can be blurred further by performing another blur pass on it. We can repeatedly blur an image until the image is blurred to the desired level.

The texture we render the scene to has the same resolution as the window client area. Therefore, we need to rebuild the off-screen texture, as well as the second texture buffer **B** used in the blur algorithm. We do this on the OnResize method:

```
void BlurApp::OnResize()
{
  D3DApp::OnResize();

  // The window resized, so update the aspect ratio and
  // recompute the projection matrix.
  XMMATRIX P = XMMatrixPerspectiveFovLH(
    0.25f*MathHelper::Pi, AspectRatio(),
    1.0f, 1000.0f);
  XMStoreFloat4x4(&mProj, P);

  if(mBlurFilter != nullptr)
  {
    mBlurFilter->OnResize(mClientWidth, mClientHeight);
  }
}

void BlurFilter::OnResize(UINT newWidth, UINT newHeight)
{
  if((mWidth != newWidth) || (mHeight != newHeight))
  {
    mWidth = newWidth;
    mHeight = newHeight;

    // Rebuild the off-screen texture resource with new dimensions.
    BuildResources();

    // New resources, so we need new descriptors to that resource.
    BuildDescriptors();
  }
}
```

The `mBlur` variable is an instance of a `BlurFilter` helper class we make. This class encapsulates the texture resources to textures **A** and **B**, encapsulates SRVs and UAVs to the textures, and provides a method that kicks off the actual blur operation on the compute shader, the implementation of which we will see in a moment.

The `BlurFilter` class encapsulates texture resources. To bind these resources to the pipeline to use for a draw/dispatch command, we are going to need to create descriptors to these resources. That means we will have to allocate extra room in the `D3D12_DESCRIPTOR_HEAP_TYPE_CBV_SRV_UAV` descriptor heap to store these descriptors. The `BlurFilter::BuildDescriptors` method takes descriptor handles to the starting location in the descriptor heap to store the descriptors used by

BlurFilter. The method caches the handles for all the descriptors it needs and then creates the corresponding descriptors. The reason it caches the handles is so that it can recreate the descriptors when the resources change, which happens when the screen is resized:

```
void BlurFilter::BuildDescriptors(
  CD3DX12_CPU_DESCRIPTOR_HANDLE hCpuDescriptor,
  CD3DX12_GPU_DESCRIPTOR_HANDLE hGpuDescriptor,
  UINT descriptorSize)
{
  // Save references to the descriptors.
  mBlur0CpuSrv = hCpuDescriptor;
  mBlur0CpuUav = hCpuDescriptor.Offset(1, descriptorSize);
  mBlur1CpuSrv = hCpuDescriptor.Offset(1, descriptorSize);
  mBlur1CpuUav = hCpuDescriptor.Offset(1, descriptorSize);

  mBlur0GpuSrv = hGpuDescriptor;
  mBlur0GpuUav = hGpuDescriptor.Offset(1, descriptorSize);
  mBlur1GpuSrv = hGpuDescriptor.Offset(1, descriptorSize);
  mBlur1GpuUav = hGpuDescriptor.Offset(1, descriptorSize);

  BuildDescriptors();
}

void BlurFilter::BuildDescriptors()
{
  D3D12_SHADER_RESOURCE_VIEW_DESC srvDesc = {};
  srvDesc.Shader4ComponentMapping = D3D12_DEFAULT_SHADER_4_COMPONENT_
    MAPPING;
  srvDesc.Format = mFormat;
  srvDesc.ViewDimension = D3D12_SRV_DIMENSION_TEXTURE2D;
  srvDesc.Texture2D.MostDetailedMip = 0;
  srvDesc.Texture2D.MipLevels = 1;

  D3D12_UNORDERED_ACCESS_VIEW_DESC uavDesc = {};

  uavDesc.Format = mFormat;
  uavDesc.ViewDimension = D3D12_UAV_DIMENSION_TEXTURE2D;
  uavDesc.Texture2D.MipSlice = 0;

  md3dDevice->CreateShaderResourceView(mBlurMap0.Get(), &srvDesc,
    mBlur0CpuSrv);
  md3dDevice->CreateUnorderedAccessView(mBlurMap0.Get(),
    nullptr, &uavDesc, mBlur0CpuUav);

  md3dDevice->CreateShaderResourceView(mBlurMap1.Get(), &srvDesc,
    mBlur1CpuSrv);
  md3dDevice->CreateUnorderedAccessView(mBlurMap1.Get(),
    nullptr, &uavDesc, mBlur1CpuUav);
}

// In BlurApp.cpp...Offset to location in heap to
// store descriptors for BlurFilter
```

```
mBlurFilter->BuildDescriptors(
  CD3DX12_CPU_DESCRIPTOR_HANDLE(
    mCbvSrvUavDescriptorHeap->GetCPUDescriptorHandleForHeapStart(),
    3, mCbvSrvUavDescriptorSize),
  CD3DX12_GPU_DESCRIPTOR_HANDLE(
    mCbvSrvUavDescriptorHeap->GetGPUDescriptorHandleForHeapStart(),
    3, mCbvSrvUavDescriptorSize),
  mCbvSrvUavDescriptorSize);
```

> **Note:** *Blurring is an expensive operation and the time it takes is a function of the image size being blurred. Often, when rendering the scene to an off-screen texture, the off-screen texture will be made a quarter of the size of the back buffer. For example, if the back buffer is 800 × 600, the off-screen texture will be 400 × 30. This speeds up the drawing to the off-screen texture (less pixels to fill); moreover, it speeds up the blur (less pixels to blur), and there is additional blurring performed by the magnification texture filter when the texture is stretched from a quarter of the screen resolution to the full screen resolution.*

Suppose our image has width w and height h. As we will see in the next section when we look at the compute shader, for the horizontal 1D blur, our thread group is a horizontal line segment of 256 threads, and each thread is responsible for blurring one pixel in the image. Therefore, we need to dispatch $ceil\left(\frac{w}{256}\right)$ thread groups in the x-direction and h thread groups in the y-direction in order for each pixel in the image to be blurred. If 256 does not divide evenly into w, the last horizontal thread group will have extraneous threads (see Figure (13.8)). There is not really anything we can do about this since the thread group size is fixed. We take care of out-of-bounds with clamping checks in the shader code.

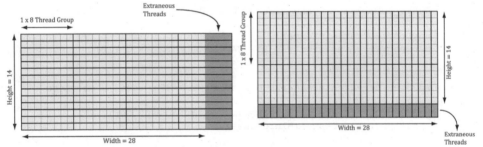

Figure 13.8. Consider a 28 × 14 texture, where our horizontal thread groups are 8 × 1 and our vertical thread groups are 1 × 8 ($X \times Y$ format). For the horizontal pass, in order to cover all the pixels we need to dispatch $ceil\left(\frac{w}{8}\right)=ceil\left(\frac{28}{8}\right)=4$ thread groups in the x-direction and 14 thread groups in the y-direction. Since 28 is not a multiple of 8, we end of with extraneous threads that do not do any work in the right-most thread groups. For the vertical pass, in order to cover all the pixels we need to dispatch $ceil\left(\frac{h}{8}\right)=ceil\left(\frac{14}{8}\right)=2$ thread groups in the y-direction and 28 thread groups in the x-direction. Since 14 is not a multiple of 8, we end up with extraneous threads that do not do any work in the bottom-most thread groups. The same concepts apply to a larger texture with thread groups of size 256.

The situation is similar for the vertical 1D blur. Again, our thread group is a vertical line segment of 256 threads, and each thread is responsible for blurring one pixel in the image. Therefore, we need to dispatch $ceil\left(\frac{h}{256}\right)$ thread groups in the *y*-direction and *w* thread groups in the *x*-direction in order for each pixel in the image to be blurred.

The code below figures out how many thread groups to dispatch in each direction, and kicks off the actual blur operation on the compute shader:

```
void BlurFilter::Execute(ID3D12GraphicsCommandList* cmdList,
              ID3D12RootSignature* rootSig,
              ID3D12PipelineState* horzBlurPSO,
              ID3D12PipelineState* vertBlurPSO,
        ID3D12Resource* input,
                int blurCount)
{
  auto weights = CalcGaussWeights(2.5f);
  int blurRadius = (int)weights.size() / 2;

  cmdList->SetComputeRootSignature(rootSig);

  cmdList->SetComputeRoot32BitConstants(0, 1, &blurRadius, 0);
  cmdList->SetComputeRoot32BitConstants(0, (UINT)weights.size(), weights.
    data(), 1);

  cmdList->ResourceBarrier(1, &CD3DX12_RESOURCE_BARRIER::Transition(input,
    D3D12_RESOURCE_STATE_RENDER_TARGET, D3D12_RESOURCE_STATE_COPY_SOURCE));

  cmdList->ResourceBarrier(1, &CD3DX12_RESOURCE_BARRIER::Transition(mBlurMap0.
    Get(),
    D3D12_RESOURCE_STATE_COMMON, D3D12_RESOURCE_STATE_COPY_DEST));

  // Copy the input (back-buffer in this example) to BlurMap0.
  cmdList->CopyResource(mBlurMap0.Get(), input);

  cmdList->ResourceBarrier(1, &CD3DX12_RESOURCE_BARRIER::Transition(mBlurMap0.
    Get(),
    D3D12_RESOURCE_STATE_COPY_DEST, D3D12_RESOURCE_STATE_GENERIC_READ));

  cmdList->ResourceBarrier(1, &CD3DX12_RESOURCE_BARRIER::Transition(mBlurMap1.
    Get(),
    D3D12_RESOURCE_STATE_COMMON, D3D12_RESOURCE_STATE_UNORDERED_ACCESS));

  for(int i = 0; i < blurCount; ++i)
  {
    //
    // Horizontal Blur pass.
    //

    cmdList->SetPipelineState(horzBlurPSO);

    cmdList->SetComputeRootDescriptorTable(1, mBlur0GpuSrv);
    cmdList->SetComputeRootDescriptorTable(2, mBlur1GpuUav);
```

```cpp
    // How many groups do we need to dispatch to cover a row of pixels, where
    // each group covers 256 pixels (the 256 is defined in the ComputeShader).
    UINT numGroupsX = (UINT)ceilf(mWidth / 256.0f);
    cmdList->Dispatch(numGroupsX, mHeight, 1);

    cmdList->ResourceBarrier(1, &CD3DX12_RESOURCE_BARRIER::Transition(
      mBlurMap0.Get(),
      D3D12_RESOURCE_STATE_GENERIC_READ,
      D3D12_RESOURCE_STATE_UNORDERED_ACCESS));

    cmdList->ResourceBarrier(1, &CD3DX12_RESOURCE_BARRIER::Transition(
      mBlurMap1.Get(),
      D3D12_RESOURCE_STATE_UNORDERED_ACCESS,
      D3D12_RESOURCE_STATE_GENERIC_READ));

    //
    // Vertical Blur pass.
    //

    cmdList->SetPipelineState(vertBlurPSO);

    cmdList->SetComputeRootDescriptorTable(1, mBlur1GpuSrv);
    cmdList->SetComputeRootDescriptorTable(2, mBlur0GpuUav);

    // How many groups do we need to dispatch to cover a column of pixels,
    // where each group covers 256 pixels (the 256 is defined in the
    // ComputeShader).
    UINT numGroupsY = (UINT)ceilf(mHeight / 256.0f);
    cmdList->Dispatch(mWidth, numGroupsY, 1);

    cmdList->ResourceBarrier(1, &CD3DX12_RESOURCE_BARRIER::Transition(
      mBlurMap0.Get(),
      D3D12_RESOURCE_STATE_UNORDERED_ACCESS,
      D3D12_RESOURCE_STATE_GENERIC_READ));

    cmdList->ResourceBarrier(1, &CD3DX12_RESOURCE_BARRIER::Transition(
      mBlurMap1.Get(),
      D3D12_RESOURCE_STATE_GENERIC_READ,
      D3D12_RESOURCE_STATE_UNORDERED_ACCESS));
  }
}
```

Figure 13.9. Left: A screenshot of the "Blur" demo where the image has been blurred two times. Right: A screen shot of the "Blur" demo where the image has been blurred eight times.

13.7.4 Compute Shader Program

In this section, we look the compute shader program that actually does the blurring. We will only discuss the horizontal blur case. The vertical blur case is analogous, but the situation transposed.

As mentioned in the previous section, our thread group is a horizontal line segment of 256 threads, and each thread is responsible for blurring one pixel in the image. An inefficient first approach is to just implement the blur algorithm directly. That is, each thread simply performs the weighted average of the row matrix (row matrix because we are doing the 1D horizontal pass) of pixels centered about the pixel the thread is processing. The problem with this approach is that it requires fetching the same texel multiple times (see Figure 13.10).

We can optimize by following the strategy described in §13.6 and take advantage of shared memory. Each thread can read in a texel value and store it in shared memory. After all the threads are done reading their texel values into shared memory, the threads can proceed to perform the blur, but where it reads the texels from the shared memory, which is fast to access. The only tricky thing about this is that a thread group of $n = 256$ threads requires $n + 2R$ texels to perform the blur, where R is the blur radius (Figure 13.11).

The solution is simple; we allocate $n + 2R$ elements of shared memory, and have $2R$ threads lookup two texel values. The only thing that is tricky about this is that it requires a little more book keeping when indexing into the shared memory; we no longer have the ith group thread ID corresponding to the ith element in the shared memory. Figure 13.12 shows the mapping from threads to shared memory for $R = 4$.

Finally, the last situation to discuss is that the left-most thread group and the right-most thread group can index the input image out-of-bounds, as shown in Figure 13.13.

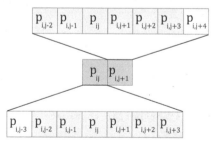

Figure 13.10. Consider just two neighboring pixels in the input image, and suppose that the blur kernel is 1 × 7. Observe that six out of the eight unique pixels are sampled twice—once for each pixel.

Figure 13.11. Pixels near the boundaries of the thread group will read pixels outside the thread group due to the blur radius.

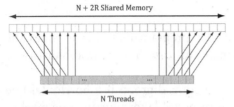
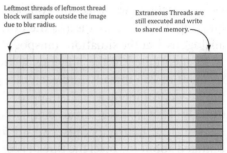

Figure 13.12. In this example, R = 4. The four leftmost threads each read two texel values and store them into shared memory. The four rightmost threads each read two texel values and store them into shared memory. Every other thread just reads one texel value and stores it in shared memory. This gives us all the texel values we need to blur N pixels with blur radius R.

Figure 13.13. Situations where we can read outside the bounds of the image.

Reading from an out-of-bounds index is not illegal—it is defined to return 0 (and writing to an out-of-bounds index results in a no-op). However, we do not want to read 0 when we go out-of-bounds, as it means 0 colors (i.e., black) will make their way into the blur at the boundaries. Instead, we want to implement something analogous to the *clamp* texture address mode, where if we read an out-of-bounds value, it returns the same value as the boundary texel. This can be implemented by clamping the indices:

```
// Clamp out of bound samples that occur at left image borders.
int x = max(dispatchThreadID.x - gBlurRadius, 0);
gCache[groupThreadID.x] = gInput[int2(x, dispatchThreadID.y)];

// Clamp out of bound samples that occur at right image borders.
int x = min(dispatchThreadID.x + gBlurRadius, gInput.Length.x-1);
gCache[groupThreadID.x+2*gBlurRadius] =
gInput[int2(x, dispatchThreadID.y)];

// Clamp out of bound samples that occur at image borders.
gCache[groupThreadID.x+gBlurRadius] =
gInput[min(dispatchThreadID.xy, gInput.Length.xy-1)];
```

The full shader code is shown below:

```
//===============================================================
// Performs a separable Guassian blur with a blur radius up to 5 pixels.
//===============================================================

cbuffer cbSettings : register(b0)
{
  // We cannot have an array entry in a constant buffer that gets
    mapped onto
  // root constants, so list each element.
  
  int gBlurRadius;
  
  // Support up to 11 blur weights.
  float w0;
```

```hlsl
    float w1;
    float w2;
    float w3;
    float w4;
    float w5;
    float w6;
    float w7;
    float w8;
    float w9;
    float w10;
};

static const int gMaxBlurRadius = 5;


Texture2D gInput            : register(t0);
RWTexture2D<float4> gOutput : register(u0);

#define N 256
#define CacheSize (N + 2*gMaxBlurRadius)
groupshared float4 gCache[CacheSize];

[numthreads(N, 1, 1)]
void HorzBlurCS(int3 groupThreadID : SV_GroupThreadID,
                int3 dispatchThreadID : SV_DispatchThreadID)
{
    // Put in an array for each indexing.
    float weights[11] = { w0, w1, w2, w3, w4, w5, w6, w7, w8, w9, w10 };

    //
    // Fill local thread storage to reduce bandwidth.  To blur 
    // N pixels, we will need to load N + 2*BlurRadius pixels
    // due to the blur radius.
    //
    
    // This thread group runs N threads.  To get the extra 2*BlurRadius 
    // pixels, have 2*BlurRadius threads sample an extra pixel.
    if(groupThreadID.x < gBlurRadius)
    {
        // Clamp out of bound samples that occur at image borders.
        int x = max(dispatchThreadID.x - gBlurRadius, 0);
        gCache[groupThreadID.x] = gInput[int2(x, dispatchThreadID.y)];
    }
    if(groupThreadID.x >= N-gBlurRadius)
    {
        // Clamp out of bound samples that occur at image borders.
        int x = min(dispatchThreadID.x + gBlurRadius, gInput.Length.x-1);
        gCache[groupThreadID.x+2*gBlurRadius] = gInput[int2(x,
          dispatchThreadID.y)];
    }
    
    // Clamp out of bound samples that occur at image borders.
    gCache[groupThreadID.x+gBlurRadius] = gInput[min(dispatchThreadID.xy,
      gInput.Length.xy-1)];
```

```
	// Wait for all threads to finish.
	GroupMemoryBarrierWithGroupSync();
	
	//
	// Now blur each pixel.
	//
	
	float4 blurColor = float4(0, 0, 0, 0);
	
	for(int i = -gBlurRadius; i <= gBlurRadius; ++i)
	{
	  int k = groupThreadID.x + gBlurRadius + i;
	  
	  blurColor += weights[i+gBlurRadius]*gCache[k];
	}
	
	gOutput[dispatchThreadID.xy] = blurColor;
}

[numthreads(1, N, 1)]
void VertBlurCS(int3 groupThreadID : SV_GroupThreadID,
				int3 dispatchThreadID : SV_DispatchThreadID)
{
	// Put in an array for each indexing.
	float weights[11] = { w0, w1, w2, w3, w4, w5, w6, w7, w8, w9, w10 };
	
	//
	// Fill local thread storage to reduce bandwidth. To blur
	// N pixels, we will need to load N + 2*BlurRadius pixels
	// due to the blur radius.
	//
	
	// This thread group runs N threads. To get the extra 2*BlurRadius
	// pixels, have 2*BlurRadius threads sample an extra pixel.
	if(groupThreadID.y < gBlurRadius)
	{
	  // Clamp out of bound samples that occur at image borders.
	  int y = max(dispatchThreadID.y - gBlurRadius, 0);
	  gCache[groupThreadID.y] = gInput[int2(dispatchThreadID.x, y)];
	}
	if(groupThreadID.y >= N-gBlurRadius)
	{
	  // Clamp out of bound samples that occur at image borders.
	  int y = min(dispatchThreadID.y + gBlurRadius, gInput.Length.y-1);
	  gCache[groupThreadID.y+2*gBlurRadius] =
	    gInput[int2(dispatchThreadID.x, y)];
	}
	
	// Clamp out of bound samples that occur at image borders.
	gCache[groupThreadID.y+gBlurRadius] = gInput[min(dispatchThreadID.xy,
	   gInput.Length.xy-1)];
	
	
	// Wait for all threads to finish.
	GroupMemoryBarrierWithGroupSync();
```

```
//
// Now blur each pixel.
//

float4 blurColor = float4(0, 0, 0, 0);

for(int i = -gBlurRadius; i <= gBlurRadius; ++i)
{
   int k = groupThreadID.y + gBlurRadius + i;

   blurColor += weights[i+gBlurRadius]*gCache[k];
}

gOutput[dispatchThreadID.xy] = blurColor;
}
```

For the last line

```
gOutput[dispatchThreadID.xy] = blurColor;
```

it is possible in the right-most thread group to have extraneous threads that do not correspond to an element in the output texture (Figure 13.13). That is, the `dispatchThreadID.xy` will be an out-of-bounds index for the output texture. However, we do not need to worry about handling this case, as an out-of-bound write results in a no-op.

13.8 FURTHER RESOURCES

Compute shader programming is a subject in its own right, and there are several books on using GPUs for compute programs:

1. *Programming Massively Parallel Processors: A Hands-on Approach* by David B. Kirk and Wen-mei W. Hwu.
2. *OpenCL Programming Guide* by Aaftab Munshi, Benedict R. Gaster, Timothy G. Mattson, James Fung, and Dan Ginsburg.

Technologies like CUDA and OpenCL are just different APIs for accessing the GPU for writing compute programs. Best practices for CUDA and OpenCL programs are also best practices for Direct Compute programs, as the programs are all executed on the same hardware. In this chapter, we have shown the majority of Direct Compute syntax, and so you should have no trouble porting a CUDA or OpenCL program to Direct Compute.

Chuck Walbourn has posted a blog page consisting of links to many Direct Compute presentations:

http://blogs.msdn.com/b/chuckw/archive/2010/07/14/directcompute.aspx

In addition, Microsoft's Channel 9 has a series of lecture videos on Direct Compute programming:
   http://channel9.msdn.com/tags/DirectCompute-Lecture-Series/
Finally, NVIDIA has a whole section on CUDA training.
   http://developer.nvidia.com/cuda-training
In particular, there are full video lectures on CUDA programming from the University of Illinois, which we highly recommend. Again, we emphasize that CUDA is just another API for accessing the compute functionality of the GPU. Once you understand the syntax, the hard part about GPU computing is learning how to write efficient programs for it. By studying these lectures on CUDA, you will get a better idea of how GPU hardware works so that you can write optimal code.

13.9 SUMMARY

1. The `ID3D12GraphicsCommandList::Dispatch` API call dispatches a grid of thread groups. Each thread group is a 3D grid of threads; the number of threads per thread group is specified by the `[numthreads(x,y,z)]` attribute in the compute shader. For performance reasons, the total number of threads should be a multiple of the warp size (thirty-two for NVIDIA hardware) or a multiple of the wavefront size (sixty-four ATI hardware).

2. To ensure parallelism, at least two thread groups should be dispatched per multiprocessor. So if your hardware has sixteen multiprocessors, then at least thirty-two thread groups should be dispatched so a multiprocessor always has work to do. Future hardware will likely have more multiprocessors, so the number of thread groups should be even higher to ensure your program scales well to future hardware.

3. Once thread groups are assigned to a multiprocessor, the threads in the thread groups are divided into warps of thirty-two threads on NVIDIA hardware. The multiprocessor than works on a warp of threads at a time in an SIMD fashion (i.e., the same instruction is executed for each thread in the warp). If a warp becomes stalled, say to fetch texture memory, the multiprocessor can quickly switch and execute instructions for another warp to hide this latency. This keeps the multiprocessor always busy. You can see why there is the recommendation of the thread group size being a multiple of the warp size; if it were not then when the thread group is divided into warps, there will be warps with threads that are not doing anything.

4. Texture resources can be accessed by the compute shader for input by creating a SRV to the texture and binding it to the compute shader. A read-write texture (`RWTexture`) is a texture the compute shader can read and write output to. To set a texture for reading and writing to the compute shader, a UAV (unordered access view) to the texture is created and bound to the compute shader. Texture elements can be indexed with operator [] notation, or sampled via texture coordinates and sampler state with the `SampleLevel` method.

5. A structured buffer is a buffer of elements that are all the same type, like an array. The type can be a user-defined type defined by a struct for example. Read-only structured buffers are defined in the HLSL like this:

```
StructuredBuffer<DataType> gInputA;
```

Read-write structured buffers are defined in the HLSL like this:

```
RWStructuredBuffer<DataType> gOutput;
```

Read-only buffer resources can be accessed by the compute shader for input by create a SRV to a structured buffer and binding it to the compute shader. Read-write buffer resources can be accessed by the compute shader for reading and writing by creating a UAV to a structured buffer and binding it to the compute shader.

6. Various thread IDs are passed into the compute shader via the system values. These IDs are often used to index into resources and shared memory.

7. Consume and append structured buffers are defined in the HLSL like this:

```
ConsumeStructuredBuffer<DataType> gInput;
AppendStructuredBuffer<DataType> gOutput;
```

Consume and append structured buffers are useful if you do not care about the order in which data elements are processed and written to the output buffer, as it allows you to avoid indexing syntax. Note that append buffers do not automatically grow, and they must have be large enough to store all the data elements you will append to it.

8. Thread groups are given a section of so-called shared memory or thread local storage. Accessing this memory is fast and can be thought of being as fast as a hardware cache. This shared memory cache can be useful for optimizations or needed for algorithm implementations. In the compute shader code, shared memory is declared like so:

```
groupshared float4 gCache[N];
```

The array size N can be whatever you want, but the maximum size of group shared memory is 32kb. Assuming a multiprocessor supports the maximum of 32kb for shared memory, for performance, a thread group should not use more than 16kb of shared memory; otherwise it is impossible to fit two thread groups on a single multiprocessor.

9. Avoid switching between compute processing and rendering when possible, as there is overhead required to make the switch. In general, for each frame try to do all of your compute work first, then do all of your rendering work.

13.10 EXERCISES

1. Write a compute shader that inputs a structured buffer of sixty-four 3D vectors with random magnitudes contained in [1, 10]. The compute shader computes the length of the vectors and outputs the result into a floating-point buffer. Copy the results to CPU memory and save the results to file. Verify that all the lengths are contained in [1, 10].

2. Redo the previous exercise using typed buffers; that is, `Buffer<float3>` for the input buffer and `Buffer<float>` for the output buffer.

3. Assume that in the previous exercises that we do not care the order in which the vectors are normalized. Redo Exercise 1 using Append and Consume buffers.

4. Research the bilateral blur technique and implement it on the compute shader. Redo the "Blur" demo using the bilateral blur.

5. So far in our demos we have done a 2D wave equation on the CPU with the `Waves` class in Waves.h/.cpp. Port this to a GPU implementation. Use textures of `floats` to store the previous, current, and next height solutions. Because UAVs are read/write, we can just use UAVs throughout and not bother with SRVs:

```
RWTexture2D<float> gPrevSolInput : register(u0);
RWTexture2D<float> gCurrSolInput : register(u1);
RWTexture2D<float> gOutput       : register(u2);
```

Use the compute shader to perform the wave update computations. A separate compute shader can be used to disturb the water to generate waves. After you have update the grid heights, you can render a triangle grid with the same vertex resolution as the wave textures (so there is a texel corresponding to each grid vertex), and bind the current wave solution texture to a new "waves" vertex shader. Then in the vertex shader, you can sample the solution texture to offset the heights (this is called *displacement mapping*) and estimate the normal.

```
VertexOut VS(VertexIn vin)
{
  VertexOut vout = (VertexOut)0.0f;


#ifdef DISPLACEMENT_MAP
  // Sample the displacement map using non-transformed [0,1]^2 tex-coords.
  vin.PosL.y += gDisplacementMap.SampleLevel(gsamLinearWrap, vin.TexC, 1.0f).r;
  // Estimate normal using finite difference.
  float du = gDisplacementMapTexelSize.x;
  float dv = gDisplacementMapTexelSize.y;
  float l = gDisplacementMap.SampleLevel( gsamPointClamp,
    vin.TexC-float2(du, 0.0f), 0.0f ).r;
  float r = gDisplacementMap.SampleLevel( gsamPointClamp,
    vin.TexC+float2(du, 0.0f), 0.0f ).r;
  float t = gDisplacementMap.SampleLevel( gsamPointClamp,
    vin.TexC-float2(0.0f, dv), 0.0f ).r;
  float b = gDisplacementMap.SampleLevel( gsamPointClamp,
    vin.TexC+float2(0.0f, dv), 0.0f ).r;

  vin.NormalL = normalize( float3(-r+l, 2.0f*gGridSpatialStep, b-t) );

#endif


  // Transform to world space.
  float4 posW = mul(float4(vin.PosL, 1.0f), gWorld);
  vout.PosW = posW.xyz;

  // Assumes nonuniform scaling; otherwise, need to use inverse-transpose of
  // world matrix.
  vout.NormalW = mul(vin.NormalL, (float3x3)gWorld);

  // Transform to homogeneous clip space.
  vout.PosH = mul(posW, gViewProj);

  // Output vertex attributes for interpolation across triangle.
  float4 texC = mul(float4(vin.TexC, 0.0f, 1.0f), gTexTransform);
  vout.TexC = mul(texC, gMatTransform).xy;

  return vout;
}
```

Compare your performance results (time per frame) to a CPU implementation with 512 × 512 grid points in release mode.

6. The *Sobel Operator* measures edges in an image. For each pixel, it estimates the magnitude of the gradient. A pixel with a large gradient magnitude means the color difference between the pixel and its neighbors has high variation, and so that pixel must be on an edge. A pixel with a small gradient magnitude means

the color difference between the pixel and its neighbors has low variation, and so that pixel is not on an edge. Note that the Sobel Operator does not return a binary result (on edge or not on edge); it returns a grayscale value in the range [0, 1] that denotes an edge "steepness" amount, where 0 denotes no edge (the color is not changing locally about a pixel) and 1 denotes a very steep edge or discontinuity (the color is changing a lot locally about a pixel). The inverse Sobel image $(1 - c)$ is often more useful, as white denotes no edge and black denotes edges (see Figure 13.14).

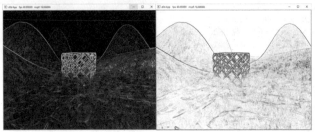

Figure 13.14. Left: In image after applying Sobel Operator, the white pixels denote edges. In the inverse image of the Sobel Operator, the black pixels denote edge.

If you color multiply the original image by the inverse of the image generated by the Sobel Operator, then you get a stylized cartoon/comic book like effect by making edges look like black pen strokes (see Figure 13.15). You can take this stylized cartoon/comic book effect even further by first blurring the original image to wash out details, then applying the Sobel Operator on the blurred image to build the edge detection image, and finally multiplying the blurred image by the inverse of the edge detection image.

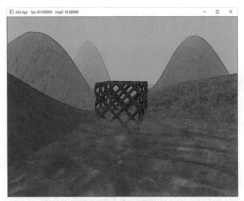

Figure 13.15. Multiplying the original image by the inverse of the edge detection image to produce a stylized look where edge look like black pen strokes.

Use render-to-texture and a compute shader to implement the *Sobel Operator*. After you have generated the edge detection image, multiply the original image with the inverse of the image generated by the Sobel Operator to get the results shown in Figure 13.15. The necessary shader code is included below:

```
//=====================================================================
// Performs edge detection using Sobel operator.
//=====================================================================

Texture2D gInput         : register(t0);
RWTexture2D<float4> gOutput : register(u0);


// Approximates luminance ("brightness") from an RGB value. These weights are
// derived from experiment based on eye sensitivity to different wavelengths
// of light.
float CalcLuminance(float3 color)
{
  return dot(color, float3(0.299f, 0.587f, 0.114f));
}

[numthreads(16, 16, 1)]
void SobelCS(int3 dispatchThreadID : SV_DispatchThreadID)
{
  // Sample the pixels in the neighborhood of this pixel.
  float4 c[3][3];
  for(int i = 0; i < 3; ++i)
  {
    for(int j = 0; j < 3; ++j)
    {
      int2 xy = dispatchThreadID.xy + int2(-1 + j, -1 + i);
      c[i][j] = gInput[xy];
    }
  }

  // For each color channel, estimate partial x derivative using Sobel scheme.
  float4 Gx = -1.0f*c[0][0] - 2.0f*c[1][0] - 1.0f*c[2][0] +
    1.0f*c[0][2] + 2.0f*c[1][2] + 1.0f*c[2][2];

  // For each color channel, estimate partial y derivative using Sobel scheme.
  float4 Gy = -1.0f*c[2][0] - 2.0f*c[2][1] - 1.0f*c[2][1] +
    1.0f*c[0][0] + 2.0f*c[0][1] + 1.0f*c[0][2];

  // Gradient is (Gx, Gy). For each color channel, compute magnitude to
  // get maximum rate of change.
  float4 mag = sqrt(Gx*Gx + Gy*Gy);

  // Make edges black, and nonedges white.
  mag = 1.0f - saturate(CalcLuminance(mag.rgb));

  gOutput[dispatchThreadID.xy] = mag;
}

//*********************************************************************
// Composite.hlsl by Frank Luna (C) 2015 All Rights Reserved.
//
```

```
// Combines two images.
//***************************************************************************

Texture2D gBaseMap : register(t0);
Texture2D gEdgeMap : register(t1);

SamplerState gsamPointWrap        : register(s0);
SamplerState gsamPointClamp       : register(s1);
SamplerState gsamLinearWrap       : register(s2);
SamplerState gsamLinearClamp      : register(s3);
SamplerState gsamAnisotropicWrap  : register(s4);
SamplerState gsamAnisotropicClamp : register(s5);

static const float2 gTexCoords[6] =
{
    float2(0.0f, 1.0f),
    float2(0.0f, 0.0f),
    float2(1.0f, 0.0f),
    float2(0.0f, 1.0f),
    float2(1.0f, 0.0f),
    float2(1.0f, 1.0f)
};

struct VertexOut
{
    float4 PosH : SV_POSITION;
    float2 TexC : TEXCOORD;
};

VertexOut VS(uint vid : SV_VertexID)
{
    VertexOut vout;

    vout.TexC = gTexCoords[vid];

    // Map [0,1]^2 to NDC space.
    vout.PosH = float4(2.0f*vout.TexC.x - 1.0f, 1.0f - 2.0f*vout.TexC.y, 0.0f,
     1.0f);

    return vout;
}

float4 PS(VertexOut pin) : SV_Target
{
    float4 c = gBaseMap.SampleLevel(gsamPointClamp, pin.TexC, 0.0f);
    float4 e = gEdgeMap.SampleLevel(gsamPointClamp, pin.TexC, 0.0f);

    // Multiple edge map with original image.
    return c*e;
}
```

Chapter 14
THE TESSELLATION STAGES

The tessellation stages refer to three stages in the rendering pipeline involved in tessellating geometry. Simply put, tessellation refers to subdividing geometry into smaller triangles and then offsetting the newly generated vertices in some way. The motivation to increase the triangle count is to add detail to the mesh. But why not just create a detailed high-poly mesh to start with and be done? Below are three reasons for tessellation.

1. Dynamic LOD on the GPU. We can dynamically adjust the detail of a mesh based on its distance from the camera and other factors. For example, if a mesh is very far away, it would be wasteful to render a high-poly version of it, as we would not be able to see all that detail anyway. As the object gets closer to the camera, we can continuously increase tessellation to increase the detail of the object.
2. Physics and animation efficiency. We can perform physics and animation calculations on the low-poly mesh, and then tessellate to the higher polygon version. This saves computation power by performing the physics and animation calculations at a lower frequency.
3. Memory savings. We can store lower polygon meshes in memory (on disk, RAM, and VRAM), and then have the GPU tessellate to the higher polygon version on the fly.

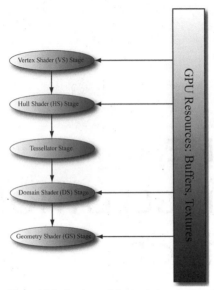

Figure 14.1. A subset of the rendering pipeline showing the tessellation stages.

Figure 14.1 shows that the tessellation stages sit between the vertex shader and geometry shader. These stages are optional, as we have not been using them in this book so far.

Objectives:

1. To discover the patch primitive types used for tessellation.
2. To obtain an understanding of what each tessellation stage does, and what the expected inputs and outputs are for each stage.
3. To be able to tessellate geometry by writing hull and domain shader programs.
4. To become familiar with different strategies for determining when to tessellate and to become familiar with performance considerations regarding hardware tessellation.
5. To learn the mathematics of Bézier curves and surfaces and how to implement them in the tessellation stages.

14.1 TESSELLATION PRIMITIVE TYPES

When we render for tessellation, we do not submit triangles to the IA stage. Instead, we submit *patches* with a number of *control points*. Direct3D supports patches with 1-32 control points, and these are described by the following primitive types:

```
D3D_PRIMITIVE_TOPOLOGY_1_CONTROL_POINT_PATCHLIST = 33,
D3D_PRIMITIVE_TOPOLOGY_2_CONTROL_POINT_PATCHLIST = 34,
D3D_PRIMITIVE_TOPOLOGY_3_CONTROL_POINT_PATCHLIST = 35,
D3D_PRIMITIVE_TOPOLOGY_4_CONTROL_POINT_PATCHLIST = 36,
.
.
.
D3D_PRIMITIVE_TOPOLOGY_31_CONTROL_POINT_PATCHLIST = 63,
D3D_PRIMITIVE_TOPOLOGY_32_CONTROL_POINT_PATCHLIST = 64,
```

A triangle can be thought of a triangle patch with three control points (D3D_PRIMITIVE_3_CONTROL_POINT_PATCH), so you can still submit your usual triangle meshes to be tessellated. A simple quad patch can be submitted with four control points (D3D_PRIMITIVE_4_CONTROL_POINT_PATCH). These patches are eventually tessellated into triangles by the tessellation stages.

Note: *When passing control point primitive types to* ID3D12GraphicsCommandList::IASetPrimitiveTopology, *you need to set the* D3D12_GRAPHICS_PIPELINE_STATE_DESC::PrimitiveTopologyType *field to* D3D12_PRIMITIVE_TOPOLOGY_TYPE_PATCH:

opaquePsoDesc.PrimitiveTopologyType = D3D12_PRIMITIVE_TOPOLOGY_TYPE_PATCH;

So what about the patches with a higher number of control points? The idea of control points comes from the construction of certain kinds of mathematical curves and surfaces. If you have ever worked with Bézier curves in a drawing program like Adobe Illustrator, then you know that you mold the shape of the curve via control points. The mathematics of Bézier curves can be generalized to Bézier surfaces. For example, you can create a Bézier quad patch that uses nine control points to shape it or sixteen control points; increasing the number of control points gives you more degrees of freedom in shaping the patch. So the motivation for all these control type primitives is to provide support for these kinds of curved surfaces. We give an explanation and demo of Bézier quad patches in this chapter.

14.1.1 Tessellation and the Vertex Shader

Because we submit patch control points to the rendering pipeline, the control points are what get pumped through the vertex shader. Thus, when tessellation is enabled, the vertex shader is really a "vertex shader for control points," and we can do any control point work we need before tessellation starts. Typically, animation or physics calculations are done in the vertex shader at the lower frequency before the geometry is tessellated.

14.2 THE HULL SHADER

In the following subsections, we explore the hull shader, which actually consists of two shaders:

1. Constant Hull Shader
2. Control Point Hull Shader

14.2.1 Constant Hull Shader

This *constant hull shader* is evaluated per patch, and is tasked with outputting the so-called *tessellation factors* of the mesh. The tessellation factors instruct the tessellation stage how much to tessellate the patch. Here is an example of a *quad patch* with four control points, where we tessellate it uniformly three times.

```
struct PatchTess
{
  float EdgeTess[4]   : SV_TessFactor;
  float InsideTess[2] : SV_InsideTessFactor;

  // Additional info you want associated per patch.
};

PatchTess ConstantHS(InputPatch<VertexOut, 4> patch,
         uint patchID : SV_PrimitiveID)
{
  PatchTess pt;

  // Uniformly tessellate the patch 3 times.

  pt.EdgeTess[0] = 3; // Left edge
  pt.EdgeTess[1] = 3; // Top edge
  pt.EdgeTess[2] = 3; // Right edge
  pt.EdgeTess[3] = 3; // Bottom edge

  pt.InsideTess[0] = 3; // u-axis (columns)
  pt.InsideTess[1] = 3; // v-axis (rows)

  return pt;
}
```

The constant hull shader inputs all the control points of the patch, which is defined by the type `InputPatch<VertexOut, 4>`. Recall that the control points are first pumped through the vertex shader, so their type is determined by the output type of the vertex shader `VertexOut`. In this example, our patch has four control points, so we specify 4 for the second template parameter of `InputPatch`. The system also provides a patch ID value via the `SV_PrimitiveID` semantic that can be used if needed; the ID uniquely identifies the patches in a draw call. The constant hull shader must output the tessellation factors; the tessellation factors depend on the topology of the patch.

Besides the tessellation factors (`SV_TessFactor` *and* `SV_InsideTessFactor`*), you can output other patch information from the constant hull shader. The domain shader receives the output from the constant hull shader as input, and could make use of this extra patch information.*

Tessellating a quad patch consists of two parts:

1. Four edge tessellation factors control how much to tessellate along each edge.
2. Two interior tessellation factors indicate how to tessellate the quad patch (one tessellation factor for the horizontal dimension of the quad, and one tessellation factor for the vertical dimension of the quad).

Figure 14.2 shows examples of different quad patch configurations we can get when the tessellation factors are not the same. Study these figures until you are comfortable with how the edge and interior tessellation factors work.

Tessellating a *triangle patch* also consists of two parts:

1. Three edge tessellation factors control how much to tessellate along each edge.
2. One interior tessellation factor indicates how much to tessellate the triangle patch.

Figure 14.3 shows examples of different triangle patch configurations we can get when the tessellation factors are not the same.

The maximum tessellation factor supported by Direct3D 11 hardware is 64. If all the tessellation factors are zero, the patch is rejected from further processing. This allows us to implement optimizations such as frustum culling and backface culling on a per patch basis.

1. If a patch is not visible by the frustum, then we can reject the patch from further processing (if we did tessellate it, the tessellated triangles would be rejected during triangle clipping).
2. If a patch is backfacing, then we can reject the patch from further processing (if we did tessellate it, the tessellated triangles would be rejected in the backface culling part of rasterization).

A natural question to ask is how much should you tessellate. So remember that the basic idea of tessellation is to add detail to your meshes. However, we do not want to unnecessarily add details if they cannot be appreciated by the user. The following are some common metrics used to determine the amount to tessellate:

1. **Distance from the camera:** The further an object is from the eye, the less we will notice fine details; therefore, we can render a low-poly version of the object when it is far away, and tessellate more as it gets closer to the eye.
2. **Screen area coverage:** We can estimate the number of pixels an object covers on the screen. If this number is small, then we can render a low-poly version of the object. As its screen area coverage increases, we can tessellate more.
3. **Orientation:** The orientation of the triangle with respect to the eye is taken into consideration with the idea that triangles along silhouette edges will be more refined than other triangles.
4. **Roughness:** Rough surfaces with lots of details will need more tessellation than smooth surfaces. A roughness value can be precomputed by examining the surface textures, which can be used to decide how much to tessellate.

[Story10] gives the following performance advice:

1. If the tessellation factors are 1 (which basically means we are not really tessellating), consider rendering the patch without tessellation, as we will be wasting GPU overhead going through the tessellation stages when they are not doing anything.
2. For performance reasons related to GPU implementations, do not tessellate such that the triangles are so small they cover less than eight pixels.
3. Batch draw calls that use tessellation (i.e., turning tessellation on and off between draw calls is expensive).

14.2.2 Control Point Hull Shader

The control point hull shader inputs a number of control points and outputs a number of control points. The control point hull shader is invoked once per control point output. One application of the hull shader is to change surface representations, say from an ordinary triangle (submitted to the pipeline with three control points) to a cubic Bézier triangle patch (a patch with ten control points). For example, suppose your mesh is modeled as usual by triangles (three control points); you can use the hull shader to augment the triangle to a higher order cubic Bézier triangle patch with 10 control points, then detail can be added with the additional control points and the triangle patch tessellated to the desired amount. This strategy is the so-called *N-patches scheme or PN triangles* scheme [Vlachos01]; it is convenient because it uses tessellation to improve existing triangle meshes with no modification to the art pipeline. For our first demo, it will be a simple *pass-through* shader, where we just pass the control point through unmodified.

> **Note:** *Drivers can detect and optimize pass-through shaders [Bilodeau10b].*

```
struct HullOut
{
    float3 PosL : POSITION;
};

[domain("quad")]
[partitioning("integer")]
[outputtopology("triangle_cw")]
[outputcontrolpoints(4)]
[patchconstantfunc("ConstantHS")]
[maxtessfactor(64.0f)]
HullOut HS(InputPatch<VertexOut, 4> p,
       uint i : SV_OutputControlPointID,
       uint patchId : SV_PrimitiveID)
{
    HullOut hout;

    hout.PosL = p[i].PosL;

    return hout;
}
```

The hull shader inputs all of the control points of the patch via the `InputPatch` parameter. The system value `SV_OutputControlPointID` gives an index identifying the output control point the hull shader is working on. Note that the input patch control point count does *not* need to match the output control point count; for example, the input patch could have 4 control points and the output patch could have sixteen control points; the additional control points could be derived from the four input control points.

The control point hull shader introduces a number of attributes:

1. `domain`: The patch type. Valid arguments are `tri`, `quad`, or `isoline`.
2. `partitioning`: Specifies the subdivision mode of the tessellation.
   a. `integer`: New vertices are added/removed only at integer tessellation factor values. The fractional part of a tessellation factor is ignored. This creates a noticeable "popping" when a mesh changes is tessellation level.
   b. Fractional tessellation (`fractional_even`/`fractional_odd`): New vertices are added/removed at integer tessellation factor values, but "slide" in gradually based on the fractional part of the tessellation factor. This is useful when you want to smoothly transition from a coarser version of the mesh to a finer version through tessellation, rather than abruptly at integer steps. The difference between integer and fractional tessellation is best understood by an animation, so the exercises at the end of this chapter will have you experiment to see the difference first hand.
3. `outputtopology`: The winding order of the triangles created via subdivision.
   a. `triangle_cw`: clockwise winding order.

b. `triangle_ccw`: counterclockwise winding order.
c. `line`: For line tessellation.
4. `outputcontrolpoints`: The number of times the hull shader executes, outputting one control point each time. The system value `SV_OutputControlPointID` gives an index identifying the output control point the hull shader is working on.
5. `patchconstantfunc`: A string specifying the constant hull shader function name.
6. `maxtessfactor`: A hint to the driver specifying the maximum tessellation factor your shader uses. This can potentially enable optimizations by the hardware if it knows this upper bound, as it will know how much resources are needed for the tessellation. The maximum tessellation factor supported by Direct3D 11 hardware is 64.

14.3 THE TESSELLATION STAGE

As programmers, we do not have control of the tessellation stage. This stage is all done by the hardware, and tessellates the patches based on the tessellation factors output from the constant hull shader program. The following figures illustrate different subdivisions based on the tessellation factors.

14.3.1 Quad Patch Tessellation Examples

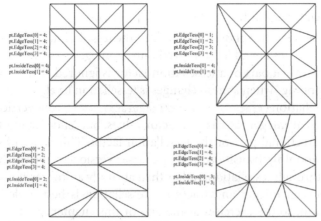

Figure 14.2. Quad subdivisions based on edge and interior tessellation factors.

14.3.2 Triangle Patch Tessellation Examples

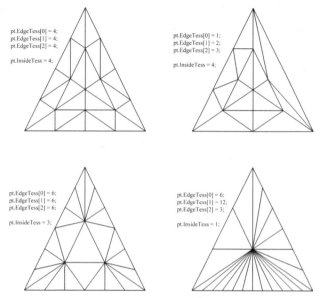

Figure 14.3. Triangle subdivisions based on edge and interior tessellation factors.

14.4 THE DOMAIN SHADER

The tessellation stage outputs all of our newly created vertices and triangles. The domain shader is invoked for each vertex created by the tessellation stage. With tessellation enabled, whereas the vertex shader acts as a vertex shader for each control point, the hull shader is essentially the vertex shader for the tessellated patch. In particular, it is here that we project the vertices of the tessellated patch to homogeneous clip space.

For a quad patch, the domain shader inputs the tessellation factors (and any other per patch information you output from the constant hull shader), the parametric (u, v) coordinates of the tessellated vertex positions, and all the patch control points output from the control point hull shader. Note that the domain shader does not give you the actual tessellated vertex positions; instead it gives you the parametric (u, v) coordinates (Figure 14.4) of these points in the patch domain space. It is up to you to use these parametric coordinates and the control points to derive the actual 3D vertex positions; in the code below, we do this via bilinear interpolation (which works just like texture linear filtering).

```
struct DomainOut
{
```

```
    float4 PosH : SV_POSITION;
};

// The domain shader is called for every vertex created by the tessellator.
// It is like the vertex shader after tessellation.
[domain("quad")]
DomainOut DS(PatchTess patchTess,
        float2 uv : SV_DomainLocation,
        const OutputPatch<HullOut, 4> quad)
{
  DomainOut dout;
  
  // Bilinear interpolation.
  float3 v1 = lerp(quad[0].PosL, quad[1].PosL, uv.x);
  float3 v2 = lerp(quad[2].PosL, quad[3].PosL, uv.x);
  float3 p  = lerp(v1, v2, uv.y);
  
  float4 posW = mul(float4(p, 1.0f), gWorld);
  dout.PosH = mul(posW, gViewProj);
  
  return dout;
}
```

> **Note:** As shown in Figure 14.4, the ordering of the quad patch control points is row-by-row.

The domain shader for a triangle patch is similar, except that instead of the parametric (u, v) values being input, the `float3` barycentric (u, v, w) coordinates of the vertex are input (see §C.3) for an explanation of barycentric coordinates. The reason for outputting barycentric coordinates for triangle patches is probably due to the fact that Bézier triangle patches are defined in terms of barycentric coordinates.

14.5 TESSELLATING A QUAD

For our one of the demos in this chapter, we submit a quad patch to the rendering pipeline, tessellate it based on the distance from the camera, and displace the

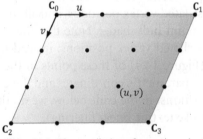

Figure 14.4. The tessellation of a quad patch with 4 control points generating 16 vertices in the normalized uv-space, with coordinates in $[0, 1]^2$.

generated vertices by a mathematic function that is similar to the one we have been using for this "hills" in our past demos.

Our vertex buffer storing the four control points is created like so:

```cpp
void BasicTessellationApp::BuildQuadPatchGeometry()
{
  std::array<XMFLOAT3,4> vertices =
  {
    XMFLOAT3(-10.0f, 0.0f, +10.0f),
    XMFLOAT3(+10.0f, 0.0f, +10.0f),
    XMFLOAT3(-10.0f, 0.0f, -10.0f),
    XMFLOAT3(+10.0f, 0.0f, -10.0f)
  };

  std::array<std::int16_t, 4> indices = { 0, 1, 2, 3 };

  const UINT vbByteSize = (UINT)vertices.size() * sizeof(Vertex);
  const UINT ibByteSize = (UINT)indices.size() * sizeof(std::uint16_t);

  auto geo = std::make_unique<MeshGeometry>();
  geo->Name = "quadpatchGeo";

  ThrowIfFailed(D3DCreateBlob(vbByteSize, &geo->VertexBufferCPU));
  CopyMemory(geo->VertexBufferCPU->GetBufferPointer(), vertices.data(),
    vbByteSize);

  ThrowIfFailed(D3DCreateBlob(ibByteSize, &geo->IndexBufferCPU));
  CopyMemory(geo->IndexBufferCPU->GetBufferPointer(), indices.data(),
    ibByteSize);

  geo->VertexBufferGPU = d3dUtil::CreateDefaultBuffer(md3dDevice.Get(),
    mCommandList.Get(), vertices.data(), vbByteSize,
    geo->VertexBufferUploader);

  geo->IndexBufferGPU = d3dUtil::CreateDefaultBuffer(md3dDevice.Get(),
    mCommandList.Get(), indices.data(), ibByteSize,
    geo->IndexBufferUploader);

  geo->VertexByteStride = sizeof(XMFLOAT3);
  geo->VertexBufferByteSize = vbByteSize;
  geo->IndexFormat = DXGI_FORMAT_R16_UINT;
  geo->IndexBufferByteSize = ibByteSize;

  SubmeshGeometry quadSubmesh;
  quadSubmesh.IndexCount = 4;
  quadSubmesh.StartIndexLocation = 0;
  quadSubmesh.BaseVertexLocation = 0;

  geo->DrawArgs["quadpatch"] = quadSubmesh;

  mGeometries[geo->Name] = std::move(geo);
}
```

Our render-item for the quad patch is created as follows:

```
void BasicTessellationApp::BuildRenderItems()
{
  auto quadPatchRitem = std::make_unique<RenderItem>();
  quadPatchRitem->World = MathHelper::Identity4x4();
  quadPatchRitem->TexTransform = MathHelper::Identity4x4();
  quadPatchRitem->ObjCBIndex = 0;
  quadPatchRitem->Mat = mMaterials["whiteMat"].get();
  quadPatchRitem->Geo = mGeometries["quadpatchGeo"].get();
  quadPatchRitem->PrimitiveType = D3D_PRIMITIVE_TOPOLOGY_4_CONTROL_
    POINT_PATCHLIST;
  quadPatchRitem->IndexCount = quadPatchRitem->Geo-
    >DrawArgs["quadpatch"].IndexCount;
  quadPatchRitem->StartIndexLocation =
    quadPatchRitem->Geo->DrawArgs["quadpatch"].StartIndexLocation;
  quadPatchRitem->BaseVertexLocation =
    quadPatchRitem->Geo->DrawArgs["quadpatch"].BaseVertexLocation;
  mRitemLayer[(int)RenderLayer::Opaque].push_back(quadPatchRitem.get());

  mAllRitems.push_back(std::move(quadPatchRitem));
}
```

We will now turn attention to the hull shader. The hull shader is similar to what we showed in §14.2.1 and §14.2.2, except that we now determine the tessellation factors based on the distance from the eye. The idea behind this is to use a low-poly mesh in the distance, and increase the tessellation (and hence triangle count) as the mesh approaches the eye (see Figure 14.5). The hull shader is simply a pass-through shader.

```
struct VertexIn
{
  float3 PosL : POSITION;
};

struct VertexOut
{
  float3 PosL : POSITION;
};

VertexOut VS(VertexIn vin)
{
  VertexOut vout;
  vout.PosL = vin.PosL;
  return vout;
```

Figure 14.5. The mesh is tessellated more as the distance to the eye decreases.

```
}

struct PatchTess
{
  float EdgeTess[4]   : SV_TessFactor;
  float InsideTess[2] : SV_InsideTessFactor;
};

PatchTess ConstantHS(InputPatch<VertexOut, 4> patch, uint patchID :
    SV_PrimitiveID)
{
  PatchTess pt;

  float3 centerL = 0.25f*(patch[0].PosL +
             patch[1].PosL +
             patch[2].PosL +
             patch[3].PosL);

  float3 centerW = mul(float4(centerL, 1.0f), gWorld).xyz;

  float d = distance(centerW, gEyePosW);

  // Tessellate the patch based on distance from the eye such that
  // the tessellation is 0 if d >= d1 and 64 if d <= d0. The interval
  // [d0, d1] defines the range we tessellate in.

  const float d0 = 20.0f;
  const float d1 = 100.0f;
  float tess = 64.0f*saturate( (d1-d)/(d1-d0) );

  // Uniformly tessellate the patch.

  pt.EdgeTess[0] = tess;
  pt.EdgeTess[1] = tess;
  pt.EdgeTess[2] = tess;
  pt.EdgeTess[3] = tess;

  pt.InsideTess[0] = tess;
  pt.InsideTess[1] = tess;

  return pt;
}

struct HullOut
{
  float3 PosL : POSITION;
};

[domain("quad")]
[partitioning("integer")]
[outputtopology("triangle_cw")]
[outputcontrolpoints(4)]
[patchconstantfunc("ConstantHS")]
[maxtessfactor(64.0f)]
HullOut HS(InputPatch<VertexOut, 4> p,
     uint i : SV_OutputControlPointID,
```

```
         uint patchId : SV_PrimitiveID)
{
  HullOut hout;
  hout.PosL = p[i].PosL;
  return hout;
}
```

Simply tessellating is not enough to add detail, as the new triangles just lie on the patch that was subdivided. We must offset those extra vertices in some way to better approximate the shape of the object we are modeling. This is done in the domain shader. In this demo, we offset the *y*-coordinates by the "hills" function we introduced in §7.7.3.

```
struct DomainOut
{
  float4 PosH : SV_POSITION;
};

// The domain shader is called for every vertex created by the
//   tessellator.
// It is like the vertex shader after tessellation.
[domain("quad")]
DomainOut DS(PatchTess patchTess,
       float2 uv : SV_DomainLocation,
       const OutputPatch<HullOut, 4> quad)
{
  DomainOut dout;

  // Bilinear interpolation.
  float3 v1 = lerp(quad[0].PosL, quad[1].PosL, uv.x);
  float3 v2 = lerp(quad[2].PosL, quad[3].PosL, uv.x);
  float3 p  = lerp(v1, v2, uv.y);

  // Displacement mapping
  p.y = 0.3f*( p.z*sin(p.x) + p.x*cos(p.z) );

  float4 posW = mul(float4(p, 1.0f), gWorld);
  dout.PosH = mul(posW, gViewProj);

  return dout;
}

float4 PS(DomainOut pin) : SV_Target
{
  return float4(1.0f, 1.0f, 1.0f, 1.0f);
}
```

14.6 CUBIC BÉZIER QUAD PATCHES

In this section, we describe cubic Bézier quad patches to show how surfaces are constructed via a higher number of control points. Before we get to surfaces, however, it helps to first start with Bézier curves.

14.6.1 Bézier Curves

Consider three noncollinear points $\mathbf{p}_0$, $\mathbf{p}_1$, and $\mathbf{p}_2$ which we will call the control points. These three control points define a Bézier curve in the following way. A point $\mathbf{p}(t)$ on the curve is first found by linearly interpolating between $\mathbf{p}_0$ and $\mathbf{p}_1$ by t, and $\mathbf{p}_1$ and $\mathbf{p}_2$ by t to get the intermediate points:

$$\mathbf{p}_0^1 = (1-t)\mathbf{p}_0 + t\mathbf{p}_1$$

$$\mathbf{p}_1^1 = (1-t)\mathbf{p}_1 + t\mathbf{p}_2$$

Then $\mathbf{p}(t)$ is found by linearly interpolating between $\mathbf{p}_0^1$ and $\mathbf{p}_1^1$ by t:

$$\begin{aligned}\mathbf{p}(t) &= (1-t)\mathbf{p}_0^1 + t\mathbf{p}_1^1 \\ &= (1-t)\big((1-t)\mathbf{p}_0 + t\mathbf{p}_1\big) + t\big((1-t)\mathbf{p}_1 + t\mathbf{p}_2\big) \\ &= (1-t)^2\mathbf{p}_0 + 2(1-t)t\mathbf{p}_1 + t^2\mathbf{p}_2\end{aligned}$$

In other words, this construction by repeated interpolation leads to the parametric formula for a quadratic (degree 2) Bézier curve:

$$\mathbf{p}(t) = (1-t)^2\mathbf{p}_0 + 2(1-t)t\mathbf{p}_1 + t^2\mathbf{p}_2$$

In a similar manner, four control points $\mathbf{p}_0$, $\mathbf{p}_1$, $\mathbf{p}_2$, and $\mathbf{p}_3$ define a cubic (degree 3) Bézier curve, and a point $\mathbf{p}(t)$ on the curve is found again by repeated interpolation. Figure 14.6 shows the situation. First linearly interpolate along each line segment the four given control points define to get three first generation intermediate points:

$$\mathbf{p}_0^1 = (1-t)\mathbf{p}_0 + t\mathbf{p}_1$$
$$\mathbf{p}_1^1 = (1-t)\mathbf{p}_1 + t\mathbf{p}_2$$
$$\mathbf{p}_2^1 = (1-t)\mathbf{p}_2 + t\mathbf{p}_3$$

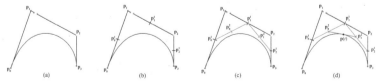

Figure 14.6. Repeated linear interpolation defined points on the cubic Bézier curve. The figure uses $t = 0.5$. (a) The four control points and the curve they define. (b) Linearly interpolate between the control points to calculate the first generation of intermediate points. (c) Linearly interpolate between the first generation intermediate points to get the second generation intermediate points. (d) Linearly interpolate between the second generation intermediate points to get the point on the curve.

Next, linearly interpolate along each line segment these first generation intermediate points define to get two second generation intermediate points:

$$\mathbf{p}_0^2 = (1-t)\mathbf{p}_0^1 + t\mathbf{p}_1^1$$
$$= (1-t)^2 \mathbf{p}_0 + 2(1-t)t\mathbf{p}_1 + t^2\mathbf{p}_2$$
$$\mathbf{p}_1^2 = (1-t)\mathbf{p}_1^1 + t\mathbf{p}_2^1$$
$$= (1-t)^2 \mathbf{p}_1 + 2(1-t)t\mathbf{p}_2 + t^2\mathbf{p}_3$$

Finally, **p**(t) is found by linearly interpolating between these last generation intermediate pints:

$$\mathbf{p}(t) = (1-t)\mathbf{p}_0^2 + t\mathbf{p}_1^2$$
$$= (1-t)\left((1-t)^2 \mathbf{p}_0 + 2(1-t)t\mathbf{p}_1 + t^2\mathbf{p}_2\right) + t\left((1-t)^2 \mathbf{p}_1 + 2(1-t)t\mathbf{p}_2 + t^2\mathbf{p}_3\right)$$

which simplifies to the parametric formula for a cubic (degree 3) Bézier curve:

$$\mathbf{p}(t) = (1-t)^3 \mathbf{p}_0 + 3t(1-t)^2 \mathbf{p}_1 + 3t^2(1-t)\mathbf{p}_2 + t^3 \mathbf{p}_3 \qquad \text{(eq. 14.1)}$$

Generally, people stop at cubic curves, as they give enough smoothness and degrees of freedom for controlling the curve, but you can keep going to higher-order curves with the same recursive pattern of repeated interpolation.

It turns out, that the formula for Bézier curves of degree n can be written in terms of the *Bernstein basis functions*, which are defined by:

$$B_i^n(t) = \frac{n!}{i!(n-i)!} t^i (1-t)^{n-i}$$

For degree 3 curves, the Bernstein basis functions are:

$$B_0^3(t) = \frac{3!}{0!(3-0)!} t^0 (1-t)^{3-0} = (1-t)^3$$

$$B_1^3(t) = \frac{3!}{1!(3-1)!} t^1 (1-t)^{3-1} = 3t(1-t)^2$$

$$B_2^3(t) = \frac{3!}{2!(3-2)!} t^2 (1-t)^{3-2} = 3t^2(1-t)$$

$$B_3^3(t) = \frac{3!}{3!(3-3)!} t^3 (1-t)^{3-3} = t^3$$

Compare these values to the factors in Equation 14.1. Therefore, we can write a cubic Bézier curve as:

$$\mathbf{p}(t) = \sum_{j=0}^{3} B_j^3(t)\mathbf{p}_j = B_0^3(t)\mathbf{p}_0 + B_1^3(t)\mathbf{p}_1 + B_2^3(t)\mathbf{p}_2 + B_3^3(t)\mathbf{p}_3$$

The derivatives of the cubic Bernstein basis functions can be found by application of the power and product rules:

$$B_0^{3\prime}(t) = -3(1-t)^2$$
$$B_1^{3\prime}(t) = 3(1-t)^2 - 6t(1-t)$$
$$B_2^{3\prime}(t) = 6t(1-t) - 3t^2$$
$$B_3^{3\prime}(t) = 3t^2$$

And the derivative of the cubic Bézier curve is:

$$\mathbf{p}'(t) = \sum_{j=0}^{3} B_j^{3\prime}(t)\mathbf{p}_j = B_0^{3\prime}(t)\mathbf{p}_0 + B_1^{3\prime}(t)\mathbf{p}_1 + B_2^{3\prime}(t)\mathbf{p}_2 + B_3^{3\prime}(t)\mathbf{p}_3$$

Derivatives are useful for computing the tangent vector along the curve.

Note: *There are Bézier curve applets online that allow you to set and manipulate the control points to see how the curves are shaped interactively.*

14.6.2 Cubic Bézier Surfaces

Refer to Figure 14.7 throughout this section. Consider a patch of 4 × 4 control points. Each row, therefore, contains 4 control points that can be used to define cubic Bézier curve; the Bézier curve of the *ith row is given by:*

$$\mathbf{q}_i(u) = \sum_{j=0}^{3} B_j^3(u)\mathbf{p}_{i,j}$$

If we evaluate each of these Bézier curves at say u_0, then we get a "column" of 4 points, one along each curve. We can use these 4 points to define another Bézier curve that lies on the *Bézier surface* at u_0:

$$\mathbf{p}(v) = \sum_{i=0}^{3} B_i^3(v)\mathbf{q}_i(u_0)$$

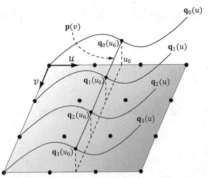

Figure 14.7. Constructing a Bézier surface. Some simplifications were made to make the figure easier to understand—the control points do not all lie in the plane, all the $\mathbf{q}_i(u)$ need not be the same as the figure suggests (they would only be the same if the control points were the same for each row to give the same curves), and $\mathbf{p}(v)$ generally would not be a straight line but a cubic Bézier curve.

Now, if we let u vary as well, we sweep out a family of cubic Bézier curves that form the *cubic Bézier surface*:

$$\mathbf{p}(u,v) = \sum_{i=0}^{3} B_i^3(v) \mathbf{q}_i(u)$$

$$= \sum_{i=0}^{3} B_i^3(v) \sum_{j=0}^{3} B_j^3(u) \mathbf{p}_{i,j}$$

The partial derivatives of a Bézier surface are useful for computing tangent and normal vectors:

$$\frac{\partial \mathbf{p}}{\partial u}(u,v) = \sum_{i=0}^{3} B_i^3(v) \sum_{j=0}^{3} \frac{\partial B_j^3}{\partial u}(u) \mathbf{p}_{i,j}$$

$$\frac{\partial \mathbf{p}}{\partial v}(u,v) = \sum_{i=0}^{3} \frac{\partial B_i^3}{\partial v}(v) \sum_{j=0}^{3} B_j^3(u) \mathbf{p}_{i,j}$$

14.6.3 Cubic Bézier Surface Evaluation Code

In this section, we give code to evaluate a cubic Bézier surface. To help understand the code that follows, we expand out the summation notation:

$$\mathbf{q}_0(u) = B_0^3(u)\mathbf{p}_{0,0} + B_1^3(u)\mathbf{p}_{0,1} + B_2^3(u)\mathbf{p}_{0,2} + B_3^3(u)\mathbf{p}_{0,3}$$

$$\mathbf{q}_1(u) = B_0^3(u)\mathbf{p}_{1,0} + B_1^3(u)\mathbf{p}_{1,1} + B_2^3(u)\mathbf{p}_{1,2} + B_3^3(u)\mathbf{p}_{1,3}$$

$$\mathbf{q}_2(u) = B_0^3(u)\mathbf{p}_{2,0} + B_1^3(u)\mathbf{p}_{2,1} + B_2^3(u)\mathbf{p}_{2,2} + B_3^3(u)\mathbf{p}_{2,3}$$

$$\mathbf{q}_3(u) = B_0^3(u)\mathbf{p}_{3,0} + B_1^3(u)\mathbf{p}_{3,1} + B_2^3(u)\mathbf{p}_{3,2} + B_3^3(u)\mathbf{p}_{3,3}$$

$$\begin{aligned}\mathbf{p}(u,v) &= B_0^3(v)\mathbf{q}_0(u) + B_1^3(v)\mathbf{q}_1(u) + B_2^3(v)\mathbf{q}_2(u) + B_3^3(v)\mathbf{q}_3(u) \\ &= B_0^3(v)\left[B_0^3(u)\mathbf{p}_{0,0} + B_1^3(u)\mathbf{p}_{0,1} + B_2^3(u)\mathbf{p}_{0,2} + B_3^3(u)\mathbf{p}_{0,3}\right] \\ &+ B_1^3(v)\left[B_0^3(u)\mathbf{p}_{1,0} + B_1^3(u)\mathbf{p}_{1,1} + B_2^3(u)\mathbf{p}_{1,2} + B_3^3(u)\mathbf{p}_{1,3}\right] \\ &+ B_2^3(v)\left[B_0^3(u)\mathbf{p}_{2,0} + B_1^3(u)\mathbf{p}_{2,1} + B_2^3(u)\mathbf{p}_{2,2} + B_3^3(u)\mathbf{p}_{2,3}\right] \\ &+ B_3^3(v)\left[B_0^3(u)\mathbf{p}_{3,0} + B_1^3(u)\mathbf{p}_{3,1} + B_2^3(u)\mathbf{p}_{3,2} + B_3^3(u)\mathbf{p}_{3,3}\right]\end{aligned}$$

The code below maps directly to the formulas just given:

```
float4 BernsteinBasis(float t)
{
  float invT = 1.0f - t;

  return float4( invT * invT * invT,      // B_0^3(t)=(1-t)^3
           3.0f * t * invT * invT,        // B_1^3(t)=3t(1-t)^2
           3.0f * t * t * invT,           // B_2^3(t)=3t^2(1-t)
           t * t * t );                   // B_3^3(t)=t^3
}

float4 dBernsteinBasis(float t)
{
  float invT = 1.0f - t;

  return float4(
    -3 * invT * invT,                     // B_0^{3'}(t)=-3(1-t)^2
    3 * invT * invT - 6 * t * invT,       // B_1^{3'}(t)=3(1-t)^2-6t(1-t)
    6 * t * invT - 3 * t * t,             // B_2^{3'}(t)=6t(1-t)-3t^2
    3 * t * t );                          // B_3^{3'}(t)=3t^2
}

float3 CubicBezierSum(const OutputPatch<HullOut, 16> bezpatch,
        float4 basisU, float4 basisV)
{
  float3 sum = float3(0.0f, 0.0f, 0.0f);
  sum = basisV.x * (basisU.x*bezpatch[0].PosL +
          basisU.y*bezpatch[1].PosL +
          basisU.z*bezpatch[2].PosL +
          basisU.w*bezpatch[3].PosL );

  sum += basisV.y * (basisU.x*bezpatch[4].PosL +
          basisU.y*bezpatch[5].PosL +
          basisU.z*bezpatch[6].PosL +
          basisU.w*bezpatch[7].PosL );

  sum += basisV.z * (basisU.x*bezpatch[8].PosL +
          basisU.y*bezpatch[9].PosL +
          basisU.z*bezpatch[10].PosL +
          basisU.w*bezpatch[11].PosL);
```

```
        sum += basisV.w * (basisU.x*bezpatch[12].PosL +
                    basisU.y*bezpatch[13].PosL +
                    basisU.z*bezpatch[14].PosL +
                    basisU.w*bezpatch[15].PosL);

        return sum;
}
```
The above functions can be utilized like so to evaluate p(u, v) and compute the partial derivatives:
```
float4 basisU = BernsteinBasis(uv.x);
float4 basisV = BernsteinBasis(uv.y);

// p(u,v)
float3 p = CubicBezierSum(bezPatch, basisU, basisV);

float4 dBasisU = dBernsteinBasis(uv.x);
float4 dBasisV = dBernsteinBasis(uv.y);

// ∂p/∂u (u,v)
float3 dpdu = CubicBezierSum(bezPatch, dbasisU, basisV);

// ∂p/∂v (u,v)
float3 dpdv = CubicBezierSum(bezPatch, basisU, dbasisV);
```

Note: *Observe that we pass the evaluated basis function values to* `CubicBezierSum`. *This enables us to use* `CubicBezierSum` *for evaluating both* **p**(u, v) *and the partial derivatives, as the summation form is the same, the only differencing being the basis functions.*

14.6.4 Defining the Patch Geometry

Our vertex buffer storing the sixteen control points is created like so:
```
void BezierPatchApp::BuildQuadPatchGeometry()
{
  std::array<XMFLOAT3,16> vertices =
  {
    // Row 0
    XMFLOAT3(-10.0f, -10.0f, +15.0f),
    XMFLOAT3(-5.0f, 0.0f, +15.0f),
    XMFLOAT3(+5.0f, 0.0f, +15.0f),
    XMFLOAT3(+10.0f, 0.0f, +15.0f),

    // Row 1
    XMFLOAT3(-15.0f, 0.0f, +5.0f),
    XMFLOAT3(-5.0f, 0.0f, +5.0f),
    XMFLOAT3(+5.0f, 20.0f, +5.0f),
    XMFLOAT3(+15.0f, 0.0f, +5.0f),
```

Figure 14.8. Screenshot of the Bézier surface demo.

```cpp
    // Row 2
    XMFLOAT3(-15.0f, 0.0f, -5.0f),
    XMFLOAT3(-5.0f,  0.0f, -5.0f),
    XMFLOAT3(+5.0f,  0.0f, -5.0f),
    XMFLOAT3(+15.0f, 0.0f, -5.0f),

    // Row 3
    XMFLOAT3(-10.0f, 10.0f, -15.0f),
    XMFLOAT3(-5.0f,  0.0f,  -15.0f),
    XMFLOAT3(+5.0f,  0.0f,  -15.0f),
    XMFLOAT3(+25.0f, 10.0f, -15.0f)
};

std::array<std::int16_t, 16> indices =
{
  0, 1, 2, 3,
  4, 5, 6, 7,
  8, 9, 10, 11,
  12, 13, 14, 15
};

const UINT vbByteSize = (UINT)vertices.size() * sizeof(Vertex);
const UINT ibByteSize = (UINT)indices.size() * sizeof(std::uint16_t);

auto geo = std::make_unique<MeshGeometry>();
geo->Name = "quadpatchGeo";

ThrowIfFailed(D3DCreateBlob(vbByteSize, &geo->VertexBufferCPU));
CopyMemory(geo->VertexBufferCPU->GetBufferPointer(), vertices.data(),
  vbByteSize);

ThrowIfFailed(D3DCreateBlob(ibByteSize, &geo->IndexBufferCPU));
CopyMemory(geo->IndexBufferCPU->GetBufferPointer(), indices.data(),
  ibByteSize);

geo->VertexBufferGPU = d3dUtil::CreateDefaultBuffer(md3dDevice.Get(),
  mCommandList.Get(), vertices.data(), vbByteSize, geo-
  >VertexBufferUploader);

geo->IndexBufferGPU = d3dUtil::CreateDefaultBuffer(md3dDevice.Get(),
  mCommandList.Get(), indices.data(), ibByteSize, geo-
  >IndexBufferUploader);
```

```
geo->VertexByteStride = sizeof(XMFLOAT3);
geo->VertexBufferByteSize = vbByteSize;
geo->IndexFormat = DXGI_FORMAT_R16_UINT;
geo->IndexBufferByteSize = ibByteSize;

SubmeshGeometry quadSubmesh;
quadSubmesh.IndexCount = (UINT)indices.size();
quadSubmesh.StartIndexLocation = 0;
quadSubmesh.BaseVertexLocation = 0;

geo->DrawArgs["quadpatch"] = quadSubmesh;

mGeometries[geo->Name] = std::move(geo);
}
```

 There is no restriction that the control points need to be equidistant to form a uniform grid.

Our render-item for the quad patch is created as follows:

```
void BezierPatchApp::BuildRenderItems()
{
    auto quadPatchRitem = std::make_unique<RenderItem>();
    quadPatchRitem->World = MathHelper::Identity4x4();
    quadPatchRitem->TexTransform = MathHelper::Identity4x4();
    quadPatchRitem->ObjCBIndex = 0;
    quadPatchRitem->Mat = mMaterials["whiteMat"].get();
    quadPatchRitem->Geo = mGeometries["quadpatchGeo"].get();
    quadPatchRitem->PrimitiveType = D3D11_PRIMITIVE_TOPOLOGY_16_CONTROL_
      POINT_PATCHLIST;
    quadPatchRitem->IndexCount = quadPatchRitem->Geo-
      >DrawArgs["quadpatch"].IndexCount;
    quadPatchRitem->StartIndexLocation =
      quadPatchRitem->Geo->DrawArgs["quadpatch"].StartIndexLocation;
    quadPatchRitem->BaseVertexLocation =
      quadPatchRitem->Geo->DrawArgs["quadpatch"].BaseVertexLocation;
    mRitemLayer[(int)RenderLayer::Opaque].push_back(quadPatchRitem.
      get());

    mAllRitems.push_back(std::move(quadPatchRitem));
}
```

14.7 SUMMARY

1. The tessellation stages are optional stages of the rendering pipeline. They consist of the hull shader, the tessellator, and the domain shader. The hull and domain shaders are programmable, and the tessellator is completely controlled by the hardware.

2. Hardware tessellation provides memory benefits, as a low-poly asset can be stored and then detail can be added on the fly via tessellation. Additionally, computations such as animation and physics can be done on the low-poly mesh frequency before tessellation. Finally, continuous LOD algorithms can now be implemented completely on the GPU, which always had to be implemented on the CPU before hardware tessellation was available.

3. New primitive types are used only with tessellation to submit control points to the rendering pipeline. Direct3D 12 supports between one and thirty-two control points, which are represented by the enumerated types `D3D_PRIMITIVE_1_CONTROL_POINT_PATCH... D3D_PRIMITIVE_32_CONTROL_POINT_PATCH`.

4. With tessellation, the vertex shader inputs control points and generally animates or performs physics computations per control point. The hull shader consists of the constant hull shader and the control point hull shader. The constant hull shader operates per patch and outputs the tessellation factors of the patch, which instruct the tessellator how much to tessellate the patch, as well as any other optional per patch data. The control point hull shader inputs a number of control points and outputs a number of control points. The control point hull shader is invoked once per control point output. Typically, the control point hull shader changes the surface representation of the input patch. For example, this stage might input a triangle with three control points, and output a Bézier triangle surface patch with ten control points.

5. The domain shader is invoked for each vertex created by the tessellation stage. Whereas the vertex shader acts as a vertex shader for each control point, with tessellation enabled the hull shader is essentially the vertex shader for the tessellated patch vertices. In particular, it is here that we project the vertices of the tessellated patch to homogeneous clip space and do other per vertex work.

6. If you are not going to tessellate an object (e.g., tessellation factors are close to 1), then do not render the object with the tessellation stages enabled, as there is overhead. Avoid tessellating so much that triangles are smaller than eight pixels. Draw all your tessellated objects together to avoid turning tessellation on and off during a frame. Use back face culling and frustum culling in the hull shader to discard patches that are not seen from being tessellated.

7. Bézier curves and surfaces, specified by parametric equations, can be used to describe smooth curves and surfaces. They are "shaped" via control points. In addition to allowing us to draw smooth surfaces directly, Bézier surfaces are used in many popular hardware tessellation algorithms such as PN Triangles and Catmull-Clark approximations.

14.8 EXERCISES

1. Redo the "Basic Tessellation" demo, but tessellate a triangle patch instead of a quad patch.
2. Tessellate an iscoahedron into a sphere based on distance.
3. Modify the "Basic Tessellation" demo so that it does fixed tessellation of a flat quad. Experiment with different edge/interior tessellation factors until you are comfortable with how the tessellation factors work.
4. Explore fractional tessellation. That is, try the "Basic Tessellation" demo with:
   ```
   [partitioning("fractional_even")]
   [partitioning("fractional_odd")]
   ```
5. Compute the Bernstein basis functions $B_0^2(t), B_1^2(t), B_2^2(t)$ for a quadratic Bézier curve, and compute the derivatives $B_0^{2'}(t), B_1^{2'}(t), B_2^{2'}(t)$. Derive the parametric equation for a quadratic Bézier surface.
6. Experiment with the "Bézier Patch" demo by changing the control points to change the Bézier surface.
7. Redo the "Bézier Patch" demo to use a quadratic Bézier surface with nine control points.
8. Modify the "Bézier Patch" demo to light and shade the Bézier surface. You will need to compute vertex normals in the domain shader. A normal at a vertex position can be found by taking the cross product of the partial derivatives at the position.
9. Research and implement Bézier triangle patches.

Part 3 TOPICS

In this part, we focus on applying Direct3D to implement several 3D applications, demonstrating techniques such as sky rendering, ambient occlusion, character animation, picking, environment mapping, normal mapping, and shadow mapping. A brief description of the chapters in this part follows.

Chapter 15, Building a First Person Camera and Dynamic Indexing: In this chapter, we show how to design a camera system that behaves more as you would expect in a first person game. We show how to control the camera via keyboard and mouse input. In addition, we introduce a new Direct3D 12 technique called dynamic indexing, where we can dynamically index an array of texture objects in a shader.

Chapter 16, Instancing and Frustum Culling: Instancing is a hardware supported technique that optimizes the drawing of the same geometry multiple times with different properties (say at different positions in the scene and with different colors). Frustum culling is an optimization technique where we discard an entire object from being submitted to the rendering pipeline if it lies completely outside the virtual camera's field of view. We also show how to compute the bounding box and sphere of a mesh.

Chapter 17, Picking: This chapter shows how to determine the particular 3D object (or 3D primitive) that the user has selected with the mouse. Picking is often a necessity in 3D games and applications where the user interacts with the 3D world with the mouse.

Chapter 18, Cube Mapping: In this chapter, we show how to reflect environments onto arbitrary meshes with environment mapping; in addition, we use an environment map to texture a sky-sphere.

Chapter 19, Normal Mapping: This chapter shows how to get more detailed real-time lighting results by using normal maps, which are textures that store normal vectors. This gives surface normals at a finer granularity than per-vertex normals resulting in more realistic lighting.

Chapter 20, Shadow Mapping: Shadow mapping is a real-time shadowing technique, which shadows arbitrary geometry (it is not limited to planar shadows). In addition, we learn how projective texturing works.

Chapter 21, Ambient Occlusion: Lighting plays an important role in making our scenes look realistic. In this chapter, we improve the ambient term of our lighting equation by estimating how occluded a point in our scene is from incoming light.

Chapter 22, Quaternions: In this chapter, we study mathematical objects called quaternions. We show that unit quaternions represent rotations and can be interpolated in a simple way, thereby giving us a way to interpolate rotations. Once we can interpolate rotations, we can create 3D animations.

Chapter 23, Character Animation: This chapter covers the theory of character animation and show how to animate a typical human game character with a complex walking animation.

Chapter 15 BUILDING A FIRST PERSON CAMERA AND DYNAMIC INDEXING

In this chapter, we cover two separate short topics. First, we design a camera system that behaves more as you would expect in a first person game. This camera system will replace the orbiting camera system we have been using thus far in the demos. Second, we introduce a new Direct3D 12 technique called dynamic indexing (new to shader model 5.1), where we can dynamically index an array of texture objects `(Texture2D gDiffuseMap[n])`. This is similar to how we indexed the special texture array object `(Texture2DArray)` in Chapter 12, but unlike `Texture2DArray` the textures in this array can be different sizes and formats, making it more flexible than `Texture2DArrays`.

Objectives:

1. To review the mathematics of the view space transformation.
2. To be able to identify the typical functionality of a first person camera.
3. To learn how to implement a first person camera.
4. To understand how to dynamically index into an array of textures.

15.1 VIEW TRANSFORM REVIEW

View space is the coordinate system attached to the camera as shown in Figure 15.1. The camera sits at the origin looking down the positive z-axis, the x-axis aims to the right of the camera, and the y-axis aims above the camera. Instead of describing our scene vertices relative to the world space, it is convenient for later stages of the rendering pipeline to describe them relative to the camera coordinate system. The change of coordinate transformation from world space to view space is called the *view transform*, and the corresponding matrix is called the *view matrix*.

If $\mathbf{Q}_W = (Q_x, Q_y, Q_z, 1)$, $\mathbf{u}_W = (u_x, u_y, u_z, 0)$, $\mathbf{v}_W = (v_x, v_y, v_z, 0)$, and $\mathbf{w}_W = (w_x, w_y, w_z, 0)$ describe, respectively, the origin, x-, y-, and z-axes of view space with homogeneous coordinates relative to world space, then we know from §3.4.3 that the change of coordinate matrix from view space to world space is:

$$\mathbf{W} = \begin{bmatrix} u_x & u_y & u_z & 0 \\ v_x & v_y & v_z & 0 \\ w_x & w_y & w_z & 0 \\ Q_x & Q_y & Q_z & 1 \end{bmatrix}$$

However, this is not the transformation we want. We want the reverse transformation from world space to view space. But recall from §3.4.5 that reverse transformation is just given by the inverse. Thus $\mathbf{W}^{-1}$ transforms from world space to view space.

The world coordinate system and view coordinate system generally differ by position and orientation only, so it makes intuitive sense that $\mathbf{W} = \mathbf{RT}$ (i.e., the world matrix can be decomposed into a rotation followed by a translation). This form makes the inverse easier to compute:

$$\mathbf{V} = \mathbf{W}^{-1} = (\mathbf{RT})^{-1} = \mathbf{T}^{-1}\mathbf{R}^{-1} = \mathbf{T}^{-1}\mathbf{R}^T$$

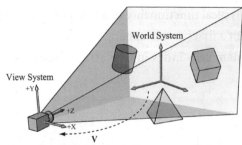

Figure 15.1. The camera coordinate system. Relative to its own coordinate system, the camera sits at the origin looking down the positive z-axis.

$$= \begin{bmatrix} 1 & 0 & 0 & 0 \\ 0 & 1 & 0 & 0 \\ 0 & 0 & 1 & 0 \\ -Q_x & -Q_y & -Q_z & 1 \end{bmatrix} \begin{bmatrix} u_x & v_x & w_x & 0 \\ u_y & v_y & w_y & 0 \\ u_z & v_z & w_z & 0 \\ 0 & 0 & 0 & 1 \end{bmatrix} = \begin{bmatrix} u_x & v_x & w_x & 0 \\ u_y & v_y & w_y & 0 \\ u_z & v_z & w_z & 0 \\ -\mathbf{Q} \cdot \mathbf{u} & -\mathbf{Q} \cdot \mathbf{v} & -\mathbf{Q} \cdot \mathbf{w} & 1 \end{bmatrix}$$

So the view matrix has the form:

$$\mathbf{V} = \begin{bmatrix} u_x & v_x & w_x & 0 \\ u_y & v_y & w_y & 0 \\ u_z & v_z & w_z & 0 \\ -\mathbf{Q} \cdot \mathbf{u} & -\mathbf{Q} \cdot \mathbf{v} & -\mathbf{Q} \cdot \mathbf{w} & 1 \end{bmatrix} \quad \text{(eq. 15.1)}$$

As with all change-of-coordinate transformations, we are not moving anything in the scene. The coordinates change because we are using the camera space frame of reference instead of the world space frame of reference.

15.2 THE CAMERA CLASS

To encapsulate our camera related code, we define and implement a `Camera` class. The data of the camera class stores two key pieces of information. The *position, right, up,* and look vectors of the camera defining, respectively, the origin, *x*-axis, *y*-axis, and *z*-axis of the view space coordinate system in world coordinates, and the properties of the frustum. You can think of the lens of the camera as defining the frustum (its field of view and near and far planes). Most of the methods are trivial (e.g., simple access methods). See the comments below for an overview of the methods and data members. We review selected methods in the next section.

```
class Camera
{
public:

    Camera();
    ~Camera();

    // Get/Set world camera position.
    DirectX::XMVECTOR GetPosition()const;
    DirectX::XMFLOAT3 GetPosition3f()const;
    void SetPosition(float x, float y, float z);
    void SetPosition(const DirectX::XMFLOAT3& v);

    // Get camera basis vectors.
    DirectX::XMVECTOR GetRight()const;
    DirectX::XMFLOAT3 GetRight3f()const;
```

```cpp
    DirectX::XMVECTOR GetUp()const;
    DirectX::XMFLOAT3 GetUp3f()const;
    DirectX::XMVECTOR GetLook()const;
    DirectX::XMFLOAT3 GetLook3f()const;

    // Get frustum properties.
    float GetNearZ()const;
    float GetFarZ()const;
    float GetAspect()const;
    float GetFovY()const;
    float GetFovX()const;

    // Get near and far plane dimensions in view space coordinates.
    float GetNearWindowWidth()const;
    float GetNearWindowHeight()const;
    float GetFarWindowWidth()const;
    float GetFarWindowHeight()const;

    // Set frustum.
    void SetLens(float fovY, float aspect, float zn, float zf);

    // Define camera space via LookAt parameters.
    void LookAt(DirectX::FXMVECTOR pos,
         DirectX::FXMVECTOR target,
         DirectX::FXMVECTOR worldUp);
    void LookAt(const DirectX::XMFLOAT3& pos,
         const DirectX::XMFLOAT3& target,
         const DirectX::XMFLOAT3& up);

    // Get View/Proj matrices.
    DirectX::XMMATRIX GetView()const;
    DirectX::XMMATRIX GetProj()const;

    DirectX::XMFLOAT4X4 GetView4x4f()const;
    DirectX::XMFLOAT4X4 GetProj4x4f()const;

    // Strafe/Walk the camera a distance d.
    void Strafe(float d);
    void Walk(float d);

    // Rotate the camera.
    void Pitch(float angle);
    void RotateY(float angle);

    // After modifying camera position/orientation, call to rebuild the
    view matrix.
    void UpdateViewMatrix();

private:

    // Camera coordinate system with coordinates relative to world
    space.
    DirectX::XMFLOAT3 mPosition = { 0.0f, 0.0f, 0.0f };
    DirectX::XMFLOAT3 mRight = { 1.0f, 0.0f, 0.0f };
    DirectX::XMFLOAT3 mUp = { 0.0f, 1.0f, 0.0f };
    DirectX::XMFLOAT3 mLook = { 0.0f, 0.0f, 1.0f };
```

```
    // Cache frustum properties.
    float mNearZ = 0.0f;
    float mFarZ = 0.0f;
    float mAspect = 0.0f;
    float mFovY = 0.0f;
    float mNearWindowHeight = 0.0f;
    float mFarWindowHeight = 0.0f;

    bool mViewDirty = true;

    // Cache View/Proj matrices.
    DirectX::XMFLOAT4X4 mView = MathHelper::Identity4x4();
    DirectX::XMFLOAT4X4 mProj = MathHelper::Identity4x4();
};
```

The Camera.h/Camera.cpp files are in the Common directory.

15.3 SELECTED METHOD IMPLEMENTATIONS

Many of the camera class methods are trivial get/set methods that we will omit here. However, we will review a few of the important ones in this section.

15.3.1 `XMVECTOR` Return Variations

First, we want to remark that we provide `XMVECTOR` return variations for many of the "get" methods; this is just for convenience so that the client code does not need to convert if they need an `XMVECTOR`:

```
XMVECTOR Camera::GetPosition()const
{
  return XMLoadFloat3(&mPosition);
}

XMFLOAT3 Camera::GetPosition3f()const
{
  return mPosition;
}
```

15.3.2 `SetLens`

We can think of the frustum as the lens of our camera, for it controls our view of view. We cache the frustum properties and build the projection matrix is the `SetLens` method:

```
void Camera::SetLens(float fovY, float aspect, float zn, float zf)
{
  // cache properties
```

```
    mFovY = fovY;
    mAspect = aspect;
    mNearZ = zn;
    mFarZ = zf;

    mNearWindowHeight = 2.0f * mNearZ * tanf( 0.5f*mFovY );
    mFarWindowHeight  = 2.0f * mFarZ  * tanf( 0.5f*mFovY );

    XMMATRIX P = XMMatrixPerspectiveFovLH(mFovY, mAspect, mNearZ, mFarZ);
    XMStoreFloat4x4(&mProj, P);
}
```

15.3.3 Derived Frustum Info

As we just saw, we cache the vertical field of view angle, but additionally provide a method that derives the horizontal field of view angle. Moreover, we provide methods to return the width and height of the frustum at the near and far planes, which are sometimes useful to know. The implementations of these methods are just trigonometry, and if you have trouble following the equations, then review §5.6.3:

```
float Camera::GetFovX()const
{
  float halfWidth = 0.5f*GetNearWindowWidth();
  return 2.0f*atan(halfWidth / mNearZ);
}

float Camera::GetNearWindowWidth()const
{
  return mAspect * mNearWindowHeight;
}

float Camera::GetNearWindowHeight()const
{
  return mNearWindowHeight;
}

float Camera::GetFarWindowWidth()const
{
  return mAspect * mFarWindowHeight;
}

float Camera::GetFarWindowHeight()const
{
  return mFarWindowHeight;
}
```

15.3.4 Transforming the Camera

For a first person camera, ignoring collision detection, we want to be able to:

1. Move the camera along its look vector to move forwards and backwards. This can be implemented by translating the camera position along its look vector.

2. Move the camera along its right vector to strafe right and left. This can be implemented by translating the camera position along its right vector.
3. Rotate the camera around its right vector to look up and down. This can be implemented by rotating the camera's look and up vectors around its right vector using the `XMMatrixRotationAxis` function.
4. Rotate the camera around the world's *y*-axis (assuming the *y*-axis corresponds to the world's "up" direction) vector to look right and left. This can be implemented by rotating all the basis vectors around the world's *y*-axis using the `XMMatrixRotationY` function.

```
void Camera::Walk(float d)
{
  // mPosition += d*mLook
  XMVECTOR s = XMVectorReplicate(d);
  XMVECTOR l = XMLoadFloat3(&mLook);
  XMVECTOR p = XMLoadFloat3(&mPosition);
  XMStoreFloat3(&mPosition, XMVectorMultiplyAdd(s, l, p));}

void Camera::Strafe(float d)
{
  // mPosition += d*mRight
  XMVECTOR s = XMVectorReplicate(d);
  XMVECTOR r = XMLoadFloat3(&mRight);
  XMVECTOR p = XMLoadFloat3(&mPosition);
  XMStoreFloat3(&mPosition, XMVectorMultiplyAdd(s, r, p));
}

void Camera::Pitch(float angle)
{
  // Rotate up and look vector about the right vector.

  XMMATRIX R = XMMatrixRotationAxis(XMLoadFloat3(&mRight), angle);

  XMStoreFloat3(&mUp,   XMVector3TransformNormal(XMLoadFloat3(&mUp),
    R));
  XMStoreFloat3(&mLook, XMVector3TransformNormal(XMLoadFloat3(&mLook),
    R));
}

void Camera::RotateY(float angle)
{
  // Rotate the basis vectors about the world y-axis.

  XMMATRIX R = XMMatrixRotationY(angle);

  XMStoreFloat3(&mRight,   XMVector3TransformNormal(XMLoadFloat3(&mRig
    ht), R));
  XMStoreFloat3(&mUp, XMVector3TransformNormal(XMLoadFloat3(&mUp), R));
  XMStoreFloat3(&mLook, XMVector3TransformNormal(XMLoadFloat3(&mLook),
    R));
}
```

15.3.5 Building the View Matrix

The first part of the `UpdateViewMatrix` method *reorthonormalizes* the camera's right, up, and look vectors. That is to say, it makes sure they are mutually orthogonal to each other and unit length. This is necessary because after several rotations, numerical errors can accumulate and cause these vectors to become non-orthonormal. When this happens, the vectors no longer represent a rectangular coordinate system, but a skewed coordinate system, which is not what we want. The second part of this method just plugs the camera vectors into Equation 15.1 to compute the view transformation matrix.

```
void Camera::UpdateViewMatrix()
{
  if(mViewDirty)
  {
    XMVECTOR R = XMLoadFloat3(&mRight);
    XMVECTOR U = XMLoadFloat3(&mUp);
    XMVECTOR L = XMLoadFloat3(&mLook);
    XMVECTOR P = XMLoadFloat3(&mPosition);

    // Keep camera's axes orthogonal to each other and of unit length.
    L = XMVector3Normalize(L);
    U = XMVector3Normalize(XMVector3Cross(L, R));

    // U, L already ortho-normal, so no need to normalize cross
    product.
    R = XMVector3Cross(U, L);

    // Fill in the view matrix entries.
    float x = -XMVectorGetX(XMVector3Dot(P, R));
    float y = -XMVectorGetX(XMVector3Dot(P, U));
    float z = -XMVectorGetX(XMVector3Dot(P, L));

    XMStoreFloat3(&mRight, R);
    XMStoreFloat3(&mUp, U);
    XMStoreFloat3(&mLook, L);

    mView(0, 0) = mRight.x;
    mView(1, 0) = mRight.y;
    mView(2, 0) = mRight.z;
    mView(3, 0) = x;

    mView(0, 1) = mUp.x;
    mView(1, 1) = mUp.y;
    mView(2, 1) = mUp.z;
    mView(3, 1) = y;

    mView(0, 2) = mLook.x;
    mView(1, 2) = mLook.y;
    mView(2, 2) = mLook.z;
    mView(3, 2) = z;
```

```
    mView(0, 3) = 0.0f;
    mView(1, 3) = 0.0f;
    mView(2, 3) = 0.0f;
    mView(3, 3) = 1.0f;

    mViewDirty = false;
  }
}
```

15.4 CAMERA DEMO COMMENTS

We can now remove all the old variables from our application class that were related to the orbital camera system such as `mPhi`, `mTheta`, `mRadius`, `mView`, and `mProj`. We will add a member variable:

```
Camera mCam;
```

When the window is resized, we know longer rebuild the projection matrix explicitly, and instead delegate the work to the `Camera` class with `SetLens`:

```
void CameraApp::OnResize()
{
  D3DApp::OnResize();

  mCamera.SetLens(0.25f*MathHelper::Pi, AspectRatio(), 1.0f, 1000.0f);
}
```

In the `UpdateScene` method, we handle keyboard input to move the camera:

```
void CameraApp::UpdateScene(float dt)
{
  if( GetAsyncKeyState('W') & 0x8000 )
    mCamera.Walk(10.0f*dt);

  if( GetAsyncKeyState('S') & 0x8000 )
    mCamera.Walk(-10.0f*dt);

  if( GetAsyncKeyState('A') & 0x8000 )
    mCamera.Strafe(-10.0f*dt);

  if( GetAsyncKeyState('D') & 0x8000 )
    mCamera.Strafe(10.0f*dt);
```

In the `OnMouseMove` method, we rotate the camera's look direction:

```
void CameraAndDynamicIndexingApp::OnMouseMove(WPARAM btnState, int x,
    int y)
{
  if( (btnState & MK_LBUTTON) != 0 )
  {
    // Make each pixel correspond to a quarter of a degree.
    float dx = XMConvertToRadians(
      0.25f*static_cast<float>(x - mLastMousePos.x));
```

Figure 15.2. Screenshot of the camera demo. Use the 'W', 'S', 'A', and 'D' keys to move forward, backward, strafe left, and strafe right, respectively. Hold the left mouse button down and move the mouse to "look" in different directions.

```
        float dy = XMConvertToRadians(
          0.25f*static_cast<float>(y - mLastMousePos.y));

        mCamera.Pitch(dy);
        mCamera.RotateY(dx);
    }

    mLastMousePos.x = x;
    mLastMousePos.y = y;
}
```

Finally, for rendering, the view and projection matrices can be accessed from the camera instance:

```
mCamera.UpdateViewMatrix();

XMMATRIX view = mCamera.View();
XMMATRIX proj = mCamera.Proj();
```

15.5 DYNAMIC INDEXING

The idea of dynamic indexing is relatively straightforward. We dynamically index into an array of resources in a shader program; in this demo, the resources will be an array of textures. The index can be specified in various ways:

1. The index can be an element in a constant buffer.
2. The index can be a system ID like `SV_PrimitiveID`, `SV_VertexID`, `SV_DispatchThreadID`, or `SV_InstanceID`.
3. The index can be the result of come calculation.
4. The index can come from a texture.
5. The index can come from a component of the vertex structure.

The following shader syntax declares a texture array of 4 elements and shows how we can index into the texture array where the index comes from a constant buffer:

```
cbuffer cbPerDrawIndex : register(b0)
{
  int gDiffuseTexIndex;
};

Texture2D gDiffuseMap[4] : register(t0);

float4 texValue = gDiffuseMap[gDiffuseTexIndex].Sample(
  gsamLinearWrap, pin.TexC);
```

For this demo, our goal is the following: we want to minimize the number of descriptors we set on a per render-item basis. Right now we set the object constant buffer, the material constant buffer, and the diffuse texture map SRV on a per render-item basis. Minimizing the number of descriptors we need to set will make our root signature smaller, which means less overhead per draw call; moreover, this technique of dynamic indexing will prove especially useful with instancing (the topic of the next chapter). Our strategy is as follows:

1. Create a structured buffer that stores all of the material data. That is, instead of storing our material data in constant buffers, we will store it in a structured buffer. A structured buffer can be indexed in a shader program. This structured buffer will be bound to the rendering pipeline once per frame making all materials visible to the shader programs.

2. Add a `MaterialIndex` field to our object constant buffer to specify the index of the material to use for this draw call. In our shader programs, we use this to index into the material structured buffer.

3. Bind *all* of the texture SRV descriptors used in the scene once per frame, instead of binding one texture SRV per render-item.

4. Add a `DiffuseMapIndex` field to the material data that specifies the texture map associated with the material. We use this to index into the array of textures we bound to the pipeline in the previous step.

With this setup, we only need to set a per object constant buffer for each render-item. Once we have that, we use the `MaterialIndex` to fetch the material to use for the draw call, and from that we use the `DiffuseMapIndex` to fetch the texture to use for the draw call.

Recall that a structured buffer is just an array of data of some type that can live in GPU memory and be accessed by shader programs. Because we still need to be able to update materials on the fly, we use an upload buffer rather than a default buffer. The material structured buffer replaces our material constant buffer in the frame resources class and is created like so:

```
struct MaterialData
{
  DirectX::XMFLOAT4 DiffuseAlbedo = { 1.0f, 1.0f, 1.0f, 1.0f };
  DirectX::XMFLOAT3 FresnelR0 = { 0.01f, 0.01f, 0.01f };
  float Roughness = 64.0f;

  // Used in texture mapping.
  DirectX::XMFLOAT4X4 MatTransform = MathHelper::Identity4x4();

  UINT DiffuseMapIndex = 0;
  UINT MaterialPad0;
  UINT MaterialPad1;
  UINT MaterialPad2;
};

MaterialBuffer = std::make_unique<UploadBuffer<MaterialData>>(
  device, materialCount, false);
```

Other than that, the code for the material structured buffer is not much different from the code with the material constant buffer.

We update the root signature based on the new data the shader expects as input:

```
CD3DX12_DESCRIPTOR_RANGE texTable;
texTable.Init(D3D12_DESCRIPTOR_RANGE_TYPE_SRV, 4, 0, 0);

// Root parameter can be a table, root descriptor or root constants.
CD3DX12_ROOT_PARAMETER slotRootParameter[4];

// Perfomance TIP: Order from most frequent to least frequent.
slotRootParameter[0].InitAsConstantBufferView(0);
slotRootParameter[1].InitAsConstantBufferView(1);
slotRootParameter[2].InitAsShaderResourceView(0, 1);
slotRootParameter[3].InitAsDescriptorTable(1, &texTable, D3D12_SHADER_
    VISIBILITY_PIXEL);


auto staticSamplers = GetStaticSamplers();

// A root signature is an array of root parameters.
CD3DX12_ROOT_SIGNATURE_DESC rootSigDesc(4, slotRootParameter,
    (UINT)staticSamplers.size(), staticSamplers.data(),
    D3D12_ROOT_SIGNATURE_FLAG_ALLOW_INPUT_ASSEMBLER_INPUT_LAYOUT);
```

Now, before we draw any render-items, we can bind all of our materials and texture SRVs once per frame rather than per-render-item, and then each render-item just sets the object constant buffer:

```
void CameraAndDynamicIndexingApp::Draw(const GameTimer& gt)
{
  ...
  auto passCB = mCurrFrameResource->PassCB->Resource();
  mCommandList->SetGraphicsRootConstantBufferView(1, passCB-
    >GetGPUVirtualAddress());
```

```cpp
    // Bind all the materials used in this scene. For structured buffers,
    // we can bypass the heap and set as a root descriptor.
    auto matBuffer = mCurrFrameResource->MaterialBuffer->Resource();
    mCommandList->SetGraphicsRootShaderResourceView(2,
        matBuffer->GetGPUVirtualAddress());

    // Bind all the textures used in this scene. Observe
    // that we only have to specify the first descriptor in the table.
    // The root signature knows how many descriptors are expected in the
        table.
    mCommandList->SetGraphicsRootDescriptorTable(3,
        mSrvDescriptorHeap->GetGPUDescriptorHandleForHeapStart());

    DrawRenderItems(mCommandList.Get(), mOpaqueRitems);
    ...
}

void CameraAndDynamicIndexingApp::DrawRenderItems(
    ID3D12GraphicsCommandList* cmdList,
    const std::vector<RenderItem*>& ritems)
{
    ...
    // For each render item...
    for(size_t i = 0; i < ritems.size(); ++i)
    {
        auto ri = ritems[i];
        ...

        cmdList->SetGraphicsRootConstantBufferView(0, objCBAddress);

        cmdList->DrawIndexedInstanced(ri->IndexCount, 1,
            ri->StartIndexLocation, ri->BaseVertexLocation, 0);
    }
}
```

We note that the `ObjectConstants` structure has been updated to have a `MaterialIndex`. The value you set for this is the same index you would have used to offset into the material constant buffer:

```cpp
// UpdateObjectCBs...
ObjectConstants objConstants;
XMStoreFloat4x4(&objConstants.World, XMMatrixTranspose(world));
XMStoreFloat4x4(&objConstants.TexTransform, XMMatrixTranspose(texTransform));
objConstants.MaterialIndex = e->Mat->MatCBIndex;
```

The modified shader code demonstrating dynamic indexing is included below with relevant sections bolded:

```hlsl
// Include structures and functions for lighting.
#include "LightingUtil.hlsl"

struct MaterialData
{
    float4   DiffuseAlbedo;
```

```hlsl
    float3   FresnelR0;
    float    Roughness;
    float4x4 MatTransform;
    uint     DiffuseMapIndex;
    uint     MatPad0;
    uint     MatPad1;
    uint     MatPad2;
};

// An array of textures, which is only supported in shader model 5.1+. Unlike
// Texture2DArray, the textures in this array can be different sizes and
// formats, making it more flexible than texture arrays.
Texture2D gDiffuseMap[4] : register(t0);

// Put in space1, so the texture array does not overlap with these resources.
// The texture array will occupy registers t0, t1, ..., t3 in space0.
StructuredBuffer<MaterialData> gMaterialData : register(t0, space1);


SamplerState gsamPointWrap        : register(s0);
SamplerState gsamPointClamp       : register(s1);
SamplerState gsamLinearWrap       : register(s2);
SamplerState gsamLinearClamp      : register(s3);
SamplerState gsamAnisotropicWrap  : register(s4);
SamplerState gsamAnisotropicClamp : register(s5);

// Constant data that varies per frame.
cbuffer cbPerObject : register(b0)
{
    float4x4 gWorld;
    float4x4 gTexTransform;
    uint gMaterialIndex;
    uint gObjPad0;
    uint gObjPad1;
    uint gObjPad2;
};

// Constant data that varies per material.
cbuffer cbPass : register(b1)
{
    float4x4 gView;
    float4x4 gInvView;
    float4x4 gProj;
    float4x4 gInvProj;
    float4x4 gViewProj;
    float4x4 gInvViewProj;
    float3 gEyePosW;
    float cbPerObjectPad1;
    float2 gRenderTargetSize;
    float2 gInvRenderTargetSize;
    float gNearZ;
    float gFarZ;
    float gTotalTime;
    float gDeltaTime;
```

```
    float4 gAmbientLight;

    // Indices [0, NUM_DIR_LIGHTS) are directional lights;
    // indices [NUM_DIR_LIGHTS, NUM_DIR_LIGHTS+NUM_POINT_LIGHTS) are point lights;
    // indices [NUM_DIR_LIGHTS+NUM_POINT_LIGHTS,
    // NUM_DIR_LIGHTS+NUM_POINT_LIGHT+NUM_SPOT_LIGHTS)
    // are spot lights for a maximum of MaxLights per object.
    Light gLights[MaxLights];
};

struct VertexIn
{
    float3 PosL    : POSITION;
    float3 NormalL : NORMAL;
    float2 TexC    : TEXCOORD;
};

struct VertexOut
{
    float4 PosH    : SV_POSITION;
    float3 PosW    : POSITION;
    float3 NormalW : NORMAL;
    float2 TexC    : TEXCOORD;
};

VertexOut VS(VertexIn vin)
{
    VertexOut vout = (VertexOut)0.0f;

    // Fetch the material data.
    MaterialData matData = gMaterialData[gMaterialIndex];

    // Transform to world space.
    float4 posW = mul(float4(vin.PosL, 1.0f), gWorld);
    vout.PosW = posW.xyz;

    // Assumes nonuniform scaling; otherwise, need to use inverse-transpose
    // of world matrix.
    vout.NormalW = mul(vin.NormalL, (float3x3)gWorld);

    // Transform to homogeneous clip space.
    vout.PosH = mul(posW, gViewProj);

    // Output vertex attributes for interpolation across triangle.
    float4 texC = mul(float4(vin.TexC, 0.0f, 1.0f), gTexTransform);
    vout.TexC = mul(texC, matData.MatTransform).xy;

    return vout;
}

float4 PS(VertexOut pin) : SV_Target
{
    // Fetch the material data.
    MaterialData matData = gMaterialData[gMaterialIndex];
```

```
    float4 diffuseAlbedo = matData.DiffuseAlbedo;
    float3 fresnelR0 = matData.FresnelR0;
    float  roughness = matData.Roughness;
    uint diffuseTexIndex = matData.DiffuseMapIndex;

    // Dynamically look up the texture in the array.
    diffuseAlbedo *= gDiffuseMap[diffuseTexIndex].Sample(gsamLinearWrap, pin.TexC);

    // Interpolating normal can unnormalize it, so renormalize it.
    pin.NormalW = normalize(pin.NormalW);

    // Vector from point being lit to eye.
    float3 toEyeW = normalize(gEyePosW - pin.PosW);

    // Light terms.
    float4 ambient = gAmbientLight*diffuseAlbedo;

    Material mat = { diffuseAlbedo, fresnelR0, roughness };
    float4 directLight = ComputeDirectLighting(gLights, mat, pin.PosW, pin.
NormalW, toEyeW);

    float4 litColor = ambient + directLight;

    // Common convention to take alpha from diffuse albedo.
    litColor.a = diffuseAlbedo.a;

    return litColor;
}
```

> **Note:** *The above shader code demonstrated writing an explicit register space:*
>
> ```
> StructuredBuffer<MaterialData> gMaterialData : register(t0, space1);
> ```
>
> *If you do not explicitly specify a space, it defaults to* `space0`. *A space just gives you another dimension to specify a shader register and is used to prevent resource overlap. For example, we can put multiple resources in register t0 if they are in different spaces:*
>
> ```
> Texture2D gDiffuseMap : register(t0, space0);
> Texture2D gNormalMap  : register(t0, space1);
> Texture2D gShadowMap  : register(t0, space2);
> ```
>
> *They are often used when there are arrays of resources. For example, the following 4 element texture array occupies registers t0, t1, t2, and t3:*
>
> ```
> Texture2D gDiffuseMap[4] : register(t0);
> ```
>
> *We could have counted and figured out that the next free register was t4, or we could just not worry about it and introduce a new space:*
>
> ```
> // Put in space1, so the texture array does not overlap with these
> // resources.
> // The texture array will occupy registers t0, t1, ..., t3 in space0.
> StructuredBuffer<MaterialData> gMaterialData : register(t0, space1);
> ```

To conclude this section, three additional uses of dynamic indexing are given:

1. Merging nearby meshes with different textures into a single render-item so that they can be drawn with one draw call. The meshes could store the texture/material to use as an attribute in the vertex structure.
2. Multitexturing in a single rendering-pass where the textures have different sizes and formats.
3. Instancing render-items with different textures and materials using the `SV_InstanceID` value as an index. We will see an example of this in the next chapter.

15.6 SUMMARY

1. We define the camera coordinate system by specifying its position and orientation. The position is specified by a position vector relative to the world coordinate system, and the orientation is specified by three orthonormal vectors relative to the world coordinate system: a right, up, and look vector. Moving the camera amounts to moving the camera coordinate system relative to the world coordinate system.
2. We included projection related quantities in the camera class, as the perspective projection matrix can be thought of as the "lens" of the camera by controlling the field of view, and near and far planes.
3. Moving forward and backwards can be implemented simply by translating the camera position along its look vector. Strafing right and left can be implemented simply by translating the camera position along its right vector. Looking up and down can be achieved by rotating the camera's look and up vectors around its right vector. Looking left and right can be implemented by rotating all the basis vectors around the world's y-axis.
4. Dynamic indexing is new to shader model 5.1 and and allows us to dynamically index an array of texture resources, where the textures in this array can be different sizes and formats. One application of this is to bind all of our texture descriptors once per frame, and then index into the texture array in the pixel shader to use the appropriate texture for a given pixel.

15.7 EXERCISES

1. Given the world space axes and origin in world coordinates: $\mathbf{i} = (1, 0, 0)$, $\mathbf{j} = (0, 1, 0)$, $\mathbf{k} = (0, 0, 1)$ and $\mathbf{O} = (0, 0, 0)$, and the view space axes and origin in world coordinates: $\mathbf{u} = (u_x, u_y, u_z)$, $\mathbf{v} = (v_x, v_y, v_z)$, $\mathbf{w} = (w_x, w_y, w_z)$ and $\mathbf{Q} = (Q_x, Q_y, Q_z)$, derive the view matrix form

$$\mathbf{V} = \begin{bmatrix} u_x & v_x & w_x & 0 \\ u_y & v_y & w_y & 0 \\ u_z & v_z & w_z & 0 \\ -\mathbf{Q} \cdot \mathbf{u} & -\mathbf{Q} \cdot \mathbf{v} & -\mathbf{Q} \cdot \mathbf{w} & 1 \end{bmatrix}$$

using the dot product. (Remember, to find the change of coordinate matrix from world space to view space, you just need to describe the world space axes and origin with coordinates relative to view space. Then these coordinates become the rows of the view matrix.)

2. Modify the camera demo to support "roll." This is where the camera rotates around its look vector. This could be useful for an aircraft game.

3. Suppose you have a scene with five boxes at different positions and each box has a different texture. Create a single mesh that stores the geometry for the five boxes at the different positions, and create a single render-item for the five boxes. Add an additional field to the vertex structure that is an index to the texture to use. For example, the vertices of box 0 will have a texture index of 0 so that box 0 is textured with texture 0, the vertices of box 1 will have a texture index of 1 so that box 1 is textured with texture 1, etc. Bind all five textures to the pipeline once per frame, and use the vertex structure index to select the texture to use in the pixel shader. Observe that we have drawn five boxes with five different textures with one draw call. If draw calls were a bottleneck in your application, merging nearby geometries into one render item like this could be an optimization for your application.

Chapter 16: Instancing and Frustum Culling

In this chapter, we study instancing and frustum culling. Instancing refers to drawing the same object more than once in a scene. Instancing can provide significant optimization, and so there is dedicated Direct3D support for instancing. Frustum culling refers to rejecting entire groups of triangles from further processing that are outside the viewing frustum with a simple test.

Objectives:

1. To learn how to implement hardware instancing.
2. To become familiar with bounding volumes, why they are useful, how to create them, and how to use them.
3. To discover how to implement frustum culling.

16.1 HARDWARE INSTANCING

Instancing refers to drawing the same object more than once in a scene, but with different positions, orientations, scales, materials, and textures. Here are a few examples:

1. A few different tree models are drawn multiple times to build a forest.

2. A few different asteroid models are drawn multiple times to build an asteroid field.

3. A few different character models are drawn multiple times to build a crowd of people.

It would be wasteful to duplicate the vertex and index data for each instance. Instead, we store a single copy of the geometry (i.e., vertex and index lists) relative to the object's local space. Then we draw the object several times, but each time with a different world matrix and a different material if additional variety is desired.

Although this strategy saves memory, it still requires per-object API overhead. That is, for each object, we must set its unique material, its world matrix, and invoke a draw command. Although Direct3D 12 was redesigned to minimize a lot of the API overhead that existed in Direct3D 11 when executing a draw call, there is still some overhead. The Direct3D instancing API allows you to instance an object multiple times with a single draw call; and moreover, with dynamic indexing (covered in the previous chapter), instancing is more flexible than in Direct3D 11.

Why the concern about API overhead? It was common for Direct3D 11 applications to be CPU bound due to the API overhead (this means the CPU was the bottleneck, not the GPU). The reason for this is that level designers like to draw many objects with unique materials and textures, and this requires state changes and draw calls for each object. When there is a high-level of CPU overhead for each API call, scenes would be limited to a few thousand draw calls in order to still maintain real-time rendering speeds. Graphics engines would then employ batching techniques (see [Wloka03]) to minimize the number of draw calls. Hardware instancing is one aspect where the API helps perform batching.

16.1.1 Drawing Instanced Data

Perhaps surprisingly, we have already been drawing instanced data in all the previous chapter demos. However, the instance count has always been 1 (second parameter):

```
cmdList->DrawIndexedInstanced(ri->IndexCount, 1,
    ri->StartIndexLocation, ri->BaseVertexLocation, 0);
```

The second parameter, InstanceCount, specifies the number of times to instance the geometry we are drawing. If we specify ten, the geometry will be drawn 10 times.

Drawing an object ten times alone does not really help us, though. The object will be drawn in the same place using the same materials and textures. So the next step is to figure out how to specify additional per-instance data so that we can vary the instances by rendering them with different transforms, materials, and textures.

16.1.2 Instance Data

The previous version of this book obtained instance data from the input assembly stage. When creating an input layout, you can specify that data streams in per-instance rather than at a per-vertex frequency by using `D3D12_INPUT_CLASSIFICATION_PER_INSTANCE_DATA` instead of `D3D12_INPUT_CLASSIFICATION_PER_VERTEX_DATA`, respectively. You would then bind a secondary vertex buffer to the input stream that contained the instancing data. Direct3D 12 still supports this way of feeding instancing data into the pipeline, but we opt for a more modern approach.

The modern approach is to create a structured buffer that contains the per-instance data for all of our instances. For example, if we were going to instance an object 100 times, we would create a structured buffer with 100 per-instance data elements. We then bind the structured buffer resource to the rendering pipeline, and index into it in the vertex shader based on the instance we are drawing. How do we know which instance is being drawn in the vertex shader? Direct3D provides the system value identifier `SV_InstanceID` which you can use in your vertex shader. For example, vertices of the first instance will have id 0, vertices of the second instance will have id 1, and so on. So in our vertex shader, we can index into the structured buffer to fetch the per-instance data we need. The following shader code shows how this all works:

```
// Defaults for number of lights.
#ifndef NUM_DIR_LIGHTS
  #define NUM_DIR_LIGHTS 3
#endif

#ifndef NUM_POINT_LIGHTS
  #define NUM_POINT_LIGHTS 0
#endif

#ifndef NUM_SPOT_LIGHTS
  #define NUM_SPOT_LIGHTS 0
#endif

// Include structures and functions for lighting.
#include "LightingUtil.hlsl"

struct InstanceData
{
  float4x4 World;
```

```hlsl
    float4x4 TexTransform;
    uint    MaterialIndex;
    uint    InstPad0;
    uint    InstPad1;
    uint    InstPad2;
};

struct MaterialData
{
    float4   DiffuseAlbedo;
    float3   FresnelR0;
    float    Roughness;
    float4x4 MatTransform;
    uint     DiffuseMapIndex;
    uint     MatPad0;
    uint     MatPad1;
    uint     MatPad2;
};

// An array of textures, which is only supported in shader model 5.1+.
// Unlike Texture2DArray, the textures in this array can be different
// sizes and formats, making it more flexible than texture arrays.
Texture2D gDiffuseMap[7] : register(t0);

// Put in space1, so the texture array does not overlap with these.
// The texture array above will occupy registers t0, t1, ..., t6 in
// space0.
StructuredBuffer<InstanceData> gInstanceData : register(t0, space1);
StructuredBuffer<MaterialData> gMaterialData : register(t1, space1);

SamplerState gsamPointWrap        : register(s0);
SamplerState gsamPointClamp       : register(s1);
SamplerState gsamLinearWrap       : register(s2);
SamplerState gsamLinearClamp      : register(s3);
SamplerState gsamAnisotropicWrap  : register(s4);
SamplerState gsamAnisotropicClamp : register(s5);

// Constant data that varies per pass.
cbuffer cbPass : register(b0)
{
    float4x4 gView;
    float4x4 gInvView;
    float4x4 gProj;
    float4x4 gInvProj;
    float4x4 gViewProj;
    float4x4 gInvViewProj;
    float3   gEyePosW;
    float    cbPerObjectPad1;
    float2   gRenderTargetSize;
    float2   gInvRenderTargetSize;
    float    gNearZ;
    float    gFarZ;
    float    gTotalTime;
    float    gDeltaTime;
    float4   gAmbientLight;
```

```
   // Indices [0, NUM_DIR_LIGHTS) are directional lights;
   // indices [NUM_DIR_LIGHTS, NUM_DIR_LIGHTS+NUM_POINT_LIGHTS) are
     point lights;
   // indices [NUM_DIR_LIGHTS+NUM_POINT_LIGHTS,
   // NUM_DIR_LIGHTS+NUM_POINT_LIGHT+NUM_SPOT_LIGHTS)
   // are spot lights for a maximum of MaxLights per object.
   Light gLights[MaxLights];
};

struct VertexIn
{
   float3 PosL    : POSITION;
   float3 NormalL : NORMAL;
   float2 TexC    : TEXCOORD;
};

struct VertexOut
{
   float4 PosH    : SV_POSITION;
   float3 PosW    : POSITION;
   float3 NormalW : NORMAL;
   float2 TexC    : TEXCOORD;

   // nointerpolation is used so the index is not interpolated
   // across the triangle.
   nointerpolation uint MatIndex : MATINDEX;
};

VertexOut VS(VertexIn vin, uint instanceID : SV_InstanceID)
{
   VertexOut vout = (VertexOut)0.0f;

   // Fetch the instance data.
   InstanceData instData = gInstanceData[instanceID];
   float4x4 world = instData.World;
   float4x4 texTransform = instData.TexTransform;
   uint matIndex = instData.MaterialIndex;

   vout.MatIndex = matIndex;

   // Fetch the material data.
   MaterialData matData = gMaterialData[matIndex];

   // Transform to world space.
   float4 posW = mul(float4(vin.PosL, 1.0f), world);
   vout.PosW = posW.xyz;

   // Assumes nonuniform scaling; otherwise, need to use inverse-transpose
   // of world matrix.
   vout.NormalW = mul(vin.NormalL, (float3x3)world);

   // Transform to homogeneous clip space.
```

```hlsl
    vout.PosH = mul(posW, gViewProj);

    // Output vertex attributes for interpolation across triangle.
    float4 texC = mul(float4(vin.TexC, 0.0f, 1.0f), texTransform);
    vout.TexC = mul(texC, matData.MatTransform).xy;

    return vout;
}

float4 PS(VertexOut pin) : SV_Target
{
    // Fetch the material data.
    MaterialData matData = gMaterialData[pin.MatIndex];
    float4 diffuseAlbedo = matData.DiffuseAlbedo;
    float3 fresnelR0 = matData.FresnelR0;
    float roughness = matData.Roughness;
    uint diffuseTexIndex = matData.DiffuseMapIndex;

    // Dynamically look up the texture in the array.
    diffuseAlbedo *= gDiffuseMap[diffuseTexIndex].Sample(gsamLinearWrap,
      pin.TexC);

    // Interpolating normal can unnormalize it, so renormalize it.
    pin.NormalW = normalize(pin.NormalW);

    // Vector from point being lit to eye.
    float3 toEyeW = normalize(gEyePosW - pin.PosW);

    // Light terms.
    float4 ambient = gAmbientLight*diffuseAlbedo;

    Material mat = { diffuseAlbedo, fresnelR0, roughness };
    float4 directLight = ComputeDirectLighting(gLights, mat,
      pin.PosW, pin.NormalW, toEyeW);

    float4 litColor = ambient + directLight;

    // Common convention to take alpha from diffuse albedo.
    litColor.a = diffuseAlbedo.a;

    return litColor;
}
```

Note that we no longer have a per-object constant buffer. The per-object data comes from the instance buffer. Observe also how we use dynamic indexing to associate a different material for each instance, and a different texture. We are able to get quite a lot of per-instance variety in a single draw call! For completeness, the corresponding root signature description is shown below that corresponds to the above shader programs:

```
CD3DX12_DESCRIPTOR_RANGE texTable;
texTable.Init(D3D12_DESCRIPTOR_RANGE_TYPE_SRV, 7, 0, 0);
```

```cpp
// Root parameter can be a table, root descriptor or root constants.
CD3DX12_ROOT_PARAMETER slotRootParameter[4];

// Perfomance TIP: Order from most frequent to least frequent.
slotRootParameter[0].InitAsShaderResourceView(0, 1);
slotRootParameter[1].InitAsShaderResourceView(1, 1);
slotRootParameter[2].InitAsConstantBufferView(0);
slotRootParameter[3].InitAsDescriptorTable(1, &texTable, D3D12_SHADER_
    VISIBILITY_PIXEL);

auto staticSamplers = GetStaticSamplers();

// A root signature is an array of root parameters.
CD3DX12_ROOT_SIGNATURE_DESC rootSigDesc(4, slotRootParameter,
    (UINT)staticSamplers.size(), staticSamplers.data(),
    D3D12_ROOT_SIGNATURE_FLAG_ALLOW_INPUT_ASSEMBLER_INPUT_LAYOUT);
```

As in the last chapter, we bind all the scene materials and textures once per-frame, and the only per draw call resource we need to set is the structured buffer with the instanced data:

```cpp
void InstancingAndCullingApp::Draw(const GameTimer& gt)
{
    ...
    // Bind all the materials used in this scene. For structured buffers,
      we
    // can bypass the heap and set as a root descriptor.
    auto matBuffer = mCurrFrameResource->MaterialBuffer->Resource();
    mCommandList->SetGraphicsRootShaderResourceView(1, matBuffer-
        >GetGPUVirtualAddress());

    auto passCB = mCurrFrameResource->PassCB->Resource();
    mCommandList->SetGraphicsRootConstantBufferView(2, passCB-
        >GetGPUVirtualAddress());

    // Bind all the textures used in this scene.
    mCommandList->SetGraphicsRootDescriptorTable(3,
        mSrvDescriptorHeap->GetGPUDescriptorHandleForHeapStart());

    DrawRenderItems(mCommandList.Get(), mOpaqueRitems);
    ...
}

void InstancingAndCullingApp::DrawRenderItems(
    ID3D12GraphicsCommandList* cmdList,
    const std::vector<RenderItem*>& ritems)
{
    // For each render item...
    for(size_t i = 0; i < ritems.size(); ++i)
    {
        auto ri = ritems[i];

        cmdList->IASetVertexBuffers(0, 1, &ri->Geo->VertexBufferView());
        cmdList->IASetIndexBuffer(&ri->Geo->IndexBufferView());
        cmdList->IASetPrimitiveTopology(ri->PrimitiveType);
```

```cpp
    // Set the instance buffer to use for this render-item.
    // For structured buffers, we can bypass
    // the heap and set as a root descriptor.
    auto instanceBuffer = mCurrFrameResource->InstanceBuffer-
    >Resource();
    mCommandList->SetGraphicsRootShaderResourceView(
      0, instanceBuffer->GetGPUVirtualAddress());

    cmdList->DrawIndexedInstanced(ri->IndexCount,
      ri->InstanceCount, ri->StartIndexLocation,
      ri->BaseVertexLocation, 0);
  }
}
```

16.1.3 Creating the Instanced Buffer

The instance buffer stores the data that varies per-instance. It looks a lot like the data we previously put in our per-object constant buffer. On the CPU side, our instance data structure looks like this:

```cpp
struct InstanceData
{
  DirectX::XMFLOAT4X4 World = MathHelper::Identity4x4();
  DirectX::XMFLOAT4X4 TexTransform = MathHelper::Identity4x4();
  UINT MaterialIndex;
  UINT InstancePad0;
  UINT InstancePad1;
  UINT InstancePad2;
};
```

The per-instance data in system memory is stored as part of the render-item structure, as the render-item maintains how many times it should be instanced:

```cpp
struct RenderItem
{
  ...

  std::vector<InstanceData> Instances;

  ...
};
```

For the GPU to consume the instance data, we need to create a structured buffer with element type `InstanceData`. Moreover, this buffer will be dynamic (i.e., an upload buffer) so that we can update it every frame; in our demo, we copy the instanced data of only the *visible* instances into the structure buffer (this is related to frustum culling, see §16.3), and the set of visible instances will change as the camera moves/looks around. Creating a dynamic buffer is simple with our `UploadBuffer` helper class:

```cpp
struct FrameResource
{
public:

    FrameResource(ID3D12Device* device, UINT passCount,
        UINT maxInstanceCount, UINT materialCount);
    FrameResource(const FrameResource& rhs) = delete;
    FrameResource& operator=(const FrameResource& rhs) = delete;
    ~FrameResource();

    // We cannot reset the allocator until the GPU is done processing the commands.
    // So each frame needs their own allocator.
    Microsoft::WRL::ComPtr<ID3D12CommandAllocator> CmdListAlloc;

    // We cannot update a cbuffer until the GPU is done processing the commands
    // that reference it. So each frame needs their own cbuffers.
    // std::unique_ptr<UploadBuffer<FrameConstants>> FrameCB = nullptr;
    std::unique_ptr<UploadBuffer<PassConstants>> PassCB = nullptr;
    std::unique_ptr<UploadBuffer<MaterialData>> MaterialBuffer = nullptr;

    // NOTE: In this demo, we instance only one render-item, so we only have
    // one structured buffer to store instancing data. To make this more
    // general (i.e., to support instancing multiple render-items), you
    // would need to have a structured buffer for each render-item, and
    // allocate each buffer with enough room for the maximum number of
    // instances you would ever draw. This sounds like a lot, but it is
    // actually no more than the amount of per-object constant data we
    // would need if we were not using instancing. For example, if we
    // were drawing 1000 objects without instancing, we would create a
    // constant buffer with enough room for a 1000 objects. With instancing,
    // we would just create a structured buffer large enough to store the
    // instance data for 1000 instances.
    std::unique_ptr<UploadBuffer<InstanceData>> InstanceBuffer = nullptr;

    // Fence value to mark commands up to this fence point. This lets us
    // check if these frame resources are still in use by the GPU.
    UINT64 Fence = 0;
};

FrameResource::FrameResource(ID3D12Device* device,
    UINT passCount, UINT maxInstanceCount, UINT materialCount)
{
    ThrowIfFailed(device->CreateCommandAllocator(
        D3D12_COMMAND_LIST_TYPE_DIRECT,
        IID_PPV_ARGS(CmdListAlloc.GetAddressOf())));

    PassCB = std::make_unique<UploadBuffer<PassConstants>>(
        device, passCount, true);
    MaterialBuffer = std::make_unique<UploadBuffer<MaterialData>>(
        device, materialCount, false);
    InstanceBuffer = std::make_unique<UploadBuffer<InstanceData>>(
        device, maxInstanceCount, false);
}
```

Note that `InstanceBuffer` is not a constant buffer, so we specify false for the last parameter.

16.2 BOUNDING VOLUMES AND FRUSTUMS

In order to implement frustum culling, we need to become familiar with the mathematical representation of a frustum and various bounding volumes. Bounding volumes are primitive geometric objects that approximate the volume of an object—see Figure 16.1. The tradeoff is that although the bounding volume only approximates the object its form has a simple mathematical representation, which makes it easy to work with.

16.2.1 DirectX Math Collision

We use the *DirectXCollision.h* utility library, which is part of DirectX Math. This library provides fast implementations to common geometric primitive intersection tests such as ray/triangle intersection, ray/box intersection, box/box intersection, box/plane intersection, box/frustum, sphere/frustum, and much more. Exercise 3 asks you to explore this library to get familiar with what it offers.

16.2.2 Boxes

The *axis-aligned bounding box* (AABB) of a mesh is a box that tightly surrounds the mesh and such that its faces are parallel to the major axes. An AABB can be described by a minimum point $\mathbf{v}_{min}$ and a maximum point $\mathbf{v}_{max}$ (see Figure 16.2). The minimum point $\mathbf{v}_{min}$ is found by searching through all the vertices of the mesh and finding the minimum x-, y-, and z-coordinates, and the maximum point $\mathbf{v}_{max}$ is found by searching through all the vertices of the mesh and finding the maximum x-, y-, and z-coordinates.

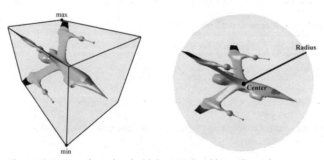

Figure 16.1. A mesh rendered with its AABB and bounding sphere.

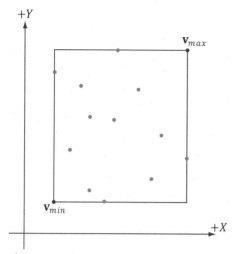

Figure 16.2. The AABB of a set of points using minimum and maximum point representation.

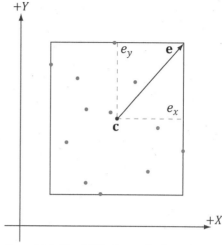

Figure 16.3. The AABB of a set of points using center and extents representation.

Alternatively, an AABB can be represented with the box center point **c** and *extents* vector **e**, which stores the distance from the center point to the sides of the box along the coordinate axes (see Figure 16.3).

The DirectX collision library uses the center/extents representation:

```
struct BoundingBox
{
    static const size_t CORNER_COUNT = 8;

    XMFLOAT3 Center;    // Center of the box.
    XMFLOAT3 Extents;   // Distance from the center to each side.
    ...
```

It is easy to convert from one representation to the other. For example, given a bounding box defined by $\mathbf{v}_{min}$ and $\mathbf{v}_{max}$, the center/extents representation is given by:

$$\mathbf{c} = 0.5\left(\mathbf{v}_{min} + \mathbf{v}_{max}\right)$$

$$\mathbf{e} = 0.5\left(\mathbf{v}_{max} - \mathbf{v}_{min}\right)$$

The following code shows how we compute the bounding box of the skull mesh in this chapter's demo:

```
XMFLOAT3 vMinf3(+MathHelper::Infinity, +MathHelper::Infinity,
    +MathHelper::Infinity);
XMFLOAT3 vMaxf3(-MathHelper::Infinity, -MathHelper::Infinity,
    -MathHelper::Infinity);
```

```cpp
XMVECTOR vMin = XMLoadFloat3(&vMinf3);
XMVECTOR vMax = XMLoadFloat3(&vMaxf3);

std::vector<Vertex> vertices(vcount);
for(UINT i = 0; i < vcount; ++i)
{
  fin >> vertices[i].Pos.x >> vertices[i].Pos.y >> vertices[i].Pos.z;
  fin >> vertices[i].Normal.x >> vertices[i].Normal.y >> vertices[i].
    Normal.z;

  XMVECTOR P = XMLoadFloat3(&vertices[i].Pos);

  // Project point onto unit sphere and generate spherical texture
    coordinates.
  XMFLOAT3 spherePos;
  XMStoreFloat3(&spherePos, XMVector3Normalize(P));

  float theta = atan2f(spherePos.z, spherePos.x);

  // Put in [0, 2pi].
  if(theta < 0.0f)
    theta += XM_2PI;

  float phi = acosf(spherePos.y);

  float u = theta / (2.0f*XM_PI);
  float v = phi / XM_PI;

  vertices[i].TexC = { u, v };

  vMin = XMVectorMin(vMin, P);
  vMax = XMVectorMax(vMax, P);
}

BoundingBox bounds;
XMStoreFloat3(&bounds.Center, 0.5f*(vMin + vMax));
XMStoreFloat3(&bounds.Extents, 0.5f*(vMax - vMin));
```

The XMVectorMin and XMVectorMax functions return the vectors:

$$\mathbf{min}(\mathbf{u},\mathbf{v}) = \left(\min(u_x,v_x), \min(u_y,v_y), \min(u_z,v_z), \min(u_w,v_w)\right)$$

$$\mathbf{max}(\mathbf{u},\mathbf{v}) = \left(\max(u_x,v_x), \max(u_y,v_y), \max(u_z,v_z), \max(u_w,v_w)\right)$$

16.2.2.1 Rotations and Axis-Aligned Bounding Boxes

Figure 16.4 shows that a box axis-aligned in one coordinate system may not be axis-aligned with a different coordinate system. In particular, if we compute the AABB of a mesh in local space, it gets transformed to an *oriented bounding box* (OBB) in world space. However, we can always transform into the local space of the mesh and do the intersection there where the box is axis-aligned.

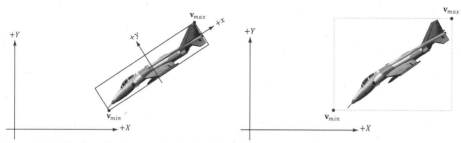

Figure 16.4. The bounding box is axis aligned with the *xy*-frame, but not with the *XY*-frame.

Figure 16.5. The bounding box is axis aligned with the *XY*-frame.

Alternatively, we can recompute the AABB in the world space, but this can result in a "fatter" box that is a poorer approximation to the actual volume (see Figure 16.5).

Yet another alternative is to abandon axis-aligned bounding boxes, and just work with oriented bounding boxes, where we maintain the orientation of the box relative to the world space. The DirectX collision library provides the following structure for representing an oriented bounding box.

```
struct BoundingOrientedBox
{
    static const size_t CORNER_COUNT = 8;

    XMFLOAT3 Center;        // Center of the box.
    XMFLOAT3 Extents;       // Distance from the center to each side.
    XMFLOAT4 Orientation;   // Unit quaternion representing rotation
      (box -> world).
    ...
```

 In this chapter, you will see mention of quaternions for representing rotations/ orientations. Briefly, a unit quaternion can represent a rotation just like a rotation matrix can. We cover quaternions in Chapter 22. For now, just think of it as representing a rotation like a rotation matrix.

An AABB and OBB can also be constructed from a set of points using the DirectX collision library with the following *static* member functions:

```
void BoundingBox::CreateFromPoints(
  _Out_ BoundingBox& Out,
  _In_ size_t Count,
  _In_reads_bytes_(sizeof(XMFLOAT3)+Stride*(Count-1)) const XMFLOAT3* pPoints,
  _In_ size_t Stride );

void BoundingOrientedBox::CreateFromPoints(
  _Out_ BoundingOrientedBox& Out,
  _In_ size_t Count,
  _In_reads_bytes_(sizeof(XMFLOAT3)+Stride*(Count-1)) const XMFLOAT3* pPoints,
  _In_ size_t Stride );
```

If your vertex structure looks like this:

```
struct Basic32
{
  XMFLOAT3 Pos;
  XMFLOAT3 Normal;
  XMFLOAT2 TexC;
};
```

And you have an array of vertices forming your mesh:

```
std::vector<Vertex::Basic32> vertices;
```

Then you call this function like so:

```
BoundingBox box;
BoundingBox::CreateFromPoints(
  box,
  vertices.size(),
  &vertices[0].Pos,
  sizeof(Vertex::Basic32));
```

The stride indicates how many bytes to skip to get to the next position element.

> In order to compute bounding volumes of your meshes, you need to have a system memory copy of your vertex list available, such as one stored in `std::vector`. This is because the CPU cannot read from a vertex buffer created for rendering. Therefore, it is common for applications to keep a system memory copy around for things like this, as well as picking (Chapter 17), and collision detection.

16.2.3 Spheres

The bounding sphere of a mesh is a sphere that tightly surrounds the mesh. A bounding sphere can be described with a center point and radius. One way to compute the bounding sphere of a mesh is to first compute its AABB. We then take the center of the AABB as the center of the bounding sphere:

$$\mathbf{c} = 0.5(\mathbf{v}_{min} + \mathbf{v}_{max})$$

The radius is then taken to be the maximum distance between any vertex **p** in the mesh from the center **c**:

$$r = \max\{\|\mathbf{c} - \mathbf{p}\| : \mathbf{p} \in mesh\}$$

Suppose we compute the bounding sphere of a mesh in local space. After the world transform, the bounding sphere may not tightly surround the mesh due to scaling. Thus the radius needs to be rescaled accordingly. To compensate for non-uniform scaling, we must scale the radius by the largest scaling component so that the sphere encapsulates the transformed mesh. Another possible strategy is to avoid scaling all together by having all your meshes modeled to the same scale of the game world. This way, models will not need to be rescaled once loaded into the application.

The DirectX collision library provides the following structure for representing a bounding sphere:

```
struct BoundingSphere
{
    XMFLOAT3 Center;    // Center of the sphere.
    float Radius;       // Radius of the sphere.
    ...
```

And it provides the following *static* member function for creating one from a set of points:

```
void BoundingSphere::CreateFromPoints(
  _Out_ BoundingSphere& Out,
  _In_ size_t Count,
  _In_reads_bytes_(sizeof(XMFLOAT3)+Stride*(Count-1)) const XMFLOAT3* pPoints,
  _In_ size_t Stride );
```

16.2.4 Frustums

We are well familiar with frustums from Chapter 5. One way to specify a frustum mathematically is as the intersection of six planes: the left/right planes, the top/bottom planes, and the near/far planes. We assume the six frustum planes are "inward" facing—see Figure 16.6.

This six plane representation makes it easy to do frustum and bounding volume intersection tests.

16.2.4.1 Constructing the Frustum Planes

One easy way to construct the frustum planes is in view space, where the frustum takes on a canonical form centered at the origin looking down the positive z-axis.

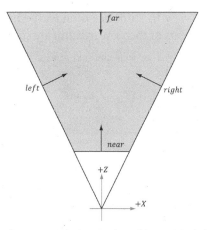

Figure 16.6. The intersection of the positive half spaces of the frustum planes defines the frustum volume.

Here, the near and far planes are trivially specified by their distances along the
z-axis, the left and right planes are symmetric and pass through the origin (see
Figure 16.6 again), and the top and bottom planes are symmetric and pass
through the origin. Consequently, we do not even need to store the full plane
equations to represent the frustum in view space, we just need the plane slopes
for the top/bottom/left/right planes, and the z distances for the near and far plane.
The DirectX collision library provides the following structure for representing a
frustum:

```
struct BoundingFrustum
{
  static const size_t CORNER_COUNT = 8;

  XMFLOAT3 Origin;          // Origin of the frustum (and projection).
  XMFLOAT4 Orientation;     // Quaternion representing rotation.

  float RightSlope;         // Positive X slope (X/Z).
  float LeftSlope;          // Negative X slope.
  float TopSlope;           // Positive Y slope (Y/Z).
  float BottomSlope;        // Negative Y slope.
  float Near, Far;          // Z of the near plane and far plane.
  ...
```

In the local space of the frustum (e.g., view space for the camera), the `Origin`
would be zero, and the `Orientation` would represent an identity transform (no
rotation). We can position and orientate the frustum somewhere in the world by
specifying an `Origin` position and `Orientation` quaternion.

If we cached the frustum vertical field of view, aspect ratio, near and far planes
of our camera, then we can determine the frustum plane equations in view space
with a little mathematical effort. However, it is also possible to derive the frustum
plane equations in view space from the projection matrix in a number of ways (see
[Lengyel02] or [Möller08] for two different ways). The XNA collision library takes
the following strategy. In NDC space, the view frustum has been warped into the
box $[-1,1] \times [-1,1] \times [0,1]$. So the eight corners of the view frustum are simply:

```
// Corners of the projection frustum in homogenous space.
static XMVECTORF32 HomogenousPoints[6] =
{
  { 1.0f, 0.0f, 1.0f, 1.0f },    // right (at far plane)
  { -1.0f, 0.0f, 1.0f, 1.0f },   // left
  { 0.0f, 1.0f, 1.0f, 1.0f },    // top
  { 0.0f, -1.0f, 1.0f, 1.0f },   // bottom

  { 0.0f, 0.0f, 0.0f, 1.0f },    // near
  { 0.0f, 0.0f, 1.0f, 1.0f }     // far
};
```

We can compute the inverse of the projection matrix (as well is invert the
homogeneous divide), to transform the eight corners from NDC space back to

view space. One we have the eight corners of the frustum in view space, some simple mathematics is used to compute the plane equations (again, this is simple because in view space, the frustum is positioned at the origin, and axis aligned). The following DirectX collision code computes the frustum in view space from a projection matrix:

```
//-----------------------------------------------------------------------
// Build a frustum from a persepective projection matrix. The matrix may only
// contain a projection; any rotation, translation or scale will cause the
// constructed frustum to be incorrect.
//-----------------------------------------------------------------------
_Use_decl_annotations_
inline void XM_CALLCONV BoundingFrustum::CreateFromMatrix(
    BoundingFrustum& Out,
    FXMMATRIX Projection )
{
    // Corners of the projection frustum in homogenous space.
    static XMVECTORF32 HomogenousPoints[6] =
    {
        {  1.0f,  0.0f, 1.0f, 1.0f },   // right (at far plane)
        { -1.0f,  0.0f, 1.0f, 1.0f },   // left
        {  0.0f,  1.0f, 1.0f, 1.0f },   // top
        {  0.0f, -1.0f, 1.0f, 1.0f },   // bottom

        {  0.0f,  0.0f, 0.0f, 1.0f },   // near
        {  0.0f,  0.0f, 1.0f, 1.0f }    // far
    };

    XMVECTOR Determinant;
    XMMATRIX matInverse = XMMatrixInverse( &Determinant, Projection );

    // Compute the frustum corners in world space.
    XMVECTOR Points[6];

    for( size_t i = 0; i < 6; ++i )
    {
        // Transform point.
        Points[i] = XMVector4Transform( HomogenousPoints[i], matInverse );
    }

    Out.Origin = XMFLOAT3( 0.0f, 0.0f, 0.0f );
    Out.Orientation = XMFLOAT4( 0.0f, 0.0f, 0.0f, 1.0f );

    // Compute the slopes.
    Points[0] = Points[0] * XMVectorReciprocal( XMVectorSplatZ( Points[0] ) );
    Points[1] = Points[1] * XMVectorReciprocal( XMVectorSplatZ( Points[1] ) );
    Points[2] = Points[2] * XMVectorReciprocal( XMVectorSplatZ( Points[2] ) );
    Points[3] = Points[3] * XMVectorReciprocal( XMVectorSplatZ( Points[3] ) );

    Out.RightSlope  = XMVectorGetX( Points[0] );
    Out.LeftSlope   = XMVectorGetX( Points[1] );
    Out.TopSlope    = XMVectorGetY( Points[2] );
    Out.BottomSlope = XMVectorGetY( Points[3] );
```

```
// Compute near and far.
Points[4] = Points[4] * XMVectorReciprocal( XMVectorSplatW( Points[4] ) );
Points[5] = Points[5] * XMVectorReciprocal( XMVectorSplatW( Points[5] ) );

Out.Near = XMVectorGetZ( Points[4] );
Out.Far  = XMVectorGetZ( Points[5] );
}
```

16.2.4.2 Frustum/Sphere Intersection

For frustum culling, one test we will want to perform is a frustum/sphere intersection test. This tells us whether a sphere intersects the frustum. Note that a sphere completely inside the frustum counts as an intersection because we treat the frustum as a volume, not just a boundary. Because we model a frustum as six inward facing planes, a frustum/sphere test can be stated as follows: If there exists a frustum plane L such that the sphere is in the negative half-space of L, then we can conclude that the sphere is completely outside the frustum. If such a plane does not exist, then we conclude that the sphere intersects the frustum.

So a frustum/sphere intersection test reduces to six sphere/plane tests. Figure 16.7 shows the setup of a sphere/plane intersection test. Let the sphere have center point c and radius r. Then the signed distance from the center of the sphere to the plane is $k = \mathbf{n} \cdot \mathbf{c} + d$ (Appendix C). If $|k| \leq r$ then the sphere intersects the plane. If $k < -r$ then the sphere is behind the plane. If $k > r$ then the sphere is in front of the plane and the sphere intersects the positive half-space of the plane. For the purposes of the frustum/sphere intersection test, if the sphere is in front of the plane, then we count it as an intersection because it intersects the positive half-space the plane defines.

The `BoundingFrustum` class provides the following member function to test if a sphere intersects a frustum. Note that the sphere and frustum must be in the same coordinate system for the test to make sense.

```
enum ContainmentType
{
    // The object is completely outside the frustum.
    DISJOINT = 0,
    // The object intersects the frustum boundaries.
```

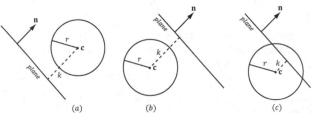

Figure 16.7. Sphere/plane intersection. (a) $k > r$ and the sphere intersects the positive half-space of the plane. (b) $k < -r$ and the sphere is completely behind the plane in the negative half-space. (c) $|k| \leq r$ and the sphere intersects the plane.

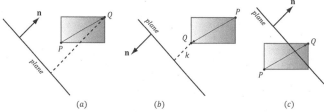

Figure 16.8. AABB/plane intersection test. The diagonal $\overrightarrow{PQ}$ is always the diagonal most directed with the plane normal.

```
    INTERSECTS = 1,
    // The object lies completely inside the frustum volume.
    CONTAINS = 2,
};
ContainmentType BoundingFrustum::Contains(
    _In_ const BoundingSphere& sphere ) const;
```

Note: BoundingSphere *contains a symmetrical member function:*

```
ContainmentType BoundingSphere::Contains(
    _In_ const BoundingFrustum& fr ) const;
```

16.2.4.3 Frustum/AABB Intersection

The frustum/AABB intersection test follows the same strategy as the frustum/sphere test. Because we model a frustum as six inward facing planes, a frustum/AABB test can be stated as follows: If there exists a frustum plane L such that the box is in the negative half-space of L, then we can conclude that the box is completely outside the frustum. If such a plane does not exist, then we conclude that the box intersects the frustum.

So a frustum/AABB intersection test reduces to six AABB/plane tests. The algorithm for an AABB/plane test is as follows. Find the box diagonal vector $\mathbf{v} = \overrightarrow{PQ}$, passing through the center of the box, that is most aligned with the plane normal $\mathbf{n}$. From Figure 16.8, (a) if P is in front of the plane, then Q must be also in front of the plane; (b) if Q is behind the plane, then P must be also be behind the plane; (c) if P is behind the plane and Q is in front of the plane, then the box intersects the plane.

Finding PQ most aligned with the plane normal vector $\mathbf{n}$ can be done with the following code:

```
// For each coordinate axis x, y, z...
for(int j = 0; j < 3; ++j)
{
    // Make PQ point in the same direction as
    // the plane normal on this axis.
    if( planeNormal[j] >= 0.0f )
    {
        P[j] = box.minPt[j];
```

```
        Q[j] = box.maxPt[j];
    }
    else
    {
        P[j] = box.maxPt[j];
        Q[j] = box.minPt[j];
    }
}
```

This code just looks at one dimension at a time, and chooses P_i and Q_i such that $Q_i - P_i$ has the same sign as the plane normal coordinate n_i (Figure 16.9).

The `BoundingFrustum` class provides the following member function to test if an AABB intersects a frustum. Note that the AABB and frustum must be in the same coordinate system for the test to make sense.

```
ContainmentType BoundingFrustum::Contains(
    _In_ const BoundingBox& box ) const;
```

Note: `BoundingBox` *contains a symmetrical member function:*

```
ContainmentType BoundingBox::Contains(
    _In_ const BoundingFrustum& fr ) const;
```

16.3 FRUSTUM CULLING

Recall from Chapter 5 that the hardware automatically discards triangles that are outside the viewing frustum in the clipping stage. However, if we have millions of triangles, all the triangles are still submitted to the rendering pipeline via draw calls (which has API overhead), and all the triangles go through the vertex shader, possibly through the tessellation stages, and possibly through the geometry shader, only to be discarded during the clipping stage. Clearly, this is wasteful inefficiency.

The idea of frustum culling is for the application code to cull groups of triangles at a higher level than on a per-triangle basis. Figure 16.10 shows a simple example. We build a bounding volume, such as a sphere or box, around each object in the scene. If the bounding volume does not intersect the frustum, then we do not need

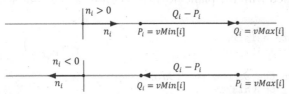

Figure 16.9. (Top) The normal component along the ith axis is positive, so we choose $P_i = vMin[i]$ and $Q_i = vMax[i]$ so that $Q_i - P_i$ has the same sign as the plane normal coordinate n_i. (Bottom) The normal component along the ith axis is negative, so we choose $P_i = vMax[i]$ and $Q_i = vMin[i]$ so that $Q_i - P_i$ has the same sign as the plane normal coordinate n_i.

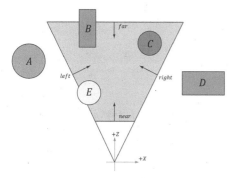
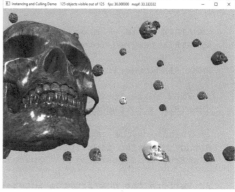

Figure 16.10. The objects bounded by volumes *A* and *D* are completely outside the frustum, and so do not need to be drawn. The object corresponding to volume *C* is completely inside the frustum, and needs to be drawn. The objects bounded by volumes *B* and *E* are partially outside the frustum and partially inside the frustum; we must draw these objects and let the hardware clip and triangles outside the frustum.

Figure 16.11. Screenshot of the "Instancing and Culling" demo.

to submit the object (which could contain thousands of triangles) to Direct3D for drawing. This saves the GPU from having to do wasteful computations on invisible geometry, at the cost of an inexpensive CPU test. Assuming a camera with a 90° field of view and infinitely far away far plane, the camera frustum only occupies $1/6^{th}$ of the world volume, so $5/6^{th}$ of the world objects can be frustum culled, assuming objects are evenly distributed throughout the scene. In practice, cameras use smaller field of view angles than 90° and a finite far plane, which means we could cull even more than $5/6^{th}$ of the scene objects.

In our demo, we render a 5 × 5 × 5 grid of skull meshes (see Figure 16.11) using instancing. We compute the AABB of the skull mesh in local space. In the `UpdateInstanceData` method, we perform frustum culling on all of our instances. If the instance intersects the frustum, then we add it to the next available slot in our structured buffer containing the instance data and increment the `visibleInstanceCount` counter. This way, the front of the structured buffer contains the data for all the visible instances. (Of course, the structured buffer is sized to match the number of instances in case all the instances are visible.) Because the AABB of the skull mesh is in local space, we must transform the view frustum into the local space of each instance in order to perform the intersection test; we could use alternative spaces, like transform the AABB to world space and the frustum to world space, for example. The frustum culling update code is given below:

```
XMMATRIX view = mCamera.GetView();
XMMATRIX invView = XMMatrixInverse(&XMMatrixDeterminant(view), view);

auto currInstanceBuffer = mCurrFrameResource->InstanceBuffer.get();
```

```cpp
for(auto& e : mAllRitems)
{
  const auto& instanceData = e->Instances;

  int visibleInstanceCount = 0;
  for(UINT i = 0; i < (UINT)instanceData.size(); ++i)
  {
    XMMATRIX world = XMLoadFloat4x4(&instanceData[i].World);
    XMMATRIX texTransform = XMLoadFloat4x4(&instanceData[i].TexTransform);

    XMMATRIX invWorld = XMMatrixInverse(&XMMatrixDeterminant(world), world);

    // View space to the object's local space.
    XMMATRIX viewToLocal = XMMatrixMultiply(invView, invWorld);

    // Transform the camera frustum from view space to the object's local space.
    BoundingFrustum localSpaceFrustum;
    mCamFrustum.Transform(localSpaceFrustum, viewToLocal);

    // Perform the box/frustum intersection test in local space.
    if(localSpaceFrustum.Contains(e->Bounds) != DirectX::DISJOINT)
    {
      InstanceData data;
      XMStoreFloat4x4(&data.World, XMMatrixTranspose(world));
      XMStoreFloat4x4(&data.TexTransform, XMMatrixTranspose(texTransform));
      data.MaterialIndex = instanceData[i].MaterialIndex;

      // Write the instance data to structured buffer for the visible objects.
      currInstanceBuffer->CopyData(visibleInstanceCount++, data);
    }
  }

  e->InstanceCount = visibleInstanceCount;

  // For informational purposes, output the number of instances
  // visible over the total number of instances.
  std::wostringstream outs;
  outs.precision(6);
  outs << L"Instancing and Culling Demo" <<
    L"    " << e->InstanceCount <<
    L" objects visible out of " << e->Instances.size();
  mMainWndCaption = outs.str();
}
```

Even though our instanced buffer has room for every instance, we only draw the visible instances which correspond to instances from 0 to `visibleInstanceCount-1`:

```cpp
cmdList->DrawIndexedInstanced(ri->IndexCount,
    ri->InstanceCount,
    ri->StartIndexLocation,
    ri->BaseVertexLocation, 0);
```

Figure 16.12 shows the performance difference between having frustum culling enabled and not. With frustum culling, we only submit eleven instances to the

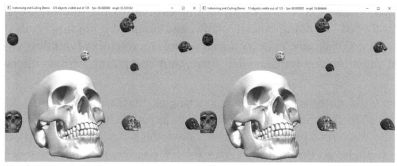

Figure 16.12. (Left) Frustum culling is turned off, and we are rendering all 125 instances, and it takes about 33.33 ms to render a frame (Right) Frustum culling is turned on, and we see that 13 out of 125 instances are visible, and our frame rate doubles.

rendering pipeline for processing. Without frustum culling, we submit all 125 instances to the rendering pipeline for processing. Even though the visible scene is the same, with frustum culling disabled, we waste computation power drawing over a 100 skull meshes whose geometry is eventually discarded during the clipping stage. Each skull has about 60K triangles, so that is a lot of vertices to process and a lot of triangles to clip per skull. By doing one frustum/AABB test, we can reject 60K triangles from even being sent to the graphics pipeline—this is the advantage of frustum culling and we see the difference in the frames per second.

16.4 SUMMARY

1. Instancing refers to drawing the same object more than once in a scene, but with different positions, orientations, scales, materials, and textures. To save memory, we can only create one mesh, and submit multiple draw calls to Direct3D with a different world matrix, material, and texture. To avoid the API overhead of issuing resource changes and multiple draw calls, we can bind an SRV to a structured buffer that contains all of our instance data and index into it in our vertex shader using the `SV_InstancedID` value. Furthermore, we can use dynamic indexing to index into arrays of textures. The number of instances to draw with one draw call is specified by the second parameter, `InstanceCount`, of the `ID3D12GraphicsCommandList::DrawIndexedInstanced` method.

2. Bounding volumes are primitive geometric objects that approximate the volume of an object. The tradeoff is that although the bounding volume only approximates the object its form has a simple mathematical representation,

which makes it easy to work with. Examples of bounding volumes are spheres, axis-aligned bounding boxes (AABB), and oriented bounding boxes (OBB). The *DirectXCollision.h* library has structures representing bounding volumes, and functions for transforming them, and computing various intersection tests.

3. The GPU automatically discards triangles that are outside the viewing frustum in the clipping stage. However, clipped triangles are still submitted to the rendering pipeline via draw calls (which has API overhead), and all the triangles go through the vertex shader, possibly through the tessellation stages, and possibly through the geometry shader, only to be discarded during the clipping stage. To fix this inefficiency, we can implement frustum culling. The idea is to build a bounding volume, such as a sphere or box, around each object in the scene. If the bounding volume does not intersect the frustum, then we do not need to submit the object (which could contain thousands of triangles) to Direct3D for drawing. This saves the GPU from having to do wasteful computations on invisible geometry, at the cost of an inexpensive CPU test.

16.5 EXERCISES

1. Modify the "Instancing and Culling" demo to use bounding spheres instead of bounding boxes.
2. The plane equations in NDC space take on a very simple form. All points inside the view frustum are bounded as follows:

$$-1 \leq x_{ndc} \leq 1$$

$$-1 \leq y_{ndc} \leq 1$$

$$0 \leq z_{ndc} \leq 1$$

In particular, the left plane equation is given by $x = -1$ and the right plane equation is given by $x = 1$ in NDC space. In homogeneous clip space before the perspective divide, all points inside the view frustum are bounded as follows:

$$-w \leq x_h \leq w$$

$$-w \leq y_h \leq w$$

$$0 \leq z_h \leq w$$

Here, the left plane is defined by $w = -x$ and the right plane is defined by $w = x$. Let $\mathbf{M} = \mathbf{VP}$ be the view-projection matrix product, and let

$\mathbf{v} = (x, y, z, 1)$ be a point in world space inside the frustum. Consider $(x_h, y_h, z_h, w) = \mathbf{vM} = (\mathbf{v}\cdot\mathbf{M}_{*,1}, \mathbf{v}\cdot\mathbf{M}_{*,2}, \mathbf{v}\cdot\mathbf{M}_{*,3}, \mathbf{v}\cdot\mathbf{M}_{*,4})$ to show that the inward facing frustum planes in world space are given by:

Left	$0 = \mathbf{v}\cdot(\mathbf{M}_{*,1} + \mathbf{M}_{*,4})$
Right	$0 = \mathbf{v}\cdot(\mathbf{M}_{*,4} - \mathbf{M}_{*,1})$
Bottom	$0 = \mathbf{v}\cdot(\mathbf{M}_{*,2} + \mathbf{M}_{*,4})$
Top	$0 = \mathbf{v}\cdot(\mathbf{M}_{*,4} - \mathbf{M}_{*,2})$
Near	$0 = \mathbf{v}\cdot\mathbf{M}_{*,3}$
Far	$0 = \mathbf{v}\cdot(\mathbf{M}_{*,4} - \mathbf{M}_{*,3})$

Note:

(a) *We ask for inward facing normals. That means a point inside the frustum has a positive distance from the plane; in other words, $\mathbf{n}\cdot\mathbf{p} + d \geq 0$ for a point $\mathbf{p}$ inside the frustum.*

(b) *Note that $v_w = 1$, so the above dot product formulas do yield plane equations of the form $Ax + By + Cz + D = 0$.*

(c) *The calculated plane normal vectors are not unit length; see Appendix C for how to normalize a plane.*

3. Examine the *DirectXCollision.h* header file to get familiar with the functions it provides for intersection tests and bounding volume transformations.

4. An OBB can be defined by a center point **C**, three orthonormal axis vectors $\mathbf{r}_0, \mathbf{r}_1$, and $\mathbf{r}_2$ defining the box orientation, and three extent lengths a_0, a_1, and a_2 along the box axes $\mathbf{r}_0, \mathbf{r}_1$, and $\mathbf{r}_2$, respectively, that give the distance from the box center to the box sides.

(a) Consider Figure 16.13 (which shows the situation in 2D) and conclude the projected "shadow" of the OBB onto the axis defined by the normal vector is $2r$, where

$$r = |a_0\mathbf{r}_0 \cdot \mathbf{n}| + |a_1\mathbf{r}_1 \cdot \mathbf{n}| + |a_2\mathbf{r}_2 \cdot \mathbf{n}|$$

(b) In the previous formula for r, explain why we must take the absolute values instead of just computing $r = (a_0\mathbf{r}_0 + a_1\mathbf{r}_1 + a_2\mathbf{r}_2)\cdot\mathbf{n}$?

(c) Derive a plane/OBB intersection test that determines if the OBB is in front of the plane, behind the plane, or intersecting the plane.

(d) An AABB is a special case of an OBB, so this test also works for an AABB. However, the formula for r simplifies in the case of an AABB. Find the simplified formula for r for the AABB case.

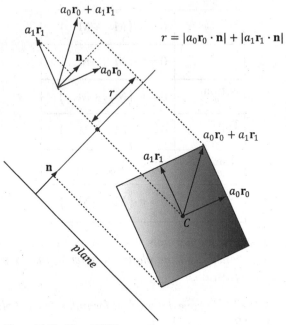

$$r = |a_0 \mathbf{r}_0 \cdot \mathbf{n}| + |a_1 \mathbf{r}_1 \cdot \mathbf{n}|$$

Figure 16.13. Plane/OBB intersection setup

Chapter 17 PICKING

In this chapter, we have the problem of determining the 3D object (or primitive) the user picked with the mouse cursor (see Figure 17.1). In other words, given the 2D screen coordinates of the mouse cursor, can we determine the 3D object that was projected onto that point? To solve this problem, in some sense, we must work backwards; that is to say, we typically transform from 3D space to screen space, but here we transform from screen space back to 3D space. Of course, we already have a slight problem: a 2D screen point does not correspond to a unique 3D point (i.e., more than one 3D point could be projected onto the same 2D projection window point—see Figure 17.2). Thus, there is some ambiguity in determining which object is really picked. However, this is not such a big problem, as the closest object to the camera is usually the one we want.

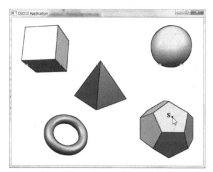

Figure 17.1. The user picking the dodecahedron.

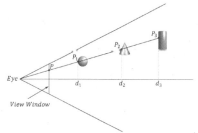

Figure 17.2. A side view of the frustum. Observe that several points in 3D space can get projected onto a point on the projection window.

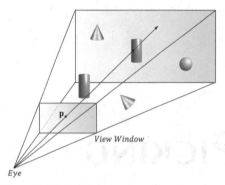

Figure 17.3. A ray shooting through **p** will intersect the object whose projection surrounds **p**. Note that the projected point **p** on the projection window corresponds to the clicked screen point s.

Consider Figure 17.3, which shows the viewing frustum. Here **p** is the point on the projection window that corresponds to the clicked screen point **s**. Now, we see that if we shoot a *picking ray*, originating at the eye position, through **p**, we will intersect the object whose projection surrounds **p**, namely the cylinder in this example. Therefore, our strategy is as follows: Once we compute the picking ray, we can iterate through each object in the scene and test if the ray intersects it. The object that the ray intersects is the object that was picked by the user. As mentioned, the ray may intersect several scene objects (or none at all—nothing was picked), if the objects are along the ray's path but with different depth values, for example. In this case, we can just take the intersected object nearest to the camera as the picked object.

Objectives:

1. To learn how to implement the picking algorithm and to understand how it works. We break picking down into the following four steps:
   (a) Given the clicked screen point **s**, find its corresponding point on the projection window and call it **p**.
   (b) Compute the picking ray in view space. That is the ray originating at the origin, in view space, which shoots through **p**.
   (c) Transform the picking ray and the models to be tested with the ray into the same space.
   (d) Determine the object the picking ray intersects. The nearest (from the camera) intersected object corresponds to the picked screen object.

17.1 SCREEN TO PROJECTION WINDOW TRANSFORM

The first task is to transform the clicked screen point to normalized device coordinates (see §5.4.3.3). Recall that the viewport matrix transforms vertices from normalized device coordinates to screen space; it is given below:

$$\mathbf{M} = \begin{bmatrix} \frac{Width}{2} & 0 & 0 & 0 \\ 0 & -\frac{Height}{2} & 0 & 0 \\ 0 & 0 & MaxDepth - MinDepth & 0 \\ TopLeftX + \frac{Width}{2} & TopLeftY + \frac{Height}{2} & MinDepth & 1 \end{bmatrix}$$

The variables of the viewport matrix refer to those of the D3D12_VIEWPORT structure:

```
typedef struct D3D12_VIEWPORT
{
  FLOAT TopLeftX;
  FLOAT TopLeftY;
  FLOAT Width;
  FLOAT Height;
  FLOAT MinDepth;
  FLOAT MaxDepth;
} D3D12_VIEWPORT;
```

Generally, for a game, the viewport is the entire backbuffer and the depth buffer range is 0 to 1. Thus, $TopLeftX = 0$, $TopLeftY = 0$, $MinDepth = 0$, $MaxDepth = 1$, $Width = w$, and $Height = h$, where w and h, are the width and height of the backbuffer, respectively. Assuming this is indeed the case, the viewport matrix simplifies to:

$$\mathbf{M} = \begin{bmatrix} w/2 & 0 & 0 & 0 \\ 0 & -h/2 & 0 & 0 \\ 0 & 0 & 1 & 0 \\ w/2 & h/2 & 0 & 1 \end{bmatrix}$$

Now let $\mathbf{p}_{ndc} = (x_{ndc}, y_{ndc}, z_{ndc}, 1)$ be a point in normalized device space (i.e., $-1 \leq x_{ndc} \leq 1$, $-1 \leq y_{ndc} \leq 1$, and $0 \leq z_{ndc} \leq 1$). Transforming $\mathbf{p}_{ndc}$ to screen space yields:

$$[x_{ndc}, y_{ndc}, z_{ndc}, 1] \begin{bmatrix} w/2 & 0 & 0 & 0 \\ 0 & -h/2 & 0 & 0 \\ 0 & 0 & 1 & 0 \\ w/2 & h/2 & 0 & 1 \end{bmatrix} = \left[\frac{x_{ndc}w + w}{2}, \frac{-y_{ndc}h + h}{2}, z_{ndc}, 1 \right]$$

The coordinate z_{ndc} is just used by the depth buffer and we are not concerned with any depth coordinates for picking. The 2D screen point $\mathbf{p}_s = (x_s, y_s)$ corresponding to $\mathbf{p}_{ndc}$ is just the transformed x- and y-coordinates:

$$x_s = \frac{x_{ndc} w + w}{2}$$

$$y_s = \frac{-y_{ndc} h + h}{2}$$

The above equation gives us the screen point $\mathbf{p}_s$ in terms of the normalized device point $\mathbf{p}_{ndc}$ and the viewport dimensions. However, in our picking situation, we are initially given the screen point $\mathbf{p}_s$ and the viewport dimensions, and we want to find $\mathbf{p}_{ndc}$. Solving the above equations for $\mathbf{p}_{ndc}$ yields:

$$x_{ndc} = \frac{2x_s}{w} - 1$$

$$y_{ndc} = -\frac{2y_s}{h} + 1$$

We now have the clicked point in NDC space. But to shoot the picking ray, we really want the screen point in view space. Recall from §5.6.3.3 that we mapped the projected point from view space to NDC space by dividing the x-coordinate by the aspect ratio r:

$$-r \leq x' \leq r$$

$$-1 \leq x'/r \leq 1$$

Thus, to get back to view space, we just need to multiply the x-coordinate in NDC space by the aspect ratio. The clicked point in view space is thus:

$$x_v = r\left(\frac{2s_x}{w} - 1\right)$$

$$y_v = -\frac{2s_y}{h} + 1$$

Note: The projected y-coordinate in view space is the same in NDC space. This is because we chose the height of the projection window in view space to cover the interval $[-1, 1]$.

Now recall from §5.6.3.1 that the projection window lies at a distance $d = \cot\left(\frac{\alpha}{2}\right)$ from the origin, where α is the vertical field of view angle. So we could shoot the

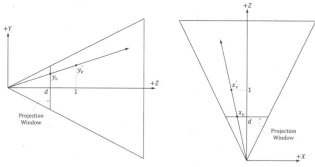

Figure 17.4. By similar triangles, $\frac{y_v}{d} = \frac{y'_v}{1}$ and $\frac{x_v}{d} = \frac{x'_v}{1}$.

picking ray through the point (x_v, y_v, d) on the projection window. However, this requires that we compute $d = \cot\left(\frac{\alpha}{2}\right)$. A simpler way is to observe from Figure 17.4 that:

$$x'_v = \frac{x_v}{d} = \frac{x_v}{\cot\left(\frac{\alpha}{2}\right)} = x_v \cdot \tan\left(\frac{\alpha}{2}\right) = \left(\frac{2s_x}{w} - 1\right) r \tan\left(\frac{\alpha}{2}\right)$$

$$y'_v = \frac{y_v}{d} = \frac{y_v}{\cot\left(\frac{\alpha}{2}\right)} = y_v \cdot \tan\left(\frac{\alpha}{2}\right) = \left(-\frac{2s_y}{h} + 1\right) \tan\left(\frac{\alpha}{2}\right)$$

Recalling that $\mathbf{P}_{00} = \dfrac{1}{r \tan\left(\frac{\alpha}{2}\right)}$ and $\mathbf{P}_{11} = \dfrac{1}{\tan\left(\frac{\alpha}{2}\right)}$ in the projection matrix, we can rewrite this as:

$$x'_v = \left(\frac{2s_x}{w} - 1\right) \Big/ \mathbf{P}_{00}$$

$$y'_v = \left(-\frac{2s_y}{h} + 1\right) \Big/ \mathbf{P}_{11}$$

Thus, we can shoot our picking ray through the point $(x'_v, y'_v, 1)$ instead. Note that this yields the same picking ray as the one shot through the point (x_v, y_v, d). The code that computes the picking ray in view space is given below:

```
void PickingApp::Pick(int sx, int sy)
{
    XMFLOAT4X4 P = mCamera.GetProj4x4f();

    // Compute picking ray in view space.
    float vx = (+2.0f*sx / mClientWidth  - 1.0f) / P(0, 0);
    float vy = (-2.0f*sy / mClientHeight + 1.0f) / P(1, 1);
```

```
// Ray definition in view space.
XMVECTOR rayOrigin = XMVectorSet(0.0f, 0.0f, 0.0f, 1.0f);
XMVECTOR rayDir = XMVectorSet(vx, vy, 1.0f, 0.0f);
```

Note that the ray originates from the origin in view space since the eye sits at the origin in view space.

17.2 WORLD/LOCAL SPACE PICKING RAY

So far we have the picking ray in view space, but this is only useful if our objects are in view space as well. Because the view matrix transforms geometry from world space to view space, the inverse of the view matrix transforms geometry from view space to world space. If $\mathbf{r}_v(t) = \mathbf{q} + t\mathbf{u}$ is the view space picking ray and $\mathbf{V}$ is the view matrix, then the world space picking ray is given by:

$$\mathbf{r}_w(t) = \mathbf{q}\mathbf{V}^{-1} + t\mathbf{u}\mathbf{V}^{-1}$$
$$= \mathbf{q}_w + t\mathbf{u}_w$$

Note that the ray origin $\mathbf{q}$ is transformed as a point (i.e., $q_w = 1$) and the ray direction $\mathbf{u}$ is transformed as a vector (i.e., $u_w = 0$).

A world space picking ray can be useful in some situations where you have some objects defined in world space. However, most of the time, the geometry of an object is defined relative to the object's own local space. Therefore, to perform the ray/object intersection test, we must transform the ray into the local space of the object. If $\mathbf{W}$ is the world matrix of an object, the matrix $\mathbf{W}^{-1}$ transforms geometry from world space to the local space of the object. Thus the local space picking ray is:

$$\mathbf{r}_L(t) = \mathbf{q}_w\mathbf{W}^{-1} + t\mathbf{u}_w\mathbf{W}^{-1}$$

Generally, each object in the scene has its own local space. Therefore, the ray must be transformed to the local space of each scene object to do the intersection test.

One might suggest transforming the meshes to world space and doing the intersection test there. However, this is too expensive. A mesh may contain thousands of vertices, and all those vertices would need to be transformed to world space. It is much more efficient to just transform the ray to the local spaces of the objects.

The following code shows how the picking ray is transformed from view space to the local space of an object:

```
// Assume nothing is picked to start, so the picked render-item is invisible.
```

```
mPickedRitem->Visible = false;

// Check if we picked an opaque render item.  A real app might keep a separate
// "picking list" of objects that can be selected.
for(auto ri : mRitemLayer[(int)RenderLayer::Opaque])
{
  auto geo = ri->Geo;

  // Skip invisible render-items.
  if(ri->Visible == false)
    continue;

  XMMATRIX V = mCamera.GetView();
  XMMATRIX invView = XMMatrixInverse(&XMMatrixDeterminant(V), V);

  XMMATRIX W = XMLoadFloat4x4(&ri->World);
  XMMATRIX invWorld = XMMatrixInverse(&XMMatrixDeterminant(W), W);

  // Tranform ray to vi space of Mesh.
  XMMATRIX toLocal = XMMatrixMultiply(invView, invWorld);

  rayOrigin = XMVector3TransformCoord(rayOrigin, toLocal);
  rayDir = XMVector3TransformNormal(rayDir, toLocal);

  // Make the ray direction unit length for the intersection tests.
  rayDir = XMVector3Normalize(rayDir);
```

The `XMVector3TransformCoord` and `XMVector3TransformNormal` functions take 3D vectors as parameters, but note that with the `XMVector3TransformCoord` function there is an understood $w = 1$ for the fourth component. On the other hand, with the `XMVector3TransformNormal` function there is an understood $w = 0$ for the fourth component. Thus we can use `XMVector3TransformCoord` to transform points and we can use `XMVector3TransformNormal` to transform vectors.

17.3 RAY/MESH INTERSECTION

Once we have the picking ray and a mesh in the same space, we can perform the intersection test to see if the picking ray intersects the mesh. The following code iterates through each triangle in the mesh and does a ray/triangle intersection test. If the ray intersects one of the triangles, then it must have hit the mesh the triangle belongs to. Otherwise, the ray misses the mesh. Typically, we want the nearest triangle intersection, as it is possible for a ray to intersect several mesh triangles if the triangles overlap with respect to the ray.

```
// If we hit the bounding box of the Mesh, then we might have
// picked a Mesh triangle, so do the ray/triangle tests.
//
// If we did not hit the bounding box, then it is impossible that we hit
// the Mesh, so do not waste effort doing ray/triangle tests.
```

```cpp
float tmin = 0.0f;
if(ri->Bounds.Intersects(rayOrigin, rayDir, tmin))
{
  // NOTE: For the demo, we know what to cast the vertex/index data to.
  // If we were mixing formats, some metadata would be needed to figure
  // out what to cast it to.
  auto vertices = (Vertex*)geo->VertexBufferCPU->GetBufferPointer();
  auto indices = (std::uint32_t*)geo->IndexBufferCPU->GetBufferPointer();
  UINT triCount = ri->IndexCount / 3;

  // Find the nearest ray/triangle intersection.
  tmin = MathHelper::Infinity;
  for(UINT i = 0; i < triCount; ++i)
  {
    // Indices for this triangle.
    UINT i0 = indices[i * 3 + 0];
    UINT i1 = indices[i * 3 + 1];
    UINT i2 = indices[i * 3 + 2];

    // Vertices for this triangle.
    XMVECTOR v0 = XMLoadFloat3(&vertices[i0].Pos);
    XMVECTOR v1 = XMLoadFloat3(&vertices[i1].Pos);
    XMVECTOR v2 = XMLoadFloat3(&vertices[i2].Pos);

    // We have to iterate over all the triangles in order to find
    // the nearest intersection.
    float t = 0.0f;
    if(TriangleTests::Intersects(rayOrigin, rayDir, v0, v1, v2, t))
    {
      if(t < tmin)
      {
        // This is the new nearest picked triangle.
        tmin = t;
        UINT pickedTriangle = i;

        // Set a render item to the picked triangle so that
        // we can render it with a special "highlight" material.
        mPickedRitem->Visible = true;
        mPickedRitem->IndexCount = 3;
        mPickedRitem->BaseVertexLocation = 0;

        // Picked render item needs same world matrix as object picked.
        mPickedRitem->World = ri->World;
        mPickedRitem->NumFramesDirty = gNumFrameResources;

        // Offset to the picked triangle in the mesh index buffer.
        mPickedRitem->StartIndexLocation = 3 * pickedTriangle;
      }
    }
  }
}
```

Observe that for picking, we use the system memory copy of the mesh geometry stored in the `MeshGeometry` class. This is because we cannot access a vertex/index buffer for reading that is going to be drawn by the GPU. It is common to store system memory copies of geometry for things like picking and collision detection. Sometimes a simplified version of the mesh is stored for these purposes to save memory and computation.

17.3.1 Ray/AABB Intersection

Observe that we first use the DirectX collision library function `BoundingBox::Intersects` to see if the ray intersects the bounding box of the mesh. This is analogous to the frustum culling optimization in the previous chapter. Performing a ray intersection test for every triangle in the scene adds up in computation time. Even for meshes not near the picking ray, we would still have to iterate over each triangle to conclude the ray misses the mesh; this is wasteful and inefficient. A popular strategy is to approximate the mesh with a simple bounding volume, like a sphere or box. Then, instead of intersecting the ray with the mesh, we first intersect the ray with the bounding volume. If the ray misses the bounding volume, then the ray necessarily misses the triangle mesh and so there is no need to do further calculations. If the ray intersects the bounding volume, then we do the more precise ray/mesh test. Assuming that the ray will miss most bounding volumes in the scene, this saves us many ray/triangle intersection tests. The `BoundingBox::Intersects` function returns true if the ray intersects the box and false otherwise; it is prototyped as follows:

```
bool XM_CALLCONV
BoundingBox::Intersects(
  FXMVECTOR Origin,    // ray origin
  FXMVECTOR Direction, // ray direction (must be unit length)
  float& Dist ); const // ray intersection parameter
```

Given the ray $\mathbf{r}(t) = \mathbf{q} + t\mathbf{u}$, the last parameter outputs the ray parameter t_0 that yields the actual intersection point $\mathbf{p}$:

$$\mathbf{p} = \mathbf{r}(t_0) = \mathbf{q} + t_0 \mathbf{u}$$

17.3.2 Ray/Sphere Intersection

There is also a ray/sphere intersection test given in the DirectX collision library:

```
bool XM_CALLCONV
BoundingSphere::Intersects(
  FXMVECTOR Origin,
  FXMVECTOR Direction,
  float& Dist ); const
```

To give a flavor of these tests, we show how to derive the ray/sphere intersection test. The points $\mathbf{p}$ on the surface of a sphere with center $\mathbf{c}$ and radius r satisfy the equation:

$$\|\mathbf{p} - \mathbf{c}\| = r$$

Let $r(t) = q + tu$ be a ray. We wish to solve for t_1 and t_2 such that $r(t_1)$ and $r(t_2)$ satisfy the sphere equation (i.e., the parameters t_1 and t_2 along the ray that yields the intersection points).

$$r = \|\mathbf{r}(t) - \mathbf{c}\|$$
$$r^2 = (\mathbf{r}(t) - \mathbf{c}) \cdot (\mathbf{r}(t) - \mathbf{c})$$
$$r^2 = (\mathbf{q} + t\mathbf{u} - \mathbf{c}) \cdot (\mathbf{q} + t\mathbf{u} - \mathbf{c})$$
$$r^2 = (\mathbf{q} - \mathbf{c} + t\mathbf{u}) \cdot (\mathbf{q} - \mathbf{c} + t\mathbf{u})$$

For notational convenience, let $\mathbf{m} = \mathbf{q} - \mathbf{c}$.

$$(\mathbf{m} + t\mathbf{u}) \cdot (\mathbf{m} + t\mathbf{u}) = r^2$$
$$\mathbf{m} \cdot \mathbf{m} + 2t\mathbf{m} \cdot \mathbf{u} + t^2 \mathbf{u} \cdot \mathbf{u} = r^2$$
$$t^2 \mathbf{u} \cdot \mathbf{u} + 2t\mathbf{m} \cdot \mathbf{u} + \mathbf{m} \cdot \mathbf{m} - r^2 = 0$$

This is just a quadratic equation with:

$$a = \mathbf{u} \cdot \mathbf{u}$$
$$b = 2(\mathbf{m} \cdot \mathbf{u})$$
$$c = \mathbf{m} \cdot \mathbf{m} - r^2$$

If the ray direction is unit length, then $a = \mathbf{u} \cdot \mathbf{u} = 1$. If the solution has imaginary components, the ray misses the sphere. If the two real solutions are the same, the ray intersects a point tangent to the sphere. If the two real solutions are distinct, the ray pierces two points of the sphere. A negative solution indicates an intersection point "behind" the ray. The smallest positive solution gives the nearest intersection parameter.

17.3.3 Ray/Triangle Intersection

For performing a ray/triangle intersection test, we use the DirectX collision library function `TriangleTests::Intersects`:

```
bool XM_CALLCONV
TriangleTests::Intersects(
  FXMVECTOR Origin,    // ray origin
  FXMVECTOR Direction, // ray direction (unit length)
  FXMVECTOR V0,  // triangle vertex v0
  GXMVECTOR V1,  // triangle vertex v1
  HXMVECTOR V2,  // triangle vertex v2
  float& Dist ); // ray intersection parameter
```

Let $\mathbf{r}(t) = \mathbf{q} + t\mathbf{u}$ be a ray and $\mathbf{T}(u, v) = \mathbf{v}_0 + u(\mathbf{v}_1 - \mathbf{v}_0) + v(\mathbf{v}_2 - \mathbf{v}_0)$ for $u \geq 0$, $v \geq 0$, $u + v \leq 1$ be a triangle (see Figure 17.5). We wish to simultaneously solve for t, u, v such that $\mathbf{r}(t) = \mathbf{T}(u, v)$ (i.e., the point the ray and triangle intersect):

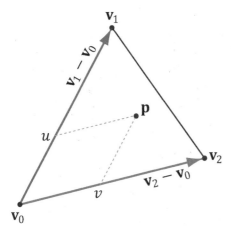

Figure 17.5. The point **p** in the plane of the triangle has coordinates (u, v) relative to the skewed coordinate system with origin $\mathbf{v}_0$ and axes $\mathbf{v}_1 - \mathbf{v}_0$ and $\mathbf{v}_2 - \mathbf{v}_0$.

$\mathbf{r}(t) = \mathbf{T}(u, v)$

$$\mathbf{q} + t\mathbf{u} = \mathbf{v}_0 + u(\mathbf{v}_1 - \mathbf{v}_0) + v(\mathbf{v}_2 - \mathbf{v}_0)$$
$$-t\mathbf{u} + u(\mathbf{v}_1 - \mathbf{v}_0) + v(\mathbf{v}_2 - \mathbf{v}_0) = \mathbf{q} - \mathbf{v}_0$$

For notational convenience, let $\mathbf{e}_1 = \mathbf{v}_1 - \mathbf{v}_0$, $\mathbf{e}_2 = \mathbf{v}_2 - \mathbf{v}_0$ and $\mathbf{m} = \mathbf{q} - \mathbf{v}$

$$-t\mathbf{u} + u\mathbf{e}_1 + v\mathbf{e}_2 = \mathbf{m}$$

$$\begin{bmatrix} \uparrow & \uparrow & \uparrow \\ -\mathbf{u} & \mathbf{e}_1 & \mathbf{e}_2 \\ \downarrow & \downarrow & \downarrow \end{bmatrix} \begin{bmatrix} t \\ u \\ v \end{bmatrix} = \begin{bmatrix} \uparrow \\ \mathbf{m} \\ \downarrow \end{bmatrix}$$

Consider the matrix equation $\mathbf{Ax} = \mathbf{b}$, where $\mathbf{A}$ is invertible. Then Cramer's Rule tells us that $x_i = \det \mathbf{A}_i / \det \mathbf{A}$, where $\mathbf{A}_i$ is found by swapping the ith column vector in $\mathbf{A}$ with $\mathbf{b}$. Therefore,

$$t = \det \begin{bmatrix} \uparrow & \uparrow & \uparrow \\ \mathbf{m} & \mathbf{e}_1 & \mathbf{e}_2 \\ \downarrow & \downarrow & \downarrow \end{bmatrix} / \det \begin{bmatrix} \uparrow & \uparrow & \uparrow \\ -\mathbf{u} & \mathbf{e}_1 & \mathbf{e}_2 \\ \downarrow & \downarrow & \downarrow \end{bmatrix}$$

$$u = \det \begin{bmatrix} \uparrow & \uparrow & \uparrow \\ -\mathbf{u} & \mathbf{m} & \mathbf{e}_2 \\ \downarrow & \downarrow & \downarrow \end{bmatrix} / \det \begin{bmatrix} \uparrow & \uparrow & \uparrow \\ -\mathbf{u} & \mathbf{e}_1 & \mathbf{e}_2 \\ \downarrow & \downarrow & \downarrow \end{bmatrix}$$

$$v = \det\begin{bmatrix} \uparrow & \uparrow & \uparrow \\ -\mathbf{u} & \mathbf{e}_1 & \mathbf{m} \\ \downarrow & \downarrow & \downarrow \end{bmatrix} \Big/ \det\begin{bmatrix} \uparrow & \uparrow & \uparrow \\ -\mathbf{u} & \mathbf{e}_1 & \mathbf{e}_2 \\ \downarrow & \downarrow & \downarrow \end{bmatrix}$$

Using the fact that $\det\begin{bmatrix} \uparrow & \uparrow & \uparrow \\ \mathbf{a} & \mathbf{b} & \mathbf{c} \\ \downarrow & \downarrow & \downarrow \end{bmatrix} = \mathbf{a} \cdot (\mathbf{b} \times \mathbf{c})$ we can reformulate this as:

$$t = -\mathbf{m} \cdot (\mathbf{e}_1 \times \mathbf{e}_2) / \mathbf{u} \cdot (\mathbf{e}_1 \times \mathbf{e}_2)$$
$$u = \mathbf{u} \cdot (\mathbf{m} \times \mathbf{e}_2) / \mathbf{u} \cdot (\mathbf{e}_1 \times \mathbf{e}_2)$$
$$v = \mathbf{u} \cdot (\mathbf{e}_1 \times \mathbf{m}) / \mathbf{u} \cdot (\mathbf{e}_1 \times \mathbf{e}_2)$$

To optimize the computations a bit, we can use the fact that every time we swap columns in a matrix, the sign of the determinant changes:

$$t = \mathbf{e}_2 \cdot (\mathbf{m} \times \mathbf{e}_1) / \mathbf{e}_1 \cdot (\mathbf{u} \times \mathbf{e}_2)$$
$$u = \mathbf{m} \cdot (\mathbf{u} \times \mathbf{e}_2) / \mathbf{e}_1 \cdot (\mathbf{u} \times \mathbf{e}_2)$$
$$v = \mathbf{u} \cdot (\mathbf{m} \times \mathbf{e}_1) / \mathbf{e}_1 \cdot (\mathbf{u} \times \mathbf{e}_2)$$

And note the common cross products that can be reused in the calculations: $\mathbf{m} \times \mathbf{e}_1$ and $\mathbf{u} \times \mathbf{e}_2$.

17.4 DEMO APPLICATION

The demo for this chapter renders a car mesh and allows the user to pick a triangle by pressing the right mouse button, and the selected triangle is rendered using a "highlight" material (see Figure 17.6). To render the triangle with a highlight, we need a render-item for it. Unlike the previous render-items in this book where we defined them at initialization time, this render-item can only be partially filled out at initialization time. This is because we do not yet know which triangle will be picked, and so we do not know the starting index location and world matrix. In addition, a triangle does not need to always be picked. Therefore, we have added a `Visible` property to the render-item structure. An invisible render-item will not be drawn. The below code, which is part of the `PickingApp::Pick` method, shows how we fill out the remaining render-item properties based on the selected triangle:

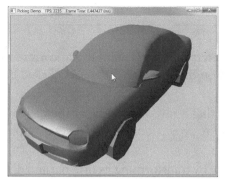

Figure 17.6. The picked triangle is highlighted green.

```
// Cache a pointer to the render-item of the picked
// triangle in the PickingApp class.
RenderItem* mPickedRitem;

if(TriangleTests::Intersects(rayOrigin, rayDir, v0, v1, v2, t))
{
  if(t < tmin)
  {
    // This is the new nearest picked triangle.
    tmin = t;
    UINT pickedTriangle = i;

    // Set a render item to the picked triangle so that
    // we can render it with a special "highlight" material.
    mPickedRitem->Visible = true;
    mPickedRitem->IndexCount = 3;
    mPickedRitem->BaseVertexLocation = 0;

    // Picked render item needs same world matrix as object picked.
    mPickedRitem->World = ri->World;
    mPickedRitem->NumFramesDirty = gNumFrameResources;

    // Offset to the picked triangle in the mesh index buffer.
    mPickedRitem->StartIndexLocation = 3 * pickedTriangle;
  }
}
```

This render-item is drawn after we draw our opaque render-items. It uses a special highlight PSO, which uses transparency blending and sets the depth test comparison function to D3D12_COMPARISON_FUNC_LESS_EQUAL. This is needed because the picked triangle will be drawn twice, the second time with the highlighted material. The second time the triangle is drawn the depth test would fail if the comparison function was just D3D12_COMPARISON_FUNC_LESS.

```
DrawRenderItems(mCommandList.Get(), mRitemLayer[(int)RenderLayer::Opaque]);
mCommandList->SetPipelineState(mPSOs["highlight"].Get());
DrawRenderItems(mCommandList.Get(), mRitemLayer[(int)RenderLayer::Highlight]);
```

17.5 SUMMARY

1. Picking is the technique used to determine the 3D object that corresponds to the 2D projected object displayed on the screen that the user clicked on with the mouse.
2. The picking ray is found by shooting a ray, originating at the origin of the view space, through the point on the projection window that corresponds to the clicked screen point.
3. We can transform a ray $\mathbf{r}(t) = \mathbf{q} + t\mathbf{u}$ by transforming its origin q and direction **u** by a transformation matrix. Note that the origin is transformed as a point ($w = 1$) and the direction is treated as a vector ($w = 0$).
4. To test if a ray has intersected an object, we perform a ray/triangle intersection test for every triangle in the object. If the ray intersects one of the triangles, then it must have hit the mesh the triangle belongs to. Otherwise, the ray misses the mesh. Typically, we want the nearest triangle intersection, as it is possible for a ray to intersect several mesh triangles if the triangles overlap with respect to the ray.
5. A performance optimization for ray/mesh intersection tests is to first perform an intersection test between the ray and a bounding volume that approximates the mesh. If the ray misses the bounding volume, then the ray necessarily misses the triangle mesh and so there is no need to do further calculations. If the ray intersects the bounding volume, then we do the more precise ray/mesh test. Assuming that the ray will miss most bounding volumes in the scene, this saves us many ray/triangle intersection tests.

17.6 EXERCISES

1. Modify the "Picking" demo to use a bounding sphere for the mesh instead of an AABB.
2. Research the algorithm for doing a ray/AABB intersection test.
3. If you had thousands of objects in a scene, you would still have to do thousands of ray/bounding volume tests for picking. Research *octrees*, and explain how they can be used to reduce ray/bounding volume intersection tests. Incidentally, the same general strategy works for reducing frustum/bounding volume intersection tests for frustum culling.

Chapter 18 CUBE MAPPING

In this chapter, we study cube maps, which are basically arrays of six textures interpreted in a special way. With cube mapping, we can easily texture a sky or model reflections.

Objectives:

1. To learn what cube maps are and how to sample them in HLSL code.
2. To discover how to create cube maps with the DirectX texturing tools.
3. To find out how we can use cube maps to model reflections.
4. To understand how we can texture a sphere with cube maps to simulate a sky and distant mountains.

18.1 CUBE MAPPING

The idea of cube mapping is to store six textures and to visualize them as the faces of a cube—hence the name cube map—centered and axis aligned about some coordinate system. Since the cube texture is axis aligned, each face corresponds with a direction along the three major axes; therefore, it is natural to a reference a particular face on a cube map based on the axis direction ($\pm X$, $\pm Y$, $\pm Z$) that intersects the face.

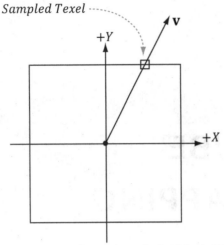

Figure 18.1. We illustrate in 2D for simplicity; in 3D the square becomes a cube. The square denotes the cube map centered and axis-aligned with some coordinate system. We shoot a vector **v** from the origin. The texel **v** intersects is the sampled texel. In this illustration, **v** intersects the cube face corresponding to the +Y axis.

In Direct3D, a cube map is represented by a texture array with six elements such that

1. index 0 refers to the +X face
2. index 1 refers to the −X face
3. index 2 refers to the +Y face
4. index 3 refers to the −Y face
5. index 4 refers to the +Z face
6. index 5 refers to the −Z face

In contrast to 2D texturing, we can no longer identify a texel with 2D texture coordinates. To identify a texel in a cube map, we use 3D texture coordinates, which define a 3D *lookup* vector **v** originating at the origin. The texel of the cube map that **v** intersects (see Figure 18.1) is the texel corresponding to the 3D coordinates of **v**. The concepts of texture filtering discussed in Chapter 9 applies in the case **v** intersects a point between texel samples.

 The magnitude of the lookup vector is unimportant, only the direction matters. Two vectors with the same direction but different magnitudes will sample the same point in the cube map.

In the HLSL, a cube texture is represented by the `TextureCube` type. The following code fragment illustrates how we sample a cube map:

```
TextureCube gCubeMap;
SamplerState gsamLinearWrap   : register(s2);
```

```
...
// in pixel shader
float3 v = float3(x,y,z); // some lookup vector
```

The lookup vector should be in the same space the cube map is relative to. For example, if the cube map is relative to the world space (i.e., the cube faces are axis aligned with the world space axes), then the lookup vector should have world space coordinates.

18.2 ENVIRONMENT MAPS

The primary application of cube maps is *environment mapping*. The idea is to position a camera at the center of some object O in the scene with a 90° field of view angle (both vertically and horizontally). Then have the camera look down the positive x-axis, negative x-axis, positive y-axis, negative y-axis, positive z-axis, and negative z-axis, and to take a picture of the scene (excluding the object O) from each of these six viewpoints. Because the field of view angle is 90°, these six images will have captured the entire surrounding environment (see Figure 18.2) from the perspective of the object O. We then store these six images of the surrounding environment in a cube map, which leads to the name environment map. In other words, an environment map is a cube map where the cube faces store the surrounding images of an environment.

The above description suggests that we need to create an environment map for each object that is to use environment mapping. While this would be more accurate, it also requires more texture memory. A compromise would be to use a few environment maps that capture the environment at key points in the scene. Then objects will sample the environment map closest to them. This simplification

Figure 18.2. An example of an environment map after "unfolding" the cube map. Imagine refolding these six faces into a 3D box, and then imagine being at the center of the box. From every direction you look, you see the surrounding environment.

Figure 18.3. Screenshot of the "Cube Map" demo.

usually works well in practice because with curved objects inaccurate reflections are hard to notice. Another simplification often taken with environment mapping is to omit certain objects from the scene. For example, the environment map in Figure 18.2 only captures the distant "background" information of the sky and mountains that are very far away. Local scene objects are omitted. Although the background environment map is, in some sense, incomplete, it works well in practice to create specular reflections. In order to capture local objects, we would have to use Direct3D to render the six images of our environment map; this is discussed in §18.5. In the demo for this chapter (Figure 18.3), all the objects in the scene share the same environment map shown in Figure 18.2.

If the axis directions the camera looked down to build the environment map images were the world space axes, then the environment map is said to be generated relative to the world space. You could, of course, capture the environment from a different orientation (say the local space of an object). However, the lookup vector coordinates must be in the space the cube map is relative to.

Because cube maps just store texture data, their contents can be pre-generated by an artist (just like the 2D textures we've been using). Consequently, we do not need to use real-time rendering to compute the images of a cube map. That is, we can create a scene in a 3D world editor, and then pre-render the six cube map face images in the editor. For outdoor environment maps, the program *Terragen* (http://www.planetside.co.uk/) is common to use (free for personal use), and can create photorealistic outdoor scenes. The environment maps we create for this book, such as the one shown in Figure 18.2, were made with *Terragen*.

> **Note:** *If you choose to try out Terragen, you need to go to the* **Camera Settings** *dialog box and set the* **zoom** *factor to 1.0 to achieve a 90° field of view. Also, be sure to set your output image dimensions to be equal so that both the vertical and horizontal field of view angles are the same, namely 90°.*

There is a nice Terragen *script on the web (https://developer.valvesoftware.com/wiki/Skybox_(2D)_with_Terragen) that will use the current camera position, and render out the six surrounding images with a 90° field of view.*

Once you have created the six cube map images using some program, we need to create a cube map texture, which stores all six. The DDS texture image format we have been using readily supports cube maps, and we can use the *texassemble* tool to build a cube map from six images. Below is an example of how to create a cube map using texassemble (taken from the *texassemble* documentation):

```
texassemble -cube -w 256 -h 256 -o cubemap.dds lobbyxposjpg lobbyxneg.
   jpg lobbyypos.jpg lobbyyneg.jpg lobbyzpos.jpg lobbyzneg.jpg
```

NVIDIA provides Photoshop plugins for saving .DDS and cubemaps in Photoshop; see http://developer.nvidia.com/nvidia-texture-tools-adobe-photoshop.

18.2.1 Loading and Using Cube Maps in Direct3D

As mentioned, a cube map is represented in Direct3D by a texture array with six elements. Our DDS texture loading code (*DDSTextureLoader.h/.cpp*) already supports loading cube maps, and we can load the texture like any other. The loading code will detect that the DDS file contains a cube map, and will create a texture array and load the face data into each element.

```
auto skyTex = std::make_unique<Texture>();
skyTex->Name = "skyTex";
skyTex->Filename = L"Textures/grasscube1024.dds";
ThrowIfFailed(DirectX::CreateDDSTextureFromFile12(md3dDevice.Get(),
    mCommandList.Get(), skyTex->Filename.c_str(),
    skyTex->Resource, skyTex->UploadHeap));
```

When we create an SRV to a cube map texture resource, we specify the dimension `D3D12_SRV_DIMENSION_TEXTURECUBE` and use the `TextureCube` property of the SRV description:

```
D3D12_SHADER_RESOURCE_VIEW_DESC srvDesc = {};
srvDesc.Shader4ComponentMapping = D3D12_DEFAULT_SHADER_4_COMPONENT_MAPPING;
srvDesc.ViewDimension = D3D12_SRV_DIMENSION_TEXTURECUBE;
srvDesc.TextureCube.MostDetailedMip = 0;
srvDesc.TextureCube.MipLevels = skyTex->GetDesc().MipLevels;
srvDesc.TextureCube.ResourceMinLODClamp = 0.0f;
srvDesc.Format = skyTex->GetDesc().Format;
md3dDevice->CreateShaderResourceView(skyTex.Get(), &srvDesc, hDescriptor);
```

18.3 TEXTURING A SKY

We can use an environment map to texture a sky. We create a large sphere that surrounds the entire scene. To create the illusion of distant mountains far in the horizon and a sky, we texture the sphere using an environment map by the method shown in Figure 18.4. In this way, the environment map is projected onto the sphere's surface.

We assume that the sky sphere is infinitely far away (i.e., it is centered about the world space but has infinite radius), and so no matter how the camera moves in the world, we never appear to get closer or farther from the surface of the sky sphere. To implement this infinitely faraway sky, we simply center the sky sphere about the camera in world space so that it is always centered about the camera. Consequently, as the camera moves, we are getting no closer to the surface of the sphere. If we did not do this, and we let the camera move closer to the sky surface, the whole illusion would break down, as the trick we use to simulate the sky would be obvious.

The shader file for the sky is given below:

```
//***********************************************************************
// Sky.hlsl by Frank Luna (C) 2015 All Rights Reserved.
//***********************************************************************

// Include common HLSL code.
#include "Common.hlsl"
```

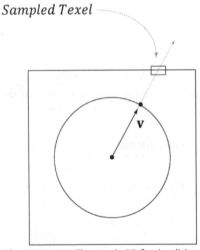

Figure 18.4. We illustrate in 2D for simplicity; in 3D the square becomes a cube and the circle becomes a sphere. We assume that the sky and environment map are centered about the same origin. Then to texture a point on the surface of the sphere, we use the vector from the origin to the surface point as the lookup vector into the cube map. This projects the cube map onto the sphere.

```hlsl
struct VertexIn
{
    float3 PosL    : POSITION;
    float3 NormalL : NORMAL;
    float2 TexC    : TEXCOORD;
};

struct VertexOut
{
    float4 PosH : SV_POSITION;
    float3 PosL : POSITION;
};

VertexOut VS(VertexIn vin)
{
    VertexOut vout;
    
    // Use local vertex position as cubemap lookup vector.
    vout.PosL = vin.PosL;
    
    // Transform to world space.
    float4 posW = mul(float4(vin.PosL, 1.0f), gWorld);
    
    // Always center sky about camera.
    posW.xyz += gEyePosW;
    
    // Set z = w so that z/w = 1 (i.e., skydome always on far plane).
    vout.PosH = mul(posW, gViewProj).xyww;
    
    return vout;
}

float4 PS(VertexOut pin) : SV_Target
{
    return gCubeMap.Sample(gsamLinearWrap, pin.PosL);
}
```

The sky shader programs are significantly different than the shader programs for drawing our objects (*Default.hlsl*). However, it shares the same root signature so that we do not have to change root signatures in the middle of drawing. The code that is common to both *Default.hlsl* and *Sky.hlsl* has been moved to *Common.hlsl* so that the code is not duplicated. For reference, *Common.hlsl* looks like this:

```hlsl
//***************************************************************************************
// Common.hlsl by Frank Luna (C) 2015 All Rights Reserved.
//***************************************************************************************

// Defaults for number of lights.
#ifndef NUM_DIR_LIGHTS
    #define NUM_DIR_LIGHTS 3
#endif

#ifndef NUM_POINT_LIGHTS
    #define NUM_POINT_LIGHTS 0
```

```
#endif

#ifndef NUM_SPOT_LIGHTS
  #define NUM_SPOT_LIGHTS 0
#endif

// Include structures and functions for lighting.
#include "LightingUtil.hlsl"

struct MaterialData
{
  float4   DiffuseAlbedo;
  float3   FresnelR0;
  float    Roughness;
  float4x4 MatTransform;
  uint     DiffuseMapIndex;
  uint     MatPad0;
  uint     MatPad1;
  uint     MatPad2;
};

TextureCube gCubeMap : register(t0);

// An array of textures, which is only supported in shader model 5.1+. Unlike
// Texture2DArray, the textures in this array can be different sizes and
// formats, making it more flexible than texture arrays.
Texture2D gDiffuseMap[4] : register(t1);

// Put in space1, so the texture array does not overlap with these resources.
// The texture array will occupy registers t0, t1, ..., t3 in space0.
StructuredBuffer<MaterialData> gMaterialData : register(t0, space1);


SamplerState gsamPointWrap        : register(s0);
SamplerState gsamPointClamp       : register(s1);
SamplerState gsamLinearWrap       : register(s2);
SamplerState gsamLinearClamp      : register(s3);
SamplerState gsamAnisotropicWrap  : register(s4);
SamplerState gsamAnisotropicClamp : register(s5);

// Constant data that varies per frame.
cbuffer cbPerObject : register(b0)
{
  float4x4 gWorld;
  float4x4 gTexTransform;
  uint gMaterialIndex;
  uint gObjPad0;
  uint gObjPad1;
  uint gObjPad2;
};

// Constant data that varies per material.
cbuffer cbPass : register(b1)
{
  float4x4 gView;
```

```
    float4x4 gInvView;
    float4x4 gProj;
    float4x4 gInvProj;
    float4x4 gViewProj;
    float4x4 gInvViewProj;
    float3 gEyePosW;
    float cbPerObjectPad1;
    float2 gRenderTargetSize;
    float2 gInvRenderTargetSize;
    float gNearZ;
    float gFarZ;
    float gTotalTime;
    float gDeltaTime;
    float4 gAmbientLight;

    // Indices [0, NUM_DIR_LIGHTS) are directional lights;
    // indices [NUM_DIR_LIGHTS, NUM_DIR_LIGHTS+NUM_POINT_LIGHTS) are point lights;
    // indices [NUM_DIR_LIGHTS+NUM_POINT_LIGHTS,
    // NUM_DIR_LIGHTS+NUM_POINT_LIGHT+NUM_SPOT_LIGHTS)
    // are spot lights for a maximum of MaxLights per object.
    Light gLights[MaxLights];
};
```

Note: *In the past, applications would draw the sky first and use it as a replacement to clearing the render target and depth/stencil buffer. However, the "ATI Radeon HD 2000 Programming Guide" (http://developer.amd.com/media/gpu_assets/ATI_Radeon_HD_2000_programming_guide.pdf) now advises against this for the following reasons. First, the depth/stencil buffer needs to be explicitly cleared for internal hardware depth optimizations to perform well. The situation is similar with render targets. Second, typically most of the sky is occluded by other geometry such as buildings and terrain. Therefore, if we draw the sky first, then we are wasting resources by drawing pixels that will only get overridden later by geometry closer to the camera. Therefore, it is now recommended to always clear, and to draw the sky last.*

Drawing the sky requires different shader programs, and hence a new PSO. Therefore, we draw the sky as a separate layer in our drawing code:

```
    // Draw opaque render-items.
    mCommandList->SetPipelineState(mPSOs["opaque"].Get());
    DrawRenderItems(mCommandList.Get(), mRitemLayer[(int)
        RenderLayer::Opaque]);

    // Draw the sky render-item.
    mCommandList->SetPipelineState(mPSOs["sky"].Get());
    DrawRenderItems(mCommandList.Get(), mRitemLayer[(int)
        RenderLayer::Sky]);
```

In addition, rendering the sky requires some different render states. In particular, because the camera lies inside the sphere, we need to disable back face culling (or making counterclockwise triangles front facing would also work), and we need to change the depth comparison function to `LESS_EQUAL` so that the sky will pass the depth test:

```
D3D12_GRAPHICS_PIPELINE_STATE_DESC skyPsoDesc = opaquePsoDesc;

// The camera is inside the sky sphere, so just turn off culling.
skyPsoDesc.RasterizerState.CullMode = D3D12_CULL_MODE_NONE;

// Make sure the depth function is LESS_EQUAL and not just LESS.
// Otherwise, the normalized depth values at z = 1 (NDC) will
// fail the depth test if the depth buffer was cleared to 1.
skyPsoDesc.DepthStencilState.DepthFunc = D3D12_COMPARISON_FUNC_LESS_EQUAL;
skyPsoDesc.pRootSignature = mRootSignature.Get();
skyPsoDesc.VS =
{
        reinterpret_cast<BYTE*>(mShaders["skyVS"]->GetBufferPointer()),
        mShaders["skyVS"]->GetBufferSize()
};
skyPsoDesc.PS =
{
        reinterpret_cast<BYTE*>(mShaders["skyPS"]->GetBufferPointer()),
        mShaders["skyPS"]->GetBufferSize()
};
ThrowIfFailed(md3dDevice->CreateGraphicsPipelineState(
  &skyPsoDesc, IID_PPV_ARGS(&mPSOs["sky"])));
```

18.4 MODELING REFLECTIONS

In Chapter 8, we learned that specular highlights come from light sources where the emitted light strikes a surface and can reflect into the eye based on the Fresnel effect and surface roughness. However, due to light scattering and bouncing, light really strikes a surface from all directions above the surface, not just along the rays from direct light sources. We have modeled indirect diffuse light with our ambient term in our lighting equation. In this section, we show how to use environment maps to model *specular reflections* coming from the surrounding environment. By specular reflections, we mean that we are just going to look at the light that is reflected off a surface due to the Fresnel effect. An advanced topic we do not discuss uses cube maps to compute diffuse lighting from the surrounding environment as well (e.g., see *http://http.developer.nvidia.com/GPUGems2/ gpugems2_chapter10.html*).

When we render a scene about a point O to build an environment map, we are recording light values coming in from all directions about the point O. In other words, the environment map stores the light values coming in from every direction about the point O, and we can think of every texel on the environment map as a source of light. We use this data to approximate specular reflections of

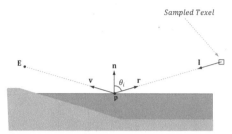

Figure 18.5. Here **E** is the eye point, and **n** is the surface normal at the point **p**. The texel that stores the light that reflects off **p** and enters the eye is obtained by sampling the cube map with the vector **r**.

light coming from the surrounding environment. To see this, consider Figure 18.5. Light from the environment comes in with incident direction I and reflects off the surface (due to the Fresnel effect) and enters the eye in the direction $\mathbf{v} = \mathbf{E} - \mathbf{p}$. The light from the environment is obtained by sampling the environment cube map with the lookup vector $\mathbf{r} = \text{reflect}(-\mathbf{v}, \mathbf{n})$. This makes the surface have mirror like properties: the eye looks at **p** and sees the environment reflected off **p**.

We compute the reflection vector per-pixel and then use it to sample the environment map:

```
const float shininess = 1.0f - roughness;

// Add in specular reflections.
float3 r = reflect(-toEyeW, pin.NormalW);
float4 reflectionColor = gCubeMap.Sample(gsamLinearWrap, r);
float3 fresnelFactor = SchlickFresnel(fresnelR0, pin.NormalW, r);
litColor.rgb += shininess * fresnelFactor * reflectionColor.rgb;
```

Because we are talking about reflections, we need to apply the Fresnel effect, which determines how much light is reflected from the environment into the eye based on the material properties of the surface and the angle between the light vector (reflection vector) and normal. In addition, we scale the amount of reflection based on the shininess of the material—a rough material should have a low amount of reflection, but still some reflection.

Figure 18.6 shows that reflections via environment mapping do not work well for flat surfaces.

This is because the reflection vector does not tell the whole story, as it does not incorporate position; we really need a reflection ray and to intersect the ray with the environment map. A ray has position and direction, whereas a vector just has direction. From the figure, we see that the two reflection rays, $\mathbf{q}(t) = \mathbf{p} + t\mathbf{r}$ and $\mathbf{q}'(t) = \mathbf{p}' + t\mathbf{r}$, intersect different texels of the cube map, and thus should be colored differently. However, because both rays have the same direction vector **r**, and the direction vector **r** is solely used for the cube map lookup, the same texel gets mapped to **p** and **p**′ when the eye is at **E** and **E**′, respectively. For flat objects

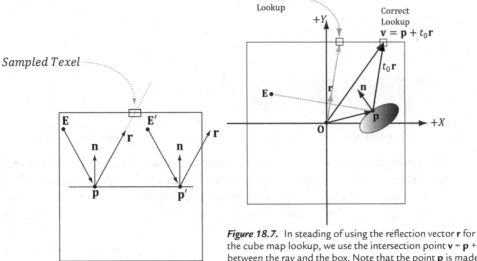

Figure 18.6. The reflection vector corresponding to two different points **p** and **p′** when the eye is at positions **E** and **E′**, respectively.

Figure 18.7. In steading of using the reflection vector **r** for the cube map lookup, we use the intersection point $v = p + t_0 r$ between the ray and the box. Note that the point **p** is made relative to the center of the bounding box proxy geometry so that the intersection point can be used as a lookup vector for the cube map.

this defect of environment mapping is very noticeable. For curvy surfaces, this shortcoming of environment mapping goes largely unnoticed, since the curvature of the surface causes the reflection vector to vary.

One solution is to associate some proxy geometry with the environment map. For example, suppose we have an environment map for a square room. We can associate an axis-aligned bounding box with the environment map that has approximately the same dimensions as the room. Figure 18.7 then shows how we can do a ray intersection with the box to compute the vector **v** which gives a better lookup vector than the reflection vector **r**. If the bounding box associated with the cube map is input into the shader (e.g., via a constant buffer), then the ray/box intersection test can be done in the pixel shader, and we can compute the improved lookup vector in the pixel shader to sample the cube map.

The following function shows how the cube map look up vector can be computed.

```
float3 BoxCubeMapLookup(float3 rayOrigin, float3 unitRayDir,
         float3 boxCenter, float3 boxExtents)
{
    // Based on slab method as described in Real-Time Rendering
    // 16.7.1 (3rd edition).

    // Make relative to the box center.
    float3 p = rayOrigin - boxCenter;

    // The ith slab ray/plane intersection formulas for AABB are:
```

```
    //
    // t1 = (-dot(n_i, p) + h_i)/dot(n_i, d) = (-p_i + h_i)/d_i
    // t2 = (-dot(n_i, p) - h_i)/dot(n_i, d) = (-p_i - h_i)/d_i

    // Vectorize and do ray/plane formulas for every slab together.
    float3 t1 = (-p+boxExtents)/unitRayDir;
    float3 t2 = (-p-boxExtents)/unitRayDir;

    // Find max for each coordinate. Because we assume the ray is inside
    // the box, we only want the max intersection parameter.
    float3 tmax = max(t1, t2);

    // Take minimum of all the tmax components:
    float t = min(min(tmax.x, tmax.y), tmax.z);

    // This is relative to the box center so it can be used as a
    // cube map lookup vector.
    return p + t*unitRayDir;
}
```

18.5 DYNAMIC CUBE MAPS

So far we have described static cube maps, where the images stored in the cube map are premade and fixed. This works for many situations and is relatively inexpensive. However, suppose that we want animated actors moving in our scene. With a pre-generated cube map, you cannot capture these animated objects, which means we cannot reflect animated objects. To overcome this limitation, we can build the cube map at runtime. That is, every frame you position the camera in the scene that is to be the origin of the cube map, and then *render the scene six times into each cube map face* along each coordinate axis direction (see Figure 18.8). Since the cube map is rebuilt every frame, it will capture animated objects in the environment, and the reflection will be animated as well (see Figure 18.9).

> **Note:** *Rendering a cube map dynamically is expensive. It requires rendering the scene to six render targets! Therefore, try to minimize the number of dynamic cube maps needed in a scene. For example, perhaps only use dynamic reflections for key objects in your scene that you want to show off or accentuate. Then use static cube maps for the less important objects were dynamic reflections would probably go unnoticed or not be missed. Normally, low resolution cube maps are used for dynamic cube maps, such as 256 × 256, to save on pixel processing (i.e., fill rate).*

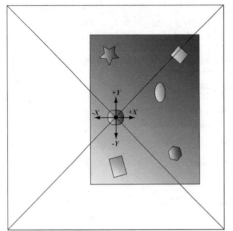

Figure 18.8. The camera is placed at position O in the scene, centered about the object we want to generate the dynamic cube map relative to. We render the scene six times along each coordinate axis direction with a field of view angle of 90° so that the image of the entire surrounding environment is captured.

Figure 18.9. Screenshot of the "Dynamic CubeMap" demo showing off dynamic reflections. The skull orbits the center sphere, and its reflection in the sphere animates accordingly. Moreover, because we are drawing the cube maps ourselves, we can model the reflections of the local objects as well, such as the columns, spheres, and floor.

18.5.1 Dynamic Cube Map Helper Class

To help render to a cube map dynamically, we create the following `CubeRenderTarget` class, which encapsulates the actual `ID3D12Resource` object of the cube map, the various descriptors to the resource, and other useful data for rendering to the cube map:

```
class CubeRenderTarget
{
public:
  CubeRenderTarget(ID3D12Device* device,
    UINT width, UINT height,
    DXGI_FORMAT format);

  CubeRenderTarget(const CubeRenderTarget& rhs)=delete;
  CubeRenderTarget& operator=(const CubeRenderTarget& rhs)=delete;
  ~CubeRenderTarget()=default;

  ID3D12Resource* Resource();
  CD3DX12_GPU_DESCRIPTOR_HANDLE Srv();
  CD3DX12_CPU_DESCRIPTOR_HANDLE Rtv(int faceIndex);

  D3D12_VIEWPORT Viewport()const;
  D3D12_RECT ScissorRect()const;

  void BuildDescriptors(
    CD3DX12_CPU_DESCRIPTOR_HANDLE hCpuSrv,
    CD3DX12_GPU_DESCRIPTOR_HANDLE hGpuSrv,
    CD3DX12_CPU_DESCRIPTOR_HANDLE hCpuRtv[6]);

  void OnResize(UINT newWidth, UINT newHeight);
```

```
private:
  void BuildDescriptors();
  void BuildResource();

private:

  ID3D12Device* md3dDevice = nullptr;

  D3D12_VIEWPORT mViewport;
  D3D12_RECT mScissorRect;

  UINT mWidth = 0;
  UINT mHeight = 0;
  DXGI_FORMAT mFormat = DXGI_FORMAT_R8G8B8A8_UNORM;

  CD3DX12_CPU_DESCRIPTOR_HANDLE mhCpuSrv;
  CD3DX12_GPU_DESCRIPTOR_HANDLE mhGpuSrv;
  CD3DX12_CPU_DESCRIPTOR_HANDLE mhCpuRtv[6];

  Microsoft::WRL::ComPtr<ID3D12Resource> mCubeMap = nullptr;
};
```

18.5.2 Building the Cube Map Resource

Creating a cube map texture is done by creating a texture array with six elements (one for each face). Because we are going to render to the cube map, we must set the D3D12_RESOURCE_FLAG_ALLOW_RENDER_TARGET flag. Below is the method that builds the cube map resource:

```
void CubeRenderTarget::BuildResource()
{
  D3D12_RESOURCE_DESC texDesc;
  ZeroMemory(&texDesc, sizeof(D3D12_RESOURCE_DESC));
  texDesc.Dimension = D3D12_RESOURCE_DIMENSION_TEXTURE2D;
  texDesc.Alignment = 0;
  texDesc.Width = mWidth;
  texDesc.Height = mHeight;
  texDesc.DepthOrArraySize = 6;
  texDesc.MipLevels = 1;
  texDesc.Format = mFormat;
  texDesc.SampleDesc.Count = 1;
  texDesc.SampleDesc.Quality = 0;
  texDesc.Layout = D3D12_TEXTURE_LAYOUT_UNKNOWN;
  texDesc.Flags = D3D12_RESOURCE_FLAG_ALLOW_RENDER_TARGET;

  ThrowIfFailed(md3dDevice->CreateCommittedResource(
    &CD3DX12_HEAP_PROPERTIES(D3D12_HEAP_TYPE_DEFAULT),
    D3D12_HEAP_FLAG_NONE,
    &texDesc,
    D3D12_RESOURCE_STATE_GENERIC_READ,
    nullptr,
    IID_PPV_ARGS(&mCubeMap)));
}
```

18.5.3 Extra Descriptor Heap Space

Rendering to a cube map requires six additional render target views, one for each face, and one additional depth/stencil buffer. Therefore, we must override the `D3DApp::CreateRtvAndDsvDescriptorHeaps` method and allocate these additional descriptors:

```
void DynamicCubeMapApp::CreateRtvAndDsvDescriptorHeaps()
{
  // Add +6 RTV for cube render target.
  D3D12_DESCRIPTOR_HEAP_DESC rtvHeapDesc;
  rtvHeapDesc.NumDescriptors = SwapChainBufferCount + 6;
  rtvHeapDesc.Type = D3D12_DESCRIPTOR_HEAP_TYPE_RTV;
  rtvHeapDesc.Flags = D3D12_DESCRIPTOR_HEAP_FLAG_NONE;
  rtvHeapDesc.NodeMask = 0;
  ThrowIfFailed(md3dDevice->CreateDescriptorHeap(
    &rtvHeapDesc, IID_PPV_ARGS(mRtvHeap.GetAddressOf())));

  // Add +1 DSV for cube render target.
  D3D12_DESCRIPTOR_HEAP_DESC dsvHeapDesc;
  dsvHeapDesc.NumDescriptors = 2;
  dsvHeapDesc.Type = D3D12_DESCRIPTOR_HEAP_TYPE_DSV;
  dsvHeapDesc.Flags = D3D12_DESCRIPTOR_HEAP_FLAG_NONE;
  dsvHeapDesc.NodeMask = 0;
  ThrowIfFailed(md3dDevice->CreateDescriptorHeap(
    &dsvHeapDesc, IID_PPV_ARGS(mDsvHeap.GetAddressOf())));

  mCubeDSV = CD3DX12_CPU_DESCRIPTOR_HANDLE(
    mDsvHeap->GetCPUDescriptorHandleForHeapStart(),
    1,
    mDsvDescriptorSize);
}
```

In addition, we will need one extra SRV so that we can bind the cube map as a shader input after it has been generated.

The descriptor handles are passed into the `CubeRenderTarget::BuildDescriptors` method which saves a copy of the handles and then actually creates the views:

```
auto srvCpuStart = mSrvDescriptorHeap->GetCPUDescriptorHandleForHeapStart();
auto srvGpuStart = mSrvDescriptorHeap->GetGPUDescriptorHandleForHeapStart();
auto rtvCpuStart = mRtvHeap->GetCPUDescriptorHandleForHeapStart();

// Cubemap RTV goes after the swap chain descriptors.
int rtvOffset = SwapChainBufferCount;

CD3DX12_CPU_DESCRIPTOR_HANDLE cubeRtvHandles[6];
for(int i = 0; i < 6; ++i)
  cubeRtvHandles[i] = CD3DX12_CPU_DESCRIPTOR_HANDLE(
    rtvCpuStart, rtvOffset + i, mRtvDescriptorSize);

mDynamicCubeMap->BuildDescriptors(
  CD3DX12_CPU_DESCRIPTOR_HANDLE(
    srvCpuStart, mDynamicTexHeapIndex, mCbvSrvDescriptorSize),
```

```
    CD3DX12_GPU_DESCRIPTOR_HANDLE(
      srvGpuStart, mDynamicTexHeapIndex, mCbvSrvDescriptorSize),
    cubeRtvHandles);

void CubeRenderTarget::BuildDescriptors(CD3DX12_CPU_DESCRIPTOR_HANDLE hCpuSrv,
                    CD3DX12_GPU_DESCRIPTOR_HANDLE hGpuSrv,
                    CD3DX12_CPU_DESCRIPTOR_HANDLE hCpuRtv[6])
{
  // Save references to the descriptors.
  mhCpuSrv = hCpuSrv;
  mhGpuSrv = hGpuSrv;

  for(int i = 0; i < 6; ++i)
    mhCpuRtv[i] = hCpuRtv[i];

  // Create the descriptors
  BuildDescriptors();
}
```

18.5.4 Building the Descriptors

In the previous section, we allocated heap space for our descriptors and cached references to the descriptors, but we did not actually create any descriptors to resources. We now need to create an SRV to the cube map resource so that we can sample it in a pixel shader after it is built, and we also need to create a render target view to each element in the cube map texture array, so that we can render onto each cube map face one-by-one. The following method creates the necessary views:

```
void CubeRenderTarget::BuildDescriptors()
{
  D3D12_SHADER_RESOURCE_VIEW_DESC srvDesc = {};
  srvDesc.Shader4ComponentMapping = D3D12_DEFAULT_SHADER_4_COMPONENT_
    MAPPING;
  srvDesc.Format = mFormat;
  srvDesc.ViewDimension = D3D12_SRV_DIMENSION_TEXTURECUBE;
  srvDesc.TextureCube.MostDetailedMip = 0;
  srvDesc.TextureCube.MipLevels = 1;
  srvDesc.TextureCube.ResourceMinLODClamp = 0.0f;

  // Create SRV to the entire cubemap resource.
  md3dDevice->CreateShaderResourceView(mCubeMap.Get(), &srvDesc,
    mhCpuSrv);

  // Create RTV to each cube face.
  for(int i = 0; i < 6; ++i)
  {
    D3D12_RENDER_TARGET_VIEW_DESC rtvDesc;
    rtvDesc.ViewDimension = D3D12_RTV_DIMENSION_TEXTURE2DARRAY;
    rtvDesc.Format = mFormat;
    rtvDesc.Texture2DArray.MipSlice = 0;
    rtvDesc.Texture2DArray.PlaneSlice = 0;
```

```
        // Render target to ith element.
        rtvDesc.Texture2DArray.FirstArraySlice = i;

        // Only view one element of the array.
        rtvDesc.Texture2DArray.ArraySize = 1;

        // Create RTV to ith cubemap face.
        md3dDevice->CreateRenderTargetView(mCubeMap.Get(), &rtvDesc,
            mhCpuRtv[i]);
    }
}
```

18.5.5 Building the Depth Buffer

Generally, the cube map faces will have a different resolution than the main back buffer. Therefore, for rendering to the cube map faces, we need a depth buffer with dimensions that matches the resolution of a cube map face. However, because we render to the cube faces one at a time, we only need one depth buffer for the cube map rendering. We build an additional depth buffer and DSV with the following code:

```
void DynamicCubeMapApp::BuildCubeDepthStencil()
{
    // Create the depth/stencil buffer and view.
    D3D12_RESOURCE_DESC depthStencilDesc;
    depthStencilDesc.Dimension = D3D12_RESOURCE_DIMENSION_TEXTURE2D;
    depthStencilDesc.Alignment = 0;
    depthStencilDesc.Width = CubeMapSize;
    depthStencilDesc.Height = CubeMapSize;
    depthStencilDesc.DepthOrArraySize = 1;
    depthStencilDesc.MipLevels = 1;
    depthStencilDesc.Format = mDepthStencilFormat;
    depthStencilDesc.SampleDesc.Count = 1;
    depthStencilDesc.SampleDesc.Quality = 0;
    depthStencilDesc.Layout = D3D12_TEXTURE_LAYOUT_UNKNOWN;
    depthStencilDesc.Flags = D3D12_RESOURCE_FLAG_ALLOW_DEPTH_STENCIL;

    D3D12_CLEAR_VALUE optClear;
    optClear.Format = mDepthStencilFormat;
    optClear.DepthStencil.Depth = 1.0f;
    optClear.DepthStencil.Stencil = 0;
    ThrowIfFailed(md3dDevice->CreateCommittedResource(
        &CD3DX12_HEAP_PROPERTIES(D3D12_HEAP_TYPE_DEFAULT),
        D3D12_HEAP_FLAG_NONE,
        &depthStencilDesc,
        D3D12_RESOURCE_STATE_COMMON,
        &optClear,
        IID_PPV_ARGS(mCubeDepthStencilBuffer.GetAddressOf())));

    // Create descriptor to mip level 0 of entire resource using
    // the format of the resource.
    md3dDevice->CreateDepthStencilView(
```

```
    mCubeDepthStencilBuffer.Get(), nullptr, mCubeDSV);

// Transition the resource from its initial state to be used as a
   depth buffer.
mCommandList->ResourceBarrier(1,
    &CD3DX12_RESOURCE_BARRIER::Transition(
    mCubeDepthStencilBuffer.Get(),
    D3D12_RESOURCE_STATE_COMMON,
    D3D12_RESOURCE_STATE_DEPTH_WRITE));
}
```

18.5.6 Cube Map Viewport and Scissor Rectangle

Because the cube map faces will have a different resolution than the main back buffer, we need to define a new viewport and scissor rectangle that covers a cube map face:

```
CubeRenderTarget::CubeRenderTarget(ID3D12Device* device,
                UINT width, UINT height,
                DXGI_FORMAT format)
{
  md3dDevice = device;

  mWidth = width;
  mHeight = height;
  mFormat = format;

  mViewport = { 0.0f, 0.0f, (float)width, (float)height, 0.0f, 1.0f };
  mScissorRect = { 0, 0, width, height };

  BuildResource();
}

D3D12_VIEWPORT CubeRenderTarget::Viewport()const
{
    return mViewport;
}

D3D12_RECT CubeRenderTarget::ScissorRect()const
{
    return mScissorRect
}
```

18.5.7 Setting up the Cube Map Camera

Recall that to generate a cube map idea is to position a camera at the center of some object O in the scene with a 90° field of view angle (both vertically and horizontally). Then have the camera look down the positive *x*-axis, negative *x*-axis, positive *y*-axis, negative *y*-axis, positive *z*-axis, and negative *z*-axis, and to take a picture of the scene (excluding the object O) from each of these six viewpoints.

To facilitate this, we generate six cameras, one for each face, centered at the given position (*x, y, z*):

```
Camera mCubeMapCamera[6];
void DynamicCubeMapApp::BuildCubeFaceCamera(float x, float y, float z)
{
  // Generate the cube map about the given position.
  XMFLOAT3 center(x, y, z);
  XMFLOAT3 worldUp(0.0f, 1.0f, 0.0f);

  // Look along each coordinate axis.
  XMFLOAT3 targets[6] =
  {
    XMFLOAT3(x + 1.0f, y, z), // +X
    XMFLOAT3(x - 1.0f, y, z), // -X
    XMFLOAT3(x, y + 1.0f, z), // +Y
    XMFLOAT3(x, y - 1.0f, z), // -Y
    XMFLOAT3(x, y, z + 1.0f), // +Z
    XMFLOAT3(x, y, z - 1.0f)  // -Z
  };

  // Use world up vector (0,1,0) for all directions except +Y/-Y. In
    these cases, we
  // are looking down +Y or -Y, so we need a different "up" vector.
  XMFLOAT3 ups[6] =
  {
    XMFLOAT3(0.0f, 1.0f, 0.0f),  // +X
    XMFLOAT3(0.0f, 1.0f, 0.0f),  // -X
    XMFLOAT3(0.0f, 0.0f, -1.0f), // +Y
    XMFLOAT3(0.0f, 0.0f, +1.0f), // -Y
    XMFLOAT3(0.0f, 1.0f, 0.0f),  // +Z
    XMFLOAT3(0.0f, 1.0f, 0.0f)   // -Z
  };

  for(int i = 0; i < 6; ++i)
  {
    mCubeMapCamera[i].LookAt(center, targets[i], ups[i]);
    mCubeMapCamera[i].SetLens(0.5f*XM_PI, 1.0f, 0.1f, 1000.0f);
    mCubeMapCamera[i].UpdateViewMatrix();
  }
}
```

Because rendering to each cube map face utilizes a different camera, each cube face needs its own set of `PassConstants`. This is easy enough, as we just increase our `PassConstants` count by six when we create our frame resources.

```
void DynamicCubeMapApp::BuildFrameResources()
{
  for(int i = 0; i < gNumFrameResources; ++i)
  {
    mFrameResources.push_back(std::make_unique<FrameResource>(md3dDevice.Get(),
      7, (UINT)mAllRitems.size(), (UINT)mMaterials.size()));
  }
}
```

Element 0 will correspond to our main rendering pass, and elements 1-6 will correspond to our cube map faces.

We implement the following method to set the constant data for each cube map face:

```
void DynamicCubeMapApp::UpdateCubeMapFacePassCBs()
{
  for(int i = 0; i < 6; ++i)
  {
    PassConstants cubeFacePassCB = mMainPassCB;

    XMMATRIX view = mCubeMapCamera[i].GetView();
    XMMATRIX proj = mCubeMapCamera[i].GetProj();

    XMMATRIX viewProj = XMMatrixMultiply(view, proj);
    XMMATRIX invView = XMMatrixInverse(&XMMatrixDeterminant(view),
    view);
    XMMATRIX invProj = XMMatrixInverse(&XMMatrixDeterminant(proj),
    proj);
    XMMATRIX invViewProj = XMMatrixInverse(&XMMatrixDeterminant(viewPr
    oj), viewProj);

    XMStoreFloat4x4(&cubeFacePassCB.View, XMMatrixTranspose(view));
    XMStoreFloat4x4(&cubeFacePassCB.InvView,
    XMMatrixTranspose(invView));
    XMStoreFloat4x4(&cubeFacePassCB.Proj, XMMatrixTranspose(proj));
    XMStoreFloat4x4(&cubeFacePassCB.InvProj,
    XMMatrixTranspose(invProj));
    XMStoreFloat4x4(&cubeFacePassCB.ViewProj,
    XMMatrixTranspose(viewProj));
    XMStoreFloat4x4(&cubeFacePassCB.InvViewProj, XMMatrixTranspose(inv
    ViewProj));
    cubeFacePassCB.EyePosW = mCubeMapCamera[i].GetPosition3f();
    cubeFacePassCB.RenderTargetSize =
      XMFLOAT2((float)CubeMapSize, (float)CubeMapSize);
    cubeFacePassCB.InvRenderTargetSize =
      XMFLOAT2(1.0f / CubeMapSize, 1.0f / CubeMapSize);

    auto currPassCB = mCurrFrameResource->PassCB.get();

    // Cube map pass cbuffers are stored in elements 1-6.
    currPassCB->CopyData(1 + i, cubeFacePassCB);
  }
}
```

18.5.8 Drawing into the Cube Map

For this demo we have three render layers:

```
enum class RenderLayer : int
{
  Opaque = 0,
  OpaqueDynamicReflectors,
```

```
    Sky,
    Count
};
```

The `OpaqueDynamicReflectors` layer contains the center sphere in Figure () which will use the dynamic cube map to reflect local dynamic objects. Our first step is to draw the scene to each face of the cube map, but not including the center sphere; this means we just need to render the opaque and sky layers to the cube map:

```
void DynamicCubeMapApp::DrawSceneToCubeMap()
{
  mCommandList->RSSetViewports(1, &mDynamicCubeMap->Viewport());
  mCommandList->RSSetScissorRects(1, &mDynamicCubeMap->ScissorRect());

  // Change to RENDER_TARGET.
  mCommandList->ResourceBarrier(1,
    &CD3DX12_RESOURCE_BARRIER::Transition(
    mDynamicCubeMap->Resource(),
    D3D12_RESOURCE_STATE_GENERIC_READ,
    D3D12_RESOURCE_STATE_RENDER_TARGET));

   UINT passCBByteSize = d3dUtil::CalcConstantBufferByteSize(sizeof(PassConstants));

  // For each cube map face.
  for(int i = 0; i < 6; ++i)
  {
    // Clear the back buffer and depth buffer.
    mCommandList->ClearRenderTargetView(
      mDynamicCubeMap->Rtv(i), Colors::LightSteelBlue, 0, nullptr);
    mCommandList->ClearDepthStencilView(mCubeDSV,
      D3D12_CLEAR_FLAG_DEPTH | D3D12_CLEAR_FLAG_STENCIL,
      1.0f, 0, 0, nullptr);

    // Specify the buffers we are going to render to.
    mCommandList->OMSetRenderTargets(1, &mDynamicCubeMap->Rtv(i),
      true, &mCubeDSV);

    // Bind the pass constant buffer for this cube map face so we use
    // the right view/proj matrix for this cube face.
    auto passCB = mCurrFrameResource->PassCB->Resource();
    D3D12_GPU_VIRTUAL_ADDRESS passCBAddress =
      passCB->GetGPUVirtualAddress() + (1+i)*passCBByteSize;
    mCommandList->SetGraphicsRootConstantBufferView(1, passCBAddress);

    DrawRenderItems(mCommandList.Get(), mRitemLayer[(int)
    RenderLayer::Opaque]);

    mCommandList->SetPipelineState(mPSOs["sky"].Get());
    DrawRenderItems(mCommandList.Get(), mRitemLayer[(int)
    RenderLayer::Sky]);

    mCommandList->SetPipelineState(mPSOs["opaque"].Get());
  }
```

```
    // Change back to GENERIC_READ so we can read the texture in a
      shader.
    mCommandList->ResourceBarrier(1,
        &CD3DX12_RESOURCE_BARRIER::Transition(
        mDynamicCubeMap->Resource(),
        D3D12_RESOURCE_STATE_RENDER_TARGET,
        D3D12_RESOURCE_STATE_GENERIC_READ));
}
```

Finally, after we rendered the scene to the cube map, we set our main render targets and draw the scene as normal, but with the dynamic cube map applied to the center sphere:

```
...
DrawSceneToCubeMap();

// Set main render target settings.

mCommandList->RSSetViewports(1, &mScreenViewport);
mCommandList->RSSetScissorRects(1, &mScissorRect);

// Indicate a state transition on the resource usage.
mCommandList->ResourceBarrier(1,
    &CD3DX12_RESOURCE_BARRIER::Transition(
    CurrentBackBuffer(),
    D3D12_RESOURCE_STATE_PRESENT,
    D3D12_RESOURCE_STATE_RENDER_TARGET));

// Clear the back buffer and depth buffer.
mCommandList->ClearRenderTargetView(CurrentBackBufferView(),
    Colors::LightSteelBlue, 0, nullptr);
mCommandList->ClearDepthStencilView(
    DepthStencilView(),
    D3D12_CLEAR_FLAG_DEPTH | D3D12_CLEAR_FLAG_STENCIL,
    1.0f, 0, 0, nullptr);

// Specify the buffers we are going to render to.
mCommandList->OMSetRenderTargets(1,
    &CurrentBackBufferView(), true, &DepthStencilView());

auto passCB = mCurrFrameResource->PassCB->Resource();
mCommandList->SetGraphicsRootConstantBufferView(1,
    passCB->GetGPUVirtualAddress());


// Use the dynamic cube map for the dynamic reflectors layer.
CD3DX12_GPU_DESCRIPTOR_HANDLE dynamicTexDescriptor(
    mSrvDescriptorHeap->GetGPUDescriptorHandleForHeapStart());
dynamicTexDescriptor.Offset(mSkyTexHeapIndex + 1,
    mCbvSrvDescriptorSize);
mCommandList->SetGraphicsRootDescriptorTable(3, dynamicTexDescriptor);

DrawRenderItems(mCommandList.Get(),
mRitemLayer[(int)RenderLayer::OpaqueDynamicReflectors]);
```

```cpp
// Use the static "background" cube map for the other objects 
    (including the sky)
mCommandList->SetGraphicsRootDescriptorTable(3, skyTexDescriptor);

DrawRenderItems(mCommandList.Get(), mRitemLayer[(int)
    RenderLayer::Opaque]);

mCommandList->SetPipelineState(mPSOs["sky"].Get());
DrawRenderItems(mCommandList.Get(), mRitemLayer[(int)
    RenderLayer::Sky]);

// Indicate a state transition on the resource usage.
mCommandList->ResourceBarrier(1,
    &CD3DX12_RESOURCE_BARRIER::Transition(
    CurrentBackBuffer(),
    D3D12_RESOURCE_STATE_RENDER_TARGET,
    D3D12_RESOURCE_STATE_PRESENT));
...
```

18.6 DYNAMIC CUBE MAPS WITH THE GEOMETRY SHADER

In the previous section, we redrew the scene six times to generate the cube map—once for each cube map face. Draw calls are not free, and we should work to minimize them. There is a Direct3D 10 sample called "CubeMapGS," which uses the geometry shader to render a cube map by drawing the scene only once. In this section, we highlight the main ideas of how this sample works. Note that even though we show the Direct3D 10 code, the same strategy can be used in Direct3D 12 and porting the code is straightforward.

First, it creates a render target view to the *entire* texture array (not each individual face texture):

```cpp
// Create the 6-face render target view
D3D10_RENDER_TARGET_VIEW_DESC DescRT;
DescRT.Format = dstex.Format;
DescRT.ViewDimension = D3D10_RTV_DIMENSION_TEXTURE2DARRAY;
DescRT.Texture2DArray.FirstArraySlice = 0;
DescRT.Texture2DArray.ArraySize = 6;
DescRT.Texture2DArray.MipSlice = 0;
V_RETURN( pd3dDevice->CreateRenderTargetView(
    g_pEnvMap, &DescRT, &g_pEnvMapRTV ) );
```

Moreover, this technique requires a cube map of depth buffers (one for each face). The depth stencil view to the *entire* texture array of depth buffers is creates as follows:

```cpp
// Create the depth stencil view for the entire cube
D3D10_DEPTH_STENCIL_VIEW_DESC DescDS;
```

```
DescDS.Format = DXGI_FORMAT_D32_FLOAT;
DescDS.ViewDimension = D3D10_DSV_DIMENSION_TEXTURE2DARRAY;
DescDS.Texture2DArray.FirstArraySlice = 0;
DescDS.Texture2DArray.ArraySize = 6;
DescDS.Texture2DArray.MipSlice = 0;
V_RETURN( pd3dDevice->CreateDepthStencilView(
 g_pEnvMapDepth, &DescDS, &g_pEnvMapDSV ) );
```

It then binds this render target and depth stencil view to the OM stage of the pipeline:

```
ID3D10RenderTargetView* aRTViews[ 1 ] = { g_pEnvMapRTV };
pd3dDevice->OMSetRenderTargets(sizeof(aRTViews)/sizeof(aRTViews[0]),
 aRTViews, g_pEnvMapDSV );
```

That is, we have bound a view to an array of render targets and a view to an array of depth stencil buffers to the OM stage, and we are going to render to each array slice simultaneously.

Now, the scene is rendered once and an array of six view matrices (one to look in the corresponding direction of each cube map face) is available in the constant buffers. The geometry shader replicates the input triangle six times, and assigns the triangle to one of the six render target array slices. Assigning a triangle to a render target array slice is done by setting the system value SV_RenderTargetArrayIndex. This system value is an integer index value that can only be set as an output from the geometry shader to specify the index of the render target array slice the primitive should be rendered onto. This system value can only be used if the render target view is actually a view to an array resource.

```
struct PS_CUBEMAP_IN
{
  float4 Pos : SV_POSITION;    // Projection coord
  float2 Tex : TEXCOORD0;      // Texture coord
  uint RTIndex : SV_RenderTargetArrayIndex;
};

[maxvertexcount(18)]
void GS_CubeMap( triangle GS_CUBEMAP_IN input[3],
 inout TriangleStream<PS_CUBEMAP_IN> CubeMapStream )
{
  // For each triangle
  for( int f = 0; f < 6; ++f )
  {
    // Compute screen coordinates
    PS_CUBEMAP_IN output;

    // Assign the ith triangle to the ith render target.
    output.RTIndex = f;

    // For each vertex in the triangle
    for( int v = 0; v < 3; v++ )
    {
```

```
    // Transform to the view space of the ith cube face.
    output.Pos = mul( input[v].Pos, g_mViewCM[f] );

    // Transform to homogeneous clip space.
    output.Pos = mul( output.Pos, mProj );

    output.Tex = input[v].Tex;
    CubeMapStream.Append( output );
   }
   CubeMapStream.RestartStrip();
 }
}
```

Thus we see that we have rendered the scene to each cube map face by rendering the scene only once instead of six times.

We have summarized the main idea of this sample, but refer to the "CubeMapGS" Direct3D 10 sample for the full source code to fill in any details.

This strategy is interesting and demonstrates simultaneous render targets and the `SV_RenderTargetArrayIndex` system value; however, it is not a definite win. There are two issues that make this method unattractive:

1. It uses the geometry shader to output a large set of data. Recall from Chapter 12 that we mentioned the geometry shader acts inefficiently when outputting a large set of data. Therefore, using a geometry shader for this purpose could hurt performance.

2. In a typical scene, a triangle will not overlap more than one cube map face (see again Figure 18.9). Therefore, the act of replicating a triangle and rendering it onto each cube face when it will be clipped by five out of six of the faces is wasteful. Admittedly, our demo for this chapter also renders the entire scene to each cube map face for simplicity. However, in real applications (non-demo), we would use frustum culling (Chapter 16), and only render the objects visible to a particular cube map face. Frustum culling at the object level cannot be done by a geometry shader implementation.

On the other hand, a situation where this strategy does work well would be rendering a mesh that surrounds the scene. For example, suppose that you had a dynamic sky system where the clouds moved and the sky color changed based on the time of day. Because the sky is changing, we cannot use a prebaked cube map texture to reflect the sky, so we have to use a dynamic cube map. Since the sky mesh surrounds the entire scene, it *is visible by all six* cube map faces. Therefore, the second bullet point above does not apply, and the geometry shader method could be a win by reducing draw calls from six to one, assuming usage of the geometry shader does not hurt performance too much.

Note: *Recent optimizations available in NVIDIA's Maxwell architecture enables geometry to be replicated to multiple render targets with without the penalties of using a geometry shader (see http://docs.nvidia.com/gameworks/content/gameworkslibrary/graphicssamples/opengl_samples/cascadedshadowmapping.htm, which uses the Viewport Multicast and Fast Geometry Shader features). At the time of this writing, these features are not exposed by Direct3D 12, but will probably be in a future update.*

18.7 SUMMARY

1. A cube map consists of six textures that we visualize as the faces of a cube. In Direct3D 12, a cube map can be represented by the `ID3D12Resource` interface as a texture array with six elements. In the HLSL, a cube map is represented by the `TextureCube` type. To identify a texel in a cube map, we use 3D texture coordinates, which define a 3D *lookup* vector **v** originating at the center of the cube map. The texel of the cube map that **v** intersects is the texel corresponding to the 3D coordinates of **v**.

2. An environment map captures the surrounding environment about a point with six images. These images can then be stored in a cube map. With environment maps we can easily texture a sky or approximate reflections.

3. Cube maps can be made from six individual images using the *texassemble* tool. Cube maps can then be saved to file with the DDS image format. Because cube maps store six 2D textures, which can consume a lot of memory, a compressed DDS format should be used.

4. Prebaked cube maps do not capture objects that move or objects in the scene that did not exist when the cube map was generated. To overcome this limitation, we can build the cube map at runtime. That is, every frame you position the camera in the scene that is to be the origin of the cube map, and *then render the scene six times into each cube map* face along each coordinate axis direction. Since the cube map is rebuilt every frame, it will capture animated objects and every object in the environment. Dynamic cube maps are expensive and their use should be minimized to key objects.

5. We can bind a render target view to a texture array to the OM stage. Moreover, we can render to each array slice in the texture array simultaneously. Assigning a triangle to a render target array slice is done by setting the system value `SV_RenderTargetArrayIndex`. A render target view to a texture array, along with the `SV_RenderTargetArrayIndex` system value allows generating a cube map

dynamically by rendering the scene once instead of six times. However, this strategy might not always be a win over rendering the scene six times with frustum culling.

18.8 EXERCISES

1. Experiment with different `FresnelR0` and Roughness material values in the "Cube Map" demo. Also try to make the cylinders and box reflective.
2. Find six image that capture an environment (either find cube map images online or use a program like *Terragen* to make them), and assemble them into a cube map using the *texassemble* tool. Test your cube map out in the "Cube Map" demo.
3. A *dielectric* is a transparent material that refracts light; see Figure 18.11. When a ray strikes a dielectric, some light reflects and some light refracts based on *Snell's Law of Refraction*. The indices of refraction n_1 and n_2 determine how much the light bends:
   1. If $n_1 = n_2$, then $\theta_1 = \theta_2$ (no bending).
   2. If $n_2 > n_1$, then $\theta_2 < \theta_1$ (ray bends toward normal).
   3. If $n_1 > n_2$, then $\theta_2 > \theta_1$ (ray bends away from normal).

   Thus, in Figure 18.11, $n_2 > n_1$ since the ray bends toward the normal when we enter the block. Physically, the light ray refracts again when leaving the block, but for real-time graphics, typically only the first refraction is modeled. The HLSL provides the intrinsic `refract` function to calculate the refraction vector:

   ```
   float3 refract(float3 incident, float3 normal, float eta);
   ```

   The incident vector is the incoming light ray vector ($\mathbf{v}_0$ in Figure 18.10), and the normal vector is the outward surface normal (**n** in Figure 18.10). The third parameter is the ratio of the indices of refraction n_1/n_2. The index of refraction of a vacuum is 1.0; some other index of refactions: water—1.33; glass—1.51. For this exercise, modify the "Cube Map" demo to do refraction instead of reflection (see Figure 18.11); you may need to adjust the `Material::Reflect` values. Try out `eta = 1.0`, `eta = 0.95`, `eta = 0.9`.

Cube Mapping   625

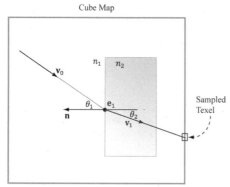

Figure 18.10. The incident vector v0 travels through a medium with index of refraction n_1. The ray strikes a transparent material with index of refraction n_2, and refracts into the vector $\mathbf{v}_1$. We use the refracted vector $\mathbf{v}_1$ as a look up into the cube map. This is almost like alpha blending transparency, except alpha blending transparency does not bend the incident vector.

Figure 18.11. "Cube Demo" with refraction instead of reflection.

4. Just like with specular highlights from light sources, roughness will cause the specular reflections to spread out. Thus rougher surfaces will have blurry reflections as multiple samples from the environment map will average and scatter into the same direction into the eye. Research techniques for modeling blurry reflections with environment maps.

Chapter 19 NORMAL MAPPING

In Chapter 9, we introduced texture mapping, which enabled us to map fine details from an image onto our triangles. However, our normal vectors are still defined at the coarser vertex level and interpolated over the triangle. For part of this chapter, we study a popular method for specifying surface normals at a higher resolution. Specifying surface normals at a higher resolution increases the detail of the lighting, but the mesh geometry detail remains unchanged.

Objectives:

1. To understand why we need normal mapping.
2. To discover how normal maps are stored.
3. To learn how normal maps can be created.
4. To find out the coordinate system the normal vectors in normal maps are stored relative to and how it relates to the object space coordinate system of a 3D triangle.
5. To learn how to implement normal mapping in a vertex and pixel shader.

19.1 MOTIVATION

Consider Figure 19.1 from the Cube Mapping demo of the preceding chapter. The specular highlights on the cone shaped columns do not look right—they look unnaturally smooth compared to the bumpiness of the brick texture. This is because the underlying mesh geometry is smooth, and we have merely applied the image of bumpy bricks over the smooth cylindrical surface. However, the lighting calculations are performed based on the mesh geometry (in particular, the interpolated vertex normals), and not the texture image. Thus the lighting is not completely consistent with the texture.

Ideally, we would tessellate the mesh geometry so much that the actual bumps and crevices of the bricks could be modeled by the underlying geometry. Then the lighting and texture could be made consistent. Hardware tessellation could help in this area, but we still need a way to specify the normals for the vertices generated by the tessellator (using interpolated normals does not increase our normal resolution).

Another possible solution would be to bake the lighting details directly into the textures. However, this will not work if the lights are allowed to move, as the texel colors will remain fixed as the lights move.

Thus our goal is to find a way to implement dynamic lighting such that the fine details that show up in the texture map also show up in the lighting. Since textures provide us with the fine details to begin with, it is natural to look for a texture mapping solution to this problem. Figure 19.2 shows the same scene shown in Figure 19.1 with normal mapping; we can see now that the dynamic lighting is much more consistent with the brick texture.

Figure 19.1. Smooth specular highlights.

Figure 19.2. Bumpy specular highlights.

19.2 NORMAL MAPS

A *normal map* is a texture, but instead of storing RGB data at each texel, we store a compressed *x*-coordinate, *y*-coordinate, and *z*-coordinate in the red component, green component, and blue component, respectively. These coordinates define a normal vector; thus a normal map stores a normal vector at each pixel. Figure 19.3 shows an example of how to visualize a normal map.

For illustration, we will assume a 24-bit image format, which reserves a byte for each color component, and therefore, each color component can range from 0-255. (A 32-bit format could be employed where the alpha component goes unused or stores some other scalar value such as a heightmap or specular map. Also, a floating-point format could be used in which no compression is necessary, but this requires more memory.)

Note: As Figure 19.3 shows, the vectors are generally mostly aligned with the *z*-axis. That is, the *z*-coordinate has the largest magnitude. Consequently, normal maps usually appear mostly blue when viewed as a color image. This is because the *z*-coordinate is stored in the blue channel and since it has the largest magnitude, this color dominates.

So how do we compress a unit vector into this format? First note that for a unit vector, each coordinate always lies in the range $[-1, 1]$. If we shift and scale this range to $[0, 1]$ and multiply by 255 and truncate the decimal, the result will be an integer in the range 0-255. That is, if x is a coordinate in the range $[-1, 1]$, then the integer part of $f(x)$ is an integer in the range 0-255, where f is defined by

$$f(x) = (0.5x + 0.5) \cdot 255$$

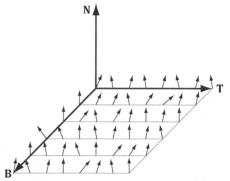

Figure 19.3. Normals stored in a normal map relative to a texture space coordinate system defined by the vectors **T** (*x*-axis), **B** (*y*-axis), and **N** (*z*-axis). The **T** vector runs right horizontally to the texture image; the **B** vector runs down vertically to the texture image; and **N** is orthogonal to the texture plane.

So to store a unit vector in 24-bit image, we just apply f to each coordinate and write the coordinate to the corresponding color channel in the texture map.

The next question is how to reverse the compression process; that is, given a compressed texture coordinate in the range 0-255, how can we recover its true value in the interval $[-1, 1]$. The answer is to simply invert the function f, which after a little thought, can be seen to be:

$$f^{-1}(x) = \frac{2x}{255} - 1$$

That is, if x is an integer in the range 0-255, then $f^{-1}(x)$ is a floating-point number in the range $[-1, 1]$.

We will not have to do the compression process ourselves, as we will use a Photoshop plug-in to convert images to normal maps. However, when we sample a normal map in a pixel shader, we will have to do part of the inverse process to uncompress it. When we sample a normal map in a shader like this:

```
float3 normalT = gNormalMap.Sample( gTriLinearSam, pin.Tex );
```

The color vector `normalT` will have normalized components (r, g, b) such that $0 \leq r, g, b \leq 1$.

Thus, the method has already done part of the uncompressing work for us (namely the divide by 255, which transforms an integer in the range 0-255 to the floating-point interval $[0, 1]$). We complete the transformation by shifting and scaling each component in $[0, 1]$ to $[-1, 1]$ with the function $g: [0, 1] \to [-1, 1]$ defined by:

$$g(x) = 2x - 1$$

In code, we apply this function to each color component like this:

```
// Uncompress each component from [0,1] to [-1,1].
    normalT = 2.0f*normalT - 1.0f;
```

This works because the scalar 1.0 is augmented to the vector (1, 1, 1) so that the expression makes sense and is done componentwise.

Note: The Photoshop plug-in is available at http://developer.nvidia.com/nvidia-texture-tools-adobe-photoshop. There are other tools available for generating normal maps such as http://www.crazybump.com/ and http://shadermap.com/home/. Also, there are tools that can generate normal maps from high resolution meshes (see http://www.nvidia.com/object/melody_home.html).

If you want to use a compressed texture format to store normal maps, then use the BC7 (`DXGI_FORMAT_BC7_UNORM`) format for the best quality, as it significantly reduces the errors caused by compressing normal maps. For BC6 and BC7 formats, the

DirectX SDK has a sample called "BC6HBC7EncoderDecoder11." This program can be used to convert your texture files to `BC6` or `BC7`.

19.3 TEXTURE/TANGENT SPACE

Consider a 3D texture mapped triangle. For the sake of discussion, suppose that there is no distortion in the texture mapping; in other words, mapping the texture triangle onto the 3D triangle requires only a rigid body transformation (translation and rotation). Now, suppose that the texture is like a decal. So we pick the decal up, translate it, and rotate it onto the 3D triangle. Now Figure 19.4 shows how the texture space axes relate to the 3D triangle: they are tangent to the triangle and lie in the plane of the triangle. The texture coordinates of the triangle are, of course, relative to the texture space coordinate system. Incorporating the triangle face normal **N**, we obtain a 3D *TBN-basis* in the plane of the triangle that we call *texture space* or *tangent space*. Note that the tangent space generally varies from triangle-to-triangle (see Figure 19.5).

Now, as Figure 19.3 shows, the normal vectors in a normal map are defined relative to the texture space. But our lights are defined in world space. In order to do lighting, the normal vectors and lights need to be in the same space. So our first step is to relate the tangent space coordinate system with the object space coordinate system the triangle vertices are relative to. Once we are in object space, we can use the world matrix to get from object space to world space (the details of this are covered in the next section). Let $\mathbf{v}_0$, $\mathbf{v}_1$, and $\mathbf{v}_2$ define the three vertices of a 3D triangle with corresponding texture coordinates (u_0, v_0), (u_1, v_1), and

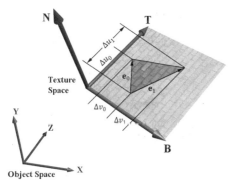

Figure 19.4. The relationship between the texture space of a triangle and the object space. The 3D tangent vector **T** aims in the *u*-axis direction of the texturing coordinate system, and the 3D tangent vector **B** aims in the *v*-axis direction of the texturing coordinate system.

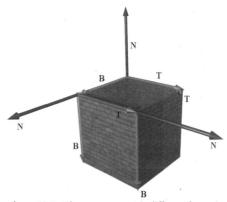

Figure 19.5. The texture space is different for each face of the box.

(u_2, v_2) that define a triangle in the texture plane relative to the texture space axes (i.e., **T** and **B**). Let $\mathbf{e}_0 = \mathbf{v}_1 - \mathbf{v}_0$ and $\mathbf{e}_1 = \mathbf{v}_2 - \mathbf{v}_0$ be two edge vectors of the 3D triangle with corresponding texture triangle edge vectors $(\Delta u_0, \Delta v_0) = (u_1 - u_0, v_1 - v_0)$ and $(\Delta u_1, \Delta v_1) = (u_2 - u_0, v_2 - v_0)$. From Figure 19.4, it is clear that

$$\mathbf{e}_0 = \Delta u_0 \mathbf{T} + \Delta v_0 \mathbf{B}$$
$$\mathbf{e}_1 = \Delta u_1 \mathbf{T} + \Delta v_1 \mathbf{B}$$

Representing the vectors with coordinates relative to object space, we get the matrix equation:

$$\begin{bmatrix} e_{0,x} & e_{0,y} & e_{0,z} \\ e_{1,x} & e_{1,y} & e_{1,z} \end{bmatrix} = \begin{bmatrix} \Delta u_0 & \Delta v_0 \\ \Delta u_1 & \Delta v_1 \end{bmatrix} \begin{bmatrix} T_x & T_y & T_z \\ B_x & B_y & B_z \end{bmatrix}$$

Note that we know the object space coordinates of the triangle vertices; hence we know the object space coordinates of the edge vectors, so the matrix

$$\begin{bmatrix} e_{0,x} & e_{0,y} & e_{0,z} \\ e_{1,x} & e_{1,y} & e_{1,z} \end{bmatrix}$$

is known. Likewise, we know the texture coordinates, so the matrix

$$\begin{bmatrix} \Delta u_0 & \Delta v_0 \\ \Delta u_1 & \Delta v_1 \end{bmatrix}$$

is known. Solving for the **T** and **B** object space coordinates we get:

$$\begin{bmatrix} T_x & T_y & T_z \\ B_x & B_y & B_z \end{bmatrix} = \begin{bmatrix} \Delta u_0 & \Delta v_0 \\ \Delta u_1 & \Delta v_1 \end{bmatrix}^{-1} \begin{bmatrix} e_{0,x} & e_{0,y} & e_{0,z} \\ e_{1,x} & e_{1,y} & e_{1,z} \end{bmatrix}$$

$$= \frac{1}{\Delta u_0 \Delta v_1 - \Delta v_0 \Delta u_1} \begin{bmatrix} \Delta v_1 & -\Delta v_0 \\ -\Delta u_1 & \Delta u_0 \end{bmatrix} \begin{bmatrix} e_{0,x} & e_{0,y} & e_{0,z} \\ e_{1,x} & e_{1,y} & e_{1,z} \end{bmatrix}$$

In the above, we used the fact that the inverse of a matrix $\mathbf{A} = \begin{bmatrix} a & b \\ c & d \end{bmatrix}$ is given by:

$$\mathbf{A}^{-1} = \frac{1}{ad - bc} \begin{bmatrix} d & -b \\ -c & a \end{bmatrix}$$

Note that the vectors **T** and **B** are generally not unit length in object space, and if there is texture distortion, they will not be orthonormal either.

The **T**, **B**, and **N** vectors are commonly referred to as the *tangent*, *binormal* (or *bitangent*), and *normal* vectors, respectively.

19.4 VERTEX TANGENT SPACE

In the previous section, we derived a tangent space per triangle. However, if we use this texture space for normal mapping, we will get a triangulated appearance since the tangent space is constant over the face of the triangle. Therefore, we specify tangent vectors per vertex, and we do the same averaging trick that we did with vertex normals to approximate a smooth surface:

1. The tangent vector **T** for an arbitrary vertex **v** in a mesh is found by averaging the tangent vectors of every triangle in the mesh that shares the vertex **v**.

2. The bitangent vector **B** for an arbitrary vertex **v** in a mesh is found by averaging the bitangent vectors of every triangle in the mesh that shares the vertex **v**.

Generally, after averaging, the TBN-bases will generally need to be orthonormalized, so that the vectors are mutually orthogonal and of unit length. This is usually done using the Gram-Schmidt procedure. Code is available on the web for building a per-vertex tangent space for an arbitrary triangle mesh: *http://www.terathon.com/code/tangent.html*.

In our system, we will not store the bitangent vector **B** directly in memory. Instead, we will compute $\mathbf{B} = \mathbf{N} \times \mathbf{T}$ when we need **B**, where **N** is the usual averaged vertex normal. Hence, our vertex structure looks like this:

```
struct Vertex
{
  XMFLOAT3 Pos;
  XMFLOAT3 Normal;
  XMFLOAT2 Tex;
  XMFLOAT3 TangentU;
};
```

Recall that our procedurally generated meshes created by `GeometryGenerator` compute the tangent vector **T** corresponding to the *u*-axis of the texture space. The object space coordinates of the tangent vector **T** is easily specified at each vertex for box and grid meshes (see Figure 19.5). For cylinders and spheres, the tangent vector **T** at each vertex can be found by forming the vector-valued function of two variables $\mathbf{P}(u, v)$ of the cylinder/sphere and computing $\partial \mathbf{p}/\partial u$, where the parameter u is also used as the *u*-texture coordinate.

19.5 TRANSFORMING BETWEEN TANGENT SPACE AND OBJECT SPACE

At this point, we have an orthonormal TBN-basis at each vertex in a mesh. Moreover, we have the coordinates of the TBN vectors relative to the object space of the mesh. So now that we have the coordinate of the TBN-basis relative to the object space coordinate system, we can transform coordinates from tangent space to object space with the matrix:

$$\mathbf{M}_{object} = \begin{bmatrix} T_x & T_y & T_z \\ B_x & B_y & B_z \\ N_x & N_y & N_z \end{bmatrix}$$

Since this matrix is orthogonal, its inverse is its transpose. Thus, the change of coordinate matrix from object space to tangent space is:

$$\mathbf{M}_{tangent} = \mathbf{M}_{object}^{-1} = \mathbf{M}_{object}^{T} = \begin{bmatrix} T_x & B_x & N_x \\ T_y & B_y & N_y \\ T_z & B_z & N_z \end{bmatrix}$$

In our shader program, we will actually want to transform the normal vector from tangent space to world space for lighting. One way would be to transform the normal from tangent space to object space first, and then use the world matrix to transform from object space to world space:

$$\mathbf{n}_{world} = \left(\mathbf{n}_{tangent} \mathbf{M}_{object} \right) \mathbf{M}_{world}$$

However, since matrix multiplication is associative, we can do it like this:

$$\mathbf{n}_{world} = \mathbf{n}_{tangent} \left(\mathbf{M}_{object} \mathbf{M}_{world} \right)$$

And note that

$$\mathbf{M}_{object} \mathbf{M}_{world} = \begin{bmatrix} \leftarrow \mathbf{T} \rightarrow \\ \leftarrow \mathbf{B} \rightarrow \\ \leftarrow \mathbf{N} \rightarrow \end{bmatrix} \mathbf{M}_{world} = \begin{bmatrix} \leftarrow \mathbf{T}' \rightarrow \\ \leftarrow \mathbf{B}' \rightarrow \\ \leftarrow \mathbf{N}' \rightarrow \end{bmatrix} = \begin{bmatrix} T'_x & T'_y & T'_z \\ B'_x & B'_y & B'_z \\ N'_x & N'_y & N'_z \end{bmatrix}$$

where $\mathbf{T}' = \mathbf{T} \cdot \mathbf{M}_{world}$, $\mathbf{B}' = \mathbf{B} \cdot \mathbf{M}_{world}$, and $\mathbf{N}' = \mathbf{N} \cdot \mathbf{M}_{world}$. So to go from tangent space directly to world space, we just have to describe the tangent basis in world coordinates, which can be done by transforming the TBN-basis from object space coordinates to world space coordinates.

We will only be interested in transforming vectors (not points). Thus, we only need a 3×3 matrix. Recall that the fourth row of an affine matrix is for translation, but we do not translate vectors.

19.6 NORMAL MAPPING SHADER CODE

We summarize the general process for normal mapping:

1. Create the desired normal maps from some art program or utility program and store them in an image file. Create 2D textures from these files when the program is initialized.
2. For each triangle, compute the tangent vector **T**. Obtain a per-vertex tangent vector for each vertex **v** in a mesh by averaging the tangent vectors of every triangle in the mesh that shares the vertex **v**. (In our demo, we use simply geometry and are able to specify the tangent vectors directly, but this averaging process would need to be done if using arbitrary triangle meshes made in a 3D modeling program.)
3. In the vertex shader, transform the vertex normal and tangent vector to world space and output the results to the pixel shader.
4. Using the interpolated tangent vector and normal vector, we build the TBN-basis at each pixel point on the surface of the triangle. We use this basis to transform the sampled normal vector from the normal map from tangent space to the world space. We then have a world space normal vector from the normal map to use for our usual lighting calculations.

To help us implement normal mapping, we have added the following function to *Common.hlsl*:

```
//---------------------------------------------------------------
// Transforms a normal map sample to world space.
//---------------------------------------------------------------
float3 NormalSampleToWorldSpace(float3 normalMapSample,
               float3 unitNormalW,
               float3 tangentW)
{
    // Uncompress each component from [0,1] to [-1,1].
    float3 normalT = 2.0f*normalMapSample - 1.0f;

    // Build orthonormal basis.
    float3 N = unitNormalW;
    float3 T = normalize(tangentW - dot(tangentW, N)*N);
    float3 B = cross(N, T);

    float3x3 TBN = float3x3(T, B, N);

    // Transform from tangent space to world space.
    float3 bumpedNormalW = mul(normalT, TBN);

    return bumpedNormalW;
}
```

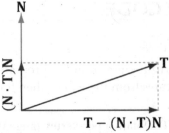

Figure 19.6. Since $||\mathbf{N}||=1$, $\text{proj}_\mathbf{N}(\mathbf{T}) = (\mathbf{T}\cdot\mathbf{N})\mathbf{N}$. The vector $\mathbf{T}\text{-proj}_\mathbf{N}(\mathbf{T})$ is the portion of $\mathbf{T}$ orthogonal to $\mathbf{N}$.

This function is used like this in the pixel shader:

```
float3 normalMapSample = gNormalMap.Sample(samLinear, pin.Tex).rgb;
float3 bumpedNormalW = NormalSampleToWorldSpace(
normalMapSample,
pin.NormalW,
pin.TangentW);
```

Two lines that might not be clear are these:

```
float3 N = unitNormalW;
float3 T = normalize(tangentW - dot(tangentW, N)*N);
```

After the interpolation, the tangent vector and normal vector may not be orthonormal. This code makes sure **T** is orthonormal to **N** by subtracting off any component of **T** along the direction **N** (see Figure 19.6). Note that there is the assumption that `unitNormalW` is normalized.

Once we have the normal from the normal map, which we call the "bumped normal," we use it for all the subsequent calculation involving the normal vector (e.g., lighting, cube mapping). The entire normal mapping effect is shown below for completeness, with the parts relevant to normal mapping in bold.

```
//***************************************************************
// Default.hlsl by Frank Luna (C) 2015 All Rights Reserved.
//***************************************************************

// Defaults for number of lights.
#ifndef NUM_DIR_LIGHTS
    #define NUM_DIR_LIGHTS 3
#endif

#ifndef NUM_POINT_LIGHTS
    #define NUM_POINT_LIGHTS 0
#endif

#ifndef NUM_SPOT_LIGHTS
    #define NUM_SPOT_LIGHTS 0
#endif

// Include common HLSL code.
```

```
#include "Common.hlsl"

struct VertexIn
{
    float3 PosL     : POSITION;
    float3 NormalL  : NORMAL;
    float2 TexC     : TEXCOORD;
    float3 TangentU : TANGENT;
};

struct VertexOut
{
    float4 PosH     : SV_POSITION;
    float3 PosW     : POSITION;
    float3 NormalW  : NORMAL;
    float3 TangentW : TANGENT;
    float2 TexC     : TEXCOORD;
};

VertexOut VS(VertexIn vin)
{
    VertexOut vout = (VertexOut)0.0f;

    // Fetch the material data.
    MaterialData matData = gMaterialData[gMaterialIndex];

    // Transform to world space.
    float4 posW = mul(float4(vin.PosL, 1.0f), gWorld);
    vout.PosW = posW.xyz;

    // Assumes nonuniform scaling; otherwise, need to use
    // inverse-transpose of world matrix.
    vout.NormalW = mul(vin.NormalL, (float3x3)gWorld);

    vout.TangentW = mul(vin.TangentU, (float3x3)gWorld);

    // Transform to homogeneous clip space.
    vout.PosH = mul(posW, gViewProj);

    // Output vertex attributes for interpolation across triangle.
    float4 texC = mul(float4(vin.TexC, 0.0f, 1.0f), gTexTransform);
    vout.TexC = mul(texC, matData.MatTransform).xy;

    return vout;
}

float4 PS(VertexOut pin) : SV_Target
{
    // Fetch the material data.
    MaterialData matData = gMaterialData[gMaterialIndex];
    float4 diffuseAlbedo = matData.DiffuseAlbedo;
    float3 fresnelR0 = matData.FresnelR0;
    float  roughness = matData.Roughness;
    uint diffuseMapIndex = matData.DiffuseMapIndex;
```

```
uint normalMapIndex = matData.NormalMapIndex;

// Interpolating normal can unnormalize it, so renormalize it.
pin.NormalW = normalize(pin.NormalW);

float4 normalMapSample = gTextureMaps[normalMapIndex].Sample(
  gsamAnisotropicWrap, pin.TexC);
float3 bumpedNormalW = NormalSampleToWorldSpace(
  normalMapSample.rgb, pin.NormalW, pin.TangentW);

// Uncomment to turn off normal mapping.
//bumpedNormalW = pin.NormalW;

// Dynamically look up the texture in the array.
diffuseAlbedo *= gTextureMaps[diffuseMapIndex].Sample(
  gsamAnisotropicWrap, pin.TexC);

// Vector from point being lit to eye.
float3 toEyeW = normalize(gEyePosW - pin.PosW);

// Light terms.
float4 ambient = gAmbientLight*diffuseAlbedo;

// Alpha channel stores shininess at per-pixel level.
const float shininess = (1.0f - roughness) * normalMapSample.a;
Material mat = { diffuseAlbedo, fresnelR0, shininess };
float3 shadowFactor = 1.0f;
float4 directLight = ComputeLighting(gLights, mat, pin.PosW,
  bumpedNormalW, toEyeW, shadowFactor);

float4 litColor = ambient + directLight;

// Add in specular reflections.
float3 r = reflect(-toEyeW, bumpedNormalW);
float4 reflectionColor = gCubeMap.Sample(gsamLinearWrap, r);
float3 fresnelFactor = SchlickFresnel(fresnelR0, bumpedNormalW, r);
litColor.rgb += shininess * fresnelFactor * reflectionColor.rgb;

// Common convention to take alpha from diffuse albedo.
litColor.a = diffuseAlbedo.a;

return litColor;
}
```

Observe that the "bumped normal" vector is use in the light calculation, but also in the reflection calculation for modeling reflections from the environment map. In addition, in the alpha channel of the normal map we store a shininess mask, which controls the shininess at a per-pixel level (see Figure 19.7).

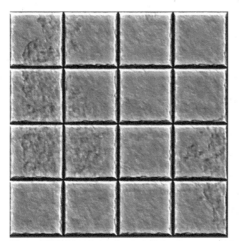

Figure 19.7. The alpha channel of the *tile_nmap.dds* image from the book's DVD. The alpha channel denotes the shininess of the surface. White values indicate a shininess value of 1.0 and black values indicate a shininess value of 0.0. This gives us per-pixel control of the shininess material property.

19.7 SUMMARY

1. The strategy of normal mapping is to texture our polygons with normal maps. We then have per-pixel normals, which capture the fine details of a surface like bumps, scratches, and crevices. We then use these per-pixel normals from the normal map in our lighting calculations, instead of the interpolated vertex normal.

2. A normal map is a texture, but instead of storing RGB data at each texel, we store a compressed *x*-coordinate, *y*-coordinate, and *z*-coordinate in the red component, green component, and blue component, respectively. We use various tools to generate normal maps such as the ones located at *http://developer.nvidia.com/nvidia-texture-tools-adobe-photoshop*, *http://www.crazybump.com/*, and *http://shadermap.com/home/*.

3. The coordinates of the normals in a normal map are relative to the texture space coordinate system. Consequently, to do lighting calculations, we need to transform the normal from the texture space to the world space so that the lights and normals are in the same coordinate system. The TBN-bases built at each vertex facilitates the transformation from texture space to world space.

19.8 EXERCISES

1. Download the NVIDIA normal map plug-in (*http://developer.nvidia.com/object/nv_texture_tools.html*) and experiment with making different normal maps with it. Try your normal maps out in this chapter's demo application.

2. Download the trial version of *CrazyBump* (*http://www.crazybump.com/*). Load a color image, and experiment making a normal and displacement map. Try your maps in this chapter's demo application.

3. If you apply a rotation texture transformation, then you need to rotate the tangent space coordinate system accordingly. Explain why. In particular, this means you need to rotate **T** about **N** in world space, which will require expensive trigonometric calculations (more precisely, a rotation transform about an arbitrary axis **N**). Another solution is to transform **T** from world space to tangent space, where you can use the texture transformation matrix directly to rotate **T**, and then transform back to world space.

4. Instead of doing lighting in world space, we can transform the eye and light vector from world space into tangent space and do all the lighting calculations in that space. Modify the normal mapping shader to do the lighting calculations in tangent space.

5. The idea of displacement mapping is to utilize an additional map, called a *heightmap*, which describes the bumps and crevices of a surface. Often it is combined with hardware tessellation, where it indicates how newly added vertices should be offset in the normal vector direction to add geometric detail to the mesh. Displacement mapping can be used to implement ocean waves. The idea is to scroll two (or more) heightmaps over a flat vertex grid at different speeds and directions. For each vertex of the grid, we sample the heightmaps, and add the heights together; the summed height becomes the height (i.e., *y*-coordinate) of the vertex at this instance in time. By scrolling the heightmaps, waves continuously form and fade away giving the illusion of ocean waves (see Figure 19.8). For this exercise, implement the ocean wave effect just described using the two ocean wave heightmaps (and corresponding normal maps) available to download for this chapter (Figure 19.9). Here are a few hints to making the waves look good:

    (a) Tile the heightmaps differently so that one set can be used to model broad low frequency waves with high amplitude and the other can be used to model high frequency small choppy waves with low amplitude. So you will need two sets of texture coordinates for the heightmaps maps and two texture transformations for the heightmaps.

(b) The normal map textures should be tiled more than the heightmap textures. The heightmaps give the shape of the waves, and the normal maps are used to light the waves per pixel. As with the heightmaps, the normal maps should translate over time and in different directions to give the illusion of new waves forming and fading. The two normals can then be combined using code similar to the following:

```
float3 normalMapSample0 = gNormalMap0.Sample(samLinear, pin.WaveNormalTex0).rgb;
float3 bumpedNormalW0 = NormalSampleToWorldSpace(
normalMapSample0, pin.NormalW, pin.TangentW);

float3 normalMapSample1 = gNormalMap1.Sample(samLinear, pin.WaveNormalTex1).rgb;
float3 bumpedNormalW1 = NormalSampleToWorldSpace(
normalMapSample1, pin.NormalW, pin.TangentW);

float3 bumpedNormalW = normalize(bumpedNormalW0 + bumpedNormalW1);
```

(c) Modify the waves' material to make it more ocean blue, and keep some reflection in from the environment map.

Figure 19.8. Ocean waves modeled with heightmaps, normal maps, and environment mapping.

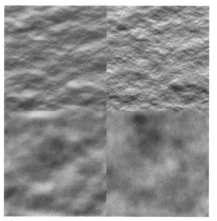

Figure 19.9. (Top Row) Ocean waves normal map and heightmap for high frequency choppy waves. (Bottom Row) Ocean waves normal map and heightmap for low frequency broad waves

Chapter 20 Shadow Mapping

Shadows indicate to the observer where light originates and helps convey the relative locations of objects in a scene. This chapter provides an introduction to the basic shadow mapping algorithm, which is a popular method for modeling dynamic shadows in games and 3D applications. For an introductory book, we focus only on the basic shadow mapping algorithm; more sophisticated shadowing techniques, such as cascading shadow maps [Engel06] which give better quality results, are built by extending the basic shadow mapping algorithm.

Objectives:

1. To discover the basic shadow mapping algorithm.
2. To learn how projective texturing works.
3. To find out about orthographic projections.
4. To understand shadow map aliasing problems and common strategies for fixing them.

20.1 RENDERING SCENE DEPTH

The shadow mapping algorithm relies on rendering the scene depth from the viewpoint of the light source—this is essentially a variation of render-to-texture, which was first described in §13.7.2. By "rendering scene depth" we mean building the depth buffer from the viewpoint of the light source. Thus, after we have rendered the scene from the viewpoint of the light source, we will know the pixel fragments nearest to the light source—such fragments cannot be in shadow. In this section we review a utility class called ShadowMap that helps us store the scene depth from the perspective of the light source. It simply encapsulates a depth/stencil buffer, necessary views, and viewport. A depth/stencil buffer used for shadow mapping is called a *shadow map*.

```
class ShadowMap
{
public:
  ShadowMap(ID3D12Device* device,
    UINT width, UINT height);

  ShadowMap(const ShadowMap& rhs)=delete;
  ShadowMap& operator=(const ShadowMap& rhs)=delete;
  ~ShadowMap()=default;

  UINT Width()const;
  UINT Height()const;
  ID3D12Resource* Resource();
  CD3DX12_GPU_DESCRIPTOR_HANDLE Srv()const;
  CD3DX12_CPU_DESCRIPTOR_HANDLE Dsv()const;

  D3D12_VIEWPORT Viewport()const;
  D3D12_RECT ScissorRect()const;

  void BuildDescriptors(
    CD3DX12_CPU_DESCRIPTOR_HANDLE hCpuSrv,
    CD3DX12_GPU_DESCRIPTOR_HANDLE hGpuSrv,
    CD3DX12_CPU_DESCRIPTOR_HANDLE hCpuDsv);

  void OnResize(UINT newWidth, UINT newHeight);

private:
  void BuildDescriptors();
```

```
    void BuildResource();

private:

    ID3D12Device* md3dDevice = nullptr;

    D3D12_VIEWPORT mViewport;
    D3D12_RECT mScissorRect;

    UINT mWidth = 0;
    UINT mHeight = 0;
    DXGI_FORMAT mFormat = DXGI_FORMAT_R24G8_TYPELESS;

    CD3DX12_CPU_DESCRIPTOR_HANDLE mhCpuSrv;
    CD3DX12_GPU_DESCRIPTOR_HANDLE mhGpuSrv;
    CD3DX12_CPU_DESCRIPTOR_HANDLE mhCpuDsv;

    Microsoft::WRL::ComPtr<ID3D12Resource> mShadowMap = nullptr;
};
```

The constructor creates the texture of the specified dimensions and viewport. The resolution of the shadow map affects the quality of our shadows, but at the same time, a high resolution shadow map is more expensive to render into and requires more memory.

```
ShadowMap::ShadowMap(ID3D12Device* device, UINT width, UINT height)
{
    md3dDevice = device;

    mWidth = width;
    mHeight = height;

    mViewport = { 0.0f, 0.0f, (float)width, (float)height, 0.0f, 1.0f };
    mScissorRect = { 0, 0, (int)width, (int)height };

    BuildResource();
}

void ShadowMap::BuildResource()
{
    D3D12_RESOURCE_DESC texDesc;
    ZeroMemory(&texDesc, sizeof(D3D12_RESOURCE_DESC));
    texDesc.Dimension = D3D12_RESOURCE_DIMENSION_TEXTURE2D;
    texDesc.Alignment = 0;
    texDesc.Width = mWidth;
    texDesc.Height = mHeight;
    texDesc.DepthOrArraySize = 1;
```

```
texDesc.MipLevels = 1;
texDesc.Format = mFormat;
texDesc.SampleDesc.Count = 1;
texDesc.SampleDesc.Quality = 0;
texDesc.Layout = D3D12_TEXTURE_LAYOUT_UNKNOWN;
texDesc.Flags = D3D12_RESOURCE_FLAG_ALLOW_DEPTH_STENCIL;

D3D12_CLEAR_VALUE optClear;
optClear.Format = DXGI_FORMAT_D24_UNORM_S8_UINT;
optClear.DepthStencil.Depth = 1.0f;
optClear.DepthStencil.Stencil = 0;

ThrowIfFailed(md3dDevice->CreateCommittedResource(
    &CD3DX12_HEAP_PROPERTIES(D3D12_HEAP_TYPE_DEFAULT),
    D3D12_HEAP_FLAG_NONE,
    &texDesc,
    D3D12_RESOURCE_STATE_GENERIC_READ,
    &optClear,
    IID_PPV_ARGS(&mShadowMap)));
}
```

As we will see, the shadow mapping algorithm requires two render passes. In the first one, we render the scene depth from the viewpoint of the light into the shadow map; in the second pass, we render the scene as normal to the back buffer from our "player" camera, but use the shadow map as a shader input to implement the shadowing algorithm. We provide a method to access the shader resource and its views:

```
ID3D12Resource* ShadowMap::Resource()
{
  return mShadowMap.Get();
}

CD3DX12_GPU_DESCRIPTOR_HANDLE ShadowMap::Srv()const
{
   return mhGpuSrv;
}

CD3DX12_CPU_DESCRIPTOR_HANDLE ShadowMap::Dsv()const
{
   return mhCpuDsv;
}
```

20.2 ORTHOGRAPHIC PROJECTIONS

So far in this book we have been using a perspective projection. The key property of perspective projection is that objects are perceived as getting smaller as their distance from the eye increases. This agrees with how we perceive things in real life. Another type of projection is an orthographic projection. Such projections

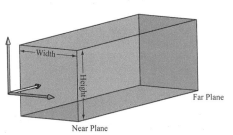

Figure 20.1. The orthographic viewing volume is a box that is axis aligned with the view coordinate system.

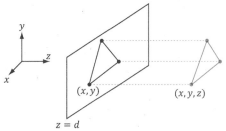

Figure 20.2. The orthographic projection of points onto the projection plane. The lines of projection are parallel to the view space z-axis with an orthographic projection.

are primarily used in 3D science or engineering applications, where it is desirable to have parallel lines remain parallel after projection. However, orthographic projections will enable us to model shadows that parallel lights generate. With an orthographic projection, the viewing volume is a box axis-aligned with the view space with width w, height h, near plane n and far plane f that looks down the positive z-axis of view space (see Figure 20.1). These numbers, defined relative to the view space coordinate system, define the box view volume.

With an orthographic projection, the lines of projection are parallel to the view space z-axis (Figure 20.2). And we see that the 2D projection of a vertex (x, y, z) is just (x, y).

As with perspective projection, we want to maintain relative depth information, and we want normalized device coordinates. To transform the view volume from view space to NDC space, we need to rescale and shift to map the view space view volume $\left[-\frac{w}{2}, \frac{w}{2}\right] \times \left[-\frac{h}{2}, \frac{h}{2}\right] \times [n, f]$ to the NDC space view volume $[-1, 1] \times [-1, 1] \times [0, 1]$. We can determine this mapping by working coordinate-by-coordinate. For the first two coordinates, it is easy to see that the intervals differ only by a scaling factor:

$$\frac{2}{w} \cdot \left[-\frac{w}{2}, \frac{w}{2}\right] = [-1, 1]$$

$$\frac{2}{h} \cdot \left[-\frac{h}{2}, \frac{h}{2}\right] = [-1, 1]$$

For the third coordinate, we need to map $[n, f] \to [0, 1]$. We assume the mapping takes the form $g(z) = az + b$ (i.e., a scaling and translation). We have the conditions $g(n) = 0$ and $g(f) = 1$, which allow us to solve for a and b:

$$an + b = 0$$
$$af + b = 1$$

The first equation implies $b = -an$. Plugging this into the second equation we get:

$$af - an = 1$$

$$a = \frac{1}{f - n}$$

And so:

$$-\frac{n}{f - n} = b$$

Thus,

$$g(z) = \frac{z}{f - n} - \frac{n}{f - n}$$

The reader may wish to graph $g(z)$ over the domain $[n, f]$ for various n and f such that $f > n$.

Finally, the orthographic transformation from view space coordinates (x, y, z) to NDC space coordinates (x', y', z') is:

$$x' = \frac{2}{w} x$$

$$y' = \frac{2}{h} y$$

$$z' = \frac{z}{f - n} - \frac{n}{f - n}$$

Or in terms of matrices:

$$[x', y', z', 1] = [x, y, z, 1] \begin{bmatrix} \frac{2}{w} & 0 & 0 & 0 \\ 0 & \frac{2}{h} & 0 & 0 \\ 0 & 0 & \frac{1}{f - n} & 0 \\ 0 & 0 & \frac{n}{n - f} & 1 \end{bmatrix}$$

The 4 × 4 matrix in the above equation is the *orthographic projection matrix*.

Recall that with the perspective projection transform, we had to split it into two parts: a linear part described by the projection matrix, and a nonlinear part described by the divide by w. In contrast, the orthographic projection transformation is completely linear—there is no divide by w. Multiplying by the orthographic projection matrix takes us directly into NDC coordinates.

20.3 PROJECTIVE TEXTURE COORDINATES

Projective texturing is so called because it allows us to project a texture onto arbitrary geometry, much like a slide projector. Figure 20.3 shows an example of projective texturing.

Projective texturing can be useful on its own for modeling slide projector lights, but as we will see in §20.4, it is also used as an intermediate step for shadow mapping.

The key to projective texturing is to generate texture coordinates for each pixel in such a way that the applied texture looks like it has been projected onto the geometry. We will call such generated texture coordinates *projective texture coordinates*.

From Figure 20.4, we see that the texture coordinates (u, v) identify the texel that should be projected onto the 3D point **p**. But the coordinates (u, v) precisely identify the projection of **p** on the projection window, relative to a texture space coordinate system on the projection window. So the strategy of generating projective texture coordinates is as follows:

1. Project the point **p** onto the light's projection window and transform the coordinates to NDC space.
2. Transform the projected coordinates from NDC space to texture space, thereby effectively turning them into texture coordinates.

Step 1 can be implemented by thinking of the light projector as a camera. We define a view matrix **V** and projection matrix **P** for the light projector. Together, these matrices essentially define the position, orientation, and frustum of the light projector in the world. The matrix **V** transforms coordinates from world space to

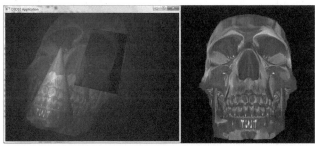

Figure 20.3. The skull texture (right) is projected onto the scene geometry (left).

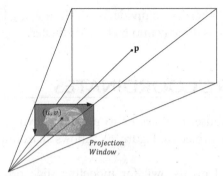

Figure 20.4. The texel identified by the coordinates (u, v) relative to the texture space on the projection window is projected onto the point **p** by following the line of sight from the light origin to the point **p**.

the coordinate system of the light projector. Once the coordinates are relative to the light coordinate system, the projection matrix, along with the homogeneous divide, are used to project the vertices onto the projection plane of the light. Recall from §5.6.3.5 that after the homogeneous divide, the coordinates are in NDC space.

Step 2 is accomplished by transforming from NDC space to texture space via the following change of coordinate transformation:

$$u = 0.5x + 0.5$$
$$v = -0.5y + 0.5$$

Here, $u, v \in [0, 1]$ provided $x, y \in [-1, 1]$. We scale the y-coordinate by a negative to invert the axis because the positive y-axis in NDC coordinates goes in the direction opposite to the positive v-axis in texture coordinates. The texture space transformations can be written in terms of matrices (recall Exercise 21 from Chapter 3):

$$\begin{bmatrix} x & y & 0 & 1 \end{bmatrix} \begin{bmatrix} 0.5 & 0 & 0 & 0 \\ 0 & -0.5 & 0 & 0 \\ 0 & 0 & 1 & 0 \\ 0.5 & 0.5 & 0 & 1 \end{bmatrix} = \begin{bmatrix} u & v & 0 & 1 \end{bmatrix}$$

Let us call the above matrix **T** for "texture matrix" that transforms from NDC space to texture space. We can form the composite transform **VPT** that takes us from world space directly to texture space. After we multiply by this transform, we still need to do the perspective divide to complete the transformation; see Chapter 5 Exercise 8 for why we can do the perspective divide after doing the texture transform.

20.3.1 Code Implementation

The code for generating projective texture coordinates is shown below:

```
struct VertexOut
{
    float4 PosH     : SV_POSITION;
    float3 PosW     : POSITION;
    float3 TangentW : TANGENT;
    float3 NormalW  : NORMAL;
    float2 Tex      : TEXCOORD0;
    float4 ProjTex  : TEXCOORD1;
};

VertexOut VS(VertexIn vin)
{
    VertexOut vout;

    [...]

    // Transform to light's projective space.
    vout.ProjTex = mul(float4(vIn.posL, 1.0f),
      gLightWorldViewProjTexture);

    [...]

    return vout;
}

float4 PS(VertexOut pin) : SV_Target
{
    // Complete projection by doing division by w.
    pin.ProjTex.xyz /= pin.ProjTex.w;

    // Depth in NDC space.
    float depth = pin.ProjTex.z;

    // Sample the texture using the projective tex-coords.
    float4 c = gTextureMap.Sample(sampler, pin.ProjTex.xy);

    [...]
}
```

20.3.2 Points Outside the Frustum

In the rendering pipeline, geometry outside the frustum is clipped. However, when we generate projective texture coordinates by projecting the geometry from the point of view of the light projector, no clipping is done—we simply project vertices. Consequently, geometry outside the projector's frustum receives projective texture coordinates outside the [0, 1] range. Projective texture coordinates outside the [0, 1] range function just like normal texture coordinates outside the [0, 1] range based on the enabled address mode (see (§9.6) used when sampling the texture.

Generally, we do not want to texture any geometry outside the projector's frustum because it does not make sense (such geometry receives no light from the projector). Using the border color address mode with a zero color is a common solution. Another strategy is to associate a spotlight with the projector so that anything outside the spotlight's field of view cone is not lit (i.e., the surface receives no projected light). The advantage of using a spotlight is that the light intensity from the projector is strongest at the center of the spotlight cone, and can smoothly fade out as the angle ϕ between $-\mathbf{L}$ and $\mathbf{d}$ increases (where $\mathbf{L}$ is the light vector to the surface point and $\mathbf{d}$ is the direction of the spotlight).

20.3.3 Orthographic Projections

So far we have illustrated projective texturing using perspective projections (frustum shaped volumes). However, instead of using a perspective projection for the projection process, we could have used an orthographic projection. In this case, the texture is projected in the direction of the z-axis of the light through a box.

Everything we have talked about with projective texture coordinates also applies when using an orthographic projection, except for a couple things. First, with an orthographic projection, the spotlight strategy used to handle points outside the projector's volume does not work. This is because a spotlight cone approximates the volume of a frustum to some degree, but it does not approximate a box. However, we can still use texture address modes to handle points outside the projector's volume. This is because an orthographic projection still generates NDC coordinates and a point (x, y, z) is inside the volume if and only if:

$$-1 \leq x \leq 1$$
$$-1 \leq y \leq 1$$
$$0 \leq z \leq 1$$

Second, with an orthographic projection, we do not need to do the divide by w; that is, we do not need the line:

```
// Complete projection by doing division by w.
pin.ProjTex.xyz /= pin.ProjTex.w;
```

This is because after an orthographic projection, the coordinates are already in NDC space. This is faster, because it avoids the per-pixel division required for perspective projection. On the other hand, leaving in the division does not hurt because it divides by 1 (an orthographic projection does not change the w-coordinate, so w will be 1). If we leave the division by w in the shader code, then the shader code works for both perspective and orthographic projections uniformly. Though, the tradeoff for this uniformity is that you do a superfluous division with an orthographic projection.

20.4 SHADOW MAPPING

20.4.1 Algorithm Description

The idea of the shadow mapping algorithm is to render-to-texture the scene depth from the viewpoint of the light into a depth buffer called a *shadow map*. After this is done, the shadow map will contain the depth values of all the visible pixels from the perspective of the light. (Pixels occluded by other pixels will not be in the shadow map because they will fail the depth test and either be overwritten or never written.)

To render the scene from the viewpoint of the light, we need to define a light view matrix that transforms coordinates from world space to the space of the light and a light projection matrix, which describes the volume that light emits through in the world. This can be either a frustum volume (perspective projection) or box volume (orthographic projection). A frustum light volume can be used to model spotlights by embedding the spotlight cone inside the frustum. A box light volume can be used to model parallel lights. However, the parallel light is now bounded and only passes through the box volume; therefore, it may only strike a subset of the scene (see Figure 20.5). For a light source that strikes the entire scene (such as the sun), we can make the light volume large enough to contain the entire scene.

Once we have built the shadow map, we render the scene as normal from the perspective of the "player" camera. For each pixel p rendered, we also compute its depth from the light source, which we denote by $d(p)$. In addition, using projective texturing, we sample the shadow map along the line of sight from the light source to the pixel p to get the depth value $s(p)$ stored in the shadow map; this value is the depth of the pixel closest to the light along the line of sight from the position of the light to p. Then, from Figure 20.6, we see that a pixel p is in shadow if and only if $d(p) > s(p)$. Hence a pixel is not in shadow if and only if $d(p) \leq s(p)$.

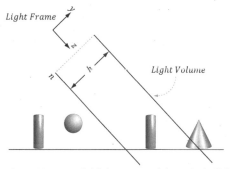

Figure 20.5. Parallel light rays travel through the light volume, so only a subset of the scene inside the volume receives light. If the light source needs to strike the entire scene, we can set the light volume size to contain the entire scene.

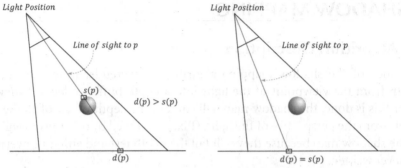

Figure 20.6. On the left, the depth of the pixel p from the light is $d(p)$. However, the depth of the pixel nearest to the light along the same line of sight has depth $s(p)$, and $d(p) > s(p)$. We conclude, therefore, that there is an object in front of p from the perspective of the light and so p is in shadow. On the right, the depth of the pixel p from the light is $d(p)$ and it also happens to be the pixel nearest to the light along the line of sight, that is, $s(p) = d(p)$, so we conclude p is not in shadow.

Note: *The depth values compared are in NDC coordinates. This is because the shadow map, which is a depth buffer, stores the depth values in NDC coordinates. How this is done exactly will be clear when we look at the code.*

20.4.2 Biasing and Aliasing

The shadow map stores the depth of the nearest visible pixels with respect to its associated light source. However, the shadow map only has some finite resolution. So each shadow map texel corresponds to an area of the scene. Thus, the shadow map is just a discrete sampling of the scene depth from the light perspective. This causes aliasing issues known as *shadow acne* (see Figure 20.7).

Figure 20.7. Notice the aliasing on the floor plane with the "stair-stepping" alternation between light and shadow. This aliasing error is often called shadow acne.

Shadow Mapping   655

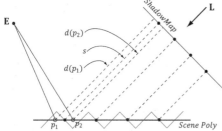

Figure 20.8. The shadow map samples the depth of the scene. Observe that due to finite resolution of the shadow map, each shadow map texel corresponds to an area of the scene. The eye **E** sees two points on the scene p_1 and p_2 that correspond to different screen pixels. However, from the viewpoint of the light, both points are covered by the same shadow map texel (that is, $s(p_1) = s(p_2) = s$). When we do the shadow map test, we have $d(p_1) > s$ and $d(p_2) \leq s$. Thus, p_1 will be colored as if it were in shadow, and p_2 will be colored as if it were not in shadow. This causes the shadow acne.

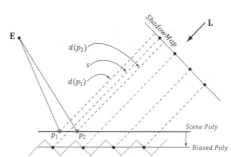

Figure 20.9. By biasing the depth values in the shadow map, no false shadowing occurs. We have that $d(p_1) \leq s$ and $d(p_2) \leq s$. Finding the right depth bias is usually done by experimentation.

Figure 20.8 shows a simple diagram to explain why shadow acne occurs. A simple solution is to apply a constant bias to offset the shadow map depth. Figure 20.9 shows how this corrects the problem.

Too much biasing results in an artifact called *peter-panning*, where the shadow appears to become detached from the object (see Figure 20.10).

Unfortunately, a fixed bias does not work for all geometry. In particular, Figure 20.11 shows that triangles with large slopes (with respect to the light source) need a larger bias. It is tempting to choose a large enough depth bias to handle all slopes. However, as Figure 20.10 showed, this leads to peter-panning.

Figure 20.10. Peter-panning—the shadow becomes detached from the column due to a large depth bias.

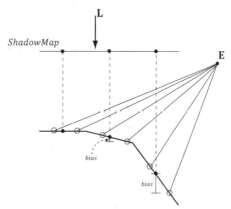

Figure 20.11. Polygons with large slopes, relative to the light source, require more bias than polygons with small slopes relative to the light source.

What we want is a way to measure the polygon slope with respect to the light source, and apply more bias for larger sloped polygons. Fortunately, graphics hardware has intrinsic support for this via the so-called *slope-scaled-bias* rasterization state properties:

```
typedef struct D3D12_RASTERIZER_DESC {
  [...]
  INT         DepthBias;
  FLOAT       DepthBiasClamp;
  FLOAT       SlopeScaledDepthBias;
  [...]
} D3D12_RASTERIZER_DESC;
```

1. `DepthBias`: A fixed bias to apply; see comments below for how this integer value is used for a UNORM depth buffer format.
2. `DepthBiasClamp`: A maximum depth bias allowed. This allows us to set a bound on the depth bias, for we can imagine that for very steep slopes, the bias slope-scaled-bias would be too much and cause peter-panning artifacts.
3. `SlopeScaledDepthBias`: A scale factor to control how much to bias based on the polygon slope; see comments below for the formula.

Note that we apply the slope-scaled-bias *when we are rendering the scene to the shadow map*. This is because we want to bias based on the polygon slope *with respect to the light source*. Consequently, we are biasing the shadow map values. In our demo we use the values:

```
// [From MSDN]
// If the depth buffer currently bound to the output-merger stage
// has a UNORM format or no depth buffer is bound the bias value
// is calculated like this:
//
// Bias = (float)DepthBias * r + SlopeScaledDepthBias * MaxDepthSlope;
//
// where r is the minimum representable value > 0 in the
// depth-buffer format converted to float32.
// [/End MSDN]
//
// For a 24-bit depth buffer, r = 1 / 2^24.
//
// Example: DepthBias = 100000 ==> Actual DepthBias = 100000/2^24 = .006

// These values are highly scene dependent, and you will need
// to experiment with these values for your scene to find the
// best values.
D3D12_GRAPHICS_PIPELINE_STATE_DESC smapPsoDesc = opaquePsoDesc;
smapPsoDesc.RasterizerState.DepthBias = 100000;
smapPsoDesc.RasterizerState.DepthBiasClamp = 0.0f;
smapPsoDesc.RasterizerState.SlopeScaledDepthBias = 1.0f;
```

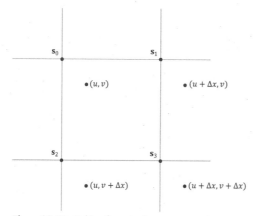

Figure 20.12. Taking four shadow map samples.

 Depth bias happens during rasterization (after clipping), so does not affect geometry clipping.

 For the complete details of depth bias, search the SDK documentation for "Depth Bias," and it will give all the rules for how it is applied, and how it works for floating-point depth buffers.

20.4.3 PCF Filtering

The projective texture coordinates (u, v) used to sample the shadow map generally will not coincide with a texel in the shadow map. Usually, it will be between four texels. With color texturing, this is solved with bilinear interpolation (§9.5.1). However, [Kilgard01] points out that we should not average depth values, as it can lead to incorrect results about a pixel being flagged in shadow. (For the same reason, we also cannot generate mipmaps for the shadow map.) Instead of interpolating the depth values, we interpolate the results—this is called *percentage closer filtering (PCF)*. That is, we use point filtering (MIN_MAG_MIP_POINT) and sample the texture with coordinates (u, v), $(u + \Delta x, v)$, $(u, v + \Delta x)$, $(u + \Delta x, v + \Delta x)$, where $\Delta x = 1/\text{SHADOW\_MAP\_SIZE}$. Since we are using point sampling, these four points will hit the nearest four texels s_0, s_1, s_2, and s_3, respectively, surrounding (u, v), as shown in Figure 20.12. We then do the shadow map test for each of these sampled depths and bilinearly interpolate the shadow map results:

```
static const float SMAP_SIZE = 2048.0f;
static const float SMAP_DX = 1.0f / SMAP_SIZE;

...

    // Sample shadow map to get nearest depth to light.
    float s0 = gShadowMap.Sample(gShadowSam,
```

```
                projTexC.xy).r;
float s1 = gShadowMap.Sample(gShadowSam,
        projTexC.xy + float2(SMAP_DX, 0)).r;
float s2 = gShadowMap.Sample(gShadowSam,
        projTexC.xy + float2(0, SMAP_DX)).r;
float s3 = gShadowMap.Sample(gShadowSam,
        projTexC.xy + float2(SMAP_DX, SMAP_DX)).r;

// Is the pixel depth <= shadow map value?
float result0 = depth <= s0;
float result1 = depth <= s1;
float result2 = depth <= s2;
float result3 = depth <= s3;

// Transform to texel space.
float2 texelPos = SMAP_SIZE*projTexC.xy;

// Determine the interpolation amounts.
float2 t = frac( texelPos );

// Interpolate results.
return lerp( lerp(result0, result1, t.x),
        lerp(result2, result3, t.x), t.y);
```

In this way, it is not an all-or-nothing situation; a pixel can be partially in shadow. For example, if two of the samples are in shadow and two are not in shadow, then the pixel is 50% in shadow. This creates a smoother transition from shadowed pixels to non-shadows pixels (see Figure 20.13).

The HLSL `frac` *function returns the fractional part of a floating-point number (i.e., the mantissa). For example, if* `SMAP_SIZE = 1024` *and* `projTex.xy = (0.23, 0.68)`, *then* `texelPos = (235.52, 696.32)` *and* `frac(texelPos) = (0.52, 0.32)`. *These fractions tell us how much to interpolate between the samples. The HLSL* `lerp(x, y, s)` *function is the linear interpolation function and returns* $x + s(y - x) = (1 - s)x + sy$.

Figure 20.13. In the top image, observe the "stair-stepping" artifacts on the shadow boundary. On the bottom image, these aliasing artifacts are smoothed out a bit with filtering.

Note: *Even with our filtering, the shadows are still very hard and the aliasing artifacts can still be unsatisfactory close up. More aggressive methods can be used; see [Uralsky05], for example. We also note that using a higher-resolution shadow map helps, but can be cost prohibitive.*

The main disadvantage of PCF filtering as described above is that it requires four texture samples. Sampling textures is one of the more expensive operations on a modern GPU because memory bandwidth and memory latency have not improved as much as the raw computational power of GPUs [Möller08]. Fortunately, Direct3D 11+ graphics hardware has built in support for PCF via the `SampleCmpLevelZero` method:

```
Texture2D gShadowMap : register(t1);
SamplerComparisonState gsamShadow : register(s6);

// Complete projection by doing division by w.
shadowPosH.xyz /= shadowPosH.w;

// Depth in NDC space.
float depth = shadowPosH.z;

// Automatically does a 4-tap PCF.
gShadowMap.SampleCmpLevelZero(gsamShadow,
   shadowPosH.xy, depth).r;
```

The `LevelZero` part of the method name means that it only looks at the top mipmap level, which is fine because that is what we want for shadow mapping (we do not generate a mipmap chain for the shadow map). This method does not use a typical sampler object, but instead uses a so-called *comparison sampler.* This is so that the hardware can do the shadow map comparison test, which needs to be done before filtering the results. For PCF, you need to use the filter `D3D12_FILTER_COMPARISON_MIN_MAG_LINEAR_MIP_POINT` and set the comparison function to `LESS_EQUAL` (`LESS` also works since we bias the depth). The first and second parameters are the comparison sampler and texture coordinates, respectively. The third parameter is the value to compare against the shadow map samples. So settings the compare value to `depth`, and the comparison function to `LESS_EQUAL` we are doing the comparisons:

```
float result0 = depth <= s0;
float result1 = depth <= s1;
float result2 = depth <= s2;
float result3 = depth <= s3;
```

Then the hardware bilinearly interpolates the results to finish the PCF.

The following code shows how we describe the comparison sampler for shadow mapping:

```
const CD3DX12_STATIC_SAMPLER_DESC shadow(
   6, // shaderRegister
   D3D12_FILTER_COMPARISON_MIN_MAG_LINEAR_MIP_POINT, // filter
```

```
D3D12_TEXTURE_ADDRESS_MODE_BORDER, // addressU
D3D12_TEXTURE_ADDRESS_MODE_BORDER, // addressV
D3D12_TEXTURE_ADDRESS_MODE_BORDER, // addressW
0.0f,                              // mipLODBias
16,                                // maxAnisotropy
D3D12_COMPARISON_FUNC_LESS_EQUAL,
D3D12_STATIC_BORDER_COLOR_OPAQUE_BLACK);
```

From the SDK documentation, only the following formats support comparison filters: R32_FLOAT_X8X24_TYPELESS, R32_FLOAT, R24_UNORM_X8_TYPELESS, R16_UNORM.

So far in this section, we used a 4-tap PCF kernel. Larger kernels can be used to make the edges of shadows larger and even smoother, at the expensive of extra SampleCmpLevelZero calls. In our demo, we call SampleCmpLevelZero in a 3 × 3 box filter pattern. Since each SampleCmpLevelZero call performs a 4-tap PCF, we are using 4 × 4 unique sample points from the shadow map (based on our pattern there is some overlap of sample points). Using large filtering kernels can cause the shadow acne problem to return; we explain why and describe a solution in §20.5.

An observation is that PCF really only needs to be performed at the shadow edges. Inside the shadow, there is no blending, and outside the shadow there is no blending. Based on this observation, methods have been devised to only do PCF at the shadow edges. [Isidoro06b] describes one way to do this. Such a technique requires a dynamic branch in the shader code: "If we are on a shadow edge, do expensive PCF, otherwise just take one shadow map sample."

Note that the extra expensive of doing such a method makes it only worthwhile if your PCF kernel is large (say 5 × 5 or greater); however, this is just general advice and you will need to profile to verify the cost/benefit.

One final remark is that your PCF kernel need not be a box filter grid. Many articles have been written about randomly picking points to be in the PCF kernel.

20.4.4 Building the Shadow Map

The first step in shadow mapping is building the shadow map. To do this, we create a ShadowMap instance:

```
mShadowMap = std::make_unique<ShadowMap>(
    md3dDevice.Get(), 2048, 2048);
```

We then define a light view matrix and projection matrix (representing the light frame and view volume). The light view matrix is derived from the primary light source, and the light view volume is computed to fit the bounding sphere of the entire scene.

```
DirectX::BoundingSphere mSceneBounds;

ShadowMapApp::ShadowMapApp(HINSTANCE hInstance)
```

```cpp
    : D3DApp(hInstance)
{
    // Estimate the scene bounding sphere manually since we know how the
    // scene was constructed.
    // The grid is the "widest object" with a width of 20 and depth of
    // 30.0f, and centered at
    // the world space origin. In general, you need to loop over every
    // world space vertex
    // position and compute the bounding sphere.
    mSceneBounds.Center = XMFLOAT3(0.0f, 0.0f, 0.0f);
    mSceneBounds.Radius = sqrtf(10.0f*10.0f + 15.0f*15.0f);
}

void ShadowMapApp::Update(const GameTimer& gt)
{
    [...]

    //
    // Animate the lights (and hence shadows).
    //

    mLightRotationAngle += 0.1f*gt.DeltaTime();

    XMMATRIX R = XMMatrixRotationY(mLightRotationAngle);
    for(int i = 0; i < 3; ++i)
    {
        XMVECTOR lightDir = XMLoadFloat3(&mBaseLightDirections[i]);
        lightDir = XMVector3TransformNormal(lightDir, R);
        XMStoreFloat3(&mRotatedLightDirections[i], lightDir);
    }

    AnimateMaterials(gt);
    UpdateObjectCBs(gt);
    UpdateMaterialBuffer(gt);
    UpdateShadowTransform(gt);
    UpdateMainPassCB(gt);
    UpdateShadowPassCB(gt);
}

void ShadowMapApp::UpdateShadowTransform(const GameTimer& gt)
{
    // Only the first "main" light casts a shadow.
    XMVECTOR lightDir = XMLoadFloat3(&mRotatedLightDirections[0]);
    XMVECTOR lightPos = -2.0f*mSceneBounds.Radius*lightDir;
    XMVECTOR targetPos = XMLoadFloat3(&mSceneBounds.Center);
    XMVECTOR lightUp = XMVectorSet(0.0f, 1.0f, 0.0f, 0.0f);
    XMMATRIX lightView = XMMatrixLookAtLH(lightPos, targetPos, lightUp);

    XMStoreFloat3(&mLightPosW, lightPos);

    // Transform bounding sphere to light space.
    XMFLOAT3 sphereCenterLS;
    XMStoreFloat3(&sphereCenterLS, XMVector3TransformCoord(targetPos,
        lightView));
```

```cpp
    // Ortho frustum in light space encloses scene.
    float l = sphereCenterLS.x - mSceneBounds.Radius;
    float b = sphereCenterLS.y - mSceneBounds.Radius;
    float n = sphereCenterLS.z - mSceneBounds.Radius;
    float r = sphereCenterLS.x + mSceneBounds.Radius;
    float t = sphereCenterLS.y + mSceneBounds.Radius;
    float f = sphereCenterLS.z + mSceneBounds.Radius;

    mLightNearZ = n;
    mLightFarZ = f;
    XMMATRIX lightProj = XMMatrixOrthographicOffCenterLH(l, r, b, t, n,
       f);

    // Transform NDC space [-1,+1]^2 to texture space [0,1]^2
    XMMATRIX T(
      0.5f, 0.0f, 0.0f, 0.0f,
      0.0f, -0.5f, 0.0f, 0.0f,
      0.0f, 0.0f, 1.0f, 0.0f,
      0.5f, 0.5f, 0.0f, 1.0f);

    XMMATRIX S = lightView*lightProj*T;
    XMStoreFloat4x4(&mLightView, lightView);
    XMStoreFloat4x4(&mLightProj, lightProj);
    XMStoreFloat4x4(&mShadowTransform, S);
}
```

Rendering the scene into the shadow map is done like so:

```cpp
void ShadowMapApp::DrawSceneToShadowMap()
{
  mCommandList->RSSetViewports(1, &mShadowMap->Viewport());
  mCommandList->RSSetScissorRects(1, &mShadowMap->ScissorRect());

  // Change to DEPTH_WRITE.
  mCommandList->ResourceBarrier(1, &CD3DX12_RESOURCE_BARRIER::Transition(
    mShadowMap->Resource(),
    D3D12_RESOURCE_STATE_GENERIC_READ,
    D3D12_RESOURCE_STATE_DEPTH_WRITE));

  UINT passCBByteSize = d3dUtil::CalcConstantBufferByteSize(sizeof
    (PassConstants));

  // Clear the back buffer and depth buffer.
  mCommandList->ClearDepthStencilView(mShadowMap->Dsv(),
    D3D12_CLEAR_FLAG_DEPTH | D3D12_CLEAR_FLAG_STENCIL, 1.0f, 0, 0, nullptr);

  // Set null render target because we are only going to draw to
  // depth buffer. Setting a null render target will disable color writes.
  // Note the active PSO also must specify a render target count of 0.
  mCommandList->OMSetRenderTargets(0, nullptr, false, &mShadowMap->Dsv());

  // Bind the pass constant buffer for the shadow map pass.
  auto passCB = mCurrFrameResource->PassCB->Resource();
  D3D12_GPU_VIRTUAL_ADDRESS passCBAddress = passCB->GetGPUVirtualAddress()
    + 1*passCBByteSize;
```

```
mCommandList->SetGraphicsRootConstantBufferView(1, passCBAddress);

mCommandList->SetPipelineState(mPSOs["shadow_opaque"].Get());

DrawRenderItems(mCommandList.Get(), mRitemLayer[(int)RenderLayer::Opaque]);

// Change back to GENERIC_READ so we can read the texture in a shader.
mCommandList->ResourceBarrier(1, &CD3DX12_RESOURCE_BARRIER::Transition(
    mShadowMap->Resource(),
    D3D12_RESOURCE_STATE_DEPTH_WRITE,
    D3D12_RESOURCE_STATE_GENERIC_READ));
}
```

Observe that we set a null render target, which essentially disables color writes. This is because when we render the scene to the shadow map, all we care about is the depth values of the scene relative to the light source. Graphics cards are optimized for only drawing depth; a depth only render pass is significantly faster than drawing color and depth. The active pipeline state object must also specify a render target count of 0:

```
D3D12_GRAPHICS_PIPELINE_STATE_DESC smapPsoDesc = opaquePsoDesc;
smapPsoDesc.RasterizerState.DepthBias = 100000;
smapPsoDesc.RasterizerState.DepthBiasClamp = 0.0f;
smapPsoDesc.RasterizerState.SlopeScaledDepthBias = 1.0f;
smapPsoDesc.pRootSignature = mRootSignature.Get();
smapPsoDesc.VS =
{
    reinterpret_cast<BYTE*>(mShaders["shadowVS"]->GetBufferPointer()),
    mShaders["shadowVS"]->GetBufferSize()
};
smapPsoDesc.PS =
{
    reinterpret_cast<BYTE*>(mShaders["shadowOpaquePS"]->GetBufferPointer()),
    mShaders["shadowOpaquePS"]->GetBufferSize()
};

// Shadow map pass does not have a render target.
smapPsoDesc.RTVFormats[0] = DXGI_FORMAT_UNKNOWN;
smapPsoDesc.NumRenderTargets = 0;
ThrowIfFailed(md3dDevice->CreateGraphicsPipelineState(
    &smapPsoDesc, IID_PPV_ARGS(&mPSOs["shadow_opaque"])));
```

The shader programs we use for rendering the scene from the perspective of the light is quite simple because we are only building the shadow map, so we do not need to do any complicated pixel shader work.

```
//***************************************************************
// Shadows.hlsl by Frank Luna (C) 2015 All Rights Reserved.
//***************************************************************

// Include common HLSL code.
#include "Common.hlsl"
```

```hlsl
struct VertexIn
{
  float3 PosL  : POSITION;
  float2 TexC  : TEXCOORD;
};

struct VertexOut
{
  float4 PosH  : SV_POSITION;
  float2 TexC  : TEXCOORD;
};

VertexOut VS(VertexIn vin)
{
   VertexOut vout = (VertexOut)0.0f;

   MaterialData matData = gMaterialData[gMaterialIndex];

   // Transform to world space.
   float4 posW = mul(float4(vin.PosL, 1.0f), gWorld);

   // Transform to homogeneous clip space.
   vout.PosH = mul(posW, gViewProj);

   // Output vertex attributes for interpolation across triangle.
   float4 texC = mul(float4(vin.TexC, 0.0f, 1.0f), gTexTransform);
   vout.TexC = mul(texC, matData.MatTransform).xy;

   return vout;
}

// This is only used for alpha cut out geometry, so that shadows
// show up correctly. Geometry that does not need to sample a
// texture can use a NULL pixel shader for depth pass.
void PS(VertexOut pin)
{
   // Fetch the material data.
   MaterialData matData = gMaterialData[gMaterialIndex];
   float4 diffuseAlbedo = matData.DiffuseAlbedo;
   uint diffuseMapIndex = matData.DiffuseMapIndex;

   // Dynamically look up the texture in the array.
   diffuseAlbedo *= gTextureMaps[diffuseMapIndex].
     Sample(gsamAnisotropicWrap, pin.TexC);

#ifdef ALPHA_TEST
   // Discard pixel if texture alpha < 0.1. We do this test as soon
   // as possible in the shader so that we can potentially exit the
   // shader early, thereby skipping the rest of the shader code.
   clip(diffuseAlbedo.a - 0.1f);
#endif
}
```

Figure 20.14. Leaf texture.

Notice that the pixel shader does not return a value because we only need to output depth values. The pixel shader is solely used to clip pixel fragments with zero or low alpha values, which we assume indicate complete transparency. For example, consider the tree leaf texture in Figure 20.14; here, we only want to draw the pixels with white alpha values to the shadow map. To facilitate this, we provide two techniques: one that does the alpha clip operation, and one that does not. If the alpha clip does not need to be done, then we can bind a null pixel shader, which would be even faster than binding a pixel shader that only samples a texture and performs a clip operation.

> **Note:** *Although not shown for brevity, the shaders for rendering the depth for tessellated geometry are slightly more involved. When drawing tessellated geometry into the shadow map, we need to tessellate the geometry the same way we tessellate it when being drawn into the back buffer (i.e., based on the distance to the player's eye). This is for consistency; the geometry the eye sees should be the same that the light sees. That being said, if the tessellated geometry is not displaced too much, the displacement might not even be noticeable in the shadows; therefore, a possible optimization may be not to tessellate the geometry when rendering the shadow map. This optimization trades accuracy for speed.*

20.4.5 The Shadow Factor

The shadow factor is a new factor we add to the lighting equation. The shadow factor is a scalar in the range 0 to 1. A value of 0 indicates a point is in shadow, and a value of 1 indicates a point is not in shadow. With PCF (§20.4.3), a point can also be partially in shadow, in which case the shadow factor will be between 0 and 1. The `CalcShadowFactor` implementation is in *Common.hlsl*.

```
float CalcShadowFactor(float4 shadowPosH)
{
  // Complete projection by doing division by w.
  shadowPosH.xyz /= shadowPosH.w;
```

```
    // Depth in NDC space.
    float depth = shadowPosH.z;

    uint width, height, numMips;
    gShadowMap.GetDimensions(0, width, height, numMips);

    // Texel size.
    float dx = 1.0f / (float)width;

    float percentLit = 0.0f;
    const float2 offsets[9] =
    {
      float2(-dx, -dx), float2(0.0f, -dx), float2(dx, -dx),
      float2(-dx, 0.0f), float2(0.0f, 0.0f), float2(dx, 0.0f),
      float2(-dx, +dx), float2(0.0f, +dx), float2(dx, +dx)
    };

    [unroll]
    for(int i = 0; i < 9; ++i)
    {
      percentLit += gShadowMap.SampleCmpLevelZero(gsamShadow,
        shadowPosH.xy + offsets[i], depth).r;
    }

    return percentLit / 9.0f;
}
```

In our model, the shadow factor will be multiplied against the direct lighting (diffuse and specular) terms:

```
// Only the first light casts a shadow.
float3 shadowFactor = float3(1.0f, 1.0f, 1.0f);
shadowFactor[0] = CalcShadowFactor(pin.ShadowPosH);

const float shininess = (1.0f - roughness) * normalMapSample.a;
Material mat = { diffuseAlbedo, fresnelR0, shininess };
float4 directLight = ComputeLighting(gLights, mat, pin.PosW,
    bumpedNormalW, toEyeW, shadowFactor);


float4 ComputeLighting(Light gLights[MaxLights], Material mat,
          float3 pos, float3 normal, float3 toEye,
          float3 shadowFactor)
{
  float3 result = 0.0f;

  int i = 0;

#if (NUM_DIR_LIGHTS > 0)
  for(i = 0; i < NUM_DIR_LIGHTS; ++i)
  {
    result += shadowFactor[i] * ComputeDirectionalLight(gLights[i],
      mat, normal, toEye);
  }
#endif
```

```
#if (NUM_POINT_LIGHTS > 0)
  for(i = NUM_DIR_LIGHTS; i < NUM_DIR_LIGHTS+NUM_POINT_LIGHTS; ++i)
  {
    result += ComputePointLight(gLights[i], mat, pos, normal, toEye);
  }
#endif

#if (NUM_SPOT_LIGHTS > 0)
  for(i = NUM_DIR_LIGHTS + NUM_POINT_LIGHTS; i < NUM_DIR_LIGHTS +
    NUM_POINT_LIGHTS + NUM_SPOT_LIGHTS; ++i)
  {
    result += ComputeSpotLight(gLights[i], mat, pos, normal, toEye);
  }
#endif

  return float4(result, 0.0f);
}
```

The shadow factor does not affect ambient light since that is indirect light, and it also does not affect reflective light coming from the environment map.

20.4.6 The Shadow Map Test

After we have built the shadow map by rendering the scene from the perspective of the light, we can sample the shadow map in our main rendering pass to determine if a pixel is in shadow or not. The key issue is computing $d(p)$ and $s(p)$ for each pixel p. The value $d(p)$ is found by transforming the point to the NDC space of the light; then the z-coordinate gives the normalized depth value of the point from the light source. The value $s(p)$ is found by projecting the shadow map onto the scene through the light's view volume using projective texturing. Note that with this setup, both $d(p)$ and $s(p)$ are measured in the NDC space of the light, so they can be compared. The transformation matrix `gShadowTransform` transforms from world space to the shadow map texture space (§20.3).

```
// Generate projective tex-coords to project shadow map onto scene
// in vertex shader.
vout.ShadowPosH = mul(posW, gShadowTransform);

// Do the shadow map test in pixel shader.
float3 shadowFactor = float3(1.0f, 1.0f, 1.0f);
shadowFactor[0] = CalcShadowFactor(pin.ShadowPosH);
```

The `gShadowTransform` matrix is stored as a per-pass constant.

20.4.7 Rendering the Shadow Map

For this demo, we also render the shadow map onto a quad that occupies the lower-right corner of the screen. This allows us to see what the shadow map looks like for each frame. Recall that the shadow map is just a depth buffer texture and we can create an SRV to it so that it can be sampled in a shader program. The shadow map

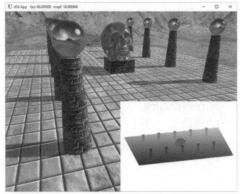

Figure 20.15. Screenshot of the shadow map demo.

is rendered as a grayscale image since it stores a one-dimensional value at each pixel (a depth value). Figure 20.15 shows a screenshot of the "Shadow Map" demo.

20.5 LARGE PCF KERNELS

In this section, we discuss problem occurs when using a large PCF kernel. Our demos do not use a large PCF kernel, so this section is in some sense optional, but it introduces some interesting ideas.

Refer to Figure 20.16, where we are computing the shadow test for a pixel p visible by the eye. With no PCF, we compute the distance $d = d(p)$ and compare it to the corresponding shadow map value $s_0 = s(p)$. With PCF, we also compare neighboring shadow map values s_{-1} and s_1 against d. However, it is not valid to compare d with s_{-1} and s_1. The texels s_{-1} and s_1 describe the depths of different areas of the scene that may or may not be on the same polygon as p.

The scenario in Figure 20.16 actually results in an error in the PCF. Specifically, when we do the shadow map test we compute:

$$lit_0 = d \leq s_0 \quad (true)$$
$$lit_{-1} = d \leq s_{-1} \quad (true)$$
$$lit_1 = d \leq s_1 \quad (false)$$

When the results are interpolated, we get that p is is 1/3rd in shadow, which is incorrect as nothing is occluding p.

Observe from Figure 20.16 that more depth biasing would fix the error. However, in this example, we are only sampling the next door neighbor texels in the shadow map. If we widen the PCF kernel, then even more biasing is needed. Thus for small PCF kernels, simply doing the depth bias as explained in §20.4.2 is enough to counter this problem and it is nothing to worry about. But for large

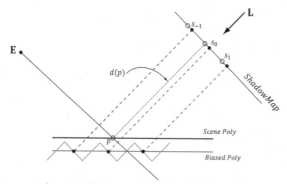

Figure 20.16. Comparing the depth $d(p)$ with s_0 is correct, since the texel s_0 covers the scene area p is contained in. However, it is not correct to compare $d(p)$ with s_{-1} and s_1, as those texels cover areas of the scene that are unrelated to p.

PCF kernels such as 5×5 or 9×9, which are used to make soft shadows, this can become a real problem.

20.5.1 The DDX and DDY Functions

Before we can look at an approximate solution to this problem, we first need to discuss the `ddx` and `ddy` HLSL functions. These functions estimate $\partial \mathbf{p}/\partial x$ and $\partial \mathbf{p}/\partial y$, respectively, where x is the screen space x-axis and y is the screen space y-axis. With these functions you can determine how per pixel quantities $\mathbf{p}$ vary from pixel to pixel. Examples of what the derivative functions could be used for:

1. Estimate how colors are changing pixel by pixel.
2. Estimate how depths are changing pixel by pixel.
3. Estimate how normals are changing pixel by pixel.

How the hardware estimates these partial derivatives is not complicated. The hardware processes pixels in 2×2 quads at a time in parallel. Then the partial derivative in the x-direction can be estimated by the forward difference equation $q_{x+1,y} - q_{x,y}$ (estimates how the quantity q changes from pixel (x, y) to pixel $(x + 1, y)$), and similarly for the partial derivative in the y direction.

20.5.2 Solution to the Large PCF Kernel Problem

The solution we describe is from [Tuft10]. The strategy is to make the assumption the neighboring pixels of p lie on the same plane as p. This assumption is not always true, but it is the best we have to work with.

Let $\mathbf{p} = (u, v, z)$ be the coordinates in light space. The coordinates (u, v) are used to index into the shadow map, and the value z is the distance from the light source used in the shadow map test. We can compute the vectors $\frac{\partial \mathbf{p}}{\partial x} = \left(\frac{\partial u}{\partial x}, \frac{\partial v}{\partial x}, \frac{\partial z}{\partial x} \right)$ and

$\frac{\partial \mathbf{p}}{\partial y} = \left(\frac{\partial u}{\partial y}, \frac{\partial v}{\partial y}, \frac{\partial z}{\partial y}\right)$ with ddx and ddy, which lie in the tangent plane of the polygon. This tells us how we move in light space when we move in screen space. In particular, if we move $(\Delta x, \Delta y)$ units in screen space, we move $\Delta x \left(\frac{\partial u}{\partial x}, \frac{\partial v}{\partial x}, \frac{\partial z}{\partial x}\right) + \Delta y \left(\frac{\partial u}{\partial y}, \frac{\partial v}{\partial y}, \frac{\partial z}{\partial y}\right)$ units in light space in the directions of the tangent vectors. Ignoring the depth term for the moment, if we move $(\Delta x, \Delta y)$ units in screen space, we move $\Delta x \left(\frac{\partial u}{\partial x}, \frac{\partial v}{\partial x}\right) + \Delta y \left(\frac{\partial u}{\partial y}, \frac{\partial v}{\partial y}\right)$ units in light space *on the uv-plane*; this can be expressed by the matrix equation:

$$[\Delta x, \Delta y] \begin{bmatrix} \frac{\partial u}{\partial x} & \frac{\partial v}{\partial x} \\ \frac{\partial u}{\partial y} & \frac{\partial v}{\partial y} \end{bmatrix} = \Delta x \left(\frac{\partial u}{\partial x}, \frac{\partial v}{\partial x}\right) + \Delta y \left(\frac{\partial u}{\partial y}, \frac{\partial v}{\partial y}\right) = [\Delta u, \Delta v]$$

Therefore,

$$[\Delta x, \Delta y] = [\Delta u, \Delta v] \begin{bmatrix} \frac{\partial u}{\partial x} & \frac{\partial v}{\partial x} \\ \frac{\partial u}{\partial y} & \frac{\partial v}{\partial y} \end{bmatrix}^{-1}$$

(eq. 20.1)

$$= [\Delta u, \Delta v] \frac{1}{\frac{\partial u}{\partial x}\frac{\partial v}{\partial y} - \frac{\partial v}{\partial x}\frac{\partial u}{\partial y}} \begin{bmatrix} \frac{\partial v}{\partial y} & -\frac{\partial v}{\partial x} \\ -\frac{\partial u}{\partial y} & \frac{\partial u}{\partial x} \end{bmatrix}$$

Note: Recall from Chapter 2 that

$$\begin{bmatrix} A_{11} & A_{12} \\ A_{21} & A_{22} \end{bmatrix}^{-1} = \frac{1}{A_{11}A_{22} - A_{12}A_{21}} \begin{bmatrix} A_{22} & -A_{12} \\ -A_{21} & A_{11} \end{bmatrix}$$

This new equation tells us that if we move $(\Delta u, \Delta v)$ units in light space on the uv-plane, then we move $(\Delta x, \Delta y)$ units in screen space. So why is Equation 20.1 important to us? Well, when we build our PCF kernel, we offset our texture coordinates to sample neighboring values in the shadow map:

```
// Texel size.
    const float dx = SMAP_DX;

    float percentLit = 0.0f;
    const float2 offsets[9] =
    {
        float2(-dx, -dx), float2(0.0f, -dx), float2(dx, -dx),
        float2(-dx, 0.0f), float2(0.0f, 0.0f), float2(dx, 0.0f),
        float2(-dx, +dx), float2(0.0f, +dx), float2(dx, +dx)
    };
```

```
// 3x3 box filter pattern.  Each sample does a 4-tap PCF.
[unroll]
for(int i = 0; i < 9; ++i)
{
    percentLit += shadowMap.SampleCmpLevelZero(samShadow,
            shadowPosH.xy + offsets[i], depth).r;
}
```

In other words, we know how much we are displacing in light space in the *uv-plane*—we know $(\Delta u, \Delta v)$. Equation 20.1 tells us that when we move $(\Delta u, \Delta v)$ units in light space we are moving $(\Delta x, \Delta y)$ in screen space.

Now, let us return to the depth term we have been ignoring. If we move $(\Delta x, \Delta y)$ units in screen space, then the light space depth moves by $\Delta z = \Delta x \frac{\partial z}{\partial x} + \Delta y \frac{\partial z}{\partial y}$. Thus, when we offset our texture coordinates to do the PCF, we can modify the depth value used in the depth test accordingly: $z' = z + \Delta z$ (see Figure 20.17).

Let us summarize:

1. In our PCF implementation, we offset our texture coordinates to sample neighboring values in the shadow map. So for each sample, we know $(\Delta u, \Delta v)$.
2. We can use Equation 20.1 to find the screen space offset $(\Delta x, \Delta y)$ when we offset $(\Delta u, \Delta v)$ units in light space.
3. With $(\Delta x, \Delta y)$ solved for, apply $\Delta z = \Delta x \frac{\partial z}{\partial x} + \Delta y \frac{\partial z}{\partial y}$ to figure out the light space depth change.

The "CascadedShadowMaps11" demo in the DirectX 11 SDK implements this method in the `CalculateRightAndUpTexelDepthDeltas` and `CalculatePCFPercentLit` functions.

20.5.3 An Alternative Solution to the Large PCF Kernel Problem

This solution presented in [Isidoro06] is in the same spirit as the previous section, but takes a slightly different approach.

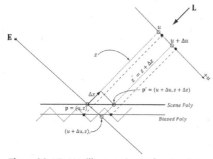

Figure 20.17. We illustrate in 2D for simplicity. If we offset from **p** = (u, z) by Δu in the *u*-direction to get $(u + \Delta u, z)$, then we need to offset by Δz in order to remain on the polygon to get **p′** = $(u + \Delta u, z + \Delta z)$.

Let $\mathbf{p} = (u, v, z)$ be the coordinates in light space. The coordinates (u, v) are used to index into the shadow map, and the value z is the distance from the light source used in the shadow map test. We can compute $\frac{\partial \mathbf{p}}{\partial x} = \left(\frac{\partial u}{\partial x}, \frac{\partial v}{\partial x}, \frac{\partial z}{\partial x}\right)$ and $\frac{\partial \mathbf{p}}{\partial y} = \left(\frac{\partial u}{\partial y}, \frac{\partial v}{\partial y}, \frac{\partial z}{\partial y}\right)$ with `ddx` and `ddy`.

In particular, the fact that we can take these derivatives means $u = u(x, y)$, $v = v(x, y)$ and $z = z(x, y)$ are all functions of x and y. However, we can also think of z as a function of u and v—that is, $z = z(u, v)$; as we move in light space in the u- and v-directions, the depth z changes along the polygon plane. By the chain rule, we have:

$$\frac{\partial z}{\partial x} = \frac{\partial z}{\partial u}\frac{\partial u}{\partial x} + \frac{\partial z}{\partial v}\frac{\partial v}{\partial x}$$

$$\frac{\partial z}{\partial y} = \frac{\partial z}{\partial u}\frac{\partial u}{\partial y} + \frac{\partial z}{\partial v}\frac{\partial v}{\partial y}$$

Or in matrix notation:

$$\begin{bmatrix} \frac{\partial z}{\partial x} & \frac{\partial z}{\partial y} \end{bmatrix} = \begin{bmatrix} \frac{\partial z}{\partial u} & \frac{\partial z}{\partial v} \end{bmatrix} \begin{bmatrix} \frac{\partial u}{\partial x} & \frac{\partial u}{\partial y} \\ \frac{\partial v}{\partial x} & \frac{\partial v}{\partial y} \end{bmatrix}$$

Taking the inverse yields:

$$\begin{bmatrix} \frac{\partial z}{\partial u} & \frac{\partial z}{\partial v} \end{bmatrix} = \begin{bmatrix} \frac{\partial z}{\partial x} & \frac{\partial z}{\partial y} \end{bmatrix} \begin{bmatrix} \frac{\partial u}{\partial x} & \frac{\partial u}{\partial y} \\ \frac{\partial v}{\partial x} & \frac{\partial v}{\partial y} \end{bmatrix}^{-1}$$

$$= \frac{\begin{bmatrix} \frac{\partial z}{\partial x} & \frac{\partial z}{\partial y} \end{bmatrix} \begin{bmatrix} \frac{\partial v}{\partial y} & -\frac{\partial u}{\partial y} \\ -\frac{\partial v}{\partial x} & \frac{\partial u}{\partial x} \end{bmatrix}}{\frac{\partial u}{\partial x}\frac{\partial v}{\partial y} - \frac{\partial u}{\partial y}\frac{\partial v}{\partial x}}$$

We now have solved for $\frac{\partial z}{\partial u}$ and $\frac{\partial z}{\partial v}$ directly (everything on the right-side of the equation is known). If we move $(\Delta u, \Delta v)$ units in light space on the *uv-plane*, then the light space depth moves by $\Delta z = \Delta u \frac{\partial z}{\partial u} + \Delta v \frac{\partial z}{\partial v}$.

So with this approach, we do not have to transform to screen space, but can stay in light space—the reason being that we figured out directly how depth changes when u and v change, whereas in the previous section, we only knew how depth changed when x and y changed in screen space.

20.6 SUMMARY

1. The back buffer need not always be the render target; we can render to a different texture. Rendering to texture provides an efficient way for the GPU to update the contents of a texture at runtime. After we have rendered to a texture, we can bind the texture as a shader input and map it onto geometry. Many special effects require render to texture functionality like shadow maps, water simulations, and general purpose GPU programming.

2. With an orthographic projection, the viewing volume is a box (see Figure 20.1) with width w, height h, near plane n and far plane f, and the lines of projection are parallel to the view space z-axis. Such projections are primarily used in 3D science or engineering applications, where it is desirable to have parallel lines remain parallel after projection. However, we can use orthographic projections to model shadows that parallel lights generate.

3. Projective texturing is so called because it allows us to project a texture onto arbitrary geometry, much like a slide projector. The key to projective texturing is to generate texture coordinates for each pixel in such a way that the applied texture looks like it has been projected onto the geometry. Such texture coordinates are called *projective texture coordinates*. We obtain the projective texture coordinates for a pixel by projecting it onto the projection plane of the projector, and then mapping it to the texture coordinate system.

4. Shadow mapping is a real-time shadowing technique, which shadows arbitrary geometry (it is not limited to planar shadows). The idea of shadow mapping is to render the depth of the scene from the light's viewpoint into a shadow map; thus, after which, the shadow map stores the depth of all pixels visible from the light's perspective. We then render the scene again from the camera's perspective, and we project the shadow map onto the scene using projective texturing. Let $s(p)$ be the depth value projected onto a pixel p from the shadow map and let $d(p)$ be the depth of the pixel from the light source. Then p is in shadow if $d(p) > s(p)$; that is, if the depth of the pixel is greater than the projected pixel depth $s(p)$, then there must exist a pixel closer to the light which occludes p, thereby casting p in shadow.

5. Aliasing is the biggest challenge with shadow maps. The shadow map stores the depth of the nearest visible pixels with respect to its associated light source. However, the shadow map only has some finite resolution. So each shadow map texel corresponds to an area of the scene. Thus, the shadow map is just a discrete sampling of the scene depth from the light perspective. This causes aliasing issues known as *shadow acne*. Using the graphics hardware intrinsic support for *slope-scaled-bias* (in the rasterization render state) is a common

strategy to fix shadow acne. The finite resolution of the shadow map also causes aliasing at the shadow edges. PCF is a popular solution to this. More advanced solutions utilized for the aliasing problem are *cascaded shadow maps* and *variance shadow maps*.

20.7 EXERCISES

1. Write a program that simulates a slide projector by projecting a texture onto the scene. Experiment with both perspective and orthographic projections.
2. Modify the solution to the previous exercise by using texture address modes so that points outside the projector's frustum do not receive light.
3. Modify the solution to Exercise 1 by using a spotlight so that points outside the spotlight cone do not receive any light from the projector.
4. Modify this chapter's demo application by using a perspective projection. Note that the slope-scaled-bias that worked for an orthographic projection might not work well for a perspective projection. When using a perspective projection, notice that the depth map is heavily biased to white (1.0). Does this make sense considering the graph in Figure 5.25?
5. Experiment with the following shadow map resolutions: 4096 × 4096, 1024 × 1024, 512 × 512, 256 × 256.
6. Derive the matrix that maps the box $[l,r] \times [b,t] \times [n,f] \rightarrow [-1,1] \times [-1,1] \times [0,1]$. This is an "off center" orthographic view volume (i.e., the box is not centered about the view space origin). In contrast, the orthographic projection matrix derived in §20.2 is an "on center" orthographic view volume.
7. In Chapter 17, we learned about picking with a perspective projection matrix. Derive picking formulas for an off-centered orthographic projection.
8. Modify the "Shadow Demo" to use a single point sampling shadow test (i.e., no PCF). You should observe hard shadows and jagged shadow edges.
9. Turn off the slope-scaled-bias to observe shadow acne.
10. Modify the slope-scaled-bias to have a very large bias to observe the peter-panning artifact.
11. An orthographic projection can be used to generate the shadow map for directional lights, and a perspective projection can be used to generate the shadow map for spotlights. Explain how cube maps and six 90° field of view perspective projections can be used to generate the shadow map for a point light.

 Hint: (Recall how dynamic cube maps were generated in Chapter 18.) Explain how the shadow map test would be done with a cube map.

Chapter 21 Ambient Occlusion

Due to performance constraints, it is common for real-time lighting models not to take indirect light (i.e., light that has bounced off other objects in the scene) into consideration. However, much light we see in the real world is indirect. In Chapter 8 we introduced the ambient term to the lighting equation:

$$c_a = A_L \otimes m_d$$

The color A_L specifies the total amount of indirect (ambient) light a surface receives from a light source, and the diffuse albedo m_d specifies the amount of incoming light that the surface reflects due to diffuse reflectance. All the ambient term does is uniformly brighten up the object a bit so that it does not go completely black in shadow—there is no real physics calculation at all. The idea is that the indirect light has scattered and bounced around the scene so many times that it strikes the object equally in every direction. Figure 21.1 shows that if we draw a model using only the ambient term, it is rendered out as a constant color.

Figure 21.1 makes it clear that our ambient term could use some improvement. In this chapter, we discuss the popular technique of ambient occlusion to improve our ambient term.

676 Topics

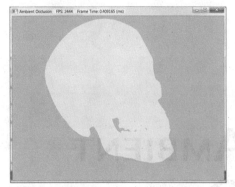

Figure 21.1. A mesh rendered with only the ambient term appears as a solid color.

Objectives:

1. To understand the basic idea behind ambient occlusion and how to implement ambient occlusion via ray casting.
2. To learn how to implement a real-time approximation of ambient occlusion in screen space called screen space ambient occlusion.

21.1 AMBIENT OCCLUSION VIA RAY CASTING

The idea of ambient occlusion is that the amount of indirect light a point **p** on a surface receives is proportional to how occluded it is to incoming light over the hemisphere about **p**—see Figure 21.2.

One way to estimate the occlusion of a point **p** is via ray casting. We randomly cast rays over the hemisphere about **p**, and check for intersections against the mesh (Figure 21.3). If we cast N rays, and h of them intersect the mesh, then the point has the occlusion value:

$$\text{occlusion} = \frac{h}{N} \in [0,1]$$

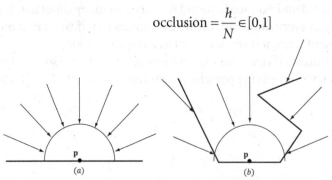

Figure 21.2. (a) A point **p** is completely unoccluded and all incoming light over the hemisphere about **p** reaches **p**. (b) Geometry partially occludes **p** and blocks incoming light rays over the hemisphere about **p**.

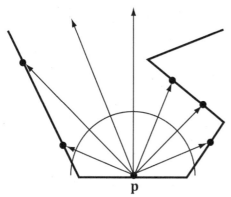

Figure 21.3. Estimating ambient occlusion via ray casting.

Only rays with an intersection point **q** whose distance from **p** is less than some threshold value *d* should contribute to the occlusion estimate; this is because an intersection point **q** far away from **p** is too far to occlude it.

The occlusion factor measures how occluded the point is (i.e., how much light it does not receive). For the purposes of calculations, we like to work with the inverse of this. That is, we want to know how much light the point does receive—this is called *accessibility* (or we call it ambient-access) and is derived from occlusion as:

$$accessiblity = 1 - occlusion \in [0,1]$$

The following code performs the ray cast per triangle, and then averages the occlusion results with the vertices that share the triangle. The ray origin is the triangle's centroid, and we generate a random ray direction over the hemisphere of the triangle.

```
void AmbientOcclusionApp::BuildVertexAmbientOcclusion(
    std::vector<Vertex::AmbientOcclusion>& vertices,
    const std::vector<UINT>& indices)
{
    UINT vcount = vertices.size();
    UINT tcount = indices.size()/3;

    std::vector<XMFLOAT3> positions(vcount);
    for(UINT i = 0; i < vcount; ++i)
        positions[i] = vertices[i].Pos;

    Octree octree;
    octree.Build(positions, indices);

    // For each vertex, count how many triangles contain the vertex.
    std::vector<int> vertexSharedCount(vcount);

    // Cast rays for each triangle, and average triangle occlusion
    // with the vertices that share this triangle.
    for(UINT i = 0; i < tcount; ++i)
```

```cpp
{
  UINT i0 = indices[i*3+0];
  UINT i1 = indices[i*3+1];
  UINT i2 = indices[i*3+2];

  XMVECTOR v0 = XMLoadFloat3(&vertices[i0].Pos);
  XMVECTOR v1 = XMLoadFloat3(&vertices[i1].Pos);
  XMVECTOR v2 = XMLoadFloat3(&vertices[i2].Pos);

  XMVECTOR edge0 = v1 - v0;
  XMVECTOR edge1 = v2 - v0;

  XMVECTOR normal = XMVector3Normalize(
    XMVector3Cross(edge0, edge1));

  XMVECTOR centroid = (v0 + v1 + v2)/3.0f;

  // Offset to avoid self intersection.
  centroid += 0.001f*normal;

  const int NumSampleRays = 32;
  float numUnoccluded = 0;
  for(int j = 0; j < NumSampleRays; ++j)
  {
    XMVECTOR randomDir = MathHelper::RandHemisphereUnitVec3(normal);

    // Test if the random ray intersects the scene mesh.
    //
    // TODO: Technically we should not count intersections
    // that are far away as occluding the triangle, but
    // this is OK for demo.
    if( !octree.RayOctreeIntersect(centroid, randomDir) )
    {
      numUnoccluded++;
    }
  }

  float ambientAccess = numUnoccluded / NumSampleRays;

  // Average with vertices that share this face.
  vertices[i0].AmbientAccess += ambientAccess;
  vertices[i1].AmbientAccess += ambientAccess;
  vertices[i2].AmbientAccess += ambientAccess;

  vertexSharedCount[i0]++;
  vertexSharedCount[i1]++;
  vertexSharedCount[i2]++;
}

// Finish average by dividing by the number of samples we added,
// and store in the vertex attribute.
for(UINT i = 0; i < vcount; ++i)
```

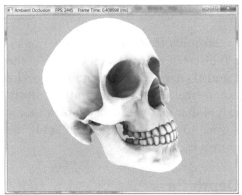

Figure 21.4. The mesh is rendered only with ambient occlusion—there are no scene lights. Notice how the crevices are darker; this is because when we cast rays out they are more likely to intersect geometry and contribute to occlusion. On the other hand, the skull cap is white (unoccluded) because when we cast rays out over the hemisphere for points on the skull cap, they will not intersect any geometry of the skull.

```
    {
       vertices[i].AmbientAccess /= vertexSharedCount[i];
    }
}
```

> **Note:** *The demo uses an octree to speed up the ray/triangle intersection tests. For a mesh with thousands of triangles, it would be very slow to test each random ray with every mesh triangle. An octree sorts the triangles spatially, so we can quickly find only the triangles that have a good chance of intersecting the ray; this reduces the number of ray/triangle intersection tests substantially. An octree is a classic spatial data structure, and Exercise 1 asks you to research them further.*

Figure 21.4 shows a screenshot of a model rendered only with ambient occlusion generated by the previous algorithm (there are no light sources in the scene). The ambient occlusion is generated as a precomputation step during initialization and stored as vertex attributes. As we can see, it is a huge improvement over Figure 21.1—the model actually looks 3D now.

Precomputing ambient occlusion works well for static models; there are even tools (*http://www.xnormal.net*) that generate *ambient occlusion maps*—textures that store ambient occlusion data. However, for animated models these static approaches break down. If you load and run the "Ambient Occlusion" demo, you will notice that it takes a few seconds to precompute the ambient occlusion for just one model. Hence, casting rays at runtime to implement dynamic ambient occlusion is not feasible. In the next section, we examine a popular technique for computing ambient occlusion in real-time using screen space information.

21.2 SCREEN SPACE AMBIENT OCCLUSION

The strategy of *screen space ambient occlusion* (SSAO) is, for every frame, render the scene view space normals to a full screen render target and the scene depth to the usual depth/stencil buffer, and then estimate the ambient occlusion at each pixel using only the view space normal render target and the depth/stencil buffer as input. Once we have a texture that represents the ambient occlusion at each pixel, we render the scene as usual to the back buffer, but apply the SSAO information to scale the ambient term at each pixel.

21.2.1 Render Normals and Depth Pass

First we render the view space normal vectors of the scene objects to a screen sized `DXGI_FORMAT_R16G16B16A16_FLOAT` texture map, while the usual depth/stencil buffer is bound to lay down the scene depth. The vertex/pixel shaders used for this pass are as follows:

```
// Include common HLSL code.
#include "Common.hlsl"

struct VertexIn
{
  float3 PosL    : POSITION;
  float3 NormalL : NORMAL;
  float2 TexC    : TEXCOORD;
  float3 TangentU : TANGENT;
};

struct VertexOut
{
  float4 PosH     : SV_POSITION;
  float3 NormalW  : NORMAL;
  float3 TangentW : TANGENT;
  float2 TexC     : TEXCOORD;
};

VertexOut VS(VertexIn vin)
{
  VertexOut vout = (VertexOut)0.0f;

  // Fetch the material data.
  MaterialData matData = gMaterialData[gMaterialIndex];

  // Assumes nonuniform scaling; otherwise, need to use
  // inverse-transpose of world matrix.
  vout.NormalW = mul(vin.NormalL, (float3x3)gWorld);
  vout.TangentW = mul(vin.TangentU, (float3x3)gWorld);

  // Transform to homogeneous clip space.
  float4 posW = mul(float4(vin.PosL, 1.0f), gWorld);
```

```
  vout.PosH = mul(posW, gViewProj);

  float4 texC = mul(float4(vin.TexC, 0.0f, 1.0f), gTexTransform);
  vout.TexC = mul(texC, matData.MatTransform).xy;

  return vout;
}

float4 PS(VertexOut pin) : SV_Target
{
  // Fetch the material data.
  MaterialData matData = gMaterialData[gMaterialIndex];
  float4 diffuseAlbedo = matData.DiffuseAlbedo;
  uint diffuseMapIndex = matData.DiffuseMapIndex;
  uint normalMapIndex = matData.NormalMapIndex;

  // Dynamically look up the texture in the array.
  diffuseAlbedo *= gTextureMaps[diffuseMapIndex].
    Sample(gsamAnisotropicWrap, pin.TexC);

#ifdef ALPHA_TEST
  // Discard pixel if texture alpha < 0.1. We do this test as soon
  // as possible in the shader so that we can potentially exit the
  // shader early, thereby skipping the rest of the shader code.
  clip(diffuseAlbedo.a - 0.1f);
#endif

  // Interpolating normal can unnormalize it, so renormalize it.
  pin.NormalW = normalize(pin.NormalW);

  // NOTE: We use interpolated vertex normal for SSAO.

  // Write normal in view space coordinates
  float3 normalV = mul(pin.NormalW, (float3x3)gView);
  return float4(normalV, 0.0f);
}
```

As the code shows, the pixel shader outputs the normal vector in view space. Observe that we are writing to a floating-point render target, so there is no problem writing out arbitrary floating-point data.

21.2.2 Ambient Occlusion Pass

After we have laid down the view space normals and scene depth, we disable the depth buffer (we do not need it for generating the ambient occlusion texture), and draw a full screen quad to invoke the SSAO pixel shader at each pixel. The pixel shader will then use the normal texture and depth buffer to generate an ambient accessibility value at each pixel. We call the generated texture map in this pass the *SSAO map*. Although we render the normal/depth map at full screen resolution (i.e., the resolution of our back buffer), we render to the SSAO map at half the width and height of the back buffer for performance

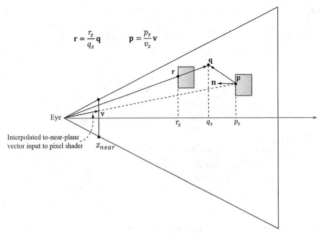

Figure 21.5. The points involved in SSAO. The point **p** corresponds to the current pixel we are processing, and it is reconstructed from the depth value stored in the depth buffer and the vector **v** that passes through the near plane at this pixel. The point **q** is a random point in the hemisphere of **p**. The point **r** corresponds to the nearest visible point along the ray from the eye to **q**. The point **r** contributes to the occlusion of **p** if $|p_z - r_z|$ is sufficiently small and the angle between **r** − **p** and **n** is less than 90°. In the demo, we take 14 random sample points and average the occlusion from each to estimate the ambient occlusion in screen space.

reasons. Rendering at half the dimensions does not affect quality too much, as ambient occlusion is a low frequency effect. Refer to Figure 21.5 throughout the following subsections.

21.2.2.1 Reconstruct View Space Position

When we draw the full screen quad to invoke the SSAO pixel shader at each pixel of the SSAO map, we can use the inverse of the projection matrix to transform the quad corner points in NDC space to points on the near projection plane window:

```
static const float2 gTexCoords[6] =
{
  float2(0.0f, 1.0f),
  float2(0.0f, 0.0f),
  float2(1.0f, 0.0f),
  float2(0.0f, 1.0f),
  float2(1.0f, 0.0f),
  float2(1.0f, 1.0f)
};

// Draw call with 6 vertices
VertexOut VS(uint vid : SV_VertexID)
{
    VertexOut vout;

    vout.TexC = gTexCoords[vid];

    // Quad covering screen in NDC space.
    vout.PosH = float4(2.0f*vout.TexC.x - 1.0f, 1.0f - 2.0f*vout.TexC.y,
       0.0f, 1.0f);
```

```
    // Transform quad corners to view space near plane.
    float4 ph = mul(vout.PosH, gInvProj);
    vout.PosV = ph.xyz / ph.w;

    return vout;
}
```

These to-near-plane vectors are interpolated across the quad and give us a vector $\mathbf{v}$ (Figure 21.5) from the eye to the near plane for each pixel. Now, for each pixel, we sample the depth buffer so that we have the z-coordinate p_z of the nearest visible point to the eye in NDC coordinates. The goal is to reconstruct the view space position $\mathbf{p} = (p_x, p_y, p_z)$ from the sampled NDC z-coordinate p_z and the interpolated to-near-plane vector $\mathbf{v}$. This reconstruction is done as follows. Since the ray of $\mathbf{v}$ passes through $\mathbf{p}$, there exists a t such that $\mathbf{p} = t\mathbf{v}$. In particular, $p_z = tv_z$ so that $t = p_z/v_z$. Thus $\mathbf{p} = \frac{p_z}{v_z}\mathbf{v}$. The reconstruction code in the pixel shader is as follows:

```
float NdcDepthToViewDepth(float z_ndc)
{
    // We can invert the calculation from NDC space to view space for the
    // z-coordinate. We have that
    // z_ndc = A + B/viewZ, where gProj[2,2]=A and gProj[3,2]=B.
    // Therefore...
    float viewZ = gProj[3][2] / (z_ndc - gProj[2][2]);
    return viewZ;
}

float4 PS(VertexOut pin) : SV_Target
{
    // Get z-coord of this pixel in NDC space from depth map.
    float pz = gDepthMap.SampleLevel(gsamDepthMap, pin.TexC, 0.0f).r;
    // Transform depth to view space.
    pz = NdcDepthToViewDepth(pz);

    // Reconstruct the view space position of the point with depth pz.
    float3 p = (pz/pin.PosV.z)*pin.PosV;

    [...]
}
```

21.2.2.2 Generate Random Samples

This step is analogous to the random ray cast over the hemisphere. We randomly sample N points $\mathbf{q}$ about $\mathbf{p}$ that are also in front of $\mathbf{p}$ and within a specified occlusion radius. The occlusion radius is an artistic parameter to control how far away from $\mathbf{p}$ we want to take the random sample points. Choosing to only sample points in front of $\mathbf{p}$ is analogous to only casting rays over the hemisphere instead of the whole sphere when doing ray casted ambient occlusion.

The next question is how to generate the random samples. We can generate random vectors and store them in a texture map, and then sample this texture map at *N* different positions to get *N* random vectors. However, since they are random we have no guarantee that the vectors we sample will be uniformly distributed—they may all clump together in roughly the same direction, which would give a bad occlusion estimate. To overcome this, we do the following trick. In our implementation, we use $N = 14$ samples, and we generate fourteen equally distributed vectors in the C++ code:

```
void Ssao::BuildOffsetVectors()
{
    // Start with 14 uniformly distributed vectors. We choose the
    // 8 corners of the cube and the 6 center points along each
    // cube face. We always alternate the points on opposite sides
    // of the cubes. This way we still get the vectors spread out
    // even if we choose to use less than 14 samples.

    // 8 cube corners
    mOffsets[0] = XMFLOAT4(+1.0f, +1.0f, +1.0f, 0.0f);
    mOffsets[1] = XMFLOAT4(-1.0f, -1.0f, -1.0f, 0.0f);

    mOffsets[2] = XMFLOAT4(-1.0f, +1.0f, +1.0f, 0.0f);
    mOffsets[3] = XMFLOAT4(+1.0f, -1.0f, -1.0f, 0.0f);

    mOffsets[4] = XMFLOAT4(+1.0f, +1.0f, -1.0f, 0.0f);
    mOffsets[5] = XMFLOAT4(-1.0f, -1.0f, +1.0f, 0.0f);

    mOffsets[6] = XMFLOAT4(-1.0f, +1.0f, -1.0f, 0.0f);
    mOffsets[7] = XMFLOAT4(+1.0f, -1.0f, +1.0f, 0.0f);

    // 6 centers of cube faces
    mOffsets[8] = XMFLOAT4(-1.0f, 0.0f, 0.0f, 0.0f);
    mOffsets[9] = XMFLOAT4(+1.0f, 0.0f, 0.0f, 0.0f);

    mOffsets[10] = XMFLOAT4(0.0f, -1.0f, 0.0f, 0.0f);
    mOffsets[11] = XMFLOAT4(0.0f, +1.0f, 0.0f, 0.0f);

    mOffsets[12] = XMFLOAT4(0.0f, 0.0f, -1.0f, 0.0f);
    mOffsets[13] = XMFLOAT4(0.0f, 0.0f, +1.0f, 0.0f);

    for(int i = 0; i < 14; ++i)
    {
        // Create random lengths in [0.25, 1.0].
        float s = MathHelper::RandF(0.25f, 1.0f);

        XMVECTOR v = s * XMVector4Normalize(XMLoadFloat4(&mOffsets[i]));

        XMStoreFloat4(&mOffsets[i], v);
    }
}
```

We use 4D homogeneous vectors just so we do not have to worry about any alignment issues when setting the array of offset vectors to the effect.

Now, in the pixel shader we just sample the random vector texture map once, and use it to reflect our fourteen equally distributed vectors. This results in 14 *equally distributed random vectors*.

21.2.2.3 Generate the Potential Occluding Points

We now have random sample points **q** surrounding **p**. However, we know nothing about them—whether they occupy empty space or a solid object; therefore, we cannot use them to test if they occlude **p**. To find potential occluding points, we need depth information from the depth buffer. So what we do is generate projective texture coordinates for each **q** with respect to the camera, and use these to sample the depth buffer to get the depth in NDC space, and then transform to view space to obtain the depth r_z of the nearest visible pixel along the ray from the eye to **q**. With the z-coordinates r_z known, we can reconstruct the full 3D view space position **r** in an analogous way we did in §21.2.2.1. Because the vector from the eye to **q** passes through **r** there exists a t such that $\mathbf{r} = t\mathbf{q}$. In particular, $r_z = tq_z$ so $t = r_z/q_z$. Therefore, $\mathbf{r} = \frac{r_z}{q_z}\mathbf{q}$. The points **r**, one generated for each random sample point **q**, are our potential occluding points.

21.2.2.4 Perform the Occlusion Test

Now that we have our potential occluding points **r**, we can perform our occlusion test to estimate if they occlude **p**. The test relies on two quantities:

1. The view space depth distance $|p_z - r_z|$. We linearly scale down the occlusion as the distance increases since points farther away from have less of an occluding effect. If the distance is beyond some specified maximum distance, then no occlusion occurs. Also, if the distance is very small, then we assume **p** and **q** are on the same plane so **q** cannot occlude **p**.

2. The angle between **n** and $\mathbf{r} - \mathbf{p}$ measured by $\max\left(\mathbf{n} \cdot \left(\frac{\mathbf{r}-\mathbf{p}}{\|\mathbf{r}-\mathbf{p}\|}\right), 0\right)$. This is to prevent self-intersection (see Figure 21.6).

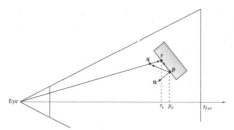

Figure 21.6. If **r** lies on the same plane as **p**, it can pass the first condition that the distance $|p_z - r_z|$ is small enough that **r** occludes **p**. However, the figure shows this is incorrect as **r** does not occlude **p** since they lie on the same plane. Scaling the occlusion by $\max\left(\mathbf{n} \cdot \left(\frac{\mathbf{r}-\mathbf{p}}{\|\mathbf{r}-\mathbf{p}\|}\right), 0\right)$ prevents this situation.

21.2.2.5 Finishing the Calculation

After we have summed the occlusion from each sample, we compute the average occlusion by dividing by the sample count. Then we compute the ambient-access, and finally raise the ambient-access to a power to increase the contrast. You may also wish to increase the brightness of the ambient map by adding some number to increase the intensity. You can experiment with different contrast/brightness values.

```
occlusionSum /= gSampleCount;

float access = 1.0f - occlusionSum;

// Sharpen the contrast of the SSAO map to make the SSAO affect more dramatic.
return saturate(pow(access, 4.0f));
```

21.2.2.6 Implementation

The previous section outlined the key ingredients for generating the SSAO map. Below are the HLSL programs:

```
//===========================================================================
// Ssao.hlsl by Frank Luna (C) 2015 All Rights Reserved.
//===========================================================================

cbuffer cbSsao : register(b0)
{
    float4x4 gProj;
    float4x4 gInvProj;
    float4x4 gProjTex;
    float4   gOffsetVectors[14];

    // For SsaoBlur.hlsl
    float4 gBlurWeights[3];

    float2 gInvRenderTargetSize;

    // Coordinates given in view space.
    float  gOcclusionRadius;
    float  gOcclusionFadeStart;
    float  gOcclusionFadeEnd;
    float  gSurfaceEpsilon;
};

cbuffer cbRootConstants : register(b1)
{
    bool gHorizontalBlur;
};

// Nonnumeric values cannot be added to a cbuffer.
Texture2D gNormalMap    : register(t0);
Texture2D gDepthMap     : register(t1);
Texture2D gRandomVecMap : register(t2);

SamplerState gsamPointClamp : register(s0);
```

```
SamplerState gsamLinearClamp : register(s1);
SamplerState gsamDepthMap : register(s2);
SamplerState gsamLinearWrap : register(s3);

static const int gSampleCount = 14;

static const float2 gTexCoords[6] =
{
  float2(0.0f, 1.0f),
  float2(0.0f, 0.0f),
  float2(1.0f, 0.0f),
  float2(0.0f, 1.0f),
  float2(1.0f, 0.0f),
  float2(1.0f, 1.0f)
};

struct VertexOut
{
  float4 PosH : SV_POSITION;
  float3 PosV : POSITION;
  float2 TexC : TEXCOORD0;
};

VertexOut VS(uint vid : SV_VertexID)
{
  VertexOut vout;

  vout.TexC = gTexCoords[vid];

  // Quad covering screen in NDC space.
  vout.PosH = float4(2.0f*vout.TexC.x - 1.0f, 1.0f - 2.0f*vout.TexC.y,
    0.0f, 1.0f);

  // Transform quad corners to view space near plane.
  float4 ph = mul(vout.PosH, gInvProj);
  vout.PosV = ph.xyz / ph.w;

  return vout;
}

// Determines how much the sample point q occludes the point p as a
    function
// of distZ.
float OcclusionFunction(float distZ)
{
  //
  // If depth(q) is "behind" depth(p), then q cannot occlude p.
    Moreover, if
  // depth(q) and depth(p) are sufficiently close, then we also assume
    q cannot
  // occlude p because q needs to be in front of p by Epsilon to
    occlude p.
  //
  // We use the following function to determine the occlusion.
  //
```

```
//
//      1.0    --------------\
//              |       | \
//              |       |  \
//              |       |   \
//              |       |    \
//              |       |     \
//              |       |      \
// ------|------|-------------|--------------|---------|--> zv
//       0    Eps      z0             z1
//

    float occlusion = 0.0f;
    if(distZ > gSurfaceEpsilon)
    {
      float fadeLength = gOcclusionFadeEnd - gOcclusionFadeStart;

      // Linearly decrease occlusion from 1 to 0 as distZ goes
      // from gOcclusionFadeStart to gOcclusionFadeEnd.
      occlusion = saturate( (gOcclusionFadeEnd-distZ)/fadeLength );
    }

    return occlusion;
}

float NdcDepthToViewDepth(float z_ndc)
{
  // z_ndc = A + B/viewZ, where gProj[2,2]=A and gProj[3,2]=B.
  float viewZ = gProj[3][2] / (z_ndc - gProj[2][2]);
  return viewZ;
}

float4 PS(VertexOut pin) : SV_Target
{
  // p -- the point we are computing the ambient occlusion for.
  // n -- normal vector at p.
  // q -- a random offset from p.
  // r -- a potential occluder that might occlude p.

  // Get viewspace normal and z-coord of this pixel.
  float3 n = gNormalMap.SampleLevel(gsamPointClamp, pin.TexC, 0.0f).
    xyz;
  float pz = gDepthMap.SampleLevel(gsamDepthMap, pin.TexC, 0.0f).r;
  pz = NdcDepthToViewDepth(pz);

  //
  // Reconstruct full view space position (x,y,z).
  // Find t such that p = t*pin.PosV.
  // p.z = t*pin.PosV.z
  // t = p.z / pin.PosV.z
  //
  float3 p = (pz/pin.PosV.z)*pin.PosV;

  // Extract random vector and map from [0,1] --> [-1, +1].
  float3 randVec = 2.0f*gRandomVecMap.SampleLevel(
    gsamLinearWrap, 4.0f*pin.TexC, 0.0f).rgb - 1.0f;
```

```
float occlusionSum = 0.0f;

// Sample neighboring points about p in the hemisphere oriented by n.
for(int i = 0; i < gSampleCount; ++i)
{
  // Are offset vectors are fixed and uniformly distributed (so that
  // our offset vectors do not clump in the same direction). If we
  // reflect them about a random vector then we get a random uniform
  // distribution of offset vectors.
  float3 offset = reflect(gOffsetVectors[i].xyz, randVec);

  // Flip offset vector if it is behind the plane defined by (p, n).
  float flip = sign( dot(offset, n) );

  // Sample a point near p within the occlusion radius.
  float3 q = p + flip * gOcclusionRadius * offset;

  // Project q and generate projective tex-coords.
  float4 projQ = mul(float4(q, 1.0f), gProjTex);
  projQ /= projQ.w;

  // Find the nearest depth value along the ray from the eye to q
  // (this is not the depth of q, as q is just an arbitrary point
  // near p and might occupy empty space). To find the nearest depth
  // we look it up in the depthmap.

  float rz = gDepthMap.SampleLevel(gsamDepthMap, projQ.xy, 0.0f).r;
  rz = NdcDepthToViewDepth(rz);

  // Reconstruct full view space position r = (rx,ry,rz). We know r
  // lies on the ray of q, so there exists a t such that r = t*q.
  // r.z = t*q.z ==> t = r.z / q.z

  float3 r = (rz / q.z) * q;

  //
  // Test whether r occludes p.
  //   * The product dot(n, normalize(r - p)) measures how much in
  //     front of the plane(p,n) the occluder point r is. The more in
  //     front it is, the more occlusion weight we give it. This also
  //     prevents self shadowing where a point r on an angled plane (p,n)
  //     could give a false occlusion since they have different depth
  //     values with respect to the eye.
  //   * The weight of the occlusion is scaled based on how far the
  //     occluder is from the point we are computing the occlusion of. If
  //     the occluder r is far away from p, then it does not occlude it.
  //

  float distZ = p.z - r.z;
  float dp = max(dot(n, normalize(r - p)), 0.0f);
  float occlusion = dp * OcclusionFunction(distZ);

  occlusionSum += occlusion;
}
```

Figure 21.7. SSAO appears noisy due to the fact that we have only taken a few random samples.

```
    occlusionSum /= gSampleCount;

    float access = 1.0f - occlusionSum;

    // Sharpen the contrast of the SSAO map to make the SSAO affect more
    // dramatic.
    return saturate(pow(access, 2.0f));
}
```

 For scenes with large viewing distances, rendering errors can result due to the limited accuracy of the depth buffer. A simple solution is to fade out the affect of SSAO with distance.

21.2.3 Blur Pass

Figure 21.7 shows what our ambient occlusion map currently looks like. The noise is due to the fact that we have only taken a few random samples. Taking enough samples to hide the noise is impractical for real-time. The common solution is to apply an edge preserving blur (i.e., bilateral blur) to the SSAO map to smooth it out. If we used a non-edge preserving blur, then we lose definition in the scene as sharp discontinuities become smoothed out. The edge preserving blur is similar to the blur we implemented in Chapter 13, except we add a conditional statement so that we do not blur across edges (edges are detected from the normal/depth map):

```
//=============================================================
// SsaoBlur.hlsl by Frank Luna (C) 2015 All Rights Reserved.
//
// Performs a bilateral edge preserving blur of the ambient map. We use
// a pixel shader instead of compute shader to avoid the switch from
// compute mode to rendering mode. The texture cache makes up for some
// of the loss of not having shared memory. The ambient map uses 16-bit
// texture format, which is small, so we should be able to fit a lot of
// texels in the cache.
```

```hlsl
//===========================================================================
cbuffer cbSsao : register(b0)
{
  float4x4 gProj;
  float4x4 gInvProj;
  float4x4 gProjTex;
  float4   gOffsetVectors[14];

  // For SsaoBlur.hlsl
  float4 gBlurWeights[3];

  float2 gInvRenderTargetSize;

  // Coordinates given in view space.
  float gOcclusionRadius;
  float gOcclusionFadeStart;
  float gOcclusionFadeEnd;
  float gSurfaceEpsilon;


};

cbuffer cbRootConstants : register(b1)
{
  bool gHorizontalBlur;
};

// Nonnumeric values cannot be added to a cbuffer.
Texture2D gNormalMap : register(t0);
Texture2D gDepthMap  : register(t1);
Texture2D gInputMap  : register(t2);

SamplerState gsamPointClamp  : register(s0);
SamplerState gsamLinearClamp : register(s1);
SamplerState gsamDepthMap    : register(s2);
SamplerState gsamLinearWrap  : register(s3);

static const int gBlurRadius = 5;

static const float2 gTexCoords[6] =
{
  float2(0.0f, 1.0f),
  float2(0.0f, 0.0f),
  float2(1.0f, 0.0f),
  float2(0.0f, 1.0f),
  float2(1.0f, 0.0f),
  float2(1.0f, 1.0f)
};

struct VertexOut
{
  float4 PosH : SV_POSITION;
  float2 TexC : TEXCOORD;
};
```

```
VertexOut VS(uint vid : SV_VertexID)
{
  VertexOut vout;

  vout.TexC = gTexCoords[vid];

  // Quad covering screen in NDC space.
  vout.PosH = float4(2.0f*vout.TexC.x - 1.0f, 1.0f - 2.0f*vout.TexC.y,
    0.0f, 1.0f);

  return vout;
}

float NdcDepthToViewDepth(float z_ndc)
{
  // z_ndc = A + B/viewZ, where gProj[2,2]=A and gProj[3,2]=B.
  float viewZ = gProj[3][2] / (z_ndc - gProj[2][2]);
  return viewZ;
}

float4 PS(VertexOut pin) : SV_Target
{
  // unpack into float array.
  float blurWeights[12] =
  {
    gBlurWeights[0].x, gBlurWeights[0].y, gBlurWeights[0].z,
    gBlurWeights[0].w,
    gBlurWeights[1].x, gBlurWeights[1].y, gBlurWeights[1].z,
    gBlurWeights[1].w,
    gBlurWeights[2].x, gBlurWeights[2].y, gBlurWeights[2].z,
    gBlurWeights[2].w,
  };

    float2 texOffset;
    if(gHorizontalBlur)
    {
       texOffset = float2(gInvRenderTargetSize.x, 0.0f);
    }
    else
    {
       texOffset = float2(0.0f, gInvRenderTargetSize.y);
    }

    // The center value always contributes to the sum.
    float4 color   = blurWeights[gBlurRadius] * gInputMap.SampleLevel(
      gsamPointClamp, pin.TexC, 0.0);
    float totalWeight = blurWeights[gBlurRadius];

  float3 centerNormal = gNormalMap.SampleLevel(gsamPointClamp, pin.
    TexC, 0.0f).xyz;
  float centerDepth = NdcDepthToViewDepth(
    gDepthMap.SampleLevel(gsamDepthMap, pin.TexC, 0.0f).r);

  for(float i = -gBlurRadius; i <=gBlurRadius; ++i)
    {
```

```
    // We already added in the center weight.
    if( i == 0 )
      continue;

    float2 tex = pin.TexC + i*texOffset;

    float3 neighborNormal = gNormalMap.SampleLevel(gsamPointClamp, tex,
     0.0f).xyz;
    float neighborDepth = NdcDepthToViewDepth(
      gDepthMap.SampleLevel(gsamDepthMap, tex, 0.0f).r);

    //
    // If the center value and neighbor values differ too much
    // (either in normal or depth), then we assume we are
    // sampling across a discontinuity. We discard such
    // samples from the blur.
    //

    if( dot(neighborNormal, centerNormal) >= 0.8f &&
      abs(neighborDepth - centerDepth) <= 0.2f )
    {
      float weight = blurWeights[i + gBlurRadius];

      // Add neighbor pixel to blur.
      color += weight*gInputMap.SampleLevel(
        gsamPointClamp, tex, 0.0);

      totalWeight += weight;
    }
  }

  // Compensate for discarded samples by making total weights sum to 1.
  return color / totalWeight;
}
```

Figure 21.8 shows the ambient map after an edge preserving blur.

Figure 21.8. An edge preserving blur smoothes out the noise. In our demo, we blur the image four times.

21.2.4 Using the Ambient Occlusion Map

Thus far we have constructed the ambient occlusion map. The final step is to apply it to the scene. One might think to use alpha blending and modulate the ambient map with the back buffer. However, if we do this, then the ambient map modifies not just the ambient term, but also the diffuse and specular term of the lighting equation, which is incorrect. Instead, when we render the scene to the back buffer, we bind the ambient map as a shader input. We then generate projective texture coordinates (with respect to the camera), sample the SSAO map, and apply it only to the ambient term of the lighting equation:

```
// In Vertex shader, generate projective tex-coords
// to project SSAO map onto scene.
vout.SsaoPosH = mul(posW, gViewProjTex);

// In pixel shader, finish texture projection and sample SSAO map.
pin.SsaoPosH /= pin.SsaoPosH.w;
float ambientAccess = gSsaoMap.Sample(gsamLinearClamp, pin.SsaoPosH.xy,
    0.0f).r;

// Scale ambient term of lighting equation.
float4 ambient = ambientAccess*gAmbientLight*diffuseAlbedo;
```

Figure 21.9 shows the scene with the SSAO map applied. The SSAO can be subtle, and your scene has to reflect enough ambient light so that scaling it by the ambient-access makes enough of a noticeable difference. The advantage of SSAO is most apparent when objects are in shadow. For when objects are in shadow, the diffuse and specular terms are killed; thus only the ambient term shows up. Without SSAO, objects in shadow will appear flatly lit by a constant ambient term, but with SSAO they will keep their 3D definition.

When we render the scene view space normals, we also build the depth buffer for the scene. Consequently, when we render the scene the second time with the

Figure 21.9. Screenshot of the demo. The affects are subtle as they only affect the ambient term, but you can see darkening at the base of the columns and box, under the spheres, and around the skull.

SSAO map, we modify the depth comparison test to "EQUALS." This prevents any overdraw in the second rendering pass, as only the nearest visible pixels will pass this depth comparison test. Moreover, the second rendering pass does not need to write to the depth buffer because we already wrote the scene to the depth buffer in the normal render target pass.

```
opaquePsoDesc.DepthStencilState.DepthFunc = D3D12_COMPARISON_FUNC_
    EQUAL;
opaquePsoDesc.DepthStencilState.DepthWriteMask = D3D12_DEPTH_WRITE_
    MASK_ZERO;
ThrowIfFailed(md3dDevice->CreateGraphicsPipelineState(
    &opaquePsoDesc, IID_PPV_ARGS(&mPSOs["opaque"])));
```

21.3 SUMMARY

1. The ambient term of the lighting equation models indirect light. In our lighting model, the ambient term is simply a constant value. Therefore, when an object is in shadow and only ambient light is applied to the surface, the model appears very flat with no solid definition. The goal of ambient occlusion is to find a better estimate for the ambient term so that the object still looks 3D even with just the ambient term applied.

2. The idea of ambient occlusion is that the amount of indirect light a point **p** on a surface receives is proportional to how occluded it is to incoming light over the hemisphere about **p**. One way to estimate the occlusion of a point **p** is via ray casting. We randomly cast rays over the hemisphere about **p**, and check for intersections against the mesh. If the rays do not intersect any geometry, then the point is completely unoccluded; however, the more intersections there are, the more occluded **p** must be.

3. Ray casted ambient occlusion is too expensive to do in real-time for dynamic objects. Screen space ambient occlusion (SSAO) is a real-time approximation that is based on the view space normal/depth values. You can definitely find flaws and situations where it gives wrong results, but the results are very good in practice with the limited information it has to work with.

21.4 EXERCISES

1. Research on the web: KD-Trees, quadtrees, and octrees.
2. Modify the "Ssao" demo to do a Gaussian blur instead of an edge preserving blur. Which one do you like better?

3. Can SSAO be implemented on the compute shader? If yes, sketch out an implementation.
4. Figure 21.10 shows what happens to the SSAO map if we do not include a check for self-intersection (§21.2.2.4). Modify the "Ssao" demo to remove the self-intersection check and reproduce the results in Figure 21.10.

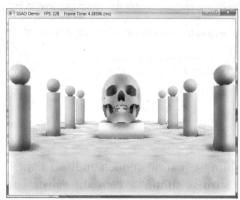

Figure 21.10. False occlusions everywhere.

Chapter 22 QUATERNIONS

In Chapter 1, we introduced a new class of mathematical objects called vectors. In particular, we learned that a 3D vector consists of an ordered 3-tuple of real numbers, and we defined operators on vectors that are useful geometrically. Likewise, in Chapter 2 we introduced matrices, which are rectangular tables of real numbers with operations defined on them that are useful; for example, we saw how matrices can represent linear and affine transformations, and how matrix multiplication corresponds to transformation composition. In this chapter, we learn about another type of mathematical objects called quaternions. We will see that a unit quaternion can be used to represent a 3D rotation, and has convenient interpolation properties. For readers looking for a comprehensive treatment of quaternions (and rotations), we like the book devoted to the topic by [Kuipers99].

Objectives:

1. To review the complex numbers and recall how complex number multiplication performs a rotation in the plane.
2. To obtain an understanding of quaternions and the operations defined on them.
3. To discover how the set of unit quaternions represent 3D rotations.
4. To find out how to convert between the various rotation representations.

5. To learn how to interpolate between unit quaternions, and understand that this is geometrically equivalent to interpolating between 3D orientations.
6. To become familiar with the DirectX Math library's quaternion functions and classes.

22.1 REVIEW OF THE COMPLEX NUMBERS

The quaternions can be viewed as a generalization of the complex numbers; this motivates us to study complex numbers before quaternions. In particular, our main goal in this section is to show that multiplying a complex number **p** (thought of as a 2D vector or point) by a unit complex number results in a rotation of **p**. We will then show in §22.3 that a special quaternion product involving a unit quaternion results in a 3D rotation of a vector or point **p**.

22.1.1 Definitions

There are different ways to introduce complex numbers. We introduce them in such a way that they immediately cause us to think of complex numbers as 2D points or vectors.

An ordered pair of real numbers $\mathbf{z} = (a, b)$ is a complex number. The first component is called the *real* part and the second component is called the *imaginary* part. Moreover, equality, addition, subtraction, multiplication and division are defined as follows:

1. $(a, b) = (c, d)$ if and only if $a = c$ and $b = d$.
2. $(a, b) \pm (c, d) = (a \pm c, b \pm d)$.
3. $(a, b)(c, d) = (ac - bd, ad + bc)$.
4. $\frac{(a,b)}{(c,d)} = \left(\frac{ac+bd}{c^2+d^2}, \frac{bc-ad}{c^2+d^2} \right)$ if $(c,d) \neq (0,0)$.

It is easy to verify that the usual arithmetic properties of real numbers also hold for complex arithmetic (e.g., commutativity, associativity, distributive laws); see Exercise 1.

If a complex number is of the form $(x, 0)$, then it is customary to identify it by the real number x and write $x = (x, 0)$; thus any real number can be thought of as a complex number with a zero imaginary component. Observe then that a real number times a complex number is given by $x(a, b) = (x, 0)(a, b) = (xa, xb) = (a, b)(x, 0) = (a, b)x$, which is reminiscent of scalar-vector multiplication.

We define the *imaginary unit* $i = (0, 1)$. Using our definition of complex multiplication, observe that $i^2 = (0, 1)(0, 1) = (-1, 0) = -1$, which implies $i = \sqrt{-1}$. This tells us that i solves the equation $x^2 = -1$.

The *complex conjugate* of a complex number $\mathbf{z} = (a, b)$ is denoted by $\bar{\mathbf{z}}$ and given by $\bar{\mathbf{z}} = (a, -b)$. A simple way to remember the complex division formula is to multiply the numerator and denominator by the conjugate of the denominator so that the denominator becomes a real number:

$$\frac{(a,b)}{(c,d)} = \frac{(a,b)}{(c,d)} \frac{(c,-d)}{(c,-d)} = \frac{(ac+bd, bc-ad)}{c^2+d^2} = \left(\frac{ac+bd}{c^2+d^2}, \frac{bc-ad}{c^2+d^2} \right)$$

Next, we show that a complex number (a, b) can be written in the form $a + ib$. We have $a = (a, 0), b = (b, 0)$ and $i = (0, 1)$, so

$$a + ib = (a,0) + (0,1)(b,0) = (a,0) + (0,b) = (a,b)$$

Using the form $a + ib$, we can recast the formulas for addition, subtraction, multiplication and division as follows:

1. $a + ib \pm c + id = (a \pm c) + i(b \pm d)$.
2. $(a+ib)(c+id) = (ac-bd) + i(ad+bc)$.
3. $\dfrac{a+ib}{c+id} = \dfrac{ac+bd}{c^2+d^2} + i \dfrac{bc-ad}{c^2+d^2}$ if $(c,d) \neq (0,0)$

Furthermore, in this form, the complex conjugate of $\mathbf{z} = a + ib$ is given by $\bar{\mathbf{z}} = a - ib$.

22.1.2 Geometric Interpretation

The ordered pair form $a + ib = (a, b)$ of a complex number naturally suggests that we think of a complex number geometrically as a 2D point or vector in the complex plane. In fact, our definition of complex number addition matches our definition of vector addition; see Figure 22.1. We will give a geometric interpretation to complex number multiplication in the next section.

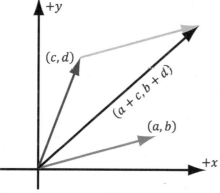

Figure 22.1. Complex addition is reminiscent of vector addition in the plane.

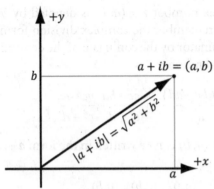

Figure 22.2. The magnitude of a complex number.

The *absolute value*, or *magnitude*, of the complex number $a + ib$ is defined as the length of the vector it represents (Figure 22.2), which we know is given by:

$$|a+ib| = \sqrt{a^2 + b^2}$$

We say that a complex number is a *unit complex number* if it has a magnitude of one.

22.1.3 Polar Representation and Rotations

Because complex numbers can be viewed as just points or vectors in the 2D complex plane, we can just as well express their components using polar coordinates (see Figure 22.3):

$$r = |a+ib|$$
$$a + ib = r\cos\theta + ir\sin\theta = r(\cos\theta + i\sin\theta)$$

The right-hand-side of the equation is called the *polar representation* of the complex number $a + ib$.

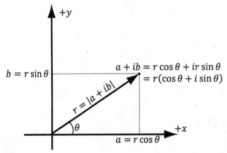

Figure 22.3. Polar representation of a complex number.

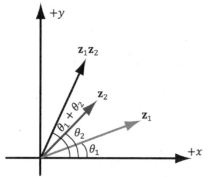

Figure 22.4. $z_1 = r_1(\cos\theta_1 + i\sin\theta_1)$, $z_2 = (\cos\theta_2 + i\sin\theta_2)$. The product $z_1 z_2$ rotates z_1 by the angle θ_2.

Let us multiply two complex numbers in polar form. Let $z_1 = r_1(\cos\theta_1 + i\sin\theta_1)$ and $z_2 = r_2(\cos\theta_2 + i\sin\theta_2)$. Then

$$z_1 z_2 = r_1 r_2 (\cos\theta_1 \cos\theta_2 - \sin\theta_1 \sin\theta_2 + i(\cos\theta_1 \sin\theta_2 + \sin\theta_1 \cos\theta_2))$$
$$= r_1 r_2 (\cos(\theta_1 + \theta_2) + i\sin(\theta_1 + \theta_2))$$

where we employed the trigonometric identities

$$\sin(\alpha + \beta) = \sin\alpha \cos\beta + \cos\alpha \sin\beta$$
$$\cos(\alpha + \beta) = \cos\alpha \cos\beta - \sin\alpha \sin\beta$$

Thus, geometrically, the product $z_1 z_2$ is the complex number representing the vector with magnitude $r_1 r_2$ and which makes an angle $\theta_1 + \theta_2$ with the real axis. In particular, if $r_2 = 1$, then $z_1 z_2 = r_1(\cos(\theta_1 + \theta_2) + i\sin(\theta_1 + \theta_2))$, which, geometrically, rotates z_1 by the angle θ_2; see Figure 22.4. Therefore, multiplying a complex number z_1 (thought of as a 2D vector or point) by a unit complex number z_2 results in a rotation of z_1.

22.2 QUATERNION ALGEBRA

22.2.1 Definition and Basic Operations

An ordered 4-tuple of real numbers $\mathbf{q} = (x, y, z, w) = (q_1, q_2, q_3, q_4)$ is a quaternion. This is commonly abbreviated as $\mathbf{q} = (\mathbf{u}, w) = (x, y, z, w)$, and we call $\mathbf{u} = (x, y, z)$ the imaginary vector part and w the real part. Moreover, equality, addition, subtraction, multiplication, and division are defined as follows:

1. $(\mathbf{u}, a) = (\mathbf{v}, b)$ if and only if $\mathbf{u} = \mathbf{v}$ and $a = b$.
2. $(\mathbf{u}, a) \pm (\mathbf{v}, b) = (\mathbf{u} \pm \mathbf{v}, a \pm b)$.
3. $(\mathbf{u}, a)(\mathbf{v}, b) = (a\mathbf{v} + b\mathbf{u} + \mathbf{u} \times \mathbf{v}, ab - \mathbf{u} \cdot \mathbf{v})$

The definition of multiplication may seem "weird," but these operations are definitions, so we can *define* them however we want—and this definition turns out to be useful. The definition of matrix multiplication may have seemed weird at first, but it turned out to be useful.

Let $\mathbf{p} = (\mathbf{u}, p_4) = (p_1, p_2, p_3, p_4)$ and $\mathbf{q} = (\mathbf{v}, q_4) = (q_1, q_2, q_3, q_4)$. Then $\mathbf{u} \times \mathbf{v} = (p_2 q_3 - p_3 q_2, p_3 q_1 - p_1 q_3, p_1 q_2 - p_2 q_1)$ and $\mathbf{u} \cdot \mathbf{v} = p_1 q_1 + p_2 q_2 + p_3 q_3$. Now, in component form, the quaternion product $\mathbf{r} = \mathbf{pq}$ takes on the form:

$$r_1 = p_4 q_1 + q_4 p_1 + p_2 q_3 - p_3 q_2 = q_1 p_4 - q_2 p_3 + q_3 p_2 + q_4 p_1$$
$$r_2 = p_4 q_2 + q_4 p_2 + p_3 q_1 - p_1 q_3 = q_1 p_3 + q_2 p_4 - q_3 p_1 + q_4 p_2$$
$$r_3 = p_4 q_3 + q_4 p_3 + p_1 q_2 - p_2 q_1 = -q_1 p_2 + q_2 p_1 + q_3 p_4 + q_4 p_3$$
$$r_4 = p_4 q_4 - p_1 q_1 - p_2 q_2 - p_3 q_3 = -q_1 p_1 - q_2 p_2 - q_3 p_3 + q_4 p_4$$

This can be written as a matrix product:

$$\mathbf{pq} = \begin{bmatrix} p_4 & -p_3 & p_2 & p_1 \\ p_3 & p_4 & -p_1 & p_2 \\ -p_2 & p_1 & p_4 & p_3 \\ -p_1 & -p_2 & -p_3 & p_4 \end{bmatrix} \begin{bmatrix} q_1 \\ q_2 \\ q_3 \\ q_4 \end{bmatrix}$$

Note: *If you prefer row vector-matrix multiplication, simply take the transpose:*

$$\left(\begin{bmatrix} p_4 & -p_3 & p_2 & p_1 \\ p_3 & p_4 & -p_1 & p_2 \\ -p_2 & p_1 & p_4 & p_3 \\ -p_1 & -p_2 & -p_3 & p_4 \end{bmatrix} \begin{bmatrix} q_1 \\ q_2 \\ q_3 \\ q_4 \end{bmatrix} \right)^T = \begin{bmatrix} q_1 \\ q_2 \\ q_3 \\ q_4 \end{bmatrix}^T \begin{bmatrix} p_4 & -p_3 & p_2 & p_1 \\ p_3 & p_4 & -p_1 & p_2 \\ -p_2 & p_1 & p_4 & p_3 \\ -p_1 & -p_2 & -p_3 & p_4 \end{bmatrix}^T$$

22.2.2 Special Products

Let $\mathbf{i} = (1, 0, 0, 0)$, $\mathbf{j} = (0, 1, 0, 0)$, $\mathbf{k} = (0, 0, 1, 0)$ be quaternions. Then we have the special products, some of which are reminiscent of the behavior of the cross product:

$$\mathbf{i}^2 = \mathbf{j}^2 = \mathbf{k}^2 = \mathbf{ijk} = -1$$
$$\mathbf{ij} = \mathbf{k} = -\mathbf{ji}$$
$$\mathbf{jk} = \mathbf{i} = -\mathbf{kj}$$
$$\mathbf{ki} = \mathbf{j} = -\mathbf{ik}$$

These equations follow directly from our definition of quaternion multiplication. For example,

$$\mathbf{ij} = \begin{bmatrix} 0 & 0 & 0 & 1 \\ 0 & 0 & -1 & 0 \\ 0 & 1 & 0 & 0 \\ -1 & 0 & 0 & 0 \end{bmatrix} \begin{bmatrix} 0 \\ 1 \\ 0 \\ 0 \end{bmatrix} = \begin{bmatrix} 0 \\ 0 \\ 1 \\ 0 \end{bmatrix} = \mathbf{k}$$

22.2.3 Properties

Quaternion multiplication is *not* commutative; for instance, §22.2.2 showed that $\mathbf{ij} = -\mathbf{ji}$. Quaternion multiplication is associative, however; this can be seen from the fact that quaternion multiplication can be written using matrix multiplication and matrix multiplication is associative. The quaternion $\mathbf{e} = (0, 0, 0, 1)$ serves as a multiplicative identity:

$$\mathbf{pe} = \mathbf{ep} = \begin{bmatrix} p_4 & -p_3 & p_2 & p_1 \\ p_3 & p_4 & -p_1 & p_2 \\ -p_2 & p_1 & p_4 & p_3 \\ -p_1 & -p_2 & -p_3 & p_4 \end{bmatrix} \begin{bmatrix} 0 \\ 0 \\ 0 \\ 1 \end{bmatrix} = \begin{bmatrix} 1 & 0 & 0 & 0 \\ 0 & 1 & 0 & 0 \\ 0 & 0 & 1 & 0 \\ 0 & 0 & 0 & 1 \end{bmatrix} \begin{bmatrix} p_1 \\ p_2 \\ p_3 \\ p_4 \end{bmatrix} = \begin{bmatrix} p_1 \\ p_2 \\ p_3 \\ p_4 \end{bmatrix}$$

We also have that quaternion multiplication distributes over quaternion addition: $\mathbf{p}(\mathbf{q} + \mathbf{r}) = \mathbf{pq} + \mathbf{pr}$ and $(\mathbf{q} + \mathbf{r})\mathbf{p} = \mathbf{qp} + \mathbf{rp}$. To see this, write the quaternion multiplication and addition in matrix form, and note that matrix multiplication distributes over matrix addition.

22.2.4 Conversions

We relate real numbers, vectors (or points), and quaternions in the following way: Let s be a real number and let $\mathbf{u} = (x, y, z)$ be a vector. Then

1. $s = (0, 0, 0, s)$

2. $\mathbf{u} = (x, y, z) = (\mathbf{u}, 0) = (x, y, z, 0)$

In other words, any real number can be thought of as a quaternion with a zero vector part, and any vector can be thought of as a quaternion with zero real part. In particular, note that for the identity quaternion, $1 = (0, 0, 0, 1)$. A quaternion with zero real part is called a *pure quaternion*.

Observe, using the definition of quaternion multiplication, that a real number times a quaternion is just "scalar multiplication" and it is commutative:

$$s(p_1, p_2, p_3, p_4) = (0,0,0,s)(p_1, p_2, p_3, p_4) = \begin{bmatrix} s & 0 & 0 & 0 \\ 0 & s & 0 & 0 \\ 0 & 0 & s & 0 \\ 0 & 0 & 0 & s \end{bmatrix} \begin{bmatrix} p_1 \\ p_2 \\ p_3 \\ p_4 \end{bmatrix} = \begin{bmatrix} sp_1 \\ sp_2 \\ sp_3 \\ sp_4 \end{bmatrix}$$

Similarly,

$$(p_1, p_2, p_3, p_4)s = (p_1, p_2, p_3, p_4)(0,0,0,s) = \begin{bmatrix} p_4 & -p_3 & p_2 & p_1 \\ p_3 & p_4 & -p_1 & p_2 \\ -p_2 & p_1 & p_4 & p_3 \\ -p_1 & -p_2 & -p_3 & p_4 \end{bmatrix} \begin{bmatrix} 0 \\ 0 \\ 0 \\ s \end{bmatrix} = \begin{bmatrix} sp_1 \\ sp_2 \\ sp_3 \\ sp_4 \end{bmatrix}$$

22.2.5 Conjugate and Norm

The conjugate of a quaternion $\mathbf{q} = (q_1, q_2, q_3, q_4) = (\mathbf{u}, q_4)$ is denoted by $\mathbf{q}^*$ and defined by

$$\mathbf{q}^* = -q_1 - q_2 - q_3 + q_4 = (-\mathbf{u}, q_4)$$

In other words, we just negate the imaginary vector part of the quaternion; compare this to the complex number conjugate. The conjugate has the following properties:

1. $(\mathbf{pq})^* = \mathbf{q}^* \mathbf{p}^*$
2. $(\mathbf{p} + \mathbf{q})^* = \mathbf{p}^* + \mathbf{q}^*$
3. $(\mathbf{q}^*)^* = \mathbf{q}$
4. $(s\mathbf{q})^* = s\mathbf{q}^*$ for $s \in \mathbb{R}$
5. $\mathbf{q} + \mathbf{q}^* = (\mathbf{u}, q_4) + (-\mathbf{u}, q_4) = (0, 2q_4) = 2q_4$
6. $\mathbf{qq}^* = \mathbf{q}^*\mathbf{q} = q_1^2 + q_2^2 + q_3^2 + q_4^2 = \|\mathbf{u}\|^2 + q_4^2$

In particular, note that $\mathbf{q} + \mathbf{q}^*$ and $\mathbf{qq}^* = \mathbf{q}^*\mathbf{q}$ evaluate to *real* numbers.

The *norm* (or *magnitude*) of a quaternion is defined by:

$$\|\mathbf{q}\| = \sqrt{\mathbf{qq}^*} = \sqrt{q_1^2 + q_2^2 + q_3^2 + q_4^2} = \sqrt{\|\mathbf{u}\|^2 + q_4^2}$$

We say that a quaternion is a *unit quaternion* if it has a norm of one. The norm has the following properties:

1. $\|\mathbf{q}^*\| = \|\mathbf{q}\|$
2. $\|\mathbf{pq}\| = \|\mathbf{p}\|\|\mathbf{q}\|$

In particular, property 2 tells us that the product of two unit quaternions is a unit quaternion; also if $\|\mathbf{p}\| = 1$, then $\|\mathbf{pq}\| = \|\mathbf{q}\|$.

The conjugate and norm properties can be derived straightforwardly from the definitions. For example,

$$(\mathbf{q}^*)^* = (-\mathbf{u}, q_4)^* = (\mathbf{u}, q_4) = \mathbf{q}$$

$$\|\mathbf{q}^*\| = \|(-\mathbf{u}, q_4)\| = \sqrt{\|-\mathbf{u}\|^2 + q_4^2} = \sqrt{\|\mathbf{u}\|^2 + q_4^2} = \|\mathbf{q}\|$$

$$\begin{aligned}
\|\mathbf{pq}\|^2 &= (\mathbf{pq})(\mathbf{pq})^* \\
&= \mathbf{pqq}^*\mathbf{p}^* \\
&= \mathbf{p}\|\mathbf{q}\|^2\mathbf{p}^* \\
&= \mathbf{pp}^*\|\mathbf{q}\|^2 \\
&= \|\mathbf{p}\|^2\|\mathbf{q}\|^2
\end{aligned}$$

The reader ought to try and derive the other properties (see Exercises).

22.2.6 Inverses

As with matrices, quaternion multiplication is not commutative, so we cannot define a division operator. (We like to reserve division only for when multiplication is commutative so that we have: $\frac{a}{b} = ab^{-1} = b^{-1}a$) However, every nonzero quaternion has an inverse. (The zero quaternion has zeros for all its components.) Let $\mathbf{q} = (q_1, q_2, q_3, q_4) = (\mathbf{u}, q_4)$ be a nonzero quaternion, then the inverse is denoted by $\mathbf{q}^{-1}$ and given by:

$$\mathbf{q}^{-1} = \frac{\mathbf{q}^*}{\|\mathbf{q}\|^2}$$

It is easy to check that this is indeed the inverse, for we have:

$$\mathbf{qq}^{-1} = \frac{\mathbf{qq}^*}{\|\mathbf{q}\|^2} = \frac{\|\mathbf{q}\|^2}{\|\mathbf{q}\|^2} = 1 = (0,0,0,1)$$

$$\mathbf{q}^{-1}\mathbf{q} = \frac{\mathbf{q}^*\mathbf{q}}{\|\mathbf{q}\|^2} = \frac{\|\mathbf{q}\|^2}{\|\mathbf{q}\|^2} = 1 = (0,0,0,1)$$

Observe that if $\mathbf{q}$ is a unit quaternion, then $\|\mathbf{q}\|^2 = 1$ and so $\mathbf{q}^{-1} = \mathbf{q}^*$.

The following properties hold for the quaternion inverse:

1. $\left(\mathbf{q}^{-1}\right)^{-1} = \mathbf{q}$
2. $(\mathbf{pq})^{-1} = \mathbf{q}^{-1}\mathbf{p}^{-1}$

22.2.7 Polar Representation

If $\mathbf{q} = (q_1, q_2, q_3, q_4) = (\mathbf{u}, q_4)$ is a unit quaternion, then

$$\|\mathbf{q}\|^2 = \|\mathbf{u}\|^2 + q_4^2 = 1$$

This implies $q_4^2 \leq 1 \Leftrightarrow |q_4| \leq 1 \Leftrightarrow -1 \leq q_4 \leq 1$. Figure 22.5 shows there exists an angle $\theta \in [0, \pi]$ such that $q_4 = \cos\theta$. Employing the trigonometric identity $\sin^2\theta + \cos^2\theta = 1$, we have that

$$\sin^2\theta = 1 - \cos^2\theta = 1 - q_4^2 = \|\mathbf{u}\|^2$$

This implies

$$\|\mathbf{u}\| = |\sin\theta| = \sin\theta \quad \text{for} \quad \theta \in [0, \pi]$$

Now label the unit vector in the same direction as $\mathbf{u}$ by $\mathbf{n}$:

$$\mathbf{n} = \frac{\mathbf{u}}{\|\mathbf{u}\|} = \frac{\mathbf{u}}{\sin\theta}$$

Hence, $\mathbf{u} = \sin\theta\,\mathbf{n}$ and, we may therefore write the unit quaternion $\mathbf{q} = (\mathbf{u}, q_4)$ in the following *polar representation* where $\mathbf{n}$ is a unit vector:

$$\mathbf{q} = (\sin\theta\,\mathbf{n}, \cos\theta) \quad \text{for} \quad \theta \in [0, \pi]$$

For example, suppose we are given the quaternion . To convert to polar representation, we find $\theta = \arccos\frac{\sqrt{3}}{2} = \frac{\pi}{6}$, $\mathbf{n} = \frac{\left(0, \frac{1}{2}, 0\right)}{\sin\frac{\pi}{6}} = (0, 1, 0)$. So $\mathbf{q} = \left(\sin\frac{\pi}{6}(0,1,0), \cos\frac{\pi}{6}\right)$.

> **Note:** The restriction of $\theta \in [0, \pi]$ is for when converting a quaternion $\mathbf{q} = (q_1, q_2, q_3, q_4)$ to polar representation. That is, we need the angle restriction in order to associate a unique angle with the quaternion $\mathbf{q} = (q_1, q_2, q_3, q_4)$. Nothing

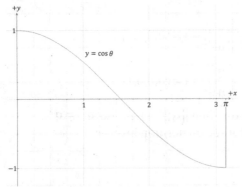

Figure 22.5. For a number $y \in [-1, 1]$ there exists an angle θ such that $y = \cos\theta$

stops us, however, from constructing a quaternion **q** = *(sinθ***n**, *cosθ) from any angle θ, but observe that* **q** = *(sin(θ + 2πn)***n**, *cos(θ + 2πn)) for all integers n. So the quaternion does not have a unique polar representation without the angle restriction θ ∈ [0, π].*

Observe that substituting $-\theta$ for θ is equivalent to negating the vector part of the quaternion:

$$(\mathbf{n}\sin(-\theta), \cos(-\theta)) = (-\mathbf{n}\sin\theta, \cos\theta) = \mathbf{p}^*$$

In the next section we will see that **n** represents the axis of rotation, and so we can rotate in the other direction by negating the axis of rotation.

22.3 UNIT QUATERNIONS AND ROTATIONS

22.3.1 Rotation Operator

Let $\mathbf{q} = (\mathbf{u}, w)$ be a unit quaternion and let **v** be a 3D point or vector. Then we can think of **v** as the pure quaternion $\mathbf{p} = (\mathbf{v}, 0)$. Also recall that since **q** is a unit quaternion, we have that $\mathbf{q}^{-1} = \mathbf{q}^*$. Recall the formula for quaternion multiplication:

$$(\mathbf{m}, a)(\mathbf{n}, b) = (a\mathbf{n} + b\mathbf{m} + \mathbf{m} \times \mathbf{n}, ab - \mathbf{m} \cdot \mathbf{n})$$

Now consider the product:

$$\begin{aligned}
\mathbf{qpq}^{-1} &= \mathbf{qpq}^* \\
&= (\mathbf{u}, w)(\mathbf{v}, 0)(-\mathbf{u}, w) \\
&= (\mathbf{u}, w)(w\mathbf{v} - \mathbf{v} \times \mathbf{u}, \mathbf{v} \cdot \mathbf{u})
\end{aligned}$$

Simplifying this is a little lengthy, so we will do the real part and vector part separately. We make the symbolic substitutions:

$$a = w$$
$$b = \mathbf{v} \cdot \mathbf{u}$$
$$\mathbf{m} = \mathbf{u}$$
$$\mathbf{n} = w\mathbf{v} - \mathbf{v} \times \mathbf{u}$$

<u>Real Part</u>

$$\begin{aligned}
ab &- \mathbf{m} \cdot \mathbf{n} \\
&= w(\mathbf{v} \cdot \mathbf{u}) - \mathbf{u} \cdot (w\mathbf{v} - \mathbf{v} \times \mathbf{u}) \\
&= w(\mathbf{v} \cdot \mathbf{u}) - \mathbf{u} \cdot w\mathbf{v} + \mathbf{u} \cdot (\mathbf{v} \times \mathbf{u}) \\
&= w(\mathbf{v} \cdot \mathbf{u}) - w(\mathbf{v} \cdot \mathbf{u}) + 0 \\
&= 0
\end{aligned}$$

Note that $\mathbf{u} \cdot (\mathbf{v} \times \mathbf{u}) = 0$ because $(\mathbf{v} \times \mathbf{u})$ is orthogonal to $\mathbf{u}$ by the definition of the cross product.

Vector Part

$$a\mathbf{n} + b\mathbf{m} + \mathbf{m} \times \mathbf{n}$$
$$= w(w\mathbf{v} - \mathbf{v} \times \mathbf{u}) + (\mathbf{v} \cdot \mathbf{u})\mathbf{u} + \mathbf{u} \times (w\mathbf{v} - \mathbf{v} \times \mathbf{u})$$
$$= w^2\mathbf{v} - w\mathbf{v} \times \mathbf{u} + (\mathbf{u} \cdot \mathbf{v})\mathbf{u} + \mathbf{u} \times w\mathbf{v} + \mathbf{u} \times (\mathbf{u} \times \mathbf{v})$$
$$= w^2\mathbf{v} + \mathbf{u} \times w\mathbf{v} + (\mathbf{u} \cdot \mathbf{v})\mathbf{u} + \mathbf{u} \times w\mathbf{v} + \mathbf{u} \times (\mathbf{u} \times \mathbf{v})$$
$$= w^2\mathbf{v} + 2(\mathbf{u} \times w\mathbf{v}) + (\mathbf{u} \cdot \mathbf{v})\mathbf{u} + \mathbf{u} \times (\mathbf{u} \times \mathbf{v})$$
$$= w^2\mathbf{v} + 2(\mathbf{u} \times w\mathbf{v}) + (\mathbf{v} \cdot \mathbf{u})\mathbf{u} + (\mathbf{u} \cdot \mathbf{v})\mathbf{u} - (\mathbf{u} \cdot \mathbf{v})\mathbf{v}$$
$$= (w^2 - \mathbf{u} \cdot \mathbf{u})\mathbf{v} + 2w(\mathbf{u} \times \mathbf{v}) + 2(\mathbf{u} \cdot \mathbf{u})\mathbf{v}$$
$$= (w^2 - \mathbf{u} \cdot \mathbf{u})\mathbf{v} + 2(\mathbf{u} \cdot \mathbf{v})\mathbf{u} + 2w(\mathbf{u} \times \mathbf{v})$$

Where we applied the triple product identity $\mathbf{a} \times (\mathbf{b} \times \mathbf{c}) = (\mathbf{a} \cdot \mathbf{c})\mathbf{b} - (\mathbf{a} \cdot \mathbf{b})\mathbf{c}$ to $\mathbf{u} \times (\mathbf{u} \times \mathbf{v})$.

We have shown:

$$\mathbf{qpq}^* = \left((w^2 - \mathbf{u} \cdot \mathbf{u})\mathbf{v} + 2(\mathbf{u} \cdot \mathbf{v})\mathbf{u} + 2w(\mathbf{u} \times \mathbf{v}), 0\right) \quad \text{(eq. 22.1)}$$

Observe that this results in a vector or point since the real component is zero (which is necessary if this operator is to rotate a vector or point—it must evaluate to a vector or point). Therefore, in the subsequent equations, we drop the real component.

Now, because $\mathbf{q}$ is a unit quaternion, it can be written as

$$\mathbf{q} = (\sin\theta \mathbf{n}, \cos\theta) \quad \text{for} \quad \|\mathbf{n}\| = 1 \quad \text{and} \quad \theta \in [0, \pi]$$

Substituting this into Equation 22.1 yields:

$$\mathbf{qpq}^* = (\cos^2\theta - \sin^2\theta)\mathbf{v} + 2(\sin\theta \mathbf{n} \cdot \mathbf{v})\sin\theta \mathbf{n} + 2\cos\theta(\sin\theta \mathbf{n} \times \mathbf{v})$$
$$= (\cos^2\theta - \sin^2\theta)\mathbf{v} + 2\sin^2\theta(\mathbf{n} \cdot \mathbf{v})\mathbf{n} + 2\cos\theta\sin\theta(\mathbf{n} \times \mathbf{v})$$

To simplify this further, we apply the trigonometric identities:

$$\cos^2\theta - \sin^2\theta = \cos(2\theta)$$
$$2\cos\theta\sin\theta = \sin(2\theta)$$
$$\cos(2\theta) = 1 - 2\sin^2\theta$$

$$\mathbf{qpq}^* = (\cos^2\theta - \sin^2\theta)\mathbf{v} + 2\sin^2\theta(\mathbf{n} \cdot \mathbf{v})\mathbf{n} + 2\cos\theta\sin\theta(\mathbf{n} \times \mathbf{v})$$
$$= \cos(2\theta)\mathbf{v} + (1 - \cos(2\theta))(\mathbf{n} \cdot \mathbf{v})\mathbf{n} + \sin(2\theta)(\mathbf{n} \times \mathbf{v}) \quad \text{(eq. 22.2)}$$

Now, compare Equation 22.2 with the axis-angle rotation Equation 3.5 to see that this is just the rotation formula $\mathbf{R_n(v)}$; that is, it rotates the vector (or point) $\mathbf{v}$ about the axis $\mathbf{n}$ by an angle 2θ.

$$\mathbf{R_n(v)} = \cos\theta \mathbf{v} + (1-\cos\theta)(\mathbf{n}\cdot\mathbf{v})\mathbf{n} + \sin\theta(\mathbf{n}\times\mathbf{v})$$

Consequently, we define the quaternion rotation operator by:

$$\begin{aligned} R_q(\mathbf{v}) &= \mathbf{qvq}^{-1} \\ &= \mathbf{qvq}^* \\ &= \cos(2\theta)\mathbf{v} + (1-\cos(2\theta))(\mathbf{n}\cdot\mathbf{v})\mathbf{n} + \sin(2\theta)(\mathbf{n}\times\mathbf{v}) \end{aligned} \quad \text{(eq. 22.3)}$$

We have shown that the quaternion rotation operator $R_q(\mathbf{v}) = \mathbf{qvq}^{-1}$ rotates a vector (or point) $\mathbf{v}$ about the axis $\mathbf{n}$ by an angle 2θ.

So suppose you are given an axis $\mathbf{n}$ and angle θ to rotate about the axis $\mathbf{n}$. You construct the corresponding rotation quaternion by:

$$\mathbf{q} = \left(\sin\left(\frac{\theta}{2}\right)\mathbf{n}, \cos\left(\frac{\theta}{2}\right)\right)$$

Then apply the formula $R_q(\mathbf{v})$. The division by 2 is to compensate for the 2θ because we want to rotate by the angle θ, not 2θ.

22.3.2 Quaternion Rotation Operator to Matrix

Let $\mathbf{q} = (\mathbf{u}, w) = (q_1, q_2, q_3, q_4)$ be a unit quaternion. From Equation 22.1, we know

$$\mathbf{r} = R_q(\mathbf{v}) = \mathbf{qvq}^* = (w^2 - \mathbf{u}\cdot\mathbf{u})\mathbf{v} + 2(\mathbf{u}\cdot\mathbf{v})\mathbf{u} + 2w(\mathbf{u}\times\mathbf{v})$$

Note that $q_1^2 + q_2^2 + q_3^2 + q_4^2 = 1$ implies that $q_4^2 - 1 = -q_1^2 - q_2^2 - q_3^2$, and so

$$\begin{aligned}(w^2 - \mathbf{u}\cdot\mathbf{u})\mathbf{v} &= (q_4^2 - q_1^2 - q_2^2 - q_3^2)\mathbf{v} \\ &= (2q_4^2 - 1)\mathbf{v}\end{aligned}$$

The three terms in $R_q(\mathbf{v})$ can be written in terms of matrices:

$$(w^2 - \mathbf{u}\cdot\mathbf{u})\mathbf{v} = \begin{bmatrix} v_x & v_y & v_z \end{bmatrix} \begin{bmatrix} 2q_4^2 - 1 & 0 & 0 \\ 0 & 2q_4^2 - 1 & 0 \\ 0 & 0 & 2q_4^2 - 1 \end{bmatrix}$$

$$2(\mathbf{u}\cdot\mathbf{v})\mathbf{u} = \begin{bmatrix} v_x & v_y & v_z \end{bmatrix} \begin{bmatrix} 2q_1^2 & 2q_1q_2 & 2q_1q_3 \\ 2q_1q_2 & 2q_2^2 & 2q_2q_3 \\ 2q_1q_3 & 2q_2q_3 & 2q_3^2 \end{bmatrix}$$

$$2w(\mathbf{u}\times\mathbf{v}) = \begin{bmatrix} v_x & v_y & v_z \end{bmatrix} \begin{bmatrix} 0 & 2q_4q_3 & -2q_4q_2 \\ -2q_4q_3 & 0 & 2q_4q_1 \\ 2q_4q_2 & -2q_4q_1 & 0 \end{bmatrix}$$

Summing the terms yields:

$$R_\mathbf{q}(\mathbf{v}) = \mathbf{vQ} = \begin{bmatrix} v_x & v_y & v_z \end{bmatrix} \begin{bmatrix} 2q_1^2+2q_4^2-1 & 2q_1q_2+2q_3q_4 & 2q_1q_3-2q_2q_4 \\ 2q_1q_2-2q_3q_4 & 2q_2^2+2q_4^2-1 & 2q_2q_3+2q_1q_4 \\ 2q_1q_3+2q_2q_4 & 2q_2q_3-2q_1q_4 & 2q_3^2+2q_4^2-1 \end{bmatrix}$$

The unit length property $q_1^2+q_2^2+q_3^2+q_4^2=1$ of $\mathbf{q}$ implies:

$$2q_1^2+2q_4^2 = 2-2q_2^2-2q_3^2$$
$$2q_2^2+2q_4^2 = 2-2q_1^2-2q_3^2$$
$$2q_3^2+2q_4^2 = 2-2q_1^2-2q_2^2$$

We can, therefore, rewrite this matrix equation as:

$$R_\mathbf{q}(\mathbf{v}) = \mathbf{vQ} = \begin{bmatrix} v_x & v_y & v_z \end{bmatrix} \begin{bmatrix} 1-2q_2^2-2q_3^2 & 2q_1q_2+2q_3q_4 & 2q_1q_3-2q_2q_4 \\ 2q_1q_2-2q_3q_4 & 1-2q_1^2-2q_3^2 & 2q_2q_3+2q_1q_4 \\ 2q_1q_3+2q_2q_4 & 2q_2q_3-2q_1q_4 & 1-2q_1^2-2q_2^2 \end{bmatrix} \quad \textbf{(eq. 22.4)}$$

Note: Many graphics books use matrix-column vector ordering for transforming vectors. Hence you will see the transpose of the matrix $\mathbf{Q}$ in many graphics books: $R_\mathbf{q}(\mathbf{v}) = \mathbf{Q}^T \mathbf{v}^T$.

22.3.3 Matrix to Quaternion Rotation Operator

Given the rotation matrix

$$\mathbf{R} = \begin{bmatrix} R_{11} & R_{12} & R_{13} \\ R_{21} & R_{22} & R_{23} \\ R_{31} & R_{32} & R_{33} \end{bmatrix}$$

we want to find the quaternion $\mathbf{q}=(q_1,q_2,q_3,q_4)$ such that if we build the Equation 22.4 matrix $\mathbf{Q}$ from $\mathbf{q}$ we get $\mathbf{R}$. So our strategy is to set:

$$\begin{bmatrix} R_{11} & R_{12} & R_{13} \\ R_{21} & R_{22} & R_{23} \\ R_{31} & R_{32} & R_{33} \end{bmatrix} = \begin{bmatrix} 1-2q_2^2-2q_3^2 & 2q_1q_2+2q_3q_4 & 2q_1q_3-2q_2q_4 \\ 2q_1q_2-2q_3q_4 & 1-2q_1^2-2q_3^2 & 2q_2q_3+2q_1q_4 \\ 2q_1q_3+2q_2q_4 & 2q_2q_3-2q_1q_4 & 1-2q_1^2-2q_2^2 \end{bmatrix}$$

and solve for q_1, q_2, q_3, q_4. Note that we are given $\mathbf{R}$, so all the elements on the left-hand-side of the equation are known.

We start by summing the diagonal elements (which is called the *trace* of a matrix):

$$\begin{aligned} \text{trace}(\mathbf{R}) &= R_{11}+R_{22}+R_{33} \\ &= 1-2q_2^2-2q_3^2+1-2q_1^2-2q_3^2+1-2q_1^2-2q_2^2 \\ &= 3-4q_1^2-4q_2^2-4q_3^2 \\ &= 3-4(q_1^2+q_2^2+q_3^2) \\ &= 3-4(1-q_4^2) \\ &= -1+4q_4^2 \\ \therefore q_4 &= \frac{\sqrt{\text{trace}(\mathbf{R})+1}}{2} \end{aligned}$$

Now we combine diagonally opposite elements to solve for q_1, q_2, q_3 (because we eliminate terms):

$$\begin{aligned} R_{23}-R_{32} &= 2q_2q_3+2q_1q_4-2q_2q_3+2q_1q_4 \\ &= 4q_1q_4 \\ \therefore q_1 &= \frac{R_{23}-R_{32}}{4q_4} \end{aligned}$$

$$\begin{aligned} R_{31}-R_{13} &= 2q_1q_3+2q_2q_4-2q_1q_3+2q_2q_4 \\ &= 4q_2q_4 \\ \therefore q_2 &= \frac{R_{31}-R_{13}}{4q_4} \end{aligned}$$

$$\begin{aligned} R_{12}-R_{21} &= 2q_1q_2+2q_3q_4-2q_1q_2+2q_3q_4 \\ &= 4q_3q_4 \\ \therefore q_3 &= \frac{R_{12}-R_{21}}{4q_4} \end{aligned}$$

If $q_4 = 0$ then these equations are undefined. In this case, we will find the largest diagonal element of $\mathbf{R}$ to divide by, and choose other combinations of matrix elements. Suppose R_{11} is the maximum diagonal:

$$R_{11} - R_{22} - R_{33} = 1 - 2q_2^2 - 2q_3^2 - 1 + 2q_1^2 + 2q_3^2 - 1 + 2q_1^2 + 2q_2^2$$

$$= -1 + 4q_1^2$$

$$\therefore q_1 = \frac{\sqrt{R_{11} - R_{22} - R_{33} + 1}}{2}$$

$$R_{12} + R_{21} = 2q_1q_2 + 2q_3q_4 + 2q_1q_2 - 2q_3q_4$$

$$= 4q_1q_2$$

$$\therefore q_2 = \frac{R_{12} + R_{21}}{4q_1}$$

$$R_{13} + R_{31} = 2q_1q_3 - 2q_2q_4 + 2q_1q_3 + 2q_2q_4$$

$$= 4q_1q_3$$

$$\therefore q_3 = \frac{R_{13} + R_{31}}{4q_1}$$

$$R_{23} - R_{32} = 2q_2q_3 + 2q_1q_4 - 2q_2q_3 + 2q_1q_4$$

$$= 4q_1q_4$$

$$\therefore q_4 = \frac{R_{23} - R_{32}}{4q_1}$$

A similar pattern is taken if R_{22} or R_{33} is the maximum diagonal.

22.3.4 Composition

Suppose **p** and **q** are unit quaternions with corresponding rotational operators given by R_p and R_q, respectively. Letting $\mathbf{v}' = R_p(\mathbf{v})$, the composition is given by:

$$R_q(R_p(\mathbf{v})) = R_q(\mathbf{v}') = \mathbf{q}\mathbf{v}'\mathbf{q}^{-1} = \mathbf{q}(\mathbf{p}\mathbf{v}\mathbf{p}^{-1})\mathbf{q}^{-1} = (\mathbf{qp})\mathbf{v}(\mathbf{p}^{-1}\mathbf{q}^{-1}) = (\mathbf{qp})\mathbf{v}(\mathbf{qp})^{-1}$$

Because **p** and **q** are both unit quaternions, the product **pq** is also a unit quaternion since $\|\mathbf{pq}\| = \|\mathbf{p}\|\|\mathbf{q}\| = 1$; thus, the quaternion product **pq** also represents a rotation; namely, the net rotation given by the composition $R_q(R_p(\mathbf{v}))$.

22.4 QUATERNION INTERPOLATION

Since quaternions are 4-tuples of real numbers, geometrically, we can visualize them as 4D vectors. In particular, unit quaternions are 4D unit vectors that lie on the 4D unit sphere. With the exception of the cross product (which is only defined for 3D vectors), our vector math generalizes to 4-space—and even n-space. Specifically, the dot product holds for quaternions. Let $\mathbf{p} = (\mathbf{u}, s)$ and $\mathbf{q} = (\mathbf{v}, t)$, then:

$$\mathbf{p} \cdot \mathbf{q} = \mathbf{u} \cdot \mathbf{v} + st = \|\mathbf{p}\|\|\mathbf{q}\|\cos\theta$$

where θ is the angle between the quaternions. If the quaternions $\mathbf{p}$ and $\mathbf{q}$ are unit length, then $\mathbf{p} \cdot \mathbf{q} = \cos\theta$ The dot product allows us to talk about the angle between two quaternions, as a measure of how "close" they are to each other on the unit sphere.

For the purposes of animation, we want to interpolate from one orientation to another orientation. To interpolate quaternions, we want to interpolate on the arc of the unit sphere so that our interpolated quaternion is also a unit quaternion. To derive such a formula, consider Figure 22.6, where we want to interpolate between $\mathbf{a}$ to $\mathbf{b}$ by an angle $t\theta$. We want to find weights c_1 and c_2 such that $\mathbf{p} = c_1\mathbf{a} + c_2\mathbf{b}$, where $\|\mathbf{p}\| = \|\mathbf{a}\| = \|\mathbf{b}\|$. We setup two equations for the two unknowns as follows:

$$\mathbf{a} \cdot \mathbf{p} = c_1 \mathbf{a} \cdot \mathbf{a} + c_2 \mathbf{a} \cdot \mathbf{b}$$
$$\cos(t\theta) = c_1 + c_2 \cos(\theta)$$

$$\mathbf{p} \cdot \mathbf{b} = c_1 \mathbf{a} \cdot \mathbf{b} + c_2 \mathbf{b} \cdot \mathbf{b}$$
$$\cos((1-t)\theta) = c_1 \cos(\theta) + c_2$$

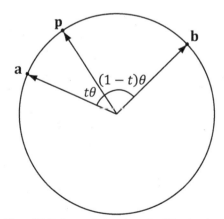

Figure 22.6. Interpolating along the 4D unit sphere from $\mathbf{a}$ to $\mathbf{b}$ by an angle $t\theta$. The angle between $\mathbf{a}$ and $\mathbf{b}$ is θ, the angle between $\mathbf{a}$ and $\mathbf{p}$ is $t\theta$, and the angle between $\mathbf{p}$ and $\mathbf{b}$ is $(1-t)\theta$.

This yields the matrix equation:

$$\begin{bmatrix} 1 & \cos(\theta) \\ \cos(\theta) & 1 \end{bmatrix} \begin{bmatrix} c_1 \\ c_2 \end{bmatrix} = \begin{bmatrix} \cos(t\theta) \\ \cos((1-t)\theta) \end{bmatrix}$$

Consider the matrix equation $\mathbf{Ax} = \mathbf{b}$, where $\mathbf{A}$ is invertible. Then Cramer's Rule tells us that $x_i = \det \mathbf{A}_i / \det \mathbf{A}$, where $\mathbf{A}_i$ is found by swapping the ith column vector in $\mathbf{A}$ with $\mathbf{b}$. Therefore:

$$c_1 = \frac{\det \begin{bmatrix} \cos(t\theta) & \cos(\theta) \\ \cos((1-t)\theta) & 1 \end{bmatrix}}{\det \begin{bmatrix} 1 & \cos(\theta) \\ \cos(\theta) & 1 \end{bmatrix}} = \frac{\cos(t\theta) - \cos(\theta)\cos((1-t)\theta)}{1 - \cos^2(\theta)}$$

$$c_2 = \frac{\det \begin{bmatrix} 1 & \cos(t\theta) \\ \cos(\theta) & \cos((1-t)\theta) \end{bmatrix}}{\det \begin{bmatrix} 1 & \cos(\theta) \\ \cos(\theta) & 1 \end{bmatrix}} = \frac{\cos((1-t)\theta) - \cos(\theta)\cos(t\theta)}{1 - \cos^2(\theta)}$$

From the trigonometric Pythagorean identity and addition formulas, we have:

$$1 - \cos^2(\theta) = \sin^2(\theta)$$
$$\cos((1-t)\theta) = \cos(\theta - t\theta) = \cos(\theta)\cos(t\theta) + \sin(\theta)\sin(t\theta)$$
$$\sin((1-t)\theta) = \sin(\theta - t\theta) = \sin(\theta)\cos(t\theta) - \cos(\theta)\sin(t\theta)$$

Therefore,

$$c_1 = \frac{\cos(t\theta) - \cos(\theta)\left[\cos(\theta)\cos(t\theta) + \sin(\theta)\sin(t\theta)\right]}{\sin^2(\theta)}$$

$$= \frac{\cos(t\theta) - \cos(\theta)\cos(\theta)\cos(t\theta) - \cos(\theta)\sin(\theta)\sin(t\theta)}{\sin^2(\theta)}$$

$$= \frac{\cos(t\theta)\left(1 - \cos^2(\theta)\right) - \cos(\theta)\sin(\theta)\sin(t\theta)}{\sin^2(\theta)}$$

$$= \frac{\cos(t\theta)\sin^2(\theta) - \cos(\theta)\sin(\theta)\sin(t\theta)}{\sin^2(\theta)}$$

$$= \frac{\sin(\theta)\cos(t\theta) - \cos(\theta)\sin(t\theta)}{\sin(\theta)}$$

$$= \frac{\sin((1-t)\theta)}{\sin(\theta)}$$

and

$$c_2 = \frac{\cos(\theta)\cos(t\theta) + \sin(\theta)\sin(t\theta) - \cos(\theta)\cos(t\theta)}{\sin^2(\theta)}$$

$$= \frac{\sin(t\theta)}{\sin(\theta)}$$

Thus we define the spherical interpolation formula:

$$\text{slerp}(\mathbf{a},\mathbf{b},t) = \frac{\sin((1-t)\theta)\mathbf{a} + \sin(t\theta)\mathbf{b}}{\sin\theta} \quad \text{for} \quad t \in [0,1]$$

Thinking of unit quaternions as 4D unit vectors allows us to solve for the angle between the quaternions: $\theta = \arccos(\mathbf{a} \cdot \mathbf{b})$.

If θ, the angle between **a** and **b** is near zero, $\sin\theta$ is near zero, and the division can cause problems due to finite numerical precision. In this case, perform linear interpolation between the quaternions and normalize the result, which is actually a good approximation for small θ (see Figure 22.7).

Observe from Figure 22.8 that linear interpolation followed by projecting the interpolated quaternion back on to the unit sphere results in a nonlinear rate of rotation. Thus is you used linear interpolation for large angles, the speed of rotation will speed up and slow down. This effect is often undesirable, and one reason why spherical interpolation is preferred (which rotates at a constant speed).

We now point out an interesting property of quaternions. Note that since $(s\mathbf{q})^* = s\mathbf{q}^*$ and scalar-quaternion multiplication is commutative, we have that:

$$R_{-\mathbf{q}}(\mathbf{v}) = -\mathbf{q}\mathbf{v}(-\mathbf{q})^*$$
$$= (-1)\mathbf{q}\mathbf{v}(-1)\mathbf{q}^*$$
$$= \mathbf{q}\mathbf{v}\mathbf{q}^*$$

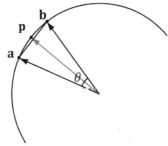

Figure 22.7. For small angles θ between **a** and **b**, linear interpolation is a good approximation for spherical interpolation. However, when using linear interpolation, the interpolated quaternion no longer lies on the unit sphere, so you must normalize the result to project it back on to the unit sphere.

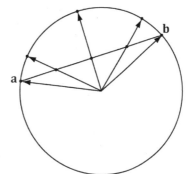

Figure 22.8. Linear interpolation results in nonlinear interpolation over the unit sphere after normalization. This means the rotation speeds up and slows down as it interpolates, rather than moving at a constant speed.

We therefore have **q** and −**q** representing the same rotation. To see this another way, if $q = \left(\mathbf{n}\sin\frac{\theta}{2}, \cos\frac{\theta}{2}\right)$, then

$$-\mathbf{q} = \left(-\mathbf{n}\sin\frac{\theta}{2}, -\cos\frac{\theta}{2}\right)$$

$$= \left(-\mathbf{n}\sin\left(\pi - \frac{\theta}{2}\right), \cos\left(\pi - \frac{\theta}{2}\right)\right)$$

$$= \left(-\mathbf{n}\sin\left(\frac{2\pi - \theta}{2}\right), \cos\left(\frac{2\pi - \theta}{2}\right)\right)$$

That is, R_q rotates θ about the axis **n**, and R_{-q} rotates $2\pi - \theta$ about the axis −**n**. Geometrically, a unit quaternion **q** on the 4D unit sphere and its polar opposite −**q** represent the same orientation. Figure 22.9 shows that these two rotations take us to the same place. However, we see that one will take the shorter angle around and the other will take the longer angle around.

Because **b** and −**b** representing the same orientation, we have two choices for interpolation: slerp(**a**, **b**, t) or slerp(**a**, −**b**, t). One will interpolate between the orientations in the most direct way that minimizes spinning (analogous to Figure 22.9a), and one will take the long way around (analogous to Figure 22.9b). Referring to Figure 22.10, we want to choose **b** or −**b** based on which one interpolates over a shorter arc on the 4D unit sphere. Choosing the shorter arc results in interpolating through the most direct path; choosing the longer arc results in extra spinning of the object [Eberly01], as it rotates the long way around.

From [Watt92], to find the quaternion that gives the shortest arc around the 4D unit sphere, we compare $||\mathbf{a} - \mathbf{b}||^2$ and $||\mathbf{a} - (-\mathbf{b})||^2 = ||\mathbf{a} + \mathbf{b}||^2$. If $||\mathbf{a} + \mathbf{b}||^2 < ||\mathbf{a} - \mathbf{b}||^2$ then we choose −**b** for interpolation instead of **b** because −**b** is closer to **a**, and thus will give the shorter arc.

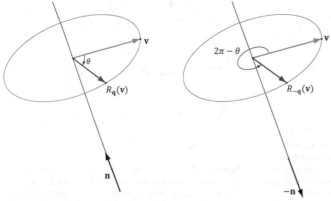

Figure 22.9. R_q rotates θ about the axis **n**, and R_{-q} rotates $2\pi - \theta$ about the axis −**n**.

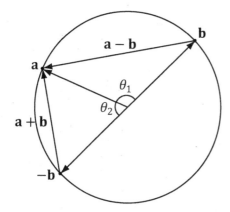

Figure 22.10. Interpolating from **a** to **b** results in interpolating over the larger arc θ_1 on the 4D unit sphere, whereas interpolating from **a** to **−b** results in interpolating over the shorter arc θ_2 on the 4D unit sphere. We want to choose the shortest arc on the 4D unit sphere.

```
// Linear interpolation (for small theta).
public static Quaternion LerpAndNormalize(Quaternion p, Quaternion q,
    float s)
{
  // Normalize to make sure it is a unit quaternion.
  return Normalize((1.0f - s)*p + s*q);
}

public static Quaternion Slerp(Quaternion p, Quaternion q, float s)
{
  // Recall that q and -q represent the same orientation, but
  // interpolating between the two is different: One will take the
  // shortest arc and one will take the long arc. To find
  // the shortest arc, compare the magnitude of p-q with the
  // magnitude p-(-q) = p+q.

  if(LengthSq(p-q) > LengthSq(p+q))
    q = -q;

  float cosPhi = DotP(p, q);

  // For very small angles, use linear interpolation.
  if(cosPhi > (1.0f - 0.001))
    return LerpAndNormalize(p, q, s);

  // Find the angle between the two quaternions.
  float phi = (float)Math.Acos(cosPhi);

  float sinPhi = (float)Math.Sin(phi);

  // Interpolate along the arc formed by the intersection of the 4D
  // unit sphere and the plane passing through p, q, and the origin of
  // the unit sphere.
```

```
    return ((float)Math.Sin(phi*(1.0-s))/sinPhi)*p +
        ((float)Math.Sin(phi*s)/sinPhi)*q;
}
```

22.5 DIRECTX MATH QUATERNION FUNCTIONS

The DirectX math library supports quaternions. Because the "data" of a quaternion is four real numbers, DirectX math uses the XMVECTOR type for storing quaternions. Then some of the common quaternion functions defined are:

// Returns the quaternion dot product $Q_1 \cdot Q_2$.
```
XMVECTOR XMQuaternionDot(XMVECTOR Q1, XMVECTOR Q2);
```

// Returns the identity quaternion (0, 0, 0, 1).
```
XMVECTOR XMQuaternionIdentity();
```

// Returns the conjugate of the quaternion **Q**.
```
XMVECTOR XMQuaternionConjugate(XMVECTOR Q);
```

// Returns the norm of the quaternion **Q**.
```
XMVECTOR XMQuaternionLength(XMVECTOR Q);
```

// Normalizes a quaternion by treating it as a 4D vector.
```
XMVECTOR XMQuaternionNormalize(XMVECTOR Q);
```

// Computes the quaternion product $Q_1 Q_2$.
```
XMVECTOR XMQuaternionMultiply(XMVECTOR Q1, XMVECTOR Q2);
```

// Returns a quaternions from axis-angle rotation representation.
```
XMVECTOR XMQuaternionRotationAxis(XMVECTOR Axis, FLOAT Angle);
```

// Returns a quaternions from axis-angle rotation representation, where the axis
// vector is normalized—this is faster than XMQuaternionRotationAxis.
```
XMVECTOR XMQuaternionRotationNormal(XMVECTOR NormalAxis,FLOAT Angle);
```

// Returns a quaternion from a rotation matrix.
```
XMVECTOR XMQuaternionRotationMatrix(XMMATRIX M);
```

// Returns a rotation matrix from a unit quaternion.
```
XMMATRIX XMMatrixRotationQuaternion(XMVECTOR Quaternion);
```

// Extracts the axis and angle rotation representation from the quaternion **Q**.
```
VOID XMQuaternionToAxisAngle(XMVECTOR *pAxis, FLOAT *pAngle, XMVECTOR Q);
```

// Returns slerp($\mathbf{Q}_1$, $\mathbf{Q}_2$, t)
```
XMVECTOR XMQuaternionSlerp(XMVECTOR Q0, XMVECTOR Q1, FLOAT t);
```

22.6 ROTATION DEMO

For this chapter's demo, we animate a skull mesh around a simple scene. The position, orientation, and scale of the mesh are animated. We use quaternions to represent the orientation of the skull, and use slerp to interpolate between orientations. We use linear interpolation to interpolate between position and scale. This demo also serves as an animation "warm up" to the next chapter on character animation.

A common form of animation is called key frame animation. A *key frame* specifies the position, orientation, and scale of an object at an instance in time. In our demo (in *AnimationHelper.h/.cpp*), we define the following key frame structure:

```
struct Keyframe
{
  Keyframe();
  ~Keyframe();

  float TimePos;
  XMFLOAT3 Translation;
  XMFLOAT3 Scale;
  XMFLOAT4 RotationQuat;
};
An animation is a list of key frames sorted by time:
struct BoneAnimation
{
  float GetStartTime()const;
  float GetEndTime()const;

  void Interpolate(float t, XMFLOAT4X4& M)const;

  std::vector<Keyframe> Keyframes;
};
```

The reason for using the term "bone" will be made clear in the next section. For now, you can just think of animating a single bone as animating a single object. The method `GetStartTime` just returns the time of the first key frame. For example, maybe the object does not start animating until after ten seconds relative to some timeline. Similarly, the method `GetEndTime` returns the time of the last key frame. This is useful to know when the animation ends, and we can stop animating it.

We now have a list of key frames, which define the rough overall look of the animation. So how will the animation look at time between the key frames? This is where interpolation comes in. For times t between two key frames, say K_i and K_{i+1}, we interpolate between the two key frames K_i and K_{i+1}.

```cpp
void BoneAnimation::Interpolate(float t, XMFLOAT4X4& M)const
{
  // t is before the animation started, so just return the first key
  //   frame.
  if( t <= Keyframes.front().TimePos )
  {
    XMVECTOR S = XMLoadFloat3(&Keyframes.front().Scale);
    XMVECTOR P = XMLoadFloat3(&Keyframes.front().Translation);
    XMVECTOR Q = XMLoadFloat4(&Keyframes.front().RotationQuat);

    XMVECTOR zero = XMVectorSet(0.0f, 0.0f, 0.0f, 1.0f);
    XMStoreFloat4x4(&M, XMMatrixAffineTransformation(S, zero, Q, P));
  }
  // t is after the animation ended, so just return the last key frame.
  else if( t >= Keyframes.back().TimePos )
  {
    XMVECTOR S = XMLoadFloat3(&Keyframes.back().Scale);
    XMVECTOR P = XMLoadFloat3(&Keyframes.back().Translation);
    XMVECTOR Q = XMLoadFloat4(&Keyframes.back().RotationQuat);

    XMVECTOR zero = XMVectorSet(0.0f, 0.0f, 0.0f, 1.0f);
    XMStoreFloat4x4(&M, XMMatrixAffineTransformation(S, zero, Q, P));
  }
  // t is between two key frames, so interpolate.
  else
  {
    for(UINT i = 0; i < Keyframes.size()-1; ++i)
    {
      if( t >= Keyframes[i].TimePos && t <= Keyframes[i+1].TimePos )
      {
        float lerpPercent = (t - Keyframes[i].TimePos) /
          (Keyframes[i+1].TimePos - Keyframes[i].TimePos);

        XMVECTOR s0 = XMLoadFloat3(&Keyframes[i].Scale);
        XMVECTOR s1 = XMLoadFloat3(&Keyframes[i+1].Scale);

        XMVECTOR p0 = XMLoadFloat3(&Keyframes[i].Translation);
        XMVECTOR p1 = XMLoadFloat3(&Keyframes[i+1].Translation);

        XMVECTOR q0 = XMLoadFloat4(&Keyframes[i].RotationQuat);
        XMVECTOR q1 = XMLoadFloat4(&Keyframes[i+1].RotationQuat);

        XMVECTOR S = XMVectorLerp(s0, s1, lerpPercent);
        XMVECTOR P = XMVectorLerp(p0, p1, lerpPercent);
        XMVECTOR Q = XMQuaternionSlerp(q0, q1, lerpPercent);

        XMVECTOR zero = XMVectorSet(0.0f, 0.0f, 0.0f, 1.0f);
        XMStoreFloat4x4(&M, XMMatrixAffineTransformation(S, zero, Q, P));
```

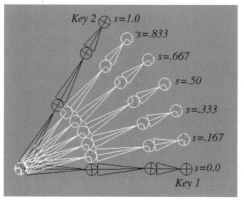

Figure 22.11. Key frame interpolation. The key frames define the "key" poses of the animation. The interpolated values represent the values between the key frames.

```
            break;
        }
    }
  }
}
```

Figure 22.11 shows the in-between frames generated by interpolating from *Key 1* to *Key 2*.

 Figure 22.11 appeared in the book by Frank D. Luna, Introduction to 3D Game Programming with DirectX 9.0c: A Shader Approach, 2006: Jones and Bartlett Learning, Burlington, MA. www.jblearning.com. Reprinted with permission.

After interpolation, we construct a transformation matrix because ultimately we use matrices for transformations in our shader programs. The XMMatrixAffineTransformation function is declared as follows:

```
XMMATRIX XMMatrixAffineTransformation(
    XMVECTOR Scaling,
    XMVECTOR RotationOrigin,
    XMVECTOR RotationQuaternion,
    XMVECTOR Translation);
```

Now that our simple animation system is in place, the next part of our demo is to define some key frames:

```
// Member data

float mAnimTimePos = 0.0f;
BoneAnimation mSkullAnimation;

//
// In constructor, define the animation keyframes
```

```
//
void QuatApp::DefineSkullAnimation()
{
  //
  // Define the animation keyframes
  //

  XMVECTOR q0 = XMQuaternionRotationAxis(
    XMVectorSet(0.0f, 1.0f, 0.0f, 0.0f), XMConvertToRadians(30.0f));
  XMVECTOR q1 = XMQuaternionRotationAxis(
    XMVectorSet(1.0f, 1.0f, 2.0f, 0.0f), XMConvertToRadians(45.0f));
  XMVECTOR q2 = XMQuaternionRotationAxis(
    XMVectorSet(0.0f, 1.0f, 0.0f, 0.0f), XMConvertToRadians(-30.0f));
  XMVECTOR q3 = XMQuaternionRotationAxis(
    XMVectorSet(1.0f, 0.0f, 0.0f, 0.0f), XMConvertToRadians(70.0f));

  mSkullAnimation.Keyframes.resize(5);
  mSkullAnimation.Keyframes[0].TimePos = 0.0f;
  mSkullAnimation.Keyframes[0].Translation = XMFLOAT3(-7.0f, 0.0f,
    0.0f);
  mSkullAnimation.Keyframes[0].Scale = XMFLOAT3(0.25f, 0.25f, 0.25f);
  XMStoreFloat4(&mSkullAnimation.Keyframes[0].RotationQuat, q0);

  mSkullAnimation.Keyframes[1].TimePos = 2.0f;
  mSkullAnimation.Keyframes[1].Translation = XMFLOAT3(0.0f, 2.0f,
    10.0f);
  mSkullAnimation.Keyframes[1].Scale = XMFLOAT3(0.5f, 0.5f, 0.5f);
  XMStoreFloat4(&mSkullAnimation.Keyframes[1].RotationQuat, q1);

  mSkullAnimation.Keyframes[2].TimePos = 4.0f;
  mSkullAnimation.Keyframes[2].Translation = XMFLOAT3(7.0f, 0.0f,
    0.0f);
  mSkullAnimation.Keyframes[2].Scale = XMFLOAT3(0.25f, 0.25f, 0.25f);
  XMStoreFloat4(&mSkullAnimation.Keyframes[2].RotationQuat, q2);

  mSkullAnimation.Keyframes[3].TimePos = 6.0f;
  mSkullAnimation.Keyframes[3].Translation = XMFLOAT3(0.0f, 1.0f,
    -10.0f);
  mSkullAnimation.Keyframes[3].Scale = XMFLOAT3(0.5f, 0.5f, 0.5f);
  XMStoreFloat4(&mSkullAnimation.Keyframes[3].RotationQuat, q3);

  mSkullAnimation.Keyframes[4].TimePos = 8.0f;
  mSkullAnimation.Keyframes[4].Translation = XMFLOAT3(-7.0f, 0.0f,
    0.0f);
  mSkullAnimation.Keyframes[4].Scale = XMFLOAT3(0.25f, 0.25f, 0.25f);
  XMStoreFloat4(&mSkullAnimation.Keyframes[4].RotationQuat, q0);
}
```

Our key frames position the skull at different locations in the scene, at different orientations, and at different scales. You can have fun experimenting with this demo by adding your own key frames or changing the key frame values. For example, you can set all the rotations and scaling to identity, to see what the animation looks like when only position is animated.

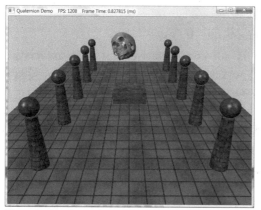

Figure 22.12. Screenshot of the quaternion demo.

The last step to get the animation working is to perform the interpolation to get the new skull world matrix, which changes over time:

```
void QuatApp::UpdateScene(float dt)
{
  ...

  // Increase the time position.
  mAnimTimePos += dt;
  if(mAnimTimePos >= mSkullAnimation.GetEndTime())
  {
    // Loop animation back to beginning.
    mAnimTimePos = 0.0f;
  }

  // Get the skull's world matrix at this time instant.
  mSkullAnimation.Interpolate(mAnimTimePos, mSkullWorld);

  ...
}
```

The skull's world matrix is now changing every frame in order to animate the skull.

22.7 SUMMARY

1. An ordered 4-tuple of real numbers $\mathbf{q} = (x, y, z, w) = (q_1, q_2, q_3, q_4)$ is a quaternion. This is commonly abbreviated as $\mathbf{q} = (\mathbf{u}, w) = (x, y, z, w)$, and we call $\mathbf{u} = (x, y, z)$ the imaginary vector part and w the real part. Moreover, equality, addition, subtraction, multiplication and division are defined as follows:

   (a) $(\mathbf{u}, a) = (\mathbf{v}, b)$ if and only if $\mathbf{u} = \mathbf{v}$ and $a = b$.

(b) $(\mathbf{u}, a) \pm (\mathbf{v}, b) = (\mathbf{u} \pm \mathbf{v}, a \pm b)$.

(c) $(\mathbf{u}, a)(\mathbf{v}, b) = (a\mathbf{v} + b\mathbf{u} + \mathbf{u} \times \mathbf{v}, ab - \mathbf{u} \cdot \mathbf{v})$.

2. Quaternion multiplication is *not* commutative, but it is associative. The quaternion $\mathbf{e} = (0, 0, 0, 1)$ serves as a multiplicative identity. Quaternion multiplication distributes over quaternion addition: $\mathbf{p}(\mathbf{q} + \mathbf{r}) = \mathbf{pq} + \mathbf{pr}$ and $(\mathbf{q} + \mathbf{r})\mathbf{p} = \mathbf{qp} + \mathbf{rp}$.

3. We can convert a real number s to quaternion space by writing $s = (0, 0, 0, s)$, and we can convert a vector $\mathbf{u}$ to quaternion space by writing $\mathbf{u} = (\mathbf{u}, 0)$. A quaternion with zero real part is called a *pure quaternion*. It is then possible to multiply a scalar and a quaternion, and the result is $s(p_1, p_2, p_3, p_4) = (sp_1, sp_2, sp_3, sp_4) = (p_1, p_2, p_3, p_4)s$. The special case of scalar multiplication is commutative.

4. The conjugate of a quaternion $\mathbf{q} = (q_1, q_2, q_3, q_4) = (\mathbf{u}, q_4)$ is denoted by $\mathbf{q}^*$ and defined by $\mathbf{q}^* = -q_1 - q_2 - q_3 + q_4 = (-\mathbf{u}, q_4)$. The *norm* (or *magnitude*) of a quaternion is defined by: $\|\mathbf{q}\| = \sqrt{\mathbf{qq}^*} = \sqrt{q_1^2 + q_2^2 + q_3^2 + q_4^2} = \sqrt{\|\mathbf{u}\|^2 + q_4^2}$. We say that a quaternion is a *unit quaternion* if it has a norm of one.

5. Let $\mathbf{q} = (q_1, q_2, q_3, q_4) = (\mathbf{u}, q_4)$ be a nonzero quaternion, then the inverse is denoted by $\mathbf{q}^{-1}$ and given by: $\mathbf{q}^{-1} = \frac{\mathbf{q}^*}{\mathbf{q}^2}$. If $\mathbf{q}$ is a unit quaternion, then $\mathbf{q}^{-1} = \mathbf{q}^*$.

6. A unit quaternion $\mathbf{q} = (\mathbf{u}, q_4)$ can be written in the *polar representation* $\mathbf{q} = (\sin\theta \mathbf{n}, \cos\theta)$, where $\mathbf{n}$ is a unit vector.

7. If $\mathbf{q}$ is a unit quaternion, then $\mathbf{q} = (\sin\theta \mathbf{n}, \cos\theta)$ for $\|\mathbf{n}\| = 1$ and $\theta \in [0, \pi]$. The quaternion rotation operator is defined by $R_\mathbf{q}(\mathbf{v}) = \mathbf{qvq}^{-1} = \mathbf{qvq}^*$ and rotates the point/vector $\mathbf{v}$ around the axis $\mathbf{n}$ by an angle 2θ. $R_\mathbf{q}$ has a matrix representation, and any rotation matrix can be converted to a quaternion representing the rotation.

8. A common task in animation is to interpolate between two orientations. Representing each orientation by a unit quaternion, we can use spherical interpolation to interpolate the unit quaternions to find the interpolated orientation.

22.8 EXERCISES

1. Perform the indicated complex number operation.

    (a) $(3 + 2i) + (-1 + i)$

(b) $(3+2i) - (-1+i)$
(c) $(3+2i)(-1+i)$
(d) $4(-1+i)$
(e) $(3+2i)/(-1+i)$
(f) $(3+2i)^*$
(g) $|3+2i|$

2. Write the complex number $(-1, 3)$ in polar notation.
3. Rotate the vector $(2, 1)$ 30° using complex number multiplication.
4. Show using the definition of complex division that $\frac{a+ib}{a+ib} = 1$
5. Let $z = a + ib$. Show $|z|^2 = z\bar{z}$.
6. Let $\mathbf{M}$ be a 2×2 matrix. Prove that $\det \mathbf{M} = 1$ and $\mathbf{M}^{-1} = \mathbf{M}^T$ if and only if $\mathbf{M} = \begin{bmatrix} \cos\theta & \sin\theta \\ -\sin\theta & \cos\theta \end{bmatrix}$. That is, if and only if $\mathbf{M}$ is a rotation matrix. This gives us a way of testing if a matrix is a rotation matrix.
7. Let $\mathbf{p} = (1, 2, 3, 4)$ and $\mathbf{q} = (2, -1, 1, -2)$ be quaternions. Perform the indicated quaternion operations.
   (a) $\mathbf{p} + \mathbf{q}$
   (b) $\mathbf{p} - \mathbf{q}$
   (c) $\mathbf{pq}$
   (d) $\mathbf{p}^*$
   (e) $\mathbf{q}^*$
   (f) $\mathbf{p}^*\mathbf{p}$
   (g) $\|\mathbf{p}\|$
   (h) $\|\mathbf{q}\|$
   (i) $\mathbf{p}^{-1}$
   (j) $\mathbf{q}^{-1}$
8. Write the unit quaternion $\mathbf{q} = \left(\frac{1}{2}, \frac{1}{2}, 0, \frac{1}{\sqrt{2}}\right)$ in polar notation.
9. Write the unit quaternion $\mathbf{q} = \left(\frac{\sqrt{3}}{2}, 0, 0, -\frac{1}{2}\right)$ in polar notation.
10. Find the unit quaternion that rotates 45° about the axis $(1, 1, 1)$.
11. Find the unit quaternion that rotates 60° about the axis $(0, 0, -1)$.
12. Let $\mathbf{p} = \left(\frac{1}{2}, 0, 0, \frac{\sqrt{3}}{2}\right)$ and $\mathbf{q} = \left(\frac{\sqrt{3}}{2}, 0, 0, \frac{1}{2}\right)$. Compute $\text{slerp}\left(\mathbf{p}, \mathbf{q}, \frac{1}{2}\right)$ and verify it is a unit quaternion.

13. Show that a quaternion (x, y, z, w) can be written in the form $x\mathbf{i} + y\mathbf{j} + z\mathbf{k} + w$.
14. Prove that $\mathbf{qq}^* = \mathbf{q}^*\mathbf{q} = q_1^2 + q_2^2 + q_3^2 + q_4^2 = \|\mathbf{u}\|^2 + q_4^2$
15. Let $\mathbf{p} = (\mathbf{u}, 0)$ and $\mathbf{q} = (\mathbf{v}, 0)$ be pure quaternions (i.e., real part 0). Show $\mathbf{pq} = (\mathbf{p} \times \mathbf{q}, -\mathbf{p} \cdot \mathbf{q})$.
16. Prove the following properties:
    (a) $(\mathbf{pq})^* = \mathbf{q}^*\mathbf{p}^*$
    (b) $(\mathbf{p}+\mathbf{q})^* = \mathbf{p}^* + \mathbf{q}^*$
    (c) $(s\mathbf{q})^* = s\mathbf{q}^*$ for $s \in \mathbb{R}$
    (d) $\mathbf{qq}^* = \mathbf{q}^*\mathbf{q} = q_1^2 + q_2^2 + q_3^2 + q_4^2$
    (e) $\|\mathbf{pq}\| = \|\mathbf{p}\|\|\mathbf{q}\|$
17. Prove $\mathbf{a} \cdot \dfrac{\sin((1-t)\theta)\mathbf{a} + \sin(t\theta)\mathbf{b}}{\sin\theta} = \cos(t\theta)$ algebraically.
18. Let $\mathbf{a}, \mathbf{b}, \mathbf{c}$ be 3D vectors. Prove the identities:
    (a) $\mathbf{a} \times (\mathbf{b} \times \mathbf{c}) = (\mathbf{a} \cdot \mathbf{c})\mathbf{b} - (\mathbf{a} \cdot \mathbf{b})\mathbf{c}$
    (b) $(\mathbf{a} \times \mathbf{b}) \times \mathbf{c} = -(\mathbf{c} \cdot \mathbf{b})\mathbf{a} + (\mathbf{c} \cdot \mathbf{a})\mathbf{b}$

Chapter 23 Character Animation

 Portions of this chapter appeared in the book by Frank D. Luna, Introduction to 3D Game Programming with DirectX 9.0c: A Shader Approach, 2006: Jones and Bartlett Learning, Burlington, MA. www.jblearning.com. Reprinted with permission.

In this chapter, we learn how to animate complex characters like a human or animal. Characters are complex because they have many moving parts that all move at the same time. Consider a human running—every bone is moving in some way. Creating such complicated animations is not practical by hand, and there are special modeling and animation tools for this task. Assuming we already have a character and its corresponding animation data created, in this chapter we will learn how to animate and render it using Direct3D.

Objectives:

1. To become familiar with the terminology of animated skinned meshes.
2. To learn the mathematics of mesh hierarchy transformations and how to traverse tree-based mesh hierarchies.
3. To understand the idea and mathematics of vertex blending.
4. To find out how to load animation data from file.
5. To discover how to implement character animation in Direct3D.

23.1 FRAME HIERARCHIES

Many objects are composed of parts, with a parent-child relationship, where one or more child objects can move independently on their own (with possible physical motion constraints—e.g., human joints have a particular range of motion), but are also forced to move when their parent moves. For example, consider an arm divided into the parts: upper arm, forearm, and hand. The hand can rotate in isolation about its wrist joint; however, if the forearm rotates about its elbow joint, then the hand must rotate with it. Similarly, if the upper arm rotates about the shoulder joint, the forearm rotates with it, and if the forearm rotates, then the hand rotates with it (see Figure 23.1). Thus we see a definite object hierarchy: The hand is a child of the forearm; the forearm is a child of the upper arm, and if we extended our situation, the upper arm would be a child of the torso, and so on and so forth, until we have completed the skeleton (Figure 23.2 shows a more complex hierarchy example).

The aim of this section is to show how to place an object in the scene based on its position, and also the position of its *ancestors* (i.e., its parent, grandparent, great-grandparent, etc.).

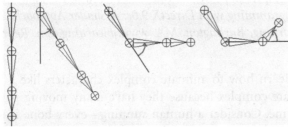

Figure 23.1. Hierarchy transforms; observe that the parent transformation of a bone influences itself and all of its children.

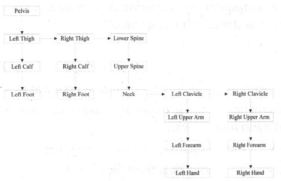

Figure 23.2. A more complex tree hierarchy to model a bipedal humanoid character. Down arrows represent "first child" relationships, and right arrows represent "sibling" relationships. For example, "Left Thigh," "Right Thigh," and "Lower Spine" are all children of the "Pelvis" bone.

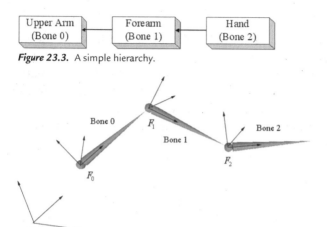

Figure 23.3. A simple hierarchy.

Figure 23.4. The geometry of each bone is described relative to its own local coordinate system. Furthermore, because all the coordinate systems exist in the same universe, we can relate them to one another.

23.1.1 Mathematical Formulation

 The reader may wish to review Chapter 3 of this book, specifically the topic of change-of-coordinate transformations.

To keep things simple and concrete, we work with the upper arm (the root), forearm, and hand hierarchy, which we label as Bone 0, Bone 1, and Bone 2, respectively (see Figure 23.3).

Once the basic concept is understood, a straightforward generalization is used to handle more complex situations. So given an object in the hierarchy, how do we correctly transform it to world space? Obviously, we cannot just transform it directly into the world space because we must also take into consideration the transformations of its ancestors since they also influence its placement in the scene.

Each object in the hierarchy is modeled about its own local coordinate system with its pivot joint at the origin to facilitate rotation (see Figure 23.4).

Because all the coordinate systems exist in the same universe, we can relate them; in particular, for an arbitrary instant in time (we fix time and study a snapshot because, in general, these mesh hierarchies are animated and so these relationships change as a function of time), we describe each coordinate system relative to its parent coordinate system. (The parent coordinate system of the root frame F_0 is the world space coordinate system W; that is, the coordinate system F_0 is described relative to the world coordinate system.) Now that we have related the child and parent coordinate systems, we can transform from a child's space to its parent's space with a transformation matrix. (This is the same idea as the local-to-world transformation. However, instead of transforming from local space to world space, we transform from the local space to the space of the parent.) Let A_2 be a matrix that transforms geometry from frame F_2 into F_1, let A_1 be a matrix that transform geometry from frame F_1 into F_0, and let A_0 be a matrix that transform geometry from frame F_0 into W. (We call A_i a *to-parent* matrix since it transforms geometry from a child's coordinate system into its parent's coordinate system.) Then, we can transform the *i*th object in the arm hierarchy into world space by the matrix M_i defined as follows:

$$M_i = A_i A_{i-1} \cdots A_1 A_0 \qquad \text{(eq. 23.1)}$$

Specifically, in our example, $M_2 = A_2 A_1 A_0$, $M_1 = A_1 A_0$ and $M_0 = A_0$ transforms the hand into world space, the forearm into world space, and the upper arm into world space, respectively. Observe that an object inherits the transformations of its ancestors; this is what will make the hand move if the upper arm moves, for example.

Figure 23.5 illustrates what Equation 23.1 says graphically; essentially, to transform an object in the arm hierarchy, we just apply the to-parent transform of the object and all of its ancestors (in ascending order) to percolate up the coordinate system hierarchy until the object arrives in the world space.

The example we have been working with is a simple linear hierarchy. But the same idea generalizes to a tree hierarchy; that being, for any object in the hierarchy, its world space transformation is found by just applying the to-parent transform of the object and all of its ancestors (in ascending order) to percolate up the coordinate system hierarchy until the object arrives in the world space (we

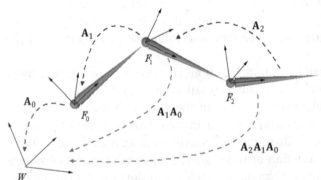

Figure 23.5. Because the coordinate systems exist in the same universe we can relate them, and therefore, transform from one to the other. In particular, we relate them by describing each bone's coordinate system relative to its parent's coordinate system. From that, we can construct a *to-parent* transformation matrix that transforms the geometry of a bone from its local coordinate system to its parent's coordinate system. Once in the parent's coordinate system, we can then transform by the parent's to-parent matrix to transform to the grandparent's coordinate system, and so on and so forth, until we have visited each ancestor's coordinate system and finally reached the world space.

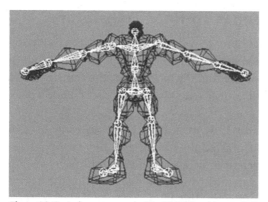

Figure 23.6. A character mesh. The highlighted bone chain represents the character's skeleton. The dark colored polygons represent the character's skin. The skin vertices are relative to the *bind space*, which is the coordinate system the mesh was modeled in.

again stipulate that the parent coordinate system of the root is the world space). The only real difference is that we have a more complicated tree data structure to traverse instead of a linear list.

As an example, consider the left clavicle in Figure 23.2. It is a sibling of the neck bone, and therefore a child of the upper spine. The upper spine is a child of the lower spine, and the lower spine is a child of the pelvis. Therefore, the world transform of the left clavicle it formed by concatenating the left clavicle's to-parent transform, followed by the upper spine's to-parent transform, followed by the lower spine's to-parent transform, followed by the pelvis' to-parent transform.

23.2 SKINNED MESHES

23.2.1 Definitions

Figure 23.6 shows a character mesh. The highlighted chain of bones in the figure is called a *skeleton*. A skeleton provides a natural hierarchal structure for driving a character animation system. The skeleton is surrounded by an exterior *skin*, which we model as 3D geometry (vertices and polygons). Initially, the skin vertices are relative to the *bind space*, which is the local coordinate system that the entire skin is defined relative to (usually the root coordinate system). Each bone in the skeleton influences the shape and position of the subset of skin it influences (i.e., the vertices it influences), just like in real life. Thus, as we animate the skeleton, the attached skin is animated accordingly to reflect the current pose of the skeleton.

23.2.2 Reformulating the Bones To-Root Transform

One difference from §23.1 is that here we will transform from the root coordinate system to the world coordinate system in a separate step. So rather than finding the to-world matrix for each bone, we find the *to-root* (i.e., the transformation that transforms from the bone's local coordinate system to the root bone's coordinate system) matrix for each bone.

A second difference is that in §23.1, we traversed the ancestry of a node in a bottom-up fashion, where we started at a bone and moved up its ancestry. However, it is actually more efficient to take a top-down approach (see Equation 23.2), where we start at the root and move down the tree. Labeling the n bones with an integer number $0, 1, \ldots, n-1$, we have the following formula for expressing the ith bone's to-root transformation:

$$toRoot_i = toParent_i \cdot toRoot_p \qquad \text{(eq. 23.2)}$$

Here, p is the bone label of the parent of bone i. Does this make sense? Indeed, $toRoot_p$ gives us a direct map that sends geometry from the coordinate system of bone p to the coordinate system of the root. So to get to the root coordinate system, it follows that we just need to get geometry from the coordinate system of bone i to the coordinate system of its parent bone p, and $toParent_i$ does that job.

The only issue is that for this to work, when we go to process the ith bone, we must have already computed the to-root transformation of its parent. However, if we traverse the tree top-down, then a parent's to-root transformation will always be computed before its children's to-root transformation.

We can also see why this is more efficient. With the top-down approach, for any bone i, we already have the to-root transformation matrix of its parent; thus, we are only *one* step away from the to-root transformation for bone i. With a bottoms-up technique, we'd traverse the entire ancestry for each bone, and many matrix multiplications would be duplicated when bones share common ancestors.

23.2.3 The Offset Transform

There is a small subtlety that comes from the fact that the vertices influenced by a bone are not relative to the coordinate system of the bone (they are relative to the *bind space*, which is the coordinate system the mesh was modeled in). So before we apply Equation 15.2, we first need to transform the vertices from bind space to the space of the bone that influences the vertices. A so-called *offset transformation* does this; see Figure 23.7.

Thus, by transforming the vertices by the offset matrix of some arbitrary bone B, we move the vertices from the bind space to the bone space of B. Then, once we have the vertices in bone space of B, we can use B's to-root transform to position it back in character space in its current animated pose.

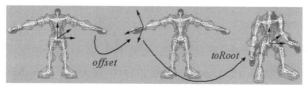

Figure 23.7. We first transform the vertices influenced by a bone from bind space to the space of the influencing bone via the offset transform. Then, once in the space of the bone, we apply the bone's to-root transformation to transform the vertices from the space of the bone to the space of the root bone. The final transformation is the combination of the offset transform, followed by the to-root transform.

We now introduce a new transform, call it the *final transform*, which combines a bone's offset transform with its to-root transform. Mathematically, the final transformation matrix of the ith bone $\mathbf{F}_i$ is given by:

$$\mathbf{F}_i = \textit{offset}_i \cdot \textit{toRoot}_i \qquad \text{(eq. 23.3)}$$

23.2.4 Animating the Skeleton

In the demo of the last chapter, we showed how to animate a single object. We defined that a *key frame* specifies the position, orientation, and scale of an object at an instance in time, and that an *animation* is a list of key frames sorted by time, which roughly define the look of the overall animation. We then showed how to interpolate between key frames to calculate the placement of the object at times between key frames. We now extend our animation system to animating skeletons. These animation classes are defined in *SkinnedData.h/.cpp* in the "Skinned Mesh" demo of this chapter.

Animating a skeleton is not much harder than animating a single object. Whereas we can think of a single object as a single bone, a skeleton is just a collection of connected bones. We will assume that each bone can move independently. Therefore, to animate a skeleton, we just animate each bone locally. Then after each bone has done its local animation, we take into consideration the movement of its ancestors, and transform it to the root space.

We define an *animation clip* to be a list of animations (one for each bone in the skeleton) that work together to form a specific animation of the skeleton. For example, "walking," "running," "fighting," "ducking," and "jumping" are examples of animation clips.

```
///<summary>
/// Examples of AnimationClips are "Walk", "Run", "Attack", "Defend".
/// An AnimationClip requires a BoneAnimation for every bone to form
/// the animation clip.
///</summary>
struct AnimationClip
{
  // Smallest end time over all bones in this clip.
  float GetClipStartTime()const;
```

```
    // Largest end time over all bones in this clip.
    float GetClipEndTime()const;

    // Loops over each BoneAnimation in the clip and interpolates
    // the animation.
    void Interpolate(float t, std::vector<XMFLOAT4X4>& boneTransforms)
      const;

    // Animation for each bone.
    std::vector<BoneAnimation> BoneAnimations;
};
```

A character will generally have several animation clips for all the animations the character needs to perform in the application. All the animation clips work on the same skeleton, however, so they use the same number of bones (although some bones may be stationary for a particular animation). We can use an unordered_map data structure to store all the animation clips and to refer to an animation clip by a readable name:

```
std::unordered_map<std::string, AnimationClip> mAnimations;
AnimationClip& clip = mAnimations["attack"];
```

Finally, as already mentioned, each bone needs an offset transform to transform the vertices from bind space to the space of the bone; and additionally, we need a way to represent the skeleton hierarchy (we use an array—see the next section for details). This gives us our final data structure for storing our skeleton animation data:

```
class SkinnedData
{
public:

  UINT BoneCount()const;

  float GetClipStartTime(const std::string& clipName)const;
  float GetClipEndTime(const std::string& clipName)const;

  void Set(
    std::vector<int>& boneHierarchy,
    std::vector<DirectX::XMFLOAT4X4>& boneOffsets,
    std::unordered_map<std::string, AnimationClip>& animations);

  // In a real project, you'd want to cache the result if there was a
  // chance that you were calling this several times with the same
  // clipName at the same timePos.
  void GetFinalTransforms(const std::string& clipName, float timePos,
    std::vector<DirectX::XMFLOAT4X4>& finalTransforms)const;

private:
  // Gives parentIndex of ith bone.
  std::vector<int> mBoneHierarchy;
```

```
  std::vector<DirectX::XMFLOAT4X4> mBoneOffsets;

  std::unordered_map<std::string, AnimationClip> mAnimations;
};
```

23.2.5 Calculating the Final Transform

Our frame hierarchy for a character will generally be a tree, similar to the one in Figure 23.2. We model the hierarchy with an array of integers such that the ith array entry gives the parent index of the ith bone. Moreover, the ith entry corresponds to the ith `BoneAnimation` in the working animation clip and the ith entry corresponds to the ith offset transform. The root bone is always at element 0 and it has no parent. So for example, the animation and offset transform of the grandparent of bone i is obtained by:

```
int parentIndex = mBoneHierarchy[i];
int grandParentIndex = mBoneHierarchy[parentIndex];

XMFLOAT4X4 offset = mBoneOffsets[grandParentIndex];

AnimationClip& clip = mAnimations["attack"];
BoneAnimation& anim = clip.BoneAnimations[grandParentIndex];
```

We can therefore compute the final transform for each bone like so:

```
void SkinnedData::GetFinalTransforms(const std::string& clipName,
    float timePos, std::vector<XMFLOAT4X4>& finalTransforms)const
{
  UINT numBones = mBoneOffsets.size();

  std::vector<XMFLOAT4X4> toParentTransforms(numBones);

  // Interpolate all the bones of this clip at the given time instance.
  auto clip = mAnimations.find(clipName);
  clip->second.Interpolate(timePos, toParentTransforms);

  //
  // Traverse the hierarchy and transform all the bones to the
  // root space.
  //

  std::vector<XMFLOAT4X4> toRootTransforms(numBones);

  // The root bone has index 0. The root bone has no parent, so
  // its toRootTransform is just its local bone transform.
  toRootTransforms[0] = toParentTransforms[0];

  // Now find the toRootTransform of the children.
  for(UINT i = 1; i < numBones; ++i)
  {
    XMMATRIX toParent = XMLoadFloat4x4(&toParentTransforms[i]);
```

```
        int parentIndex = mBoneHierarchy[i];
        XMMATRIX parentToRoot = XMLoadFloat4x4(&toRootTransforms[parentInd
        ex]);

        XMMATRIX toRoot = XMMatrixMultiply(toParent, parentToRoot);

        XMStoreFloat4x4(&toRootTransforms[i], toRoot);
    }

    // Premultiply by the bone offset transform to get the final
      transform.
    for(UINT i = 0; i < numBones; ++i)
    {
        XMMATRIX offset = XMLoadFloat4x4(&mBoneOffsets[i]);
        XMMATRIX toRoot = XMLoadFloat4x4(&toRootTransforms[i]);
        XMStoreFloat4x4(&finalTransforms[i], XMMatrixMultiply(offset,
        toRoot));
    }
}
```

There is one requirement needed to make this work. When we traverse the bones in the loop, we look up the to-root transform of the bone's parent:

```
int parentIndex = mBoneHierarchy[i];
XMMATRIX parentToRoot = XMLoadFloat4x4(&toRootTransforms[parentIndex]);
```

This only works if we are guaranteed that the parent bone's to-root transform has already been processed earlier in the loop. We can, in fact, make this guarantee if we ensure that the bones are always ordered in the arrays such that a parent bone always comes before a child bone. Our sample 3D data has been generated such that this is the case. Here is some sample data of the first ten bones in the hierarchy array of some character model:

```
ParentIndexOfBone0: -1
ParentIndexOfBone1: 0
ParentIndexOfBone2: 0
ParentIndexOfBone3: 2
ParentIndexOfBone4: 3
ParentIndexOfBone5: 4
ParentIndexOfBone6: 5
ParentIndexOfBone7: 6
ParentIndexOfBone8: 5
ParentIndexOfBone9: 8
```

So take Bone9. Its parent is Bone8, the parent of Bone8 is Bone5, the parent of Bone5 is Bone4, the parent of Bone4 is Bone3, the parent of Bone3 is Bone2, and the parent of Bone2 is the root node Bone0. Notice that a child bone never comes before its parent bone in the ordered array.

23.3 VERTEX BLENDING

We have showed how to animate the skeleton. In this section we will focus on animating the skin of vertices that cover the skeleton. The algorithm for doing this is called *vertex blending*.

The strategy of vertex blending is as follows. We have an underlying bone hierarchy, but the skin itself is one continuous mesh (i.e., we do not break the mesh up into parts to correspond with each bone and animate them individually). Moreover, one or more bones can influence a vertex of the skin; the net result being determined by a weighted average of the influencing bones' final transforms (the weights are specified by an artist when the model is being made and saved to file). With this setup, a smooth transitional blend can be achieved at joints (which are typically the troubled areas), thereby making the skin feel elastic; see Figure 23.8.

In practice, [Möller08] notes that we usually do not need more than four bone influences per vertex. Therefore, in our design we will consider a maximum of four influential bones per vertex. So to implement vertex blending, we model the character mesh's skin as one continuous mesh. Each vertex contains up to four indices that index into a *bone matrix palette*, which is the array of final transformation matrices (one entry for each bone in the skeleton). Additionally, each vertex also has up to four weights that describe the respective amount of influence each of the four influencing bones has on that vertex. Thus we have the following vertex structure for vertex blending (Figure 23.9):

A continuous mesh whose vertices have this format is ready for vertex blending, and we call it a *skinned mesh*.

The *vertex-blended position* $\mathbf{v}'$ of any vertex $\mathbf{v}$, relative to the root frame (remember we perform the world transformation as a last step once we have everything in the root coordinate system), can be calculated with the following weighted average formula:

$$\mathbf{v}' = w_0 \mathbf{v} \mathbf{F}_0 + w_1 \mathbf{v} \mathbf{F}_1 + w_2 \mathbf{v} \mathbf{F}_2 + w_3 \mathbf{v} \mathbf{F}_3$$

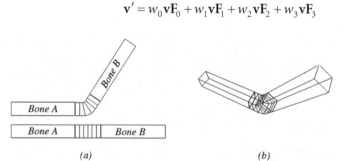

Figure 23.8. The skin is one continuous mesh that covers both bones. Observe that the vertices near the joint are influenced by both bone *A* and bone *B* to create a smooth transitional blend to simulate a flexible skin.

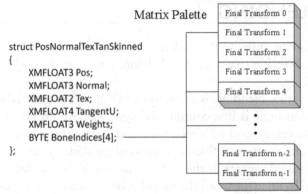

Figure 23.9. The matrix palette stores the final transformation for each bone. Observe how the four bone indices index into the matrix palette. The bone indices identify the bones of the skeleton that influence the vertex. Note that the vertex is not necessarily influenced by four bones; for instance, only two of the four indices might be used, thereby indicating that only two bones influence the vertex. We can set a bone weight to zero to effectively remove the bone from influencing the vertex.

Where $w_0 + w_1 + w_2 + w_3 = 1$; that is, the sum of the weights sums to one.

Observe that in this equation, we transform a given vertex v individually by all of the final bone transforms that influence it (i.e., matrices $\mathbf{F}_0$, $\mathbf{F}_1$, $\mathbf{F}_2$, $\mathbf{F}_3$). We then take a weighted average of these individually transformed points to compute the final vertex blended position $\mathbf{v}'$.

Transforming normals and tangents are done similarly:

$$\mathbf{n}' = \text{normalize}(w_0 \mathbf{nF}_0 + w_1 \mathbf{nF}_1 + w_2 \mathbf{nF}_2 + w_3 \mathbf{nF}_3)$$
$$\mathbf{t}' = \text{normalize}(w_0 \mathbf{tF}_0 + w_1 \mathbf{tF}_1 + w_2 \mathbf{tF}_2 + w_3 \mathbf{tF}_3)$$

Here we *assume* that the transformation matrices $\mathbf{F}_i$ do not contain any nonuniform scaling. Otherwise, we need to use the inverse-transpose $(\mathbf{F}_i^{-1})^T$ when transforming the normals (see §8.2.2).

The following vertex shader fragment shows the key code that does vertex blending with a maximum of four bone influences per vertex:

```
cbuffer cbSkinned : register(b1)
{
  // Max support of 96 bones per character.
  float4x4 gBoneTransforms[96];
};

struct VertexIn
{
  float3 PosL     : POSITION;
  float3 NormalL  : NORMAL;
  float2 TexC     : TEXCOORD;
  float4 TangentL : TANGENT;
#ifdef SKINNED
  float3 BoneWeights : WEIGHTS;
  uint4 BoneIndices  : BONEINDICES;
```

```
#endif
};

struct VertexOut
{
    float4 PosH       : SV_POSITION;
    float4 ShadowPosH : POSITION0;
    float4 SsaoPosH   : POSITION1;
    float3 PosW       : POSITION2;
    float3 NormalW    : NORMAL;
    float3 TangentW   : TANGENT;
    float2 TexC       : TEXCOORD;
};

VertexOut VS(VertexIn vin)
{
    VertexOut vout = (VertexOut)0.0f;

    // Fetch the material data.
    MaterialData matData = gMaterialData[gMaterialIndex];

#ifdef SKINNED
    float weights[4] = { 0.0f, 0.0f, 0.0f, 0.0f };
    weights[0] = vin.BoneWeights.x;
    weights[1] = vin.BoneWeights.y;
    weights[2] = vin.BoneWeights.z;
    weights[3] = 1.0f - weights[0] - weights[1] - weights[2];

    float3 posL = float3(0.0f, 0.0f, 0.0f);
    float3 normalL = float3(0.0f, 0.0f, 0.0f);
    float3 tangentL = float3(0.0f, 0.0f, 0.0f);
    for(int i = 0; i < 4; ++i)
    {
        // Assume no nonuniform scaling when transforming normals, so
        // that we do not have to use the inverse-transpose.

        posL += weights[i] * mul(float4(vin.PosL, 1.0f),
            gBoneTransforms[vin.BoneIndices[i]]).xyz;
        normalL += weights[i] * mul(vin.NormalL,
            (float3x3)gBoneTransforms[vin.BoneIndices[i]]);
        tangentL += weights[i] * mul(vin.TangentL.xyz,
            (float3x3)gBoneTransforms[vin.BoneIndices[i]]);
    }

    vin.PosL = posL;
    vin.NormalL = normalL;
    vin.TangentL.xyz = tangentL;
#endif

    // Transform to world space.
    float4 posW = mul(float4(vin.PosL, 1.0f), gWorld);
    vout.PosW = posW.xyz;

    // Assumes nonuniform scaling; otherwise, need to
    // use inverse-transpose of world matrix.
```

```
    vout.NormalW = mul(vin.NormalL, (float3x3)gWorld);

    vout.TangentW = mul(vin.TangentL, (float3x3)gWorld);

    // Transform to homogeneous clip space.
    vout.PosH = mul(posW, gViewProj);

    // Generate projective tex-coords to project SSAO map onto scene.
    vout.SsaoPosH = mul(posW, gViewProjTex);

    // Output vertex attributes for interpolation across triangle.
    float4 texC = mul(float4(vin.TexC, 0.0f, 1.0f), gTexTransform);
    vout.TexC = mul(texC, matData.MatTransform).xy;

    // Generate projective tex-coords to project shadow map onto scene.
    vout.ShadowPosH = mul(posW, gShadowTransform);

    return vout;
}
```

If the above vertex shader does vertex blending with a maximum of four bone influences per vertex, then why do we only input three weights per vertex instead of four? Well, recall that the total weight must sum to one; thus, for four weights we have: $w_0 + w_1 + w_2 + w_3 = 1 \Leftrightarrow w_3 = 1 - w_0 - w_1 - w_2$.

23.4 LOADING ANIMATION DATA FROM FILE

We use a text file to store a 3D skinned mesh with animation data. We call this an .m3d file for "model 3D." The format has been designed for simplicity in loading and readability—not for performance—and the format is just used for this book.

23.4.1 Header

At the beginning, the .m3d format defines a header which specifies the number of materials, vertices, triangles, bones, and animations that make up the model:

```
***************m3d-File-Header***************
#Materials 3
#Vertices 3121
#Triangles 4062
#Bones 44
#AnimationClips 15
```

1. `#Materials`: The number of distinct materials the mesh uses.
2. `#Vertices`: The number of vertices of the mesh.
3. `#Triangles`: The number of triangles in the mesh.

4. `#Bones`: The number of bones in the mesh.
5. `#AnimationClips`: The number of animation clips in the mesh.

23.4.2 Materials

The next "chunk" in the .m3d format is a list of materials. Below is an example of the first two materials in the soldier.m3d file:

```
***************Materials********************
Name: soldier_head
Diffuse: 1 1 1
Fresnel0: 0.05 0.05 0.05
Roughness: 0.5
AlphaClip: 0
MaterialTypeName: Skinned
DiffuseMap: head_diff.dds
NormalMap: head_norm.dds

Name: soldier_jacket
Diffuse: 1 1 1
Fresnel0: 0.05 0.05 0.05
Roughness: 0.8
AlphaClip: 0
MaterialTypeName: Skinned
DiffuseMap: jacket_diff.dds
NormalMap: jacket_norm.dds
```

The file contains the material data we are familiar with (diffuse, roughness, etc.), but also contains additional information such as the textures to apply, whether alpha clipping needs to be applied, and the material type name. The material type name is used to indicate which shader programs are needed for the given material. In the example above, the "Skinned" type indicates that the material will need to be rendered with shader programs that support skinning.

23.4.3 Subsets

A mesh consists of one or more subsets. A *subset* is a group of triangles in a mesh that can all be rendered using the same material. Figure 23.10 illustrates how a mesh representing a car may be divided into several subsets.

There is a subset corresponding to each material and the *i*th subset corresponds to the *i*th material. The ith subset defines a contiguous block of geometry that should be rendered with the ith material.

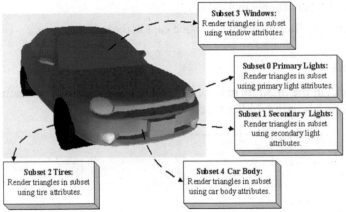

Figure 23.10. A car broken up by subset. Here only the materials per subset differ, but we could also imagine textures being added and differing as well. In addition, the render states may differ; for example, the glass windows may be rendered with alpha blending for transparency.

```
***************SubsetTable******************
SubsetID: 0 VertexStart:     0 VertexCount: 3915 FaceStart:     0 FaceCount: 7230
SubsetID: 1 VertexStart:  3915 VertexCount: 2984 FaceStart:  7230 FaceCount: 4449
SubsetID: 2 VertexStart:  6899 VertexCount: 4270 FaceStart: 11679 FaceCount: 6579
SubsetID: 3 VertexStart: 11169 VertexCount: 2305 FaceStart: 18258 FaceCount: 3807
SubsetID: 4 VertexStart: 13474 VertexCount:  274 FaceStart: 22065 FaceCount:  442
```

In the above example, the first 7230 triangles of the mesh (which reference vertices [0, 3915)) should be rendered with material 0, and the next 4449 triangles of the mesh (which reference vertices [3915, 6899)) should be rendered with material 1.

23.4.4 Vertex Data and Triangles

The next two chunks of data are just lists of vertices and indices (3 indices per triangle):

```
***************Vertices*********************
Position: -14.34667 90.44742 -12.08929
Tangent: -0.3069077 0.2750875 0.9111171 1
Normal: -0.3731041 -0.9154652 0.150721
Tex-Coords: 0.21795 0.105219
BlendWeights: 0.483457 0.483457 0.0194 0.013686
BlendIndices: 3 2 39 34

Position: -15.87868 94.60355 9.362272
Tangent: -0.3069076 0.2750875 0.9111172 1
Normal: -0.3731041 -0.9154652 0.150721
Tex-Coords: 0.278234 0.091931
BlendWeights: 0.4985979 0.4985979 0.002804151 0
BlendIndices: 39 2 3 0
 ...

***************Triangles********************
```

```
0  1  2
3  4  5
6  7  8
9 10 11
12 13 14
...
```

23.4.5 Bone Offset Transforms

The bone offset transformation chunk, just stores a list of 4×4 matrices, one for each bone.

```
***************BoneOffsets******************
BoneOffset0 -0.8669753 0.4982096 0.01187624 0
0.04897417 0.1088907 -0.9928461 0
-0.4959392 -0.8601914 -0.118805 0
-10.94755 -14.61919 90.63506 1

BoneOffset1 1 4.884964E-07 3.025227E-07 0
-3.145564E-07 2.163151E-07 -1 0
4.884964E-07 0.9999997 -9.59325E-08 0
3.284225 7.236738 1.556451 1
...
```

23.4.6 Hierarchy

The hierarchy chunk stores the hierarchy array—an array of integers such that the ith array entry gives the parent index of the ith bone.

```
***************BoneHierarchy****************
ParentIndexOfBone0: -1
ParentIndexOfBone1: 0
ParentIndexOfBone2: 1
ParentIndexOfBone3: 2
ParentIndexOfBone4: 3
ParentIndexOfBone5: 4
ParentIndexOfBone6: 5
ParentIndexOfBone7: 6
ParentIndexOfBone8: 7
ParentIndexOfBone9: 7
ParentIndexOfBone10: 7
ParentIndexOfBone11: 7
ParentIndexOfBone12: 6
ParentIndexOfBone13: 12
...
```

23.4.7 Animation Data

The last chunk we need to read are the animation clips. Each animation has a readable name and a list of key frames for each bone in the skeleton. Each key frame stores the time position, the translation vector specifying the position of the bone, the scaling vector specifying the bone scale, and the quaternion specifying the orientation of the bone.

```
***************AnimationClips****************
AnimationClip run_loop
{
    Bone0 #Keyframes: 18
    {
       Time: 0 Pos: 2.538344 101.6727 -0.52932
       Scale: 1 1 1
       Quat: 0.4042651 0.3919331 -0.5853591 0.5833637
       Time: 0.0666666
       Pos: 0.81979 109.6893 -1.575387
       Scale: 0.9999998 0.9999998 0.9999998
       Quat: 0.4460441 0.3467651 -0.5356012 0.6276384
       ...
    }

    Bone1 #Keyframes: 18
    {
       Time: 0
       Pos: 36.48329 1.210869 92.7378
       Scale: 1 1 1
       Quat: 0.126642 0.1367731 0.69105 0.6983587
       Time: 0.0666666
       Pos: 36.30672 -2.835898 93.15854
       Scale: 1 1 1
       Quat: 0.1284061 0.1335271 0.6239273 0.7592083
       ...
    }
    ...
}

AnimationClip walk_loop
{
    Bone0 #Keyframes: 33
    {
       Time: 0
       Pos: 1.418595 98.13201 -0.051082
       Scale: 0.9999985 0.999999 0.9999991
       Quat: 0.3164562 0.6437552 -0.6428624 0.2686314
       Time: 0.0333333
       Pos: 0.956079 96.42985 -0.047988
       Scale: 0.9999999 0.9999999 0.9999999
       Quat: 0.3250651 0.6395872 -0.6386833 0.2781091
       ...
    }

    Bone1 #Keyframes: 33
    {
       Time: 0
       Pos: -5.831432 2.521564 93.75848
       Scale: 0.9999995 0.9999995 1
       Quat: -0.033817 -0.000631005 0.9097761 0.4137191
       Time: 0.0333333
```

```
            Pos:   -5.688324 2.551427 93.71078
            Scale: 0.9999998 0.9999998 1
            Quat:  -0.033202 -0.0006390021 0.903874 0.426508
            ...
        }
        ...
}
```

...

The following code shows how we read the animation clips from file:
```
void M3DLoader::ReadAnimationClips(
  std::ifstream& fin,
  UINT numBones,
  UINT numAnimationClips,
  std::unordered_map<std::string,
  AnimationClip>& animations)
{
  std::string ignore;
  fin >> ignore; // AnimationClips header text
  for(UINT clipIndex = 0; clipIndex < numAnimationClips; ++clipIndex)
  {
    std::string clipName;
    fin >> ignore >> clipName;
    fin >> ignore; // {

    AnimationClip clip;
    clip.BoneAnimations.resize(numBones);

    for(UINT boneIndex = 0; boneIndex < numBones; ++boneIndex)
    {
      ReadBoneKeyframes(fin, numBones, clip.BoneAnimations[boneIndex]);
    }
    fin >> ignore; // }

    animations[clipName] = clip;
  }
}

void M3DLoader::ReadBoneKeyframes(
  std::ifstream& fin,
  UINT numBones,
  BoneAnimation& boneAnimation)
{
  std::string ignore;
  UINT numKeyframes = 0;
  fin >> ignore >> ignore >> numKeyframes;
  fin >> ignore; // {

  boneAnimation.Keyframes.resize(numKeyframes);
  for(UINT i = 0; i < numKeyframes; ++i)
  {
    float t    = 0.0f;
    XMFLOAT3 p(0.0f, 0.0f, 0.0f);
    XMFLOAT3 s(1.0f, 1.0f, 1.0f);
    XMFLOAT4 q(0.0f, 0.0f, 0.0f, 1.0f);
```

```
            fin >> ignore >> t;
            fin >> ignore >> p.x >> p.y >> p.z;
            fin >> ignore >> s.x >> s.y >> s.z;
            fin >> ignore >> q.x >> q.y >> q.z >> q.w;

            boneAnimation.Keyframes[i].TimePos     = t;
            boneAnimation.Keyframes[i].Translation = p;
            boneAnimation.Keyframes[i].Scale       = s;
            boneAnimation.Keyframes[i].RotationQuat = q;
        }

        fin >> ignore; // }
    }
```

23.4.8 M3DLoader

The code to load the data from an .m3d file is contained in *LoadM3D.h/.cpp*, in particular, the `LoadM3d` function:

```
bool M3DLoader::LoadM3d(
  const std::string& filename,
  std::vector<SkinnedVertex>& vertices,
  std::vector<USHORT>& indices,
  std::vector<Subset>& subsets,
  std::vector<M3dMaterial>& mats,
  SkinnedData& skinInfo)
{
  std::ifstream fin(filename);

  UINT numMaterials = 0;
  UINT numVertices  = 0;
  UINT numTriangles = 0;
  UINT numBones     = 0;
  UINT numAnimationClips = 0;

  std::string ignore;

  if( fin )
  {
    fin >> ignore; // file header text
    fin >> ignore >> numMaterials;
    fin >> ignore >> numVertices;
    fin >> ignore >> numTriangles;
    fin >> ignore >> numBones;
    fin >> ignore >> numAnimationClips;

    std::vector<XMFLOAT4X4> boneOffsets;
    std::vector<int> boneIndexToParentIndex;
    std::unordered_map<std::string, AnimationClip> animations;

    ReadMaterials(fin, numMaterials, mats);
    ReadSubsetTable(fin, numMaterials, subsets);
    ReadSkinnedVertices(fin, numVertices, vertices);
    ReadTriangles(fin, numTriangles, indices);
```

```
    ReadBoneOffsets(fin, numBones, boneOffsets);
    ReadBoneHierarchy(fin, numBones, boneIndexToParentIndex);
    ReadAnimationClips(fin, numBones, numAnimationClips, animations);

    skinInfo.Set(boneIndexToParentIndex, boneOffsets, animations);

    return true;
  }
  return false;
}
```

The helper functions `ReadMaterials`, and etc., are straightforward text file parsing using `std::ifstream`. We leave it to the read to examine the source code for the implementation details.

23.5 CHARACTER ANIMATION DEMO

As we saw in the skinned mesh shader code, the final bone transforms are stored in a constant buffer where they are accessed in the vertex shader to do the animation transformations.

```
cbuffer cbSkinned : register(b1)
{
  // Max support of 96 bones per character.
  float4x4 gBoneTransforms[96];
};
```

We therefore need to add these new constant buffers, one for each skinned mesh object, to our frame resources:

```
struct SkinnedConstants
{
  DirectX::XMFLOAT4X4 BoneTransforms[96];
};

std::unique_ptr<UploadBuffer<SkinnedConstants>> SkinnedCB = nullptr;

SkinnedCB = std::make_unique<UploadBuffer<SkinnedConstants>>(
    device, skinnedObjectCount, true);
```

We will need one `SkinnedConstants` for each instance of an animated character. An animated character instance will generally be composed of multiple render-items (one per material), but all render-items for the same character instance can share the same `SkinnedConstants` since they all use the same underlying animated skeleton.

To represent an animated character instance at an instance in time, we define the following structure:

```
struct SkinnedModelInstance
{
```

```
    SkinnedData* SkinnedInfo = nullptr;

    // Storage for final transforms at the given time position.
    std::vector<DirectX::XMFLOAT4X4> FinalTransforms;

    // Current animation clip.
    std::string ClipName;

    // Animation time position.
    float TimePos = 0.0f;

    // Call every frame to increment the animation.
    void UpdateSkinnedAnimation(float dt)
    {
      TimePos += dt;

      // Loop animation
      if(TimePos > SkinnedInfo->GetClipEndTime(ClipName))
        TimePos = 0.0f;

      // Called every frame and increments the time position,
      // interpolates the animations for each bone based on
      // the current animation clip, and generates the final
      // transforms which are ultimately set to the effect
      // for processing in the vertex shader.
      SkinnedInfo->GetFinalTransforms(ClipName, TimePos,
        FinalTransforms);
    }
};
```

Then we add the following data members to our render-item structure:

```
struct RenderItem
{
  [...]
  // Index to bone transformation constant buffer.
  // Only applicable to skinned render-items.
  UINT SkinnedCBIndex = -1;

  // Pointer to the animation instance associated with this render
    item.
  // nullptr if this render-item is not animated by skinned mesh.
  SkinnedModelInstance* SkinnedModelInst = nullptr;  [...]
};
```

Every frame we update the animated character instances (in our demo we only have one):

```
void SkinnedMeshApp::UpdateSkinnedCBs(const GameTimer& gt)
{
  auto currSkinnedCB = mCurrFrameResource->SkinnedCB.get();

  // We only have one skinned model being animated.
  mSkinnedModelInst->UpdateSkinnedAnimation(gt.DeltaTime());
```

```
SkinnedConstants skinnedConstants;
std::copy(
  std::begin(mSkinnedModelInst->FinalTransforms),
  std::end(mSkinnedModelInst->FinalTransforms),
  &skinnedConstants.BoneTransforms[0]);

currSkinnedCB->CopyData(0, skinnedConstants);
}
```

And when we draw the render-items, we bind the associated final bone transforms if the render-item is animated by a skinned mesh:

```
if(ri->SkinnedModelInst != nullptr)
{
  D3D12_GPU_VIRTUAL_ADDRESS skinnedCBAddress =
    skinnedCB->GetGPUVirtualAddress() +
    ri->SkinnedCBIndex*skinnedCBByteSize;
  cmdList->SetGraphicsRootConstantBufferView(1, skinnedCBAddress);
}
else
{
  cmdList->SetGraphicsRootConstantBufferView(1, 0);
}
```

Figure 23.10 shows a screenshot or our demo. The original animated model and textures were taken from the DirectX SDK and converted to the .m3d format for demoing purposes. This sample model only has one animation clip called *Take1*.

Figure 23.10. Screenshot of the "Skinned Mesh" demo.

23.6 SUMMARY

1. Many real world objects we wish to model graphically in a computer program consist of parts with a parent-children relationship, where a child object can move independently on its own, but is also forced to move when its parent moves. For example, a tank turret can rotate independently of the tank, but it is still fixed to the tank and moves with the tank. Another classic example is skeletons, in which bones are attached to other bones and must move when they move. Consider game characters on a train. The characters can move independently inside the train, but they also move as the train moves. This example illustrates how, in a game, the hierarchy can change dynamically and must be updated. That is, before a character enters a train, the train is not part of the character's hierarchy, but once the player does enter a train, the train does become part of the character's hierarchy (the character inherits the train transformation).

2. Each object in a mesh hierarchy is modeled about its own local coordinate system with its pivot joint at the origin to facilitate rotation. Because the coordinate systems exist in the same universe we can relate them, and therefore, transform from one to the other. In particular, we relate them by describing each object's coordinate system relative to its parent's coordinate system. From that, we can construct a *to-parent* transformation matrix that transforms the geometry of an object from its local coordinate system to its parent's coordinate system. Once in the parent's coordinate system, we can then transform by the parent's to-parent matrix to transform to the grandparent's coordinate system, and so on and so forth, until we have visited each ancestor's coordinate system and finally reach the world space. Stated in other words, to transform an object in a mesh hierarchy from its local space to world space, we apply the to-parent transform of the object and all of its ancestors (in ascending order) to percolate up the coordinate system hierarchy until the object arrives in the world space. In this way, the object inherits the transformations of its parents and moves when they move.

3. We can express the to-root transformation of the ith bone with the recurrence relation: $toRoot_i = toParent_i \cdot toRoot_p$ where p refers to the parent bone of the ith bone.

4. The bone-offset transformation transforms vertices from bind space to the space of the bone. There is an offset transformation for each bone in the skeleton.

5. In vertex blending, we have an underlying bone hierarchy, but the skin itself is one continuous mesh, and one or more bones can influence a vertex. The

magnitude in which a bone influences a vertex is determined by a bone weight. For four bones, the transformed vertex **v**′, relative to the root of the skeleton, is given by the weighted averaging formula $\mathbf{v}' = w_0\mathbf{vF}_0 + w_1\mathbf{vF}_1 + w_2\mathbf{vF}_2 + w_3\mathbf{vF}_3$, where $w_0 + w_1 + w_2 + w_3 = 1$. By using a continuous mesh, and several weighted bone influences per vertex, a more natural elastic skin effect is achieved.

6. To implement vertex blending, we store an array of final transformation matrices for each bone (the array is called a *matrix palette*). (The ith bone's final transformation is defined as $\mathbf{F}_i = \mathit{offset}_i \cdot \mathit{toRoot}_i$ —that is, the bone's offset transformation followed by its to-root transformation.) Then, for each vertex, we store a list of vertex weights and matrix palette indices. The matrix palette indices of a vertex identify the final transformations of the bones that influence the vertex.

23.7 EXERCISES

1. Model and render an animated linear hierarchy by hand. For example, you might model a simple robot arm built from sphere and cylinder meshes; the sphere could model a joint and the cylinder an arm.

2. Model and render an animated tree hierarchy by hand such as the one shown in Figure 23.11. You can again use spheres and cylinders.

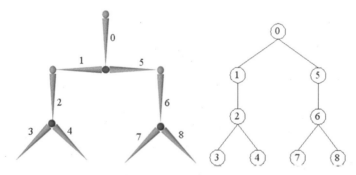

Figure 23.11. Simple mesh hierarchy.

3. If you have access to an animation package (*Blender http://www.blender.org/* is free), try learning how to model a simple animated character using bones and blend weights. Export your data to the .x file format which supports vertex blending, and try to convert the file data to the .m3d format for rendering in the "Skinned Mesh" demo. This is not a short project.

Appendix A

INTRODUCTION TO WINDOWS PROGRAMMING

To use the Direct3D API (Application Programming Interface), it is necessary to create a Windows (Win32) application with a main window, upon which we will render our 3D scenes. This appendix serves as an introduction to writing Windows applications using the native Win32 API. Loosely, the Win32 API is a set of low-level functions and structures exposed to us in the C programming language that enables us to create Windows applications. For example, to define a window class, we fill out an instance of the Win32 API `WNDCLASS` structure; to create a window, we use the Win32 API `CreateWindow` function; to notify Windows to show a particular window, we use the Win32 API function `ShowWindow`.

Windows programming is a huge subject, and this appendix introduces only the amount necessary for us to use Direct3D. For readers interested in learning more about Windows programming with the Win32 API, the book *Programming Windows* by Charles Petzold, now in its fifth edition, is the standard text on the subject. Another invaluable resource when working with Microsoft technologies is the MSDN library, which is usually included with Microsoft's Visual Studio but can also be read online at *www.msdn.microsoft.com*. In general, if you come upon a Win32 function or structure that you would like to know more about, go to MSDN and search for that function or structure for its full documentation. If we mention a Win32 function or structure in this appendix and do not elaborate on it, it is an implicit suggestion that the reader look the function up in MSDN.

Objectives:

1. To learn and understand the event driven programming model used in Windows programming.
2. To learn the minimal code necessary to create a Windows application that is necessary to use Direct3D.

 To avoid confusion, we will use a capital 'W' to refer to Windows the OS and we will use a lower case 'w' to refer to a particular window running in Windows.

A.1 OVERVIEW

As the name suggests, one of the primary themes of Windows programming is programming windows. Many of the components of a Windows application are windows, such as, the main application window, menus, toolbars, scroll bars, buttons, and other dialog controls. Therefore, a Windows application typically consists of several windows. These next subsections provide a concise overview of Windows programming concepts we should be familiar with before beginning a more complete discussion.

A.1.1 Resources

In Windows, several applications can run concurrently. Therefore, hardware resources such as CPU cycles, memory, and even the monitor screen must be shared amongst multiple applications. In order to prevent chaos from ensuing due to several applications accessing/modifying resources without any organization, Windows applications do not have direct access to hardware. One of the main jobs of Windows is to manage the presently instantiated applications and handle the distribution of resources amongst them. Thus, in order for our application to do something that might affect another running application, it must go through Windows. For example, to display a window you must call the Win32 API function ShowWindow; you cannot write to video memory directly.

A.1.2 Events, the Message Queue, Messages, and the Message Loop

A Windows application follows an *event-driven programming model*. Typically, a Windows application sits and waits1 for something to happen—an *event*. An

---

[1] We note that an application can perform idle processing; that is, perform a certain task when no events are occurring.

event can be generated in a number of ways; some common examples are key presses, mouse clicks, and when a window is created, resized, moved, closed, minimized, maximized, or becomes visible.

When an event occurs, Windows sends a *message* to the application the event occurred for, and adds the message to the application's *message queue*, which is simply a priority queue that stores messages for an application. The application constantly checks the message queue for messages in a *message loop* and, when it receives one, it dispatches the message to the *window procedure* of the particular window the message is for. (Remember, an application can contain several windows within it.) Every window has with it an associated function called a window procedure.2 Window procedures are functions we implement which contain code that is to be executed in response to specific messages. For instance, we may want to destroy a window when the Escape key is pressed. In our window procedure we would write:

```
case WM_KEYDOWN:
     if( wParam == VK_ESCAPE )
          DestroyWindow(ghMainWnd);
     return 0;
```

The messages a window does not handle should be forwarded to the default window procedure, which then handles the message. The Win32 API supplies the default window procedure, which is called `DefWindowProc`.

To summarize, the user or an application does something to generate an event. The OS finds the application the event was targeted towards, and it sends that application a message in response. The message is then added to the application's message queue. The application is constantly checking its message queue for messages. When it receives a message, the application dispatches it to the window procedure of the window the message is targeted for. Finally, the window procedure executes instructions in response to the message.

Figure (A.1) summarizes the event driven programming model.

A.1.3 GUI

Most Windows programs present a GUI (Graphical User Interface) that users can work from. A typical Windows application has one main window, a menu, toolbar, and perhaps some other controls. Figure A.2 shows and identifies some common GUI elements. For Direct3D game programming, we do not need a fancy GUI. In fact, all we need is a main window, where the client area will be used to render our 3D worlds.

---

[2] Every window has a window procedure, but several windows can share the same window procedure; therefore, we do not necessarily have to write a unique window procedure for each window. Two different windows would have different window procedures if we wanted them to respond to messages differently.

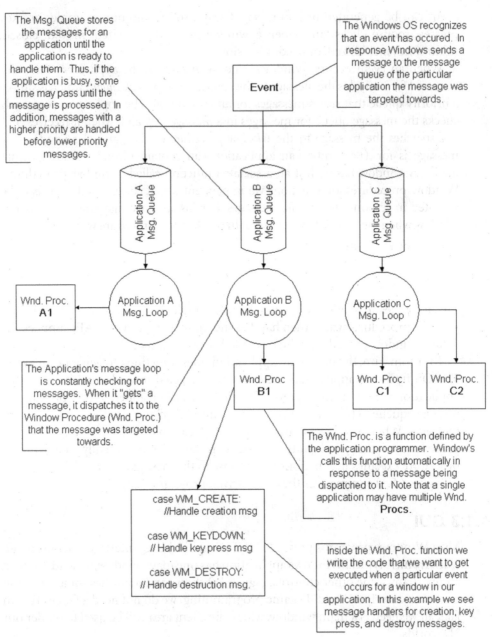

A.1. The event driven programming model.

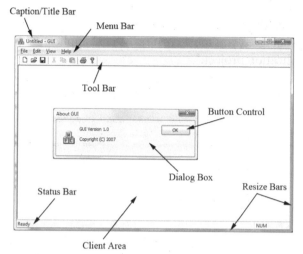

A.2. The A typical Windows application GUI. The client area is the entire large white rectangular space of the application. Typically, this area is where the user views most of the program output. When we program our Direct3D applications, we render our 3D scenes into the client area of a window.

A.1.4 Unicode

Essentially, Unicode (*http://unicode.org/*) uses 16-bit values to represent a character. This allows us to represent a larger character set to support international characters, and other symbols. For Unicode in C++, we use the *wide-characters* type wchar_t. In 32- and 64-bit Windows, a wchar_t is 16-bits. When using wide characters, we must prefix a string literal with a capital L; for example:

```
const wchar_t* wcstrPtr = L"Hello, World!";
```

The L tells the compiler to treat the string literal as a string of wide-characters (i.e., as wchar_t instead of char). The other important issue is that we need to use the wide-character versions of the string functions. For example, to get the length of a string we need to use wcslen instead of strlen; to copy a string we need to use wcscpy instead of strcpy; to compare two strings we need to use wcscmp instead of strcmp. The wide-character versions of these functions work with wchar_t pointers instead of char pointers. The C++ standard library also provides a wide-character version of its string class: std::wstring. The Windows header file WinNT.h also defines:

```
typedef wchar_t WCHAR; // wc, 16-bit UNICODE character
```

A.2 BASIC WINDOWS APPLICATION

Below is the code to a fully functional, yet simple, Windows program. Follow the code as best you can, and read the explanatory comments. The next section will explain the code a bit at a time. It is recommended that you create a project with your development tool, type the code in by hand, compile it and execute it as an exercise. Note that for Visual C++, you must create a "Win32 application project," *not* a "Win32 console application project."

```cpp
//=====================================================================
// Win32Basic.cpp by Frank Luna (C) 2008 All Rights Reserved.
//
// Illustrates the minimal amount of the Win32 code needed for
// Direct3D programming.
//=====================================================================

// Include the windows header file; this has all the Win32 API
// structures, types, and function declarations we need to program
// Windows.
#include <windows.h>

// The main window handle; this is used to identify a
// created window.
HWND ghMainWnd = 0;

// Wraps the code necessary to initialize a Windows
// application. Function returns true if initialization
// was successful, otherwise it returns false.
bool InitWindowsApp(HINSTANCE instanceHandle, int show);

// Wraps the message loop code.
int Run();

// The window procedure handles events our window receives.
LRESULT CALLBACK
WndProc(HWND hWnd, UINT msg, WPARAM wParam, LPARAM lParam);

// Windows equivalant to main()
int WINAPI
WinMain(HINSTANCE hInstance, HINSTANCE hPrevInstance,
    PSTR pCmdLine, int nShowCmd)
{
    // First call our wrapper function (InitWindowsApp) to create
    // and initialize the main application window, passing in the
    // hInstance and nShowCmd values as arguments.
    if(!InitWindowsApp(hInstance, nShowCmd))
        return 0;

    // Once our application has been created and initialized we
    // enter the message loop. We stay in the message loop until
    // a WM_QUIT mesage is received, indicating the application
    // should be terminated.
    return Run();
}

bool InitWindowsApp(HINSTANCE instanceHandle, int show)
{
```

```cpp
    // The first task to creating a window is to describe some of its
    // characteristics by filling out a WNDCLASS structure.
    WNDCLASS wc;

    wc.style         = CS_HREDRAW | CS_VREDRAW;
    wc.lpfnWndProc   = WndProc;
    wc.cbClsExtra    = 0;
    wc.cbWndExtra    = 0;
    wc.hInstance     = instanceHandle;
    wc.hIcon         = LoadIcon(0, IDI_APPLICATION);
    wc.hCursor       = LoadCursor(0, IDC_ARROW);
    wc.hbrBackground = (HBRUSH)GetStockObject(WHITE_BRUSH);
    wc.lpszMenuName  = 0;
    wc.lpszClassName = L"BasicWndClass";


    // Next, we register this WNDCLASS instance with Windows so
    // that we can create a window based on it.
    if(!RegisterClass(&wc))
    {
        MessageBox(0, L"RegisterClass FAILED", 0, 0);
        return false;
    }

    // With our WNDCLASS instance registered, we can create a
    // window with the CreateWindow function. This function
    // returns a handle to the window it creates (an HWND).
    // If the creation failed, the handle will have the value
    // of zero. A window handle is a way to refer to the window,
    // which is internally managed by Windows. Many of the Win32 API
    // functions that operate on windows require an HWND so that
    // they know what window to act on.

    ghMainWnd = CreateWindow(
        L"BasicWndClass", // Registered WNDCLASS instance to use.
        L"Win32Basic",    // window title
        WS_OVERLAPPEDWINDOW, // style flags
        CW_USEDEFAULT,    // x-coordinate
        CW_USEDEFAULT,    // y-coordinate
        CW_USEDEFAULT,    // width
        CW_USEDEFAULT,    // height
        0,       // parent window
        0,       // menu handle
        instanceHandle,   // app instance
        0);      // extra creation parameters

    if(ghMainWnd == 0)
    {
        MessageBox(0, L"CreateWindow FAILED", 0, 0);
        return false;
    }

    // Even though we just created a window, it is not initially
    // shown. Therefore, the final step is to show and update the
```

```cpp
    // window we just created, which can be done with the following
    // two function calls. Observe that we pass the handle to the
    // window we want to show and update so that these functions know
    // which window to show and update.
    ShowWindow(ghMainWnd, show);
    UpdateWindow(ghMainWnd);

    return true;
}

int Run()
{
    MSG msg = {0};

    // Loop until we get a WM_QUIT message. The function
    // GetMessage will only return 0 (false) when a WM_QUIT message
    // is received, which effectively exits the loop. The function
    // returns -1 if there is an error. Also, note that GetMessage
    // puts the application thread to sleep until there is a
    // message.
    BOOL bRet = 1;
    while( (bRet = GetMessage(&msg, 0, 0, 0)) != 0 )
    {
        if(bRet == -1)
        {
            MessageBox(0, L"GetMessage FAILED", L"Error", MB_OK);
            break;
        }
        else
        {
            TranslateMessage(&msg);
            DispatchMessage(&msg);
        }
    }

    return (int)msg.wParam;
}

LRESULT CALLBACK
WndProc(HWND hWnd, UINT msg, WPARAM wParam, LPARAM lParam)
{
    // Handle some specific messages. Note that if we handle a
    // message, we should return 0.
    switch( msg )
    {
        // In the case the left mouse button was pressed,
        // then display a message box.
    case WM_LBUTTONDOWN:
        MessageBox(0, L"Hello, World", L"Hello", MB_OK);
        return 0;

        // In the case the escape key was pressed, then
        // destroy the main application window.
    case WM_KEYDOWN:
        if( wParam == VK_ESCAPE )
```

```
            DestroyWindow(ghMainWnd);
        return 0;

        // In the case of a destroy message, then send a
        // quit message, which will terminate the message loop.
        case WM_DESTROY:
            PostQuitMessage(0);
            return 0;
    }

    // Forward any other messages we did not handle above to the
    // default window procedure. Note that our window procedure
    // must return the return value of DefWindowProc.
    return DefWindowProc(hWnd, msg, wParam, lParam);
}
```

A.3. A screenshot of the above program. Note that the message box appears when you press the left mouse button in the window's client area. Also try exiting the program by pressing the Escape key.

A.3 EXPLAINING THE BASIC WINDOWS APPLICATION

We will examine the code from top to bottom, stepping into any function that gets called along the way. Refer back to the code listing in the "Basic Windows Application" section throughout the following subsections.

A.3.1 Includes, Global Variables, and Prototypes

The first thing we do is include the windows.h header file. By including the windows.h file we obtain the structures, types, and function declarations needed for using the basic elements of the Win32 API.

```
#include <windows.h>
```

The second statement is an instantiation of a global variable of type HWND. This stands for "handle to a window" or "window handle." In Windows programming, we often use handles to refer to objects maintained internally by Windows. In this sample, we will use an HWND to refer to our main application window maintained by Windows. We need to hold onto the handles of our windows because many calls to the API require that we pass in the handle of the window we want the API call to act on. For example, the call UpdateWindow takes one argument that is of type HWND that is used to specify the window to update. If we did not pass in a handle to it, the function would not know which window to update.

```
HWND ghMainWnd = 0;
```

The next three lines are function declarations. Briefly, InitWindowsApp creates and initializes our main application window; Run encapsulates the message loop for our application; and WndProc is our main window's window procedure. We will examine these functions in more detail when we come to the point where they are called.

```
bool InitWindowsApp(HINSTANCE instanceHandle, int show);
int Run();
LRESULT CALLBACK
WndProc(HWND hWnd, UINT msg, WPARAM wParam, LPARAM lParam);
```

A.3.2 WinMain

WinMain is the Windows equivalent to the main function in normal C++ programming. WinMain is prototyped as follows:

```
int WINAPI
WinMain(HINSTANCE hInstance, HINSTANCE hPrevInstance,
    PSTR pCmdLine, int nShowCmd)
```

1. hInstance: Handle to the current application instance. It serves as a way of identifying and referring to this application. Remember there may be several Windows applications running concurrently, so it is useful to be able to refer to each one.
2. hPrevInstance: Not used in Win32 programming and is zero.
3. pCmdLine: The command line argument string used to run the program.
4. nCmdShow: Specifies how the application should be displayed. Some common commands that show the window in its current size and position, maximized, and minimized, respectively, are SW_SHOW, SW_SHOWMAXIMIZED, and SW_SHOWMINIMIZED. See the MSDN library for a complete list of show commands.

If WinMain succeeds, it should return the wParam member of the WM_QUIT message. If the function exits without entering the message loop, it should return zero. The WINAPI identifier is defined as:

```
#define WINAPI    __stdcall
```

This specifies the calling convention of the function, which means how the function arguments get placed on the stack.

A.3.3 WNDCLASS and Registration

Inside `WinMain` we call the function `InitWindowsApp`. As you can guess, this function does all the initialization of our program. Let us take a closer look at this function and its implementation. `InitWindowsApp` returns either `true` or `false`: `true` if the initialization was a success and false otherwise. In the `WinMain` definition, we pass as arguments a copy of our application instance and the show command variable into `InitWindowsApp`. Both are obtained from the `WinMain` parameter list.

```
if(!InitWindowsApp(hInstance, nShowCmd))
```

The first task at hand in initialization of a window is to describe some basic properties of the window by filling out a WNDCLASS (window class) structure. Its definition is:

```
typedef struct _WNDCLASS {
        UINT style;
        WNDPROC lpfnWndProc;
        int    cbClsExtra;
        int    cbWndExtra;
        HANDLE hInstance;
        HICON hIcon;
        HCURSOR hCursor;
        HBRUSH hbrBackground;
        LPCTSTR lpszMenuName;
        LPCTSTR lpszClassName;
} WNDCLASS;
```

1. `style`: Specifies the class style. In our example we use `CS_HREDRAW` combined with `CS_VREDRAW`. These two bit flags indicate that the window is to be repainted when either the horizontal or vertical window size is changed. For the complete list of the various styles with description, see the MSDN library.

   ```
   wc.style = CS_HREDRAW | CS_VREDRAW;
   ```

2. `lpfnWndProc`: Pointer to the window procedure function to associate with this WNDCLASS instance. Windows that are created based on this `WNDCLASS` instance will use this window procedure. Thus, to create two windows with the same window procedure, you just create the two windows based on the same `WNDCLASS` instance. If you want to create two windows with different window procedures, you will need to fill out a different `WNDCLASS` instance for each of the two windows. The window procedure function is explained in section A.3.6.

   ```
   wc.lpfnWndProc = WndProc;
   ```

3. `cbClsExtra` and `cbWndExtra`: These are extra memory slots you can use for your own purpose. Our program does not require any extra space and therefore sets both of these to zero.

   ```
   wc.cbClsExtra = 0;
   wc.cbWndExtra = 0;
   ```

4. `hInstance`: This field is a handle to the application instance. Recall the application instance handle is originally passed in through `WinMain`.

   ```
   wc.hInstance = instanceHandle;
   ```

5. `hIcon`: Here you specify a handle to an icon to use for the windows created using this window class. You can use your own designed icon, but there are several built-in icons to choose from; see the MSDN library for details. The following uses the default application icon:

   ```
   wc.hIcon = LoadIcon(0, IDI_APPLICATION);
   ```

6. `hCursor`: Similar to `hIcon`, here you specify a handle to a cursor to use when the cursor is over the window's client area. Again, there are several built-in cursors; see the MSDN library for details. The following code uses the standard "arrow" cursor.

   ```
   wc.hCursor = LoadCursor(0, IDC_ARROW);
   ```

7. `hbrBackground`: This field is used to specify a handle to brush which specifies the background color for the client area of the window. In our sample code, we call the Win32 function `GetStockObject`, which returns a handle to a prebuilt white colored brush; see the MSDN library for other types of built in brushes.

   ```
   wc.hbrBackground = (HBRUSH)GetStockObject(WHITE_BRUSH);
   ```

8. `lpszMenuName`: Specifies the window's menu. Since we have no menu in our application so, we set this to zero.

   ```
   wc.lpszMenuName = 0;
   ```

9. `lpszClassName`: Specifies the name of the window class structure we are creating. This can be anything you want. In our application, we named it "BasicWndClass". The name is simply used to identify the class structure so that we can reference it later by its name.

   ```
   wc.lpszClassName = L"BasicWndClass";
   ```

Once we have filled out a `WNDCLASS` instance, we need to register it with Windows so that we can create windows based on it. This is done with the `RegisterClass` function which takes a pointer to a `WNDCLASS` structure. This function returns zero upon failure.

```
if(!RegisterClass(&wc))
```

```
        {
                MessageBox(0, L"RegisterClass FAILED", 0, 0);
                return false;
        }
```

A.3.4 Creating and Displaying the Window

After we have registered a WNDCLASS variable with Windows, we can create a window based on that class description. We can refer to a registered WNDCLASS instance via the class name we gave it (lpszClassName). The function we use to create a window is the CreateWindow function, which is declared as follows:

```
HWND CreateWindow(
        LPCTSTR lpClassName,
        LPCTSTR lpWindowName,
        DWORD dwStyle,
        int x,
        int y,
        int nWidth,
        int nHeight,
        HWND hWndParent,
        HMENU hMenu,
        HANDLE hInstance,
        LPVOID lpParam
);
```

1. lpClassName: The name of the registered WNDCLASS structure that describes some of the properties of the window we want to create.

2. lpWindowName: The name we want to give our window; this is also the name that appears in the window's caption bar.

3. dwStyle: Defines the style of the window. WS_OVERLAPPEDWINDOW is a combination of several flags: WS_OVERLAPPED, WS_CAPTION, WS_SYSMENU, WS_THICKFRAME, WS_MINIMIZEBOX, and WS_MAXIMIZEBOX. The names of these flags describe the characteristics of the window they produce. See the MSDN library for the complete list of styles.

4. x: The x position at the top left corner of the window relative to the screen. You can specify CW_USEDEFAULT for this parameter, and Windows will choose an appropriate default.

5. y: The y position at the top left corner of the window relative to the screen. You can specify CW_USEDEFAULT for this parameter, and Windows will choose an appropriate default.

6. nWidth: The width of the window in pixels. You can specify CW_USEDEFAULT for this parameter, and Windows will choose an appropriate default.

7. nHeight: The height of the window in pixels. You can specify CW_USEDEFAULT for this parameter, and Windows will choose an appropriate default.

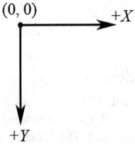

A.4. Screen space.

8. `hWndParent`: Handle to a window that is to be the parent of this window. Our window has no relationship with any other windows, and therefore we set this value to zero.

9. `hMenu`: A handle to a menu. Our program does not use a menu, so we specify 0 for this field.

10. `hInstance`: Handle to the application the window will be associated with.

11. `lpParam`: A pointer to user-defined data that you want to be available to a WM_CREATE message handler. The `WM_CREATE` message is sent to a window when it is being created, but before `CreateWindow` returns. A window handles the `WM_CREATE` message if it wants to do something when it is created (e.g., initialization).

 When we specify the (x, y) coordinates of the window's position, they are relative to the upper-left corner of the screen. Also, the positive x-axis runs to the right as usual but the positive y-axis runs downward. Figure (A.4) shows this coordinate system, which is called screen coordinates, or screen space.

`CreateWindow` returns a handle to the window it creates (an `HWND`). If the creation failed, the handle will have the value of zero (null handle). Remember that the handle is a way to refer to the window, which is managed by Windows. Many of the API calls require a `HWND` so that it knows what window to act on.

```
ghMainWnd = CreateWindow(L"BasicWndClass", L"Win32Basic",
    WS_OVERLAPPEDWINDOW,
    CW_USEDEFAULT, CW_USEDEFAULT,
    CW_USEDEFAULT, CW_USEDEFAULT,
    0, 0, instanceHandle, 0);
if(ghMainWnd == 0)
{
    MessageBox(0, L"CreateWindow FAILED", 0, 0);
    return false;
}
```

The last two function calls in the `InitWindowsApp` function have to do with displaying the window. First we call `ShowWindow` and pass in the handle of our newly created window so that Windows knows which window to show. We also pass in an integer value that defines how the window is to be initially shown (e.g., minimized, maximized, etc.). This value should be `nShowCmd`, which is a parameter of `WinMain`. After showing the window, we should refresh it. `UpdateWindow` does this; it takes one argument that is a handle to the window we wish to update.

```
ShowWindow(ghMainWnd, show);
    UpdateWindow(ghMainWnd);
```

If we made it this far in `InitWindowsApp`, then the initialization is complete; we return true to indicate everything went successfully.

A.3.5 The Message Loop

Having successfully completed initialization we can begin the heart of the program—the message loop. In our Basic Windows Application, we have wrapped the message loop in a function called `Run`.

```
int Run()
{
    MSG msg = {0};

    BOOL bRet = 1;
    while( (bRet = GetMessage(&msg, 0, 0, 0)) != 0 )
    {
        if(bRet == -1)
        {
            MessageBox(0, L"GetMessage FAILED", L"Error", MB_OK);
            break;
        }
        else
        {
            TranslateMessage(&msg);
            DispatchMessage(&msg);
        }
    }

    return (int)msg.wParam;
}
```

The first thing done in Run is an instantiation of a variable called `msg` of type `MSG`, which is the structure that represents a Windows message. Its definition is as follows:

```
typedef struct tagMSG {
        HWND hwnd;
        UINT message;
        WPARAM wParam;
        LPARAM lParam;
        DWORD time;
        POINT pt;
} MSG;
```

1. `hwnd`: The handle to the window whose window procedure is to receive the message.
2. `message`: A predefined constant value identifying the message (e.g., `WM_QUIT`).
3. `wParam`: Extra information about the message. This is dependent upon the specific message.
4. `lParam`: Extra information about the message. This is dependent upon the specific message.
5. `time`: The time the message was posted.
6. `pt`: The (x, y) coordinates of the mouse cursor, in screen coordinates, when the message was posted.

Next, we enter the message loop. The `GetMessage` function retrieves a message from the message queue, and fills out the `msg` argument with the details of the message. The second, third, and fourth parameters of `GetMessage` may be set to zero, for our purposes. If an error occurs in `GetMessage`, then `GetMessage` returns -1. If a `WM_QUIT` message is received, then GetMessage returns 0, thereby terminating the message loop. If `GetMessage` returns any other value, then two more functions get called: `TranslateMessage` and `DispatchMessage`. `TranslateMessage` has Windows perform some keyboard translations; specifically, virtual key to character messages. `DispatchMessage` finally dispatches the message off to the appropriate window procedure.

If the application successfully exits via a `WM_QUIT` message, then the `WinMain` function should return the `wParam` of the `WM_QUIT` message (exit code).

A.3.6 The Window Procedure

We mentioned previously that the window procedure is where we write the code that we want to execute in response to a message our window receives. In the Basic Windows Application program, we name the window procedure `WndProc` and it is prototyped as:

```
LRESULT CALLBACK
WndProc(HWND hWnd, UINT msg, WPARAM wParam, LPARAM lParam);
```

This function returns a value of type `LRESULT` (defined as an integer), which indicates the success or failure of the function. The `CALLBACK` identifier specifies that the function is a *callback* function, which means that Windows will be calling this function outside of the code space of the program. As you can see from the Basic Windows Application source code, we never explicitly call the window procedure ourselves—Windows calls it for us when the window needs to process a message.

The window procedure has four parameters in its signature:

1. `hWnd`: The handle to the window receiving the message.
2. `msg`: A predefined value that identifies the particular message. For example, a quit message is defined as `WM_QUIT`. The prefix WM stands for "Window Message." There are over a hundred predefined window messages; see the MSDN library for details.
3. `wParam`: Extra information about the message which is dependent upon the specific message.
4. `lParam`: Extra information about the message which is dependent upon the specific message.

Our window procedure handles three messages: `WM_LBUTTONDOWN`, `WM_KEYDOWN`, and `WM_DESTROY` messages. A `WM_LBUTTONDOWN` message is sent when the user clicks the left mouse button on the window's client area. A `WM_KEYDOWN` message is sent to a window in focus when a key is pressed. A `WM_DESTROY` message is sent when a window is being destroyed.

Our code is quite simple; when we receive a `WM_LBUTTONDOWN` message we display a message box that prints out "Hello, World":

```
case WM_LBUTTONDOWN:
    MessageBox(0, L"Hello, World", L"Hello", MB_OK);
    return 0;
```

When our window gets a `WM_KEYDOWN` message, we test if the Escape key was pressed, and if it was, we destroy the main application window using the `DestroyWindow` function. The `wParam` passed into the window procedure specifies the *virtual key code* of the specific key that was pressed. Think of virtual key codes as an identifier for a particular key. The Windows header files have a list of virtual key code constants we can use to then test for a particular key; for example to test if the escape key was pressed, we use the virtual key code constant `VK_ESCAPE`.

```
case WM_KEYDOWN:
    if( wParam == VK_ESCAPE )
        DestroyWindow(ghMainWnd);
    return 0;
```

Remember, the `wParam` and `lParam` parameters are used to specify extra information about a particular message. For the `WM_KEYDOWN` message, the `wParam` specifies the *virtual key code* of the specific key that was pressed. The MSDN library will specify the information the `wParam` and `lParam` parameters carry for each Windows message.

When our window gets destroyed, we post a `WM_QUIT` message with the `PostQuitMessage` function (which terminates the message loop):

```
case WM_DESTROY:
    PostQuitMessage(0);
    return 0;
```

At the end of our window procedure, we call another function named `DefWindowProc`. This function is the default window procedure. In our Basic Windows Application program, we only handle three messages; we use the default behavior specified in `DefWindowProc` for all the other messages we receive but do not necessarily need to handle ourselves. For example, the Basic Windows Application program can be minimized, maximized, resized, and closed. This functionality is provided to us through the default window procedure, as we did not handle the messages to perform this functionality.

A.3.7 The MessageBox Function

There is one last API function we have not yet covered, and that is the `MessageBox` function. This function is a very handy way to provide the user with information and to get some quick input. The declaration to the MessageBox function looks like this:

```
int MessageBox(
  HWND hWnd,       // Handle of owner window, may specify null.
  LPCTSTR lpText,  // Text to put in the message box.
  LPCTSTR lpCaption,// Text to put for the title of the message box.
  UINT uType       // Style of the message box.
);
```

The return value for the `MessageBox` function depends on the type of message box. See the MSDN library for a list of possible return values and styles; one possible style is a Yes/No message box; see Figure A.5.

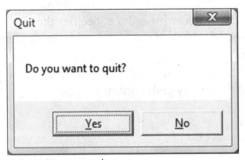

A.5. Yes/No message box.

A.4 A BETTER MESSAGE LOOP

Games are very different application than traditional Windows applications such as office type applications and web browsers. Typically, games do not sit around waiting for a message, but are constantly being updated. This presents a problem, because if there are no messages in the message queue, the function `GetMessage` puts the thread to sleep and waits for a message. For a game, we do not want this behavior; if there are no Windows messages to be processed, then we want to run our own game code. The fix is to use the `PeekMessage` function instead of `GetMessage`. The `PeekFunction` message returns immediately if there are no messages. Our new message loop is as follows:

```
int Run()
{
    MSG msg = {0};

    while(msg.message != WM_QUIT)
    {
        // If there are Window messages then process them.
        if(PeekMessage( &msg, 0, 0, 0, PM_REMOVE ))
        {
    TranslateMessage( &msg );
    DispatchMessage( &msg );
        }
        // Otherwise, do animation/game stuff.
        else
    {


    }
    }
    return (int)msg.wParam;
}
```

After we instantiate `msg`, we enter into an endless loop. We first call the API function `PeekMessage`, which checks the message queue for a message. See MSDN for the parameter descriptions. If there is a message it returns true and we handle the message. If there are no messages, `PeekMessage` returns false and we execute our own specific game code.

A.5 SUMMARY

1. To use Direct3D we must create a Windows application that has a main window onto which we can render our 3D scenes. Furthermore, for games we create a special message loop that checks for messages. If there are messages, it processes them; otherwise, it executes our game logic.
2. Several Windows applications can be running concurrently, and therefore Windows must manage resource between them and direct messages to the applications for which they were intended. Messages are sent to an application's message queue when an event (key press, mouse click, timer, etc.) has occurred for that application.

3. Every Windows application has a message queue in which messages an application receives are stored. The application's message loop constantly checks the queue for messages and dispatches them off to their intended window procedure. Note that a single application can have several windows within it.

4. The window procedure is a special callback function we implement that Windows calls when a window in our application receives a message. In the window procedure, we write the code we want to be executed when a window in our application receives a particular message. Messages we do not specifically handle are forwarded to a default window procedure for default handling.

A.6 EXERCISES

1. Modify the program in §A.2 to use a different icon, cursor, and background color.

Hint: Look up the `LoadIcon`, `LoadCursor`, *and* `GetStockObject` *functions in MSDN.)*

2. Modify the program in §A.2 by handling the `WM_CLOSE` message. This message is sent to a window or application indicating that the window or application should close. Use the message box function to ask the user if they really want to exit by displaying a Yes/No styled message box. If the user chooses "Yes," then destroy the window; otherwise do not destroy the window. You could also use this technique to ask the user if they want to save their work before closing.

3. Modify the program in §A.2 by handling the `WM_CREATE` message. This message is sent to a window when it is being created, but before `CreateWindow` returns. Output a message, via the message box function, indicating that the window has been created.

4. Look up the `Sleep` function in MSDN and summarize, in your own words, what the function does.

5. Look up the messages `WM_SIZE` and `WM_ACTIVATE` in MSDN and summarize, in your own words, when the messages are sent.

Appendix B

HIGH LEVEL SHADER LANGUAGE REFERENCE

VARIABLE TYPES

Scalar Types

1. `bool`: True or false value. Note that the HLSL provides the `true` and `false` keywords like in C++.
2. `int`: 32-bit signed integer.
3. `half`: 16-bit floating point number.
4. `float`: 32-bit floating point number.
5. `double`: 64-bit floating point number.

Some platforms might not support `int`, `half`, and `double`. If this is the case these types will be emulated using `float`.

Vector Types

1. `float2`: 2D vector, where the components are of type `float`.
2. `float3`: 3D vector, where the components are of type `float`.
3. `float4`: 4D vector, where the components are of type `float`.

Note: *You can create vectors where the components are of a type other than* `float`. *For example:* `int2, half3, bool4`.

We can initialize a vector using an array like syntax or constructor like syntax:

```
float3 v = {1.0f, 2.0f, 3.0f};
float2 w = float2(x, y);
float4 u = float4(w, 3.0f, 4.0f); // u = (w.x, w.y, 3.0f, 4.0f)
```

We can access a component of a vector using an array subscript syntax. For example, to set the *i*th component of a vector `vec` we would write:

```
vec[i] = 2.0f;
```

In addition, we can access the components of a vector `vec`, as we would access the members of a structure, using the defined component names `x, y, z, w, r, g, b,` and `a`.

```
vec.x = vec.r = 1.0f;
vec.y = vec.g = 2.0f;
vec.z = vec.b = 3.0f;
vec.w = vec.a = 4.0f;
```

The names `r, g, b,` and `a` refer to the exact same component as the names `x, y, z,` and `w`, respectively. When using vectors to represent colors, the RGBA notation is more desirable since it reinforces the fact that the vector is representing a color.

Swizzles

Consider the vector $\mathbf{u} = (u_x, u_y, u_z, u_w)$ and suppose we want to copy the components of $\mathbf{u}$ to a vector $\mathbf{v}$ such that $\mathbf{v} = (u_w, u_y, u_y, u_x)$. The most immediate solution would be to individually copy each component of $\mathbf{u}$ over to $\mathbf{v}$ as necessary. However, the HLSL provides a special syntax for doing these kinds of out of order copies called *swizzles*:

```
float4 u = {1.0f, 2.0f, 3.0f, 4.0f};
float4 v = {0.0f, 0.0f, 5.0f, 6.0f};

v = u.wyyx; // v = {4.0f, 2.0f, 2.0f, 1.0f}
```

Another example:

```
float4 u = {1.0f, 2.0f, 3.0f, 4.0f};
float4 v = {0.0f, 0.0f, 5.0f, 6.0f};

v = u.wzyx; // v = {4.0f, 3.0f, 2.0f, 1.0f}
```

When copying vectors, we do not have to copy every component over. For example, we can only copy the *x*- and *y*-components over as this code snippet illustrates:

```
float4 u = {1.0f, 2.0f, 3.0f, 4.0f};
```

```
float4 v = {0.0f, 0.0f, 5.0f, 6.0f};

v.xy = u; // v = {1.0f, 2.0f, 5.0f, 6.0f}
```

Matrix Types

We can define an $m \times n$ matrix, where m and n are between 1 and 4, using the following syntax:

```
floatmxn matmxn;
```

 Examples:

1. `float2x2`: 2×2 matrix, where the entries are of type `float`.
2. `float3x3`: 3×3 matrix, where the entries are of type `float`.
3. `float4x4`: 4×4 matrix, where the entries are of type `float`.
4. `float3x4`: 3×4 matrix, where the entries are of type `float`.

Note: *You can create matrices where the components are of a type other than float. For example:* `int2x2`, `half3x3`, `bool4x4`.

We can access an entry in a matrix using a double array subscript syntax. For example, to set the *ij*th entry of a matrix M we would write:

```
M[i][j] = value;
```

In addition, we can refer to the entries of a matrix M as we would access the members of a structure. The following entry names are defined:

One-Based Indexing:

```
M._11 = M._12 = M._13 = M._14 = 0.0f;
M._21 = M._22 = M._23 = M._24 = 0.0f;
M._31 = M._32 = M._33 = M._34 = 0.0f;
M._41 = M._42 = M._43 = M._44 = 0.0f;
```

Zero-Based Indexing:

```
M._m00 = M._m01 = M._m02 = M._m03 = 0.0f;
M._m10 = M._m11 = M._m12 = M._m13 = 0.0f;
M._m20 = M._m21 = M._m22 = M._m23 = 0.0f;
M._m30 = M._m31 = M._m32 = M._m33 = 0.0f;
```

Sometimes we want to refer to a particular row vector in a matrix. We can do so using a single array subscript syntax. For example, to extract the *i*th row vector in a 3×3 matrix M, we would write:

```
float3 ithRow = M[i]; // get the ith row vector in M
```

In this next example, we insert three vectors into the first, second and third row of a matrix:

```
float3 N = normalize(pIn.normalW);
float3 T = normalize(pIn.tangentW - dot(pIn.tangentW, N)*N);
float3 B = cross(N,T);
float3x3 TBN;
TBN[0] = T; // sets row 1
TBN[1] = B; // sets row 2
TBN[2] = N; // sets row 3
```

We can also construct a matrix from vectors:

```
float3 N = normalize(pIn.normalW);
float3 T = normalize(pIn.tangentW - dot(pIn.tangentW, N)*N);
float3 B = cross(N,T);

float3x3 TBN = float3x3(T, B, N);
```

Instead of using float4 *and* float4x4 *to represent 4D vectors and 4 × 4 matrices, you can equivalently use the* vector *and* matrix *type:*

```
vector u = {1.0f, 2.0f, 3.0f, 4.0f};
matrix M; // 4x4 matrix
```

Arrays

We can declare an array of a particular type using familiar C++ syntax, for example:

```
float M[4][4];
half  p[4];
float3 v[12]; // 12 3D vectors
```

Structures

Structures are defined exactly as they are in C++. However, structures in the HLSL cannot have member functions. Here is an example of a structure in the HLSL:

```
struct SurfaceInfo
{
  float3 pos;
  float3 normal;
  float4 diffuse;
  float4 spec;
};

SurfaceInfo v;
litColor += v.diffuse;
dot(lightVec, v.normal);
float specPower = max(v.spec.a, 1.0f);
```

The `typedef` Keyword

The HLSL `typedef` keyword functions exactly the same as it does in C++. For example, we can give the name `point` to the type `vector<float, 3>` using the following syntax:

```
typedef float3 point;
```

Then instead of writing:

```
float3 myPoint;
```

We can just write:

```
point myPoint;
```

Here is another example showing how to use the `typedef` keyword with the HLSL `const` keyword (which works as in C++):

```
typedef const float CFLOAT;
```

Variable Prefixes

The following keywords can prefix a variable declaration.

1. `static`: Essentially the opposite of `extern`; this means that the shader variable will not be exposed to the C++ application.
   ```
   static float3 v = {1.0f, 2.0f, 3.0f};
   ```
2. `uniform`: This means that the variable does not change per vertex/pixel—it is constant for all vertices/pixels until we change it at the C++ application level. Uniform variables are initialized from outside the shader program (e.g., by the C++ application).
3. `extern`: This means that the C++ application can see the variable (i.e., the variable can be accessed outside the shader file by the C++ application code. Global variables in a shader program are, by default, uniform and extern.
4. `const`: The `const` keyword in the HLSL has the same meaning it has in C++. That is, if a variable is prefixed with the `const` keyword then that variable is constant and cannot be changed.
   ```
   const float pi = 3.14f;
   ```

Casting

The HLSL supports a very flexible casting scheme. The casting syntax in the HLSL is the same as in the C programming language. For example, to cast a `float` to a `matrix` we write:

```
float f = 5.0f;
float4x4 m = (float4x4)f; // copy f into each entry of m.
```

What this scalar-matrix cast does is copy the scalar into each entry of the matrix. Consider the following example:

```
float3 n = float3(...);
float3 v = 2.0f*n - 1.0f;
```

The `2.0f*n` is just scalar-vector multiplication, which is well defined. However, to make this a vector equation, the scalar `1.0f` is augmented to the vector `(1.0f, 1.0f, 1.0f)`. So the above statement is like:

```
float3 v = 2.0f*n - float3(1.0f, 1.0f, 1.0f);
```

For the examples in this book, you will be able to deduce the meaning of the cast from the syntax. For a complete list of casting rules, search the SDK documentation index for "Casting and Conversion").

KEYWORDS AND OPERATORS

Keywords

For reference, here is a list of the keywords the HLSL defines:

```
asm, bool, compile, const, decl, do,
double, else, extern, false, float, for,
half, if, in, inline, inout, int,
matrix, out, pass, pixelshader, return, sampler,
shared, static, string, struct, technique, texture,
true, typedef, uniform, vector, vertexshader, void,
volatile, while
```

This next set of keywords displays identifiers that are reserved and unused, but may become keywords in the future:

```
auto, break, case, catch, char, class,
const_cast, continue, default, delete, dynamic_cast, enum,
explicit, friend, goto, long, mutable, namespace,
new, operator, private, protected, public, register,
reinterpret_cast, short, signed, sizeof, static_cast, switch,
template, this, throw, try, typename, union,
unsigned, using, virtual
```

Operators

HLSL supports many familiar C++ operators. With a few exceptions noted below, they are used exactly the same way as they are in C++. The following table, lists the HLSL operators:

[ ]	.	>	<	<=	>=	!=	==	!
&&	||	? :	+	+=	-	-=	*	*=
/	/=	%	%=	++	--	=	( )	,

Although the operators' behavior is very similar to C++, there are some differences. First of all, the modulus % operator works on both integer and floating-point types. And in order to use the modulus operator, both the left hand side value and right hand side value must have the same sign (e.g., both sides must be positive or both sides must be negative).

Secondly, observe that many of the HLSL operations work on a per component basis. This is due to the fact that vectors and matrices are built into the language and these types consist of several components. By having the operations work on a component level, operations such as vector/matrix addition, vector/matrix subtraction, and vector/matrix equality tests can be done using the same operators we use for scalar types. See the following examples.

 The operators behave as expected for scalars, that is, in the usual C++ way.

```
float4 u = {1.0f, 0.0f, -3.0f, 1.0f};
float4 v = {-4.0f, 2.0f, 1.0f, 0.0f};

// adds corresponding components
float4 sum = u + v; // sum = (-3.0f, 2.0f, -2.0f, 1.0f)
```

Incrementing a vector increments each component:

```
// before increment: sum = (-3.0f, 2.0f, -2.0f, 1.0f)

sum++; // after increment: sum = (-2.0f, 3.0f, -1.0f, 2.0f)
```

Multiplying vectors component wise:

```
float4 u = {1.0f, 0.0f, -3.0f, 1.0f};
float4 v = {-4.0f, 2.0f, 1.0f, 0.0f};

// multiply corresponding components
float4 product = u * v; // product = (-4.0f, 0.0f, -3.0f, 0.0f)
```

If you have two matrices:

```
float4x4 A;
float4x4 B;
```

The syntax `A*B` *does componentwise multiplication, not matrix multiplication. You need to use the* `mul` *function for matrix multiplication.*

Comparison operators are also done per component and return a vector or matrix where each component is of type `bool`. The resulting "`bool`" vector contains the results of each compared component. For example:

```
float4 u = { 1.0f, 0.0f, -3.0f, 1.0f};
float4 v = {-4.0f, 0.0f, 1.0f, 1.0f};

float4 b = (u == v); // b = (false, true, false, true)
```

Finally, we conclude by discussing variable promotions with binary operations:

1. For binary operations, if the left hand side and right hand side differ in dimension, then the side with the smaller dimension is promoted (cast) to have the same dimension as the side with the larger dimension. For example, if x is of type `float` and y is of type `float3`, in the expression `(x + y)`, the variable x is promoted to `float3` and the expression evaluates to a value of type `float3`. The promotion is done using the defined cast, in this case we are casting Scalar-to-Vector, therefore, after x is promoted to `float3`, x = (x, x, x) as the Scalar-to-Vector cast defines. Note that the promotion is not defined if the cast is not defined. For example, we can't promote `float2` to `float3` because there exists no such defined cast.
2. For binary operations, if the left hand side and right hand side differ in type. Then the side with the lower type resolution is promoted (cast) to have the same type as the side with the higher type resolution. For example, if x is of type `int` and y is of type `half`, in the expression `(x + y)`, the variable x is promoted to a `half` and the expression evaluates to a value of type `half`.

PROGRAM FLOW

The HLSL supports many familiar C++ statements for selection, repetition, and general program flow. The syntax of these statements is exactly like C++.

The *Return* Statement:

```
return (expression);
```

The *If* and *If...Else* Statements:

```
if( condition )
{
   statement(s);
}

if( condition )
{
   statement(s);
}
else
{
   statement(s);
}
```

The *for* statement:

```
for(initial; condition; increment)
{
   statement(s);
```

}
```

The while statement:

```
while( condition )
{
  statement(s);
}
```

The *do...while* statement:

```
do
{
  statement(s);
}while( condition );
```

FUNCTIONS

User Defined Functions

Functions in the HLSL have the following properties:

1. Functions use a familiar C++ syntax.
2. Parameters are always passed by value.
3. Recursion is not supported.
4. Functions are always inlined.

Furthermore, the HLSL adds some extra keywords that can be used with functions. For example, consider the following function written in the HLSL:

```
bool foo(in const bool b, // input bool
    out int r1,    // output int
    inout float r2) // input/output float
{
  if( b ) // test input value
  {
    r1 = 5; // output a value through r1
  }
  else
  {
    r1 = 1; // output a value through r1
  }

  // since r2 is inout we can use it as an input
  // value and also output a value through it
  r2 = r2 * r2 * r2;

  return true;
}
```
```

The function is almost identical to a C++ function except for the `in`, `out`, and `inout` keywords.

1. `in`: Specifies that the *argument* (particular variable we pass into a parameter) should be copied to the parameter before the function begins. It is not necessary to explicitly specify a parameter as `in` because a parameter is `in` by default. For example, the following are equivalent:

   ```
   float square(in float x)
   {
     return x * x;
   }
   ```

   And without explicitly specifying `in`:
   ```
   float square(float x)
   {
     return x * x;
   }
   ```

2. `out`: Specifies that the parameter should be copied to the argument when the function returns. This is useful for returning values through parameters. The `out` keyword is necessary because the HLSL doesn't allow us to pass by reference or to pass a pointer. We note that if a parameter is marked as `out` the argument is not copied to the parameter before the function begins. In other words, an `out` parameter can only be used to output data—it can't be used for input.

   ```
   void square(in float x, out float y)
   {
     y = x * x;
   }
   ```

   Here we input the number to be squared through `x` and return the square of `x` through the parameter `y`.

3. `inout`: Shortcut that denotes a parameter as both `in` and `out`. Specify `inout` if you wish to use a parameter for both input and output.

   ```
   void square(inout float x)
   {
     x = x * x;
   }
   ```

   Here we input the number to be squared through `x` and also return the square of `x` through `x`.

Built-in Functions

The HLSL has a rich set of built in functions that are useful for 3D graphics. The following table describes an abridged list of them.

S. No.	Function	Description
1.	`abs(x)`	Returns $|x|$.
2.	`ceil(x)`	Returns the smallest integer $\geq x$.
3.	`cos(x)`	Returns the cosine of x, where x is in radians.
4.	`clamp(x, a, b)`	Clamps x to the range [a, b] and returns the result.
5.	`clip(x)`	This function can only be called in a pixel shader, and it discards the current pixel from further processing if `x < 0`.
6.	`cross(u, v)`	Returns $\mathbf{u} \times \mathbf{v}$.
7.	`ddx(p)`	Estimates screen space partial derivative $\partial \mathbf{p}/\partial x$. This allows you can determine how per pixel quantities **p** vary from pixel to pixel in the screen space x-direction.
8.	`ddy(p)`	Estimates screen space partial derivative $\partial \mathbf{p}/\partial y$. This allows you can determine how per pixel quantities **p** vary from pixel to pixel in the screen space y-direction.
9.	`degrees(x)`	Converts x from radians to degrees.
10.	`determinant(M)`	Returns the determinant of a matrix.
11.	`distance(u, v)`	Returns the distance $\|\mathbf{v} - \mathbf{u}\|$ between the points **u** and **v**.
12.	`dot(u, v)`	Returns $\mathbf{u} \cdot \mathbf{v}$.
13.	`floor(x)`	Returns the greatest integer $\leq x$.
14.	`frac(x)`	This function returns the fractional part of a floating-point number (i.e., the mantissa). For example, if `x = (235.52, 696.32)` and `frac(x) = (0.52, 0.32)`.
15.	`length(v)`	Returns **v**.
16.	`lerp(u, v, t)`	Linearly interpolates between **u** and **v** based on the parameter $t \in [0, 1]$.
17.	`log(x)`	Returns $\ln(x)$.
18.	`log10(x)`	Returns $\log_{10}(x)$.
19.	`log2(x)`	Returns $\log_2(x)$.
20.	`max(x, y)`	Returns x if $x \geq y$, else returns y.
21.	`min(x, y)`	Returns x if $x \leq y$, else returns y.

S. No.	Function	Description
22.	`mul(M, N)`	Returns the matrix product **MN**. Note that the matrix product **MN** must be defined. If **M** is a vector, it is treated as a row vector so that the vector-matrix product is defined. Likewise, if **N** is a vector, it is treated as a column vector so that the matrix-vector product is defined.
23.	`normalize(v)`	Returns $\mathbf{v}/\|\mathbf{v}\|$.
24.	`pow(b, n)`	Returns b^n.
25.	`radians(x)`	Converts x from degrees to radians.
26.	`saturate(x)`	Returns `clamp(x, 0.0, 1.0)`.
27.	`sin(x)`	Returns the sine of x, where x is in radians.
28.	`sincos(in x, out s, out c)`	Returns the sine and cosine of x, where x is in radians.
29.	`sqrt(x)`	Returns $\sqrt{x}$.
30.	`reflect(v, n)`	Computes the reflection vector given the incident vector **v** and the surface normal **n**.
31.	`refract(v, n, eta)`	Computes the refraction vector given the incident vector **v**, the surface normal **n**, and the ratio of the two indices of refraction of the two materials `eta`.
32.	`rsqrt(x)`	Returns $\dfrac{1}{\sqrt{x}}$.
33.	`tan(x)`	Returns the tangent of x, where x is in radians.
34.	`transpose(M)`	Returns the transpose $\mathbf{M}^T$.
35.	`Texture2D::Sample(S, texC)`	Returns a color from a 2D texture map based on the `SamplerState` object `S`, and 2D texture coordinates `texC`.
36.	`Texture2D::SampleLevel(S, texC, mipLevel)`	Returns a color from a 2D texture map based on the `SamplerState` object `S`, 2D texture coordinates `texC`, and mipmap level `mipLevel`. This function differs from `Texture2D::Sample` in that the third parameter manually specifies the mipmap level to use. For example, we would specify 0 to access the topmost mipmap LOD.
37.	`TextureCube::Sample(S, v)`	Returns a color from a cube map based on the `SamplerState` object `S`, and 3D lookup vector `v`.

S. No.	Function	Description
38.	`Texture2DArray::Sample (S, texC)`	Returns a color from a 2D texture array based on the `SamplerState` object `S` (recall a sampler state specifies texture filters and texture address modes), and 3D texture coordinates `texC`, where the first two coordinates are the usual 2D texture coordinates, and the third coordinate specifies the array index.

Most of the functions are overloaded to work with all the built-in types that the function makes sense for. For instance, `abs` makes sense for all scalar types and so is overloaded for all of them. As another example, the cross product `cross` only makes sense for 3D vectors so it is only overloaded for 3D vectors of any type (e.g., 3D vectors of `int`s, `float`s, `double`s etc.). On the other hand, linear interpolation, `lerp`, makes sense for scalars, 2D, 3D, and 4D vectors and therefore is overloaded for all types.

If you pass in a non-scalar type into a "scalar" function, that is a function that traditionally operates on scalars (e.g., `cos(x)`), the function will act per component. For example, if you write:

```
float3 v = float3(0.0f, 0.0f, 0.0f);
v = cos(v);
```

Then the function will act per component: **v** *= (cos(x), cos(y), cos(z)).*

For further reference, the complete list of the built in HLSL functions can be found in the DirectX documentation. Search the index for "HLSL Intrinsic Functions").

Constant Buffer Packing

In the HLSL, constant buffer padding occurs so that elements are packed into 4D vectors, with the restriction that a single element cannot be split across two 4D vectors. Consider the following example:

```
// HLSL
cbuffer cb : register(b0)
{
  float3 Pos;
  float3 Dir;
};
```

If we have to pack the data into 4D vectors, you might think it is done like this:

```
vector 1: (Pos.x, Pos.y, Pos.z, Dir.x)
vector 2: (Dir.y, Dir.z, empty, empty)
```

However, this splits the element `dir` across two 4D vectors, which is not allowed by the HLSL rules—an element is not allowed to straddle a 4D vector boundary. Therefore, it has to be packed like this in shader memory:

```
vector 1: (Pos.x, Pos.y, Pos.z, empty)
vector 2: (Dir.x, Dir.y, Dir.z, empty)
```

Now suppose our C++ structure that mirrors the constant buffer was defined like so:

```
// C++
struct Data
{
  XMFLOAT3 Pos;
  XMFLOAT3 Dir;
};
```

If we did not pay attention to these packing rules, and just blindly called copied the bytes over when writing to the constant buffer with a `memcpy`, then we would end up with the incorrect first situation and the constant values would be wrong:

```
vector 1: (Pos.x, Pos.y, Pos.z, Dir.x)
vector 2: (Dir.y, Dir.z, empty, empty)
```

Thus we must define our C++ structures so that the elements copy over correctly into the HLSL constants based on the HLSL packing rules; we use "pad" variables for this. We redefine the constant buffer to make the padding explicit:

```
cbuffer cb : register(b0)
{
  float3 Pos;
  float  __pad0;
  float3 Dir;
  float  __pad1;
};
```

Now we can define a C++ structure that matches the constant buffer exactly:

```
// C++
struct Data
{
  XMFLOAT3 Pos;
  float    __pad0;
  XMFLOAT3 Dir;
  float    __pad1;
};
```

If we do a `memcpy` now, the data gets copied over correctly to the constant buffer:

```
vector 1: (Pos.x, Pos.y, Pos.z, __pad0)
vector 2: (Dir.x, Dir.y, Dir.z, __pad1)
```

We use padding variables in our constant buffers when needed in this book. In addition, when possible we order our constant buffer elements to reduce empty space to avoid padding. For example, we define our Light structure as follows so that we do not need to pad the *w*-coordinates—the structure elements are ordered so that the scalar data naturally occupies the *w*-coordinates:

```
struct Light
{
  DirectX::XMFLOAT3 Strength;
  float FalloffStart = 1.0f;
  DirectX::XMFLOAT3 Direction;
  float FalloffEnd = 10.0f;
  DirectX::XMFLOAT3 Position;
  float SpotPower = 64.0f;
};
```

When written to a constant buffer, these data elements will tightly pack three 3D vectors:

```
vector 1: (Strength.x, Strength.y, Strength.z, FalloffStart)
vector 2: (Direction.x, Direction.y, Direction.z, FalloffEnd)
vector 3: (Position.x, Position.y, Position.z, SpotPower).
```

You should define your C++ constant buffer data structures to match the memory layout of the constant buffer in shader memory so that you can do a simple memory copy.

Just to make the HLSL packing/padding clearer, let us look at a few more examples of how HLSL constants are packed. If we have a constant buffer like this:

```
cbuffer cb : register(b0)
{
  float3 v;
  float s;
  float2 p;
  float3 q;
};
```

The structure would be padded and the data will be packed into three 4D vectors like so:

```
vector 1: (v.x, v.y, v.z, s)
vector 2: (p.x, p.y, empty, empty)
vector 3: (q.x, q.y, q.z, empty)
```

Here we can put the scalar s in the fourth component of the first vector. However, are are not able to fit all of q in the remaining slots of vector 2, so q has to get its own vector.

As another example, consider the constant buffer:

```
cbuffer cb : register(b0)
{
    float2 u;
```

```
        float2 v;
        float a0;
        float a1;
        float a2;
};
```

This would be padded and packed like so:

```
vector 1: (u.x, u.y, v.x, v.y)
vector 2: (a0, a1, a2, empty)
```

Arrays are handled differently. From the SDK documentation, "every element in an array is stored in a four-component vector." So for example, if you have an array of float2*:*

```
float2 TexOffsets[8];
```

you might assume that two float2 *elements will be packed into one* float4 *slot, as the examples above suggest. However, arrays are the exception, and the above is equivalent to:*

```
float4 TexOffsets[8];
```

Therefore, from the C++ code you would need to set an array of 8 XMFLOAT4s, *not an array of 8* XMFLOAT2s *for things to work properly. Each element wastes two floats of storage since we really just wanted a* float2 *array. The SDK documentation points out that you can use casting and additional address computation instructions to make it more memory efficient:*

```
float4 array[4];
static float2 aggressivePackArray[8] = (float2[8])array;
```

Appendix C

SOME ANALYTIC GEOMETRY

In this appendix, we use vectors and points as building blocks for more complicated geometry. These topics are used in the book, but not as frequently as vectors, matrices, and transformations; hence, we have put them in an appendix, rather than the main text.

C.1 RAYS, LINES, AND SEGMENTS

A line can be described by a point $\mathbf{p}_0$ on the line and a vector $\mathbf{u}$ that aims parallel to the line (see Figure C.1). The vector line equation is:

$$\mathbf{p}(t) = \mathbf{p}_0 + t\mathbf{u} \text{ for } t \in \mathbb{R}$$

By plugging in different values for t (t can be any real number) we obtain different points on the line.

If we restrict t to nonnegative numbers, then the graph of the vector line equation is a ray with origin $\mathbf{p}_0$ and direction $\mathbf{u}$ (see Figure C.2).

Now suppose we wish to define a line segment by the endpoints $\mathbf{p}_0$ and $\mathbf{p}_1$. We first construct the vector $\mathbf{u} = \mathbf{p}_1 - \mathbf{p}_0$ from $\mathbf{p}_0$ to $\mathbf{p}_1$; see Figure C.3. Then, for $t \in [0, 1]$, the graph of the equation $\mathbf{p}(t) = \mathbf{p}_0 + t\mathbf{u} = \mathbf{p}_0 + (\mathbf{p}_1 - \mathbf{p}_0)$ is the line segment defined by $\mathbf{p}_0$ and $\mathbf{p}_1$. Note that if you go outside the range $t \in [0, 1]$, then you get a point on the line that coincides with the segment, but which is not on the segment.

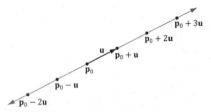

Figure C.1. A line described by a point $\mathbf{p}_0$ on the line and a vector $\mathbf{u}$ that aims parallel to the line. We can generate points on the line by plugging in any real number t.

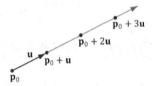

Figure C.2 A ray described by an origin $\mathbf{p}_0$ and direction $\mathbf{u}$. We can generate points on the ray by plugging in scalars for t that are greater than or equal to zero.

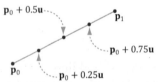

Figure C.3. We generate points on the line segment by plugging in different values for t in $[0, 1]$. For example, the midpoint of the line segment is given at $t = 0.5$. Also note that if $t = 0$, we get the endpoint $\mathbf{p}_0$ and if $t = 1$, we get the endpoint $\mathbf{p}_1$.

C.2 PARALLELOGRAMS

Let $\mathbf{q}$ be a point, and $\mathbf{u}$ and $\mathbf{v}$ be two vectors that are not scalar multiples of one another (i.e., $\mathbf{u} \neq k\mathbf{v}$ for any scalar k). Then the graph of the following function is a parallelogram (see Figure C.4):

$$\mathbf{p}(s,t) = \mathbf{q} + s\mathbf{u} + t\mathbf{v} \quad \text{for} \quad s,t \in [0,1]$$

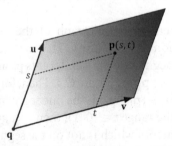

Figure C.4. Parallelogram. By plugging in different $s, t \in [0, 1]$ we generate different points on the parallelogram.

The reason for the "$\mathbf{u} \neq k\mathbf{v}$ for any scalar k" requirement can be seen as follows: If $\mathbf{u} = k\mathbf{v}$ then we could write:

$$\mathbf{p}(s,t) = \mathbf{q} + s\mathbf{u} + t\mathbf{v}$$
$$= \mathbf{q} + sk\mathbf{v} + t\mathbf{v}$$
$$= \mathbf{q} + (sk+t)\mathbf{v}$$
$$= \mathbf{q} + \bar{t}\mathbf{v}$$

which is just the equation of a line. In other words, we only have one degree of freedom. To get a 2D shape like a parallelogram, we need two degrees of freedom, so the vectors $\mathbf{u}$ and $\mathbf{v}$ must not be scalar multiples of each another.

C.3 TRIANGLES

The vector equation of a triangle is similar to that of the parallelogram equation, except that we restrict the domain of the parameters further:

$$\mathbf{p}(s,t) = \mathbf{p}_0 + s\mathbf{u} + t\mathbf{v} \quad \text{for} \quad s \geq 0, t \geq 0, s+t \leq 1$$

Observe from Figure C.5 that if any of the conditions on s and t do not hold, then $\mathbf{p}(s,t)$ will be a point "outside" the triangle, but on the plane of the triangle.

We can obtain the above parametric equation of a triangle given three points defining a triangle. Consider a triangle defined by three vertices $\mathbf{p}_0, \mathbf{p}_1, \mathbf{p}_2$. Then for that $s \geq 0, t \geq 0, s+t \leq 1$ a point on the triangle can be given by:

$$\mathbf{p}(s,t) = \mathbf{p}_0 + s(\mathbf{p}_1 - \mathbf{p}_0) + t(\mathbf{p}_2 - \mathbf{p}_0)$$

We can take this further and distribute the scalars:

$$\mathbf{p}(s,t) = \mathbf{p}_0 + s\mathbf{p}_1 - s\mathbf{p}_0 + t\mathbf{p}_2 - t\mathbf{p}_0$$
$$= (1-s-t)\mathbf{p}_0 + s\mathbf{p}_1 + t\mathbf{p}_2$$
$$= r\mathbf{p}_0 + s\mathbf{p}_1 + t\mathbf{p}_2$$

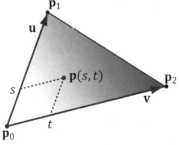

Figure C.5. Triangle. By plugging in different s, t such that $s \geq 0$, $t \geq 0$, $s+t \leq 1$, we generate different points on the triangle.

where we have let $r = (1 - s - t)$. The coordinates (r, s, t) are called *barycentric coordinates*. Note that $r + s + t = 1$ and the barycentric combination $\mathbf{p}(r, s, t) = r\mathbf{p}_0 + s\mathbf{p}_1 + t\mathbf{p}_2$ expresses the point $\mathbf{p}$ as a weighted average of the vertices of the triangle. There are interesting properties of barycentric coordinates, but we do not need them for this book; the reader may wish to further research barycentric coordinates.

C.4 PLANES

A plane can be viewed as an infinitely thin, infinitely wide, and infinitely long sheet of paper. A plane can be specified with a vector $\mathbf{v}$ and a point $\mathbf{p}_0$ on the plane. The vector $\mathbf{n}$, not necessarily unit length, is called the plane's *normal vector* and is perpendicular to the plane; see Figure C.6. A plane divides space into a *positive half-space* and a *negative half-space*. The positive half space is the space in front of the plane, where the front of the plane is the side the normal vector emanates from. The negative half space is the space behind the plane.

By Figure C.6, we see that the graph of a plane is all the points $\mathbf{p}$ that satisfy the *plane equation*:

$$\mathbf{n} \cdot (\mathbf{p} - \mathbf{p}_0) = 0$$

When describing a particular plane, the normal $\mathbf{n}$ and a known point $\mathbf{p}_0$ on the plane are fixed, so it is typical to rewrite the plane equation as:

$$\mathbf{n} \cdot (\mathbf{p} - \mathbf{p}_0) = \mathbf{n} \cdot \mathbf{p} - \mathbf{n} \cdot \mathbf{p}_0 = \mathbf{n} \cdot \mathbf{p} + d = 0$$

where $d = -\mathbf{n} \cdot \mathbf{p}_0$. If $\mathbf{n} = (a, b, c)$ and $\mathbf{p} = (x, y, z)$, then the plane equation can be written as:

$$ax + by + cz + d = 0$$

If the plane's normal vector $\mathbf{n}$ is of unit length, then $d = -\mathbf{n} \cdot \mathbf{p}_0$ gives the shortest *signed* distance from the origin to the plane (see Figure C.7).

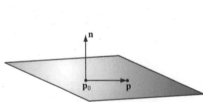

Figure C.6. A plane defined by a normal vector $\mathbf{n}$ and a point $\mathbf{p}_0$ on the plane. If $\mathbf{p}_0$ is a point on the plane, then the point $\mathbf{p}$ is also on the plane if and only if the vector $\mathbf{p} - \mathbf{p}_0$ is orthogonal to the plane's normal vector.]

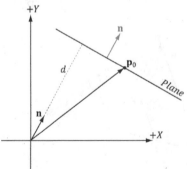

Figure C.7. Shortest distance from a plane to the origin.

To make the pictures easier to draw, we sometimes draw our figures in 2D and use a line to represent a plane. A line, with a perpendicular normal, can be thought of as a 2D plane since the line divides the 2D space into a positive half space and negative half space.

C.4.1 DirectX Math Planes

When representing a plane in code, it suffices to store only the normal vector **n** and the constant d. It is useful to think of this as a 4D vector, which we denote as $(\mathbf{n}, d) = (a, b, c, d)$. Therefore, because the XMVECTOR type stores a 4-tuple of floating-point values, the DirectX Math library overloads the XMVECTOR type to also represent planes.

C.4.2 Point/Plane Spatial Relation

Given any point **p**, observe from Figure C.6 and Figure C.8 that

1. If $\mathbf{n} \cdot (\mathbf{p} - \mathbf{p}_0) = \mathbf{n} \cdot \mathbf{p} + d > 0$ then **p** is in front of the plane.
2. If $\mathbf{n} \cdot (\mathbf{p} - \mathbf{p}_0) = \mathbf{n} \cdot \mathbf{p} + d < 0$ then **p** is behind the plane.
3. If $\mathbf{n} \cdot (\mathbf{p} - \mathbf{p}_0) = \mathbf{n} \cdot \mathbf{p} + d = 0$ then **p** is on the plane.

These tests are useful for testing the spatial location of points relative to a plane.

This next DirectX Math function evaluates $\mathbf{n} \cdot \mathbf{p} + d$ for a particular plane and point:

```
XMVECTOR XMPlaneDotCoord(// Returns n·p+d replicated in each coordinate
    XMVECTOR P, // plane
    XMVECTOR V); // point with w = 1

// Test the locality of a point relative to a plane.
XMVECTOR p = XMVectorSet(0.0f, 1.0f, 0.0f, 0.0f);

XMVECTOR v = XMVectorSet(3.0f, 5.0f, 2.0f);

float x = XMVectorGetX( XMPlaneDotCoord(p, v) );
```

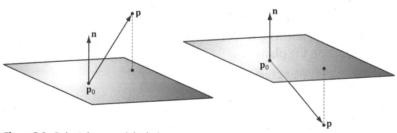

Figure C.8. Point/plane spatial relation.

```
if( x approximately equals 0.0f ) // v is coplanar to the plane.
if( x > 0 )    // v is in positive half-space.
if( x < 0 )    // v is in negative half-space.
```

 We say approximately equals due to floating point imprecision.

A similar function is:

```
XMVECTOR XMPlaneDotNormal(XMVECTOR Plane, XMVECTOR Vec);
```

This returns the dot product of the plane normal vector and the given 3D vector.

C.4.3 Construction

Besides directly specifying the plane coefficients $(\mathbf{n}, d) = (a, b, c, d)$, we can calculate these coefficients in two other ways. Given the normal $\mathbf{n}$ and a known point on the plane $\mathbf{p}_0$ we can solve for the d component:

$$\mathbf{n} \cdot \mathbf{p}_0 + d = 0 \Rightarrow d = -\mathbf{n} \cdot \mathbf{p}_0$$

The DirectX Math library provides the following function to construct a plane from a point and normal in this way:

```
XMVECTOR XMPlaneFromPointNormal(
    XMVECTOR Point,
    XMVECTOR Normal);
```

The second way we can construct a plane is by specifying three distinct points on the plane.

Given the points $\mathbf{p}_0, \mathbf{p}_1, \mathbf{p}_2$, we can form two vectors on the plane:

$$\mathbf{u} = \mathbf{p}_1 - \mathbf{p}_0$$
$$\mathbf{v} = \mathbf{p}_2 - \mathbf{p}_0$$

From that we can compute the normal of the plane by taking the cross product of the two vectors on the plane. (Remember the left hand thumb rule.)

$$\mathbf{n} = \mathbf{u} \times \mathbf{v}$$

Then, we compute $d = -\mathbf{n} \cdot \mathbf{p}_0$.

The DirectX Math library provides the following function to compute a plane given three points on the plane:

```
XMVECTOR XMPlaneFromPoints(
    XMVECTOR Point1,
    XMVECTOR Point2,
    XMVECTOR Point3);
```

C.4.4 Normalizing a Plane

Sometimes we might have a plane and would like to normalize the normal vector. At first thought, it would seem that we could just normalize the normal vector as we would any other vector. But recall that the d component also depends on the normal vector: $d = -\mathbf{n} \cdot \mathbf{p}_0$. Therefore, if we normalize the normal vector, we must also recalculate d. This is done as follows:

$$d' = \frac{d}{\|\mathbf{n}\|} = -\frac{\mathbf{n}}{\|\mathbf{n}\|} \cdot \mathbf{p}_0$$

Thus, we have the following formula to normalize the normal vector of the plane $(\mathbf{n}, d)$:

$$\frac{1}{\|\mathbf{n}\|}(\mathbf{n},d) = \left(\frac{\mathbf{n}}{\|\mathbf{n}\|}, \frac{d}{\|\mathbf{n}\|} \right)$$

We can use the following DirectX Math function to normalize a plane's normal vector:

```
XMVECTOR XMPlaneNormalize(XMVECTOR P);
```

C.4.5 Transforming a Plane

[Lengyel02] shows that we can transform a plane $(\mathbf{n}, d)$ by treating it as a 4D vector and multiplying it by the inverse-transpose of the desired transformation matrix. Note that the plane's normal vector must be normalized first. We use the following DirectX Math function to do this:

```
XMVECTOR XMPlaneTransform(XMVECTOR P, XMMATRIX M);
```

Sample Code:
```
XMMATRIX T(...); // Initialize T to a desired transformation.
XMMATRIX invT = XMMatrixInverse(XMMatrixDeterminant(T), T);
XMMATRIX invTransposeT = XMMatrixTranspose(invT);

XMVECTOR p = (...); // Initialize Plane.
p = XMPlaneNormalize(p); // make sure normal is normalized.

XMVECTOR transformedPlane = XMPlaneTransform(p, &invTransposeT);
```

C.4.6 Nearest Point on a Plane to a Given Point

Suppose we have a point $\mathbf{p}$ in space and we would like to find the point $\mathbf{q}$ on the plane $(\mathbf{n}, d)$ that is closest to $\mathbf{p}$. From Figure C.9, we see that

$$\mathbf{q} = \mathbf{p} - \text{proj}_\mathbf{n}(\mathbf{p} - \mathbf{p}_0)$$

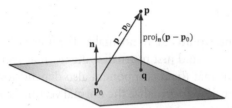

Figure C.9. The nearest point on a plane to a point **p**. The point $\mathbf{p}_0$ is a point on the plane.

Assuming $\|\mathbf{n}\| = 1$ so that $\text{proj}_\mathbf{n}(\mathbf{p}-\mathbf{p}_0) = \left[(\mathbf{p}-\mathbf{p}_0)\cdot\mathbf{n}\right]\mathbf{n}$, we can rewrite this as:

$$\mathbf{q} = \mathbf{p} - \left[(\mathbf{p}-\mathbf{p}_0)\cdot\mathbf{n}\right]\mathbf{n}$$
$$= \mathbf{p} - (\mathbf{p}\cdot\mathbf{n} - \mathbf{p}_0\cdot\mathbf{n})\mathbf{n}$$
$$= \mathbf{p} - (\mathbf{p}\cdot\mathbf{n} + d)\mathbf{n}$$

C.4.7 Ray/Plane Intersection

Given a ray $\mathbf{p}(t) = \mathbf{p}_0 + t\mathbf{u}$ and the equation of a plane $\mathbf{n}\cdot\mathbf{p} + d = 0$, we would like to know if the ray intersects the plane and also the point of intersection. To do this, we plug the ray into the plane equation and solve for the parameter t that satisfies the plane equation, thereby giving us the parameter that yields the intersection point:

$\mathbf{n}\cdot\mathbf{p}(t) + d = 0$	Plug ray into plane equation
$\mathbf{n}\cdot(\mathbf{p}_0 + t\mathbf{u}) + d = 0$	Substitute
$\mathbf{n}\cdot\mathbf{p}_0 + t\mathbf{n}\cdot\mathbf{u} + d = 0$	Distributive property
$t\mathbf{n}\cdot\mathbf{u} = -\mathbf{n}\cdot\mathbf{p}_0 - d$	Add $-\mathbf{n}\cdot\mathbf{p}_0 - d$ to both sides
$t = \dfrac{-\mathbf{n}\cdot\mathbf{p}_0 - d}{\mathbf{n}\cdot\mathbf{u}}$	Solve for t

If $\mathbf{n}\cdot\mathbf{u} = 0$ then the ray is parallel to the plane and there are either no solutions or infinite many solutions (infinite if the ray coincides with the plane). If t is not in the interval $[0,\infty)$, the ray does not intersect the plane, but the line coincident with the ray does. If t is in the interval $[0,\infty)$, then the ray does intersect the plane and the intersection point is found by evaluating the ray equation at $t_0 = \dfrac{-\mathbf{n}\cdot\mathbf{p}_0 - d}{\mathbf{n}\cdot\mathbf{u}}$.

The ray/plane intersection test can be modified to a segment/plane test. Given two points defining a line segment **p** and **q**, then we form the ray $\mathbf{r}(t) = \mathbf{p} + t(\mathbf{q} - \mathbf{p})$. We use this ray for the intersection test. If $t \in [0, 1]$, then the segment intersects the plane, otherwise it does not. The DirectX Math library provides the following function:

```
XMVECTOR XMPlaneIntersectLine(
    XMVECTOR P,
    XMVECTOR LinePoint1,
    XMVECTOR LinePoint2);
```

C.4.8 Reflecting Vectors

Given a vector **I** we wish to reflect it about a plane with normal **n**. Because vectors do not have positions, only the plane normal is involved when reflecting a vector. Figure C.10 shows the geometric situation, from which we conclude the reflection vector is given by:

$$\mathbf{r} = \mathbf{I} - 2(\mathbf{n} \cdot \mathbf{I})\mathbf{n}$$

C.4.9 Reflecting Points

Points reflect differently from vectors since points have position. Figure C.11 shows that the reflected point **q** is given by:

$$\mathbf{q} = \mathbf{p} - 2\mathrm{proj}_\mathbf{n}(\mathbf{p} - \mathbf{p}_0)$$

C.4.10 Reflection Matrix

Let $(\mathbf{n}, d) = (n_x, n_y, n_z, d)$ be the coefficients of a plane, where $d = -\mathbf{n} \cdot \mathbf{p}_0$. Then, using homogeneous coordinates, we can reflect both points and vectors about this plane using a single 4 × 4 reflection matrix:

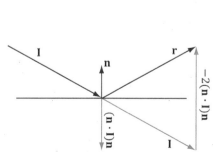

Figure C.10. Geometry of vector reflection.

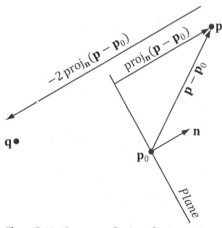

Figure C.11. Geometry of point reflection.

$$\mathbf{R} = \begin{bmatrix} 1-2n_x n_x & -2n_x n_y & -2n_x n_z & 0 \\ -2n_x n_y & 1-2n_y n_y & -2n_y n_z & 0 \\ -2n_x n_z & -2n_y n_z & 1-2n_z n_z & 0 \\ -2dn_x & -2dn_y & -2dn_z & 1 \end{bmatrix}$$

This matrix assumes the plane is normalized so that

$$\text{proj}_{\mathbf{n}}(\mathbf{p}-\mathbf{p}_0) = [\mathbf{n} \cdot (\mathbf{p}-\mathbf{p}_0)]\mathbf{n}$$
$$= [\mathbf{n} \cdot \mathbf{p} - \mathbf{n} \cdot \mathbf{p}_0]\mathbf{n}$$
$$= [\mathbf{n} \cdot \mathbf{p} + d]\mathbf{n}$$

If we multiply a point by this matrix, we get the point reflection formula:

$$[p_x, p_y, p_z, 1] \begin{bmatrix} 1-2n_x n_x & -2n_x n_y & -2n_x n_z & 0 \\ -2n_x n_y & 1-2n_y n_y & -2n_y n_z & 0 \\ -2n_x n_z & -2n_y n_z & 1-2n_z n_z & 0 \\ -2dn_x & -2dn_y & -2dn_z & 1 \end{bmatrix}$$

$$= \begin{bmatrix} p_x - 2p_x n_x n_x - 2p_y n_x n_y - 2p_z n_x n_z - 2dn_x \\ -2p_x n_x n_y + p_y - 2p_y n_y n_y - 2p_z n_y n_z - 2dn_y \\ -2p_x n_x n_z - 2p_y n_y n_z + p_z - 2p_z n_z n_z - 2dn_z \\ 1 \end{bmatrix}^T$$

$$= \begin{bmatrix} p_x \\ p_y \\ p_z \\ 1 \end{bmatrix}^T + \begin{bmatrix} -2n_x(p_x n_x + p_y n_y + p_z n_z + d) \\ -2n_y(p_x n_x + p_y n_y + p_z n_z + d) \\ -2n_z(p_x n_x + p_y n_y + p_z n_z + d) \\ 0 \end{bmatrix}^T$$

$$= \begin{bmatrix} p_x \\ p_y \\ p_z \\ 1 \end{bmatrix}^T + \begin{bmatrix} -2n_x(\mathbf{n} \cdot \mathbf{p} + d) \\ -2n_y(\mathbf{n} \cdot \mathbf{p} + d) \\ -2n_z(\mathbf{n} \cdot \mathbf{p} + d) \\ 0 \end{bmatrix}^T$$

$$= \mathbf{p} - 2[\mathbf{n} \cdot \mathbf{p} + d]\mathbf{n}$$
$$= \mathbf{p} - 2\text{proj}_{\mathbf{n}}(\mathbf{p}-\mathbf{p}_0)$$

Note: We take the transpose to turn row vectors into column vectors. This is just to make the presentation neater—otherwise, we would get very long row vectors.

And similarly, if we multiply a vector by this matrix, we get the vector reflection formula:

$$[v_x, v_y, v_z, 0] \begin{bmatrix} 1-2n_x n_x & -2n_x n_y & -2n_x n_z & 0 \\ -2n_x n_y & 1-2n_y n_y & -2n_y n_z & 0 \\ -2n_x n_z & -2n_y n_z & 1-2n_z n_z & 0 \\ -2dn_x & -2dn_y & -2dn_z & 1 \end{bmatrix} = \mathbf{v} - 2(\mathbf{n} \cdot \mathbf{v})\mathbf{n}$$

The following DirectX Math function can be used to construct the above reflection matrix given a plane:

```
XMMATRIX XMMatrixReflect(XMVECTOR ReflectionPlane);
```

C.5 EXERCISES

1. Let $\mathbf{p}(t) = (1, 1) + t(2, 1)$ be a ray relative to some coordinate system. Plot the points on the ray at $t = 0.0, 0.5, 1.0, 2.0,$ and 5.0.

2. Let $\mathbf{p}_0$ and $\mathbf{p}_1$ define the endpoints of a line segment. Show that the equation for a line segment can also be written as $\mathbf{p}(t) = (1 - t)\mathbf{p}_0 + t\mathbf{p}_1$ for $t \in [0, 1]$.

3. For each part, find the vector line equation of the line passing through the two points.
   (a) $\mathbf{p}_1 = (2, -1), \mathbf{p}_2 = (4, 1)$
   (b) $\mathbf{p}_1 = (4, -2, 1), \mathbf{p}_2 = (2, 3, 2)$

4. Let $\mathbf{L}(t) = \mathbf{p} + t\mathbf{u}$ define a line in 3-space. Let $\mathbf{q}$ be any point in 3-space. Prove that the distance from $\mathbf{q}$ to the line can be written as:

$$d = \frac{\|(\mathbf{q} - \mathbf{p}) \times \mathbf{u}\|}{\|\mathbf{u}\|}$$

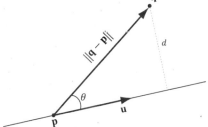

Figure C.12. Distance from **q** to the line.

5. Let $\mathbf{L}(t) = (4, 2, 2) + t(1, 1, 1)$ be a line. Find the distance from the following points to the line:
   (a) $\mathbf{q} = (0, 0, 0)$
   (b) $\mathbf{q} = (4, 2, 0)$
   (c) $\mathbf{q} = (0, 2, 2)$

6. Let $\mathbf{p}_0 = (0, 1, 0)$, $\mathbf{p}_1 = (-1, 3, 6)$, and $\mathbf{p}_2 = (8, 5, 3)$ be three points. Find the plane these points define.

7. Let $\left(\dfrac{1}{\sqrt{3}}, \dfrac{1}{\sqrt{3}}, \dfrac{1}{\sqrt{3}}, -5\right)$ be a plane. Define the locality of the following points relative to the plane: $\left(3\sqrt{3}, 5\sqrt{3}, 0\right)$, $\left(2\sqrt{3}, \sqrt{3}, 2\sqrt{3}\right)$, and $\left(\sqrt{3}, -\sqrt{3}, 0\right)$.

8. Let $\left(-\dfrac{1}{\sqrt{2}}, \dfrac{1}{\sqrt{2}}, 0, \dfrac{5}{\sqrt{2}}\right)$ be a plane. Find the point on the plane nearest to the point $(0, 1, 0)$.

9. Let $\left(-\dfrac{1}{\sqrt{2}}, \dfrac{1}{\sqrt{2}}, 0, \dfrac{5}{\sqrt{2}}\right)$ be a plane. Find the reflection of the point $(0, 1, 0)$ about the plane.

10. Let $\left(\dfrac{1}{\sqrt{3}}, \dfrac{1}{\sqrt{3}}, \dfrac{1}{\sqrt{3}}, -5\right)$ be a plane, and let $\mathbf{r}(t) = (-1, 1, -1) + t(1, 0, 0)$ be a ray. Find the point at which the ray intersects the plane. Then write a short program using the `XMPlaneIntersectLine` function to verify your answer.

Appendix D

SOLUTIONS TO SELECTED EXERCISES

Solutions (including figures) to selected exercises in the text may be found on the companion DVD.

Appendix E

Bibliography and Further Reading

[Angel00] Angel, Edward, *Interactive Computer Graphics: A Top-Down Approach with OpenGL*, Second Edition, Addison-Wesley, 2000.

[ATI1] ATI. "Dark Secrets of Shader Development or What Your Mother Never Told You About Shaders" Presentation available at *http://amd-dev.wpengine.netdna-cdn.com/wordpress/media/2012/10/Dark_Secrets_of_shader_Dev-Mojo.pdf*

[Bilodeau10] Bilodeau, Bill. "Efficient Compute Shader Programming," *Game Developers Conference*, AMD slide presentation, 2010. (*http://developer.amd.com/gpu_assets/Efficient%20Compute%20Shader%20Programming.pps*)

[Bilodeau10b] Bilodeau, Bill. "Direct3D 11 Tutorial: Tessellation," *Game Developers Conference*, AMD slide presentation, 2010. (*http://developer.amd.com/gpu_assets/Direct3D%2011%20Tessellation%20Tutorial.ppsx*)

[Blinn78] Blinn, James F., and Martin E. Newell. "Clipping using Homogeneous Coordinates." In *Computer Graphics (SIGGRAPH '78 Proceedings)*, pages 245-251, New York, 1978.

[Blinn96] Blinn, Jim, *Jim Blinn's Corner: A Trip Down the Graphics Pipeline*, Morgan Kaufmann Publishers, Inc, San Francisco CA, 1996.

[Boyd08] Boyd, Chas. "DirectX 11 Compute Shader," Siggraph slide presentation, 2008. (http://s08.idav.ucdavis.edu/boyd-dx11-compute-shader.pdf)

[Boyd10] Boyd, Chas. "DirectCompute Lecture Series 101: Introduction to DirectCompute," 2010. (*http://channel9.msdn.com/Blogs/gclassy/DirectCompute-Lecture-Series-101-Introduction-to-DirectCompute*)

[Brennan02] Brennan, Chris. "Accurate Reflections and Refractions by Adjusting for Object Distance," *Direct3D ShaderX: Vertex and Pixel Shader Tips and Tricks.*
Wordware Publishing Inc., 2002.

[Burg10] Burg, John van der, "Building an Advanced Particle System." *Gamasutra*, June 2000. (*http://www.gamasutra.com/features/20000623/vanderburg_01.htm*)

[Crawfis12] Crawfis, Roger. "Modern GPU Architecture." Course notes available at *http://web.cse.ohio-state.edu/~crawfis/cse786/ReferenceMaterial/CourseNotes/Modern%20GPU%20Architecture.ppt*

[De berg00] de Berg, M., M. van Kreveld, M. Overmars, and O. Schwarzkopf. *Computational Geometry: Algorithms and Applications Second Edition.* Springer-Verlag Berlin Heidelberg, 2000.

[Dietrich] Dietrich, Sim. "Texture Space Bump Maps." (*http://developer.nvidia.com/object/texture_space_bump_mapping.html*)

[Dunlop03] Dunlop, Robert. "FPS Versus Frame Time," 2003. (*http://www.mvps.org/directx/articles/fps_versus_frame_time.htm*)

[DirectXMath] DirectXMath Online Documentation, Microsoft Corporation. *http://msdn.microsoft.com/en-us/library/windows/desktop/hh437833(v=vs.85).aspx*

[DXSDK] Microsoft DirectX June 2010 SDK Documentation, Microsoft Corporation.

[Eberly01] Eberly, David H., *3D Game Engine Design*, Morgan Kaufmann Publishers, Inc, San Francisco CA, 2001.

[Engel02] Engel, Wolfgang (Editor), *Direct3D ShaderX: Vertex and Pixel Shader Tips and Tricks*, Wordware Publishing, Plano TX, 2002.

[Engel04] Engel, Wolfgang (Editor), *ShaderX2: Shader Programming Tips & Tricks with DirectX 9*, Wordware Publishing, Plano TX, 2004.

[Engel06] Engel, Wolfgang (Editor), *ShaderX5: Shader Advanced Rendering Techniques*, Charles River Media, Inc., 2006.

[Engel08] Engel, Wolfgang (Editor), *ShaderX6: Shader Advanced Rendering Techniques*, Charles River Media, Inc., 2008.

[Farin98] Farin, Gerald, and Dianne Hansford. *The Geometry Toolbox: For Graphics and Modeling.* AK Peters, Ltd., 1998.

[Fernando03] Fernando, Randima, and Mark J. Kilgard. *The CG Tutorial: The Definitive Guide to Programmable Real-Time Graphics.* Addison-Wesley, 2003.

[Fraleigh95] Fraleigh, John B., and Raymond A. Beauregard. *Linear Algebra 3rd Edition.* Addison-Wesley, 1995.

[Friedberg03] Friedberg, Stephen H., Arnold J. Insel, and Lawrence E. Spence. *Linear Algebra Fourth Edition*. Pearson Education, Inc., 2003.

[Fung10] Fung, James. "DirectCompute Lecture Series 210: GPU Optimizations and Performance," 2010. (*http://channel9.msdn.com/Blogs/gclassy/DirectCompute-Lecture-Series-210-GPU-Optimizations-and-Performance*)

[Halliday01] Halliday, David, Robert Resnick, and Jearl Walker. *Fundamentals of Physics: Sixth Edition*. John Wiley & Sons, Inc, 2001.

[Hausner98] Hausner, Melvin. *A Vector Space Approach to Geometry*. Dover Publications, Inc. (*www.doverpublications.com*), 1998

[Hoffmann75] Hoffmann, Banesh. *About Vectors*. Dover Publications, Inc. (*www.doverpublications.com*), 1975.

[Isidoro06] Isidoro, John R. "Shadow Mapping: GPU-based Tips and Techniques," *Game Developers Conference*, ATI slide presentation, 2006. (http://developer.amd.com/media/gpu_assets/Isidoro-ShadowMapping.pdf)

[Isidoro06b] Isidoro, John R. "Edge Masking and Per-Texel Depth Extent Propagation for Computation Culling During Shadow Mapping," *ShaderX 5: Advanced Rendering Techniques*. Charles River Media, 2007.

[Kilgard99] Kilgard, Mark J., "Creating Reflections and Shadows Using Stencil Buffers," *Game Developers Conference*, NVIDIA slide presentation, 1999. (http://developer.nvidia.com/docs/IO/1407/ATT/stencil.ppt)

[Kilgard01] Kilgard, Mark J. "Shadow Mapping with Today's OpenGL Hardware," Computer Entertainment Software Association's CEDEC, NVIDIA presentation, 2001. (*http://developer.nvidia.com/object/cedec_shadowmap.html*)

[Kryachko05] Kryachko, Yuri. "Using Vertex Texture Displacement for Realistic Water Rendering," *GPU Gems 2: Programming Techniques for High-Performance Graphics and General Purpose Computation*. Addison-Wesley, 2005.

[Kuipers99] Kuipers, Jack B. *Quaternions and Rotation Sequences: A Primer with Applications to Orbits, Aerospace, and Virtual Reality*. Princeton University Press, 1999.

[Lengyel02] Lengyel, Eric, *Mathematics for 3D Game Programming and Computer Graphics*. Charles River Media, Inc., 2002.

[Möller08] Möller, Tomas, and Eric Haines. *Real-Time Rendering: Third Edition*. AK Peters, Ltd., 2008.

[Mortenson99] Mortenson, M.E. *Mathematics for Computer Graphics Applications*. Industrial Press, Inc., 1999.

[NVIDIA05] Antialiasing with Transparency, NVIDIA Corporation, 2005. (*ftp://download.nvidia.com/developer/SDK/Individual_Samples/DEMOS/Direct3D9/src/AntiAliasingWithTransparency/docs/AntiAliasingWithTransparency.pdf*)

[NVIDIA08] GPU Programming Guide GeForce 8 and 9 Series, NVIDIA Corporation, 2008. (http://developer.download.nvidia.com/GPU_Programming_Guide/GPU_Programming_Guide_G80.pdf)

[NVIDIA09] NVIDIA's Next Generation CUDA Compute Architecture: Fermi, NVIDIA Corporation, 2009. (*http://www.nvidia.com/content/PDF/fermi_white_papers/NVIDIA_Fermi_Compute_Architecture_Whitepaper.pdf*)

[NVIDIA10] DirectCompute Programming Guide, NVIDIA Corporation, 2007–2010 (*http://developer.download.nvidia.com/compute/DevZone/docs/html/DirectCompute/doc/DirectCompute_Programming_Guide.pdf*)

[Thibieroz13] Thibieroz, Nick and Holger Gruen. "DirectX Performance Reloaded." Presentation at Game Developers Conference 2013.

[Oliveira10] Oliveira, Gustavo. "Designing Fast Cross-Platform SIMD Vector Libraries," 2010. (*http://www.gamasutra.com/view/feature/4248/designing_fast_crossplatform_simd_.php*)

[Parent02] Parent, Rick. *Computer Animation: Algorithms and Techniques*. Morgan Kaufmann Publishers (*www.mkp.com*), 2002.

[Pelzer04] Pelzer, Kurt. "Rendering Countless Blades of Waving Grass," *GPU Gems: Programming Techniques, Tips, and Tricks for Real-Time Graphics*. Addison-Wesley, 2004.

[Pettineo12] Pettineo, Matt. "A Closer Look at Tone Mapping," 2012. (*https://mynameismjp.wordpress.com/2010/04/30/a-closer-look-at-tone-mapping/*)

[Petzold99] Petzold, Charles, *Programming Windows*, Fifth Edition, Microsoft Press, Redmond WA, 1999.

[Prosise99] Prosise, Jeff, *Programming Windows with MFC*, Second Edition, Microsoft Press, Redmond WA, 1999.

[Reinhard10] Reinhard, Erik, et al, *High Dynamic Range Imaging*, Second Edition, Morgan Kaufmann, 2010.

[Santrock03] Santrock, John W. *Psychology 7*. The McGraw-Hill Companies, Inc., 2003.

[Savchenko00] Savchenko, Sergei, *3D Graphics Programming: Games and Beyond*, Sams Publishing, 2000.

[Schneider03] Schneider, Philip J., and David H. Eberly. *Geometric Tools for Computer Graphics*. Morgan Kaufmann Publishers (*www.mkp.com*), 2003.

[Snook03] Snook, Greg. *Real-Time 3D Terrain Engines using C++ and DirectX9*. Charles River Media, Inc., 2003.

[Story10] Story, Jon, and Cem Cebenoyan, "Tessellation Performance," *Game Developers Conference*, NVIDIA slide presentation, 2010. (*http://developer.download.nvidia.com/presentations/2010/gdc/Tessellation_Performance.pdf*)

[Sutherland74] Sutherland, I. E., and G. W. Hodgeman. Reentrant Polygon Clipping. *Communications of the ACM*, 17(1):32-42, 1974.

[Tuft10] Tuft, David. "Cascaded Shadow Maps," 2010. (*http://msdn.microsoft.com/en-us/library/ee416307%28v=vs.85%29.aspx*)

[Uralsky05] Uralsky, Yuri. "Efficient Soft-Edged Shadows Using Pixel Shader Branching," *GPU Gems 2: Programming Techniques for High-Performance Graphics and General Purpose Computation.* Addison-Wesley, 2005.

[Verth04] Verth, James M. van, and Lars M. Bishop. *Essential Mathematics for Games & Interactive Applications: A Programmer's Guide.* Morgan Kaufmann Publishers (*www.mkp.com*), 2004.

[Vlachos01] Vlachos, Alex, Jörg Peters, Chas Boyd, and Jason L. Mitchell, "Curved PN Triangles," *ACM Symposium on Interactive 3D Graphics 2001*, pp. 159-166, 2001. (http://alex.vlachos.com/graphics/CurvedPNTriangles.pdf)

[Watt92] Watt, Alan, and Mark Watt, *Advanced Animation and Rendering Techniques: Theory and Practice*, Addison-Wesley, 1992.

[Watt00] Watt, Alan, *3D Computer Graphics*, Third Edition, Addison-Wesley, 2000.

[Watt01] Watt, Alan, and Fabio Policarpo, *3D Games: Real-time Rendering and Software Technology*, Addison-Wesley, 2001.

[Weinreich98] Weinreich, Gabriel, *Geometrical Vectors*. The University of Chicago Press, Chicago, 1998.

[Whatley05] Whatley, David. "Toward Photorealism in Virtual Botany," *GPU Gems 2: Programming Techniques for High-Performance Graphics and General Purpose Computation.* Addison-Wesley, 2005.

[Wloka03] Wloka, Matthias. "Batch, Batch, Batch: What Does It Really Mean? " Presentation at Game Developers Conference 2003. *http://developer.nvidia.com/docs/IO/8230/BatchBatchBatch.pdf*

INDEX

8-bit color components, 166–167
24-bit depth buffer, 96, 420
32-bit color values, 165, 262
32-bit floating-point components, 92, 360
128-bit color values, 165, 262

A

AABB (axis-aligned bounding box), 566–580, 608
AABB/plane tests, 574, 575
acceleration, 90, 487
adapters, default, 94, 118, 127
address modes, 360, 376, 378, 394
affine transformations, 59, 66–68, 84
aliasing, 98–100, 446, 463, 654–658
alpha channel, 92, 403, 408–417, 452, 639
alpha component, 92, 165, 197, 365, 398, 629
alpha-to-coverage, 402, 463–465
alpha-to-coverage blend state object, 402, 446, 463–465
alpha value, 399, 408–10, 665
ambient-access, 677, 686, 694
ambient light, 326–327
ambient map, 686, 693–694
ambient occlusion, 494, 537–538, 675–696
ambient occlusion demo, 679
ambient occlusion map, 679, 694–695
ambient term, 327, 341 346, 538,675–676
angle
    acute, 10–11
    obtuse, 11

angle restriction, 706–707
animating, 719, 733–735
animation, 93, 131–139, 393, 538, 719–724
    entire frame of, 93, 155
    frames of, 131, 134
    given frame of, 93, 155
    next frame of, 93, 155
API overhead, 214, 558, 576
application code, 146–147, 298, 384, 576
application-defined masking value, 421
application instance, 142, 762–764
application message loop, 135, 139, 142
application window, main, 139, 143–144
array, 58, 91–92, 106–109, 124–130, 233, 245, 259
aspect ratio, 142, 183–186, 572, 586
assembly code, 239
attribute values, 196
average, weighted, 18, 319, 411, 489, 490, 501
average frames, 143, 156
averaged pixel color, 98
axis-aligned bounding box *see* AABB
axis directions, 600

B

backface culling, 194–195
background color, 764
basic input/output system (BIOS), 133
basic tessellation demo, 536
basis, per-triangle, 576

basis vectors, 62, 71, 85, 554–555
   standard, 60, 62, 71–72
   transformed, 71–2
Bernstein basis functions, 528
Bézier curves, 514–515, 527–529
Bézier Patch demo, 536
Bézier quad patches, 526
Bézier surfaces, 515, 529
   cubic, 88, 526
   quadratic, 536
Bézier triangle patches, 522
Bézier triangle surface patch, 535
biasing, 654–56
binding, 211, 233, 235, 370
BIOS (basic input/output system), 133
bird's eye, 451, 493–494
blend, 88, 397
blend demo, 410–411, 439, 441
blend factor color, 401
blend factors, 400–401
   destination, 398, 403–406
blend operations, 399–400
blend operator, 400, 404–406
blend state, 244, 400–403
   default, 401
blender, 163, 400, 751
blending, 88, 197, 397–417
blending equation, 398–399
blending method, 406–407
blending operators, 401
blending transparency, 625
BlendState, 244,
blocks, 95, 126
blur, 376, 410, 489–494
   preserving, 690, 693,
   vertical, 490, 495,
blur radius, 490, 501,
blurred result, 494–495
blurring, 489, 498
blurring algorithm, 489, 495,
bone influences, 728, 740, 751
bone space, 732
bounding box, 428, 537, 566–569
bounding sphere, 566, 570–571
bounding volumes, 557, 566–575, 579
branching, dynamic, 239, 341
buffer, 31, 88, 93–98, 121, 124–130, 143–144, 152, 155,
   168, 207–212, 224–235, 309
   32-bit floating-point depth, 96, 420
   allocated, 167
   depth stencil, 96, 125, 420, 422, 425
   entire, 129, 209,
   floating-point, 30, 92
   floating-point depth, 96, 420,
   normal/depth, 681, 690
   off-screen, 93, 155, 419, 438, 493
   raw, 481
   second texture, 460
   static, 310
buffer alpha values, 399,
buffer definitions, 240
buffer dimensions, 147, 183
buffer form, 93, 155, 438
buffer of elements, 480, 507
buffer pixel color, 407
buffer pixels, 427, 436
   mirror stencil, 436
buffer resources, 122–126, 224, 479, 507
buffer textures, 93
buffer width, 142
buffering, double, 87, 93, 121, 155

C

camera, 17, 87, 144, 155, 160, 179, 181–182, 261,
   411–412, 452–453, 494, 518, 537, 539–555, 600, 615
   first person, 537, 539, 545
   void, 21
camera basis vectors, 541
camera class, 541–542
camera coordinate system, 180–181, 540
camera demo, 547–548
camera frustum, 577
camera position, 160, 181, 411, 601
camera space, 179, 541
camera system, 537, 539, 547
camera vectors, 546
cast, 361, 432–434, 679
cast rays, 676, 679
character, 208, 358, 538, 558, 727–751
character animation, 538, 727–751
character mesh, 731
clamp, 165, 376, 377
clip, 182, 191, 733, 783,
clip function, 88, 222, 409
clipping, 191–193, 408, 657
color
   32-bit, 165–168
   128-bit, 165
   blue, 92, 163
   border, 376–377
   destination, 398, 405
   fog, 410–416
   fogged, 411–413
   green, 92, 99, 163–168, 595
   lit, 412
   new, 163–164, 398
   per-vertex, 356, 538
   pixel's, 385
color channels, 365–367, 418
color ck, 441

INDEX   811

color component, 163–167, 629–630
    additional, 165, 197
color elements, 261
color image, 629, 640
color information, 92–93,
color intensity, 443
color operations, 164–165
color pixels, 362
color texturing, 657
color value, 167, 257, 262, 345
color vectors, 164, 197, 398
    single, 442
colored cube, 260
COM (Component Object Model), 90–91, 155
COM interfaces, 90–91, 155
COM objects, 90–91
comparison function, 422–424, 441
compiler, 22, 52, 236, 239, 757
complex numbers, 657, 698–700
complicated pixel shader work, 663
component object model *see* COM
components
    bit floating point, 92
    floating-point, 30
    normal, 576
    unsigned integer, 92, 96
composition, 72
compressed formats, 365
compressed texture formats, 365
Compute shader 88, 310, 311, 470
ComputeBoundingAxisAligned
    BoxFromPoints, 519–20
ComputeBoundingSphereFromPoints, 520
ComputeFrustumFromProjection, 523
constant acceleration, 487
constant buffer values, 430
constant buffer variable, 262, 389
constant buffers, 97, 224–234
    omit, 385, 600
constant color, 196, 675
constant hull shader, 516–518
constant interpolation, 373–374
constant vectors, 23–24, 32
constant XMVECTOR instances, 23
control point output, 518, 535
control points, 172, 514–516
    additional, 518
    vertex shader inputs, 445, 535
convert spherical to Cartesian coordinates, 230, 252
coordinate matrices, 76–77
coordinate matrix, change of, 76–78
coordinate representation, 5–7, 73
coordinates
    barycentric, 83, 522
    floating-point, 30–31
    ith, 433
    normal, 576
    normalized device, 185–189, 585, 647
    object's, 175
    u-texture, 633
    vector's, 5
corner to-far-plane vector,
crate demo, 359, 385, 390, 395
crate pixels, 397
creating vertex buffers, 454
crevices, 628, 679
cube map, 365, 367, 494, 538, 597–625
    dynamic, 609–620, 674,
cube map demo, 600, 624
cube map faces, 614–615
cube map texture, 598, 601, 622
cube mapping, 538, 597–625
cube texture, 369, 597
CUDA, 469,
CUDA cores, 471
current time value, 132, 156
CXMVECTOR, 22, 32

D

D3D_DRIVER_TYPE_HARDWARE, 142
D3D_FEATURE_LEVEL, 101
D3D11_BLEND, 402,
D3D11_BLEND_DESC, 402
D3D11_INPUT_ELEMENT_DESC, 205, 217
D3D11_MAX_MULTISAMPLE_SAMPLE_COUNT, 100
D3D11_RENDER_TARGET_BLEND_DESC, 402
data elements, 91, 155, 226, 360, 469, 507
    array of, 91
    matrix of, 91, 360
data members, 19, 21
data structures, 486, 787
DDS file, 366–367, 461
DDS texture image format, 601
debug output window, 221
depth bias, 655–657
depth buffer, 87, 93–96, 100, 125, 161
depth buffer range, 585
depth buffering, 87, 93–96
depth buffering algorithm, 187, 188, 195
depth comparison test, 695
depth complexity, 420, 440–443
depth coordinates, 188, 586
depth in NDC space, 651, 685
DepthStencilState, 244–246, 419
depth settings, 423
depth stencil, 96, 125–129, 245, 420, 422, 425, 429
depth/stencil buffer, 96, 117, 125–129, 207, 404
depth/stencil buffering, 420
depth/stencil state, 245, 422, 425, 429
depth/stencil state block, 425

depth/stencil texture, 128, 460
depth test, 95, 223, 407, 420, 440, 442, 671
depth values, 93, 95, 188, 195, 442, 584, 654, 655
    corresponding, 95
    normalized, 187–189, 667
    pixel shader modifies, 442
derivatives, partial, 353, 530, 669
destination blend factor Fdst, 403
destination pixel colors, 398
diffuse light, 325–326, 334
diffuse light color, 326
diffuse lighting, 325–326
diffuse lighting calculation, 326
diffuse material, 351, 408
diffuse material color, 326
Direct3D functions, 153, 155
Direct3D resources, 88, 155, 470
direction vector, 339, 607
directional lights, 88, 316, 342, 346
directional shadow matrix, 433
DirectX SDK, 23, 631, 749
DirectX Texture Tool, 394
displacement mapping, 175, 509, 526, 640
displacements, 2, 4, 68, 175, 509, 526, 640, 665
distance
    fog start, 411, 417
    function of, 340, 412
domain, 168, 376, 391, 514, 517, 519, 521
    normalized texture space, 391
domain shader, 168, 236, 244, 514, 517, 521, 536
dot product, 10–12, 32, 40, 67, 164, 345, 581, 713
dot product properties, 34
driver, 90, 518, 520
DXGI_FORMAT R32G32_UINT, 92, 360
DXGI_FORMAT_D16_UNORM, 96
DXGI_FORMAT_D24_UNORM_S8_UINT, 96, 142, 420, 438
DXGI_FORMAT_D32_FLOAT, 96
DXGI_FORMAT_D32_FLOAT_S8X24_UINT, 96
DXGI_FORMAT_R16G16B16A16_ UNORM, 92, 360
DXGI_FORMAT_R32_UINT, 213
DXGI_FORMAT_R8G8B8A8_SINT, 92, 205, 361
DXGI_FORMAT_R8G8B8A8_SNORM, 92, 360
DXGI_SAMPLE_DESC structure, 99
DXGI_SWAP_CHAIN_DESC, 120–122
DXGI_SWAP_CHAIN_FLAG_ALLOW_MODE_ SWITCH, 121
dynamic buffers, 310–312

E

edge vectors, 632
    corresponding texture triangle, 632
edges
    triangle's, 34, 319, 677
elements, vertex shader output, 217, 222–223

environment map, 599–601
environment mapping, 537, 599–601
equation, parametric, 136, 163, 536, 791,
eye position, 270, 323, 326, 346

F

far plane, 183, 192, 199–201
far plane values, 199
fetch, vertex texture, 311, 553, 559–562
fetching texture samples, 492
field, horizontal, 184
filtering, 374–376, 657–659
    anisotropic, 376
    linear, 374–376, 380
filters, 375, 394, 785
final transformation matrices, 751
flashlight, 341, 356
flatten, 239, 436
float
    16-bit, 773
    32-bit, 773
    lookup vector, 598
    return, 349, 526, 531
    static, 145, 310, 777
    texture, 371
float access, 686, 690
float occlusion, 687, 689
float offset, 80
floating-point imprecision, 30
floating-point number, 30, 630
floating-point numbers, 30
floating-point values, 362, 793
forces, 2, 4, 8–9, 143
format, 143, 155, 167, 169, 205, 213, 221, 245, 352, 360, 365–370,
    depth-buffer, 656
format DXGI, 32-bit pixel, 92, 96, 361
FPS (frames per second), 134, 143, 156, 316, 579
frame
    camera space, 541
    complete, 93, 112, 155
    origin of, 75
    previous, 134–136
    y-axes of, 74–75
    z-axes of, 74–75, 81
frame F0, 729
frame matrix, change of, 76, 81
frame of reference, 5–6, 73, 79, 81, 136, 541
frame rate, 131, 146, 156, 579
frames per second *see* FPS
framework, 139–154
    vector algebra, 2, 18
framework functions, 139, 149
    virtual, 139,
framework methods, 143–145

front buffer, 93, 153
frustum, 94, 182–185, 191–201, 411, 517
    projector's, 651, 674
frustum culling, 517, 537, 557–582
frustum plane equations, 193, 572
frustum planes, 571, 581
frustum properties, 542, 543
function
    interpolating, 374
    vector-valued, 633
functionality, vertex texture fetch, 310, 311

G

GameTimer, 133–134
Gaussian blur, 490, 492
Gaussian function, 490, 491
geometric interpretation, 8, 12, 44, 70, 395, 699–700
geometric primitives, 88, 168–169
geometric transformations, 2, 37, 59, 72
geometry
    arbitrary, 538, 649
    blended, 407
    non-blended, 407–8
    object's, 175
geometry buffers, 282
geometry resolution, projected screen, 375
geometry shader, 88, 168, 171–172, 191, 219, 244, 311, 445–467
    optional, 445, 464
geometry shader body, 446, 448
geometry shader implementation, 447, 622
geometry shader inputs, 176, 399
geometry shader outputs, 445
geometry shader programs, 445, 454
geometry shader signatures, 448
geometry shader stage, 168, 191
geosphere, 279
GPGPU programming, 469–471, 485
GPU (graphics processing unit), 88, 90
GPU memory, 107, 167, 175, 191, 208, 259, 310, 365
GPU resources, 96, 126, 156, 168, 470
grass texture, 390, 392
green light, 164
grid, using triangle, 301
grid points, 309, 509
grid texture coordinate generation, 391–392
grid triangles, 304
grid vertex, 391
    ijth, 302, 391
grid vertices, 302–304
ground plane, 181, 436

H

hardware instancing, 557–558
hardware tessellation, 311, 535, 628, 640

height
    proper, 607, 610, 627
    wave, 309
height function, 305–307
heightmap, 629, 640–641
hemisphere, 676, 678, 679, 689, 695
high level shading language *see* HLSL
highlight, 332, 345, 594, 595, 628, 731
hills, 265, 305, 336, 390, 523, 526
HLSL (high level shading language), 216
HLSL function outputs, 346–347
HLSL shader compiler, 240
homogeneous clip space, 182–183, 189, 191, 193, 445
homogeneous coordinates, 66–67
hull shader, 168, 244, 516–520, 535
    control point, 516, 518–520

I

icosahedron, 279, 465–466
identity matrix, 43–44, 55, 67, 77, 321, 390
IDXGIFactory, 102
IDXGISwapChain::GetBuffer, 124
IDXGISwapChain::Present, 93, 144, 153, 493
IDXGISwapChain::Present method, 144, 153, 493
IDXGISwapChain::ResizeBuffers, 93
IDXGISwapChain interface, 93, 102, 155
illusion, 159, 160–162, 393, 420, 602
image
    blurred, 490, 495, 510
    grayscale, 366, 668
image borders, 502–504
image color, 99
image data, 88, 91, 93, 155, 359–370
image file, 364, 365, 393–395, 635
implementation, 133–135, 143–146, 216, 342–346, 453, 469
incident, 187, 218, 323, 327, 596, 607
increment, 113, 275, 290, 312, 425, 436, 577
index, linear, 462, 486
index buffer stores indices, 212
index buffers, 172, 212–216, 230, 282, 311, 474, 480
    large, 215, 262
index of refraction, 316, 327–328, 624–625
indexing, 477–479, 537, 539, 548, 558, 775
indexing and sampling textures, 477–479
indices, matrix palette, 737
indices of refraction, 327
indirect light, 318, 326, 333, 341, 357, 667, 675, 695
information, real-time using screen space, 679
initialization code, 139, 143–144
input assembler, 168–174, 211, 459, 465
input assembler stage, 168–174
input buffer, 484, 508
input image, 461, 492, 501
input layout, 203–206, 219–221, 379,

using, 206
input layout description, 204, 219–221
input parameters, 23, 216–222
input primitives, 447
input registers, 221, 293, 312
input signature, 204, 217, 219–221
input slots, 206, 211, 261
    single, 261
input texture, 389–390, 474
input texture coordinates, 389–390
input texture resources, 474
input triangle, 621
instanced buffer, 564–566, 578
    dynamic, 564
instancing, 177, 206, 212, 282, 537, 555, 557–581
instancing, advanced technique of, 206
integer indices, 478
    using, 478
integer tessellation factor values, 519
integers, unsigned, 92, 96, 166, 205, 360, 420, 458
intensity of red light, 163–164
interchanging, 42, 55
intermediate points, 527–528
interpolate rotations, 538
interpolate texture coordinates, 449
interpolated to-near-plane vector input, 683
interpolation
    bilinear, 373, 521, 657,
    repeated, 527–528
    spherical, 715, 724
intersection, nearest triangle, 589, 596
intersection points, 192, 433, 435, 592
intersection tests, 566, 571, 580, 679
    frustum/AABB, 575
    frustum/sphere, 574
    ray/sphere, 591
    ray/triangle, 566, 589, 592–594
inverses and change of coordinate matrices, 77–78
inward facing planes, 574–575
iterate, 275, 304–305, 348, 591

K
key frames, 720–723
    first, 719
    last, 719
    list of, 719, 743
key texturing topics, 88

L
Lambert's Cosine Law, 323–325, 334
large PCF kernels, 668–672
layers, 617–618
light
    array of, 354
    blue, 163–164, 316, 326
    first, 666
    incoming, 316–317, 325–334, 624
    key, 357
    spot, 339, 342–355
    using colored, 357
light colors, 316
light intensity, 316, 340, 652
light mixture, 163–164
light projector, 649–651
light rays, 317–318, 339, 435, 653, 676
light receptors, 317
light scatters, 325–326, 333, 357
light source, 88, 161–162, 197, 261, 316–318, 326, 333, 339–357, 426, 432–434
light source emits, 316–7
light space, 662, 669–672
light space depth, 671–672
light strikes, 316–317, 328, 356, 606
light vector, 323–334, 339–357, 607, 640, 652
light vector aims, 333, 339, 346
lighting
    direct, 318, 357, 666
    dynamic, 628
    specular, 327–333
lighting calculations, 341, 352–356, 628
lighting demo, 351–356
lighting equation, 164, 316, 327, 333
lighting models, 315, 317, 334, 675
    real-time, 538, 675
line segment, 4–9, 31, 86, 162, 319, 466–467, 790, 799
line strip, 170, 172
linear combination, 37, 42, 56, 61, 71–2, 83
linear interpolation, 196, 373–376, 521, 527, 657
linear transformation, 45, 60–2, 65, 67–8, 70, 72, 83–4
load time, 364, 394
location, base vertex, 215
loop, 113, 135–142, 277, 661, 754
    ray/triangle intersection, 566
low intensity colors, 443

M
magnification, 330, 373–375, 394, 463
magnitude, 4, 6, 9–10, 18, 31, 67, 83
map, normal/depth, 681, 690, 695
map vertex shader outputs, 217, 222
maps frame, 76, 81, 83, 85
match vertex elements, 217, 222
material mat, 337–351, 458
material values, 335, 356, 370
mathematical objects, 2, 538, 697
matrices row vectors, 38
matrix
    initialize, 50
    orthogonal, 64, 81, 85

row, 501
square, 43–5, 48, 55
to-parent, 730–731, 750
matrix addition, 39, 55, 703, 779
matrix algebra, 2, 37, 39, 41, 43, 45, 47–9, 51, 53, 55, 57
matrix-column vector ordering, 710
matrix elements, 712
matrix equation, 48, 55, 59, 435, 593, 632
matrix equation Ax, 593, 714
matrix inverses, 47, 48
matrix-matrix multiplication, 59, 72–3, 78, 83
matrix minors, 45
matrix multiplication, 37–48, 55–68, 72–3, 78, 81–85, 186, 218, 272, 321
matrix of pixels, 98–100, 489–490
matrix product, 40–42, 55–56, 72–76
matrix representation, 60–61, 65, 67–77, 186, 201, 724
standard, 82–85
matrix types, 50–51
maxtessfactor, 51–520, 525
memory
   run-time, 149, 250
   video, 470, 754
mesh
   continuous, 737, 750–751
   land, 353, 390–392
   skull, 313, 567, 577, 719
mesh geometry, 590, 627–628
mesh hierarchies, 727, 729
mesh index buffer, 590, 595
mesh surface, 318, 339, 356, 392
mesh triangles, 589, 596
mesh vertices, 282, 309
messages, 118, 145–157, 238, 754–755
meters, 4–5
minification, 375, 380
minimum point, 62–69, 566
mipmap chain, 375, 394–395, 462, 659
mipmap levels, 92, 126, 360, 367, 369–370, 375, 380, 394
mipmaps, 92, 126, 360, 367, 369–370, 375, 380, 394
mirror, 607, 786, 327, 330, 336, 343, 344
mirror demo, 432, 436, 439, 443
mirror pixels, 419–20
   visible, 653–4, 673
mirror plane, 426
mode
   debug, 117, 118, 149, 157, 221
   full-screen, 101, 104, 121, 129, 494,
   wireframe, 203, 242, 243, 262
model formats
   custom, 203
   standard, 753
model reflections, 597
modelers, 162
mountains, distant, 597, 602,

multiplication, 7, 8, 778
multiprocessor, 133, 469, 471, 488
multisampling, 87, 98–101, 105, 207
   using, 209, 211

N

name, 659, 734–5, 741, 743, 745, 754, 764–5, 768, 770, 774–5, 777
NDC coordinates, 186, 649–54, 683
NDC space, 186, 193, 200, 512, 572, 580, 586, 647–52, 652, 662, 666
nearest ray/triangle intersection, 590
non-xMVECTOR parameters, 23
normal/depth, 681, 690
normal mapping, 91, 360, 371, 537–8, 627–39
normal maps, 366, 538, 573, 627–30
normal vector direction, 640
normal vector visualization technique, 466
normal vectors, 530, 538, 631, 680, 318–19
   sampled, 581
   transformed, 321
normalized range, 130, 335, 164, 187
normalized texture-coordinates, 478
normals, per-pixel, 639
null depth/stencil buffer, 207, 230, 245,404
null pixel shader, 664–5
number, random, 683
numthreads, 473, 477–9, 482, 486
NVIDIA hardware, 506, 472
NVIDIA texture tools, 601

O

OBB (oriented bounding box), 568, 580–2,
object space, 631
object space coordinates, 627–634
objects
   animated, 609, 623
   blend state, 401–3
   blended, 436, 442, 737
   cbuffer, 413–14, 455, 472, 478, 502
   child, 728–735
   distant, 410–11
   effect, 114,
   geometric, 566, 579
   global illumination models light, 318
   group of, 94, 161
   key, 609, 623
   multiple, 281,
   output XMVECTOR, 23, 25, 28, 35, 53
   sampler, 378–9
   semi-transparent, 397, 416
   single, 719, 733
   solid, 194, 685
   state, 120, 784, 785
   state group, 243–45

transparent, 316, 328, 406–7
tree, 176,
occludes, 673, 676, 685, 687, 689
    front-facing triangles, 194, 242,
occluding points, potential, 685
occlusion, 494, 537, 538, 675
    average triangle, 677
offset transform, 732–37,
offset transformation, 732,
offset vectors, 684, 689
OM *see* Output Merger
OM stage, 124, 167, 197–8, 400, 442, 656
one-by-one, texture animation frames, 191, 216, 262, 613
opacity, 165, 197, 406
opaque, 617–620, 656, 660, 663
opaque scene objects, 155
operations, 360, 372,395, 399
operator, 399–406,417, 422
    overloaded, 24,27, 51, 785
oriented bounding box *see* OBB,568–9, 580–2
origin, 275, 279, 326, 339,
orthogonalization, 13, 14, 16, 17
orthogonalize, 13–14, 16, 17
orthographic projections, 643, 646–7, 652–3, 673
orthonormal set, 13–14
output buffer, 487, 507–8
output control point, 419–20
output image, 495,600
output merger, 124, 167–8, 197, 400,442
output merger (OM), 197–8
output merger stage, 124, 556, 167, 197
output parameters, 216–7, 223
output primitives, 445, 464
output resources, 473–4,
output signature, 240, 400
output texture, 505
output triangle lists, 448
output vertex attributes, 664, 740, 389. 415, 509
output window, 118, 157, 221, 238
output XMVECTOR, 23, 25, 28, 35, 53
outputcontrolpoints, 519–20, 525,
outputtopology, 519–20, 525,

P

parallel light rays, 339, 435, 653
parallel lights, 339, 435, 647, 553, 673
parallelogram, 35, 58, 71, 85, 790, 791
parameter passing, 21, 23, 346
parameters
    attenuation, 340, 341
    first, 348, 644, 646, 648, 652, 660, 661, 669,680, 685, 702, 719, 720, 728, 732, 733, 736, 771
    second, 100, 106, 107, 129, 227, 385, 401, 558, 579, 659,
particle systems, 88, 309, 469

partitioning, 519, 525, 536
pass vertex color, 216–218, 223, 224, 272
patch
    tessellated, 190, 515, 517, 518, 521, 535, 665
patch control points, 515, 521, 522
patch vertices, tessellated, 535
patchconstantfunc, 519, 520, 525.
paused time, 136–8
    track of, 6, 131
PCF (percentage closer filtering), 657
PCF kernel, 660, 668–671
per-vertex materials, 556
percentage closer filtering *see* PCF, 657
performance, peak 446
performance counter, 87, 89, 132–4, 156
performance timer, 132, 156
perspective projection, 182, 189, 199, 200, 434, 555, 647–8, 652–3, 674
perspective projection matrix, 189, 199, 200, 555, 674
picking, 6, 70, 247, 537, 570, 583
picking ray, 584–9,596
ping-ponging vertex buffers, 207
pipeline, rendering, 230, 232, 234, 237, 242, 269, 361, 366, 425, 464, 470, 493, 493, 495,513, 515, 522, 534, 535, 540
pipeline stages, 88, 97, 156, 167–8,180
pixel block colors, 98
pixel center, 463, 99
pixel color, 193, 262
    final, 694, 733–38
    lit, 161
    resolved, 98, 99
pixel colors,193, 262, 398,
    object's, 265, 269
pixel formats, 87, 365–6
pixel fragments,407, 419, 438, 440, 443, 664, 665, 197,
pixel nearest, 654
pixel shader,272, 294, 319, 346–7, 358, 400, 403, 408–10, 417–8, 442, 459
    simple, 223
pixel shader alpha, 463
pixel shader body, 459
pixel shader input, 222–3
pixel shader input parameters, 222
pixel shader instructions, 410
pixel shader modifies, 433, 694
pixel shader stage, 167–8, 196
pixels
    changing, 366, 669
    clipping408, 410
    current, 682,783
    discard, 222, 409, 410, 415, 458, 664
    edge, 463,
    extra, 504

ijth, 40, 47, 475,55, 94,302, 391, 398, 419, 440, 490
less, 518
neighbor, 501, 510–11, 669
neighboring, 501,669
opaque, 463
particular, 95
reject, 421, 438, 442
rendering, 409, 417
single, 440
time processing, 440
transparent, 417
visible, 427, 653–4, 685, 695
Pixel Shader, 87–8, 167, 196
plane
   bottom, 571, 572
   complex, 699, 700
plane equations, 572–3, 581–82, 193,
player, 646, 653, 750, 4, 107, 130–1, 136
PN triangles and Catmull-clark approximations, 535
PN triangles scheme, 518
point filtering, 375, 380, 657
point light source, 340, 346, 434
point lights, 316, 339, 340, 346
point list, 170, 447, 171, 261
point primitives, 453, 466,
point/vector, 69, 724, 73
points, vanishing, 160–1, 182, 197
polar representation, 700, 706, 707, 724
polygon slope, 656
polygons, convex, 192
position
   given, 616
   particle, 309 487
   standard, 5, 17, 32, 86
   vertex-blended, 737
position element, 260, 442, 570
position vector, 17, 66, 71, 81, 465, 555
primitive IDs, 88, 446, 459, 460–467, 468
primitive topologies, 170
primitives, geometry shader outputs, 445
problem, depth buffer precision, 188
product, vector-matrix, 702, 784, 37, 41, 61, 72, 218, 272
program geometry shaders, 88, 446
programming geometry shaders, 446–447
project vertices, 651, 281
projection frustum, 572–3
projection matrix, 555, 572–3, 580, 587, 648–50, 653, 660,682, 144, 186–9
   orthographic, 643, 646–49, 652, 673–4
projection plane, , 647, 650, 673, 682, 182–4
projection transformation, 182, 186
projection window, 649–50, 182–7, 196, 440–1, 583–7, 596
projective texturing, 643, 649,652, 667, 673, 200, 538

using, 652
PS *see* Pixel Shader

Q

quad patch, 88, 515–6, 521–22, 524, 527–34
   cubic Bézier, 526
quad vertices, 452
quality levels, 100, 105–6, 116, 119, 121, 126, 245
quantities, vector-valued, 4–5
quaternion multiplication, 703–5, 707, 715, 724
quaternion rotation operator, 709–10, 724
quaternion space, 724
quaternions, 538, 569, 701–05, 712, 713, 715, 718, 719, 724, 725, 726
   interpolated, 713, 715
   nonzero, 705, 724
QueryPerformanceCounter, 132, 134–35, 137
   using, 132
QueryPerformanceCounter function, 132, 156

R

random vectors, 683, 684
ray casting, 676, 695
ray direction, 434, 588, 592, 677
ray intersects, 584, 589, 591–92, 596, 796, 800
ray misses, 589, 591–92, 596
ray origin, 339, 584, 588, 677,
ray/triangle intersection, 566, 589, 591, 592–594, 596, 679
real numbers, 7, 30, 33, 38, 40, 44, 54, 55, 697, 698, 699, 701, 703, 704, 713, 718, 723, 789,
   properties of, 33
real part, 698, 701, 703, 707, 723, 724, 726
rebuild, 213, 457, 500, 505
rectangles, 117, 131, 246, 373, 421
   scissor, 131, 246
red light, 164, 317, 326, 357
reference vectors, 64
reference vertices, 198
reflectance, 327, 333, 344, 675
reflection, 88, 196, 323, 327, 328–29, 335, 420, 426, 428, 431, 494, 607, 609, 623, 625, 638, 784, 797, 799
   dynamic, 494, 610
   specular, 606–9
reflection vector, 323, 784
reflection vector per-pixel, 607
reinterpret, 92, 98, 221, 227–28, 245–46, 258, 361, 362, 410, 451, 483, 606, 663, 778
render-to-texture, 361, 489, 493–95, 510, 644, 653,
rendering effects, 114, 169, 259, 260
rendering pass, 270, 271, 273, 355, 555, 617, 667
   second, 695
representation, axis-angle rotation, 718
resolution textures, 374
resource, single, 155
resource bindings, 234

818 INDEX

resource format, 97, 362
result, short distances, 463
RGB components, 398, 399, 417
RGBA color vector, 197, 352, 398
right-handed coordinate systems, 6–7
rotation matrices, 64, 70, 81, 85
rotation matrix, 65, 72, 82, 85, 177, 569, 710, 718, 724, 725
    general, 84, 87
rotation transformation, 71, 88
row vector-matrix multiplication, 702
row vectors, 40–2, 49, 55, 64, 67, 70, 71, 81, 177

S

sample
    bound, 379,
    random, 684–85, 690,
    thread, 449–50
sample code, 134, 139, 764, 795
sample count, 100, 121, 245, 686
sample framework, 121, 156, 348, 464
sample framework code, 89
sample neighboring value, 670–1
sample points, random, 683, 685
sample texture, 379, 477
sampler, 97, 232, 378–384, 659, 785
    comparison, 659
sampler states, 385, 507, 784–785,
scalar multiplication, 7–8, 24, 28, 32–3, 39–40, 55, 164–5, 703, 724
scaling 2-units, 86
scaling matrix, 62, 72, 79, 82, 83, 85, 177
scaling transformation, 61, 321
scene, entire, 93, 116, 129, 155, 440, 602, 622, 653, 660
scene depth, 443, 644–46, 653–54, 673, 680–81
scene geometry, 281, 649,
scene lights, 175, 356, 431, 679
scene objects, 116, 155, 317, 577, 584, 600, 680
scene vertices, 180, 540
screen pixels, 375, 394
screen point, clicked, 533–5, 546
screen point ps, 586
screen quad, 494, 681–2
screen resolution, 98–99, 126, 498, 681
screen space, 195, 494, 583, 585, 669–72, 676, 680–695
screen space ambient occlusion *see* SSAO
shader
    compiled, 235, 238, 242, 418, 451
    specialized, 259–60, 389, 409,
    vertex/pixel, 680
shader code, 205, 236, 335, 409, 413, 415, 458, 487, 498, 502, 507, 511, 551, 554, 559, 635–39, 652, 660, 664, 681, 747
shader generator mechanism, 226–7

shader input, 191, 204, 217, 219, 222–23, 232, 259, 293, 312, 361, 445, 518, 519, 612, 646, 673, 694,
    control point hull, 516, 518–20, 521, 535
shader programs, 224, 230, 232–33, 235, 241, 259, 270, 293, 301, 312, 341, 356, 368, 372, 381, 386, 514, 549, 562, 603, 605, 663, 721, 741
shader resource, 97, 114, 230, 361–62, 371, 470, 474, 646,
    corresponding, 400
shader variations, 242
shades, 163, 165,
shadow, planar, 88, 162, 432–438, 538, 673
shadow acne, 654–5, 660, 673–74,
shadow cast, 433,
shadow edges, 660, 674,
shadow factor, 665–67
shadow map, 494, 537, 643–6, 649, 653–74, 740,
shadow map demo, 668
shadow map samples, 655, 657
shadow map stores, 654, 673
shadow map test, 655, 657, 667–68, 672, 674
shadow map texel, 654–5, 673
shadow map texture space, 667
shadow map values, 656, 668
shadow mapping, 261, 380, 494, 537, 643–6, 649, 653–68, 673
shadow mapping algorithm, basic, 643
shadow matrix, 434, 436, 439
    general, 435,
shadow plane, 433, 435
shadowing techniques, 538, 643
    real-time, 673
shared memory, 471–2, 487–9, 501–2, 507
shared memory array, 488
shares, 98, 99, 173, 320, 463, 603, 633, 635,
shear transform, 201, 322
SIMD, 18–20, 27, 32, 50–1, 55, 165, 197, 471, 506,
SIMD instructions, 18–19
size, wavefront, 472, 473, 506,
sized triangles, 449
    equal, 279
skin vertices, 731
skinned mesh demo, 733, 749, 751,
skull, 162, 313, 420, 426, 427, 430, 436–38, 443, 567, 577, 579, 649, 679, 694, 719, 722–23
    reflected, 426–9
slices, 275, 279, 621
slope-scaled-bias, 656, 673–4
SMAP, 679–80, 686–7, 694, 698
source, parallel light, 339–40, 443, 435, 647, 653,
source alpha component, 406, 408
source blend factor, 398, 403, 405–6,
source data, 96–97,
source image, 489,
source pixels, 397–8, 404–8, 416–417
space

homogeneous, 177, 180, 182–83, 193, 200, 217, 223, 434, 445, 464
homogenous, 219, 572–3
positive half, 191, 571, 574, 792–3
volume of, 160, 179, 182
space coordinate system, 175–6, 541, 627, 631, 634, 639–640, 647, 649, 729
space coordinates, 179, 391, 599, 632, 633–34, 648
space depth, 671, 685
space normals, 680–81, 694
space position, 682–3, 685
space z-axis, 647, 673
spaceship, 162
specify DXGI, 121
specifying texture coordinates, 385
specular, 316, 328, 600, 606, 625, 628, 666, 694,
specular light, 327–333, 357,
amount of, 323, 326–28, 330–31, 333,
specular term, 666, 694
sphere
lit, 161, 315
unlit, 144, 315
sphere intersects, 574
sphere vertices box vertices cylinder vertices, 215
spotlight, 88, 316, 341–2, 347, 356, 358, 652, 653, 674
spotlight cone, 342, 652–3, 674
spotlight factor, 342
square, 63, 65, 68, 71, 82, 84, 85, 178, 340, 598, 602, 608, 782
square matrices, 47, 49, 55
SRC, 350, 353–4, 356
SRT, 72, 161–2
SRV, 419, 435–6, 440–2, 456–7, 467–8, 562, 665
SSAO (screen space ambient occlusion), 680–82, 686, 690, 694–6
SSAO map, 681–2, 686, 690, 694–6, 740
SSAO pixel shader, 681–82
SSE2, 18–19, 21, 23, 32, 52
stacks, 275, 279
stage, clipping, 198, 576, 579–80
stencil, 88, 96–7, 99, 117, 122, 398, 404, 419–22
stencil buffer, 88, 96, 117, 122, 125–29, 143, 147, 152, 167, 197, 223, 230, 245, 404, 419–21, 424, 426–29, 432, 436–37, 605, 612, 621, 644, 680
8-bit, 425
updated, 427
stencil buffer entry, 425, 427–8, 436–437, 440
corresponding, 428, 437, 440
stencil buffer operation, 441
stencil buffer pixels, 427, 436
stencil buffer tests, 197, 223
stencil buffer to prevent double blending, 432, 436–7
stencil buffer value, 436
stencil test, 99, 245, 398, 421–8, 436–38, 463
strikes, 163–4, 316–8, 324–28, 333, 339, 356–7, 606, 624, 653, 675
string, 154, 204, 236, 238, 520, 757, 762,
strips, 173, 447,
structure
output vertex type, 446
structured buffer resources, 479–81
structured buffers, 479, 481–82, 487, 507
subdivide, 99, 279, 448, 465–6, 526
subpixels, 98–9, 463,
visible, 99
subrectangle, 129–30
supersampling, 98–9
surface, smooth, 330–32, 335, 342, 518, 535, 633
surface colors, 356
surface normals, 318, 356, 538, 627
specifying, 627
surface point, 323, 333–34, 353–54, 356, 411, 413, 417, 602, 652,
surface textures, 518
SV_DispatchThreadID, 473, 477–79, 482, 486, 488–89, 503–04, 511, 548
SV_GroupID, 485
SV_GroupIndex, 486
SV_GroupThreadID, 485–6, 488–89, 503–4
SV_InstanceID, 548, 555, 559, 561
SV_PrimitiveID, 454, 456–59, 464, 516, 519, 525–26, 548
SV_RenderTargetArrayIndex, 621–23
SV_TessFactor, 516–17, 525
SWAP, 153, 171,
swap chain, 93, 100–1, 116, 118, 120–22, 124–25, 143–44, 153, 155, 493
switch, 95, 121, 133, 404, 409, 471, 488, 495, 506, 508, 690, 778
system
three-point lighting, 357–58
system memory, 208–9, 227, 247, 259, 273, 336–37, 470, 482, 564, 570, 590–91
system memory buffer, 482
system memory copy, 570, 590
system memory resource, 482
system values, 217, 507, 566

T

tangent, 261, 318, 321–22, 353–4, 529–30, 592, 738, 784
tangent plane, 318, 353, 356, 670
tangent space, 631–35, 640
tangent vectors, 261, 353–54, 385, 633, 635, 670
per-vertex, 356
transformed, 631
target array slice, 621, 623
target point, 181
TBN-bases, 633, 639,
technique
advanced, 91, 130–31, 144, 152, 191, 206, 212, 214, 244, 360, 403

820 INDEX

billboard, 451
multi-texturing, 395
multiple, 131, 144, 152
render-to-texture, 489
rendering, 144
terragen, 600–1, 624
terrain, 208, 301, 307, 397, 605
terrain surface, 353
tessellate, 88, 190, 311, 513–14, 516–18, 520, 522, 535, 628
tessellated geometry, 665
tessellating, 280, 466, 513, 517–18, 526, 535,
tessellation, 88, 172, 190–91, 198, 279, 311, 445, 464, 513, 514, 516, 520–21, 524, 535, 576, 580, 628, 640
    fractional, 519, 536
tessellation factors, 516–8, 520–1, 524, 535
    interior, 517, 520, 536
tessellation stages, 88, 190–1, 198, 311, 445, 464, 513–15, 518, 534–35, 576, 580
tessellator, 522, 526, 534–35, 628
    ray/triangle, 589
test scene, 443, 466,
tex-coords, 509, 651, 667, 689, 694, 740, 742
texel points, 373–74
texel values, 501–2
texture alpha, 409, 415, 458, 664, 681
texture animation, 360, 393
texture array, 88, 126, 365, 367, 446, 454, 459–62, 465, 539, 549, 554–55, 598, 601, 604, 611, 613, 620, 623, 785
    entire, 620–2
texture array index, 462
texture array stores, 459, 465
texture artists, 364
texture atlas, 364, 372
texture buffers, 93, 495
texture color, 375,
texture coordinate system, 362, 673
texture coordinate transformations, 390
texture coordinates
    compressed, 630
    corresponding, 363, 631
    generated, 649
    generating projective, 649, 651
    interpolated, 373, 385
    normal, 651
    normalized, 373, 478
    pair of, 363, 373
    projective, 649, 651–3, 667, 673, 685, 694
    respective, 363, 395
    transforming, 394
    unique, 373
    using, 478
texture data, 367, 369, 378, 385, 600
texture dimensions, 362, 369
texture distortion, 364, 632

texture elements, 460, 465, 507
texture files, 631
texture filtering, 378, 394, 477, 598
texture format, 100, 105, 365, 630
texture function, 376
texture functionality, 311, 673
texture geometry, 476
texture gOutput, 477
texture image, 477, 601, 628
    entire, 364, 385
texture map, 370–1, 373, 375, 380, 385, 417, 549, 628, 630, 680–1, 683, 685, 784
    random vector, 685
texture mapping, 88, 336, 359, 364, 627–8, 631
texture matrix, 390, 393, 650
    water's, 391
texture objects, 360, 537, 539
texture outputs and unordered access, 474–77
texture plane, 390, 393, 629, 632
texture resolution, 373, 378
texture resources, 125, 167, 207, 360, 367–9, 372, 379, 474–5, 496, 507, 555, 601
texture samples, 488, 659
    reducing, 492
texture size, 478
texture space, 363, 391, 393, 631–33, 639, 649–50, 667
texture space axes, 631–2
texture space coordinates, 391
texture space plane, 393
texture stores, 91, 360, 460
texture subresources, 462
texture tiling, 88, 332
texture transform, 650
texture transformation matrix, 392, 640
texture transformations, 640
    animated, 88
texture triangle, 363, 631
texture values, 374, 488
texture vertex, 363
Texture2D, 126, 128, 208, 232, 296, 299, 360, 369–70, 384, 387, 413, 460, 472–5, 478, 486, 488–9, 497, 503, 511, 539, 549, 554, 560, 611, 645, 659, 686, 691, 784
TextureCube, 369, 598, 601, 604, 614, 623, 784
texturing, 88, 97, 126, 169, 200, 295, 335, 370–1, 374–5, 387, 538, 597–8, 602, 643, 649, 652–3, 657, 667, 673
texturing coordinate system, 631
thread group sizes, 472, 485, 498, 506
thread groups, 471–3, 477, 482, 485–9, 495, 498–99, 501, 505–8
thread ID values, 486
thread IDs, 471, 477, 485–6, 507
threads, 116, 471–3, 477, 482, 485–6, 489, 498–9, 501,
    extraneous, 498, 505
    main rendering, 113
thumb points, 6, 15

time, 131–9, 144–7, 156, 160, 176, 208, 225, 237–9, 264, 281–2, 285, 301, 309, 327, 360, 362, 367, 394, 402, 428, 436, 440, 448, 464, 489, 495, 501, 506, 516, 558, 5776, 588, 645, 719,
    current, 132, 135–6
    function of, 136, 262, 357, 390–1, 393, 395, 466, 729
    initialization, 98, 110, 116, 246, 375, 386, 404, 594
    real number, 697, 698
    total, 136–7, 139
time intervals, 131, 156
time position, 743
timer, 89, 131–3, 137, 147, 156
    to-near-plane vectors, 683
    interpolated, 683
to-parent transform, 730–1, 750
transform, 69–70, 72, 79, 81, 86, 130, 175–6, 179–80, 187, 193, 195, 200–1, 217, 225, 279, 316, 321–2, 356, 389–90, 434, 445, 540, 559, 569–70, 572, 577, 583–5, 588, 596, 634–5, 639–40, 647–50, 653, 672, 682, 685, 729–38, 750, 795
transform coordinates, 2, 634
transform geometry, 730
transform quad vertices, 457
transformation matrices, 59, 80, 175, 281, 390, 737, 751,
    constructing, 59
    creating multiple world, 281
transformation matrix, 69, 81, 200, 262, 321, 392, 546, 596, 640, 667, 721, 719, 729, 732–3, 795
    affine, 67, 70, 185–6
    net, 59, 72
    single, 82
    to-parent, 730, 750
    translation affine, 78
transformations, 1–2, 37, 45, 59, 60, 66, 69–72, 75, 84, 88, 175, 177, 179, 390, 541, 581, 640, 650, 697, 721, 727, 729–30, 789
    active, 78–9, 81
    body, 70, 631
    change-of-coordinate, 541, 729
    final, 733, 735, 747, 751
    identity, 67
    reverse, 180, 540
    rotation texture, 640
    sequence of, 177–8
    texture space, 650
    to-root, 732–3, 736, 750–51
transformed normal vector nA, 321
transformed point, 71, 738
transformed tangent vector, 321
    associated, 322
transforming normal vectors, 322
transforming normals, 738–9
transitions, smooth, 334, 358, 463, 519, 658, 737,
translation, 2, 37, 59, 66–8, 70, 72–3, 78–79, 81–3, 86, 177, 180, 188, 201, 322, 540, 631, 434, 647, 743, 768

translation matrix, 68, 72, 82–83, 86, 177, 201, 322
translation transformations, 68, 79
transparency, 88, 92, 195, 197, 316, 336, 398, 406, 408, 410, 428, 432, 436, 463, 595, 625, 665, 742
transpose, 37, 42–3, 47, 55–6, 58, 65, 81, 322, 634, 702, 710, 738, 795, 798
traverse, 727, 731–2, 736
tree billboard demo, 451–4, 461, 463, 467
trees, 208, 451, 460, 464
triangle centroid, 677
triangle clipping, 517
triangle count, 88, 513, 524
    low, 190
triangle density, 275
triangle duplicates, 173
triangle grid, 508
triangle grid mesh, 301, 309
triangle grid mesh vertices, 309
triangle input, 466
triangle lists, 170, 172–4, 191, 212, 445, 448
    using, 172, 174
triangle mesh, 162, 197, 318, 320, 336, 339, 356, 515, 518, 591, 596, 633, 635
    arbitrary, 308, 579
    using arbitrary, 581
triangle mesh approximation, 162
triangle patch, 515–8, 521–2, 536
    cubic Bézier, 518
    order cubic Bézier, 518
triangle patch configurations, 517
triangle patch tessellation examples, 521
triangle shares, 321
triangle strip, 170–73, 261, 447,
    using, 171
triangle strip vertices, 457
triangle subdivisions, 521
triangle-to-triangle, 631
triangle topology, 311
triangle vertex, 592
triangle vertices, 194, 466, 631–2
triangles
    acute angled, 364
    adjacent, 170–2
    back-facing, 194–5, 242
    clipped, 192, 500
    corresponding, 363
    discards, 576, 580
    extra, 190
    facing, 424–5
    flattened, 436
    front-facing, 194, 242–3
    left, 194
    mapped, 631
    neighboring, 171
    new, 190, 526

ordinary, 518
overlapping, 436
picked, 590, 594–5
right, 194
right angled, 364
slice, 278
subdivided, 448
tessellated, 515
top, 450
translating, 466
using, 279
triangles form, 162
triple buffering, 93
trivial access function, 142
typeless formats, 92, 361–2

U

UAV (Unordered Access Views), 474–77, 480–82, 495, 496, 507, 508
unit length, 10, 12–14, 64, 81, 85, 322, 331, 333, 354, 466, 546, 581, 592, 632, 633, 710, 713, 792
unit quaternions, 538, 697–98, 705, 707–12, 715, 724
unit sphere, 280, 354, 465, 713, 715–16
unordered access views *see* UAV
UNORM depth buffer format, 656
UNORM format, 263, 630, 656
updating, 227, 271, 354–55, 453

V

valid depth/stencil buffer formats, 438
valleys, 265, 307, 309
values
    approximate, 373
    decremented, 425
    incremented, 425
    maximum, 425
    stencil, 152
vector addition, 7–8, 19, 24, 28, 32
    geometric interpretation of, 8, 12, 70–71, 395
vector coordinates, 6, 600
    lookup, 598–609, 623, 784
vector dot product function, 345
vector functions, 3, 26–30, 165, 197
vector-matrix multiplications, 72, 77
vector operations, 7, 26, 33, 164, 197
vector part, 701–708
    imaginary, 701, 704
vector/point, 75, 81
vector properties, 33
vector subtraction, 8, 28
vectors
    32-bit float, 205
    bitangent, 633
    column, 38–41, 55
    coordinate, 61

displacement, 68, 70
distributed, 684–685
first, 15, 787
incident, 624–625, 784
incoming light ray, 624
ith column, 593, 714
jth column, 40, 55
lookup, 598–609, 623, 784
normalized, 30, 487
orthogonal, 12, 16, 34
orthogonal set of, 13–14
orthonormal, 17, 555
orthonormal axis, 581
returned, 15, 27
right, 545, 555
signed integer, 205
texture coordinate, 390
transform, 322, 589
transforming, 80, 634, 710
translation, 67, 743
unsigned integer, 205
using, 9, 17–18
vectors and coordinate systems, 5–6
velocities, 2, 4
vertex
    arbitrary, 320, 633
    first, 212, 215
    ijth, 391
    last, 277
    middle, 320
    object's, 176
vertex arrays, 172
vertex attributes, 195–6, 222, 415
vertex basis, 259, 335
vertex buffer storing, 523, 532
vertex buffers, 207–212
    array of, 211
    concatenated, 282
    corresponding, 214
    corresponding local, 215
    dynamic, 265, 309–311
    global, 214
    ith, 213
    large, 262
    special initialization, 000
    start binding, 211
    static, 453,312
    using, 214
    using dynamic, 265, 311–12
vertex buffer's memory, 212
vertex colors, 316, 336, 356
vertex component, 206
vertex data, 309, 311, 352, 363
vertex depth values, 195
vertex elements, 205, 206, 217, 221, 284

vertex formats, 169, 204
  custom, 203, 259
vertex heights change, 311
vertex IDs, 459, 465, 467
vertex/index buffers, 172, 286
vertex index values, 459, 465, 467
vertex level, 339, 352, 627
vertex lighting calculation, 319
vertex list, 174, 198, 445, 570
vertex normals, 318–321, 339, 352, 466
vertex points, 318–19, 356
vertex positions, 191, 265, 445, 521
  first sphere, 215
  tessellated, 521
vertex shader, simple, 472–73
vertex shader acts, 521, 535, 622
vertex shader body, 459
vertex shader fragment, 738
vertex shader function, 175, 416
vertex shader input parameters, 217
vertex shader input signature, 204, 259
vertex shader output, 222–23
vertex shader parameters, 217, 222
vertex shader signature, 459, 465
vertex shader stage, 175
vertex shader structure order, corresponding, 263
vertex structure, 204–7, 453–54
  custom, 217
vertex structure order, 263
vertex texture coordinates, 363, 373, 395
vertex type, 210, 446–47
vertex vertices, 210
vertical field, 183–84
vertices
  array of, 173–174
  duplicate, 173
  generated, 88, 513, 523
  list of, 169, 445, 447
  maximum number of, 446, 457
  new, 279, 311, 465, 519
  object's, 433, 435
  outgoing, 447, 459
  unique, 174, 275
  vertex shader inputs, 445, 535
vertices output, 448
viewer, 93–96, 155–161, 179, 194–195, 317, 464
viewpoint, 194, 326, 328, 599, 615, 646, 653, 655, 673
viewport, 109, 117, 129–131, 150, 193–194, 246, 263, 585–586, 611–623, 644–645
viewport matrix, 585
virtual camera, 17, 87, 159, 167, 179, 198
vM, vector-matrix product, 80

W

w-coordinate, negative, 434

wall, 88, 318, 326, 373–375, 408, 420, 426–427
water, 6, 73, 301, 316, 329, 354, 391
water geometry, 391
water pixels, 397
water texture, 391, 393
waves, 301–302, 307–311, 351, 390, 508, 640–641
waves demo, 301–302, 307–311, 351, 390
waves vertex shader, 508
weights, 83, 320, 490–491
winding order, 171, 173, 195, 431–432
wireframe, 203, 243, 302, 466
work
  computation, 488–489
  specialized, 259–260
world, combined, 225, 229
world coordinate system, 176, 179–180, 198
world coordinates, 541, 556, 634
world matrices, 282
world matrix, 176–180, 229, 271, 438, 540, 631, 634
  skull's, 723
world space axes, 556, 599, 600
world space coordinates, 179, 599, 634
world space float, 351
world transform, 176–179, 262, 279, 281, 434, 570, 730, 731, 737
world transformation matrix, 262
world-view-projection matrix, combined, 229
world y-axis, 181, 545

X

XM_NO_OPERATOR_OVERLOADS, 24–28, 50–55
XMCOLOR, 166–69, 197, 260,
XMColorModulate, 165
XMConvertToDegrees, 25, 29
XMConvertToRadians, 25, 229, 254, 547–48, 722
XMFLOAT, 20
XMFLOAT2, 19–21
XMFLOAT3, 19–21
XMFLOAT4, 19–21
XMFLOAT4X4 ,51, 55
XMLoadColor, 167
XMMATRIX ViewProj, 272, 617
XMMATRIX world, 230, 252, 271, 578
XMMATRIX class, 50, 53, 55
XMMatrixAffineTransformation, 720–21
XMMatrixDeterminant, 52, 54–55, 272, 577–78, 617, 795
XMMatrixIdentity, 52–3, 55
XMMatrixInverse, 52, 54, 55, 272, 322, 573, 577–78, 617, 795
XMMatrixIsIdentity, 52
XMMatrixLookAtLH, 181–2,230, 661
XMMatrixMultiply, 52,55, 272, 578, 589,617, 736
XMMatrixPerspectiveFovLH, 189–90, 252, 469, 544
XMMatrixReflect, 431, 799
XMMatrixRotationAxis, 80, 545

XMMatrixRotationAxis function, 545
XMMatrixRotationX, 79
XMMatrixRotationY, 79, 545, 661
XMMatrixRotationZ, 79
XMMatrixScaling, 79, 286, 393
XMMatrixScalingFromVector, 79
XMMatrixShadow, 436,
XMMatrixTranslation, 80, 286–7, 438
XMMatrixTranslationFromVector, 80
XMMatrixTranspose, 52–4, 230, 252, 271, 501, 617
XMPlaneDotCoord, 793
XMPlaneDotNormal, 794
XMPlaneFromPointNormal, 794
XMPlaneFromPoints, 794
XMPlaneIntersectLine, 797, 800
XMPlaneNormalize, 794–5
XMPlaneTransform, 794–5
XMQuaternionConjugate, 718
XMQuaternionIdentity, 718
XMQuaternionLength, 718
XMQuaternionMultiply, 718
XMQuaternionNormalize, 718
XMQuaternionRotationAxis, 718, 722
XMQuaternionRotationNormal, 718
XMQuaternionSlerp, 719–20
XMStoreColor, 167

XMStoreFloat, 21
XMStoreFloat2, 21
XMStoreFloat3, 281, 354–55, 431, 545
XMStoreFloat4, 21, 36, 722,
XMStoreFloat4x4, 55, 230, 272, 287, 393, 438, 496, 544, 617, 720
XMVector3AngleBetweenVectors, 27, 29
XMVector3ComponentsFromNormal, 27, 29
XMVector3Cross, 27–8, 32, 276, 319, 546, 678
XMVector3Dot, 27–8, 32, 546
XMVector3Equal, 27, 29
XMVector3Length, 26–8, 30, 32
XMVector3LengthSq, 27, 32,
XMVector3Normalize, 27–8, 30, 32, 276, 218, 319, 354, 546, 568, 589, 678
XMVector3NotEqual, 27, 29
XMVector3Orthogonal, 27
XMVector3Transform, 80
XMVector3TransformCoord, 80, 589, 661
XMVector3TransformNormal, 80, 431, 545, 589, 661
XMVectorReplicate, 25–6, 545
XMVectorSet, 21, 26, 28, 30, 36, 182, 230, 252, 322, 431, 438, 588, 661, 720, 722, 793
XMVectorSplatOne, 25–6
XNA collision library, 572